Praise for the Reformation Commentary on Scripture

"Protestant reformers were fundamentally exegetes as much as theologians, yet (except for figures like Luther and Calvin) their commentaries and sermons have been neglected because these writings are not available in modern editions or languages. That makes this new series of Reformation Commentary on Scripture most welcome as a way to provide access to some of the wealth of biblical exposition of the sixteenth and seventeenth centuries. The editor's introduction explains the nature of the sources and the selection process; the intended audience of modern pastors and students of the Bible has led to a focus on theological and practical comments. Although it will be of use to students of the Reformation, this series is far from being an esoteric study of largely forgotten voices; this collection of reforming comments, comprehending every verse and provided with topical headings, will serve contemporary pastors and preachers very well."

Elsie Anne McKee, *Retired Archibald Alexander Professor of Reformation Studies and the History of Worship, Princeton Theological Seminary*

"This series provides an excellent introduction to the history of biblical exegesis in the Reformation period. The introductions are accurate, clear and informative, and the passages intelligently chosen to give the reader a good idea of methods deployed and issues at stake. It puts precritical exegesis in its context and so presents it in its correct light. Highly recommended as reference book, course book and general reading for students and all interested lay and clerical readers."

Irena Backus, *Professeure Ordinaire, Institut d'histoire de la Réformation, Université de Genève*†

"The Reformation Commentary on Scripture is a major publishing event—for those with historical interest in the founding convictions of Protestantism, but even more for those who care about understanding the Bible. As with IVP Academic's earlier Ancient Christian Commentary on Scripture, this effort brings flesh and blood to 'the communion of saints' by letting believers of our day look over the shoulders of giants from the past. By connecting the past with the present, and by doing so with the Bible at the center, the editors of this series perform a great service for the church. The series deserves the widest possible support."

Mark A. Noll, *Professor Emeritus, University of Notre Dame*

"For those who preach and teach Scripture in the church, the Reformation Commentary on Scripture is a significant publishing event. Pastors and other church leaders will find delightful surprises, challenging enigmas and edifying insights in this series, as many Reformational voices are newly translated into English. The lively conversation in these pages can ignite today's pastoral imagination for fresh and faithful expositions of Scripture."

J. Todd Billings, *Gordon H. Girod Research Professor of Reformed Theology, Western Theological Seminary*

"The reformers discerned rightly what the church desperately needed in the sixteenth century—the bold proclamation of the Word based on careful study of the sacred Scriptures. We need not only to hear that same call again for our own day but also to learn from the Reformation how to do it. This commentary series is a godsend!"

Richard J. Mouw, *President Emeritus and Senior Professor of Faith and Public Life, Fuller Theological Seminary*

"Like the Ancient Christian Commentary on Scripture, the Reformation Commentary on Scripture does a masterful job of offering excellent selections from well-known and not-so-well-known exegetes. The editor's introductory survey is, by itself, worth the price of the book. It is easy to forget that there were more hands, hearts and minds involved in the Reformation than Luther and Calvin. Furthermore, encounters even with these figures are often limited to familiar quotes on familiar topics. However, the Reformation Commentary helps us to recognize the breadth and depth of exegetical interests and skill that fueled and continue to fuel faithful meditation on God's Word. I heartily recommend this series as a tremendous resource not only for ministry but for personal edification."

Michael S. Horton, *J. Gresham Machen Professor of Systematic Theology and Apologetics, Westminster Seminary, California*

"The Reformation was ignited by a fresh reading of Scripture. In this series of commentaries, we contemporary interpreters are allowed to feel some of the excitement, surprise and wonder of our spiritual forebears. Luther, Calvin and their fellow revolutionaries were masterful interpreters of the Word. Now, in this remarkable series, some of our very best Reformation scholars open up the riches of the Reformation's reading of the Scripture."

William H. Willimon, *Professor of the Practice of Christian Ministry, Duke Divinity School*

"The Reformation Scripture principle set the entirety of Christian life and thought under the governance of the divine Word, and pressed the church to renew its exegetical labors. This series promises to place before the contemporary church the fruit of those labors, and so to exemplify life under the Word."

John Webster, *Professor of Divinity, University of St. Andrews†*

"Since Gerhard Ebeling's pioneering work on Luther's exegesis seventy years ago, the history of biblical interpretation has occupied many Reformation scholars and become a vital part of study of the period. The Reformation Commentary on Scripture provides fresh materials for students of Reformation-era biblical interpretation and for twenty-first-century preachers to mine the rich stores of insights from leading reformers of the sixteenth century into both the text of Scripture itself and its application in sixteenth-century contexts. This series will strengthen our understanding of the period of the Reformation and enable us to apply its insights to our own days and its challenges to the church."

Robert Kolb, *Professor Emeritus, Concordia Theological Seminary*

"The multivolume Ancient Christian Commentary on Scripture is a valuable resource for those who wish to know how the Fathers interpreted a passage of Scripture but who lack the time or the opportunity to search through the many individual works. This new Reformation Commentary on Scripture will do the same for the reformers and is to be warmly welcomed. It will provide much easier access to the exegetical treasures of the Reformation and will hopefully encourage readers to go back to some of the original works themselves."

Anthony N. S. Lane, *Professor of Historical Doctrine, Lecturer in Doctrine, London School of Theology*

"This volume of the RCS project is an invaluable source for pastors and the historically/biblically interested that provides unparalleled access not only to commentaries of the leading Protestant reformers but also to a host of nowadays unknown commentaters on Galatians and Ephesians. The RCS is sure to enhance and enliven contemporary exegesis. With its wide scope, the collection will enrich our understanding of the variety of Reformation thought and biblical exegesis."

Sigrun Haude, *Associate Professor of Reformation and Early Modern European History, University of Cincinnati*

"This grand project sets before scholars, pastors, teachers, students and growing Christians an experience that can only be likened to stumbling into a group Bible study only to discover that your fellow participants include some of the most significant Christians of the Reformation and post-Reformation (for that matter, of any) era. Here the Word of God is explained in a variety of accents: German, Swiss, French, Dutch, English, Scottish and more. Each one vibrates with a thrilling sense of the living nature of God's Word and its power to transform individuals, churches and even whole communities. Here is a series to anticipate, enjoy and treasure."

Sinclair Ferguson, *Professor of Systematic Theology, Reformed Theological Seminary*

"I strongly endorse the Reformation Commentary on Scripture. Introducing how the Bible was interpreted during the age of the Reformation, these volumes will not only renew contemporary preaching, but they will also help us understand more fully how reading and meditating on Scripture can, in fact, change our lives!"

Lois Malcolm, *Professor and Olin and Amanda Fjelstad Registad Chair for Systematic Theology, Luther Seminary*

"Discerning the true significance of movements in theology requires acquaintance with their biblical exegesis. This is supremely so with the Reformation, which was essentially a biblical revival. The Reformation Commentary on Scripture will fill a yawning gap, just as the Ancient Christian Commentary did before it, and the first volume gets the series off to a fine start, whetting the appetite for more. Most heartily do I welcome and commend this long overdue project."

J. I. Packer, *Board of Governors' Professor of Theology, Regent College*†

"There is no telling the benefits to emerge from the publication of this magnificent Reformation Commentary on Scripture series! Now exegetical and theological treasures from Reformation era commentators will be at our fingertips, providing new insights from old sources to give light for the present and future. This series is a gift to scholars and to the church; a wonderful resource to enhance our study of the written Word of God for generations to come!"

Donald K. McKim, *Executive Editor of Theology and Reference, Westminster John Knox Press*

"Why was this not done before? The publication of the Reformation Commentary on Scripture should be greeted with enthusiasm by every believing Christian—but especially by those who will preach and teach the Word of God. This commentary series brings the very best of the Reformation heritage to the task of exegesis and exposition, and each volume in this series represents a veritable feast that takes us back to the sixteenth century to enrich the preaching and teaching of God's Word in our own time."

R. Albert Mohler Jr., *President, The Southern Baptist Theological Seminary*

"Today more than ever, the Christian past is the church's future. InterVarsity Press has already brought the voice of the ancients to our ears. Now, in the Reformation Commentary on Scripture, we hear a timely word from the first Protestants as well."

Bryan Litfin, *Moody Publishers*

"I am delighted to see the Reformation Commentary on Scripture. The editors of this series have done us all a service by gleaning from these rich fields of biblical reflection. May God use this new life for these old words to give him glory and to build his church."

Mark Dever, *Senior Pastor, Capitol Hill Baptist Church, and President of 9Marks Ministries*

"Monumental and magisterial, the Reformation Commentary on Scripture, edited by Timothy George, is a remarkably bold and visionary undertaking. Bringing together a wealth of resources, these volumes will provide historians, theologians, biblical scholars, pastors and students with a fresh look at the exegetical insights of those who shaped and influenced the sixteenth-century Reformation. With this marvelous publication, InterVarsity Press has reached yet another plateau of excellence. We pray that this superb series will be used of God to strengthen both church and academy."

David S. Dockery, *President of the International Alliance for Christian Education*

"Detached from her roots, the church cannot reach the world as God intends. While every generation must steward the scriptural insights God grants it, only arrogance or ignorance causes leaders to ignore the contributions of those faithful leaders before us. The Reformation Commentary on Scripture roots our thought in great insights of faithful leaders of the Reformation to further biblical preaching and teaching in this generation."

Bryan Chapell, *President Emeritus, Covenant Theological Seminary*

"After reading several volumes of the Reformation Commentary on Scripture, I exclaimed, 'Hey, this is just what the doctor ordered—I mean Doctor Martinus Lutherus!' The church of today bearing his name needs a strong dose of the medicine this doctor prescribed for the ailing church of the sixteenth century. The reforming fire of Christ-centered preaching that Luther ignited is the only hope to reclaim the impact of the gospel to keep the Reformation going, not for its own sake but to further the renewal of the worldwide church of Christ today. This series of commentaries will equip preachers to step into their pulpits with confidence in the same living Word that inspired the witness of Luther and Calvin and many other lesser-known reformers."

Carl E. Braaten, *Cofounder of the Center for Catholic and Evangelical Theology*

"As a pastor, how does one cultivate a knowledge of the history of interpretation? That's where IVP's Reformation Commentary on Scripture and its forerunner, the Ancient Christian Commentary on Scripture, come in. They do an excellent job in helping pastors become more aware of the history of exegesis for the benefit of their congregations. Every pastor should have access to a set of each."

Carl R. Trueman, *Professor of Biblical and Religious Studies, Grove City College*

Reformation Commentary on Scripture

Old Testament

IX

Proverbs, Ecclesiastes, Song of Songs

Edited by

David C. Fink

General Editor

Timothy George

Associate General Editor

Scott M. Manetsch

IVP Academic

An imprint of InterVarsity Press

Downers Grove, Illinois

InterVarsity Press
P.O. Box 1400 | Downers Grove, IL 60515-1426
ivpress.com | email@ivpress.com

InterVarsity Press® is the publishing division of InterVarsity Christian Fellowship/USA®. For more information, visit intervarsity.org.

Cover design: Cindy Kiple
Interior design: Daniel van Loon

ISBN 978-0-8308-2959-0 (print) | ISBN 978-0-8308-4253-7 (digital)

Printed in the United States of America ♾

Library of Congress Cataloging-in-Publication Data
A catalog record for this book is available from the Library of Congress.

29 28 27 26 25 24 23 | 10 9 8 7 6 5 4 3 2 1

Reformation Commentary on Scripture
Project Staff

Project Editor
David W. McNutt

Executive Editor
Elissa Schauer

Assistant Managing Editor
Zachary Gordon

Copyeditor
Jeffrey A. Reimer

Assistant Project Editor
Travis Ables

Editorial and Research Assistants
David J. Hooper
Alberto I. Bonilla-Giovanetti

Assistants to the General Editors
Evan Musgraves
Bryan Just
Christopher Gow

Design
Cindy Kiple

Proofreader
Michael LeFebvre

CONTENTS

ACKNOWLEDGMENTS

It has been over a decade now since I first agreed to edit this volume for the Reformation Commentary on Scripture. I was still in graduate school at the time, and I remember well the dubious expression on my Doktorvater's face when I told him I was thinking about taking it on. "I hope you realize," he warned, "this is going to be a lot of work." He was right. It has been. But with the wisdom (or perhaps simply the exhaustion) of hindsight, I can say that it was worth the effort.

When friends and sympathetic colleagues asked what it is that I was working on, I typically responded with some variation of the following: my job is to read through a stack of sermons, commentaries, pamphlets, and treatises from the Reformation era on Wisdom literature of the Hebrew Bible, then pick out the interesting bits, translate them into English, and make them accessible to a wider audience. Easier said than done. But I have had lots of help.

To begin with, I have had considerable help in tracking down the relevant texts. A generation ago, this would have required trips to at least a dozen major research libraries in Europe. Alas, due to the wonders of digitization, such trips are no longer needed. But the assistance of skilled research librarians is still essential, and I have been helped by some of the best. At Duke University, where this project began, I had help from numerous members of the staff in digging up materials from some of the mustier corners of the Divinity School Library, and Andy Keck was unreasonably patient in teaching me how to use the microfilm reader. At Furman University, where I have taught since 2013, the library staff have been tenacious in helping me track down copies of rare manuscripts at libraries in Paris, Rome, Berlin, and Warsaw, and my special thanks are due to Caroline Mills, Libby Young, and the late Jenny Colvin. Finally, the staff at InterVarsity Press made heroic efforts to secure a copy of Melchior Hoffmann's commentary on the Song of Songs, after several years of effort on my part had gotten me nowhere.

Once I had the texts in hand—or, more typically, on my hard drive—I needed more help in making sense of them. John Slotemaker was my go-to authority on late medieval paleography, and he helpfully responded to dozens of queries about cryptic abbreviations, funny-looking ligatures, and indecipherable handwriting. My colleagues in the Religion Department, Tim Wardle and Brian Bibb, have been unfailingly helpful when I've found myself at a loss on questions of text criticism and biblical philology. Christopher Blackwell, Randall Childree, Eunice Kim, and Chiara Palladino all helped me at various points when I was in over my head with Greek or Latin. Ilke Rasch was always *schlagfertig* when I found myself bogged down in German. Occasionally I even found myself behipt (whatever that means!) by some of my sources' early modern English, and when this happened, Margaret Oakes and Melinda Menzer helped me avoid making a fool of myself in my native tongue.

One of the most time-consuming aspects of this project has been tracking down the voluminous citations and allusions to ancient sources, especially in the commentaries by humanistically trained writers like Philipp Melanchthon. When they gave me direct quotes in Greek or Latin, the job was usually pretty easy, thanks to digital resources like the online TLG or Loeb Library. Often, however, I had to work with an author's imperfectly remembered paraphrase, or a loose translation into a second language (usually from Greek to Latin), or simply a casual allusion to a text the author knew much better than I did. In cases like this, I have not hesitated to reach out to friends, colleagues, or even complete strangers for help in identifying sources, and I've been gratified at how frequently they have been willing to share their time and expertise. I know I haven't remembered them all, but thanks to Esther Chung-Kim, Valeria Cinaglia, Jonathan Dean, Nathan Eubank, Craig Farmer, Ralph Keen, Gregory Lee, Mickey Mattox, Sujin Pak, J. Warren Smith, Matt Thiessen, and Edwin Woodruff Tait.

I would like to express my deep gratitude to Timothy George and Scott Manetsch, who first invited me to be a part of this project, and to the dedicated editorial team at InterVarsity Press. David Noe, James Kellerman, and Christina Moss provided expert help in translating materials from Cajetan, Johann Gerhard, and Melchior Hoffman. A succession of RCS project editors and assistant project editors have offered their encouragement and assistance at every stage, beginning with Joel Scandrett, Mike Gibson, Brannon Ellis, and Todd Hains; and David McNutt was steadfast in his role as Samwise Gamgee, spurring/dragging me up the final slope of Mount Doom as the project wound to its completion.

Even though it has been six years now since his passing, I still feel the loss of David Steinmetz quite keenly. This volume could never have gotten off the ground without his guidance, friendship, and cautious encouragement. But I would like to dedicate the work to Virginia, who for so many of us has been and continues to be a source of blessing and encouragement:

She openeth her mouth with wisdom;
and in her tongue is the law of kindness. (Prov 31:26)

ABBREVIATIONS

ACCS	Ancient Christian Commentary on Scripture. 29 vols. Edited by Thomas Oden. Downers Grove, IL: InterVarsity, 1998–2010.
ANF	Ante-Nicene Fathers, 10 vols. Edited by Philip Schaff et al. New York, 1885–1887. Several reprints; also available online at www.ccel.org.
CCSL	Corpus Christianorum, Series Latina. Turnhout, Belgium: Brepols, 1981–.
CO	Ioannis Calvini Opera quae supersunt omnia. 59 vols. Corpus Reformatorum 29-88. Edited by G. Baum, E. Cunitz, and E. Reuss. Berlin: C. A. Schwetschke, 1863–1900. Digital copies online at http://archive-ouverte.unige.ch/unige:650.
CR	Corpus Reformatorum. 101 vols. Edited by C. G. Bretschneider. Halle, 1834–1860.
CRR	Classics of the Radical Reformation. 12 vols. Waterloo, ON, and Scottdale, PA: Herald Press, 1973–.
CWE	Collected Works of Erasmus. 86 vols. planned. Toronto: University of Toronto Press, 1969–.
DCOO	D. Dionysii Cartusiani Opera Omnia. 42 vols. Montreuil-sur-Mer, 1896–1913.
EEBO	Early English Books Online. Subscription database, eebo.chadwyck.com.
LCC	The Library of Christian Classics. 26 vols. Edited by John Baillie et al. Philadelphia: Westminster, 1953–1966.
LCL	Loeb Classical Library. Cambridge, MA: Harvard University Press, 1911–. Digital copies online at www.loebclassics.com.
LW	Luther's Works ["American Edition"]. 82 vols. planned. St. Louis: Concordia, www.cph.org; Philadelphia: Fortress, 1955–1986; 2009–. Used by permission. All rights reserved.
LXX	Septuagint
NPNF	A Select Library of the Nicene and Post-Nicene Fathers of the Christian Church. 28 vols. in two series, denoted as NPNF[1] and NPNF[2]. Edited by Philip Schaff et al. Buffalo, NY: Christian Literature, 1887–1894. Several reprints; also available online at www.ccel.org.
PG	Patrologia cursus completus. Series Graeca. 166 vols. Edited by J.-P. Migne. Paris: Migne, 1857–1886.
PL	Patrologia cursus completus. Series Latina. 221 vols. Edited by J.-P. Migne. Paris: Migne, 1844–1864. Digital copies online at http://books.google.com.
SChr	Sources Chrétiennes. 607 vols. Paris: Cerf, 1942–.

WA	D. Martin Luthers Werke: Kritische Gesamtausgabe. 66 vols. Weimar: Hermann Böhlaus Nachfolger, 1883–1987.
WA, DB	D. Martin Luthers Werke: Kritische Gesamtausgabe: Deutsche Bibel. 12 vols. Weimar: Hermann Böhlaus Nachfolger, 1906–1961.
WA, Tr	D. Martin Luthers Werke: Kritische Gesamtausgabe: Tischreden. 6 vols. Weimar: Hermann Böhlaus Nachfolger, 1912–1921.
WSA	The Works of Saint Augustine: A New Translation for the 21st Century. 44 vols. Hyde Park, NY: New City Press, 1990–.

A GUIDE TO USING THIS COMMENTARY

Several features have been incorporated into the design of this commentary. The following comments are intended to assist readers in making full use of this volume.

Pericopes of Scripture

The scriptural text has been divided into pericopes, or passages, usually several verses in length. Each of these pericopes is given a heading, which appears at the beginning of the pericope. For example, the first section in this commentary is Proverbs 1:1-7, "The Beginning of Knowledge." This heading is followed by the Scripture passage quoted in the English Standard Version (ESV). The Scripture passage is provided for the convenience of readers, but it is also in keeping with Reformation-era commentaries, which often followed the patristic and medieval commentary tradition, in which the citations of the reformers were arranged according to the text of Scripture.

Overviews

Following each pericope of text is an overview of the Reformation authors' comments on that pericope. The format of this overview varies among the volumes of this series, depending on the requirements of the specific book(s) of Scripture. The function of the overview is to identify succinctly the key exegetical, theological, and pastoral concerns of the Reformation writers arising from the pericope, providing the reader with an orientation to Reformation-era approaches and emphases. It tracks a reasonably cohesive thread of argument among reformers' comments, even though they are derived from diverse sources and generations. Thus, the summaries do not proceed chronologically or by verse sequence. Rather, they seek to rehearse the overall course of the reformers' comments on that pericope.

We do not assume that the commentators themselves anticipated or expressed a formally received cohesive argument but rather that the various arguments tend to flow in a plausible, recognizable pattern. Modern readers can thus glimpse aspects of continuity in the flow of diverse exegetical traditions representing various generations and geographical locations.

Topical Headings

An abundance of varied Reformation-era comment is available for each pericope. For this reason we have broken the pericopes into two levels. First is the verse with its topical heading.

The reformers' comments are then focused on aspects of each verse, with topical headings summarizing the essence of the individual comment by evoking a key phrase, metaphor, or idea. This feature provides a bridge by which modern readers can enter into the heart of the Reformation-era comment.

Identifying the Reformation Authors, Texts, and Events

Following the topical heading of each section of comment, the name of the Reformation commentator is given. An English translation (where needed) of the reformer's comment is then provided. This is immediately followed by the title of the original work rendered in English.

Readers who wish to pursue a deeper investigation of the reformers' works cited in this commentary will find full bibliographic detail for each Reformation title provided in the bibliography at the back of the volume. Information on English translations (where available) and standard original-language editions and critical editions of the works cited is found in the bibliography. The Biographical Sketches section provides brief overviews of the life and work of each commentator, and each confession or collaborative work, appearing in the present volume (as well as in any previous volumes). Finally, a Timeline of the Reformation offers broader context for people, places, and events relevant to the commentators and their works.

Footnotes and Back Matter

To aid the reader in exploring the background and texts in further detail, this commentary utilizes footnotes. The use and content of footnotes may vary among the volumes in this series. Where footnotes appear, a footnote number directs the reader to a note at the bottom of the page, where one will find annotations (clarifications or biblical cross references), information on English translations (where available) or standard original-language editions of the work cited.

Where original-language texts have remained untranslated into English, we provide new translations. Where there is any serious ambiguity or textual problem in the selection, we have tried to reflect the best available textual tradition. Wherever current English translations are already well rendered, they are utilized, but where necessary they are stylistically updated. A single asterisk (*) indicates that a previous English translation has been updated to modern English or amended for easier reading. We have standardized spellings and made grammatical variables uniform so that our English references will not reflect the linguistic oddities of the older English translations. For ease of reading we have in some cases removed superfluous conjunctions.

GENERAL INTRODUCTION

The Reformation Commentary on Scripture (RCS) is a twenty-eight-volume series of exegetical comment covering the entire Bible and gathered from the writings of sixteenth-century preachers, scholars and reformers. The RCS is intended as a sequel to the highly acclaimed Ancient Christian Commentary on Scripture (ACCS), and as such its overall concept, method, format, and audience are similar to the earlier series. Both series are committed to the renewal of the church through careful study and meditative reflection on the Old and New Testaments, the charter documents of Christianity, read in the context of the worshiping, believing community of faith across the centuries. However, the patristic and Reformation eras are separated by nearly a millennium, and the challenges of reading Scripture with the reformers require special attention to their context, resources and assumptions. The purpose of this general introduction is to present an overview of the context and process of biblical interpretation in the age of the Reformation.

Goals

The Reformation Commentary on Scripture seeks to introduce its readers to the depth and richness of exegetical ferment that defined the Reformation era. The RCS has four goals: the enrichment of contemporary biblical interpretation through exposure to Reformation-era biblical exegesis; the renewal of contemporary preaching through exposure to the biblical insights of the Reformation writers; a deeper understanding of the Reformation itself and the breadth of perspectives represented within it; and a recovery of the profound integration of the life of faith and the life of the mind that should characterize Christian scholarship. Each of these goals requires a brief comment.

Renewing contemporary biblical interpretation. During the past half-century, biblical hermeneutics has become a major growth industry in the academic world. One of the consequences of the historical-critical hegemony of biblical studies has been the privileging of contemporary philosophies and ideologies at the expense of a commitment to the Christian church as the primary reading community within which and for which biblical exegesis is done. Reading Scripture with the church fathers and the reformers is a corrective to all such imperialism of the present. One of the greatest skills required for a fruitful interpretation of the Bible is the ability to listen. We rightly emphasize the importance of listening to the voices of contextual theologies today, but in doing so we often marginalize or ignore another crucial context—the community of believing Christians through the centuries. The serious study of Scripture requires more than the latest

Bible translation in one hand and the latest commentary (or niche study Bible) in the other. John L. Thompson has called on Christians today to practice the art of "reading the Bible with the dead."[1] The RCS presents carefully selected comments from the extant commentaries of the Reformation as an encouragement to more in-depth study of this important epoch in the history of biblical interpretation.

Strengthening contemporary preaching. The Protestant reformers identified the public preaching of the Word of God as an indispensible means of grace and a sure sign of the true church. Through the words of the preacher, the living voice of the gospel (*viva vox evangelii*) is heard. Luther famously said that the church is not a "pen house" but a "mouth house."[2] The Reformation in Switzerland began when Huldrych Zwingli entered the pulpit of the Grossmünster in Zurich on January 1, 1519, and began to preach a series of expositional sermons chapter by chapter from the Gospel of Matthew. In the following years he extended this homiletical approach to other books of the Old and New Testaments. Calvin followed a similar pattern in Geneva. Many of the commentaries represented in this series were either originally presented as sermons or were written to support the regular preaching ministry of local church pastors. Luther said that the preacher should be a *bonus textualis*—a good one with a text—well-versed in the Scriptures. Preachers in the Reformation traditions preached not only about the Bible but also from it, and this required more than a passing acquaintance with its contents. Those who have been charged with the office of preaching in the church today can find wisdom and insight—and fresh perspectives—in the sermons of the Reformation and the biblical commentaries read and studied by preachers of the sixteenth century.

Deepening understanding of the Reformation. Some scholars of the sixteenth century prefer to speak of the period they study in the plural, the European Reformations, to indicate that many-diverse impulses for reform were at work in this turbulent age of transition from medieval to modern times.[3] While this point is well taken, the RCS follows the time-honored tradition of using *Reformation* in the singular form to indicate not only a major moment in the history of Christianity in the West but also, as Hans J. Hillerbrand has put it, "an essential cohesiveness in the heterogeneous pursuits of religious reform in the sixteenth century."[4] At the same time, in developing guidelines to assist the volume editors in making judicious selections from the vast amount of commentary material available in this period, we have stressed the multifaceted character of the Reformation across many confessions, theological orientations, and political settings.

Advancing Christian scholarship. By assembling and disseminating numerous voices from such a signal period as the Reformation, the RCS aims to make a significant contribution to the ever-growing stream of Christian scholarship. The post-Enlightenment split between the study of the Bible as an academic discipline and the reading of the Bible as spiritual nurture was foreign

[1]John L. Thompson, *Reading the Bible with the Dead* (Grand Rapids: Eerdmans, 2007).

[2]WA 10,2:48.

[3]See Carter Lindberg, *The European Reformations*, 2nd ed. (Malden, MA: Wiley-Blackwell, 2010).

[4]Hans J. Hillerbrand, *The Division of Christendom* (Louisville, KY: Westminster John Knox, 2007), x. Hillerbrand has also edited the standard reference work in Reformation studies, *OER*. See also Diarmaid MacCulloch, *The Reformation* (New York: Viking, 2003), and Patrick Collinson, *The Reformation: A History* (New York: Random House, 2004).

to the reformers. For them the study of the Bible was transformative at the most basic level of the human person: *coram deo.*

The reformers all repudiated the idea that the Bible could be studied and understood with dispassionate objectivity, as a cold artifact from antiquity. Luther's famous Reformation breakthrough triggered by his laborious study of the Psalms and Paul's letter to the Romans is well known, but the experience of Cambridge scholar Thomas Bilney was perhaps more typical. When Erasmus's critical edition of the Greek New Testament was published in 1516, it was accompanied by a new translation in elegant Latin. Attracted by the classical beauty of Erasmus's Latin, Bilney came across this statement in 1 Timothy 1:15: "Christ Jesus came into the world to save sinners." In the Greek this sentence is described as *pistos ho logos,* which the Vulgate had rendered *fidelis sermo,* "a faithful saying." Erasmus chose a different word for the Greek *pistos—certus,* "sure, certain." When Bilney grasped the meaning of this word applied to the announcement of salvation in Christ, he tells us that "immediately, I felt a marvellous comfort and quietness, insomuch as 'my bruised bones leaped for joy.'"[5]

Luther described the way the Bible was meant to function in the minds and hearts of believers when he reproached himself and others for studying the nativity narrative with such cool unconcern:

> I hate myself because when I see Christ laid in the manger or in the lap of his mother and hear the angels sing, my heart does not leap into flame. With what good reason should we all despise ourselves that we remain so cold when this word is spoken to us, over which everyone should dance and leap and burn for joy! We act as though it were a frigid historical fact that does not smite our hearts, as if someone were merely relating that the sultan has a crown of gold.[6]

It was a core conviction of the Reformation that the careful study and meditative listening to the Scriptures, what the monks called *lectio divina,* could yield transformative results for *all* of life. The value of such a rich commentary, therefore, lies not only in the impressive volume of Reformation-era voices that are presented throughout the course of the series but in the many particular fields for which their respective lives and ministries are relevant. The Reformation is consequential for historical studies, both church as well as secular history. Biblical and theological studies, to say nothing of pastoral and spiritual studies, also stand to benefit and progress immensely from renewed engagement today, as mediated through the RCS, with the reformers of yesteryear.

Perspectives

In setting forth the perspectives and parameters of the RCS, the following considerations have proved helpful.

Chronology. When did the Reformation begin, and how long did it last? In some traditional accounts, the answer was clear: the Reformation began with the posting of Luther's Ninety-five

[5]John Foxe, *The Acts and Monuments of John Foxe: A New and Complete Edition,* 8 vols., ed. Stephen Reed Cattley (London: R. B. Seeley & W. Burnside, 1837), 4:635; quoting Ps 51:8; cited in A. G. Dickens, *The English Reformation,* 2nd ed. (University Park, PA: The Pennsylvannia State University Press, 1991), 102.

[6]WA 49:176-77, quoted in Roland Bainton, "The Bible in the Reformation," in *CHB,* 3:23.

Theses at Wittenberg in 1517 and ended with the death of Calvin in Geneva in 1564. Apart from reducing the Reformation to a largely German event with a side trip to Switzerland, this perspective fails to do justice to the important events that led up to Luther's break with Rome and its many reverberations throughout Europe and beyond. In choosing commentary selections for the RCS, we have adopted the concept of the long sixteenth century, say, from the late 1400s to the mid-seventeenth century. Thus we have included commentary selections from early or pre-Reformation writers such as John Colet and Jacques Lefèvre d'Étaples to seventeenth-century figures such as Henry Ainsworth and Johann Gerhard.

Confession. The RCS concentrates primarily, though not exclusively, on the exegetical writings of the Protestant reformers. While the ACCS provided a compendium of key consensual exegetes of the early Christian centuries, the Catholic/Protestant confessional divide in the sixteenth century tested the very idea of consensus, especially with reference to ecclesiology and soteriology. While many able and worthy exegetes faithful to the Roman Catholic Church were active during this period, this project has chosen to include primarily those figures that represent perspectives within the Protestant Reformation. For this reason we have not included comments on the apocryphal or deuterocanonical writings.

We recognize that "Protestant" and "Catholic" as contradistinctive labels are anachronistic terms for the early decades of the sixteenth century before the hardening of confessional identities surrounding the Council of Trent (1545–1563). Protestant figures such as Philipp Melanchthon, Johannes Oecolampadius and John Calvin were all products of the revival of sacred letters known as biblical humanism. They shared an approach to biblical interpretation that owed much to Desiderius Erasmus and other scholars who remained loyal to the Church of Rome. Careful comparative studies of Protestant and Catholic exegesis in the sixteenth century have shown surprising areas of agreement when the focus was the study of a particular biblical text rather than the standard confessional debates.

At the same time, exegetical differences among the various Protestant groups could become strident and church-dividing. The most famous example of this is the interpretive impasse between Luther and Zwingli over the meaning of "This is my body" (Mt 26:26) in the words of institution. Their disagreement at the Colloquy of Marburg in 1529 had important christological and pastoral implications, as well as social and political consequences. Luther refused fellowship with Zwingli and his party at the end of the colloquy; in no small measure this bitter division led to the separate trajectories pursued by Lutheran and Reformed Protestantism to this day. In Elizabethan England, Puritans and Anglicans agreed that "Holy Scripture containeth all things necessary to salvation: so that whatsoever is not read therein, nor may be proved thereby, is not to be required of any man" (article 6 of the Thirty-Nine Articles of Religion), yet on the basis of their differing interpretations of the Bible they fought bitterly over the structures of the church, the clothing of the clergy and the ways of worship. On the matter of infant baptism, Catholics and Protestants alike agreed on its propriety, though there were various theories as to how a practice not mentioned in the Bible could be justified biblically. The Anabaptists were outliers on this subject. They rejected infant baptism altogether. They appealed to the example of the baptism of Jesus and to his final words as recorded in the Gospel of Matthew (Mt 28:19-20): "Go therefore, and make disciples of all nations, baptizing them in the name of the Father, and of the Son, and of the Holy Spirit, teaching them to observe all that I have commanded you." New Testament Christians, they argued, are to follow not only the commands of Jesus in the Great Commission, but also the exact order in which they were given: evangelize, baptize, catechize.

These and many other differences of interpretation among the various Protestant groups are reflected in their many sermons, commentaries and public disputations. In the RCS, the volume editors' introduction to each volume is intended to help the reader understand the nature and significance of doctrinal conversations and disputes that resulted in particular, and frequently clashing, interpretations. Footnotes throughout the text will be provided to explain obscure references, unusual expressions and other matters that require special comment. Volume editors have chosen comments on the Bible across a wide range of sixteenth-century confessions and schools of interpretation: biblical humanists, Lutheran, Reformed, Anglican, Puritan, and Anabaptist. We have not pursued passages from post-Tridentine Catholic authors or from radical spiritualists and antitrinitarian writers, though sufficient material is available from these sources to justify another series.

Format. The design of the RCS is intended to offer reader-friendly access to these classic texts. The availability of digital resources has given access to a huge residual database of sixteenth-century exegetical comment hitherto available only in major research universities and rare book collections. The RCS has benefited greatly from online databases such as Alexander Street Press's Digital Library of Classical Protestant Texts (DLCPT) and Early English Books Online as well as freely accessible databases like the Post-Reformation Digital Library (prdl.org). Through the help of RCS editorial advisor Herman Selderhuis, we have also had access to the special Reformation collections of the Johannes a Lasco Bibliothek in Emden, Germany. In addition, modern critical editions and translations of Reformation sources have been published over the past generation. Original translations of Reformation sources are given unless an acceptable translation already exists.

Each volume in the RCS will include an introduction by the volume editor placing that portion of the canon within the historical context of the Protestant Reformation and presenting a summary of the theological themes, interpretive issues and reception of the particular book(s). The commentary itself consists of particular pericopes identified by a pericope heading; the biblical text in the English Standard Version (ESV), with significant textual variants registered in the footnotes; an overview of the pericope in which principal exegetical and theological concerns of the Reformation writers are succinctly noted; and excerpts from the Reformation writers identified by name according to the conventions of the *Oxford Encyclopedia of the Reformation*. Each volume will also include a bibliography of sources cited, as well as an appendix of authors and source works.

The Reformation era was a time of verbal as well as physical violence, and this fact has presented a challenge for this project. Without unduly sanitizing the texts, where they contain anti-Semitic, sexist or inordinately polemical rhetoric, we have not felt obliged to parade such comments either. We have noted the abridgement of texts with ellipses and an explanatory footnote.

While this procedure would not be valid in the critical edition of such a text, we have deemed it appropriate in a series whose primary purpose is pastoral and devotional. When translating *homo* or similar terms that refer to the human race as a whole or to individual persons without reference to gender, we have used alternative English expressions to the word *man* (or derivative constructions that formerly were used generically to signify humanity at large), whenever such substitutions can be made without producing an awkward or artificial construction.

As is true in the ACCS, we have made a special effort where possible to include the voices of women, though we acknowledge the difficulty of doing so for the early modern period when for a variety of social and cultural reasons few theological and biblical works were published by women. However, recent scholarship has focused on a number of female leaders whose literary remains show us how they understood and interpreted the Bible. Women who made significant contributions to the Reformation include Marguerite d'Angoulême, sister of King Francis I, who supported French reformist evangelicals including Calvin and who published a religious poem influenced by Luther's theology, *The Mirror of the Sinful Soul*; Argula von Grumbach, a Bavarian noblewoman who defended the teachings of Luther and Melanchthon before the theologians of the University of Ingolstadt; Katharina Schütz Zell, the wife of a former priest, Matthias Zell, and a remarkable reformer in her own right—she conducted funerals, compiled hymnbooks, defended the downtrodden, and published a defense of clerical marriage as well as composing works of consolation on divine comfort and pleas for the toleration of Anabaptists and Catholics alike; and Anne Askew, a Protestant martyr put to death in 1546 after demonstrating remarkable biblical prowess in her examinations by church officials. Other echoes of faithful women in the age of the Reformation are found in their letters, translations, poems, hymns, court depositions, and martyr records.

Lay culture, learned culture. In recent decades, much attention has been given to what is called "reforming from below," that is, the expressions of religious beliefs and churchly life that characterized the popular culture of the majority of the population in the era of the Reformation. Social historians have taught us to examine the diverse pieties of townspeople and city folk, of rural religion and village life, the emergence of lay theologies, and the experiences of women in the religious tumults of Reformation Europe.[7] Formal commentaries by their nature are artifacts of learned culture. Almost all of them were written in Latin, the lingua franca of learned discourse well past the age of the Reformation. Biblical commentaries were certainly not the primary means by which the Protestant Reformation spread so rapidly across wide sectors of sixteenth-century society. Small pamphlets and broadsheets, later called *Flugschriften* ("flying writings"), with their graphic woodcuts and cartoon-like depictions of Reformation personalities and events, became the means of choice for mass communication in the early age of printing. Sermons and works of devotion were also printed with appealing visual aids. Luther's early writings were often accompanied by drawings and sketches from Lucas Cranach and other artists. This was done "above all for the sake of children and simple folk," as Luther

[7]See Peter Matheson, ed., *Reformation Christianity* (Minneapolis: Fortress, 2007).

put it, "who are more easily moved by pictures and images to recall divine history than through mere words or doctrines."[8]

We should be cautious, however, in drawing too sharp a distinction between learned and lay culture in this period. The phenomenon of preaching was a kind of verbal bridge between scholars at their desks and the thousands of illiterate or semiliterate listeners whose views were shaped by the results of Reformation exegesis. According to contemporary witness, more than one thousand people were crowding into Geneva to hear Calvin expound the Scriptures every day.[9] An example of how learned theological works by Reformation scholars were received across divisions of class and social status comes from Lazare Drilhon, an apothecary of Toulon. He was accused of heresy in May 1545 when a cache of prohibited books was found hidden in his garden shed. In addition to devotional works, the French New Testament and a copy of Calvin's Genevan liturgy, there was found a series of biblical commentaries, translated from the Latin into French: Martin Bucer's on Matthew, François Lambert's on the Apocalypse and one by Oecolampadius on 1 John.[10] Biblical exegesis in the sixteenth century was not limited to the kind of full-length commentaries found in Drilhon's shed. Citations from the Bible and expositions of its meaning permeate the extant literature of sermons, letters, court depositions, doctrinal treatises, records of public disputations and even last wills and testaments. While most of the selections in the RCS will be drawn from formal commentary literature, other sources of biblical reflection will also be considered.

Historical Context

The medieval legacy. On October 18, 1512, the degree *Doctor in Biblia* was conferred on Martin Luther, and he began his career as a professor in the University of Wittenberg. As is well known, Luther was also a monk who had taken solemn vows in the Augustinian Order of Hermits at Erfurt. These two settings—the university and the monastery—both deeply rooted in the Middle Ages, form the background not only for Luther's personal vocation as a reformer but also for the history of the biblical commentary in the age of the Reformation. Since the time of the Venerable Bede (d. 735), sometimes called "the last of the Fathers," serious study of the Bible had taken place primarily in the context of cloistered monasteries. The Rule of St. Benedict brought together *lectio* and *meditatio*, the knowledge of letters and the life of prayer. The liturgy was the medium through which the daily reading of the Bible, especially the Psalms, and the sayings of the church fathers came together in the spiritual formation of the monks.[11] Essential to this understanding was a belief in the unity of the people of God throughout time as well as space, and an awareness that life in this world was a preparation for the beatific vision in the next.

[8]Martin Luther, "Personal Prayer Book," LW 43:42-43* (WA 10,2:458); quoted in R. W. Scribner, *For the Sake of Simple Folk: Popular Propaganda for the German Reformation* (Cambridge: Cambridge University Press, 1981), xi.

[9]Letter of De Beaulieu to Guillaume Farel (1561) in *Theodor Beza nach handschriftlichen und anderen gleichzeitigen Quellen*, ed. J. W. Baum (Leipzig: Weidmann, 1851), 2:92.

[10]Francis Higman, "A Heretic's Library: The Drilhon Inventory" (1545), in Francis Higman, *Lire et Découvrire: la circulation des idées au temps de la Réforme* (Geneva: Droz, 1998), 65-85.

[11]See the classic study by Jean Leclercq, *The Love of Learning and the Desire for God* (New York: Fordham University Press, 1961).

The source of theology was the study of the sacred page *(sacra pagina)*; its object was the accumulation of knowledge not for its own sake but for the obtaining of eternal life. For these monks, the Bible had God for its author, salvation for its end and unadulterated truth for its matter, though they would not have expressed it in such an Aristotelian way. The medieval method of interpreting the Bible owed much to Augustine's *On Christian Doctrine*. In addition to setting forth a series of rules (drawn from an earlier work by Tyconius), Augustine stressed the importance of distinguishing the literal and spiritual or allegorical senses of Scripture. While the literal sense was not disparaged, the allegorical was valued because it enabled the believer to obtain spiritual benefit from the obscure places in the Bible, especially in the Old Testament. For Augustine, as for the monks who followed him, the goal of scriptural exegesis was freighted with eschatological meaning; its purpose was to induce faith, hope, and love and so to advance in one's pilgrimage toward that city with foundations (see Heb 11:10).

Building on the work of Augustine and other church fathers going back to Origen, medieval exegetes came to understand Scripture as possessed of four possible meanings, the famous *quadriga*. The literal meaning was retained, of course, but the spiritual meaning was now subdivided into three senses: the allegorical, the moral, and the anagogical. Medieval exegetes often referred to the four meanings of Scripture in a popular rhyme:

The letter shows us what God and our fathers did;
The allegory shows us where our faith is hid;
The moral meaning gives us rules of daily life;
The anagogy shows us where we end our strife.[12]

In this schema, the three spiritual meanings of the text correspond to the three theological virtues: faith (allegory), hope (anagogy), and love (the moral meaning). It should be noted that this way of approaching the Bible assumed a high doctrine of scriptural inspiration: the multiple meanings inherent in the text had been placed there by the Holy Spirit for the benefit of the people of God. The biblical justification for this method went back to the apostle Paul, who had used the words *allegory* and *type* when applying Old Testament events to believers in Christ (Gal 4:21-31; 1 Cor 10:1-11). The problem with this approach was knowing how to relate each of the four senses to one another and how to prevent Scripture from becoming a nose of wax turned this way and that by various interpreters. As G. R. Evans explains, "Any interpretation which could be put upon the text and was in keeping with the faith and edifying, had the warrant of God himself, for no human reader had the ingenuity to find more than God had put there."[13]

With the rise of the universities in the eleventh century, theology and the study of Scripture moved from the cloister into the classroom. Scripture and the Fathers were still important, but they came to function more as footnotes to the theological questions debated in the schools and brought together in an impressive systematic way in works such as Peter Lombard's *Books of Sentences* (the standard theology textbook of the Middle Ages) and the great scholastic *summae* of the thirteenth

[12]Robert M. Grant, *A Short History of the Interpretation of the Bible* (New York: Macmillan, 1963), 119. A translation of the well-known Latin quatrain: *Littera gesta docet/Quid credas allegoria/Moralis quid agas/Quo tendas anagogia.*

[13]G. R. Evans, *The Language and Logic of the Bible: The Road to Reformation* (Cambridge: Cambridge University Press, 1985), 42.

century. Indispensible to the study of the Bible in the later Middle Ages was the *Glossa ordinaria*, a collection of exegetical opinions by the church fathers and other commentators. Heiko Oberman summarized the transition from devotion to dialectic this way: "When, due to the scientific revolution of the twelfth century, Scripture became the *object* of study rather than the *subject* through which God speaks to the student, the difference between the two modes of speaking was investigated in terms of the texts themselves rather than in their relation to the recipients."[14] It was possible, of course, to be both a scholastic theologian and a master of the spiritual life. Meister Eckhart, for example, wrote commentaries on the Old Testament in Latin and works of mystical theology in German, reflecting what had come to be seen as a division of labor between the two.

An increasing focus on the text of Scripture led to a revival of interest in its literal sense. The two key figures in this development were Thomas Aquinas (d. 1274) and Nicholas of Lyra (d. 1340). Thomas is best remembered for his *Summa Theologiae*, but he was also a prolific commentator on the Bible. Thomas did not abandon the multiple senses of Scripture but declared that all the senses were founded on one—the literal—and this sense eclipsed allegory as the basis of sacred doctrine. Nicholas of Lyra was a Franciscan scholar who made use of the Hebrew text of the Old Testament and quoted liberally from works of Jewish scholars, especially the learned French rabbi Salomon Rashi (d. 1105). After Aquinas, Lyra was the strongest defender of the literal, historical meaning of Scripture as the primary basis of theological disputation. His *Postilla*, as his notes were called—the abbreviated form of *post illa verba textus*, meaning "after these words from Scripture"—were widely circulated in the late Middle Ages and became the first biblical commentary to be printed in the fifteenth century. More than any other commentator from the period of high scholasticism, Lyra and his work were greatly valued by the early reformers. According to an old Latin pun, *Nisi Lyra lyrasset, Lutherus non saltasset*, "If Lyra had not played his lyre, Luther would not have danced."[15] While Luther was never an uncritical disciple of any teacher, he did praise Lyra as a good Hebraist and quoted him more than one hundred times in his lectures on Genesis, where he declared, "I prefer him to almost all other interpreters of Scripture."[16]

Sacred philology. The sixteenth century has been called a golden age of biblical interpretation, and it is a fact that the age of the Reformation witnessed an explosion of commentary writing unparalleled in the history of the Christian church. Kenneth Hagen has cataloged forty-five commentaries on Hebrews between 1516 (Erasmus) and 1598 (Beza).[17] During the sixteenth century, more than seventy new commentaries on Romans were published, five of them by Melanchthon alone, and nearly one hundred commentaries on the Bible's prayer book, the Psalms.[18] There were two developments in the fifteenth century that presaged this development and without which it

[14]Heiko Oberman, *Forerunners of the Reformation* (Philadelphia: Fortress, 1966), 284.

[15]Nicholas of Lyra, *The Postilla of Nicolas of Lyra on the Song of Songs*, trans. and ed. James George Kiecker (Milwaukee: Marquette University Press, 1998), 19.

[16]LW 2:164 (WA 42:377).

[17]Kenneth Hagen, *Hebrews Commenting from Erasmus to Bèze, 1516–1598* (Tübingen: Mohr, 1981).

[18]R. Gerald Hobbs, "Biblical Commentaries," *OER* 1:167-71. See in general David C. Steinmetz, ed., *The Bible in the Sixteenth Century* (Durham: Duke University Press, 1990).

could not have taken place: the invention of printing and the rediscovery of a vast store of ancient learning hitherto unknown or unavailable to scholars in the West.

It is now commonplace to say that what the computer has become in our generation, the printing press was to the world of Erasmus, Luther, and other leaders of the Reformation. Johannes Gutenberg, a goldsmith by trade, developed a metal alloy suitable for type and a machine that would allow printed characters to be cast with relative ease, placed in even lines of composition and then manipulated again and again, making possible the mass production of an unbelievable number of texts. In 1455, the Gutenberg Bible, the masterpiece of the typographical revolution, was published at Mainz in double columns in gothic type. Forty-seven copies of the beautiful Gutenberg Bible are still extant, each consisting of more than one thousand colorfully illuminated and impeccably printed pages. What began at Gutenberg's print shop in Mainz on the Rhine River soon spread, like McDonald's or Starbucks in our day, into every nook and cranny of the known world. Printing presses sprang up in Rome (1464), Venice (1469), Paris (1470), the Netherlands (1471), Switzerland (1472), Spain (1474), England (1476), Sweden (1483), and Constantinople (1490). By 1500, these and other presses across Europe had published some twenty-seven thousand titles, most of them in Latin. Erasmus once compared himself with an obscure preacher whose sermons were heard by only a few people in one or two churches while his books were read in every country in the world. Erasmus was not known for his humility, but in this case he was simply telling the truth.[19]

The Italian humanist Lorenzo Valla (d. 1457) died in the early dawn of the age of printing, but his critical and philological studies would be taken up by others who believed that genuine reform in church and society could come about only by returning to the wellsprings of ancient learning and wisdom—*ad fontes,* "back to the sources!" Valla is best remembered for undermining a major claim made by defenders of the papacy when he proved by philological research that the so-called Donation of Constantine, which had bolstered papal assertions of temporal sovereignty, was a forgery. But it was Valla's *Collatio Novi Testamenti* of 1444 that would have such a great effect on the renewal of biblical studies in the next century. Erasmus discovered the manuscript of this work while rummaging through an old library in Belgium and published it at Paris in 1505. In the preface to his edition of Valla, Erasmus gave the rationale that would guide his own labors in textual criticism. Just as Jerome had translated the Latin Vulgate from older versions and copies of the Scriptures in his day, so now Jerome's own text must be subjected to careful scrutiny and correction. Erasmus would be *Hieronymus redivivus,* a new Jerome come back to life to advance the cause of sacred philology. The restoration of the Scriptures and the writings of the church fathers would usher in what Erasmus believed would be a golden age of peace and learning. In 1516, the Basel publisher Froben brought out Erasmus's *Novum Instrumentum,* the first published edition of the Greek New Testament. Erasmus's Greek New Testament would go through five editions in his lifetime, each one with new emendations to the text and a growing section of annotations that expanded to include not only technical notes about the text but also theological comment. The influence of Erasmus's Greek New

[19]E. Harris Harbison, *The Christian Scholar in the Age of the Reformation* (New York: Charles Scribner's Sons, 1956), 80.

Testament was enormous. It formed the basis for Robert Estienne's *Novum Testamentum Graece* of 1550, which in turn was used to establish the Greek *Textus Receptus* for a number of late Reformation translations including the King James Version of 1611.

For all his expertise in Greek, Erasmus was a poor student of Hebrew and only published commentaries on several of the psalms. However, the renaissance of Hebrew letters was part of the wider program of biblical humanism as reflected in the establishment of trilingual colleges devoted to the study of Hebrew, Greek and Latin (the three languages written on the *titulus* of Jesus' cross [Jn 19:20]) at Alcalá in Spain, Wittenberg in Germany, Louvain in Belgium, and Paris in France. While it is true that some medieval commentators, especially Nicholas of Lyra, had been informed by the study of Hebrew and rabbinics in their biblical work, it was the publication of Johannes Reuchlin's *De rudimentis hebraicis* (1506), a combined grammar and dictionary, that led to the recovery of *veritas Hebraica*, as Jerome had referred to the true voice of the Hebrew Scriptures. The pursuit of Hebrew studies was carried forward in the Reformation by two great scholars, Konrad Pellikan and Sebastian Münster. Pellikan was a former Franciscan friar who embraced the Protestant cause and played a major role in the Zurich reformation. He had published a Hebrew grammar even prior to Reuchlin and produced a commentary on nearly the entire Bible that appeared in seven volumes between 1532 and 1539. Münster was Pellikan's student and taught Hebrew at the University of Heidelberg before taking up a similar position in Basel. Like his mentor, Münster was a great collector of Hebraica and published a series of excellent grammars, dictionaries and rabbinic texts. Münster did for the Hebrew Old Testament what Erasmus had done for the Greek New Testament. His *Hebraica Biblia* offered a fresh Latin translation of the Old Testament with annotations from medieval rabbinic exegesis.

Luther first learned Hebrew with Reuchlin's grammar in hand but took advantage of other published resources, such as the four-volume Hebrew Bible published at Venice by Daniel Bomberg in 1516 to 1517. He also gathered his own circle of Hebrew experts, his *sanhedrin* he called it, who helped him with his German translation of the Old Testament. We do not know where William Tyndale learned Hebrew, though perhaps it was in Worms, where there was a thriving rabbinical school during his stay there. In any event, he had sufficiently mastered the language to bring out a freshly translated Pentateuch that was published at Antwerp in 1530. By the time the English separatist scholar Henry Ainsworth published his prolix commentaries on the Pentateuch in 1616, the knowledge of Hebrew, as well as Greek, was taken for granted by every serious scholar of the Bible. In the preface to his commentary on Genesis, Ainsworth explained that "the literal sense of Moses's Hebrew (which is the tongue wherein he wrote the law), is the ground of all interpretation, and that language hath figures and properties of speech, different from ours: These therefore in the first place are to be opened that the natural meaning of the Scripture, being known, the mysteries of godliness therein implied, may be better discerned."[20]

The restoration of the biblical text in the original languages made possible the revival of scriptural exposition reflected in the floodtide of sermon literature and commentary work. Of even

[20]Henry Ainsworth, *Annotations upon the First Book of Moses Called Genesis* (Amsterdam, 1616), preface (unpaginated).

more far-reaching import was the steady stream of vernacular Bibles in the sixteenth century. In the introduction to his 1516 edition of the New Testament, Erasmus had expressed his desire that the Scriptures be translated into all languages so that "the lowliest women" could read the Gospels and the Pauline epistles and "the farmer sing some portion of them at the plow, the weaver hum some parts of them to the movement of his shuttle, the traveler lighten the weariness of the journey with stories of this kind."[21] Like Erasmus, Tyndale wanted the Bible to be available in the language of the common people. He once said to a learned divine that if God spared his life he would cause the boy who drives the plow to know more of the Scriptures than he did![22] The project of allowing the Bible to speak in the language of the mother in the house, the children in the street and the cheesemonger in the marketplace was met with stiff opposition by certain Catholic polemists such as Johann Eck, Luther's antagonist at the Leipzig Debate of 1519. In his *Enchiridion* (1525), Eck derided the "inky theologians" whose translations paraded the Bible before "the untutored crowd" and subjected it to the judgment of "laymen and crazy old women."[23] In fact, some fourteen German Bibles had already been published prior to Luther's September Testament of 1522, which he translated from Erasmus's Greek New Testament in less than three months' time while sequestered in the Wartburg. Luther's German New Testament became the first best-seller in the world, appearing in forty-three distinct editions between 1522 and 1525 with upward of one hundred thousand copies issued in these three years. It is estimated that 5 percent of the German population may have been literate at this time, but this rate increased as the century wore on due in no small part to the unmitigated success of vernacular Bibles.[24]

Luther's German Bible (inclusive of the Old Testament from 1534) was the most successful venture of its kind, but it was not alone in the field. Hans Denck and Ludwig Hätzer, leaders in the early Anabaptist movement, translated the prophetic books of the Old Testament from Hebrew into German in 1527. This work influenced the Swiss-German Bible of 1531 published by Leo Jud and other pastors in Zurich. Tyndale's influence on the English language rivaled that of Luther on German. At a time when English was regarded as "that obscure and remote dialect of German spoken in an off-shore island," Tyndale, with his remarkable linguistic ability (he was fluent in eight languages), "made a language for England," as his modern editor David Daniell has put it.[25] Tyndale was imprisoned and executed near Brussels in 1536, but the influence of his biblical work among the common people of England was already being felt. There is no reason to doubt the authenticity of John Foxe's recollection of how Tyndale's New Testament was received in England during the 1520s and 1530s:

[21]John C. Olin, *Christian Humanism and the Reformation* (New York: Fordham University Press, 1987), 101.

[22]This famous statement of Tyndale was quoted by John Foxe in his *Acts and Monuments of Matters Happening in the Church* (London, 1563). See Henry Wansbrough, "Tyndale," in *The Bible in the Renaissance*, ed. Richard Griffith (Aldershot, UK: Ashgate, 2001), 124.

[23]John Eck, *Enchiridion of Commonplaces*, trans. Ford Lewis Battles (Grand Rapids: Baker, 1979), 47-49.

[24]The effect of printing on the spread of the Reformation has been much debated. See the classic study by Elizabeth L. Eisenstein, *The Printing Press as an Agent of Change* (Cambridge: Cambridge University Press, 1979). More recent studies include Mark U. Edwards Jr., *Printing, Propaganda and Martin Luther* (Minneapolis: Fortress, 1994), and Andrew Pettegree and Matthew Hall, "The Reformation and the Book: A Reconsideration," *Historical Journal* 47 (2004): 1-24.

[25]David Daniell, *William Tyndale: A Biography* (New Haven: Yale University Press, 1994), 3.

> The fervent zeal of those Christian days seemed much superior to these our days and times; as manifestly may appear by their sitting up all night in reading and hearing; also by their expenses and charges in buying of books in English, of whom some gave five marks, some more, some less, for a book: some gave a load of hay for a few chapters of St. James, or of St. Paul in English.[26]

Calvin helped to revise and contributed three prefaces to the French Bible translated by his cousin Pierre Robert Olivétan and originally published at Neuchâtel in 1535. Clément Marot and Beza provided a fresh translation of the Psalms with each psalm rendered in poetic form and accompanied by monophonic musical settings for congregational singing. The Bay Psalter, the first book printed in America, was an English adaptation of this work. Geneva also provided the provenance of the most influential Italian Bible published by Giovanni Diodati in 1607. The flowering of biblical humanism in vernacular Bibles resulted in new translations in all of the major language groups of Europe: Spanish (1569), Portuguese (1681), Dutch (New Testament, 1523; Old Testament, 1527), Danish (1550), Czech (1579–1593/94), Hungarian (New Testament, 1541; complete Bible, 1590), Polish (1563), Swedish (1541), and even Arabic (1591).[27]

Patterns of Reformation

Once the text of the Bible had been placed in the hands of the people, in cheap and easily available editions, what further need was there of published expositions such as commentaries? Given the Protestant doctrine of the priesthood of all believers, was there any longer a need for learned clergy and their bookish religion? Some radical reformers thought not. Sebastian Franck searched for the true church of the Spirit "scattered among the heathen and the weeds" but could not find it in any of the institutional structures of his time. *Veritas non potest scribi, aut exprimi*, he said, "truth can neither be spoken nor written."[28] Kaspar von Schwenckfeld so emphasized religious inwardness that he suspended external observance of the Lord's Supper and downplayed the readable, audible Scriptures in favor of the Word within. This trajectory would lead to the rise of the Quakers in the next century, but it was pursued neither by the mainline reformers nor by most of the Anabaptists. Article 7 of the Augsburg Confession (1530) declared the one holy Christian church to be "the assembly of all believers among whom the Gospel is purely preached and the holy sacraments are administered according to the Gospel."[29]

Historians of the nineteenth century referred to the material and formal principles of the Reformation. In this construal, the matter at stake was the meaning of the Christian gospel: the liberating insight that helpless sinners are graciously justified by the gift of faith alone, apart from any works or merits of their own, entirely on the basis of Christ's atoning work on the cross. For Luther especially, justification by faith alone became the criterion by which all other doctrines and

[26]Foxe, *Acts and Monuments*, 4:218.

[27]On vernacular translations of the Bible, see *CHB* 3:94-140 and Jaroslav Pelikan, *The Reformation of the Bible/The Bible of the Reformation* (New Haven: Yale University Press, 1996), 41-62.

[28]Sebastian Franck, *280 Paradoxes or Wondrous Sayings*, trans. E. J. Furcha (Lewiston, NY: Edwin Mellen Press, 1986), 10, 212.

[29]BoC 42 (BSLK 61).

practices of the church were to be judged. The cross proves everything, he said at the Heidelberg disputation in 1518. The distinction between law and gospel thus became the primary hermeneutical key that unlocked the true meaning of Scripture.

The formal principle of the Reformation, *sola Scriptura,* was closely bound up with proper distinctions between Scripture and tradition. "Scripture alone," said Luther, "is the true lord and master of all writings and doctrine on earth. If that is not granted, what is Scripture good for? The more we reject it, the more we become satisfied with human books and human teachers."[30] On the basis of this principle, the reformers challenged the structures and institutions of the medieval Catholic Church. Even a simple layperson, they asserted, armed with Scripture should be believed above a pope or a council without it. But, however boldly asserted, the doctrine of the primacy of Scripture did not absolve the reformers from dealing with a host of hermeneutical issues that became matters of contention both between Rome and the Reformation and within each of these two communities: the extent of the biblical canon, the validity of critical study of the Bible, the perspicuity of Scripture and its relation to preaching, and the retention of devotional and liturgical practices such as holy days, incense, the burning of candles, the sprinkling of holy water, church art, and musical instruments. Zwingli, the Puritans, and the radicals dismissed such things as a rubbish heap of ceremonials that amounted to nothing but tomfoolery, while Lutherans and Anglicans retained most of them as consonant with Scripture and valuable aids to worship.

It is important to note that while the mainline reformers differed among themselves on many matters, overwhelmingly they saw themselves as part of the ongoing Catholic tradition, indeed as the legitimate bearers of it. This was seen in numerous ways including their sense of continuity with the church of the preceding centuries; their embrace of the ecumenical orthodoxy of the early church; and their desire to read the Bible in dialogue with the exegetical tradition of the church.

In their biblical commentaries, the reformers of the sixteenth century revealed a close familiarity with the preceding exegetical tradition, and they used it respectfully as well as critically in their own expositions of the sacred text. For them, *sola Scriptura* was not *nuda Scriptura.* Rather, the Scriptures were seen as the book given to the church, gathered and guided by the Holy Spirit. In his restatement of the Vincentian canon, Calvin defined the church as "a society of all the saints, a society which, spread over the whole world, and existing in all ages, and bound together by the one doctrine and the one spirit of Christ, cultivates and observes unity of faith and brotherly concord. With this church we deny that we have any disagreement. Nay, rather, as we revere her as our mother, so we desire to remain in her bosom." Defined thus, the church has a real, albeit relative and circumscribed, authority since, as Calvin admits, "We cannot fly without wings."[31] While the reformers could not agree with the Council of Trent (though some recent Catholic theologians have challenged this interpretation) that Scripture and tradition were two separate and equal sources of divine revelation,

[30]LW 32:11-12* (WA 7:317).

[31]John C. Olin, ed., *John Calvin and Jacopo Sadoleto: A Reformation Debate* (New York: Harper Torchbooks, 1966), 61-62, 77.

they did believe in the coinherence of Scripture and tradition. This conviction shaped the way they read and interpreted the Bible.[32]

Schools of Exegesis

The reformers were passionate about biblical exegesis, but they showed little concern for hermeneutics as a separate field of inquiry. Niels Hemmingsen, a Lutheran theologian in Denmark, did write a treatise, *De methodis* (1555), in which he offered a philosophical and theological framework for the interpretation of Scripture. This was followed by the *Clavis Scripturae Sacrae* (1567) of Matthias Flacius Illyricus, which contains some fifty rules for studying the Bible drawn from Scripture itself.[33] However, hermeneutics as we know it came of age only in the Enlightenment and should not be backloaded into the Reformation. It is also true that the word *commentary* did not mean in the sixteenth century what it means for us today. Erasmus provided both annotations and paraphrases on the New Testament, the former a series of critical notes on the text but also containing points of doctrinal substance, the latter a theological overview and brief exposition. Most of Calvin's commentaries began as sermons or lectures presented in the course of his pastoral ministry. In the dedication to his 1519 study of Galatians, Luther declared that his work was "not so much a commentary as a testimony of my faith in Christ."[34] The exegetical work of the reformers was embodied in a wide variety of forms and genres, and the RCS has worked with this broader concept in setting the guidelines for this compendium.

The Protestant reformers shared in common a number of key interpretive principles such as the priority of the grammatical-historical sense of Scripture and the christological centeredness of the entire Bible, but they also developed a number of distinct approaches and schools of exegesis.[35] For the purposes of the RCS, we note the following key figures and families of interpretation in this period.

Biblical humanism. The key figure is Erasmus, whose importance is hard to exaggerate for Catholic and Protestant exegetes alike. His annotated Greek New Testament and fresh Latin translation challenged the hegemony of the Vulgate tradition and was doubtless a factor in the decision of the Council of Trent to establish the Vulgate edition as authentic and normative. Erasmus believed that the wide distribution of the Scriptures would contribute to personal spiritual renewal and the reform of society. In 1547, the English translation of Erasmus's *Paraphrases* was ordered to be placed in every parish church in England. John Colet first encouraged Erasmus

[32]See Timothy George, "An Evangelical Reflection on Scripture and Tradition," *Pro Ecclesia* 9 (2000): 184-207.

[33]See Kenneth G. Hagen, "'*De Exegetica Methodo*': Niels Hemmingsen's *De Methodis* (1555)," in *The Bible in the Sixteenth Century*, ed. David C. Steinmetz (Durham: Duke University Press, 1990), 181-96.

[34]LW 27:159 (WA 2:449). See Kenneth Hagen, "What Did the Term *Commentarius* Mean to Sixteenth-Century Theologians?" in *Théorie et pratique de l'exégèse*, eds. Irena Backus and Francis M. Higman (Geneva: Droz, 1990), 13-38.

[35]I follow here the sketch of Irena Backus, "Biblical Hermeneutics and Exegesis," *OER* 1:152-58. In this work, Backus confines herself to Continental developments, whereas we have noted the exegetical contribution of the English Reformation as well. For more comprehensive listings of sixteenth-century commentators, see Gerald Bray, *Biblical Interpretation* (Downers Grove, IL: InterVarsity Press, 1996), 165-212; and Richard A. Muller, "Biblical Interpretation in the Sixteenth and Seventeenth Centuries," *DMBI* 22-44.

to learn Greek, though he never took up the language himself. Colet's lectures on Paul's epistles at Oxford are reflected in his commentaries on Romans and 1 Corinthians.

Jacques Lefèvre d'Étaples has been called the "French Erasmus" because of his great learning and support for early reform movements in his native land. He published a major edition of the Psalter, as well as commentaries on the Pauline Epistles (1512), the Gospels (1522), and the General Epistles (1527). Guillaume Farel, the early reformer of Geneva, was a disciple of Lefèvre, and the young Calvin also came within his sphere of influence.

Among pre-Tridentine Catholic reformers, special attention should be given to Thomas de Vio, better known as Cajetan. He is best remembered for confronting Martin Luther on behalf of the pope in 1518, but his biblical commentaries (on nearly every book of the Bible) are virtually free of polemic. Like Erasmus, he dared to criticize the Vulgate on linguistic grounds. His commentary on Romans supported the doctrine of justification by grace applied by faith based on the "alien righteousness" of God in Christ. Jared Wicks sums up Cajetan's significance in this way: "Cajetan's combination of passion for pristine biblical meaning with his fully developed theological horizon of understanding indicates, in an intriguing manner, something of the breadth of possibilities open to Roman Catholics before a more restrictive settlement came to exercise its hold on many Catholic interpreters in the wake of the Council of Trent."[36] Girolamo Seripando, like Cajetan, was a cardinal in the Catholic Church, though he belonged to the Augustinian rather than the Dominican order. He was an outstanding classical scholar and published commentaries on Romans and Galatians. Also important is Jacopo Sadoleto, another cardinal, best known for his 1539 letter to the people of Geneva beseeching them to return to the Church of Rome, to which Calvin replied with a manifesto of his own. Sadoleto published a commentary on Romans in 1535. Bucer once commended Sadoleto's teaching on justification as approximating that of the reformers, while others saw him tilting away from the Augustinian tradition toward Pelagianism.[37]

Luther and the Wittenberg School. It was in the name of the Word of God, and specifically as a doctor of Scripture, that Luther challenged the church of his day and inaugurated the Reformation. Though Luther renounced his monastic vows, he never lost that sense of intimacy with *sacra pagina* he first acquired as a young monk. Luther provided three rules for reading the Bible: prayer, meditation, and struggle *(tentatio)*. His exegetical output was enormous. In the American edition of Luther's works, thirty out of the fifty-five volumes are devoted to his biblical studies, and additional translations are planned. Many of his commentaries originated as sermons or lecture notes presented to his students at the university and to his parishioners at Wittenberg's parish church of St. Mary. Luther referred to Galatians as his bride: "The Epistle to the Galatians is my dear epistle. I have betrothed myself to it. It is my Käthe von Bora."[38] He considered his 1535 commentary on Galatians his greatest exegetical work, although his massive commentary on Genesis

[36]Jared Wicks, "Tommaso de Vio Cajetan (1469-1534)," *DMBI* 283-87, here 286.

[37]See the discussion by Bernard Roussel, "Martin Bucer et Jacques Sadolet: la concorde possible," *Bulletin de la Société de l'histoire de protestantisme français* (1976): 525-50, and T. H. L. Parker, *Commentaries on the Epistle to the Romans, 1532–1542* (Edinburgh: T&T Clark, 1986), 25-34.

[38]WATR 1:69 no. 146; cf. LW 54:20 no. 146. I have followed Rörer's variant on Dietrich's notes.

(eight volumes in LW), which he worked on for ten years (1535–1545), must be considered his crowning work. Luther's principles of biblical interpretation are found in his *Open Letter on Translating* and in the prefaces he wrote to all the books of the Bible.

Philipp Melanchthon was brought to Wittenberg to teach Greek in 1518 and proved to be an able associate to Luther in the reform of the church. A set of his lecture notes on Romans was published without his knowledge in 1522. This was revised and expanded many times until his large commentary of 1556. Melanchthon also commented on other New Testament books including Matthew, John, Galatians, and the Petrine epistles, as well as Proverbs, Daniel, and Ecclesiastes. Though he was well trained in the humanist disciplines, Melanchthon devoted little attention to critical and textual matters in his commentaries. Rather, he followed the primary argument of the biblical writer and gathered from this exposition a series of doctrinal topics for special consideration. This method lay behind Melanchthon's *Loci communes* (1521), the first Protestant theology textbook to be published. Another Wittenberger was Johannes Bugenhagen of Pomerania, a prolific commentator on both the Old and New Testaments. His commentary on the Psalms (1524), translated into German by Bucer, applied Luther's teaching on justification to the Psalter. He also wrote a commentary on Job and annotations on many of the books in the Bible. The Lutheran exegetical tradition was shaped by many other scholar-reformers including Andreas Osiander, Johannes Brenz, Caspar Cruciger, Erasmus Sarcerius, Georg Maior, Jacob Andreae, Nikolaus Selnecker, and Johann Gerhard.

The Strasbourg-Basel tradition. Bucer, the son of a shoemaker in Alsace, became the leader of the Reformation in Strasbourg. A former Dominican, he was early on influenced by Erasmus and continued to share his passion for Christian unity. Bucer was the most ecumenical of the Protestant reformers seeking rapprochement with Catholics on justification and an armistice between Luther and Zwingli in their strife over the Lord's Supper. Bucer also had a decisive influence on Calvin, though the latter characterized his biblical commentaries as longwinded and repetitious.[39] In his exegetical work, Bucer made ample use of patristic and medieval sources, though he criticized the abuse and overuse of allegory as "the most blatant insult to the Holy Spirit."[40] He declared that the purpose of his commentaries was "to help inexperienced brethren [perhaps like the apothecary Drilhon, who owned a French translation of Bucer's *Commentary on Matthew*] to understand each of the words and actions of Christ, and in their proper order as far as possible, and to retain an explanation of them in their natural meaning, so that they will not distort God's Word through age-old aberrations or by inept interpretation, but rather with a faithful comprehension of everything as written by the Spirit of God, they may expound to all the churches in their firm upbuilding in faith and love."[41] In addition to writing commentaries on all four Gospels, Bucer published commentaries on Judges, the Psalms, Zephaniah, Romans, and Ephesians. In the early years of the Reformation, there was a great deal of back and forth between Strasbourg and Basel, and both

[39]CNTC 8:3 (CO 10:404).

[40]*DMBI* 249; P. Scherding and F. Wendel, eds., "Un Traité d'exégèse pratique de Bucer," *Revue d'histoire et de philosophie religieuses* 26 (1946): 32-75, here 56.

[41]Martin Bucer, *Enarrationes perpetuae in sacra quatuor evangelia*, 2nd ed. (Strasbourg: Georg Ulrich Andlanus, 1530), 10r; quoted in D. F. Wright, "Martin Bucer," *DMBI* 290.

were centers of a lively publishing trade. Wolfgang Capito, Bucer's associate at Strasbourg, was a notable Hebraist and composed commentaries on Hosea (1529) and Habakkuk (1527).

At Basel, the great Sebastian Münster defended the use of Jewish sources in the Christian study of the Old Testament and published, in addition to his famous Hebrew grammar, an annotated version of the Gospel of Matthew translated from Greek into Hebrew. Oecolampadius, Basel's chief reformer, had been a proofreader in Froben's publishing house and worked with Erasmus on his Greek New Testament and his critical edition of Jerome. From 1523 he was both a preacher and professor of Holy Scripture at Basel. He defended Zwingli's eucharistic theology at the Colloquy of Marburg and published commentaries on 1 John (1524), Romans (1525), and Haggai–Malachi (1525). Oecolampadius was succeeded by Simon Grynaeus, a classical scholar who taught Greek and supported Bucer's efforts to bring Lutherans and Zwinglians together. More in line with Erasmus was Sebastian Castellio, who came to Basel after his expulsion from Geneva in 1545. He is best remembered for questioning the canonicity of the Song of Songs and for his annotations and French translation of the Bible.

The Zurich group. Biblical exegesis in Zurich was centered on the distinctive institution of the *Prophezei*, which began on June 19, 1525. On five days a week, at seven o'clock in the morning, all of the ministers and theological students in Zurich gathered into the choir of the Grossmünster to engage in a period of intense exegesis and interpretation of Scripture. After Zwingli had opened the meeting with prayer, the text of the day was read in Latin, Greek, and Hebrew, followed by appropriate textual or exegetical comments. One of the ministers then delivered a sermon on the passage in German that was heard by many of Zurich's citizens who stopped by the cathedral on their way to work. This institute for advanced biblical studies had an enormous influence as a model for Reformed academies and seminaries throughout Europe. It was also the seedbed for sermon series in Zurich's churches and the extensive exegetical publications of Zwingli, Leo Jud, Konrad Pellikan, Heinrich Bullinger, Oswald Myconius, and Rudolf Gwalther. Zwingli had memorized in Greek all of the Pauline epistles, and this bore fruit in his powerful expository preaching and biblical exegesis. He took seriously the role of grammar, rhetoric, and historical research in explaining the biblical text. For example, he disagreed with Bucer on the value of the Septuagint, regarding it as a trustworthy witness to a proto-Hebrew version earlier than the Masoretic text.

Zwingli's work was carried forward by his successor Bullinger, one of the most formidable scholars and networkers among the reformers. He composed commentaries on Daniel (1565), the Gospels (1542–1546), the Epistles (1537), Acts (1533), and Revelation (1557). He collaborated with Calvin to produce the *Consensus Tigurinus* (1549), a Reformed accord on the nature of the Lord's Supper, and produced a series of fifty sermons on Christian doctrine, known as *Decades*, which became required reading in Elizabethan England. As the *Antistes* ("overseer") of the Zurich church for forty-four years, Bullinger faced opposition from nascent Anabaptism on the one hand and resurgent Catholicism on the other. The need for a well-trained clergy and scholarly resources, including Scripture commentaries, arose from the fact that the Bible was "difficult or obscure to the unlearned, unskillful, unexercised, and malicious or corrupted wills." While forswearing papal claims to infallibility, Bullinger and other leaders of the magisterial Reformation saw the need for a kind of Protestant magisterium as a check against the tendency to read the Bible in "such sense as everyone shall be persuaded in himself to be most convenient."[42]

Two other commentators can be treated in connection with the Zurich group, though each of them had a wide-ranging ministry across the Reformation fronts. A former Benedictine monk, Wolfgang Musculus, embraced the Reformation in the 1520s and served briefly as the secretary to Bucer in Strasbourg. He shared Bucer's desire for Protestant unity and served for seventeen years (1531–1548) as a pastor and reformer in Augsburg. After a brief time in Zurich, where he came under the influence of Bullinger, Musculus was called to Bern, where he taught the Scriptures and published commentaries on the Psalms, the Decalogue, Genesis, Romans, Isaiah, 1 and 2 Corinthians, Galatians and Ephesians, Philippians, Colossians, 1 and 2 Thessalonians, and 1 Timothy. Drawing on his exegetical writings, Musculus also produced a compendium of Protestant theology that was translated into English in 1563 as *Commonplaces of Christian Religion.*

Peter Martyr Vermigli was a Florentine-born scholar and Augustinian friar who embraced the Reformation and fled to Switzerland in 1542. Over the next twenty years, he would gain an international reputation as a prolific scholar and leading theologian within the Reformed community. He lectured on the Old Testament at Strasbourg, was made regius professor at Oxford, corresponded with the Italian refugee church in Geneva and spent the last years of his life as professor of Hebrew at Zurich. Vermigli published commentaries on 1 Corinthians, Romans, and Judges during his lifetime. His biblical lectures on Genesis, Lamentations, 1 and 2 Samuel, and 1 and 2 Kings were published posthumously. The most influential of his writings was the *Loci communes (Commonplaces)*, a theological compendium drawn from his exegetical writings.

The Genevan reformers. What Zwingli and Bullinger were to Zurich, Calvin and Beza were to Geneva. Calvin has been called "the father of modern biblical scholarship," and his exegetical work is without parallel in the Reformation. Because of the success of his *Institutes of the Christian Religion* Calvin has sometimes been thought of as a man of one book, but he always intended the *Institutes*, which went through eight editions in Latin and five in French during his lifetime, to serve as a guide to the study of the Bible, to show the reader "what he ought especially to seek in Scripture and to what end he ought to relate its contents." Jacob Arminius, who modified several principles of Calvin's theology, recommended his commentaries next to the Bible, for, as he said, Calvin "is incomparable in the interpretation of Scripture."[43] Drawing on his superb knowledge of Greek and Hebrew and his thorough training in humanist rhetoric, Calvin produced commentaries on all of the New Testament books except 2 and 3 John and Revelation. Calvin's Old Testament commentaries originated as sermon and lecture series and include Genesis, Psalms, Hosea, Isaiah, minor prophets, Daniel, Jeremiah and Lamentations, a harmony of the last four books of Moses,

[42]Euan Cameron, *The European Reformation* (Oxford: Oxford University Press, 1991), 120.
[43]Letter to Sebastian Egbert (May 3, 1607), in *Praestantium ac eruditorum virorum epistolae ecclesiasticae et theologicae varii argumenti*, ed. Christiaan Hartsoeker (Amsterdam: Henricus Dendrinus, 1660), 236-37. Quoted in A. M. Hunter, *The Teaching of Calvin* (London: James Clarke, 1950), 20.

Ezekiel 1–20, and Joshua. Calvin sought for brevity and clarity in all of his exegetical work. He emphasized the illumination of the Holy Spirit as essential to a proper understanding of the text. Calvin underscored the continuity between the two Testaments (one covenant in two dispensations) and sought to apply the plain or natural sense of the text to the church of his day. In the preface to his own influential commentary on Romans, Karl Barth described how Calvin worked to recover the mind of Paul and make the apostle's message relevant to his day:

> How energetically Calvin goes to work, first scientifically establishing the text ("what stands there?"), then following along the footsteps of its thought; that is to say, he conducts a discussion with it until the wall between the first and the sixteenth centuries becomes transparent, and until there in the first century Paul speaks and here the man of the sixteenth century hears, until indeed the conversation between document and reader becomes concentrated upon the substance (which must be the same now as then).[44]

Beza was elected moderator of Geneva's Company of Pastors after Calvin's death in 1564 and guided the Genevan Reformation over the next four decades. His annotated Latin translation of the Greek New Testament (1556) and his further revisions of the Greek text established his reputation as the leading textual critic of the sixteenth century after Erasmus. Beza completed the translation of Marot's metrical Psalter, which became a centerpiece of Huguenot piety and Reformed church life. Though known for his polemical writings on grace, free will, and predestination, Beza's work is marked by a strong pastoral orientation and concern for a Scripture-based spirituality.

Robert Estienne (Stephanus) was a printer-scholar who had served the royal household in Paris. After his conversion to Protestantism, in 1550 he moved to Geneva, where he published a series of notable editions and translations of the Bible. He also produced sermons and commentaries on Job, Ecclesiastes, the Song of Songs, Romans and Hebrews, as well as dictionaries, concordances, and a thesaurus of biblical terms. He also published the first editions of the Bible with chapters divided into verses, an innovation that quickly became universally accepted.

The British Reformation. Commentary writing in England and Scotland lagged behind the continental Reformation for several reasons. In 1500, there were only three publishing houses in England compared with more than two hundred on the Continent. A 1408 statute against publishing or reading the Bible in English, stemming from the days of Lollardy, stifled the free flow of ideas, as was seen in the fate of Tyndale. Moreover, the nature of the English Reformation from Henry through Elizabeth provided little stability for the flourishing of biblical scholarship. In the sixteenth century, many "hot-gospel" Protestants in England were edified by the English translations of commentaries and theological writings by the Continental reformers. The influence of Calvin and Beza was felt especially in the Geneva Bible with its "Protestant glosses" of theological notes and references.

During the later Elizabethan and Stuart church, however, the indigenous English commentary came into its own. Both Anglicans and Puritans contributed to this outpouring of biblical studies.

---

[44]Karl Barth, *Die Römerbrief* (Zurich: TVZ, 1940), 11, translated by T. H. L. Parker as the epigraph to *Calvin's New Testament Commentaries*, 2nd ed. (Louisville, KY: Westminster John Knox, 1993).

The sermons of Lancelot Andrewes and John Donne are replete with exegetical insights based on a close study of the Greek and Hebrew texts. Among the Reformed authors in England, none was more influential than William Perkins, the greatest of the early Puritan theologians, who published commentaries on Galatians, Jude, Revelation, and the Sermon on the Mount (Mt 5–7). John Cotton, one of his students, wrote commentaries on the Song of Songs, Ecclesiastes, and Revelation before departing for New England in 1633. The separatist pastor Henry Ainsworth was an outstanding scholar of Hebrew and wrote major commentaries on the Pentateuch, the Psalms, and the Song of Songs. In Scotland, Robert Rollock, the first principal of Edinburgh University (1585), wrote numerous commentaries including those on the Psalms, Ephesians, Daniel, Romans, 1 and 2 Thessalonians, John, Colossians, and Hebrews. Joseph Mede and Thomas Brightman were leading authorities on Revelation and contributed to the apocalyptic thought of the seventeenth century. Mention should also be made of Archbishop James Ussher, whose *Annals of the Old Testament* was published in 1650. Ussher developed a keen interest in biblical chronology and calculated that the creation of the world had taken place on October 26, 4004 B.C. As late as 1945, the Scofield Reference Bible still retained this date next to Genesis 1:1, but later editions omitted it because of the lack of evidence on which to fix such dates.[45]

Anabaptism. Irena Backus has noted that there was no school of "dissident" exegesis during the Reformation, and the reasons are not hard to find. The radical Reformation was an ill-defined movement that existed on the margins of official church life in the sixteenth century. The denial of infant baptism and the refusal to swear an oath marked radicals as a seditious element in society, and they were persecuted by Protestants and Catholics alike. However, in the RCS we have made an attempt to include some voices of the radical Reformation, especially among the Anabaptists. While the Anabaptists published few commentaries in the sixteenth century, they were avid readers and quoters of the Bible. Numerous exegetical gems can be found in their letters, treatises, martyr acts (especially *The Martyrs' Mirror*), hymns, and histories. They placed a strong emphasis on the memorizing of Scripture and quoted liberally from vernacular translations of the Bible. George H. Williams has noted that "many an Anabaptist theological tract was really a beautiful mosaic of Scripture texts."[46] In general, most Anabaptists accepted the apocryphal books as canonical, contrasted outer word and inner spirit with relative degrees of strictness and saw the New Testament as normative for church life and social ethics (witness their pacifism, nonswearing, emphasis on believers' baptism and congregational discipline).

We have noted the Old Testament translation of Ludwig Hätzer, who became an antitrinitarian, and Hans Denck that they published at Worms in 1527. Denck also wrote a notable commentary on Micah. Conrad Grebel belonged to a Greek reading circle in Zurich and came to his Anabaptist convictions while poring over the text of Erasmus's New Testament. The only Anabaptist leader with university credentials was Balthasar Hubmaier, who was made a doctor of theology (Ingolstadt, 1512) in the same year as Luther. His reflections on the Bible are found in his numerous

[45]*The New Scofield Reference Bible* (New York: Oxford University Press, 1967), vi.
[46]George H. Williams, *The Radical Reformation*, 3rd ed. (Kirksville, MO: Sixteenth Century Journal Publishers, 1992), 1247.

writings, which include the first catechism of the Reformation (1526), a two-part treatise on the freedom of the will and a major work *(On the Sword)* setting forth positive attitudes toward the role of government and the Christian's place in society. Melchior Hoffman was an apocalyptic seer who wrote commentaries on Romans, Revelation, and Daniel 12. He predicted that Christ would return in 1533. More temperate was Pilgram Marpeck, a mining engineer who embraced Anabaptism and traveled widely throughout Switzerland and south Germany, from Strasbourg to Augsburg. His "Admonition of 1542" is the longest published defense of Anabaptist views on baptism and the Lord's Supper. He also wrote many letters that functioned as theological tracts for the congregations he had founded dealing with topics such as the fruits of repentance, the lowliness of Christ, and the unity of the church. Menno Simons, a former Catholic priest, became the most outstanding leader of the Dutch Anabaptist movement. His masterpiece was the *Foundation of Christian Doctrine* published in 1540. His other writings include *Meditation on the Twenty-fifth Psalm* (1537); *A Personal Exegesis of Psalm Twenty-five* modeled on the style of Augustine's *Confessions; Confession of the Triune God* (1550), directed against Adam Pastor, a former disciple of Menno who came to doubt the divinity of Christ; *Meditations and Prayers for Mealtime* (1557); and the *Cross of the Saints* (1554), an exhortation to faithfulness in the face of persecution. Like many other Anabaptists, Menno emphasized the centrality of discipleship *(Nachfolge)* as a deliberate repudiation of the old life and a radical commitment to follow Jesus as Lord.

Reading Scripture with the Reformers

In 1947, Gerhard Ebeling set forth his thesis that the history of the Christian church is the history of the interpretation of Scripture. Since that time, the place of the Bible in the story of the church has been investigated from many angles. A better understanding of the history of exegesis has been aided by new critical editions and scholarly discussions of the primary sources. The *Cambridge History of the Bible*, published in three volumes (1963–1970), remains a standard reference work in the field. The ACCS built on, and itself contributed to, the recovery of patristic biblical wisdom of both East and West. Beryl Smalley's *The Study of the Bible in the Middle Ages* (1940) and Henri de Lubac's *Medieval Exegesis: The Four Senses of Scripture* (1959) are essential reading for understanding the monastic and scholastic settings of commentary work between Augustine and Luther. The Reformation took place during what has been called "le grand siècle de la Bible."[47] Aided by the tools of Renaissance humanism and the dynamic impetus of Reformation theology (including permutations and reactions against it), the sixteenth century produced an unprecedented number of commentaries on every book in the Bible. Drawing from this vast storehouse of exegetical treasures, the RCS allows us to read Scripture along with the reformers. In doing so, it serves as a practical homiletic and devotional guide to some of the greatest masters of biblical interpretation in the history of the church.

The RCS gladly acknowledges its affinity with and dependence on recent scholarly investigations of Reformation-era exegesis. Between 1976 and 1990, three international colloquia on the

[47]J-R. Aarmogathe, ed., *Bible de tous les temps*, 8 vols.; vol. 6, *Le grand siècle de la Bible* (Paris: Beauchesne, 1989).

history of biblical exegesis in the sixteenth century took place in Geneva and in Durham, North Carolina.[48] Among those participating in these three gatherings were a number of scholars who have produced groundbreaking works in the study of biblical interpretation in the Reformation. These include Elsie McKee, Irena Backus, Kenneth Hagen, Scott H. Hendrix, Richard A. Muller, Guy Bedouelle, Gerald Hobbs, John B. Payne, Bernard Roussel, Pierre Fraenkel, and David C. Steinmetz (1936–2015). Among other scholars whose works are indispensible for the study of this field are Heinrich Bornkamm, Jaroslav Pelikan, Heiko A. Oberman, James S. Preus, T. H. L. Parker, David F. Wright, Tony Lane, John L. Thompson, Frank A. James, and Timothy J. Wengert.[49] Among these scholars no one has had a greater influence on the study of Reformation exegesis than David C. Steinmetz. A student of Oberman, he emphasized the importance of understanding the Reformation in medieval perspective. In addition to important studies on Luther and Staupitz, he pioneered the method of comparative exegesis showing both continuity and discontinuity between major Reformation figures and the preceding exegetical traditions (see his *Luther in Context* and *Calvin in Context*). From his base at Duke University, he spawned what might be called a Steinmetz school, a cadre of students and scholars whose work on the Bible in the Reformation era continues to shape the field. Steinmetz served on the RCS Board of Editorial Advisors, and a number of our volume editors pursued doctoral studies under his supervision.

In 1980, Steinmetz published "The Superiority of Pre-critical Exegesis," a seminal essay that not only placed Reformation exegesis in the context of the preceding fifteen centuries of the church's study of the Bible but also challenged certain assumptions underlying the hegemony of historical-critical exegesis of the post-Enlightenment academy.[50] Steinmetz helps us to approach the reformers and other precritical interpreters of the Bible on their own terms as faithful witnesses to the church's apostolic tradition. For them, a specific book or pericope had to be understood within the scope of the consensus of the canon. Thus the reformers, no less than the Fathers and the schoolmen, interpreted the hymn of the Johannine prologue about the preexistent Christ in consonance with the creation narrative of Genesis 1. In the same way, Psalm 22, Isaiah 53, and Daniel 7 are seen as part of an overarching storyline that finds ultimate fulfillment in Jesus Christ. Reading the Bible with the resources of the new learning, the reformers challenged the exegetical conclusions of their medieval predecessors at many points. However, unlike Alexander Campbell in the nineteenth century, their aim was not to "open the New Testament as if mortal man had never seen it before."[51]

---

[48]Olivier Fatio and Pierre Fraenkel, eds., *Histoire de l'exégèse au XVIe siècle: texts du colloque international tenu à Genève en 1976* (Geneva: Droz, 1978); David C. Steinmetz, ed., *The Bible in the Sixteenth Century* [Second International Colloquy on the History of Biblical Exegesis in the Sixteenth Century] (Durham: Duke University Press, 1990); Irena Backus and Francis M. Higman, eds., *Théorie et pratique de l'exégèse. Actes du troisième colloque international sur l'histoire de l'exégèse biblique au XVIe siècle, Genève, 31 août–2 septembre 1988* (Geneva: Droz, 1990); see also Guy Bedouelle and Bernard Roussel, eds., *Bible de tous les temps*, 8 vols.; vol. 5, *Le temps des Réformes et la Bible* (Paris: Beauchesne, 1989).

[49]For bibliographical references and evaluation of these and other contributors to the scholarly study of Reformation-era exegesis, see Richard A. Muller, "Biblical Interpretation in the Era of the Reformation: The View From the Middle Ages," in *Biblical Interpretation in the Era of the Reformation: Essays Presented to David C. Steinmetz in Honor of His Sixtieth Birthday*, ed. Richard A. Muller and John L. Thompson (Grand Rapids: Eerdmans, 1996), 3-22.

[50]David C. Steinmetz, "The Superiority of Pre-Critical Exegesis," *Theology Today* 37 (1980): 27-38.

[51]Alexander Campbell, *Memoirs of Alexander Campbell*, ed. Robert Richardson (Cincinnati: Standard Publishing Company, 1872), 97.

Rather, they wanted to do their biblical work as part of an interpretive conversation within the family of the people of God. In the reformers' emphatic turn to the literal sense, which prompted their many blasts against the unrestrained use of allegory, their work was an extension of a similar impulse made by Thomas Aquinas and Nicholas of Lyra.

This is not to discount the radically new insights gained by the reformers in their dynamic engagement with the text of Scripture; nor should we dismiss in a reactionary way the light shed on the meaning of the Bible by the scholarly accomplishments of the past two centuries. However, it is to acknowledge that the church's exegetical tradition is an indispensible aid for the proper interpretation of Scripture. And this means, as Richard Muller has said, that "while it is often appropriate to recognize that traditionary readings of the text are erroneous on the grounds offered by the historical-critical method, we ought also to recognize that the conclusions offered by historical-critical exegesis may themselves be quite erroneous on the grounds provided by the exegesis of the patristic, medieval, and reformation periods."[52] The RCS wishes to commend the exegetical work of the Reformation era as a program of retrieval for the sake of renewal—spiritual réssourcement for believers committed to the life of faith today.

George Herbert was an English pastor and poet who reaped the benefits of the renewal of biblical studies in the age of the Reformation. He referred to the Scriptures as a book of infinite sweetness, "a mass of strange delights," a book with secrets to make the life of anyone good. In describing the various means pastors require to be fully furnished in the work of their calling, Herbert provided a rationale for the history of exegesis and for the Reformation Commentary on Scripture:

> The fourth means are commenters and Fathers, who have handled the places controverted, which the parson by no means refuseth. As he doth not so study others as to neglect the grace of God in himself and what the Holy Spirit teacheth him, so doth he assure himself that God in all ages hath had his servants to whom he hath revealed his Truth, as well as to him; and that as one country doth not bear all things that there may be a commerce, so neither hath God opened or will open all to one, that there may be a traffic in knowledge between the servants of God for the planting both of love and humility. Wherefore he hath one comment[ary] at least upon every book of Scripture, and ploughing with this, and his own meditations, he enters into the secrets of God treasured in the holy Scripture.[53]

Timothy George
General Editor

[52]Richard A. Muller and John L. Thompson, "The Significance of Precritical Exegesis: Retrospect and Prospect," in *Biblical Interpretation in the Era of the Reformation: Essays Presented to David C. Steinmetz in Honor of His Sixtieth Birthday*, ed. Richard A. Muller and John L. Thompson (Grand Rapids: Eerdmans, 1996), 342.
[53]George Herbert, *The Complete English Poems* (London: Penguin, 1991), 205.

INTRODUCTION TO PROVERBS, ECCLESIASTES, AND SONG OF SONGS

The Reformation of the sixteenth century was a complex set of allied, competing, and at times antagonistic movements that erupted onto the European landscape over the course of a single generation, decisively altering the shape of Western Christendom for centuries to come. Although these movements differed significantly in their aims and origins, they were united by a common conviction that the renewal of church and society was inextricably linked with the renewal of biblical interpretation. Martin Luther's attack on the indulgence trade and subsequent confrontation with ecclesiastical and imperial authorities was sparked by a revolutionary new way of understanding certain themes in Paul's writings. No scene in the early history of the Reformation is more iconic than Luther's unyielding insistence at Worms in 1521 that his conscience was bound to the Word of God, and his recollections later in life of his own intellectual and spiritual development up to that point describe the turning point as hinging on a shift in his understanding of the Bible. Thus, in a passage familiar to most students of the Reformation, Luther relates that he "beat importunately upon Paul" until suddenly "a totally other face of the entire Scripture showed itself" to him, a moment that sparked for Luther a dramatic reconfiguration not only of that one passage in Paul but of the entire Bible itself. Similar stories can be told about analogous "breakthrough" events in other early Reformation movements: a conviction that the veneration of images ran afoul of the prohibitions against "graven images" in the Decalogue, or that the entanglement of church and state in the polities of Christendom represented a deep betrayal of the radical form of community life modeled by Jesus in the Gospels.[1]

The books of Proverbs, Ecclesiastes, and Song of Songs were not the focal point in any of these debates. If the controversies over justification by faith or the purification of Christian worship from idolatry were earthquakes that shook the tectonic plates of dogma and devotion, these books from the Hebrew Bible's Wisdom literature were miles away from the epicenters of seismic activity in the Pauline letters, the Torah, or John's Gospel. This does not mean, however, that Reformation-era interpretation of these books was static or lacking in innovation. The shockwaves of

[1]Accounts of Luther's intellectual development between the onset of the indulgence controversy and the Diet of Worms feature prominently in most critical biographies; see, for example, Scott H. Hendrix, *Martin Luther: Visionary Reformer* (New Haven, CT: Yale University Press, 2015). The quoted passage in which Luther recalls his "breakthrough" moment is from the 1545 preface to his collected Latin works (LW 34:336-38; WA 54:185-86). For a succinct account of how biblical exegesis drove resistance to idolatry among the early Reformed movements, see David C. Steinmetz, "The Reformation and the Ten Commandments," *Interpretation* 43, no. 3 (1989): 256-66.

controversy reverberated through every part of the Bible as exegetes from all the major and emerging traditions set about the work of rethinking settled verities and exegetical assumptions in light of new theological insights. Where Luther "ran through the Bible from memory" in the immediate blaze of discovery, later Protestant exegetes combed through the text methodically in search of analogy, congruence, and confirmation, reconfiguring the shape of the biblical canon to meet the needs of confessional polemic and catechetical instruction. Readers of this commentary will not have to look far to find evidence of familiar reformational themes—justification by faith alone, *sola Scriptura*, the critique of images in worship, controversies over the nature and number of the sacraments, and so on—surfacing in the exegesis of these ancient books of wisdom.

Christian Hebraism

Sixteenth-century interpreters, however, did not merely rewrite the Bible to suit their own doctrinal tastes. On the contrary, the Reformation was from its earliest stages an outgrowth of the Renaissance imperative to return to the sources—in this case, the sources of Christian teaching, especially the Greek and Hebrew of the original texts. For our purposes, this means understanding the commentary tradition of the Reformation in the context of the emerging Christian Hebraism of the sixteenth century. A movement that often cut across confessional lines in its aims and sensibilities, Christian Hebraism was "an offshoot of Renaissance humanism whose devotees—biblical scholars, theologians, lawyers, physicians, scientists, philosophers, and teachers in Latin schools—borrowed and adapted texts, literary forms, and ideas from Jewish scholarship and tradition to meet Christian cultural and religious needs."[2] These needs included the polemical demands of the moment—demonstrating, for example, that the *Hebraica veritas* supported a reformational reading of a particular text, as opposed to the distortions of the Latin Vulgate or "monkish glosses"—but were by no means exhausted by them. Several of the writers featured prominently in this volume, such as Konrad Pellikan, Sebastian Münster, and Ludwig Lavater, were pioneers in the recovery of the Hebrew language and rabbinic biblical scholarship for Christian readers, and virtually all the other scholars sampled here were influenced by their labors to one degree or another.

At the beginning of the sixteenth century, Christian Hebraism was still very much in its embryonic stages. Despite periodic calls for a recovery of scholarship in the biblical languages, few Christian theologians in the Middle Ages could read Hebrew with any real facility. In the fifteenth century, Italian humanists Marco Lippomanno, Giannozzo Manetti, and Pico della Mirandola had devoted themselves to serious study of the language with an eye toward producing more accurate translations of the Old Testament and tapping the wealth of Jewish commentary and scholarship for a Christian readership. But these efforts were slow in forming the necessary academic infrastructure for widespread dissemination, and they were often met with hostility

[2]Stephen G. Burnett and Seth Jerchower, *Hebraica Veritas? An Exhibition from the Collection of the Center for Judaic Studies Library* (Philadelphia: University of Pennsylvania Library, 2000), 5, quoted in Burnett, "Philosemitism and Christian Hebraism in the Reformation Era (1500–1620)," in *Geliebter Feind, gehasster Freund: Antisemitismus und Philosemitismus in Geschichte und Gegenwart*, ed. Irene Diekmann and Elka-Vera Kotowski (Berlin: Verlag für Berlin-Brandenburg, 2009), 136.

from ecclesiastical authorities, as in the celebrated case of Johannes Reuchlin.[3] Both Reuchlin and the Basel humanist Konrad Pellikan learned Hebrew through a combination of self-study and hiring Jewish tutors on an ad hoc basis, but starting around 1515, Hebrew language instruction was integrated into the academic curriculum at a number of universities, including Paris (1517), Wittenberg (1518), Louvain (1520), Ingolstadt (1520), Freiburg im Briesgau (1521), Strasbourg (1523), Basel (1524), Rome (1524), Zurich (1525), Bern (1527), Marburg (1527), and Salamanca (1530).[4]

By the middle of the sixteenth century, most major commentators were at least attempting to reckon with advances in linguistic and textual scholarship, and the interpretive landscape was starting to evolve rapidly as new editions, translations, and exegetical tools began to flood the marketplace. It is difficult to make broad generalizations about how Reformation-era interpreters made use of these new tools, so widely varied was the practice. For some, such as the German Lutheran pastor Lucas Osiander, the Latin Vulgate remained the point of departure for exegesis: his commentary on Ezra, Nehemiah, Esther, Job, the Psalter, the Proverbs of Solomon, Ecclesiastes, and the Song of Songs, first published in 1576, printed the received text in Latin type with his own commentary in italics, and despite the subtitle (*Emended According to the Hebrew Truth*), the corrections were minimal. At the other end of the spectrum, Konrad Pellikan's massive commentary on the entire Old Testament (including the Greek deuterocanonical books), published in four volumes between 1534 and 1538, was based on the author's own translation from the original languages, with only scarce (and usually polemical) reference to the Vulgate. Others, like Philipp Melanchthon, seem to have adopted a more eclectic practice. In his commentaries on Proverbs and Ecclesiastes, Melanchthon gave his own idiosyncratic translation, one that often preserved the wording of the Vulgate, but informed both by the Hebrew and by the Greek Septuagint. The same is also true of the commentaries written by Tommaso de Vio, Cardinal Cajetan. More commonly known today as Luther's nemesis at Augsburg, Cajetan was one of the foremost exponents of Thomism in his generation. But he was also a serious student of the new biblical philology, a fact that belies the simplistic juxtaposition of humanism and scholastic theology.[5]

[3]Johannes Reuchlin (1455–1522) was a German lawyer and humanist, and one of the early transmitters of Christian Hebraism to northern Europe. He published a Hebrew grammar in 1506 and several subsequent works on the kabbalistic tradition and promoted publication of the Talmud and other sources of rabbinic biblical scholarship. These publications, combined with Reuchlin's championing of Jewish rights in the imperial court, led to heresy charges for being "impermissibly favorable to the Jews." Several of Reuchlin's works were eventually condemned, and he was forced into retirement, though by recanting his views he was able to avoid harsher penalties. His case eventually became a cause célèbre for the humanists, who portrayed Reuchlin as a champion of the new learning against the backward obscurantism of the scholastic theological establishment. For an excellent treatment of the affair, see David H. Price, *Johannes Reuchlin and the Campaign to Destroy Jewish Books* (New York: Oxford University Press, 2011).

[4]Stephen G. Burnett, "Christian Hebraism," in *The Oxford Encyclopedia of Martin Luther*, ed. Derek R. Nelson and Paul R. Hinlicky, Vol. 1 (New York: Oxford University Press, 2017), 255. For developments in Christian study of the Hebrew Bible more broadly during this period, see Alastair Hamilton, "The Study of Tongues: The Semitic Languages and the Bible in the Renaissance," in *The New Cambridge History of the Bible*, vol. 3, *From 1450 to 1750*, ed. Euan Cameron, 17-36 (New York: Oxford University Press, 2016).

[5]Michael O'Connor, *Cajetan's Biblical Commentaries: Motive and Method*, St. Andrews Studies in Reformation History (Leiden: Brill, 2019).

This period also saw a proliferation of different types of commentary, or at least of commentaries tailored for particular purposes. At one end of the spectrum, we have highly specialized works of scholarship aimed at an academic readership conversant in Latin, Hebrew, and Greek, and engaging in matters of philology and textual criticism. So, for example, in 1525 Sebastian Münster provided the Hebrew text of the Song of Songs along with his own Latin translation on the facing pages, followed by extensive textual, grammatical, and lexical annotations, a format similar to the annotations of earlier humanists such as Lorenzo Valla and Erasmus.[6] Münster's work proved to be foundational for later Christian Hebraists, commentators, and preachers, but given the narrowly philological focus of his annotations, with little development of the literary or theological significance of his scholarship, its influence remains largely in the background in the present volume. At the other end of the spectrum is an array of publications aimed at a more popular readership, including commentaries focused on theological and pastoral aims, collections of sermons (on entire books or selected passages thereof), verse and prose paraphrases, and other works more difficult to define by genre. In keeping with the aims of the Reformation Commentary on Scripture series, I have tended to favor selections engaging in theological and ethical reflection on the text rather than the purely textual or topical, though when appropriate I have tried to highlight selections that demonstrate how advances in biblical philology influenced theological exegesis.

Between Ancient and Modern

The humanists, biblical scholars, and reformers collected in this volume stood at the onset of an intellectual movement that would have far-reaching effects for the ways in which modern readers understand the Bible. The Renaissance impulse to return to the sources (*ad fontes*) and the Reformation insistence on the Bible as the ultimate norm for theology and practice (*sola Scriptura*) unleashed tremendous intellectual energy directed toward understanding the text in its original, historical contexts. In the centuries to come, these impulses would lead to increasingly critical approaches, as well as a divergence between historical study of the Bible on the one hand and theological interpretation on the other.[7] Both the Protestant reformers and their Catholic opponents stood squarely on the same side of the gap that subsequently would open up between ancient and modern interpretation. The biblical scholar James Kugel has summarized this "ancient" or "precritical" approach to biblical interpretation as bounded by four assumptions: (1) The Bible is a fundamentally cryptic text, with multivalent levels of meaning. Often when the text says one thing, it means another, and the job of the interpreter is to move beyond the surface to penetrate the hidden depths of its meaning. (2) The Bible contains spiritual and ethical guidance of abiding relevance beyond its immediate historical context. The Bible may not have been written *to* later

[6]Sebastian Münster, שִׁיר הַשִּׁירִים *Canticum Canticorum Salomonis, Latine iuxta Hebraicum contextum per Sebastianum Munsterum translatum, atque annotationibus aliquot nonnihil illustratum* (Basil, 1525).

[7]See, for instance, Keith D. Stanglin, *The Letter and Spirit of Biblical Interpretation: From the Early Church to Modern Practice* (Grand Rapids, MI: Baker Academic, 2018); Michael C. Legaspi, *The Death of Scripture and the Rise of Biblical Studies* (New York: Oxford University Press, 2011).

generations of Christians, but it was certainly written *for* their guidance and instruction. (3) The Bible is a perfectly harmonious text, with no contradictions or mistakes; it may be an anthology of texts written by different human authors at different times and places, but despite apparent contradictions its constituent parts are bound together by an underlying unity of purpose. This is because (4) the Bible is a divinely inspired book, by which God speaks to humanity through his prophets.[8]

The Song of Songs: A cryptic text. Taken as a whole, these four assumptions are as much characteristic of the reformers in the sixteenth century as they were of the rabbis and church fathers of antiquity, or the monastic commentators in the Middle Ages. However, subtle differences were beginning to emerge. Consider the first of these assumptions, the notion that the Bible is a cryptic text. It is still widely believed in many quarters that the Reformation represented a rejection of allegorical or spiritual interpretation in favor of the literal or historical sense of the text. To be sure, there is abundant evidence of Reformation polemic against the supposed excesses of medieval allegorization, and if one limits one's purview to exegesis of the Pauline letters, for example, or certain passages in the Gospels, this characterization might appear to be well founded.[9] But the illusion quickly dissipates upon first contact with Protestant exegesis of other portions of the canon, such as the Song of Songs. Without exception, all of the sources collected in this volume agree that the Song is, in its first and primary valence, an allegorical representation of spiritual realities that transcend or even occlude altogether the poem's ostensible meaning at the literal level—that is, as a celebration of human sexuality and erotic desire. I am aware of no published commentary or preaching on this text from the sixteenth century that insists on a purely literal interpretation of the Song, and the few instances we know of when such a suggestion was tendered resulted in considerable scandal—most famously in the case of Sebastian Castellio, who was dismissed from his teaching post in Geneva owing in part to his rejection of the Song from the biblical canon on grounds that it was "a malicious and obscene song in which Solomon describes his shameless acts of lovemaking."[10] Several years earlier, Erasmus had been pilloried by Luther for describing the poem as an "amatory song," even though (unlike Castellio) he did not regard this as undermining the book's authority or its place in the canon. "Is it not an amatory Song?" Erasmus asked plaintively in his defense. "Does 'amatory' always have bad connotations?"[11] For Luther, such a characterization was not only inadmissible but offensive. Other exegetes, like the French Lutheran François Lambert or the Dutch scholar Hugo Grotius, allowed that the

[8]James Kugel, *How to Read the Bible: A Guide to Scripture, Then and Now* (New York: Free Press, 2007), 14-15.

[9]One instance from a mountain of similar statements must suffice here. Commenting on Daniel 10:6, Calvin writes, "I am aware of the plausible nature of allegories, but when we reverently weigh the teachings of the Holy Spirit, those speculations which at first sight pleased us exceedingly vanish from our view. I am not captivated by these enticements myself, and I wish all my hearers to be persuaded of this—nothing can be better than a sober treatment of Scripture. We ought never to fetch from a distance subtle explanations, for the true sense will, as I have previously expressed it, flow naturally from a passage when it is weighted with maturer deliberation." CTS 13:242.

[10]Or so Calvin characterized Castellio's views (CO 11:675); cited in James Alfred Loader, "Calvin and the Canticles," *Studia Historiae Ecclesiasticae* 35, no. 2 (2009): 57-75, at 58.

[11]CWE 76:291.

poem did contain erotic themes, but that these were in turn the bearers of a deeper spiritual meaning, pointing to the ravishing love of God for his people.[12]

How shall we reconcile the reformers' frequent polemics against allegory with their lockstep insistence that the Song be read allegorically? In part, the difficulty lies in the inconsistent use of terminology, both then and now. There simply were no clearly universally agreed-on definitions for terms like *allegory*, *type*, or even *literal sense*.[13] There were, however, broad patterns of usage that can help clarify common interpretive practices. At the risk of anachronism, I shall describe these different modes using a distinction introduced two centuries prior to the Reformation by the Italian poet and theologian Dante Alighieri. Writing in his *Convivio*, Dante sets out a distinction between two kinds of allegory, that of the poets and that of the theologians. Allegory of the poets Dante describes as "a truth hidden under the beautiful lie." This type of allegory is a conscious literary device employed by authors to say one thing while meaning another, "as when Ovid says that Orpheus calmed beasts with his lyre, and made the trees and rocks to move toward him."[14] Nobody supposes that any of this really happened—not even Ovid. The real meaning is that "the wise man with the instrument of his voice makes cruel hearts mild and humble, and moves at will those who have no life of knowledge and art."[15] Notice that with the allegory of the poets, the literal sense is patently false and textual meaning is monovalent: this *for* that. By contrast, the allegory of the theologians is an interpretive strategy employed by readers uniquely in the case of holy Scripture. In this case, the literal sense points to historical realities, and these in turn are interpreted as pointing to transcendent realities beyond themselves.[16] Here the literal sense is presumed to be true, and textual meaning is multivalent: this *and* that. As an example of this second kind of allegory, Dante gives a compact demonstration of the medieval "fourfold method" for Psalm 114, which begins, "When Israel came out of Egypt."

> For if we inspect the letter alone, the departure of the children of Israel from Egypt in the time of Moses is presented to us; if the allegory, our redemption wrought by Christ; if the moral sense, the conversion of the soul from the grief and misery of sin to the state of grace is presented to us; if the anagogical, the departure of the holy soul from the slavery of this corruption to the liberty of

---

[12]Lambert, *In Cantica Canticorum Salomonis*, 1r-2v.

[13]As Deeana Copeland Klepper observes, "Sixteenth-century exegetes were able to abandon the fourfold sense of Scripture in favour of a 'purely' literal sense to whatever degree they did, largely because the innovations of the thirteenth century had provided a model for incorporating figurative language and prophecy within the literal sense." "Theories of Interpretation: The Quadriga and Its Successors," in *The New Cambridge History of the Bible*, vol. 3, *From 1450 to 1750*, ed. Euan Cameron (New York: Oxford University Press, 2016), 437.

[14]My summary in this paragraph follows the exposition by Charles S. Singleton in his celebrated essay "Allegory," in *Dante's "Commedia": Elements of Structure* (Baltimore: Johns Hopkins University Press, 1954), 1-17.

[15]Dante, *Convivio: A Dual-Language Critical Edition*, ed. Andrew Frisardi (New York: Cambridge University Press, 2018), 59.

[16]A classic statement of this view can be found in Thomas Aquinas: "The author of Holy Scripture is God, in whose power it is to signify His meaning, not by words only (as man also can do) but also by things themselves. So, whereas in every other science things are signified by words, this science has the property that the things signified by the words have themselves also a signification. Therefore that first signification whereby words signify things belongs to the first sense, the historical or literal. That signification whereby things signified by words have themselves also a signification is called the spiritual sense, which is based on the literal and presupposes it." Thomas Aquinas, *Summa theologiae* I, q.1, a.10, resp. In *Summa Theologiae Prima Pars, 1-49*, trans. Laurence Shapcote (Lander, WY: Aquinas Institute for the Study of Sacred Doctrine, 2012), 14-15.

> eternal glory is presented to us. And although these mystic senses have each their special denominations, they may all in general be called allegorical, since they differ from the literal and historical.[17]

This distinction between the allegory of the poets and the allegory of the theologians, while never (to my knowledge) employed specifically by Reformation-era writers, can nevertheless go a long way in helping us understand what they were actually doing. When Luther rejects any hint of the Song's "amatory" character while at the same time insisting that he is doing nothing more than getting "at the simplest sense and real character of this book," he is not being inconsistent; he is reading it as an allegory of the poets.[18] That is, he is interpreting the poem as a self-conscious literary device on the part of the author to say one thing while meaning another: "For this is the custom with kings and princes: they compose and sing amatory ballads *which the crowd takes* to be songs about a bride or a sweetheart, *when in fact* they portray the condition of their state and people with their songs."[19] Thus, for Luther the meaning is monovalent: this *for* that. Anyone who fixates on the amatory nature of the song makes the same vulgar mistake as the crowd, mistaking form for reality. Contrast this with Lambert, who insists that Scripture often represents spiritual realities under the "type" of bodily—even sexual—realities: "Indeed, if according to the opinion of Paul in Ephesians 5 the pure marriage bed holds a great mystery in Christ and the Church, and if kisses, the womb, the navel, and other such things belong to the sanctity of marriage, then it was necessary to be mindful of all of these in order that the truth signified may fully be opened."[20] Thus, for Lambert the meaning is multivalent: this *and* that; anyone who excludes the bodily and physical risks tearing the Scripture apart. In response to critics who blush at what all this talk of "kisses, breasts, the womb, the navel, flower beds, and all the rest call to mind," Lambert asks in exasperation why they don't also seek to expunge other racy passages, like this one: "You grew and arrived at the flower of womanhood. Your breasts grew large, and your hair sprouted" (Ezek 16:7)! There is no use being squeamish about such things, Lambert argues; they are persistent themes in Scripture, and as such they are both good in themselves and capable of bearing a higher order of meaning.

The reformers thus regarded the Song of Songs as a cryptic text, but they differed dramatically among themselves as to *how* they thought its hidden meanings should be unlocked. In this they were heirs to a long tradition of allegorical interpretation stretching back to the earliest centuries of the Christian era. Though varying considerably in scope and execution, three main trajectories of interpretation may be discerned in the centuries prior to the Reformation. The first, and perhaps the most dominant, was the ecclesiological reading, first expounded by Origen of Alexandria in the third century and brought to classic expression by Gregory the Great at the end of the sixth. This line of interpretation took its point of departure in the ancient rabbinic practice of

[17]This from the "Letter to Can Grande," cited in Singleton, "Allegory," 14.
[18]LW 15:191 (WA 31.2:586).
[19]LW 15:193 (emphasis added).
[20]Lambert, *In Cantica Canticorum Salomonis*, 1r.

reading the Song as a figural representation of God's love for his chosen people, the Jews. Christian exegetes either redirected this referent to the church or argued that the ancient synagogue itself pointed to the consummation of God's jealous and electing love in the Christian community. This mode of interpretation, as E. Ann Matter has shown, was the basic default for Christian interpretation of the Song and lay latent in the other main readings even when not the explicit focus of exposition.[21] The second major interpretive tradition was the tropological (or mystical), a mode of reading that focused on the relationship between God and the individual Christian soul. This approach is most characteristic of the monastic commentaries of the ninth through the twelfth centuries, and is epitomized in the preaching and commentary of Bernard of Clairvaux. Finally, a minor theme building on the first two and arising first in liturgical contexts was the Mariological reading. This interpretation, developed most fully by Rupert of Deutz early in the twelfth century, viewed the Blessed Virgin Mary as the female interlocutor in the poem's dialogue. As the lover addressed directly by Christ, she was both the historical source and embodiment of the church, as well as the ideal "model of monastic virtues: virginity, humility, and obedience."[22]

Early Protestant exegetes embraced the first two of these modes and rejected the third—that is, they tended to interpret the Song either as an allegory of Christ's love for the church or as a figure of the individual soul's growth in intimacy with Christ. Unsurprisingly, given Reformation polemics against medieval monasticism and the veneration of the saints, there was little interest in the Mariological mode of interpretation. Despite these objections, however, there was no shortage of creative approaches to allegorizing the Song. Two particularly ingenious approaches deserve mention. The first is Luther's strategy of reading the poem as an "an encomium of the political order" in poetic form, a text that "deals with matters of the loftiest and greatest kind, namely with divinely ordained governments, or with the people of God."[23] Reading the text as a coded treatise on political theory has struck many later readers as bizarre, and though certain of his insights were picked up and repeated by later Lutheran exegetes, such as Lucas Osiander and Johann Gerhard, Luther's rather idiosyncratic approach seems not to have been widely adopted outside confessional Lutheranism. There was, however, an equally novel and ingenious mode of interpretation among Reformed writers in the commentaries of Thomas Brightman and John Cotton. These English Puritan pastors read the Song as an apocalyptic text, one that unfolds the history of God's people in symbolic form from the earliest stages of biblical history up through their own era, a continuous narrative building up to the consummation of salvation history in the establishment of God's millennial kingdom on earth—an event they regarded as imminent. Modern readers will likely find such interpretive approaches to be overly schematic or fanciful, but both may rightly be regarded as an extension of the earlier ecclesiological mode of allegory, in that

[21]E. Ann Matter, *The Voice of My Beloved: The Song of Songs in Western Medieval Christianity* (Philadelphia: University of Pennsylvania Press, 1990), 86.
[22]Matter, *The Voice of My Beloved*, 163.
[23]LW 15:195, 192.

the aim was to shed light on the intimate and mysterious ways in which God's grace worked itself out in wooing and preserving his chosen people.

Proverbs: A relevant text. The creativity of Protestant exegesis of the Song of Songs during this period only underscores the imperative to read the Bible as a text that speaks to the moral and spiritual needs of its readers. Read allegorically, the Song could lead the faithful into deeper intimacy with Christ or provide comfort for congregations of persecuted dissenters unsure of their place in the turbulent flow of redemptive history. But other texts seemed to bear on the ordinary lives of congregants and citizens in a much clearer and more direct manner. The book of Proverbs, in particular, was viewed as the manual for practical ethics par excellence, and no one did more to establish it in this role for Protestant congregations than Philipp Melanchthon, Luther's right-hand man in Wittenberg. Melanchthon is more widely known for his systematic theology (the *Loci Communes*) and for his exegesis of the Greek New Testament—indeed, his academic appointment was as a professor of Greek at the University of Wittenberg, and he never developed the same mastery of the Hebrew language as he did of Greek. But Melanchthon invested tremendous energy in expounding the book of Proverbs; according to Timothy Wengert, "Next to Romans and Colossians, there was no book of the Bible on which Melanchthon produced more commentaries than Proverbs."[24] Why did Melanchthon invest so much time and effort on this book? At first blush, the choice seems rather strange; we might expect that he would have had more pressing exegetical work in other parts of the biblical canon, where the new humanistic learning and Luther's revolutionary theological insights were forcing the reevaluation of central Christian doctrines and practices. Lecturing and writing on the Proverbs may seem like a retreat into a relative biblical backwater, but set in the context of humanist educational reforms, Melanchthon's interest in the Proverbs makes perfect sense.

By the time Melanchthon took up his teaching post in Wittenberg in 1518, Erasmus had just released the third edition of his celebrated *Adages*, a work intended to harvest the practical wisdom and literary elegance of pagan antiquity for a revivified curriculum of Christian moral formation. Erasmus was convinced that these pagan proverbs, more so than the ancient myths or fables, lent themselves most readily to adaptation and assimilation in a wider body of Christian learning. According to one scholar, Erasmus felt that the legacy of classical antiquity was most clearly captured "in proverbs, in excerpts, in gemlike and durable fragments, or in texts which, like Homer's, seem made to be weighed and assimilated in fragments."[25] Melanchthon's commentary on the Proverbs seems to be an attempt to do for the Wisdom literature of the Hebrew Bible what Erasmus had done for the adages of pagan antiquity: to demonstrate the abiding value of these gemlike fragments of ancient wisdom for the renewal of Western Christendom. But unlike the *Adages*

[24]Timothy J. Wengert, "The Biblical Commentaries of Philip Melanchthon," in *Philip Melanchthon (1497–1560) and the Commentary*, ed. Timothy J. Wengert and M. Patrick Graham (Sheffield: University of Sheffield Press, 1997), 55. A total of three separate commentaries were published under Melanchthon's name during his lifetime, the first of which was a pirated set of student notes on his class lectures published without his permission.

[25]Daniel Kinney, "Erasmus' *Adagia*: Midwife to the Rebirth of Learning," *Journal of Medieval and Renaissance Studies* 11, no. 2 (1981): 169-92, at 172.

of Erasmus, Melanchthon's commentary on the Proverbs contains a harder theological edge. Though clearly appreciative of the political, economic, and social wisdom contained in the proverbs of pagan antiquity, Melanchthon was at pains to demonstrate the superiority of the wisdom revealed to Solomon. The biblical Proverbs are superior, he observes, not only because of their origin but also on account of their subject matter. Writing in the prologue to his 1529 *Nova Scholia*, Melanchthon contrasted the writings of ancient writers such as Hesiod, Theognis, and Phocylides, who collected proverbs illuminating "the customs of civic life." The Proverbs of Solomon deal with these matters at length, of course, but what makes them different is that they also touch on higher things: "on the will of God, the fear of God, faith, and the cross."[26]

Melanchthon was one of the first, and perhaps the most influential, early Protestant interpreters of the Proverbs, but he was by no means unusual in the way he found contemporary relevance for the text by reading it against the backdrop of the wisdom of pagan antiquity. In fact, one of the most striking features of early modern commentary on the Bible's Wisdom literature is the eagerness of exegetes to coordinate revealed wisdom with secular. Nor should we assume that the contrast was always negative. For many early modern writers—especially those, like Melanchthon, who had been schooled in the texts and methods of Renaissance humanism—the writers of ancient Greece and Rome represented the best of what human wit and wisdom could accomplish on its own, unaided by God's saving grace. Such accomplishments may be incomplete or even at times opposed to the saving knowledge of God imparted in the gospel, but they were of undeniable value in organizing a degree of relative peace, justice, and prosperity in worldly affairs. Seen in this light, it comes as no surprise to find early modern exegetes weighing the biblical wisdom carefully against the harvest of antiquity. When secular writers could be found expressing similar sentiments, it could be taken as evidence that the biblical text was expressing a truth widely available to human reason, and thus one that could serve as a basis for ordering justice in the secular world. When the biblical wisdom was found to stand in tension with the secular, it could be taken as an indication of a revealed truth that transcended the wisdom of this world.

Consider, for example, Melanchthon's exegesis of Proverbs 29:18, "Where there is no prophetic vision the people cast off restraint." He begins by identifying "prophetic vision" with the advice given to rulers by godly prophets, citing the examples of Elisha and Isaiah, who during their lifetimes curbed the worst instincts of the kings of Samaria and Judah. The beneficial effects of their advice can be seen, Melanchthon observes, in the way that each kingdom slid precipitously into ruin after the prophets' deaths. The biblical proverb does not identify the underlying reason for this decline, but Melanchthon sees a corollary principle in some lines from the Roman poet Claudian, who attributed the enduring rule of Rome to the restraint of its laws, in contrast with other fallen empires of the ancient world, which had lacked such restraint:

> Nor will there ever be a limit to the empire of Rome, *for luxury and its attendant vices, and pride with sequent hate have brought to ruin all kingdoms else.* 'Twas thus that Sparta laid low the foolish

[26]Philipp Melanchthon, *Nova Scholia in Proverbia Salomonis* (Hagenau, 1531), 4r.

> pride of Athens but to fall herself a victim to Thebes; thus that the Mede deprived the Assyrian of empire and the Persian the Mede. Macedonia subdued Persia and was herself to yield to Rome. But Rome found her strength in the oracles of the Sibyl, her vigour in the hallowed laws of Numa.[27]

Melanchthon cites only the italicized lines above in his commentary, lines that fill out the contrast implied in the Solomonic proverb: prophetic guidance preserves a kingdom, while luxury, pride, and hate bring it to ruin. The wider context of the original text, which I have quoted above, goes on to attribute Rome's avoidance of these vices to the prophetic guidance of the Sibyl and the laws of Numa. Melanchthon, however, pivots back to the second line of the proverb: "But Solomon goes further, telling what sort of prophetic guidance is needed when he says, 'blessed is the one who keeps the law,' as if to say that prophetic guidance is such that it holds on to true doctrine and true rites of worship, and gives counsels which are congruent with the word of God."[28] In other words, the first line of the Solomonic proverb expresses the exact same insight the sages of ancient Rome had learned from bitter experience, while the second half redirects the content of their piety and doctrine back to the sources of divine revelation in the word of God. Like centuries of Christian readers before them, Melanchthon and the other early modern interpreters believed strongly that the Bible was a source of moral and spiritual wisdom that could guide human behavior in all facets of life, and in the aftermath of the humanist recovery of the wisdom of ancient Greece and Rome they sought to bring the Bible's guidance into conversation with as wide a literary field as possible.

Ecclesiastes: A harmonious text? The Reformation was in large part a battle over the meaning of the Bible—*who* should read it, *how* it should be read, and *whose* judgments counted in applying its teaching or settling disputes over its meaning. But all sides in the disputes of this period more or less took for granted that the Bible was both true and ultimately coherent in its teachings. The rapid diffusion of textual and linguistic expertise championed by the humanists during the fifteenth and sixteenth centuries was accompanied by a shifting set of sensibilities as to how best to understand texts as products, each of a unique historical context. The result was that students of ancient literature became more deeply attuned to the ways in which language itself changed over time, and more wary of anachronism in interpretation.

These new critical sensibilities were on striking display in Lorenzo Valla's *Declamation on the Forged Donation of Constantine* of 1440, which demonstrated conclusively on the basis of internal evidence that the emperor Constantine's purported "donation" of imperial lands and power to the church at the end of his reign was a later forgery.[29] So subversive of papal claims to power was Valla's work that it was placed on the Index of Forbidden Books in 1559—more than a century after its publication!—but there was no stopping the dissemination of the critical questions Valla asked or the demands for historical corroboration. For example, if Constantine had really transferred

[27]LCL 136:54-55.
[28]CR 14:79.
[29]For a succinct account of this incident, see Charles G. Nauert Jr., *Humanism and the Culture of the Renaissance* (New York: Cambridge University Press, 1995), 38-40.

authority over the Western empire to Pope Sylvester I as the document claimed, where were the imperial edicts issued in Sylvester's name? Where were the coins minted with his likeness? Why were there no other documents in the imperial or papal registries attesting to such a momentous political transformation? Moreover, Valla deployed his superior knowledge of classical Latin to demonstrate that the style and vocabulary of the *Donation* could not possibly date to the age of Constantine, but used terminology and forms of address that only developed centuries later. The effect of these arguments on the status of the *Donation* itself was devastating. Apologists for papal power were quick to point out that the jurisdictional claims of the Petrine see did not stand or fall with this one text, nor was Valla himself attempting to overthrow papal power altogether. But the kinds of questions he was asking and the new awareness of language itself as a cultural artifact had implications far beyond the study of papal registries in the Vatican libraries. The implications for the study of the Bible were real and apparent, as Valla himself slyly let drop in one passage: "When I was a boy, I remember asking someone who had written the Book of Job. When he answered, 'Job himself,' I asked the further question of how therefore he managed to mention his own death. This can be said of many other books, although it is not appropriate to discuss them here."[30]

The three books traditionally attributed to Solomon in the Hebrew Bible raised similar, uncomfortable questions. The narrative frame for this attribution was 1 Kings 1–11, which describes the struggle over succession following the death of King David; God's gift of wisdom to Solomon and the fame, wealth, and power that this gift brought to his reign; his construction and dedication of the temple in Jerusalem; and finally his fall into idolatry, led astray by his many foreign wives. This narrative in itself was deeply unsettling: if God had indeed granted Solomon "a wise and discerning mind, so that none like you has been before you and none like you shall arise after you" (1 Kings 3:12), then why was this wisdom insufficient to preserve Solomon from idolatry? True, his father David had sinned spectacularly, but David's lapses had always been presented as isolated incidents, quickly followed by sincere and humble repentance. Not so with Solomon: the Scripture only relates that "his heart was not wholly true to the Lord his God" (1 Kings 11:4), with no mention of any subsequent change of heart. The ambiguous legacy of Solomon is stated concisely by the prophet Nehemiah: "Did not Solomon king of Israel sin on account of such women? Among the many nations there was no king like him, and he was beloved by his God, and God made him king over all Israel. Nevertheless, foreign women made even him to sin" (13:26).

This ambiguity raised a difficult problem for premodern interpreters of the books traditionally associated with Solomon: if they were written prior to his fall into sin, they would seem to be relics of an earlier, immature character, a wisdom as yet untested by all that the world would throw at it. Moreover, at least two of the books in question, Ecclesiastes and the Song of Songs, give strong evidence of the writer's firsthand experience with the delights of the flesh. Is it likely that a young man who had said to himself, "Come now, I will test you with pleasure; enjoy yourself" (Eccles 2:1), only to find in it nothing but vanity, would return later in life to

[30]Lorenzo Valla, *On the Donation of Constantine*, trans. G. W. Bowersock, I Tatti Renaissance Library 24 (Cambridge, MA: Harvard University Press, 2007), 113.

have his hard-won wisdom overthrown by the delights of the harem? On the other hand, if Solomon had written these words after his fall, why is there no account of his restoration in 1 Kings? And why would he have failed to mention the wives and concubines who had led him astray in Ecclesiastes?[31]

Early modern interpreters wrestled with these questions of authorship and the canonical setting of Proverbs, Ecclesiastes, and Song of Songs at some length. Most were content to take at face value the authorial ascriptions and read these texts as products of the same inspired author, albeit at different periods of life. Luther, however, seems to have been one of the first Christian interpreters to introduce doubts on this score. In his published commentary on Ecclesiastes, Luther attributes the text to Solomon, but suggests that he is speaking in a persona, rather than merely relating his own personal experience in unvarnished form:

> I think that these words were spoken by Solomon in some assembly of his retinue, perhaps after dinner or even during dinner to some great and prominent men who were present. He spoke this way after he had thought long and hard to himself about the condition and the vanity of human affairs, or rather of human affections. Then he poured this out to those who were present, as usually happens, and afterwards what he said was put down and assembled by the leaders of the community or of the church. . . . This is, then, a public sermon which they heard from Solomon, on the basis of which it seemed appropriate to call this book Qoheleth—not in the sense that Solomon himself was a preacher but that this book was preached as though it had been a public sermon.[32]

Some decades earlier, Denis the Carthusian had also described Solomon's narrative voice in Ecclesiastes as a shifting set of personas adopted as a literary convention, so both Luther and Denis appear to be introducing a degree of literary distance between Solomon the character (Ecclesiastes) and Solomon the historical figure (1 Kings). Luther had been more explicit on this point two years earlier in the preface to his German translation: "Now this book was certainly not written or set down by King Solomon with his own hand. Instead scholars put together what others had heard from Solomon's lips. . . . That is to say, certain persons selected by the kings and the people were at that time appointed to fix and arrange this and other books that were handed down by Solomon, the one shepherd."[33] But in a dinner-table speech of his own several years later (1533), Luther went even further, suggesting that Ecclesiastes may have been written "by Sirach in the time of the Maccabees," and he compared it to the Talmud as a derivative work stitched together from an assembly of earlier sources.[34]

Even more forceful in his rejection of the tradition of Solomonic authorship was Hugo Grotius, writing a century later. Grotius argued on the basis of Hebrew lexicography that the ascription

[31]For an explicit elaboration of these questions, see the comments of Johann Gerhard on the superscription to the Song of Songs.

[32]LW 15:12 (WA 20:14-15).

[33]WA DB 11.1:23; LW 35:263.

[34]WA Tr 1:207, no. 698. Scott Jones has argued forcefully that the transcriber of Luther's *Tischreden* mistook "Ecclesiastes" for "Ecclesiasticus" in this instance, with the result that Luther is better understood as offering comment on the authorship of Sirach, not "the Preacher." Jones, "Solomon's Table Talk: Martin Luther on the Authorship of Ecclesiastes," *Scandinavian Journal of the Old Testament* 28, no. 1 (2014): 81-90.

"Qoheleth" was better translated as "the Gatherer" than "the Preacher," with the result that the book ought to be viewed, like Job, as a largely fictional construct assembled for the purpose of showcasing the full range of opinions on what makes for human happiness offered by the various philosophical schools current at the time of its writing. And like Valla with the *Donation of Constantine* two centuries earlier, for Grotius it was the linguistic arguments that clinched the case: "For my part, however, I do not think that it is Solomon's; rather, it was written later under the name of that king, as though he had been led to repentance. In support of this argument I can point to many words which you will not find anywhere else but in Daniel, Esdras, and other Chaldean translations."[35] It is important to note that for none of the interpreters discussed above did these considerations regarding authorship undermine the essential truth of the text or the appropriateness of canonical interpretation. Whether or not Solomon was the *literal* author of Ecclesiastes (or of Proverbs or the Song of Songs), he was clearly the implied *literary* author, which meant that the text was best understood within the broad narrative sweep of the Israelite monarchy at apogee, and even authors like Luther and Grotius who expressed doubts as to Solomonic authorship continued to read the text within this canonical narrative framework.

Three inspired texts. The biblical scholars and commentators who appear in the following pages were united by a common love and veneration for the Bible as God's word for humanity, and the assiduous efforts they lavished on its every word and turn of phrase bear witness to their conviction that here, above all other places, is where the highest wisdom can be found. In the sermons, commentaries, treatises, and paraphrases produced by these early modern pastors and scholars, we can catch a sense of the urgency that infused their reading of Scripture, their sense of answering the critical demands of a moment when careful exegesis of the Bible mattered. It mattered because they stood at a critical junction in history, when old habits of thought and speech and worship were being reconfigured in light of a fresh understanding of Scripture's message. Far from being a sterile academic exercise or a futile gesture of protest against an indifferent secular world, Reformation engagement with Scripture responded to a swiftly changing landscape and set the agenda for congregations and for kingdoms.

The books of Proverbs, Ecclesiastes, and Song of Songs cover a wide range of literary genres and an even wider range of thematic topics. The book of Proverbs alone is a veritable encyclopedia of practical ethics, touching on matters of politics and the common good; money and economic justice; marriage, sex, and family life; private virtue and public justice. Ecclesiastes had long been read as a treatise urging *contemptus mundi*—that is, a demonstration of the vanity of earthly pleasures and a commendation of the higher, spiritual duties. It retained this character for many early modern exegetes, but when it came in contact with the Reformation theology of salvation by faith alone, and its consequent rejection of monastic asceticism, it was reinterpreted as a commendation of those same worldly goods, received as gifts from the God who gives all things freely. The Song of Songs, as I have already observed, was often read as a cipher pointing to the mysteries of

[35]Grotius, *Annotationes in Vetus Testamentum*, 258.

God's love for his people, but increasingly it came to be acknowledged (even if only tacitly) that even the most intimate delights of the body could also be received as God's good gifts.

Given the staggering diversity of subject matter covered in these books, it is impossible to do justice to the breadth, depth, and creative brilliance of exegetical insight stretching over the roughly two centuries this commentary series aims to cover. I make no pretense at having presented a complete or even representative sampling of the exegetical perspectives on offer. The reader will no doubt notice that I have played favorites from time to time: Cardinal Cajetan, Philipp Melanchthon, and Michel Cop on the Proverbs; Martin Luther and Jean de Serres on Ecclesiastes; Theodore Beza, Melchior Hoffman, and the English Puritans on the Song of Songs. In each section of the commentary these "mainstays" seemed to me to have set the agenda for other interpreters, who often responded to their exegesis. When possible, I have tried to give my readers a sense of the lively cut and thrust of exegetical debate as it developed around certain passages—for example, debates over the nature of work and vocation in Proverbs 6 or Christology in Proverbs 8; the propriety of usury in Proverbs 28 or slavery in Ecclesiastes 2; the nature of allegory and figural interpretation running all through the Song. But on the whole, I have followed my own judgment in presenting selections that struck me as particularly insightful, novel, influential, or just plain eyebrow-raising. I hope readers will find themselves as captivated as I have been in watching these early modern interpreters at work and be drawn—as were they themselves—back to the sources.

COMMENTARY ON PROVERBS

Overview: The book of Proverbs presented Reformation-era commentators with both a challenge and an opportunity: the challenge was to find common themes within what often seemed to be disparate or loosely-held-together pieces of advice and admonition; the opportunity was to apply this biblical wisdom to their ministries, their theologies, and the lives of those they served. In their introductory comments on the book, they considered several questions that resonate throughout their interpretation of the text: What exactly is a proverb? What is the place of this book among the works often ascribed to Solomon? And, most importantly, what is the nature of biblical wisdom, how does it compare to other forms of wisdom, and how does it apply to the Christian life?

Three Kinds of Wisdom. Denis the Carthusian: "The Lord said to Solomon: 'Because you have asked for wisdom. . . . Behold! I have given you a wise and understanding heart, in so much as there has been no one like you before, nor will there arise after you.'" In these words three things are mentioned: first, the excellence of the wisdom granted to Solomon; second, in what way or from whom he received it; and third, the meritorious cause of this generous infusion of wisdom—namely, that when given the option to ask for whatever he wanted, he asked for wisdom rather than riches, long life, or fame, or triumph.

In short, wisdom was given to Solomon that was both wide-ranging and supernaturally infused. First of all, there is that wisdom which is numbered first among the seven gifts of the Holy Spirit, and it consists of a supernaturally infused habit by which the created mind discerns and contemplates divine things with an internal sense; also, it judges accurately the highest and unchanging Good by virtue of participation in its nature, and by the conformity of its affections to that knowledge. And so it is by this wisdom that a person discerns—not with a bare and unformed knowledge, but with formed knowledge and an engaged will—that God alone is to be enjoyed, and that he must devote himself wholly to God and cling to him to the very end. This is what he feels and senses with an internal sensibility. This wisdom cannot be formless; indeed, it is inseparably linked with charity, so that whoever exists in a state of salvation (that is, in charity and grace) has this wisdom to some degree. And the more one grows in charity, the more do they grow in that wisdom. . . .

The second type of supernatural wisdom is the gift and habit of the gift freely given [*gratia gratis data*], by which a person knows and can do those things which pertain to faith—proclaiming, proving, and defending it. As Augustine writes in this connection, "You have faith itself, but you do not have the ability and the resources to defend the faith."† This wisdom can be unformed; that is, it can exist apart from charity and saving grace [*gratia gratum faciente*]; it is common among both the virtuous and the vicious, just like the other freely given gifts. Concerning these, the apostle writes, "To one is given through the Spirit the utterance of wisdom, and to another the utterance of knowledge." This wisdom, although given by infusion to the glorious apostles and to many other saints, can nevertheless be obtained by reading, by listening, and by study of the sacred Scriptures and other theological texts; indeed, it is continually learned by students and by the studious. This wisdom was also infused by grace into Solomon in great abundance. . . .

The third type of wisdom is natural, or philosophical. This kind of wisdom can be found and obtained by natural light and by study, even though it is granted to some by an infusion of grace. And this kind of wisdom is sometimes taken more broadly in reference to all true knowledge that can be acquired and discovered by natural reason. Thus, it comprehends both knowledge [*scientiam*] and prudence [*prudentiam*]. Sometimes it is taken more strictly for the knowledge of divine and immaterial things. But this wisdom (in the broader sense) seems to have been infused into Solomon to an exceptional degree, such that there has been none greater than him before or after, excepting only Christ and the first-created human (Adam). (Though Jerome says of Aristotle that he was certainly a great miracle among the whole human race, since whatever could be known by nature seems to have been infused into him.[‡] Let this be understood in the most pious sense.)

Moreover, the Scripture seems to imply that Solomon was preeminent in all these types of wisdom—in natural knowledge, moral, and rational—all at the same time. For we read in 1 Kings that "God gave to Solomon wisdom, and understanding exceeding much, and greatness of heart, as the sand that is on the sea shore. And the wisdom of Solomon surpassed the wisdom of all the Orientals, and of the Egyptians; and he was wiser than all men. . . . Solomon also spoke three thousand parables, and his poems were five thousand. And he treated about trees, from the cedar that is in Lebanon to the hyssop that grows out of the wall; and he spoke of beasts, and of fowls, and of creeping things, and of fishes." And again, in the person of Solomon the following is said: "God gave me the true knowledge of things that exist: to know the disposition of the whole world and the virtues of the elements; the beginning and ending, and the middle of times, the alterations of their courses, and the changes of seasons; the revolutions of the year and the dispositions of the stars; the natures of living creatures and rage of wild beasts; the force of winds and the reasonings of people; the diversities of plants and the virtues of roots." Since, therefore, Solomon's wisdom was so great, it is clear that his words contain the highest wisdom and ought to be studied with great diligence. EXPOSITION OF THE BOOK OF PROVERBS.[1]

THE PLACE OF PROVERBS IN SOLOMON'S TRILOGY. FRANCIS TAYLOR: Three works there are of Solomon's in Scripture, arguments of that large wisdom which God gave him resembling his people: the one like the sand on the seashore; the other like the dust of the earth; [the third] that he begged and received. . . . The Proverbs set out true wisdom; Ecclesiastes, worldly vanity; and Canticles, heavenly love. The first teaches us how to live in the world. The second, how to wean us from the world. The third, how to rejoice in the love of Christ. And Solomon varies the title suitably to the occasion. In the beginning of the Proverbs, he writes himself "king of Israel," that he might teach all his people. In Ecclesiastes he calls himself "king in Jerusalem," that the people who had seen his vanity there might not imitate it. In the Canticles, he takes no kingly title at all—nothing but bare Solomon: "He is content with his own name, taking no notice that he was a king."[†] He had no

[1]DCOO 7:3-4; citing 1 Kings 3:11-12; Is 11:2; 1 Cor 12:8; 1 Kings 4:29-33; Wis 7:17-20. [†]A loose paraphrase of the following passage in Augustine's *Sermon* 240: "Those who know how to defend this case are more learned than the rest, not more faithful. They have faith, they have the ability to defend the faith. Others lack this ability and the resources and learning to defend the faith, but have the faith itself" (240.1; PL 38:1151; WSA 3.7:65). Denis is using this passage as warrant for the scholastic distinction between saving grace (*gratia gratum faciens*) and the spiritual gifts that God bestows according to his own counsel (*gratia gratis data*). [‡]The source of the quotation is obscure. Maarten Hoenen notes a parallel citation in another work of Denis (*Epistola de cursu puerorum*), suggesting that it may be an allusion to Jerome's *Commentary on Jonah*, cap. (s. s.) 3, 6/9 (CCSL 76:408), though Hoenen also observes that the wording more closely resembles a passage in Averroes (*In de anima* 3, comm. 14). Hoenen, "Denys the Carthusian and Heymeric de Campo on the Pilgrimages of Children to Mont-Saint-Michel," *Archives d'histoire doctrinale et littéraire du moyen âge* 61 (1994): 387-418.

title to Christ's love as a king. Every good subject of his had as much title to it as he. An Exposition with Practical Observations.[2]

What Is a Proverb? Desiderius Erasmus: There are two things that are peculiar to the character of a proverb: common usage and novelty. This means that it must be well known and in popular currency; for this is the origin of the word *paroimia* in Greek (from *oimos*, a road, as though well-polished in use and circulating), that which travels everywhere on the lips of men and women, and of *adagium* in Latin, as if you should say "something passed round," following Varro. And then it must be shrewd, so as to have some mark, as it were, to distinguish it from ordinary talk. But we cannot immediately rank in this category everything that has passed into popular speech or contains an unusual image; it must be recommended by its antiquity and erudition alike, for that is what I call shrewd.

Proverbs get into popular speech, either from the oracles of the gods, like "Neither the third nor the fourth,"[†] or from the sayings of sages, which indeed circulated in antiquity as if they were oracles, such as "Good things are difficult."[‡] Or else they come from some very ancient poet, as for instance Homer's "When a thing is done, a fool can see it,"[§] or Pindar's "To kick against the goad,"[◊] or from Sappho, "No bees, no honey";[Δ] for at a time when tongues were as yet uncorrupted, the verses of the poets were also sung at feasts. Or they may come from the stage—that is, from tragedies and comedies, like this from Euripides: "Upwards flow the streams,"[††] or this from Aristophanes: "Off with you to the crows!"[‡‡] It is comedy especially which by a mutual give-and-take, adopts many of the expressions in constant use among the common people, and in turn gives birth to others that are passed on to them for constant use. Some are derived from the subjects of legend, such as the great jar that cannot be filled from the story of the daughters of Danaus,[§§] or the helmet of Orcus from the tale of Perseus.[◊◊] Some arise from fables, among which we find "But we see not what is in the wallet behind."[ΔΔ] Occasionally they are born from an actual occurrence: "Leucon carries some things; his ass carries others."[†††] Several are borrowed from history: "Rome wins by sitting still."[‡‡‡] Others come from apothegms—that is, from quick witty replies, like that remark "Who does not own himself would Samos own."[§§§] There are some that are snatched from a word rashly spoken, such as "Hippocleides doesn't care."[◊◊◊] In a word, the behavior, the natural qualities of any race or individual or even of an animal, or last, any power belonging even to a thing, if remarkable and commonly known—all these have given occasion for an adage. . . .

Now in case anyone should impatiently thrust aside this aspect of learning as too humble, perfectly easy and almost childish, I will explain in a few words how much respect was earned by these apparent trivialities among the ancients. . . . To start with, that an acquaintance with adages was held to be not unimportant by the greatest men is sufficiently proved, I think, by the fact that authors of the first distinction have thought them a worthy subject for a number of volumes diligently compiled. . . . But why should I be talking of these people, when the Hebrew sages themselves did not hesitate to bring out more than one book with this title, and to enclose the venerable mysteries of the unsearchable deity in proverbs which the intellects of so many and such great theologians have struggled to elucidate, as they are struggling to this day? . . .

Then who would dare to despise this mode of speech, when they saw that some of the oracles of the holy prophets are made of proverbs? One example of this is "The fathers have eaten sour grapes, and the children's teeth are set on edge." Who would not revere them as an almost holy thing, fit to express the mysteries of religion, since Christ himself, whom we ought to imitate in all things, seems to have taken a particular delight in

[2]Taylor, *An Exposition with Practicall Observations upon the First Three Chapters of the Proverbs*, 1-2; citing 1 Kings 4:29; 2 Chron 1:9-12; Eccles 1:1; Song 1:1. [†]Jerome, *Commentary on Ecclesiastes* (PL 23:1013).

this way of speaking? An adage is current in Greek: "I judge the tree by its fruit."[ΔΔΔ] In Luke we read the same thing: "A good tree does not bear corrupt fruit, neither does a corrupt tree bear good fruit." . . . Christ cites a proverb from children playing in the marketplace: "We have piped to you and you have not danced; we have mourned to you, and you have not wept." This is very like that saying in Theognis, if one may compare sacred with profane: "For Jove himself may not content us all, / Whether he holds rain back or lets it fall."[††††] Adages.[3]

[3]CWE 34:4-5, 9-10, 13*; citing Jer 31:29; Lk 6:43; Mt 11:17. [†]"The Megarians are neither the third nor the fourth." Erasmus explains, "This used to be said in old days of exceptionally idle and worthless people who had no claims to respect at all." *Adagia* 2.1.79 (CWE 33:61). [‡]Plato, *Cratylus* 384b; *Adagia* 2.1.12. [§]Homer, *Iliad* 17.31-2; 20.197-98; *Adagia* 1.1.30 [◊]Terence, *Phormio* 77-78; *Adagia* 1.3.46. Oddly, Erasmus omits mention of the fact that Paul reports a voice from heaven speaking these words in Aramaic in Acts 26:14. [Δ]Diogenianus, *Paroemiographi Graeci* 6.58; *Adagia* 1.6.62. [††]Euripides, *Medea* 410-13; *Adagia* 1.3.15. [‡‡]Aristophanes, *Nubes* 133, *Plutus* 394, 604; *Adagia* 2.1.96. [§§]"He draws water from a sieve": Plautus, *Pseudolus* 102; *Adagia* 1.4.60. [◊◊]Zenobius, 1.41; *Adagia* 2.10.74. [ΔΔ]"The proverb," Erasmus explains, "took its rise from one of Aesop's fables, which is told as follows by Stobaeus: Aesop said that each of us carries two wallets, one in front and the other behind hanging from our shoulders; and in the front one we put what other men do wrong and our own failings into the back one." *Adagia* 1.6.90 (CWE 33:59). [†††]Zenobius, 1.74; Diogenianus, *Paroemiographi Graeci* 2.21; *Adagia* 2.2.86. [‡‡‡]Varro, *De re rustica* 1.2.2; *Adagia* 1.10.29. [§§§]"This will suit people who demand something outrageous, or who concern themselves with details and neglect the larger issues. Derived from an anecdote preserved by Plutarch in his 'Sayings of Spartans.' When the Athenians had surrendered their city to the victor, they asked that he should at least let them keep Samos, and his reply took the form 'When you are not your own masters, do you expect to master other men?'" Plutarch, *Moralia* 233D; *Adagia* 1.7.83 (CWE 33:117). [◊◊◊]"This adage was used to convey that they were neglecting something and not greatly concerned. It is derived from a story told at some length by Herodotus in the *Erato*. To put it briefly, this Hippocleides was a son of Teisander, who along with many other young men sought the hand of a daughter of Cleisthenes of Sicyon. Cleisthenes tested the suitors for a whole year, during which there was a party at which Hippocleides gave an unseemly exhibition by dancing on his hands with his feet in the air. The father took great offence at the young man's improper levity, and said, 'Son of Teisander, you have danced yourself out of your marriage.' To which he promptly replied, 'Hippocleides doesn't care'; and the remark, as Herodotus tells us, passed into a proverb." Zenobius, 5.31; Diogenianus, *Paroemiographi Graeci* 7.21; *Adagia* 1.10.12 (CWE 33:239).

Theology in Lowly Form. Konrad Pellikan: Proverbs, or comparisons [*similitudines*], which are called parables in Greek, are not the same as adages, which are commonly repeated aphorisms [*sententiae*] enveloped in a comparison—that is, they signify something different from what they say.[†] Rather, they are discourses [*sermones*] and pregnant aphorisms [*sententiae*] conducive to every aspect of faithful living. Though wrapped in lowly form, they contain within themselves much that is of use, such as certain first principles of genuine theology, of which we can make use in understanding the common topics of faith and ethics, as well the whole of sacred Scripture. A Succinct and Universal Commentary on the Bible.[4]

Solomon's Wisdom Excels That of the Pagans. Philipp Melanchthon: Regarding the two modes of speaking, it is customary on the one hand for the dialectical method to proceed in an orderly manner, rendering a universal doctrine much the same way one might erect a building. Or, for example, the way a doctor first speaks concerning the structure of the body, distinguishing its members from its fluids, then moving on to a discussion of birth and the causes of diseases, and finally to speak of treatments. The other mode of speaking involves delivering brief opinions in the form of aphorisms, and it often happens that these are given indiscriminately, with no great concern for order, as for example in the moral precepts given by Phocylides, Theognis, and others. This book by Solomon is a collection of such aphorisms [*sententiae*], and its Latin title is *Proverbia*, though there is a distinction in Greek

[ΔΔΔ]Diogenianus, *Paroemiographi Graeci* 5.15; *Adagia* 1.9.39. [††††]The adage, drawn from the quoted lines in Theognis, is, "Even Jupiter does not please everybody." *Adagia* 2.7.55 (CWE 20:27).

[4]Pellikan, *Commentaria bibliorum et illa brevia quidem ac catholica*, 198v. [†]In his introduction to the *Adagia*, Erasmus considered the definition of a proverb among several Greek authorities as "a manner of speaking which wraps up in obscurity an obvious truth" (CWE 31:3). Although allowing that some proverbs have such "allegorical" character, he rejected the definition as too narrow.

between aphorisms [*gnōmas*] and proverbs [*paroimías*], and also in Latin between *sententiae* and *proverbia*; in Hebrew this is signified by a variety of terms.

An aphorism [*sententia*], or *gnome*, is a brief saying containing a moral precept, or a warning concerning reward and punishment, or a description of good fortune in life, consideration of which is a useful reminder. Examples of such aphorisms are: "Scorn voluptuousness, for cheap pleasures are bought with pain."[†] Or "Remember to disbelieve."[‡] Or "Know thyself."[§] Of rewards and punishments: "Good things come to the children of the pious, not to those of the impious."[◊] Of good fortune: "Pride often runs riot in prosperity."[Δ] Or "Fortune makes fools of her favorites."[††]

A proverb, however, is a widely celebrated saying and generally involves some sort of figure of speech, whether a metaphor, or comparison, or imagery, or hyperbole, or irony signifying something else, whether it contains an aphorism [*sententia*] or some other kind of description. For example: "A leaky jar."[‡‡] Or "Until the Greek calends."[§§] Or "He is going to the crows."[◊◊] Or "An ever-shifting channel."[ΔΔ] These and many other proverbs communicate no aphorism [*sententia*], but they are adapted to signify different things in different circumstances.

Even though there is a distinction between proverbs and aphorisms, many proverbs contain the latter—for example, "You have obtained Sparta; now adorn it."[†††] This is an aphorism, reminding each individual of their own vocation (as we call it): let them understand what is contained within its limits and rightly perform the duties required of them. But it is also a proverb, because it is adorned by a figure and widely known. "We do not see the knapsack on our own back."[‡‡‡] This is an aphorism reprehending an evil self-love that judges others harshly. But it is also a proverb, because it is communicated in figurative terms and is widely known. The following are aphorisms and proverbs: "The censor pardons the crows and convicts the doves."[§§§] "Tortoises conquer both virtue and wisdom."[◊◊◊]

With so many sayings in this book that are both aphorisms and proverbs, the title of Proverbs is not a bad fit; however, whether the title be aphorisms or proverbs, it must still be known that this is a collected treasury of the sweetest aphorisms, which are precepts concerning all the virtues.[ΔΔΔ]

But we ought always to bear in mind that the chief summary of teaching on the virtues, adapted for our comprehension, is contained in the Decalogue. Here also [in Proverbs] is taught what must be done, and the various types of maxims may be divided up in accordance with the commandments of the Decalogue. These types can be given as follows: some are theological, and these address matters concerning God and the precepts of the first table; others are political, addressing the duties of governance; others are ethical, giving instruction on mores common to everyone; still others are economic, speaking on matters of marriage and domestic affairs. . . .

But it is necessary even at the outset to be reminded that there is a great difference between the pagan *gnomologias*—for example, of Phocylides or Theognis—and those handed down by Solomon in the church of God, just as there is said to be a difference in kind between philosophy and the teaching which resounds in the church. Even as philosophy retains a fragment of the law, so also Phocylides says something about the wrath of God and the penalties of crime. But concerning the Mediator, the remission of sins, reconciliation, true prayer, faith and hope, the nearness of God in our calamities, he says nothing, even though he recites many precepts pertaining to the second table of the Decalogue. But Solomon often addresses the true knowledge of God and how to approach him, as well as the other virtues pertaining to the first table of the law; for example: "the beginning of wisdom of is the fear of the Lord." And: "Trust in the Lord with all your heart, and do not lean on your own wisdom, in all your ways acknowledge him, and he will direct your paths." Concerning the cross: "The Lord chastises the one he loves, that he not fall away from him." And concerning salvation after this life: "The righteous hopes in his death."

The emperor Julian rated Phocylides higher than Solomon when he argued that there was no greater wisdom handed down in the prophetic and apostolic books than what could be found among the pagans.[‡‡‡‡] Now Cyril points out in refutation of Julian that Solomon is greatly to be preferred [to the pagans] because he preceded them by an age. For Phocylides, who was from Miletus, and Theognis, who was from Megara, lived in the age of Cyrus and Thales. But this puerile response does not satisfy an argument of this gravity. For he should have spoken instead about the true sources of their teaching, whether it be the doctrine of the law or that of the gospel. Granted that Phocylides recited a good part of the law, but of that teaching which is unique to the church—namely, those teachings concerning the revelation of God, both in deed and in testimony, concerning the great promises which make up the gospel, announcing the remission of sins and offering eternal life on account of the Son, or concerning the consolation in the cross—on these high matters the pagan scribes are silent. This difference must always be kept in view, so that we know the doctrine which is unique to the church.

This also must be added by way of preface: because this book was written for the true church of God, in which the promise of the Messiah was known, we recognize him and desire that, with faith lighting the way, we may contemplate the Messiah by experience in every aphorism, whether it speaks of faith or of works. For example, when in chapter 3 it says, "Trust in the Lord with your whole heart," understand "on account of the Mediator," just as David himself had previously pointed out: "Kiss the Son. . . . Blessed are all who trust in him." Indeed, Solomon expressly commands that this teaching, which was given by God to this people, be embraced. And where mention is made of faith, it is necessary to contemplate the promises. Likewise when it speaks concerning marriage: "Rejoice in the wife of your youth," understand (with faith lighting the way) that the statutes are accepted by God on account of the Mediator, and on account of him are works divinely ordained pleasing to God. Thus the teaching concerning the Messiah is to be grasped everywhere, though it is delivered with greater clarity in the Psalms and Prophets. But indeed, it is indicated here also, because mention is made of the wisdom of God proclaimed in human fashion, which is the Son sent to the church. EXPOSITION OF THE PROVERBS OF SOLOMON.[5]

[5]CR 14:1-6; citing Prov 9:10; 3:5-6; 3:12; 14:32; 3:5; Ps 2:12; Prov 5:18. [†]Horace, *Epistle* 1.2.55. [‡]Lucian, *Hermotimus* 47.23. This proverb—"not mine, it comes from one of the sages"—is followed in the text of Lucian's play by the following explanation: "For if we are not prepared to believe everything we hear, but rather to act like judges and let the next man have his say, perhaps we may escape the labyrinths with ease." (LCL 430:350-51). [§]An ancient Greek aphorism attributed to various sources, including Socrates. [◊]Theocritus, *Idyll* 26.32. [Δ]Ovid, *Ars amatoria* 2.437. [††]Publilius Syrus, *Sententia* 203. [‡‡]Melanchthon appears to be quoting Erasmus's Latin version of Diogenianus's Greek proverb, one that carries two meanings. As Erasmus explains, "The first of these is used of the greedy and rapacious. The second refers to those who are very forgetful; every piece of learning that is poured into them immediately flows away. The same myth is also the origin of the saying that even today continues to be in common use: 'to draw water with a sieve'" (CWE 30:221). [§§]Suetonius wrote of Caesar Augustus that "when he wished to indicate that certain men will never pay, [he said] that 'they will pay on the Greek Kalends.'" *Divus Augustus* 87.1. The Greeks did not divide their year into kalends. [◊◊]The origin of this expression is obscure, but it seems to be the equivalent of "going to the dogs." [ΔΔ]Another obscure image, but Cicero uses similar language in describing the unstable whims of the voting public: "What sea, what channel (*euripo*) do you think exists, which is liable to such commotions—to such great and various agitations of waves, as the storms and tides by which the public is influenced?" *Ad Murena* 17.35, in *The Orations of Marcus Tullius Cicero*, trans. Yonge (London: Bohn, 1856). Whatever the origin, the image clearly refers to an unstable person. [†††]Versions of this saying can be found in Cicero (*Epistulae ad Atticum* 4.6.2) and Plutarch (*Moralia* 602b). In Erasmus's commentary (n°1401), this adage is an exhortation to rulers to content themselves with their own lands and apply themselves diligently to the task of governing. [‡‡‡]Catullus, *Carmina* 22.21. [§§§]Juvenal, *Satires* 2.63. The censor was an ancient Roman office wielding judicial authority—unjustly, in the satirist's view. [◊◊◊]Julius Pollux, *Onomasticon* 8.74.6. The proverb is also found in the writings of one of the early desert fathers, Arsenius the Great (*Apophthegmata* 12.31b), who explains that "the ancients would also stamp a tortoise on coins; whence the expression, 'Tortoises conquer virtue and wisdom.'" I am grateful to my colleague Eunice Kim for help with the translation of this passage from the Doric dialect. [ΔΔΔ]Melanchthon had titled an earlier edition of his commentary *Sententiae*, or "maxims," but in

HEAVENLY WISDOM TEACHING CHRIST. MICHEL COP: Although we are not kings or worldly princes, nor do we have public office, yet we ought to follow the wisdom of good kings and princes, as they are given to us by God for an example. And even though we do not always have wise superiors, as experience teaches us, we still need at all times to be wise, unless we want to perish with the foolish. For neither the folly of the great nor that of the small will be excused from guilt of damnation, if we follow it and delight in it. And for this reason, Solomon was not only content to be a mirror of wisdom to those of his own time, but he also desired to be a profit to all ages, so long as the world should last, and so he has written these notable proverbs and excellent sayings, profitable to teach one to govern oneself wisely in all holiness and honesty, in all righteousness and innocence, in all modesty and sobriety, in the faith and fear of God, as it will be understood by those who hear and read them. . . .

Therefore we must be neither deaf nor negligent, but ready and diligent to hear the Proverbs of King Solomon, in which he promises above all to teach us wisdom—not the wisdom of this world, nor of the princes of this world, which passes away. Such wisdom is foolishness before God, who gave Solomon the wisdom that he teaches in these proverbs. If we learn them truly, and delight in what they teach, we shall be endued with heavenly wisdom. This wisdom has always been one and the same, so let us not think that Solomon here teaches anything new, for it is said, "You shall neither add anything to what I command you, nor take anything away." The wisdom he teaches here is simply this: to hold fast to the word of God, and to walk in his commandments. This is the same wisdom Moses taught the children of Israel, saying, "Behold, I have taught you laws and ordinances, as the Lord my God commanded me."

But here it might be objected that Solomon need not have written, seeing that Moses had before him already written and that he is teaching no different wisdom but what Moses taught. It may be answered that what Moses taught briefly and obscurely, adapted for the capacity of the people, Solomon expands upon and amplifies, and so in this way he serves as an interpreter to Moses. But it may be objected again that if Solomon teaches no other wisdom than what Moses taught, he does not teach Jesus Christ, whom God has made for us wisdom and righteousness; therefore his teaching does not apply to us, who should aspire to know nothing but Jesus Christ and him crucified. I answer that Moses has indeed spoken of Jesus Christ: "If you had believed Moses, you would also have believed me." And "The law was our schoolmaster, to bring us to Christ."

But Solomon does not merely teach the law but faith as well, for he sets forth for us various promises of God, and then teaches us Jesus Christ, of whom he also was a figure, for all the promises of God are "yes" and "amen" in Jesus Christ. Therefore, when we hear the Proverbs of Solomon, let us not expect that he will lead us only to perform the works of the law outwardly, but that he primarily intends to conform our character to the fear and reverence of God, and this cannot be done without faith. ON THE PROVERBS OF SOLOMON.[6]

NO DISCERNABLE PATTERN. PETER MOFFETT: Proverbs are certain general, short, and pithy sayings, used, or [intended] to be used, in every person's mouth. Even though various parables are set down in the writings of the prophets, the evangelists, and the apostles, yet this is the only

the final edition he reverted to the more traditional title of *Proverbiorum*. Here he seems to be reminding the reader that no matter the title, the content is the same. ††††See the commentary on Prov 5:18-19. ‡‡‡‡"Is their [that is, the Christians'] 'wisest' man Solomon at all comparable with Phocylides or Theognis or Isocrates among the Hellenes? Certainly not. At least, if one were to compare the exhortations of Isocrates with Solomon's proverbs, you would I am very sure, find that the son of Theodorus is superior to their 'wisest' king." Julian, *Against the Galileans* 224c (LCL 157:383).

[6]Cop, *Sur les Proverbes de Salomon*, 1-2; citing 1 Cor 2:6; Deut 4:2; 4:5; 1 Cor 2:2; Jn 5:46; Gal 3:24; 2 Cor 1:20.

book of Scripture titled by the name of Proverbs, because in it alone proverbial sentences are continued without ceasing or intermission, and without mingling of stories, prayers, or other matters. For in this little volume a great heap of grave and most prudent sayings is so nearly couched and so briefly comprised, such that proverbs, like drifts of snow, seem to lie thick together and, like grapes of the same bunch, to cluster one upon another. As concerning the arrangement of this book, neither are the proverbs so confusedly shuffled but that some of them, now and then, have affinity and coherence together; nor yet are they so suitably sorted but that even those often that are placed as very near neighbors differ greatly in substance, and have no dependence upon one another. A Commentary upon the Book of the Proverbs of Solomon.[7]

A Collection Made by Royal Decree. Hugo Grotius: In Greek this book is called *Paroimíai*, though the Hebrew title, *mashal*, signifies in particular a comparison or a parable. But since Proverbs is full of such compact comparisons, eventually the term came to be used for all *gnōmē*, or pithy sayings. I will not repeat here what I said about this in my prologue to Stobaeus's *Sayings of the Poets*, or in my comments on Matthew 13:3.[†] But it seems that this book is a selection of the best sayings from many different writers who preceded Solomon, in much the same way that many of the emperors of Constantinople had anthologies drawn up for their own use. But all the sayings collected here are about ethics—that is, they relate either to character or to instruction in prudence, but always in relation to the worship of God, for this virtue begets all the rest of itself. Having been neglected by many nations, this was the special study of the Hebrew sages, as Josephus has observed.[‡] Annotations on the Old Testament.[8]

[7]Moffett, *A Commentary upon the Book of the Proverbs of Solomon*, 2*.

[8]Grotius, *Annotationes in Vetus Testamentum*, 247. [†]Ioannes Stobaeus (John of Stobi) was a fifth-century Greek writer who compiled a massive collection, *Selections, Sayings, and Admonitions*, culled from the writings of more than five hundred ancient Greek writers, from Homer to Themistius. In 1623, Grotius published a partial translation of Stobaeus into Latin, the *Dicta Poetarum*, to which he refers the reader here. [‡]The reference is uncertain, but the treatise *Against Apion* argues a similar point (see esp. 2.17-18).

1:1-7 THE BEGINNING OF KNOWLEDGE

[1]*The proverbs of Solomon, son of David, king of Israel:*

[2]*To know wisdom and instruction,*
to understand words of insight,

[3]*to receive instruction in wise dealing,*
in righteousness, justice, and equity;

[4]*to give prudence to the simple,*
knowledge and discretion to the youth—

[5]*Let the wise hear and increase in learning,*
and the one who understands obtain guidance,

[6]*to understand a proverb and a saying,*
the words of the wise and their riddles.

[7]*The fear of the* LORD *is the beginning of knowledge;*
fools despise wisdom and instruction.

OVERVIEW: The opening verses of Proverbs, among the best known in the whole book, sound out the primary themes of the book: wisdom and the fear of the Lord. The Reformation commentators focus on the meaning of the many synonyms the biblical author uses, distinguishing *wisdom* from *knowledge, insight, instruction,* and other Hebrew terms. The exegetes especially stress the relationship of wisdom and virtue, and distinguish godly understanding from worldly ways of knowing. In particular, they contemplate the meaning of the fear of the Lord, noting the difference between biblical wisdom and that of the Greeks and other ancients.

1:1-6 *To Know Wisdom and Instruction*

KNOWLEDGE FOR RIGHT ACTION. CARDINAL CAJETAN: This is clearly the goal toward which Solomon's parables are aimed, and the parables supplied are directed toward two tasks: knowing and understanding. And so the mere statement of the text is itself inadequate, but there is instead a specific prayer in these words. "The fear of the Lord. . . ." The meaning is that the parables of Solomon son of David King of Israel are comparisons for understanding wisdom. . . . But still, these two tasks are set out in two different ways: first by division into sections by genus, and later by species. "And instruction." According to the Hebrew this is "and knowledge." Thus the first benefit of these parables is described as "knowing wisdom and knowledge." And this lesson concerns practical knowledge—namely, the sure conception by which we know. This is not just that we might know something, but that we might engage in works, which is moral knowledge. But wisdom is not undertaken as an intellectual practice distinguished by philosophers from knowledge as opposed to understanding, skill, and prudence. It is instead the correct explanation of human actions according to their highest cause—namely, God (as Solomon made clear further on in the work). Knowledge, moreover, is not restricted to learning and teaching, but as it entails an appetitive element, and applies both to what one does and experiences, so also they include those external things by which we are corrected. The text itself will supply evidence of this. THE PARABLES OF SOLOMON, CORRECTED BY THE ORIGINAL HEBREW.[1]

WISDOM AND PRUDENCE. LUDWIG LAVATER: This book of aphorisms [*sententiae*] was written and published so that we may learn wisdom from it. Wisdom is defined by the philosophers as the knowledge [*scientia*] of divine and human things,

[1]Cajetan, *Parabolae Salomonis ad veritatem Hebraicam castigatae*, 2.

and the understanding of what causes them. Or, more simply put, it is by wisdom that we are able to understand the true knowledge of God, which is true wisdom. This is why Paul says, "We speak the wisdom of God in a mystery, which is hidden, which God ordained before the age." And indeed, there are many aphorisms set down in this book that cast light upon the nature of God. And from this we may learn *mûsār*, that is, discipline, reproof, or correction, to which is added instruction. For this book teaches us how we ought to act, if we should receive correction either from God or from human beings. And it also shows us how to give correction to children and to others, so that they might be called back from sin. "Words of understanding and prudence." The Hebrew *bînâ* (insight) indicates a judgment that is born from wisdom, by which one may distinguish between good and bad, true and false, what is to be desired and what to be fled from. This differs from *ḥokmâ* (wisdom); the latter refers to knowledge, while the former indicates a power of discernment or judgment. On the Book of Proverbs, or Sayings, of Solomon the Most-Wise King.[2]

A Straight Line Leading to Repentance. Peter Moffett: In this second verse, two ends or uses of the parables of this book are noted for us. The former end is *the knowing of wisdom and instruction. Wisdom* is an effectual knowledge of things that are to be believed or practiced, wrought by the light of God's Word and Spirit clearing and directing the mind and understanding. As concerning *instruction*, it is a virtue consisting in the right use of wisdom, whereby, through the Lord's working and training, the hearts and lives of men and women are reformed. The second use of these parables is to understand the words of prudence (or skillful speech). These words of prudence are those holy doctrines or divine instructions whereby people may reform that which is amiss in them, and govern themselves aright in the whole course of their lives. For how else should a young person—indeed, any person!—redress their way, but ruling themselves after the word of God, every sentence of which is like a straight line leading to repentance? And it is especially so with the sentences of this excellent book. A Commentary upon the Book of the Proverbs of Solomon.[3]

Heavenly Wisdom for the Simple and the Wise. Lucas Osiander: I have written down these sayings, says Solomon, so that simpler folk and those who have the task of training the young (that is, those who are not yet sufficiently established in the word of God) may learn true wisdom and prudence. Thus, if they have any vices or defects of character, they may correct them and govern their habits with honorable discipline. So also they may come to understand what is just, equitable, and honest, by which one may live rightly and (if their calling requires) govern others rightly. And since these parables teach about not only civil but also heavenly things, it is clear that the reading of the sacred literature is the means or organ by which our hearts are enlightened by heavenly wisdom. But lest anyone should think themselves so prudent that they have no need of this training, Solomon adds, "the wise will hear and become wiser." Proverbs.[4]

Understanding the Truth and Living by It. Michael Jermin: In Homer, it is the smoke of his country that Odysseus longed for and wished to see,[†] and this is the wish of many who (as seaweed cleaves to the rocks, so are their hearts fastened by love to this world) desire still to enjoy the smoky ignorance of the earth, and do not care for the light of heaven, nor pay any attention to wisdom and instruction. And to show that this verse is to be referred to such people, some of the rabbis tell us that the original word *mûsār*, translated here "instruction," is nothing else but that

[2]Lavater, *In librum Proverbiorum siue Sententiarum Solomonis Regis sapientissimi*, 3; citing 1 Cor 2:7.

[3]Moffett, *A Commentary upon the Book of the Proverbs of Solomon*, 4.

[4]Osiander, *Esdras, Nehemias, Esther, Iob, Psalterium, Prouerbia Salomonis, Ecclesiastes, & Canticum Canticorum*, 1021.

knowledge by which the ignorant multitude is taught. . . . There is much false wisdom, much vain instruction spoken about in the world, for as Athanasius says, "the Greeks promise wisdom, and heretics think they have instruction,"[‡] but it is true wisdom, right instruction that here the wise man promises, and that here he gives. And to distinguish the diversity of words here used, by "wisdom" we may understand the truth of those things that are to be known; by "instruction" the framing of our lives according to our knowledge; by "words of understanding" the proficiency of goodness in us, by a continual learning. The difference that Levi Gershom[§] makes between wisdom in the first place and understanding in the last place is this: that wisdom is the knowledge of a thing by its proper and intrinsic causes, and that understanding is that knowledge that is got by causes that are not proper and intrinsic. Paraphrastic Meditations.[5]

Wearing Away the Veil. John Trapp: Tertullian calls the Bible (and the Proverbs especially) "our digest" from the lawyers, and others "our pandects" from them also.[†] Is there not a thin veil laid over them, which is more rarefied by reading, and at last wholly worn away? Surely, as by much reading in the statute book people grow worldly wise, and as a friend (it is Chrysostom's comparison) that is acquainted with his friend will work out the meaning of a letter or phrase that a stranger could not understand, so it is in Scripture.[‡] And here, as one often observes, the poorest idiot who is a sound Christian goes beyond the most profound clerics that are not sanctified, because he has his own heart instead of a commentary to help him to understand even the more needful points of the Scripture. Solomon's Book of All Virtues.[6]

Types of Wisdom and Their Source. The English Annotations: We may note, the word *ḥokmâ* in Scripture is a very general word and comprehends all types of wisdom, as does the word *sophia* in the Greek authors. Sometimes it imports a mechanical craft and wisdom, which, though of an inferior degree, yet is from God too, as we are taught. Sometimes worldly wisdom, whether practical, which we call policy, prudence, or speculative, as the knowledge of things natural. Last, heavenly sanctifying wisdom, of which we see more in the seventh verse of this chapter. All these kinds are from God, so they all may concur and meet in one person. One and the same may excel in mechanical craft, whether by practice and actual operation, or by showing their ready fancy, quick apprehension, and sound judgment in all such things; and may be very prudent and skillful in worldly things both at home and abroad; and besides all this, a very godly person too. Annotations of Proverbs 1:2.[7]

Wisdom as Enjoying God's Kindness. Michel Cop: By his sayings we shall learn to be well-governed, and also we will listen willingly to those who show us our own faults—chiefly those who are wise and experienced, and who know how to give reproof in its proper time and place so that we may correct our way of life and become wise. And so by these sayings he works to draw us away from death, where the obstinate and incorrigible are headed. "Or do you despise the riches of his kindness, patience, and long-suffering, not knowing that the kindness of God leads you to repentance?" Finally, they serve so to frame our hearts that we should delight to give to our neighbors what is theirs, to allow no one to do

[5]Jermin, *Paraphrasticall Meditations*, 642-43. [†]Homer, *Odyssey* 1.55-60. [‡]Jermin is quoting the *Synopsis of the Sacred Scriptures*, a text attributed to Athanasius by premodern scholars but now thought to date from the sixth century. [§]Levi ben Gershom (1288–1344), also known as Gersonides, was a Jewish mathematician, astronomer, philosopher, and biblical scholar.

[6]Trapp, *Solomonis ΠΑΝΑΡΕΤΟΣ*, 2. [†]Tertullian describes the canonical Gospels as "our digests" in his treatise against Marcion (*Adversus Marcionem* 4.3). The terms "digest" and "pandect" are derived from Roman law, and they refer to the collections of case law that illustrate the application of the statutes in practice. [‡]As Chrysostom observes, "The inexperienced reader who picks up a letter will consider it to be merely papyrus and ink, but the experienced reader will hear a voice and converse with an absent interlocutor" (*Hom. 1 Cor.* 7:2; PG 61.56).

[7]Downame, ed., *English Annotations*, 6Q1r*; citing Ex 28:3; 31:3; Is 8:23, 24; 1 Kings 4:30; Deut 4:6; Job 28:28; Ps 111.

them wrong, and to govern ourselves in such a manner that no one can find anything in us worthy of blame or reproach. We learn then by these sayings to do well by all people, to hurt no one, and to be a good example rather than a scandal to our neighbors. In doing this, we set out on the blessed life, to possess the kingdom of heaven, which is ever on our lips. Both those who do the contrary enter into their own hell even now. Therefore, so far as we can see, these sayings teach us to fear and serve God, to get along with our neighbors, and to work out our salvation. ON THE PROVERBS OF SOLOMON.[8]

THE GRAMMAR OF WISDOM. PHILIPP MELANCHTHON: The proposition is evident in what he says, that collecting these proverbs is of great advantage in admonishing and teaching the young and uncultivated, and in bending them to diligence by forming their character, both with respect to God and with respect to people. He describes these advantages using many words, but the following terms deserve special consideration:

Wisdom [*sapientia*] signifies the recognition of God, which shines in the heart with true fear and true faith.

Discipline [*disciplina*] or instruction refers to preparation or education in general.

Prudence [*prudendia*] signifies the formation of character.

Understanding [*intelligentia*] refers to good judgment, the ability to make a difficult choice from among a range of (apparently) more attractive options, as when Jeremiah urged surrender [to the king of Babylon], contrary the opinion of [King Zedekiah's] other counselors. So also, Zechariah urged that servitude must be endured, and that the people must not be moved to rebellion.[†]

Justice [*iusticia*] signifies general obedience to all the commandments.

Judgment [*iudicium*] refers to accusation, condemnation, and penalty.

Rectitude is the opposite of hypocrisy, and is also called sincerity.

Circumspection is the opposite of brutish insensibility, which rashly rushes ahead without deliberation.

Knowledge [*scientia*] signifies discriminating judgment.

Consideration is the same as deliberation, which takes into account what is appropriate for the diversity of place, time, and persons. EXPOSITION OF THE PROVERBS OF SOLOMON.[9]

1:7 *The Fear of the Lord Is the Beginning of Wisdom*

FEAR AND AFFECTIVE KNOWLEDGE. CARDINAL CAJETAN: The difference in the Hebrew text, "the fear of Jehovah is the foundation of knowledge," is minimal. This is where the argument of the book begins. The preceding verses are a kind of introduction to the whole title and serve to state the author's purpose. And so he begins his treatise on knowledge with his subject as the kind that exists among human beings, stating that knowledge is found in those who fear God and not among fools. At the same time he fulfills three duties. He distinguishes between one type of knowledge and another. In saying that the fear of Jehovah is the beginning of knowledge, he makes it clear that this is not a discourse on the knowledge that resides in a hypothetical aspect. For that kind of knowledge is also found in Gentiles who do not fear God and is acquired by careful investigation. The knowledge that is the topic of this treatise, from the very fact that it is acquired by the one who fears God, is very different from that just mentioned. And from the fact that the fear of God is the beginning of knowledge, it is obvious that it must apply to the affective aspect of the person and functions with respect to God as judge and ruler of the universe. For one does not fear God as the object of fear (since he is the highest good and takes no part in

[8]Cop, *Sur les Proverbes de Salomon*, 2-3; citing Rom 2:4.

[9]CR 14:6-7; citing Jer 38. [†]It is not entirely clear whether Melanchthon has in mind the Zechariah associated with the canonical prophet or the figured mentioned in 2 Chron 24:20-22.

evil whatsoever), but as the one capable of inflicting harm. This knowledge also makes clear who the men are who approximate knowledge, since it says that "the fear of God is the beginning of knowing." It is significant that the phrase is not "the beginning of knowledge" but "the beginning of knowing." So we understand that it is not talking about the beginning of knowledge taken absolutely, but about that beginning by which we come to possess knowledge. For knowledge taken absolutely is a type of analogue to divine and human knowledge. Therefore, taken absolutely it does not have the fear of God as its foundation, but merely with respect to what pertains to us it begins from the fear of God. Likewise, fear of God is not limited to a kind of abject fear. Because fear as it embarks upon a course of knowledge from the subject's perspective (i.e., of the one who is acquiring it) is not divorced from that actual knowledge but is rather brought to its fulfillment, as in the statement in the Gospel: "I will show you whom you should fear. Fear the one who, after he kills you, has the authority to consign you to Gehenna." And so the beginning of knowing (i.e., of possessing the proper understanding of all human affairs with respect to God) is to fear Jehovah as the very source of being from whom we have being, life, and all other goods. And therefore, knowledge of this type can be attained and exist only in those who fear God. The Parables of Solomon, Corrected by the Original Hebrew.[10]

The Fear of the Lord Is a Gift of the Spirit. Dirk Philips: The sixth gift of the Holy Spirit is the fear of the Lord, about which the holy Scripture has much to say. Ecclesiasticus in particular writes much about it in his book, as may be briefly summarized as follows: The fear of the Lord is the beginning of wisdom and is the foundation of the heart alone with the righteous and the believers. The fear of the Lord is the true worship of God. It keeps and makes the heart pious and happy, gives joy and blessing eternally. Fearing God is the wisdom that makes one rich and brings every good thing with it. It fills the whole house with its gifts, and all the rooms with its treasures. The fear of the Lord is a crown of wisdom and gives peace and righteousness abundantly. This wisdom makes people truly wise. To fear the Lord is the true root of wisdom, and its branches grow or bloom eternally. The fear of the Lord drives out sin, but the one who is without this fear is not loved by God.

The true fear of the Lord consists in a serious questioning, reflecting on, and seeking for the good, holy, and perfect will of God, and it requires that the people watch themselves carefully in all their thoughts, words, and deeds, so that they may be pleasing to their God. For the nature and character of the fear of the Lord is to avoid evil and pursue the good. Such fear of the Lord brings the clean and perfectly pure recognition of the only and eternal Almighty God and his divine being—that is, it leads one truly to recognize God the Father and his only born son Jesus Christ, our Lord, and his Holy Spirit in name, power, office, and activity. Out of such acknowledgment comes faith—that is, that blessed, dear, and firm faith in God and his Word, a certain comprehension of heavenly and invisible matters, through which we become God's children, formed according to him through Jesus Christ in the Holy Spirit and made partakers of the divine nature. And when we are thus united with God, we must love him as the highest good, in certain confidence and living hope that God is the rewarder of all those who seek him in truth.

Therefore the fear of the Lord is truly the beginning of wisdom. It teaches people to deny themselves and, with childlike reverence, worship, and obedience, to serve God in holiness and righteousness, which is pleasing to him, and in complete surrender to set their entire hope on the living God and to wait patiently for what God will do and work. Just as Abraham did when he offered his son to the Lord out of the fear of God through his faith in an undoubting hope, that he, because of the promise of God, would receive him back again.

[10]Cajetan, *Parabolae Salomonis ad veritatem Hebraicam castigatae*, 6; citing Mt 10:28.

Therefore God gave Isaac back to him as an example of the resurrection, with such witness that he certainly feared the Lord, since he had not spared his only son for the Lord's sake. Out of all this it is now easy to notice how much good the fear of the Lord accomplishes. ANSWER TO SEBASTIAN FRANCK.[11]

TO FEAR GOD IS TO LOVE GOD. MICHEL COP: In the beginning of this preface he teaches us the way to attain true knowledge. For just as the true knowledge in which we must glory is to know God, when we are instructed in his law and delight to follow it, so we must understand that the fear of the Lord, about which Solomon speaks here, is a humility and reverence, by which we tremble at God's word. This fear does not mean that we ought to mistrust his goodness; rather, we should diligently beware of displeasing him, and set ourselves to do that which makes him happy. This is the fear that the angel attributed to Abraham, and this is the fear that God requires of his people: "So now, O Israel, what does the Lord your God require of you? Only to fear the Lord your God, to walk in all his ways, to love him, to serve the Lord your God with all your heart and with all your soul, and to keep the commandments of the Lord your God and his decrees that I am commanding you today, for your own well-being." . . . It might also be said that the fear of the Lord is the chief part of knowledge, for if in all our doings we have not this fear, we know nothing. Without it, we are void of wisdom and understanding, like ignorant, rude, sottish, blind beasts. . . .

This word which Solomon uses indicates the *beginning,* or principal part. And this fear is joined both with the love of God and of his word, as Moses teaches us in the passage cited above. Likewise, in Deuteronomy 29 and Deuteronomy 6, the holy Scripture often points us to this fear, with the aim that learning to recognize our own frailty and weakness, we might distrust ourselves and lean more strongly on the mercy of God alone, always submitting ourselves to him with humility and an earnest desire to obey him in everything. This kind of fear leads us to repentance, and so overwhelms us with a sense of how angry God is with us for our sins; and yet, although this fear does beat us down in ourselves, it also serves to make us certain and assured that God is merciful to us. . . . This is not then that fear about which St. John speaks, when he says, "There is no fear in love, but perfect love casts out fear." Therefore the papists have here no foundation for their doctrine—or false opinion, rather—whereby they argue that we cannot be certain whether God loves us or not. For if we fear God, we know him; if we know him, we love him; and if we love him, we can be sure that he loves us: for we cannot love him first. If we know God truly in this way, we would rather suffer any kind of death than give him offense—even if there were no hell. ON THE PROVERBS OF SOLOMON.[12]

TRUE WISDOM, NOT ALCHEMY. JOHN TRAPP: "The fear of the Lord" is the chief and principal point of wisdom (as the word is used here); indeed, it is wisdom itself. This Solomon learned by the instruction of his father, who had taught him when he was a child, and therefore he sets it here in the beginning of his works, as the beginning of all, just as in the end he makes it the end of all. . . . Heathen sages, such as Seneca and Socrates, were wise in their generations and had many excellent gifts, but they missed the main point of wisdom: there was no fear of God before their eyes. In this they were like alchemists, who fail in their goal, but yet find many excellent things by the way. These merchants found goodly pearls, but the pearl of great price they failed to discover. But the prophet calls the fear of God "our treasure." SOLOMON'S BOOK OF ALL VIRTUES.[13]

---

[11]CRR 6:453-53*; citing Sir 2; Rom 12:1-2; Heb 11:1; Gal 3; Eph 4; Deut 6:5; Mt 22:37; Heb 11:6; Mt 16:24; Lk 1; 1 Pet 1:14; Gen 22:9; Heb 11:17.

[12]Cop, *Sur les Proverbes de Salomon*, 5-6; citing Jer 9:24; Gen 22:12; Deut 10:12-13; 1 Jn 4:18; 4:10.

[13]Trapp, *Solomonis ΠΑΝΆΡΕΤΟΣ*, 4; citing Job 28:28; Prov 4:4; Ps 111:10; Eccles 12:13; Mt 13:45-46; Is 33:6.

1:8-19 THE ENTICEMENT OF SINNERS

[8]Hear, my son, your father's instruction,
and forsake not your mother's teaching,

[9]for they are a graceful garland for your head
and pendants for your neck.

[10]My son, if sinners entice you,
do not consent.

[11]If they say, "Come with us, let us lie in wait
for blood;
let us ambush the innocent without reason;

[12]like Sheol let us swallow them alive,
and whole, like those who go down to the pit;

[13]we shall find all precious goods,
we shall fill our houses with plunder;

[14]throw in your lot among us;
we will all have one purse"—

[15]my son, do not walk in the way with them;
hold back your foot from their paths,

[16]for their feet run to evil,
and they make haste to shed blood.

[17]For in vain is a net spread
in the sight of any bird,

[18]but these men lie in wait for their own blood;
they set an ambush for their own lives.

[19]Such are the ways of everyone who is greedy
for unjust gain;
it takes away the life of its possessors.

Overview: Our commentators take the admonition at the beginning of this passage ("My son") as an occasion to dwell on the values of Christian parenting and the godly household, though they also discuss the symbolic meaning of the church as a mother. The latter part of the passage concerns the wicked, and the reformers take this opportunity to ponder the dangers of temptation as well as the ultimate fate of the ungodly in hell. The writers conclude by noting one of the key themes of Jewish Wisdom literature, which was also a concern of theirs during their own time, not least in light of the abuses of the Roman church: the dangers of wealth and greed.

1:8-9 *Hear, My Son*

The Ornaments of Wisdom. Philipp Melanchthon: Earlier he said that the chief point of doctrine and worship was this: "The fear of the Lord is the beginning of wisdom." Now he points out who it is doing the teaching, and he commands that they be heard. For it is necessary that there be a ministry of teaching, and necessary that the minister be heard. The first rank in the order of those [who teach] is that of parents, and first among their duties is to teach their children about God, as it is written in the letter to the Ephesians: "Educate children in the teaching and discipline of the Lord." But attached to this is the prior command: "Hear your father's instruction"—that is, teaching about the fear of the Lord. The church of Israel resounds with this instruction, which is also called "the law of your mother" (the church), for it was handed down by God with firm and clear testimonies in Israel. Therefore we know for certain that we are bound by this type of instruction, when it says, "do not forsake your mother's teaching." For by the title "mother" is signified the church of Israel. But clearly this command is often repeated, so that we may esteem this unique kind of instruction about God that is handed on to us by the church in the writings of the prophets and apostles. For in the same way, the eternal Father says concerning the Son, "Hear him," and the Lord says, "If anyone loves me, he will keep my teaching, and my Father will love him"[†] But just as the Lord adds the greatest promise of all to this precept concerning the knowledge and profession of his teaching, so here Solomon adds a promise that, in order to make it more appealing, he clothes it in the ornaments of his childhood. A "crown" signifies royal power or authority; this is what it means: God will establish you among the good rulers, and he will support and assist your plans (insofar as they are life-giving for you and for the people), and he will make you an instrument of mercy to yourself and to the people, like Samuel, David, Jehoshaphat, and Hezekiah were, and not an instrument of wrath, like Saul and Absalom. "An ornament for your neck" signifies the eloquence of teaching and counsels which give life. God will adorn you with these great gifts, if you give ear to the law of your mother. EXPOSITION OF THE PROVERBS OF SOLOMON.[1]

FEAR OF THE LORD BEGINS AT HOME. CARDINAL CAJETAN: Sticking to the Hebrew, it should read "learning" [rather than "teaching"]. As Solomon is going to make two definitive statements, he first deals with the duties of home, then those of public life. In other words, he handles first the instruction of the home, then what pertains to civil life. For the instruction that takes place at home he begins with his first injunction: parents deserve honor. The fear of God, by natural consequence, descends through parents to their children. Parents are obligated not only to nourish their children's bodies but also to shape their souls. Thus in order to instill within children this fear of God, the beginning of becoming wise, Solomon speaks to them, saying, "Listen, my son, to your father's learning." This is the first commandment in the second table. The first aspect of the honor owed to parents is both to listen to a father's precepts, and then to preserve a mother's rules. Furthermore, he mentioned here each parent not only because a son owes obedience to each, but also so that from the cradle the son might be instilled with a kind of fear of God from his mother's precepts. For the child spends most of his early life with his mother rather than with his father. THE PARABLES OF SOLOMON, CORRECTED BY THE ORIGINAL HEBREW.[2]

HONORING GOD AS FATHER MEANS OBEYING THE CHURCH AS MOTHER. MICHEL COP: In this exhortation, Solomon speaks as a father to his child, with the aim that he may be heard with more reverence and fear. Here we may say that Solomon speaks in the person of God, who is the only father of all, or in the person of the pastor and teacher of the church, who calls those whom he teaches his children, because he begets them to God and to his church through the word. David uses this manner of speaking, and so also do St. Paul and St. John. In doing so, they attribute nothing to themselves, nor do they detract from the fatherhood of God, for it has pleased God to make them partakers in this honor, when he uses them as instruments to increase his church and to conceive spiritual children for himself. For this reason, Solomon urges us to obey God, who is our only father and teacher, . . . and when he calls us to "hear," he also requires us to obey. And we must obey if we are to be accounted wise by God; otherwise, we enter into destruction with the foolish. . . . And along with this, he immediately answers a question that might be raised: How shall we hear God, seeing that he is an invisible and incomprehensible spirit? He gives us, I say, the solution, admonishing us not to forsake the teaching of our "mother." It is just as though he says, "If you will hear God's instructions for you, be obedient to the church, in which he has conceived you, and in which he continues to teach you by the ministry of his apostles and prophets, his

[1]CR 14:7-8; citing Eph 6:4; Lk 9:35; Jn 14:15. [†]Melanchthon is quoting from an earlier edition of the Vulgate, which reads, "If anyone loves me, he will keep my word, and my Father will love him, and we will come to him and make our abode with him." Erasmus's edition of the Greek New Testament in 1519 had omitted the longer reading: "If you love me, keep my commands." Luther had followed Erasmus in preferring the shorter reading beginning with his *Septembertestament* of 1522, so it is curious that Melanchthon here quotes the longer Vulgate reading.

[2]Cajetan, *Parabolae Salomonis ad veritatem Hebraicam castigatae*, 7.

evangelists, pastors, and teachers. Furthermore, we must understand that God calls them his children, whom he exhorts by his word and gives to his spouse, which is the church, to be taught. For the church is the pillar and strength of truth—not the popish church, which rejects the word of God and does not acknowledge Jesus Christ as its head, but rather serves antichrist, and is the enemy of God. But insofar as we ourselves cannot discern the church of the wicked from that of the faithful, we must ask for the spirit of wisdom and discretion from the heavenly Father, and he will surely give it to us." On the Proverbs of Solomon.[3]

1:10-16 *Do Not Listen to the Wicked*

Enticing the Saints. John Trapp: The dragon bites the elephant's ear, and thence sucks his blood, because he knows that to be the only place he cannot reach with his trunk to defend. So deals the red dragon and his angels: with good words and fair speeches they deceive the hearts of the simple. . . . But if sinners have their "Come," should not the saints much more so? "Come, let us go to the house of the Lord." "Come, let us walk in the light of the Lord." "Let us go speedily to pray before the Lord, and to seek the Lord of hosts: I will go also." Should we not incite, entice, whet, and provoke one another? Should we not sharpen one another? Should we not rouse and stir each other up to love and good works? Solomon's Book of All Virtues.[4]

No Safety in Numbers. Michel Cop: Here Solomon begins to uncover their persuasions, along with their wicked and pernicious deeds. . . . The beginning of their persuasion is to say, "Come with us," as if to say, "We are the greater number, and so obviously we are also the strongest and the wisest; if you wish to proceed in good company, forsake the others (who are but a handful in comparison) and join with us." This is a great temptation, and the unsteady are easily shaken by it. For this reason, we must beware of such temptation, for we naturally desire to follow the greatest number, and think that if we be on that side, we cannot perish. But the Holy Spirit teaches us the opposite, both by examples and admonitions. Noah was not drowned by the waters of the flood; Lot did not perish in the overthrow of Sodom; Joshua and Caleb did not die in the desert. It is also written, "You shall not follow a multitude to evil." And again: "Enter in at the narrow gate, for wide is that gate and broad the way that leads to destruction, and many there be that go that way." The multitude is one of the arguments which the papists set against us, to show that we are in the way of perdition. But if the multitude be the best, it follows that the Turks and pagans are more honorable than the papists, for theirs is the greater number. On the Proverbs of Solomon.[5]

The Living Death of the Wicked. Cardinal Cajetan: In the Hebrew this reads, "We will swallow them alive like the pit, and whole like those who go down to a well." This means, "We will not kill them, nor shall we strike and wound them. But rather, according to the image of a pit we will swallow them alive." Or one could interpret the pit as a prison. That is, as a prison into which someone falls while still alive and unharmed. Likewise "we will swallow them" up whole, without wounds and bruises of blows, like those who descend in a well. This means, "like those who go down into a prison after they have been robbed of their belongings." For sinful young men are urging them on, and so they will lie in ambush like men who are going to beat and murder others. And yet they will not murder or strike them, but rather they will catch the men alive and unharmed in their persons, like a young man who, though he shrinks back from committing murders is pulled toward violent looting as a lesser evil. The Parables of Solomon, Corrected by the Original Hebrew.[6]

[3]Cop, *Sur les Proverbes de Salomon*, 6-7.
[4]Trapp, *Solomonis ΠΑΝΆΡΕΤΟΣ*, 5; citing Rom 16:18; Is 2:3; 2:5; Zech 8:21; Heb 10:24; Prov 27:17; 2 Pet 1:13.
[5]Cop, *Sur les Proverbes de Salomon*, 9; citing Ex 23:2; Mt 7:13.
[6]Cajetan, *Parabolae Salomonis ad veritatem Hebraicam castigatae*, 8.

An Image of the Devil's Malice. Michael Jermin: The ready eagerness of the wicked to sin is still further set forth: "Let us swallow them up alive," let us not wait until death swallows them up, but let us be the grave in which they are devoured. . . . In general, the speech is boastful hyperbole, which commonly exceeds the truth, but here it is less than the truth, and the comparison falls short in expressing the malice of the wicked. For the grave swallows not the living, but the dead, and it is not the whole person, but the body only that goes into the pit. Indeed, wide is the grave's mouth and large the devouring stomach of the pit, but wider and larger is a bloody and malicious heart. Surely if Sheol (*šĕʾôl*) may anywhere almost be taken for hell, then it may be here. And the words may be applied fitly to the devil, for it is on account of their likeness to him that wicked people truly are known. For it is the devil that seeks to swallow people alive, and he it is that labors to bring them into the dungeon of eternal torments. But though this roaring lion may have got any into his ravenous mouth, yet if only two legs are hanging out, by which they may go into the Lord's house, or if only a piece of an ear, by which they may hear God's Word, and the shepherds of the church take hold of them, they may yet happily be delivered. For as St. Chrysostom speaks, "There is nothing that so causes holiness of life and corrects unholiness as steady church attendance and an earnest desire to hear the word of God."[†] Those whom the devil has shut out from the church are those whom he has shut up in the pit of destruction, and it is the whole swallowing up of people in a hellish security that makes them to be swallowed up whole in hell. Paraphrastic Meditations.[7]

1:17-19 *The Fate of the Wicked*

Clear Advance Warning. Philipp Melanchthon: Even if the wicked believe that they lurk hidden from view, they swallow themselves up in their own snares, and they do not remain concealed. For God, who is the defender of the weak, sees everything, "and surely there is a God who judges men on the earth." So also, "you render to each according to his deeds." Therefore Solomon exhorts us, and describes the threat of punishment against those who act against God, lest we be agitated by examples of the wicked who prosper. And among those punishments this is the most sorrowful: "Then they will call on me, and I will not answer them." God does not desire that those who have fallen into wickedness should be unable to turn back to repentance, nor that their repentance be useless. Indeed, he calls us all to repentance, and he promises both to lighten our present punishments and to forgive our eternal ones, as is said in the prophet Isaiah: "Though your sins be as scarlet, they shall be white as snow." The intent of the saying is that giving heed, the wicked might repent before being punished, but when punishment comes, it will be too late. If it comes while still in the body, it may be mitigated by repentance, but if it is the eternal punishment, there is no entreaty, as in the destruction of Saul and Judas. In short: hear and obey to rest secure. Exposition of the Proverbs of Solomon.[8]

Avarice as Bad as Murder. Michel Cop: The world greatly prizes those who profit themselves and gather up many goods. On the other hand, those who are not cunning for gain are held in disdain and reputed to be idiots. This is a great temptation to the simpleminded and those who lack in discretion, leading them into covetousness, that they might be held in higher esteem. . . . In the meanwhile, they do not consider into what a gulf of wickedness they are falling, when they greedily pursue gain. But Solomon desires to draw us up out of this gulf, and to make us detest and abhor the great toil of greed to follow after gain. So he explains to us here that the avaricious have the mindset, affections, enterprises, and business described above, when he says, "Such are the

[7]Jermin, *Paraphrasticall Meditations*, 642-43; citing Amos 3:12.
[†]Chrysostom, *Contra Anomoeos* 11.3, in PG 48:800-801.

[8]CR 14:8-9; citing Ps 58:11; 62:12; Prov 1:28; Is 1:18.

ways. . . ." It is as though he said, "Just as you would not lay in wait for innocent blood, the avaricious do exactly that. And rather than give up their business, they would take the lives of the innocent and murder those who possess the goods they desire. So you must flee avarice, and choose rather to be poor than to desire an abundance of riches, unless you would be counted as murderers before God and his angels." I say expressly before God and his angels that the most avaricious people are not held by the world to be murderers and homicides, but honorable people of good reputation. And so when Solomon says that "it takes away the life of its possessors," he does not mean that they always kill those who possess the goods they want. But rather by subtlety and guile, by sharp practice and illicit means, by force and extortion they plunder their neighbors and bring about their undoing. And it is no thanks to them if their neighbors do not die, when they take away from them those things their lives depend upon. . . . And so before God they are murderers, even though in the eyes of the world they are held to be men of good repute, because they manage their business well, or are good stout men, because they always clean their plates. On the Proverbs of Solomon.[9]

The Audacity of Covetousness. John Trapp: The greater the wealth, the greater spoil awaits a person. As a tree with thick and large boughs, every person desires to lop him. Trithemius writes that the Templars at the request of King Philip of France were put down and suppressed upon the pretext of heresy, but in fact it was because they were rich and Philip greatly longed for their possessions.[†] Cyprus for its great wealth became spoil for the Romans. . . . Covetousness is daring and desperate: it rides without reins, as Balaam did after the wages of wickedness, the Mammon of iniquity. Solomon's Book of All Virtues.[10]

[9]Cop, *Sur les Proverbes de Salomon*, 11-12.

[10]Trapp, *Solomonis ΠΑΝΆΡΕΤΟΣ*, 7; citing Lk 16:9. [†]Johannes Trithemius (1462–1516) was a German humanist and polymath who was active across a wide range of scholarly fields. The incident in question is related in Trithemius, *Annales Hirsaugienses* (St. Gall, 1690), 2:112-13; originally published 1509–1514.

1:20–2:22 THE CALL AND VALUE OF WISDOM

[20] *Wisdom cries aloud in the street,*
in the markets she raises her voice;

[21] *at the head of the noisy streets she cries out;*
at the entrance of the city gates she speaks:

[22] *"How long, O simple ones, will you love being simple?*
How long will scoffers delight in their scoffing
and fools hate knowledge?

[23] *If you turn at my reproof,*[a]
behold, I will pour out my spirit to you;
I will make my words known to you.

[24] *Because I have called and you refused to listen,*
have stretched out my hand and no one has heeded,

[25] *because you have ignored all my counsel*
and would have none of my reproof,

[26] *I also will laugh at your calamity;*
I will mock when terror strikes you,

[27] *when terror strikes you like a storm*
and your calamity comes like a whirlwind,
when distress and anguish come upon you.

[28] *Then they will call upon me, but I will not answer;*
they will seek me diligently but will not find me.

[29] *Because they hated knowledge*
and did not choose the fear of the LORD,

[30] *would have none of my counsel*
and despised all my reproof,

[31] *therefore they shall eat the fruit of their way,*
and have their fill of their own devices.

[32] *For the simple are killed by their turning away,*
and the complacency of fools destroys them;

[33] *but whoever listens to me will dwell secure*
and will be at ease, without dread of disaster."

2 *My son, if you receive my words*
and treasure up my commandments with you,

[2] *making your ear attentive to wisdom*
and inclining your heart to understanding;

[3] *yes, if you call out for insight*
and raise your voice for understanding,

[4] *if you seek it like silver*
and search for it as for hidden treasures,

[5] *then you will understand the fear of the LORD*
and find the knowledge of God.

[6] *For the LORD gives wisdom;*
from his mouth come knowledge and understanding;

[7] *he stores up sound wisdom for the upright;*
he is a shield to those who walk in integrity,

[8] *guarding the paths of justice*
and watching over the way of his saints.

[9] *Then you will understand righteousness and justice*
and equity, every good path;

[10] *for wisdom will come into your heart,*
and knowledge will be pleasant to your soul;

[11] *discretion will watch over you,*
understanding will guard you,

[12] *delivering you from the way of evil,*
from men of perverted speech,

[13] *who forsake the paths of uprightness*
to walk in the ways of darkness,

[14] *who rejoice in doing evil*
and delight in the perverseness of evil,

[15] *men whose paths are crooked,*
and who are devious in their ways.

[16]*So you will be delivered from the forbidden*[b]
woman,
from the adulteress[c] *with her smooth words,*

[17]*who forsakes the companion of her youth*
and forgets the covenant of her God;

[18]*for her house sinks down to death,*
and her paths to the departed;[d]

[19]*none who go to her come back,*
nor do they regain the paths of life.

[20]*So you will walk in the way of the good*
and keep to the paths of the righteous.

[21]*For the upright will inhabit the land,*
and those with integrity will remain in it,

[22]*but the wicked will be cut off from the land,*
and the treacherous will be rooted out of it.

a Or *Will you turn away at my reproof?* **b** Hebrew *strange* **c** Hebrew *foreign woman* **d** Hebrew *to the Rephaim*

OVERVIEW: The first chapter of Proverbs concludes with the well-known personification of Wisdom calling out to people on the street. The Reformation commentators tend to interpret this as a reference to the preincarnate Son of God speaking as the Father's Word and Wisdom. Rather than dwelling on trinitarian questions, though, the exegetes stick to the moral admonitions of this section, pondering the nature of the simple and discussing both the severity and the mercy of God even in the face of foolish and sinful humanity. As the commentators turn to the next chapter, they discuss their reading of the Bible's plea to receive wisdom from God the Father as contained within the church. With the moralizing portrait of the adulteress woman, another motif of Proverbs, Michel Cop returns to the issues of marriage and the household that arose in the first chapter.

1:20-33 *Wisdom Cries Aloud*

GOD'S WISDOM ON PUBLIC DISPLAY. CARDINAL CAJETAN: Wisdom cries aloud in public. In the Hebrew this reads, "wisdoms will sing out loud." After he has explained the subject of wisdom (which of course means fearing God) in light of the teaching that takes place at home, he then goes on to explain it according to public life, that fools despise wisdom and learning, which was the second of the two propositions. And first of course he speaks generally: "wisdoms will sing out loud." This means not only that wisdom is learned at home when it is handed down by parents but also that many elements of wisdom, measured out in different ways at different stages of a person's life, will cry aloud in public, outside the home. That is, they will speak with a clear and alluring voice. But the manner of speech is not evident in the phrase itself and is threefold, whether through natural works or through miracles. For through works of nature wisdom speaks to the wise, who although they had known God they did not worship him as God. But wisdom also spoke to the Egyptians and the Canaanites, the enemies of the Israelites, through miraculous works. Or by means of teachers or prophets, as we often read and see, or through internal inspiration that some follow and others do not. Next, by distinguishing between different types he identifies three separate types under this one category that he called "in public." The first of these is, "She raises her voice in the streets." The Hebrew expression varies hardly at all, "In the broad paths she will raise her voice." Second is, "She shouts aloud at the head of the crowds." According to the Hebrew it reads, "She will call at the head of the noisy crowds." But the third expression is, "At the doors of the city gates she speaks, expressing her own words." Here as well there is little difference in the

Hebrew phrasing, "At the entrances of the gates in the city she will state her thoughts." And with these three he has included all the classes of people, because people dwell in the streets, in the towns, and in their tents. In crowded groups people gather for war and for other such activities. Among those who are entering the gates, the citizens are designated in the first instance (that is, the judges and the elders who sit at the city gate). Consequently, no one is exempt from listening to wisdom so that these lessons can be learned, and wisdom excludes no one from her instruction. The Parables of Solomon, Corrected by the Original Hebrew.[1]

Christ's Warning to the Wicked. Lucas Osiander: Now Solomon utters a complaint in the persona of the Son of God (who is the wisdom of the Father), that even though true wisdom (i.e., the knowledge of God and of true piety) is lavishly made manifest in the Word of God, both in public and in private, nevertheless most of those who hear are foolish, taking greater pleasure in impiety. And to these hardened despisers of God's Word he threatens a terrible punishment, that they will certainly be abandoned by God in their dangers. For "Wisdom," says Solomon, "preaches abroad, she raises her voice in the streets; at the head of the multitude," that is, where many people gather, there she preaches and "cries out in the entrance of the gates" (where the people convene to see justice handed down), "she utters her words," that is, the Son of God eloquently drives home the Word of God everywhere. Usually when God reveals his word he broadcasts it widely, and sends down a most generous shower of his word, so that the impenitent may be rendered inexcusable. And so in this way Wisdom cries out, saying, "How long will you little ones delight in infantile things?" Or more properly, how long will you fools love folly? For he calls "fools" those who neglect the Word of God and have no taste for it, and "folly" their impious life, which is not regulated and governed by the same. Such fools take pleasure in their unscrupulousness. Proverbs[2]

Three Types of Folly. Michel Cop: Wisdom cries after three types of people who occupy the world: the slow-witted, the scornful, and fools. The slow-witted are those who are poorly taught, and therefore easily deceived; also, they are easily taken in by appearances, and follow after whatever seems good to the understanding of the flesh. What these people love is but foolishness, even though the world may praise and esteem it. For God has also made the wisdom of this world foolish. The scornful are those whose hearts are so swelled with pride and presumption, their minds so malicious and wicked, that they can be taught nothing, nor can they be rebuked or set straight. They scorn all discipline and correction, and in this scornfulness they take pleasure and delight, just as Solomon observes when he says, "Scoffers delight in their scoffing." The Pharisees showed themselves to be such, and there are also those who act this way now. Fools are much like the slow-witted, but they have this in common with the scorners, that they hate knowledge which is contrary to their scorn and foolishness. For those who delight in the knowledge of God and of his Word, which is the true knowledge, set no store in those things that please the flesh, and they submit themselves to be taught more and more, and they receive in humility all discipline and correction, so that they may mortify the flesh. Not only do fools not do this, but they hate anything that does not delight the flesh, and they persecute by word and deed those who labor to instruct them. Such was St. Paul before his conversion. Such are idolaters, of whom the world is full: for among ten million, scarcely may one be found who is not either slow-witted, scornful, or a fool. The ministers of the Word will thus take nothing upon themselves, but knowing that it is God who works by his wisdom, they will carry out their ministry in fear and trembling, without promising anything of

[1]Cajetan, *Parabolae Salomonis ad veritatem Hebraicam castigatae*, 12.

[2]Osiander, *Esdras, Nehemias, Esther, Iob, Psalterium, Prouerbia Salomonis, Ecclesiastes, & Canticum Canticorum*, 1024.

themselves, and they will confess the great and inestimable goodness of God, who has not disdained to abase himself so low as to warn the slow-witted, the scornful, and the fools by his wisdom—even though his wisdom is so outraged that it is thought to be foolishness. For St. Paul says, "The preaching of the cross is foolishness to those who are perishing." ON THE PROVERBS OF SOLOMON.[3]

THE LEAST BAD MEN. JOHN TRAPP: The *fatuelli* (little fools) that are easily persuaded into a fool's paradise. These are the best sort of bad men; the apostle calls them *akakōn* (naive). "Those are thought to be very good popes," writes Papirius Massonius, a popish writer, "who are only moderately bad, or that have any good at all in them."[†] These simpletons are much better than scorners, who delight in their scorning, but far beyond those fools who hate knowledge. See a similar gradation in Psalm 1:1. All sins are not equally sinful, and wicked people grow worse and worse. SOLOMON'S BOOK OF ALL VIRTUES.[4]

UNIVERSAL JUDGMENT. LUDWIG LAVATER: We are speaking here about the Word of God, that is, the very Son of God himself, our Lord Jesus Christ, who cries aloud in the forum, the streets, and in other places where people gather; he expostulates with them, but they care nothing for wisdom. They laugh and hold him in contempt, even though he offers them ample opportunity to repent. Now again we see what benefits he bestows on those who are guided by wisdom, and what punishments await those who reject it. To summarize in a few words, he says that great evils will befall you, which you will not be able to explain. This teaching does not apply to only a particular people or time, but it applies equally to all places and eras. Certainly, if we compare our life, pursuits, and character (both public and private) with these words of wisdom, we shall see that eventually God, who is most just, will render us an account. ON THE BOOK OF PROVERBS, OR SAYINGS, OF SOLOMON THE MOST-WISE KING.[5]

GOD REJOICES IN THE MISERY OF THE WICKED. JOHN TRAPP: "If God laughs, you have good reason to cry."[†] Note here the venomous nature of sin, so offensive to God, as it makes him (against his ordinary wont) merry at his creatures' misery, who otherwise delights in mercy. SOLOMON'S BOOK OF ALL VIRTUES.[6]

WISDOM ONLY SEEMS TO REJOICE IN THE DESTRUCTION OF SINNERS. MICHEL COP: Having complained about hardness of the slow-witted, the scornful, and the foolish, and of their unrepentant hearts, Wisdom threatens to laugh at them and mock them, when the destruction they fear shall fall on their own heads. It may indeed be thought that the wicked and obstinate fear nothing, because they seem to have such strength in numbers, and so often do they succeed in their purposes; also, they live at their ease, enjoying much in the way of temporal riches, and for this reason they are esteemed and held in high regard. Notwithstanding all this, their evil consciences often still reprove them, and they feel themselves guilty and afraid of God's judgment. Most of all do they fear eternal death, which is their last destruction. And therefore any time the least trouble comes into their way, they are greatly afraid. It is the destruction and fear at which Wisdom will laugh and mock. But insofar as destruction and mockery are the acts of dissolute and riotous persons, it might here be asked whether it is fitting for the Wisdom of God to deride and mock, and whether it is lawful to

[3]Cop, *Sur les Proverbes de Salomon*, 13-14; citing 1 Cor 1:20; 1:8.
[4]Trapp, *Solomonis ΠΑΝΆΡΕΤΟΣ*, 7; citing Rom 16:18. [†]Massonius was a sixteenth-century Catholic writer whose frank remarks on the state of the papacy were widely repeated by Protestant polemicists.
[5]Lavater, *In librum Proverbiorum siue Sententiarum Solomonis Regis sapientissimi*, 11.
[6]Trapp, *Solomonis ΠΑΝΆΡΕΤΟΣ*, 8; citing Mic 7:18. [†]A marginal note indicates Augustine as the author of this quotation, and a nineteenth-century editor of Trapp's works identifies *De Genesi ad litteram* (*On the Literal Meaning of Genesis*) as its source.

attribute any such things to her. I answer that Wisdom does not laugh and mock in the way that people do, nor is it lawful for us to attribute to her such derision and mockery, for this would be to make her like the most wicked imps of this world. But the holy Scripture, accommodating itself to our rudeness and willing to express how Wisdom appears to the understanding and opinion of the hard-hearted and the obstinate, does indeed attribute to her mockery and derision. ON THE PROVERBS OF SOLOMON.[7]

NO POSTMORTEM REPRIEVE. CARDINAL CAJETAN: The phrase "They will rise up in the morning" should be translated, according to the Hebrew reading, as "They will search for me." Read the Gospel and you will find the rich man as he cries out in his torments, "Father Abraham, have mercy." Then you will understand that what is written here is true about the damned: "Then they will call and I will not hear. They will look for me and will not find me." The rich man sought for wisdom, for the sake of his brothers at least, and he did not find it. And they considered discipline hateful. These four phrases according to the Hebrew should be read as follows, instead of wisdom they found knowledge hateful, and they did not choose the fear of the Lord. They did not desire my counsel, and they disregarded all my correction. An explanation is given for why Wisdom does not listen after death—namely, that they persevered in these four attacks on Wisdom. As a consequence of this, due to past sins, a reason is provided for why she does not hear those who call on and seek her. It is because the discussion concerns those who call on her after death and seek her after death. For past sins do not suffice to prevent the hearing of those who call on Wisdom in this life, because no matter in what hour the sinner cries out for help, mercy is offered. Therefore they shall eat. The punishment of loss is set forth, and the punishment of feeling is added to it by saying, "And they will eat from the fruit of their ways" (i.e., they will not eat from the fruit of Wisdom's paths, but from the fruit of their own wicked paths). And they will be glutted with the fruit of their plans. Or as they eat they will receive punishment until they are stuffed. THE PARABLES OF SOLOMON, CORRECTED BY THE ORIGINAL HEBREW.[8]

ON HARD AND SOFT ANSWERS. MICHEL COP: It might be said that God does answer the wicked after their death. For when the rich man is lying in hell he receives a far stronger answer from Abraham than ever he received in this life. In the same way, our Lord answers the goats. I answer that according to Solomon's way of thinking these here have not yet received an answer, for they have only a hard and sharp answer, such as a man would make to his enemy, resisting him to his face, or denying his intent. This is the sort of answer a judge gives to whose on whom he pronounces sentence, sending them to the gallows. But Solomon is speaking here of a soft and favorable answer, the sort a man might make to his friend, agreeing to what is asked of him. He says that God denies such answer to the fools and scorners who are obstinate and hardened; he hides himself from them and will not help them in any way. This is what Solomon means when he says, "They shall not find me." But it may be objected again that Solomon does not appear to speak with the same spirit as David his father did, when he wrote, "Call on me in the time of trouble, and I will deliver you." I answer that David speaks of those sinners who are not yet hardened in their wickedness, but with all their heart they truly turn and seek the Lord. And God promises always to hear such persons. But Solomon speaks here of those who have no intention of repenting, and who harden their hearts more and more against all holy admonitions and corrections. Such persons are not heard, nor do they experience God as favorable to them, for they do not really call on God. They do not seek him for the love they bear him, nor even for the

[7]Cop, *Sur les Proverbes de Salomon*, 16.

[8]Cajetan, *Parabolae Salomonis ad veritatem Hebraicam castigatae*, 14; citing Lk 16:24.

hatred and unpleasantness they have for their sin, but only because they are afraid of God's judgment, and they feel that their own destruction is at hand. On the Proverbs of Solomon.[9]

Don't Turn Your Hearts Away. Denis the Carthusian: "The turning away of the little ones."[†] The sense here is the same as in the verse above, "How long, O children, how long will you love childishness?" (1:22). This "turning away will kill them," for such people have turned their hearts away from God, by preferring transitory and carnal things to charity and the love of God. And this very turning away kills their souls with a spiritual destruction, for it is death in a state of guilt and mortal sin by which they died spiritually in the sight of God. Our Savior says of this death, "Let the dead bury their own dead." And in the Apocalypse: "You have a name of being alive, but you are dead." And this turning away will also kill them after this life, with the death of eternal damnation: "They shall have their portion in the pool burning with fire and brimstone, which is the second death." "And the prosperity of fools shall destroy them"; that is, the earthly prosperity of the wicked, by which in the present age they follow after riches, enjoyments, and honors, will be the cause or occasion of their perpetual damnation in the future, because they abuse the good gifts of God and are puffed up with present prosperity. The psalmist says of such people, "As the dream of those who awake, O Lord; so in your city you shall bring their image to nothing." And Job says that the wicked are advanced and secure in their riches, and the rod of God is not on them: "They spend their days in wealth, and in a moment they go down to hell." Exposition of the Book of Proverbs.[10]

2:1-22 *Receiving the Word of Wisdom*

God Helps Those Who Seek Wisdom. Philipp Melanchthon: The entire second chapter is an exhortation to hear and understand this doctrine, which God has delivered to us through the church. He binds us to this, and commands us to flee from all other wisdom that is at variance with this teaching. And the adulterous woman is understood to be a figure for any purported wisdom that draws our minds away from God. And in particular he says that that roving woman must be handed over to her master, to whom she had been betrothed. For such a mind is like an adulteress who scorns and abandons her true master, to whom she had been betrothed, wandering about most insolently and laughing at impious opinions. They delight themselves with the audacity of Epicurus, and in the worship of idols, and they suppose that it is because of these that they have great success and every good thing. But this chapter imparts both promises and warnings, just as it is said, "Seek first the kingdom of God, and all these things will be added to you." So also, "Blessed is the man who does not walk in the counsel of the wicked." It also reminds us how we can make progress by connecting its two causes: divine assistance and our own effort, just as elsewhere it is said, "How much more will [the Father] give the Holy Spirit to those who ask for him!" Again: "Ask, and it will be given to you, seek and you will find." And in the book of Wisdom it is written, "Wisdom is easily found by those who love her, and she anticipates those who seek her out." These sayings promise help to those who learn wisdom. Exposition of the Proverbs of Solomon.[11]

Bearing Fruit Openly. Michel Cop: With the intention that we not deceive ourselves by thinking that it is enough only to hear Wisdom, Solomon shows here that we should not be like the seed which fell by the wayside, but rather like that

[9]Cop, *Sur les Proverbes de Salomon*, 17-18; citing Lk 16:19-31; Mt 25:41; Ps 50:15.
[10]DCOO 7:16; citing Mt 8:22; Rev 3:1; 21:8; Ps 73:22; Job 21:7, 9, 13. [†]Vulgate: *parvulorum*.

[11]CR 14:9; citing Mt 6:33; Ps 1:1; Lk 11:13; Mt 7:7; Wis 6:13-14.

which fell upon the good soil, and that by so doing we shall obtain the former promise. And to show this, he explains in greater length what he had said earlier only briefly: because we do not easily at first understand things that are spoken concerning God, at the beginning of this passage, God shows himself to us as our Father, and he calls everyone who gives heed to his Wisdom his son. He does this so that we may more eagerly follow his desires, and that we may understand that he demands nothing of us but what a loving and gentle father ought and may require of his children. That which he desires for us is that when we hear his words, which are the seed of life, we should receive them in such a way that we should not allow the birds of the air to come and peck up this seed. When he urges us to "receive" and "hide," he is teaching us that we fulfill his commandments not merely by performing outward works, but in order to obey them truly we must imprint them on our hearts, so that the external works may proceed from the inward desire of our hearts, which is first and foremost the glory of God. Even though God requires us to "hide within us his commandments," this should not be understood to imply that it is lawful for us to become false Nicodemites,† making ourselves believe that our hearts are right before God, even as we dissemble before men and conceal our confession, nor also that we seem to go along with superstition and idolatry. The wise man does not teach us that, for just as the Jews were bound to declare themselves to be the people of God by the outward observance of the law, the feasts, the sacrifices, and the other ceremonies, so must we make profession of our Christian religion by bringing forth fruits worthy of repentance. ON THE PROVERBS OF SOLOMON.[12]

THE DEVIL SEEKS TO DISGUISE TRUE KNOWLEDGE. THE ENGLISH ANNOTATIONS: If people could be persuaded that all true knowledge is in the fear of the Lord and that all other knowledge without the fear of the Lord is mere vanity and folly, it would be a very strong motive to induce people (rational people) to the pursuit of piety and religion and to bring them to a good opinion of it. Whence the devil, on the other side, labors what he can, to possess all people with the opinion that religion turns wise people into fools and idiots. ANNOTATIONS ON PROVERBS 2:5.[13]

WISDOM IS GOD'S GIFT. CARDINAL CAJETAN: According to the Hebrew reading this would be, "because Jehovah will give wisdom, from his mouth knowing and understanding." The manner in which these fruits are acquired is then made clear, so that no one might think that these fruits arise naturally in a person as a consequence of human effort, as though from a sufficient cause. Rather, the writer wants us to know that human effort contributes to the fruits of wisdom as preparation and ordering, but it is God who acts as the bestower. For this reason he says that Jehovah will grant wisdom by working it in us. And again, because from his mouth (i.e., from the revelation of God himself) proceed both human knowledge and understanding. For if God had not revealed those things that belong to his providence and eternal life, as well as eternal punishment, we would not know them, and we would not have the capacity to know or understand with respect to God. THE PARABLES OF SOLOMON, CORRECTED BY THE ORIGINAL HEBREW.[14]

KNOWLEDGE OF GOD COMES FROM GOD. MICHAEL JERMIN: It is the saying of Aristotle, "It belongs to a wise man to consider the highest cause, by which there is the most certain judgment of all other things, and according to which it behooves all things to be ordered."† Now who can consider the highest cause, unless it be by the influence of the highest cause? Who can be wise in the knowledge

[12]Cop, *Sur les Proverbes de Salomon*, 22-23; citing Mt 13:4.
†"Nicodemite" was a derisive term used by Calvin and his followers to describe "closet Protestants," those who clandestinely frequented evangelical worship while publicly conforming to Catholic practices.

[13]Downame, ed., *English Annotations*, 6Q4r*.
[14]Cajetan, *Parabolae Salomonis ad veritatem Hebraicam castigatae*, 18.

of the Lord, unless the Lord give him wisdom? Theodoret observes that although the three captive children were brought up in all the learning of the Chaldeans, yet it is said of them that the Lord gave them wisdom, "for it was not the instruction of the Chaldeans but the grace of God that made them to be wise."[‡] And "if anyone lacks wisdom, let him ask it of God, who gives to all liberally, and does not upbraid." Gregory of Nazianzus, applying to this purpose that passage in Isaiah, "Come, everyone who thirsts, come to the waters; and he who has no money, come, buy and drink," speaks thus: "O readiness of his mercy! Only be willing, and you have bought this treasure. He thirsts after those who thirst, and to them that will drink, he gives drink!"[§] And how God gives wisdom we may learn from this verse. For the hands of God are the works of his hands, and the mouth of God is the mouth of his ministers: with the one he gives wisdom, "out of his mouth comes knowledge and understanding." Paraphrastic Meditations.[15]

Wisdom Must Penetrate the Heart. The English Annotations: A person may talk of wisdom, yea, and be able to discourse on it, its nature and properties, largely and learnedly, and to write of it too, with commendation. As we know there are those who preach, very plausibly, who are or have been known to be very lewd (the more the pity such should be suffered) in their lives and conversations. The reason is because they have wisdom well in their tongues and in their brains, but nothing in their hearts. And so long as that is not affected, our wisdom may do good to others by chance, but sometimes more hurt than good. As to ourselves, there is nothing done yet, nay our case is more lamentable and dangerous, than if we had no knowledge at all. Annotations on Proverbs 2:10.[16]

Adultery Condemned. Michel Cop: When a path is frequently trodden, there is no consideration given to its danger, and when a thing is often done, even though it is wicked, people may make themselves believe that there is no evil in it. This is the case with those who rashly swear, or who give themselves to lascivious and dissolute talk, or avarice, usury, sharp practice, sloth, or idleness. In the same way, there are many who are faithless and think nothing of breaking their marriage vows, having no pangs of conscience in becoming adulterers. And the world is full of those who mock and despise the institution of holy marriage, which God ordained from the beginning of the world, and would rather consort with prostitutes than take to themselves an honest companion or wife in marriage, which is honorable among all people. For this reason, it seems to most people that there is no danger in following the ways of adulterers and whoremongers, and that they commit no evil in being defiled and polluted with whoredom and fornication. But when the Holy Spirit declares to us by the mouth of Solomon that we may be delivered "from the strange woman," he shows us well that it is not as the world judges, for if there were no danger, there would be no need for God to give us counsel and understanding to deliver us from her. . . .

The unfaithfulness of the adulterous woman consists in this, that she leaves and forsakes her husband. Not that she forsakes him utterly, leaving him forever and not returning to him anymore; for unfaithfulness consists not only in that, but primarily in that she joins herself to another, separating herself from her husband and making one flesh of two; and yet she still returns to her husband, covering her unfaithfulness. So also it is with an adulterer who is unfaithful to his wife. And to show that the adulterous woman is not only unfaithful but also disobedient, rebellious,

[15]Jermin, *Paraphrasticall Meditations*, 642-43; citing Jas 1:5; Is 55:1. [†]Jermin appears to be quoting a Latin translation of Aristotle's *Metaphysics* widely cited among the medieval theologians (e.g., Thomas Aquinas, *Summa Theologiae* II-II, q. 45, a. 1). The indicated passage in the original is as follows: "The knowledge of everything must necessarily belong to him who in the highest degree possesses knowledge of the universal, because he knows in a sense all the particulars which it comprises." *Metaphysics* 1.2.4; LCL 271:11. [‡]Theodoret of Cyrus, *Commentary on Daniel* (1:17), in PG 80:1280. [§]Gregory of Nazianzus, *Oration* 40.27, in NPNF[2] 7:370.

[16]Downame, ed., *English Annotations*, 6R1r*.

and ungrateful, Solomon calls her husband the prince, teacher, and guide of his wife's youth, and in doing so he shows that the husband is the head and the governor, having prerogative above her. For this reason, she ought to fear and reverence him, and faithfully obey him. . . . Likewise, the adulterous man is not only unfaithful to his wife but also cruel, for he does not govern her youthfulness, her weakness, and her frailty, bearing with her and tenderly loving her. But Solomon teaches husbands to do this when he describes a husband as the guide of his wife's youth. ON THE PROVERBS OF SOLOMON.[17]

[17]Cop, *Sur les Proverbes de Salomon*, 30-31.

3:1-35 TRUST IN THE LORD

[1]*My son, do not forget my teaching,*
but let your heart keep my commandments,

[2]*for length of days and years of life*
and peace they will add to you.

[3]*Let not steadfast love and faithfulness forsake you;*
bind them around your neck;
write them on the tablet of your heart.

[4]*So you will find favor and good success*[a]
in the sight of God and man.

[5]*Trust in the LORD with all your heart,*
and do not lean on your own understanding.

[6]*In all your ways acknowledge him,*
and he will make straight your paths.

[7]*Be not wise in your own eyes;*
fear the LORD, and turn away from evil.

[8]*It will be healing to your flesh*[b]
and refreshment[c] *to your bones.*

[9]*Honor the LORD with your wealth*
and with the firstfruits of all your produce;

[10]*then your barns will be filled with plenty,*
and your vats will be bursting with wine.

[11]*My son, do not despise the LORD's discipline*
or be weary of his reproof,

[12]*for the LORD reproves him whom he loves,*
as a father the son in whom he delights.

[13]*Blessed is the one who finds wisdom,*
and the one who gets understanding,

[14]*for the gain from her is better than gain from silver*
and her profit better than gold.

[15]*She is more precious than jewels,*
and nothing you desire can compare with her.

[16]*Long life is in her right hand;*
in her left hand are riches and honor.

[17]*Her ways are ways of pleasantness,*
and all her paths are peace.

[18]*She is a tree of life to those who lay hold of her;*
those who hold her fast are called blessed.

[19]*The LORD by wisdom founded the earth;*
by understanding he established the heavens;

[20]*by his knowledge the deeps broke open,*
and the clouds drop down the dew.

[21]*My son, do not lose sight of these—*
keep sound wisdom and discretion,

[22]*and they will be life for your soul*
and adornment for your neck.

[23]*Then you will walk on your way securely,*
and your foot will not stumble.

[24]*If you lie down, you will not be afraid;*
when you lie down, your sleep will be sweet.

[25]*Do not be afraid of sudden terror*
or of the ruin[d] *of the wicked, when it comes,*

[26]*for the LORD will be your confidence*
and will keep your foot from being caught.

[27]*Do not withhold good from those to whom it is due,*[e]
when it is in your power to do it.

[28]*Do not say to your neighbor, "Go, and come again,*
tomorrow I will give it"—when you have it with you.

[29]*Do not plan evil against your neighbor,*
who dwells trustingly beside you.

[30]*Do not contend with a man for no reason,*
when he has done you no harm.

[31]*Do not envy a man of violence*
and do not choose any of his ways,

[32]for the devious person is an abomination to
the Lord,
but the upright are in his confidence.

[33]The Lord's curse is on the house of the
wicked,
but he blesses the dwelling of the righteous.

[34]Toward the scorners he is scornful,
but to the humble he gives favor.[f]

[35]The wise will inherit honor,
but fools get[g] *disgrace.*

a Or *repute* **b** Hebrew *navel* **c** Or *medicine* **d** Hebrew *storm* **e** Hebrew *Do not withhold good from its owners* **f** Or *grace* **g** The meaning of the Hebrew word is uncertain

Overview: The third chapter of Proverbs begins with another appeal from father to son, this time to trust in the Lord. The commentators enlarge on this call, discussing the rewards of wisdom—long life, spiritual health, and eternal welfare—and considering what it means to trust God. They also reflect on belief in biblical teaching, affective faith responses to God, and the importance of generosity. A major theme that resonates with the reformers is the importance of discipline or reproof from God, which some Protestants regarded as a mark of the "true church," and they relate it to the Christian concept of bearing the cross as embodied in Jesus Christ. The interpreters dwell on the blessings of wisdom in the second half of the chapter, arguing that true rewards are heavenly. Once again, they see wisdom personified in Jesus Christ, perceiving in the reference to a "tree of life" in Proverbs 3:18 as nothing less than redemption from the fall in the Garden of Eden. Finally, our commentators discuss several practical matters, which will be a theme of the biblical material throughout the book and were among the reformers' pastoral concerns, including neighborly practices of justice and mercy.

3:1-12 *Trust in God, Not Your Own Understanding*

Long Life, Peace, and Grace. Cardinal Cajetan: "They set before you length of days, long life, and peace." Three points are listed as constituting the reward for remembering this. The first is that God has promised long life to those who honor their parents. No doubt the son who remembers to preserve his parents' practical instruction is counted among them. And so length of days is promised in the present life. Now to prevent anyone from fearing that the length of days will prove unhappy, by way of explanation "long life" is also added. These years are not merely delaying of death, like years of sicknesses, bondage, oppression, and hardship. And so that "length of days," together with "long life," may contain all that is needed, this is added as well: "and peace." The Hebrews by the word "peace" summarize all that is good.

"Mercy and truth do not abandon you." The term translated as "mercy" should be understood as grace. This term has become quite common. It does not mean the experience of mercy, but properly speaking grace, as I have explained elsewhere. The practice of preserving the practical commands of a father in one's memory is described, by coming down to the particular injunctions of what is morally good. Now the first consists in the genus, and the second in the species. In the genus, moreover, two very broad commands are given. The first concerns grace, by which we perform some kindness to another of our own free purpose. The other concerns truth, by which—disregarding all that is false—we make our actions conform to what we say, our words to our heartfelt intention, and our heartfelt intention to our obligations. Therefore, grace is that by which we show gracious actions, and truth that by which we show what is obligatory. The inseparable combination of these two virtues and the careful practice of them is revealed as the skill of practical memory with respect to what is morally good, when the author says, "Grace and truth do not abandon you." THE PARABLES OF SOLOMON, CORRECTED BY THE ORIGINAL HEBREW.[1]

THE PROMISE OF HEAVENLY PROSPERITY. MICHEL COP: Here Solomon promises nothing that is not often repeated in the Law and in the Prophets. Therefore, seeing that we have so great a number of witnesses, let us in no way doubt this promise. Even though now we are encircled by evils and walk in the midst of the shadow of death, we should not fear that God (who is always present with us) will fail to accomplish his promise. And this is so chiefly in regard to our spiritual health, and the eternal prosperity to which we must aspire, for we must not content ourselves with days and years of peace in this temporal life, or with earthly prosperity. And although the Lord is our life and the length of our days, still Solomon attributes it to the law and to the commandments, because God communicates both himself and his riches to those who do not forsake his law, but keep his commandments. ON THE PROVERBS OF SOLOMON.[2]

TRUSTING GOD MEANS TRUSTING IN GOD'S SELF-DISCLOSURE. PHILIPP MELANCHTHON: Three precepts follow from this. The first relates to the knowledge of God, faith, and fear; the second relates to keeping intact the ministry of teaching; the third concerns the cross—there is so much doctrine in one single verse! First it teaches about faith, and adds its antithesis: "Do not lean on your own understanding." This is understood in a threefold sense as referring to the knowledge of God, to morals, and to judgments of a practical nature. If you acknowledge God, as he is disclosed in this doctrine, you will not wander about as the heathens do, inventing various names, cults, and opinions about God. Instead, I want you to conform your character to these precepts, and not follow your own imagination, as the Spartans did in allowing men to bargain with one another for their wives.[†] The pope forbids [clerical] marriage. But I want you to follow my precepts in choosing useful things: do what needs to be done, but don't be a busybody, and avoid both hope or fear for anything outside your calling. Remember what is said in Ezekiel: "Walk in my ways." EXPOSITION OF THE PROVERBS OF SOLOMON.[3]

TRUSTING GOD MEANS LOVING GOD. MICHEL COP: In this Solomon teaches the same thing Moses taught with the first commandments, that our hearts must not be divided, so as to give one portion to God and the other part somewhere else. For that would be to assign a companion to God, something he will not endure. And because many do not esteem the Word of God (which ought to be the wisdom and understanding of his children and servants), they dream up and fashion in their imaginations divine services, and they think to honor God by laboring away in them. But in order to pull us away from this foolish presumption and abuse, Solomon warns us that trusting in God with our hearts requires that we not lean on our own wisdom, just as Moses warned the children of Israel. . . . Moreover, considering that we cannot trust a person unless we love them, Solomon exhorting us to trust in God depends on us loving him, as Moses says. Now if we do love God, we will worship him in spirit and in truth, and will call on him alone in our spiritual necessities, knowing that it is he alone who can and will provide for all our needs. ON THE PROVERBS OF SOLOMON.[4]

[1]Cajetan, *Parabolae Salomonis ad veritatem Hebraicam castigatae*, 23-24.
[2]Cop, *Sur les Proverbes de Salomon*, 35*.

[3]CR 14:10; citing Ezek 36:27. [†]Melanchthon is apparently referring to the Spartan custom of plural marriage, whereby multiple men might father children by the same woman (e.g., Xenophon, *Respublica Lacedaemoniorum* 1.7-10; Plutarch, *Lycurgus* 15.6-10). Given that his next remark concerns the Catholic prohibition of clerical marriage, it seems that he is presenting these as opposing extremes of human moral invention.
[4]Cop, *Sur les Proverbes de Salomon*, 38-39.

Maturity Means Continuing to Lean on God. The English Annotations: This is a seasonable caveat and admonition, lest having set forth the praise of wisdom and understanding as effects of the fear of God, foolish people, upon a persuasion of godliness and religion, should ascribe these to their own wit and prudence and grow presumptuous as they grow (or persuade themselves that they grow) religious. Neither is it enough for us to trust in God (not in ourselves) for the means, that is, that in case things fall out as we wished and endeavored, we give him thanks, but also for the events, whether so or so, that in case it proves contrary to our desires or endeavors, yet to believe God is wiser than we, and orders all events for the best, though we cannot penetrate into the depths of his counsels. Annotations on Proverbs 3:5.[5]

Support the Ministry of the Word. Philipp Melanchthon: In this passage he bids each one assist according to his own means in maintaining the ministry of teaching in the temples and schools, and the sweetest promise is added, just as in Matthew 10:42 it is written, "Whoever gives a drink of water to one of the least of mine because of the teaching will have a reward." Exposition of the Proverbs of Solomon.[6]

Instructions on Generosity. Michel Cop: The fourth commandment has respect to that which God has ordained in Exodus 23:19: "The best of the firstfruits of your ground you shall bring into the house of the Lord your God." And again: "Speak to the people of Israel, that they take for me a contribution. From every man whose heart moves him you shall receive the contribution for me." And also the first two chapters of Leviticus. And therefore at first glance, it may appear that this commandment has nothing to do with us, but only applied to the Jews, until the time that Jesus Christ came and appeared in the flesh. For, if they will receive Jesus Christ, they have the truth of the ancient figures and shadows. But Jesus Christ, who is the true interpreter of the law (and the one who fulfills it, not destroys it), has shown us clearly that we always ought to observe this commandment. For he says to his disciples, "And the King will answer them, 'Truly, I say to you, as you did it to one of the least of these my brothers, you did it to me.'" And St. Paul stirs up his readers to the same end, saying, "I have received full payment, and more. I am well supplied, having received from Epaphroditus the gifts you sent, a fragrant offering, a sacrifice acceptable and pleasing to God."

To obey this commandment we must be merciful, helping the needy from that which is ours, as Solomon explicitly teaches us here, saying, "with your wealth." We must not give alms at the cost of another, nor from our neighbor's goods, as do manservants and maidservants, and hirelings; so also do the avaricious, usurers, and thieves, who despoil their neighbors' property for the sake of giving alms, and do no honor to the Lord thereby. For just as in old times the Lord refused the sacrifices of such people, even so alms given from robbery do not please him.[†] Added to this category are those priests, monks, and nuns who under guise of long prayers and their beautiful divine service said so devoutly devour the houses of simple folk, who are easily deceived. . . . And therefore, let us not apply ourselves to anything more than to obey the Word of God, for it alone shall put enough in our hands to bestow. . . .

But when we hear that it is said, "The earth is the Lord's, and all that is in it" . . . the question may be raised whether it is lawful to call anything ours that we possess. I answer that we neither have nor can deserve that anything should be ours; otherwise, our Lord would not need to teach us to ask of God that he would give our daily bread. But all creatures are ours, and we may use them as our own, with thanksgiving, even though they are not ours by right, but rather they come to us by the goodness of God, who gives us all things abundantly for us to use. Thus does God make them "ours," showing us a wonderful fatherly goodness. And we, in turn, should not be grieved to honor the

[5]Downame, ed., *English Annotations*, 6R2v*.
[6]CR 14:10.

Lord with these gifts, but acknowledging his great generosity, we should distribute them gladly and generously to our needy brethren and neighbors. For it is said that "God loves a cheerful giver." . . . But we must spend our substance reasonably, as stewards, sparing nothing where necessity requires it. And this is the way we honor God with our substance, for though it be divided up many ways, eaten and consumed, yet shall we always have enough, and even great abundance, as Solomon promises us, saying, "So shall your barns be filled with plenty." On the Proverbs of Solomon.[7]

God's Reproof Is Good. Balthasar Hubmaier: No one may resist the will of God where God does not himself graciously offer freedom of will. However, where he offers the same to a person, his will once again takes place, either for good or for punishment, which is also good to the one who recognizes its goodness. Freedom of the Will.[8]

Bearing the Cross Versus Philosophic Patience. Philipp Melanchthon: Here the entire doctrine of the cross is summed up, and the distinction between philosophy and the gospel must be considered. Philosophy and human reason offer a different account of death and human calamity than does the voice of the gospel. But it is imperative that we know the reason why the church is subjected to the cross, and only then can the consolations offered by philosophy and the gospel be compared, and Christian forms of patience be distinguished from philosophic patience. Exposition of the Proverbs of Solomon.[9]

Don't Ignore the Lord's Reproof. Dirk Philips: "Therefore we also," says the apostle, "since we have such a crowd of witnesses around us, let us put off the sin that always sticks to us and makes us slothful, and let us run with patience in the struggle that is ordained for us and look on Jesus, the beginner and perfecter of faith, who, when he certainly might have had happiness, endured the cross and did not pay attention to the shame and has placed himself at the right hand of the throne of God. Consider him who had to bear such opposition from sinners against him, so that you do not becomes slothful in your mind and cease and forget the comfort that speaks to you as to children: my son, do not deem the punishment of the Lord as small, and do not despair if you are punished by him, for whom the Lord loves, those he punishes; he scourges every son whom he receives." The Enchiridion.[10]

The Elect Experience Afflictions as God's Fatherly Discipline. Michel Cop: Those among God's children who are weak are tempted to impatience when they see things in confusion, such that those who walk uprightly suffer affliction, while the wicked prosper; indeed, they may even be tempted to follow after the wicked, so that they might enjoy the same prosperity, as Psalm 73 suggests. But Solomon resists this temptation when he says, "My son, do not despise. . . ." In this fifth commandment he warns the children of God that if in this world they suffer poverty and afflictions they should receive them from the hand of God, who in all things acts justly and from necessity. Therefore, they should receive these things with patience, knowing that by these means God corrects and rebukes them, just as they have deserved, with the goal that they should acknowledge their faults and endeavor more and more to amend their ways, and to improve from good to better. But even though it is profitable for us to be afflicted, as the Holy Spirit teaches us by Solomon, who commands that we should not refuse correction, yet our flesh, which is impatient and desires nothing but pleasure and ease, tempts

[7] Cop, *Sur les Proverbes de Salomon*, 43-44; citing Ex 25:2; Mt 25:40; Phil 4:18; Ps 24:1; 2 Cor 9:7. †Medieval Catholic teaching had long maintained strictures against giving alms from ill-gotten goods (e.g., Thomas Aquinas, *Summa Theologiae* II-II, q. 32, a. 7-8). Cop gives this teaching a distinctively Reformation twist by associating the service of monks and nuns with this prohibition.
[8] CRR 5:467*; citing Ps 76:8; Rom 9:19; Heb 12:6.
[9] CR 14:10-11.

[10] CRR 6:38-88*; citing Heb 12.

us to reject the yoke of the Lord, discouraging and making us despair, as though God persecuted us to destroy us, and as though he hated us like an enemy or an adversary. . . .

"For the Lord reproves him whom he loves." If we receive this reason as true, as indeed it is, we will understand that the discipline, corrections, calamities, and afflictions that God sends upon us are witnesses that he loves us, and that we are pleasing and agreeable to him, and that it is only for our salvation that he disciplines us. We must not then conclude or say when we are afflicted that God hates us, but rather the contrary. One might say that the reason Solomon gives is not sufficient to compel us not to be grieved at our afflictions; for we see that God seems to make no difference in punishing the reprobate as well as the elect, and by his punishments more often he declares his anger than his love. Also the Scripture speaks in this matter, and experience confirms it. I answer that when the faithful are threatened with any punishment, they receive it from the hand of God, and know that it is their Father who disciplines them for their profit, and in so doing he shows his fatherly love. The reprobate, on the other hand, do not know that they are governed by God's hand when they are afflicted, so more often they assume that it comes by chance, and being strangers from God and his family, they do not understand that the hand of God can touch them. Let us then remember when we are disciplined that we cannot feel the taste of God's love for us unless we firmly believe that the afflictions we experience are fatherly corrections, by which he disciplines our sins. The reprobate can never think so, for their thoughts stray, and fly hither and thither. ON THE PROVERBS OF SOLOMON.[11]

3:13-35 *Blessed Is the One Who Finds Wisdom*

PURSUING THE HIGHEST GOOD. CARDINAL CAJETAN: After the commandments that pertain to God have been carefully explained, there then follows an explanation of the reward that was mentioned above. He had previously said that "length of days" and "long life" as well as "peace" are set before you. Developing this further he explains the blessings of the man who has already found the wisdom that he sought. Now here understand the "blessed" person as he who is now so in hope, and at some time shall be in substance. Moreover, the aspects of blessedness that are here recounted surpass the good things of this present life. But here the goodness of wisdom is developed, because it is here—as the concept of the morally good is situated among moral goods generally—that the highest good [*summum bonum*] is described as something to be remembered. "And the one who abounds in prudence." According to the Hebrew this should be taken as, "and of the man who will apply his understanding." This means: and of the man who finds wisdom such that he makes application to some understanding from things that are hidden. Because not only does he know what he has learned, but he also—from the things which he knows—applies this to the understanding of other things. And again, "Blessed is he who applies his understanding to some work." THE PARABLES OF SOLOMON, CORRECTED BY THE ORIGINAL HEBREW.[12]

DIVINE AND HUMAN WISDOM CONTRASTED. PHILIPP MELANCHTHON: Here the text returns to common exhortations and instructs us, that we may learn the doctrine given by God and obey it, preferring neither our own wisdom nor shrewdness, and to this end it adds both promises and warnings. All of these are opposed by human wisdom, which impudently fools about with its own invented opinions about God, religious practices, and forms of worship, and does not want to be bound to the word of God. Likewise, it seeks safety in the counsels of life from its own shrewdness, and does not remain within the bounds set

[11]Cop, *Sur les Proverbes de Salomon*, 44-45; citing Eccles 9:1.

[12]Cajetan, *Parabolae Salomonis ad veritatem Hebraicam castigatae*, 28.

down by the word of God. And all of these exhortations are in keeping with the entire Psalm, *Beati immaculati*, "Blessed are they who are undefiled in the way. . . ." But these commendations of wisdom are rightly understood as referring to revealed wisdom, that is, to the Word of God disclosed in the church, to the Decalogue and the Gospel. Nor is this anything other than antiquity accommodating its praises of wisdom to the person of the Son of God, who discloses the Word resounding in the church. The church is brought into being by that Word, and in him is revealed the nature of God and his will. Exposition of the Proverbs of Solomon.[13]

The Blessings of Wisdom Are Eternal. Michel Cop: To show how the wise man is blessed, Solomon uses a circumlocution and a comparison. The circumlocution goes like this, in that he does *not* say, "blessed is the wise person," but "blessed is the person who finds. . . ." And he uses the comparison to show that the wise one is like a person who grows rich by his labor. For just as the latter is careful in working to find riches and treasures, and having found these, takes them for himself and guards them, and is accounted wealthy, so he who by yielding himself attentively to the Word of God gets wisdom and abides therein, keeping the Lord's commandments, and is wise. And just as the rich man judges himself to be blessed and is thought to be so by the world, so the wise man is assured that he is blessed before God. But even though the wise man and the rich man are here set side by side, this is not to say that the blessedness of the one is equal to the other, for the riches that are got by wisdom do not change, except to go from good to better. For this reason the wise man is blessed forever, and without end. On the Proverbs of Solomon.[14]

Spiritual and Temporal Blessings. John Donne: The person to whom Solomon attributes this right and left hand is Wisdom; and a wise person may reach out with their right and left hand to receive blessings of both sorts. And the person whom Solomon represents by Wisdom there is Christ himself. So that not only a worldly wise person, but a Christian wise person, may reach out with both hands, to both kinds of blessings, left and right, temporal and spiritual. Sermon on Psalm 144:15.[15]

Wisdom Restores Fruit Lost in the Fall. Francis Taylor: Solomon goes on to set out a commendation of Wisdom, so that he may allure men to seek the more earnestly after her. He had set out her excellence by [comparison to] silver, gold, pearls: "She is silver to poor men, gold to noble men, and pearls to princes."[†] . . . Now he sets out Wisdom's excellence (1) by comparing her to the tree of life, and (2) by promising happiness to those who get and keep her. . . . "Is a tree of life," like to a living tree that brings forth stores of pleasant fruit to delight and preserve the life of the eaters. Or more particularly, as most writers agree, it is an allusion to the tree of life in Paradise, which was a sign to Adam that he should live forever in health, strength, and comfort on the earth—if he did not sin. So wisdom restores us to that which we lost in Adam, eternal life, but in a better place in heaven. . . .

Wisdom not only preserves people's lives, as a tree of life, but also makes them happy. But this happiness is not to everyone, as fruit does not do good to those who only look on it, or touch it, or smell it, but to those who gather, eat, and digest it. So Wisdom's fruit does no good to those who seek it casually, or think on it only a little; it goes rather to those who take pains to get it and keep it, who will not let her go till they have found out the depth of her treasure, who observe all her commands, even the very least, and persevere in doing so to the very last. An Exposition with Practical Observations.[16]

---

[13]CR 14:11; citing Ps 118.

[14]Cop, *Sur les Proverbes de Salomon*, 46-47.

[15]Donne, *Works*, 3:329*.

[16]Taylor, *An Exposition with Practicall Observations upon the First Three Chapters of the Proverbs*, 473-74*; citing Gen 2:9. [†]The text

An Expansive View of the Tree of Life. The English Annotations: Not elsewhere mentioned in the Old Testament, except in Genesis and this book, it seems by comparing uses that it was a proverb in Solomon's time applicable to anything that is much desired, and longed for, and brings great joy and comfort when it comes, whether it has any relation to life (in the proper sense) or not. Annotations on Proverbs 3:18.[17]

The World Is God's College. Michael Jermin: It is a saying that Justin Martyr cites out of Plato: "God himself as the old word is, possesses the beginning, end, and middle of all things."[†] And in the book of Wisdom it is said that "Wisdom reaches from one end to the other mightily." Here God and Wisdom are joined together, and "the Lord by wisdom" is said to have "founded the earth, by understanding" to have "established the heavens." But as Jerome notes, "It is not that the earth has any foundations laid in great deepness; but the will and power of God, in which all things are contained, are to be called its foundations."[‡] And therefore in Job it is said that "God hangs the earth upon nothing." Now as God has founded the earth and established the heavens, so we, while we are on the earth, must be founded by faith, that so in heaven we may be established in glory. In a more full understanding of the words, by "the earth" we may conceive not only the earth in itself, but all things that are on or in the earth; by "the heavens" not only the heavens themselves but all things that are contained in them, as they are taken in their largest sense. For so in this verse and the next, the wise man shows all the works of God to have been made by wisdom, and then the founding and establishing of them is nothing but the settling of everything in that nature and condition that God has given and appointed to it. And if I shall not seem too lightly to mark the works: the whole earth is but God's college, founded by his wisdom. The officers of this college are the magistrates of the world; its statutes are the commandments; its studies are the several professions of the world; its several degrees of students are the several ranks of men; its treasury is God's mercy; its revenues are God's blessings; its library, in which all books are contained, is God's Word. Paraphrastic Meditations.[18]

Holding Fast to the Eternal Word. Michel Cop: Solomon does not want us to think that the Wisdom he so earnestly commends to us here, and to which he attributes such great virtues and excellent graces, is a thing dreamed up in human minds, to perish with them, so that we should mistrust and despise her. Therefore he declares to us her eternity, divinity, and power. For if the Lord has built the earth by Wisdom, it follows that she is before all creatures, and so she is eternal. Forasmuch as there is no one but God that is everlasting, we must understand that Wisdom is of the same divine essence with God, and consequently of the same power. When Solomon speaks in this way of Wisdom, he attributes the creation, ordering, and government of all things, both heavenly and earthly, to her, and he shows that it is the same eternal world of which Moses speaks. Therefore we must understand that this Wisdom is the everlasting Son of God, our Lord Jesus Christ. And so by these words, Solomon entices us to put all our happiness, all the hope of our salvation, all our joy and pleasure in Jesus Christ, that he alone should be our sustenance and true contentment, and that we should not desire other riches or treasures, but that he should be to us all in all, since he alone has created all things, ordered all things, and holds all things in his power. Therefore if we receive him in this way and hold

cites Aeneas Silvius (the humanist writer who became Pope Pius II, 1405–1464) in English, most likely Taylor's own paraphrase.
[17]Downame, ed., *English Annotations*, 6R3r*.

[18]Jermin, *Paraphrasticall Meditations*, 54-55; citing Wis 8:1; Job 26:7. [†]The *Exhortation to the Greeks* (*Cohortatio ad Graecos*) from which Jermin here quotes is regarded by modern scholars as pseudonymous. For the original passage in Plato (which has a rather different sense), see *Parmenides* 165A. [‡]Jerome, *Commentariorum in Isaiam Prophetam* 6.13 (PL 24:219).

fast to him, then we are richly blessed and shall lack nothing. On the Proverbs of Solomon.[19]

Justice Requires Lending a Hand. Cardinal Cajetan: According to the Hebrew this reads, "you shall not hold back some good from the one to whom it is due when it is within your power to perform it." As he has explained above with respect to God the particular and specific precepts of truth and of grace, so as a consequence he now explains five precepts of truth and grace in their species with respect to human beings. He does this so that the memory of divine law can easily be preserved under these five safeguards. For it is in keeping with a treatise on the acquisition of wisdom, insofar as it is the highest good, to descend to the species of moral precepts, both with respect to God and with respect to human beings. These precepts, moreover, are all negative, such that instruction proceeds from more simple concepts, because it is easier not to do wrong than to do good. And to the benefit of wisdom, which preserves men and women from the harm of punishment (harm inflicted by one's neighbors), are properly joined those precepts that prohibit the wrong of guilt against one's neighbor. The first precept is that of justice—namely, that one does not refuse (so long as it is within his power to restore it) to return a possession to its owner. And he refers to one's possession as a good, so as to differentiate it from giving back his sword to someone who is insane. He does not say, "Give it back," but "You will not withhold," in order to possess them, everything that has been entrusted to you that you might keep them for yourself. This would prevent the owner from having what belongs to him or what is owed him. This in fact entails the notion that one is commanded to return the belonging with interest. For he is commanded not to refuse help to his neighbor who is trying to recover his possession. And consequently, when it is in your power to do this, if your strength is adequate (if you have the opportunity) to supply your neighbor with helpful support, then you must do so, both in the work of truth and in the intention of grace. The Parables of Solomon, Corrected by the Original Hebrew.[20]

Avoiding Scandal for the Sake of Vocation. Philipp Melanchthon: Do not get in the way of other people's calling [*vocationem*], and fulfill the demands of your own faithfully and with diligence. "Do not say to your neighbor, 'Go and return; tomorrow I will give to you,' when you can give now. Do not plot evil against your neighbor, who lives near you in security." This precept and the following pertain to the commandment, "Do not kill." Now there are two ways in which evil against others can be construed: on the one hand, there is outright violence; on the other, there is fraud, calumny, theft, and so on. John [the Baptist] prohibits both types when he says, "Do violence to no one, neither accuse falsely." "Do not quarrel with another without reason, when he has done you no evil." This verse prohibits an entire species of calumny, unjust contention. "Do not envy the unjust man, and do not follow his ways." The general principle is that we not take offense at the scandal of the cross or the successes of the wicked, and so fall away from God and imitate the wicked, who put their hope in power, wealth, tranquility, and other commodities. Often it seems that the church is subjected to the cross and the wicked rule over everything; an entire psalm warns us about this scandal: "Do not envy the wicked." Exposition of the Proverbs of Solomon.[21]

Mercy Not Optional for Christians. Michel Cop: At the beginning of this third chapter, Solomon commends to us the law of God in general, and its division between mercy and faithfulness. For our instruction in faithfulness, he has given us many commandments pertaining to the first table of Moses, from which we receive

[19]Cop, *Sur les Proverbes de Salomon*, 46-47; citing Gen 1:3; Jn 1:1.

[20]Cajetan, *Parabolae Salomonis ad veritatem Hebraicam castigatae*, 32-33.

[21]CR 14:11-12; citing Ex 20:13; Lk 3:14; Ps 36.

most excellent promises to give us courage in keeping the commandments. But now to teach us mercy, he gives us commandments belonging to the second table, which shows us how we ought to live with our neighbors, and what duty we owe them. First of all, he forbids theft—not only that for which thieves are punished by the magistrates, but primarily that for which some people actually pride themselves and expect to be held in high regard by those who extol covetousness and think nothing of hurting their neighbors so that they can get ahead. They do this because they think they will encounter no resistance, nor any avenging power. And there are many kinds of such thieves, who not only go unpunished, but are honored among people. Yet even though they are full of cruelty, they should not think to escape punishment, for as it is said, "Blessed are the merciful, for they shall be shown mercy," so also cursed are the cruel and unmerciful, for "judgment without mercy shall fall on him that shows no mercy." So they shall buy their honors very dearly. It would be much better for them to have confessed their faults, and to be punished in this world with shame, than to hear this fearful sentence, "Depart from me, you that are accursed." We say "with shame," because since they say they are Christians, it should be a foul shame for them to suffer the gibbet, as St. Peter shows us: "See to it that none of you suffers as a murderer, or thief, or evildoer." But we shall avoid both punishment and shame, if being merciful and charitable, we do to our neighbors as we would be done to in return, and do not withhold the good from the one who owns it. For to do this well, it is not enough merely to forsake all evil trades, all unlawful and unreasonable means of drawing to ourselves the goods of our neighbors; beyond this, we must renounce all enterprises, purposes, and schemes to enrich ourselves at our neighbors' expense, and we must do our duty to preserve our neighbor in what he possesses. We must readily pay the worker his wages, and give alms to the poor when we are in possession of worldly goods, for they belong to such as these, and not to us only. Therefore whatever legal right we may have to possess them, they are entrusted to us to use them as God has taught us by his Word. ON THE PROVERBS OF SOLOMON.[22]

[22]Cop, *Sur les Proverbes de Salomon*, 56-57; citing Mt 5:7; Jas 2:13; Mt 25:41; 1 Pet 4:15; Mt 7:12.

4:1-27 A FATHER'S WISE INSTRUCTION

1 *Hear, O sons, a father's instruction,*
and be attentive, that you may gain[a] *insight,*

2 *for I give you good precepts;*
do not forsake my teaching.

3 *When I was a son with my father,*
tender, the only one in the sight of my mother,

4 *he taught me and said to me,*

"Let your heart hold fast my words;
keep my commandments, and live.

5 *Get wisdom; get insight;*
do not forget, and do not turn away from
the words of my mouth.

6 *Do not forsake her, and she will keep you;*
love her, and she will guard you.

7 *The beginning of wisdom is this: Get wisdom,*
and whatever you get, get insight.

8 *Prize her highly, and she will exalt you;*
she will honor you if you embrace her.

9 *She will place on your head a graceful garland;*
she will bestow on you a beautiful crown."

10 *Hear, my son, and accept my words,*
that the years of your life may be many.

11 *I have taught you the way of wisdom;*
I have led you in the paths of uprightness.

12 *When you walk, your step will not be hampered,*
and if you run, you will not stumble.

13 *Keep hold of instruction; do not let go;*
guard her, for she is your life.

14 *Do not enter the path of the wicked,*
and do not walk in the way of the evil.

15 *Avoid it; do not go on it;*
turn away from it and pass on.

16 *For they cannot sleep unless they have done*
wrong;
they are robbed of sleep unless they have
made someone stumble.

17 *For they eat the bread of wickedness*
and drink the wine of violence.

18 *But the path of the righteous is like the light of*
dawn,
which shines brighter and brighter until full
day.

19 *The way of the wicked is like deep darkness;*
they do not know over what they stumble.

20 *My son, be attentive to my words;*
incline your ear to my sayings.

21 *Let them not escape from your sight;*
keep them within your heart.

22 *For they are life to those who find them,*
and healing to all their[b] *flesh.*

23 *Keep your heart with all vigilance,*
for from it flow the springs of life.

24 *Put away from you crooked speech,*
and put devious talk far from you.

25 *Let your eyes look directly forward,*
and your gaze be straight before you.

26 *Ponder*[c] *the path of your feet;*
then all your ways will be sure.

27 *Do not swerve to the right or to the left;*
turn your foot away from evil.

a Hebrew *know* **b** Hebrew *his* **c** Or *Make level*

Overview: As with the previous addresses from father to son, the Reformation commentators interpret this as an admonition from God the Father to gain true wisdom. Michel Cop in particular sees in the father's monologue a model for Christian ministry and how preachers and teachers should instruct Christians according to the law of God. With the images of a shield and a crown, the reformers note the rewards of wisdom to those who embrace it. This discussion of rewards continues in the second section of the chapter, where our commentators see an important teaching on long life given to the wise, similar to that enjoyed by Solomon. The exegetes conclude by considering warnings to keep good company and maintain focus on the ultimate "prize" of the Christian life.

4:1-9 *Listen, My Sons*

Disposing Oneself to Receive Wisdom. Denis the Carthusian: Solomon again exhorts his readers to love and desire wisdom, and here he offers himself as an example: "Hear, children, the instruction of a father"—a heavenly Father, God Almighty; or me, who am your father by virtue of my preeminent wisdom. For indeed, he could in a literal sense call himself "father" with regard to his subjects on account of his royal dignity. "And attend"—that is, diligently pay attention to my words "that you may know prudence," because first one must know; only then can one work. And even though wisdom is an infused virtue, which comes immediately and entirely from God, still one can dispose oneself for this infusion and progress in it through diligence and experience. Exposition of the Book of Proverbs.[1]

Different Terms for the Same Wisdom. Lucas Osiander: Solomon again exhorts his readers to preserve the true wisdom of the Word of God, for this can never be sufficiently commended to us, since the world and human reason are wont to reject it. "Hear, children, the discipline"—that is, my teaching—"of your father"—that is, of one who has a father's heart and desires to teach you things that will make you happy. "Attend" to me "so that you may know prudence," to learn the true heavenly wisdom (for Solomon indiscriminately varies his terminology, with the terms *prudence, wisdom, knowledge, intellect, discipline, counsel,* but all refer to one and the same thing). Proverbs.[2]

Children Must Be Obedient to Their Parents. Swiss Brethren Confession of Hesse: We believe, acknowledge, and confess that children are responsible to follow their biological parents, father and mother, to listen to them, to be obedient and subject to them, and to hold them in honor. Concerning the Obedience of Children.[3]

A Model for Preachers and Listeners. Michel Cop: Solomon accommodates himself to our simplicity, as a father to the weakness, slowness, and forgetfulness of his child. He repeats again the same exhortations that he has made to us previously, and seeing that we well deserve to be sharply reproved, he speaks to us as children. But instead of threatening us as a judge, he calls us to hear the instruction of the father of spirits, with the hope the we may be made attentive hearers and be delivered from ignorance. . . .

"For I give you." For this reason he would have us know that all teaching which turns us from the law of God is not good; or rather, it is unprofitable and harmful. Therefore we should not desire to be instructed in any other teaching than that which our heavenly Father gives us: this alone is good because he alone is good. This teaching is none other than his law, which in no way should we despise, as he shows us when he concludes, "therefore forsake not my law."† He speaks here in the name and the authority of God, whose servant

[1]DCOO 7:34.

[2]Osiander, *Esdras, Nehemias, Esther, Iob, Psalterium, Prouerbia Salomonis, Ecclesiastes, & Canticum Canticorum,* 1036.

[3]CRR 11:81*; citing Ex 20:12; Deut 5:16; Lev 19:2-3; Sir 3:13; Prov 4:3-4; Mt 15:3-6; Eph 6:1-3; Col 3:20; Heb 12:7-9; 2 Jn 4.

he was, and he committed to instruct his people. Therefore he affirms that his teaching is good, and that it is the law of God, and so we are bound to hear his instruction, and to learn the knowledge that he teaches us. In doing this, he shows ministers what they ought to bring to the people—that is, the pure word of God from the divinely inspired Scripture, which is profitable to teach. . . . It is the instruction of our Father; it is the learning to which all people ought to apply their minds, to obtain true knowledge. It is the teaching that is profitable and necessary for us; it is the law of God, which we should never forsake, but continually be trained in. But here he also shows the people how they ought to conduct themselves. First of all, they should listen as though they were being taught not by men but by our heavenly Father. He is the only teacher, for men who speak are but his organs and instruments. Second, they ought to be attentive and give diligent heed, that they may be delivered from the dungeon of ignorance, to receive light and learn the true knowledge. Third, they should confess the goodness and faithfulness of God, who will not allow them to be deceived by fables and lies, or by vain and fruitless doctrines, but sets before them the wholesome teaching of his Law, his Prophets, and his Gospel. . . . Fourth, they should not be negligent in doing good, as the law commands. And so in this manner we should apply our hearts and bodies to the service of God, as he requires, and so we shall not receive the preaching of the Word of God in vain, nor to our condemnation, as they do who come to hear only under compulsion, or for the sake of habit. On the Proverbs of Solomon.[4]

God Draws Those Who Seek Him. Philipp Melanchthon: There appears to be an obscurity in one saying here: "the beginning of wisdom is to acquire wisdom." But the idea is clear from the way in which conversion to God begins in the soul: one hears the teaching, and one truly desires it and prays for guidance from God, according to his teaching, and this is the beginning of conversion, as is also said elsewhere: "He gives the Holy Spirit to those who ask." So also the prophet says, "Return to me, and I will return to you." And in Wisdom: "She is found by those who seek her, and she hastens to those who desire her." Likewise, Proverbs 2 can be summarized as follows: if you seek Wisdom, you will find her. Finally, in the epistle of James: "If anyone is lacking in wisdom, let him ask God." To sum up: it is God who draws us, but he only draws those who are willing. Exposition of the Proverbs of Solomon.[5]

Keeping the Main Thing the Main Thing. Michael Jermin: The original says nothing more than "wisdom is the beginning," or, "the beginning of wisdom." If we read it the first way, the meaning is that wisdom is the first thing to be gotten; that is, the beginning for doing anything well, and therefore whatsoever you desire to get, first "get wisdom." If we read it the second way, the meaning is that the beginning of wisdom is to set our minds to get it, and to prioritize the acquisition of wisdom above any other thing. The Syriac reads, "in the beginning of wisdom," and so the meaning may be this: as soon as you have entered upon wisdom and begun to be acquainted with it, make it your primary aim, and go after it so that you may be sure to have it, and therefore get it with all your strength. But our translation expresses very well the sense of the Hebrew: "Wisdom is the main thing." Getting the main thing wrong is the principal disorder of the human heart. One thinks pleasure to be the main thing, and goes after it with all his desire, seeking it alone; another thinks greatness of command to be the main thing, and he seeks to get it by any way he can; another thinks that abundance of riches is the main thing, and with all the engines of getting he works to that end. But as it is light that shows us what light is, so it is the main thing that shows us the main thing—and

[4]Cop, *Sur les Proverbes de Salomon*, 61-62; citing 1 Tim 3:16. †The Hebrew *tôrātî* can be rendered "my law" or "my teaching." Modern translations favor the latter, but the LXX and Vulgate favored the former.

[5]CR 14:12; citing Lk 11:13; Mal 3:7; Wis 6:12-13; Jas 1:5.

it is wisdom alone that does this. Therefore let us "get" wisdom with all our care "of getting," for with wisdom we shall get even heaven itself. Paraphrastic Meditations.[6]

Wisdom's Shield of Protection. Cardinal Cajetan: "She will honor you because you embrace her." I understand from this the precepts that are attached to the purchase. It was not sufficient to say, "buy wisdom," by spending all one's resources to have it. But he added this, "love her, exalt her, embrace her." Many things are purchased not from love but from necessity. Or the things that are bought are not loved. Also many items that were purchased and loved are not exalted, and some things that were exalted sometimes become loathsome. And therefore one is commanded to embrace wisdom, together with the reward of honor, which is the greatest of human rewards. "She will bestow upon your head the increase of grace." In the Hebrew this is taken as the companionship of grace. This means it will make you lovable and welcome to others, and so will not only cause you to receive honor but also love. And through this companionship, a blessing is bestowed on your head, inasmuch as the rational element—which is accomplished through wisdom—is conceived of as residing in the head. And a glorious crown will guard you. Or according to the Hebrew, "a crown of glory will defend you." The word translated as "defend" is reminiscent (if I may be permitted to say so) of functioning as a shield. For the word is derived from the figure of a shield. And this is the meaning: a crown of glory will serve as your shield. That is, the crown of glory that adorns you as a glorious king will not pull you toward wickedness by abusing the glory of your kingdom. Instead it will serve as a defensive shield protecting you from injustice. So the glory of many kings, because they lacked wisdom, ended up being the reason for their destruction. As you, on the other hand, embrace wisdom, this will be your shield against the projectiles both of others' words and deeds. The Parables of Solomon, Corrected by the Original Hebrew.[7]

Striving for the Crown of Glory. Michel Cop: Solomon here explains how Wisdom exalts those who magnify her, and how she glorifies those who embrace her. He does this by a comparison with the doings of kings and great princes, who exalt to honor and glory those who honor them, seeking the profit and preservation of their persons and their kingdoms. So Pharaoh took the ring from his finger and put it on the hand of Joseph, and Mordecai departed from the king in royal robes of blue and white, with a great crown of gold. Or else the comparison is taken from the reward that is given to those who fight and run a race. For the one who fights or runs best receives the crown. But however it is interpreted, this declaration has two parts, with the second explaining the first: for the increase of grace is a crown of glory, which is given to the wise in this life, and that in two ways. First of all, they are praised and honored so by God that he causes the world to marvel at them, and even though the foolish and scorners may persecute and revile them, they do this against their own consciences, which convict them that they act wickedly. Second, by faith and hope they have eternal life, and this is the crown of glory which in the end they will wholly and fully possess, and so they may say, "A crown of righteousness is kept for me." The persecutions of this world shall not deprive us of this crown; on the contrary, "Blessed is the one who endures temptation, for when he has been tried, he shall receive the crown of life." On the Proverbs of Solomon.[8]

4:10-27 *These Words Are Life*

Wisdom's Tangible Rewards. Peter Moffett: Wisdom is indeed the good gift of God, as we have heard before; but, as the

[6]Jermin, *Paraphrasticall Meditations*, 73.

[7]Cajetan, *Parabolae Salomonis ad veritatem Hebraicam castigatae*, 38-39.

[8]Cop, *Sur les Proverbes de Salomon*, 66; citing Gen 41:42; Esther 8:15; 2 Sam 5:8; 1 Cor 9:24; 2 Tim 2:5; 4:8; Jas 1:12.

common proverb has it, "The Lord sells all things for man's labor," so that it may be bought and purchased after a certain sort. And there is good reason why wisdom should not only be followed after, but be held first as a most precious jewel; for, says David, "Do not forsake her, and she will keep you; love her, and she will preserve you." If you do this, wisdom and prudence will guard you like trusty watchmen, so that you shall not come into any danger; or, if perchance you may fall into any trouble, they will preserve and deliver you from destruction. Therefore it is not without cause that in the next verse this admonition is given: "First of all, seek wisdom; purchase wisdom and with your whole possession purchase prudence," for before all things we are to labor after the kingdom of God, being ready to part with our sweetest delights and richest commodities so that we may obtain the understanding of God's will. Therefore those who chiefly and principally seek after the transitory treasures of this life take a preposterous course and set the cart before the horse, as it were, being less careful for the good and salvation of their souls than they are for those things that appertain to the use or preservation of their bodies. But to conclude, everyone is to know that the labor they take in following after Wisdom is not lost, and that she is indeed a good mistress to serve, for "magnify her, and she will advance you; if you will embrace her, she will honor you. She will set on your head a comely attire, and she will put on you a crown of glory." To "magnify" Wisdom is to count all things as dung in comparison with her, and to have her in singular reverence; to "embrace her" is to love her entirely, and to make much of her. Thus if you will exalt and entertain Wisdom, she as a queen will make you honorable, and as it were a knight or a lord, so that you shall be preferred to some good living, or be lifted up to such dignity in the commonwealth or church of God that you shall seem very gracious and glorious to men and angels. Nor shall the glory to which you shall be advanced be mean, but exceedingly great and princely, so that it may be compared to an ornament that is put on the head, or to the diadem with which kings and emperors are crowned. For wisdom will either bring you to some office of rule and government in this world, or it will make you a spiritual king, and inheritor of eternal glory. These promises of David were fulfilled in Solomon, for since he chose wisdom above all other things, in this way he obtained great honor and fame, and because of this he was with the general consent and joy of all the Israelites received and lifted up to the kingdom. A Commentary upon the Whole Book of the Proverbs of Solomon.[9]

God's Commandments Keep Us Safe. Lucas Osiander: "Listen, my son," says Solomon, "and accept my words" (just as I listened to and carried out the teaching and admonition of my parents), "that the years of your life may be multiplied." For those who shun crimes that are prohibited by the Word of God avoid capital punishment, and God extends life to those who are zealous for true piety. "I have shown you the way of wisdom, and I have led you in the paths of equity"; or better: "of uprightness"—that is, I taught you to walk wisely and justly in the ways, or commandments, of the Lord, "which, when you have entered them, your steps will not be hemmed in, and in running you will not meet a stumbling block." That is, you will not be forced into narrow straits, nor will you stumble disgracefully or fall to the ground when you listen to my teaching and obey me. But those who enter the crooked ways of wickedness entangle themselves in their own deceits, are struck down, and are brought to shame. "Take hold of instruction, and leave it not: keep it, because it is your life." Go on to observe the commandments of God steadfastly, because their observance will prolong your life. We must persevere in obedience to God's commandments, for it is not enough to have begun well. Proverbs.[10]

[9]Moffett, *A Commentary upon the Whole Booke of the Proverbs of Salomon*, 23-24; citing Mt 6:33.

[10]Osiander, *Esdras, Nehemias, Esther, Iob, Psalterium, Prouerbia Salomonis, Ecclesiastes, & Canticum Canticorum*, 1038.

Years of Life Extended Beyond Death. Michel Cop: Solomon often repeats to us this one lesson, as anyone can tell who hears or reads his teaching, and this is to help the ignorance of those who have a genuine will to learn and become obedient. For owing to the corruption of our flesh, we are very sluggish in receiving and remembering good teaching, because the affections of our fleshly nature provoke us to rebellion and enmity against God. . . . For as the repetitions of this one doctrine make it easier to grasp for those who are willing to learn, they also serve to make the heedless and the rebellious inexcusable. And although the Word is only directed to the children of God, yet it still resounds in the ears of those strangers who are mingled with the household of God. But because they hear it with contempt (as they demonstrate by not receiving it with faith and obedience), it works their condemnation and death. On the other hand, to those who do receive it, it gives life.

Solomon affirms exactly this when he tells his son that his words shall increase the years of his life. If then we desire long life, let us yield ourselves willingly to learn, and diligently to hear the preaching of the Word. Let us submit ourselves with true obedience, striving to perform that which it commands us by the reverence we bear for God, who is our Father, and through the fear we have to disobey him. This is the manner in which our years shall be prolonged: not that we can live in this world beyond the term that God has ordained from eternity, but however short our life may be, it shall be so long as is expedient for the salvation of our souls. And we should content ourselves with this, knowing that our years are not shortened by temporal death, but rather we shall enter into the true length of life, and this shall be without end. On the Proverbs of Solomon.[11]

Fleeing Wicked Habits. Cardinal Cajetan: "Take no delight in the paths of the wicked." According to the Hebrew this reads, "You shall not walk in the paths of the unrighteous, and you shall not rejoice in the way of the wicked." He had explained the fruit of his father's instruction on this understanding, that he ascribed it to walking wisely, and running wisely, by moving through the paths of upright living. He now explains the paths of upright living by their opposites—namely, the paths of the wicked. For when opposites are held in contrast they are better illuminated, and one understands what this means in all these paths. "I have instructed you." The writer proceeds by recalling the lessons he has taught the listener, by teaching him the path of wisdom and upright living. But the best safeguard for avoiding wicked habits and depraved behaviors (that locate happiness in evil) is provided by the metaphor of entering, when he says, "Do not enter into the path of the unrighteous." You shall not go into them. So it will come to pass that you will not consider yourself or others happy in the path of the wicked. It is impossible, or very difficult, for those who enter into the path of the unrighteous to avoid the moral pattern on that same path, or the practice of living wickedly. The one who does this, consequently, will find his happiness on the path of the wicked. As each individual exists according to the condition of his soul, so does his moral end present itself to him. "Flee from it." According to the Hebrew this reads, "Turn away from it." When the entrance has been blocked so as to avoid the pursuit of wickedness, then he next advises how to avoid entering onto the path of wickedness by saying, turn from her and do not trust only in passing her by, as though merely passing by would cause no harm. Because passing along the path of the unrighteous is poisonous, turn from it, and you shall not pass through it nor imperil yourself. The Parables of Solomon, Corrected by the Original Hebrew.[12]

An Emphatic Warning Against Bad Company. The English Annotations: Solomon, by this reiterated language (which is

[11]Cop, *Sur les Proverbes de Salomon*, 66-67.

[12]Cajetan, *Parabolae Salomonis ad veritatem Hebraicam castigatae*, 41.

natural in such cases), would have us understand the eminence and imminence of the danger that young men are in through ill company. As if passing by in the streets we should decry fire breaking out in a house which had not been taken notice of, or, on the highways, we should observe some ignorant traveler, at full speed, coming to some terrible precipice. Nobody would wonder to hear us often repeat the same words as "fire, fire" or "a precipice, a precipice," "take heed, look to yourself," and the like. So is this unusual repetition of words here of purpose, to make us more sensible of that which, though it be so true as nothing can be more, yet it is so little believed that more young men laugh at it when they are told of it than are persuaded that there is any danger in it. And in what age or place in the world did any people, whether heathens or Christians (so called), both men and women, indulge themselves more freely in this way than they do now, in these times, which we are taught to call (so little we make of mocking God) blessed and happy times, and times of reformation? ANNOTATIONS ON PROVERBS 4:14.[13]

EYES ON THE PRIZE. JOHN TRAPP: Let "your eyes" be fixed on right objects. Get that stoic eye of our Savior; get a patriarch's eye; be well skilled in Moses's optics; have "eyes on the prize," which was Ludovico Vives's motto.[†] Do as mariners who have their eye on the star, their hand on the stern. A person may not look intently on that which he may not love. The disciples were set agog by beholding the beauty of the temple. If therefore your eye offends you, or causes you to offend, pull it out of the old Adam, and set it in the new man. If you do not use it well, you will wish that you had indeed pulled it out, as Democritus did.[‡] "Ponder the path of your feet"—that is, by the weights of the Word. Look to your affections, for by these maids Satan woos the mistress. Take heed where you set gunpowder, since fire is in your hearts. Augustine thanks God that his heart and the temptation did not meet together. Walk accurately, tread rightly, step warily; lift not up one foot till you find firm footing for another, as those in Psalms 35:6. The way of this world is like the vale of Siddim, slimy and slippery, so beware. We have an Eve, a tempter within each one of us, our own flesh, says Bernard.[§] And "No one searches out his own steps; each one is his own Satan," says another father. We have enough to watch for our halting; the devil also casts his club at us that we "may stumble and fall, and be broken, and snared, and taken." SOLOMON'S BOOK OF ALL VIRTUES.[14]

[13]Downame, ed., *English Annotations*, 6R4r*.

[14]Trapp, *Solomonis ΠΑΝΆΡΕΤΟΣ*, 227; citing Heb 12:1-2; 11:23-29; Mt 24:2; 5:29; Eph 5:15; Is 8:15. [†]*Oculum in metam*, lit.: "eye on the goal." Juan Luis Vives (1493–1540) was a Spanish humanist and polymath; the maxim Trapp quotes comes from his *Sattelitium Animi*, a collection of proverbs similar in arrangement Erasmus's *Adages*. [‡]According to the Roman writer Aulus Gelius, the Greek philosopher Democritus "of his own accord deprived himself of eyesight," not to avoid sexual temptation, but "because he believed that the thoughts and meditations of his mind in examining nature's laws would be more vivid and exact, if he should free them from the allurements of sight and the distractions offered by the eyes" (*Noctes Atticae* 10.17; LCL 200:261). [§]Bernard of Clairvaux (1090–1153), a medieval writer regarded by many of the reformers as the "last church father." Trapp does not cite the original Latin, but a similar idea is expressed in one of Bernard's sermons on the Song of Songs: "Eve still lives on in our flesh, through whose hereditary concupiscence our serpent lusts eagerly to seek the consent of his party" (PL 183:1132).

5:1-23 Warning Against Adultery

1My son, be attentive to my wisdom;
incline your ear to my understanding,

2that you may keep discretion,
and your lips may guard knowledge.

3For the lips of a forbidden[a] woman drip honey,
and her speech[b] is smoother than oil,

4but in the end she is bitter as wormwood,
sharp as a two-edged sword.

5Her feet go down to death;
her steps follow the path to[c] Sheol;

6she does not ponder the path of life;
her ways wander, and she does not know it.

7And now, O sons, listen to me,
and do not depart from the words of my mouth.

8Keep your way far from her,
and do not go near the door of her house,

9lest you give your honor to others
and your years to the merciless,

10lest strangers take their fill of your strength,
and your labors go to the house of a foreigner,

11and at the end of your life you groan,
when your flesh and body are consumed,

12and you say, "How I hated discipline,
and my heart despised reproof!

13I did not listen to the voice of my teachers
or incline my ear to my instructors.

14I am at the brink of utter ruin
in the assembled congregation."

15Drink water from your own cistern,
flowing water from your own well.

16Should your springs be scattered abroad,
streams of water in the streets?

17Let them be for yourself alone,
and not for strangers with you.

18Let your fountain be blessed,
and rejoice in the wife of your youth,
19a lovely deer, a graceful doe.

Let her breasts fill you at all times with delight;
be intoxicated[d] always in her love.

20Why should you be intoxicated, my son, with a forbidden woman
and embrace the bosom of an adulteress?[e]

21For a man's ways are before the eyes of the Lord,
and he ponders[f] all his paths.

22The iniquities of the wicked ensnare him,
and he is held fast in the cords of his sin.

23He dies for lack of discipline,
and because of his great folly he is led astray.

a Hebrew *strange*; also verse 20 b Hebrew *palate* c Hebrew *lay hold of* d Hebrew *be led astray*; also verse 20 e Hebrew *a foreign woman* f Or *makes level*

Overview: This chapter returns to the theme of the adulterous woman, and our commentators do not shy away from depictions of the "harlotry" of lust and faithlessness, both spiritual and literal. Demonstrating their willingness to perceive multiple senses or meanings in the text, the reformers understand the fountain in Proverbs 5:18 as both a call to frugality and generosity and an image of marital fidelity. Melanchthon in particular takes the occasion to discuss romantic love, with allusions to classical literature, in order to highlight the biblical teaching on marriage.

5:1-14 *A Forbidden Woman*

Lust Destroys Body and Soul. Denis the Carthusian: "For the lips of a harlot are like a honeycomb dripping"—that is, they are like the drippings of the honeycomb. "And her throat is smoother than oil," because she polishes and adorns it, so as to make herself more attractive. "But her end is as bitter as wormwood," for many are the pangs of guilt and painful punishments that attend lust, both in body and in soul, not only in this life but also in eternal damnation, as it is said in the Apocalypse: "As much as she has glorified herself and lived in delicacies, so much torment and sorrow give to her." "And sharp as a two-edged sword," for they afflict both body and soul: the one leading to sensible punishments and the other to damnation. Exposition of the Book of Proverbs.[1]

The High Price of Repentance. Michael Jermin: To make clearer the coherence of this verse with the former part of the chapter, the Latin Vulgate adds here, "Mind not the deceitfulness of a woman,"[†] as if the connection were this: attend to my wisdom, not to her falsehood. Or else, since this is not found in the Hebrew, we may suppose the wise man from the end of the verse before to have taken his hint of beginning this matter, and that having spoken of keeping knowledge in the lips, he shows how the lips of a harlot keep cunning and subtlety. "For the lips of a strange woman drop as a honeycomb." The lips "drop" well "as a honeycomb" when the bees that make it are honest, virtuous, and pious thoughts. Then is the "mouth" well "smoother than oil" when the heart also is softened with grace. But the lips of a harlot do not drop so sweetly, since her heart devises falsely; her mouth is not so smooth, since her face is rough and hardened with impudence. Origen therefore says truly that "a harlot cannot love, she can only entice; her kiss has venom in it, and her mouth pernicious poison."[‡] And yet the force of her mischievous enchantment is great. St. Jerome relates a story concerning the Corinthian [courtesan] Lais, whose prerogative beauty allowed only the embrace of kings and princes, that setting upon Demosthenes she endeavored by conquering the miracle of his known chastity to set out the triumph of her beauty, as being able to move stones with it. Now as the father says, "Having drawn him to her with flatteries, she led him along sweetly," and when now Demosthenes was wantonly softened to her bed, she demanded of him a hundred talents for her hire. But the answer Demosthenes gave her was witty and virtuous: "I will not buy repentance so dear."[§] Paraphrastic Meditations.[2]

Lack of Pondering Leads to Perdition. The English Annotations: There is much weight in that word [i.e., "ponder"]. It is not bare pondering that can do good alone, unless afterward follows consent, or assent and resolution. But by pondering, he comprehends these also, as supposing that no person can be so mad or senseless (the desire for happiness being natural to all), as that after they have seriously, again and again, considered (which is understood by pondering, a thing not to be done without care and diligence) of their case and of the ends and consequences of these courses they are in, that they should continue in them to their apparent destruction, both body and soul, temporal and eternal. . . . Certainly, want of this sober, serious consideration and ratiocination (the proper work of the rational creature) is the greatest cause of most people's perdition. Annotations on Proverbs 5:6.[3]

---

[1]DCOO 7:40; citing Rev 18:7.

[2]Jermin, *Paraphrasticall Meditations*, 642-43*. [†]A textual variant common in medieval manuscripts. [‡]Chrysostom, *Homilies on the Statutes* 14.10 (PG 49:149; NPNF[2] 9:435); Jermin incorrectly attributes this work to Origen. [§]The *Letter of Valerius to Rufinus, Dissuading Him from Taking a Wife* was spuriously attributed to Jerome in sixteenth-century editions of his writings. Modern scholarship has identified the English writer Walter Map (1130–c. 1210) as the author. Map's source for this anecdote appears to be Aulus Gellius, *Attic Nights* 1.8.

[3]Downame, ed., *English Annotations*, 6R4v*; citing Rom 8:18.

5:15-23 *Rejoice in Your Wife*

Adulterers Lose Control over What Is Theirs. Cardinal Cajetan: "Drink water from your own cistern." According to the Hebrew this is, "Drink water from your own well." Up to this point the father has warned his son to guard himself from the strange woman, both because she is deceptive and because she is harmful to him personally and to his possessions. And also because she will cause him regret. Consequently he gives the same warning by showing all the good things that accompany avoiding the woman who is not his. And first he shows the good benefits, using the example of fresh waters. Now the proverb consists in this: the man who has his own well or fountain drinks water with his companions from his private supply. Likewise, he drinks the water that bubbles up from the fountain's center, and then disperses it so abundantly around that he produces, so to speak, a puddle in the flat, open space. But he keeps back his own water for himself, not allowing others to possess along with him his private source of water. So a man must be master of his own resources, and use them freely, distributing them also abroad to the poor and pilgrims. But he must not grant strangers access to control of his own resources. But this, however, is the very thing he does when he shares them with someone else's wife. The Parables of Solomon, Corrected by the Original Hebrew.[4]

Work Hard, Consume Frugally, Give Generously. Michel Cop: In order to teach us that we should not give our honor to strangers, lest we be forced to lament the consumption of our flesh and of our strength, Solomon exhorts us to drink the waters of our own cistern. By this image he evokes the description of the land of Judah, where there were mountains and valleys watered by the rains from heaven; therefore, the people made wells and cisterns to hold and preserve water, which was necessary for them. So when Abraham came and dwelt in this land his servants dug wells. Regarding this situation he commands that we should drink water, by which he means all the fruits we gather from our labor and travail. He indicates this when he says not simply "of cisterns and wells," but "of your cisterns" and "out of your own wells"; that is, the ones you have made, dug, and maintained. Now since Solomon here uses an image of that which is of least value and estimation in the provision of a house (for there is nothing that is spilled more often than water, or that has less value as merchandise), he seems to include all the necessities of the house. First, he shows that we must keep great sobriety and temperance, and not desire to make excessive or superfluous expenditure, or fall into gluttony or drunkenness. And when he says, "drink," this is not an invitation to imbibe, but rather he shows that we should be careful to nourish our household, and not to spend our goods prodigally making good cheer among frivolous company, or with prostitutes, or with those whose mouths and bellies are insatiable. Rather, we should be sober and temperate, easily satisfied with simple drinks and meats (even though it is lawful for us to use all kinds). . . . Second, whatever license is given to us to use all things for our benefit, we must abstain from those that belong to our neighbor, as we have two express commands against it. And Solomon says the same here, when he says, "of your cisterns" and "out of your own wells." Third, since cisterns and wells tend to fall into decay and ruin when they are not maintained with investments of cost and labor, so Solomon puts us on notice that we shall have to work, and implicitly forbids begging, from which much evil comes. Fourth, even though the wells and cisterns are our own, and Solomon bids us drink their water, yet we ought not to be so partial, nor so given over to our own profit that we do not take care of our neighbors, and try to communicate a part of what is ours to relieve their need.

We must not be such penny-pinchers as to eat our bread alone, but must distribute what we have into diverse parts, as Solomon says when he

[4]Cajetan, *Parabolae Salomonis ad veritatem Hebraicam castigatae*, 48.

continues, "Let your fountain flow forth." Just as one who has one or many fountains is never in need of water, though they overrun their streams here and there, so the one who distributes the goods that God has given him shall always have enough, and never be in need. Even when we were papists, we used to say, "To give for God's sake does not make a man poor." If in such darkness of ignorance, of superstition and idolatry, of all wickedness and abomination, we spoke and felt so rightly, what ought we to say and feel now, when God by his grace has delivered us . . . ? "But let them be yours." Solomon is not satisfied simply to have said "yours," but repeats again, "yours," and even adds an exclusive term: "only." But let us not think that he would exclude the poor members of Jesus Christ, who are not only our brothers, but also flesh of our flesh, and bone of our bones, for we are all one body in Jesus Christ, and every one of us one another's members. And just as Jesus Christ with all that is his is ours through grace, even so among Christians and the faithful there ought to be such followship that no one should say that anything is their own, but should be prepared to give it for the profit of their neighbors as need shall require, just as the early church has given us an example. ON THE PROVERBS OF SOLOMON.[5]

AN ALLEGORY OF MARITAL FIDELITY. PETER MOFFETT: Often in Scripture the state and use of wedlock is shadowed out by the allegory or borrowed speech of waters. If, then, the same thing is here also represented by similitudes, of which opinion divines and Hebraists of most excellent judgment are, this is the natural sense of this passage: Quench the thirst of your desire, not by abusing those who belong to another, but by enjoying your own wife, even as it is fitting that one having a well or pit of his own should drink from it, and not from that of another man. The fruit of this lawful intercourse will be sweet and great, for you shall have children begotten in honest wedlock, of whom you may be sure that they are your own, and who may be an ornament to the commonwealth, and a refreshing to you in the streets of the city. Let, therefore, your wife become a fruitful vine and, forsaking all others, keep yourself only to her and delight in her. A COMMENTARY UPON THE WHOLE BOOK OF THE PROVERBS OF SOLOMON.[6]

THE DELIGHTS OF YOUNG LOVE. PHILIPP MELANCHTHON: The fifth chapter pertains to two commandments: "Do not commit adultery," and "Do not steal." The first part of the chapter forbids adultery and all wandering lusts, and it adds a warning regarding the penalties for such things. For without a doubt, this will be the outcome according to the divine law: God will punish fornicators and adulterers. The adulterer will destroy his own soul, as both private and public histories demonstrate: David, Troy, Thebes. . . .[†] And even though God may mitigate the punishments for those who repent, yet there is always some punishment accompanying, and often sins in seed are punished in their issue—that is, in their offspring.

A most sweet exhortation is inserted here, in approbation of marriage and mutual love, and the charms of marriage over adultery. The commendation of marriage and mutual love comes in verse 18: "Take delight in the wife of your youth"—that is, the wife you marry in your youth. Next, it depicts this mutual love with remarkable images, as a stag and a hind, or rather as a she goat and a mule. It is a burning love, without pretense or constraint; it is agreeable, without peevishness or fastidiousness; it is sincere, without suspicions and without pride. In this mutual love the husband and wife may rest content, not parting company or longing for anyone else. A description of this ardor is given in the poet Oppian:

> But the hind runs and the stag running with
> swift feet

[5]Cop, *Sur les Proverbes de Salomon*, 85-87*; citing Gen 26:15; Rom 12:3.

[6]Moffett, *A Commentary upon the Whole Booke of the Proverbs of Salomon*, 67; citing Num 24:7; Deut 33:28; Is 48:1; Ps 68:27; Is 51:1.

Overtakes her and seizes the fugitive and
embraces her for his bride.[‡]

The antithesis of this love may be seen in many examples. Tiberius was led against his will to marry Julia, and this deception and constraint rendered the marriage odious to both parties.[§] So also Pomponia was only made more miserable by her marriage to Quintus Cicero.[◊] Many men and women are by nature mistrustful, proud, diffident, not maintaining equality in their manner of life. But all such defects are removed by considering the sincere and sweet affection of the she goat and mule, or the hind and the stag. And the text reiterates the sweetest approbation of love and conjugal marriage, when it says, "Let her breasts intoxicate you." Clearly this is a true and burning love, not a passing fancy. Consider the emphases in this passage: breasts signify affection (*storgē*); inebriation signifies great desire (*amorem*).[Δ] And following this, the text goes on to warn against being led away into the love of another. The point of all this is as follows: love your wife, and be content with her alone, just as this same law concerning marriage was immediately ordained in Paradise: "The two will become one flesh"—that is, one man and one woman inseparably joined. For even if human nature had remained intact, God would have wanted humans to know chastity, and to exercise the discipline of obedience so as to preserve self-control against wandering lusts. EXPOSITION OF THE PROVERBS OF SOLOMON.[7]

SINS HAVE NATURAL CONSEQUENCES. THE ENGLISH ANNOTATIONS: Having spoken of God's judgments and secret knowledge in the former verses as the chief thing that should keep people in awe, if all have faith to believe it, or prudence to consider it in time, he proceeds to that which is more present and visible: the punishment that (besides the torments of an evil conscience common to all sins, which by heathens themselves, upon good observation and experience, are set out as very hell) attends every sin, arising from the sin itself. For example, drunkenness leads to such and such diseases, untimely deaths and so forth, and most particularly, adultery. Besides bodily diseases innumerable, and a general consumption of the flesh and body, . . . and adulterers also expose themselves to many dangers. ANNOTATIONS ON PROVERBS 5:22.[8]

---

[7]CR 14:12-14; citing Gen 2:24. [†]As he so often does, Melanchthon interweaves *exempla* from both sacred and secular history: David's adultery with Bathsheba is understood to have precipitated the later rebellion of David's sons, especially Absalom (2 Sam 11–20); Helen's adultery with Paris was understood as the *casus belli* of the Trojan War (e.g., Sappho, frag. 16; other ancient sources characterize the liaison as abduction or rape, however). Perhaps most flagrant of all, Jupiter's repeated infidelities with various Theban women (Semele, Alcmena, and Europa) was the source of Juno's hostility to that city, and ultimately led to its destruction. [‡]Oppian, *Cynegetica* 2.200-201 (LCL 219:73). Melanchthon cites two lines from a longer passage that describes the amorous habits of these creatures, a passage that begins thus: "But there is a rough passion among stags and much venery [literally, "much of Aphrodite"], and a heart that burns for mating all the day" (ll. 186-87). Melanchthon's purpose in citing these lines is presumably to illuminate the biblical imagery with reference to perceptions of the same beast in other ancient cultures. [§]In 11 BC, the emperor Augustus forced his daughter Julia to marry his stepson Tiberius, an arrangement designed to secure the latter's future succession. By all accounts, the two despised one another, and the failure of their marriage eventually led to Julia's exile and untimely death, an episode that cast a long shadow over both emperors in the estimation of the ancient historians Suetonius and Tacitus. [◊]Marcus Tullius Cicero, the Roman statesman and orator, arranged for his brother Quintus to marry Pomponia, sister to one of the most illustrious noblemen in Rome, but the two constantly quarreled, and the marriage was notoriously unhappy. [Δ]Melanchthon explicates the biblical imagery here using the more precise vocabulary of classical poetry. It may surprise modern readers that he associates the imagery of breasts with the nonsexual character of the Greek *storgē*, but he pairs this with the Latin *amor*, often personified as the god of (sexual) love, Cupid (Eros, in Greek). However intuitive the associations may be, it is clear that Melanchthon's understanding of married love involves both strong sexual desire *and* companionable friendship.

[8]Downame, ed., *English Annotations*, 6S1v*.

6:1–7:27 PRACTICAL WARNINGS

[1]*My son, if you have put up security for your neighbor,*
have given your pledge for a stranger,

[2]*if you are snared in the words of your mouth,*
caught in the words of your mouth,

[3]*then do this, my son, and save yourself,*
for you have come into the hand of your neighbor:
go, hasten,[a] *and plead urgently with your neighbor.*

[4]*Give your eyes no sleep*
and your eyelids no slumber;

[5]*save yourself like a gazelle from the hand of the hunter,*[b]
like a bird from the hand of the fowler.

[6]*Go to the ant, O sluggard;*
consider her ways, and be wise.

[7]*Without having any chief,*
officer, or ruler,

[8]*she prepares her bread in summer*
and gathers her food in harvest.

[9]*How long will you lie there, O sluggard?*
When will you arise from your sleep?

[10]*A little sleep, a little slumber,*
a little folding of the hands to rest,

[11]*and poverty will come upon you like a robber,*
and want like an armed man.

[12]*A worthless person, a wicked man,*
goes about with crooked speech,

[13]*winks with his eyes, signals*[c] *with his feet,*
points with his finger,

[14]*with perverted heart devises evil,*
continually sowing discord;

[15]*therefore calamity will come upon him suddenly;*
in a moment he will be broken beyond healing.

[16]*There are six things that the* LORD *hates,*
seven that are an abomination to him:

[17]*haughty eyes, a lying tongue,*
and hands that shed innocent blood,

[18]*a heart that devises wicked plans,*
feet that make haste to run to evil,

[19]*a false witness who breathes out lies,*
and one who sows discord among brothers.

[20]*My son, keep your father's commandment,*
and forsake not your mother's teaching.

[21]*Bind them on your heart always;*
tie them around your neck.

[22]*When you walk, they*[d] *will lead you;*
when you lie down, they will watch over you;
and when you awake, they will talk with you.

[23]*For the commandment is a lamp and the teaching a light,*
and the reproofs of discipline are the way of life,

[24]*to preserve you from the evil woman,*[e]
from the smooth tongue of the adulteress.[f]

[25]*Do not desire her beauty in your heart,*
and do not let her capture you with her eyelashes;

[26]*for the price of a prostitute is only a loaf of bread,*[g]
but a married woman[h] *hunts down a precious life.*

[27]*Can a man carry fire next to his chest*
and his clothes not be burned?

[28]*Or can one walk on hot coals*
and his feet not be scorched?

[29]*So is he who goes in to his neighbor's wife;*
none who touches her will go unpunished.

[30]*People do not despise a thief if he steals*
to satisfy his appetite when he is hungry,

[31]*but if he is caught, he will pay sevenfold;*
he will give all the goods of his house.

[32]*He who commits adultery lacks sense;*
he who does it destroys himself.

[33]*He will get wounds and dishonor,*
and his disgrace will not be wiped away.

[34]*For jealousy makes a man furious,*
and he will not spare when he takes revenge.

[35]*He will accept no compensation;*
he will refuse though you multiply gifts.

7 *My son, keep my words*
and treasure up my commandments with you;

[2]*keep my commandments and live;*
keep my teaching as the apple of your eye;

[3]*bind them on your fingers;*
write them on the tablet of your heart.

[4]*Say to wisdom, "You are my sister,"*
and call insight your intimate friend,

[5]*to keep you from the forbidden*[i] *woman,*
from the adulteress[j] *with her smooth words.*

[6]*For at the window of my house*
I have looked out through my lattice,

[7]*and I have seen among the simple,*
I have perceived among the youths,
a young man lacking sense,

[8]*passing along the street near her corner,*
taking the road to her house

[9]*in the twilight, in the evening,*
at the time of night and darkness.

[10]*And behold, the woman meets him,*
dressed as a prostitute, wily of heart.[k]

[11]*She is loud and wayward;*
her feet do not stay at home;

[12]*now in the street, now in the market,*
and at every corner she lies in wait.

[13]*She seizes him and kisses him,*
and with bold face she says to him,

[14]*"I had to offer sacrifices,*[l]
and today I have paid my vows;

[15]*so now I have come out to meet you,*
to seek you eagerly, and I have found you.

[16]*I have spread my couch with coverings,*
colored linens from Egyptian linen;

[17]*I have perfumed my bed with myrrh,*
aloes, and cinnamon.

[18]*Come, let us take our fill of love till morning;*
let us delight ourselves with love.

[19]*For my husband is not at home;*
he has gone on a long journey;

[20]*he took a bag of money with him;*
at full moon he will come home."

[21]*With much seductive speech she persuades him;*
with her smooth talk she compels him.

[22]*All at once he follows her,*
as an ox goes to the slaughter,
or as a stag is caught fast[m]

[23] *till an arrow pierces its liver;*
as a bird rushes into a snare;
he does not know that it will cost him his life.

[24]*And now, O sons, listen to me,*
and be attentive to the words of my mouth.

[25]*Let not your heart turn aside to her ways;*
do not stray into her paths,

[26]*for many a victim has she laid low,*
and all her slain are a mighty throng.

[27]*Her house is the way to Sheol,*
going down to the chambers of death.

a Or *humble yourself* **b** Hebrew lacks *of the hunter* **c** Hebrew *scrapes* **d** Hebrew *it*; three times in this verse **e** Revocalization (compare Septuagint) yields *from the wife of a neighbor* **f** Hebrew *the foreign woman* **g** Or (compare Septuagint, Syriac, Vulgate) *for a prostitute leaves a man with nothing but a loaf of bread* **h** Hebrew *a man's wife* **i** Hebrew *strange* **j** Hebrew *the foreign woman* **k** Hebrew *guarded in heart* **l** Hebrew *peace offerings* **m** Probable reading (compare Septuagint, Vulgate, Syriac); Hebrew *as a chain to discipline a fool*

OVERVIEW: With its sixth chapter, Proverbs begins to move into matters of the miscellaneous practicalities that characterize much of the book, though the reformers still find much to comment on in these verses. First is the question of surety, or taking a pledge on behalf of another. They collectively warn against the practice, arguing both that this usurps one's trust in God and that it can unwisely yoke one together with another, potentially immoral person. With the example of the ant, the commentators discuss the value of work and the vice of sloth, though Melanchthon balances these considerations with warnings against the opposing vice, that of being a busybody. Our commentators further examine the evils that the Lord "hates," and in the latter part of Proverbs 6 and 7, they return to the dangers of literal and spiritual adultery, alluding to the lessons of Solomon and his wives. Importantly, we also find a woman's perspective offered by Arcangela Tarabotti, who points out the courage and wisdom of women found in Scripture.

6:1–19 *Advice About Daily Life*

NO SURETY BUT GOD. MARTIN LUTHER: There is a common error, which has become a widespread custom not only among merchants but throughout the world, by which one man becomes surety for another. Although this practice seems to be without sin and looks like a virtue springing from love, nevertheless it causes the ruin of many and brings them irrevocable injury. King Solomon often forbade this practice and condemned it in his Proverbs. In Proverbs 6 he says, "My son, if you stand surety for your neighbor. . . ." So also in Proverbs 20:16: "Take his garment that becomes surety for a stranger and take a pledge of him for the stranger's sake." Likewise in Proverbs 22:26: "Do not be one of those who strike hands and become surety for debts." . . . See with what strictness and vehemence the wise king forbids in holy Scripture that one become surety for another, and the German proverb agrees with him: "To the gallows with guarantors!" It serves the guarantor right when he is caught and has to pay, for he acts thoughtlessly and foolishly in standing surety. Therefore it is decreed in Scripture that no one shall become surety for another unless he is able and entirely willing to assume the debt and pay it.

It seems strange that this practice should be wrong and be condemned, though many have discovered the folly of it when it has made them scratch their heads. Why, then, is it condemned? Let us see. Standing surety is a work that is too lofty for a man. It is unseemly, for it is presumptuous, and an invasion of God's rights. For in the first place, the Scriptures forbid us to put our trust and reliance in anyone but God, for human nature is false, vain, deceitful, and unreliable, as the Scriptures say and as experience teaches daily. But he who becomes surety puts his trust in a man, and risks life and property on a false and insecure foundation; therefore, it serves him right when he falls and goes to ruin.

In the second place, a man puts his trust in himself and makes himself God, for that on which a man puts his trust and reliance is his god. But of his life and property a man is not sure and certain for a single moment, any more than he is certain of the man for whom he becomes surety, but everything is in God's hand alone, and he will not allow us a hair's breadth of power or right over the future, or have us for a single moment sure or certain of it. Therefore the man who becomes surety acts in an unchristian manner, and deserves what he gets, because he pledges and promises what is not his and is not in his power, but in the hands of God alone. Thus, we read in Genesis 43:9 and 44:32 how the patriarch Judah became surety to his father Jacob for his brother Benjamin, promising that he would bring him back or bear the blame forever. But God justly punished his presumption so that he could not bring Benjamin back until he gave himself up in exchange for him, and afterward he was freed only by grace. It served him right too, for these guarantors act as though they did not need to be on speaking terms with God, or to consider whether they were sure of a tomorrow for their life and property.

Moreover, God has condemned this presumption about the future and disregard of himself in other passages, such as Luke 12:16 and Acts 1:7. In Proverbs 27:1 he says, "Do not boast about tomorrow, for you do not even know what may happen today." For this reason, he has urged us in the Lord's Prayer to ask for nothing more than our daily bread for today, so that we may live and act in fear and know that at no hour are we sure of either life or property, but may await and receive everything from his hands. This is what true faith does. Indeed, we see daily in many of God's works that things must happen in this way, whether it suits us or not. ON TRADING AND USURY.[1]

SURETY AND THE VIRTUE OF CANDOR. PHILIPP MELANCHTHON: In the sixth chapter, the first proverb warns against standing surety, recounting its dangers. Many who do this are cheated, as is written in the famous inscription in the temple at Delphi: "Destruction is at hand for the one who pledges."[†] And Homer says in *The Odyssey*, "A pledge for a worthless man is a worthless pledge indeed"[‡]—that is, evil is assured to the one who stands surety to evildoers. Moreover, this proverb warns that as a general rule credit arrangements are rarely carried out with sincerity and fidelity. But on the contrary, so many are inconstant, painted, faithless, and deceitful that all too often people complain that "nowhere is faith secure."[§] "Fly those whom you deem faithful, and you will be safe."[◊] And as Epicharmus says, "Don't get drunk or trust your neighbor; there's the kernel of good sense."[Δ] Again, in the Psalms we read, "Trust not in princes, nor in the sons of men, in whom there is no salvation." And according to Jeremiah, "Cursed is the one who trusts in man."

This raises the question of whether anything is to be trusted. I answer: First, doctrine about God is to be trusted on the basis of the Word of God, to which God has added certain clear testimonies, such as raising people from the dead. . . . But human declarations about God, apart from the doctrine handed down by God himself, are rash presumptions, and not to be trusted, as it is written: "You shall add or subtract nothing." In the next place, there is reliable doctrine established in the arts by rational demonstration and other causes of certainty, because the faculties of judgment (*kritēria*) and demonstrations are also established in the divine order, which God desired to be conspicuous to human minds. But there are many changes in things, and a great many changes in human intentions, which often are deceitful; therefore, careful judgment must be used in this place, and it must be considered when and to what extent assent should be given to human promises, and when they should not be agreed to.

For this is the virtue which is called candor; its job is to discern intentions, avoiding the extremes of false accusation [*calumnia*] and foolish credulity.[†] For candor is a virtue related to honesty, approving the purposes of others upon probable reason, and not giving birth to vain suspicions from malevolence or bad character (*kakoētheia*). Candor also views any ambiguities in the better light, and indeed it hopes well, but nevertheless it recognizes that human purposes can be changed, and that people may vacillate from one purpose to another, when they do not thoroughly inspect the hidden recesses of their hearts. Thus David thought well of Jonathan, for he had probable reason for hoping that his purpose was firm, because he knew that he feared God and honored the divine testimony. He did not think well of Ahithophel, for he noticed that he did not fear God. So in this way we must understand that passage in 1 Corinthians 13:7: "Love believes all things," that is, love is candid, not suspicious; it does not think evil of another without serious probable reason. EXPOSITION OF THE PROVERBS OF SOLOMON.[2]

[1]WA:15:298-300; ET adapted from C. M. Jacobs, trans., *Works of Martin Luther* (Philadelphia: Muhlenberg Press, 1943), 4:12-14.

[2]CR 14:15-16; citing Ps 146:3; Jer 17:5; Deut 12:32. [†]In the ancient world, this Delphic inscription was often interpreted as an expression of philosophical skepticism. So, for example, Diogenes Laertius quotes the saying in his genealogy of the school of the skeptics: "The maxims of the Seven Wise Men, too, [are called] skeptical; for instance, 'observe the golden mean,' and 'a pledge is a

Do Not Be Hasty in Standing Pledge. Michel Cop: It seems at first glance that Solomon sets out to dissuade us from agreeing to stand in pledge or surety for our neighbors. For no one wants to become entangled or in bondage to another, but all naturally desire to be free, and to use the powers that God has given us at our own will. But Solomon here tells us that we are captives, if it happens that we become pledges or sureties for our neighbor. But so that we should not misunderstand Solomon, and charge him with dissuading us from works of charity, we must carefully make note of the condition he would not have us agree to in becoming pledge for the stranger, and also of the reason why we should not redeem our neighbors. For the first part, we must not be ignorant of the fact that every person, no matter how strange or unknown they may be to us, is our neighbor. Now he has already exhorted us above that we should keep our way far from [the forbidden woman], lest our honor go to a stranger. And it may happen that if we are not discreet, we shall be surety for the sort of person who borrows money to go a-whoring, and in this manner we should give our honor to strangers, and our fountains will no longer be ours, but the strangers' with us. Therefore we must understand that Solomon intends to put us on our guard by these words, that we not be hasty in pledging our neighbor unless we know him well, and also know that it is needful, and that by so doing we shall not bring our own family into such extremity as it should be compelled to beg their bread, and that we ourselves should not be unduly troubled. For although it is commanded that we love our neighbor as ourselves, and to assist him with what is ours, we are not commanded to put ourselves in distress so that others may live at their ease. On the Proverbs of Solomon.[3]

Be Wise When Binding Yourself to Another. The English Annotations: He does not forbid us to become sureties for our friends, according to the rule of charity, but he wills that we consider for whom, to whom, and on what terms we do it, so that the creditor is not defrauded, and we are not indemnified. Annotations on Proverbs 6:2.[4]

Storing Up Spiritual Goods. Denis the Carthusian: "Go to the ant, O sluggard," so that you who do not obey the Scripture, nor the exhortation of your elders, may at least be instructed by the example of irrational beasts and so be ashamed of your foolishness and laziness. "Consider its ways," that is, the responsibility, activity, and foresight ants display; "and learn wisdom; which, although it has no leader" from whom to receive instructions . . . "gathers its food in the harvest." Because they collect grains in the harvest and carry other things into their nest, when it gets cold they do not need to go outside. And they do all this by natural instinct, impressed upon them by the Author of nature, who is the supreme and universal Leader of all, the Teacher and Ruler, outside of and transcending every genus and order. For, as a commentator on Aristotle observes, "A work of nature is a work of intelligence," and this is true above all for the First Cause [*primae causae*], whose work is also the work of intelligence.[†] Hence, as the Damascene points out, brute and soulless animals are more driven in such things than actually acting.[‡] Therefore we (and especially those

curse at one's elbow,' meaning that whoever plights his troth steadfastly and trustfully brings a curse on his own head." Diogenes Laertius, *Lives of Eminent Philosophers* 9.11 (LCL 185:485). [†]Homer *Odyssey* 8.351; ET: Robert Fagles (New York: Penguin, 1999), 202. [§]*Nusquam tuta fides*, a famous line from Dido's lament after she was abandoned by Aeneas. Virgil, *Aeneid* 4.373 (LCL 63:446-47). [◊]Ovid, *Ars amatoria* 1.752 (LCL 232:64-65). [Δ]Quoted in Cicero, *Epistulae ad Atticum* 1.19.8 (LCL 7:116-17). [†]Here, as in the comments in the next passage on the virtue of sedulousness, Melanchthon follows the Aristotelian convention of defining virtue as the mean between vicious extremes. Candor as such was not typically enumerated by ancient writers in the lists of standard virtues; however, it is often used in the sense that Melanchthon gives it here, as a cognate of truthfulness, indicating an open disposition free from mean suspicion.

[3]Cop, *Sur les Proverbes de Salomon*, 93-94; citing Lev 19:18; 2 Cor 8:13.

[4]Downame, ed., *English Annotations*, 6S2r*.

who are in positions of leadership) ought to exercise good works during the summer—that is, in youth, in health, and in vigor—and so gather plenty of spiritual nourishment for ourselves and for our neighbors. And "in the harvest," that is, in the time when we are able to earn merits, and to grow and be enriched spiritually, even in the midst of our trials we should run with charity and zeal to gather together the necessities of our salvation, by which we may be enabled "in winter," that is, in the hour of our death and on the day of judgment—to be refreshed, assisted, and saved, as the apostle warns: "Therefore, while we have time, let us do good to all," and, "Behold, now is the acceptable time: behold, now is the day of salvation." But contrast this with those who act improvidently in bodily goods, who consume and fritter away their patrimony in their youth, and afterward, when they are in need, must suffer the pangs of poverty. Exposition of the Book of Proverbs.[5]

Work and the Virtue of Sedulousness. Philipp Melanchthon: In this sixth chapter the second teaching concerns labor, which the author illustrates by means of an example, commanding us to consider the ants and imitate their sedulousness. First let us learn both that God has ordained positions of office or vocation, and that God has mandated that each one work in his own vocation. He must not thrust himself into a strange vocation, but should strive to excel in his own with diligence and faith. This is taught in many passages throughout the Scriptures. . . .[†] As often, however, as mention is made of labor, at the same time let it be understood as an invocation for God's help, as it is written: "I know, Lord, that a man's way is not his own." And, "Unless the Lord builds the house, [the laborers work in vain]." And, "Commit your way to the Lord and hope in him, and he will act." And, "How much more will the heavenly Father give the Holy Spirit to those who ask." Also, "God gives wisdom to the wise," and, "In all that you do, whether in word or deed, do all in the name of our Lord Jesus." And above, in Proverbs 3, "In all your ways acknowledge him, and he will make your paths straight."

There should always be a joining together of prayer and labor. This virtue is called "sedulousness," and this is its definition: sedulousness is that virtue by which firmly and consistently we desire, on account of God and the common good, to perform the duties appropriate to our vocation as commanded by God, who promises help to those who ask for it. Thus, David is a sedulous soldier; Paul is a sedulous teacher. The extremes of this virtue are idleness [*ignavia*] and *polypragmosynē*, or busybody.[‡] The idler is excessively inactive; the *polypragmōn* toils away after many unnecessary and pointless tasks, and takes upon himself callings that are not his own [*alienis vocationibus*]. Thus, Achan, Pericles, and Demosthenes stirred up by means of unnecessary strife wars that could have been avoided. So also the church is often thrown into confusion by unnecessary disputes and contentions when its teachers obtrude themselves into affairs of civil business, as though having one foot in the court and the other in the temple.

This I have said briefly concerning sedulousness. But those who are keen to do so may find many similar ideas in the prophetic and evangelical Scriptures, as well as in other wise sayings; for example, "You have obtained Sparta; adorn it."[§] This also teaches sedulousness, and warns against being a busybody. Against this, Nazianzus reminds us to focus our efforts on what is necessary: "By no means do I call busywork work."[◊] Exposition of the Proverbs of Solomon.[6]

---

[5]DCOO 7:44-45; citing Gal 6:10; 2 Cor 6:2. [†]The unnamed commentator is Albert the Great, whose observation that "every act of nature is an act of intelligence" (*De mineralibus* I, tr. 1, c. 8) became axiomatic in late medieval theology. [‡]John of Damascus, *On the Orthodox Faith* 2.12.

[6]CR 14:16-17; citing Jer 10:23; Ps 127:1; 37:5; Lk 11:13; Dan 2:21; Col 3:17; Prov 3:6. [†]Melanchthon here cites a number of standard prooftexts: 1 Thess 4:10-11; Eccl 9:10; Rom 12–13; 1 Cor 12; 1 Cor 7:17. [‡]Translation of both of these terms is problematic, for different reasons. The Latin *ignavia* might be taken to mean "laziness" or "sloth," but I have chosen "idleness" for reasons of context, as well as to highlight the difference between this term and the traditional medieval term for "sloth," *acedia*. The latter is a Greek term (*polypragmosynē*) that I have chosen simply to

The Sluggard's Shame. Michel Cop: The sluggards ought to have great shame and bashfulness when Solomon urges them to learn from a beast so small and weak, almost as if he were making them subject to this little creature, which ought to be subject to them—indeed, as should all the beasts of the world, be they never so wild and cruel, as the Word of God teaches us. But the image of God has been effaced in us through sin, and we do not have such dominion and lordship over the beasts as was given to us at the beginning, for there are now those that rise up against human beings, as the great wild beasts, and those very small that trouble human beings in both their bodies and their goods. So if for no other reason than that they are made in the image of God and that the ant is a little, feeble beast, the sluggards ought to be ashamed that the wise man here sends them to consider God's workmanship, to learn wisdom and good governance over their households and families. For inasmuch as this tiny creature goes about its business without constraint and without orders from another, it makes provision for those things it needs, following its own natural inclination and the instinct it has received from God, and by these it works with all diligence. But the sluggish not only have the natural sense they have received from God, and by which they ought to be motivated to work and set themselves to useful labor, but they also have their parents and neighbors, whose example and counsel they should follow. They also have master workers and laborers, from whom they may learn to do the work necessary for this present life. In addition, there are the laws of the magistrate that compel them to work. The ants have no such guidance. This ought to confound the sluggish and, make them ashamed, not having the audacity to appear before other men. For though they have so many different guides, they follow none of them, but this little beast and ant has no guides, yet it follows its natural inclination. On the Proverbs of Solomon.[7]

There's Winking, and There's Winking. The English Annotations: We must distinguish between a natural kind of winking, which may proceed from weakness of the eyes or some such bodily cause . . . that has no dependency on the heart and mind, and that which is occasioned by the motions and suggestions of the mind and inward thoughts. Certainly, when there is much winking in company, there is just cause to suspect it is not right, and at the best, if there is no wickedness in the mind, there is incivility in carriage, especially if it is in company as good as or better than ourselves. But it must be remembered, as has been said recently, that these outward signs are probable . . . but not necessary. To speak roughly and to be full of gesticulation in company is, of itself, a bad sign and to be avoided, yet it is possible that both may occur when the heart is well affected. And on the contrary, none are often more dangerous and pernicious than those that are most silent, or most smooth, in both tongue and carriage, when in company. Annotations on Proverbs 6:13.[8]

What God Hates. Cardinal Cajetan: Now that the evil man has been described, the author then describes the evil things that are hateful to God Most High. "And a seventh that his soul abhors." According to the Hebrew this reads, "and seven things that are abominations to his soul." The meaning, however, is the same. For the author wants to say that there are six things that are hateful to God, and if a seventh is added, there will be seven things abominable to the soul of God. The language here is metaphorical, likened to the revulsion we feel in our souls. And so the addition

---

transliterate, since there exists no precise English equivalent. According to the classicist William Arrowsmith, "in political terms, *polupragmosúne* is the very spirit of Athenian imperialism, its remorseless need to expand, the *hybris* of power and energy in a spirited people; in moral terms, it is a divine discontent and an impatience with necessity, a disease whose symptoms are disorder, corruption, and the hunger for change." Arrowsmith, ed., *Three Comedies by Aristophanes* (Ann Arbor: University of Michigan Press, 1969), 3. [5]See Melanchthon's introduction of this adage in the preface, above. [6]Gregory of Nazianzus, *Poemata moralia* 1.2.32 (PG 37:926.9).

[7]Cop, *Sur les Proverbes de Salomon*, 95.
[8]Downame, ed., *English Annotations*, 6S2v*.

of the seventh makes it so that not only are they hateful but also abominable. "Haughty eyes." This is the first hateful thing. And the discussion is not about the eyes of the body, but those of the mind. The beginning of arrogance is described as haughty eyes. This is because it is typical of the arrogant man to gaze longingly at what is too high and inappropriate for him. By the phrase "haughty eyes" we can also understand definitions of lofty subjects that surpass the understanding of those who provide such definitions. This is because those who deny divine providence over human actions possess arrogant eyes. Such people deny the immortality of the soul and things of that sort. The eyes of those Christians who deny the mystery of the Trinity, and similar doctrines that the Catholic faith confesses are arrogant. "A lying tongue." This is true universally about every kind of falsehood, for deception is inherently depraved, and cannot be spoken no matter how holy the motive that attaches to it. And for this reason, by its very nature, a lying tongue is hateful to God. "Hands that shed innocent blood." The third item that is hateful to God needs no explanation. "A heart that meditates on the worst thoughts." According to the Hebrew the last phrase should be read "iniquity." This expression is also obvious. "Feet that are swift to run into evil." This is the fifth thing the Lord hates. By the expression "feet" is meant those who are quick in their execution of evil. "A false witness who spreads lies." In the Hebrew this means, "the man who will contrive to speak lies as the testimony of falsehood." This is counted as the sixth thing hateful to God, to act as someone who is lying, to give false testimony. This frequently happens in judicial cases, to the serious harm of one's neighbor. "And the one who sows disagreement among brothers." The meaning is plain enough, and this is the seventh thing so hateful to God that he stops at the seven abominations, that is, to make all things abominable in the sight of God. Clearly it is very much against nature and morality to introduce quarrels among brothers, among those who enjoy a natural kind of harmony. The Parables of Solomon, Corrected by the Original Hebrew.[9]

God "Hates" Sin, but Without Passion. Michel Cop: It cannot be doubted that something which does not please God cannot long endure; thus, it should come as no surprise that the ruin of depraved and wicked people should fall on them suddenly, and without remedy. . . . To show why this cannot be otherwise, Solomon explains to us more amply their manners and customs, to show us just how displeasing they are to God. And so to begin, he says, "There are six things that God hates"; and then, as if he had not expressed a sufficient number, he corrects himself, saying that there are seven. And as if that hatred were not enough to show that the wicked and depraved well deserve to be destroyed, and that their lives are not agreeable to God, he adds that "they are an abomination." For insofar as "in God we live, and move, and have our being," it is necessary that what God hates and abhors must not endure. . . . When he says that God "hates" and "abhors" these things, it is not that God is driven by passionate emotions, as human beings are often led as their emotions carry them. God never changes, but in all things he works according to what he has eternally determined from before the foundation of the world was laid. So he does not proceed by hatred and anger to destroy the wicked; rather, those whom he destroys according to their just deserts experience him as if he hated them. In this way, the Scripture attributes hatred to God in the same way that the criminal who is sent to the gallows attributes it to the judge who sends him there. On the Proverbs of Solomon.[10]

6:20–7:27 *More Warnings About Adultery*

On the Dangers of Whoring. Peter Moffett: Now Solomon comes to warn his son

[9]Cajetan, *Parabolae Salomonis ad veritatem Hebraicam castigatae*, 54-56.

[10]Cop, *Sur les Proverbes de Salomon*, 99; citing Acts 17:28.

not to be drawn to go astray by any provocations to unchastity. "Desire not her beauty in your heart"; even though she is fair, yet do not look on her to lust after her. "Neither let her catch you with her eyelids." Neither allow her wanton or pleasant looks to be a net to entangle you, or a fire to inflame you. Two great hurts arising to men by following after strange women are here specified, as sufficient reasons to dissuade everyone from the foul sin of adultery. One is the loss of goods: "For by a whorish woman one is brought to a morsel of bread." Through whoring, men come to extreme poverty, for the harlots have one part of their substance who frequent their company, bawds and ruffians another part, officers before whom they are often arraigned another part, and the rest is consumed through a secret curse of the Lord, and thus at last all comes to nothing. Another mischief is the loss of life itself, for "the adulteress hunts for life, which is precious." The vile harlot brings a man not only to beggary but to death and destruction, being in this respect like hunters who seek after the life of a poor beast; for the adulteress seeks by all means to draw her companion to commit folly with her, whereby it comes to pass that he is laid open to her husband's rage, the magistrate's sword, and God's wrath. Now, because she uses craft and deceit to entangle her lovers, it is not only here said of her that she hunts, but in the book of the Preacher, that her heart is as nets and her hands as snares. A Commentary upon the Whole Book of the Proverbs of Solomon.[11]

Theft and Adultery Contrasted. Cardinal Cajetan: "No one despises a thief because he steals to satisfy his heart because he is hungry." Therefore, the author likens theft to adultery, both with respect to its causes and to the harm it occasions, by demonstrating that adultery is far more serious. And to be sure he explains the underlying causes of theft—namely, to keep oneself alive if there is no food available. In addition, he removes the disrepute from the bad consequences of this same activity by declaring that bad consequences of theft are to restore sevenfold.[†] And if it should prove necessary, to give all of one's possessions in restitution. The Parables of Solomon, Corrected by the Original Hebrew.[12]

Laws Must Yield to Human Necessity. Martin Luther: The vow of chastity is a purely bodily affair that concerns absolutely nothing but the flesh. Therefore, it can be abolished with absolute confidence. In fact, it was never binding, nor could it ever be binding where it imperiled soul or body. A vow never demanded that you lose your soul and body. According to Christ's own interpretation, the vow of chastity means this: "I vow chastity insofar as it is possible to do so without danger to the body or soul." If afterward you feel the surge of passion, then the vow is void and you may safely follow Paul's advice: "If they cannot be continent, let them marry," and again, "It is better to marry than burn." . . . I will break the law of the vow of chastity on the ground of a greater necessity as well as a greater danger to the soul. Fear not; Christ will not fail you. You are not really breaking the vow; you are laying hold of a sound interpretation of what the vow really means.

At this point some stupid fellow will say, "By the same argument adultery will be allowed, if necessity demands. Or, for that matter, murder or theft. All the precepts of God could be broken!" I reply, Such a necessity does not come about in practice. There are women, and there are men: marry, take a wife [or a husband]. There is danger neither to body nor possessions if you are gentle and control your temper. "But can you make out such a case for stealing?" I reply: If necessity demands, stealing is permissible. Then the proverb is shown to be true—namely, "In necessity all things are common." How foolish it would be, even godless, if you were

[11]Moffett, *A Commentary upon the Whole Booke of the Proverbs of Salomon*, 84-85; citing Eccles 7:26.

[12]Cajetan, *Parabolae Salomonis ad veritatem Hebraicam castigatae*, 54-56. [†]Cajetan here follows the teaching of Aquinas, who held that in cases of extreme need, theft of basic sustenance was no sin (*Summa Theologiae* II-II, q. 66, a. 7).

to kill yourself by hunger for fear of the law when you could steal food from the abundance of another and thereby save your life. You are just as foolish if you do not take a wife when passion stirs and you remain continent to the danger of your soul. Under the stress of a consuming passion you must interpret the law of the vow as though the vow of chastity were not required, just as under the stress of hunger you would regard the law about stealing as if it did not exist. It seems that this was laid down even by Solomon in Proverbs 6, where the Hebrew literally says, "Men do not condemn a thief if he steals to feed himself because he is hungry. But if he be found, he shall restore sevenfold and shall give all the substance of his house. But whoever commits adultery with a woman is lacking in understanding and will destroy his soul." This means that a thief will not be condemned even if caught and punished before the law by someone determined to be without mercy, provided that the thief steals under the necessity of hunger. The Judgment of Martin Luther on Monastic Vows.[13]

Adultery Worse than Theft. Michel Cop: He demonstrates here that the adulterer well deserves to be despised, in that he is only led to this filthiness by wickedness, and not by necessity: he is "destitute of understanding," and so he attributes to the adulterer a particular infamy, from which he exempts the thief. He also points out that he "destroys his soul," a charge he also does not lay against the thief. In this we may see that the world is greatly lacking in sound judgment, for a thief nowadays is pursued with all diligence, and is even punished with death, while the adulterer is pardoned, and suffers nothing worse than laughter at the horrible abomination he has committed, as if it were a harmless hobby or child's play. In speaking thus, we do not acquit the thief, or excuse them from punishment, for we know what is written in Romans 13. But we would say that those who punish the thief more harshly than the adulterer do an injury to God, who has appointed a more grievous penalty for the adulterer than the thief. . . . They are wicked judges to favor the wicked so, but one day they shall appear before the righteous judge, who will not favor their ungodliness, but will punish them with all severity, and without any forgiveness. On the Proverbs of Solomon.[14]

How to Understand Sevenfold? The English Annotations: Of a sevenfold restoration, we do not read anything in the law, though it does speak of double and fourfold in some cases and in others, fivefold. Therefore, as seven is often taken for many, so sevenfold here for manifold, by which word all those different restitutions appointed by law are comprehended. Some by sevenfold understand *septies*, or seven times; that is, they say, as often as one is convicted, whether it is seven times or more often, they can be put to restitution and their life is not in danger. Sevenfold may also be taken for plentiful, restitution with good advantage, such as is prescribed by the law. Subtlety is not to be slighted either, as those who join Exodus 22 verse 1 and verse 4 together, that is, five and two, which is there appointed for restitution, which would make up the sevenfold pattern of Solomon's words. Annotations on Proverbs 6:31.[15]

A Parable for Foolish Men. Michel Cop: Here we see the fatherly care God has for us, when so often he admonishes us by Solomon that we should keep his Word—not only by external works, as the hypocrites do, but that it should adorn our very hearts. And it is well for us that he takes such care to admonish us, for he has no need of our service, but we have great need of his. Indeed, we cannot obey him without it. We have seen it before now in various places, where Solomon has shown us the profit that comes from obeying the Word, and the hurt of disobedience. . . .

[13]LW 44:390-92 (WA 8:663); citing 1 Cor 7:9.

[14]Cop, *Sur les Proverbes de Salomon*, 107.

[15]Downame, ed., *English Annotations*, 6S3r*; citing Ex 22:1, 4; Ps 12:6.

And so to turn us away from whoredom and adultery, he uses a parable, in which he displays the foolishness of those who allow themselves to be deceived. In this they are not so much ignorant, but rather they know full well that they do evil, for they wish to avoid being seen. He shows also the subtleties and craftiness, the flatteries and sweet words of those who labor to entice others to go along with their wicked desires. When he attributes the subtleties and crafty dealings, the flattering speeches and sweet words to an adulterous woman, he only speaks according to what is most commonly the case: for if there were no women who sold themselves and advertised their charms, there would not be so many men in open adultery, nor so many whoremongers. On the Proverbs of Solomon.[16]

The Fruit of Bitter Experience. Robert Cleaver: In this chapter Solomon confirms from his own experience that which in the two former chapters (and elsewhere) he had testified concerning the fraudulent and pernicious practices of the harlot. The parts are three: first, an instigation to the studious keeping of wisdom and knowledge (7:1-5); second, a narration of those things that he had seen and observed in her impudent behavior, and answerable success (7:6-24); third, an application to his readers, as an admonition and warning to them (7:25-28). . . . "Keep my commandments and live, and my laws as the apple of your eye." To set an edge on his exhortation, that it might prevail the better with us, he adds a promise of life, and he does this in a most emphatic manner, commanding us to "live"; by doing this he teaches how immediate and certain is the happiness that comes with keeping his precepts. Then he expresses the manner how he would have us keep his doctrine by a similitude—as "the apple of the eye," as that which is most precious to you. For a person will ward and keep off violence from their head before all other parts of the body, and regard their face more than any other part of their head, and respect the eye more than any other part of their face, for the eye is the light of the whole body, and therein the black, or "apple of the eye," is most dear to him. This is also apparent in other Scriptures, such as Psalm 17:8: "Keep me as the apple of your eye," and "he that touches you touches the apple of my eye." A Brief Explanation.[17]

What Is the Peace Offering? The English Annotations: Some interpreters would have the peace offerings mentioned here to have reference to the young man, as though she intended to say that she had made a vow to God concerning him, either for his good health, or her meeting with him, or both, and should now acknowledge or congratulate herself, that she has achieved her wish, or something to that effect. But they are certainly mistaken to think so. In ancient times, when sacrifices were in use, both among the Jews and elsewhere, almost all the world over, they seldom made any feast (not sober housekeepers at least), but when they did sacrifice, then it is that as the word "feast", which properly signifies a "holy day," is taken for an invitation and merry meeting. Thus sacrifices in Scripture are sometimes taken for good cheer. . . . Now sacrifices among the Hebrews were of several kinds. In some (as in holocausts) nothing was reserved, but all was consumed in smoke and ashes. In others, the priest had all the flesh that was left; it was his due by law. In some others again (of which were those that were properly called peace offerings), the greatest part went to the offerer himself, who was in charge of the sacrifice. Those were the sacrifices that caused invitations and good cheer. Here, therefore, "I have a peace offering with me" is, in effect, "I have good provision at home, and this day I make a feast." Annotations on Proverbs 7:14.[18]

Do Not Underestimate Women's Fortitude. Arcangela Tarabotti: Women proved

[16]Cop, *Sur les Proverbes de Salomon*, 107.

[17]Cleaver, *A Brief Explanation of the Whole Booke of the Proverbs of Salomon*, 112-13; citing Zech 2:8.

[18]Downame, ed., *English Annotations*, 6S4v*; citing Prov 17:1; Lev 7.

themselves the courageous sex at Christ's death, when the apostles fled. . . . How can they be weak when they faced death itself, when they have always been strong not only in suffering but in every other necessity? Who will deny Judith's courage? With striking fearlessness she severed the head of Holofernes and freed her country from a deadly siege. What about Tamiris, queen of the Scythians, whose valor brought about a victory against proud King Cyrus?[†] . . . Feminine courage shines out, documented in infinite histories; by it we have subordinated kings, emperors, and powerful armies. As to whether the greatest wise men fell prey to irresistible feminine beauty, let David, Samson, and Solomon tell their tales. The latter in his book of Proverbs says about one of us, "For she has cast down many wounded, and the strongest have been slain by her." Paternal Tyranny.[19]

[19]Tarabotti, *Paternal Tyranny*, 141; citing Judith 12–13. [†]Tamiris (fl. c. 550–530 BC) was a Scythian queen and ruler of the nomadic Massagetae people in ancient Persia. According to Herodotus, she spurned an offer of marriage from King Cyrus and later repelled his invading army, resulting in the latter's death in 530 BC (Herodotus, *Persian Wars* 1.204-15).

8:1-36 THE BLESSINGS OF WISDOM

1 *Does not wisdom call?*
Does not understanding raise her voice?

2 *On the heights beside the way,*
at the crossroads she takes her stand;

3 *beside the gates in front of the town,*
at the entrance of the portals she cries aloud:

4 *"To you, O men, I call,*
and my cry is to the children of man.

5 *O simple ones, learn prudence;*
O fools, learn sense.

6 *Hear, for I will speak noble things,*
and from my lips will come what is right,

7 *for my mouth will utter truth;*
wickedness is an abomination to my lips.

8 *All the words of my mouth are righteous;*
there is nothing twisted or crooked in them.

9 *They are all straight to him who understands,*
and right to those who find knowledge.

10 *Take my instruction instead of silver,*
and knowledge rather than choice gold,

11 *for wisdom is better than jewels,*
and all that you may desire cannot compare with her.

12 *"I, wisdom, dwell with prudence,*
and I find knowledge and discretion.

13 *The fear of the LORD is hatred of evil.*
Pride and arrogance and the way of evil
and perverted speech I hate.

14 *I have counsel and sound wisdom;*
I have insight; I have strength.

15 *By me kings reign,*
and rulers decree what is just;

16 *by me princes rule,*
and nobles, all who govern justly.[a]

17 *I love those who love me,*
and those who seek me diligently find me.

18 *Riches and honor are with me,*
enduring wealth and righteousness.

19 *My fruit is better than gold, even fine gold,*
and my yield than choice silver.

20 *I walk in the way of righteousness,*
in the paths of justice,

21 *granting an inheritance to those who love me,*
and filling their treasuries.

22 *"The LORD possessed*[b] *me at the beginning of his work,*[c]
the first of his acts of old.

23 *Ages ago I was set up,*
at the first, before the beginning of the earth.

24 *When there were no depths I was brought forth,*
when there were no springs abounding with water.

25 *Before the mountains had been shaped,*
before the hills, I was brought forth,

26 *before he had made the earth with its fields,*
or the first of the dust of the world.

27 *When he established the heavens, I was there;*
when he drew a circle on the face of the deep,

28 *when he made firm the skies above,*
when he established[d] *the fountains of the deep,*

29 *when he assigned to the sea its limit,*
so that the waters might not transgress his command,

when he marked out the foundations of the earth,
30 *then I was beside him, like a master workman,*

and I was daily his[e] delight,
rejoicing before him always,

[31]*rejoicing in his inhabited world*
and delighting in the children of man.

[32]*"And now, O sons, listen to me:*
blessed are those who keep my ways.

[33]*Hear instruction and be wise,*
and do not neglect it.

[34]*Blessed is the one who listens to me,*
watching daily at my gates,
waiting beside my doors.

[35]*For whoever finds me finds life*
and obtains favor from the Lord,

[36]*but he who fails to find me injures himself;*
all who hate me love death."

a Most Hebrew manuscripts; many Hebrew manuscripts, Septuagint *govern the earth* **b** Or *fathered*; Septuagint *created* **c** Hebrew *way* **d** The meaning of the Hebrew is uncertain **e** Or *daily filled with*

Overview: The call of personified Wisdom returns in this chapter, and the reformers read this as both an appearance of the preincarnate Son of God and an encomium on the richness of biblical teaching. In both cases, the address of Wisdom leads to repentance. True wisdom, write the commentators, leads to embracing good and rejecting evil, and imparts power and strength of character. Our exegetes also note the legitimacy of human rule as appointed by God. Finally, Scripture's mention of a Wisdom possessed by the Lord at the beginning introduces an occasion for explicit trinitarian discussion. The reformers discuss Nicene teaching, note Arian errors, and point out the importance of precise exegesis and translation to preserve the teaching of the eternal nature of the second person of the Trinity and the triune God's work for creation.

The Praise of Wisdom. The English Annotations: This whole chapter contains nothing else but the praises of wisdom: human and created to verse 22, divine and uncreated to verse 32. It begins, for conclusion, with an exhortation to all, to embrace so useful and heavenly a thing—Wisdom herself—by a *prosopopeia*,[†] under the person of a woman, being made to commend herself. Though among people this is not allowable, because we have nothing we have not received and because the most perfect, in strict judgment, are but unprofitable servants. In God it is quite another thing. Whatever we can say by way of praise speaks to his nature, rather than what we call praise among people, whom we cannot praise properly, as that may bring us to some conceit of nature by way of praise and admiration. Besides, the benefit of divine praises does not redound to God but to people, who by those praises come to the knowledge and love of God, wherein is their felicity. Annotations on Proverbs 8:1.[1]

8:1-11 *The Call of Wisdom*

Wisdom's Persistent Call. Cardinal Cajetan: "Does not Wisdom keep crying aloud?" The word here that has been translated as "keep shouting" should be taken as "will call." Moreover what follows, "and Prudence raises her voice," according to the Hebrew should read, "and Understanding will raise her voice." Because in the preceding verses Solomon had introduced the notion of the wanton woman, summoning young men to all this passion with her flattering and impatient speech, consequently he introduces Wisdom inviting men to virtue. And so to demonstrate the point that men are no less invited by Wisdom than by that wicked woman, he portrays Wisdom as equal to the wicked woman in this

[1]Downame, ed., *English Annotations*, 6S4v-6S5r*; citing Prov 27:2; 1 Cor 4:7; Lk 17:10. [†]Another term for personification, or literary anthropomorphism.

respect: Wisdom herself also calls aloud, and in a similar fashion Understanding persists in raising her voice. Now to call means to stir up, and to turn those who have been called to listen as Wisdom speaks, just as the one who calls with an audible voice stirs up and converts the one who has been called to listen as she speaks. First she introduces wisdom as it exists in men, calling one another, then wisdom as it is found speaking in the divine mind. The Parables of Solomon, Corrected by the Original Hebrew.[2]

The Voice of the Father's Wisdom. Lucas Osiander: Now Solomon introduces the Son of God (who is the Wisdom of the Father) speaking and commending his teaching, which is truly the Word of God. For he is wisdom itself, and thereby he teaches us how to believe truly and to act justly. "Does not Wisdom cry aloud, and Prudence put forth her voice?" The voice of the Son of God is heard in the ministry of the Word. "On the high places," "beside the way," where many people walk, "in the middle of the paths, beside the gates of the city," where the people frequent, "in the very doors" of the city "she speaks," for there the people usually flock together to listen to public debates. That is, freely and bountifully the Son of God gives out his word, by which he exhorts people to repent, so that they might cast aside the folly of impiety and embrace the true wisdom of piety, leaving no one with excuse. (And today we indeed have the word of God in great abundance; therefore let us see to it that we do not hear it to our judgment!) For Wisdom exhorts her listeners to repentance, "saying: O men, to you I call" (by the ministry of my word) "and my voice" is directed "to the sons of men," whom I desire to save. "Understand, you little ones," or more properly, you fools, "grasp understanding"; that is, learn my word, which can make you truly astute (that is, truly wise), and put it into practice; "take heed, you fools," or more rightly, understand in your heart, gain understanding, you who hitherto have been ignorant of divine things; learn now the true wisdom for I am showing you the way to true salvation. Proverbs.[3]

Wisdom Cries Out in the Voices of Preachers. Michel Cop: In order to prove that the foolish and indiscreet cannot be excused for having followed the lusts and desires of their flesh, Solomon here sets out for us an interrogation to show that if these foolish and indiscreet people have yielded to temptation, following their own untamed lusts, it has not been for want of teaching, exhortation, and correction. Rather, they have shown contempt for wisdom and understanding, not wishing to give their hearts and attentions to holy sermons, which are given by the church's pastors both in public and in private. These are the ones by whom Wisdom cries, who raises understanding and thunders with her voice, when they purely handle the Scriptures, seeking only the glory of God and the edification of their neighbors. And so that no one may claim that they have not heard this proclamation, nor understood this calling, Solomon shows us that Gad has not imparted his wisdom to his ministers with the intent that they should hide themselves, or stop their mouths, but rather that they may openly show it and preach it plainly. On the Proverbs of Solomon.[4]

8:12-36 *Wisdom Speaks*

Foreshadowing the Fullness of Wisdom. Michael Jermin: It has been but a *pedagogica sapientia*, a wisdom of training up children, as Gregory of Nazianzus says, of which Solomon hitherto has spoken, and by which he has spoken to us.[†] But now he teaches the ripest in knowledge, and it is the highest "Wisdom that cries," the most glorious "Understanding that utters her voice." Or else as Lyra paraphrases it, before Solomon taught

[2]Cajetan, *Parabolae Salomonis ad veritatem Hebraicam castigatae*, 65-66.

[3]Osiander, *Esdras, Nehemias, Esther, Iob, Psalterium, Prouerbia Salomonis, Ecclesiastes, & Canticum Canticorum*, 1053.

[4]Cop, *Sur les Proverbes de Salomon*, 116.

domestically, as a father to his son; now he teaches scholastically, as a teacher to his students.[‡] Or rather, he teaches now prophetically, as a prophet instructing the church, as the Messiah would when he came in the flesh. It is therefore the uncreated Wisdom of God, his eternal Wisdom that is here described to us, and it is the earnestness of his care to teach us, the vehemence of his desire to bring us to knowledge, which "by crying and putting forth his voice" is here set before us. But seeing that this whole passage is to be understood of Christ, let me have leave to apply this first part of it to his forerunner. For since Abraham saw the days of Christ, so Solomon heard his voice. First his voice is heard, and then himself. Now his voice was John the Baptist, who was the voice crying in the wilderness. He was but the voice; Christ was the Word, the glorious Word of God, who was made flesh and dwelt among us, and spoke with us. And as acquaintance with the voice makes the words more easily understood, so the Baptist prepared acquaintance for Christ to be received into human hearts. All those musical instruments that King David invented, and that were used in the service of God, signified this voice. Those trumpets at the sounding of which Jericho fell down signified this voice. PARAPHRASTIC MEDITATIONS.[5]

WE MUST HATE WHAT GOD HATES. DAVID JORIS: You must progress so far until you hate—in words, works, and thoughts—every kind of sin that the old being clings to or permits. For the vain thoughts must be completely removed and opposed, for from these grow all manner of evil. This must be so if anyone desires to obtain victory and complete perfection. We must regard all things in which we still live as abominations, and not admire them. . . . Take heed. We must likewise hate all of God's enemies from the ground of our hearts. We must feel the Father's heart in us and not love or be favorably inclined to whatever he hates. Each one who wishes to remain unspoiled and free of sin, see to this. O take this to heart indeed. HEAR, HEAR, HEAR, GREAT WONDER, GREAT WONDER, GREAT WONDER.[6]

THE SPIRIT PREPARES THE HEART TO RECEIVE GOOD AND REJECT EVIL. ANDREAS BODENSTEIN VON KARLSTADT: The spirit of the fear of God lays the foundation in the soul and renders the heart receptive toward all treasures from God. That same spirit implants in the heart such noble, gentle thoughts and intense desires for God and creates disgust for all that is evil. REGARDING THE TWO GREATEST COMMANDMENTS.[7]

WISDOM IMPARTS POWER. CARDINAL CAJETAN: "Prudence is mine, strength is mine." According to the Hebrew it should be rendered, "I possess understanding, and power belongs to me." Because (as has often been written before) these efforts bear witness that to be wise cannot be separated from understanding. Thus Wisdom says, "I am understanding," so that all perfection of knowledge for living rightly is understood to reside comprehensively in wisdom. What is added, "power belongs to me." This is the beginning of some corollary statements. Wisdom moreover boasts, because the power is her own. This is not only because power should attach to wisdom (only the wise ought to have authority over others), but especially because power arises from wisdom of its own accord. For this reason natural scientists (*physici*) say that those who are strong of character naturally rule over others.[†] THE PARABLES OF SOLOMON, CORRECTED BY THE ORIGINAL HEBREW.[8]

[5]Jermin, *Paraphrasticall Meditations*, 151-152. [†]Gregory of Nazianzus, *Oration* 11. [‡]Nicholas of Lyra (1270–1349) was a late medieval biblical scholar unusual among Latin Christians for his knowledge of biblical Hebrew.

[6]CRR 7:132*; citing Ps 31:6.

[7]CRR 8:237*.

[8]Cajetan, *Parabolae Salomonis ad veritatem Hebraicam castigatae*, 70. [†]Cajetan likely has in mind Aristotle, who argued that some human beings were "natural" slaves, since they lacked the rational capacity to govern their own affairs (e.g., *Politics* 1.5, 1254b21-23; 1.13, 1260a12-13).

Human Laws Must Conform to God's Law. Konrad Pellikan: Nothing happens without the wisdom, counsel, will, and decree of God, which are all-powerful among men. Therefore the rule of every king depends on the providence of God, so that who reigns, how well he reigns, for how long he reigns, and in what manner all depend on the will of God. "The heart of the king is in the hand of the Lord, and he turns it wherever he wills" (and see the many good works in chapter 20). Apart from divine wisdom human laws are unjust, and so it is necessary that human traditions be brought into conformity with the laws in the Word of God, for law cannot be just apart from God's approval. A Succinct and Universal Commentary on the Bible.[9]

Rulers Are Appointed by God. Swiss Brethren Confession of Hesse: We believe, acknowledge, and confess that the office and authority to govern is ordained by God for the good of humankind. It is divinely ordained to rule and to preserve. Servants of God should do nothing else except advance justice, protect the righteous, and punish the evildoer. Concerning Authority.[10]

Christ, the First Act of God. Dirk Philips: Where Daniel points toward Christ and his kingdom, he speaks of the stone that is hewn without hands out of the great mountain and itself becomes a great mountain that fulfills all. This is a basic prophecy and an incontrovertible testimony of the true divinity of our Lord Jesus Christ. For that the stone was hewn out of the mountains without hands signifies to us the marvelous, incomprehensible, and inexpressible birth of the Son of God, Jesus Christ, out of God his heavenly Father, which took place before the beginning of all creatures. The Enchiridion.[11]

[9]Pellikan, *Commentaria bibliorum et illa brevia quidem ac catholica*, 211r; citing Prov 21:1.
[10]CRR 11:75*; citing Gen 9:6; Ex 18:21; 1 Sam 10:24; Dan 2:21-22; 4:25; Ps 82:1-4; Prov 21:1; Wis 6:10-11; Jn 19:11; Rom 13:1, 4.
[11]CRR 6:155*; citing Dan 2:34-35; Is 53:2; Acts 8:32.

A Rational Account of God's Wisdom. Cardinal Cajetan: "The Lord possessed me at the beginning of his ways." According to the Hebrew it reads, "Jehovah acquired me as the foundation of his path." Lift up your mind, wise reader. It is not simply moral lessons that are recorded here, but very marvelous things. After Wisdom portrays herself with respect to how she dwells among human beings, she flies aloft by ascending to a description of herself as she exists with God, the reason of his divine works. Actually, Wisdom is described analogically both with respect to human wisdom and then with respect to divine wisdom. Note how this is organized: after a contrast is drawn between consorting with the shameful woman, and the alluring speech by which she invites young men, the author depicts Wisdom as dwelling among wise men, calling and inviting others to her virtue. Now, consequently, in contrast to the wanton woman who had boasted that she made a vow to God, and that she had been heard by God, the author introduces Wisdom as describing her union with God Most High. Now we can talk about divine wisdom in two different ways: absolutely, and thus without verification that it has been acquired by God. For God's essence is per se his wisdom. And there are no degrees of increase found between essence and wisdom. Or we can speak of it as determined with respect to the performance of God's works. So wisdom has been acquired by God, through the mediation of divine choice. For this does not occur naturally, but according to his choice God has set apart his wisdom for this purpose, that there might be a rational account of those works that he has performed, does perform, and will perform. If you find it hard to understand these distinctions, then recall the difference between natural power and rational power. According to the former, that power is innately determined toward one end, as heat is to making warm and cold to causing something to be cold. But rational power can achieve opposite effects, as medical skill can both heal and produce sickness. Likewise, the art of fabrication can produce an object either beautiful or unsightly. Now unless it is determined by the choice of the doctor or the craftsman, nothing will ever be accomplished. There will be no foundation for either of these opposite tasks. Likewise, divine wisdom would have no foundation for either work unless it had been determined by the choice of God himself to that which is its foundation, both the reason for these works and for other kinds. Therefore, Wisdom describes herself here not absolutely, but with respect to the foundation of the whole divine workmanship when she says, "Jehovah acquired me as the foundation of his path." This means, of all his work. THE PARABLES OF SOLOMON, CORRECTED BY THE ORIGINAL HEBREW.[12]

A PLURALITY OF PERSONS IN THE GODHEAD. MARTIN LUTHER: Here Solomon shows that he understood the doctrine of our religion that was revealed by Moses, but he does it in such a way that the uneducated people heard and read his words and yet did not understand them. If Solomon had not understood this mystery, he could not have spoken thus. But he drew it all from Moses, as also that question, "What is his name, and what is his Son's name, if you know?" But I think there were similar writings of other holy men as well, like Enoch or Elijah, in which many testimonies of this kind were prominent. But all this remains hidden even nowadays; although it has been revealed ever so clearly in the New Testament, still it is not accepted by the majority but opposed. This same thing happened much more among the Jewish people, since the holy patriarchs set their testimonies even before the learned in rather mysterious form and did not write them down in very blunt language.

But for us it is a great comfort to know that ever since the beginning of the world, there have been such indications that in the divine being there is a plurality of persons and nevertheless a unity of the divine nature and essence. But if there are some who do not believe this or who oppose it, what do we care? Abraham saw three, and he worshiped one. Likewise, the Holy Spirit says in Genesis, "And the Lord rained fire from the heaven from the Lord." Even if the fanatics do not understand or pay attention to these words, we still know that they are the words, not of a drunken person but of God. LECTURES ON GENESIS.[13]

THE WORD REVEALED TO THE CHURCH. PHILIPP MELANCHTHON: In the eighth chapter, after repeating the initial precepts of the Decalogue, now he returns to the general exhortation, so that we may learn this wisdom and obey it. For this wisdom from God has been revealed and displayed for us, and he binds us to it. This is not said concerning the wisdom of Pericles or Alcibiades, or some such ones, who were skillful in increasing their power and wealth in any circumstance, whether justly or unjustly. Nor indeed can it be doubted that Solomon speaks of the word revealed to the church, concerning the law of God and the gospel, when he says, "Wisdom calls in the gates of the city." But when the eternal and immovable wisdom that is God himself is revealed in the voice of the law and the gospel, it is revealed through the Son himself, through whom the Father speaks his decrees regarding the creation and the restoration of humanity: Antiquity understood this passage to refer to the wisdom which is the Son speaking to the church; I agree with this interpretation, rightly understood.

But the Arians falsely picked out certain snippets to confirm their view that the Son is a created being. For when Solomon says, "The Lord possessed me at the beginning of his way," the Arians read, "The Lord created me at the beginning of their ways."[†] But in the Hebrew text the word is "possessed," not "created," and this word indicates a continuous sense, which clearly refutes the Arians. For so also in John it is written: "In the beginning was the Word," and this says exactly the same thing very nicely: "The Lord possessed me at the start."

[12]Cajetan, *Parabolae Salomonis ad veritatem Hebraicam castigatae*, 73-74.

[13]LW 1:20-21 (WA 42:16); citing Prov 30:4; Gen 18:2; 19:24.

So also, "Before the ages I was set up." And this Wisdom says that he himself was the craftsman or founder, just as John 1 says, "All things were made through him." Likewise, "He upholds all things by the word of his power." This is because the Son is the same one through whom the decree is spoken for the establishment of creation and the restoration of humanity. Therefore he calls this by the same name as that wisdom that creates and sends forth the law and the gospel. Exposition of the Proverbs of Solomon.[14]

The Importance of Original-Language Exegesis. Ludwig Lavater: This passage is most appropriately understood in conjunction with the beginning of the first chapter of John's Gospel: "In the beginning was the Word, and the Word was with God, and the Word was God." The Son of God is said to be the Word because it was by him that God wanted to make himself known to us, as well as by whom all the ancients spoke. But Justin Martyr adduces this passage in his *Dialogue with Trypho the Jew* in establishing the divinity of the Son of God.[†] This testimony, "The Lord possessed me from the beginning," the Arians have twisted in defense of their own erroneous doctrines, perversely reading it as "The Lord created me" (*ektise*) instead of "possessed me" (*ektēse*). From this they have gathered that the Wisdom of God is a creature (*ktisma*), and not true God from eternity. They spread this error far and wide, and when they had gained authority and power, they at length persecuted the orthodox with much more cruelty than the Roman emperors had done. Epiphanius, in defending this dictum of Solomon against Arius, first teaches that this expression may refer to the incarnate economy (*ton ensarkon oikonomian*), but then he renders the Hebrew word "created" and explicates it metaphorically, as it is used in Sirach.[‡] . . . There are also others among the fathers who read it thus: "The Lord created me at the beginning of his ways," understanding this with reference to the incarnation—see, for example, the beginning of Gregory of Nazianzus's fourth *Theological Oration*.[§] . . . Understand, then, that he was "created" according to the flesh, not according to his divinity.[◊] According to the form of God it is said, "before all the hills he begot me"—that is, before all the heights of creation. And, "before the daystar I begot you"—that is, before all time and temporality. But according to the form of a servant, it is said, "The Lord created me in the beginning of his works. . . ."

But in passing we can see here how useful is the study of languages for understanding and explicating the sacred books. For if the ancients had been adept in the Hebrew language, they would never have read this passage as "the Lord created me." There are in our day some who say that the study of languages is not only useless but indeed very harmful, generating heresies. On the contrary, it is when the sacred languages are unknown or neglected that the worst heresies arise and are accepted, and so it is clear that the gift of understanding their languages is a special benefaction of the Holy Spirit for helping us to understand the sacred writings. On the Book of Proverbs, or Sayings, of Solomon the Most-Wise King.[15]

Textual Change Leads to Much Ado About the Trinity. The English Annotations: Much ado, there has been, of old, about these words, as cannot be unknown to those who are not altogether unacquainted with ecclesiastical

[14]CR 14:18-19; citing Jn 1:1; 1:3; Heb 1:3. [†]Arius (d. 336) and his followers were condemned at the Council of Nicaea (325) for preaching that the Son of God was neither co-essential nor co-eternal with the Father, but rather preeminent among God's creatures. His heresy remained influential until the late sixth century.

[15]Lavater, *In librum Proverbiorum siue Sententiarum Solomonis Regis sapientissimi*, 73-74; citing Jn 1:1; Sir 1:4-10; Ps 109:3 LXX. [†]Justin Martyr, *Dialogue with Trypho* 61. [‡]Epiphanius, *Panarion* 2.24.1. [§]A celebrated passage laying down an exegetical principle that would become axiomatic for pro-Nicene interpretation of Scripture: "Whatever we find joined with a cause we are to refer to the manhood, but all that is absolute and unoriginated we are to reckon to the account of his Godhead." Gregory of Nazianzus, *Theological Oration* 4.2 (ET: *Christology of the Later Fathers*, ed. Edward R. Hardy [Louisville: Westminster John Knox, 1954], 178). [◊]Augustine, *On the Trinity* 1.12.

histories and heresies. For what is here in the Hebrew *qānānî*, well rendered as "possessed me," was by the Septuagint translated *ektisen mē*, that is, "created me," which the Arians, who denied the eternal deity of Christ, took hold of and made great boast of this authority. The Fathers, most of them for want of the Hebrew tongue, were much put to it to answer them. Many answers were devised, but among them all, not many solid and satisfactory. Since the Hebrew text has been better understood, most people have been of the opinion that the Greek translation was right enough at first, but since depraved, either on purpose or accidentally because of the affinity of the words—that is, where they had rendered it *ektēse mē* (with an *ē* from [*ktēō*] "possession"), it was made afterward *ektise mē* (with an *i* from *ktizō*, that is, "created me"). . . . For my part, I could be content to believe that the Hebrew word *qnh* had anciently both significations, to possess and to create . . . but "to possess" is the more proper signification in this place, yet if it were granted the word might be "created" also, I think we should grant no more than what might be conveniently enough interpreted according to St. Paul's expression of Christ, "the image of the living God, the firstborn of every creature." . . .

"Possessed me" is a very proper word to express the eternal generation of Christ the Son of God. Of a temporal but mystical generation it is used where Moses speaks to the Israelites, "Is he not God your Father?" . . . . "In the beginning of his ways, before his works of old." Because the Hebrews have no proper word to express eternity . . . , they are wont to set it out by times and things before the creation, which, though improper of itself, yet is most suitable (eternity being a thing incomprehensible to people) to people's apprehensions and capacities. ANNOTATIONS ON PROVERBS 8:22.[16]

GOD DOES NOTHING WITHOUT HIS WISDOM. MICHEL COP: With the aim of ensuring that we should not think that Wisdom, who has so extolled herself from the beginning of this chapter, should not in truth be as she has declared, and that it is not simply a fantasy framed in the human brain, Solomon takes proper care to describe her eternal power. Therefore, he says, "The Lord has possessed Wisdom in the beginning of his way." With this he wants us to understand that God has never purposed or ordained anything in his eternal decree without Wisdom—that is, with this Wisdom that was already in existence before God put into execution any of his purposes and ordinances. This was indeed necessary, for it follows that if it was in the beginning of the way of the Lord, that it was before all things, and consequently, that it is no creature who has taken its essence from created things. For this reason we must conclude that this being is eternal, and likewise is his power. And since there is no eternal being or eternal power, except in God, it therefore follows that this Wisdom is in God, and that it is nothing distinct from or separate from God, and consequently, that this Wisdom is God. ON THE PROVERBS OF SOLOMON.[17]

A MEDIATOR FROM THE BEGINNING. PETER MOFFETT: Here the Son of God entreats concerning his being, and concerning his calling to the office of a Mediator. "Jehovah possessed me in the beginning." I, the eternal Word of God, was with God the Father at the beginning, being of one and the selfsame essence with him and the Spirit. "Before the world was anointed," I was appointed to the office of a mediator between God and humanity from all eternity. "While yet there were no depths I was born," I had my person from the person of my Father from all eternity, being begotten before all creatures, and to continue forever. A COMMENTARY UPON THE WHOLE BOOK OF THE PROVERBS OF SOLOMON.[18]

---

[16]Downame, ed., *English Annotations*, 6T1v-6T2r*; citing Deut 3:6.

[17]Cop, *Sur les Proverbes de Salomon*, 122-23.

[18]Moffett, *A Commentary upon the Whole Booke of the Proverbs of Salomon*, 98-99; citing Jn 1:1; Heb 1:2.

Creation by the Father Through the Son. John Donne: We used to ascribe creation to the Father, but the Father created by the Word, and his Word is his Son, Christ. "When he prepared the heavens, I was there," says Christ of himself in the person of Wisdom, "and when he appointed the foundations of the earth, then was I by him, as one brought up with him." It is not as one brought in to him or brought in by him, but with him; one as old, that is, eternal—as much God as he. Sermon on John 5:28-29.[19]

Wisdom Rejoices to Guide the Plans of Kings. Philipp Melanchthon: He writes that Wisdom was "rejoicing before him at all times, rejoicing in the orb of the earth, and delighting myself with the sons of men." First of all, this Wisdom delights in the Father; in the next place it reveals the Father to angels and to humans in marveling at the order of the created world; then, it reveals and glorifies the Father in the proclamation of the Word, in the assumption of human nature, in the resurrection, in the restoration of humanity, and in the preservation of the whole church, from the flood of Noah, to [the crossing of] the Red Sea, and to all the other miraculous events. All these marvelous works are here described as the rejoicing and delighting of the Wisdom of God. Let devout readers pay special attention to this sweetest idea, and to this Wisdom itself—that is, the Son teaches the church externally by the proclamation of the Word, and internally he supports, teaches, and illuminates it. And since he watches over every human race because of the church, to the extent they become just in their politics, they are made so by [Wisdom] himself, who sustains and teaches their rulers by the word breathed out, and governs them in a secret manner. Thus he says, "Through me kings reign and judges render just judgments," and distinguishes this Wisdom of God, which rules through the word made known by public proclamation, from human shrewdness. The divine wisdom is fruitful, efficacious, and life-giving, and eventually carries us to a happy outcome, even if this is delayed a while. Indeed, the shrewdness of Pericles, Alcibiades, Demosthenes, and others like them is destructive to society and to those who practice it.[†] For this reason the Wisdom of God says, "Counsel and success[‡] are with me"; that is, those counsels are just that are congruent with the Word of God, and these will finally have a happy outcome, helped by the Son of God, who desires to be present for those who persist in the word he gives them and who call on him, as it is written, "Commit your way to God and hope in him, and he will do it." And in Proverbs 3: "In all your ways acknowledge him, and he will direct your steps." And again: "It is God who works, so that you may will and act [according to his good will]." But punishments do indeed pursue the unrighteous, even if for a while in the present they enjoy their pleasures and increase in power. Exposition of the Proverbs of Solomon.[20]

Trinitarian Delight in Creation. Robert Cleaver: Having thus set forth and proved his eternity, he proceeds to set forth his felicity, partly in the delight which he both gave to his Father and received from him before the world (in which also is to be understood that the Holy Spirit, the third person in the Trinity, communicates with them both), and partly in the delight that since the world was made he takes in the world generally, and especially in the sons of men. The former is set down in borrowed speeches, accommodated to our capacity, in which he compares himself to a baby smiling and laughing with his nurse, and to a little child sporting and playing before his father. The latter is set down first in one of the same borrowed

[19]Donne, *Works*, 1:358*.

[20]CR 14:19-20; citing Ps 37:5; Prov 3:6; Phil 2:13. [†]Alcibiades (c. 450–404 BC) was a statesmen and demagogue whom Thucydides blamed for the downfall of Athens during the Peloponnesian War; the reputations of Pericles and Demosthenes are perhaps less polarizing, though Melanchthon regarded them as overly ambitious figures whose *polypragmosynē* undermined the peace of their lands. For more on Melanchthon's critique of this vice, see his comments on Prov 6:6-11, above. [‡]Melanchthon here renders the Hebrew *tôšîh* with the Latin *successus* (compare with the Vulgate's *aequitas*).

speeches, "laughing" and "sporting in the habitual part of the earth"—that is, taking pleasure in the creatures, beholding in them the fruit of the most absolute wisdom, power, and goodness of the whole Trinity. And second, in plainer speech, "my delight"—indeed, my double delight is in the sons of men, as they were at first formed and fashioned in Adam, bearing before his fall the stamp and print of God's image, for wisdom, holiness, and righteousness; and foreseeing, and preordaining the glorious estate to which they were to be restored after humanity's fall, to be made like himself, and to be incorporated into him, and with him, by the merit of his suffering, and obedience, together with the efficacy of his spirit, and grace to inherit holiness, honor, and immortality forever. A BRIEF EXPLANATION.[21]

[21]Cleaver, *A Brief Explanation of the Whole Booke of the Proverbs of Salomon*, 138-39.

9:1–11:31 THE WAY OF WISDOM AND THE WAY OF FOLLY

1 Wisdom has built her house;
she has hewn her seven pillars.

2 She has slaughtered her beasts; she has mixed her wine;
she has also set her table.

3 She has sent out her young women to call
from the highest places in the town,

4 "Whoever is simple, let him turn in here!"
To him who lacks sense she says,

5 "Come, eat of my bread
and drink of the wine I have mixed.

6 Leave your simple ways,[a] and live,
and walk in the way of insight."

7 Whoever corrects a scoffer gets himself abuse,
and he who reproves a wicked man incurs injury.

8 Do not reprove a scoffer, or he will hate you;
reprove a wise man, and he will love you.

9 Give instruction[b] to a wise man, and he will be still wiser;
teach a righteous man, and he will increase in learning.

10 The fear of the LORD is the beginning of wisdom,
and the knowledge of the Holy One is insight.

11 For by me your days will be multiplied,
and years will be added to your life.

12 If you are wise, you are wise for yourself;
if you scoff, you alone will bear it.

13 The woman Folly is loud;
she is seductive[c] and knows nothing.

14 She sits at the door of her house;
she takes a seat on the highest places of the town,

15 calling to those who pass by,
who are going straight on their way,

16 "Whoever is simple, let him turn in here!"
And to him who lacks sense she says,

17 "Stolen water is sweet,
and bread eaten in secret is pleasant."

18 But he does not know that the dead[d] are there,
that her guests are in the depths of Sheol.

10 *The proverbs of Solomon.*

A wise son makes a glad father,
but a foolish son is a sorrow to his mother.

2 Treasures gained by wickedness do not profit,
but righteousness delivers from death.

3 The LORD does not let the righteous go hungry,
but he thwarts the craving of the wicked.

4 A slack hand causes poverty,
but the hand of the diligent makes rich.

5 He who gathers in summer is a prudent son,
but he who sleeps in harvest is a son who brings shame.

6 Blessings are on the head of the righteous,
but the mouth of the wicked conceals violence.[e]

7 The memory of the righteous is a blessing,
but the name of the wicked will rot.

8 The wise of heart will receive commandments,
but a babbling fool will come to ruin.

9 Whoever walks in integrity walks securely,
but he who makes his ways crooked will be found out.

10 Whoever winks the eye causes trouble,
and a babbling fool will come to ruin.

[11]*The mouth of the righteous is a fountain of life,*
but the mouth of the wicked conceals violence.

[12]*Hatred stirs up strife,*
but love covers all offenses.

[13]*On the lips of him who has understanding,*
wisdom is found,
but a rod is for the back of him who lacks sense.

[14]*The wise lay up knowledge,*
but the mouth of a fool brings ruin near.

[15]*A rich man's wealth is his strong city;*
the poverty of the poor is their ruin.

[16]*The wage of the righteous leads to life,*
the gain of the wicked to sin.

[17]*Whoever heeds instruction is on the path to*
life,
but he who rejects reproof leads others astray.

[18]*The one who conceals hatred has lying lips,*
and whoever utters slander is a fool.

[19]*When words are many, transgression is not*
lacking,
but whoever restrains his lips is prudent.

[20]*The tongue of the righteous is choice silver;*
the heart of the wicked is of little worth.

[21]*The lips of the righteous feed many,*
but fools die for lack of sense.

[22]*The blessing of the LORD makes rich,*
and he adds no sorrow with it.[f]

[23]*Doing wrong is like a joke to a fool,*
but wisdom is pleasure to a man of
understanding.

[24]*What the wicked dreads will come upon him,*
but the desire of the righteous will be granted.

[25]*When the tempest passes, the wicked is no*
more,
but the righteous is established forever.

[26]*Like vinegar to the teeth and smoke to the*
eyes,
so is the sluggard to those who send him.

[27]*The fear of the LORD prolongs life,*
but the years of the wicked will be short.

[28]*The hope of the righteous brings joy,*
but the expectation of the wicked will perish.

[29]*The way of the LORD is a stronghold to the*
blameless,
but destruction to evildoers.

[30]*The righteous will never be removed,*
but the wicked will not dwell in the land.

[31]*The mouth of the righteous brings forth wisdom,*
but the perverse tongue will be cut off.

[32]*The lips of the righteous know what is*
acceptable,
but the mouth of the wicked, what is perverse.

11 *A false balance is an abomination to the LORD,*
but a just weight is his delight.

[2]*When pride comes, then comes disgrace,*
but with the humble is wisdom.

[3]*The integrity of the upright guides them,*
but the crookedness of the treacherous
destroys them.

[4]*Riches do not profit in the day of wrath,*
but righteousness delivers from death.

[5]*The righteousness of the blameless keeps his*
way straight,
but the wicked falls by his own wickedness.

[6]*The righteousness of the upright delivers them,*
but the treacherous are taken captive by their lust.

[7]*When the wicked dies, his hope will perish,*
and the expectation of wealth[g] *perishes too.*

[8]*The righteous is delivered from trouble,*
and the wicked walks into it instead.

[9]*With his mouth the godless man would*
destroy his neighbor,
but by knowledge the righteous are delivered.

[10]*When it goes well with the righteous, the city*
rejoices,

and when the wicked perish there are shouts
of gladness.

11 *By the blessing of the upright a city is exalted,*
but by the mouth of the wicked it is
overthrown.

12 *Whoever belittles his neighbor lacks sense,*
but a man of understanding remains silent.

13 *Whoever goes about slandering reveals secrets,*
but he who is trustworthy in spirit keeps a
thing covered.

14 *Where there is no guidance, a people falls,*
but in an abundance of counselors there is
safety.

15 *Whoever puts up security for a stranger will*
surely suffer harm,
but he who hates striking hands in pledge is
secure.

16 *A gracious woman gets honor,*
and violent men get riches.

17 *A man who is kind benefits himself,*
but a cruel man hurts himself.

18 *The wicked earns deceptive wages,*
but one who sows righteousness gets a sure reward.

19 *Whoever is steadfast in righteousness will live,*
but he who pursues evil will die.

20 *Those of crooked heart are an abomination to*
the LORD,
but those of blameless ways are his delight.

21 *Be assured, an evil person will not go*
unpunished,
but the offspring of the righteous will be
delivered.

22 *Like a gold ring in a pig's snout*
is a beautiful woman without discretion.

23 *The desire of the righteous ends only in good,*
the expectation of the wicked in wrath.

24 *One gives freely, yet grows all the richer;*
another withholds what he should give, and
only suffers want.

25 *Whoever brings blessing will be enriched,*
and one who waters will himself be watered.

26 *The people curse him who holds back grain,*
but a blessing is on the head of him who sells it.

27 *Whoever diligently seeks good seeks favor,*[h]
but evil comes to him who searches for it.

28 *Whoever trusts in his riches will fall,*
but the righteous will flourish like a green leaf.

29 *Whoever troubles his own household will*
inherit the wind,
and the fool will be servant to the wise of heart.

30 *The fruit of the righteous is a tree of life,*
and whoever captures souls is wise.

31 *If the righteous is repaid on earth,*
how much more the wicked and the sinner!

a Or *Leave the company of the simple* **b** Hebrew lacks *instruction* **c** Or *full of simpleness* **d** Hebrew *Rephaim* **e** Or *but violence covers the mouth of the wicked*; also verse 11 **f** Or *and toil adds nothing to it* **g** Or *of his strength*, or *of iniquity* **h** Or *acceptance*

OVERVIEW: This section represents a transition in the book of Proverbs, moving from an introductory discussion of wisdom in Proverbs 9 and turning to give examples of how this principle is applied in real-world contexts. The way the text draws this overview to a close elicits little comment from our commentators, though the exposition of the seven pillars of Wisdom's house from the *English Annotations* is noteworthy, as they move away from the tendency of patristic and Jewish exegetes to give each pillar a specific referent and instead settle on a generic interpretation.[1] The reformers instead focus on the fear of the Lord and the ways it functions in the lives of believers. For Martin Luther and Pilgram Marpeck, this fear leads to repentance, though Marpeck emphasizes that the believer must move beyond fear to experience grace and freedom. For Peter Moffett on the other hand, fear must remain as a reminder for believers to shun vice and embrace virtue. As the text turns to aphorisms that apply the introductory teachings on wisdom and folly to particular situations, our commentators find much to discuss in these examples. Seeking to encourage virtue in their readers and deter them from vice, many of them emphasize the ways in which God's work stands above human actions, as his favor, blessing, and providence animate his followers and provide for their needs, whatever their circumstances.

9:1-18 *Wisdom Versus Folly*

What Are the Seven Pillars? The English Annotations: Christ the supreme wisdom, or wisdom in general, as opposed to folly, is a heavenly thing. Even so, heathens themselves speak of it, though they know nothing of Christ, either as God or man.

He has prepared himself a church. Or, if wisdom in general is understood, the building of a house and hewing of pillars may serve to set out the firmness and stability, yea, and the glory of true wisdom, in its own nature, though it does not always fall out to wise people in this world, according to their wisdom, as observed by Solomon, "I returned and saw under the sun, 'the race is not to the swift.'" . . .

"Seven pillars" [may refer to] the chief supports and principal parts of his church, as were the patriarchs, prophets, apostles, pastors, and doctors. Some rabbis by the seven pillars understand the seven liberal arts. Others, the seven gifts of the Holy Ghost. Others, the seven first days of the creation of the world. Many such allegories can be devised, which may have some ground of application. But the most literal interpretation is, to take seven here, as is ordinary in Scripture, *pro numero perfectionis*, as a perfect number, so that by seven pillars, we understand many pillars, so many, both in number and variety, as might be sufficient to both uphold and adorn the building. Annotations on Proverbs 9:1.[2]

Wisdom's Temple Is the Human Body. Hugo Grotius: "Wisdom has built herself a home": the human body. "And has hewn them from seven pillars": this is how many posts there were in the temple under the treasuries. Or it may be understood with reference to the five senses, with two others added: voice and memory. Annotations on the Old Testament.[3]

The Wise Press On to Perfection. Cardinal Cajetan: Teach a righteous man and he will be quick to receive your instruction. According to the Hebrew this reads, "Cause the righteous man to know and he will add to his learning." For the righteous, no matter how recently they have learned something, they add this as well to their supply of knowledge, and they provide others with instruction and information. And therefore, as righteous as they are wise, they derive benefit from the new knowledge they acquire. In contrast to the wicked, they are described as righteous, just as in contrast to mockers they are described as wise. And indeed these fruitless persons are forsaken, but those are called to perfection. . . . For simpletons are those of little wisdom, but mockers claim for themselves the right to criticize others. The wise, however, judge according to the truth. . . . For those who are weak in heart lack moral virtue, but the wicked are evil in character from their excess, as

[1]For examples of patristic interpretations, see J. Robert Wright, ed., *Psalms, Proverbs, Ecclesiastes*, ACCS OT 9 (Downers Grover, IL: InterVarsity Press, 2005), 72.

[2]Downame, ed., *English Annotations*, 6T2r-v*; citing Prov 8:1; Eccles 9:11; Is 11:2.

[3]Grotius, *Annotationes in Vetus Testamentum*, 249.

those who sin with malice. The righteous, however, choose the truly good. The Parables of Solomon, Corrected by the Original Hebrew.[4]

Consuming the Word and Sacraments. The English Annotations: By meat and drink is meant the Word of God and the ministration of the sacraments, whereby God nourishes his servants in his house, which is the church. More generally and probably by "bread" here we may understand any variety of fish or flesh that may probably be supposed in a sumptuous feast with plentiful entertainment. Annotations on Proverbs 9:5.[5]

Evildoers Seek to Hide from the Discipline of the Word. Dirk Philips: Since God's Word pierces, disciplines, and judges, evildoers hate the light of the divine Word so that they may neither be disciplined nor judged by it. For the godless hate discipline, and seek corners to slip into in order to hide themselves. They love darkness and are not eager to be seen, since what they do secretly is a shame to say, as the apostle writes to the Ephesians. The Enchiridion.[6]

Forsake Those Who Are Incorrigible. Michel Cop: Even though we must forsake fools and their folly, nevertheless we must be diligent to reprove and correct them, as we have seen that Noah, Lot, Moses, the prophets, and apostles all have done. So also has our Lord reproved them, as we may see in the Gospel histories, and he has commanded that they be reproved. And as St. Paul says, "Have nothing to do with the fruitless deeds of darkness, but rather reprove them." And, "Rebuke openly those who persist in sin, that the rest also may fear." Even so, there are some who are so depraved and incorrigible that we can gain nothing by correcting them. With such people we only appear to share in their dishonesty, and so are considered as being like them. For those who are of corrupt judgment and led by evil intentions will condemn the ministers, judging them to be of the same sort as those with whom they associated and whom they cannot set straight. Solomon knew this well, and therefore he says as a complaint, "He who reproves a scorner. . . ." It is not that such reproof is evil in itself, but that scorners, so much as they can, bring shame on the ones who reprove and correct them, for they slander and dishonor them, and attempt to make it appear that the one giving correction is no better esteemed among others than they are. Thus not only do we waste our time in correcting scorners, but we also get blame and censure. On the Proverbs of Solomon.[7]

Godly Fear Prepares Our Hearts for Salvation. Martin Luther: The "beginning of wisdom," or the highest wisdom, is the fear of God—to know God's wrath and, as a result, to live and to perform everything we do with humble hearts. Scripture thus exalts the fear of God. It impresses on people so to live that they fear God's wrath at all times and feel that they have merited death. This is the first element of salvation, when, because of sin, we see no deliverance. This is the highest wisdom: to go about our tasks in full awareness of God's wrath. In this way we are made ready, like the earth for the plow, to receive the divine seed, the fruit of which is eternal life. Pharaoh, Sennacherib, and others lacked this wisdom. Therefore they perished before they realized that they were perishing. They were blinded by their power and by the strength of their armed forces. On the other hand, Hezekiah, though besieged in Jerusalem, was rescued. Moses and the Jews experienced a certain and glorious deliverance at the Red Sea. Therefore we should cling to the truth that it is not a damnable thing to feel God's wrath, but that this feeling is the beginning of deliverance, which cannot be gained without constant prayer. This feeling is a singular gift of God, which reason

[4]Cajetan, *Parabolae Salomonis ad veritatem Hebraicam castigatae*, 88.
[5]Downame, ed., *English Annotations*, 6T2v*; citing Jn 6:27; Gen 31:54.
[6]CRR 6:231*; citing Eph 5:12.
[7]Cop, *Sur les Proverbes de Salomon*, 135; citing Mt 18:15; Eph 5:11; 1 Tim 5:20.

does not grasp or understand. Commentary on Psalm 90.[8]

Repentance Must Grow Beyond Fear. Pilgram Marpeck: Where commandment or prohibition rule conscience, heart, and even God's law, one is not free but in bondage to sin and wickedness. There is no free grace, peace, or joy in the Holy Spirit, but rather the threat of punishment, fear, sorrowing, and anxiety about the vengeance on sin through the coming wrath of God. Because of this fear, external works and fruits of sin are at times abstained from. Such fear of God is the beginning of repentance, the hope to become free of the law of sin and to become free through faith in Jesus Christ, in the word of grace. This fear is the beginning of wisdom and the knowledge of God in his Son, who is the wisdom of his Father. In this manner, Jesus Christ, the Son of God, sets one free. Concerning Hasty Judgments and Verdicts.[9]

The Necessity of Fear for Ethical Action. Peter Moffett: I think that this sentence is very excellent, and not without cause so often repeated, not only in this book, but in other places of the Scripture. . . . For take away the fear of God, engendered by the Word of God, and who will abstain from doing wickedness whenever they think they may lie hidden? Who will shun those vices which by law are not punished? Who will fear an oath who does not fear God? Who will of conscience shun evil and do that which is good? Because the fear of God is in the wise and just, they profit by instructions and reproofs. The foolish and simple can never become wise till they have begun to fear the Lord. So, likewise, the knowledge of holy things is understanding; for what good would it do a person to be a cunning lawyer and yet condemned everlastingly? And to be a skillful physician and yet not able to salve the sores of one's soul? And to be passingly well seen in music and yet always troubled with a jarring conscience? Or, to conclude, to be learned in all the arts and sciences and yet ignorant of Christ? For if you know him, it does not matter if you know nothing else. A Commentary upon the Whole Book of the Proverbs of Solomon.[10]

10:1-32 *Walking in Integrity*

Providence and the Cross. Philipp Melanchthon: The common doctrine of providence is often repeated throughout this whole book. For God distinguishes the righteous from the unrighteous with eternal rewards and punishments, because this is the order of justice: the righteous are preserved and the unrighteous are destroyed, as it is written, "God is a consuming fire." For God intends that, at the mention of punishments and rewards, the difference between righteousness and unrighteousness may be brought more clearly into view. For the righteous are those who are conformed to God and to his law, but the unrighteous are at war with both.

But temporal punishments must be distinguished from eternal. The former are imposed primarily to call people back to repentance, but when they fall on those who do not repent, they are the beginning of their destruction, as were the sufferings of Saul, Judas, Nero, and all others who fall into eternal punishments. Likewise, bodily goods may be distinguished from eternal. The church, indeed, will have eternal goods. Indeed, it is for that reason that rational creatures were made, that they might in some way be organs through which God communicates himself—his light, his wisdom, his justice, his life and eternal joy. But in this mortal life the church is still subjected to the cross, for many of its members are sternly trained, some more, some less. However, since God desires that the church be the minister of his voice in this life, it could not be otherwise; for the church

[8]LW 13:129-30 (WA 40.3:574-75); citing Ex 5:2; 2 Kings 18:35; 19:35; Ex 14:27.
[9]CRR 12:143-44; citing Rom 7:23; 14:17; Sir 1:16.
[10]Moffett, *A Commentary upon the Whole Booke of the Proverbs of Salomon*, 107; citing Job 28:28; Ps 111:10.

always acts to give succor to any group of people which, without food, drink, or hospitality, cannot live. Thus it lightens the cross, for it gives them not only those things that are necessary for preserving bodily life, but it also preserves among them these laws regarding eternal life: harsh offenses are accompanied by harsh punishments. Thus the adultery of David and the wickedness of Manasseh were followed by horrible punishments, though indeed many of these punishments are lightened for the faithful, and the course of many is made more tranquil. Thus are driven home promises both eternal and bodily, as is said in this passage: "The Lord will not allow the soul of the righteous to go hungry," and in Psalm 33, "Lions will go hungry, but those who fear the Lord will not lack any good thing." Exposition of the Proverbs of Solomon.[11]

God Will Not Let His Faithful Starve. Michel Cop: We may see the wicked prosper and so abound in wealth that they have ease and pleasures, spend their time joyfully, and have rest and quiet, while the faithful who strive for justice are poor and endure much evil. This is common and ordinary through all the world, and so it happens that the children of God may become envious or sorrowful, and be tempted to forsake all justice and innocence and follow wickedness, to enjoy the ease of the wicked and to prosper for a time with them. Those who do not flatter themselves in their infirmities and imperfections, if they truly know what they are, will know and feel that they are tossed with such temptations. David makes it plain in his psalms that he has felt this way, and confesses it. . . . He warns us not to vex ourselves over the wicked, nor to envy them. And by the discourse of his psalms, he shows us that the good show put on by the wicked is nothing but vanity, and that the poor condition of the faithful is much better and more profitable than it seems or is thought to be. In following this doctrine, Solomon would not have fathers and mothers to fear that their children (whom they should instruct in wisdom and justice) should perish or starve, even though they may gather no great treasures for them. He also instructs us all generally, that we should not put our trust in goods, even if we abound in them, and that we should not be discouraged whether we have little or much, provided that we delight to walk in a safe conscience, as God teaches us by his Word. . . .

When Solomon promises us things that we do not see with our bodily eyes, and that appear to run contrary to the senses of the flesh, he is teaching us that we have need of faith, with which we may be fortified against the scandals of the cross. For when we see that the wicked prosper, and that the good are afflicted, the flesh takes offense and judges that God does not care to help them. But the promises of God require faith, whereby we believe that God does help and defend us, even though for a little time he allows us to be exercised by various kinds of afflictions; moreover, he defends us not only in preserving us in this life but also in giving us possession of the life to come. For since his gifts and his callings are irrevocable, it follows that his promises reach beyond this world, as the holy patriarchs understood full well. . . .

Finally, Solomon does not promise the righteous great comfort, and abundance of goods or money to live at their ease in carnal delight, but only that they shall not starve. For we must eat to satisfy our hunger and quench our thirst, not to fill ourselves in gluttony and drunkenness. And so we are taught to desire our daily bread, and to content ourselves with food and clothing. And the apostle also admonishes us, saying, "Let your manner of living be free from avarice." On the Proverbs of Solomon.[12]

Deception Never Pays. Cardinal Cajetan: "A deceitful hand makes a man poor, but the hand of the diligent will make him rich." This is proved true with respect to God as well, that a deceitful

[11]CR 14:20-21; citing Heb 12:29; Ps 33:10.

[12]Cop, *Sur les Proverbes de Salomon*, 135; citing Ps 73:2; Rom 11:29; 1 Tim 6:8; Heb 13:5.

hand (i.e., deceptive action) makes a man poor, inasmuch as he heaps up for someone else what does not belong to him. And then he is obligated to give back those possessions by which he enriched himself, and in restoring them he remains poor. This is true of the one who does not toil to acquire his own wealth but someone else's. In contrast to this is added the fact that the hand of the diligent will enrich them. The action of those who are excellent for the sharpness of their understanding, and of those who do not waste their effort with the task at hand makes them rich. Because by lawful activity they acquire the skills which some acquire through deceit, cunning, or other unlawful activities. THE PARABLES OF SOLOMON, CORRECTED BY THE ORIGINAL HEBREW.[13]

LAZINESS AND DECEPTION GO HAND IN HAND. MICHAEL JERMIN: The original is most directly translated thus: "The hand of deceit makes poor; the hand of the diligent makes rich." And so it shows that there are two ways whereby people seek and get riches: deceit and diligence. It is poverty that deceit obtains, even though it seeks riches. Indeed, even if it gets riches, it is not riches that it has because it does not have God's blessing with it. But as diligence gets that which it seeks, so that which it gets is riches, being enriched with the comfort of God's favor. But to follow our translation [KJV: "He becommeth poore, that dealeth with a slacke hand."], Plutarch relates that by a law of the Athenians, idleness was punished with death.[†] But though the law of God is not so severe, yet by God it is punished with poverty, which he deals out to those who "deal with a slack hand." A "slack hand" therefore is like a slack knot, for just as the one deceives the one who holds it, so the other will deceive the one who thinks to live by it. Therefore rightly does the original call it a "hand of deceit," not only because it is false to the hope that relies on it, false to the business that is undertaken by it, but also because for the most part, the lazy hand being not able to sustain itself, it betakes itself for relief to cozening and deceit. PARAPHRASTIC MEDITATIONS.[14]

THE VIRTUE OF CLEMENCY. PHILIPP MELANCHTHON: This is a precept concerning clemency (*epieikeia*) and candor, and it pertains to the fifth and eighth commandments.[†] Here first it is necessary to know the common definitions and distinctions of justice. "Particular justice" [*iusticia particularis*] is the virtue of rendering to each their due.[‡] Thus for a judge, justice means maintaining the rights of the innocent and punishing the guilty. There are indeed degrees of crime, such that the wickedness of Satan is more heinous than that of Adam, and that of Judas worse than that of Peter; there are distinctions and degrees for the just judge, severity and clemency, and both are just, but their extreme forms are cruelty and indulgence. Sulla was cruel, for after victory he wantonly slaughtered a great number of people, and so (as the poet says): "The medicine exceeded the limit."[§] Julius Caesar, on the other hand, spared Cicero, Marcellus, and others, and he carried out no brutality in the city.[◊]

For these things may be seen in this saying of Solomon that "love covers all offenses," and this is true both for the judge and for the private person. The judge is compelled by divine mandate to use severity against those who do heinous wrongs, such as those who commit blasphemy, perjury, and homicide, and those who are polluted by adultery and incestuous desires. It is written in Deuteronomy 19: "You shall remove the evil from your midst," and "you shall not show him mercy," but "it shall be life for life," because God desires the punishments for evil to be made conspicuous, so that it may be

[13]Cajetan, *Parabolae Salomonis ad veritatem Hebraicam castigatae*, 94.

[14]Jermin, *Paraphrasticall Meditations*, 195-96. [†]Plutarch does indeed describe such legislation, but he also relates that Solon repealed the laws of his predecessor Draco as being too harsh: "For one penalty was assigned to almost all transgressions—namely, death—so that even those convicted of idleness were put to death, and those who stole salad or fruit received the same punishment as those who committed sacrilege or murder. Therefore Demades, in later times, made a hit when he said that Draco's laws were written not with ink, but blood" (Plutarch, *Solon* 17; LCL 46:448-51).

recognized that he distinguishes the just from the unjust, and judges and punishes crimes, with the aim of defending the common good. But the same judge will also realize when he must show leniency in punishment, just as the laws themselves make assassination to be more heinous than accidental manslaughter.[△] This moderating virtue is called clemency (*epieikeia*), and it is a form of justice that mitigates some laws and penalties on the basis of prudential reason. Many examples of this mitigation have been handed down with the greatest wisdom—for example, when David was hungry, he made use of the consecrated bread, and Thrasybulus enacted amnesty (*amnēstian*), forbearing to drive those in possession from their properties and precipitate a new war. . . .[††]

But regarding private persons and private offenses, first of all it must be understood that self-defense (*necessaria defensio*) is permitted, but aside from this case, private injuries must be forgiven, just as it is said, "Forgive, and it will be forgiven you."[‡‡] But when so many injuries in human custom befall so many, it is madness to hope for a life in which many do not attack you. For I do not suppose that this commandment speaks only of rare offenses, for we know that this gift is necessary in many areas of life when private offenses are given and received. And this gift [of forgiveness] must be given, first on account of God, and second on account of the common peace. For not only does God command this virtue but he desires us to be a visible reminder of his gift; thus he says, "Forgive, and it will be forgiven you." He also desires that we meditate on this virtue and that we exercise ourselves in remembering his mercy in the gospel, by which is offered so great a legal clemency, that even our incomplete, meager, and shabby obedience receives it, and our many infirmities are forgiven, and daily the punishments [for our sins] are relaxed, as it is written, "It is by the mercy of the Lord that we are not consumed." Exposition of the Proverbs of Solomon.[15]

God's Blessings Meet Our Necessities. Michel Cop: People naturally want to be rich and to abound in temporal goods, not only to maintain themselves in this life at a middling condition, but also to nourish themselves on delicacies, to make merry and be sumptuously appareled, to cut a grand figure, and to enjoy all the pleasures this world has to offer. To attain these ends we labor with body and soul, and set our minds to work on how we may become rich. And because we commonly see that it is the fools and idiots, the

[15]CR 14:22-23; citing Deut 19:19; 1 Sam 21:6; Lk 6:37; Lam 3:22. [†]Melanchthon's exposition often relates specific moral teachings in the Proverbs to specific commandments in the Decalogue. For Lutherans, the fifth and eighth commandments prohibited murder and bearing false witness, respectively. Aristotle had defined *epieikeia* as "a diminution of the expedient and the just" (*Topics* 141a16). Melanchthon returns to discuss this virtue in his comments on Prov 27:3. [‡]This basic notion that justice on a personal level involves the equitable distribution of goods goes back at least as far as the first book of Plato's *Republic*, where such an understanding is already understood to be conventional. The precise terms of Melanchthon's definition here echo the usage of Cicero (*De legibus* 1.15) and the *Corpus Iuris Civilis* of Justinian (1.1).[§]Lucan, *Pharsalia* 2.142. Lucius Cornelius Sulla Felix (132–78 BC) was a Roman general who seized power in the republic at the end of the so-called Social War (91–88 BC). [◊]Cicero and Marcellus were both supporters of Pompei against Caesar, but were allowed to return home unmolested after Caesar's victory (Plutarch, *Cicero* 39; Cicero, *Pro Marcello* and *Epistulae ad familiars* 4.4.3, 7-12). [△]*Caedes ex insidiis* and *caedes fortuita* are legal terms Melanchthon uses to illustrate the spectrum of possible intentions that demand a judge's careful discernment. [††]The Greek speechwriter Andocides records the famed "Athenian Amnesty" of 403, when after the defeat of Sparta at Piraeus, the Athenian exiles who had fled the city under the reign of the Thirty Tyrants were allowed to return, but only after taking an oath of reconciliation in which they pledged to refrain from taking vengeance on their former oppressors (*On the Mysteries* 81-87). [‡‡]Medieval jurists and theologians generally allowed that private individuals had a right to self-defense, but there was disagreement as to its legitimacy by degrees of imminence. The case of *necessaria defensio* represented an immediate physical attack, as opposed to *utilis defensio*, which represented an attack in preparation. By limiting the right of self-defense to the former, Melanchthon is opting for the most restrictive interpretation of this right. However even this, it may be noted, puts him at odds with Luther, who explicitly insisted that the Sermon on the Mount prohibits Christians from responding to a personal assault with violence. See, for example, Luther's short treatise *On Secular Authority*: "In what concerns you and yours, you govern yourself by the gospel and suffer injustice toward yourself as a true Christian; in what concerns the person or property of others, you govern yourself according to love and tolerate no injustice toward your neighbor" (LW 45:96).

negligent and the slothful, the weak and the infirm who are poor and have great need, it seems to us that we make ourselves rich by dint of our own wisdom and industry, force, and strength, by our own labor and travail. For this reason people tend to chalk up whatever goods or riches they possess to their own powers, and think that they are due them as their just deserts.

But this view is nothing but vanity. "I made great works," says Solomon in Ecclesiastes, but then "I considered all that my hands had done and the toil I had spent in doing it, and again, all was vanity and vexation of mind." For in this way of life, people do not recognize God, as is fitting. When they see themselves abounding in riches, they ought not be like the pigs who always have their snouts in the ground till they find acorns, and who never look up from the spot where they fall to the ground. But they ought to lift up the eyes of their mind, and behold the heavens, and confess that the goods they have, even though they found them in the earth and they are brought out of the earth, yet they have descended from heaven, and are given to them by the sheer generosity of God, who makes all things to grow for the use of his people. God said, "Let the earth bring forth green herbs," and, "He blessed them, and said, 'grow and increase.'" And later, "I have given every green thing to be food for you." The holy patriarchs also acknowledged this power and liberality. . . . Now also Solomon confesses it when he says, "The blessing of the Lord makes rich." If anyone is rich, it is only because God has extended his blessing on them. Thus riches ought not to be attributed either to the labor, wisdom, industry, diligence, or care of people, nor to fortune or chance (as the infidels do), but rather we should acknowledge and confess that as God is the Creator of both heaven and earth, and of all things they contain, and that the earth and all it contains is his, so he distributes the things of this world as he pleases, and to whom he pleases. . . .

Insofar as it is the blessing of the Lord that makes people rich, let us first of all know that we possess nothing, however small it be, for which we should not give thanks to God. David says much the same thing in Psalm 34, and St. Paul admonishes us to give thanks for all things. Second, since no evil comes from the blessing of God, it follows that riches are good, and that it is lawful to possess them, and to use them with joy and gladness. For everything made by God is good, and nothing from him ought to be refused, so long as it is received with thanksgiving. Nevertheless, we must take heed that we do not abuse God's blessing. And to ensure this, we must take care that we possess nothing unjustly gotten; otherwise, we would be little more than petty thieves, brigands, highwaymen, avaricious usurers, or other shady swindlers. But instead of snatching up profits and carrying away whatever we can, we ought to be distributing part of what we possess, so that we walk uprightly and faithfully in all our affairs. For to come right to the point, we must follow the counsel of the psalmist: "Put no trust in extortion; set no vain hopes on robbery; if riches increase, set not your heart on them." . . .

We must also take care that we do not use the riches God has given us dissolutely or intemperately, like gluttons and drunkards, or other arrogant and pompous fellows, who are not content to rejoice with sobriety and moderation, but display a brutish and arrogant joy. But we must use these gifts with rejoicing as in the presence of the Lord. And to do this well, we must not eat so much meat, nor deck ourselves out in costly and sumptuous apparel; rather, we should think on the needy, and "especially those of the household of faith." For if it is required of us to do good to our enemies that we may be like our Father in heaven, how much more must we have care for those who love us in Jesus Christ! For such as these, we should spare the morsel from our own mouths to give them, and do it with a good heart from our own free will.

Third, as it is his blessing that makes rich, it follows that we may ask riches from God, but only insofar as it is needful to help our necessity. This is what our Lord teaches us when he commands us to ask our daily bread. But also we must consider that when he adds "this day," he does not want us to desire to become rich, but rather as St. Paul teaches, "If we have food and clothing, with these we will be content." And, "Let your conversation be free from covetousness, being content with what you have already." Therefore it is lawful for us to ask riches of God sufficient to keep us in this life, that having what is necessary for us we may better follow our vocation, but it is not lawful for us to covet riches. On the Proverbs of Solomon.[16]

Human Efforts Do Not Guarantee Success. Philipp Melanchthon: Profane people think that riches and victories are obtained only by human industry and labors. So, for example, they suppose that Alexander the Great was victorious because of his strategy and industry, and because the strength of his arms exceeded that of the Persian hordes, as is commonly said: "Hard work conquers all."[†] And Plato says, "Happy is the one whose fortune does not depend on others, but who makes for himself all that is necessary for happiness."[‡] And thus says Nebuchadnezzar, "I made Babylon to be so great."[§] Such fancies only confirm that we place our faith in our own cleverness and strength, pridefully ignoring God and stirring up what is best left alone. For example, because Mark Antony thought that he was better prepared than Augustus, and hoped to overthrow him, he stirred up an unjust war.[◊] Many of the sad errors people make are of this sort.

But the divine voice teaches that the causes of good fortune are not only human labors, but God's assistance in just labor and the obedience of people in their calling. This same idea is expressly given elsewhere in negative form: "Unless the Lord builds the building, the one who builds it labors in vain."[Δ] . . . These testimonies do not prohibit us from working in our calling, but they teach that every good outcome has its cause not only in human wisdom and labor, and they condemn placing faith in ourselves. Exposition of the Proverbs of Solomon.[17]

11:1-31 *Living in Honesty and Generosity*

Justice in Trade. John Dod: Under false balances are comprehended all unjust weights, lines, and measures. And also included is a condemnation of any kind of guile or deceit, either from the buyer or the seller, as when that which is sold is defective, either in quantity or in quality, not being fit for the use that it is bought for, or not corresponding to the price that is paid for, or not accurately described by its advertising. For Amos charges the wicked wealthy men of his age with the same: "They make the epha [or measure] small and the shekel [or price] great," and falsify the weights of deceit, that they may "buy the poor for silver and the needy for shoes," and sell the refuse of their wheat. So on the other side with the buyer, when he shall fail of all due proportion between the price that he pays and the goods that he buys, giving far less than the worth and value of it. A Plain and Familiar Exposition.[18]

Just Scales Are God's Work. Philipp Melanchthon: This precept concerns particular justice,[†] and truthfulness in contracts, and it pertains to the sixth commandment: "You shall not steal." And the threat [of punishment] is often repeated, and here it is also understood: flagrant transgressions are punished with harsh penalties, even in this life. Thus it is said, "He who takes up the sword, dies by the sword," and, "Woe to you who plunder, for you shall be plundered." And in considering this order of affairs, God desires that we recognize his

[16]Cop, *Sur les Proverbes de Salomon*, 164-67; citing Eccles 2:4; 2:11; Gen 1:11; 1:28; 9:3, 14, 20; 18:3; Ps 24:1; 1 Thess 5:8; Ps 62:10; Gal 6:10; Mt 5:44; Mt 6:11; 1 Tim 6:8; Heb 13:5.

[17]CR 14:24-25; citing Ps 127:1. [†]Virgil, *Georgics* 1.145-146. [‡]I have been unable to locate the source, which appears to be Melanchthon's own translation (or paraphrase) in Latin. [§]Paraphrasing Dan 4:30. [◊]Mark Antony (83-40 BC) was a Roman politician and general. Following the death of Julius Caesar, he became part of the Second Triumvirate, but infighting led to his eventual defeat by Octavian's forces at the Battle of Actium. [Δ]Melanchthon cites a number of other texts illustrating the same idea: Eccl 9:11; Ps 33:17; Ps 44:9; Jer 10:23; Jn 3:27; 15:5.

[18]Dod, *A Plaine and Familiar Exposition of the Eleventh and Twelfth Chapters of the Proverbs of Solomon*, 136-37; citing Amos 8:5; 2:6.

divinely ordained sanction. And we know that marriage, politics, contracts, judicial judgment, and punishment are works of the wisdom and justice of God, and in whatever degree of order they remain, they are effectually preserved by God, even if at times they are thrust into great tumult by the devil and his devices. Just as the keeper of the flock watches over the whole herd, so the wolves snatch whatever sheep they can. Thus the following saying is also given among the political ordinances in chapter 16: "Weight and balance are judgments of the Lord, and all the stones of the measuring pan are his work." This admonition is necessary against the ravings of the Manichaeans and Anabaptists, as has often been explained by others at greater length. EXPOSITION OF THE PROVERBS OF SOLOMON.[19]

PERFECT WEIGHTS SHOW GOD'S FAVOR. MICHEL COP: The world is replete with fraud and deception, with usury and rapine, with larceny and fraud, with counterfeiting and swindling, and these evils endure from generation to generation; thus it is no surprise that no one gives heed to the commandment, "You shall do no wrong in judgment, weight, or measure." Or, "You shall not have in your bag two kinds of weights, a large and a small." Nor is there any reckoning made of the promise that God adds to this commandment: "that your days may be long on the earth." Nor of the threat that follows: "for all who do such things will be abhorred by the Lord." In this way we judge less of God than of mortals. If a rich and powerful man makes a promise regarding anything, people will trust to receive according to his promise, and in the meantime, be diligent to please him. If he threatens, they will fear him, and take heed not to do anything that might displease him. But although God is true—indeed, he himself is the only truth (otherwise he would not be God!) and has testified to this by various witnesses—yet we do not trust his promises, as we demonstrate when we make no account to labor in such a way as to please him. . . .

"False balances are an abomination to the Lord," and he threatens those who use them with eternal ruin and perdition. . . . But so that we may know who they are that God abhors, and that we also should abhor them (for nothing that displeases God ought to please us, but rather we should hate and condemn it), we must consider what a false balance consists in, and who they are that use them. Therefore we should know that the false balance is taken for all weights, measures, and rules in all arts, sciences, laws, and habits we use in relations with our neighbors, as we may understand in the passages quoted from Moses above. Likewise, the Lord attributes rule and balance to those things he does for his church in restoring it. Judgment, also, I will include with the rule, and righteousness with the balance. It is then a false and deceptive balance, when we do not faithfully behave in relation to our neighbor, when we are slack and negligent in paying our duty, or when we attempt to trample them underfoot, or deceive in any matter whatever. And from experience we know that there are false balances in all walks of life, as between merchants, citizens, artisans, and laborers. But they are most damaging when they fall into the hands of false teachers, who by fair words and flattering speech deceive the hearts of the simple and the innocent. Next may be said the same for wicked magistrates, who are placed in the seat of God, who is just, and yet their houses are filled with the spoils of the poor.

Now the perfection that is required of us is that we should not devise any evil against our neighbors, that we should not labor to become rich by their loss, but that in simplicity and uprightness of conscience we should work to increase their wealth with all our power. This is the "perfect weight" that pleases the Lord, as Solomon says. They who use this weight are acceptable to God, and as the weight which they use is perfect, so God reckons them as perfect, and does not impute to them the remnants of imperfection that remain in them. And insofar as they please God, he will never be displeased with them so as to destroy them. This is why Solomon says that "a perfect weight pleases

---

[19]CR 14:26-27; citing Ex 20:15; Mt 26:52; Is 33:1; Prov 16:11. †See Melanchthon's comments on Prov 10:2.

the Lord"—that is, he promises everlasting life to those who use it. Even if they are poor common folk and wretched in the eyes of the world, yet they are rich enough and blessed, for they are the heirs of the heavenly kingdom, and wonderful riches. On the Proverbs of Solomon.[20]

Pride and Humility Defined. Philipp Melanchthon: Let the definitions of humility and pride be noted here. Humility (*tapeinophrosynē*) is recognizing and acknowledging our own weakness in the fear of God, and not breaking out from our calling, but serving God in hope of divine help within the bounds of our calling, and not despising it. Humility does not pursue other callings, but allows to each the position in which they have been called in due order, and it understands also that these can be God's tools for their salvation, and not punishments resulting from God's anger. A clear example of this virtue can be found in Jonathan, but of course the greatest of all is the Son of God himself, who, obedient in his calling, says, "Learn from me, for I am mild and humble in heart." But pride is being free from care, without the fear of God, and placing confidence in one's own strength, and breaking faith by exceeding the bounds of one's own calling, desiring rather to augment one's own power. Pride despises and oppresses others, pertinaciously preferring one's own wisdom to the good advice of others, and it rages at God and human beings when the outcome is unfortunate, like Pharaoh, Goliath, Saul, Ahithophel, and the like. Exposition of the Proverbs of Solomon.[21]

Pursuing Righteousness Leads to Perfection. Cardinal Cajetan: "The righteousness of the simple will direct their path, but the wicked will be corrupted by their own wickedness." The expression translated here as "simple" means "perfect." For by pursuing righteousness the perfect person has righteousness as the guide of their works, as we read of David when he fled from Saul. On the other hand, the wicked person is corrupted in their own wickedness as Saul was. "The righteousness of the upright will set them free, and the unjust will be caught in their own schemes." The second phrase in the Hebrew means this: they will be caught by the dissolution of liars. And from this is obvious that the escape mentioned in the first phrase is an escape from captivity. So this is attributed to the righteousness of the upright. It will allow them to escape so they are not bound in chains, in prison, or in captivity. By contrast, when the time for the dissolution of liars has arrived (i.e., of those who have broken the divine law that they profess), those who tell lies will be caught and led away to captivity. Simply read the histories of the Old Testament and you will find this proven true over and over. The Parables of Solomon, Corrected by the Original Hebrew.[22]

On the Necessity of Good Counsel. John Trapp: "Where no counsel is, the people fall." As where no pilot is, the ship founders. The Vulgate renders it, "Where there is no governor, the people shall fall." Tyranny is better than anarchy. And yet, "Woe also to you, O land, whose king is a child"; that is, willful and unwilling to hear counsel—like Rehoboam, who was a child at forty years old, though his father was a man at twenty. Age is no just measure of wisdom, and royalty without wisdom is but eminent dishonor. Solomon the wise chose himself an excellent council of state, whom Rehoboam refused to hear, being as much more willful than his father, as less wise—all head, no heart, losing those ten tribes with a churlish breath, and returning to Jerusalem lighter by a crown than he went forth. He and his green-headed council was like Alcibiades and his army, where all would be leaders and none followers.† Or it may be it was then in Israel as once it was in

[20]Cop, *Sur les Proverbes de Salomon*, 179-80; citing Lev 19:35; Deut 25:13, 15-16; Is 3:14.
[21]CR 14:27-28; citing Mt 11:29.
[22]Cajetan, *Parabolae Salomonis ad veritatem Hebraicam castigatae*, 103; citing Eccles 10:16.

Persia, and as now it is in Turkey, when the great Turk stands at the dangerous door, where if any counselor delivered anything contrary to the king's mind he was chastised with rods. Or as in the kingdom of the Cyclops, where "they are solitaries: no one is anyone's subject"; where no one cared for better counsel, but "each one did what was good in his own eyes."‡ Such cannot long subsist. "But in the multitude of counselors . . ." So long as they are good counselors—better than Balaam was, better than Ahithophel, better than those of Aurelius, by whom the good emperor was even bought and sold. One special thing the primitive Christians prayed for the emperor was, that God would send him a *Senatum fidelem*, a faithful council.§ There were in Josiah's days horrible abominations—and why? "The princes were as roaring lions, the judges wolves." Queen Elizabeth was fortunate in her council, by whom she was mostly ruled, and grew amiable to her friends and formidable to her enemies, both at home and abroad. "Wisdom is better than strength," says Solomon; and, *Romani sedendo vincunt*, "The Romans conquer by being settled," they said they of old.◊ The welfare of a state is procured and preserved, not so much by a multitude of worthy warriors as of wise counselors, as Cleon in Thucydides long since observed,△ and as we have blessedly found in this present blessed parliament. SOLOMON'S BOOK OF ALL VIRTUES.[23]

INDUSTRIOUS, NOT RUTHLESS. THE ENGLISH ANNOTATIONS: Some, because *ārîṣ* [forceful] is commonly taken in a bad sense, would have the meaning that as violence and oppression is the way for men to get wealth, so meekness and gentleness lead to honor for women, their primary wealth. This might do, if Solomon did not seem to so approve violence in men as he does meekness in women, or if there were no way, at least no surer way (which Solomon elsewhere contradicts), for men to get wealth than by violence and oppression. It is more probable, therefore, that *ārîṣ* is here used in a good sense, for an industrious, active, stout man, and that Solomon, by these words, intends to set down the commendation of the properties as well of the man, that is the master, as of the woman, that is the mistress, of a house and family. Of the woman: she must be kind, affable, meek, and gracious; this is her primary care and credit. Of the man: he must be painstaking, laborious, resolute, undaunted, and the like, as also to provide for the safekeeping of his goods against any violence. ANNOTATIONS ON PROVERBS 11:16.[24]

ADORNMENT MUST BE MATCHED BY VIRTUE. PILGRAM MARPECK: Those who lay claim to natural nobility must be gifted with natural virtues, if they are to wear the elemental gems with justification, because these are only a sign of natural virtues. In the natural nobility, it is a scandal to wear too much gold and too many chains, gems, and noble garments and to lack with these the natural honors and virtues. Nobility without virtue is like a sow bedecked with gold and gems. She immediately drags it all through the dirt rather than wearing it honorably. Now if one were to inscribe virtue on the coat of arms of the fleshly nobility, one would find few true nobles. CONCERNING THREE KINDS OF PEOPLE.[25]

JUSTICE DELAYED IS NOT JUSTICE DENIED. PHILIPP MELANCHTHON: This is a notable admonition, from which Peter's pronouncement that "it is time for judgment to begin at the household of God" takes its departure. "And if judgment begins with us, what will be the end for those who do not believe in the gospel? And if the

[23]Trapp, *Solomonis ΠΑΝΆΡΕΤΟΣ*, 102-3; citing Zeph 3:3; Eccles 9:16. †Alcibiades was a leading Athenian statesman and general who fell from prominence during the Peloponnesian War. ‡The quotation on the kingdom of the Cyclops comes from Euripides, *Cyclops* 120 (LCL 12:72-73), combined with ominous refrain of the Deuteronomistic history (e.g., Deut 12:8; Judg 17:6; 21:25). §See, for example, Tertullian, *Apologia* 30.4. ◊More properly: "The Roman wins by standing still." Varro, *De re rustica* 2.2 (LCL 283:168-69). △Perhaps a loose summation of Cleon's speech in the Mytilene debate (Thucydides, *History of the Peloponnesian War* 3.37-40).

[24]Downame, ed., *English Annotations*, 6V1r*.
[25]CRR 12:642.

just person is scarcely saved, where will the faithless person and the sinner be found?" This teaching concerns repentance and the coming punishment of the wicked, and it offers consolation regarding the scandal of the cross. But the argument is set up *a minore*:[†] when the just, who are striving to mend their ways, are afflicted in this life, how much more is it necessary for the impious, who contumaciously and furiously persist in their crimes, to be punished; thus, it is necessary for there to remain a judgment after this life. For example, although David was punished for his adultery and murder, other worse offenders, such as Dionysius and Tiberius, get off scot-free;[‡] even if they end their lives in peace, there remains another judgment.

But this passage combines two rules, and their connection may be considered. The first is this: dreadful crimes are punished with dreadful punishments in this life, and this is consistent with the order of justice in God. . . . The second rule is that the church is subjected to the cross, and tyrants exercise their cruelty against her. This seems not to cohere with the order of justice, for reason disputes whether human events are indeed guided by God's providence. But the church responds as follows: first, that it is consistent with the order of justice in God also to punish the church insofar as she still clings to her sin. And the church knows many reasons why she may be subjected to the cross. In the next place, regarding tyrants, there remains indeed the other rule, for they themselves are often dragged off to punishment in this life, as it is said: "Few indeed are the kings who descend to the son-in-law of Ceres but by murder and bloodshed; few are the tyrants who die a bloodless death."[§] Though they may flourish for a time, eventually they are cast off from power.

Second, the church knows that the justice of God is consistent, such that crimes are punished for a time not only in the here-and-now, but also in eternity. Thus she responds to this argument as follows: Justice is consistent with well-being; injustice is not. The church is just; tyrants are unjust. Therefore, the church fares well, while tyrants fare badly. The church responds to the major premise as follows: Justice is consistent with well-being, injustice is not, according to the declaration of the gospel, which teaches that although the church is subjected to the cross in this life, she is preserved by God in every condition, and afterward she will take hold of eternal goods, while the impious will suffer eternal punishments. This is indeed borne out by examples testifying to future judgment. Because Abel is killed by Cain, and God, who is just, had previously shown that he loves Abel, therefore, another judgment remains, in which the unlikeness between Cain and Abel will be demonstrated. Next, to the minor premise, the following response may be given: The church is clearly just, but inchoately and by imputation, and not yet in consummation. Therefore she is exercised in time, and she recognizes the judgment of God against her sin, as is said in the prophet Isaiah: "O Lord, in distress they sought you; they poured out a whispered prayer when your discipline was on them."[◊] Therefore, the conclusion follows that tyrants are often punished in this life, but afterward they will universally suffer eternal punishments. And if the church is here afflicted, even in this life she perceives God's mitigation, and afterward she will have eternal goods. EXPOSITION OF THE PROVERBS OF SOLOMON.[26]

[26]CR 14:28-29; citing 1 Pet 4:17; Is 26:16. [†]Short for *a minore ad maius*: from the smaller to the greater. [‡]Dionysius was a common name in the ancient world, so it is unclear to whom Melanchthon is referring. He may perhaps have in mind Dionysius I of Syracuse, whose long reign was characterized by paranoia and brutality (405–367 BC). Ancient sources are divided on the cause of his death, but at least one source records that he died of natural causes. Tiberius, of course, was the reigning emperor at the time of Christ's crucifixion, and he lived nearly to the age of seventy-eight. [§]Juvenal, *Satires* 10.112-13. The "son-in-law of Ceres" is a circumlocution for Plutus, god of the underworld. [◊]Melanchthon cites only a fragment of the verse, doubtless with the expectation that his readers would supply the rest.

12:1–14:35 PROVERBS ON A VIRTUOUS LIFE

1 *Whoever loves discipline loves knowledge,*
but he who hates reproof is stupid.

2 *A good man obtains favor from the* Lord,
but a man of evil devices he condemns.

3 *No one is established by wickedness,*
but the root of the righteous will never be moved.

4 *An excellent wife is the crown of her husband,*
but she who brings shame is like rottenness in his bones.

5 *The thoughts of the righteous are just;*
the counsels of the wicked are deceitful.

6 *The words of the wicked lie in wait for blood,*
but the mouth of the upright delivers them.

7 *The wicked are overthrown and are no more,*
but the house of the righteous will stand.

8 *A man is commended according to his good sense,*
but one of twisted mind is despised.

9 *Better to be lowly and have a servant*
than to play the great man and lack bread.

10 *Whoever is righteous has regard for the life of his beast,*
but the mercy of the wicked is cruel.

11 *Whoever works his land will have plenty of bread,*
but he who follows worthless pursuits lacks sense.

12 *Whoever is wicked covets the spoil of evildoers,*
but the root of the righteous bears fruit.

13 *An evil man is ensnared by the transgression of his lips,*[a]
but the righteous escapes from trouble.

14 *From the fruit of his mouth a man is satisfied with good,*
and the work of a man's hand comes back to him.

15 *The way of a fool is right in his own eyes,*
but a wise man listens to advice.

16 *The vexation of a fool is known at once,*
but the prudent ignores an insult.

17 *Whoever speaks*[b] *the truth gives honest evidence,*
but a false witness utters deceit.

18 *There is one whose rash words are like sword thrusts,*
but the tongue of the wise brings healing.

19 *Truthful lips endure forever,*
but a lying tongue is but for a moment.

20 *Deceit is in the heart of those who devise evil,*
but those who plan peace have joy.

21 *No ill befalls the righteous,*
but the wicked are filled with trouble.

22 *Lying lips are an abomination to the* Lord,
but those who act faithfully are his delight.

23 *A prudent man conceals knowledge,*
but the heart of fools proclaims folly.

24 *The hand of the diligent will rule,*
while the slothful will be put to forced labor.

25 *Anxiety in a man's heart weighs him down,*
but a good word makes him glad.

26 *One who is righteous is a guide to his neighbor,*[c]
but the way of the wicked leads them astray.

27 *Whoever is slothful will not roast his game,*
but the diligent man will get precious wealth.[d]

28 *In the path of righteousness is life,*
and in its pathway there is no death.

13 *A wise son hears his father's instruction,*
but a scoffer does not listen to rebuke.

2 *From the fruit of his mouth a man eats what is good,*
but the desire of the treacherous is for violence.

3 *Whoever guards his mouth preserves his life;*
he who opens wide his lips comes to ruin.

4 *The soul of the sluggard craves and gets nothing,*
while the soul of the diligent is richly supplied.

5 *The righteous hates falsehood,*
but the wicked brings shame[e] *and disgrace.*

6 *Righteousness guards him whose way is blameless,*
but sin overthrows the wicked.

7 *One pretends to be rich,*[f] *yet has nothing;*
another pretends to be poor,[g] *yet has great wealth.*

8 *The ransom of a man's life is his wealth,*
but a poor man hears no threat.

9 *The light of the righteous rejoices,*
but the lamp of the wicked will be put out.

10 *By insolence comes nothing but strife,*
but with those who take advice is wisdom.

11 *Wealth gained hastily*[h] *will dwindle,*
but whoever gathers little by little will increase it.

12 *Hope deferred makes the heart sick,*
but a desire fulfilled is a tree of life.

13 *Whoever despises the word*[i] *brings destruction on himself,*
but he who reveres the commandment[j] *will be rewarded.*

14 *The teaching of the wise is a fountain of life,*
that one may turn away from the snares of death.

15 *Good sense wins favor,*
but the way of the treacherous is their ruin.[k]

16 *Every prudent man acts with knowledge,*
but a fool flaunts his folly.

17 *A wicked messenger falls into trouble,*
but a faithful envoy brings healing.

18 *Poverty and disgrace come to him who ignores instruction,*
but whoever heeds reproof is honored.

19 *A desire fulfilled is sweet to the soul,*
but to turn away from evil is an abomination to fools.

20 *Whoever walks with the wise becomes wise,*
but the companion of fools will suffer harm.

21 *Disaster*[l] *pursues sinners,*
but the righteous are rewarded with good.

22 *A good man leaves an inheritance to his children's children,*
but the sinner's wealth is laid up for the righteous.

23 *The fallow ground of the poor would yield much food,*
but it is swept away through injustice.

24 *Whoever spares the rod hates his son,*
but he who loves him is diligent to discipline him.[m]

25 *The righteous has enough to satisfy his appetite,*
but the belly of the wicked suffers want.

14 *The wisest of women builds her house,*
but folly with her own hands tears it down.

2 *Whoever walks in uprightness fears the LORD,*
but he who is devious in his ways despises him.

3 *By the mouth of a fool comes a rod for his back,*[n]
but the lips of the wise will preserve them.

4 *Where there are no oxen, the manger is clean,*
but abundant crops come by the strength of the ox.

5 *A faithful witness does not lie,*
but a false witness breathes out lies.

6 *A scoffer seeks wisdom in vain,*
but knowledge is easy for a man of understanding.

7 *Leave the presence of a fool,*
for there you do not meet words of knowledge.

8 *The wisdom of the prudent is to discern his way,*
but the folly of fools is deceiving.

9 *Fools mock at the guilt offering,*
but the upright enjoy acceptance.[o]

10 *The heart knows its own bitterness,*
and no stranger shares its joy.

11 *The house of the wicked will be destroyed,*
but the tent of the upright will flourish.

12 *There is a way that seems right to a man,*
but its end is the way to death.[p]

13 *Even in laughter the heart may ache,*
and the end of joy may be grief.

14 *The backslider in heart will be filled with the fruit of his ways,*
and a good man will be filled with the fruit of his ways.

15 *The simple believes everything,*
but the prudent gives thought to his steps.

16 *One who is wise is cautious*[q] *and turns away from evil,*
but a fool is reckless and careless.

17 *A man of quick temper acts foolishly,*
and a man of evil devices is hated.

18 *The simple inherit folly,*
but the prudent are crowned with knowledge.

19 *The evil bow down before the good,*
the wicked at the gates of the righteous.

20 *The poor is disliked even by his neighbor,*
but the rich has many friends.

21 *Whoever despises his neighbor is a sinner,*
but blessed is he who is generous to the poor.

22 *Do they not go astray who devise evil?*
Those who devise good meet[r] *steadfast love and faithfulness.*

23 *In all toil there is profit,*
but mere talk tends only to poverty.

24 *The crown of the wise is their wealth,*
but the folly of fools brings folly.

25 *A truthful witness saves lives,*
but one who breathes out lies is deceitful.

26 *In the fear of the* LORD *one has strong confidence,*
and his children will have a refuge.

27 *The fear of the* LORD *is a fountain of life,*
that one may turn away from the snares of death.

28 *In a multitude of people is the glory of a king,*
but without people a prince is ruined.

29 *Whoever is slow to anger has great understanding,*
but he who has a hasty temper exalts folly.

30 *A tranquil*[s] *heart gives life to the flesh,*
but envy[t] *makes the bones rot.*

31 *Whoever oppresses a poor man insults his Maker,*
but he who is generous to the needy honors him.

32 *The wicked is overthrown through his evildoing,*
but the righteous finds refuge in his death.

33 *Wisdom rests in the heart of a man of understanding,*
but it makes itself known even in the midst of fools.[u]

34 *Righteousness exalts a nation,*
but sin is a reproach to any people.

35 *A servant who deals wisely has the king's favor,*
but his wrath falls on one who acts shamefully.

a Or *In the transgression of the lips, there is an evil snare* **b** Hebrew *breathes out* **c** Or *The righteous chooses his friends carefully* **d** Or *but diligence is precious wealth* **e** Or *stench* **f** Or *One makes himself rich* **g** Or *another makes himself poor* **h** Or *by fraud* **i** Or *a word* **j** Or *a commandment* **k** Probable reading (compare Septuagint, Syriac, Vulgate); Hebrew *is rugged,* or *is an enduring rut* **l** Or *Evil* **m** Or *who loves him disciplines him early* **n** Or *In the mouth of a fool is a rod of pride* **o** Hebrew *but among the upright is acceptance* **p** Hebrew *ways of death* **q** Or *fears* [the LORD] **r** Or *show* **s** Or *healing* **t** Or *jealousy* **u** Or *Wisdom rests quietly in the heart of a man of understanding, but makes itself known in the midst of fools*

Overview: This section continues the proverbs of Solomon, as the biblical author's teaching on wisdom and folly are applied to specific situations. Our Reformation-era commentators find few unifying themes in these statements and prefer to see each aphorism as a distinct unit of meaning. A number of themes emerge from their commentary, however. Many of the proverbs address wealth and other signs of temporal success, and the reformers take these as opportunities to focus their readers' attention on the importance of spiritual riches and the pitfalls of worldly achievement. Justice is another common consideration, as Cardinal Cajetan and John Dod express concern for the poor and oppressed, while John Donne provides an interesting counterpoint, arguing that even ill-gotten gains can bring glory to God. The nature of human limitations also draws comment. For example, Erhart Hegenwald recognizes that human reason is not necessarily a true guide and can lead one away from God's will, while Philipp Melanchthon argues that human judgment is open to deception from many directions. Michel Cop extends this to examine the wisdom of groups, as he considers how social conventions and customs can function like law.

12:1-28 *Loving Discipline and Speaking the Truth*

The Mark of Those Who Love Knowledge. Michel Cop: From the time that Adam first sinned, darkness entered into the world, and people loved darkness more than light. And so they have walked in ignorance, and from this were given over to all sorts of wickedness, and have deprived themselves of life and are fallen into death. But it is not enough to boast about our knowledge of such things; the chief point is that we should abhor ignorance and love knowledge—not the way some people make a vain show of knowledge, and only love to praise it to others. Rather, we should love that knowledge which is acceptable in the sight of God, and be diligent to receive it, the knowledge he gives us when he teaches us by his Word. And so that we should not deceive ourselves, persuading ourselves that we love knowledge when in fact we abhor it, Solomon gives us a certain mark by which we can rightly judge whether we love knowledge or not: this is instruction, when it is pleasing and agreeable to our hearts. For he says, "He who loves instruction loves knowledge." Therefore even if we frequently attend sermons and read the holy Scriptures and become knowledgeable in it, yet if we have so high an opinion of ourselves that we think we can learn no more, and will not suffer ourselves to be admonished, or to be taught, corrected, and reproved when necessary, then we do not love knowledge. On the Proverbs of Solomon.[1]

Temporal and Eternal Wealth. The English Annotations: People who have no grounds in them of piety and godliness and live for the present only, which when they see the prosperity of the wicked and how they thrive in their bloody designs—taking up others as fishes with the angle, catching them in their net, and gathering them in their dragnet—they envy them and eagerly desire to be one of their society, that they may share with them. The root of the righteous, which has its growth underground, is not seen by fleshly eyes, but God's constant and secret blessing yields to abundance without any such violent indirect means. In this way, we expound it of temporal blessings, but it is more likely that the fruits here intended are the mystical fruits of eternal life to the righteous themselves, and the spiritual fruits of good instruction and example for the conversion and spiritual improvement of many others. Annotations on Proverbs 12:12.[2]

The Gift of a Noble Wife. Cardinal Cajetan: "A noble wife is her husband's crown, and like rot in his bones is the one who causes him shame." A wife of strong character is praised as her husband's crown. This means that she bestows on

[1]Cop, *Sur les Proverbes de Salomon*, 217.
[2]Downame, ed., *English Annotations*, 6V1v*.

her husband honor and glory. On the other hand, the wife who causes her husband shame not only makes her husband and herself ashamed but also makes his soul in his very bones (i.e., deep down) as though filled with rot. This means with decaying qualities. So she is putrid not only on the outside but also within. THE PARABLES OF SOLOMON, CORRECTED BY THE ORIGINAL HEBREW.[3]

BE HUMBLE AND SUPPORT A FAMILY. PETER MOFFETT: "Better is he who debases himself and has a servant than he who boasts himself and wants bread." That person who, setting his hand to all works and carrying a low port, has somewhat about him, and one to do his business is more to be commended and in better estate than is he who, carrying the countenance of a great gentlemen, ruffles it out in brave apparel but has not a penny in his purse—or indeed, sometimes not even sufficient food to put in his belly. Thus much is meant when it is said, "Better is he who debases himself and has a servant"—that is, is able to maintain a family—"than he that boasts himself and wants bread." The son of Sirach, who may well be called an interpreter of this book of the Proverbs, has a very similar saying to this, where he says as follows: "Better is he who works and abounds with all things than he that boasts himself and wants bread." A COMMENTARY UPON THE WHOLE BOOK OF THE PROVERBS OF SOLOMON.[4]

HONEST WORK, HONEST PAY. CARDINAL CAJETAN: "From the fruit of his mouth each one will be filled with good things, and he will be repaid according to the works of his hands." In the Hebrew this reads, "From the fruit of his mouth he will be satisfied with good, and the reward of one's hands will be given to him." Notice the difference that is described between the mouth and the hands, as between the fruit of speech and the fruit of labors. It lies in this, that the fruit of speaking well is something good for others, but the fruit of the hands (i.e., of one's labors) is one's own good. The fruit of the mouth lies in persuasion, instruction, and giving counsel. In this respect the other things that satisfy (i.e., things that are productive of satisfaction for others) are good food to the soul. But what the hands earn (i.e., one's works) these provide a man who works with what he deserves. But this, no doubt, takes place before the divine tribunal.† THE PARABLES OF SOLOMON, CORRECTED BY THE ORIGINAL HEBREW.[5]

RENDERING THE SACRIFICE OF PRAISE. MICHEL COP: Solomon urges us to use our mouths well, and to employ them in speaking truth: to thank, praise, and call on God our Father by prayer. This is what he means when he promises that a person will be "satisfied with good." And in doing so, he alludes in a way to the ancient sacrifices. For just as [the priests] who offered sacrifices were permitted to eat of them by the permission and ordinance of God, in the same way by following the counsel of the prophet Hosea, if we carry the words with us, and return to the Lord and offer the sacrifice of praise to God every day; if, I say, we follow the teaching of these holy men and apply our mouths to speak truth, giving good counsel to our neighbors, admonishing, exhorting, correcting, and warning them, to bring them to true repentance and strengthen them in the faith; if sensing our neighbors' needs we open our mouths to call on God for help, and truly confessing that he is the author of all goodness, we employ our tongues in giving thanks to him and singing his praises; if we use our mouths in this manner, he will not suffer us to lack anything, but will supply our daily needs and give us contentment. The ancient Levites and those who offered sacrifice by God's ordinance were nourished and sustained by their ministry. David appointed them to supervise the art of singing, as was commanded in the law of

[3]Cajetan, *Parabolae Salomonis ad veritatem Hebraicam castigatae*, 113.

[4]Moffett, *A Commentary upon the Whole Booke of the Proverbs of Salomon*, 144; citing Sir 10:30.

[5]Cajetan, *Parabolae Salomonis ad veritatem Hebraicam castigatae*, 115. †An implicit acknowledgment that in human affairs, those who work with their hands do not always receive what they have earned.

Moses. And Psalm 81, having respect to this order of the service of God, bids us to sing joyfully: "Open your mouth wide, and I will fill it." But to do this properly, it is not enough for the mouth alone to be occupied . . . ; the song must come from the spirit. . . .

Now this proverb is part promise and part warning, as we see in many other places. And both shall be fulfilled primarily on the last day. Yet even though we await its fulfillment, the Lord does show some proofs in advance, for even in this present life, the good are often so well-recompensed that they experience contentment, and conversely, we often see that fearful punishments fall upon the wicked, who are paid out according to their deserts. But that which is given to the good comes of mere grace, as is shown above. On the Proverbs of Solomon.[6]

Hard-Won Knowledge Concealed by Modesty. Michael Jermin: What a prudent person knows is not known hastily; what they have found out is, as it were, lost again, as St. Gregory says: "Not only do they not seek glory above their condition, but they also are unwilling for their merits to be seen." What they have discovered by their study and industry is "concealed" and hidden by their modesty. As it is found out by them, so it is lost as it were in them; as it is discovered to them, so it is concealed by them. They open nothing until good occasion and just reason turn the key. . . . And if for the benefit of others they show themselves, they are still careful, as St. Gregory again puts it, "lest while they raise up others from earthly heaviness they themselves be drowned in the desire of earthly praise."[†] But as the tongue of fools could not do it loud enough, their "heart proclaims their foolishness." Their heart is in their mouth, and as fast as they can open the one, they show the folly of the other. Paraphrastic Meditations.[7]

Speaking to Build Up. The English Annotations: Those who are wise reveal their knowledge only when they may do good with it, but fools by prattling show their folly. Some of the ancients have excellent sayings to the purpose that we should not conceal knowledge, but freely and ingeniously impart it to others. Their meaning is that we should not conceal it out of envy, not that we should make brags out of it or prostitute it to the contempt of those who are not likely to be benefited by it, which is to conceal it, in Solomon's sense. Annotations on Proverbs 12:23.[8]

13:1-25 *Righteousness and True Riches*

Everyone Has Their Price. Cardinal Cajetan: "The ransom of a person's soul is their wealth, but the one who is poor cannot bear rebuke." The word that is translated here as "ransom" means "price." And the word translated "bear" means "heed." And so this is the meaning of the proverb, that a person is valued according to their wealth, and so a person's wealth is so to speak their price. And so we assign value to a person according to the extent of their wealth, though this is not something we should immediately do. On the other hand, the poor are always regarded as worthless, so they are not allowed to listen to a rebuke. For they are rejected by others, and pointedly prevented from listening to others' affairs. The Parables of Solomon, Corrected by the Original Hebrew.[9]

The Rich Live in Fear of Extortion. Michel Cop: When we hear Solomon say this, we should take care to avoid blaspheming as the papists do, who say that we must make satisfaction for our sins, and win paradise by our alms given to the poor. Or that by distributing our goods to churches and convents we participate in their prayers and intercessions, and share in the good

[6]Cop, *Sur les Proverbes de Salomon*, 230; citing Deut 12:7; 14:23; Heb 13:15; Num 18:9; Deut 10:9; 18:1; 1 Chron 6:31; Num 10:10; Ps 81:10; Is 29:3; Mt 23; Eph 5:18-19; Col 3:16; Prov 11:18.
[7]Jermin, *Paraphrasticall Meditations*, 253. [†]Gregory the Great, *Moralia in Job* 28.61.

[8]Downame, ed., *English Annotations*, 6V2r*.
[9]Cajetan, *Parabolae Salomonis ad veritatem Hebraicam castigatae*, 121.

service to God and works of supererogation performed by the priests and monks. It is too horrible a blasphemy, by which the papists deny the power of Christ's passion and death, insofar as they can. And it is no thanks to them if the world is not already damned, seeing that there is no salvation in any other.

Now it seems that at first glance Solomon is leading people to put their trust in their riches, and (in a manner of speaking) to make them their god and savior. But we should know that Solomon never had any such thought, for the Holy Spirit, by whom he has spoken, does not contradict himself. Now the Holy Spirit attributes to God the ransom of life, and it is to God that we cry out for the redemption of our souls. . . .† Let us then understand that Solomon is not speaking here of this spiritual ransom, by which the souls of the faithful are eternally redeemed, but rather that if a person should be taken in any crime that deserves corporal punishment, or if they find themselves in the hands of their enemies, who desire nothing but their death, they will not spare their goods if they think that by them they may escape and save their life. That this is what Solomon means is clear when in contrast he says, "but the poor cannot hear the reproach." The reason for this is that because whatever danger they may be in, or whatever threats are made against them, they cannot redeem themselves for want of riches. It is said that "they cannot hear the reproach," because they cannot answer the desires of those who have them in their power.

Thieves and robbers chiefly seek after other people's purses, and for the most part the judges of the earth are like them, for they will pardon great thieves, and hang the small. And thus we may know that by their threats and reproaches they say, "Pay up, and you shall be absolved, and shall redeem your life." Those who have the wherewithal may give heed to this, but the poor, who have nothing, cannot obey.

Let us also understand that Solomon is not teaching the rich that they should deliver themselves by their riches from the punishments they have earned by their misdeeds. Nor does he teach the poor to be rebels, or to despise correction, but he simply describes for us what often happens in this world. If anyone concludes from this that the rich often must pay ransom, and that the poor fear no such exactions, there is no problem. And from this, we may learn that the poor who are content with their poverty and lowly condition have greater tranquility than the rich, who experience much more care and worry in heaping up riches and guarding them—it is the rich who are most in fear that thieves and robbers may get hold of their treasure and put their lives in danger. And since these rich worldlings and carnal people place their hope and confidence in their riches, it is a great burden and trouble always to live in fear of robbery and ransom. ON THE PROVERBS OF SOLOMON.[10]

RANSOM OF THE SOUL. MICHAEL JERMIN: Jansen, asking the question why riches are said to be "the ransom of a person's life," gives this answer: "because riches bring this benefit to their possessor, that often they free them from bondage, from calumnies, from injuries, from poverty, and from death."† And surely it is just that "riches" should be "the ransom of a person's life," for it is by them that a person's life is brought into danger. One who has much wealth has much envy, and envy will not spare your life to spend your wealth. Besides, there are many who love your riches so well as to hate you, and to quiet their malice you must quit yourself of your wealth. But those who are poor, since they have no money so also have no envy; as they have nothing, so they hear of nothing laid against their charge. Their poverty, as it gets them few friends, so it makes them few enemies. St. Ambrose takes the meaning of this verse in another way: "Riches are the ransom of a person's soul, because by them mercy is exercised, helping the poor at their own cost."† But then St. Jerome notes that it is said here "their riches," that is, he says,

[10]Cop, *Sur les Proverbes de Salomon*, 255-56; citing Acts 4:12; Ps 49:15; 130:1-3. †Cop proceeds to cite numerous other biblical texts in this connection: Mt 20:28; Heb 9:11-12; 1 Pet 1:18-19; Jn 3:16; 5:24; 1 Jn 4:9-10; Rom 3:24-25.

"their own riches, which are not gathered by iniquity, but by honest labor."§ And if we take the former part of the verse thus, then in the latter part it is said "that the poor hear no rebuke," because if they do not give what they do not have, they are not blamed for it. But St. Jerome tells us, "The better understanding of the passage is to take the 'riches' here for those hidden riches of godliness, which neither the thief can steal away secretly, nor the robber take away violently."◊ . . . According to the sense of the former part of this verse, St. Jerome expounds the latter part thus: "The poor man is that righteous man who, not having attained to the knowledge of the Scriptures, but being contented with a plain simplicity, performs those commandments which are enjoined by God."Δ And surely such a one shall not "hear rebuke" for not doing those things they do not know. The proverbial force of the verse is that many are the troubles and dangers of the rich, from which the poor are free. PARAPHRASTIC MEDITATIONS.[11]

THE DECEPTION OF RICHES. THE ENGLISH ANNOTATIONS: These words have a double sense, one economic and one philosophical, so to speak, taking philosophy here for a speculative science, though economics itself is a part of moral philosophy. The first, economic sense, and most literal, tends to warn us that the world is full of dissimulation, and that we not judge people's estates in our mutual dealings and commerces by what they show. This is of dangerous consequence, because, for example, some will make themselves poor on purpose, so that they may be able to receive support from those who are better able to relieve or gratify. Others, very beggars or in a sinking condition, may make themselves rich, that they may, by their supposed wealth and ability, have credit to take up where they will and borrow, through whose dissimulation many are undone.

The philosophical sense is that some people (truly virtuous and godly), though outwardly they appear poor . . . yet are in truth very rich, rich in their souls, the best riches. Others who appear rich (vicious and ungodly people) are in very truth poor, naked, and starved in their souls. ANNOTATIONS ON PROVERBS 13:7.[12]

THE VIRTUE OF GENTLENESS. PHILIPP MELANCHTHON: "Among the proud there is contention, and among those who deliberate there is wisdom." There is a Greek saying: "Mountains never meet," which signifies that two men of equally exalted station do not often agree.† But though there are many causes of discord, most often the cause is pride, for it is known that people who by nature admire themselves, and desire to excel others, turn every occasion into a competition. Nor are they moved by the greatness or smallness of the matter, but they fight for their reputation and for popular applause, and public discord afterward follows. Thus it is said that "some have brought a country down, through need for aspiration and renown."‡

Therefore, since these two are the fiercest of passions—the lust for glory and irascibility (or the lust for vengeance), as was the case with Marius and Sulla, with Pompey and Julius Caesar, and others—the Son of God expressly warns in the most serious terms that these two passions must be restrained: "Learn from me, for I am mild and humble in heart." The latter of these virtues is opposed to pride, while the former is opposed to the lust for vengeance. Gentleness [*mansuetudo*] is the virtue that first embraces justice, lest one fights when not necessary. But when fighting is necessary, gentleness moderates anger, and it makes use of any probable cause to placate the demands of justice or punishment. Moreover, it is also opposed to contentious deliberation, which characterizes souls burdened by ambition, wrath, and other passions, and by the desire (whether one is aware

[11]Jermin, *Paraphrasticall Meditations*, 262-63*. †Cornelius Jansen (1585–1638) was a Flemish bishop and theologian whose strong Augustinian bent and perceived affinities with Protestantism led to his condemnation in 1653. *Commentaria Proverbia Solomonis* (Antwerp, 1614), 81. ‡Ambrose, *Epistle* 7.3 (PL 16:905). §Jerome, *Commentaria in Jeremiam Prophetam* 2.6 (PL 26:753). ◊Jerome, *Epistola* 71.4 (PL 22:671). ΔJerome, *Commentaria in Amos Prophetam* 1.2 (PL 25:1006).

[12]Downame, ed., *English Annotations*, 6V2v*.

of it or not) not to be seen to suffer defeat, just as it is said, "Many a friend will give gold and riches and [surety], but one prepared to yield in talent will be found but seldom."[§] Exposition of the Proverbs of Solomon.[13]

The Wicked Seek Earthly Accomplishments. The English Annotations: Some interpret that God accomplishes the desires of good people to their joy but not those of the wicked, because they cannot be drawn to leave their sins. The most obvious and more immediate exposition is that all people (it being the nature of people to be in pursuit of something or other) have their desires, the accomplishment of which is the chief comfort of their lives, whence it is that fools or wicked people can so hardly be reclaimed. This is because, being full of desires, they have found so much sweetness (not considering that it will be bitterness in the end) in the accomplishment as they cannot promise themselves from honest ends and desires—the sweetness of which, for want of experience, they are altogether strangers. They are therefore not easily persuaded to forsake their desired courses. Annotations on Proverbs 13:9.[14]

Even Ill-Gotten Gains Can Glorify God. John Donne: Great contributions have been raised, and great sums given, to build, to endow seminaries and schools and colleges in foreign parts; but that has a superstitious end. . . . But these are not your works, if what you give is not your own. Nor is it your own if it was ill-gotten at first. . . .

If we should [scrutinize] worldly people's estates (their fraudulent, unjust gain), it would abridge and attenuate many a swelling inventory. Until this embezzlement and this scrutiny is made, so that you know what's your own and what belongs to others, your tomb shall be a monument of your rotten bones, however much gold or marble be bestowed on it, so that hospital, that free school, that college that you shall build and endow will be but a monument of your bribery, your extortion, your oppression; and God, who will not be in debt . . . may be pleased to give the reward of all that to them from whom that which was spent on it was unjustly taken. For "the wealth of the sinner is laid up for the righteous," says Solomon. The sinner may do pious works, and the righteous may be rewarded for them; the world may think of one founder, and God knows another. Sermon on Matthew 5:16.[15]

The Inefficiency of Injustice. Cardinal Cajetan: "There is much food in the unplowed fields of one's ancestors, but others gather it unjustly." In the Hebrew this reads, "There is much food in the furrows of the heads, and it is consumed by injustice." The word here translated "heads" means "headless" as concerns heads, or "the poor." Whichever way it is read, the meaning of the parable is that any given field can produce much fruit and any given field is found consumed unjustly and without reason. Therefore, some are consumed and some are not, and it is a commentary on human judgment. For God makes no distinction among persons unjustly, as we often see happen. The Parables of Solomon, Corrected by the Original Hebrew.[16]

Contentment with Mediocrity. Philipp Melanchthon: "There is a multitude of food in the furrows of the poor, and others gather it without measure." This is an economic precept concerning moderation [*mediocritate*] and diligence in looking after one's modest resources, in agreement with the saying, "Praise a large estate, but

[13]CR 14:30. [†]CWE 34:296. [‡]Juvenal, *Satires* 10.142-43 (Christopher Kelk, trans., *The Satires of Juvenal: A Verse Translation* [Lewiston, NY: Edwin Mellen Press, 2010], 243). [§]Martial, *Epigrams* 8.18.9-10 (LCL 95:168-69). Melanchthon slightly misquotes the original, which reads, "gold or wealth or *estates* [*rura*]." It may be that he was thinking of his earlier discussion of standing surety and the virtue of candor (see comments on 6:1-5).

[14]Downame, ed., *English Annotations*, 6V2v*; citing Mt 11:29.

[15]Donne, *Works*, 1:162-63*.

[16]Cajetan, *Parabolae Salomonis ad veritatem Hebraicam castigatae*, 125.

cultivate a small one."† And this is the idea, that it is better to possess modest resources and administer them properly, and enjoy them with piety and tranquility, than it is to accumulate great wealth, which cannot be accomplished without stumbling. This relates to the pronouncement of Paul, "Those who desire to become rich fall into foolish lusts and dangers." The saying may be restated as follows: It is better to be in control of little and to improve on it than it is to attain the highest peak of abundance and not be able to sustain it. Also to be noted here is a short passage in which Aristotle cites Phocylides in book four of the *Politics*: "In many things the middling sort have the best; let mine be a middle station."‡ Exposition of the Proverbs of Solomon.[17]

14:1-35 *Wise Building, Not Oppression of Others*

Wisdom Builds Up, Folly Tears Down. Cardinal Cajetan: "The wise woman has built her house, but the foolish one will destroy with her own hands what she has built." In the Hebrew these first two expressions are plural. So it reads, "Wise women have built . . ." And the meaning is that those women are wise who have built their own home. A comparison is thus drawn between wise women and the one who has constructed her own home, in that the wise woman capably manages her domestic responsibilities and concerns. By contrast, the foolish woman destroys her domestic responsibilities and the order of her belongings with her own hands (i.e., with her works). Therefore, she is likened to one who destroys her own home. The Parables of Solomon, Corrected by the Original Hebrew.[18]

Wise Women Are Rare. Michel Cop: Women with any natural sense and wit desire that all things may prosper in their houses, and that nothing should fall into decay or disrepair, but that all things should increase and be maintained for the comfort of the household. And even when there is lack, they will work so well with their hands so as to make a good and plentiful house, if at all possible. But whatever their desires may be, or whatever efforts they may make to raise their condition, yet their plans do not always come to fruition, as our first mother, Eve, has demonstrated. It is not enough then to desire and do labor, but to gain our desires we must eschew and fly from folly, abhor it, and be endued with wisdom. Now if a woman must be wise in order to build up her house, it follows that the number of them who do so is very small, seeing that it is very hard to find a wise woman: "One man among a thousand I have found, but a woman among them all I have not found." He speaks in this way to show that wise women are rare, not that there are none at all. For we see that the Scripture does attribute wisdom to some women, as to Sarah, Abigail, and Deborah. If the women and daughters of this age will be the equal of those holy women, they must labor to be wise by diligently resorting to sermons, and imprinting the pure Word of God on their hearts. On the Proverbs of Solomon.[19]

A Good Provider Cares for their Animals. The English Annotations: Solomon's aim is not to commend oxen for their strength, but the care and labor of people by which oxen become serviceable for such necessary work, plowing and so forth. By this, people's lives are chiefly maintained. It is a good sign of a careful and provident person when either oxen or horses employed in that work are well kept. Annotations on Proverbs 14:4.[20]

What Is Reasonable May Not Be Right. Erhart Hegenwald: You know, dear brethren, how all of us need and lack nothing more than the

[17]CR 14:31; citing 1 Tim 6:9. †Virgil, *Georgics* 2.412-13. ‡Aristotle, *Politics* 1295b-34.

[18]Cajetan, *Parabolae Salomonis ad veritatem Hebraicam castigatae*, 126.

[19]Cop, *Sur les Proverbes de Salomon*, 273-74; citing Eccles 7:28.

[20]Downame, ed., *English Annotations*, 6V3r*.

fear of God and the knowledge of him that is called *pietas*. For a person does their human thing, what pleases them well, what seems to them to be reasonable, right, and godly, which, however, may be quite against God's will, knowledge, fear, as it is written, "There is a way that pleases people well and that they think is good; but the end of it leads to death." We can also read this about Manasseh and other kings of Israel who burned their daughters for the glory of God. Letter to Conrad Grebel.[21]

The Frailty of Human Judgment. Philipp Melanchthon: This is an admonition concerning the haziness and infirmity of human judgment, and the many great errors of deliberation into which human beings are prone to wander. For they are deceived either through their own imaginations, or by the examples of others, or by common custom, and so on, and fall into great deceptions, bewitched by the devil, just as it is written about Judas that Satan entered into his heart. So a great multitude approved and complied with impious worship practices, and tenaciously held fast to monstrous heretical dogmas. Both Pompey and Josiah erred in their deliberations during wartime.[†] And there are many complaints on record regarding this infirmity that is common to so many: "The number of fools is infinite." And, "Every man is a liar." And, "No one on their own is skilled in everything."[‡] And, "Appearances often mislead judgment."[§] And Simonides: "Appearance forces even truth."[◊] Against these evils there is this one remedy: faithfully to acknowledge the Word of God, and according to the Word of God to do what is necessary with prayer, as it is written: "Your word is a lamp to my feet." And again, "Commend your way to the Lord, and hope in him, and he will do it." And again in Deuteronomy 4: this is your wisdom, to walk in my precepts.[Δ] Exposition of the Proverbs of Solomon.[22]

Human Custom Is No Safe Guide. Michel Cop: When something becomes customary according to the world's use, it may seem that there is no evil in it, and so it follows that it seems good and right. . . . In almost all walks of life custom is made law, even when it goes against the honor of God or against the love of our neighbor. We may see the same when it comes to superstitions and idolatries, in the crafts and occupations, in the arts and trades, in commerce and in business. Because it has always been done thus, therefore it seems as though it must be right. But people who carry on this way will come to discover at the last that they have wandered and gone astray in various ways, to their great harm. This is what Solomon signifies when he says, "Its end is the ways of death." In saying this, he teaches the same thing that Moses taught the children of Israel, when he said, "You shall not do according to all that we are doing here today, everyone doing whatever is right in their own eyes." And immediately after, he warns that if we follow that which is right in our own mind and opinion, we shall die—and not just temporally and bodily, which is common both to humans and to beasts, to the just and the unjust. Moreover, we can see that those who walk rightly in the judgment of the world are not in so great danger of corporal death as are those who seek to please God, according to his Word, who are counted as sheep to be slaughtered. But chiefly what he warns of here is eternal death, when the wicked shall know that the way which they have taken was not the right way. Such knowledge will not be of any profit to them, but shall only further torment them. Therefore, let us understand that Solomon urges us to walk contrary to our own opinion and fantasy if we wish to avoid death and obtain life. Furthermore, he shows us that we all have a tendency toward death, if left to our own devices, for we think that we are so wise, that we alone can guide ourselves. This is common to all people, until they are regenerated

[21]CRR 4:325*; citing 2 Kings 21; 2 Chron 33.
[22]CR 14:31; citing Lk 22:3; Eccles 1:15; Ps 114:2; 119:105; 37:5. [†]Pompey's missteps in the war against Julius Caesar were well-known to students of ancient history. The reference to Josiah is most likely in reference to 2 Chron 35:22. [‡]Theognis, *Elegies* 902 (LCL 258:305). [§]Theognis, *Elegies* 128. [◊]Simonides, *Poetae Melici Graeci*, fr. 598; cf. Plato, *Republic* 365C. [Δ]A paraphrase of Deut 4:5-6.

and sanctified by the Spirit of God, who by his anointing teaches and guides them. On the Proverbs of Solomon.[23]

Oppression Mocks God. Cardinal Cajetan: "The one who falsely accuses the person in need disowns their Creator, but the one who honors them has mercy on the poor person." The word here translated "falsely accuses" suggests the notion of oppressing by theft or deceit. And the word translated "disowns" suggests ridicule. And these statements are not understood absolutely as they suggest, but about the one who is oppressing the poor person, as though they needed someone to help. For in oppressing someone, one acts as though God has no concern for protecting the cause of the poor. But it is written, "The poor person is abandoned to you, you will help the orphan." On the contrary, the one who pities the poor honors God, because in helping the poor they act on God's behalf. For it has already been stated that care of the poor has been left to God. The Parables of Solomon, Corrected by the Original Hebrew.[24]

A Double Offense in Wronging the Poor. John Dod: By "poor" he means not only those who live in want and penury but those who are under the burden of any other afflictions, and unable to defend themselves; and by "oppression" he understands all kinds of hard dealing, whether it be by craft or force, or false accusation and slanders, or bitter and contumelious speeches to bring them into contempt or hate. Those who thus wrong any distressed person "reproach him who made them"—that is, the Lord who allotted to him that poor estate. "But those who show mercy to the poor," who do good and minister comfort to those who are in misery, by helping the Lord's servants, declare their love and estimation of the Lord their Master. Doctrine: all the wrong that is offered to the poor the Lord takes as done to himself. . . .

First, his commandment is thereby violated and broken, for in many places he strictly forbids all, however great, to grieve the poor, and calls on everyone to show them pity. One place for this purpose may serve, instead of many that may be brought, for confirmation of this point. Zechariah tells the people of his time what duty the Lord required, by the former prophets before the captivity, and what message was committed to him now after their return, and that was: "execute true judgment, and show mercy and compassion, every person to their brother and sister. And do not oppress the widow or the fatherless, the stranger or the poor." Second, he has undertaken to be their guardian and keeper, and they have become his wards and pupils; therefore whoever deals injuriously with them regards God either to be so unfaithful that he has no regard for the safety of his charge, or so weak and feeble that he is not able to protect and defend them. Third, our text yields a forcible reason why those who oppress the poor also despise the Lord, because he is their Creator: in respect of their persons, they are the work of his hands; and in respect of their condition, they are also his handiwork, as Hannah sang, "The Lord makes poor and makes rich; he brings low and he exalts." Thus if they wrong them as human beings, they misuse his creatures, who have their form and being from him; if as poor people, they disgrace his workmanship in shaping them with such a state. A Plain and Familiar Exposition.[25]

[23]Cop, *Sur les Proverbes de Salomon*, 284; citing Deut 12:8; Eccles 3:19; 9:2; Rom 8:36; Sir 5:1-7.
[24]Cajetan, *Parabolae Salomonis ad veritatem Hebraicam castigatae*, 133; citing Ps 10:14.
[25]Dod, *A Plaine and Familiar Exposition of the Thirteenth and Fourteenth Chapters of the Proverbs of Salomon*, 136-37; citing Zech 7:9-10; 1 Sam 2:7.

15:1–17:28 MORE PROVERBS ON THE GOOD LIFE

1 *A soft answer turns away wrath,*
but a harsh word stirs up anger.

2 *The tongue of the wise commends knowledge,*
but the mouths of fools pour out folly.

3 *The eyes of the* LORD *are in every place,*
keeping watch on the evil and the good.

4 *A gentle*[a] *tongue is a tree of life,*
but perverseness in it breaks the spirit.

5 *A fool despises his father's instruction,*
but whoever heeds reproof is prudent.

6 *In the house of the righteous there is much treasure,*
but trouble befalls the income of the wicked.

7 *The lips of the wise spread knowledge;*
not so the hearts of fools.[b]

8 *The sacrifice of the wicked is an abomination to the* LORD,
but the prayer of the upright is acceptable to him.

9 *The way of the wicked is an abomination to the* LORD,
but he loves him who pursues righteousness.

10 *There is severe discipline for him who forsakes the way;*
whoever hates reproof will die.

11 *Sheol and Abaddon lie open before the* LORD;
how much more the hearts of the children of man!

12 *A scoffer does not like to be reproved;*
he will not go to the wise.

13 *A glad heart makes a cheerful face,*
but by sorrow of heart the spirit is crushed.

14 *The heart of him who has understanding seeks knowledge,*
but the mouths of fools feed on folly.

15 *All the days of the afflicted are evil,*
but the cheerful of heart has a continual feast.

16 *Better is a little with the fear of the* LORD
than great treasure and trouble with it.

17 *Better is a dinner of herbs where love is*
than a fattened ox and hatred with it.

18 *A hot-tempered man stirs up strife,*
but he who is slow to anger quiets contention.

19 *The way of a sluggard is like a hedge of thorns,*
but the path of the upright is a level highway.

20 *A wise son makes a glad father,*
but a foolish man despises his mother.

21 *Folly is a joy to him who lacks sense,*
but a man of understanding walks straight ahead.

22 *Without counsel plans fail,*
but with many advisers they succeed.

23 *To make an apt answer is a joy to a man,*
and a word in season, how good it is!

24 *The path of life leads upward for the prudent,*
that he may turn away from Sheol beneath.

25 *The* LORD *tears down the house of the proud*
but maintains the widow's boundaries.

26 *The thoughts of the wicked are an abomination to the* LORD,
but gracious words are pure.

27 *Whoever is greedy for unjust gain troubles his own household,*
but he who hates bribes will live.

28 *The heart of the righteous ponders how to answer,*
but the mouth of the wicked pours out evil things.

29 *The* LORD *is far from the wicked,*
but he hears the prayer of the righteous.

[30]*The light of the eyes rejoices the heart,*
and good news refreshes[c] *the bones.*

[31]*The ear that listens to life-giving reproof*
will dwell among the wise.

[32]*Whoever ignores instruction despises himself,*
but he who listens to reproof gains intelligence.

[33]*The fear of the LORD is instruction in wisdom,*
and humility comes before honor.

16 *The plans of the heart belong to man,*
but the answer of the tongue is from the LORD.

[2]*All the ways of a man are pure in his own eyes,*
but the LORD weighs the spirit.[d]

[3]*Commit your work to the LORD,*
and your plans will be established.

[4]*The LORD has made everything for its purpose,*
even the wicked for the day of trouble.

[5]*Everyone who is arrogant in heart is an abomination to the LORD;*
be assured, he will not go unpunished.

[6]*By steadfast love and faithfulness iniquity is atoned for,*
and by the fear of the LORD one turns away from evil.

[7]*When a man's ways please the LORD,*
he makes even his enemies to be at peace with him.

[8]*Better is a little with righteousness*
than great revenues with injustice.

[9]*The heart of man plans his way,*
but the LORD establishes his steps.

[10]*An oracle is on the lips of a king;*
his mouth does not sin in judgment.

[11]*A just balance and scales are the LORD's;*
all the weights in the bag are his work.

[12]*It is an abomination to kings to do evil,*
for the throne is established by righteousness.

[13]*Righteous lips are the delight of a king,*
and he loves him who speaks what is right.

[14]*A king's wrath is a messenger of death,*
and a wise man will appease it.

[15]*In the light of a king's face there is life,*
and his favor is like the clouds that bring the spring rain.

[16]*How much better to get wisdom than gold!*
To get understanding is to be chosen rather than silver.

[17]*The highway of the upright turns aside from evil;*
whoever guards his way preserves his life.

[18]*Pride goes before destruction,*
and a haughty spirit before a fall.

[19]*It is better to be of a lowly spirit with the poor*
than to divide the spoil with the proud.

[20]*Whoever gives thought to the word*[e] *will discover good,*
and blessed is he who trusts in the LORD.

[21]*The wise of heart is called discerning,*
and sweetness of speech increases persuasiveness.

[22]*Good sense is a fountain of life to him who has it,*
but the instruction of fools is folly.

[23]*The heart of the wise makes his speech judicious*
and adds persuasiveness to his lips.

[24]*Gracious words are like a honeycomb,*
sweetness to the soul and health to the body.

[25]*There is a way that seems right to a man,*
but its end is the way to death.[f]

[26]*A worker's appetite works for him;*
his mouth urges him on.

[27]*A worthless man plots evil,*
and his speech[g] *is like a scorching fire.*

[28]*A dishonest man spreads strife,*
and a whisperer separates close friends.

[29]*A man of violence entices his neighbor*
and leads him in a way that is not good.

[30]*Whoever winks his eyes plans*[h] *dishonest things;*
he who purses his lips brings evil to pass.

[31]*Gray hair is a crown of glory;*
it is gained in a righteous life.

[32]*Whoever is slow to anger is better than the mighty,*
and he who rules his spirit than he who takes a city.

[33]*The lot is cast into the lap,*
but its every decision is from the LORD.

17 *Better is a dry morsel with quiet*
than a house full of feasting[i] *with strife.*

[2]*A servant who deals wisely will rule over a son who acts shamefully*
and will share the inheritance as one of the brothers.

[3]*The crucible is for silver, and the furnace is for gold,*
and the LORD tests hearts.

[4]*An evildoer listens to wicked lips,*
and a liar gives ear to a mischievous tongue.

[5]*Whoever mocks the poor insults his Maker;*
he who is glad at calamity will not go unpunished.

[6]*Grandchildren are the crown of the aged,*
and the glory of children is their fathers.

[7]*Fine speech is not becoming to a fool;*
still less is false speech to a prince.

[8]*A bribe is like a magic*[j] *stone in the eyes of the one who gives it;*
wherever he turns he prospers.

[9]*Whoever covers an offense seeks love,*
but he who repeats a matter separates close friends.

[10]*A rebuke goes deeper into a man of understanding*
than a hundred blows into a fool.

[11]*An evil man seeks only rebellion,*
and a cruel messenger will be sent against him.

[12]*Let a man meet a she-bear robbed of her cubs*
rather than a fool in his folly.

[13]*If anyone returns evil for good,*
evil will not depart from his house.

[14]*The beginning of strife is like letting out water,*
so quit before the quarrel breaks out.

[15]*He who justifies the wicked and he who condemns the righteous*
are both alike an abomination to the LORD.

[16]*Why should a fool have money in his hand to buy wisdom*
when he has no sense?

[17]*A friend loves at all times,*
and a brother is born for adversity.

[18]*One who lacks sense gives a pledge*
and puts up security in the presence of his neighbor.

[19]*Whoever loves transgression loves strife;*
he who makes his door high seeks destruction.

[20]*A man of crooked heart does not discover good,*
and one with a dishonest tongue falls into calamity.

[21]*He who sires a fool gets himself sorrow,*
and the father of a fool has no joy.

[22]*A joyful heart is good medicine,*
but a crushed spirit dries up the bones.

[23]*The wicked accepts a bribe in secret*[k]
to pervert the ways of justice.

[24]*The discerning sets his face toward wisdom,*
but the eyes of a fool are on the ends of the earth.

[25]*A foolish son is a grief to his father*
and bitterness to her who bore him.

[26]*To impose a fine on a righteous man is not good,*
nor to strike the noble for their uprightness.

[27]*Whoever restrains his words has knowledge,*
and he who has a cool spirit is a man of
understanding.

[28]*Even a fool who keeps silent is considered wise;*
when he closes his lips, he is deemed
intelligent.

a Or *healing* **b** Or *the hearts of fools are not steadfast* **c** Hebrew *makes fat* **d** Or *spirits* **e** Or *to a matter* **f** Hebrew *ways of death* **g** Hebrew *what is on his lips* **h** Hebrew *to plan* **i** Hebrew *sacrifices* **j** Or *precious* **k** Hebrew *a bribe from the bosom*

Overview: As our exegetes continue to apply the wisdom of Solomon's proverbs, a number of matters draw their attention. Cardinal Cajetan and Michel Cop both meditate on the nature of anger, with Cajetan considering its relationship to sadness and Cop recognizing that there are situations in which this emotion is an appropriate response. God's sovereignty is also discussed, and while the Lutheran Philipp Melanchthon and the Reformed Cop both emphasize God's control, with Cop in particular giving a detailed rebuttal of human self-sufficiency, the radical reformer Jan Cents argues that God's admonitions are a sign that he gave us free will. Meanwhile, as opposed to caricatures of his exegesis and theology, John Calvin recognizes the tension between divine sovereignty and human freedom and argues that while God is in control, he nevertheless has entrusted people with a degree of freedom that they are expected to exercise with wisdom. Reflecting the tendency of radical reformers to reject taking oaths as unbiblical, Peter Riedemann argues that handshakes should not be used for this purpose, but rather are an appropriate alternative to an embrace, as they can be shared between men and women as a seal of unity and a sign of the peace that marks the people of God.

15:1-33 *Wise Tongues and Understanding Hearts*

Anger Proceeds from Harshness. Cardinal Cajetan: "A gentle answer dissipates anger, but a harsh word provokes wrath." The word translated here "dissipates" suggests causing one to yield. The second expression according to the Hebrew goes like this: "Fury flares up at a hurtful word." We know that a gentle answer causes an angry person to withdraw their anger. On the other hand, if the answer is a word that brings injury, the wrath of the angered person will be overwhelming, and anger will grow to rage. The reason for this is obvious: the cause for anger is multiplied when one speaks a hurtful word. Clearly, anger proceeds from harshness, but the source of anger is lessened by the gentle response. The angry person, when they see the one with whom they are angry humbled, withdraws their anger as though they stopped being angry with that person. The Parables of Solomon, Corrected by the Original Hebrew.[1]

Peacemaking and the Lust for Strife. Philipp Melanchthon: The whole law of God is a description of what God is like, and it has been revealed to humanity in order that we may know what God is like and because he desires to conform us to himself. So, for example, he commands us not to kill, for he himself is not a God of destruction but of salvation, just as he calls himself to witness: "As I live, says the Lord, I do not desire the death of the wicked, but that he should turn and live." Therefore he gives us many precepts concerning peace, which pertain to the commandment "Do not kill," and those who disturb the peace without just cause violate that law. Also of note in this connection are the sayings "Blessed are the peacemakers, for they will be called the sons of God" and "Insofar as it is in you, keep the peace with all people."

[1]Cajetan, *Parabolae Salomonis ad veritatem Hebraicam castigatae*, 134.

There are also precepts that are handed down concerning the manner in which peace must be preserved. In the first place, let no one cause injury to another. Next, it is not enough simply to avoid entering into unjust disputes, but additionally the manner of repelling injuries in self-defense should not be so as to inflict a more savage counterattack than the original injury—just as it is said, "Let not the defense be offensive." If it is a battle of words, and there are harsh accusations, respond with moderate words; if there are no harsh accusations, often it is a virtue to ignore them, and give way for the common tranquility, refuting them by the testimony of one's life, rather than by recriminations, as Cicero says, "I should be in a sorry way if my oratory, rather than my way of life, should have to excuse me."[†] . . . And David says, "They accused me, but I gave myself to prayer."

This moderation pertains to these virtues: gentleness, patience, and a sense of duty owed to the church or the public tranquility. But the extremes are *philoneikia*—that is, the lust for strife—and laxity [*lenitas*]. But more sin through *philoneikia*, an evil far more dangerous. For whether it be in those who are driven to strife, injustice, or to inflaming unnecessary contention (either through pride, ambition, a morose nature, or through imitation, irascibility, or superstition), or whether it be in those whose response is never to yield, never to give an inch, but who always wish to conquer with harshness and always fan the flames of hatred, there is *philoneikia*, just as Lucan says, "She seeks an excuse for drawing the sword."[‡] And again, "[She] moves to and fro around the ranks, and adds fuel to the fire of their passions."[§] And Stobaeus cites an ancient saying that signifies that the lust for contention is the cause of great calamity: "The greatest evils arise from nothing else but the love of strife (*philoneikia*)."[◊]

Therefore, in order that we may shun this vice, Solomon gives us an admonition to show us how: "A soft answer turns away wrath"—that is, not only should you not respond in kind to one who has caused you injury, but you should strive to respond by easing tensions, if you can. And there are also many similar proverbs, which teach that one ought not to contend with those who are angry. For example, "Do not poke the fire with a sword."[Δ] And these verses are also praiseworthy: "When two are speaking and one is angry, the one who does not strive with words is the wiser."[††] EXPOSITION OF THE PROVERBS OF SOLOMON.[2]

JUST OR UNJUST ANGER. MICHEL COP: By "a soft answer" let us understand a humble confession of the faults and offenses that we have committed, with requests and prayers to obtain pardon from God and reconciliation with the one whom we have offended—and this chiefly when we are rebuked and admonished. And also let us include every soft and gentle word whereby we attempt to quiet those who are angry—whether rightly or wrongly—and to obtain their favor. Jacob knew well that such words were useful in turning away wrath, and this is why he spoke as he did to his brother Esau. He had not been the cause of offense to Esau, and yet he knew that Esau had threatened to kill him. And David also used a soft answer to turn away the wrath of Saul, who had wrongfully persecuted him. Likewise our Lord Jesus Christ teaches us, "If you are offering your gift at the altar and there remember that your brother has something against you, leave your gift there before the altar and go. First be reconciled to your brother, and then come and offer your gift." And "Love your enemies, and pray for those who persecute you." And if we must use a soft answer to those who do us wrong, how much more should we answer softly when we have offended God and our neighbors! ON THE PROVERBS OF SOLOMON.[3]

[2]CR 14:32-33; citing Ezek 33:11; Mt 5:9; Rom 12:18; Ps 109:4. [†]Melanchthon appears to be paraphrasing a passage in Cicero's fourteenth *Phillipic* (6, 10). [‡]Lucan, *Civil War* 1.265. [§]Lucan, *Civil War* 7.559. The original quotation describes the actions of Caesar preparing his troops for battle. [◊]Stobaeus, *Eclogae* 4.121. [Δ]Diogenes Laertius, *Lives of Eminent Philosophers* 8.1.7. [††]A verse fragment attributed to Euripides, cited in Stobaeus (*Eclogae* 3.19.3).
[3]Cop, *Sur les Proverbes de Salomon*, 312; citing Gen 32:1-5; 33:5; 1 Sam 24:9; Mt 5:23-24; 5:44.

The Wealth of the Wicked. The English Annotations: A wicked person may get much wealth, but they have much care and trouble with it, whereas a good person's treasure may be their strength and without trouble through God's blessing. It is not always so. Some wicked, wealthy people enjoy themselves (in the way of the world) and their plenty quietly enough, even to the last. But it has often been said that no moral sentence or observation can be absolute among people because of the variety of circumstances, the perfect knowledge of which is above the reach of any person. We shall only say, first, that some may be accounted wicked among people (especially when judged by people different from them) who are not so in the eyes of God, and the contrary is also true. This made the apostle refer all judgment concerning people to the great day, when the hidden counsels of every heart will be made manifest. Second, God sometimes rewards wicked people whom he has used to accomplish his will in some things with temporal blessings. Annotations on Proverbs 15:6.[4]

God Has Regard for the Person, Not the Gifts. Cardinal Cajetan: "The sacrifices of the wicked are detestable to the Lord, but the prayers of the righteous can please him." The name of the Lord is the tetragrammaton, and the second phrase according to the Hebrew reads, "and the prayer of the upright is his will." God had regard for Abel and for his gifts; it does not say that God had regard for the gifts of Abel and for Abel. So we understand that because of the person the gifts are pleasing to God and not vice versa.[†] This principle makes it all the more obvious that the sacrifice of the unrighteous not only displeases God but is also detestable to God Most High. Yes, it is noxious for the wicked person to pretend to be righteous in God's presence, just as it is the privilege of the righteous to sacrifice to God. On the contrary, the prayer of an upright person is the will of God Most High, and is pleasing to God Most High. Sacrifice is an outward offering, but prayer is inward, seeing that it is raising the mind toward God. This is what innately pleases God, what can be offered by the upright alone. But sacrifice, for its simple performance, this is something shared by the wicked and the upright like. The Parables of Solomon, Corrected by the Original Hebrew.[5]

On the Right Use of Ceremonies. Philipp Melanchthon: This teaching is often repeated in the Prophets, and it concerns three kinds of works: ceremonial, moral, and those related to faith. . . .[†] The first of these, ceremonies, are external signs. For God has instituted certain ceremonies for two reasons: first, that they may be signs pointing to his promises; second, that they may be the public harp strings of the congregation, for God does not want the church to lie hidden, but to be visible and recognizable to other people by the voice of her ceremonies.

For this reason, careful consideration must be given to the manner in which ceremonies must be used, for people are prone to false worship, and above all to the abuse of ceremonies. Having lost sight of the promises and extinguished the light of faith, they turn their eyes on ceremonies, and they think that by means of these they merit forgiveness of sins before God and are just. This conviction roams very widely among humankind at all times. The Gentiles thought this away about their sacrifices, and so did the greater part of the people of Israel. This is what the Pharisees taught, and also the monks regarding the Mass, vows, and all the other ceremonies.

The prophets sharply rebuked this common error, as may be seen in Psalm 49 and in other witnesses. Moreover, even the pagans abhorred this

[4]Downame, ed., *English Annotations*, 6V4r-v*; citing 1 Tim 6:10; 1 Cor 4:5; Ps 17:13.

[5]Cajetan, *Parabolae Salomonis ad veritatem Hebraicam castigatae*, 136. [†]This formulation is very close to Luther's famous axiom in *The Freedom of a Christian* that "it is always necessary that the substance or person himself be good before there can be any good works, and that good works follow and proceed from the good person" (LW 31:361).

superstition that ceremonies could save one, without morally good deeds, for as Plato says, worshiping God requires "that people contrive no life of pretense, but truly honor virtue."‡ But pagan abhorrence [of pretense] is not enough. For although indeed it is needful for humanity to be good and just in their consciences, yet in the church we know that it is not enough simply to assert the teachings of the law, but we must also speak of the Mediator, of the promise of grace, and of faith. For it is necessary that in all our moral and ceremonial works, an intimate knowledge of the Mediator and his promises should shine forth, with the result that we believe with our hearts what we have received and heard on account of the Mediator: that although we are unworthy, through this faith we may draw near to God, just as the Lord says, "No one comes to the Father except through the Son." . . .

After this, morally good works are pleasing to God for this purpose: not that we merit the remission of sins, but that we act in obedience to God, and learn his teaching, and rejoice in God, and that the devil may not triumph against God through us. The ceremonies that have been instituted by God are pleasing to him when they are done not with the aim of earning forgiveness, but because they are signs that call to mind the promise and enkindle faith. Likewise, because they are signs of confession, and because they are the harp strings of the congregation. The church must recognize these as the true aims of ceremonial works, and remove all other impious views. Exposition of the Proverbs of Solomon.[6]

The Joy of the Lord Adorns the Face. Michel Cop: We are very glad when our neighbors show us a friendly face, and if we love them truly we wish to respond in kind, so as not to grieve them. Now, insofar as "a joyful heart," as Solomon says, "makes a cheerful countenance," it follows first of all that we ought to work to give cheer to our neighbors—not in a worldly and carnal manner, as with idle chatter, foolish talk, or flattering their vanity. Rather, we should endeavor to make them glad not in doing them wrong, but in procuring their good before God, as much as we can to the utmost of our power, and chiefly with regard to their spiritual wealth, for there is no true joy in the heart without this. . . .

Second, it follows from this proverb that if for the love we bear our neighbors we ought to show them a cheerful countenance, we must have a cheerful heart—not cheerful with worldly and carnal joy, but with spiritual delight, as befits the children of God. We shall enjoy this if whatever may happen to us, we are content to take it in stride as coming from the hand of God, being assured that he loves us, and that he sends us nothing but what is expedient for us. . . . Such joy will adorn our faces and make us acceptable to God, and those of our neighbors who know and love the truth will think us lovely and pleasant. Therefore if we want to have shining faces, we should not seek to paint them, or to deck ourselves after the fashions of the world, but instead let us rejoice our hearts in the Lord. On the Proverbs of Solomon.[7]

Admonishment Implies Human Freedom. Jan Cents: Both before and after the fall, the Lord gave free will to human beings so that they could accept or reject the offered grace of God through faith in the promised Savior. This can be seen not only in the sending of his prophets, apostles, and disciples but also through the friendly urging of his beloved Son. This was fitting so that he could be a just judge and have proper reasons to punish his despisers with the pains of hell and reward his obedient sheep with heavenly joy at the Last Day. Confession.[8]

[6]CR 14:33-35; citing Jn 14:6. †Melanchthon cites a string of passages illustrating the priority of righteousness over ceremonial correctness: Ps 49:13; Jer 7:22-23; Is 22:13; Eccl 4:17; Hos 6:6; Jn 4:23. ‡Plato, *Epinomis* 989C (LCL 201:476-77).

[7]Cop, *Sur les Proverbes de Salomon*, 326.

[8]CRR 11:272*; citing Deut 30:15; Mt 28:18; Mk 16:16; Acts 17:30; Mt 11:29; 22:9; 1 Tim 1:15; Tit 2:11; 2 Thess 1:8; Acts 13:46; Rom 2:5; Jn 3:16, 36; 2 Thess 1:7; Heb 6:10.

The Power of Friendship. Michel Cop: Every person wants to make good cheer, and to live merrily. To do this, it seems to many—the sort who are addicted to eating and are slaves to their bellies—that they need no more than to have a table thoroughly furnished with a number of dishes, and good wine, and to eat and drink till they burst, without a care for whether those they eat and drink with are well disposed toward them, nor what love they bear for those who lay the table, or serve them. It is enough for them to satisfy their bellies, and to devour and swill at their pleasure, so much like animals are they. But Solomon shows us here that great cheer consists not in the abundance of dainty meats, nor in strong and sweet wines that please the palate, for he says, "Better is a dinner of herbs . . ." By this he indicates a simple meal that is quickly and easily prepared, and that does not consist in many dishes, nor of great cost; rather, it is simple and light fare, showing sobriety and temperance. Solomon makes a great deal of such a meal, if they who eat it are friends. Friendship then is the sauce that makes the meat good, and not only a meal—this is also the rule after which all our works ought to be wrought, if they are to be worth anything. . . . Now, although he speaks this way, preferring a small thing with love to very great things with hatred, let us not think that he would make charterhouse monks of us all, and forbid us the use of meats.[†] Meat is good, of course, but the point is to show the excellency and power of friendship, which makes even the most meager fare, and that which appears vile and contemptible in comparison to other nourishments, to be highly esteemed. On the Proverbs of Solomon.[9]

The Wicked Are Preserved Until the Evil Day. Balthasar Hubmaier: Whatever my opposition shouts, the simple understanding of this verse is: God does not want to kill the godless immediately, but out of the mercifulness of his heart he tolerates them longer until the evil day, which is evil not in itself, but will be evil to the godless because of their punishment on it. On that day God will carry out the punishment of the godless to demonstrate his glory and for the sake of our salvation, and he will give them the wages of their sin as they deserve it. However, that God has made the godless person for evil is not so. For he has made everything very good, even Lucifer. But out of his free wantonness he himself turned away from the eternal God and good. Therefore God preserves them until the evil day—that is, to the day of punishment, when he will give them all the more to the punishment of eternal pain. The devil and his gang fear that day highly. Therefore he says to Christ, "Jesus, Son of the Highest, why did you come before the time to cause us pain?" Freedom of the Will II.[10]

Diligence Defined by Justice. Michel Cop: Like a pilgrim who meets with a very thick hedge of thorns that stops him from going any further, and is grieved at the delay to his journey, so the slothful person regards the work God has set him to do in his estate and vocation to be grievous and troublesome, preferring instead to take his ease and live in idleness, without a care but for his own sleep and rest. Solomon calls this "the way of the slothful," not because he walks in it, but because following the ordinance of God, he *should* walk in it. He compares it to a hedge of thorns, not to gainsay that which is written in the law of the Lord, nor to contradict what our Lord says, but rather he speaks after the manner of the slothful themselves. They are called "slothful" here, not because they abstain from all kinds of work, but because they do not want to walk in justice, according to the Word of the Lord, but turn their backs on him and strive to do the contrary. Solomon makes this clear when in contrast to the slothful person he sets the righteous: "The path of the righteous is a level highway. . . ." For just as the traveler who finds his way

[9]Cop, *Sur les Proverbes de Salomon*, 331. [†]Charterhouse monks (Carthusians) are an enclosed order famed for the austerity of their rule, which usually forbade the consumption of meat.

[10]CRR 5:485-86*; citing Rom 9:22; Gen 1:31; Mt 8:29; 2 Pet 2:4; Jude 5.

free from all hindrances delights in his way, so justice is what causes the upright person to take pleasure in doing his work diligently and carefully executing the duties of his office. Let the thieves, covetous, usurers, deceivers, and con men work themselves to death; let them be daily at work without ceasing day or night; still they do not deserve to be called diligent. For since they are without justice, there is nothing in them but slothfulness. And so when we carefully consider their ways, we shall see that they are never contented, but always complaining that they cannot achieve their aims. And so their way is a hedge of thorns. ON THE PROVERBS OF SOLOMON.[11]

GOD AVENGES OPPRESSION. PETER MOFFETT: This sentence commends the justice of God in terrifying mighty oppressors and in comforting poor people, who are insinuated in the name of the "widow," whose estate is of all others most grievous, because having been deprived of her husband she lies open to all wrongs, but especially to the injuries of great and wealthy men. See the root of this in Exodus 22:22: "The Lord will then destroy the house of the proud." God often overthrows their families—indeed, he pulls them up by the roots—who in the pride of their hearts have oppressed the poor, taking from them either their lands or their goods. "But he will establish the border of the widow." The Lord will restore the poor to their right, or else, by some means or other, he will so defend their possessions and fields against the power of the mighty that they shall not be able to pull them out of their hands. A COMMENTARY UPON THE WHOLE BOOK OF THE PROVERBS OF SOLOMON.[12]

THREEFOLD LIGHT. DENIS THE CARTHUSIAN: This passage can be understood first of all with reference to sensible light—that is, how pleasant it is to gaze admiringly with the eyes of the body, as is said in Ecclesiastes: "The light is sweet, and it is delightful for the eyes to see the sun." In like manner, visual light existing in the pupil lights up the soul, because vision is effected through it, and the soul learns many things through outward sight. For the sight of things, according to the philosopher, shows us the greatest differences. Thus the blinded Tobit: "What manner of joy shall be to me, who sit in darkness and see not the light of heaven?" Second, the passage may be understood with reference to intelligible light—that is, regarding the grace of God, truth, and divine illumination, which rejoices the interior eyes—for contemplation of the truth gives great delight. Concerning this light Micah says, "When I sit in darkness, the Lord is my light." Thus he adds, "He will bring me forth into the light, and I shall behold his justice." Third, the passage may be expounded with regard to the light of glory, uncreated Light, whose bright and beatific vision supremely exhilarates and fully satisfies the soul, as the psalmist says, "You will fill me with joy at your countenance." These expositions agree with the ancient translation, which reads, "The eye that sees good things delights the heart." In other words, pleasure arises from the union of a power with a suitable object. EXPOSITION OF THE BOOK OF PROVERBS.[13]

SACRAMENTAL USE OF THE BODY'S SENSES. JOHN DOD: "The light of the eyes." The beholding of delightful aspects "rejoices the heart," bringing sound gladness to the soul that is seasoned with grace and looks on God's favor with his blessings. "And a good hearing," where this is a comfortable matter related, and an attentive care to listen to it "makes the bones fat"—that is, procures health and a good disposition for the whole body. In this way the bones are replenished with marrow within, and well stored with flesh and fatness without. Not that seeing serves only for the comfort of the heart, and hearing for the health of the body, but each of them is profitable in both ways. And the same may

[11]Cop, *Sur les Proverbes de Salomon*, 333; citing Mt 11:19.
[12]Moffett, *A Commentary upon the Whole Booke of the Proverbs of Salomon*, 190.
[13]DCOO 7:104; citing Eccles 11:7; Tob 5:12; Mic 7:8-9; Ps 16:10.

be understood also, in due proportion, of the other senses.

Doctrine: The Lord has ordained human senses for the use and benefit of both soul and body. He offers goodly prospects and ornaments to the sight both above and beneath, to please the eyes; pleasant speeches, besides music and other sweet sounds, to content the ears; delicious food, to sweeten the palate; and redolent smells, to refresh the nostrils. In all these he allows us a natural delight as well as a spiritual one. Moreover, he has consecrated diverse objects specially for holy uses, as under the law, and especially in Solomon's days and afterward, were to be seen in Jerusalem: the sumptuous building of the temple, the gorgeous garments of the priests, with gold and silver, and many precious jewels and vessels, then used in that house. So there were also melodious instruments and songs to be heard, sweet-smelling ointments and perfumes to be inhaled, feasts in which much meat was dressed to be tasted. And so have we in the time of the gospel our own hearing, handling, seeing, and tasting exercised in the Lord's Supper, and many joyful messages are brought to us by the ministry of the Word. In all of these, the Lord respects the good of our souls and makes our senses like tunnels, through which he pours his grace into our hearts. A PLAIN AND FAMILIAR EXPOSITION.[14]

16:1-33 *Love and Justice Instead of Pride*

THE NECESSITY OF GOD'S GUIDANCE. PHILIPP MELANCHTHON: A similar proverb follows soon after in this same chapter: "The heart of man plans his way, but the Lord confirms his steps." These sayings do not remove the freedom of the human will (or choice), but they signify that there are certain choices of the human will, not only in those who have not been reborn (such as Pompey), but also in those who have (such as Joshua, David . . .). But in these choices people sometimes err, as when Josiah unnecessarily provoked war with Egypt. In this instance, his will had its choice, but he chose poorly, and the result was not a success.

And we must diligently observe that choice in us is one thing and the outcome another. For though one may make a good decision, it is necessary for God's help to be added, and this doubly so: first, in the act of judgment, and afterward, in guiding events. For unless judgment is directed by the Word of God, and by divine light, many errors will befall, as was the cases when Josiah, Zedekiah, Demosthenes, Pompey, and Cicero acted wrongly in choosing to go to war, and horrifying events followed, because they were not assisted by God.† And sometimes, even when the mind does not err in judgment, God chooses for other reasons not to assist the one who acts, as when sorrowful events followed the battles against Benjamin, because the Israelites trusted in their own strength. EXPOSITION OF THE PROVERBS OF SOLOMON.[15]

AN IRONIC REBUKE OF SELF-SUFFICIENCY. MICHEL COP: Insofar as it is from the abundance of the heart that the mouth speaks, it follows that he who gives speech is ruler of the heart, and so governs it as to make it utter with the tongue what he desires. Even so, Solomon says that "the preparations of the heart" are from the person. It seems at first glance that that there are three problems with this. First, it seems by this saying that a person has power to prepare or dispose their own heart as they will, and from this it follows that

[14]Dod, *A Plaine and Familiar Exposition of the Fifteenth, Sixteenth, and Seventeenth Chapters of the Proverbs of Salomon*, 40.

[15]CR 14:33-35. †Although his reign is portrayed positively in the biblical accounts, Josiah inexplicably chose to support Carchemish against King Neco of Egypt, and was slain in battle (2 Chron 35:20-27). Zedekiah was the last king of Judah before the destruction of Jerusalem by Nebuchadnezzar, a disaster provoked by his decision to rebel against the king of Babylon (2 Kings 24:20). Demosthenes (384–322 BC) was a Greek orator and statesman who stirred up the Athenians to revolt against Alexander the Great, with disastrous results. Melanchthon regarded him as a prime exemplar of the vice of *polypragmosynē*, on which, see his comments on Prov 6:6 and 8:31. More remarkable here is Melanchthon's rebuke of Pompey and Cicero for resisting the tyranny of Julius Caesar. For the slaughter of the Benjaminites, see Judg 20:29–21:25.

we have no need of the promises God makes to us regarding the reforming of our hearts and minds, nor that we have any need to pray God for the ordering of our hearts, and so it would seem that the holy fathers, such as David, have prayed for these things in vain.

Second, it seems that he attributes to the creature what belongs solely to the Creator, for since "the answer of the tongue is of the Lord," it follows also that it is he who prepares the heart in causing the tongue to speak. If he has need of meddling with the governance of the tongue, it is very necessary that he have in his power the rule of the heart as well, to dispose it according to his pleasure. David understood this well, which is why he first asks for the reformation of his heart and the renewal of his spirit, before then asking that God would open his lips. And again, "O Lord, you hear the desire of the afflicted; you will strengthen their heart; you will incline your ear."

Third, it seems that he prefers the creature to the Creator, attributing more to him than to the Lord. For even though the tongue is a member very hard to control, it is nothing in comparison to the heart—indeed, it is on account of the heart itself that the tongue is so difficult to govern! And so we may point to a fourth difficulty, that it seems Solomon is attributing free will to human beings with regard to the inward operations, but denying it with regard to the outward, which are not of so great excellence—as God himself makes clear to us when he claims to have knowledge of these inner things. . . .

For these reasons, let us not think that Solomon pronounced the first part of this sentence affirmatively, as though he were attributing to a person the power of disposing of his own heart as he would. Rather, let us understand that he speaks in a human and carnal sense, so as to deride the foolish confidence of those who have the rashness to think, consult, deliberate, and undertake everything by themselves, without calling on God, seeing that without him they cannot pronounce the smallest word that might be spoken. And so still less can they purpose, consult, or undertake anything on their own. . . . We must then understand that Solomon is speaking ironically in this passage against the arrogance of those who dare to take so much in hand. On the Proverbs of Solomon.[16]

God Is Not the Cause of Evil, Only of Its Punishment. Philipp Melanchthon: The proverbs above were given to teach us to ask for God's help. This saying addresses providence, about which there are many sad doubts in people's minds. Moreover, there are two kinds of reality: the reality of good, in which order is observed, and the reality of evil, which is the order of destruction (e.g., crimes and calamities). Now, whenever the mind is moved to consider good things, it does not suppose that these arise by chance, or are maintained by chance, and yet still assent is thrown into confusion. And many philosophers have argued that the matter of heaven and earth is of such a kind as to be governed by necessity, and always has been, such that whatever bodies are generated from this matter are neither freely fashioned by an eternal mind, nor do they retain any freedom of their own.

But the very first article of Christian faith, regarding creation, warns us away from these cyclopean frenzies. On the contrary, it says that reality is not such as to come about by chance, but rather by the wisdom and goodness of God, who freely establishes and preserves all that is good—that is, heaven and earth, the seasons, the fruitfulness of the land, the generation of life in particular species, human society, the political order, the church, as well as the gifts of mind he gives to individuals: wisdom and the virtues, and the many promises of deliverance he gives to those who pray—all these things are ordained by God himself. These things all exist and are freely brought about by God for this purpose, that they may be testimonies that God exists, and that he creates and

[16] Cop, *Sur les Proverbes de Salomon*, 347-48; citing Lk 6:45; Deut 30:6; Jer 24:7; 31:33; Ezek 11:19; Ps 51:12; 51:15; 10:17; 1 Sam 16:7; Ps 7:9; Jer 17:10.

sustains with wisdom and goodness. Therefore we say that God creates for the sake of himself.

But the Epicureans† offer many inordinate objections: if God wills order, where do evil, wickedness, and calamity come from? Solomon responds with a word about punishment, for these are testimonies concerning God's providence, which is universal. Severe crimes are punished with severe penalties, even in this life, as it is said, "The one who takes up the sword will die by the sword." And more broadly, death and all calamities are punishments for original sin, as well as for other sins, as Paul says, "Through sin death entered the world." Nevertheless, it is not the case, either that God wills sin, or that he brings it about, or that he approves of it; but after human beings abuse their proper freedom, the justice of God is discerned in this ordering, that there be compensation by means of punishment.

But also the syntax of the verb "has made" must be observed. For he does not simply say, "God made the wicked," but he adds the following predicate: "He made the wicked for the day of evil"—that is, the wicked, who sin with no desire for God, he seizes for punishment. And this also is a testimony to God's providence, just as when I say that a sculptor fashioned the figure of Alexander out of marble. This sculptor does not produce the marble, but he is the artist who gives it its form; so also God is not the cause of wickedness, but by ordering justice he punishes and destroys the wicked. Exposition of the Proverbs of Solomon.[17]

Arrogance Is an Abomination. Swiss Brethren Confession of Hesse: We believe, acknowledge, and confess that all the arrogance, pride, and pomp of this world are an abomination and hated by God. For this reason the believing, newborn Christians and chosen children of God should avoid arrogance in words, works, dress, and in manners. Concerning Pride.[18]

Faith Atones for Sin. Philipp Melanchthon: "By mercy and truth sin is atoned for, and by the fear of the Lord one is turned away from evil." This is a repetition of the warning that draws a clear distinction in worship: "The sacrifice of the wicked is an abomination to the Lord." And in Hosea 6, "The knowledge of God I desire, not burnt offering, and mercy, not sacrifice." This is just another way of saying that people are not just on account of sacrifice, but only if they possess the fear of God, mercy, and truthfulness. A typical way of summarizing this teaching is: "Fight the good fight," keeping faith and a good conscience.

The "fear of the Lord" signifies a true conversion to God, in which there is fear and faith, as elsewhere is often said expressly concerning faith. The phrase is a common Hebraism, indicating sincere and unfeigned love for people, as for example Jonathan showed mercy and kept faith with David—that is, he did good to him, and he did this faithfully, consistently, and without pretense. Thus, below in chapter 20: "Mercy and truthfulness preserve a king, and his throne is supported by clemency"—that is, kindness and faithfulness are the sinews of his power. But if this is understood as a truth in respect to God, it signifies the true recognition of God, which is faith. Exposition of the Proverbs of Solomon.[19]

God's Providence Does Not Excuse Us from Acting Wisely. John Calvin: With respect to future events, Solomon easily brings

[17]CR 14:36-37; citing Mt 26:52; Rom 5:12. †Epicurus (341–270 BC) was an ancient Greek philosopher who held that the universe was infinite and eternal, and the actions of agents therein determined by the motion of atoms moving in space, a view that effectively foreclosed on the notion of divine providence. Epicurus's views were known mainly by reputation throughout the Middle Ages, but in 1417 a copy of his treatise *De rerum natura* was discovered by the Italian humanist Poggio Bracciolini, and led to a revival of interest in his views. Melanchthon uses the term "Epicurean" to describe a general tendency to downplay or deny the doctrine of God's providential ordering of human affairs.

[18]CRR 11:90*; citing Sir 10:7, 9, 12; Tob 4:14; Jdt 9:13; Is 3:18-23; 14:11; Jn 2:16; 2 Tim 3:1-2; 1 Pet 5:5.

[19]CR 14:38; citing Prov 15:8; Hos 6:6; 1 Tim 6:12; Prov 20:28.

human deliberations into agreement with God's providence. For just as he laughs at the dullness of those who boldly undertake something or other without the Lord, as though they were not ruled by his hand, so elsewhere he says, "The human heart plans its way, but the Lord will direct its steps." This means that we are not at all hindered by God's eternal decrees either from looking ahead for ourselves or from putting all our affairs in order, but always in submission to his will. The reason is obvious. For he who has set the limits to our life has at the same time entrusted to us its care; he has provided means and helps to preserve it; he has also made us able to foresee dangers; that they may not overwhelm us unaware, he has offered precautions and remedies. Now it is very clear what our duty is: thus, if the Lord has committed to us the protection of our life, our duty is to protect it; if he offers helps, to use them; if he forewarns us of dangers, not to plunge headlong; if he makes remedies available, not to neglect them. Institutes of the Christian Religion.[20]

The King Speaks God's Wisdom. Philipp Melanchthon: These sayings (vv. 10-11) affirm that the entire political order, including the magistracy, laws, separation of powers, contracts, jurisdiction, and punishment, are all ordained in God's wisdom for humankind. And even though the devil and many people rage with terrible fury against this order, unless the entire human race were to be utterly wiped out, some sort of political order would have to remain intact. For we know that it is preserved by God to good effect, just as Daniel says, "God removes and establishes kingdoms." Since we know, then, that the political order is a work of God, we obey it in due measure on account of God, and we give thanks to God for preserving it, and we know that the furies of the devil and human beings that trouble the political order are displeasing to God, as the whole teaching of Romans 13 sets out at length.

But why does it say, "An oracle [*divinatio*] is on the lips of the king, in judgment his mouth does not err?" These two clauses must be kept together: the passage speaks of the king and of his judgments, not of a tyrant and of his calumnies. The voice of the king is an oracle—that is, when he renders judgment according to the laws. For the laws themselves are called oracles, and so are the king's judgments when they are congruent with the laws, because laws are divine wisdom made manifest. For the source of all law worthy of honor is the Decalogue, which is itself a summary of natural law. And it is for this reason first and foremost that God has appointed the magistrate over humankind, that he may sing out with the voice of the Decalogue and carry out its punishments. Secondarily, God has also armed them with the power of establishing their own laws, not at variance with the Decalogue, but as extensions from it, or clarifications, or applications on the basis of sound judgment. Exposition of the Proverbs of Solomon.[21]

Solomon Derides Human Pride. John Calvin: Solomon here derides the audacious confidence of human beings when there is no plan that they will not consider, no effort that they will not dare to undertake apart from God, though they cannot even utter a word (which is a much lesser thing) except through him. It is humankind's work to prepare the heart—and it is God's to guide the tongue! Who cannot see that [this statement] is an ironical description of human pride, which claims for itself all the greatest things when it does not even have the smallest thing in its power? The Bondage and Liberation of the Will.[22]

Beware Pride and Its Fruits. Michel Cop: Let us not despise this diligence and care [in repeating this warning], and since we desire to avoid destruction, let us take heed to flee from pride, which lies not only in our outward speech

[20]LCC 20:215-16.

[21]CR 14:38-39.

[22]Lane, trans., *The Bondage and Liberation of the Will*, 223.

but chiefly in our inward affections, as Solomon indicates when he calls it a "haughty spirit." Haughty speech, and that which is bold or magniloquent, is not properly pride, but it is the fruit of pride. Therefore in order to flee from pride, let us reform our affections, becoming not only humble and lowly in our bearing, but above all humble in mind. In doing so we shall not be beaten down but raised up, for whoever humbles himself shall be exalted—not by human beings, but by God, and so the exaltation shall be eternal. And insofar as pride goes before destruction, if we are forced to undergo some destruction, let us confess that we have not walked in humility, but that pride has taken and beaten us down. Therefore we should consider that it is our own thoughts and affections which have destroyed us, and not the visible adversaries or accidents which happen without foresight. ON THE PROVERBS OF SOLOMON.[23]

IN BUSINESS, BE DELIBERATE, BE WISE, AND TRUST GOD. THE ENGLISH ANNOTATIONS: Those who will bring their affairs to a good end must have an understanding of their business and trust in God. Or thus: it is good and commendable for a person, when they go about any business, to use deliberation, and to make use of their best discretion concerning how they carry it out. There is a better hope of a good result when that is done. Nevertheless, let no person trust their own wisdom and discretion, but they should put their trust in God and depend on him for the event, which for one to do in all things is the chiefest happiness. ANNOTATIONS ON PROVERBS 16:20.[24]

AGE IS A CROWN OF REVERENCE. JOHN DONNE: Even in nature, age was the center of reverence—the channel, the valley, to which all reverence flowed. Temporal jurisdiction and spiritual jurisdiction, the magistracy and the priesthood, were appropriated to the eldest; almost in all vulgar languages, the name of a lord or a magistrate has no other derivation than so, an elder; *senior noster* is a word that passes freely through the authors of the Middle Ages, for our lord or our king, and the same derivation has the name of priest, in a holy language, *presbyter*, an elder. So evermore in the course of Scripture, all counsel and all government is placed in the elders, and all the service of God is expressed so, even in heaven too, by the four-and-twenty elders. Your Creator will be remembered in the days of your youth, but God has had longer experience of that person, and longer conversation with that person, who has come to a holy age. That wise king, who could carry nothing to a higher pitch in any comparison than to a crown, says, "Age is a crown of glory, when it is found in the ways of the righteous"; but in the ways of righteousness, no blessing is a blessing; and in the ways of righteousness, wealth may be a crown of labors, and health may be a crown of temperance, but age is the crown of reverence, of glory. SERMON ON LUKE 2:29-30.[25]

SEEKING GOD'S GUIDANCE IN PRAYER. CARDINAL CAJETAN: "Lots are thrown into the lap, but they are determined by the Lord." The second phrase according to the Hebrew reads, "and their entire judgment is from Jehovah." Among the Hebrews the casting of lots was common, and people used to throw the lots into the lap. This practice served them in place of legal judgment, but they waited for the outcome of the lots not from human beings but from God Most High. And so the lots were assigned not to chance or luck but to the judgment of divine providence. So God would guide a good lot to the one who pleased his majesty more. Therefore people cast their lots in the presence of God (i.e., with sacrifices or prayers). THE PARABLES OF SOLOMON, CORRECTED BY THE ORIGINAL HEBREW.[26]

[23]Cop, *Sur les Proverbes de Salomon*, 362; citing Mt 23:12.
[24]Downame, ed., *English Annotations*, 6X1r*.
[25]Donne, *Works*, 1:63*; citing Rev 4:9.
[26]Cajetan, *Parabolae Salomonis ad veritatem Hebraicam castigatae*, 152.

17:1-28 *On Friendship, Joy, and Discernment*

We Need God's Help to Judge Ourselves. The English Annotations: People can find out other things, but not other people's thoughts. Indeed, it is a work for a person to know their own heart. Nothing is more deceitful, and wherein people are more subject to be beguiled, than in judging themselves. Without great diligence and humility and seeking after God in prayer, it is not to be done. Hence it is that most people live securely because they are so insensible and ignorant of their condition, as has been observed more than once. The words may be understood of trials and afflictions by which God usually cleanses and purifies those whom he has destined to glory. Annotations on Proverbs 17:3.[27]

We Insult the Poor by Neglect. Michel Cop: All the world boasts that it honors God, and they persuade themselves that they are in no way displeasing to him. For there is no people so barbarous, superstitious, and idolatrous, nor so debauched and dissolute, excessive and intemperate, that they have not some manner of practice by which they think to serve God. Indeed, every individual makes effort in some degree to govern themselves so that others think that they seek the honor of God, or at least that they may persuade themselves that they do so. And yet we still despise the stranger, the fatherless, the widow, and others who are poor and needy. To be sure, they are wronged and oppressed against the express ordinance of God, who has commanded, "You shall not do injury to a stranger, nor oppress him, for you were strangers in the land of Egypt. You shall not trouble any widow, nor fatherless child." In so doing, we mock the poor, and such mockery is not ultimately directed against a human being but against God, and does him grave dishonor. . . .

This is all too common in popery. For although they persuade themselves that they intend no such injury to God, when we make no account of the poor in comparison to images and ceremonies—and even tax the poor to maintain them!—the effect demonstrates the contrary. Would to God that they who preen themselves as being "reformed" by the gospel were not given to such mockery—or even worse! But what? To maintain themselves at their ease and pleasure, to win credit and authority, they will use cruelty toward the poor, or at least will make themselves companions with those who oppress them, so they hold up their chin (as it were) and make them all the more bold. All such people who make it their sport and pastime to abuse the poor in this manner do so to their own destruction. For they will not escape unpunished.

This is what Solomon declares when he says, "The one who rejoices in their destruction will not go unpunished." He calls "destruction" the sorrow and vexation, the damage and detriment, the ruin and desolation that the poor suffer because they are without human help, and are tormented and molested with no one lifting a finger to help, as they ought—or rather, those who ought to help plunder what little the poor do have. This violence may well be called "destruction," when they who do it care not what misery and desolation they bring on the poor, and would rather put them to death than to fail in devouring them—even to the point of forcing them to beg their bread. This is why the Scripture calls them murderers and manslayers. And so they well deserve punishment, in accordance with the threats contained in many different passages of Scripture, which show that God will execute judgment. And just as there is no one of sound judgment who would wish to be accounted a mocker, nor to hold God in contempt, nor a destroyer of the poor, nor one deserving of God's punishment, we must "weep with those who weep," and have compassion on our poor members who suffer, showing mercy by unfeigned charity to the needy. For "I desire mercy, and not sacrifice." In doing this, we honor God. For the good we do to the poor is reckoned as

[27]Downame, ed., *English Annotations*, 6X2r*.

having been done to God. On the Proverbs of Solomon.[28]

On Giving and Receiving Counsel. Philipp Melanchthon: The proverbs in this section (17:9-12) all relate to the ordering of judgment, which is comprehended by the saying of Christ: "If your brother sins against you, reprove him between yourselves alone." Pastors and others who especially have the duty of teaching, when they learn of some error or unjust deed that has been committed, should first admonish the person in private. If they will not mend their ways, then let there be a public accusation. But there should be truth and candor in those who give counsel, and they should not seek to cast blame on others with calumny. The one who receives a warning should be gentle, not contumacious, and on neither side let there be *philoneikia*—that is, a lust for contention.† Thus this passage gives guidance both to those who counsel others, and to those who receive it. . . .

But one may ask, how is it possible for a person to be convinced? I answer: in public affairs, a person is convinced by legitimate judgment and judicial opinion. In philosophy, there are three common norms, which are called criteria: universal experience, practical principles, and knowledge of logical consequences. In church doctrine concerning the law and the articles of faith, one is convinced by the testimonies of the prophets and apostles (properly cited), and by the creeds. For there is no ambiguous doctrine in the church when it comes to the foundational matters. Exposition of the Proverbs of Solomon.[29]

Beware Perverting Justice. Ludwig Lavater: This proverb pertains primarily to judges, whose official duties require (among other things) passing sentence [on criminals]. But a judge sins in settling on a penalty if he causes the death of the innocent, or if he sets free those whom God commands must be killed. [The Hebrew] *maṣdiq* means "to justify," that is, "to absolve," the opposite of which is *maršîaʿ*, "to declare guilty," if one may speak so, or "to condemn" and so hand over to God for execution. The sense of the passage is this: the one who damns the innocent and absolves the guilty, both are equally hated by God.

From this we may inquire what Paul means when he writes concerning the manner by which a person can be justified—that is, how they are absolved and set free from eternal death. We stand before the judgment seat of God, and we are accused not only by the devil but also by our own consciences, and convicted of sin, for which we deserve eternal death. The question now is: How can we be saved? Paul responds: by faith in Christ, who by his death has taken away eternal death.

To injure an innocent person, even with a word, is a great sin; how much worse is it to rob someone of their life? This is especially so when done under a pretext of justice, as happened to Naboth, and to many people today who are subjected to various punishments for the sake of true religion, as though they were heretics of destructive people. For the magistrate has received a sword from God to protect the good and to cut down the bad, as Romans 13 explains. It is a great benefit to the entire commonwealth if there are many honest citizens in any state, but if the magistrates remove such people, they are an abomination to God. What we abhor we can neither bear to look at nor even to hear about with equanimity; in the same way God averts his eyes from those people and does not deign to hear their prayers, unless they repent. But even though those who condemn the righteous sin most grievously, yet they also sin who acquit the unjust. For they transgress the first commandment of God, which not only commands the killing of criminals for grave offenses but also threatens execution to the judges, unless they kill those whom he commands them to kill. Nor does any guilt cling to the magistrate who inflicts

[28]Cop, *Sur les Proverbes de Salomon*, 376-77; citing Ex 22:21-22; cf., Lev 19:33; Is 1:21; Hos 4:1-2; Ps 94:3; Zech 11:4-5; 1 Jn 3:15; Rom 12:15; 1 Cor 12:26; Mt 9:13; Prov 14:31; Mt 25:40.

[29]CR 14:39-41; citing Mt 18:15. †On *philoneikia*, see Melanchthon's comments on Prov 15:1.

punishments on criminals according to good laws, and for this reason the maxim is often repeated: their blood be on their own heads. But if he neglects the duties of his calling and grants pardon to the wicked, he himself has become vicious. On the Book of Proverbs, or Sayings, of Solomon the Most-Wise King.[30]

Flattery Whitewashes Evil. Michael Jermin: When Jacob blessed the sons of Joseph, Manasseh and Ephraim, he put his hands across and laid his right hand on Ephraim's head (who was the younger), and his left hand on the head of Manasseh (the older). This displeased Joseph, and he say, "Not so, my father!" But Jacob refused to have his hands removed. Now what Jacob did in blessing his grandchildren, this very same thing is the cursed deed of many who in the world are seated in the place of justice. For those whom God sets on his right hand they set on the left; those whom God sets on his left hand, they set on the right. Those whom God justifies, they condemn; those whom God condemns, they justify. And though God himself calls to them, "Not so!" still they refuse to alter their sentence. But if Joseph were displeased that his father did this, much more is God displeased with their doings. And though their hands in justifying and condemning go across, yet being joined together in wickedness they are both an abomination to the Lord. For how great is the wickedness of the one who justifies the wicked? How great shall their condemnation be who condemn the just? The prophet Ezekiel speaks of some who, when one has built up a wall, paints it with whitewash, about which St. Gregory says, "By the name of a wall the hardness of sin is signified, and to build this wall is for anyone to set up against himself the obstacles of sin; but those who paint it, who flatter those who commit the sin, or else do (as it were) by their flattering adorn that which those others have built in doing wickedly."† But woe to those who call evil good and good evil. Paraphrastic Meditations.[31]

Handshakes, Not Oaths. Peter Riedemann: To shake hands and embrace are signs of peace, love, and unity in God, signs by which those who are in the church community show that they are of one mind, one heart, and one soul. . . . When hands are clasped within each other, people show that their hearts are likewise knit together. The same is true of embracing. Just as people put their arms around one another, so each enfolds the other in their heart. Because these two signs are of peace, they should be observed strictly and firmly in the church in the fear of God, and in a way that expresses their inner meaning. One member of the church should receive another with this reverence.

However, if one person acts in this way towards another without having one's heart turned in that direction, that person is a hypocrite and the truth is not within them. In the world, where handshakes are a sign of friendliness, a Christian may use the handshake as such with the people of the world. When a handshake, however, is a sign of swearing an oath, it should not be used.

However, since both shaking hands and embracing mean the same thing, therefore, in order not to offend, and also to avoid a situation where flesh might be tempted to sin, a brother should only embrace his brother and a sister embrace her sisters. In this way they express what is in their heart. Between brothers and sisters, this love should only be expressed by shaking hands and not by embracing, because nothing should be allowed to bring the teaching of Christ into disrepute or dishonor. The Hutterite Confession of Faith.[32]

[30]Lavater, *In librum Proverbiorum siue Sententiarum Solomonis Regis sapientissimi*, 176.

[31]Jermin, *Paraphrasticall Meditations*, 374-75. †Gregory the Great, *Moralia, sive Expositio in Job* 18.4.8; citing Gen 48:18, Ezek 13:10.

[32]CRR 9:144*; citing Acts 2:42-46; 4:32; Gal 2:9; Phil 2:29; Rom 12:1-10; 1 Pet 1:22; Jn 3:16-18; Mt 18:6-10.

18:1–19:29 JUDGMENT, DISCERNMENT, AND JUSTICE

1 *Whoever isolates himself seeks his own desire;*
he breaks out against all sound judgment.

2 *A fool takes no pleasure in understanding,*
but only in expressing his opinion.

3 *When wickedness comes, contempt comes also,*
and with dishonor comes disgrace.

4 *The words of a man's mouth are deep waters;*
the fountain of wisdom is a bubbling brook.

5 *It is not good to be partial to*[a] *the wicked*
or to deprive the righteous of justice.

6 *A fool's lips walk into a fight,*
and his mouth invites a beating.

7 *A fool's mouth is his ruin,*
and his lips are a snare to his soul.

8 *The words of a whisperer are like delicious morsels;*
they go down into the inner parts of the body.

9 *Whoever is slack in his work*
is a brother to him who destroys.

10 *The name of the LORD is a strong tower;*
the righteous man runs into it and is safe.

11 *A rich man's wealth is his strong city,*
and like a high wall in his imagination.

12 *Before destruction a man's heart is haughty,*
but humility comes before honor.

13 *If one gives an answer before he hears,*
it is his folly and shame.

14 *A man's spirit will endure sickness,*
but a crushed spirit who can bear?

15 *An intelligent heart acquires knowledge,*
and the ear of the wise seeks knowledge.

16 *A man's gift makes room for him*
and brings him before the great.

17 *The one who states his case first seems right,*
until the other comes and examines him.

18 *The lot puts an end to quarrels*
and decides between powerful contenders.

19 *A brother offended is more unyielding than a strong city,*
and quarreling is like the bars of a castle.

20 *From the fruit of a man's mouth his stomach is satisfied;*
he is satisfied by the yield of his lips.

21 *Death and life are in the power of the tongue,*
and those who love it will eat its fruits.

22 *He who finds a wife finds a good thing*
and obtains favor from the LORD.

23 *The poor use entreaties,*
but the rich answer roughly.

24 *A man of many companions may come to ruin,*
but there is a friend who sticks closer than a brother.

19 *Better is a poor person who walks in his integrity*
than one who is crooked in speech and is a fool.

2 *Desire*[b] *without knowledge is not good,*
and whoever makes haste with his feet misses his way.

3 *When a man's folly brings his way to ruin,*
his heart rages against the LORD.

4 *Wealth brings many new friends,*
but a poor man is deserted by his friend.

5 *A false witness will not go unpunished,*
and he who breathes out lies will not escape.

6 *Many seek the favor of a generous man,*[c]
and everyone is a friend to a man who gives gifts.

7 All a poor man's brothers hate him;
how much more do his friends go far from him!

He pursues them with words, but does not have them.[d]

8 Whoever gets sense loves his own soul;
he who keeps understanding will discover good.

9 A false witness will not go unpunished,
and he who breathes out lies will perish.

10 It is not fitting for a fool to live in luxury,
much less for a slave to rule over princes.

11 Good sense makes one slow to anger,
and it is his glory to overlook an offense.

12 A king's wrath is like the growling of a lion,
but his favor is like dew on the grass.

13 A foolish son is ruin to his father,
and a wife's quarreling is a continual dripping of rain.

14 House and wealth are inherited from fathers,
but a prudent wife is from the Lord.

15 Slothfulness casts into a deep sleep,
and an idle person will suffer hunger.

16 Whoever keeps the commandment keeps his life;
he who despises his ways will die.

17 Whoever is generous to the poor lends to the Lord,
and he will repay him for his deed.

18 Discipline your son, for there is hope;
do not set your heart on putting him to death.

19 A man of great wrath will pay the penalty,
for if you deliver him, you will only have to do it again.

20 Listen to advice and accept instruction,
that you may gain wisdom in the future.

21 Many are the plans in the mind of a man,
but it is the purpose of the Lord that will stand.

22 What is desired in a man is steadfast love,
and a poor man is better than a liar.

23 The fear of the Lord leads to life,
and whoever has it rests satisfied;
he will not be visited by harm.

24 The sluggard buries his hand in the dish
and will not even bring it back to his mouth.

25 Strike a scoffer, and the simple will learn prudence;
reprove a man of understanding, and he will gain knowledge.

26 He who does violence to his father and chases away his mother
is a son who brings shame and reproach.

27 Cease to hear instruction, my son,
and you will stray from the words of knowledge.

28 A worthless witness mocks at justice,
and the mouth of the wicked devours iniquity.

29 Condemnation is ready for scoffers,
and beating for the backs of fools.

a Hebrew *to lift the face of* **b** Or *A soul* **c** Or *of a noble* **d** The meaning of the Hebrew sentence is uncertain

Overview: Judges and judgment are themes many of our Reformation-era commentators find reason to elaborate on in this section of proverbs. John Donne argues that the hand is the tool of the tongue, executing judgment after a sentence has been pronounced, while Philipp Melanchthon provides two lengthy comments on judgment, reminding believers to consider their own faults before judging those of others and teaching them that God's punishment is necessary to restore justice after the fall. Michel Cop, on the other hand, is concerned for fairness in human courts, warning his readers about crooked judges and the ways that wealth can be used to exploit the justice system. Financial justice is another concern for our exegetes, and both Martin Luther and Ludwig Lavater consider the nature of loans and the need for generosity toward the poor, while Melanchthon provides a meditation on the ways in which wealth can lead to foolishness, arguing that prosperity leads to laziness and neglect, and so prescribes a life of disciplined work in one's calling as the solution. Other commentators consider the nature of human relationships, with Konrad Pellikan and Lavater warning against those who seek to stir up trouble, while Cardinal Cajetan and Melanchthon reflect on the nature of courtship and marriage.

18:1-24 *A Fool's Mouth and the Name of the Lord*

Looking for Trouble. Konrad Pellikan: In Hebrew the passage reads, "For desire separation is sought; against everything that stands, calumny is found." According to this sense, "desire" refers to vain pleasure, and so an excuse for withdrawing from a friend or from society is sought on the basis of any trifling desire or pretext; so it is easy to latch on to an excuse for leaving a friend. And to everything that happens to be within reach, whatever the matter or the amount, an enemy discovers reason for contempt or calumny. For no one lives so well, or teaches so truly, that such a person is not driven by malice and obloquy to invent a reason for speaking ill of them. But conversely, those who are good and simple always seek a reason to forgive evil, so that good may be done and justice promoted. Thus it would not be inept to render the translation as follows: "When discord is sought on thin pretext, it is discovered in everything." A Succinct and Universal Commentary on the Bible.[1]

Beware Lovers of Strife. Ludwig Lavater: This proverb is difficult to understand, so I simply follow the ancient version and render the sense according to the Septuagint's interpretation: "The person who is isolated follows their passion, and they will embroil themselves in every matter." The person whose mind is alienated from everyone seeks the occasion to withdraw from them according to their desire, and they will certainly find it. *Tûšîâ* is interpreted variously as a good work, thing, cause, success, wisdom, religion, and so on. *Gāla*, found thus in the *hithpael*, indicates to be mixed, or to embroil oneself, become involved or implicated. Reckoned according to this sense, it refers to those who break apart a friendship without just causes.

We often find that our friends who have become alienated in mind from us will fabricate many reasons why they have withdrawn from us. And this also holds true in matters of greater import. There are those who abhor true religion, and they allege many reasons for doing so: they throw before us the discord among the church's ministers, or their dissolute lives, and so they tell us that they reject the gospel, because evangelicals are in the habit of separating. The Anabaptists, when they fled from holy society, had their own pretexts. Not wanting it to seem that they were acting from fear, they said that the preachers did not live up to what they taught, they accepted remuneration, there was no discipline. . . . The Pharisees and scribes were alienated in mind from Christ, and so they hurled calumnies against everything he said and did. Thus it can be seen that the sense of this passage is not so different from what is noted elsewhere, that those who separate themselves from others in mind are led by passion: strife is always dear to them, and wars and fighting.[†] These people will always tangle themselves up in every matter, even the most insuperable, violently hurling accusations without end. To this effect people are

[1]Pellikan, *Commentaria bibliorum et illa brevia quidem ac catholica*, 228v. The Vulgate reads, "He who wants to depart from a friend seeks opportunities; he will always be subject to reproach." The sense of the Hebrew is difficult, as the commentators' exegesis suggests. One modern commentator has translated the verse as follows: "The misfit seeks pretexts; he attacks all competence." Michael V. Fox, *Proverbs 10–31: A New Translation with Introduction and Commentary*, Anchor Bible 18B (New Haven: Yale University Press, 2008), 637.

reckoned lovers of strife (*philonikeis*) who are easily roused to combat for any reason at all.[‡] On the Book of Proverbs, or Sayings, of Solomon the Most-Wise King.[2]

Bribery Distorts Justice. Michel Cop: Solomon has already rebuked the avarice and injustice of magistrates, judges, and rulers of the earth. And because such wickedness reigns and abounds throughout the whole world and is rooted so deeply in people's hearts, so that at all times and in all lands they have spread forth their branches and brought forth their wicked fruits, he is not satisfied with the previous reprehensions. But to make these greedy, ungodly, and wicked thieves who occupy the seat of God all the more inexcusable, he reproves them for this: that the poor who bring them no gifts are trodden down and oppressed. Only those who bring gifts are given a warm welcome, but they do this only under compulsion, since free access to the seat of justice is not otherwise open to them. On the Proverbs of Solomon.[3]

The Innocent Speak Up Quickly. Cardinal Cajetan: "The one to accuse first is right, then his friend comes and will question him." The first phrase here according to the Hebrew reads, "the first man in his lawsuit is righteous." No mention is made here of the accusation, and it is also employs a future tense, "and he will come." It is, moreover, a proverb that when a lawsuit or complaint comes against a righteous man and generally when some accusation is made against him, the first righteous person to speak does not wait for the accuser or witnesses, but knows that he is righteous. The first person speaks confidently of his own innocence. But he speaks the truth, and does not wait to be examined and to answer objections. But there must be someone to question him who is not an enemy, and therefore the author adds, and his friend will come, who does not behave from hatred or some passion toward the righteous man. It is not the friend of just any person, I say, who comes, but of a righteous man, and will question him by examining his case. Because if the judge were not a friend of righteousness his judgment could be easily corrupted. The Parables of Solomon, Corrected by the Original Hebrew.[4]

Judge Yourself First. Philipp Melanchthon: "The just person is his own first accuser; afterward he searches for another."[†] Among all humankind, self-regard (*philautia*) and pride (*superbia*) are the sources of idiocy. We flatter ourselves and raise ourselves up above others, and in this way we are deluded. We love parasites who fawn on us, and we turn a blind eye on our own faults, preferring instead for others to seem inferior. Thus we judge harshly the faults of others, showing great forbearance to ourselves, even as we set ourselves up as critics and Momos of others.[‡] We are blind to our own vices, even as we spot the vices of others with the keenness of a Lynceus.[§] We are wise abroad, and foolish at home. Hence it is said, "To each their own beauty."[◊] And Cicero says to Atticus, "To each his own bride, but give me mine. To each his own love, but give me mine."[Δ] Hence the fable of the two knapsacks, concerning which Catullus says, "Each person has their own fault to bear, but we do not see the bag that hangs on our back."[††] And Horace: "When you look at your own sins your eyes are dim and feeble; how is it that you spot the vices of your friend so clearly?"[‡‡] . . .

But set against this self-regard and perversity of judgment is the admonition that is handed down in this proverb: "The just person is their own first accuser"—that is, they inquire into themselves; they know their own infirmity and their own faults, and because they are just, they are the first to lay

[2]Lavater, *In librum Proverbiorum siue Sententiarum Solomonis Regis sapientissimi*, 182-83. [†]Lavater here paraphrases Zeus's harsh critique of Ares (Homer, *Iliad* 5.891). [‡]Melanchthon also elaborates on the vice of *philoneikia* in this comments on Prov 15:1.

[3]Cop, *Sur les Proverbes de Salomon*, 402; citing Prov 17:8, 23.

[4]Cajetan, *Parabolae Salomonis ad veritatem Hebraicam castigatae*, 163.

charges against themselves. This accords with the saying, "It is disgraceful for a teacher when they are refuted by their own guilt."[§§] Moreover, even the just have their warts, as it is written: "There is no just person on earth who does good and does not sin." But because they are just, they truly confess their sins. They do not defend their faults and errors, but are the first to find fault with themselves, and amend their ways. And only after this do they give any thought to how they ought to judge others: not on the basis of frivolous suspicion, but only with sound reason. . . .

The Greek interpreter of Solomon's text used a significant term in this passage: the just accuse themselves in a *prōtologia*. Now *prōtologia* is a term drawn from courtroom jargon, and it refers to an accusatory statement lodged against a defendant. But it is difficult afterward to uproot from the mind an opinion it has first conceived, as Demosthenes says. Now consider how many censorious people there are everywhere, and how well he describes the picture of the hypocrite, who having a beam in his own eye seeks to remove the mote from that of another.

But many other vices accompany this perversity of judgment: self-regard, pride, being a busybody, cruelty, and when they are not constrained by hypocrisy they only exercise themselves in other forms of savagery. But if we recognize our own peculiar vices, we should be moved by mercy toward the cure, and be diligent to be healed in keeping with our vocation. So we remember that saying of Gregory of Nazianzus: "If you are truly aware of what you owe, seek mercy above all else, for the merciful will be repaid by God with mercy."[◊◊] Exposition of the Proverbs of Solomon.[5]

A Warning Against Crooked Judges. Michel Cop: "Those who are first in their own cause are just; then come their neighbors to make inquiries of them." It is a very dangerous thing to have dealings with an ignorant judge, one who does not know their office or is easily inclined to believe one party, and then does not care to hear the other side of the case, but condemns a defendant out of hand, even if they have the law on their side. With a judge like this, the one who gets their say in first will win the day, even though their case is weaker, regardless of the defense given by the other party. . . . For this reason, Solomon complains, saying, "Those who are first in their own cause are just. . . ." It is not without reason that he makes this complaint, for the office of a judge requires them to hear the poor as well as the rich, the stranger as well as his own father, and the last as well as the first, and to judge every person rightly. He must have an equal balance for all people, for judges sit in the seat of God, as King Jehoshaphat says, "Take care what you do, for you judge not for humans but for the Lord." . . . Some interpret this text to mean that just persons accuse themselves first, and then are judged by others, as Jesus Christ teaches. But we must add to this view that just people allow their neighbors to teach, admonish, and correct them, because he then goes on to say, "their neighbor comes to make inquiries of them." So we are admonished not to take it upon ourselves to be masters, but rather to allow ourselves to be corrected, like young students, as James exhorts us. And needless to say, this does not mean that we should fail to reprove those who sin against us, as Christ has commanded us to do. On the Proverbs of Solomon.[6]

---

[5]CR 14:39-41; citing Eccles 7:21. [†]Melanchthon's rendering of this verse reflects the Septuagint reading. [‡]Momos (*Mōmos*) was a figure who personified fault-finding in Greek literature. See, for example, Hesiod, *Theogony* 214; Lucian, *Juppiter tragoedus* 19. [§]Lynkeus, one of the Argonauts, was famed for his sharp eyes (Horace, *Satires* 1.2.90; Cicero, *Epistulae ad familiares* 9.2.2). [◊]Cicero, *Tusculanae disputationes* 5.22.63. [Δ]Cicero, *Epistulae ad Atticum* 14.20.3. [††]Catullus, *Poems* 22.20-21. Modern readers may be more familiar with the version told by Aesop: "Every man carries two bags about with him, one in front and one behind, and both are packed full of faults. The bag in front contains his neighbors' faults, the one behind his own." [‡‡]Horace, *Satires* 1.3.25-26. [§§]*Catonis Disticha* 1.521. [◊◊]Gregory of Nazianzus, *Carminum* 1.2.33; PG 37:939.159-60.

[6]Cop, *Sur les Proverbes de Salomon*, 403-4; citing 2 Chron 19:6; Mt 7:1; Jas 3:1; Mt 18:15.

TONGUE, WHERE ARE YOU GOING? DESIDERIUS ERASMUS: "Tongue, where are you going?" [*Lingua quo vadis?*] To build a city, and then again to overthrow it. Recorded by Suidas, Zenodotus, and Diogenianus.† Its message is that the tongue can be the greatest benefit to mortals and again can bring on them the greatest disasters, although as a member of the body it is very small indeed. Hence the apostle St. James compares it to a nail in a ship's timbers, which is a very small part of the whole and yet either keeps the ship safe and sound or destroys it. Plutarch in his essay *On How to Study* tells a story of Bias, which recurs in his *On Garrulity*;† when Amasis, tyrant of Egypt, told Bias to bring him the best and worst pieces of meat in the victim that he sent him, Bias cut out the tongue and sent that, indicating that it was the outstanding instrument, whether you wish to do good or harm. There is much point in Solomon's remark in chapter 18, that "Death and life are in the power of the tongue." ADAGES.[7]

THE HAND EXECUTES THE SENTENCE OF THE TONGUE. JOHN DONNE: Solomon puts both hand and tongue together: "Death and life are in the hand of the tongue." God's tongue has a hand; where his sentence goes before, the execution follows. Nay, in the execution of the last judgment, we shall feel the hand before we hear the tongue; it is "Go you accursed." First you must go, go out of the presence of God, and by that being gone, you shall know that you are accursed. In other proceedings, the sentence denounces the execution, but here, the execution denounces the sentence. SERMON ON ISAIAH 65:20.[8]

ON TAKING CARE IN COURTSHIP. CARDINAL CAJETAN: "He who finds a good wife finds blessing, and he will draw happiness from the Lord." The Hebrew does not have the adjective "good" with "wife." And the word translated "happiness" means "will," or "goodwill." . . . And so the first phrase is, "He who finds a woman finds a blessing." "To find" is properly taken as distinct from "to discover." For we find things that we sought, but we discover things that just come to us. So the meaning is that the one who finds a wife after a careful search finds a blessing. By this Solomon teaches that one should not promise to marry a woman unless a careful search has first been conducted. For if he then finds a wife he finds a blessing because he has spent time carefully looking into the woman's circumstances, and he agrees to marry only a good woman. Therefore, this part is added, and he has acquired good favor (or what he wanted from Jehovah), because he obtained what he wanted from God Most High. And so the author teaches that taking a wife requires two things: first, engaging in a careful search; and second, acknowledging that this benefit—finding the sort of woman he has described—comes from God Most High. THE PARABLES OF SOLOMON, CORRECTED BY THE ORIGINAL HEBREW.[9]

MAINTAINING PURITY IN MARRIAGE. PHILIPP MELANCHTHON: Consider the word choice in this passage. The word "to find" means "to lead happily." "To find a wife," therefore, means to lead her happily into marriage, or as the Greeks have it, *eutychōs eutychōn*. This language thus signifies a unique gift from God: the happiness, gentleness, and pious unity in which the lover and his wife are joined is in harmony at once with the church and with God, according to that verse which reads, "[May your marriage be happy in the divine will of Christ,] and may there be one mind and one love in God."†

Therefore, in the following chapter we read that "a prudent wife is from the Lord." For both of these proverbs illustrate and bear witness that marriage is pleasing to God. And with singular emphasis it is added that "he draws pleasure from the Lord," as if to say, "There are many dangers in life, and a

[7]CWE 33:93; Jas 3:4-5. †Zenodotus, *Greek Anthology* 2.99; Diogenianus, *Paroemiographi Graeci* 4.9; *Suidas*, Γ 296. †Plutarch, *Moralia* 38B; 506C. The story is told of Pittacus, not Bias. [8]Donne, *Works*, 4:464*.

[9]Cajetan, *Parabolae Salomonis ad veritatem Hebraicam castigatae*, 165.

multitude of common miseries; nevertheless, in this God will guard the marriage of those who together call on him and who rejoice in God, because they know that he cares for them." Such was the marriage of Zechariah and Elizabeth, and other pious folk whom God marvelously protected when armies of the cruelest nations continually ravaged the land of Judea. And when Lamyrus slaughtered thirty thousand Jews and forced the captives to eat the corpses of their murdered dead, even then God protected Zechariah, Elizabeth, Mary, and her parents, just as he saved the three men in the Babylonian furnace.[†] But the word "drawing" typically alludes to fountains or flowing waters, and this signifies numerous, powerful, and sweet consolations—almost as it were a re-creation.

Moreover, one may discover here a whole doctrine of purity (*castitas*) and marriage. God brings male and female together, because he desires the human race to be the church.[§] And he joined male and female together by a firm law, and circumscribed boundaries, and prohibited wandering lusts so that human beings might have an understanding of purity. For God wanted it to be understood that our minds must be pure, and so it is by thinking that we discern in prayer the nature of impurity. For it is necessary that we understand what it is that we pray for. And because we cannot embrace God with our arms, but must rather address him with our minds, we must understand this how and where he makes it clear to us. And so we say, "Almighty God, eternal Father of our Lord Jesus Christ, Maker of heaven and earth, of angels and of humans, one with your Son, our Lord Jesus Christ, and with your Holy Spirit, wise, good , true, just, merciful, judge, pure and free: have mercy on us for the sake of your Son Jesus Christ, whom you desired to be a sacrifice for us, a Mediator and Intercessor, and justify us on his account, and through him; and sanctify us by your Holy Spirit in truth and purity."

Therefore let it be understood regarding this teaching about purity that we are to preserve the most severe divine threats, as they are elaborated in Leviticus 18 and 1 Corinthians 6: it is not possible for fornicators, adulterers, and murderers, and so on to inherit the kingdom of God. And in the letter to the Hebrews: God will judge fornicators and adulterers. And in witness to this, there are examples of punishment expressly stated in Leviticus, where the Canaanites are destroyed on account of the chaos of their lustful desires.[◊] Therefore let us burn in our prayers for purity from God, because however great was God's anger against the iniquities of the nations, and however much the devil inflames people to evil, so great is God's desire to preserve us when we pray for purity. Exposition of the Proverbs of Solomon.[10]

19:1-29 *Desire Without Knowledge*

Be Careful What You Wish For. Michel Cop: Those who are not instructed by the Word of God, but led by the sense of their own corrupt nature, and according to the appetites of the flesh, have various desires, and they hasten (as much as they can) to attain their ends and to enjoy them. They still think that there is no harm in desiring that which they have in their imaginations, though they do not know what the end will be, nor if it is profitable for them to obtain what they desire. Even if the world does not reprove and condemn such desires, this does not mean that the Holy

[10]CR 14:43-44; citing 1 Cor 6:9; Heb 13:4.[†]Melanchthon is quoting an epigram that he himself wrote for his friend Johannes Stigelius on the occasion of his wedding in 1544 (CR 5:399). Oddly, he only quotes the second line of the doublet in this context, but I have supplied the first half, for the sake of clarity. [†]The historical reference is obscure. Josephus records an incident in which Ptolomy IX Soter (r. 116–81 BC), nicknamed Lathyrus, slaughtered the inhabitants of some unnamed Judean villages and forced his own soldiers to cook and eat the corpses (*Antiquities of the Jews* 13.345-47). If Melanchthon has some version of this account in mind, he may be suggesting that God's providence preserved the ancestors of Zachariah, etc. [§]A wordplay on the original meaning of the Greek *ekklēsia*: a body gathered or assembled together. The idea is that just as the church is a gathering of believers, this reflects the reality that God desires the human race to be constituted by the compound of male and female. [◊]Apparently a reference to Leviticus 18, where a lengthy catalog of illicit sexual practices concludes with the warning, "Do not make yourselves unclean by any of these things, for by all these the nations I am driving out before you have become unclean" (Lev 18:24).

Spirit ceases to blame and reject them as unprofitable and wicked, saying by Solomon, "Desire without understanding is not good," for this is to press after that which God forbids. "You shall not covet your neighbor's house; you shall not covet your neighbor's wife, or his male servant, or his female servant, or his ox, or his donkey, or anything that is your neighbor's."

Therefore, since God has given such a commandment, it is not without reason that Solomon lays blame on those who break it. For it is not lawful to approve that which God forbids, for it is his will alone that should suffice for our perfect rule of justice and equity. Likewise, we naturally perceive that our desires often provoke us to strife and debate, when we do not obtain them and enjoy them at our pleasure. And therefore St. James rightly rebukes the covetous. But we see that the ancient holy fathers (such as Abraham) had desires that were not reproved—indeed, they often obtained much more than they asked for! So Abraham desired an heir, but his desire was in accordance with understanding, which was made manifest according to the promises. Jacob desired that the Lord God should assist him, as he had been promised, and David often desired to be delivered from his enemies, for he knew that God willed that he should reign in Israel. Also, seeing that it is God's will that we should call on him, and that our Lord God has taught us to pray, and that he promises to hear us, we ought to understand that Solomon is not impugning all desire, for he himself had asked and obtained. And so in this place he does not say absolutely, "Desire is not good," but he adds "without understanding," as if to say that when we wish for anything for which we do not have certain testimony in our consciences that the Word of God allows it, the wish is not good. It is without faith, which is the foundation of all goodness, even the goodness of our desires, and without this it is impossible to please God. On the Proverbs of Solomon.[11]

[11]Cop, *Sur les Proverbes de Salomon*, 409; citing Ex 20:17; Jas 4:1; Gen 15:2; 13:14; 28:20-22; Ps 50:15.

Make Fools Work for a Living. Philipp Melanchthon: All people share in common this weakness, that in fortunate circumstances they become more neglectful, just as it is commonly said, "The soul becomes enfeebled by an excess of prosperity."[†] And, "Fortune makes fools of her favorites."[‡] And, "The people sat down to eat and drink, and they rose up to play." To sum up, this warning is repeated in many writings, that when people do not experience any distress, they pray to God less frequently and they are less attentive in attending to necessary matters. For since it is not in our nature to be completely idle, we are prone to pleasure and to vice, and those who are not occupied with necessary responsibilities rush headlong into corruption, as Cato says: "By doing nothing, people learn to do ill."[§] And, "Take away leisure and Cupid's bow is broken, and his torch lies extinguished and despised."[◊] And, "Leisure is deceptive, and harms the unwary."[△] For it was when David was at leisure that he gave in and fanned the flames of passion [for Bathsheba].

This is why it is said, "Luxuries are not fitting for a fool"—that is, when they are not conquered and tamed beforehand, they become worse and more audacious in fortunate circumstances, just as Rehoboam became more insolent when he became king in a time of such tranquility. And in Alexander, many vices sprang up after he had won so many victories. Therefore what was taught in Sirach regarding discipline is universal: "Fodder and the rod and burdens for an ass." Likewise, bread and discipline and work for a servant—that is, people should not be idle, but should certainly labor in an honest occupation. And this is the way to do it: let them have bread, but let them also have taskmasters and those who oversee their labors, urging them to work and punishing those who are stiff-necked, so that the rest may be held to their duties by the fear of their punishments. This precept is a reminder in governing the body, the household, or in administering the law: authority should not so much be the work of an executioner to the people but rather that of one who removes a mote from among the citizenry. Its concern should be in ensuring that people are occupied with honest labors, and in punishing those who are stiff-necked.

But nowadays discipline is mostly neglected, and civic resources are drained by immoderate plunder, so that the average person [*mediocres homines*] lacks the necessities of life, and cannot afford the costs of educating and providing for their children. But the divine voice has foretold that in this senile dotage of the world the authorities will be ever more degraded, and it commands us to ask God for the mitigation of public and private punishments, and for the preservation of respectable society and the church in a middling state. EXPOSITION OF THE PROVERBS OF SOLOMON.[12]

THE GRACE OF MERIT. CARDINAL CAJETAN: "He who has mercy on the poor man gives to the Lord at interest, and the Lord will repay him in kind." The phrase translated "gives at interest" suggests that we are dealing with loans. . . . But the second phrase according to the Hebrew means, "and God will repay him his due." This is the disclosure of great grace: while we must exercise mercy toward the poor man in giving to a man, one is actually loaning something to God. But you are loaning to someone who will repay you according to your merit. THE PARABLES OF SOLOMON, CORRECTED BY THE ORIGINAL HEBREW.[13]

LAWS CONCERNING THE RELEASE OF LOANS. MARTIN LUTHER: "If your brother, a Hebrew man or a Hebrew woman, is sold to you, they shall serve you six years, and in the seventh year you shall let them go free from you."[†] Moses recalls the law of Exodus 21:2-6. and refers it to this law concerning the release of loans, because this also speaks of the poor who, under the compulsion of poverty, sold themselves and received a loan, as it were, since they made themselves debtors with their own bodies. However, he adds at this place that they are not to send him away empty-handed when he is set free. . . .

Moses always adds magnificent promises. God has blessed, blesses, and will bless those who do these things, to keep them from doubting that they will be richly compensated if they either give something or lend something, as Christ says: "Give, and it will be given you." Hence also that proverb of Solomon: "The one who has pity on the poor lends to the Lord"; and again, "That one honors the Lord who has pity on the poor"; and many others. On the other hand, the Scriptures are full of threats against those who do not have pity. However, this means nothing to that deaf godlessness and unbelief which imagines that God is either joking or lying with such words, and which deserves to be robbed of the good things both of this life and of the life to come, just as that fool Nabal on Carmel withheld from David, was soon deprived of his life, and kept nothing. LECTURES ON DEUTERONOMY.[14]

GOD'S NOTE OF BOND. LUDWIG LAVATER: "He lends money at interest with Jehovah, who is gracious to the poor, and God will render to him his reward." This proverb commends kindness and liberality to the poor, and each individual word has weight. "He who shows mercy," that is, who not only is affected by the poverty of others but also gives generously out of compassion for the poor and the afflicted. The Hebrew *ḥānan* signifies to receive someone back into favor, or to give something freely. The Latin expression for "alms" (*eleemosynae*) indicates nothing other than mercy, and we also give the name "kindness" (*beneficium*) to that which is given to the poor out of

[12]CR 14:44-45; citing 1 Cor 10:7; Sir 33:25. [†]Ovid, *Ars amatoria* 2.437. [‡]Publilius Syrus, *Sententia* 203. [§]Columella, *De re rustica* 11.26. [◊]Ovid, *Remedia amoris* 139-40 (LCL 232:187). [△]Source unknown. A similar version of the proverb replaces *insidiosa* with *invidiosa*: "Leisure, so much envied, harms the unwary."

[13]Cajetan, *Parabolae Salomonis ad veritatem Hebraicam castigatae*, 170.

[14]LW 9:148-49 (WA 14:658); citing Deut 15:12-18; Lk 6:38; Prov 14:31; 1 Sam 25. [†]Luther did not preach or write a commentary on the book of Proverbs, but his comments on a related passage in Deuteronomy, which cites Proverbs, give us a clear indication of how he might have interpreted this passage.

compassion. By "poor" is indicated not merely those who are forced to beg their bread door to door but all those who need our help. The Hebrew *dōl* indicates an exhaustion of one's means, or bodily strength, a person who has become a hostage of fortune. The one who is generous to these not only does not lose what they have given but will receive it back with interest. For God commits himself as a cosignatory, and gives us his handwritten note of bond: people often default on their obligations, but God never does. We gladly invest our money with those whom we know to be honest and truthful; then why, having so often received from God promises of the surest gain, do we expect to receive nothing? The Hebrew word *lāvâ* properly signifies "something added or compounded," as when a loan or contract is undertaken; because, according to Forsterus,[†] those who accept the loan bind and obligate themselves, and pledge their faith to the ones who give them the loan. But it is not to be supposed that our alms earn eternal life. God promises rewards for our good works, but from pure grace. After all, we confer nothing on the poor that God has not made: "The earth is the Lord's, and the fullness thereof." Let us learn from this proverb to be kind to the poor. For if we show kindness to the poor, we show kindness to God himself. ON THE BOOK OF PROVERBS, OR SAYINGS, OF SOLOMON THE MOST-WISE KING.[15]

LENDING TO THE LORD. JOHN TRAPP: This is a second fruit that comes from shaking off sloth and working with the hands that which is good: that one may have to give to one who is in need. They do not give it but lend it. God accepts it, "both as a gift and as a loan," says Basil[†]—nay, they lend it at usury, and that to the Lord, who both binds himself to repay, and gives us security for it under his own hand: "He will pay him again, be sure of it!" The Hebrew here indicates[‡] that he will fully and abundantly repay the person, mostly in this world, but infallibly in the world to come. According to Cedrenus, Evagrius bequeathed three hundred pounds to the poor in his will, but insisted on a bond from the hand of Synesius the bishop, to be repaid in the next life. And the very next night, says the history, after his departure Evagrius appeared to the bishop in his own form and delivered the canceled bond, fully discharged.[§] SOLOMON'S BOOK OF ALL VIRTUES.[16]

WISDOM AT THE END OF LIFE. THE ENGLISH ANNOTATIONS: Some read this as if he meant "that you may be wise at the last" and no more. But I rather take it that Solomon had a further aim: that you may be wise in your latter end—that is, provide wisdom against the time of death, when most needful, so that you may not die a fool. Much to this is the prayer of the psalmist, "So teach us to number our days, that we may apply our hearts unto wisdom." Those who have wisdom enough to die well need care for no more. But it is a great chance if those who have been strangers to it all their lives find it at their death, if a wicked life begets a godly death. Then those who pray for

---

[15]Lavater, *In librum Proverbiorum siue Sententiarum Solomonis Regis sapientissimi*, 197-98; citing Ps 24:1. [†]Johann Förster (1498–1556), a German Lutheran Hebraist and author of a widely used Hebrew lexicon, *Dictionarium hebraicum novum* (Basil, 1557).

[16]Trapp, *Solomonis ΠΑΝΆΡΕΤΟΣ*, 227; citing Eph 4:28. [†]Trapp here quotes the Greek from St. Basil's *Homilia in psalmum* 14 (PG 29:277): "When you are about to give to a poor person on the Lord's account, that same gift is also a loan [*[kai] dōron [esti] kai daneisma*]: it is a gift because you do not hope to receive it back again, but a loan because the Master in his great beneficence undertakes to make repayment to the poor person. He receives little in the guise of the poor, but gives back much on their behalf. 'The one who has mercy on the poor lends to God.' Would you not like to have the Master of all as your guarantor for full repayment?" Basil of Caesarea, *On Social Justice*, trans. C. Paul Schroder (Crestwood, NY: St. Vladimir's Seminary Press, 2009), 97-98. [‡]The Hebrew verb in question (*šlm*) is the *piel* cognate of *šālôm*. [§]Trapp here relates a charming story first attested (according to Adler) in the sixth-century *Pratum spirituale* of the Syrian monk John Moschus (PG 87:3077). The story was repeated by the later Byzantine chroniclers George the Monk (ninth century) and Cedrenus (eleventh century). In the earlier version, the bishop Synesius opens Evagrius's tomb and finds the receipt clutched in his hand, with an added note from the deceased indicating that Christ had paid the debt in full. William Adler, "The Heartless Rich Man and the Precious Stone," in *Old Testament Pseudepigrapha: More Noncanonical Scriptures*, ed Bauckham, et al. (Grand Rapids, MI: Eerdmans, 2013), 1:360-61.

wisdom at death, and those who use the consideration of death to live wisely, in effect pray the same, though they seem to differ in their words. Annotations on Proverbs 19:20.[17]

Punishment in the Order of God's Justice. Philipp Melanchthon: After the human mind was sunk into sin, it was led into destruction (that is, death), because human nature ceased to dwell in God as it had done before, as it was said, "in him was life"—that is, humanity lived on account of the Word living in humanity, but in casting away his Word, they cast away God, the guide and giver of life, and death followed. But because God desired the Son to gather his eternal church from among humankind, our first parents were not immediately destroyed, but instead were brought back to life once more, with the Word again dwelling in them, according to the promise God had given.

With this sort of a nature, sins multiplied, the punishments piled up, and death was preceded by innumerable calamities. The material cause of physical death and of this multitude of calamities, they say, is now located in human nature itself, like a fruit that has become desiccated and rotten. They also say that other miseries were brought on by their errors and by the depraved desires of humanity. All this is rightly said concerning the immediate causes, but why is human nature itself in this condition? Where does human ignorance and the depravity of the will come from?

This doctrine of the church demonstrates the principal causes of sin. Having cast aside the Word of God, humanity cast aside God's guidance. Sin followed, and from this original sin, innumerable actual sins emerged. For it is the order of justice in God that the corruption of human nature should be destroyed, just as it is written: "Our God is a consuming fire." This is the reason that punishments follow, for there are four causes of punishment to consider. The first is the order of justice in God, according to which it is just to destroy that which corrupts nature. Next comes a consideration of final causes. God desired that the distinction between honorable and shameful things be known, and he wanted it to be known of which sort he himself is—that is, he wanted to be recognized as the judge and avenger of crimes. Therefore the second reason for punishments is that they may be a reminder of what sort of God we have to deal with. For example, because he destroyed Sodom, we know that God is pure, a lover of purity, and one who is grievously angered by polluted lusts. The third reason is utility, that humankind may be preserved; for there would be no end of villainy if there were no punishments for sin. The fourth reason is that some may be turned to God by seeing the example of others and being coerced by fear. And it is this reason that the proverb addresses: "strike scoffers and the simple will become more cautious," just like the Gibeonites became more cautious after the destruction of their neighbors [in Jericho], and sued for peace. So also the punishment of Sisamnes made Otanes more cautious when he was installed in the office from which his father had been removed, as Herodotus relates.[†]

In particular, it says, "strike scoffers," by which is meant severe delinquents who, when punishment is withheld, deride admonition with Epicurean contempt, and rage with ever great fury unless punishment is held out clearly in front of their faces, as it is said: "He is raised aloft that he may be hurled down in more headlong ruin."[‡] And the other part of the proverb says, "Correction before a prudent person increases knowledge," which indicates that although not everyone is corrected by examples of reprimand, there are others who are not crazy, and these will listen to admonitions and submit to the reminder. Exposition of the Proverbs of Solomon.[18]

[17]Downame, ed., *English Annotations*, 6X3v*; citing Ps 90:12.

[18]CR 14:45-47; citing Jn 1:4; Heb 12:29; Gen 19; Josh 9. [†]The scene is too memorable to omit: "So said Darius; and appointing Artaphrenes his father's son to be viceroy of Sardis, he rode away to Susa, taking Histiaeus with him. But first he made Otanes governor of the people on the sea-coast. Otanes' father Sisamnes had been one of the royal judges; Cambyses had cut his throat and flayed off all his skin because he had been bribed to give an

Resist the Proud, Correct the Humble. Michel Cop: It is often said that it is best to beat the dog before the lion.† The idea is that in order to warn or deter the haughty, proud, and arrogant, as well as those who are stiff-necked and obstinate, it is best to chastise the feeble, even though they have done little or nothing wrong. And when we so speak contrary to reason and justice, we often put such wickedness into practice. Thus it is said that "censure acquits the ravens and convicts the doves."‡ For one may see, as is common custom, that kings, princes, magistrates, and judges will more grievously punish some simple person who has not given much offense. They are not taught to do this by God, who strongly resists the proud, and gives grace to the humble, as he showed during the flood, the ruin of Sodom, the destruction of Pharaoh, and other desolations where he smote the scornful and spared the lowly. He did this so that the simple and the ignorant, who were not well taught, should fear and learn to walk wisely. Therefore, since the "great" of the earth sit in the seat of God, they ought to follow his lead in punishing those who have no fear of God, nor reverence for his word (as indicated by their dissolute life and indolence); those who create great scandals and give offense to their neighbors with wrongs, outrages, and violence. . . . But those who are teachable and of good capacity ought not to be handled so roughly, as the incorrigible, the scornful, and the contemptuous—although one may have to use sharp words and severe speech, as is indicated by the word "reprove." On the Proverbs of Solomon.[19]

unjust judgment; and he had then cut leather strips of the skin which had been torn away and covered therewith the seat whereon Sisamnes had sat to give judgment; which having done, Cambyses appointed the son of this slain and flayed Sisamnes to be judge in his place, admonishing him to remember what was the judgment-seat whereon he sat." Herodotus, *The Persian Wars* 5.25 (LCL 119:27). ‡Claudian, *In Rufinum* 1.21-23.

[19]Cop, *Sur les Proverbes de Salomon*, 432-33; citing Prov 3:34. †A common folk proverb, first appearing in English in Chaucer's "Squire's Tale" (*Canterbury Tales* 1.491). ‡Juvenal, *Satires* 2.63.

20:1–21:31 MORE MISCELLANEOUS PROVERBS

1 *Wine is a mocker, strong drink a brawler,*
and whoever is led astray by it is not wise.[a]

2 *The terror of a king is like the growling of a lion;*
whoever provokes him to anger forfeits his life.

3 *It is an honor for a man to keep aloof from strife,*
but every fool will be quarreling.

4 *The sluggard does not plow in the autumn;*
he will seek at harvest and have nothing.

5 *The purpose in a man's heart is like deep water,*
but a man of understanding will draw it out.

6 *Many a man proclaims his own steadfast love,*
but a faithful man who can find?

7 *The righteous who walks in his integrity—*
blessed are his children after him!

8 *A king who sits on the throne of judgment*
winnows all evil with his eyes.

9 *Who can say, "I have made my heart pure;*
I am clean from my sin"?

10 *Unequal*[b] *weights and unequal measures*
are both alike an abomination to the LORD.

11 *Even a child makes himself known by his acts,*
by whether his conduct is pure and upright.[c]

12 *The hearing ear and the seeing eye,*
the LORD *has made them both.*

13 *Love not sleep, lest you come to poverty;*
open your eyes, and you will have plenty of bread.

14 *"Bad, bad," says the buyer,*
but when he goes away, then he boasts.

15 *There is gold and abundance of costly stones,*
but the lips of knowledge are a precious jewel.

16 *Take a man's garment when he has put up security for a stranger,*
and hold it in pledge when he puts up security for foreigners.[d]

17 *Bread gained by deceit is sweet to a man,*
but afterward his mouth will be full of gravel.

18 *Plans are established by counsel;*
by wise guidance wage war.

19 *Whoever goes about slandering reveals secrets;*
therefore do not associate with a simple babbler.[e]

20 *If one curses his father or his mother,*
his lamp will be put out in utter darkness.

21 *An inheritance gained hastily in the beginning*
will not be blessed in the end.

22 *Do not say, "I will repay evil";*
wait for the LORD, *and he will deliver you.*

23 *Unequal weights are an abomination to the* LORD,
and false scales are not good.

24 *A man's steps are from the* LORD;
how then can man understand his way?

25 *It is a snare to say rashly, "It is holy,"*
and to reflect only after making vows.

26 *A wise king winnows the wicked*
and drives the wheel over them.

27 *The spirit*[f] *of man is the lamp of the* LORD,
searching all his innermost parts.

28 *Steadfast love and faithfulness preserve the king,*
and by steadfast love his throne is upheld.

29 *The glory of young men is their strength,*
but the splendor of old men is their gray hair.

30 *Blows that wound cleanse away evil;*
strokes make clean the innermost parts.

21 *The king's heart is a stream of water in the hand of the LORD;*
he turns it wherever he will.

2 *Every way of a man is right in his own eyes,*
but the LORD weighs the heart.

3 *To do righteousness and justice*
is more acceptable to the LORD than sacrifice.

4 *Haughty eyes and a proud heart,*
the lamp[g] *of the wicked, are sin.*

5 *The plans of the diligent lead surely to abundance,*
but everyone who is hasty comes only to poverty.

6 *The getting of treasures by a lying tongue*
is a fleeting vapor and a snare of death.[h]

7 *The violence of the wicked will sweep them away,*
because they refuse to do what is just.

8 *The way of the guilty is crooked,*
but the conduct of the pure is upright.

9 *It is better to live in a corner of the housetop*
than in a house shared with a quarrelsome wife.

10 *The soul of the wicked desires evil;*
his neighbor finds no mercy in his eyes.

11 *When a scoffer is punished, the simple becomes wise;*
when a wise man is instructed, he gains knowledge.

12 *The Righteous One observes the house of the wicked;*
he throws the wicked down to ruin.

13 *Whoever closes his ear to the cry of the poor*
will himself call out and not be answered.

14 *A gift in secret averts anger,*
and a concealed bribe,[i] *strong wrath.*

15 *When justice is done, it is a joy to the righteous*
but terror to evildoers.

16 *One who wanders from the way of good sense*
will rest in the assembly of the dead.

17 *Whoever loves pleasure will be a poor man;*
he who loves wine and oil will not be rich.

18 *The wicked is a ransom for the righteous,*
and the traitor for the upright.

19 *It is better to live in a desert land*
than with a quarrelsome and fretful woman.

20 *Precious treasure and oil are in a wise man's dwelling,*
but a foolish man devours it.

21 *Whoever pursues righteousness and kindness*
will find life, righteousness, and honor.

22 *A wise man scales the city of the mighty*
and brings down the stronghold in which they trust.

23 *Whoever keeps his mouth and his tongue*
keeps himself out of trouble.

24 *"Scoffer" is the name of the arrogant, haughty man*
who acts with arrogant pride.

25 *The desire of the sluggard kills him,*
for his hands refuse to labor.

26 *All day long he craves and craves,*
but the righteous gives and does not hold back.

27 *The sacrifice of the wicked is an abomination;*
how much more when he brings it with evil intent.

28 *A false witness will perish,*
but the word of a man who hears will endure.

29 *A wicked man puts on a bold face,*
but the upright gives thought to[j] *his ways.*

30 *No wisdom, no understanding, no counsel*
can avail against the LORD.

31 *The horse is made ready for the day of battle,*
but the victory belongs to the LORD.

a Or *will not become wise* **b** Or *Two kinds of*; also verse 23 **c** Or *Even a child can dissemble in his actions, though his conduct seems pure and upright* **d** Or *for an adulteress* (compare 27:13) **e** Hebrew *with one who is simple in his lips* **f** Hebrew *breath* **g** Or *the plowing* **h** Some Hebrew manuscripts, Septuagint, Latin; most Hebrew manuscripts *vapor for those who seek death* **i** Hebrew *a bribe in the bosom* **j** Or *establishes*

Overview: Our commentators' minds are drawn to a number of questions in this selection of Solomon's proverbs, but perhaps none more so than the way in which God's sovereignty interacts with human will and responsibility. We see, for example, the Roman Catholic Cardinal Cajetan and the Reformed Michel Cop argue that God's lordship even over kings demonstrates the absolute sovereignty of God, while the Anabaptist Balthasar Hubmaier dissents, teaching that there are situations in which the absolute freedom of the human will is not to be compromised. Philipp Melanchthon sees providence behind human actions, such as the desire to grow in virtue, while the *English Annotations* maintain that even knowledge of oneself is a divine gift. Our exegetes are also concerned with people using the freedom they have been given wisely. Primary among these concerns is the way wealth is used, with Ludwig Lavater concerned about the ways bribery perverts justice, Cop about ostentatious almsgiving, and Melanchthon about the need for the wealthy to be grateful for what they have. Other topics of common concern are drunkenness and the dangers of alcohol, as well as the binding effects of vows, which are addressed by Cajetan and Cop.

20:1-30 *Fair Dealings and Steadfast Love*

The Inherent Danger in Strong Drink. Cardinal Cajetan: "Wine is excessive, and drunkenness a troublemaker. Whoever is enamored of these will not be wise." According to the Hebrew it reads, "Wine is a mocker, liquor is a troublemaker; and everyone who gets lost in them will not be wise." And so the meaning is that too much wine drinking makes one a mocker, as experience proves. Those who drink too much start mocking other people, and they mock the laws and the troublemakers themselves. The Hebrew word *šēkār* is derived from intoxication, and it means every strong drink that intoxicates, no matter what it is made of. And so by these two terms, wine and liquor, the author includes every drink able to make one drunk. One should not suppose that Solomon is speaking merely about wine and liquor, because he adds everyone who gets lost in it (in wine as in liquor) will not be wise. The discussion therefore deals with the mistake[†] inherent in the drinking of wine or liquor. And the expression is universal, that those will be less wise who get lost in drinking this sort of thing. The extent of their separation from wisdom is equal to the extent of their dissipation. The Parables of Solomon, Corrected by the Original Hebrew.[1]

Drunkards Give Wine a Bad Name. Michel Cop: "Wine is a mocker, and beer is a tempest; and whoever misuses them is not wise." God created wine and other drinks, which have great odor and savor, and he gives them to us not only to sustain and fortify us but also to rejoice and delight us, as may be seen in Moses. . . . But this is not to say that one should drink so abundantly as to be drunk, as Noah and Lot did. Nor is it lawful to delight in taking too much, even though one stops short of drunkenness. For excessive consumption does not always make one drunk; for it happens that many, when they have drunk to excess one time, and found it pleasing, will return twice or thrice, and afterward continue and persevere in the habit, as long as the occupation agrees with them, and there is nothing that delights them more than funneling wine down their throats. And so they greatly abuse the good creations of God, against whom they are very ungrateful, not acknowledging that God gives us meat and drink to use in all sobriety and temperance. . . .

In this passage wine is not taken for the liquor that God brings forth from the vines, but for the person who is addicted to it, and has such a great delight in it. For as one may call a person by the virtue and grace with which they are endued, so they may also be named by the vice to which they are given, and in which they are entangled. For

[1]Cajetan, *Parabolae Salomonis ad veritatem Hebraicam castigatae*, 173. [†]There is a play on words here between *errans*, getting lost, and *errore*, which I have translated "mistake."

example, a person is called "flesh" because they are given to fleshly lusts; or, the faithful are called "light." Therefore Solomon uses the term "wine" for the one who abuses it and is corrupted by it, and says that such a drunkard is scornful; by this he means that they are delivered up to a reprobate sense, and all that has been said of the scornful may be understood as applying to the drunkard. . . . Therefore drunkards ought to feel great shame, since it is on account of their vice that this good creation of God is so reproached. ON THE PROVERBS OF SOLOMON.[2]

GOD GIVES ALL MANNER OF INSIGHT. PHILIPP MELANCHTHON: When it comes to good governance, both of the following must converge: the good judgment of authorities and the obedience of the people. And Solomon says that both are a gift from God. Thus, Jeremiah was a good adviser, but king Zedekiah did not follow his advice, and thus Jerusalem was destroyed. Hezekiah, on the other hand, obeyed Isaiah, and the city was saved. This is the main idea in this sweetest of sayings: "The hearing ear and the seeing eye, God made them both." For it reminds us not only that human wisdom has its place in political and household management, but also that we must seek help from God and he will give us counsel; also, that human will may be bent to obedience and that God will guide the course of events, just as Jeremiah says: "I know, Lord, that a man's way is not in himself." And, "Unless the Lord builds the house [those who build it labor in vain]." And, "Commend your way to the Lord and hope in him, and he will do it." And this proverb of Solomon can also be applied to all the preeminent arts, in which minds guided by God invent and discover many things which others do not perceive, just as Daniel says: "God gives wisdom to the wise and knowledge to those who have understanding." EXPOSITION OF THE PROVERBS OF SOLOMON.[3]

SUBJECTS MUST BE OBEDIENT TO RULERS. SWISS BRETHREN CONFESSION OF HESSE: We believe, acknowledge, and confess that subjects owe obedience to the authority and are to give them their dues, customs, rents, tribute, as well as in every respect everything that is not against God; to be subject to them, to serve them, and to pray for them. CONCERNING THE SUBJECTS.[4]

RESTLESSNESS IN PROSPERITY. PHILIPP MELANCHTHON: "'It is bad, it is bad,' they say, 'when they are in possession, but after they lose them, they sing their praises.'" As much as possible, we ought to consider our weaknesses, with an eye to improving them, for all of us are born with many defects. Among these is a restlessness (*fastidium*) with regard to the good things we already have, which arises from the inconstancy and fickleness of our souls, or from a propensity to fatigue, or from impatience, when we take umbrage at any inconvenience and seek for a change of circumstances. Many proverbs censure this restlessness: "The lazy ox covets the padded saddle, and the pack horse the plow."[†] See also the fable of Aesop, about the ass who continually changed his condition for the worse.[‡] And then there are these verses of Sophocles, in *Ajax*: "Foolish men often ignore the good that lies within their hands, until they have lost it."[§] But in the end, every person discovers within themselves this fastidiousness in regard to their current condition, just as Terence says: "We are ever discontented with our lot."[◊] And it is the most common habit of speaking to say that whoever is now in power is incapable of governing, and thus someone else is wanted, just as Thucydides says: "The present yoke is always heavy to subjects."[Δ] . . .

Now, this proverb of Solomon refers to that teaching by which one exercises a certain restlessness with regard to present goods, and it signifies that when they are lost, they will be desired and demanded. And this teaching, in turn, refers to the

[2]Cop, *Sur les Proverbes de Salomon*, 437; citing Deut 7:13; Prov 3:10; Gen 6:3; 2 Cor 5:21.

[3]CR 14:47; citing Jer 32; 2 Kings 19; Jer 10:23; Ps 127:1; Ps 37:5; Dan 2:21.

[4]CRR 11:76-77*; citing Jer 2:6-8; Bar 1:11-12; Eccles 10:20; Mt 22:21; Rom 13:1, 5-6; 1 Tim 2:1-2; Tit 3:1; 1 Pet 2:13-14.

virtue of patience, which means the desire to be obedient to God even in the midst of onerous circumstances, which he commands us to bear, and at the same time praying to God in expectation of his help, just as Paul commands: "Rejoice always, give thinks always, pray always." Exposition of the Proverbs of Solomon.[5]

Don't Push Too Hard for a Deal. Michel Cop: Just as there are wicked sellers who disguise their wares, extolling and praising them, and demanding far more than they ought and sometimes even lying or swearing so as to get as high a price as they can, . . . so also there are buyers who are little better, for they will do nothing but watch how they may deceive the sellers. Chiefly they do this when they think the sellers are not skillful and wily, but proceed in simplicity, or do not understand what their wares are worth; or else, when they are so needy that they are constrained to sell that which they have at a small price. Then the subtle and crafty buyers know how to belittle their goods, saying that they know where to find the same thing at a better price; or they haggle so much that they make the seller forget the number, or else will have more weight or measure than was agreed on; or they will offer some ready money, with the rest on credit—with no intention of paying. Experiences of this sort are all too well-known, and Solomon does not hold back from pointing out when he says, "'Bad, bad,' says the buyer."

He speaks in this way to show buyers, who want to have their goods almost for nothing, that the Holy Spirit knows their malice, and that against their own consciences they disparage the very thing they want to buy, which they know to be of good value. For after they have obtained it at a low price, they scoff and mock the seller behind his back, and glorify themselves in the deceit they have practiced on him. . . . By this they should understand that Solomon censures those who are not content with their estate and condition, and can never speak well about it—unless, that is, they fall into a worse condition, and only then do they acknowledge how good they had it. Then according to this second sense, let us learn to content ourselves with our calling, even if it be poor and onerous, knowing that we have nothing, be it good or evil, unless it comes by the will of God our Father, to whom we owe all obedience. And we should take what he gives in good part from his hands, praising it and giving him thanks for it. For in whatever manner he may afflict us, he never deprives us of those things which he knows are needful to us. On the Proverbs of Solomon.[6]

The Binding Character of Vows. Cardinal Cajetan: "It is a man's ruin to mark other men as holy and afterward to retract his vows." According to the Hebrew this means, "It is the snare of a man to devour holiness and afterward ask about his vows." The man who, contrary to the law, consumed the firstfruits and the other things that belonged to the priests and the Levites (i.e., took them for himself), this man swallowed up holiness. This proverb is written about him: it is the snare of a man that he devoured holiness. This holiness he had ensnared by ensnaring God's law, by his own trick of sacrilege. And likewise, it is a snare of sacrilege to ask questions after one has taken vows. A man who hesitates asks questions, but after vows have been made they cannot be overturned because of doubt but must be fulfilled. The Parables of Solomon, Corrected by the Original Hebrew.[7]

When Vows Become Stumbling Blocks. Konrad Pellikan: The Hebrew reads, "It is ruinous to a person to devour what is holy, and then afterward to seek out vows." In this reading, it

[5]CR 14:47-49; citing 1 Thess 5:16-18. [†]Horace, *Epistle* 1.14.43. [‡]Melanchthon is most likely referring to the fable known in English as "The Ass and His Masters," in which a foolish ass exchanges one master for a succession of others, each worse than the last. [§]Sophocles, *Ajax* 964-65. [◊]Terence, *Phormio* 1.3.20. [Δ]Thucydides, *History of the Peloponnesian War* 1.77.6.

[6]Cop, *Sur les Proverbes de Salomon*, 448-49.
[7]Cajetan, *Parabolae Salomonis ad veritatem Hebraicam castigatae*, 179.

is pernicious and sinful for anyone to think they can expiate a sacrilege they have committed by means of vows or other sacred rites. In former times, sacrifices were consumed in God's honor (the priests and Levites having received their share in accordance with the law concerning sacrifices), in the forecourts of the temple, with reverence and thanksgiving. But they sinned who did so insolently, without discipline, or unfaithfully, and not according to the stipulations of the law. But they were continually trying to expiate sin by means of other vows, which is forbidden. For God is not served by a multitude of vows and sacrifices, but by faith, devotion, religion, and by a devout spirit. Therefore we should not seek to repay God by multiplying unworthy ceremonies, as hitherto the clerics have done, devoting themselves to the canonical hours, multiplying vain murmurings, chantings, and repetitions, until faith, love, devotion, and all the fruits of piety have been utterly wiped out. . . . In the end these become stumbling blocks, turning us away from those holy duties that God has truly commanded, and encouraging us to set up works we have chosen for ourselves, apart from the Word of God. A Succinct and Universal Commentary on the Bible.[8]

True and False Worship. Philipp Melanchthon: "It is ruinous for a person to treat holy things with contempt, and then afterward to make vows." The Latin version of the text has been corrupted, and this has given occasion for all sorts of strange and contrived interpretations, which accommodate the text to support monastic vows.[†] But the meaning of Solomon's proverb is perfectly clear: it refers to that superstition, most common among the greater part of humankind, who, polluted by impiety, hatred of the gospel, and other crimes against conscience, anxiously perform all manner of ceremonies. They lull themselves into believing that these are pleasing to God, and they boil over with passion above all others—just like these Spanish adulterers and assassins who look to the Mass for great comfort, or carry on in public by lashing their hides in flagellation. But a proverb above instructs us in distinguishing between true and false worship: "The sacrifices of the wicked are an abomination, but the prayer of the just is pleasing to God." And in Ecclesiastes it is said, "Obedience is better than the sacrifice of fools, who do not know how much evil they do." Exposition of the Proverbs of Solomon.[9]

The Snare of External Works. Ludwig Lavater: The Hebrew *qōdeš* refers to holiness, or to things consecrated to God, such as sacrificial victims, sacred vessels, vestments, and other things pertaining to the divine cultus, which the priests used. *Yāla*ʿ signifies greedily and precipitately swallowing or devouring. Others read *lûa*ʿ, however, which means to overwhelm, destroy, corrupt, and this is the *hiphil* form. Among the Hebrew doctors, *lûa*ʿ means "to speak." Thus there is more than one sense in which this proverb may be exposited. The Vulgate edition renders the passage in the following manner: "It is ruin to a person to devour holy ones" (though some texts read, "holy things"), "and after vows to retract." Lyra interprets the sense as follows: "The one who makes a vow and does not fulfill it falls into sin, unless they are excused by inability to perform it."[†] But this interpretation cuts against the very words of Solomon, and other passages in Scripture. The Septuagint interprets it thus: "It is a snare hastily to consecrate one's own property, because after one utters the vow, one regrets it." That is to say, one should beware the trap of making vows hastily, and placing oneself under an obligation that afterward one may have difficulty in honoring. . . .

The sense of this passage is difficult and obscure, and for this reason it has rarely been diligently examined. In the Old Testament there were many sacred objects, that is, things

[8]Pellikan, *Commentaria bibliorum et illa brevia quidem ac catholica*, 232r.

[9]CR 14:49; citing Prov 15:8; Eccles 5:1. [†]The Latin Vulgate edition of this verse reads, "It is ruin to a man to devour holy ones, and after vows to retract" (Douay-Rheims).

consecrated to God, just like the sacrificial offerings. Some of these offerings were consumed by the priests and the Levites, but others were given as a burnt offering to God, and of these it was a sin to eat. . . . It is called a crime, as well as a sacrilege (and other terms as well), in order to indicate that crimes are not expiated by external things. The Jews labored under this superstition, that when a sacrilege was committed, or homicide or idolatry, they believed themselves immune if only they had taken a vow to God, that they should offer such and such a sacrifice. But the prophets always reproached them for this, for God is not placated by external things. Today there are also Christians who labor away with the same weak superstition, for there are many who devour both holy things and holy people (i.e., they commit sacrilege or murder). They think they can absolve themselves by means of external things if they fuss about painted pictures and vestments for the altar, or if they dangle anathemas before the saints or enter into a monastery. And so they fall into a snare. For God does not pay heed to such things; he only requires faith and true repentance. And certainly these people sin more gravely than the Jews, for they seek to win favor from God by means of works which he has not asked for. On the Book of Proverbs, or Sayings, of Solomon the Most-Wise King.[10]

The Divine Origin of Human Self-Knowledge. The English Annotations: There are sundry kinds of knowledge (as philosophers are wont to distinguish) in humanity, though all proceed from one single and simple foundation. Of all knowledge, that which they call *reflexam cognitionem*, whereby humans reflect on themselves and are able to reason concerning themselves, both of their nature and actions, whether they are natural or moral, is the most admirable and a great evidence of the soul's immortality. It is called here the "candle" or "lamp" of the Lord because of the divine origin of the soul (whereof this is a principal faculty), which is as it were a sparkle of the divine nature, and because of the office it has under God, as it were, in humanity, to see and oversee the whole person, to search into the most inmost and secret thoughts and actions, to guide and govern, and in sum, to be a light, both in matters of practice and speculation. If a person might suspect that the ancient heathens had anything out of Solomon, I should expect this as soon as anything. Annotations on Proverbs 20:27.[11]

21:1-31 *Do Not Succumb to Violence or Pleasure*

The Lord Does Not Take All Freedom, Always. Balthasar Hubmaier: Here my friend Zophar is of the opinion that what the king does he does out of necessity, for his heart is not in his own power but in the hand of the Lord. I am most amazed that he and others of my friends cite such Scriptures that do not serve them at all. For it is well known that Solomon here masters and kills the wrath and anger of the queen, teaching her to be merciful and mild, for, as the general proverb states, if they want to tyrannize too strongly then Jesus will appear to them on the way and knock them down himself, as happened also to Paul and the prophet Balaam. Therefore, however, freedom of the will is not taken away from all people or in all things, for the exceptional case does not rob the general truth of the Scriptures. Freedom of the Will II.[12]

The Power of Obedience. Cardinal Cajetan: "Like the different waters, so the heart of the king is in the Lord's hand. He bends it wherever he wants." The translator† added the words "like" and "so" for increased clarity. Solomon describes the simultaneous effectiveness and ability

[10]Lavater, *In librum Proverbiorum siue Sententiarum Solomonis Regis sapientissimi*, 214. †Nicholas of Lyra (1270–1349) was a late medieval biblical scholar unusual among Latin Christians for his knowledge of biblical Hebrew.

[11]Downame, ed., *English Annotations*, 6X4v*.

[12]CRR 5:486.

of divine action to bend the heart of humankind wherever God pleases using the image of dividing the waters into multiple streams. Dividing water into multiple streams is very easy so long as the water does not oppose that division. Human work is very effective for dividing up water into multiple streams, and no labor is needed for this kind of division, although effort would be needed to form the channels through which the water is led. Just like that, by the simplest effort, God moves the heart and bends it wherever he, as the Most High God, wishes. No labor is involved; there is no resistance when God decides to act. In every creature and not only in the human heart there exists what theologians call the power of obedience as it relates to God. For whatsoever God wills he does without resistance, just as he wills. The Parables of Solomon, Corrected by the Original Hebrew.[13]

Kings Demonstrate the Rule of Providence. Michel Cop: Kings should not glory in their powers, for although rivers swell sometimes, and overflow with an impetuousness that threatens to carry all away with them, and although kings have haughty and stubborn hearts, thinking themselves so mighty that no one may resist them, but that they may cut down and carry away all at their pleasure; nevertheless, by sluices, dams, and other devices one may arrest a great river, and stop it from doing harm. In the same way, it is easy for God to set a limit for kings, so that they do not make a nuisance of themselves with their pride and haughtiness. Solomon clearly indicates this when he compares their hearts not to great rivers, but only to little running brooks, whose courses are easily turned at will. Nor is it fit that they should boast in their free will, for just as rivers do not turn themselves this way or that, but are so directed in their courses as it seems good to humans, so Solomon says that "God turns the heart of the king whither he will." He does not say that he turns it to this or to that, but "whither he will," for as the Scriptures show us, he inclines one to one thing and another to another thing—one now to one thing, and later to the contrary. He turned the heart of the king of Egypt in Joseph's time to do well by Jacob and his kindred. This inclining ought to be well known, when God said to Moses, "I am sure that the king of Egypt will not let you go, unless compelled by a mighty hand," and still more clearly when God said, "I will harden his heart." He turned David's heart to goodness, as is clear when it says that "the Spirit of the Lord rushed upon David from that day forward"; and yet afterward, it was inclined to evil.

But here one might make two objections. The first is that if God inclines their hearts to evil, then kings are not culpable for their evil deeds; the second is that God is the cause and author of sin. In answer to the first, although God does turn the hearts of kings to evil, they are still culpable, for God by his just judgment, which is incomprehensible to us, provokes them to evil, either to punish their former sins by other sins, thus making them more guilty, or to punish and chastise those whom he thinks good (as when he stirred up Sennacherib and other kings against his people Israel), or to test and train his chosen ones in patience (as by the minister of Satan he stirred up the Chaldeans and Sabeans against Job). But the wicked have no knowledge of these divine judgments, no reverence for the providence of God, nor any fear of his Word, and so are carried away by their passions. Likewise, the wicked do not confess their faults to God, but being reproved by their own consciences, are forced to prove their wickedness, just as Pharaoh well knew he was an offender, and Saul made a very similar admission. David, who had been chosen by God, did not lay the blame on God after he hand numbered the people but confessed his own offense, and so gives us a brief answer to the second objection (and for a fuller answer, read the *Institutes* of John Calvin[†]).

So princes and magistrates are taught to hold God in honor and reverence, craving his guidance and governance, and fearing lest they be given up to

[13]Cajetan, *Parabolae Salomonis ad veritatem Hebraicam castigatae*, 181. [†]That is, Jerome, the translator of the Vulgate.

a reprobate heart, as many before them have been. Also, their subjects are admonished to pray for their superiors; otherwise, they are in danger lest it should happen to them according to the threats that are in various passages [against those who rebel]. For the rest, if kings who are mighty (or so they think) and make themselves to be feared, have need to be governed by God, who turns their hearts at his pleasure, it is not fitting that we should promise ourselves anything contrary to the will of God. On the Proverbs of Solomon.[14]

The Spirit Reveals Our Hypocrisy. Erhart Hegenwald: Dear friends, I know well that the shameless hypocrisy, which I would call ungodliness, lies so secret and so deeply hidden in the heart of people that no person can recognize it in themselves correctly, yea, no one but the true Spirit of God, as it stands written, "He will judge the world concerning righteousness and concerning judgment." There the Lord certainly means not the outward righteousness that we call hypocrisy. For that a human being can also observe. He means the ungodliness that no one can see, not even the person themselves, unless the Spirit of God reveals it to them, because it is he who knows the hearts. Letter to Conrad Grebel.[15]

Beware the Power of Bribery. Ludwig Lavater: This proverb describes the power and efficacy of bribes. People who have invaded our hearts by gifts given in secret can be reconciled to us. They commonly say that there is no heart so hard that glittering gold cannot soften it. But we do not speak this way, so as to corrupt upright judges, whether the cause be good or bad. This is what impious people do. Daniel foretold concerning the antichrist that on those who worship his god Mauzim[†] he would bestow gifts, of which three kinds are described: first, he will bestow distinguished titles; so, for instance, his followers will be called obedient sons, or members of the church. . . . Next, he makes them to be princes—this one an abbot, that one a bishop, another a cardinal, and so on, whence they receive an annual income. Third, he distributes authority, elevating as princes those who followed him, deposing some and replacing them with others, and taking possession of every high office. And how many take a dim view of the papacy on account of its debased doctrine and the criminal lives of its leadership, only to vest their hopes in the pope and receive great authority at his hands? That bribery was widespread in the ancient Roman Empire, we know from Sallust.[‡] So, for example, the Roman nobles undertook to defend Jugurtha, whom they had previously despised as a parricide, on account of the corrupt bribes he later gave them. And everyone knows that among our Swiss ancestors there could be bribery, for many treaties have been signed, and many ruinous wars have been waged on account of gifts given by princes. This has been the origin of many hatreds, quarrels, and civil wars that have arisen among our cities, and thus it was with the greatest wisdom that the honorable senate of Zurich has propounded the bribery law [*lex muneralis*], which stipulates that no one may accept a gift or stipend from any ruler on whose behalf they serve in arms. But when we see what can be done by the power of bribes, do not say, "I will take the money, but still do what is right." Rather, we should beware the power bribes have to corrupt us. On the Book of Proverbs, or Sayings, of Solomon the Most-Wise King.[16]

Alms Given Discreetly. Michel Cop: When people began to multiply on the earth, it was corrupted in God's sight, and filled with extortion and outrage: the feeble and weak were oppressed,

[14]Cop, *Sur les Proverbes de Salomon*, 461-62; citing Gen 45:16; Ex 3:19; 4:21; 1 Sam 16:13; Ex 9:27; 1 Sam 24:17; 26:21; 2 Sam 24:10. [†]E.g., John Calvin, *Institutes* 3.23.4.
[15]CRR 4:325*; citing Jn 16:8; Ps 96:13; 98:9.
[16]Lavater, *In librum Proverbiorum siue Sententiarum Solomonis Regis sapientissimi*, 223v-r. [†]Or, "the god of fortresses" (ESV). The Vulgate translation rendered this Hebrew term as a proper name; the LXX and most modern translations interpret the Hebrew *mṣzym* as "fortresses." [‡]The Roman historian relates Jugurtha's cynical judgment on Rome's venality: "A city for sale and soon to perish, if it finds a buyer!" (Sallust, *Bellum jugurthinum* 35.14; LCL 116:248-49).

and the poor and the needy were despised and forgotten. For this reason, God was greatly angered, and he destroyed the whole world by the flood. Again, the Lord says, "The cry of Sodom and Gomorrah is very great, and their sins are grievous," and Ezekiel explains what it was that their crime consisted in: "She and her daughters had pride, excess of food, and prosperous ease, but did not aid the poor and needy." For this reason God's wrath was kindled against them, and he destroyed them. And so we ought to be put on notice, that if we resemble them, we also shall perish by the just vengeance of God. Now to avoid this wrath and fury, Solomon shows us what we have to do when he says, "a secret gift." . . . And Jesus Christ is the best expositor of this doctrine: "Beware of practicing your righteousness before other people in order to be seen by them, for then you will have no reward from your Father who is in heaven." If we take the present passage in this sense, we have together with the doctrine it contains the promise of everlasting life: for seeing that God restrains his anger and rage when we give to the poor for his sake, it follows that we shall not perish, but that by his grace and goodness we shall live eternally. But if we understand this sentence as referring to the sorts of bribes and gifts that the judges and rulers of the earth take to pervert the law and equity, it behooves us to say that Solomon accuses the magistrates and rulers of rapine, when they ought to be rooting out the wicked in their anger. But to spare and favor them, they confess themselves to be corrupted by gifts and bribes, in exchange for which they wrong the innocent and favor the wicked, and has already been spoken of in various other proverbs. ON THE PROVERBS OF SOLOMON.[17]

LOOK TO GOD FOR ASSURANCE AND TO YOURSELF WITH FEAR. JOHN DONNE: There is a holy fear that does not only accord with an assurance of mercy but also induces and constitutes that assurance. . . . Dread, horror, and servile fear, jealousy, and suspicion of God, diffidence and distrust in his mercy, and a bosom-prophecy of self-destruction. Destruction itself "is upon the workers of iniquity," and yet says the wise king, "Blessed is the one who always fears." Though they always hope and believe in the good that God will show them, they also fear the evils that God might justly multiply on them. Blessed is the one who looks upon God with assurance, but upon themselves with fear. SERMON ON PSALM 65:5.[18]

PROVIDENCE GUIDES VIRTUE. PHILIPP MELANCHTHON: It is a necessary rule in life that we are to perform the duties of our vocation and ask help from God: in this way with God's help our labors become useful and life-giving. But unjust business, whether undertaken out of curiosity, or simply without prayer and faith in God, is ultimately unproductive, even if it is executed with great skill. Therefore the precepts concerning vocation should always be kept in view. . . .† We must set these consolations against those difficulties that drain our souls, causing us to doubt whether our work is useful. And faith and prayer must be kindled, and with hope in divine help we must sedulously perform our labors, knowing that it is God's will to exercise us in our faith, prayer, and hope through every difficult stage in life, as the psalm says: "Be still before the Lord, and pray to him." And we also know that putting faith in our own virtues is something to be censured, prone as we are to frenetic overwork (*polypragmosynēn*) and unseemly rivalry (*kakozēlian*).† Just as these texts teach us: "No wisdom, no prudence, no counsel against the Lord." Also, "A man can take up nothing, unless it is given by God." And, "Unless the Lord builds the house, the workers labor in vain." EXPOSITION OF THE PROVERBS OF SOLOMON.[19]

[17]Cop, *Sur les Proverbes de Salomon*, 470-71; citing Gen 6; 18:20; Ezek 16:49; Mt 6:1; Rom 13.

[18]Donne, *Works*, 3:220-21*; citing Prov 28:14.

[19]CR 14:50; citing Ps 37:7; Jn 3:27; Ps 127:1. †Melanchthon quotes a cluster of texts that he routinely cites in connection with the doctrine of vocation: 1 Thess 4:11; 1 Cor 7:20; Ps 37:5; 1 Cor 15:58; Jn 15:7. †For a fuller discussion of the former, see Melanchthon's comments on Prov 6:6.

22:1–24:34 WORDS OF THE WISE

1 *A good name is to be chosen rather than great riches,*
and favor is better than silver or gold.

2 *The rich and the poor meet together;*
the LORD is the Maker of them all.

3 *The prudent sees danger and hides himself,*
but the simple go on and suffer for it.

4 *The reward for humility and fear of the LORD*
is riches and honor and life.[a]

5 *Thorns and snares are in the way of the crooked;*
whoever guards his soul will keep far from them.

6 *Train up a child in the way he should go;*
even when he is old he will not depart from it.

7 *The rich rules over the poor,*
and the borrower is the slave of the lender.

8 *Whoever sows injustice will reap calamity,*
and the rod of his fury will fail.

9 *Whoever has a bountiful*[b] *eye will be blessed,*
for he shares his bread with the poor.

10 *Drive out a scoffer, and strife will go out,*
and quarreling and abuse will cease.

11 *He who loves purity of heart,*
and whose speech is gracious, will have the king as his friend.

12 *The eyes of the LORD keep watch over knowledge,*
but he overthrows the words of the traitor.

13 *The sluggard says, "There is a lion outside!*
I shall be killed in the streets!"

14 *The mouth of forbidden*[c] *women is a deep pit;*
he with whom the LORD is angry will fall into it.

15 *Folly is bound up in the heart of a child,*
but the rod of discipline drives it far from him.

16 *Whoever oppresses the poor to increase his own wealth,*
or gives to the rich, will only come to poverty.

17 *Incline your ear, and hear the words of the wise,*
and apply your heart to my knowledge,

18 *for it will be pleasant if you keep them within you,*
if all of them are ready on your lips.

19 *That your trust may be in the LORD,*
I have made them known to you today, even to you.

20 *Have I not written for you thirty sayings*
of counsel and knowledge,

21 *to make you know what is right and true,*
that you may give a true answer to those who sent you?

22 *Do not rob the poor, because he is poor,*
or crush the afflicted at the gate,

23 *for the LORD will plead their cause*
and rob of life those who rob them.

24 *Make no friendship with a man given to anger,*
nor go with a wrathful man,

25 *lest you learn his ways*
and entangle yourself in a snare.

26 *Be not one of those who give pledges,*
who put up security for debts.

27 *If you have nothing with which to pay,*
why should your bed be taken from under you?

28 *Do not move the ancient landmark*
that your fathers have set.

29 *Do you see a man skillful in his work?*
He will stand before kings;
he will not stand before obscure men.

23 *When you sit down to eat with a ruler,*
observe carefully what[d] is before you,

[2]*and put a knife to your throat*
if you are given to appetite.

[3]*Do not desire his delicacies,*
for they are deceptive food.

[4]*Do not toil to acquire wealth;*
be discerning enough to desist.

[5]*When your eyes light on it, it is gone,*
for suddenly it sprouts wings,
flying like an eagle toward heaven.

[6]*Do not eat the bread of a man who is stingy;[e]*
do not desire his delicacies,

[7]*for he is like one who is inwardly calculating.[f]*
"Eat and drink!" he says to you,
but his heart is not with you.

[8]*You will vomit up the morsels that you have eaten,*
and waste your pleasant words.

[9]*Do not speak in the hearing of a fool,*
for he will despise the good sense of your words.

[10]*Do not move an ancient landmark*
or enter the fields of the fatherless,

[11]*for their Redeemer is strong;*
he will plead their cause against you.

[12]*Apply your heart to instruction*
and your ear to words of knowledge.

[13]*Do not withhold discipline from a child;*
if you strike him with a rod, he will not die.

[14]*If you strike him with the rod,*
you will save his soul from Sheol.

[15]*My son, if your heart is wise,*
my heart too will be glad.

[16]*My inmost being[g] will exult*
when your lips speak what is right.

[17]*Let not your heart envy sinners,*
but continue in the fear of the LORD all the day.

[18]*Surely there is a future,*
and your hope will not be cut off.

[19]*Hear, my son, and be wise,*
and direct your heart in the way.

[20]*Be not among drunkards[h]*
or among gluttonous eaters of meat,

[21]*for the drunkard and the glutton will come to poverty,*
and slumber will clothe them with rags.

[22]*Listen to your father who gave you life,*
and do not despise your mother when she is old.

[23]*Buy truth, and do not sell it;*
buy wisdom, instruction, and understanding.

[24]*The father of the righteous will greatly rejoice;*
he who fathers a wise son will be glad in him.

[25]*Let your father and mother be glad;*
let her who bore you rejoice.

[26]*My son, give me your heart,*
and let your eyes observe[i] my ways.

[27]*For a prostitute is a deep pit;*
an adulteress[j] is a narrow well.

[28]*She lies in wait like a robber*
and increases the traitors among mankind.

[29]*Who has woe? Who has sorrow?*
Who has strife? Who has complaining?

Who has wounds without cause?
Who has redness of eyes?

[30]*Those who tarry long over wine;*
those who go to try mixed wine.

[31]*Do not look at wine when it is red,*
when it sparkles in the cup
and goes down smoothly.

[32]*In the end it bites like a serpent*
and stings like an adder.

[33]*Your eyes will see strange things,*
and your heart utter perverse things.

34 *You will be like one who lies down in the*
midst of the sea,
like one who lies on the top of a mast.[k]

35 *"They struck me," you will say,*[l] *"but I was not*
hurt;
they beat me, but I did not feel it.

When shall I awake?
I must have another drink."

24 *Be not envious of evil men,*
nor desire to be with them,

2 *for their hearts devise violence,*
and their lips talk of trouble.

3 *By wisdom a house is built,*
and by understanding it is established;

4 *by knowledge the rooms are filled*
with all precious and pleasant riches.

5 *A wise man is full of strength,*
and a man of knowledge enhances his might,

6 *for by wise guidance you can wage your war,*
and in abundance of counselors there is victory.

7 *Wisdom is too high for a fool;*
in the gate he does not open his mouth.

8 *Whoever plans to do evil*
will be called a schemer.

9 *The devising*[m] *of folly is sin,*
and the scoffer is an abomination to mankind.

10 *If you faint in the day of adversity,*
your strength is small.

11 *Rescue those who are being taken away to*
death;
hold back those who are stumbling to the
slaughter.

12 *If you say, "Behold, we did not know this,"*
does not he who weighs the heart perceive it?

Does not he who keeps watch over your soul
know it,
and will he not repay man according to his
work?

13 *My son, eat honey, for it is good,*
and the drippings of the honeycomb are sweet
to your taste.

14 *Know that wisdom is such to your soul;*
if you find it, there will be a future,
and your hope will not be cut off.

15 *Lie not in wait as a wicked man against the*
dwelling of the righteous;
do no violence to his home;

16 *for the righteous falls seven times and rises*
again,
but the wicked stumble in times of calamity.

17 *Do not rejoice when your enemy falls,*
and let not your heart be glad when he
stumbles,

18 *lest the* LORD *see it and be displeased,*
and turn away his anger from him.

19 *Fret not yourself because of evildoers,*
and be not envious of the wicked,

20 *for the evil man has no future;*
the lamp of the wicked will be put out.

21 *My son, fear the* LORD *and the king,*
and do not join with those who do otherwise,

22 *for disaster will arise suddenly from them,*
and who knows the ruin that will come from
them both?

23 *These also are sayings of the wise.*

Partiality in judging is not good.

24 *Whoever says to the wicked, "You are in the right,"*
will be cursed by peoples, abhorred by nations,

25 *but those who rebuke the wicked will have*
delight,
and a good blessing will come upon them.

26 *Whoever gives an honest answer*
kisses the lips.

27 *Prepare your work outside;*
get everything ready for yourself in the field,
and after that build your house.

[28]*Be not a witness against your neighbor*
without cause,
and do not deceive with your lips.

[29]*Do not say, "I will do to him as he has done*
to me;
I will pay the man back for what he has done."

[30]*I passed by the field of a sluggard,*
by the vineyard of a man lacking sense,

[31]*and behold, it was all overgrown with thorns;*
the ground was covered with nettles,
and its stone wall was broken down.

[32]*Then I saw and considered it;*
I looked and received instruction.

[33]*A little sleep, a little slumber,*
a little folding of the hands to rest,

[34]*and poverty will come upon you like a robber,*
and want like an armed man.

a Or *The reward for humility is the fear of the LORD, riches and honor and life* **b** Hebrew *good* **c** Hebrew *strange* **d** Or *who* **e** Hebrew *whose eye is evil* **f** Or *for as he calculates in his soul, so is he* **g** Hebrew *My kidneys* **h** Hebrew *those who drink too much wine* **i** Or *delight in* **j** Hebrew *a foreign woman* **k** Or *of the rigging* **l** Hebrew lacks *you will say* **m** Or *scheming*

OVERVIEW: These chapters continue a long section of miscellaneous proverbs addressing a wide variety of practical and ethical concerns. Though there is no apparent thematic organization to these chapters, the reformers found important guidance in practical matters, demonstrating that the Reformation was not just a matter of theological dispute, but was concerned for the whole of the Christian life. For example, both Philipp Melanchthon and Michel Cop address the theme of a "good name," the former reflecting on the role a healthy concern with reputation plays in God's governance of human affairs, and the latter emphasizing more strongly the dangers of too much self-regard. Also addressed in this section are a commendation of discipline in child-rearing, the providential distribution of wealth and poverty, and reflections on the biblical prohibitions against moving boundary stones, reflections that both illustrate the socially conservative temperament of the exegetes, as well as cautions against unnecessary allegorization. In the following chapter, however, a warning against overindulgence at the dinner table provides the point of departure for a eucharistic allegory by Ulrich Zwingli, as well as a warning against the envy of the ambitious when political power is at stake. Later, a proverb enjoining deliverance of those under sentence of death elicits reflections on the positive duty of Christians not merely to avoid active evil but also to resist injustice perpetrated against the weak. The final two excerpts deal with the limits of a Christian's duty of obedience to those in political power and the virtue of diligence in one's calling.

22:1-29 *How to Train Your Child*

THE VALUE OF A GOOD REPUTATION. PHILIPP MELANCHTHON: It has rightly been said that a good conscience is needful because of God, and a good reputation because of one's neighbor.† And it must be understood that a good reputation is indeed a good thing; this is because God has ordained it that we should desire approbation, for God wants there to be public testimonials demonstrating the difference between right and wrong. And so he desires that those who act rightly gain approval and are given heed to, while those who act unjustly are disparaged and blotted out. He desires that these testimonials be conspicuous, in order that we may learn the law, and that we may know something of God's existence and of his character, and that he is the avenger of crimes. Therefore a good reputation is a divinely ordained testimony, given by the multitude of those who judge rightly, granting just approbation to those who act justly.

And by this testimonial they receive their reward, when they are given an honorable place in society, and the rest are instructed and offered an invitation to act justly.

Therefore, since a good reputation is a divinely ordained approbation, and useful in life in many different ways, it is obvious that this is a good we should desire. Thus Sirach says, "Take care of a good name, for this will be more durable than great treasure." But now let us consider the reasons: First, because God wants us to have regard for the judgments of honest people, as Sirach says in chapter 6: "Stand in the assembly of the ancients, and if any are wise, stick to them." But the arrogant and the impudent are unwilling to consider the judgments of those who are sensible. Second, he also wants there to be examples of honorable conduct given for others. This is why Paul says to do everything for the glory of God and not to give offense to the church. And in the letter to the Philippians, he urges that we take heed for "whatever is true, weighty, just, amicable, praiseworthy, and whatever is renowned for virtue."

The first term brought to our attention is "truth" (*veritas*), by which true doctrine is preserved and words and agreements in all honest business are safeguarded. Indeed, because it protects true doctrine, this is considered a virtue of the first table. "Gravitas" is that constancy in speech and actions befitting to honorable people, and it is a part of modesty. "Particular justice" is doing harm to no one. "Chastity" is avoiding forbidden lusts. "Amicability" is the name for that kindness [*beneficentiam*] or reasonableness [*epiekeia*] without which it is impossible to preserve agreement. "Praiseworthiness" describes that virtue that is diligent in avoiding those scandals that arise from ambitious rivalry (*philotimia*); it is the honorable desire of honorable people for a good reputation. Finally, Paul expressly names whatever is "renowned for virtue," which signifies acting justly, without ostentation, and not merely for the sake of establishing a good reputation. Thus in Romans Paul says, "The one who serves Christ in these things is pleasing to God, and is approved by people," which tells us that God wants us to respect and be guided by the judgments of honorable people. Those who refuse to do this are arrogant and impudent. Thus Seneca rightly says of such a person, "He is a trifler, not spurred by the attraction of renown."[‡] Let the young keep in mind the corresponding aphorisms in other writings, for example in that verse of Publilius Syrus: "An honorable reputation is a second patrimony."[§] Hesiod teaches us to flee a bad reputation, and he adds that the general report is never wholly devoid of merit: "No talk [*phēmē*] is ever entirely got rid of, once many people talk it up: it too is some god."[◊] Exposition of the Proverbs of Solomon.[1]

Seek God's Glory First. Michel Cop: Every one of us is naturally inclined to desire that which seems to them good and profitable. And there are some who are so addicted to their own desire to enrich themselves that they forget all honesty and humanity, and do not care in what sort of honor or reputation they are held. They do not care whether they are esteemed by others, so long as they can make themselves rich and powerful. They think that if they can finally reach such a state, then they shall have need of no one, but instead many shall have need of them and fawn on them, placing themselves at their beck and call. And so it is the way of worldly and carnal people to make a big deal of the rich, and call them honest, and hold them in great admiration. There are some who, though they desire to have a good reputation, still think that nothing really counts but having riches. Therefore they set their whole mind and heart on this, so that they may be exalted and praised. But such people are sadly mistaken, for it is not them we praise, but

[1]CR 14:50-52; citing Sir 41:15; 6:35; 1 Cor 10:31-32; Phil 4:8; Rom 14:18. [†]Melanchthon's exact source here is obscure, although several later Protestant sources attribute this saying to Augustine. The nearest candidate may be a passage in one of Augustine's sermons, where he writes, "You need to have two things, conscience and reputation: conscience for yourself, and reputation for your neighbor" (*Sermones* 355; PL 39:1569). [‡]Seneca, *Hercules Otaeus* 416 (LCL 78:374-75). [§]Publilius Syrus, *Sententia* (LCL 284:46-47). [◊]Hesiod, *Opera et dies* 763 (LCL 57:148-49).

their riches—as they soon discover, if they have eyes. For it is obvious that if the rich person ever becomes poor, they are despised by those very people who were their best friends in their prosperity. Therefore they are worthy to be reprehended, as Solomon does here when he says, "A good name is more to be desired than great riches." And he shows us what we ought to desire and choose above all things in this world: a good name. Not the sort of renown the giants had in the time of Noah, nor the sort of favor that jesters purchase by lies, flatteries, fables, and tall tales, but that won by discreet manners, honest conversation, justice and equity, humility and temperance, and by other fruits of a right heart and sound conscience, which cause us to get credit, and to be acceptable and worthy of praise both before God and our neighbors. We ought to desire this more than anything else one can wish for in this world, be they ever so precious, for they are fragile and transitory, and subject to vanity and corruption. But a good name and loving favor will last forever. . . .

But even though we ought value a good name and loving favor, we ought nevertheless to be careful not to be overly ambitious, or to covet that others should praise us and hold us in high esteem on account of our deeds. Rather, we ought to seek the glory of God and the edification of our neighbors, without thinking on our own good name and reputation. For it is not for us to exalt ourselves; we must wait till God chooses to do it. Indeed, he alone has the power to exalt and to humble whom he pleases. And if we walk in integrity and uprightness of conscience, although we may be a reproach to other people, yet he will make our innocence shine forth when and where he sees fit, just as he did with Joseph, David, Daniel, and others. ON THE PROVERBS OF SOLOMON.[2]

EQUALITY OF RICH AND POOR. CARDINAL CAJETAN: "The rich man and the poor man meet together, and the Lord created both of them. . . ." It is clear that the rich man and the poor man are, both as concerns themselves and their poverty and wealth, from God. But this statement is attached to the proposition of the proceeding proverb, which commended reputation and favor above wealth. Now, so that no one go wrong by supposing that wealth is not from God or that poor people are excluded from these two good things that are so exceptional, he adds that the poor and the rich, though different, were both made by God. Thus from a consideration of divine workmanship we would commit neither of these errors. THE PARABLES OF SOLOMON, CORRECTED BY THE ORIGINAL HEBREW.[3]

WEALTH, POVERTY, AND PROVIDENCE. PHILIPP MELANCHTHON: It disturbs our belief in God's providence when the wicked enjoy prosperity and the just suffer calamities. Many turn to physical causes or fate to explain such outcomes, while others look elsewhere for an explanation. Therefore we must understand that God has furnished us with testimonials of his providence in works ordinary and extraordinary, and in his express words. His ordinary works reveal God's presence—for example, in the exceedingly beautiful ordering of the heavenly bodies, the change of the seasons from winter to summer, the blossoming of the earth every year, the preservation of human society, the punishment of those who commit murder, law and the judgment of conscience in each individual, the generation and nurturing of the young. God's extraordinary works are those mighty deeds that captivate our sight—all of the miracles, leading his people out of Egypt, raising the dead, and so on. When these deeds are attested to, as indeed they are in the divine Scriptures, they become evidence in the minds of many that prosperity and adversity do not simply happen by chance, but that these also are ruled by the counsel of God. This faith shines in their hearts, and they ask and expect good results from God. Thus, Jeremiah says in

[2] Cop, *Sur les Proverbes de Salomon*, 482.

[3] Cajetan, *Parabolae Salomonis ad veritatem Hebraicam castigatae*, 189.

Lamentations, "Do not both good and evil proceed from the mouth of the Lord?" . . .[†]

Following from this, we know that we must discern the will of God according to his own Word, as it is written: "Your word is a light to my feet." Therefore, it is necessary to submit to the Word of God, even when the just are often subjected to harsh afflictions, for the cause of these is certain: God wills to subject his church to the cross. And take note of this promise: "Many are the tribulations of the just, but God will deliver them from all." Therefore, although Lazarus was destitute, he did not for that reason abandon his belief in God's providence; rather, he judged according to the Word of God, which affirms that deliverance would follow according to God's providence. And this is exactly what happens in the parable. But why it is that Lazarus himself was a poor man, and not the ruler of the Roman Empire, is a question not to be probed any further. Instead, we must hold fast to the rule given in Sirach: "Think piously on those things that God has commanded, for it is not necessary to peer with your eyes into hidden things." In this way we must discern the things that are revealed from those that are not, and submit to God in whatever vocation we find ourselves.

This, in sum, is what this proverb teaches: "Rich and poor together, God has made them both"—that is, seen in the light of God's providence, neither wealth nor poverty has any cause but the counsel of God, and therefore we should serve God faithfully in whatever station we find ourselves, just as it is written: "Let each one remain in the same calling in which they were called." Let not the poor person murmur against God, but obey this command: "Humble yourselves under the mighty hand of God," and this will be your consolation: "Blessed are the poor in spirit, for theirs is the kingdom of heaven." Exposition of the Proverbs of Solomon.[4]

The First Fruit of Repentance Is the Bitter Taste of Our Sin. Pilgram Marpeck: This is the first fruit [of true repentance]: the sinner confesses themselves guilty of eternal death under the stern, serious righteousness and wrathful vengeance of God. . . . That is the first and most bitter fruit of true repentance. Prior to all other fruit, we test and experience what kind of fruit the sin that we have committed produces—and that we taste and eat this fruit. Yes, prior to all other fruit, a true penitent must taste what they themselves (through the deceit of sin) have done and sown. Concerning Five Fruits of True Repentance.[5]

The Rod Is Useful, but Instruction Is Better. Michel Cop: Children are so corrupt by nature that they have all their affections set on malice and wickedness, on disobedience and rebellion, on dissolution and insolence, on derision and despising God, his Word, and all religion. David confesses as much regarding himself, from which follow ruin and destruction, as has been seen. And because Solomon well knew that fathers and mothers did not want their children to go to destruction, but rather that they should be preserved, he teaches them how to unbind folly from their hearts when he says, "The rod of correction will drive it away from them." Although the rod with which one beats children is very profitable, and very necessary to put them in awe and restrain them from loose and dissolute deeds, nevertheless the best correction to free the heart from folly and drive it away from the child is by the Word of the Lord: to exhort them, show them the way, and warn them, as St. Paul shows us well. On the Proverbs of Solomon.[6]

An Ordinance for Jubilee. Cardinal Cajetan: "Do not transgress the ancient boundaries that your fathers have laid down." The word

[4]CR 14:52-53; citing Lam 3:38; Ps 119:105; 34:19; Sir 3:22-23; 1 Cor 7:20; 1 Pet 5:6; Mt 5:3. [†]Melanchthon also cites Zeph 1:4-12; Ps 33:13; and Mt 10:29.

[5]CRR 12:393*.

[6]Cop, *Sur les Proverbes de Salomon*, 493; citing Ps 51:5; Eph 6:4; Col 3:21.

here translated "transgress" suggests adding to. And the encroachment on someone else's property by adding to the ancient boundaries that were established by one's fathers—to maintain property ownership in families permanently—is expressly prohibited. The word translated "ancient" implies perpetuity; changing such boundaries produced confusion in the Year of Jubilee, when fields had to be restored to their previous owners. The Parables of Solomon, Corrected by the Original Hebrew.[7]

Stability Preserves the Public Good. Philipp Melanchthon: This prohibition relates to the commandment "Do not steal," and it refers to digging up the strips of uncultivated land marking a limit and throwing boundaries into confusion, as is expressly stated in Deuteronomy: "Do not move your neighbor's landmark." And in chapter 27: "Cursed is the one who moves his neighbor's landmarks." Also, the laws of Julius [Caesar], Nerva, and Hadrian prescribed penalties for those who dug up boundary stones.

Even though there is nothing obscure about this precept, it is often interpreted allegorically, as if to say that laws that have passed from antiquity into established precedent ought not to be altered, except in case of obvious necessity. For among the precepts of political life, this also is often repeated, that ancient laws ought not rashly to be changed, just as a verse reminds us: "By its ancient way of life and its men the Roman state stands firm."[†] Also noted by everyone is the story about the Locrians recounted by Demosthenes in his oration *Against Timocrates*. The Locrians had a law such that anyone proposing a new piece of legislation was required publicly to place their neck in a noose, and if the new law was not pleasing to the citizens, they might strangle them. . . .[‡] If there were now such severity, we would not have so many new dogmatists and Lycurguses when it comes to wax tapers and little bells, and suchlike matters, insisting on changes which are totally unnecessary and bring no practical use.[§]

And sometimes those who deal in politics command that some small inconveniences are tolerated by custom, so as not to disturb the public weal, just as with those who are sick in body, in order to avoid greater evils. For this reason Xenophon is not wrong when he says that "all changes in government lead to bloodshed."[◊] Therefore this saying should often be repeated: "Do not stir up an evil that has been buried well."[Δ] But it is necessary to add a correction to this. When doctrine is impious, and the laws fortify impious and idolatrous opinions, then it is necessary to remember this rule: "If anyone teaches another gospel, let them be anathema." Again, "It is better to obey God rather than humans." Again, "Blasphemy shall not be forgiven, either in this age or in the one to come." And when it is necessary to make a correction [in the laws], this is not moving the landmarks of our fathers, but restoring them. For then the doctrine handed down from God to our first fathers is set back in place, just as Tertullian says, "That is true which is most ancient."[††] But ancient truth must be sought out with diligence, for knowing that the church has held fast to their testimonies through the succeeding ages is a great confirmation of faith, and works to preserve its foundation. Exposition of the Proverbs of Solomon.[8]

[7]Cajetan, *Parabolae Salomonis ad veritatem Hebraicam castigatae*, 197.

[8]CR 14:53-55; citing Deut 19:14; 27:19; Gal 1:8; Acts 5:29 ; Mt 12:32. [†]Ennius *Annales* 5.1 (LCL 294:192-93). "Our poet," wrote Cicero, "seems to have obtained these words, so brief and true, from an oracle" (*De republica* 5.1.1). Marcus Aurelius quoted this dictum as the "line of an excellent poet, which is in the mouths of all" (*Epistle* 5.5; LCL 113:306-7). But Augustine mocked this sentiment in *City of God*: "Those who praise it should consider whether true justice flourished in it even in the ancient days of men and morals, or whether perhaps even then it was not rather a coloured picture than a moral reality" (*De civitate Dei* 2.21; *The City of God Against the Pagans*, ed. and trans. R. W. Dyson, Cambridge Texts in the History of Political Thought [Cambridge: Cambridge University Press, 1998], 79). [‡]Demosthenes, *Against Timocrates* 139-41. [§]Lycurgus (seventh century BC) was, according to tradition, the lawgiver of ancient Sparta. [◊]Xenophon, *Hellenica* 2.32. [Δ]Erasmus, *Adages* (n°62); CWE 31:106-7. [††]Tertullian, *Adversus Praxean* 2.2.

NO NEED FOR ALLEGORY. MICHEL COP: In view of the fact that it is commanded, "You shall not move your neighbor's landmark, which the men of old have set," and a curse is pronounced on the one who moves his neighbor's landmark, it would seem that Solomon had no need of putting this aphorism in writing, since it adds nothing to what has already been said by Moses. But because we are dull and sluggish, we need to be roused by many reminders. Moreover, we are so addicted to land that we never get enough of it, and so left to ourselves, we will seek ways to make the possessions of others our own. . . . If we desire to be free from this curse, we ought to be content with our just patrimony, or with what we gain by honest labor, or acquire in equitable trade.

And if it is unlawful to transgress that which our ancestors have lawfully ordained as regards temporal goods, which serve our bodies for this present life, much less is it lawful to transgress that which God (who is above all people) has ordained by his Word for the health of our souls, without adding or subtracting anything. For just as the children of Israel were forced to wander in the desert for forty years on account of their rebellion and disobedience, their small faith and misbelief, and so died without coming into the limits that God had appointed for them in the land of Canaan, so those who transgress the laws of God shall be like Cain: fugitives and renegades in this world who will not enter into the kingdom of heaven, where our landmarks have been set from before the foundation of the world.

But we should have nothing to do with those who allegorize this proverb (chiefly the doctors of the Sorbonne), as if to make it say, "Do not transgress the boundaries of the Catholic faith, which have been ordained from the beginning by the doctors of the church and other learned men." This would not be spoken amiss, but would give us a sound precept, if by the doctors of the church they understood Moses, the prophets, Jesus Christ, and his apostles, who in order to make us faithful and obedient have taught us only the words of God, without passing their limits, or declining either to the right or the left. But these scholastic doctors make a twofold error here, for since we have sound and pure doctrine in this proverb (as we have seen), congruent with the Law and the Prophets, and that Solomon does not speak darkly or in figures, we have no need to search for allegories here, for that would be to obscure and corrupt the natural sense of the passage. Second, they err in this, that by "the fathers" they understand those who have busied themselves to teach and write since the time of the apostles, whether they have given good doctrine or not. It is enough for them simply to say, "Our fathers did it this way," or "Our fathers said so," without asking whether they have rightly followed the Word of the Lord. These people bear more reverence to people than to God, and to human doctrine than the Word of the Lord, as may clearly by seen by the articles of the Paris theologians. ON THE PROVERBS OF SOLOMON.[9]

23:1-35 *Avoiding Sorrow and Strife*

WHEN A BANQUET BECOMES A TRAP. CARDINAL CAJETAN: "When you sit down to eat with a prince, note carefully what is set before you and put a knife to your throat. But if you have self-control, do not desire his food that contains the bread of deceit." In the Hebrew this reads, "Because you will sit down to eat with your master: by understanding you will understand what is before you, and you will set a knife at your jaws if you do not have self-control. You will not desire his flavors, and even his bread is deceitful." This language is metaphorical to introduce the dangers confronting a man at banquets thrown by his masters. The meaning of the proverb is that the master's guest is risking the life of his soul, as though he were surrounded by swords at his throat. He has been exposed to bodily danger, so that he is not master of his own life. It is clear that when swords threaten one's neck one is not master of his own life but is subject to the threat of losing his physical life. This is because his life is not in his own power but the power of the swords that threaten all around his

[9]Cop, *Sur les Proverbes de Salomon*, 500-501.

throat. . . . If you want to understand what is before you, you will set a host of knives around your throat (i.e., you will take yourself to be, so to speak, surrounded by a multitude of swords threatening your throat). So you will determine whether you are in control of yourself. In considering that you have been surrounded by swords of this kind, you are not in control of your life, and therefore you will not let your desires run away with you.

Notice something here, wise reader: it is obvious where the proverb's conclusion of "deceitful bread" leads. It leads to the admonition that the guest at the master's banquet is exposed to the danger of that master's deception at that banquet. Solomon has in mind that the table is often a sharp, effective instrument for ensuring the guest reveals what he never would have disclosed elsewhere. Therefore, the master's table is a very effective instrument at which the guest lets slip many secrets that lay hidden in his heart. Food and drink have an effect on people, changing their temperaments and bringing about a new attitude of the body and mind. Therefore masters use a banquet as a means of deceiving their guest, by introducing deceptive conversation. And the guest is rendered no longer in control of himself. When the guest has been affected like this, he loses the ability to control his impulses and consequently to withhold secrets and moderate his speech. Therefore, Solomon compared him to a guest of a master with his throat exposed to swords for this reason, because neither is in control of his own life. The former has no control over his physical life, and the other is not in control of his mental life. THE PARABLES OF SOLOMON, CORRECTED BY THE ORIGINAL HEBREW.[10]

A EUCHARISTIC ALLEGORY. ULRICH ZWINGLI: Augustine in his *Tractates on John*,[†] on the words, "Greater love has no man than this, that a man lay down his life for his friends," says a little further on, "This doubtless is the thought in the Proverbs of Solomon: 'When you sit to eat at the table of a ruler, consider diligently what is set before you, and put forth your hand, knowing that you must provide the like.'[‡] For what is 'the table of a ruler' but the table from which are taken the body and blood of him who laid down his life for us? And what is 'sitting at it' but approaching it in humility? And what is 'considering diligently what is before you' but pondering worthily the great favor shown you? And what is it 'to put forth your hand knowing that you must provide the like' but what I have already said, that as Christ laid down his life for us, so we also ought to lay down our lives for the brethren? For this the apostle Peter also says: 'Christ suffered for us, leaving us an example, that we should follow his steps.'" See for what purpose Augustine says that we eat the body and blood of Christ: for the purpose, namely, of pouring out our life for the brethren just as Christ did for us. ON TRUE AND FALSE RELIGION.[11]

ON THE DANGERS OF LIFE AT COURT. PHILIPP MELANCHTHON: This is an admonition pertaining to a prince's court. Friendship with a ruler has its dangers; therefore you should be cautious and circumspect in speech, approaching as though you had a blade at your throat, and should not speak rashly, so as to bring death upon yourself—just as Alexander slew Cleitus when the latter contradicted him too freely at a banquet.[†] And there are extant many similar admonitions regarding the dangers of life at court. For example, Horace says, "Those who have never tried think it pleasant to court a friend in power; one who has tried dreads it."[‡] And then there is this elegy of Ovid's:

> Live for yourself, and shun glittering renown
> so far as you can,
> For cruel is the thunderbolt which falls from
> the gleaming heights.

[10]Cajetan, *Parabolae Salomonis ad veritatem Hebraicam castigatae*, 197-99.

[11]Zwingli, *De Vera Et Falsa Religione*, 282-83; *Commentary on the True and False Religion*, 246; citing Jn 15:13; 1 Pet 2:21. [†]Augustine, *Tractates on John* 84.1. [‡]Augustine's exegesis (and that of Zwingli) follows the Septuagint, which here differs significantly from the Hebrew text.

Although the powerful alone can be of help,
They do not; rather are they more often
wont to do harm.§

And Aesop told Solon when he was going to see Croesus that when one has to speak with a king, "Our converse should be either as rare or as pleasing as possible."◊

It is necessary that there be governors and ministers, and God has ornamented these by gradations, assigning names fit for their stations in society. "I have said you are gods"—that is, having divine office. And those called to such duties should be faithful, prudent, and modest. But it is to be lamented, that at this highest peak there are so few who carry out their duties justly, and that most are either indolent or cruel. Indeed it is a marvel that in that seat of God the devil runs riot so horribly, as can be shown by examples in every age. And because many squander their authority, they draw down tragic punishments upon themselves. Thus there are many complaints about the inconstancy of fortune at court. Consider these lines of Seneca from *Agamemnon*:

Not so does the sea in the Libyan Syrtes
roll in rage wave upon wave;
not so in the Euxine
do the waters swell from the lowest depths
—those waters close to the snowy pole
where Bootes turns his shining Wain,
never touching the azure waves—
as Fortune whirls
the fates of kings in headlong movement.△

For although there is a multitude of dangers in life at court, the most common evils are in the human propensity to ambition and haughtiness. Ambition craves elevation; thus Seneca says that human souls have a tendency to rise upward, because they are fiery.†† Haughtiness in those who hold power is an abuse of their position, for they unjustly give themselves license for which eventually they will be punished. Therefore Solomon reprimands ambition and haughtiness, giving us this admonition, by which he teaches modesty and circumspection.

But there are acknowledged rules. To seek an office for which we are reasonably suited is just. But our candidacy should not impede the judgment of those who make the selection, nor should it be advanced pugnaciously by unjust means. And such candidacy ought to be an indication that one is ready to do one's duty, and to offer oneself in service of a society subject to the most difficult labors and the greatest dangers. And concerning such candidacy it is said, "Whoever desires to be an overseer desires an honorable task." And, "God loves a cheerful giver." So also Paul urged Titus to learn honorable skills so that we could be useful in the work of governing.

But it is vicious ambition, to put oneself forward for office with a desire to impede the judgment of those who make the selection, or to fight with unjust means, or after gaining office to exceed the boundaries of one's vocation. Against this ambition it is said, "Those who exalt themselves shall be abased," and "Everyone who is proud in heart is an abomination to God." And there is a form of vicious ambition called prudery (*akkismos*), found in the those who are ambitious in high degree, and yet desire to appear wholly free from it, even though they eagerly strive for position. Aristotle calls these ones "affected humbugs" (*baukopanourgous*)—that is, those who put on a show of being fastidious.‡‡

In addition, those who are raised to high office often abuse their power for private aspirations, just as David indulged himself as king, and that far more than others. Here we recall the saying of Sirach: "The greater you are, the more humble yourself, and thus you will find grace from God." Also of note is this passage in Plutarch: "A ruler imitates the sun, which, when it mounts up in the northern sky and reaches its greatest altitude, has the least motion, thus by greater slowness ensuring the safety of its course."§§ EXPOSITION OF THE PROVERBS OF SOLOMON.[12]

[12]CR 14:55-57; citing Ps 82:6; 1 Tim 3:1; 2 Cor 9:7; Mt 23:12; Prov 16:5; Sir 3:20. †Cleitus the Black (c. 375–328 BC) was a Greek general and close friend of Alexander the Great, who killed him in a drunken rage and later grieved his death (Arrian, *Anabasis*

RESTRICT YOUR APPETITE, WITH VIOLENCE IF NECESSARY. THE ENGLISH ANNOTATIONS: Bridle your appetite, as it were, by force and violence. Or, whatever you say or do, be as careful and circumspect as you would if a sharp knife were against your throat. Every person knows when they are under the barber's hand, and the razor is about their throat, it concerns them to be careful how to behave themselves. ANNOTATIONS ON PROVERBS 23:2.[13]

WARNING TO WORKAHOLICS. PHILIPP MELANCHTHON: "Do not strangle your spirit to become rich, or lay aside your wisdom." This is a warning against avarice. And yet this maxim does not forbid sedulousness and labor in one's vocation.[†] For very often Scripture expressly commends diligence and labor, and sets forth the ant as an example.[‡] But we know that labors can be fruitful, when God's help is added, as the psalm says: "Unless the Lord builds the house, [those who build it labor in vain]." Therefore these two are bound together in the work of our vocations: invocation of God, and our diligence, as the psalm says: "Commit your way to the Lord and hope in him, and he will make it happen." But this also forbids *polypragmosynē* and unjust scheming,[§] for a person pursues these things because they do not trust in God, and by that mistrust they are tormented. It is this mistrust that is the crime, not diligence in the work with which they have been entrusted. Therefore Solomon says this, that human plans clearly undertaken outside one's vocation are unjust and useless, and thus we should flee riches as the eagles fly away. In this way he calls us back to the goals of our vocations, both in asking for God's help and in diligence and wisdom of the divine teaching. EXPOSITION OF THE PROVERBS OF SOLOMON.[14]

FEAR OF THE LORD DRIVES OUT ENVY. MICHEL COP: It often seems clear to young people that they are wise enough, if they follow the multitude, to raise themselves up and be of value, advancing themselves and working for their own profit even though it comes at their neighbor's expense. And so they become the "sinners" [spoken of us in this passage]—that is, they have had their hearts infected and corrupted by malice and wickedness, which they demonstrate in their conversation, in which they are well pleased. And behaving in this way they flourish and prosper, at least to outward appearance, satisfying their desires and living at their ease, as is seen and described elsewhere in the Scriptures. By contrast, those who are truly wise and pursue justice often have misery and calamities, and for this reason they are tempted to do as the foolish and wicked do, and so enjoy their prosperity. But Solomon shows them that if by the wisdom of the heart they will only look to that which is justly theirs, they ought not to fall for such temptations: "Let not your heart be envious against sinners." Here Solomon teaches in brief what David sets out more fully in Psalm 37, where we may note that to "be envious against sinners" means to be aggrieved at our own misery when we see their temporal prosperity, and so not to care what we do, so long as we attain their comfort. And so under this word of "envy" (or zeal, or affection), we understand that Solomon comprehends the prosperity of the wicked, and he signifies that they are only happy according to outward appearances. . . . Second, we should note that when he sets "the fear of the Lord" against

4.8; Plutarch, *Alexander* 51). [†]Horace, *Epistle* 18.86-87 (LCL 194:374-75). [§]Ovid, *Tristia* 3.5-8. [◊]Plutarch, *Solon* 28.1. [Δ]Seneca, *Agamemnon* 1.65-72 (LCL 78:132-33). [††]Seneca never puts it exactly like this. In *Epistle* 50.2 he argues that the soul is air in a most rarefied form, and elsewhere he associates rarefaction with heat. [‡‡]"Those who disclaim merely trifling or obvious distinctions are called affected humbugs [*baukopanourgoi*], and are decidedly contemptible." Aristotle, *Nicomachean Ethics* 1127b27 (LCL 73:244-45). [§§]Plutarch, *Ad principem ineruditum* 782E (LCL 321:68-69).

[13]Downame, ed., *English Annotations*, 6Y2r*.

[14]CR 14:57; citing Ps 127:1; 37:5. [†]On which, see Melanchthon's comments on Prov 6:6. [‡]As examples, Melanchthon cites Eccl 9:10; 1 Cor 4:2, and the parable of the talents, Mt 25:14-30. [§]For more on *polypragmosynē* (being a "busybody"), see Melanchthon's comments on Prov 6:6, above. The second term, *aucypia*, literally refers to bird-catching.

envy, or zeal, he makes it clear that those who allow themselves to be carried away by such envy or [misplaced] affection have no fear of the Lord, for it is by this that we withdraw ourselves from evil. And when one desires to prosper as the wicked do, there is no evil to which one will not give oneself in order to achieve one's desires. ON THE PROVERBS OF SOLOMON.[15]

FLEE THE COMPANY OF THE ENVIOUS AND THE SPITEFUL. PHILIPP MELANCHTHON: A little earlier Solomon warned against the danger of being too cozy with rulers or princely courts, then he warned us not to desire power and authority beyond our vocation. Now he warns us to flee from those who are envious. For envy causes people to be sorrowful when others excel in good things, whether it be in some ordinary gift, or in virtue, or in any good thing.[†] Cain was sorrowful when his brother excelled in this great glory, such that God honored him with a public testimonial. This sorrow is the cause of horrible evils in life, as is demonstrated by the examples of Cain, Esau, Saul, Marius, Pompey, and innumerable others.

But the source of envy is pride. For all people desire to stand out, and are lustful for power (*philarxikoi*), just as the devil said to Eve, "You will be like God." And Seneca says that the human soul is fiery in nature, and for this reason it tends to rise upward.[‡] People are sorrowful when they see others excelling themselves, and all the more do they desire to see them cast down. Thus it is written in Sirach: "Pride is the beginning of all sins." And indeed so common are these evils that there is a Greek proverb that says, "All honorable things are accompanied by envy."[§] And Cicero says that "it is a blot and blemish of this age to be envious of virtue."[Δ]

But this sorrow is an injustice, because it does not render what is due, either to God or to other people. Thus Cain did not give thanks to God for consuming the offerings he gathered from his harvest, nor was he willing that his brother's gifts be accepted by God, and afterward rose up in anger and killed him. Neither did Saul give thanks to God for all the many good things he received, such as the many victories that David attributes to his reign in the testimony he gave the church. For Saul was unwilling that David should enjoy the gifts that God had given him, and burning with anger he lay in ambush to take David's life. Closely related to envy is the vice of spite (*epichairekakia*)—that is, taking delight when calamity befalls the righteous (or even the tolerable), as the devil so clearly enjoys. This vice is condemned in this passage; we are warned to flee the society of the envious and the mistrustful. EXPOSITION OF THE PROVERBS OF SOLOMON.[16]

BEING RIGHT WITH GOD REQUIRES A RIGHT HEART. JOHN DONNE: To come to God there is a straight line for every person everywhere: but we do not do this if we do not come with our heart. . . . Was he his son and did not have his heart? That may very well be. There is a filiation without the heart; not such a filiation as shall ever make him a partaker of the inheritance, but yet a filiation. Associating ourselves with the sons of God in an outward profession of religion makes us so far the sons of God that the judgment of people cannot, and the judgment of God does not, distinguish them. Because, when the sons of God stood in his presence, Satan stood among the sons of God. God does not disavow him, God does not excommunicate him; God makes his use of him, yet God knows his heart was far from him. So when God was in council with his angels about Ahab's going up to Ramoth-gilead, a spirit came forth and offered his service, and God refuses not his service, but employs him, though he knows his heart is far from him. So no doubt many times, those to

[15]Cop, *Sur les Proverbes de Salomon*, 510-11.

[16]CR 14:58; citing Gen 3:5; Sir 10:13. [†]Melanchthon's definition closely follows that of Thomas Aquinas, who in turn quotes John of Damascus: "Envy is sorrow for another's good" (*Summa Theologiae* II-II, q. 36, a. 1). [‡]Seneca, *Epistle* 50.2; see Melanchthon's comments on Prov 23:1-2. [§]Stobaeus, *Anthology* 491 (*Ioannis Stobaei Florilegium*, ed., Meineke [Leipzig, 1855], 2:47). [Δ]Cicero, *Pro Balbo* 3.16 (LCL 447:642-43).

whom God has committed supreme government, and those who receive beams of this power by subordination and delegation from them, see Satan among the sons of God. Hypocrites and impiously disposed people come into these places of holy convocation and suffer them, nay, they employ them, nay they prefer them, and yet they know their hearts are far from them. As long as they stand among the sons of God—that is, appear and conform themselves in outward acts of religion—they are not disavowed, they are not ejected. By us here they are not. But, however, we date our excommunications against them from an overt act and apparent disobedience, yet in the records of heaven, they shall meet an excommunication and a conviction of recusancy that shall bear date from that day when they came first to church with that purpose to delude the congregation, to elude the laws in that behalf provided, to advance their treacherous designs by such disguises, or upon whatever other collateral and indirect occasion people come to this place. Though they are in the right way, when they are here at church, yet because they are not upright in heart, therefore that right way does not bring them to the right end. SERMON ON PSALM 64:10.[17]

24:1-34 *Wisdom like Honey*

STRENGTH OF SPIRIT, NOT ARMS. MICHEL COP: It may seem that those fools and wicked people who are given to rape and pillage are mighty and strong, because by outward appearances they seem to do what they will, and they have such authority that no one dare resist them. On the other hand, it seems that there is no sort of people so weak or so miserable and abject as those who are good and wise, as they themselves are often tempted to believe, when they look only at what is before their bodily eyes. But tearing our sight away from appearances, which are false and deceptive, we ought to believe in the spirit of all truth, which speaks to us by Solomon and says, "The wise man is full of strength." And so he teaches us that we ought not to think that our power and might consist in things that are present to us bodily, but in the wisdom and knowledge that we learn by the Word. . . . It is as if he said that it is by wisdom and knowledge that a person is strong and increases more and more in power—not bodily force, which is a very small thing, but force of the spirit, which consists in patience and constancy. These overcome all worldly force, and they help us escape the dangers in which the strong of the world perish. This is what happened in the time of Noah with the giants, and in the time of Moses with Pharaoh, with Joseph and his mistress, with Daniel and the envious courtiers, with David and Saul, and with many others, . . . and now in our time, with the poor faithful and their adversaries, who are the great sages of the world: the pope and his supporters, the king and his flatterers. Therefore we should understand that we ought not aspire to power and force in this world, which only make a person proud, and so cause their death by setting them against God. Rather, being feeble and abject by the world's standards, we ought to fortify ourselves in humility of spirit. Then we shall have the Almighty on our side. ON THE PROVERBS OF SOLOMON.[18]

CAN YOU IN ANY WAY PREVENT IT? CARDINAL CAJETAN: "Rescue those who are being led away to death, and do not hesitate to free those who are drawn to destruction." The word translated here "lead" suggests "captive to." The second phrase according to the Hebrew is like this: "those heading to death, if you have the opportunity to prevent it." Now the meaning of the first phrase is clear—namely, that one should rescue those who have been wrongly condemned to death, because they are going to be killed unjustly. This is because the actual violence that has caught them and condemned them to death is synonymous with injustice. But the meaning of the second phrase is less clear. Nevertheless, it means that a person should prevent those from being killed

[17]Donne, *Works*, 3:186-87*; citing 1 Kings 22:22.

[18]Cop, *Sur les Proverbes de Salomon*, 523-24.

who—although they are not captured—nevertheless have been humiliated and harmed so much that they are liable to die. Such captives need a liberator to free them from the hands of those who imprison them. The humiliated need someone to keep them from being killed. Therefore he says of them, "Can you in any way prevent it?" And he means to affirm this of those who have been wrongly oppressed. THE PARABLES OF SOLOMON, CORRECTED BY THE ORIGINAL HEBREW.[19]

RESISTING UNJUST CRUELTY. PHILIPP MELANCHTHON: The precepts, "Do not kill" and "Do not participate in the sins of others" are well known. God commands both the magistracy and private persons not to kill the innocent. He also commands that we not give assistance to unjust cruelty. But when and in what manner the magistrate ought to destroy the guilty is addressed in teachings supplemental to the Decalogue, in Deuteronomy 19 and other places. For the magistrate is the guardian of innocent life, just as it is written in Romans 13: "He is God's minister, an avenger to execute punishment on the one who does evil." And private persons also, so far as they may within their vocations, ought to oppose unjust cruelties.

A worthy example of this may be found in Jonathan, when he opposed his father not only by his testimony [to David's innocence], but also when he assisted David by other services, and this without sedition. Obadiah secretly fed the prophets, who had been driven out by Jezebel. Jeremiah was hauled up from the cistern by [Ebed-melech, the Ethiopian] eunuch. The Egyptian midwives saved the Israelite newborns. Rahab saved the Israelite scouts. In the time of Diocletian, a noble man in the city of Nicomedia in Bithynia publicly tore up an edict from the emperor ordering that the Christians must be killed, in order to demonstrate that he rejected this unjust cruelty.[†]

A counterexample is Doeg [the Edomite], who cruelly slew the innocent priests when Saul was carried away by his fury. And indeed there are many at this time who take part in unjust cruelty against our churches, confirming it either openly, or with their silence. Let these people understand this saying of Solomon and other similar passages, and calling to mind the most sorrowful condemnation of Christ, mend their ways. For it is written in Matthew 23: "On you shall come all the blood that was unjustly shed on the earth, from the blood of Abel the just to that of Zechariah." Also worth remembering is the most honorable voice of Trajan, who, when conferring a sword of knighthood on one of his magistrates, said, "This sword I give you, that you may wield it for me when I act justly; but if I act unjustly, use it against me."[‡] EXPOSITION OF THE PROVERBS OF SOLOMON.[20]

FOLLOWING GOD'S MERCIFUL EXAMPLE. MICHEL COP: It is said that "God did not make death, and he does not delight in the death of the living." This fits with what the prophet Ezekiel says: "'I do not desire the death of the one who dies,' says the Lord." And again, "As I live, declares the Lord God, I have no pleasure in the death of the wicked, but that the wicked turn from his way and live." Now, when we are God's enemies on account of our sins, he declares and reveals himself to be so very merciful. He does not seek our destruction, but calls us back to himself again and gives us access by Jesus Christ his Son, by whom he has reconciled us to himself, to give us life and salvation forever. And just as he is like this toward us, who are his enemies by nature (for the affection of the flesh is enmity against God), even so he intends that we should be merciful and show pity to those who are our enemies. . . .

But some will object that the children of Israel sang a song to the Lord rejoicing in the destruction of Pharaoh and his people. And Deborah and

[19]Cajetan, *Parabolae Salomonis ad veritatem Hebraicam castigatae*, 213.

[20]CR 14:59-60; citing Ex 20:13; 1 Tim 5:22; Rom 13:4; 1 Sam 19–20; 1 Kings 18:4; Jer 38:7-13; Ex 1:15-22; Josh 2:9-13; 1 Sam 22:6-19; Mt 23:35. [†]Eusebius, *Historia ecclesiastica* 8.5.1; Lactantius relates that he was subsequently seized, tried, and executed by being burned alive (*De mortibus persecutorum* 13.2). [‡]Dio Cassius, *Historia Romana* 68.16.

Barack sang to the Lord to celebrate the defeat of their enemies. And David rejoiced at the fall of his enemies. And God said, "I will comfort myself over my enemies, and avenge myself on my foes"; therefore, it is lawful to rejoice at the fall of the enemy. I answer that we may rejoice at the fall of our enemies only when it redounds to God's glory, and when in doing so we learn to fear the Lord and magnify him. But if our intention is to prosecute our own private injuries, or to seek our own personal profit, or if we allow those passions that we normally keep under control to enter into consideration, or if we are swifter to rejoice at the ruin of our enemies on account of self-love, then our joy is not righteous, and Solomon forbids it. ON THE PROVERBS OF SOLOMON.[21]

PUBLIC AND PRIVATE ENEMIES. THE ENGLISH ANNOTATIONS: There are private enemies, over private quarrels and differences, and there are public enemies in a public cause, whether state or religion or both. Upon the falling of a public enemy there is no question but that we may rejoice, nay, must in some measure, in thankfulness to God that he has delivered us. This is no small part of the thankfulness he expects at our hands. But even then, our joy should be in reference to God's glory (often not a little interested in our deliverance) and the public good, rather than any pleasure we take at the misery of our enemies. We must still remember they are God's creatures, of the same flesh and blood as us, descended from the same first-father, Adam, and in that respect (even though we rejoice their overthrow because of the consequence) an object of compassion in their particular persons. As for particular enemies, though we must be thankful to God for them too if they were our enemies without cause such as might do us harm, yet our joy must be moderate and wary, and if we have any generosity at all, their fall will make us forget how we have been wronged (if they have wronged us) and rather dispose us to help them in their misery than (as it does to some bad natures) provoke revenge. ANNOTATIONS ON PROVERBS 24:17.[22]

OBEDIENCE TO LEGITIMATE AUTHORITY. PHILIPP MELANCHTHON: This is one of the most important proverbs in the book, for it teaches obedience, and indeed that God commands obedience. First it commands us to obey God, and next the king, because the primary duty of the ruler in the political sphere is to be the voice of the Decalogue, and the punisher of those who violate the Decalogue. And for this reason in particular God has subjected the multitudes to the magistrates, because he wants them to hear and to understand his law, so that by it he may be known; in the next place, that human society may not be ruined utterly by tumults. But God has ratified it, and for this reason we must obey, and understand that he will punish those who are contumacious. And he also circumscribes the limits of those who hold power, lest they command what is contrary to the divine mandates. Thus above it is said, "fear God," and in this is also expressed the apostles' rule: "We must obey God rather than humans."

But this passage must be understood within a wider context of teaching on the purposes of the political order and the role of the magistrates, which is set out more fully in Romans 13 and in other places. But this particular text teaches that we should shun seditious people, and so it is necessary to distinguish between dissensions and sedition. And it is easier to decide in political matters, because regular authority has long stood out above the multitude and can be seen with the eyes. Now it is clear what the duties of the regular authority are—namely, to make the voice of the Decalogue resound, and to punish those who are contumacious. Also, to administer justice and to carry out sentences according to the laws. And these judgments are honored even in doubtful cases, not only on account of probable reason but also because divine authority has been granted to

[21]Cop, *Sur les Proverbes de Salomon*, 532; citing Wis 1:13; Ezek 18:32; 33:11; Ex 15:1-18; Judg 5:1-31; Ps 9; 13; 38; Is 1:24.

[22]Downame, ed., *English Annotations*, 6Y2v*.

the magistrates, whom God wants us to obey in civil affairs and to give them the benefit of the doubt in doubtful cases. And because God gives a more peaceful and tranquil rule to some than to others, he desires that we also bear certain heavy burdens—provided that these burdens are tolerable and are not heinous and notorious injuries, or that obedience does not to cause us to sin.

In these matters we must hold to the rule of Paul: "It is necessary to obey, not only on account of wrath, but also for the sake of conscience." For those who are contumacious sin, being unwilling to obey the legitimate government, while those who are seditious sin more gravely—that is, those who are insolent in their words against the magistrates, or who attempt to cast them off by force, either through factions or through armed revolt. This proverb threatens such people with punishment, just as the Lord says: "The one who takes up the sword will die by the sword"—that is, the one who draws the sword without legal authorization will perish like Absalom, Sheba [son of Bichri], Adonijah [son of Haggith], Joab, Cassius, Brutus, and innumerable others.

But against heinous injuries and notorious abuses there must be some defense, just as the written law allows that even a consul who is caught in the act of adultery may be slain by the woman's father.[†] [The Roman general] Marius pardoned a young man who slew a military tribune in defense of his own modesty.[‡] And [the emperor] Victorinus was slain while campaigning in Germany at the colony of Agrippina by a scribe whose wife he had seduced—and this despite the fact that in all other things he was so praised for his virtues that he was favorably compared to Nerva and Trajan.[§]

The gospel does grant legitimacy to the laws that govern political life, when they are agreeable to reason. And yet if such a defense is not presented as a concession, the effect is to transform the gospel into a political doctrine, and to prop up infinite tyranny. . . . But as regards reprehensible errors in the church, it must be known that those who resist the princes and prelates who defend these errors are by no means acting sinfully. For it is necessary to obey God in confessing the truth, just as the apostles said: "We must obey God rather than humans." By these mandates of God we confirm ourselves against the clamors of princes and prelates who cry out that we are being seditious, because in our teaching and confession we censure their errors and idolatry, just as God has instructed. For we know that ministers of the gospel do not bear the sword, and so when those who hold regular power inflict violence, they must bear up under these injuries, just as it is written, "The weapons of our warfare are not of the flesh." Also, "As the Father sent me, I am sending you." And, "My kingdom is not of this world." Exposition of the Proverbs of Solomon.[23]

Working Sedulously, and in Good Order. Michel Cop: God has ordained from the beginning that human beings should occupy themselves with labor till the end of their lives. But by the corruption into which humanity is fallen, they have gone astray, wandering from this holy ordinance into fraud, deception, violence, outrage, rapine, theft, and plunder, and by such means they have sought to raise their houses. . . . Now with the intent that we do not throw in our lot with such wicked people, Solomon warns us that each one should attend to the business to which God has called them when he says, "Prepare your work outside." He speaks here of only one kind of work:

[23]CR 14:60-62; citing Acts 5:29; Rom 13:5; Mt 26:52; 2 Sam 18:1-18; 20:1-10; 1 Kings 2:13-25; 2:28-34; Acts 5:29; Mt 10:33; Mk 3:28-29; Gal 1:9; 2 Cor 10:4; Jn 20:21; 18:36. [†]Melanchthon is most likely referring to the *lex Iulia de adulteriis coercendis*, which allowed the *pater familias* wide prerogatives in avenging crimes against the family's honor. [‡]The story is repeated in many ancient writers, but the account in Cicero briefly adduces the major elements as an example of justifiable homicide: "Once a soldier in the army of Gaius Marius suffered an indecent assault at the hands of a military tribune, a relative of the commander; and the assailant was slain by his intended victim, who, being an upright youth, preferred to act at his peril rather than to endure to his dishonor. What is more, the great general absolved the offence and acquitted the offender." Cicero, *Pro Milone* 4.9 (LCL 252:14-15); see also Plutarch, *Vita Marius* 14.3-5. [§]*Scriptores Historia Augusta, Tyranni Triginta* 6.3-8.

agricultural work—and he includes under that heading all other lawful pursuits by which one may justly gain one's daily bread. He speaks here only of one type of work so as to avoid being prolix, and he uses husbandry as the chief example because God ordained it first. Moreover, it is the most necessary for the body, for from this come all our other bodily and temporal goods, and there is nothing to be found in the towns, villages, or houses that does not first come from the field. So we have nothing without labor from the earth. It is Solomon's habit to comprehend under one kind all the rest, as we have seen before.

And when he says, "which is yours," we may here learn two things. The first is that we ought not to leave our business to do what belongs to another. For in doing this, we put both ourselves and our family in danger to beg our bread. This does not mean that one should not give their neighbor all the help and service they can—especially those who are poor and feeble, and have need of help. In doing so, one does not abandon one's business, for it is everyone's duty to cheerfully and freely assist whomever has need of it. The second is that we content ourselves with what is our own, not wanting to order our own affairs at another person's cost—as do those who shift their neighbor's landmarks and encroach on their property.[†] Otherwise, we are accursed: "Cursed is the one who removes his neighbor's landmarks."

Moreover, Solomon shows in this proverb that we ought not to eat our bread for nothing. This agrees with what St. Paul teaches. If we obey in this, we shall not lack a home, as Solomon promises us here, saying, "and after that build your house." He means by this that if we want to have a house that is ours by just title, it behooves us to apply ourselves sedulously [*songneusement*] to our business and to earn our bread by working for it, as the state to which God has called us requires. But those who think nothing of labor can neither make nor possess a house that is theirs, but must usurp like thieves and robbers all that they have, no matter what title for it they may possess. But if we take the end of this proverb as an admonition, just like the beginning (as some think), then it makes sense to say that Solomon teaches the father of the household how he ought to govern himself so as to prosper in his affairs. That is, he should be careful to employ himself first of all in things most necessary. Then, when he has done one thing, he should leave off from work, but work assiduously and in good order, so that one job does not prevent another from getting done. On the Proverbs of Solomon.[24]

---

[24]Cop, *Sur les Proverbes de Salomon*, 523-24; citing Deut 27:17; Eph 4:28; 2 Thess 3:6. [†]Cf. Cop's remarks on Prov 22:28.

25:1–27:27 MORE PROVERBS FROM SOLOMON

1These also are proverbs of Solomon which the men of Hezekiah king of Judah copied.

2It is the glory of God to conceal things,
but the glory of kings is to search things out.

3As the heavens for height, and the earth for depth,
so the heart of kings is unsearchable.

4Take away the dross from the silver,
and the smith has material for a vessel;

5take away the wicked from the presence of the king,
and his throne will be established in righteousness.

6Do not put yourself forward in the king's presence
or stand in the place of the great,

7for it is better to be told, "Come up here,"
than to be put lower in the presence of a noble.

What your eyes have seen
8do not hastily bring into court,[a]

for[b] *what will you do in the end,*
when your neighbor puts you to shame?

9Argue your case with your neighbor himself,
and do not reveal another's secret,

10lest he who hears you bring shame upon you,
and your ill repute have no end.

11A word fitly spoken
is like apples of gold in a setting of silver.

12Like a gold ring or an ornament of gold
is a wise reprover to a listening ear.

13Like the cold of snow in the time of harvest
is a faithful messenger to those who send him;
he refreshes the soul of his masters.

14Like clouds and wind without rain
is a man who boasts of a gift he does not give.

15With patience a ruler may be persuaded,
and a soft tongue will break a bone.

16If you have found honey, eat only enough for you,
lest you have your fill of it and vomit it.

17Let your foot be seldom in your neighbor's house,
lest he have his fill of you and hate you.

18A man who bears false witness against his neighbor
is like a war club, or a sword, or a sharp arrow.

19Trusting in a treacherous man in time of trouble
is like a bad tooth or a foot that slips.

20Whoever sings songs to a heavy heart
is like one who takes off a garment on a cold day,
and like vinegar on soda.

21If your enemy is hungry, give him bread to eat,
and if he is thirsty, give him water to drink,

22for you will heap burning coals on his head,
and the LORD *will reward you.*

23The north wind brings forth rain,
and a backbiting tongue, angry looks.

24It is better to live in a corner of the housetop
than in a house shared with a quarrelsome wife.

25Like cold water to a thirsty soul,
so is good news from a far country.

26Like a muddied spring or a polluted fountain
is a righteous man who gives way before the wicked.

27It is not good to eat much honey,
nor is it glorious to seek one's own glory.[c]

28A man without self-control
is like a city broken into and left without walls.

26 *Like snow in summer or rain in harvest,*
so honor is not fitting for a fool.

2 *Like a sparrow in its flitting, like a swallow in its flying,*
a curse that is causeless does not alight.

3 *A whip for the horse, a bridle for the donkey,*
and a rod for the back of fools.

4 *Answer not a fool according to his folly,*
lest you be like him yourself.

5 *Answer a fool according to his folly,*
lest he be wise in his own eyes.

6 *Whoever sends a message by the hand of a fool*
cuts off his own feet and drinks violence.

7 *Like a lame man's legs, which hang useless,*
is a proverb in the mouth of fools.

8 *Like one who binds the stone in the sling*
is one who gives honor to a fool.

9 *Like a thorn that goes up into the hand of a drunkard*
is a proverb in the mouth of fools.

10 *Like an archer who wounds everyone*
is one who hires a passing fool or drunkard.[d]

11 *Like a dog that returns to his vomit*
is a fool who repeats his folly.

12 *Do you see a man who is wise in his own eyes?*
There is more hope for a fool than for him.

13 *The sluggard says, "There is a lion in the road!*
There is a lion in the streets!"

14 *As a door turns on its hinges,*
so does a sluggard on his bed.

15 *The sluggard buries his hand in the dish;*
it wears him out to bring it back to his mouth.

16 *The sluggard is wiser in his own eyes*
than seven men who can answer sensibly.

17 *Whoever meddles in a quarrel not his own*
is like one who takes a passing dog by the ears.

18 *Like a madman who throws firebrands,*
arrows, and death

19 *is the man who deceives his neighbor*
and says, "I am only joking!"

20 *For lack of wood the fire goes out,*
and where there is no whisperer, quarreling ceases.

21 *As charcoal to hot embers and wood to fire,*
so is a quarrelsome man for kindling strife.

22 *The words of a whisperer are like delicious morsels;*
they go down into the inner parts of the body.

23 *Like the glaze*[e] *covering an earthen vessel*
are fervent lips with an evil heart.

24 *Whoever hates disguises himself with his lips*
and harbors deceit in his heart;

25 *when he speaks graciously, believe him not,*
for there are seven abominations in his heart;

26 *though his hatred be covered with deception,*
his wickedness will be exposed in the assembly.

27 *Whoever digs a pit will fall into it,*
and a stone will come back on him who starts it rolling.

28 *A lying tongue hates its victims,*
and a flattering mouth works ruin.

27 *Do not boast about tomorrow,*
for you do not know what a day may bring.

2 *Let another praise you, and not your own mouth;*
a stranger, and not your own lips.

3 *A stone is heavy, and sand is weighty,*
but a fool's provocation is heavier than both.

4 *Wrath is cruel, anger is overwhelming,*
but who can stand before jealousy?

5 *Better is open rebuke*
than hidden love.

6 *Faithful are the wounds of a friend;*
profuse are the kisses of an enemy.

7 One who is full loathes honey,
but to one who is hungry everything bitter is sweet.

8 Like a bird that strays from its nest
is a man who strays from his home.

9 Oil and perfume make the heart glad,
and the sweetness of a friend comes from his earnest counsel.[f]

10 Do not forsake your friend and your father's friend,
and do not go to your brother's house in the day of your calamity.

Better is a neighbor who is near
than a brother who is far away.

11 Be wise, my son, and make my heart glad,
that I may answer him who reproaches me.

12 The prudent sees danger and hides himself,
but the simple go on and suffer for it.

13 Take a man's garment when he has put up security for a stranger,
and hold it in pledge when he puts up security for an adulteress.[g]

14 Whoever blesses his neighbor with a loud voice,
rising early in the morning,
will be counted as cursing.

15 A continual dripping on a rainy day
and a quarrelsome wife are alike;

16 to restrain her is to restrain the wind
or to grasp[h] *oil in one's right hand.*

17 Iron sharpens iron,
and one man sharpens another.[i]

18 Whoever tends a fig tree will eat its fruit,
and he who guards his master will be honored.

19 As in water face reflects face,
so the heart of man reflects the man.

20 Sheol and Abaddon are never satisfied,
and never satisfied are the eyes of man.

21 The crucible is for silver, and the furnace is for gold,
and a man is tested by his praise.

22 Crush a fool in a mortar with a pestle
along with crushed grain,
yet his folly will not depart from him.

23 Know well the condition of your flocks,
and give attention to your herds,

24 for riches do not last forever;
and does a crown endure to all generations?

25 When the grass is gone and the new growth appears
and the vegetation of the mountains is gathered,

26 the lambs will provide your clothing,
and the goats the price of a field.

27 There will be enough goats' milk for your food,
for the food of your household
and maintenance for your girls.

a Or *presence of a noble, as your eyes have seen. 8Do not go hastily out to court* **b** Hebrew *or else* **c** The meaning of the Hebrew line is uncertain **d** Or *hires a fool or passersby* **e** By revocalization; Hebrew *silver of dross* **f** Or *and so does the sweetness of a friend that comes from his earnest counsel* **g** Hebrew *a foreign woman*; a slight emendation yields (compare Vulgate; see also 20:16) *foreigners* **h** Hebrew *to meet with* **i** Hebrew *sharpens the face of another*

Overview: These chapters contain more admonitions regarding the exercise of virtue in ordinary life. Important themes treated in the exegesis include the prerogatives of rulers in weighing their words, the role of wisdom in guarding one's speech, and the duties related to the faithful pursuit of one's vocation in worldly work. All of these were practical matters for the reformers, who had to navigate their relationships with worldly authorities and whose ministries might be called into question if they did not exercise wisdom. Cardinal Cajetan dwells on the judicial role of political authorities, arguing that although their authority mirrors that of the heavenly judge, human authorities ought to rule with transparency of judgment. Michel Cop and John Donne find occasion to commend intellectual humility in the study of Scripture, and Philipp Melanchthon defends God's providence against the scandal of the cross. Proverbs 26:4-5 presents a challenging text with its opposing pieces of advice: "Answer not a fool . . . . Answer a fool . . . ." Our commentators use this juxtaposition as an opportunity to reflect on the virtues of discretion and of the duties of admonition, and their nuanced considerations emphasize that Reformational ethics are not simply rule-based, but require wisdom and spiritual discernment. Melanchthon reflects on the limits of discipline in God's providential guidance of human affairs, and Cop warns against the evils of those who nurse private hatreds and dissemble with sweet words. The final chapter of this section showcases proverbs dealing with the duties of vocation, more warnings against busybodies, the benefits of living and working in community, and the value of humility.

25:1-28 *Using Patience and Caring for Enemies*

THE PREROGATIVE OF THE HIGHEST JUDGE. CARDINAL CAJETAN: "It is God's prerogative to conceal a word, and the glory of kings to search out what has been said." The word translated here "glory" means "honor." And God is named here Elohim. I thought that this should be noted for this reason, because the discussion concerns God insofar as he is *elohim*, that is, a judge. Note here as well that the honor of Elohim and the honor of kings are distinguished by contrast according to their respective actions: concealing a word and searching out a word. Therefore, to conceal the word is an honor that belongs to Elohim and not to kings. And on the other hand, searching out a word is the honor of kings and not of Elohim. These points must be understood before the meaning of the proverb becomes clear. Therefore, because the word of Elohim (i.e., God as judge) is judgment itself, it indicates that concealing a word means hiding the reasons for his judgments. And the meaning is, concealing the reasons for his judgments is an honor belonging to the highest judge. The reasons for the divine judgments that he often executes are, in a particular instance, utterly hidden from us. And so great is the difference between God and kings that it is actually disgraceful for kings to conceal the reasons for their judgments. They ought to reveal why they judge as they do, why they condemn someone to exile, death, and so on. But concealing the reasons for his judgments is an honor that belongs to God, because this is how he makes known that he has no superior or equal; that his lordship or justice does not depend on us. Rather, it is dependent on his own will alone. Kings have the honor of searching out or investigating a word, which means the knowledge and truth of words, deeds, and so on. Attributing this action to God is absolutely forbidden, because investigating something is what a person does when they do not know something. But God knows all things, in his own person, eternally. THE PARABLES OF SOLOMON, CORRECTED BY THE ORIGINAL HEBREW.[1]

SEEKING HIDDEN WISDOM. PHILIPP MELANCHTHON: The teaching unique to the church of God differs from human wisdom, and often preeminent men particularly go astray in governing, when they prefer political wisdom over the Word of God, just as Nebuchadnezzar did when he set up worship [of his own image], dreaming that such ceremonies would be of benefit to the harmony of his reign. Thus the heretics twist the gospel to their own fancies. Therefore this proverb reminds us that the word of God is a hidden wisdom, only to be acquired with great effort. In other words, God wants us to be disciples of his voice; he does not want us to prefer our own notions and invent new dogmas or rites. Therefore the glory of a king is,

[1]Cajetan, *Parabolae Salomonis ad veritatem Hebraicam castigatae*, 220–21.

above all else, to seek out the hidden wisdom and pay heed to it, and not be distracted by sophistries. Thus Paul teaches, "Let the wisdom of God dwell in you"†—that is, seek wisely the fountains that bear witness to it, and remember that we ought to be disciples of the divine voice, just as Solomon says: "Listening to the wise, one becomes more wise." Human wisdom commanded David to kill Saul, but the Holy Spirit did not wish to present such an example to the people of God. Exposition of the Proverbs of Solomon.[2]

Kings Must Seek Wisdom. The English Annotations: Though kings often, by a special providence, are endowed with extraordinary parts of wit and judgment above ordinary people, yet it is an honor to a king not to affect to be like God in giving no account for any of his actions nor taking any counsel. To the contrary, kings should take advice from those who are wise and inquire diligently before any resolution. Besides, it is an honor to a king also not to trust others altogether but to himself be present and insistent at the search and examination of things, to judge himself, and to deliver his opinion according to the quality of the cause. Annotations on Proverbs 25:2.[3]

A Figure of Spiritual Humility. Michel Cop: No one wants to abase themselves. Our natural inclination is to rise up and appear great, so that we may be self-sufficient and enjoy the success of our enterprises and undertakings. So Adam wanted to be like God, and the giants won for themselves great renown. The sons of men began a great tower to win fame and make themselves mighty. Saul, seeing himself despised, was angry, and so to maintain his greatness he conspired against David. Absalom coveted the kingdom and wrought treason against David his father. And because Solomon knew very well that we feared the harms we ran after, furious and enraged by our rashness, boldness, pride, and haughtiness, so he seeks to strip us of these ambitions, to induce us to humility and make us love it when he says, "Do not glory in yourself." Every one of us naturally has a king's heart, worldly and carnal, which seeks to be praised, exalted, and feared. We strive to advance ourselves ahead of our neighbors, and we are eager to be ahead of them in honor and glory. Solomon thinks that such a nature, so full of pride and loftiness, is not good; he desires instead that we outstrip one another in honor, esteeming everyone more excellent than ourselves. He shows us this well, when teaching us in general to humble ourselves toward our neighbors, he names only "kings" and "great men." Since these are the ones who ought to be preferred above all others, if we do not humble ourselves before such as these, we will easily despise the others. . . .

"For it is better to be told, 'Come up here.'" Here at first glance it seems that Solomon teaches only a modest and humble civility, but interpreting it thus we do not give it the excellence that it deserves. Therefore we should understand that under a figure of humble civility he is trying to imprint on our hearts the true spiritual humility, by which we are guided to humble behavior and a modest countenance. Our Lord Jesus Christ does the same thing. Nevertheless, neither our Lord nor Solomon condemns the first place, however high it may be; rather, what is condemned is the ambitious desire [to be in the first place]. The Evangelist demonstrates this when he says that Jesus told the invited guests a parable to warn them, "when he noticed how they chose the places of honor." Nor is there any point in allegorizing this parable further for edification. Suffice it to say that the Holy Ghost invites us here to true humility, with the aim that being lowly of heart in this world, we may at last be exalted. We shall attain this if we have the same attitude as the publican. On the Proverbs of Solomon.[4]

[2]CR 14:62-63; citing Prov 1:5. †Possibly a reference to Col 3:15: "Let the word of Christ dwell in you richly in all wisdom."
[3]Downame, ed., *English Annotations*, 6Y3r*.
[4]Cop, *Sur les Proverbes de Salomon*, 548-49; citing Gen 3:5-7; 6:1-4; 11:4; 1 Sam 18:8; 2 Sam 15-17; Lk 14:7; 18:13.

DISCERNMENT IN ADMONITION. PHILIPP MELANCHTHON: "Like vinegar on soda is one who sings a song to a depraved heart." Salt and soda have a similar nature: they both burn and corrode bodies, and it is the distinctive power of soda that it expels [impurities] and is excited by vinegar and lime, which is why Pliny says that soda is applied with lime and vinegar to spreading sores.[†] Therefore this comparison signifies that when obstinate people are admonished, they may become more agitated, just as soda reacting vigorously to an infusion of vinegar is dissipated and dissolved on account of the property it has of reciprocal replacement (*antiperistasin*). Thus having been admonished, Saul became far more cruel. And so also are many impious people, who only become more furious when they are cautioned. But this proverb does not forbid true doctrine being taught; rather, it speaks to the outcome and points out that people will respond differently: some will listen, others will be responsive, and still others will be pertinacious, unwilling to be taught, just as Romans 11 says concerning those who blaspheme: "Let their eyes be darkened so that they cannot see." But although I have said that this proverb does not forbid that instruction in the truth be given, it indicates that discernment must be exercised with regard to those who listen. Those who are teachable must be faithful and sedulous in study, as Paul says: "Accept the one whose faith is weak." But concerning those others, who blaspheme, it is said, "Do not cast what is holy before dogs." And, "Do not speak in the ears of a fool, for he will despise the wisdom of your speech." And yet even before you are able to distinguish between your hearers, sound teaching must be proclaimed to everyone; afterward, the rule of Paul applies: "A heretic, after the first or second warning, shun." EXPOSITION OF THE PROVERBS OF SOLOMON.[5]

BE WISE WITH THE HONEY OF SCRIPTURE. JOHN DONNE: Content yourself with reading those parts of the Scriptures that are clear and edify, and do not perplex yourself with prophecies not yet performed. Content yourself with hearing those sermons that rectify yourself . . . in all those things that you are bound to believe and bound to practice, and do not run after those who pretend to know those things that God has not revealed to his church. Too little or too much of this honey, of this reading and of this hearing, may be unwholesome. God has chosen ways of mediocrity. He redeemed us not by God alone, nor by man alone, but by him who was both. He instructs us not by the Holy Ghost alone, without the ministry of people, nor by the minister alone, without the assistance of the Holy Ghost. SERMON ON ACTS 10:44.[6]

THE SCANDAL OF THE CROSS. PHILIPP MELANCHTHON: It is obvious how greatly troubled the minds of all wise people are by the deformity of the church when they see authority, wealth, and wisdom in the hands of wicked people; meanwhile, the true church is meager and wretched, scattered among different peoples with no clear power. Likewise, innocent people are killed by the most repulsive tyrants: the Israelite infants by Pharaoh, John the Baptist by Herod, Paul by Nero. These awful spectacles move the wise to consider that God must not care for these wretched people.

But the divine voice teaches that here is the true church, where God is exalted by the promise and by clear testimonials, by resurrection of the dead and by other wonders. And this is the one for whom God cares, whom he hears and protects, and who will inherit eternal glory before God: whoever is small and subjected to the cross for certain reasons.

By these divine testimonials are we fortified against those spectacles that are commonly called "the scandal of the cross," and we remember these sayings: "You have hidden these things from the wise, and revealed them to little ones." "Not many of you were wise according to the flesh, not many were powerful." The whole teaching of Paul in

[5]CR 14:63; citing Rom 11:10; 14:1; Mt 7:6; Prov 23:9; Titus 3:10. [†]Pliny the Elder, *Naturalis historia* 21.70.118.

[6]Donne, *Works*, 2:24*.

Romans 9 and many of the psalms also bear on this: "Do not fret yourself because of evildoers," and "my feet had almost stumbled."

It happens thus in private. When David was driven into exile, he took delight in the calamity of the wicked, and mocked them with obvious sarcasm. This judgment is described by this image: like a muddy spring is the just before the wicked. But the faithful hold fast to true consolations; they know the character of the church, and they understand the reasons why they are subjected to the cross, and from where they are to seek secure consolations. Exposition of the Proverbs of Solomon.[7]

26:1-28 *Like Sparrows, Archers, and Dogs*

An Admonition to Modesty. Philipp Melanchthon: This saying speaks to the same event: "Fortune makes fools of her favorites."[†] For it relates that people not yet chastised or pacified who become insolent in prosperity, and they loosen the reins on various desires. So, for example, although in the beginning Alexander was very modest and mild, later he desired to become a god, and instead he became inhuman. For when people are not held in check, they become secure in themselves, and do not pray for help from God; then they become drunk on their successes, and magnify their intelligence in their own eyes. So great and so sad are the fates of heroes: Hercules, Nebuchadnezzar, Julius, Pompey, and innumerable others.

But even if it says this much concerning the event, setting down a rule for ordinary circumstances, nevertheless we should quietly embrace this admonition for ourselves as a precept relating to modesty, just as Sirach relates: "The greater you are, the more must you humble yourself; so you will find favor before the Lord." Also, "God resists the proud, but gives grace to the humble." And then there is that saying of Plutarch: "Princes imitate the sun, which, when it reaches its highest summit in the northern sky, has the slowest motion, and thus by its slowness ensures the safety of its course."[‡] Exposition of the Proverbs of Solomon.[8]

Undeserved Honors Destroy a Fool. Robert Cleaver: "As snow in summer and rain in harvest." As snow and rain do not correspond to those seasons, neither did either of them fall at those times in those countries, for it was a miracle to have rain during the wheat harvest. "So honor is unseemly for a fool." So are titles, praises, and promotions unfit for wicked people, because they should be the rewards of wisdom and virtue. Snow is not fitting for summer, because it hinders the ripening of the corn on account of its extreme cold; likewise, rain is not welcome in harvest, for it hinders the gathering of the earth's fruits on account of its dampness. Likewise, "honor is not fitting for a fool," in this respect, that he is unworthy of it: all the preferments in the world cannot make a sinful person truly honorable, no more than a gold ring in a swine's snout can make her gorgeous and beautiful. . . . Moreover, [such honors] are hurtful to him, making him proud and high-minded, and breeding a dangerous discord in his heart, advertising to the world his folly and vileness and setting these on a high stage so that all may gaze on his misbehavior. A Brief Explanation.[9]

Consolation amid Calumny. Philipp Melanchthon: Here is a rule to hold on to in life: "Fight the good fight, hold fast to the faith and a good conscience." When we hold fast to these, we will also enjoy the honorable approval of others. And this is to be expected, as Sirach says: "Have regard for your good name." But still there are always many malevolent people, who attempt to discredit those whom they envy, as Cicero says: "It is a sort of blot and blemish of this age to be envious of virtue."[†] And many people are

[7]CR 14:64.

[8]CR 14:65; citing Sir 3:18; Jas 4:6. [†]Publilius Syrus, *Sententia* 203. [‡]Plutarch, *Ad principem ineruditum* 782E.

[9]Cleaver, *A Brief Explanation of the Whole Booke of the Proverbs of Salomon*, 433; citing 1 Sam 12:1.

quarrelsome by nature, taking delight in uttering evil against others, and many make it their trade, as Plautus says: "Fools have a kind of repository in their tongue, so that they regard it as profitable to insult their betters."[‡] . . . And the histories of every age make plain that many honorable people are burdened by calumnies, such as Joseph, Palamedes, Aristides, Theramenes, Socrates, and innumerable others. And in Ecclesiastes it is said, "Calumny troubles the wise, and will weaken the strength of his heart." So experience demonstrates that good people are often stymied by calumnies.

Therefore this consolation against calumny is given us: false accusations, even if they wound for a time, will be laid bare and discredited, as it is said: "Truth can be oppressed for a time, but it cannot be destroyed."[§] The psalm adds a sweeter consolation: "Let them curse, but you will bless." And in response to the insults of Shimei, David said, "God will give me some good in return for his curses." Let us hold fast to these consolations, and at the same time uphold the integrity of our conscience, just as we have often been taught: "This is our glory, the testimony of our conscience." And in Galatians, "Let each one test his own work, for then he will have glory in himself, and not in another"; that is, act rightly so that your conscience does not condemn you, and when your conscience does not prick you, you will have glory—a glory that does not depend on the foolish applause of others, but rather one which comes from the true approbation of conscience, a work that is both necessary for believing and pleasing to God. EXPOSITION OF THE PROVERBS OF SOLOMON.[10]

RESPOND TO A FOOL WITHOUT BECOMING FOOLISH. CARDINAL CAJETAN: "Do not answer a fool according to his folly, so that you do not become like him." The Hebrew meaning here is very similar: "You shall not answer a fool in his foolishness and make yourself equal to him." There then follows immediately, "Answer a fool in keeping with his foolishness, so he does not become wise in his own eyes." The meaning of the first command is that one should not answer a fool using similar, foolish speech. In that translation the preposition "in" means, you will not reply to a fool "in his foolishness." Because not answering when he acts foolishly means that the answer is not formed using similar foolishness. For example, if a fool reproaches you, you do not answer with reproach. And Solomon supplies a reason: so you do not (even accidentally) make yourself, though wise, equal to him. If you make yourself equal to him in your speech, you risk doing what is shameful, like those who are shameful. So do not bring yourself down to his level, do not become a fool like he is. Habits are formed based on repeated action. The meaning of the second command—"answer a fool as his folly"—is that one must make use of rebuke, instruction, or clear teaching. And then the reason is given: so that he is not wise in his own eyes. The reason makes clear that this is the language of rebuke as one's answer, whether by arguing, by clear statement, or by instruction. When the fool's speech is rebuked he has no opportunity to think he is wise. And notice here that the first commandment is aimed at one's own good. But the second one looks to the good of the fool, and consequently of other persons. For not only is it harmful to the fool that he should think he is wise, but also to others. And this is especially so if he is a public figure. THE PARABLES OF SOLOMON, CORRECTED BY THE ORIGINAL HEBREW.[11]

WHEN NOT TO ANSWER FOOLS. PHILIPP MELANCHTHON: Two conflicting ideas are often related, which differ from one another: sometimes curses must be refuted, and sometimes it is not necessary to respond. Prudent judgment must be exercised in determining whether to do so. But it is actually easy to decide for pastors teaching in a public office. These men always have a diverse

[10]CR 14:65-66; citing 1 Tim 6:2; Sir 41:12; Eccles 7:8; Ps 109:28; 2 Sam 16:12; 2 Cor 1:12; Gal 6:4. [†]Cicero, *Pro Balbo* 6.16 (LCL 447:642-43). [‡]Plautus, *Poenulus* 625-26 (LCL 260:84-85). [§]Cf. Livy, *History of Rome* 22.19.

[11]Cajetan, *Parabolae Salomonis ad veritatem Hebraicam castigatae*, 231.

audience: some are faithful; some are mature, others less stable; some are teachable, and yet others are stubborn adversaries or hopeless cases. Now it is necessary for pastors that they watch over the better part, so that the voice of uncorrupted doctrine may refute its adversaries. And so pastors must distinguish between different types of revilers: some mangle doctrine, whereas others bring shame upon the person teaching.

Pastors are commanded to make doctrine clear and to defend it.[†] They should be ready to fight when it comes to necessary matters, and also be eager to accept those who are weak in faith and work to strengthen them, just as Paul says. But they should not stir up trouble by getting bogged down in endless controversy, nor should they alienate the weak by their acerbity. Rather, they should give reproof privately and refute errors modestly, or else disregard them altogether, just as the psalm says: "They have slandered me, but I gave myself to prayer."

But in other private gatherings, teachers and others should carefully consider the differences between their hearers. If they appear to be teachable, they should be instructed accordingly. But if anyone incites hopeless confusion, do as John did when he came to the bathhouse where Cerinthus and his crowd were gathered. Desiring to make his confession plain on the spot, he withdrew from them as far as he could, so that it would not seem that he was colluding with heretics. This was done in accordance with the saying, "A heretic, after the first or second warning, shun." So John immediately left the bathhouse.[‡] . . .

But it is especially proper in the case of personal insults that we refrain from responding, just as David remained silent in the face of Shimei's cursing—or else that we refute them only sparingly. There are many examples of great leaders who ignored insults, just as Pericles, Fabius, Scipio, and others have done. Herodotus relates that the Spartans kept cool heads in the face of provocation from [the Persian general] Mardonius, who acted with still greater insolence on account of their silence, and was carried away by this "semblance of victory."[§] And Herodotus also relates how Gelon the tyrant of Sicily gave a magnificent reply to the Spartan legate, saying, "The hard accusations a man hears are apt to arouse his anger; but despite the insults you have hurled at me in your speech, you will not provoke me to act shamefully by returning your accusations."[◊] Moreover, people are often driven by anger to give insult. But it is folly to enter into disputes with irrational people, as an elegant saying in Greek verse has it: "When two men speak and one of them is incensed, the other is wiser not to combat his words."[Δ]

To sum up, when it comes to personal insults, we must bear in mind the words of Peter: "not returning reviling for reviling." And we should also remember that in responding it is less important that an error be set straight than that essential doctrine should be clearly and earnestly set forth. For it is not enough simply to contradict the reviling of others in an academic manner, but also it must be made clear what is to be believed. Exposition of the Proverbs of Solomon.[12]

Wisdom Is Dangerous in the Mouth of a Fool. Peter Moffett: The ungodly abuse the places into which they are advanced and the graces with which they are indued. The fool may very fitly be compared to the drunkard, for as the drunkard wants the use of his reason, so a fool is void of discretion. A parable in a fool's mouth may also very well be compared to a thorn lifted up in the hand of a drunkard; for a thorn in the hand of a drunkard is either ridiculously tossed up and down by him, or dangerously applied to the hurt of all who are near him, when he strikes or pricks them with it, not knowing or caring what he does. In the same way, the vain and wicked person either utters some excellent sentence so absurdly that he makes all that are present laugh, or he misapplies certain true sayings so corruptly and mischievously that he

[12]CR 14:66-68; citing Rom 14:1; Ps 108:3-4; Titus 3:10; 1 Pet 3:9. [†]Melanchthon cites 2 Tim 1:13; Titus 1:9, 11; 2:15, in support of this thesis. [‡]The anecdote is first reported in Irenaeus, *Adversus haereses* 3.3.4. [§]Herodotus, *Historiae* 9.48-49. [◊] Herodotus, *Historiae* 7.160. [Δ]Euripides, *Protesilaus* no. 654 (LCL 506:114-15).

vexes all who are in his company. Thus, as the drunken man does much hurt with his thorn, or as the madman sorely wounds those that come by him with the sword in his hand, so the foolish man, instead of using his gifts aright abuses them, and instead of doing good with his speech, does great harm. Therefore the ignorant fool who has no parable in his mouth is better off than the malicious fool, who having wit and utterance at will, abuses the parable of his mouth. For being drunk with anger, or with pride, or with envy, or with some similar affection, abuses good words—yes, sometimes even God's Word, God's church, and God's people—and shoots his bolts against the truth and against uprightness, betraying the malice of his heart and the darkness of his mind. There can hardly be greater grief or a more intolerable burden than to hear the unsavory and unsanctified speeches or invectives of such a witless and wicked fool. A Commentary upon the Book of the Proverbs of Solomon.[13]

The Right Skills for the Job. Philipp Melanchthon: "As a craftsman gives form to his work, so one who hires a fool pays for his work to be destroyed." The lawyer says that there are big differences among artisans. And there are many proverbs that address how to tell the difference between real craftsmen on the one hand, and imposters and busybodies who try to pass themselves off as such on the other hand. So, for example, there are many quacks who want to pass themselves off as physicians, and there are also many ignorant preachers who seek the adulation of the crowd or of princes.

Therefore we are given this admonition, which pertains to prudence, so that competent people may be chosen in their respective fields. At the same time, it is taught that those who profess to be craftsmen should not be imposters or busybodies, but as Paul says, they should be faithful—that is, they should be skilled in the arts they profess, and apply their skill with faithfulness and diligence. All this is summed up in the virtue that is called sedulousness, which is knowing and faithfully performing the work and responsibilities proper to one's vocation. Exposition of the Proverbs of Solomon.[14]

A Dog and Its Vomit. Michael Jermin: A dog is not more greedy of his meat than a fool is of his folly: it is with a canine appetite that he devours it. And "as a dog eats again what he has vomited" shows that it was not the meat that his stomach rejected but rather some pain that he felt by it that made him to vomit, "so a sinful fool returning to his folly" shows that it was not his folly that he disliked but only some trouble he suffered by it. And as a dog, little thinking of the hurt the meat did him before, eats it again, so a fool thinks little of the mischief his folly caused him when he runs into it again. . . . The Jews say that the cause of Hezekiah's sickness was that after his unheard-of victory over the king of Assyria he did not sing to God the prayer Moses sang when Pharaoh was overthrown, as Deborah did when Sisera was discomfited, or as Hannah did when Samuel was born; and so, by his sickness he was admonished for his proud ungratefulness. But after having recovered from his sickness by a great miracle and falling again into the same folly of pride by showing off his treasures, this made God to pronounce a great judgment against him. For great indeed is the wrath of God if, when we have by his mercy escaped his anger, we provoke him again by the same iniquity. And therefore what fools are careless sinners, who so often suck up their vomited wickedness. Paraphrastic Meditations.[15]

A Warning Against Hidden Malice. Michel Cop: When those who conceive a hatred against their neighbors think that they have just cause in hating them, or if they feel themselves

[13]Moffett, *A Commentary upon the Book of the Proverbs of Solomon*, 372-73.

[14]CR 14:68; citing 1 Tim 5:18.

[15]Jermin, *Paraphrasticall Meditations*, 603-4.

strong enough to inflict harm and damage on them, they will not willingly hide it. They will openly assault their enemy—just as when Saul convinced himself that David was his enemy, he pursued him without subterfuge. The enemies of the truth, who think that they are actually serving God by killing the disciples of Jesus Christ, boldly pronounce without dissimulation a sentence of death against them. Even so, those who are not ashamed to show their evil minds have no fear of declaring themselves enemies to those who do not please them. These are not the ones Solomon is speaking about when he says, "Whoever hates." Rather, he is speaking here of those who know in their consciences that they hate their neighbors wrongfully, and yet they will not cease in their hatred. Instead, they dissemble with sweet words, and secretly devise in their hearts ways to take those whom they hunt and to harm them by deceit, without putting them on their guard to avoid them. The captain of all such people is Cain, along with the brothers of Joseph. The traitor Judas also well deserves to be set in the same order. Likewise, the scribes and Pharisees and all those who hate the truth, but put on a fair show to those whom they pursue, seek ways to destroy them.

Now we must take careful heed that we do not become like the first haters, who are proud, for then we shall not only have people for our adversaries, but God, who resists the proud. And we must also take care not to be like those of whom Solomon now speaks, for then we would be cruel hypocrites, sinning against our own consciences and with deliberate malice. Hypocrisy is marked by feigning lips, and cruelty is known by the deception that lies hid within. Both are forms of deliberate malice—that is, in the deception of the lips, and in the covering of deceit. On the Proverbs of Solomon.[16]

A Warning Against Backsliding. Philipp Melanchthon: The reasons for punishments in this life have often been stated elsewhere, but to review, the primary causes are four: first, because God is just, and on account of his justice he demolishes what opposes it. Second, because he wants us to understand that he is just, and to distinguish between justice and injustice. Third, so that dangerous elements may be removed. And fourth, so that when we remember our own punishments and those of others, we may be deterred from sin, as was explained above: "Strike a scoffer, and the simple will learn prudence." And in 1 Corinthians 10, Paul says that the punishments of the people of Israel "occurred as examples [for us]." And the Lord told Abraham that it was for this reason that he should remember the example of the destruction of Sodom, that he might warn his descendants about the judgment of God. "Once stung, [the fisherman] will be wiser."[†] And, "Disaster has been my teacher."[‡] And, "It is shameful to stumble twice on the same stone."[§] And it is said concerning the examples given by others, "By observing the mistakes others make, we are educated."[◊]

But there are many who are hardened beyond the point where their own punishments, or those suffered by others, can do anything to correct them, and many of these are carried away and become rabid in the face of correction. Some may be restrained for a while, like Saul, only to relapse into their crimes, and it is about such backsliders that this proverb speaks—just as God so often reminds us in other places, that by backsliding we only bring greater punishments down on ourselves. So in Amos we read, "For three transgressions I forbear, but for four I do not." And both Christ and Peter tell us that people like this end up in worse condition than they were to start with. Solomon here compares these backsliders to dogs, but saddest of all, the Lord says that the devil returns with seven other spirits worse than himself.

There are many horrifying examples, both public and private, that we may consider in connection with this proverb. Fury arose in Pharaoh, Saul, Absalom, and Ahab; and the citizens of Sodom, who it seemed had been liberated by God when Abraham routed the army

[16]Cop, *Sur les Proverbes de Salomon*, 576-77; citing Gen 4:8; 37.

of their enemies, soon forgot their earlier punishments and liberation, and plunged headlong into far worse crimes. The Jews, after a series of most sorrowful calamities and deliverances, slew the Maccabee brothers and set about mangling their religious doctrine most perversely, carving it up between dissenting sects, the Pharisees and the Sadducees. As a result, their kingdom was mangled by civil wars.

In these histories, as well as in our own time in Germany, we see the same pattern: even when doctrine is corrected, many return to their previous errors, and then they become utterly godless (*atheoi*). Many new errors obscure the light of true doctrine and stir up new seditions. Many teachers neglect serious inquiry into doctrine, seeking instead to gratify the most vulgar elements, who are delighted by license and relax the reins on their lustful desires. In this way, we bring down still worse punishments upon ourselves; however, there will be some remnants of the true church preserved. If we want to be members of this remnant, we must be turned wholly back to God, and pray that we may be converted, ruled, and confirmed by the Son of God, and not be permitted to fall away. Exposition of the Proverbs of Solomon.[17]

Various Ways to Understand the Lying Tongue. The English Annotations: It seeks to do more mischief to those that it has hurt before. Some, making the verb active when it is more commonly passive, read, "A lying tongue hates those who crush (or repress) it," which is very plausible. Some, turning the passive plural into a singular, invert the order, thus, "A contrite (modest) person baits a lying tongue." Indeed, lying must be very odious to a mortified person, and it is a question whether one can avoid the occasion of lying sometimes if they are not altogether dead to the world and all worldly vanities. Hence "to lie" in Scripture, or "to submit," because those who are afraid to offend superiors on whom they depend and whom they seek to please in all things are forced to this base shift often according to the old saying, "Compliance begets love; truth, enmity." Annotations on Proverbs 26:28.[18]

27:1-27 *Do Not Boast, Do Not Forsake*

Attending to the Duties of Vocation in the Present. Philipp Melanchthon: This proverb agrees with several Roman sayings: "You know not what evening may bring."[†] And, "Divine power plays with human affairs, and sure trust can scarce be placed in the present hour."[‡] And, "All human affairs hang by a slender thread; chance on a sudden brings to ruin what once was strong."[§] And again, "He becomes suddenly an Irus who was but now a Croesus."[◊] Indeed, there are books full of such admonitions concerning the inconstancy of fortune, which are set down for us to prompt us to modesty and warn us away from those two great vices: faith in ourselves, and a rashness that unnecessarily stirs things up in foolish hope. These admonitions also serve to maintain us within our proper limits, so that we may only perform those duties which are necessary for our vocation, as Paul says: "Mind your own business." And knowing our own weakness, we must certainly add prayer to God along with these admonitions, as it is written: "Be subject to the Lord, and pray to him." And, "Without me, you can do nothing." And Jeremiah says, "I know, O Lord, that the way of a man is not his own"—that is, it is a vocation. For he does not say that a man can do nothing; only that without God's help, neither his plans nor his actions will be successful.

Therefore we should always keep this rule in mind, that we must rightly do what is necessary in the present moment as the rule of our duty demands. And we must seek God's help, so that resting confidence in our own virtues or other foolish hope we may not agitate ourselves with

[17]CR 14:69-70; citing Prov 19:25; 1 Cor 10:6; Gen 18:16-19; Amos 1:3, 6, 9, 11, 13; Mt 12:45; 2 Pet 2:20-22. [†]Erasmus, *Adagia* 1.1.29 (CWE 31:77). [‡]Herodotus, *The Persian Wars* 1.207 (LCL 117:260-61). [§]Erasmus, *Adagia* 1.5.8 (CWE 31:392). [◊]Stobaeus, *Sententiae ex thesauris Graecorum delectae* (Lyons, 1609), 37.

[18]Downame, ed., *English Annotations*, 6Y4v*.

unnecessary things, like Pericles, who waged an unnecessary war on the basis of the most trifling provocations, which (in the judgment of many at that time) he might well have overlooked.[Δ] . . . Such striving (*polypragmosynē*) usually ends unhappily in the end, when we undertake unnecessary deeds in foolish hope; as the saying goes, "Vain men devise vain things from their own strong desires."[††] It is useful to consider these admonitions in life, to which also relates that saying of Christ: "Let tomorrow worry about itself; each day has enough trouble of its own." That is, do what is necessary at the present moment, which has enough difficulty in itself, and do not pile up difficulties by arguing yourself into knots and worrying about what may happen in the future. EXPOSITION OF THE PROVERBS OF SOLOMON.[19]

WORKING WITH TRUST IN GOD'S PROVIDENCE. MICHEL COP: Worldlings who neither have nor wish to have any understanding of God's providence cannot believe that all things come to pass as the Lord has ordained by his eternal counsel, which cannot change. These people attribute one part to fortune or chance, and another part to their wisdom and worldly counsel, and so they are full of arrogant boasting about their lusts and disordered affections, and they promise themselves great things in time to come. But most of the time they are frustrated in their aims and intents.

Solomon wants us not to be like these worldlings when he says, "Do not boast about tomorrow." For besides their arrogance, as we may see in the Scriptures, they guide themselves by chance, not referring themselves to the will of God. Chance is indicated when Solomon says, "for you know not what the day may bring forth." When he speaks thus, he is not rebuking us for ignorance, though we do not know what shall be done tomorrow; for only God has things to come in his presence. He desires that we should wait patiently in expectation of what it pleases him to send, and that we should be assured that all things happen according to his goodwill. But the worldlings described above do not see it that way, and therefore their ignorance is culpable, even though such guilt does not attach to the faithful, who wait on the providence of God. . . .

Nevertheless, even though we do not know what the day "shall bring forth," this does not mean that we should do nothing from which we might profit tomorrow; this would be to tempt God, who wants us to work, so that afterward we may enjoy the fruits of our labor. Having regard to this will of God, if we labor faithfully to gather goods without excessively greedy desire, not with a mind to enrich ourselves, and without a desire to hurt our neighbors, we do not "boast about tomorrow," but rather we are simply following the means by which God will give us our daily bread. ON THE PROVERBS OF SOLOMON.[20]

AVOID THE ANGER OF BRUTISH PEOPLE. PHILIPP MELANCHTHON: "A stone is heavy, and sand is weighty, but the anger of a fool is heavier than both." It is often important that we distinguish between different types of sayings: some expressly enjoin something, and others prohibit; some are divine promises or warnings, while others simply describe an outcome. This last type at the same time discretely warns us how to fortify our minds against those outcomes. Now this proverb describes an outcome, and it concerns a vice common to many who are hot-tempered, and not easily appeased. Such angry people are for the most part those who are more brutish and inexperienced, who do not take into account human infirmity, and

[19]CR 14:70-71; citing 1 Thess 4:11; Ps 36:7; Jn 15:5; Jer 10:23; Mt 6:34. [†]The title of a satire by M. Varro. [‡]Ovid, *Ex Ponto* 4.3.49-50 (LCL 151:434-35). [§]Ovid, *Ex Ponto* 4.3.35-36 (LCL 151:532-33). [◊]Ovid, *Tristia* 3.7.42 (LCL 151:130-31). Irus was a beggar in Homer's Ithaca (*Odyssey* 18.5), and Croesus was the Lydian king of legendary wealth. [Δ]Such was the judgment of Plutarch (*Pericles* 31). Melanchthon adds to this the examples of several other warlike princes: Alcibiades, Hannibal, Pompey Magnus, and the more recent career of Charles of Burgundy (1433–1477). [††]A Greek apothegm. For more on the vice of striving, or being a "busybody," see Melanchthon's exegesis of Prov 6:6.

[20]Cop, *Sur les Proverbes de Salomon*, 579-80; citing Gen 11:3; 27:41; 37:27; Ex 1:8, 14:3; 1 Sam 26:2; 15:1; 1 Kings 12; 2 Kings 18; Dan 4; Lk 12:16; Jas 4:13.

do not understand that many of the mistakes of others must gently be tolerated and corrected. Thus it is said, "There is nothing more unreasonable than a man with no experience of the world who doesn't think anything right except what he's done himself."† But God's goodness shines out all the more, in that he bears with so many diseased people in their infirmities, but he also commands, "Forgive, and it will be forgiven you." So those who are wise more readily bend their minds to goodness, and recognize this common infirmity in themselves and in others, and so they are mindful of the divine command, "Forgive, and it will be forgiven you." Nor can a clearer image of brutish implacability be painted, than is set forth in the Gospel in the image of the cruel servant who owed sixty tons of gold.‡

For although this proverb of Solomon's is only a description of an outcome, nevertheless it serves as a warning to many: he commands us to recognize human weakness and remember the teaching regarding reasonableness (*epiekeia*), and to moderate our anger.§ It also warns us to avoid brutish people, who are unable either to recognize others or show forgiveness. EXPOSITION OF THE PROVERBS OF SOLOMON.[21]

PREFER OPEN REBUKE TO FLATTERY. ROBERT CLEAVER: "Open rebuke"—that is, a check or admonition given for a fault committed—"is better than secret love." It does more good and is more to be esteemed than the hidden affection of love in the heart, which is not manifested by word or deed, nor shows itself when need requires. For they are our best friends who deal most against our sins and corruptions, for by this they show that they are not flatterers, but faithfully minded toward us; they do us the best favor and perform the greatest kindness that may be by reconciling us to our best friend—namely, to the Lord, whom by our offenses we had incensed against us. Such friends aid us against our most dangerous adversaries—namely, our transgressions, as well as Satan, into whose hands we had cast ourselves; they help us when our own power fails, and they give direction to us when we have lost our way. They give us medicines to cure our deadly diseases.

The opposition stands thus: "The wounds of a friend are faithful," and therefore to be prayed for, "but the kisses of an enemy are" deceitful, and therefore "to be prayed against." The sharp and piercing chastisements, whether by words or stripes, inflicted by a friend who sees our need and in love or compassion applies himself to say or do that which is good for us (though it be tedious for him to perform and uneasy for us to suffer) "are faithful" since they proceed from the fidelity and uprightness of his heart toward us, and from a true desire for our good and welfare. "But the kisses of an enemy" are the fair and flattering countenances of one who hates a person (for in the word "kisses" he alludes to the manner used in those countries where they used to salute one another, both men and women, with kisses, and so did they profess their kind affection to each other . . .). For Judas supped with our Savior on the night that he was betrayed, and had been in his company before, and yet he kissed him not very many hours later. "Are to be prayed against," that is to be taken heed of for our better defense. And because we are not acquainted with people's guileful purposes, we are to entreat the Lord to shield us from them. For they deal dangerously when they deal most smoothly, and the still waters are commonly the deepest. A BRIEF EXPLANATION.[22]

ON THE DANGERS OF INCONSTANCY. PHILIPP MELANCHTHON: There is no kind of life, no

[21]CR 14:70-71; citing Mt 6:14. †Terence, *Adelphi* 1.2.98-99 (LCL 23:262-63). ‡The parable of the unforgiving servant (Mt 18:21-35) describes a debt of ten thousand talents, which Melanchthon reckoned as equivalent to sixty tons of gold; for the reckoning, see the guide to ancient weights and measures published by Melanchthon, along with the humanist scholars Guillaume Budé and Joachim Camerarius, in *Vocabula rei nummariae ponderum et mensurarum graeca, latina, ebraica quorum intellectus omnibus necessarius est* (Wittenberg, 1551). §See also the comments on Prov 10:12.

[22]Cleaver, *A Brief Explanation of the Whole Booke of the Proverbs of Salomon*, 454-55.

manner of performing one's duties that does not come with dangers and irritations, and squeamish people turn up in every walk of life: "The lazy ox wants to wear a saddle, and the riding horse wants to plow."† Therefore this proverb warns us not to rashly desire to break out into a different way of life from that to which we have truly been called. Paul says, "Let each one remain before God in the calling to which he is called."

In this connection, many precepts have been handed down in opposition to inconstancy, a superficial quality by which one constantly seeks to change established ways. So, "A rolling stone gathers no moss."‡ And, "A plant which is often moved does not take root."§ And, "Whatever harsh lot falls to an ass, he will still be an ass; but the one who knows to bear his lot placidly is wise."◊ And, as Arichidamus asked Periander, "Why in the world do you yearn to be called a bad poet instead of a skillful physician?"Δ Exposition of the Proverbs of Solomon.[23]

Iron Sharpens Iron. Desiderius Erasmus: "You scratch my back and I'll scratch yours." If someone rubs you, rub them in return, as is recorded in the collections of Diogenianus.† It is only fair to oblige a person who has obliged you and to repay one kindness with another. Suidas thinks the metaphor is drawn from donkeys nibbling one another, and that it can be used in either sense, for the exchange of mutual assistance or abuse.‡ There is a well-known and rather neat moral maxim to the same effect, which is ascribed to Seneca, but wrongly: "Your neighbor will treat you as you treat him."§ . . .

It was not my intention to mingle with this series the proverbs that belong to theologians, not that I despise them, but partly because I thought this showed a proper respect for holy Writ and partly because they are universally accessible. There is however one that I shall add without hesitation because it chimes in so exactly with what I have just said. It comes in the proverbs of Solomon, chapter 27: "Iron sharpens iron; so a man sharpens the countenance of his friend." Adages.[24]

Learning in Community. Philipp Melanchthon: We should acknowledge our infirmity, and understand that each person is ignorant of many things, and often errs and goes astray, as Solomon says: "The number of fools is infinite." Also, "There is a way that seems right to a person, but in the end it leads to death." There are many such complaints in literature. Euripides says, "One man cannot see all."† And Theognis, "No one on his own is skilled in everything."‡ And this is the reason God has given us the power of speech, above all so that some may teach others, and counsels may guide our way. Thus Paul says, "Teach and admonish one another," and in Sirach we read, "If you see a wise man, stay behind to approach him; let your feet wear out his doorstep."

Indeed there are many sayings that teach us to listen to the counsels and judgments of experienced people, and to discuss our thoughts with others. And everyday experience shows how dangerous it is to follow one's own counsel (*idiobouleuein*): "Each person is his own worst master."§ . . . This is obvious in the way that doctrine is corrupted by those who do not listen to others, but rather hide themselves away like those who cannot bear the light of day. These people invent new opinions from their own minds, abhorring the proven forms of teaching. Such are many now, who glory in being self-taught (*autodidaktous*); they admire their own fantasies, without ever giving heed to the judgments of others who are of sound mind. But let us obey the precepts that command us to listen to those who are skillful,

[23]CR 14:72. †Horace, *Epistle* 1.14.43; citing 1 Cor 7:20. ‡Erasmus, *Adagia* 3.4.75. Modern usage has inverted the meaning of the saying, implying that continual motion fends off stagnation. Erasmus's interpretation is that "someone who cannot stay in the same place rarely prospers" (CWE 35:48). §Menander, fr. 230, cited by Erasmus, *Adagia* 3.4.75. ◊Johann Stigel, *Poetmatum* (Jena, 1560), *Elegy* 19. ΔPlutarch, *Apophthegmata laconica* 218F.3 (LCL 245:308-9).

[24]CWE 32:126-27. †Diogenianus, *Paroemiographi Graeci* 8.48. ‡*Suda* T 767. §Publilius Syrus, *Sententia* A 2, cited by Seneca in *Epistle* 94.43.

and confer in our thinking with others, just as Paul says: "Teach and admonish one another." EXPOSITION OF THE PROVERBS OF SOLOMON.[25]

ACTIONS AND DISPOSITIONS REFLECT THE PERSON. CARDINAL CAJETAN: "As the faces of those who gaze on it are reflected in water, so the hearts of men are revealed by their wisdom." In the Hebrew this reads, "As the face of waters is to faces, so the heart of the man is to the man." This proverb is written without any verb at all. The translators, therefore, have worked out different kinds of exegesis and inserted different verbs into the text. The proverb works to recall a man to the eyes of the mind, since the heart of each man corresponds to what the man himself does. The heart of man is then compared to the man whose heart is like the stirred waters, with reflections coming back from the faces that are reflected in the waters. And comparison consists in this: as faces in the water (i.e., likenesses of comparisons) arise from the faces that are truly so, so the heart of man (i.e., his inmost being) arises from the man himself. This comparison is proved true with respect to the inmost portion of a man, as it is the part that knows and desires. Comparisons that exist in the understanding and imagination arise within the person through the exterior senses, as he handles these impressions deep within. And likewise, the dispositions of different affections in will and desire arise from the man. In keeping with this standard his character is formed from repetitive actions. And so Solomon teaches that you should not fault your inmost thoughts but instead blame yourself. Your inmost thoughts flow from you and depend on you, as the faces reflected in the water depend on the actual faces by which the reflections are made. Moreover, he mentioned water rather than a mirror, because moisture easily takes impressions. Water, because it flows so freely, distributes moisture into the internal organs. As a consequence, it can easily form reflections, as the natural scientists affirm. THE PARABLES OF SOLOMON, CORRECTED BY THE ORIGINAL HEBREW.[26]

AN IMAGE OF THE UNSTEADY HEART. PHILIPP MELANCHTHON: "As a face in waters, so is the heart of man to man." Just as faces in water appear fleeting and evanescent, so hearts are inconstant and deceitful. For there are many extant comparisons that complain about the inconstancy of the human heart. So, for example, "Nowhere is faith secure."† And, "Loyalty stands or falls with fortune."‡ For when the inconstancy of the human heart is reckoned, we are warned against putting our trust in people heedlessly. For this reason the admonition that Cicero attributed to Epicharmus is often repeated: "Don't trust your neighbor," and he describes this as the nerve and sinew of wisdom.§ And, "Fly those whom you deem faithful, and you will be safe."◊ And Jeremiah says, "Cursed is the one who trusts in people." These sayings warn in the first place about doctrine, that we not commend dogmas about God solely on the basis of human authority, but instead we should seek out the sources of doctrine given to us by God. In the next place, we should not put our trust in human protection without necessity, because the human will so often changes. EXPOSITION OF THE PROVERBS OF SOLOMON.[27]

THE EFFECTS OF PRAISE. THE ENGLISH ANNOTATIONS: True praise is got by well-doing, as gold is made praiseworthy by the fire. Or, one may be known "by their praises"—that is, according to how they are affected when they are praised or dispraised by others. Those who admit all praises, whether deserved or undeserved, that greedily hunt after popular applause, that easily swell when they

[25]CR 14:73; citing Eccles 1:15; Prov 14:12; Col 3:16; Sir 6:36; Col 3:16. †Euripides, *Phoenician Women* 745 (LCL 11:292-93). ‡Theognis, *Elegies* 901-2 (LCL 258:304-5). §Cf. Jerome, *De viris illustribus*, prol. (PL 23:603).

[26]Cajetan, *Parabolae Salomonis ad veritatem Hebraicam castigatae*, 242-43.

[27]CR 14:74; citing Jer 17:5. †Virgil, *Aeneid* 4.373 (LCL 63:446-47). ‡Ovid, *Ed Ponto* 2.3.10 (LCL 151:332-33). See also Melanchthon's comments on Prov 6:1. §Cicero, *Epistulae ad Atticum* 1.19.8 (LCL 7:116-17). ◊Ovid, *Ars amatoria* 1.752 (LCL 232:64-65).

are commended, they are vainglorious and weak. A pusillanimous person can bear no reproach patiently, though undeserved, and the like. Some would have this be the meaning, that a person may know what they are from those by whom they are commended: those who are good and virtuous are praised by the good and virtuous; the sober or intemperate, as those are who speak well or ill of them, and the like. Some would make a more general sense of the words, that everyone knows what they are with regard to virtue and vice by common report. This too may be true sometimes, and wise people may make good use of it, but it is subject to so many limitations and restrictions, as the contrary may seem more true of the two. Nor do I believe Solomon intended it this way. ANNOTATIONS ON PROVERBS 27:21.[28]

[28]Downame, ed., *English Annotations*, 6Z1r*.

28:1–29:27 SOLOMON'S FINAL PROVERBS

1 *The wicked flee when no one pursues,*
but the righteous are bold as a lion.

2 *When a land transgresses, it has many rulers,*
but with a man of understanding and knowledge,
its stability will long continue.

3 *A poor man who oppresses the poor*
is a beating rain that leaves no food.

4 *Those who forsake the law praise the wicked,*
but those who keep the law strive against them.

5 *Evil men do not understand justice,*
but those who seek the LORD understand it completely.

6 *Better is a poor man who walks in his integrity*
than a rich man who is crooked in his ways.

7 *The one who keeps the law is a son with understanding,*
but a companion of gluttons shames his father.

8 *Whoever multiplies his wealth by interest and profit*[a]
gathers it for him who is generous to the poor.

9 *If one turns away his ear from hearing the law,*
even his prayer is an abomination.

10 *Whoever misleads the upright into an evil way*
will fall into his own pit,
but the blameless will have a goodly inheritance.

11 *A rich man is wise in his own eyes,*
but a poor man who has understanding will find him out.

12 *When the righteous triumph, there is great glory,*
but when the wicked rise, people hide themselves.

13 *Whoever conceals his transgressions will not prosper,*
but he who confesses and forsakes them will obtain mercy.

14 *Blessed is the one who fears the LORD*[b] *always,*
but whoever hardens his heart will fall into calamity.

15 *Like a roaring lion or a charging bear*
is a wicked ruler over a poor people.

16 *A ruler who lacks understanding is a cruel oppressor,*
but he who hates unjust gain will prolong his days.

17 *If one is burdened with the blood of another,*
he will be a fugitive until death;[c]
let no one help him.

18 *Whoever walks in integrity will be delivered,*
but he who is crooked in his ways will suddenly fall.

19 *Whoever works his land will have plenty of bread,*
but he who follows worthless pursuits will have plenty of poverty.

20 *A faithful man will abound with blessings,*
but whoever hastens to be rich will not go unpunished.

21 *To show partiality is not good,*
but for a piece of bread a man will do wrong.

22 *A stingy man*[d] *hastens after wealth*
and does not know that poverty will come upon him.

23 *Whoever rebukes a man will afterward find more favor*
than he who flatters with his tongue.

24 *Whoever robs his father or his mother*
and says, "That is no transgression,"
is a companion to a man who destroys.

25 *A greedy man stirs up strife,*
but the one who trusts in the LORD will be enriched.

[26]*Whoever trusts in his own mind is a fool,*
but he who walks in wisdom will be delivered.

[27]*Whoever gives to the poor will not want,*
but he who hides his eyes will get many a curse.

[28]*When the wicked rise, people hide themselves,*
but when they perish, the righteous increase.

29 *He who is often reproved, yet stiffens his neck,*
will suddenly be broken beyond healing.

[2]*When the righteous increase, the people rejoice,*
but when the wicked rule, the people groan.

[3]*He who loves wisdom makes his father glad,*
but a companion of prostitutes squanders his wealth.

[4]*By justice a king builds up the land,*
but he who exacts gifts[e] *tears it down.*

[5]*A man who flatters his neighbor*
spreads a net for his feet.

[6]*An evil man is ensnared in his transgression,*
but a righteous man sings and rejoices.

[7]*A righteous man knows the rights of the poor;*
a wicked man does not understand such knowledge.

[8]*Scoffers set a city aflame,*
but the wise turn away wrath.

[9]*If a wise man has an argument with a fool,*
the fool only rages and laughs, and there is no quiet.

[10]*Bloodthirsty men hate one who is blameless*
and seek the life of the upright.[f]

[11]*A fool gives full vent to his spirit,*
but a wise man quietly holds it back.

[12]*If a ruler listens to falsehood,*
all his officials will be wicked.

[13]*The poor man and the oppressor meet together;*
the LORD gives light to the eyes of both.

[14]*If a king faithfully judges the poor,*
his throne will be established forever.

[15]*The rod and reproof give wisdom,*
but a child left to himself brings shame to his mother.

[16]*When the wicked increase, transgression increases,*
but the righteous will look upon their downfall.

[17]*Discipline your son, and he will give you rest;*
he will give delight to your heart.

[18]*Where there is no prophetic vision the people cast off restraint,*[g]
but blessed is he who keeps the law.

[19]*By mere words a servant is not disciplined,*
for though he understands, he will not respond.

[20]*Do you see a man who is hasty in his words?*
There is more hope for a fool than for him.

[21]*Whoever pampers his servant from childhood*
will in the end find him his heir.[h]

[22]*A man of wrath stirs up strife,*
and one given to anger causes much transgression.

[23]*One's pride will bring him low,*
but he who is lowly in spirit will obtain honor.

[24]*The partner of a thief hates his own life;*
he hears the curse, but discloses nothing.

[25]*The fear of man lays a snare,*
but whoever trusts in the LORD is safe.

[26]*Many seek the face of a ruler,*
but it is from the LORD that a man gets justice.

[27]*An unjust man is an abomination to the righteous,*
but one whose way is straight is an abomination to the wicked.

a That is, profit that comes from charging interest to the poor **b** Hebrew lacks *the LORD* **c** Hebrew *until the pit* **d** Hebrew *A man whose eye is evil* **e** Or *who taxes heavily* **f** Or *but the upright seek his soul* **g** Or *the people are discouraged* **h** The meaning of the Hebrew word rendered *his heir* is uncertain

Overview: This final section of proverbs attributed to Solomon gives occasion for our interpreters to address a number of issues that were immediately pressing in the Reformation era. Warnings against faction and dissension elicit poignant and timely reflection on duties of rulers to preserve peace. The single explicit mention of usury in Proverbs (Prov 29:8) provides a point of departure for a reevaluation of the Hebrew terms *nešek* and *tarbît*. Some of our exegetes, like Konrad Pellikan and Ludwig Lavater, conclude that the terms are interchangeable, and uphold the traditional Catholic prohibition against usury in all forms. Among some of our exegetes, however, the prohibition is softened: Michel Cop, for instance, allows "multiplication" of profits, so long as it is regulated by the "golden rule" of the gospel—that is, so long as it is not of the "biting" variety. All agree, however, that those who take advantage of the poor through usury will eventually see their ill-gotten gain ripped away and redistributed to the poor by God's providential judgment. A number of politically oriented proverbs feature prominently in the concluding chapter, sayings that emphasize the virtue of just princes, the importance of honesty and transparency in governance, and the critical place of divine law as a touchstone for justice in human law.

28:1-28 *Keep the Law, Rule Wisely, Care for the Poor*

Dissension Leads to Conflict. Cardinal Cajetan: "Because of sin a land has many rulers, and because of those known for their wisdom and knowledge it will enjoy sweet peace for a long time." The second phrase according to the Hebrew reads, "and in a man of understanding and knowledge it will endure." Now the meaning of the first phrase is clear, if (as the Hebrew words indicate) by the word "sins" we understand rebellion. For the meaning is that factions promote a multitude of leaders, which is something we see today. It occurred in Israel as well, both after Saul's death and after the death of Solomon. But the meaning of the second phrase is somewhat more difficult. If we consider, however, that it is compared to the first phrase by contrast, the meaning will become clear: if knowledge and understanding belong to capable people in the land, that land will endure. This means that the land enjoys unity and is not split into multiple groups with different rulers. By contrast, if the people who live there are characterized by rebellion and strife, though they may be blessed with keen understanding, they will become the cause of evil dissension. This is so even when they know the harms that follow from this and are zealous for the land's unity and peace. For such people seek to extend their reign in this way—that is, without division. The Parables of Solomon, Corrected by the Original Hebrew.[1]

Wisdom in Leadership, Prayerfulness in Followership. Philipp Melanchthon: Complaints are common about the negligence of princes, their plunderings, and the neglect of justice and the common defense. And the people accuse their princes and their courtiers, just as these verses have it: "Whatever folly kings commit, the Achaeans [i.e., the people] pay the penalty."[†] But the divine voice accuses both sides, the princes and the people, as is written in Hosea: "like people, like priests." And it is often proclaimed that the people are not given sound rulers on account of their sins, as in Isaiah, when the Lord takes away the soldier, the judge, and the prophet.

Thus it says here, "on account of the sins of the land," clearly indicating the sins of the prince and the people, "many become princes"—that is, no one rules for very long, or many quarrels reign, and one faction drives out another. This is what has happened in Pannonia, where first John ruled, then Ferdinand, and now the Turks.[‡] Such changes do not happen without great calamities, as was so truly said by Xenophon: "It goes without saying that all political revolutions bring deaths."[§] And regarding seditions, Thucydides describes scenes in which "death in every form ensued, and whatever horrors are wont to be perpetrated at such times,

[1]Cajetan, *Parabolae Salomonis ad veritatem Hebraicam castigatae*, 245-46.

all happened then."[◊] And, "Even the base wins honor in a feud."[Δ] Thus we should recognize that the sins of the many are the cause of public calamity, while public welfare is maintained solely by the vigor with which they restrain themselves.

But the antithesis is also given here, and it provides a singular reminder necessary to both princes and the people. It says that the state [*imperium*] is made more enduring by a wise and intelligent man—that is, a wise prince sometimes yields his own authority, and suffers some disadvantage, in order to avoid greater disadvantages, just like the dictator Fabius, who consented to share authority with his master of horses.[††] Nor does a wise prince give credence to rumors ahead of the safety of the state; thus Cicero granted a province to Lucius Antonius in order that he might have a colleague who agreed with him.[‡‡]

Therefore those who give counsel to a people ought to urge them not to bring worse evils down on themselves by seditious plots, as doubtless in Judea many turbulent men raised their voices, urging that the Roman armies must be driven out, just as their fathers had driven out Antiochus. But Zechariah and Simeon understood that the times and the circumstances were different, and so they argued against the war.[§§] For they knew that the end of the Jewish state was at hand, that God with singular moderation was softening their servitude, because they had autonomy (*autonomian*) in their rites of worship, and they saw that they lacked the right leader. For Antiochus had not granted autonomy in worship, and the learned knew that it was not yet time for the Jewish state to end.

In this way competent rulers carefully consider when to fight and when not to fight: Isaiah argued against surrender, but Jeremiah in his time argued for it. So we must give heed to different examples and different circumstances. We bear servitude wisely whenever it is tolerable, and with heartfelt sighs we pray for counsel and protection from God, just as the prophets themselves did. Isaiah cried, "We are your clay; do not be exceedingly angry," and Jeremiah, "Do not reduce us to nothing." And Psalm 7, "Arise, Lord, and defend the law you have commanded, that the synagogue of your people may gather around you." That is, conserve your law and the church, that it may not be wholly scattered, just as these verses say: "O Christ, may the church always remain to serve you, and guide us whom you have grafted on by your right hand."[◊◊] Exposition of the Proverbs of Solomon.[2]

Formal and Informal Usury. Konrad Pellikan: It is called "usury" [*usura*] when one receives a greater return on one's capital by the terms of contract [*ex pacto*]. It is called "profit" [*foenus*] when one freely receives a greater return without contract stipulation [*sine pacto*]. The meaning of the passage is that the wealth of

[2]CR 14:74-76; citing Hos 4:9; Is 3:1-2; 37:1-13; Jer 38:14-23; Is 64:8-9; Jer 10:24; Ps 7:6-7. [†]Horace, *Epistle* 1.2.14 (LCL 194:262-63). [‡]Pannonia was an ancient Roman province spanning territory in present-day Hungary, Austria, and the Balkans. It was the site of protracted warfare in the sixteenth century, when sovereignty over the kingdom of Hungary was disputed between John Zápolya and Archduke Ferdinand I. After the seizure of Buda by Suleiman the Magnificent in 1541, the central and southern counties were annexed by the Ottoman Empire. [§]Xenophon, *Hellenica* 2.3.32. [◊]The Greek of Melanchthon's citation is obscure, but it seems to refer to the passage quoted, in which an uprising among the Corcyraeans leads to general slaughter (Thucydides, *History of the Peloponnesian War* 3.81.5; LCL 109:140-41). [Δ]Plutarch, *De fraterno amore* 479A (LCL 337:252-53). [††]The Roman general and statesman Quintus Fabius Maximus Verrucosus (c. 280–203 BC) was appointed dictator in 233, but the Senate appointed a political rival as Fabius's *magister equitum*, the reckless and incompetent Marcus Minucius Rufus. Bowing to this political inevitability, Fabius nevertheless skillfully deployed his forces to delay and ultimately defeat the invading Carthaginians in the Second Punic War. [‡‡]Melanchthon appears to have confused Lucius Antonius with Gaius Antonius, both brothers of Mark Antony and supporters of Julius Caesar during the civil war. The incident to which Melanchthon refers is related in Cassius Dio (*Historia Romana* 38.10.4). [§§]The reference is obscure. Josephus mentions a certain Zacharias, son of Baris, whom the Zealots executed on charges of attempting to surrender the insurgency to the Romans (*Jewish War* 4.334-44). And Eusebius notes that after the death of James, Simeon, son of Clopas, was appointed bishop of Jerusalem, and he led the Christian community out of the city in response to a divine oracle foretelling the destruction of the city (*Historia ecclesiastica*. 3.5; 3.11). The arguments adduced here are not recorded in either source, but it may be that Melanchthon is reading into ancient sources which present these characters as cooler heads who presumably spoke in opposition to war. [◊◊]Two lines from a quatrain of apparently Melanchthon's own writing.

usurers, which they have heaped up in their treasuries by iniquitous means, will be returned, little by little, to merciful and faithful people, who will invest it appropriately in the poor. God watches over his holy ones, and he does not allow them to go without what is needful: "He has filled the hungry with good things, and sent the rich away empty." Wealth rots when it is gathered and horded, but it truly bears fruit when distributed. This point is disputed by many who take their profits freely, but in vain. A SUCCINCT AND UNIVERSAL COMMENTARY ON THE BIBLE.[3]

"BITING" AND "INCREASE." CARDINAL CAJETAN: The word translated "profit" signifies "increase" [*multiplicatio*], and the word translated as "interest" signifies "biting" [*morsu*], because in the holy books of the Hebrews usury is named "biting" in detestation of usurious lucre. But the two modes of unjust profiteering go hand in hand: one by usury, and the other by profit (e.g., paying out a loan for $100, while recording a debt of $150).[†] . . . Solomon points out that when one takes interest on a loan, things may turn out the opposite from what one intends: for instance, the one who bites into the substance of the poor himself becomes needy, and by the just judgment of God his riches pass into the possession of a person who has mercy on the poor, and at length from fear of God he makes restitution to the poor or performs some other acts of mercy toward them. THE PARABLES OF SOLOMON CORRECTED BY THE ORIGINAL HEBREW.[4]

THE BITER BITE. LUDWIG LAVATER: With respect to the actual terminology: the Hebrew *nešek* means "bite" or "gnawing," from *nāšak*—that is, "to bite," or "to eat away at." Just like a serpent bites or gnaws with its teeth, so usury secretly bites or eats away at a person's wealth. Chrysostom also says, "Money borrowed at interest is like a viper's bite, for on account of it the debtor kills himself—just like someone who has been struck by a snake falls charmed into sleep, and on account of the sweetness of sleep, he dies, because the venom spreads through the body without being perceived; in the same way the one who accepts a loan with interest thinks for the moment that he has received a good thing, but the usury spreads through all his faculties and converts the whole into a debt."[†] The Hebrew *tarbît* means "increase" [*multiplicatio*]. The Hebrews also called it usury when someone received more [than the amount lent], whether measured by weight, or length, or volume. Or, if agreeing on a loan of $20, a debt of $25 was recorded. The text is not saying that one should make money by usury so that later one may give alms, but rather that it often happens that one who accumulates wealth by illicit means ends up losing it to a generous person, who then distributes it to the poor. For they themselves do not give their wealth to the poor. This proverb teaches that usurers will not long enjoy their ill-gotten gains, but will soon be forced to give them up to others. ON THE BOOK OF PROVERBS, OR SAYINGS, OF SOLOMON THE MOST-WISE KING.[5]

GOD BRINGS GOOD OUT OF EVIL. MICHAEL JERMIN: Where one takes usury from another, God takes usury from them. For as they reap where they did not sow, as they gather where they did not plant, God does the same. It was not God who sowed their unjust dealings, by which they reaped their wealth; it was not God who planted their hard exactions, by which they gathered their riches. Yet God gathers "the substance" that they have gathered: God takes it to himself, and when they will not make restitution, he restores to the

---

[3]Pellikan, *Commentaria bibliorum et illa brevia quidem ac catholica*, 243r; citing Lk 1:53.

[4]Cajetan, *Parabolae Salomonis ad veritatem Hebraicam castigatae*, 247. [†]Cajetan is employing the rabbinic distinction between *nešek* (pre-paid interest, deducted in advance from the principal of the loan) and *tarbît* (accrued interest, paid out over the life of the loan), though he seems to have reversed the terms.

[5]Lavater, *In librum Proverbiorum siue Sententiarum Solomonis Regis sapientissimi*, 284v. [†]This vivid analogy is quoted in a number of late medieval authors (e.g., Thomas Aquinas and Denis the Carthusian). I have been unable to identify the quote precisely; however, one passage in Chrysostom's *Homilies on Matthew* uses similar imagery (NPNF[1] 10:350-51).

poor what has been taken from them. Therefore an unjust dealer, by increasing their substance, only increases their wickedness, and with their wickedness, their punishment. . . .

As for their substance, they do not gather that for themselves, because it is not gathered for their comfort, but for their mischief. They do not gather their substance for themselves, because although they have possession of it, God does not account it to be theirs. Thus St. Augustine says, "If he calls it his own, it is not the voice of one who possesses it justly, but that of an impudent usurper."[†] It is therefore gathered for "the one who," by being "generous to the poor," shall make themselves rich in the comfort of their riches: it is he who is their true owner. As St. Augustine again says, "Gold and silver belong to the one person who knows how to use gold and silver; that which a person does not justly use, he does not justly possess."[‡] And though an unjust dealer in gathering and disposing of their estate and wealth does not intend it for such a person, yet such a person God will find, and he will bestow it on them. The general sense of the proverb is that from the sinful dealings of bad people, God both can and does bring forth good, and he makes the fruit of sin in some to be the matter of goodness in others. Paraphrastic Meditations.[6]

Against Those Who Rationalize Usury. Michel Cop: Riches are the good creatures of God; to acquire them and possess them is lawful. But not all ways and means of coming by them are lawful, for God censures, forbids, and condemns all profit-seeking, which leads us to distrust the Lord's providence or wound the charity of our neighbor, not helping them in their need, but rather inflicting greater pain. And this is what they do who lend their money to their poor neighbors on usury, against the commandment of God. And therefore, if we want to get our goods justly and possess them lawfully, let us beware that we not oppress our poor neighbors with usury [*usure*] or increase [*surcroist*], in taking profit from them for the money or other goods that we have lent them. Instead, let us follow the teaching of Jesus Christ. In so doing, we shall be blessed in following justice; in doing otherwise, we shall be wicked and accursed.

Nevertheless, Solomon says, "whoever multiplies his wealth by interest." It may seem at first glance that he allows usury, and that he praises the person who augments their wealth by usury and increase, seeing that it is a means by which a merciful person may acquire the wherewithal to give alms to the poor—which is a very acceptable sacrifice to God. In response, we may answer in two ways. First, God often uses wicked instruments to accomplish a good work: for example, when Joseph was sent into Egypt so that he would become the ruler of the land and sustain his father and brothers in a time of famine. In this, God used the brothers, who were wicked instruments and did a miserable thing by selling their brother [into slavery]. . . . And so usurers are wicked instruments by which God gathers riches, so as to distribute them later as alms to the poor by merciful people. But this does not justify the usurers, either in the sight of God or in the sight of people who justly attend to the truth. . . . Second, since it is not lawful to do evil so that good may come about, we should know that the Holy Spirit, in order to commend good and lawful work, does not judge on the basis of consequences, even when these are good and profitable; otherwise, he would approve all the evils that are done against his faithful servants: "And we know that for those who love God all things work together for good, for those who are called according to his purpose." And so (judging by consequences), the most wicked people should be justified before God, which we must neither think nor say. But to allow a good and lawful word, the Holy Spirit judges by the mind and intent of the one who has done it, whether their mind was wholly set to follow what God teaches in his Word, by which all our works should be governed. Without this right intention, whatever goodness may arise from our deeds, and

[6]Jermin, *Paraphrasticall Meditations*, 642-43. [†]Augustine, *Sermones* 50.2.4 (PL 38:327). [‡]Augustine, *Sermones* 50.2.4 (PL 38:327).

whatever fair color they may show, they are wicked and abominable.

Nevertheless, let us note that it is not evil to multiply our riches, provided that we do no wrong to any person and that we do not oppress the poor, but that we conduct ourselves toward our neighbors as we would them have conduct themselves toward us if the circumstances were reversed—just as Jesus Christ has admonished us. And we must be careful not to follow the opinion of those who say that they do no wrong to their neighbors when their neighbors would gladly accept the money on the terms offered, for Jesus Christ speaks of a mind well-governed by unfeigned love. ON THE PROVERBS OF SOLOMON.[7]

MONEY SHOULD BE REWARDED BY GOD, NOT INTEREST. SWISS BRETHREN CONFESSION OF HESSE: We believe, acknowledge, and confess that the newborn Christian and chosen children of God should not engage in usury with their money but that they should help the poor and needy without expecting repayment with interest—that is, to lend them money and await their reward from God. CONCERNING USURY.[8]

ALL FORMS OF PROFITEERING PROHIBITED. THOMAS CARTWRIGHT: In *nešek bĕtarbît* ("usury and profit") there is a synecdoche for all illegitimate ways of gathering wealth. The aim of this proverb is to restrain the rich from oppressing the poor. It is clear that the greedy rich seek to increase their substance to no end, nor is there any way of building themselves up or increasing their property with which they are not carried away by so great a zeal that neither reason nor humanity can restrain them from achieving what they desire. And in order to restrain these various modes of raking up more wealth, two terms are set forth here as a synecdoche. The first term indicates usury, which is enforced by means of money (and the etymology of the term here indicates nothing but a biting of the one to whom the loan is given, which is what usury is understood to be); the other term is also called usury, or increase taken from the crops or other goods necessary to sustain life, as can plainly be seen in Leviticus 25:35-37. From this it appears that just as increase by usury is prohibited from crops and everything else, so also it is prohibited from money—in contrast with those who think that only usury involving money is unjust, because it is not in money's nature to generate more money.[†] But if usury were to be permitted on all these other goods, it would be necessary to approve it as well on those things that money purchases. For which cause in this passage and in Exodus 22 and Leviticus 25, that usury is prohibited by which, on the thinnest of pretexts, the neighbor is crushed and plundered. A PLAIN AND SUCCINCT COMMENTARY ON THE PROVERBS OF SOLOMON.[9]

WITH OR WITHOUT TEETH. JOHN TRAPP: Usury is condemned by the very heathens.[†] The ancient law of the Romans makes the usurer a thief and worse; the Hebrews make him a biting thief who gnaws the debtor to the very bones. Indeed, the most toothless usury (that usual plea) has sharp gums that bite as sorely as an old dog or a hungry fly, and under pretense of licking whole, sucks out the heart's blood. Let those who plead for it consider that God makes provision for no usury, whether *nešek* or *tarbit*, biting or toothless; that the lender is not dealing as he would be dealt with; that the gospel makes these sinners worse than other sinners when it says, "Sinners lend to sinners, to get back the same amount," but usurers to receive more; that in Rome to this day all usurers are excommunicated monthly; that canon law drives them from the sacrament, denies them

[7]Cop, *Sur les Proverbes de Salomon*, 579-80; citing Ex 22:25; Lev 25:35-37; Deut 23:19; Mt 5:42; Lk 6:34-35; Ps 15:5; Ezek 18:8; Hos 5:5; Mt 12:7; Heb 13:16; Rom 8:28; Mt 7:12.

[8]CRR 11:88*; citing Lev 25:35-37; Deut 23:19; Neh 5:7-13; Ps 15:1-2, 5; Jer 15:10; Ezek 18:12-13; Lk 6:35.

[9]Cartwright, *Commentarii succincti & dilucidi in Proverbia Salomonis*, 1181. [†]This natural law argument originated with Aristotle (e.g., *Politics* 1.10) and was picked up by many of the medieval scholastic theologians (e.g., Aquinas, *Summa theologiae* II-II, q. 78) and given more vivid expression in Dante's *Inferno*, where usury is paired with sodomy as corollary sins "against nature." Note that Cartwright does not reject the natural law argument; he merely objects to using it as a pretext for an unduly restrictive interpretation of the usury prohibition.

burial, and makes their will intestate, as though their goods were not their own; that no person of note in all antiquity (with the exception of Jews and Manichees)‡ for fifteen hundred years after Christ has ever undertaken to defend usury; that Chrysostom is very fierce against it, comparing it to the sting of an asp, which casts a person into a sleep from which they die. Solomon's Book of All Virtues.[10]

Covetous Gains Will Be Redistributed. John Donne: "The one who increases their riches by usury and interest gathers them for the one who will be merciful to the poor," says Solomon. Is there a discomfort in this? There is. It is presented there for an affliction and a vexation to a rich person to be told that their money shall be employed in any other way, not only than they gathered it for, but than the way they gathered it by. . . . All ways but their own displease them in their heir, but if this heir will be giving to the poor, then here are two mischiefs met together, that they could never abide the poor, and giving. Therefore such a contemplation is a double vexation, but much more it must be so, to hear that their riches shall perish, that they shall come to nothing. If we consider it correctly, it is truly all one, whether a covetous person's wealth perishes or not, for as much as they hoard up, hide, and put to no use, it is all one whether it is a thousand pounds in their chest or nothing if they never see it, yet since they have made gold their god, they have so much devilish religion in them that they are loath that their god should perish. Sermon on Ecclesiastes 5:12-13.[11]

[10]Trapp, *Solomonis ΠΑΝΑΡΕΤΟΣ*, 320; citing Ezek 18:8; Lk 6:34. †E.g., Aristotle, *Nicomachean Ethics* 4.1. ‡Rabbinic prohibitions against usury were just as forceful as Christian. However, both Jewish and Christian scholars interpreted the exception in Deut 23:20 to allow for interest-bearing loans to those of another faith. In the context of medieval Christendom, this afforded the identically interpreted exception much wider scope for a religious minority. Manichaean devaluation of the Hebrew Bible may have led to a disregard for this precept; however, Augustine charged the Manichees with preferring usury to farming (*Enarrations on the Psalms* 140.12.2-26).
[11]Donne, *Works*, 5:521*.

If You Don't Obey, Don't Expect God to Answer. The English Annotations: Those who will not be taught by God must not think that God will supply their need. Or those who live scandalously and do not apply themselves to the keeping of the commandments, even though they often pray and make long prayers with a great show of fervency of spirit (which seduced and is seducing people, who in opposition to set prayers will not allow the Lord's Prayer, call "praying by the Spirit"), yet their prayers shall not be answered. Annotations on Proverbs 28:9.[12]

Confession and the Will to Change. Philipp Melanchthon: There clearly are some pertinacious people who persevere in their atrocious crimes, even when other people know about it. No doubt, they will be destroyed in their punishments, just as it is written: "Because of these, the wrath of God is coming on the disobedient." But this warning has to do with those who conceal their crimes—that is, with those who quibble in sophistry to support impious worship, or deck false doctrines out in a cloak of excuses. These penalties are threatened, because even if they cannot be held in check by people, eventually God will restrain them, as it is written, "Every plant that was not planted by my Father will be plucked up." . . . But in each one who turns aside, there is first contrition—that is, a recognition of where they went astray and of sin, along with sorrow and a desire to change. This is what is meant by confession, and it is such that it brings about an improvement of character, as Paul acknowledges; for once he himself had gone astray, when he was an enemy to the church, and later became a witness and a planter of the gospel. Exposition of the Proverbs of Solomon.[13]

Examine Yourself Before Speaking. David Joris: When I sought the kingdom of God and the truth, I had to examine whether I was fit or

[12]Downame, ed., *English Annotations*, 6Z1v*.
[13]CR 14:76; citing Col 3:6; Mt 15:13.

immature in true knowledge, and if I understood the mind of the Lord; then it would belong for me to speak. This may not be countered. For a rich person thinks they are wise, but a poor person examines themselves. Remember the word in your hearts and thoroughly examine yourselves. Do not proudly esteem yourselves. Do not think yourselves to be wise, but pray with me for understanding from the Lord. The Strasbourg Disputation.[14]

Against False Security. Philipp Melanchthon: The next thought is higher, for it urges people to the exercise of penitence. It commands that we be in fear, knowing the judgment and wrath of God against sin, and that we have a care to warn those who have fallen into wicked opinions, as Paul says: "Work out your salvation with fear and trembling." In other words, retain the purity of your teaching, attending to its sources with great care and concern; and take similar care to shun those who have lapsed against conscience.

This teaching does not contradict the view that faith is a consolation to the conscience, or that it produces joy in the Mediator. Rather, it insists on both, so that there may be a sorrow in our hearts that deplores our stubbornness and filth, our doubts and the many other evils that remain in us. But let faith govern fear and sorrow, for it is established in us despite our misery and indignity, and only by faith can we please God on account of the Mediator.

Therefore this saying censures carnal security, and the confident pride characteristic of the wise, the unjust, and the powerful, those who care nothing for the judgment of God, but who, like Pharaoh, rush headlong into destruction trusting in their own power. Secure Bellerophon, desiring to be born into the heavens by Pegasus, fell to his destruction. Secure Antiochus, confident in his own power, attempted to destroy the law of God. Therefore we should always keep these admonitions concerning the fear of God and the limits of our vocations before our eyes: "Blessed is the one who always is fearful," and, "Where will the Lord dwell? With those who are contrite in spirit and lowly, and who tremble at my words." Exposition of the Proverbs of Solomon.[15]

Disobedient Children Are an Abomination. Swiss Brethren Confession of Hesse: We believe, acknowledge, and confess that disobedient, unbelieving, contrary children who do not obey father and mother and who do not follow the Word of God are an abomination and cursed by God. The parents must therefore be all the more persistent, diligent, and earnest in their discipline, in order to resist their children's unrighteousness. Concerning Disobedient Children.[16]

Showing Mercy Supersedes a Vow. Andreas Bodenstein von Karlstadt: When I see that a human being (whether a believer or an unbeliever) is in distress and anguish and I am able to help or lead them out, except that the fulfilling of a vow prevents me from doing so, I am to put it on hold and assist this person, for my husband desires order in the works I do. For he says, "I desire mercy, not sacrifices." You must help orphans, widows, and the poor. There must not be a beggar or anyone suffering among you. Therefore you must open your hand and assist the poor among you. You are to turn your eyes intentionally to those in need. "Blessed is the one who gives attention to and cares for the poor." Your diligence and attention must not be obstructed by any vow. Therefore, let everyone examine themselves and look to all the people in the city where they live, whether there is someone who they might be able to help through assistance, advice, or in any other manner. Let them set aside any vow that may draw them away from showing such mercy, for our husband Jesus Christ has clearly and openly spoken his word to us. Regarding Vows.[17]

[14]CRR 7:212.

[15]CR 14:76-77; citing Phil 2:12; Is 66:2.

[16]CRR 11:82; citing Deut 21:18-21; 27:16; 1 Sam 3:13; Sir 16:1-3; 26:10; 42:11; Prov 20:20.

[17]CRR 8:92*; citing Hos 6; Isa 1; Deut 15.

29:1-27 *Do Not Become like Scoffers and the Unjust*

No Excuse for Hardness of Heart. Michel Cop: God's teaching, which consists in commandments, admonitions, exhortations, remonstrances, corrections, reprehensions, and threats, is compared to a yoke bound on the neck of oxen. Now just as there are some oxen that cannot be tamed or made to carry a yoke, so the world is filled with rebels who harden their necks—who grow obstinate against God's law and against his admonitions, reprehensions, and threats, as we may see by experience. Scripture is full of complaints against such rebels, even among the people of God. And as the oxen that refuse to bear the yoke do not live long (for when we see that we can no longer use them, then we fatten them up for slaughter), so the rebels and the obdurate have need of the yoke of correction and reprehension. And yet they reject it, thinking instead that they will play the valiant captains to defend themselves, despite those who correct and reprove them. But, the one against whom they set themselves with hardened malice, can suddenly destroy them without warning. . . . Thus we are admonished to bend our neck to the yoke of the Lord—that is, to become gentle and tractable, easily taught and humble, when in his name and by his Word we are exhorted, admonished, corrected, rebuked, and threatened—especially if we wish to be preserved from destruction. We are often admonished in this way. Therefore let us humble ourselves and become obedient, that we may not be reproached as an incorrigible people, as St. Stephen reproached the Jews. For since we have the Word more clearly and plainly than they had, we well deserve to be suddenly destroyed without remedy, if we harden our necks against the teaching. On the Proverbs of Solomon.[18]

[18]Cop, *Sur les Proverbes de Salomon*, 618-19; citing Ps 95:8-9; Heb 3:7; Acts 7:51.

The Need for Honest Rulers. Philipp Melanchthon: People are governed, in large part, by example. This is because we come to understand by seeing a pattern, and we learn by imitating it. Most powerful of all are the examples of eminent persons, such as princes and teachers. Thus the advice of this proverb is often repeated, so that princes may set an honorable example and the people may admire the same, and shun what is base. In this connection, the following verses are noteworthy:

> Indeed, their leader's example remains with the crowd;
> The world shapes itself after its ruler's pattern.
> The soldier follows not only the general's standards, but his character as well.†

The examples they set can cut both ways, but a vicious contagion springs up more quickly, especially among those with whom one lives or has regular social contact. Therefore, the ancient Greeks used to say, "A puppy is only as good as her mistress." And it is commonly said today, "The abbot first happens to throw dice in an offhand way, and now the monks think it their right to play."

Therefore Solomon says, "A prince who loves falsehood has only wicked servants." But the outstanding virtue in governance is truth [*veritas*] or honesty [*veracitas*], and this virtue is opposed to vanity, treachery, calumnies, suspicions, and sophistry. Therefore a love of lies is an extremely dangerous fault in any ruler, for many vices cluster around that evil, just as there are many different kinds of falsehood.

One obvious type of falsehood is falsehood [*vanitas*], or treachery [*perfidia*], which involves not honoring one's promises or agreements. It was on account of his treacheries that Alcibiades's name became a byword, and that Virgil described with relish the death of the Alban tyrant Mettius Fufetius, when "four-horse chariots, driven apart, had torn him asunder (but you, Alban, should have stood by your words!), and Tullus dragged the liar's body through the woods."‡

Another type of falsehood is the love of calumny. This is common among courtiers, for many delight in envious disparagement, and have ears open to every tale, as in these verses of Menander: "Yes-men do best of all, blackmailers win the second prize, and spitefulness comes third."[§] And in Plautus's *Pseudolus*: "People who spread and listen to accusations would all be hanged, if I could have my way, the spreaders by their tongues and the listeners by their ears."[◊]

A third type of falsehood is suspicion. This arises from the disparaging and faithless character of those who traffic in it, and always leads to much greater evils. So tyrants destroy many on account of their suspicions, just as Alexander had Parmenion put to death, despite his excellent service.[Δ] And because those who are suspicious by nature eagerly give heed to calumnies, they naturally will be surrounded by courtiers who are good at it.

A fourth type is sophistry, which maintains false opinions and evil intents in the prince's favor by means of bogus pretexts. This type of falsehood is praised among the courtiers as being especially wise, just as the scribes who defend impious rituals with tricks of sophistry rise to high office in the papal courts, a truly avaricious type of sophistry. Therefore, when so many horrible evils in life arise from all these kinds of falsehood, Solomon reminds us to be careful and flee such courts, just as Ulysses was commanded to pass by Scylla and Charybdis.[††] Exposition of the Proverbs of Solomon.[19]

The Restlessness of Those Who Seek Visions. Cardinal Cajetan: "When prophecy has ceased, the people will be destroyed. But the one who guards the law is blessed." The first phrase according to the Hebrew is, "Without vision the people will be stripped bare." The second phrase suggests the meaning of the first: the discussion deals with a kind of uncovering or deprivation, obviously the removal of the law's beauty. It is obvious that a people stripped of its legal customs (i.e., of what has been committed by divine law) possess no vision. This means, "when divine revelations have ceased," those received through representational or intellectual visions, whether asleep or awake. People accustomed to consulting God, and to receiving answers from him, when they are deprived of answers like this, they abandon the precepts of law and turn to soothsayers and diviners. King Saul did this near the end of his life, and so did the Jews around the time of the Maccabees. When they had deprived themselves of the beauty of divine law they went over to the practices of the Gentiles. The second phrase placed next to it for contrast makes clear this double meaning when it says, "and blessed is the people who guards the law." The one who perseveres in keeping divine law—even when visions fail—this one is specifically designated blessed, both because he is truly blessed in hope, and because his happiness shines out more by contrast. The Parables of Solomon, Corrected by the Original Hebrew.[20]

Prophecy Guides Just Rulers. Philipp Melanchthon: Prophecy here refers to prophetic rule, in which God gives fruitful counsels through some beneficial ruler—and ensures a good outcome. In other words, the state will flourish only so long as it has such rulers. Thus Elisha guided the king by his counsels for around seventy years, in the midst of the greatest calamities. Samaria was liberated from its siege, when its

[19]CR 14:77-79. [†]Melanchthon has conflated lines from two different orations of Claudian. The first and third lines are from *De consulatu Stilichonis* 168-69; the second is from *Panegyric on the Fourth Consulship of the Emperor Honorius* 299. [†]Virgil, *Aeneid* 8.642-45 (LCL 64:104-5). [§]Menander, fr. 223 (LCL 459:72-73). [◊]Plautus, *Pseudolus* 527-29 (LCL 260:290-91). [Δ]Parmenion was Philip II's best general and Alexander's second in command during the first three years of his eastern campaign. After Parmenion's son Philotas was implicated and executed in a treacherous plot, Alexander ordered the assassination of the father. [††]In Homer's *Odyssey*, the hero is forced to navigate the narrow strait between the two deadly sea monsters, Scylla and Charybdis (17.201-59); in Virgil's *Aeneid*, the travelers are warned by a former companion of "luckless Ulysses" to avoid the passage altogether (3.681-92).

[20]Cajetan, *Parabolae Salomonis ad veritatem Hebraicam castigatae*, 256.

hunger was so great that a donkey's head sold for eighty pieces of silver (that is, double drachmas), and a pint of dove's dung for five pieces. After the death of Elisha, the kingdom lasted for not much more than a hundred years, riven as it was by constant sedition. So also the guidance of Isaiah mitigated many calamities for around eighty years; afterward followed destruction, during which even then a part of the people were saved by the counsels of Jeremiah.

From examples such as these it can be known why it may be said that "when prophecy ceases, the people are scattered," because with the extinction of beneficial rulers, rivalries and seditions in the state will follow, and eventually destruction, just as it is said in this verse: "For luxury and its attendant vices, and pride with sequent hate have brought to ruin all kingdoms else."[†] But Solomon goes further, telling what sort of prophetic guidance is needed when he says, "Blessed is the one who keeps the law," as if to say that prophetic guidance is such that it holds on to true doctrine and true rites of worship, and gives counsels that are congruent with the Word of God. Exposition of the Proverbs of Solomon.[21]

Receiving God's Word. Michel Cop: It is written, "Formerly in Israel, when a man went to inquire of God, he said, 'Come, let us go to the seer,' for today's 'prophet' was formerly called a 'seer.'" And since a seer is a prophet, we will take the vision for a prophecy, the same as it is understood in Isaiah. This kind of vision has always been necessary in the world for the preservation of humanity. It greatly benefited the people of Israel when they had seers to govern them, and their lack brought great harm. For when they had the prophets, they were instructed in the will of God, which showed the way to salvation and life; but being deprived of the seers, they did not know what they should do. Therefore they gave themselves over to superstitions and idolatry, to craftiness and rapine, to extortion, violence, and other wickedness, and so provoked God to wrath against them. This was the reason he raised up enemies to plunder and destroy them, as may be seen in the book of Judges, and the other sacred histories. Likewise, all other nations without seers, or rejecting the Word of God, have suffered horrible scourges. And still now we see that the nations that do not have the pure preaching of the gospel are vexed and tormented by wars, in which a great number of people perish. And so in keeping with these experiences, Solomon says, "Without vision the people perish." So unless we receive the Word (in which God reveals himself to us and declares his will for us) with all obedience, we are cursed: for by such contempt we come to perdition, even though for a time it may seem that we prosper and flourish. Let us therefore receive the vision—that is, the wholesome doctrine by which we are instructed in God's will. And so we shall not decay, but shall be happy and blessed. On the Proverbs of Solomon.[22]

Preaching Matters, but Obedience Matters More. The English Annotations: Want of preaching may damn people, but store of it cannot save them unless they are obedient to it. Others interpret this as where there is no preaching, the church is in a manner dissolved, and the great mass of people are in great danger, yet it follows not but that those that live conscionably and follow what they have learned may do well enough and be saved. Another interpretation is not less literal—that is, where God withdraws himself from his people because of their sin so that no oracle or signs of his presence are left, it is no wonder if, through a multiplicity of public woes and confusions, many, both good and bad, perish. Yet even then this may be their comfort, that those who are pious and godly, through their perseverance in good, shall be happy in the end. Annotations on Proverbs 29:18.[23]

[21]CR 14:79; citing 2 Kings 6:25. †Claudian, *De consulatu Stilichonis* 160-61 (LCL 136:54-55).

[22]Cop, *Sur les Proverbes de Salomon*, 632; citing 1 Sam 9:9; Is 1:1.

[23]Downame, ed., *English Annotations*, 6Z2r*; citing Rom 2:13; Jas 1:22; Ps 74:9.

30:1–31:31 FINAL PROVERBS

1 *The words of Agur son of Jakeh. The oracle.*[a]

The man declares, I am weary, O God;
I am weary, O God, and worn out.[b]

2 *Surely I am too stupid to be a man.*
I have not the understanding of a man.

3 *I have not learned wisdom,*
nor have I knowledge of the Holy One.

4 *Who has ascended to heaven and come down?*
Who has gathered the wind in his fists?

Who has wrapped up the waters in a garment?
Who has established all the ends of the earth?

What is his name, and what is his son's name?
Surely you know!

5 *Every word of God proves true;*
he is a shield to those who take refuge in him.

6 *Do not add to his words,*
lest he rebuke you and you be found a liar.

7 *Two things I ask of you;*
deny them not to me before I die:

8 *Remove far from me falsehood and lying;*
give me neither poverty nor riches;
feed me with the food that is needful for me,

9 *lest I be full and deny you*
and say, "Who is the Lord*?"*

or lest I be poor and steal
and profane the name of my God.

10 *Do not slander a servant to his master,*
lest he curse you, and you be held guilty.

11 *There are those*[c] *who curse their fathers*
and do not bless their mothers.

12 *There are those who are clean in their own eyes*
but are not washed of their filth.

13 *There are those—how lofty are their eyes,*
how high their eyelids lift!

14 *There are those whose teeth are swords,*
whose fangs are knives,

to devour the poor from off the earth,
the needy from among mankind.

15 *The leech has two daughters:*
Give and Give.[d]

Three things are never satisfied;
four never say, "Enough":

16 *Sheol, the barren womb,*
the land never satisfied with water,
and the fire that never says, "Enough."

17 *The eye that mocks a father*
and scorns to obey a mother

will be picked out by the ravens of the valley
and eaten by the vultures.

18 *Three things are too wonderful for me;*
four I do not understand:

19 *the way of an eagle in the sky,*
the way of a serpent on a rock,

the way of a ship on the high seas,
and the way of a man with a virgin.

20 *This is the way of an adulteress:*
she eats and wipes her mouth
and says, "I have done no wrong."

21 *Under three things the earth trembles;*
under four it cannot bear up:

22 *a slave when he becomes king,*
and a fool when he is filled with food;

23 *an unloved woman when she gets a husband,*
and a maidservant when she displaces her mistress.

[24]Four things on earth are small,
but they are exceedingly wise:

[25]the ants are a people not strong,
yet they provide their food in the summer;

[26]the rock badgers are a people not mighty,
yet they make their homes in the cliffs;

[27]the locusts have no king,
yet all of them march in rank;

[28]the lizard you can take in your hands,
yet it is in kings' palaces.

[29]Three things are stately in their tread;
four are stately in their stride:

[30]the lion, which is mightiest among beasts
and does not turn back before any;

[31]the strutting rooster,[e] the he-goat,
and a king whose army is with him.[f]

[32]If you have been foolish, exalting yourself,
or if you have been devising evil,
put your hand on your mouth.

[33]For pressing milk produces curds,
pressing the nose produces blood,
and pressing anger produces strife.

31 *The words of King Lemuel. An oracle that his mother taught him:*

[2]What are you doing, my son?[g] What are you doing, son of my womb?
What are you doing, son of my vows?

[3]Do not give your strength to women,
your ways to those who destroy kings.

[4]It is not for kings, O Lemuel,
it is not for kings to drink wine,
or for rulers to take strong drink,

[5]lest they drink and forget what has been decreed
and pervert the rights of all the afflicted.

[6]Give strong drink to the one who is perishing,
and wine to those in bitter distress;[h]

[7]let them drink and forget their poverty
and remember their misery no more.

[8]Open your mouth for the mute,
for the rights of all who are destitute.[i]

[9]Open your mouth, judge righteously,
defend the rights of the poor and needy.

[10][j]An excellent wife who can find?
She is far more precious than jewels.

[11]The heart of her husband trusts in her,
and he will have no lack of gain.

[12]She does him good, and not harm,
all the days of her life.

[13]She seeks wool and flax,
and works with willing hands.

[14]She is like the ships of the merchant;
she brings her food from afar.

[15]She rises while it is yet night
and provides food for her household
and portions for her maidens.

[16]She considers a field and buys it;
with the fruit of her hands she plants a vineyard.

[17]She dresses herself[k] with strength
and makes her arms strong.

[18]She perceives that her merchandise is profitable.
Her lamp does not go out at night.

[19]She puts her hands to the distaff,
and her hands hold the spindle.

[20]She opens her hand to the poor
and reaches out her hands to the needy.

[21]She is not afraid of snow for her household,
for all her household are clothed in scarlet.[l]

[22]She makes bed coverings for herself;
her clothing is fine linen and purple.

[23]Her husband is known in the gates
when he sits among the elders of the land.

[24]*She makes linen garments and sells them;*
she delivers sashes to the merchant.

[25]*Strength and dignity are her clothing,*
and she laughs at the time to come.

[26]*She opens her mouth with wisdom,*
and the teaching of kindness is on her tongue.

[27]*She looks well to the ways of her household*
and does not eat the bread of idleness.

[28]*Her children rise up and call her blessed;*
her husband also, and he praises her:

[29]*"Many women have done excellently,*
but you surpass them all."

[30]*Charm is deceitful, and beauty is vain,*
but a woman who fears the Lord *is to be praised.*

[31]*Give her of the fruit of her hands,*
and let her works praise her in the gates.

a Or *Jakeh, the man of Massa* **b** Revocalization; Hebrew *The man declares to Ithiel, to Ithiel and Ucal* **c** Hebrew *There is a generation*; also verses 12, 13, 14 **d** Or *"Give, give," they cry* **e** Or *the magpie*, or *the greyhound*; Hebrew *girt-of-loins* **f** Or *against whom there is no rising up* **g** Hebrew *What, my son?* **h** Hebrew *those bitter in soul* **i** Hebrew *are sons of passing away* **j** Verses 10–31 are an acrostic poem, each verse beginning with the successive letters of the Hebrew alphabet **k** Hebrew *She girds her loins* **l** Or *in double thickness*

Overview: The final two chapters of the book of Proverbs contain some of its most memorable material, but the authorial inscriptions at the beginning of each section return our exegetes' focus to questions of literary form and canonical authorship. One exegetical decision pressed on the reader by the Hebrew text was whether to translate these ascriptions as proper names (e.g., Agur son of Jakeh, as most modern translations do), or as adjectival descriptions (e.g., "Gatherer, the son of Vomiter," as Douay-Rheims). Cardinal Cajetan defends the traditional view, extending Solomonic authorship through the end of the chapter, while Michel Cop accepts the view of medieval Jewish authorities that this section marks an authorial transition. Proverbs on virtue and vice feature prominently in this chapter, and our exegetes make use of the text's natural illustrations to develop reflections on virtue and natural law. The final chapter of Proverbs sings the praises of virtuous women. Interpreting *lĕmû ʾēl* adjectivally, Cop reads this concluding chapter as Solomonic, prompting reflections on the role of Bathsheba in forming her son's education in wisdom. Beginning in Proverbs 31:10, the celebrated encomium of the virtuous wife begins, and all of our commentators, both Protestant and Catholic alike, make use of the opportunity to commend married life and the attendant domestic virtues as positive goods. Some of these commendations reflect the common early modern prejudices against women's character as "light and inconstant" (Cop), but others, such as Lucrezia Marinella and John Trapp, seize the opportunity to argue for the equal dignity of women's roles and celebrate their virtues as comparable to those of men. All are agreed that these verses praise a woman whose virtues are rooted in faith and a clear sense of Christian vocation.

30:1-33 *The Words of Agur Son of Jakeh*

Agur Was Probably a Real Person. The English Annotations: Though these names are found nowhere else in Scripture, which makes some interpret them as mystical (so the vulgar Latin and several ancients), yet it is more probable that such a man was really famous in his time for his wisdom, and his disciples, among others, are conceived to have been the two named here, Ithiel and Ucal. When or where he lived is altogether uncertain.[†] Most rabbis have Solomon as the object of these several names and they make strange interpretations of them to that purpose, but there is no appearance of solidity in anything they deliver concerning this matter.[‡] ANNOTATIONS ON PROVERBS 30:1.[1]

THE OVERFLOW OF SOLOMON'S WISDOM. CARDINAL CAJETAN: Understand, wise reader, that the first verse of chapter 30 is its title, and many believe that in this title there are several proper names. Many of these, however, are common nouns, and therefore I thought that I should give both readings. And so the first reading is, "The words of Agur son of Jakeh, the prophecies given by the man Ithiel: Ithiel and Ucal." This is the title according to those who hold that Agar, Jakeh, Ithiel, and Ucal are the names of men. This means that Agur the son of Jakeh spoke these instructions to Ithiel and Ucal. According to this second reading Solomon inserted into his own proverbs those spoken by Agur to Ithiel and Ucal. The second reading is as the Vulgate has it, "The words of the one who harvests, the son of the one who vomits. The vision that the man spoke, the one with whom God dwells; and while God stayed with him he was comforted." But according to the literal Hebrew the rendering is, "The words of the one who was gathered, the son of the one vomiting, the prophecy of a man spoken through El-with-me. Through El-with-me I shall be able." This is the second reading corresponding word for word to the Hebrew text, taking all of the nouns as common. And this is the reading that we should prefer, because we should prefer things that are certain to those that are uncertain. It is unclear whether the aforesaid nouns are names of men. But it is clear that they can be taken as common nouns. And second, because the topics fit this reading, as will become evident. Therefore, because Solomon was going to deal with the knowledge of holy things he prefixed a particular title. By this he made clear the nature of its contents—namely, its prophetic content. And he thereby distinguishes these proverbs from those that are moral in content. He also makes clear the one from whom he had this prophecy—namely, that God was with him. He also explains the method whereby he possessed these prophetic statements—namely, by gathering all of himself inwardly. And finally, he explains the means that he used to bring them forth, comparing it to the image of one who vomits. But last of all, he sets forth the effect arising from God speaking with him, saying, "I shall be able." These are the five lessons revealed in this title. Notice the individual words that without a doubt have been joined together by the one drawn into himself. For when a man is raised up in spirit, the whole of him is gathered to himself. He withdraws from the use of external senses. Next is the phrase, "of the son of the one who vomits." As he spews forth vomit, he is called the son of the one who keeps on vomiting by typical Hebrew usage. Other examples are "the son of the bridegrooms" or "the son of iniquity." By this expression Solomon means that his own mind has been filled with divine revelations. And so, like someone overflowing with vomit he is compelled to proclaim the things that he has learned after drawing in his spirit. So we see that Solomon received these kinds of revelations to reveal them for God's glory and the benefit of human beings. THE PARABLES OF SOLOMON, CORRECTED BY THE ORIGINAL HEBREW.[2]

AUTHORSHIP UNCERTAIN. MICHEL COP: According to the Hebrews, the fourth part of this book begins at this point. The opinion of Ibn Ezra[†] was that Agur was a man who lived in the time of Solomon. He walked in righteousness, was

[1]Downame, ed., *English Annotations*, 6Z2r-v*. [†]The decision to translate or transliterate (taking as proper names) the terms in this opening superscription continues to divide modern translators and commentators. Consider the following solutions: Douay (Vulgate): "The words of Gatherer the son of Vomiter. The vision which the man spoke, with whom God is, and who being strengthened by God, abiding with him." KJV: "The words of Agur the son of Jakeh, even the prophecy: the man spake unto Ithiel, even unto Ithiel and Ucal." NRSV: "The words of Agur son of Jakeh. An oracle. Thus says the man: I am weary, O God, I am weary, O God. How can I prevail?" [‡]The *Annotations* do not identify the rabbinic writers they disparage, but for a more positive interaction with specific Jewish sources, see the comments by Cop below.

[2]Cajetan, *Parabolae Salomonis ad veritatem Hebraicam castigatae*, 259-60.

experienced in knowledge, and held in honor among those of his age, and for these reasons King Solomon included his words of wisdom in his own book. And Ithiel and Ucal were wise men, the companions or disciples of Agur. But Rabbi Levi the son of Gershon‡ says that it seems that Solomon was named Agur, because of his aphorisms or proverbs in this book: for "Agur" indicates one who gathers together, and he named himself the son of Jakeh. However it may be, the words that are set down hereafter are called a prophecy, or a charge, on account of their excellence, for they contain very weighty proverbs of great importance. ON THE PROVERBS OF SOLOMON.[3]

A LAMENT FOR HUMAN IGNORANCE. PHILIPP MELANCHTHON: This first aphorism [by "the gatherer"], in which he says, "I am the stupidest of men," is a confession of human ignorance, and a lament regarding the mental blindness that characterizes our wretched human nature. Not only by the examples of the pagans is this made manifest, who lived in horrendous darkness when it came to the knowledge of God, but also in the mind of each person, troubled as we are by waves of various doubts.

Simonides was asked, "What is God?" He asked for three days to think about it, and then replied to Hiero that the more he considered the divine nature, the less he could confidently affirm that it could be discovered.† But Simonides was wrong. For the knowledge of God and of his laws shines forth in our minds, and it is by this light that we distinguish God from evil things. And it is on that basis that the description of Plato is accepted, that God is eternal mind, the cause of the good in nature.‡ But although there is this spark in human minds, assent to it is sluggish, and people fall into doubts, especially when they see good people oppressed by the wicked. Because they do not understand the reasons for this, they begin to doubt God's providence.

For this reason, above all, human ignorance is deplored—that is, we ought to acknowledge our ignorance and lament it with groans, just as the prophets did: "Everyone is a liar." And, "The human heart is perverse, and full of trouble." And even among the pagans we find lamentations of the weaknesses besetting all humankind, lamentations that are rehearsed in order to recall people to modesty. For example, Pindar exclaims, "What is a man? What is he not? A dream of a shadow is a man."§ This saying is often helpful to bear in mind.

But human wisdom is not aware of the remedies for its own ignorance and infirmity. In the church, however, we know the divine revelations, in which both the causes of our calamities and their remedies are made clear. Therefore even here in this passage we are led to the teaching handed down by God, which instructs us to hear it and embrace it, to be moved by its warnings and yield to its consolations, not adding anything to corrupt it. EXPOSITION OF THE PROVERBS OF SOLOMON.[4]

TWOFOLD PURITY OF THE WORD. PHILIPP MELANCHTHON: In this passage it is said, "Every word of God is pure," that is, without corruptions, "and he is a shield to the one who trusts in him." Just as God sent his Son and revealed him as such by his own voice, in the immensity of his goodness, so that we might not go astray, so you ought to give heed to this voice of the Son and embrace it, along with these judgments regarding the essence and the will of God, law and gospel, the wrath of God and his grace. For these truly are given to us by God,

[3]Cop, *Sur les Proverbes de Salomon*, 641-42. †R. Abraham b. Meir Ibn Ezra (1089/1092–1164/1167) was one of the most important Jewish biblical scholars of the Middle Ages. Publication of his commentary in the 1524–1525 Rabbinic Bible made his exegesis widely available to Christian Hebraists for the first time.
‡R Levi b. Gerson (1288–1344) was a medieval Jewish polymath (he published on mathematics, philosophy, medicine, and astronomy in addition to biblical studies) whose work was also published in the 1524–1525 Rabbinic Bible.

[4]CR 14:80-81. †Melanchthon's source is likely Cicero, who recounted the often-repeated anecdote of the philosopher Simonides's interview with Hiero, the king of Syracuse, as a model for intellectual circumspection (*De natura deorum* 1.22). ‡Cf. Plato, *Phaedo* 97b-c. §Pindar, *Pythian Odes* 8.95-96 (LCL 56:346-47).

who has revealed himself in the sending of the Son, and commanded us in a clear voice to know and call on him through the Son, just as the Son himself says, "This is eternal life, that they may know you, the true God, and Jesus Christ, whom you have sent." If you rightly acknowledge and call on God, you will come to understand something of his power, by which he and none other gathers the eternal church to himself.

Consider this image, when it says, "The Word of God is a shield to those who trust in God." Paul says the same thing when he describes the "shield of faith," because it is certain that it is God's power that is at work when we are sustained in our faith by the Word of God and by prayer, just as Paul says, "that through the encouragement of the Scriptures we may have hope." Also, "The gospel is the power of God, for the salvation of all who believe." And the psalmist says, "My soul endures in your Word; my soul has hoped in God."

But these sweetest of propositions are opposed by pagans, and as well as by the impious fancies and blasphemies of the Anabaptists and the Schwenckfelders, who reject the external voice by which the teaching is given.[†] But here we are taught that both the inner and the outer must be retained in the purity of the divine Word. And purity must be understood in a twofold manner: first, as regards the Word of God itself rightly perceived, without carnal imaginations. Thus the Sadducees preserved something of the letter of the law from Moses, but they understood the promises only in as applying to the world of the flesh in this present life. So also the monks understand the law in relation to external works, and faith as a matter of historical assent.

The second way in which the purity of the Word is here understood involves not adding anything to corrupt it, as the pope has done with his prayers to the dead, the trade in Masses for profit, false acts of worship, the prohibition of [clerical] marriage, and other impious traditions. Both kinds of purity are spoken of in Psalm 12: "The words of the Lord are pure words, like silver purified in a furnace, purged seven times"—that is, in the first place the Word of God is rightly understood when we come to know it in the real practice of penitence, in the cross. For here our minds are purified, so that above all else we may know the Word of God without the fancies of our flesh, just as when Paul was accused with unjust cruelty, he learned that the prophets had spoken of Christ's eternal kingdom, not a political kingdom. That is why he said that, "The natural (*psychikos*) person does not perceive the things that are of the Spirit." In the second place, there is that purity which expressly precludes adding any traditions regarding new forms of worship. For the vanity of these is revealed in true penitence and in the cross, just as Paul says that the stubble of our teaching will be consumed by fire. EXPOSITION OF THE PROVERBS OF SOLOMON.[5]

NEITHER POVERTY NOR RICHES UNDER THE OLD LAW. DENIS THE CARTHUSIAN: The speech by Solomon that follows here seems to be given according to the persona of imperfection and under the state of the Old Testament, rather than in the persona of perfection and under the state of the law and the gospel. "Two things I have asked you," that is, the Lord God: "deny them not to me before I die. Remove far from me vanity"—that is, give me the grace to cast aside and condemn all vanity (that is, vainglory, self-complacency, a stubborn clinging to perishable creatures, and the appetite for human praise and one's own honor)—and every falsehood, especially pernicious ones. "Poverty," that is, such scarcity of worldly goods that I need to beg, "and riches," that is, an abundance of worldly goods above and beyond what is necessary and appropriate for my station in life, "do not give me," or allow me to acquire. Moreover, concerning the matter of begging, it is to be understood according to the

[5]CR 14:81-82; citing Jn 17:3; Eph 6:16; Rom 15:4; 1:16; Ps 130:5; 12:6; 1 Cor 2:14; 3:15. [†]Kaspar von Schwenckfeld (1489–1562) was a radical spiritualist reformer who repeatedly clashed with Luther and his followers from 1524 onward. At stake in this context is Schwenckfeld's distinction between the "inner word" of God, communicated ineffably and directly to the soul, and the "outer word," which can point to the former, but does not necessarily convey or complete it.

state of the Mosaic law, where it is written that "there shall be no poor nor beggar among you." Thus, "provide for my subsistence only what is necessary" for maintaining me and those who are joined to me, insofar as their provision concerns me. Thus also the apostle adds, "Having food and clothing, let us be content with these." And so with these words he asks to be taken from those things that are evils in themselves, vices such as vanity and falsehood; then he asks to be taken from those things which are commonly the occasion of vices (although they are not evil in themselves), namely beggary and wealth. Exposition of the Book of Proverbs.[6]

Bold Humility. Michel Cop: Whoever it is that speaks here, either Solomon or another, he speaks of himself with great humility, even though he was endowed with great gifts and graces, and has uttered excellent proverbs to the great edification of those who consider and store them up, as they should. Various saints, knowing that God held them in high regard, refrained from boasting of their greatness and excellence, so as not to tread others down, but have shown great humility. . . .[†] But even though these holy men had thus humbled themselves, they did not cease to show themselves excellent in following their vocation boldly and manfully, and doing their duty properly. On the Proverbs of Solomon.[7]

Contentment in Mediocrity. Philipp Melanchthon: The first and highest good is true knowledge of God, just as our Lord says: "Seek first the kingdom of God." And Solomon in his petition advances other goods, as when he says, "The fear of the Lord is the beginning of wisdom." So also, "A person does not live by bread alone." But after these, a middling condition [*mediocritas*] in life is more secure than either wealth or poverty, and so these two petitions are recited here, to be a light and rule of life for us. First let us seek the kingdom of God, and be reminded that "the one who fears the Lord will lack for no good thing." And thus in the Gospel parable we are commanded to sell all our goods to acquire the pearl. Second, let us understand what the will of God is for us: that we should engage in honest labor, each one according to their own vocation, and from our labors earn our livelihood, just as Paul says: do your own work.[†] And let us be content with a middling status, remember what is said elsewhere: "The proud in heart are an abomination before God." And Sirach says, "Do not foolishly seek what is too difficult for you. . . . Give your devotion to what is commanded you."

The pagans also knew by experience that a middling sort of life was more secure, just as these verses suggest: "There are many advantages for those who adopt a middle course; that's the course I want in the city."[‡] And many squander their power and wealth in satisfying vicious cravings, according to this saying: "The soul becomes enfeebled by an excess of prosperity, and nor is it easy to bear good fortune with equanimity of mind."[§] Exposition of the Proverbs of Solomon.[8]

Being Satisfied with What God Ordains. Michel Cop: After the wise man has asked what is necessary for the life of the soul ("Remove far from me falsehood and lying"), he asks for such things as are necessary for the body, which we may lawfully demand. For although Jesus Christ does show us by various arguments that we ought not to worry about food or the other bodily necessities of this life, and though he admonishes us to seek first the kingdom of God and its righteousness, nevertheless he does not thereby forbid us from asking for bodily necessities—otherwise he would not teach us to pray to God our Father asking for our daily bread, nor would anyone have need to plow

[6]DCOO 7:185-86; citing Deut 15:4, 1 Tim 6:8.

[7]Cop, *Sur les Proverbes de Salomon*, 642. [†]Cop illustrates the pattern with the examples of Abraham, Moses, and David.

[8]CR 14:82-83; citing Mt 6:33; Prov 9:10; Deut 8:3; Ps 34:10; Mt 13:45-46; Prov 16:5; Sir 3:21-22. [†]Cf. 1 Cor 7:20; Eph 4:28. [‡]Attributed to Phocylides by Aristotle (*Politics* 4.1295b25; LCL 258:400-401). [§]Ovid, *Ars amatoria* 2.437-38.

the earth, to plant, sow, gather, and lay up in cellars and barns the fruit that the earth has brought forth. It is then lawful for us to ask things from God's hands that are necessary for our bodies, . . . yet it must be done with care, and without mistrust, knowing that the earth is the Lord's and it obeys him, bringing forth its fruits as he commands. . . .

Therefore we must know that not only is it lawful for us to ask and seek for our bodily necessities, but also it is necessary, for it requires that we humble ourselves and confess that all riches come to us from the bounty and generosity of our heavenly Father. . . . [But in so doing] we must not follow the desires of our flesh, which are insatiable, but rather content ourselves with mediocrity, as the wise man shows us in this present text, which contains three parts. The first is that he asks God not to give him poverty. There seems to be an absurdity in this request, for although he confesses (or so it seems) that poverty is given from God, he refuses it, though if it is a gift from God, it ought to be precious. Moreover, God always holds the poor in high esteem and exalts them; and Jesus Christ also says that to them belong the kingdom of heaven—and he even calls them his "brothers"! We respond to this that as a child says to his father, "Give me no rods!" In the same way, the wise man calls poverty the gift of God even as he asks that God *not* give it to him. And this is because he knows that poverty is a rod—indeed, a curse that God sends into the world for its sins. And so we must patiently bear poverty when God gives it, and never think that God hates us, any more than a good and wise father hates his child when he gives him the rod. And we are taught this well, when God by his Word so diligently commends the poor, as has often been alleged. And although St. Paul says that "neither hunger, nor nakedness shall separate us from the love of Christ," and that in poverty we must neither be discouraged nor despair, yet it is lawful to avoid it when we can, by the means that God teaches in his Word, which are labor and prayer. For although labor is ordained by God, yet it shall not profit anyone unless God himself blesses it, and we obtain this blessing by prayer. He teaches this when he says, "Call on me in the day of trouble, and I will deliver you," and the wise man here agrees when he runs to God, beseeching him that he would not give him poverty. When he prays thus, he is really asking that God would grant him the grace to work, and that he would bless his labors, which otherwise would be in vain. . . .

The second request is that he asks God not to give him riches. It may seem at first glance that he intends to rebuke riches and reject them, as if they were evil and hurtful. But if his intent were such, it would be evil, seeing that God has created riches and given them to whom he thinks good to make them prosper. So he did with Abraham and other patriarchs, with David and other kings, with Job and various others. . . . Therefore it is not in the mind of the wise man to refuse riches as evil things, for in so doing he should do injury to God; rather, the wise man distrusts himself, knowing that he was of the same nature as those others who had and continued to abuse the riches of the world in various ways, to the dishonor of God, to their own harm, and also to the harm and contempt of their neighbors. For the rich of the world often abuse their riches in idolatry, and to maintain them they will spare no expense, as may be seen in the making of the molten calf, and when it is said that the images of the heathen are but silver and gold (although this is said to show the vanity of idols and foolishness of idolaters), and when Solomon built a high place for Chemosh the abominable idol of the Moabites and Jeroboam made two golden calves. And now also we may see this among the papists, how the rich spare no expense in maintaining their service, which they call divine. They also abuse their riches to their hurt when they distrust God, and put their trust in their wealth. For in so doing, they deprive themselves of the kingdom of God, as the rich have done. Finally, they abuse them to the contempt and hurt of their neighbor, for they care nothing to help them, like the rich fool and the rich man who would not help Lazarus, but have rather oppressed them. So St. Paul has comprehended all three abuses, from which he would have the rich to turn away—without forsaking their riches. . . .

The third is that he asks God to feed him "with the bread of his estate." In this his desires are in accord with what Jesus Christ teaches us to say, "Give us this day our daily bread." And so we must be content with this, as St. Paul teaches us. We are taught by this that every person should carefully and faithfully employ himself and labor in his vocation; otherwise he shall not be maintained with "the bread of his estate" (that is, with the food God has prepared and appointed for him), but rather with the bread of others. For here, "estate" is not taken after the manner of worldlings, who commit great abuses in order to maintain their own estates. The word here translated "estate" comes from a verb that means "to ordain and appoint." And so, when it is said, "maintain me with the bread of my estate," it is not to say "according as I think belongs to me, because of my highness and power, or worthiness and excellence." But the bread that we eat justly we call "ours" because God gives it to us, and he makes it ours by his grace. On the Proverbs of Solomon.[9]

Warnings Against Vice. Philipp Melanchthon: Several of the following aphorisms are complaints against various vices—that is, they are brief accounts that demonstrate what happens [when people act in a vicious manner]. They remind us to be more vigilant and resolute in avoiding such vices, and to flee the company of the wicked like a contagion, just as Horace says: "The man who backbites an absent friend; who fails to defend him when another finds fault; the man who courts the loud laughter of others, and the reputation of a wit; who can invent what he never saw; who cannot keep a secret—that man is black of heart; of him beware, good Roman."[†] Thus vice and its causes are narrated, just as doctors describe an injury, so that it can be seen and diagnosed. The complaints in this passage are similar: "three things trouble the earth: a slave made king, and a fool made rich and powerful." As regards the former, it is said that "nothing is more cruel than a man raised from lowly station to prosperity."[‡] And regarding the latter, no one is more insolent than one of fortune's fools.[§] And Theognis says, "In truth excess breeds insolence, whenever prosperity comes to a wicked man [who is not sound of mind.]"[◊] Exposition of the Proverbs of Solomon.[10]

Spiritual and Worldly Pride. The English Annotations: There are two kinds of pride: spiritual and worldly. Sometimes they meet together in one, as when a person has a great opinion of their own godliness and excellent parts and thereupon in ordinary conversation openly praises themselves and despises others, as the proud Pharisee did in the Gospel and those in Isaiah 65:5. Sometimes the prides are severed, if one is humble and lowly outwardly but proud within themselves, for this very humility and whatever else they fantasize good and commendable is in themselves, whether real or imaginary. For distinction's sake, we may call one internal pride and the other external, though commonly neither is without external evidences nor the other ever found but from some inward cause and distemper. The first kind seems specially intended here, and the second in the next verse. By worldly pride, we comprehend also that which is altogether grounded on external things, as wealth, honor, beauty, and the like. Annotations on Proverbs 30:12.[11]

A Little Bestiary of Virtue. Philipp Melanchthon: "Four small things are wiser than wise people." Here we have a charming collection of little creatures whom it is said possess outstanding wisdom. And yet we are reminded that we

[9]Cop, *Sur les Proverbes de Salomon*, 651-54; citing Mt 6:25; 5:3; 25:40; Rom 8:28; Gen 2:15, 3:17; Eph 4:28; 2 Thess 3:6; Ps 50:15; Ex 32:3; Ps 115:4; 1 Kings 11:7; 12:28; Mt 19:23; Lk 12:19; 16:19; Jas 2:6; 1 Tim 6:9-10; 6:17-19; Mt 6:11.

[10]CR 14:83. [†]Horace, *Satires* 1.82-85 (LCL 194:54-55). [‡]Claudian, *Against Eutropius* 1.181 (LCL 135:152-53). [§]Cf. Cicero, *De amicitia* 54. [◊]Theognis, *Elegies* 153-54 (LCL 258:194-95).

[11]Downame, ed., *English Annotations*, 6Z2v*.

ought to recognize the vast misery of human nature, which wars against itself. For human nature knows God and knows his law, but does not obey. On the contrary, and with full knowledge of its actions, it runs headlong against God and against his natural decrees, just as is described in these verses of Menander: "Most evils are the result of our choices (*ekousia*), rather than happening by chance (*automata*)."[†] But even the most excellent natural virtues are not so durable; consider the examples of David, Nebuchadnezzar, Hercules, Themistocles, Alexander, and so on. But beasts obey by nature, nor are they divided within themselves.

Therefore we must consider the weakness of our condition, and seek its remedies from what the Son of God has proposed for our healing. Here he names the ant as a model for work and sedulousness. The hare seeking a hiding place reminds those who are weak not to aggrandize themselves above those who have greater virtues. The locust, who loves gathering in large numbers, is not seditious, nor does it throw the order or coordination of the swarm into chaos. The spider excels in artistry.[‡] Moreover, against the image of the ants is set the slothful, those who lack the virtue of sedulousness. Against that of the hares is set the impudent braggart (*thrasydeilos*), who stirs up all sorts of big ideas, but cannot follow through on any of them. These lack the virtue of fortitude. Against that of the locusts is set the seditious, who agitate against order and tranquility. These lack the virtue of justice, which upholds geometric proportion in its due place, and does not disturb public order.[§] Against the spider is set the uncultivated, who are confident in their own virtues and neglect to take counsel with others. These lack the virtue of prudence. EXPOSITION OF THE PROVERBS OF SOLOMON.[12]

ENTERPRISING VIRTUES. MICHAEL JERMIN: These five quaternions here set down, Rabbi Solomon applies allegorically to the four monarchies which oppressed the Israelites.[†] But Lyra with more likelihood of reason leaving out the former quaternions applies his prophetical exposition (as he calls it) to this last quaternion only, and with some difference from Rabbi Solomon makes the Lion to be Nebuchadnezzar (since in the prophecy of Jeremiah he is called this), the greyhound to be Cyrus, the he-goat to be Alexander, and the "king against whom there is no rising up" to be the Romans. But to consider them as emblems of moral instruction, the general scope of them is in this verse proposed. . . .

The first of the four is the king of beasts, the last a king of men. Now as "the lion" is the strongest among beasts, so it is the strongest among lions of which the original speaks: it is *leis*, an old mighty lion, one grown to full strength and still abiding in his full strength. . . . And he it is that "goes well": he it is from whom courage is taught us, that our affairs may go well. . . . A lion's heart in any enterprise is the heart of the enterprise. St. Gregory understanding this verse in reference to Christ tells us that "It is Christ himself who in this place is set down to be the Lion, who is said to be most strong, because in him the weakness of God is stronger than men."[§] "Who turns not away for any," for he says, "the prince of this world comes and has nothing in me." But the proverbial sense of this verse is to exhort us in a good matter to go on with a lion-like resolution, and not to turn away for any impediment that may lie in our way, or for any opposition that may be made against us.

The second help for well going on is expressed by a well-trussed horse, or a well-knit greyhound, and is a speedy diligence that strives to carry the news of good success in that which is doing.

[12]CR 14:83-84. [†]There is no extant passage in Menander that employs these two exact terms, though he does personify Chance as a god (*Samia* 163), and in *Epitrepontes* Onesimos criticizes the view that change makes wrong unavoidable: "it's *character* that's blighting him—that, nothing else" (1105-6; LCL 132:514-15). [‡]Melanchthon here follows Luther's idiosyncratic translation (*Spinne*, spider), against the LXX (*kalabōtēs*, lizard) and the Vulgate (*stilio*, newt). [§]The definition of justice as "geometric proportion" is an ancient one (cf. Aristotle, *Nicomachean Ethics* 5.4, 1131b), but one that also may help make sense of Melanchthon's association of a swarm of locusts with order and tranquility.

Delay is often the betrayer of opportunity, and negligence cheats a person's desire. The race is best run in the course of human affairs where a wise diligence is the greyhound. The third help is expressed by the he-goat, and is a patient hardiness, which does not shrink for a little wetting, nor give over for a craggy rock that must be climbed. A soft tenderness that sinks under a heavy burden is not fit to carry a business, nor likely to make it go well or carry through with it. The fourth help is expressed by "a king against whom there is no rising up," and indicates a command of needful and useful means. For courage is but rash hardiness, speedy diligence is but lost labor, patient suffering is but senseless stupidity, unless requisite means be afforded wherein they may be exercised. But he that has means to effect his business may with these helps even reign in it. Paraphrastic Meditations.[13]

The Insatiability of Concupiscence. Michel Cop: If in these two sentences (vv. 15-16) we understand nothing but what is offered at first sight by the letter, then they shall give us no instruction. And if the wise man intended to teach us nothing else but what the words sound out, then he has set down in them no excellent thing, nor anything worthy of admiration. But we ought not either to think or say such a thing. Therefore it is necessary to understand that the wise man speaks here in parables and by comparison, and his aim is to sharply censure thieves and brigands, the avaricious and usurers, swindlers and extortioners, whoremongers and adulterers, gluttons and drunkards, and all who allow themselves to be carried away by their unbridled concupiscence. He calls them "horseleeches," for these have a forked tongue, and with these two forks (which the wise man calls the "two daughters") she sucks a man's blood, and will not leave the skin until she is full, even ready to burst. In the same way, these people are not easy to please, but having "two daughters," that is, diverse ways and means to harm and oppress their neighbors, and to vex themselves—they do not stop wanting more and more to follow their own lusts. On the Proverbs of Solomon.[14]

On Not Digging Deeper in Error. Philipp Melanchthon: This proverb teaches us about penitence and correcting our mistakes. When you slip up, do not defend your error, but receive correction and understand where you went wrong. Lament your mistake and embrace the truth; make clear by your confession that you understand what you did wrong, lest you confirm your error in others. This is what Paul did when he confessed that he had erred when he was an enemy to the gospel. More is said concerning these things above, when it is said that "a just person is their own first accuser." And in Zechariah it says that the one who corrects their ways receives these wounds in the house of their friend.

If anyone who has been admonished stubbornly defends their error, Paul commands that such a person be abandoned, and he calls them "self-condemned." That is, having already been convicted, such a person knows that they fight against conscience, and so they are condemned by their own judgment. Such a blasphemer then rushes headlong into eternal destruction. About such as these it is said that "to err is human, but to persevere in error is diabolical."† But many will yield only with great difficulty, as it is said, "Many a friend will give gold and riches and land, but one prepared to yield in talent will be found but seldom."‡

And here mention must be made of pride, which is placing confidence in one's own wisdom or power rather than in God. From such confidence many overweening people have

[13]Jermin, *Paraphrasticall Meditations*, 701-2; citing Jer 4:7; 1 Cor 1:25; Jn 14:30. †That is, the kingdoms of Edom, Babylon, Persia, and Greece (ET in A. Cohen, *Proverbs* [London: Soncino, 1952]). Rabbi Solomon Isaac of Troyes (1040–1105), also known by the popular acronym "Rashi," was perhaps the most influential Jewish commentator on Hebrew Bible and the Babylonian Talmud during the Middle Ages. ‡Gregory, *Moralia in Job* 30.3.9.

[14]Cop, *Sur les Proverbes de Salomon*, 660-61.

dreamed up new dogmas, or set up new rituals of worship, and then defended their own opinions through sheer pride and self-admiration, just as it is said that "opinion becomes truth by force." And it is sad that many rush out to fight for their errors with cunning interrogations and feats of legerdemain, adding falsehood to falsehood. From these horrible sins we must flee upon recognition. Exposition of the Proverbs of Solomon.[15]

A Warning Against Pressing Too Hard. Philipp Melanchthon: This proverb primarily signifies that authority ought to be wielded with moderation, just as Plato says when he explains that the best condition involves either moderate liberty or moderate servitude, but that the excess of either leads to the very worst outcomes.[†] And then there are these verses from Solon:

> But thus will the people best the voice of their leaders obey,
> When neither too slack is the rein, nor violence holdeth sway.[‡]

Now the measure [of such moderation] is established in the Decalogue. John the Baptist says, "Be content with your wages," and "do violence to no one, nor make false accusations." And it is written in Sirach, "Burdens, fodder, and the rod for an ass; labor, bread, and discipline for a servant."

After this is added a warning against reprimands given in anger, lest public discords arise. For it is often later the case that when great catastrophes result, they originate from trivial provocations, which might have been mitigated or even cured altogether by a more moderate response. Exposition of the Proverbs of Solomon.[16]

31:1-9 *The Words of King Lemuel*

The Value of a Mother's Teaching. Michel Cop: Following the Hebrew and Latin expositors, Solomon is called Lemuel—that is to say, "Of God." For although David had older sons than Solomon, none of them was ordained king but Solomon, just as God had foretold by the prophet Nathan. Now he calls the following proverbs "his words" because having heard them from his mother, it was he who reduced them to writing. In this he shows that even though he had been a student of the prophet Nathan, he did not despise the teaching of his mother, but held her in great esteem, as he shows when he calls it a prophecy—that is, a doctrine by which his mother expounded to him the will of God as he has declared it in his word. (The term is taken in the same sense in 1 Corinthians 14:1.) And so his mother sets an example for all the great ladies and mothers, that they ought not to spend their time with the children in talking of vain things, but that they should have the Word of God in their hearts, to be able to teach their children both by mouth and by example, as the apostle Paul demonstrates. But even when women are very learned, they ought not to take it upon themselves to teach publicly as ministers of the church. And although we do not find it written in any other place that Solomon's mother taught him, it ought to be enough for us that he himself confesses it here.

We must also conclude that David, who was a great prophet, must have diligently instructed Bathsheba, Solomon's mother, with great care, so as to correct the fault they had committed together during the life of Uriah, her first husband. We might also say that Solomon called "his mother" the church, in which he had been instructed by Nathan the prophet, by the priests. However this may be, when Solomon gathered together and wrote down what had been taught him, he showed us how careful and diligent we should be to hold on to what we are taught, to frame our manners and conversation so that we may teach our

[15]CR 14:84; citing Zech 13:6; Prov 18:17; Titus 3:11. [†]A medieval proverb with no unambiguous source in antiquity (cf. Cicero, *Orationes philippicae* 12.2.5: "To err is human, but only a fool persists in error"). [‡]Martial, *Epigrams* 8.18.9-10 (LCL 95:168-69).
[16]CR 14:85; citing Lk 3:14; Sir 33:25. [†]Cf. Plato, *Republic* 8.562b-c. [‡]Frag., cited in Aristotle *Constitution of Athens* 12.1.

neighbors by good doctrine and holy conversation. ON THE PROVERBS OF SOLOMON.[17]

DO NOT COLLUDE WITH OPPRESSIVE REGIMES. PHILIPP MELANCHTHON: The last chapter is an addition that contains three aphorisms. The first is a prohibition of inebriation (31:2-7). The second is a mandate regarding confession against those who oppress the innocent. This is significant in our time, when many in princely courts understand true doctrine but do not openly display what they believe, and as a result the innocent are dragged off to punishment. Here those who understand true doctrine are commanded to protect the innocent by their own confession, and not to support this unjust cruelty by their own silence or collusion. All by himself, Jonathan openly pled for David before Saul, while Doeg [the Edomite] and his cronies incited the king to fury. So also Calisthenes and Clitus openly rebuked the extravagance of Alexander to his face, even though others supported it by their assent.† EXPOSITION OF THE PROVERBS OF SOLOMON.[18]

31:10-31 *A Woman Who Fears the Lord*

MARRIAGE IS A GOD-GIVEN GOOD. SWISS BRETHREN CONFESSION OF HESSE: We believe, acknowledge, and confess that marriage is a good, God-given ordinance, that there should be one husband and one wife living in matrimonial love and faithfulness with each other. The husband as the head should with good common sense be the leader; and the wife should be subordinate and obedient to the husband; and the two should be one flesh. CONCERNING THE STATE OF MATRIMONY.[19]

NOBILITY OF MIND. CARDINAL CAJETAN: "A noble woman who will find?" According to the Hebrew this means, "Who will find an excellent wife?" The discussion here is not about women generally, but about a wife. This is now the fifth maternal statement dealing with Solomon's wife. She describes the qualities of a wife in general so her son can learn how to find one, and to have a wife who possesses such characteristics. The result is that his wives would not lack the alluring delights of women at leisure and so on, but possess whatsoever serves for the care of her family. And so the woman who is noble and fears God possesses the remaining qualities as well. And because such a woman is rarely or in fact very rarely found (like the highly unusual orator whom Cicero describes†), he begins with this question: "Who will find an excellent wife?" The discussion here is about that nobility of mind necessary for preserving one's modesty with steadfast intention, and about the nobility of works that are appropriate for the female head of the family. THE PARABLES OF SOLOMON, CORRECTED BY THE ORIGINAL HEBREW.[20]

A BACKHANDED TRIBUTE. MICHEL COP: Women are light and inconstant by nature, and they mess up everything if left to their own devices. This is proved by experience in our first mother, whose daughters women have at all times shown themselves to be in following her—indeed, in doing worse: think of Delilah, Jezebel, and Herodias. And therefore it was not without reason that the wise man, as though marveling and amazed at the uselessness or malice of women, asks, "Who shall find a virtuous women?"—that is, a woman who has good courage, diligently applies herself to her duty in the fear of the Lord, submitting herself to please her husband and govern her family in the way of holiness and justice, in sobriety and temperance, with diligence and care. A husband who finds such a wife ought not to hate, reject, or despise her, unless he is out of his mind! But if the worldlings take great delight when they

[17]Cop, *Sur les Proverbes de Salomon*, 668-69; citing 2 Sam 7:12-13; 1 Tim 5:14; Titus 2:3; 1 Cor 14:34; 1 Tim 2:11.

[18]CR 14:85; citing 1 Sam 21–22. †Cf. Plutarch, *Alexander* 51-53.

[19]CRR 11:78*; citing Gen 2:18, 24; Mt 19:4-5; 1 Cor 7:2, 28, 29; Eph 5:33; 1 Tim 3:12; Heb 13:4.

[20]Cajetan, *Parabolae Salomonis ad veritatem Hebraicam castigatae*, 282. †As described in *De Oratore*.

have things of great price, like gold and precious stones, and if they value these things greatly, how much more ought the husband to esteem a virtuous and valiant wife? For as the wise man says here, "her price is different from pearls"—that is, it surpasses them by far. And for good reason should the husband of so valiant a wife account all the world's riches as less than her. First of all, she is created in the image and likeness of God. Second, without the woman, man does not have a good disposition. Third, she is flesh of his flesh and bone of his bones. Fourth (and most important), is that the woman is bought with as a great a price as is the man: with the precious blood of the spotless Lamb. From this reason follows a fifth: that she is heir of the heavenly kingdom, where there is neither male nor female, but all are one in Jesus Christ.

Now concerning the state between man and wife, it is this: they ought to be careful to walk in all modesty and gentleness with one another. Let the wife behave herself virtuously and in all subjection and obedience, that she may compel her husband to love her greatly; and let the husband for his part be so gentle, and show her such love that he may give her occasion to be virtuous. And let them edify their family in this way, by good example, and cause them to live holy lives. On the Proverbs of Solomon.[21]

Bathsheba's Teaching. John Trapp: Good wives are rare commodities, and therefore precious and highly to be prized, even above rubies. . . . It is easy to observe that the New Testament affords more store of good women than the Old. When Paul came first to Philippi, few or none came to hear him except women, but they drew in their husbands and it soon became a famous church. What a rare jewel was Priscilla, who better instructed Apollos, ventured her life for Paul, and was such a singular help to her husband that she is mentioned before him, as the more forward of the two. So also was Manoah's wife, and Nazianzen's mother.† Solomon's mother was behind none of them, as appears by this poem, either composed by Solomon as a character of her (as some have thought) or else by herself, for his direction in the choice of a good wife, which would be worthy of his pains, though he should fetch her as far as men do rubies. Solomon's Book of All Virtues.[22]

Praise the Womanly Arts. Lucrezia Marinella: A woman is not to be seen idle, but rather always at work, so that her household may be rich in cloth and other things that pertain to cleanliness and civility. She will make her household abundant in beautiful and delicate cloth, so that everyone may enjoy it. Even if she is noble, she will not disdain lending her hand to the needle and spindle. She will find ingenious ways to draw images of the wild beasts with the subtle thread and endow them with as much spirit and life as possible by adorning them with wonderful white shades. People who admire them will be as surprised as those who saw Nausicaa's beautiful and rich robes.† This daughter of Alcinous and Arete had decorated and made them more precious with her own hands.

This is how wise and honorable women become famous and laudable. The handling of the needle, the spindle, and the loom is suitable not only to common women but also to queens and goddesses. Although some fools disregard this art, every woman must know its excellence and praise nature, which has bestowed such happiness on them. . . .

[21]Cop, *Sur les Proverbes de Salomon*, 673-74; citing Gen 1:27; 2:18; 2:23; Gal 3:28.

[22]Trapp, *Solomonis ΠΑΝΆΡΕΤΟΣ*, 367; citing Acts 6:13; Rom 16:3-4; Ex 18:24-25. †Gregory of Nazianzus (c. 329–390), archbishop of Constantinople and one of the Cappadocian fathers who helped ensure the triumph of the pro-Nicene theology at the Council of Constantinople (381). Gregory describes his mother, Nonna, as a woman of forceful character who led his father to Christian faith and impelled him to leadership in the church. Of her he writes, "a woman in body, yes, but in character she eclipsed any man" (*De Vita Sua* 61; PG 37:1034; cited in John McGuckin, *Saint Gregory of Nazianzus: An Intellectual Biography* [Crestwood, NY: St. Vladimir's Seminary Press, 2001], 20).

By this he means that this laudable woman sought wool and linen and transformed it with the industriousness of her hands. Thus he shows us that she did not waste her time in idleness. And by adding that "her fingers grasp the spindle," he means that she spun the fine wool herself because she wanted to do something useful and good. . . . We cannot praise enough the divine industriousness of such a woman, and we should lift her industriousness to the stars. The woman Solomon describes was famous, wise, and mature, but she received praise in particular for her womanly art. From these words we can understand how useful and noble this art is, if such a wise king praises this lady for her womanly occupations. EXHORTATIONS TO WOMEN.[23]

INDUSTRIOUS PROVIDENCE. MICHEL COP: It is a very profitable thing to have merchants who send ships to sea and to the rivers to fetch provision from far countries, to support the country when it is in need. Indeed, this is the reason God has made the sea and the rivers navigable, just as we see in another way when God gave man lordship over the fishes in the sea. But merchants greatly abuse these powers when they risk danger on rivers and at sea on account of ambition, curiosity, or avarice, and primarily desiring to grow rich, without any intent of helping the needy either in their own country or another; it is enough for them simply to make money, and so they are rebuked by James. And because their affections are so evil, God frequently overthrows their enterprises and destroys their riches, beating down their pride, as he threatens in his Word. For although the trades they use are profitable, their intention is wicked. But the wise man does not here compare the virtuous woman to merchants who send their ships to the waters, but only to the ships themselves, which are laden and directed. In the same way, the virtuous woman receives the charge and office that it pleases God to lay on her, and she allows herself to be directed by God through his Holy Spirit, and by this direction (not of herself), "she brings her food from afar." That is, she does not wait to work until her family be in extreme need, but she provides "from afar," and labors to prevent poverty, without distrusting in God. For he would have us to labor, to sow, to reap, and to store away; and he also gives us first and convenient seasons for doing these things. Those who despise them are so far from trusting in God that rather they tempt him because they would live without the means that he has ordained. And if women, who are weaker vessels, must be such providers, all the more so should men be most vigilant, and yet without caring for tomorrow, as they are admonished. ON THE PROVERBS OF SOLOMON.[24]

THE ADVANTAGES OF EARLY RISING. MICHEL COP: In order to show that it is not from avarice, nor from a desire to be well that the virtuous wife "brings her food from afar," the sage declares how vigilant and careful she is, when she does not lie in bed till the day is come, but rises while it is yet night. He declares also that she does not hold back whatever is necessary and expedient for her household, not only for her own children, but also those who serve her and perform the business of the house. In this we must note, first of all, that in praising the virtuous woman for rising before dawn, he admonishes all strong persons and those who are in good health, not to be in the habit of loving sleep, but to be ready to rise up early, after having taken what is necessary and convenient to make them more able to endure throughout the day in their vocation, and not grow slothful or negligent, as do those who sleep too long. This admonition ought to be received and obeyed by all persons of good health, unless they want to be regarded as slothful, or fall into danger of poverty. But even though they may not be in such danger, they should still love to rise very early in the morning: not only has this practice been praised in all times

[23]Marinella, *Exhortations to Women*, 82-83. †Nausicaa is a Phaeacian princess appearing in Homer, *Odyssey* 6.1.

[24]Cop, *Sur les Proverbes de Salomon*, 675-76; citing Gen 1:28; Ps 107:23; Jas 4:13; Is 23:1; Mt 6:25.

and by all people of sound judgment as being healthful for the body, and not only does it all for more time and leisure in the performance of one's business, but also (and this is far better) rising early allows one to meditate on the works of God, to call on him, to give him thanks, and to sing his praises, as we may see in various psalms. And it also affords more time to do pleasure and service to our neighbors. But although the sage praises rising before day, and attributes this habit to the virtuous woman, yet this is not to say that he blames all those who do not. For we ought not to make a law or apply the same measure to all persons, whose constitutions are not the same. For one person may need less sleep than another. Nevertheless, those who are healthy and strong in constitution ought to take care of persuading themselves that they would ruin themselves if they rose so early in the morning, for then they should not be virtuous women, but very slothful. ON THE PROVERBS OF SOLOMON.[25]

ADMIRATION FOR STRONG WOMEN. JOHN TRAPP: "She girds up her loins with strength." She flies about her work, and sets on it with courage. We have read of women in whom, besides their sex, there was nothing womanlike or weak, such as Semiramis, Zenobia, Blandina, and that brave Hungarian woman who, in an assault at the siege of Buda, thrusting in among the soldiers upon the top of the fort, with a great scythe in her hand, at one blow struck off two of the Turks' heads as they were climbing up the rampart. The like is reported of Marulla, a maid of Lemnos, who seeing her father slain in the gates of the city by the Turks, who hoped to have surprised it, took up the weapons that lay by him and like a fierce Amazon notably avenged his death.† SOLOMON'S BOOK OF ALL VIRTUES.[26]

BEDTIME, THE BEST TIME TO THINK. THE ENGLISH ANNOTATIONS: She considers it on her pillow (which is the best time for consideration), and finding that all matters thrive with her, according to her heart's desire, she reaps this fruit of her labors, prospers to herself, and, greater than any other, enjoys a complacency within herself and sweet contentment of mind. This is likely to be in the night especially, when the thoughts are most free. This, as I conceive, gave Solomon occasion immediately upon it to mention her candle burning in the night. Most others make this to be the meaning (which is very good too), that finding how all things thrive with her, she is thereby encouraged to increase her industry and to labor night and day, which nevertheless must be understood to be spoken hyperbolically or figuratively, implying no more in effect than that she plies her business with great constancy and alacrity. Were it not for the coherence of both members of this verse, her "tasting of her merchandise" might very literally be understood both of her skill and care in tasting and trying her several wares and commodities before she paid for them, no contemptible commendation in point of economy and domestic providence. ANNOTATIONS ON PROVERBS 31:18.[27]

DIVISION OF LABOR? MICHEL COP: When a married wife is virtuous and is known to be such, her husband is not despised, unless he be a complete fool and utterly useless. For insofar as it is for the man, who is the head, to direct his wife, both by teaching and by example, when it is seen

[25]Cop, *Sur les Proverbes de Salomon*, 676-77.

[26]Trapp, *Solomonis ΠΑΝΆΡΕΤΟΣ*, 369. †Semiramis was a legendary queen of ancient Assyria or Babylon (depending on the source). According to Plutarch, "though a woman, she equipped great expeditions, armed her ranks, established the Babylonian Empire, and sailed about the Persian Gulf subduing the Ethiopians and Arabs." *Moralia. On the Fortune or the Virtue of Alexander* 336C (LCL 305:437-39). Zenobia (AD 240–c. 274) was queen of the Palmyrene Empire in Syria. She led an invasion of the Roman Empire in the east that culminated in the conquest of Egypt, though she was eventually defeated by the emperor Aurelian and led captive to Rome. Blandina (c. AD 162–177) was an early Christian martyr who remained steadfast through horrific tortures, as recounted with gusto by Eusebius (*Ecclesiastical History* 5.1.18). The last two accounts are drawn from Ralph Carr, *The Mahumatane or Turkish Historie* (London, 1600), fol. 741 and 413. A statue of Marulla (Maroula), sword in hand, continues to draw tourists to the Greek Orthodox church on the isle of Limnos.

[27]Downame, ed., *English Annotations*, 6Z3v*.

that his wife acts virtuously, he is praised and honored, he is raised up to dignity and authority, and has a good name among the great. . . . Now although no one ought to affect such a place of preeminence, everyone ought to aspire to make himself capable of duly exercising his office, if it should please God to give him a seat among the elders. For it is by the wisdom of God that kings reign and counselors decree justice. And we may even say (as some do) that the sage understands that the husband, knowing that his wife is virtuous, keeps good and continual residence in the judgment seat, so as to handle such affairs as shall be dealt with there, and does not hasten home; so, taking care of public matters, he commits all the household affairs to his wife. By doing this, he gets a good name, and is held in high esteem. Nevertheless, this is not to say that we ought to thrust ourselves in to meddle with public affairs, unless we are called. Rather, let every man remain in a lowly condition until it pleases God to raise him up. ON THE PROVERBS OF SOLOMON.[28]

PUT ON COURAGE AND GRACE. LUDWIG LAVATER: "Strength and dignity are her clothing." He said earlier that her raiment was "fine linen and purple"; the use of fine clothing is not described as being unique to women; however, at the same time they ought to consider what is appropriate to their age and station in life. Pride and luxury must be avoided, but care must be taken above all to ensure that they are adorned with virtues. . . . But with what things ought women to adorn themselves? Two things are put forward here: courage (*fortitudo*) and grace (*decor*), or renown (*gloria*). "Courage," as Cicero writes, "is the knowledge of enduring vicissitudes or a disposition of soul in suffering and enduring, obedient to the supreme law of our being without fear."[†] This definition cleaves to the middle way between fear and rashness. Women are by nature timid and fearful, and so many labors and troubles best them, and so courage is required, which is a great ornament in women. But courage is most characteristic of men, and indeed it is necessary for them as well.

Another thing that is proposed here is renown, which as Cicero says is "the agreed approval of good people, the unbiased verdict of judges deciding honestly the question of preeminent merit."[‡] These two things sum up all the virtues with which women ought to be endowed; virtues which are recited in part in this encomium, and in part elsewhere, set forth by the various example of godly matrons—especially in 1 Peter 3, 1 Timothy chapter 2, which also speak of the spiritual and interior worship of women. ON THE BOOK OF PROVERBS, OR SAYINGS, OF SOLOMON THE MOST-WISE KING.[29]

WOMEN SPEAK OF GOD. JOHN TRAPP: "She opens her mouth with wisdom." Her mouth is not always open, but duly shut, and discreetly opened; her words are few, true, and ponderous; the stream and current of her conference tends either to wisdom or kindness; that is, to duties either of piety or charity. The Jesuits forbid women to speak of God and his ways, either in good sort or in bad, and to meddle only with the distaff.[†] But the good women in both Testaments, Abigail, Hannah, Esther, the Virgin Mary, Priscilla, Lois, and others never heard of this new doctrine. Tatianus tells us that in the primitive church every age and sex among the Christians were Christian philosophers—indeed, that the very virgins and maids, as they sat at their work in wool, were wont to speak of God's Word.[‡] SOLOMON'S BOOK OF ALL VIRTUES.[30]

[28]Cop, *Sur les Proverbes de Salomon*, 680; citing Prov 8:15.

[29]Lavater, *In librum Proverbiorum siue Sententiarum Solomonis Regis sapientissimi*, 326-27. [†]Cicero, *Tusculan Disputations* 4.24 (LCL 141:386-87). [‡]Cicero, *Tusculan Disputations* 3.2 (LCL 141:228-29).

[30]Trapp, *Solomonis ΠΑΝΆΡΕΤΟΣ*, 371. [†]It is not clear where Trapp is getting this. It is true that Ignatius of Loyola wrote to Pope Paul III asking to "be freed from the responsibility for women"; however, this likely was directed only in reference to women seeking entry into the order. The Society of Jesus numbered several prominent women among its supporters, and its model of active mission continued to draw interest among Catholic women throughout the sixteenth and seventeenth centuries.

The Virtues of the Matron Rooted in Faith. Philipp Melanchthon: The third section of this chapter is a song about the virtues of the upright matron of the household [*materfamilias*]. And because the Decalogue ought to be the rule of life for each individual person, so it is that in this song of praise her virtues are assigned according to the Decalogue, and the line that sums up this passage pertains especially to the first tablet: "A woman who fears God is to be praised." Now "fear" is here understood as the entirety of true worship, including the true knowledge of God, fear, faith, prayer, love of God, and other related virtues, just as the prophets always employ the term "fear of God" for the whole manner of worship [*toto cultu*], which is pleasing to God. For example: "Blessed is the one who fears the Lord."

In the next place are rehearsed her other virtues: marital chastity; a love for her husband, without peevishness; sedulousness in all her household labors; thrift, frugality, and gentleness in governing the family; diligence in educating her children; assiduousness in domestic affairs; beneficence to the poor. The definitions of all these virtues are well known, and it ought to be considered that each individual virtue is rooted in a part of the Decalogue.

Now the whole of this account ought to be understood in a straightforward manner, without allegory, as the mirror of a respectable matron, just as Simonides says: happy is the man who marries a woman like the bee.[†] But this whole teaching is most sweetly summarized in what Paul says to Timothy: "The woman will be saved through childbearing, if she continues in faith, love, holiness, and temperance." And here also the preeminent virtues and duties of her vocation are recounted. Paul expressly names faith, by which he indicates a true knowledge of God and faith and God's Son, which ought to outshine all the other virtues. For it is by this faith that we are accepted and our sins forgiven, and it is by this faith that we inherit eternal life. At the same time a new light, life, and righteousness is kindled within our hearts, just as it is written: "We are being transformed into his image, for this comes from the Spirit of the Lord." Therefore when God is known by faith, and the mercy of God (which was promised on account of the Mediator) is made manifest, at the same time a love for God is enflamed within our hearts, and true prayer—just as both light and heat are simultaneously radiated by the sun. And the Son of God is called the Son of Righteousness, because he makes manifest the true God and his light (that is, he conveys true awareness of God's mercy). And true awareness of God's mercy is accompanied by a love for God, and by a willingness to call on his name, and by the rest of the virtues. David, when he heard the voice of the prophet say, "God has put away your sin," was revived in his spirit, recognized God, and submitted himself, loving God and calling on his name. In the same way Paul wants faith (that is, the true knowledge of God and trust in his mercy) to shine in matrons.

In the next place Paul considers the remaining virtues: Love of God and of neighbor for God's sake, as well as love for husband and children. Holiness, which he describes as that virtue commonly called chastity. But chastity (which is spoken of more fully in its proper place) is that virtue which shuns all sexual intercourse or effusion of semen prohibited by God, and by which the husband and wife protect one another's rights within marriage. Temperance, which is that moderation in food and drink fitting to the body's nature.

Therefore Paul hands down this sweetest consolation in opposition to the hypocrisy of the monks, for he expressly affirms that matrons in marriage, when they retain faith and a good conscience, will be saved. And it is necessary to emphasize this teaching in the church against those fanatical people who condemn marriage.

[†]Tatian (c. AD 120–c. 180) was an early Christian apologist who compiled a harmonized version of the Gospels, the *Diatessaron*. In his *Address to the Greeks*, Tatian responded with indignation to critics who "treat the women with scorn who among us pursue philosophy" (*Oratio ad Graecos* 33; ANF 2:78-79).

Also to be set aside is the other quibble of those who misapply Paul's word in confirming the opinion of the monks, that good works are meritorious, and that they are the price of eternal life, because he says that "the woman will be saved through childbearing." But Paul never says that these duties of women are meritorious, nor that they are the price of eternal life, but this is why mention is made immediately of faith. For when he says, "if she continues in faith," that is, in the knowledge of God and trust in the Mediator, he then excludes the view that works are meritorious. EXPOSITION OF THE PROVERBS OF SOLOMON.[31]

INNER BEAUTY OVER OUTER. MICHEL COP: By virtue of their corrupted natures, women and daughters are curious, and they desire to see things that profit them nothing, but rather bring them injury and dishonor, as with Dinah and Tamar. Likewise, they desire to be seen, and to please the eyes of worldlings. To do this, they color and paint themselves to appear beautiful, with a lovely bearing and pleasing countenance. This is what the sage calls "favor" and "beauty." And such painting and bearing is fitting for worldlings, whose eyes are fully of adultery: they praise and commend those women who can disguise and trim themselves up, and in their minds and fantasies they appear to be fine and honorable, whereas those who walk faithfully and plainly, are accounted foul and uncomely. In this they are deceived, as the sage shows when he calls favor "deceitful" and beauty "vanity," declaring that those who color themselves with such favor and beauty are deceived. In so doing, he says nothing that has not always been proven by experience, even from the beginning of the world. Adam found favor in his wife when he agreed to take the forbidden fruit from her hand. The sons of God saw great beauty in the daughters of men. Shechem saw that Dinah was fair. But they were all deceived, and they did not find what they were looking for; instead of finding happiness, they fell into great troubles, as the outcome has shown. And it is written that "many have been seduced by a woman's beauty, and by it passion is kindled like a fire." From this we may see that the sage, accommodating himself to our manner of speaking, here uses the word "favor" improperly. For properly speaking, "favor" is the goodwill that we bear to one another, without its being deserved. And such women who seek to be found fair do not seek to show or to bear favor, but more often sell themselves to whoever will give the most. . . . The women, therefore, who labor to make themselves appear beautiful are not to be praised or commended, but rather those whose virtues are hidden in hearts without corruption, with a mild and quiet spirit. For although the voluptuous worldlings may not esteem such virtuous women, they are highly esteemed by God—and so must they be by us. ON THE PROVERBS OF SOLOMON.[32]

MULTIFACETED RADIANCE. JOHN TRAPP: "Give her the fruit of her hands." God would have the desert dignified, and the good parts praised. Here he seals up his approbation and good liking of what her husband and children had said of her in the former verses. He takes it well when we speak good of his people, and holds himself honored in their

[31]CR 14:85-87; citing Ps 112:1; 1 Tim 2:15; 2 Cor 3:18; 2 Sam 12:13. †Semonides of Amorgos (whom Melanchthon here apparently confuses with Simonides of Ceos, a later Greek poet) was the author of misogynistic satire "The Types of Women." According to the poet, Zeus created women after the pattern of ten different models from the natural world (eight animals and two elements). Of the ten resulting "types" of women, only those patterned after the bee are depicted favorably, and Melanchthon seems to have thought Semonides's description had some resonance with that of Proverbs 31: "The one who gets her is lucky, since on her alone blame does not settle. Under her management his livelihood flourishes and increases, and she grows old in love with a loving husband, the mother of a handsome and distinguished family. She stands out among all women and a divine grace surrounds her. She takes no pleasure in sitting among women in places where they talk about sex. Such women are the best and the most sensible whom Zeus bestows as a favor on men." Semonides 7 (LCL 259:310-11).

[32]Cop, *Sur les Proverbes de Salomon*, 683; citing Gen 34; 38; 3; 6; 34; Sir 9:8.

just praises. "Give her her full due," says God, both within doors and without; let her eat of the vineyard she has planted, live off the land she has purchased, enjoy the fruit of her own labors, have both the comfort and the credit of her worthy qualities and practice, she being (as she here stands described) not unlike that precious stone among the Troglodytes which is therefore called Hexacontalithos [Sixtystone], because within its own little compass it has the radiant colors of threescore other stones of price.[†] SOLOMON'S BOOK OF ALL VIRTUES.[33]

[33]Trapp, *Solomonis ΠΑΝΆΡΕΤΟΣ*, 374. [†]This charming detail comes from the third-century geographer Solinus, whose compendium *On the Wonders of the World* (*De mirabilis mundi*), or *Polyhistor*, documented the peculiarities of various ancient cultures. In addition to boasting of a sixty-hued gemstone, Solinus also reports that the Troglodytes of Libya "compel their wives to commit adultery on the first nights of their marriage; then they bind them to perpetual chastity by the most severe laws," an omission that demonstrates Trapp's judicious use of his sources. *Polyhistor* (Vienna, 1520), 101.

COMMENTARY ON ECCLESIASTES

Overview: The book of Ecclesiastes presents special challenges for readers committed to interpreting the book as canonical Scripture, due to its skeptical tone, moral relativism, and apparent denial of core Christian teachings, such as the immortality of the soul. Most Reformation-era interpreters take time at the outset to address the overall plan of the work and frame the book's rhetoric in terms of its literary and theological aims. Virtually all of our commentators agree that these aims are summarized in the book's penultimate verse: "Fear God and keep his commandments" (Eccles 12:13), but there is considerable difference of opinion on how the book's rhetoric builds to this conclusion.

The question of the author of the book, commonly referred to as "the Preacher," also draws attention. Denis the Carthusian is typical of many medieval interpreters who, following the advice of Gregory the Great, held that Solomon spoke in a variety of assumed personas, giving voice to various forms of worldly wisdom, all of which fail to escape the vanity characteristic of the human condition. Interpreting the book properly, therefore, requires careful attention to the shifting personas employed by the authorial voice, and the cumulative effect of these successive dead-ends is a contempt for the world and all its hollow pleasures, whether sensual or intellectual. This theme of *contemptus mundi* is carried forward by a number of Protestant exegetes, particularly in the Reformed tradition (e.g., Johannes Oecolampadius, Konrad Pellikan, and John Cotton). Following Martin Luther, however, a number of early modern commentators reject this view, holding instead that the book condemns human striving for wisdom and righteousness, but not the earthly pleasures God has given for our comfort; received in faith, these can be enjoyed in moderation with a clear conscience.

Several other more idiosyncratic approaches materialize in these prefaces: for example, Philipp Melanchthon's view that Ecclesiastes offers a sustained argument in defense of God's providence, in contrast to ancient and modern skepticism, or Jean de Serres's view that the book presents a comprehensive treatment of humanity's highest good (*summum bonum*). Despite these various approaches in understanding the book's rhetoric and structure, all of our commentators agree that Ecclesiastes presents a complex dialogue of perspectives in which faith triumphs over the vanity to which human life has been subjected.

Solomon's Varied Personas. Denis the Carthusian: In order to understand this book and all it contains more clearly, we must attend to the words of St. Gregory, who says in his fourth *Dialogue* that Ecclesiastes is properly called "The Preacher" in Greek: "for truly, in preaching one expresses ideas to silence a noisy crowd. And when there are many people holding diverse opinions, they are brought to one mind by the reasoning of the preacher. This book, therefore, is called 'The Preacher' because in it Solomon takes various conflicting views as though they were his own, and he expresses these ignorant opinions for the purpose of interrogating them. For the views he expresses in his inquiry are as diverse as the personas he assumes; but like a true preacher, he opens wide his arms to calm the troubled spirits of the gathered people, and he calls them back to one way of thinking—which is what we see him do at the end of the book, when he says: 'Let us all hear together the conclusion of the discourse. Fear God and keep his commandments: for this is man's all.' For if in this book he did *not* assume multiple personas, why did he urge all of them to listen together at the end of the discourse?"[†] So it is that some things in this book are said by way of inquiry, while others are displayed that satisfy reason; some opinions are uttered under the persona of carnal men, while others are advanced on the basis of rational judgment, so that the soul may be filled with delightful things. So for example, he says, "This therefore has seemed good to me, that a man should eat and drink, and enjoy the fruit of his labor, wherewith he has labored under the sun, all the days of his life, which God has given him: and this is his portion"; yet later he adds, "It is better to go to the house of mourning than to the house of feasting." Now if it is good to eat and drink, and to enjoy one's good things, then surely it is better to go to the house of feasting than to that of mourning. And from this we can conclude that the former is the expression of a diseased and carnal persona, whereas the latter in fact appends a rational argument. For the second passage gives us the reason why it is better, when it says, "for in so doing we are put in mind of the end of all, and the living think about what is to come." . . . Therefore, since the opinions of the human mind are so diverse, let the reader of this book diligently consider to which persona each passage pertains, and not fall into the error of the Epicureans, who acknowledged the pleasures of the flesh as the highest human good. Exposition of the Book of Ecclesiastes.[1]

Fear God and Keep His Commands. Sebastian Münster: The Hebrew scribes have preserved three books from the wisdom of Solomon: the Song [of Songs], Proverbs, and Ecclesiastes, each written during a different period [of the author's life]. They say the book of Songs, for instance, was written when he was still *qāṭān*—"small," that is, in his minority, before his twentieth year. Proverbs, on the other hand, was written in his old age, and Ecclesiastes he wrote during the prime of life, when everything that is and happens under the sun had become for him vanity and an affliction of spirit. His aim was not to defame as evil or pointless those creatures of God—the heavens, earth, the sea, and all that are contained in their bounds—since God had created them all good, but rather to bear witness (just as our Paul does) that all creatures have been subjected to vanity by the perversity of people who misuse them, either by setting them on the same level as God, or in being misled by their constant changing and variety until they are brought to perfection. And so even though it seems that in this sermon we are led to the conclusion that everything leads to emptiness, and that in passing to that place we may as well enjoy the delights of food and drink, in the end the entire book is a disputation on the vanity of vanities, and its thesis may be boiled down to the following: we should fear God and follow his commands. For indeed, it says that the time of judgment is coming, in which all that we have done in the body must stand judgment, and so we must anticipate the coming sentence, in which a just reward will be meted out to each person for the works they have done, whether good or evil. Annotations on Ecclesiastes.[2]

An Extension of the Law. Johannes Brenz: This book is a sort of elaboration on, or appendix to, the law of Moses. Now the law teaches that whenever a person undertakes to keep and fulfill the righteousness [of the law], they prove themselves wholly unskilled and unprepared, and whatever they do of their own will, no matter how much zeal and effort they have brought to the struggle, eventually it becomes clear that they are merely sporting with righteousness. And the more they strive to attain righteousness by their own

[1]DCOO 7:212-13; citing Eccles 12:13; 5:18; 7:2. [†]The quotation is from Gregory the Great, whose *Dialogues* set out an approach to reading Ecclesiastes that was immensely influential in the Middle Ages and early modernity (PL 77:324).

[2]Münster, *Annotationes in Ecclesiasten*, proem; citing Rom 8:20.

works and inventions, the less they are able to grasp it. Now this little book perfectly agrees with that doctrine, and teaches that all human powers—their wisdom, reasoning, and intentions—grievously deviate from the design for which they were created. Indeed, there is not one who, if left to their own devices, could boast of being in the slightest degree capable, either of acquiring righteousness before God, or of living in happy and prosperous relations with his fellow creatures. The Ecclesiastes of Solomon.[3]

Contempt for the World. Johannes Oecolampadius: What can I say regarding the usefulness of this little book? Can anything be more worthy or more fruitful for a person than contempt of earthly things and a desire for heavenly? If there is anything to be drawn from this slender volume, it is most certainly that. For in a few words it teaches that riches, patronage, connections, pleasure, and glory are all empty things [*vana*], even if they affect us most favorably, and to the highest degree. This is because they are under God, and were fashioned such by the Creator that we should advance to seek out more solid things. And this is essentially what Ecclesiastes does, teaching us a true natural philosophy, as Ambrose observes.[†] Metaphrases of Saint Gregory on Ecclesiastes.[4]

The Vanity of Life Apart from God. Konrad Pellikan: This book Ecclesiastes is said to be not unlike the teaching handed down to the son described in the book of Proverbs. For both are in large part collections of Solomon's wisest sayings, piled up without any special consideration for their ordering, or so it seems to simpler minds. And therefore those who have treated of this book have had difficulty in expounding it, irrationally straining to find continuity and connection with the proverbs, and often dragging the words kicking and screaming to force them into a sense bearing only scant resemblance to their genuine meaning. But of all the things that are discussed and debated in this book, a single thesis runs like a plumb line from beginning to end: the vanity of all things, and from this the vanity of all pursuits that are set before us and all worldly occupations whatever, apart from the fear of God and obedience to his commandments. Likewise, for those who live without a pure and religious fear of God, and in obedience to his commandments, everything they do in the world is utterly pointless. Whatever people undertake without piety and charity ends up becoming nothing but an inane affliction to their spirit, which accomplishes nothing without grace and the providence of God. For it is on God we know ourselves to be wholly dependent, whose providence governs all things, to whom we must commit everything that is ours, and to whose plan everything done by humans eventually returns, so that we ought to consider God in all our actions and make every effort urgently to fulfill what he teaches us. A Succinct and Universal Commentary on the Bible.[5]

On Living Contentedly in the Present World. Martin Luther: Because this book has been translated obscurely from the Hebrew, all sorts of learned men have taken it upon themselves to expound it. All of them have striven to apply various of its statements to their own profession, or rather to their own opinion. This may have been due to their curiosity, which delights in things that are obscure and novel or unusual, or it may have been because it is easy to make up whatever one pleases and to set it forth on the basis of writings that are obscure. The philosophers imagined that what the Preacher says at the very beginning, "All things are full of weariness; a man cannot utter it," applied to them, as though Solomon were speaking about their inane and speculative philosophy. Others, offended at Solomon's saying, "As the beast

[3]Brenz, *Ecclesiastes Solomonis, cum commentariis*, Pro. 1-2.
[4]Oecolampadius, *In Ecclesiastem Solomonis Metaphrasis Divi Gregorii Neocaesariensis Episcopi*, 5-6. [†]Cf. Ambrose, *De excessu fratris sui Satyri* 2.30-32 (NPNF[2] 10:178).

[5]Pellikan, *Commentaria bibliorum et illa brevia quidem ac catholica*, 249v.

dies, so dies man. They all have the same fate and the same breath," suspect him of having been an Epicurean, or at any rate of having spoken in the person of the Epicureans. . . .

No less noxious for a proper understanding of this book has been the influence of many of the saintly and illustrious theologians in the church, who thought that in this book Solomon was teaching what they call "the contempt of the world"—that is, the contempt of things that have been created and established by God. Among these is St. Jerome, who by writing a commentary on this book urged Blesilla to accept the monastic life. From this source there arose and spread over the entire church, like a flood, that theology of the religious orders or monasteries. It was taught that to be a Christian meant to forsake the household, the political order, even the episcopal (or, rather, the apostolic) office, to flee to the desert, to isolate oneself from human society, to live in stillness and silence; for it was impossible to serve God in the world. As though Solomon were calling "vanity" the very marriage, political office, and office of the ministry of the Word that he praises here in such a wonderful way and calls gifts of God! Although Solomon teaches that people themselves and their counsels are vain, some reverse everything; and, following their notions completely contrary to Solomon, they call the things themselves vain, while they regard themselves and their ideas as correct and solid. In short, all they have produced from this very beautiful and useful book are their own monstrosities. They have obviously used the gold of God to fashion abominable idols. . . .

It would, therefore, be more correct to call this book of Ecclesiastes the Politics or the Economics of Solomon. He does not, indeed, legislate or prescribe laws for the governance of the state or the family. This is taken care of in great detail by the natural law or human reason, to which, according to Genesis 1:28, earthly things have been subjected; this has been, is, and must remain the source, the criterion, and the end of all laws, whether political or domestic. But this book can give counsel to a person involved in the state or the household as they deal with difficult problems, and it can instruct and encourage their mind as they bear the troubles of such a position. . . .

The summary and aim of this book, then, is as follows: Solomon wants to put us at peace and to give us a quiet mind in the everyday affairs and business of this life, so that we live contentedly in the present without care and yearning about the future and are, as Paul says, without care and anxiety. It is useless to plague oneself with anxiety about the future. By a sort of continuing induction from particulars, Solomon concludes that the efforts and endeavors of human beings are vain and useless, so that he draws a universal conclusion from particulars and shows that the efforts of all men are vain. He denies that bread is to the wise or the race to the swift or the battle to the strong. In fact, the wiser or holier or busier someone claims to be, the less they accomplish, and their wisdom, their righteousness, and their work are useless. And so if none of these things nor anything else amounts to anything, it follows that everything is vain and useless. Annotations on Ecclesiastes.[6]

A Defense of God's Providence. Philipp Melanchthon: Now after the reader of these sermons of Solomon has considered the counsels this book contains, they will know that this whole book, which is titled Ecclesiastes, is primarily concerned with affirming the doctrine of providence. It clearly affirms that God is wise and truthful, a just judge and a most liberal advocate, that he is to be honored in accordance with the teaching he himself has handed down and none other; that he punishes those who hold him in contempt, but shows mercy and watches over those who call on him and undertake to obey him. And therefore the primary work of this book is dogmatic—that is, it asserts God's providence against the Epicureans, Pyrrhonians, Stoics, and other thinkers who seek to undermine belief in

[6]LW 15:3-8 (WA 7:7-10); citing Eccles 1:8; 3:19; Phil 4:6; Eccles 9:11.

providence.[†] These affirmations are expressed in these words in the last chapter, where it says that "God will bring every deed into judgment, and every hidden thing, whether good or evil." Likewise, in chapter 11, "Know that for all these things God will lead you into judgment." And in chapter 3, "God will judge the righteous and the wicked." In these words and in others like them the main point of the whole sermon is set forth and reiterated.

Following from this assertion is the doctrine concerning obedience. When God gave the law he attached threats, but in his great mercy he also scattered [among the commandments] great promises, the voice of the gospel concerning reconciliation. And although he certainly inflicts punishment on those who treat his law with contempt, he also receives and watches over those who flee to his Son, the Mediator. It is necessary to obey his teaching. Where there is fear of God's dread judgment, faith rests in the Mediator, and standing in him you are received, heard, helped, protected, and saved, and none of your members will come to harm apart from God's command. So this teaching is put into practice when obedience follows from belief in God's providence, and in that obedience hearts are sustained with divine comfort, liberated from eternal fear, and established in the heavenly life, which is the final goal after which we must long. Enarration on Ecclesiastes.[7]

True Happiness Contrasted with Its Imitation. Jean de Serres: Some have expounded the scope of this book as follows, saying that by demonstrating the vanity of this life (that is, of human ways and counsels) Solomon intended to make us content and quiet of mind in the midst of this life's common affairs and chances; thus, with gratitude we should use the creatures of God, which are given to us with his blessing, content with things in the present and without undue concern for the future. Those who expound the book in this way certainly say something worthwhile, but they do not set the matter out with sufficient clarity. Neither do those who think that the main point of the whole sermon is an affirmation of the doctrine of providence and a refutation of objections that might be raised against it. There are comforts in this view that fortify our souls against confusion, and warnings against those outrages of the wicked, who in this life wander blindly, as if without any fear of punishment. Indeed, such matters are handled beautifully here, and yet they are not deemed to be the first and foremost end of the discourse; rather, they are suitably applied as illustrations of the main theme. . . .

Therefore I take the main point of this discussion to be the highest good [*de summo bono*], brilliantly expounded by comparison with its opposite. For although happiness is the chief and highest end of our whole life, and all people strive for happiness with their entire will and devotion, yet despite the common agreement and desire for this same thing there are so many and conflicting opinions among all sorts of people that in the meantime the greatest part are led far away from happiness. Therefore it is necessary that clear teaching should be set down concerning true happiness, in which we can rest with certainty, so that we do not cling to an image (*eidōlon*) or shadow of happiness instead of the real thing. This will certainly be the result if we follow the auspices of human wit, seeking happiness in the anxious, accidental, and uncertain wandering of human affairs. So skillfully does Solomon (a well-suited arbiter of these questions!) set out these human foibles and anxieties, that the boiling passion of these arguments cannot be more clearly represented to us. For first he teaches that happiness is not to be found in human affairs—that is, he shows us *what happiness is not*, in opposition to the arguments of human reason, which vainly imagines a false simulacrum of true happiness. Then, having

[7]CR 14:94-95; citing Eccles 12:14; 11:9; 3:17. [†]Melanchthon is of course well aware that Ecclesiastes predated all of these Greek philosophical schools by some time, and that it was not therefore written with the express intent of refuting their teachings. Rather, he deploys these terms as shorthand for archetypal denials of belief in the immortality of the soul, radical skepticism, and a fatalistic denial of God's providential ordering of human affairs, whether in the ancient world or in the sixteenth century.

refuted the errors of this corrupt reasoning, he teaches *what happiness is*: and just as he had contrasted it and distinguished it from all the counsels and customs of human life, so here he establishes it entirely in the fear of God—that is, in the true knowledge of the true God, and in the sincere worship of the same. COMMENTARY ON SOLOMON'S ECCLESIASTES.[8]

THE TESTAMENT OF A PENITENT KING. JOHANNES PISCATOR: The Ecclesiastes of Solomon contains both doctrine and admonitions. The doctrine it teaches concerns human happiness in this life: where indeed can it be found, or in what does human happiness in this life consist? And it teaches that this does not consist in the mere possession or enjoyment of earthly goods, but first and foremost in that tranquility of mind, or spiritual happiness, which comes from a filial fear of God; and then only partly in the cheerful enjoyment of the earthly goods that have fallen to each person from heaven. And the warnings are twofold, just as the doctrine is in two parts. Some are exhortations against anxiety in acquiring earthly goods, and some are exhortations to a filial fear of God and the pursuit of good works, along with the cheerful enjoyment of the earthly goods that have fallen to each person from heaven. For it seems that Solomon wrote this book in his old age, to give counsel and bear witness to the people of God of his repentance and conversion from idolatry. So it can be inferred from this that he disapproves of and condemns the vanity of the various pursuits by which he had sought after happiness before, and that on the contrary, he exhorts all to the right worship of God and the observance of God's commandments. COMMENTARY ON ALL THE BOOKS OF THE OLD TESTAMENT.[9]

WISDOM GATHERED AND SCATTERED. HUGH BROUGHTON: Solomon was born about the time that Adonijah deflowered Tamar, as the story shows, and is thought by the rabbis and the Greeks to have been twelve years old when David died.[†] His father and his mother and the prophet Nathan instructed him in the ways of God, and he craved wisdom from God, and had it above all kings. And the more he increased in wisdom, he taught the people knowledge, and fitted many proverbs. Three books he left: the Song of Songs, showing the joy of the church that truly follows Christ; the Proverbs, warning the tribes that they will fall away from God; . . . and Qoheleth is his third book. The Qoheleth had four names: Solomon, Jedidiah, Lemuel, and Qoheleth. The definition of the last should here be explained: *qāhal* the verb means "to gather," and the noun *ecclesia* is a company gathered into one assembly. . . . The best thing to gather is wisdom, and so according to Ibn Ezra, "he is called Qoheleth on account of the wisdom that he gathered," finding by experience that all things under the sun are vain and commonwealths full of folly and madness, and that therefore people should look to the kingdom of Christ in heaven. The seventy made a new term of their own: Ecclesiastes, a wise doctor. And this book comments on Nathan's prophecy, cited above,[‡] and teaches clearly that many kings of his posterity in their foolishness would break the hedge, that serpents should bite them, and would speak great words, as did Rehoboam, so foolish as one that knew not the way to the city. And he himself was entangled by his wives to build idols for them. But he proclaims their wickedness, and how Jedidiah, the beloved of God, was delivered from them. No one should doubt whether he is in the kingdom of heaven, seeing that all the prophets are there, and he spent all his life to teach the vanities of this world.[§] A COMMENT UPON COHELETH.[10]

[8]Serres, *Commentarius, in Solomonis Ecclesiasten*, 5-8.
[9]Piscator, *Commentariis in omnes libros Veteris Testamenti*, 404.

[10]Broughton, *A Comment upon Coheleth, or, Ecclesiastes*, 11-12; citing 2 Sam 12:25; Prov 31:1; Eccles 1:1; Lk 13:28. [†]Broughton appears to have confused Adonijah with Amnon (2 Sam 13). [‡]Broughton summarizes Nathan's prophecy (2 Sam 12:1-15) as follows: "that Solomon's household would not be upright with God, but would overthrow the temple and the nation," referencing Lev 26 and Deut 28. [§]One of the few of our commentators directly to

A Commentary on Corruption. John Cotton: This whole book is a discourse not unseasonable for this country,[†] in which people who have left all to enjoy the gospel now (as if they had forgotten the end for which they came here) are ready to leave the gospel for outward things, things which here are clearly shown to be "vanity"—indeed, "vanity of vanities."

Objection: But is it not more proper for a minister of the gospel to handle a text that speaks of Christ? Answer: the way to stir us to seek after Christ is to behold (and be convinced of) the vanity of all things here below. When Eve brought forth Cain, she hoped she had got the promised seed. But when she saw by his spirit and bearing that she was deceived in him, she called her next son Abel, which signified "vanity." And so she must see all things to be, before she bring forth Seth, the father of the promised seed. Now Abel, or vanity, expresses the state of all creatures after the fall. And Solomon takes up Eve's word and amplifies it: "vanity of vanities." So this whole book is a commentary on the state of corruption, while the Song of Songs provides a fit introduction to Christ. A Brief Exposition.[11]

address the issue of Solomon's ultimate salvation. It should be remembered that this had been much debated among ancient and medieval writers. Augustine thought no; Jerome, yes. Dante, who numbered Solomon among the blessed, nevertheless acknowledged the dispute when he remarked that "all the world below is greedy to discover how his soul fared" (*Paradiso* 10.110-11).

[11]Cotton, *A Briefe Exposition upon Ecclesiastes*, 1; citing Gen 4:1; 3:15; 4:2; Eccles 1:2; Rom 8:20. [†]Cotton was serving as pastor in the Boston meetinghouse of the Massachusetts Bay Colony at the time of writing.

1:1-18 LIFE'S VANITY

[1]The words of the Preacher,[a] the son of David, king in Jerusalem.

[2]Vanity[b] of vanities, says the Preacher,
vanity of vanities! All is vanity.

[3]What does man gain by all the toil
at which he toils under the sun?

[4]A generation goes, and a generation comes,
but the earth remains forever.

[5]The sun rises, and the sun goes down,
and hastens[c] to the place where it rises.

[6]The wind blows to the south
and goes around to the north;

around and around goes the wind,
and on its circuits the wind returns.

[7]All streams run to the sea,
but the sea is not full;

to the place where the streams flow,
there they flow again.

[8]All things are full of weariness;
a man cannot utter it;

the eye is not satisfied with seeing,
nor the ear filled with hearing.

[9]What has been is what will be,
and what has been done is what will be done,
and there is nothing new under the sun.

[10]Is there a thing of which it is said,
"See, this is new"?

It has been already
in the ages before us.

[11]There is no remembrance of former things,[d]
nor will there be any remembrance

of later things[e] yet to be
among those who come after.

[12]I the Preacher have been king over Israel in
Jerusalem. [13]And I applied my heart[f] to seek and to
search out by wisdom all that is done under heaven. It
is an unhappy business that God has given to the
children of man to be busy with. [14]I have seen
everything that is done under the sun, and behold, all
is vanity[g] and a striving after wind.[h]

[15]What is crooked cannot be made straight,
and what is lacking cannot be counted.

[16]I said in my heart, "I have acquired great
wisdom, surpassing all who were over Jerusalem
before me, and my heart has had great experience of
wisdom and knowledge." [17]And I applied my heart to
know wisdom and to know madness and folly. I
perceived that this also is but a striving after wind.

[18]For in much wisdom is much vexation,
and he who increases knowledge increases
sorrow.

a Or *Convener*, or *Collector*; Hebrew *Qoheleth* (so throughout Ecclesiastes) **b** The Hebrew term *hebel*, translated *vanity* or *vain*, refers concretely to a "mist," "vapor," or "mere breath," and metaphorically to something that is fleeting or elusive (with different nuances depending on the context). It appears five times in this verse and in 29 other verses in Ecclesiastes **c** Or *and returns panting* **d** Or *former people* **e** Or *later people* **f** The Hebrew term denotes the center of one's inner life, including mind, will, and emotions **g** The Hebrew term *hebel* can refer to a "vapor" or "mere breath" (see note on 1:2) **h** Or *a feeding on wind*; compare Hosea 12:1 (also in Ecclesiastes 1:17; 2:11, 17, 26; 4:4, 6, 16; 6:9)

OVERVIEW: The superscription in the first verse is the occasion for reflection on the authorship of the book and its significance for its overall message. Martin Luther and Hugo Grotius are among the first to question the book's direct authorship by Solomon, though this suggestion is not widely considered among other interpreters. As in the preface, there is some consideration given to identifying Ecclesiastes with a particular set of circumstances in the canonical narrative of Solomon's life: Sebastian Münster, for example, reports the view among the Jewish rabbis that the book is the product of Solomon's youth; Antonio Brucioli and Jean de Serres both connect the work with the flowering of Solomon's kingship in Jerusalem. Critical to the interpretation of the book's message is the valence given to the term "vanity" (*hebel*), a term repeated thirty-one times throughout the book. Denis the Carthusian and William Whitaker both expound the term broadly, in keeping with their common view that Ecclesiastes teaches contempt for the world in its fallen condition. Luther, however, makes much of the qualifier "under the sun," as limiting the scope of vanity to the world of human endeavors, thus exempting God's gifts and handiwork themselves from this charge. Selections from the remainder of the chapter illustrate the ways in which our commentators begin to trace these various forms of vanity across a range of examples drawn from human life and the created world.

1:1-3 *Superscription: All Is Vanity*

Solomon's Table Talk. Martin Luther: In my opinion, the title "Ecclesiastes," or "Preacher," should be applied to the name of the book itself rather than to that of the author, so that you understand that these are words that Solomon spoke publicly in some address to his princes and others.† For since he was a king, it was not part of his duty to teach; this belonged to the priests and Levites. Therefore I think that these words were spoken by Solomon in some assembly of his retinue, perhaps after dinner, or even during dinner to some great and prominent men who were present. He spoke this way after he had thought long and hard to himself about the condition and the vanity of human affairs, or rather of human affections. Then he poured this out to those who were present, as usually happens, and afterward what he said was put down and assembled by the leaders of the community or of the church. Therefore they also acknowledge at the end that they have received and gathered these things from one Shepherd. In the same way it could happen that one of us would discourse about human affairs while seated at table and others would take it down.‡ This is, then, a public sermon that they heard from Solomon, on the basis of which it seemed appropriate to call this book Qoheleth—not in the sense that Solomon himself was a preacher but that this book was preached as though it had been a public sermon. Annotations on Ecclesiastes.[1]

Solomon's Three Names. Antonio Brucioli: The Scriptures show that Solomon was known by three names: first and foremost, by the name Solomon, which means "peaceable"; also Jedidiah, which means "beloved of the Lord"; and also by Qoheleth, as he is called in this book, . which in the Greek language means "the speaker to the congregation"—that is, to the church; in other words, what we call the Preacher, who speaks to the people. And his speech is not directed to one person in particular, but is addressed generally to all. And he was called "peaceable" and "beloved of the Lord" because there was peace in his kingdom, and the Lord loved him. Now the Jews say that this book was written in penitence by Solomon, because it contains the considerations of a man

[1]LW 15:12 (WA 20:14-15); citing Eccles 12:11. †Luther was one of the first writers to question direct Solomonic authorship of Ecclesiastes, a point he made even more explicitly in the 1524 preface to his German translation: "Now this book was certainly not written or set down by King Solomon with his own hand. Instead scholars put together what others had heard from Solomon's lips. . . . That is to say, certain persons selected by the kings and the people were at that time appointed to fix and arrange this and other books that were handed down by Solomon, the one shepherd." LW 35:263 (WA DB 11.1:23). In a bit of dinner-table speculation several years later (1533), Luther went even further, suggesting that Ecclesiastes may have been written "by Sirach in the time of the Maccabees," and he compared it to the Talmud as a derivative work stitched together from an assembly of earlier sources (WA TR 1:207, no. 698). ‡Many volumes of Luther's *Tischreden* (Table Talk) were copied down by his friends, students, and colleagues in the later years of his life.

who, after he had put all his hope in studying wisdom, and in riches, was led astray from the Word of God by his wives. But the title and preface of this book assert its authority, and it commends its words as precious because they are the words of the Preacher, whose office is to proclaim the Word of God and not that of a private person, of low esteem. . . . And the sum and intention of this whole book is that Solomon aims to render us quiet and peaceful in our everyday business and in the affairs of this life, so that we may live contented with our present circumstances and without worry or concern in our labors. And when Christ says, "Each day has enough trouble of its own," he also shows us that worrying about the future afflicts us in vain. THE ECCLESIASTES OF SOLOMON.[2]

THE THEOLOGIAN-KING. JEAN DE SERRES: There is little doubt but that the title of "the Preacher" refers to Solomon as an indication of his preeminence, which is also indicated by the name of his father David, and the kingdom of Israel (of which Jerusalem was the chief city). It is not altogether certain when he actually wrote this, yet the conjecture is likely to be true that he wrote these things very late in his old age, for he writes in the manner of one who has learned this teaching by great experience and long use. . . . Yet I do not think that Solomon preached these things from the pulpit, for I agree with the conjecture of Luther that the Hebrew word which is translated "the Preacher" refers rather to the subject matter of the text itself, than to the person of Solomon. Not only did he impress this doctrine on his own people at various occasions, but he also desired it to be published so that all might understand it, and that being committed to writing it should last forever and be handed down to posterity, so that it might be of use to the church. Nor did Solomon confuse the distinct office of a king with that of a preacher. For although the sacred history does relate that Solomon preached at the dedication of the temple, this was something extraordinary, going beyond the general duty of a king to uphold and propagate true doctrine—and yet not so far as to violate the limits of his calling. How pernicious this is, the sacred history teaches in the calamitous example of Uzziah, who otherwise was not a bad king. . . .[†]

The authority of the Word does not depend on the person of the minister. And yet, provision must be made that the turpitude of the minister must not damage the dignity and splendor of the office. . . . Likewise, the chief duty of princes and of all chief magistrates is here signified, that they should doubtless be guardians of true religion and diligently apply themselves to this one end, that the people should be rightly instructed in sound doctrine, which is the true and solid foundation of the entire public good. For surely we could more justly call that commonwealth happy in which the king or prince were either a theologian or a theologian-king, rather than a philosopher—like those philosophers who were impious and unhappily erudite emperors, Marcus the Philosopher and Julian the Apostate,[‡] in whom the knowledge of philosophy and literature was a dangerous tool for the ruin and destruction of their subjects. On the other hand, the examples of David, Solomon, Hezekiah, and other godly kings have demonstrated that earnest devotion to the nurturing of religion is the most certain foundation of the common good, and that established in this it will happily flourish. COMMENTARY ON SOLOMON'S ECCLESIASTES.[3]

---

[2]Brucioli, *L'Ecclesiasto di Salomo*, A 1-2; citing 2 Chron 22:9; 2 Sam 12:25; Mt 6:34.

[3]Serres, *Commentarius, in Solomonis Ecclesiasten*, 32-35; citing 1 Kings 8:22-61. [†]When he had defeated his enemies, King Uzziah "grew proud, to his destruction." He entered the temple to make an offering himself, for which he was struck with leprosy and became a cautionary tale illustrating the danger for princes who usurp the prerogatives of clergy (2 Chron 26:16-21). [‡]Marcus Aurelius (AD 121–180) was known as the "Philosopher King" within his own lifetime, even by several early Christian writers (such as Justin Martyr and Eusebius). In *Meditations* 11, Marcus sneers at the "obstinacy" with which the Christian martyrs met their deaths. Christians were certainly persecuted during his reign, though it is not clear to what extent he directed or approved of these measures. Julian "the Apostate" (331–363) reigned fewer than two years before he was killed in battle against the Persians, but during that time he deployed his considerable

A Pseudepigraphic Compendium. Hugo Grotius: This book is *qohelet* in Hebrew. Names of this form are usually feminine, but because Hebrew lacks a case common to both masculine and feminine, names are often taken to apply to both. And so it appears to be the case here, with the masculine construction "son of David." And so the Greeks changed the name to "the Preacher" (*Ekklēsiastēn*), but better would be "the Gatherer" (*Synathroistēs*), since the word *qāhal* typically means "to assemble" (*synathroizein*). So we should understand that various opinions by people held to be wise concerning what makes for happiness (*peri tēs eudaimonias; de beatitudine*) have been summarized in this book, just as the book of Job encompasses nearly everything that has been said or could be said concerning divine governance of human affairs—and their contraries. So we ought not to wonder if we read things here that prove to be unsound, since all these various ideas with their supporting arguments are rehearsed, just as Aristotle was in the habit of breaking a subject down into pieces before then giving it definition. But since both the beginning and the end sufficiently demonstrate the writer's purpose, for these reasons (so say the Hebrews) it was rightly received into the canon. For my part, however, I do not think that it is Solomon's; rather, it was written later under the name of that king, as though he had been led to repentance. In support of this argument I can point to many words that you will not find anywhere else but in Daniel, Esdras, and other Chaldean translations. Annotations on the Old Testament.[4]

In Praise of "Vanity." Desiderius Erasmus: In his first chapter Ecclesiastes wrote, "The number of fools is infinite,"[†] and in making the number infinite, doesn't he seem to include the entire human race, except for a few poor specimens on whom I doubt if anyone ever laid eyes? . . . When he cries, "Vanity of vanities, all is vanity," what do you suppose he meant, if not, as I was saying before, that human life is a puppet show containing nothing but folly? Thus he confirms the celebrated vote cast by Cicero in my favor, and which I've already quoted, to the effect that "the world is full of fools."[‡] So too with that wise man Ecclesiasticus, who said, "The fool changes like the moon, the wise man endures unchanged like the sun"; what can he have meant, if not that the entire human race is foolish, but the word "wise" belongs to God alone? . . . Again, Solomon in his fifteenth chapter says, "Folly is joy to him that is destitute of wisdom," thereby making abundantly clear that without folly there is no joy in life. In the same vein is that other text, "He who increases knowledge increases grief, and in much understanding is vexation." And the same thing is said quite explicitly by the Preacher in his seventh chapter: "The heart of the wise is in the house of mourning, but the heart of the fool is in the house of mirth." These passages make it clear that he thought mere knowledge of wisdom insufficient without knowledge of me as well. And if you don't believe me, here are his very words, as written in his first chapter: "I gave my mind to know wisdom and to madness and folly." In this passage you must particularly note that folly is given the highest praise because she is placed last in the sentence. Ecclesiastes wrote it, and you know that the ecclesiastical ordering always places the person of highest dignity in the last place. . . .

Now consider this: the Scriptures attribute to the foolish a candid and generous mind, while the wise man thinks himself superior to everyone else. That at least is the way I interpret what Ecclesiastes wrote in his tenth chapter: "When he that is a fool walks by the way, his wisdom fails him, and he says to everyone that he is a fool." Now don't you think that a mark of exceptional candor, to think everyone your equal, and instead of puffing yourself up, to share your merits with everybody else? And so even King Solomon the Great was not ashamed of this epithet when he said in his thirtieth chapter, "I am the most foolish of men."

literary and philosophical gifts to turning back the tide of Christianization initiated in the Roman Empire by Constantine.

[4]Grotius, *Annotationes in Vetus Testamentum*, 258.

Even Paul, the teacher of the Gentiles, was not ashamed to call himself a fool when writing to the Corinthians. "I speak as a fool," he says; "I am more"—as if it were a disgrace to be outdone in stupidity. The Praise of Folly.[5]

"Vanity" Means Bitter Emptiness. Johannes Brenz: "All things are vanity." This apothegm neatly sums up the whole first chapter of this book. And to engrave it with painstaking labor in our minds, and thus make it stick there more deeply, he is not content with mentioning the word one time, but repeats it and calls us back to this term for emphasis, saying: "All things are the vainest vanity." But what exactly is "vanity"? In Hebrew the term is *hebel*, which in Latin is interpreted as "void" [*nudus*], "empty" [*inanis*], "useless" [*inutilis*], or "vanity" [*vanitas*]. And so the sense is that all things are wholly vain, all things are void, vacuous, and empty. Like the proverbial "fruit of the cypress,"[†] all human affairs eventually end in ruin, whatever their intent; nothing anywhere in all of creation is found to be solid, stable, and firm. The Ecclesiastes of Solomon.[6]

A Faithful Preacher Calls Out Vanity. Jean de Serres: By condemning all human affairs as "vanity," and doing so as a Preacher, we are taught that it especially behooves the servants of God earnestly to condemn human vanity and to thunder against human pride, so that their hearers may not rest in human cleverness, but seek happiness outside themselves. Away then with the mendacious babblings of those who by various arguments seek out human happiness in human things, for in doing so they cast their hearers down into the lowest abyss of unhappiness. For this indeed is the difference between the truth and a lie: by the one, a person pleads guilty of their infirmity, a saving self-condemnation; by the other, a person is kept within oneself by a deadly error. Commentary on Solomon's Ecclesiastes.[7]

True Happiness Cannot Be Found in Worldly Vanities. The English Annotations: The scope of the wise man is to direct us in the right way to true happiness. This he does first negatively, assuring us that it is not to be found in anything under the sun and, second, affirmatively, that it is to be found only in God and his service. For the former, this is the last issue and result of all that curious inquiry that Solomon made into the utmost excellency of creatures here below. He was furnished above all others with a variety of requisites for such a work and set himself critically about it. So done, this is the upshot, that all is nothing but very vanity. He does this in a vehement and pathetical manner, that it may be observed. He does not say all is vain, but in the abstract (which is more emphatic), "All is vanity," not vanity only but "vanity of vanities"—that is, extreme vanity. Annotations on Ecclesiastes 1:2.[8]

Contempt for the World. William Whitaker: Many formerly, as Philaster relates,[†] rejected the books of Solomon, and especially Ecclesiastes and the Song of Songs, because in the former Solomon seems to invite people to a life of pleasure, and in the latter, to relate certain amatory discourses between himself and Pharaoh's daughter. But it is plain that these people fell into a manifest and impious error. For in Ecclesiastes, Solomon

[5]Erasmus, *Praise of Folly*, 75-77; citing Sir 27:12; Eccles 1:18; 7:4; 1:17; 10:3; Prov 30:2; 2 Cor 11:21. Erasmus's *Praise of Folly* is a satire: the work is written in the voice of Folly personified, who surveys her kingdom on earth with a certain perverse pride, cataloging the achievements of the various princes, prelates, and common folk who pay her homage. Even though Folly's exegesis often lives up to the speaker's name, in passages like this it is apparent that Erasmus is only half joking. [†]Vulgate. [†]Cicero, *Epistulae ad familiares* 9.22.

[6]Brenz, *Ecclesiastes Solomonis, cum commentariis*, 15v. [†]According to Erasmus, the "fruit of the cypress" was a proverbial expression applied to "fine-sounding, but useless words. The proverb has come from the nature of the tree, which Pliny says . . . 'grows grudgingly, has useless fruit, astringent berries, butter-tasting leaves, a strong smell, and does not even afford agreeable shade.'" *Adagia* 4.3.10 (CWE 36:8).

[7]Serres, *Commentarius, in Solomonis Ecclesiasten*, 41.

[8]Downame, ed., *English Annotations*, 7A1r*.

does not allure people to enjoy the pleasures and blandishments of the world, but rather deters them from such pleasures, and exhorts them, with a divine eloquence, to despise and condemn the present world. Thus at the very commencement he exclaims, "Vanity of vanities, all is vanity," in which words he declares that all those things that are sought after in this world are uncertain, transitory, and fallacious. Whence it necessarily follows that those are mad who acquiesce in the enjoyment of such objects. And so (after having disputed through the whole book against those who pursue these pleasures so greedily, and desire to satisfy themselves with such goods, whatever they are) he at the close teaches that happiness consists not, as many suppose, in things of this kind, but in true piety, and thus concludes, "Fear God, and keep his commandments; for this is the whole of man." This is not the judgment of an Epicurus, but of a holy prophet, withdrawing foolish people from the pursuit of worthless objects, and recalling them into the true path of a pious and a happy life. A Disputation on Scripture.[9]

Vanity Seeks Treasure "Under the Sun." Denis the Carthusian: "Under the sun" regards labors concerning sensible and fleshly things, undertaken to acquire wealth, delicacies, and honors. Ultimately, these things lead to nothing but vanity. Thus it is that at the end the late penitents will say, "We wearied ourselves in the way of iniquity and destruction, and have walked through hard ways, but the way of the Lord we have not known." Indeed, all who occupy themselves thus return to vanity, and drain it to the dregs. Thus according to Jeremiah, the Lord says, "What iniquity have your fathers found in me, that they are gone far from me, and have walked after vanity, and are become vain?" And the psalmist cries out similar charges: "O sons of men, how long will you be dull of heart? Why do you love vanity, and seek after lying?" And concerning one of these it is said in the Gospel, "You fool! This night your soul is required from you. And whose shall those things be which you have provided?" To which the Savior adds, "So is he who lays up treasure for himself and is not rich toward God." Exposition of the Book of Ecclesiastes.[10]

The Vanity of Human Endeavors. Martin Luther: He is about to describe the realm of vanity and the location of this realm. He calls this entire realm of vanity existence "under the sun," a unique phrase that we do not read elsewhere in Scripture. In this way he seeks to exclude the works of God, which God himself either works in us or has commanded us to work; these are above the sun and beyond human efforts. For the sun rises, as Psalm 104:22-23 says, so that people may go forth to their work, so that it may serve as the light of the world, so that it may be of service in physical matters. Under that sun, I say, are carried on those vain strivings with which mortals are afflicted. This must be noted again, in refutation of the vain notion of the interpreters, that this applies to the vanity of the creatures. The creatures are indeed subjected to vanity, as Paul declares in Romans 8:20, but they themselves are good things. Otherwise he would have said that the sun is vain; but he makes the sun an exception, for he says, "under the sun." Therefore he is dealing not with the works of God, which are good, true, and above the sun, but with works that are under the sun, works that we carry on in this physical and earthly life. Annotations on Ecclesiastes.[11]

1:4-11 *All Streams Run to the Sea*

On Human Inconstancy. Jean de Serres: I read these four verses (4-7) together as one sequence, because they contain one simple argument aimed at demonstrating the vanity of human life. . . . And it fits with the argument hitherto explained: how can a person reap any

[9]Whitaker, *Disputatio de sacra scriptura*, 5-6; citing Eccles 12:13.
†Philaster was a fourth-century bishop and heresiologist.

[10]DCOO 7:214; citing Wis 5:8; Jer 2:5; Ps 4:2; Lk 12:20-21.
[11]LW 15:14-15 (WA 20:18).

certain fruit from their labors, when all humankind is buffeted hither and yon with a most uncertain motion? For in all of nature there are indeed some certain and set patterns that are precisely maintained: the earth stands in the middle of the whole world as its center, and the seat and dwelling place of all living things. The sun has its rising and its setting, which it keeps with an unwearied course. The wind, although it holds to its courses from various parts of the heavens, still keeps them steadily. So also the ebb and flow of rivers from sea to sea is varied and diverse, and yet it remains constant. To sum up, all things have their established and settled bounds according to the manner of their creation, and they keep themselves within them. But what is more unstable than humankind, what more weak, when one by one they daily die, and daily they are transformed by an inconstant motion, so that one age follows another with various vicissitudes, and horrible spectacles come to pass in the overthrow of cities, kingdoms, families, and in the destruction of humans themselves? Here, therefore, is a comparison of humanity with other created things, and in the strength of their condition the weakness and uncertainty of human nature is more clearly demonstrated. . . .

The rabbis and Jerome transform all these things into exotic allegories, so much so that in reckoning them up, I would be afraid to abuse the reader's patience with a rehearsal of such vain trifles. Therefore letting these things pass, I have no doubt but that the wise reader will agree with the former exposition as being both the simplest and the most accurate. In sum, the vanity of human life appears most clearly in this, that among all created things, those that are void of reason steadfastly keep the set courses of their creation, while humans are often changed by the hour, and their ages variously come and go. COMMENTARY ON SOLOMON'S ECCLESIASTES.[12]

GOD'S GRACE FLOWS INTO OPEN HEARTS. DENIS THE CARTHUSIAN: According to the spiritual sense, "all rivers run to the sea" signifies that all streams of grace descend into the human heart, which the image of the sea, with its profundity and inscrutability, illuminates. "And the sea does not overflow"—that is, the human heart does not overstep the limits set for it, vainly glorying in ostentatious display or in boastful swelling. On the contrary, it humbles itself more, and to the degree that it seeks to be subjected to the fount of graces, all the more does it receive more and greater gifts from the same source. EXPOSITION OF THE BOOK OF ECCLESIASTES.[13]

A MARK OF GOD'S IMAGE. ULRICH ZWINGLI: Now there are many ways in which we experience the divine likeness within us more specifically than we do with the three faculties, intellect, will, and memory. I do not reject the opinion of Augustine, but I think that there are many things that give us an awareness of the divine likeness apart from those that Augustine singled out as the chief. There is in particular that looking to God and to the words of God, which is a sure sign of the divine relationship, image, and similitude within us. . . . It is for this reason that we thirst after God and believe his Word above all things. For everywhere we find the universal desire for eternal blessedness after this present distress, a desire that would never have concerned us, any more than it does the beasts or plants, had it not been native to us. . . . For every human spirit looks forward to eternal joy and fears eternal loss, desiring like all else to return to its first beginning, as Solomon shows in Ecclesiastes 1: "The spirit or wind whirls about continually and searches out all things and the returns again according to its circuits. All the rivers run into the sea; yet the sea is not full; and the rivers return again to the place from which they come." OF THE CLARITY AND CERTAINTY OF THE WORD OF GOD.[14]

[12]Serres, *Commentarius, in Solomonis Ecclesiasten*, 49-52.

[13]DCOO 7:216; citing Jer 12:9.

[14]LCC 24:61-62.

Perpetual Motion. Martin Luther: He says that everything is borne along in its proper order and that one thing follows another in perpetual motion, just as the sun continually moves and never stops. Thus also the air is always in motion. The streams, too, continually run into the sea, and the sea in turn, as it were, is distilled and sweats itself out through hidden passageways of the earth and channels of the mountains into rivers and springs. The earth is a veritable bag of lye, by which water is purified. Thus you see that in a few words Solomon embraces the marvelous arrangement and interaction of the four elements, as he mentions the earth, the sun, the wind, and the streams.

I believe, however, that Solomon intends this as an allegory of these changes in nature in order to direct us to the matter he is discussing and that he applies this allegory as a comparison with us. It is as though he were saying, "Just as all those things remain in their assigned places, so our things should as well." The sun never grows weary in its continual rounds, and the waters run to the sea but are not exhausted. So it is with human beings. They do not cease imitating their ancestors, who strove after vanity. Just as they never accomplished anything, so we never accomplish anything. No one is improved by the example of others or becomes more careful because of the danger of others. Julius Caesar was occupied with the vainest of strivings. Cicero strove for eloquence, but what was the outcome of his striving? An utterly vain outcome, for he never attained what he wanted. If he had used his eloquence not for the sake of his own schemes but for the circumstances and benefit of other people, he would have been truly happy. We, too, follow their example. Therefore all the strivings of men rise and set, go and return, and remain just as they always have been. Thus, as I have said, these words contain not only a description of the realm of vanity but also an analogy and a picture of human striving. Annotations on Ecclesiastes.[15]

The Difficulty of Attaining Knowledge. Jean de Serres: "All streams run to the sea." This verse is expounded variously. Some think that it is the conclusion of the previous line of argumentation, such that if the first elements and principles are subject to vanity and perpetual alteration, how much more the things that have their source in these and are composed by them? . . . Some think that the studies of philosophers are here disparaged, studies in which they search out the nature and causes of things—as if this were evil or unsolvable. Others judge that this is the plain meaning of the words, that the vanity of humans is so diverse and manifold that it can by no means be expressed in words.

I detest the sophistical and foolish ignorance of those who condemn the study of these things in themselves—at least, if we take them to mean that the singular gifts of God, the arts and sciences, are to be refused simply because they are difficult. Nor can I embrace the other two opinions, not because they are contrary to the truth, but because they are contrary to the proper meaning of this passage. What then? Truly, I take it to be a new reason used to prove the main proposition concerning the vanity of human nature from weakness of mind. . . . For if human intelligence is unable to understand the things of nature in themselves, how then can it order them according to its own will? And yet people act as though by their counsels and efforts they were able to rule the whole world! I think therefore that Solomon here refers explicitly to the weakness of human intellectual capacity, because insofar as this is the better part of human nature, there cannot be offered a better argument in demonstration of human vanity. Commentary on Solomon's Ecclesiastes.[16]

No Contentment in Novelty. Michael Jermin: Humanity, whose fickle changeability cannot fasten on the permanence of anything, seeks to find contentment in the newness of things. But this also the Preacher declares to be vain,

[15]LW 15:17-18 (WA 20:21).

[16]Serres, *Commentarius, in Solomonis Ecclesiasten*, 62-64.

showing here that there is nothing new, neither that which shall be, nor that which is, because "that which shall be has been, and that which is shall be" (1:9). The kind of things is still the same; the contentment they yield is still the same in its nature; the vanity of things and the delight taken in them is still the same, for "there is nothing new under the sun." If we will have new things, we must go above the sun. There are indeed new things of another nature—things of eternity, things of true contentment, things in which there is no vanity. But that we may attain to these, we must be new creatures by amendment of our life: the old person must be crucified in us, that we may be glorified in these new things. COMMENTARY UPON THE WHOLE BOOKE OF ECCLESIASTES.[17]

AN ARGUMENT FROM THE WORLD'S ETERNITY. CARDINAL CAJETAN: "There is nothing new under the sun." Having described the circular motion of the parts of the universe with respect to the things themselves, he now describes them with respect to time. For he argues from the eternity of time that all things consist in circular motion, both in terms of their being and in terms of their becoming. And concerning their existence, he asks, "What is it that has been?" He answers, "The same that will be." And concerning this becoming, he indeed says, "And what is it that has been done?" And he answers, "The same that will be done." Then he adds the conclusion, "There is nothing new under the sun." Let the prudent reader notice two things: first, there is nothing said here about numerical identity, but only specific. For he does not mean that each and every individual thing that once was [will be], but rather that every *kind* of thing that once was will be again, and that every *kind* of action will happen again. And thus he concludes that "there is no new kind of thing under the sun"—that is, in the sphere of the elements. Second, Solomon speaks in this sermon of the temporal world, according to what appears most probable according to sense perception. For natural reasons suggest that the world is eternal—that is, that the world never had a beginning—and Solomon makes use of this opinion (a view that, though plausible, is false) in this passage to affirm that there is nothing new under the sun. This is what the philosophers say; nevertheless, Catholic faith holds otherwise.[†] THE PARABLES OF SOLOMON [AND ECCLESIASTES], CORRECTED BY THE ORIGINAL HEBREW.[18]

NATURE UNDERTAKES NO NEW THING. JOHN COTTON: It may seem a paradox at first sight, for it may be asked, what is it that all people (like the Athenians) enquire after? News! If there is no new thing, why are people taxed for hunting after new fashions in apparel (especially Englishmen, as unfit to be suited as the changeable moon) if there be no new thing? Will God again destroy the world with water? Was it not a new thing for God to deliver the law with a lively voice from heaven? Was it not a new thing, or shall it again be repeated, for the sun to stand still, or to go back ten degrees? A virgin to bear a son? Christ to be born, to die, to rise again, to ascend? The Holy Ghost to descend? The apostles to preach and write the New Testament? Are there not sundry inventions of art that are new, such as guns, printing, and the use of the loadstone? Was not the Gunpowder Treason new, without precedent or former example?[†]

To answer these and similar doubts, many interpretations and limitations of these words have been given that are not worth rehearsing, such as that of Cajetan concerning Solomon, to reason from the eternity of time to argue the circular motion of natural bodies, or that alleged of Origen, touching Plato's "great year" of forty-nine thousand years, in which he would have all the stars come to

[17]Jermin, *A commentary, upon the whole booke of Ecclesiastes*, 15.

[18]Cajetan, *Parabolae Salomonis ad veritatem Hebraicam castigatae*, 292-93. [†]The view that *something* (whether matter or form) has existed eternally distinct from God was widely held among ancient Greek philosophers, such as Anaxagoras, Empedocles, and Plato, though the recovery of Aristotle's writings in the thirteenth century gave added impetus to Christian theologians arguing against this view. For Aristotle's view, see for example *Physica* 1.4 (187a22-b6) and *De caelo et mundo* 3.2 (300b29-301a20).

the same position, and so all things return again in the same course. But to touch only those that come nearer to the truth: some have thought (among them Jerome) that all things now done were first in God's predestination.[†] But though this is true, it is not pertinent here, for God's predestination is above the sun, and the things done here according to it are new still under the sun, as having never been done under the son before. Besides, God's predestination was not in old time before us, but before all time.

Others understand the words as denying new arts; but what will they say of the art of printing? Others (like Pineda) understand it of new happiness, nor any new way to attain it. But Solomon seems to speak here of the lack of new objects to eye and ear, from which it comes to pass that they are not satisfied. Others (and that rightly) conceive him to speak of natural things, and their natural actions.[‡] For of these Solomon here discourses, to prove that happiness cannot be found in the knowledge of these, because they are lacking in newness and variety. As if he should say, "Nature undertakes no new thing." Though on this particular occasion he seems to reach further, in denying newness to the common affairs of men in the world. . . .

In answer therefore to the former doubts, Solomon is not speaking about God's miraculous and extraordinary actions, whether of judgment or grace, such as the drowning of the world, the standing of the sun, the birth and death of Christ, or the writing of the Scriptures. . . . Rather, he speaks of natural bodies and the whole course of nature—that is, nature works now as it has from the beginning, undertaking no new thing except on some accidental defect of superfluity in the matter. As for the artificial inventions of humanity, though they are new sometimes at first, yet in their types many of them have been before, and generally none of them continue new for long, but grow stale and old like other things. A Brief Exposition.[19]

1:12-18 *The Vanity of Wisdom*

The Burden of Governing. Antonio Brucioli: Up to this point, we have seen that the general theme or argument of the book concerns the unhappy studies and efforts of mortals, by which they strive to rule and carry out their counsels, and which God makes vain. And here he already begins to number the particulars, building up step by logical step to that universal proposition with which the book began: the vanity of vanities. And so he begins by offering himself as an example of vanity, saying, in effect, "I endeavored to establish my kingdom wisely." And so it appears in the book of 2 Kings, which bears witness to the great wisdom of this king. And yet even so wise and prudent a ruler did not accomplish everything he wanted, nor did he succeed in all his intentions, because God did not grant him wisdom to do all things. For God did not say, "I will give you wisdom that all will obey." And so Solomon actually got more frustration than success from this wisdom. He certainly took pleasure in the fact that God established his reign, but neither the people nor the princes carried out his will. This is why he says that it was an unhappy business with which he was afflicted. The Ecclesiastes of Solomon.[20]

[19]Cotton, *A Briefe Exposition upon Ecclesiastes*, 19-21; citing Acts 17:21; Gen 9:11; Deut 4:32-33; Josh 10:13-14; 2 Kings 20:11; 2 Pet 3:4-6; Ps 102:26; Heb 8:13. [*]The Gunpowder Plot was a conspiracy by a small group of radical English Catholics to assassinate King James I at a gathering of the House of Lords in 1605 and install his daughter Elizabeth as queen under a Catholic regency. The plot failed and the conspirators were executed, an event commemorated in annual burnings of Guy Fawkes, one of the chief ringleaders, in effigy. [†]For Cajetan's exegesis of this text, see above. Plato had described in his *Timaeus* (39d) a "great year," the time it takes for all the heavenly bodies to complete their rotation around the earth and return to their original position, suggesting a cyclical quality to the physical world reflecting the intelligible metaphysical reality that grounds it. Later authors calculated the period variously, ranging from 24,000 to 49,000 solar years; Origen (*On First Principles* 3.1.13) entertained the notion, but never assigned a precise number. Jerome's exegesis is closer to Cotton's, in that he reads the passage applying primarily to the course of natural cycles, though he does allow that it may also refer to God's predestination of the elect. [‡]Avicenna, Sup. q. 91 a. 1.

[20]Brucioli, *L'Ecclesiasto di Salomo*, 9-10.

Even the Best Kings Fail. Martin Luther: He begins with himself and sets himself up as an example of vanity. He says, "I tried to establish my reign wisely and brilliantly, but I failed, even though I was a king by divine right." It is well known that this king had been commended and ennobled in holy Scripture for his divine wisdom, as we read in 1 Kings 3. . . . This was a great testimony to the wisdom of this king. And yet so wise and prudent a king did not achieve what he wanted. His schemes did not meet with success, and properly so, for God did not give him this wisdom to make him capable of everything. God did not say, "I shall give a wisdom that others will hear about." Therefore Solomon had more labor and sorrow from this wisdom than he did success. He saw that God was pleased when he established his reign properly and laid down the laws for the people; but no one, neither princes nor people, followed him. . . . If a king so powerful, free, and wise, ruling over the holiest of peoples in the holiest of cities, with God and the Word of God present, still cannot carry out his good and holy plans, what shall we say about others? Annotations on Ecclesiastes.[21]

Theory and Practice Make the Best Teachers. Jean de Serres: True teachers are those who soberly and carefully combine theory (*theōrian*) with a knowledge derived from practice (*praxin*)—that is, they have the conviction of experience for what they teach. The apostles excelled greatly in this sort of teaching, for they taught that the cross should be borne by bearing it themselves. Away therefore with the inane speculations of those ghostlike masters who can only debate matters pertaining to godliness at home in their studies, who reason coldly and abstractly, as if in the schools of the philosophers! But let those teachers be considered greater among us who join doctrine with experience. Commentary on Solomon's Ecclesiastes.[22]

"Religious" People Are the Hardest to Correct. Michael Jermin: "The perverse are hard to be corrected." The Septuagint (and following them the Latin Vulgate) reads this verse in a more moral sense, and sets it down thus. Now they are properly said to be perverse who [think they] have been right, and how difficult they are to amend, St. Augustine shows, saying, "As I have hardly found any better than those who have profited in monasteries, so I have found none to be worse than those who have fallen in monasteries."[†] For such are amended with difficulty. But as for fools, as for those who were never good, the number of them is infinite. Commentary upon the Whole Booke of Ecclesiastes.[23]

Self-Knowledge Leads to Sorrow for Sin. Denis the Carthusian: It is indeed laborious to study and gain proficiency, because (as the Philosopher says), "art and virtue are surrounded by difficulties," and so it is only through these that a person acquires wisdom and learning, and understands for themselves the errors of excess and neglect.[†] For it is from these difficulties that he receives affliction, contrition, and sorrow, and for these that he afflicts himself with vices. "Because in much wisdom there is much vexation"—that is, the more a person grows in true and saving wisdom, the more indignant do they become against vice and the more do they abominate those who are subjected to it. . . . "And he who adds knowledge"—that is, who grows in moral teaching—"adds also sorrow," because from knowledge one is led to sorrow for one's own sins, and for the evils of one's neighbors and the miseries in the world, and this increases sorrow and compassion in oneself, and weeping and sadness. Exposition of the Book of Ecclesiastes.[24]

---

[21]LW 15:22-23 (WA 20:27); citing 1 Kings 3:11-12.

[22]Serres, *Commentarius, in Solomonis Ecclesiasten*, 78.

[23]Jermin, *A commentary, upon the whole booke of Ecclesiastes*, 23. [†]Augustine, *Epistolae secundum ordinem Temporum* 2.78.9 (PL 33:272).

[24]DCOO 7:220. [†]The quotation is actually from Thomas Aquinas's commentary on Aristotle's *Nichomachean Ethics* (lib. 2, l. 3, n. 14).

Experience Produces Frustration. Martin Luther: "Knowledge" does not refer to speculative knowledge, but to a practical and experiential insight, a discretion in the performance of actions, what we call experience and practice in human affairs, as in the psalm: "Teach me good judgment and knowledge." Wisdom, on the other hand, is the insight by which I know how the state ought to be established and administered; this is then modified by knowledge or experience, in accordance with things as they are at present and with circumstances, in the manner and pattern that the facts and the times warrant. . . . Anyone who sees much and who knows how it is to go cannot help becoming angry. He thinks: Oh, how miserably and dreadfully things happen in this world! What is the source of this anger and indignation except much wisdom? For anyone who is very wise has many reasons to become angry, as one who daily sees many things that are wrong. Someone whose eyes are closed knows nothing and does not become indignant. Therefore learn to keep quiet, to commit the kingdom to God, and to pray, "Lord, thy will be done." Otherwise you will wear out your heart and your body, and you will waste time and eventually your life. Annotations on Ecclesiastes.[25]

Experience of Human Affairs Produces Sorrow. Philipp Melanchthon: "In great wisdom is great indignation." In saying this, Solomon is not talking about consideration of the physical order in the creation of the world, nor of understanding the Word of God, but rather he is speaking about consideration of the counsels, actions, and human affairs that we perceive are full of confusion, vicious error, and calamity in this life. Those who are wiser and more experienced in government see more clearly the evils at hand, and they perceive the many further evils that may result from these things in the future. This is why they are tormented with great sadness on account of present and future miseries; for indeed, once changes had arisen, even greater confusions followed, just as when war broke out in the time of Pericles, there followed the destruction of nearly all the great cities in Greece. And it is very true what Pindar says, that it is easy enough to shake a city, but to establish it in tranquility, only God can do.[†]

Up to now, the first chapter has recited a complaint, without adding any consolation (this will follow later). But here is the summary: our lives seem to be beset with confusions, great errors, and many sad events. Therefore we cannot rest easy with things as they are: the confusion of events does not allow us to find peace, nor yet on account of these miseries can we turn away from God. Rather, patiently obeying him, we wait on him to defend and deliver us, and in this faith we rest easy according to his Word. This is the sum not only of this first chapter but also of the whole book, which agrees with the following sayings: "Be subject to God and pray to him." And, "Cast your cares upon God, and he will sustain you." This consolation comes later, in the third chapter, and it continues thereafter. Enarration on Ecclesiastes.[26]

---

[25]LW 15:22-23, 28 (WA 20:27, 34); citing Ps 119:66.

[26]CR 14:106-7; citing Ps 37:7; 1 Pet 5:7. [†]Pericles (495–429 BC) was an Athenian statesman and general during the "golden age" of Athens, which was brought to an end by the outbreak of the Peloponnesian War. The exact quotation from Pindar is as follows: "For easily can even weaklings shake a city; but to set it back in place again is a difficult struggle indeed, unless suddenly a god becomes a helmsman for the leaders" (*Pythian Odes* 4.272-274; LCL 56:303).

2:1-26 The Futility of Self-Indulgence

[1]I said in my heart, "Come now, I will test you with pleasure; enjoy yourself." But behold, this also was vanity.[a] [2]I said of laughter, "It is mad," and of pleasure, "What use is it?" [3]I searched with my heart how to cheer my body with wine—my heart still guiding me with wisdom—and how to lay hold on folly, till I might see what was good for the children of man to do under heaven during the few days of their life. [4]I made great works. I built houses and planted vineyards for myself. [5]I made myself gardens and parks, and planted in them all kinds of fruit trees. [6]I made myself pools from which to water the forest of growing trees. [7]I bought male and female slaves, and had slaves who were born in my house. I had also great possessions of herds and flocks, more than any who had been before me in Jerusalem. [8]I also gathered for myself silver and gold and the treasure of kings and provinces. I got singers, both men and women, and many concubines,[b] the delight of the sons of man.

[9]So I became great and surpassed all who were before me in Jerusalem. Also my wisdom remained with me. [10]And whatever my eyes desired I did not keep from them. I kept my heart from no pleasure, for my heart found pleasure in all my toil, and this was my reward for all my toil. [11]Then I considered all that my hands had done and the toil I had expended in doing it, and behold, all was vanity and a striving after wind, and there was nothing to be gained under the sun.

[12]So I turned to consider wisdom and madness and folly. For what can the man do who comes after the king? Only what has already been done. [13]Then I saw that there is more gain in wisdom than in folly, as there is more gain in light than in darkness. [14]The wise person has his eyes in his head, but the fool walks in darkness. And yet I perceived that the same event happens to all of them. [15]Then I said in my heart, "What happens to the fool will happen to me also. Why then have I been so very wise?" And I said in my heart that this also is vanity. [16]For of the wise as of the fool there is no enduring remembrance, seeing that in the days to come all will have been long forgotten. How the wise dies just like the fool! [17]So I hated life, because what is done under the sun was grievous to me, for all is vanity and a striving after wind.

[18]I hated all my toil in which I toil under the sun, seeing that I must leave it to the man who will come after me, [19]and who knows whether he will be wise or a fool? Yet he will be master of all for which I toiled and used my wisdom under the sun. This also is vanity. [20]So I turned about and gave my heart up to despair over all the toil of my labors under the sun, [21]because sometimes a person who has toiled with wisdom and knowledge and skill must leave everything to be enjoyed by someone who did not toil for it. This also is vanity and a great evil. [22]What has a man from all the toil and striving of heart with which he toils beneath the sun? [23]For all his days are full of sorrow, and his work is a vexation. Even in the night his heart does not rest. This also is vanity.

[24]There is nothing better for a person than that he should eat and drink and find enjoyment[c] in his toil. This also, I saw, is from the hand of God, [25]for apart from him[d] who can eat or who can have enjoyment? [26]For to the one who pleases him God has given wisdom and knowledge and joy, but to the sinner he has given the business of gathering and collecting, only to give to one who pleases God. This also is vanity and a striving after wind.

a The Hebrew term *hebel* can refer to a "vapor" or "mere breath"; also verses 11, 15, 17, 19, 21, 23, 26 (see note on 1:2) **b** The meaning of the Hebrew word is uncertain **c** Or *and make his soul see good* **d** Some Hebrew manuscripts, Septuagint, Syriac; most Hebrew manuscripts *apart from me*

Overview: The second chapter of Ecclesiastes opens with the Preacher's report of his headlong plunge into sensuality, a turn regarded as a cautionary tale by all of our commentators. Denis takes the author to be speaking in the persona of a "fleshly and inexperienced person," though most of the rest simply regard this as the voice of the aged Solomon reflecting on the follies of his youth. Martin Luther is one of the last commentators to rely on the Vulgate translation of Ecclesiastes 2:3, leading to an interesting juxtaposition of the corollary folly of abstinence from wine; Cardinal Cajetan's correction of the Vulgate at this place, however, illustrates how exegetes in both traditions are beginning to benefit from a better understanding of the Hebrew. The catalog of Solomon's luxuries in Ecclesiastes 2:4-8 calls forth denunciations of excessive luxury from many of our commentators, and while some express some discomfort with the report that Solomon "bought male and female slaves" (Eccles 2:7), only Michael Jermin condemns the practice of slavery outright, citing the powerful critique of the fourth-century Greek father Gregory of Nyssa. In the second half of the chapter the Preacher turns from sensuality to wisdom, but concludes that even this is vanity, since the same end awaits both the wise and the foolish (a theme explored in greater depth by most of our commentators in Eccles 9:1-5). Here Luther's comment on Ecclesiastes 2:24, affirming the value of eating, drinking, and finding happiness in labor, highlights the sharp contrast between his distinctive outlook and that of the *contemptus mundi* tradition.

2:1-11 *The Vanity of Self-Indulgence*

The Carnal Mind. Denis the Carthusian: Solomon teaches in different ways that the outcome of a life consisting in bodily goods and fleshly delights is not happiness, but vanity. And so in the persona of a fleshly and inexperienced person he speaks, saying, "Therefore, I said in my heart"; that is, since I had learned that in wisdom and knowledge there is only frustration and sorrow, and not peace or satisfaction or salvation . . . therefore I said to myself, "I will go"; that is, leaving aside my preoccupation with progress in wisdom and knowledge, I will go to the objects of fleshly delight, "and abound"; that is, I will give myself over entirely "to delights," to gluttony and lust, "and enjoy good things"—external things, adhering to them. For we enjoy the end, but we use the means. "And I saw"; that is, it quickly and easily became apparent to me "that this too is vanity," impious and brutal, turning the mind from God and completely immersing it in the lowest things. Exposition of the Book of Ecclesiastes.[1]

Seizing Upon Pleasure. Martin Luther: It is as though he were saying, "Since anxieties and my own plans cannot achieve anything, I shall refrain from them. I shall turn to the right hand and make a more tranquil life for myself. I shall create ease and tranquility, take delight in good things, let everything happen as it happens and chooses, and live a life of pleasure." But this, too, was useless and was no more successful than his earlier reliance on human wisdom and anxiety, for God resists this also. Tranquility is not attainable except from the Word and work of God. Experience itself teaches this. Often dinner parties are arranged to create a happy atmosphere, with foods and entertainment intended to make the guests happy. But usually it comes out just the opposite way, and only seldom does a good party result. Either there are gloomy and solemn faces present, or something else upsets all the arrangements, especially when there is such deliberation and planning about how much fun it will be. By contrast, it often happens that someone happens upon a most joyful dinner party by accident—that is, by the gift of God. The same thing happens in other areas of life. One seeks pleasure in love but soon experiences bitterness. Augustine also complains in his *Confessions* that he was tormented horribly in the very midst of his amorous affairs.[†]

[1]DCOO 7:221.

Thus when we seize on pleasure, it is soon covered with bitterness. ANNOTATIONS ON ECCLESIASTES.[2]

THE DANGERS OF IMMODERATE PLEASURE. JEAN DE SERRES: Such is indeed human nature that, being carried away with the rage of desires, it is driven headlong in conflicting directions by external things. So we may often see that stern severity is relaxed into a certain dissolute licentiousness, such that they who have lived a hard life, when they abandon their austere severity, licentiously give themselves over to pleasure. Daily life affords us many examples of this human inconstancy; for example, Jehoash, king of the Jews (and the first to reign from childhood), was at first well brought up by the high priest Jehoiada with care and diligence, and his reign was very firmly established.[†] In the beginning of his reign he showed a singular concern for restoring the pure worship of God, and yet by the end his life had turned in completely the opposite direction, with both his zeal and his behavior shamefully altered. The Roman Empire also experienced a pernicious change of behavior in Caligula.[‡] Themistocles,[§] Lucullus,[◊] and many others utterly abandoned care of the commonwealth and gave themselves wholly over to pleasure and ease, that they might watch Neptune raging far off from the land.[Δ]

This way of seeking happiness Solomon also describes as vanity. . . . However, we are to bear in mind that the things themselves [in which he sought pleasure] are not to be condemned—that is, pleasure, ease, joy, and so on. On the contrary, God wants there to be seen in the sweetest pleasures testimonies to his fatherly goodness, with which he would season the miseries and troubles of this mortal life. But we must use all things moderately and soberly that pertain to this earthly life—and indeed to life itself—with prayer and thanksgiving, having them as though having them not, and seeing in them the pledges of God's goodwill toward us, we must rest wholly in God, who is their author, and regard it as a most empty vanity to cling to things which are fleeting and perishable. COMMENTARY ON SOLOMON'S ECCLESIASTES.[3]

THE FOLLY OF ABSTINENCE. MARTIN LUTHER: "And I thought in my heart that I would abstain[†] from wine." Now for the third time he undertakes to experience something else, to see whether perhaps this would succeed: "In the world and in human society, where I have lived, I find success neither in the anxieties with which I trouble myself as I seek to give counsel to others nor in my own pleasures. They are all useless. Therefore I shall undertake a rigid and austere way of life, one of total abstinence and strictness." I am amazed that those false despisers of the world and of creation have not referred to this passage of Solomon, where he calls an austere way of life and severe

---

[2]LW 15:29-30 (WA 20:35-36). [†]See, especially, Augustine, *Confessions* 6.12.21–6.26.26.

[3]Serres, *Commentarius, in Solomonis Ecclesiasten*, 107-9. [†]The OT offers conflicting accounts of Jehoash's life: 2 Kings 12:2 reports that he "did what was right in the eyes of the LORD all his days, because Jehoiada the priest instructed him." A darker account is giving in 2 Chron 24, in which after the death of Jehoiada, Jehoash abandoned the house of God and refused to listen to the prophets who were sent to warn him. [‡]The Roman historian Suetonius, having cataloged the emperor Caligula's (AD 12–41) early accomplishments in office, dramatized the abruptness of his descent into cruelty and madness thus: "So much for Caligula as emperor; we must now tell of his career as a monster" (*Gaius Caligula* 22.1; LCL 31:447). [§]Themistocles (524–459 BC) was an Athenian general and politician who, following a string of early successes against the Persians, was eventually driven out of Athens by intrigue and died in exile. Unlike Caligula, his reputation was later rehabilitated by admiring historians such as Diodorus (*Bibliotheca historia* 11.58). [◊]Lucius Licinius Lucullus (118–57/56 BC) was a Roman general and optimate who achieved spectacular success in the Third Mithridatic War and returned to Italy with considerable spoils. He was generally regarded as a competent politician and a generous patron of the arts, although Plutarch reports that toward the end of his life "his understanding was affected and gradually faded away" (*Lucullus* 43.1), and it was rumored that his dementia was brought about by poisoning. [Δ]The reference to Neptune is not entirely clear. There was a tradition of popular sea ballads in seventeenth-century England titled "Neptune's Raging Fury," which contrasted the intrepid courage of common seamen with the idle security of the wealthy merchants who employed him. Whether or not Serres was familiar with such songs, he seems to be drawing a similar contrast: rulers who indulge themselves in a life of pleasure are free to contemplate the dangers faced by others from a safe distance.

rigor "vanity." Therefore he is condemning here those extremely strict observances of the monks, and especially those of the Carthusians, which the world nevertheless admires and regards as marks of piety and sanctity.[‡] This passage is like a thunderbolt against all the regulations and the religiosity of the monks, by which they subject to themselves and to their own planning such things as do not belong to them. This is not to say that abstinence is evil; what is evil is to seek it out by one's own planning and to bind oneself to it as something necessary. For time, things, and places are gifts of God, which they nevertheless want to take captive through their rules and prescriptions. Besides, all they get out of it is sorrow and misery, while they torture the flesh and torment themselves in vain. Annotations on Ecclesiastes.[4]

Where Drunkenness Leads. Cardinal Cajetan: "I thought in my heart, to withdraw my flesh from wine." But the Hebrew has it: "I searched my heart to pull my flesh into wine." This has completely the opposite sense of what is written in the Vulgate edition. For to pull one's flesh into wine indicates to inebriate oneself, and not remain sober. For people of this kind derive their life from wine, and they are deprived of the powers of a truly rational life, since they are never fully sober, and therefore they do not so much lead a life as lead a death, since they are leading their bodies to the grave. For Ecclesiastes heaps up the choices that occurred to Solomon's heart in order to demonstrate that all these things are vanities. This is why, in treating of laughter and joy, he adds drunkenness, by describing that which is the "drawing of the flesh into wine." And if drunkenness continues, the flesh is eventually drawn (as the text says) to death; but if it is only for a time, the flesh is drawn in that direction for so long as the drunkenness lasts. And because he wants to have a clear view of the effect of drunkenness, he says, "I have searched in my heart" to what end drunkenness leads. The Parables of Solomon [and Ecclesiastes], Corrected by the Original Hebrew.[5]

Practical Wisdom. Jean de Serres: When Solomon says that he "made great works," he means that he was preeminent and magnificent in the management of his affairs, and he proceeds to elaborate here on the magnificence and brilliance of his household economy: he built houses, planted vineyards, made gardens and orchards, and planted in them trees bearing all kinds of fruits; he made water ponds to irrigate his woods, he acquired menservants, maidservants, and cattle, and he had a great number of slaves born into his household; finally, he amassed great wealth for himself, and added to this magnificence a great number of male and female singers, as kings and great men are accustomed to do. All of this pertains to the administration of his family affairs so as to make them perfect in every respect, and to use them according to right reason, which Solomon says that he did: his wisdom remained with him—that is, in his desire to accumulate an abundance of wealth and plenty, he was not so foolish and frenzied as that blind Plutus usually causes rich men to be.[†] Rather, he excelled in firm and steady wisdom [*prudentia*], for not only did he administer his own affairs with keenness and industry (for this is what is called "civil wisdom"), but he also used his goods with liberality and magnificence. This is indicated by the words "Whatever my eyes desired, I did not refuse them," which means that he allowed himself the most generous use of his goods, unlike those sordid skinflints who dare not touch their food and wine, but gape covetously at the riches which they have heaped up with such great labor. . . . The upshot is that Solomon left nothing undone which

[4]LW 15:32 (WA 20:39). [†]Luther's translation of this passage differs from most modern versions in following the sense of the Vulgate, in which the speaker resolves to "withdraw my flesh from wine" (*abstrahere a vino*). The Hebrew *mšk* means "to cheer," giving this passage a very different meaning. [‡]The Carthusians are a religious order founded independently from the Rule of St. Benedict in the late eleventh century. In Luther's time, the order had a reputation for ascetic rigor.

[5]Cajetan, *Parabolae Salomonis ad veritatem Hebraicam castigatae*, 299.

might contribute to a happy life, so far as men in public life can attain it. Commentary on Solomon's Ecclesiastes.[6]

The Trappings of Kingship Are Still Vanity. The English Annotations: Having upon further deliberation declared his purpose to search for good among pleasures and bodily delights, he now shows what magnificent and royal provisions he made in order to meet that design: sumptuous diet, stately buildings, vineyards, gardens, orchards, forests, parks, fish ponds, an honorable retinue of servants, possessions, all sorts of chattel, treasures of gold, silver, and all precious things, music, vocals, instrumentals, and all these in great abundance, as far as royal wealth could procure, largeness of hearts could desire, or exquisite wisdom could contrive. In all this, he took much joy and delight, being withheld by no kind of impediment from the full enjoyment of them, yet in conclusion, he passes the same censure here as he had before, that all was vanity. Annotations on Ecclesiastes 2:4.[7]

No Tranquility in Managing a Large Household. Philipp Melanchthon: He adds to show that some business, though undertaken with diligence for the increase of the family's affairs, is often useless, or even destructive to those who will inherit a large patrimony. Concerning all these, the search for knowledge and skill (as described above), he reminds us that these are good things and must be pursued as a vocation. These necessities must be learned, so that the family estate can be maintained, but we should not expect that we should find tranquility in this business. For many spend their lives in useless occupations, and their lives are full of error. Nor do we avoid cares and sadness, when the outcome of our efforts does not meet our hopes, but rather we must patiently endure the will of God and do what is necessary. Enarration on Ecclesiastes.[8]

Luxury Rests on Exploitation. Konrad Pellikan: The fruit of such labors can only be extracted from the burdens of the unfortunate. Where there are many riches, there are many devourers; where there are many luxuries, there are many laborers. He owned or bought slaves from among those who were foreign-born, for it was not permitted that the children of Israel should be enslaved; rather, by law they labored according to honorable conditions. But in this passage "male and female slaves" are properly understood as captives who were destined for hard labor, for hauling wood and stones, serving as water bearers, and for other difficult or impure tasks. Their sons here are said to be "born in my house," or born to his domestic slaves. Or it may be this is a broad term indicating the various officers who every month served at the king's table, or whom he had placed in charge of his herds. "More than all those who had been before me in Jerusalem." Clearly vanity is engendered by excess, since it is far more fortunate and safer to abound in moderation, as he taught elsewhere, "Give me neither riches nor poverty." It was without doubt this pride and luxury, and an ever-increasing greed, which at length turned him away from the love of God, and from the uprightness of truth, faith, and piety, as an example to all rich men and kings. A Succinct and Universal Commentary on the Bible.[9]

Many Slaves, Many Detractors. Johannes Brenz: After amusing myself by cultivating the earth and various other works, I forced myself to withdraw from these vain and empty things, for I found nothing there to satisfy my heart's longing. Now I seized on a new way of life, becoming the head of a great family [*paterfamilias*]: "I acquired male and female slaves, I furnished myself with

[6]Serres, *Commentarius, in Solomonis Ecclesiasten*, 107-9. †Plutus was the Greek god of wealth, whose mythical blindness reflected the observation, surely common to every society, that the gift of prosperity is seldom distributed in proportion to virtue.
[7]Downame, ed., *English Annotations*, 7A3v*.
[8]CR 14:106-7.
[9]Pellikan, *Commentaria bibliorum et illa brevia quidem ac catholica*, 253r; citing Prov 30:8.

great numbers of sheep, I dedicated a huge weight of silver and gold to the treasury"—all to see whether I could thus gain a genuine advantage for a better life. Read in the book of 1 Kings, and you will see how magnificent and with what wisdom and expense Solomon manages his family, of which he had so great an abundance that for a single day he provided thirty cors of the finest flour, sixty of meal, ten fattened oxen, twenty oxen from the pastures, and one hundred sheep, to say nothing of the deer and gazelles, and all the expenditures on feed for his livestock. Indeed, Solomon observes that in a single year the weight of the gold that came to him was 666 talents, aside from that which came in from the traders, apothecaries,[†] and the kings and princes of neighboring lands. Moreover, silver was so abundant in Jerusalem in those days as to be valued almost like rubble. Now, therefore, if anyone has managed his household affairs with such splendor and magnificence, or stored away so many treasures, or secured a life of greater peace and tranquility, I'd like to know. For who among all mortals, I ask you, was able to search out and test these things better than Solomon? But listen to the colophon[‡] he sets under his own way of thinking: "Behold," he says, "all of that was vanity and wretchedness." Indeed, this is almost exactly the idea expressed in another ancient adage: "As many enemies as you have slaves."[§] With many servants come many plagues, and the more gold is heaped up the more anxieties multiply. So does the one draw the other: a numerous family, innumerable family enemies; many servants, many detractors; much money, many afflictions; great riches, great misery. And indeed, so pernicious a mistress is wealth that whoever possesses it is drawn into all manner of shameful excesses, as Paul says: "Those who desire riches fall into temptations and the nets of demons." Commentary on the Ecclesiastes of Solomon.[10]

Owning Slaves Devalues the Image of God. Michael Jermin: It is human folly that he delights not only in the vanity of his own eyes and his own imagination but also in the vanity of the eyes of others, and of the imagination that others have of him. The Preacher, therefore, having shown how he tried his heart with the delight of the one, here he shows how he tried himself also with the delight of the other. For what is the pleasure of a multitude of servants, and of a greater multitude of cattle, but that others look with admiration on them, and by the great number of them, imagine a great deal of happiness in the one who has them? And this imagination in others is that which much increases his own imagination of his own greatness, which the Preacher expresses here, saying that he "had servants and cattle above all that were in Jerusalem before" him. In this, human pride exceeds even that of nature, making him to imagine himself as if he were not of the same nature, but even of another nature from all that had gone before him. . . . St. Jerome reads it, "I bought servants and maidens for myself."[†] But as a Greek Father asks, "At how many pennies did you value reason? At how many half pennies did you rate the image of God?"[‡] Plainly, as if these were vanities, glory in the buying! To the servants and maidens that were bought the Preacher adds those who were born in his house, as if they had been born of his small and great cattle, it being the vain pride of too many, to reckon those who are under them no better than beasts. Commentary upon the Whole Booke of Ecclesiastes.[11]

[10]Brenz, *Ecclesiastes Salomonis, cum commentariis*, 38v-r; citing 1 Kings 4:22-23; 10:14-15; 10:21; 1 Tim 6:9. †Brenz's loose translation of this passage is idiosyncratic. Modern translations refer to "the explorers . . . and the business of the merchants" (ESV), but Brenz uses the Latin *pharmacopolis*, which might just as well be translated as "quack" or "drug dealer." ‡As with many humanistically inclined writers of this period, Brenz delights in obscure classical allusions. Here *Coronides* may refer to the curved line (colophon) used to indicate the end of a book in ancient literature, or it may refer to the daughters of Orion, Menippe and Metioche, who sacrificed themselves to save their city and were rewarded by the gods with the celestial bodies of comets (Ovid, *Metamorphoses* 13.687). Neither solution is wholly satisfying. §Seneca, *Epistle* 47.5 (LCL 75:303). Seneca adds in the next line that "they are not enemies when we acquire them; we make them our enemies."

[11]Jermin, *A commentary, upon the whole booke of Ecclesiastes*, 37-38. †Jermin is relying on Jerome's early *Commentary on Ecclesiastes* (PL 23:1079), rather than on the later Vulgate. In his earlier

Practical Wisdom Remained. Martin Luther: By "wisdom" he understands not speculative wisdom but the wisdom to govern life and all things; in this, of course, divine wisdom is included. He acknowledges that he had not only an abundance of all things but with it also the wisdom to administer, carry on, and govern all these things properly, which is the greatest gift of God. But he did not have success, because he wanted to make everything succeed by his own counsel, the things that he himself had prudently arranged, and so on, although the unanimous statement of all people on earth is "It doesn't work!" They see that many things are defined and set up prudently but still do not meet with success. Therefore the greatest part of wisdom is to know this, that success does not follow except in its own time and that things are not governed either by the counsel of the wise or by the temerity of the foolish. Annotations on Ecclesiastes.[12]

2:12-26 *The Vanity of Living Wisely*

The Contrast Between Wisdom and Folly. Jean de Serres: Intending to speak of the vanity of human wisdom, it was necessary to set down by way of preface a few things so as to avoid confusing foolishness with [true] wisdom, and in so doing give the appearance of obviating the difference between good and evil, which would be monstrous. Therefore he urges very aptly and clearly the difference between wisdom and foolishness, as though saying, "Is the study of wisdom to be cast away entirely, as though there were no difference between wisdom and folly, as if all things were mixed up and thrown into confusion?" Solomon answers that "he has seen"—that is, discovered by sound arguments which he has firmly grasped, that there is a very great difference between wisdom and folly, as great as the difference between light and darkness. He also uses a very memorable image when he compares wisdom to light and folly to darkness. For just as light, the first of all creatures and the most excellent, distinguishes and illuminates the difference between the various forms of things, and reveals them to the eyes so that they can be known according to their natures; and just as by contrast, in darkness all things are mingled together and nothing can be perceived with certainty, so the mind, being enlightened by the force and power of wisdom can distinguish good from evil, truth from falsehood, and clearly understand things as they are. But folly is unable to perceive these things, and instead stumbles about in dullness and ignorance, groping after them in futility. And just as this holds true in respect to nature, so especially in the case of human fellowship and society (of which this discourse primarily speaks). For those who deprive human life of the guidance and power of wisdom remove the sun from the world. Commentary on Solomon's Ecclesiastes.[13]

The Wise Have Eyes in Their Head. Martin Luther: Wisdom is indeed a good thing; nevertheless, it lacks power and cannot accomplish things or decide events. . . . I see that the same thing happens to both of them. Wisdom errs, and so does temerity; nevertheless, wisdom excels folly. To have "one's eyes in one's head" is a Hebraism, which we express commonly in German this way: "Whoever wants to play chess had better not hide their eyes in their pocket." By this we mean that he must not only be an expert at the game but must also be a watchful and diligent player. Thus he says here also, "The wise man has his eyes in his head." That is, they are not only prudent administrators of affairs, but circumspect, diligent, and watchful. They do indeed see how

translation, Jerome follows the Hebrew more literally, rendering *qanîtî* as *mercatus sum*, "to buy." In the Vulgate, Jerome opts for the more ambiguous *possedi* (Douay-Rheims: "I got me"), which brings his translation closer to the LXX. †Gregory of Nyssa, *Homilies on Ecclesiastes* 4 (PG 44:666). Gregory (c. 335–c. 395) was one of the few Christian writers prior to the nineteenth century to argue for the categorical abolition of slavery rooted in theological anthropology, a view seldom echoed in later theological commentary on this passage.

[12]LW 15:37 (WA 20:43-44).

[13]Serres, *Commentarius, in Solomonis Ecclesiasten*, 146-48.

affairs are to be administered, but they cannot bring about the outcome. Fools, on the other hand, do not have their eyes in their forehead, because they are carried along by temerity and boldness. Eventually the affairs of both are decided by luck and fortune—that is, by God's determination of the outcome—and not by either our counsel or our temerity. Both of them sometimes fall and sometimes prosper. But God does not want this to become the basis of rules. For the creatures are not in our hand, but in God's, who gives them to us to use and who through us does what he wishes. What we add on our own, however, when we wish to determine this use by our own counsels and efforts, is in vain. Therefore he instructs us not to trust in our own wisdom and counsel but to do what he has given us to do; if it does not succeed, we should commit it to God. Annotations on Ecclesiastes.[14]

Even the Wise Pass and Are Forgotten. The English Annotations: What he observed in general before, he now makes good in two particulars, oblivion and death, which are both alike common to wise people and fools. Wise people seem to secure their names at least, though not their bodies, from mortality by such magnificent works as Solomon here wrought and by such noble contemplations as he was conversant in, but he assures us to the contrary here and elsewhere that only piety keeps the name from rotting with the body. Time will eat out all the monuments to wisdom, or, though they continue, yet the renown of a wise person does them no good at all, as they are not sensible or comforted by it after death. New wise people who will arise in later ages will darken and eclipse the honor of those who went before them, and so will be done to them in the ages that follow. To be sure, no mere wise or great person's honor, separated from piety, will hold pace with their being. At the last day there will be so much shameful matter discovered against the wisest of the wicked, as they shall lose all their renown and appear to be vessels of dishonor and shame forevermore. Annotations on Ecclesiastes 2:16.[15]

Clinging to Life Drains Its Joy. John Trapp: "Therefore I hated life"—that is, I loved it less than I had done. I saw mortality to be a mercy, with Cato; I was neither fond of life, nor afraid of death, with Queen Elizabeth.[†] I preferred my coffin before my cradle, my burial day before my birthday. One greater than Solomon threatens those who love life with the loss of life; he has purposely set a particular vanity and vexation upon every day of our life so that we may not dote upon it, since we "die daily." "Sufficient to the day is the evil (that is, the misery) thereof." "Whatever good things we have," says Augustine, "are either past, present, or to come. If past, it is nothing; if to come, it is uncertain; if present, yet it is insufficient, unsatisfactory."[‡] So that, "while I call to mind things past," said that incomparable Queen Elizabeth, "behold things present, and expect things to come, I hold them happiest that go hence soonest."[§]

"Yea, I hated all my labor." I was sorry to think that I had been so eager and earnest in getting a great estate, which now I must leave, and to whom I know not; I am sure that it will be to those who never took any pains for it. And in this we see the corruption of our nature discover itself, in that we are so wedded to the things of this world—especially if got by our own art and industry—that we think much to be divorced from them by death, and to leave them to others, when we ourselves can enjoy them no longer. Henry Beaufort, that rich and wretched cardinal, bishop of Winchester, and chancellor of England in the reign of Henry VI, when he perceived that he must die, and that there was no remedy, murmured at death that his riches could not reprieve him till a further time. For he asked, "Why should I die, being so rich? If the whole realm would save my life, I am able either by

[14] LW 15:39-40 (WA 20:47-48).

[15] Downame, ed., *English Annotations*, 7A4v*; citing Prov 10:7; Ps 112:6; 49:11-12; Jer 17:13; 1 Cor 4:5; 2 Tim 2:20.

policy to get it, or by riches to buy it. Fie!" he says, "Will not death be hired? Will money do nothing?"[◊] A Commentary or Exposition upon Ecclesiastes.[16]

The Lord Himself Is Your God. Martin Luther: "There is nothing better than that a person should eat and drink and find enjoyment in his toil." This is the principal conclusion, in fact the point of the whole book, which he will often repeat. This is a remarkable passage, one that explains everything preceding and following it. This is how it agrees with the preceding: Those pleasures are to be condemned that we by our own counsels seek to achieve for the future, and those labors are to be condemned that we strive to carry out by our own counsels. But those pleasures and labors that God gives are good, and they are to be used for the present without anxiety about either future afflictions or future pleasures. But who is capable of such things? It is rightly said, but what is wisely set forth does not happen. Indeed, hearing we do not hear and seeing we do not see, and no one follows it. We are immersed in striving and anxiety about planning and carrying out our affairs. The heart is averse to plans, and every day it becomes more irritated and restless. Those who are pious refrain from anxiety; the rest of the human race have a restless life until they die. Therefore he says, "This also, I saw, is from the hand of God." This is a noteworthy statement and an outstanding doctrine, but he stresses it less than he did the earlier one. This is because an affirmative statement affects us less than a negative one, as, for example, even the affirmative statement "I am the Lord your God, who brought you out of the land of Egypt" is quickly said but does not affect us, while there is greater force in the negative statement "You shall have no other gods before me." Thus here also he treats the affirmative statement "It is good for a man to eat. . . ." in few words; but he uses many words in the negative statement, to prove and show us our foolishness—namely, that we accomplish nothing by all our counsels and our toil, distracted as we are by anxiety so that we do not use the things that are present. To crude people it is necessary that he speaks in crude and lengthy terms and with examples. To wise people he could have said it all in one word: "The Lord himself is your God." Annotations on Ecclesiastes.[17]

[16]Trapp, *A Commentary or Exposition upon Ecclesiastes*, 22-23; citing Eccles 7:1; Lk 17:33; 1 Cor 15:31; Mt 6:34. [*]Cato the Younger (95–46 BC) opposed Julius Caesar's party during the Roman civil war, and upon defeat killed himself rather than live under what he took to be tyranny. Later Christians were divided in their views of his character: Augustine (*City of God* 1.23) attributed his suicide to wounded pride, whereas Dante (*Purgatorio* 1) lauded him as the embodiment of natural virtue, assigning him a role as guardian of purgatory's shores. [†]This appears to be a rather loose paraphrase of a passage in *Confessions* 11.20.26. [§]William Camden, *Annales the true and royall history of the famous empresse Elizabeth* (London, 1625), 170. [◊]John Foxe, *Acts and Monuments* (London, 1833), 3:716.

[17]LW 15:46-47 (WA 20:55-57); citing Ex 20:2-3.

3:1-22 A Time for All of Life's Moments

1 For everything there is a season, and a time for every matter under heaven:

> *2 a time to be born, and a time to die;*
> *a time to plant, and a time to pluck up what is planted;*
>
> *3 a time to kill, and a time to heal;*
> *a time to break down, and a time to build up;*
>
> *4 a time to weep, and a time to laugh;*
> *a time to mourn, and a time to dance;*
>
> *5 a time to cast away stones, and a time to gather stones together;*
> *a time to embrace, and a time to refrain from embracing;*
>
> *6 a time to seek, and a time to lose;*
> *a time to keep, and a time to cast away;*
>
> *7 a time to tear, and a time to sew;*
> *a time to keep silence, and a time to speak;*
>
> *8 a time to love, and a time to hate;*
> *a time for war, and a time for peace.*

9 What gain has the worker from his toil? 10 I have seen the business that God has given to the children of man to be busy with. 11 He has made everything beautiful in its time. Also, he has put eternity into man's heart, yet so that he cannot find out what God has done from the beginning to the end. 12 I perceived that there is nothing better for them than to be joyful and to do good as long as they live; 13 also that everyone should eat and drink and take pleasure in all his toil—this is God's gift to man.

14 I perceived that whatever God does endures forever; nothing can be added to it, nor anything taken from it. God has done it, so that people fear before him. 15 That which is, already has been; that which is to be, already has been; and God seeks what has been driven away.[a]

16 Moreover, I saw under the sun that in the place of justice, even there was wickedness, and in the place of righteousness, even there was wickedness. 17 I said in my heart, God will judge the righteous and the wicked, for there is a time for every matter and for every work. 18 I said in my heart with regard to the children of man that God is testing them that they may see that they themselves are but beasts. 19 For what happens to the children of man and what happens to the beasts is the same; as one dies, so dies the other. They all have the same breath, and man has no advantage over the beasts, for all is vanity.[b] *20 All go to one place. All are from the dust, and to dust all return. 21 Who knows whether the spirit of man goes upward and the spirit of the beast goes down into the earth? 22 So I saw that there is nothing better than that a man should rejoice in his work, for that is his lot. Who can bring him to see what will be after him?*

a Hebrew *what has been pursued* **b** The Hebrew term *hebel* can refer to a "vapor" or "mere breath" (see note on 1:2)

Overview: The first eight verses of this chapter make up perhaps the most celebrated passage in Ecclesiastes, and early modern preachers and commentators were just as drawn to its beauty as modern poets and folk singers have been. Most Reformation-era commentary does not differ from ancient and medieval interpretation in taking solace from the Preacher's poetic recitation of God's providence in the orderly sequence of the turning seasons, though at least one (George Gifford) found the perpetual change disconcerting. Henry Lok's versified paraphrase may not excel the original in the poetic economy of its expression, but it does give a sense of how writers of this time worked to elaborate on the Preacher's themes and give them current application. Several of the various "seasons" that the text takes for granted raise real ethical concerns for our interpreters: for example "a time to kill" prompts John Trapp, Konrad Pellikan, and Thomas Granger to consider the workings of God's justice, while "a time to dance" is cause for concern to the Puritan John Cotton. The second half of the chapter transitions to themes of worldly work and fulfillment, where questions of the Christian's vocation come to the fore. The beautiful and puzzling statement that God has "put eternity into the human heart" (Eccles 3:11) calls forth various explanations, as does the Preacher's expressed doubts concerning the immortality of the soul beginning in Ecclesiastes 3:19. Calvin's first published work, the *Psychopannychia*, draws extensively on this passage, and though he agrees with earlier exegetes like Denis the Carthusian in affirming traditional Christian teaching, he regards this conclusion as a matter for faith rather than philosophical demonstration.

3:1-8 *A Time for Everything*

A Poem on Time. Henry Lok:

"All purposes have proper times, all things fit seasons find,
At time of birth, and death, to plant and supplant is assigned."
But for I see the worldly wise will say,
They have just cause, to study to attain
The hidden course, which nature doth bewray
In interchange of times: which doth remain
Enrolled in writ of many a learned brain,
  I will with them awhile confer, and show
  To thee the depth of all the skill they know.

Most true it is (I grant) that hidden are,
In knowledge of Philosophy indeed,
Such rules profound, by learning set so far,
As in the mind doth admiration breed:
But yet that skill doth serve to little steed,
  For God hath natures bounds prefixed so,
  That from that course art cannot make them go.

Begin we first where we begin and end,
With birth of man in mother's womb conceiv'd,
Which (forty weeks expir'd) needs forth must send,
And age compels to yield the breath receiv'd,
In both of which, the wisest are deceiv'd:
  The birth and death of diverse, diversely
  Preventing time, of birth and time to die.

And as of men, so in increase of things
The which the earth brings forth in growing kind,
Although we know the moon fit seasons brings,
To planted things to prosper, yet we find
They oft miscarry, and we change our mind,
  And (be their fruits once ripe) they gathered bee,
  And stock once rotten, we stub up the tree.

"A time to cure and kill there is, to build and overthrow,
To laugh and weep, a mournful cheer and merry heart to show."
And though it be a thing unnatural,
And most repugnant to society,
The life of man by hand of man to fall,
And to shed blood, wherein his life doth lie,
Yet justice craves that malefactors die,
  As well as that the sick, should physick have,
  Or salves employed, the wounded corps to save.

Yea though that cities first well founded were,
For safety unto men of civil sort:
Yet never monarch's seat such fame did bear,
Or city grow of much with great resort,
But time made cottages of small import
  Survive their greatness, and surpass them far,
  As Henok, Babel, Troy, true patterns are.

Though nothing be more needful to our kind,
The rigors to allay of worldly care,
Though nothing better for the health we find,
Then mirth (at times we may well for it spare)
Yet in the use of it we must beware,
  And use it so as if we ready were,
  The brunt of greatest crosses straight to bear.

For times there are, when duty doth require,
We should impart with neighbors' woe and grief,
For (partners in distress) do all desire,
And men suppose thereby they find relief
For sin, so should we mourn, as cause most chief:

When God's offended face, doth threat his rod,
Thus mirth and woe, are both requir'd by God.

Ecclesiastes, Otherwise Called the Preacher.[1]

Bodily Life Is the Time to Serve Others: Desiderius Erasmus: St. Paul frequently takes material for exhortation from the time: "Behold now is the acceptable time, behold now the day of salvation," and elsewhere, "Night has gone forward, day approaches"; similarly, in commending a celibate life to the Corinthians, he says, "Time is short," and he compares this life to the time of sowing and the life to come to the time of harvest. All things have their time. As long as we are in the body, the sowing must be done vigorously, not sparingly, as the apostle advises, but abundantly; after this life will come the time not of sowing but of harvesting what each has sown. What is it to sow abundantly or, as the apostle says, in prayers? It is to serve everyone, but most especially those who share your faith, and that wise preacher shows in many words what befits each time, how a pious man adjusts himself to every time, so long as he maintains firmly what admits no exception, namely that he persist in the fear and love of God. The Evangelical Preacher.[2]

All Good Things in God's Time. Cardinal Cajetan: "All things have their season, and in their times all things pass under heaven." Little does it matter that the Hebrew has it, "To everything a time, and a time to every desire under heaven." After differentiating among the various vanities, comparing the wise and the foolish, he continues his sermon on vanity by comparing human works with the works of God that he accomplishes among humans. And he begins this comparison from the regular interchange of time, over against the deeds performed by and among humans. And he begins first with genus, then proceeds to species; of the genera, he opposes two pairs, and then proceeds to affirm on the one hand that there is a time for every species. And because the word is interpreted as "time," it signifies that time is a fixed period; therefore the sense is that for any given thing, there is a fixed time determined for it to exist, when it will be and for how long. On the other hand, there is not lacking a proper time for any desirable thing. And so by these two is signified that no desirable thing for humanity is lacking in time, and when it occurs, it has its own period. The Parables of Solomon [and Ecclesiastes], Corrected by the Original Hebrew.[3]

God's Calling Governs Life's Seasons. Philipp Melanchthon: In the third chapter, he now expressly adds the conclusion and assertion after the complaints [about vanity]. God has made all things good in his time; that is, the use of things has been ordained by God, and their use will be good and happy in his time. Provided, that is, that we use these things according to God's ordinance and with God's assistance, just as it is written, "A person cannot receive anything unless it is given to him from above." This is why he appends a lengthy catalog—"all things have their season"—that is, it is not for the human mind to choose happy times without the aid and calling [*vocation*] of God. Brutus, Cicero, Hircius, and Pansa[†] all thought they could restore the old state of the Roman republic, and they all were mistaken. And always in this way, many have deceived and been deceived. But business proceeds when we obey our calling and rely on God's help, though at times it is more difficult, and at other times less. This relates to the saying in the psalm, "Commit your way to God, and he will do it." Enarration on Ecclesiastes.[4]

[1]Lok, *Ecclesiastes, Otherwise Called the Preacher*, 23-24.
[2]CWE 67:641; citing 2 Cor 6:2; Rom 13:2; 1 Cor 7:29; Gal 6:8-9; 2 Cor 9:6; Gal 6:10.
[3]Cajetan, *Parabolae Salomonis ad veritatem Hebraicam castigatae*, 308.
[4]CR 14:107; citing Jn 3:27; Ps 37:5. [†]The roles of Brutus and Cicero in Rome's civil wars are well known; Aulus Hirtius and Gaius Vibius Pansa Caetronianus were Roman consuls killed by Mark Antony at the Battle of Mutina in 43 BC.

No Rest in Shifting Seasons. George Gifford: If we were not such very dull scholars, blind and earthly minded, there is enough said in the two former chapters to persuade us thoroughly that humanity's estate under the sun, even at its best, is most vain and miserable. But seeing that our wickedness is such that we fasten our love and put our trust in transitory things, although we know them to be such, the wise man goes on with further arguments to recover us. . . . For if Solomon with all his glory, in the midst of his great riches and pleasures, found no good, what shall we say of the life of those (and this is by far the greatest part of the world!) that instead of their delights are laden with evils? I suppose there is no one so simple who cannot reason as follows: If the life of Solomon were vexation, what is the life of other people? . . . These griefs he observed, and some of them he notes down. But first he uses one general argument as the ground and foundation, which also serves as a confirmation of his former discourse (in chapters 1–2). This argument is taken from time: all things under heaven are in time, and therefore changeable with time. No wonder, therefore, that all creatures, all works, studies, endeavors, counsels, and desires are vain, and of no enduring profit, seeing that time eats them up entirely. . . . All things under the sun, or, as the holy apostle says, "the things that are seen," are temporal, and for this reason they alter, they vary, they change, they succeed one another, and there is nothing but a continual turning and tumbling up and down, even as times do turn and alter. There is nothing durable and constant, but it has a season and then its opposite has its turn and expels it. . . . By the way, we must not interpret this so as to think that he intends to show what is lawful and right to be done, but rather what happens by the change of time. Eight Sermons on Ecclesiastes.[5]

Enjoy Life's Good Things in Season. Michael Jermin: Having ended the former chapter with the good enjoyment of the good things of this life, and with the vanity that is yet in them, the Preacher begins this chapter by showing how they may be enjoyed well: namely, by taking them in their time and season; but also by showing their vanity, in that they have but a time and season. More generally, we may note that having above shown the vanity of human things from his own personal experience, here the Preacher goes on to show it from those things that his experience had observed in others. By this we are taught first to look on ourselves and to mark our own ways, and then to cast our eye on those things that are done by others. . . .

To consider then the verse as we read it, the first thing is to note "the season" of things, and that is of such use in the use of things, that as an ancient writer has it, "When it is in season, it is good that it should be, even if it is not a good thing in itself."[†] The other thing is the time of all things: for every thing under heaven has but a time, and such a time as is also allotted to it. . . . Now as the first point teaches that nothing in its time is to be rejected, and nothing not in its time is to be embraced, so the other teaches us to use things in their due season, and to perceive their vanity in that they have but a time. But as everything has its season, so one thing there is that has every season, and that is the business of our salvation. Commentary upon the Whole Booke of Ecclesiastes.[6]

Awareness of Providence a Remedy for Vanity. Jean de Serres: Solomon brings forth a new remedy here against the vanity of human wisdom, which, in an effort to rule itself, undertakes many needless things without call [*sine vocatione*], seeking to bring even the very times and seasons into submission. And when things do not fall out as planned, it cannot be but that she [i.e., Wisdom] is greatly dismayed. Against this thoughtless and unjust haste, the stepmother of good order, the wise man opposes grave meditation

[5]Gifford, *Eight Sermons*, 77v-78r citing 2 Cor 4:18.

[6]Jermin, *A commentary, upon the whole booke of Ecclesiastes*, 66-67. [†]Hugh of St. Victor, *In Ecclesiasten Homiliae* 19 (PL 175:207).

on the providence of God, by whose force and divine will all things are duly governed. He teaches that it does not lie in human counsel to forestall the times preordained by God; therefore, it is a true and timely remedy against the vanity of our counsels and our enterprises to rest in the providence of God and patiently to wait for those times and seasons that he himself has appointed, and not to be so foolish and crazy as to think that opportunities for doing things in due course established by God can be altered by our prudence or our industry. Commentary on Solomon's Ecclesiastes.[7]

Against Free Will. Martin Luther: Here too, as has been said before, Solomon is speaking about human works—that is, about works undertaken by human counsel. Because they do not observe this, the interpreters suppose that he is speaking here about the corruption of created things. Therefore you should understand this as follows: All human works and efforts have a certain and definite time of acting, of beginning, and of ending, beyond human control. Thus this is spoken in opposition to free will. It is not up to us to prescribe the time, the manner, or the effect of the things that are to be done; and so it is obvious that here our strivings and efforts are unreliable. Everything comes and goes at the time that God has appointed. He proves this on the basis of examples of human works whose times lie outside human choice. From this he draws the conclusion that it is useless for humans to be tormented by their strivings and that they do not accomplish anything, even though they were to burst, unless the proper time and the hour appointed by God has come. Here the statement in the Gospel is pertinent: "His hour had not yet come"; and again, "When a woman is in travail, she has sorrow, because her hour has come." So the power of God comprehends all things in definite hours, so that they cannot be hindered by anyone.

But you will say, How then have men and women been installed as the lords over things, according to Genesis 1:26, if they cannot have dominion over them according to their own will and use them in keeping with their own desire? The answer is: We are installed as lords over things in such a way that we are able to use them for the present, but we are not able to have dominion over them by our anxiety and effort. No one is able by their effort to accomplish anything for the future. For how can someone who is uncertain about the future determine something about the future? Therefore God wants us to make use of creatures, but freely, as he has provided them, without our prescribing the time, the manner, and the hour. These are in the hand of the Lord, so that we should not think that it is in our hands to use things as we wish if he does not give them. Therefore Ecclesiasticus says, "God left man in the power of his own inclination," but he added the commandments by which humankind was to regulate their inclinations and actions. Annotations on Ecclesiastes.[8]

Providence Sets the Bounds of Life. Denis the Carthusian: "A time to be born"—that is, the natural order has been set and predetermined by the Creator. And within time, the body of each one who will be born is formed and prepared to assume their own substantial form, and having received it, is begotten secretly in the womb. For begetting is the bringing forth of a thing in its being—that is, in its specific substance. And when such a thing breaks out into the light, it is called generation from the womb (or opening), but more properly this is a manifestation of a preceding generation, rather than generation properly called. "A time to die," when the complexion is completely corrupted, and the natural heat decreases. For the human constitution has been fixed for a set period—that is, it has been granted a measure of duration between birth and death. This period varies greatly in different people, whether it

[7]Serres, *Commentarius, in Solomonis Ecclesiasten*, 195-96.

[8]LW 15:49-50 (WA 20:58-59); citing Jn 7:30; 16:21; Sir 15:14.

be from natural causes, which yield a variety of physical constitutions, or from the disposition of the Creator's providence, which announces diverse measures of mercy and judgment in different people guided by the rudder of his infinite wisdom. This indeed is what holy Job was getting at when he said to God, "You have established his boundaries, beyond which he cannot pass." Exposition of the Book of Ecclesiastes.[9]

Enjoy Life in Due Season. Antonio Brucioli: This catalog, running up to the ninth verse, is drawn from experience, with the result that it can be applied to the whole course of life: thus, one acquires, the other loses badly; one sows, the other reaps. And in sum, each work of human life has its definite time, such that all that you endeavor apart from this will profit you nothing, and will be in vain. This is why it often happens that when we want to hold on to happy times, a sudden disturbance arises and our rejoicing is cut short, as experience often proves. Our counsels avail nothing outside the hour appointed by God, so we should not torment ourselves about the future, but simply enjoy the present. The Ecclesiastes of Solomon.[10]

Birth and Death Are out of Our Hands. Martin Luther: He now cites examples to prove what he has said about human affairs and human efforts. Birth, he says, has its own time, and death has its own time. And as we do not have our birth in our own hand, so we do not have our death either. Yet there is nothing that is more our own than our life and the various parts of our body—but only in the sense of use, for we have not been granted dominion over them even for a moment, and therefore it is useless for us to try to define them with laws. An infant is in the hand of God and is not born until its hour of birth comes. Women labor and are concerned about the birth of an infant, and they predict its time, but there is nothing certain about it. Nor do we die, in spite of great danger and extreme desperation, except at our appointed hour. Why then do we fear death? You cannot live any longer than the Lord has prescribed, nor die any sooner. . . . To Christians this is a great comfort, so that they know that death has not been placed into the power of tyrants nor into the hands of any creature and so that they are not extremely fearful about death but die like children when it pleases God. Annotations on Ecclesiastes.[11]

Killing in Defense of Justice. John Trapp: "A time to kill." That is, to cut off corrupt members by the sword of justice, or of war, "lest the untainted part also draw infection."[†] This is a cruel mercy, says one; a pious cruelty, says another. But "cursed be the one who does the work of the Lord negligently (in a good cause, and on a good calling), and cursed be he who keeps back his sword from blood." But that soldier can never answer before God who strikes not as a justice of the peace rather than as a soldier of fortune. A Commentary or Exposition upon Ecclesiastes.[12]

The Medicine of God's Judgment. Konrad Pellikan: There is a time for the wicked to be punished by the Lord, when their sins will be judged to have been filled to completion and the faithful will be given their deliverance. But these are medicines God applies in his own time for changing the complexion of the body, and these influences of the heavens will either benefit the sick or tell against them. The time of the law was Mosaic and ceremonial; now is the time of grace and the Spirit. Even so, let us not misuse grace in carnal and sinful liberty. The time to kill was the time of the Egyptians, the Amalekites, the Babylonians, the Greeks, and the Romans; the providence of God had long before foretold such massacres, and had arranged them by his just judgment. The

[9]DCOO 7:226; citing Job 14:5.
[10]Brucioli, *L'Ecclesiasto di Salomo*, D 2.
[11]LW 15:50-51 (WA 20:60-61).
[12]Trapp, *A Commentary or Exposition upon Ecclesiastes*, 29; citing Jer 48:10. [†]Ovid, *Metamorphoses* 1.191 (LCL 42:15).

time also was to receive all for grace through the gospel of Christ, and to cast away again for transgressions. It is also time to tear down and build up again, for good things cannot be built up unless evils are first destroyed. All things slope downward and easily dissipate, and many are the indolent, difficult, and lazy who must be built up. Once the ardor of piety built temples, altars, and monasteries; and then, exchanging piety for gain, it corrupted everything and brought all to naught. There is nothing stable, nothing that is not consumed apart from the word of faith and the fear of God. A Succinct and Universal Commentary on the Bible.[13]

No Time for Dancing. John Cotton: [The fourth use] is to take away the plea for dancing. For it is not said there is a *lawful* time to dance, but a *limited* time. Herodias's daughter, Salome, had a time to dance, to earn half a kingdom for a dance, but she got John the Baptist's head. But later she made a very different dance, when falling through the ice (if we may believe Nicephorus) her feet capered underwater and her head being cut off by the ice, it danced on the surface.[†] We read first of a religious dance, second of a civil dance to entertain conquerors, when the eyes are set on joy. But not in marriages, where there is more temptation to lust. As Cicero writes, "Hardly anyone dances except in his cups, either by himself or at any respectable party, [unless of course he is out of his mind]."[‡] It is especially inappropriate in New England, and when the churches of England are in such distress. A Brief Exposition.[14]

Speak Faithfully When Given Freedom. Lucas Osiander: "A time to keep silent, and a time to speak." When we are forced to keep silent by the oppression of a tyrannical regime. Nor can we speak freely in a republic without a certain danger to our lives, and so we understand that by speaking we often make no progress, but rather only provoke evil, which we must bear with patience. When happier times have come, allowing us to take part in public deliberations, we should do so faithfully. Ecclesiastes.[15]

The Power of Love and Hate in Human Affairs. Theodore Beza: Since humanity is bound together by the right use of true friendship, it is admirable that human strength and power is increased when we love and safeguard our friendships. And there is no less force in the contrary: that is, in discerning our enemies and either setting upon them or steering clear of them, we turn to our own use and benefit such injuries and inconveniences as may befall us. For whatever order people try to impose on their lives and their possessions, concord and discord often impinge on our personal affairs, and war often overturns the course of human affairs more generally. Ecclesiastes, or The Preacher.[16]

Love, Hate, and Cheek-Turning. Thomas Granger: Love or true friendship is the bond of human society. By the bond of love, all the members of the body are knit together into one head: it is the sinew of the church and of the commonwealth. Where love fails, all things tend toward dissolution. . . . Contrarily, there is a time to hate: to know our enemies; to confront and contend with them; to beware, and to avoid them; to encounter and fly away—yes, also to make good use to ourselves of the wrongs that are offered us. For no matter how well a person orders their life and behaves themselves in all things, still love and hatred, concord and discord, goodwill and envy shall buffet and toss their affairs. For the unclean spirit mingles himself in all things to make

[13]Pellikan, *Commentaria bibliorum et illa brevia quidem ac catholica*, 253r.

[14]Cotton, *A Briefe Exposition upon Ecclesiastes*, 58; citing Ex 15:20; 1 Sam 18:6; Lk 15:25; Ezek 21:10. [†]This morbid tale is found in the *Historia ecclesiastica* of Nicephoros Kallistos Xanthopoulos (c. 1256–c.1335), published in Basel in 1555. [‡]Cicero, *Pro Murena* 13 (LCL 324:201).

[15]Osiander, *Ecclesiastes: iuxta Veterem seu Vulgatam Translationem omnia ad Hebraeam Veritatem emendata*, 1203.

[16]Beza, *Ecclesiastes Solomonis Concio*, 16-17.

confusion and to bring destruction. Therefore Solomon says, "They who forsake the law praise the wicked, but they who keep the law contend with them." The wicked are whelps of the same litter . . . but the person of conscience who fears God will disapprove, discourage, dispraise, resist, and oppose them, and strive for the truth until death. This is why David says, "I hate them that hate you, and earnestly contend with those who rise up against you."

Objection: Christ says, "Do not resist the one who is evil. But if anyone slaps you on the right cheek, turn to them the other also." Answer: Resistance is either a lawful and harmless avoiding of evil, or else a retaliation, or rendering of like for like, wrong for wrong, revenge for revenge, and that is forbidden. Indeed, we ought so to be possessed with the spirit of patience, generosity, and goodness as to suffer a new wrong, rather than to revenge an old through hatred and ill-will. To this purpose Paul says, "Repay no one evil for evil," for this is to "be overcome by evil," but "overcome evil with good," darkness with light, corruption with grace. "If possible . . . have peace with all people." How is that? "Do not avenge yourselves, but if your enemy is hungry, give him meat, and if he thirst, give him drink, for so shall you heap coals of fire upon his head"—that is, either win him with your good deeds, or his own conscience shall witness against him, that the fire of God's wrath hangs over his head, and God will not allow the wicked to go unpunished. You must not desire the terror of his conscience, nor rejoice in any way at God's revenge, or for the ease of your own stomach, lest God turn his wrath from him to you. But rather pity him, yet so as God might have the glory.

Therefore, turning the cheek does not mean that a person should make themselves a prey to contentious, malapert, or violent people, or become a voluntary object of their cruel contempt; but rather, to be of such moderation and equity as to pacify and win them over with patience, goodness, kindness, or whatever good means sanctified reason can devise. . . . We must do good to our enemies willingly, resist their evils peaceably, make the cause God's rather than our own, contend with them lawfully, live among them warily, commit the vengeance to God, cast no stumbling blocks before them; but rather, offer the means to further their conversion, that they may glorify God in the day of visitation—that is, when it shall please God to open their eyes to see and discern the truth. To conclude: love and hatred in private persons, war and peace in public states, have always been and must always be, until the end. For throughout all nature there is an opposition of one thing to another, as well discord as concord, tares as wheat, because God will be glorified as well by judgment as by mercy. For he delights in both. A Familiar Exposition.[17]

3:9-15 *The God-Given Task*

The Human Mind Humbled. Henry Lok:

"What profit finds the toilsome man, of all his cark and care?
To humble man's ambitious mind, God did these pains prepare."
Which if so be (as so it is indeed)
Then would I have the gymnosophists wise,
The magi, druids, and stoics breed,
The sophists, and most wise of all Rabbis,
And all philosophers of every guise,
  Who moral rules, and natural skill did know,
  Or judgments supernatural did show.

Them would I have to tell to me in brief,
What profit man, most properly may say,
He has, of all his days consumed in grief,
Which he assured is with him shall stay:
The goods of fortune subject to decay,
  The strength of body, failing every hour,
  The mind's much more, which worldly cares
    devour.

I see (methinks) a labyrinth of woes
Environ man about, from day of birth

[17] Granger, *A Familiar Exposition or Commentarie on Ecclesiastes*, 77-80; citing Prov 28:4; Ps 139:21; Mt 5:39; Lev 19:17-18; Rom 12:17, 21, 18, 20; Jer 9:24.

Till hour of death, what so about he goes,
With sour face, seasoning still his feigned mirth,
Cares him accompanying upon the earth,
  For needful things for life, yet foolish he,
  With needless studies still will meddling be.

And God has justly given this plague to all,
For our forefather Adam's climbing mind,
That humbled so, we might before him fall,
Confessing that we are poor worms, most blind,
And fly to him where we may comfort find,
  Upon his providence ourselves to rest,
  As thing whereby we only may be blessed.

Ecclesiastes, Otherwise Called the Preacher.[18]

Labor Is Subordinate to Providence. The English Annotations: It is vain for a person, by any anxious toil, to go about to effect anything according to their own will if the counsel and providence of God are against it. When they build, God may pull down or put in some accident or causal event that shall divert or undo all. Yet God does not intend to restrain people from needful labor in their callings, but from trusting in or building on their labors and fretting if such fruits do not follow as intended and expected, rather than patiently submitting to the holy will of God, to whom it belongs to dispose our persons and our liberties as it pleases him. Whence observe that anxiety and caring are indeed a striving with the irresistible providence of God, which no labor of ours can alter or bend to our wills. On the other side, glorying out of our own strength or wisdom is robbing him of his honor. Labor is subordinate to providence and must never strive against it. There is no profit to anyone in their labor without God's blessing, which they therefore must pray and rejoice in without fruitless anxiety for the future. Annotations on Ecclesiastes 3:9.[19]

The Beauty of Contentment. Martin Luther: Those who do not expect their appointed time are afflicted, while those who do expect it are delighted. For everything that God makes or that happens through the gift of God in its appointed time is pleasant. That is to say, when the heart is empty of cares and yet something happens to it that is pleasant or some interesting sight comes along, this is very delightful. Therefore such people have pleasure where others have affliction, because they do things at the time which has been appointed by God. . . . "Although God has given the world into the hearts of human beings," he says, "they still cannot govern it by their own counsels." "To give into the heart" or "to speak into the heart" is a Hebraism for giving or speaking in a sweet and flattering way. He wants to say, God not only gives the world into the hand of men and women, so that they can use the things that are present, but also into their heart, so that they can use them joyfully and with pleasure and so that they have fun and delight from it. Nevertheless, humans cannot know what the beginning or the end of the work is, when or for how long they are to have these things. Therefore humans should be content that they have the world for their use. Paul speaks in similar terms in Acts 14:17: "Yet he did not leave himself without witness, for he did good and gave from heaven rains and fruitful seasons, satisfying their hearts with food and gladness." And elsewhere, "who richly furnishes everything." This happiness the Christian has, and everyone else would have it also if they could be content with the things that are present. St. Jerome says correctly in his preface to the Bible, "The believer has a world of riches, but the unbeliever does not have a penny; as the proverb says, 'the miser lacks not only what he does not have but also what he does have.'"[†] Annotations on Ecclesiastes.[20]

Making an Idol of the World. Jean de Serres: "He has set the world in their heart." These words are expounded in various ways by the

[18]Lok, *Ecclesiastes, Otherwise Called the Preacher*, 27.

[19]Downame, ed., *English Annotations*, 7B2r*; citing Is 4:1; 5:9; Jon 4:8, 9; Deut 8:17, 18; Hab 1:16.

[20]LW 15:53 (WA 20:62-63); citing 1 Tim 6:17. [†]Jerome, *Epistle* 53.10.

interpreters. I will first of all set out the plain meaning, which seems to me to be the best, and then afterward touch on the other expositions, leaving them to the reader's judgment. Intending to highlight the cause of that same pensive and laborious trouble with which the minds of men and women are entangled, he said that the providence of God had appointed a certain order and time for all things; now he teaches that the reason why people are so worn out is that they cannot rest in this wise ordinance and government of God, and that it is a matter of great folly for mortals to go about by their own counsels, seeking to prevent the wisdom of the immortal God. Therefore, since they have their minds set on these fading and fleeting things (which is what he indicates by "the world") and sink themselves up to their heads and ears in worldly lusts, the result is that they cannot earnestly think on those excellent works of God—that is, they are unable to depend upon God's providence, and to wait for his help in due season. This is why they weary themselves greatly and vex themselves with infinite labors; and even though they busy themselves with many needless things, with no calling [from God] and without faith, still they get nothing good from all their efforts, and this itself is a certain punishment for their faithless and frantic hustling. The sum and effect is that men who are blinded by too much care for the things pertaining to this life (*biōtikōn*) do not rest in the providence of God, and therefore everything they do ends badly.

The word *ʿôlām* in the Scriptures signifies either "a long period of time" [*diurnitas*] or "eternity" [*aeternitas*]—that is, everlasting time. Sometimes it refers to the world [*mundus*], as a synonym for *ḥeled* . . . or agreeing with the New Testament description of "the present evil age." Therefore, some explain this passage as referring to the love of the world, and of earthly things; others hold that it refers to a certain sense of eternity, as though they should always live here—so given are people to these earthly things and to pursue them with such great desire. Both explanations agree well with our exposition. God is said to have set love of the world, or a vain sense of their own immortality, within the hearts of people because in his just judgment he allows them to be blinded by the love of this world, and to be carried headlong in their madness, for insofar as they trust in this world, they will naturally feel more keenly its thorns, as we have explained above. This human vanity of making for themselves an idol of eternity is clearly described in Psalm 49. Solomon says that these people, besotted with a demented love for the world, "cannot perceive the workings of God from the beginning even to the very end"—that is, they see nothing, even though the works of God are most excellent and obvious, and shine forth in all the parts of our lives, yet they are so blind that they can see neither the beginning, nor the unfolding, nor the end. Or that they stubbornly remain in this blindness throughout their lives. This seems to me the true meaning of this passage. Yet others explain it as though God were to have "set the world in the hearts of mortals," because not only does he give the world into human hands, that we may use these things that are present, but also he sets them in our hearts, that we may use them joyfully, and with pleasure. And yet, we cannot tell when the beginning or end of the work may be, when or how long we shall have these things; and so the gist of it is that God has created things so that people ought to use them cheerfully, and praise him as their author, and find rest in him, but the use of these things becomes unpleasant to those who have wandering lusts, when they intermingle vain cares in distrust. . . . These things are indeed true, but in my judgment they agree neither with the words nor with the meaning of this passage. Commentary on Solomon's Ecclesiastes.[21]

God's Purposes Prevail. Antonio Brucioli: "Whatever God does endures forever." That is, I have seen that all the things God does last forever, but our works are uncertain and vain. And from this the corollary follows: only God can bring his

[21]Serres, *Commentarius, in Solomonis Ecclesiasten*, 203-6; citing Ps 17:14; Gal 1:4.

counsels to fulfilment at the time of his choosing and ensure that they always unfold according to his will. And what his counsels may be, no one can search out. When God grants life, no one can snatch it away, since the time God has granted for it is certain and enduring, and no one can change that. But all our works have their appointed hour, and this is set by God, not by us. Why, then, does he afflict humanity in this way by keeping to himself the hours he has chosen? For this reason, he says, so that God may be feared and so that we do not come to rely on our own works, laboring in pride for our own private gain. This is what Paul teaches, when he reminds us to remain in the fear of God, because "it is not from the one who wills, or the one who runs"; rather, the work and the will are from God, and he will bring them to completion. The Ecclesiastes of Solomon.[22]

Awe and Submission. The English Annotations: God's decrees and immutable providence should not drive us into despair and a willful neglect of all means, the use of which God expects that we should wait on him and in which, in the way of his providence, he uses to work good for his people. Nor do they allow us to lean on our own wisdom and deify our own counsels or burn incense to our own nets. Instead, by them we are taught, in consideration of the sovereignty, wisdom, and power of God in all things, to stand in awe of him, to submit to him, in blessings to be thankful and in sufferings to be patient, because it is still the Lord that decrees, orders, and rules over all. Annotations on Ecclesiastes 3:14.[23]

Living in the Present. Martin Luther: Earlier in chapter 1 he said, "What has been is what will be." This is quite different from what he says here: "That which has been already is." There he was speaking about the works and things of mortals, here about the deeds of God. The human heart cannot be content with the things that are present; nor can it wish for what merely is, but only for what is to be. But once it has what is to be, it is still not content but looks for something else again. The heart is not satisfied. This is the condition of the human heart, always to be looking for future things but never to be satisfied. But God works and acts in the opposite way. With him "whatever has been is present"—that is, he does not turn away to future things. For it is said of him, "He saw everything that he had made, and it was very good." God abides in the work that he does, and he does not overthrow it or run off to other and still other desires for the future, as the minds of mortals do. Those who walk according to God do this also; they are not diverted toward future things, to the neglect of the things that are present. Annotations on Ecclesiastes.[24]

3:16-22 *From Dust to Dust*

The Intractability of Human Justice. Martin Luther: Solomon is not complaining because there is wickedness in the place of justice but because the wickedness in the place of justice cannot be corrected. It is as though he were saying, "Thus all things are vain, so that even a concern about correcting the injustice of the magistrates is of no avail. When I saw wickedness, I thought I would correct it, but I realized that I could not do so until God corrected it." Thus our Prince Frederick[†] used to say, "The longer I rule, the less I know about ruling." Again, "Where shall I finally find someone whom I can trust?" You see that in all the courts of princes, regardless of how many people there are who are good, interested in the welfare of the state, and ready to give advice, you will always find others who cause plenty of trouble for all the plans of everyone and who make trouble for everything. The malice of human beings is so great that you cannot set them all straight. Therefore Solomon wants to say, "If someone torments themselves here in order to set them all straight,

[22]Brucioli, *L'Ecclesiasto di Salomo*, D3; citing Rom 9:16.

[23]Downame, ed., *English Annotations*, 7B2v*; citing Job 1:21; 1 Sam 3:18; 2 Sam 15:25, 26; Ps 36:5-7.

[24]LW 15:55-56 (WA 20:65-66); citing Eccles 1:9; Gen 1:31.

they will have nothing but affliction and sorrow." Therefore one must commit it to God. A stone that can be lifted and carried should be lifted and carried, but one that cannot be lifted should be allowed to lie there. . . . Therefore it would be best to do what God gives one to do and to commit the rest to God, who in his own time will judge the righteous and the wicked. People do not want to do so, and they cannot even if they want to very much. Annotations on Ecclesiastes.[25]

The Vanity of Human Virtue. Jean de Serres: This is clearly the beginning of a new discourse. Up to this point, he has taught that happiness is not found in knowledge, or in pleasure, nor even in human wisdom itself; now he teaches that it does not consist even in virtue itself (insofar as judgment can be made from those things that often happen to virtuous people or good causes). He is speaking of those things that happen in this life, and manifest themselves in outward appearance, and so he is speaking according to the supposition of our senses—that is, insofar as human reason can judge. And he offers three reasons why this kind of life—a life based on virtue—is a vain one (if we judged based on outward appearance). The first is that injustice and iniquity often hold sway in those very places that are regarded as sanctuaries of law and of justice. The second is that the final destination of humans and animals is the same, since all die in the same manner. The third is that even the very best of people and those who are guiltless are often used very ill at the hands of dishonest and profligate people. If judging only with the eyes and on the basis of human reason, without the Word of God, this human life would seem to be in such confusion that people were crushed like ants by the assaults of blind fortune. Commentary on Solomon's Ecclesiastes.[26]

Reason Proves the Immortality of the Soul. Denis the Carthusian: "I said in my heart concerning the sons of men, that God would prove them." That is, I thought and desired that God might search out human nature and its qualities on the basis of their various deeds and powers—not so that God might come to know them, but so that they might be made manifest to us, just as it is said in Scripture that he tests and proves people: "The Lord has tried me, I shall come out as gold," and, "For you have proved us, O God, you have tried us by fire." But then is added, "and show them to be like beasts." Solomon says this in the persona of those ignorant persons who think there is no future life, and who desire to convince others of this. Of such a sort were the Sadducees, as reported in the Acts of the Apostles, when they said that there was no resurrection from the dead, no angels, and no spirit. "Therefore the same," that is, the same in kind, similar in all respects, "is the death of humans and of beasts," that is, the death of humans and of the brutes is similar, in that the human soul perishes with the body. "And their condition is equal: just as a human dies, so they die; all thing breathe alike," that is, humans and beasts, "and humans have nothing more than beasts," that is, in nothing do they excel the dignity of brutes. This is the argumentation of foolish and uneducated people: that because humans and beasts agree in many things, therefore humans surpass the beasts in none, and fall short like brutes—even though at the same time they excel them in reason, understanding, and free will. This is why holy Job says that God "teaches us more than the beasts of the earth, and makes us wiser than the birds of the heavens." . . .

[25]LW 15:56-57 (WA 20:67-68). †Frederick III, "the Wise" (1463–1525), Elector of Saxony was Luther's patron and protector. Remarks like this one, frequent in Luther's writings, suggest an intimate familiarity with Frederick's thinking and manner of expression. In point of fact, Luther and Frederick never actually met in person. They did share views frequently, however, a relationship mediated by Frederick's privy secretary, Georg Spalatin, who exchanged hundreds of letters with Luther. For more on the unique "friendship" between the reformer and his prince, see Susan Karant-Nun, "Luther's Friendship with Frederick the Wise," in *The Personal Luther: Essays on the Reformer from a Cultural Historical Perspective* (Leiden: Brill, 2017), 46-66.

[26]Serres, *Commentarius, in Solomonis Ecclesiasten*, 220-21.

"Who knows if the spirits of the children of Adam ascend upward," that is, whether the souls of dying people are brought to the judgment of God, or to the heavenly places? And who knows "if the spirits," that is, the irrational souls, "of the beasts descend downward," that is, whether they are reduced to potential matter and from that state fall into nonbeing and the abyss of nothingness, as opposed to human souls, which excel the souls of brutes by virtue of their immortality? It is as though he were to say, no one knows for sure. But (as it is known) Solomon speaks these things in the persona of carnal and thoroughly beastly people. . . . These fools thought that all were like them in this folly; but they have erred most gravely, because from the beginning of the world the providence of God, his right to judgment, and the immortality of rational souls have become known not only to the holy patriarchs and prophets, and to their followers, but also to the foremost philosophers.

By contrast, Plato observes in *Timaeus* that the Creator-God willed that life should be just and pleasant, if souls would curb and subjugate the passions, but that if they were to be conquered by them, life would be unjust and laborious. And to those souls who are victorious over the passions is promised a return to their native stars in their heavenly abode, passing at length into the blessed life; those who are conquered by their passions, however, are changed into women. . . .[†] Moreover, Aristotle teaches very clearly that the intellect is immaterial and immortal, both in book three of *On the Soul*, and in his book *On the Generation of Animals*.[‡] And also the Platonist Proclus, in his *Elements of Theology*, proves the immortality of the soul with great subtlety, arguing that because souls are self-constituted beings capable of reverting and reflecting on themselves, they must necessarily be incorporeal and incorruptible.[§] Hence he acknowledges the following theorem: every intellect has substance in eternity, as well as power and operation; and later he says that every soul is an incorporeal substance, and separable from the body; and also that it is indestructible and incorruptible. Exposition of the Book of Ecclesiastes.[27]

Immortality of the Soul beyond the Reach of Reason. John Calvin: The fourth argument that they[†] urge against us, as their most powerful battering ram, is the passage in which Solomon thus writes in his Ecclesiastes, "I said in my heart of the children of men that God would prove them to show that they were like the brutes. As humans die, so do they also die. In like manner all things breathe, and humans have no more than a beast of burden. . . ." What if Solomon himself here answers them in one word? "Vanity of vanities, saith the Preacher, vanity of vanities, and all is vanity!" For what else does he aim at than to show the vain sense of humans, and the uncertainty of all things? Humans see that they die like the brutes, that they have life and death in common with them; and they therefore infer that their condition is on an equality with theirs: and as nothing remains to them after death, so they make nothing remain to themselves. This is the mind of human beings, this their reason, this their intellect! "For the animal man does not receive the things of the Spirit; they are foolishness to him, neither can he understand them."

Human beings look with the eyes of flesh and behold death present, and the only reflection they make is that all things have sprung from the earth, and equally return to the earth; meanwhile, they take no account of the soul. And this is the meaning of the subjoined clause, "Who knows whether the spirit of the sons of Adam ascends upward?" For if the subject of the soul is considered, human nature, wholly contracted in itself, comprehends nothing distinctly or clearly by studying, meditating, and reasoning. Therefore, when Solomon shows the vanity of human sense, from the consideration that in examining the mind

[27]DCOO 7:231-32; citing Job 23:10; Ps 65:10; Acts 23:8; Job 35:11. [†]Plato, *Timaeus* 42b-c. Denis offers several more extracts from the *Phaedo* illustrating Plato's belief in the immortality of the soul. [‡]Aristotle, *On the Soul* 3.5.430^{a}22; *On the Generation of Animals* 2.736^{b}27-28. [§]Proclus, *Elements of Theology* 186-87.

it fluctuates and is held in suspense, he by no means countenances their error, but nobly supports our faith. That which exceeds the capacity and little measure of the human mind the wisdom of God explains, assuring us that the spirit of the sons of Adam ascends upward. I will bring forward a similar passage from the same writer for the purpose of somewhat bending their stubborn neck. "Human beings do not understand either the hatred or the love of God toward humans, but all things are kept uncertain, because all things happen equally to the righteous and the wicked, the good and bad, to the one sacrificing victims and to the one not sacrificing." If all things are kept uncertain in regard to the future, shall the believer, to whom all things work together for good, regard affliction as an evidence of divine hatred? By no means. For believers have been told, "In the world you shall have tribulation; in me, consolation." Supported by this consideration, they not only endure whatever befalls them with unshaken magnanimity, but even glory in tribulation, acknowledging with blessed Job, "Though he slay us, we will hope in him."

How, then, are all things kept uncertain in regard to the future? This is only humanly speaking. But every living person is vanity. He adds, "The worst thing I have seen under the sun is that the same things happen to all; hence the hearts of the children of men are filled with malice and contempt in their life, and afterward are taken down to the lower regions. There is no man who can live always, or have expectation of such a thing. A living dog is better than a dead lion. For the living know that they shall die, but the dead no longer know anything. Nor have they further any reward; for their memory is given up to oblivion," and so on. Does he not speak thus of the gross stupidity of those who see only what is actually present, hoping neither for future life nor resurrection? For even if it were true that we are nothing after death, still the resurrection remains; if they would fix their hopes on it, they would neither feel contempt for God nor be filled with all kinds of wickedness, not to mention other things. Let us therefore conclude, with Solomon, that all these things are beyond the reach of human reason. But if we would have any certainty, let us run to the law and the testimony, where are the truth and the ways of the Lord. They declare to us, "Until the dust return to the earth from where it was, and the spirit return to God who gave it." Let no one, then, who has heard the Word of the Lord, have any doubt that the spirit of the children of Adam ascends upward. By "ascending upward" in that passage, I understand simply subsisting and retaining immortality, just as "descending downward" seems to me to mean lapsing, falling, becoming lost. On Soul Sleep.[28]

Philosophical Doubts. Hugo Grotius: In contrast to that idea about judgment in a future age in the preceding discourse, another thought arose in me: that God permits people to live among themselves in a savage manner, so that he may better declare and show that they are equal to the beasts. And to this thought he adds an argument: "Who knows if the spirits of the children of Adam ascend on high?" That is, whether they endure, in heaven. "Or whether the spirits of beasts descend below." Do they perish, as bodies that rot in the ground? Human beings have no firsthand understanding [*native ratione*] about this, and Socrates, Cicero, and Seneca all expressed doubts on this score.† Annotations on the Old Testament.[29]

[28]*Calvin's Tracts*, 3:459-62 (CO 5:208-210); citing 1 Cor 2:14; Eccles 9:1; Jn 16:33; Job 13:15; Eccles 9:3-5; Eccles 12:7. †Calvin's first theological treatise, the *Psychopannychia* (*On Soul Sleep*), was written in 1534, two years prior to the publication of his first edition of the *Institutes*. In this short work, he attacks the doctrine of the conditional immortality of the soul, along with the corollary idea that the soul remains in a state of sleep or oblivion in the intermediate state between death and the final judgment. This doctrine had been condemned by the Fifth Lateran Council (1513), but was picked up by a number of radical writers in Calvin's generation. Calvin himself never identifies his opponents by name, describing them merely as "some dregs from the Anabaptists" (CO 5:72).

[29]Grotius, *Annotationes in Vetus Testamentum*, 260. †Denis the Carthusian (above) drew on Platonic arguments in support of the soul's immortality, but in other passages (e.g., *Apology* 40c-42a) Socrates appears noncommittal. In the first book of the *Tusculun Disputations*, Cicero responded to Socrates's apparent

The Animal-Like Misery of the Human Condition. Thomas Granger: The apt coherence of these three verses (3:19-22) with the former (3:18) intimates that . . . they are a reason proving the corruption, vanity, vileness, and misery of proud humanity, by comparing them to beasts, whose frailty, corruption, and vanity is God's judgment on the human race. In them humans may behold their sin, and their corporal punishments for sin before their eyes, if they be otherwise insensible; and these are the forerunners and beginning of eternal torments, just as senselessness is a judgment of God on the reprobate. . . . There is a great difference between humans and beasts, for humans' animal nature and spirit is but the mold or vessel of the soul, which is not compounded or mixed with it, but only united to it. Therefore when this frail vessel is broken or dissolved, the immortal spirit or soul ascends to God who gave it, and the vessel again is subsumed into the elements from which it was formed. . . .

This is indeed the holy and divine truth, but now speaking of the worldly, outward, and miserable state of humanity, as it appears to human senses and reason, who can by any sign or token or skill of anatomy find out any difference between these spirits? What person can show me the ascending of the human spirit into heaven, or the descending of the beast's spirit into the earth—that is, its dispersal into the elements? If someone were to say that the spirit of a person ascends upward into the firmament, how can he let me see that? But if it does, then does that of the beast also, for the firmament is but the quintessence or prime of the elements, as the spirit is of the body, according to Plato? And even though by human reason one may easily demonstrate the immortality of the soul, as the learned heathen have all done, yet what is that to the outward worldly state of a living person? A human while human (and of humans only we speak, not of spirits) is no better than a beast. So to conclude, seeing that it is with humans as with beasts, there is no profit, no contentment, no rest, no durable prosperity, no happiness at all in this cursed, confused, brutal world, but all is vanity. A Familiar Exposition.[30]

skepticism in this passage by arguing that regardless of whether the soul passes on to life or oblivion, death itself is not an evil. Seneca's views on the matter are debated, and seem to be ambivalent: in some passages (e.g., *Epistle* 36.9, 54.4) Seneca seems to express the "Epicurean" view that death brings only oblivion; in other passages he seems content to allow an ambiguity similar to that of Cicero: "Death either annihilates us or strips us bare. If we are then released, there remains the better part, after the burden has been withdrawn; if we are annihilated, nothing remains; good and bad are alike removed" (*Epistle* 24.18, LCL 75:176-77).

[30]Granger, *A Familiar Exposition or Commentarie on Ecclesiastes*, 90-92*.

4:1-16 Evil and Good Under the Sun

1 Again I saw all the oppressions that are done under the sun. And behold, the tears of the oppressed, and they had no one to comfort them! On the side of their oppressors there was power, and there was no one to comfort them. 2 And I thought the dead who are already dead more fortunate than the living who are still alive. 3 But better than both is he who has not yet been and has not seen the evil deeds that are done under the sun.

4 Then I saw that all toil and all skill in work come from a man's envy of his neighbor. This also is vanity[a] *and a striving after wind.*

5 The fool folds his hands and eats his own flesh.

6 Better is a handful of quietness than two hands full of toil and a striving after wind.

7 Again, I saw vanity under the sun: 8 one person who has no other, either son or brother, yet there is no end to all his toil, and his eyes are never satisfied with riches, so that he never asks, "For whom am I toiling and depriving myself of pleasure?" This also is vanity and an unhappy business.

9 Two are better than one, because they have a good reward for their toil. 10 For if they fall, one will lift up his fellow. But woe to him who is alone when he falls and has not another to lift him up! 11 Again, if two lie together, they keep warm, but how can one keep warm alone? 12 And though a man might prevail against one who is alone, two will withstand him—a threefold cord is not quickly broken.

13 Better was a poor and wise youth than an old and foolish king who no longer knew how to take advice. 14 For he went from prison to the throne, though in his own kingdom he had been born poor. 15 I saw all the living who move about under the sun, along with that[b] *youth who was to stand in the king's*[c] *place. 16 There was no end of all the people, all of whom he led. Yet those who come later will not rejoice in him. Surely this also is vanity and a striving after wind.*

a The Hebrew term *hebel* can refer to a "vapor" or "mere breath"; also verses 7, 8, 16 (see note on 1:2) **b** Hebrew *the second* **c** Hebrew *his*

Overview: Ecclesiastes 4 gathers together reflections on the various oppressions suffered by the poor and the futility of labor driven by envy, and it concludes with the reflections on the solace offered by friendship and community. Johannes Brenz gives eloquent lament to the sea of troubles that afflict the poor and the powerless, making their lives a living death, and holds out the hope of eschatological judgment. Jean de Serres registers the indignation of the Preacher for the violence done against the poor, a fact that undercuts the Stoic notion that virtue is its own reward, while Luther draws on a wealth of pastoral experience to unpack the connection between envy and the human propensity to endless toil—without losing his sense of humor. When it comes to the Preacher's observation that "two are better than one" (Eccles 4:9), now an ecumenical mainstay of wedding liturgies, several of our Reformation-era interpreters acknowledge the legitimacy of this application to the companionship of husband and wife, though all root it in the deeper theological-anthropological understanding of humanity having been created for community.

4:1-8 *No End to Toil*

Injustice Makes Life a Living Death. Johannes Brenz: The poets tell of a many-headed hydra, a huge monster, which hides in the swamp, crying out loud. When one head is cut off, immediately many are reborn in its place. So also it happens in this world, that when one trouble is removed, many new ones are immediately reborn in its place. For it seems as though one misfortune or another is always ready to befall us, so that we are never not entangled in uproars and miseries. Although there is more than a little in the preceding chapters about the miseries and afflictions of this world that Solomon has enumerated, now he urges us to wait and ask for help in all our affairs from the Lord alone, and from our God. Up to this point he seems scarcely to have addressed the issue, and that obliquely; now at last he advances to the heart of the matter, saying: O unworthy deed! O what manners, O what times![†] Is it not an extreme misery in this world, that so many are found oppressed by wrong, and who, though they cry to the Lord, are not heard? There is nowhere here where those poor people can even be consoled, nor can I tell who will bring them help. There is not one of them who can vindicate himself in the courts of empire, for their adversaries are far superior to them in power.

Is not this a terrible calamity? For who is so insane that any lust of this life holds him more firmly? Even the prophets marvel at the miseries of this world, as in the first chapter of Habakkuk: "Why do you look upon the wicked and remain silent, allowing the wicked to subjugate the righteous?" And Psalm 74: "How long, O God, will the enemy taunt? Shall the adversary provoke your name indefinitely? Why do you stay your hand, keep your right hand in your bosom for so long?" Who, I ask you, can you turn a blind eye to the evil schemes of the ungodly, and to the world's immense sea of atrocities, and still maintain their attitude of patience? Is not your name blasphemed in outlandish ways? Are your people not oppressed by the wicked in a most unworthy manner? Therefore, whenever human reason, without faith and without the Word, fixes its eyes on the terrible tragedy of this world, it cannot but be greatly offended, for it thinks that God is either nonexistent, or, if it is even possible to think such a thing, that he is either asleep, or not at home, or untouched by any care for mortal things, and so they think that God winks as people riot among themselves, driven by their own lusts, while in the meantime he himself sits happy and secure in his heaven.

And so at last his line of argument comes to this, that the lot of the dead (indeed, even more that of those who were never born, nor had any taste of this calamity) is much better than that of those who live and are thus exposed to so many hardships and afflictions. But this grave and dangerous scandal must be cut off by faith in the Word of the Lord. For he teaches in the Word of God that the cross, affliction, and suffering are the straightest way to eternal salvation and the very workshop in which life, salvation, and all happiness are wrought. This is why he allows his people to be oppressed so frequently, and for the wicked to exercise tyranny over his people according to their whims, so that they may fall headlong deeper and deeper into the sewer of their impiety and crimes. And finally, by these things the faith of the pious is tested, as gold is by fire, and made firm, until the day of the last judgment, when all ambiguity will be destroyed and all things, now thrown into confusion on every side, will be made straight and level. The Ecclesiastes of Solomon.[1]

For the Oppressed, Death Seems Better than Life. Jean de Serres: Here he sets out a third doubt, why happiness does not consist in virtue itself, by reason of the appalling disorder in human affairs, in which the good and the guiltless are everywhere afflicted and oppressed. For lewd and profligate people are always looking for ways to give vent to lust and presumption against good people, inflicting all manner of injury on them in their rage, and railing with impunity against them, being devoid in themselves of all comfort and help. What trial could be devised that is sharper and bitterer than this? Now in the midst of so great a confusion and disorder, how can life truly be life? For when the affairs of the world are so tossed up and down by the storm and tempest of such great troubles, that those whose life ought to be defended by all are molested even by the very ones

[1]Brenz, *Ecclesiastes Solomonis, cum commentariis*, Pro. 75r; citing Hab 1:13; Ps 74:10-11. [†]Brenz's rhetoric echoes the famous expression of disgust from Cicero's *First Oration Against Catiline*: "O tempora, O mores!" (1.2).

who hold power and authority—when, in short, nothing is safe from the wickedness and presumption of depraved people, death seems preferable to life, since it sets us free from such agonies and harms. COMMENTARY ON SOLOMON'S ECCLESIASTES.[2]

THE RESULTS OF OPPRESSION. THE ENGLISH ANNOTATIONS: Here we may observe: (1) The sad condition of people under the power of oppressors when they have not so much abatement of their misery as to be pitied. (2)The cruelty of powerful oppressors that deters others from showing compassion to those whom they oppress. (3) The dangerous temptation that oppression exposes people to, even to be weary of life, as we see in the cases of Job, Elijah, and others. (4) The inconvenience in cases of difficulty, which relate in any way to conscience, to consult with carnal reason, which will easily lead us to extremes. ANNOTATIONS ON ECCLESIASTES 4:3.[3]

HOW TO MAKE FUN OF THE WORLD. MARTIN LUTHER: This is another kind of calamity and hindrance to the efforts and counsels of human beings. Just as slander and oppression are dominant among those who are great and powerful, so among the common people there is nothing but envy, rivalry, hatred, and so on. "Come down to the common people," he says, "and look at the craftsmen. You will find craftsmen with an evil will; you will sense their wickedness, fraud, cheating, and disparagement of one another, how they constantly hate and envy one another." If someone has ability, they arouse hostility. Anyone who is a good craftsman has a thousand people who hate them, and it happens as the poet says, "The potter envies the potter, the smith envies the smith, and the poet envies the poet."[†] This is the downfall and the normal course of all craftsmen. Imagine someone who wants to learn a craft from which they hope in the future to have a happy life or a livelihood. If they learn it well and are preeminent over others, they will have the envy and the hatred of many. What are they to do then? Should they stop? Should they not learn anything? No, they should do their work in accordance with their abilities and commit their work to God. What are we to do in our studies? Should we stop because our students do not accept this or that, or because the learned despise us? No, you do what you are doing, and meanwhile wait for the appointed time. You know that it is a good thing to teach others, and so do not pay attention to the world or to your own counsels. Wherever you look, there will be troubles. We today want to be of service to Germany through the gospel, and we used to hope that everyone would embrace it. But the very people whom we were aiding to be free from the tyranny of the pope are covering us with their excrement, and those whose helpers we thought we would be are treading us underfoot. What are we to do here? Should we not become indignant? Should we not let everything go? No. Let other people envy, despise, and persecute. We, in accordance with our abilities, will stick to our teaching, working, writing, and learning, because this is what God wills. For no one who only wants to do the right thing will ever be without envy in the world. We should not prematurely define the hour in which our labor is to succeed; God will see to that. But you just do your job and do what God places into your hands. Nor should you suppose that everything can be set right by you, that all rulers will be good and all craftsmen harmonious and honest. . . .

When I was new as a preacher, I seriously undertook to make everyone good. But people said to me, and truly, "He has too rakish a bill to be able to make old rascals pious." The same thing happens in all positions. This evil is present in every way of life. Therefore the best thing is to enjoy the things that you have in the present, to do everything in the present, and to let what is evil flow past you. This is the way to make fun of the world. In short, anyone who wants to live quietly should put the proposition to themselves that in the world they will see nothing but vanity. They

[2]Serres, *Commentarius, in Solomonis Ecclesiasten*, 244-45.
[3]Downame, ed., *English Annotations*, 7B3r*.

should not be sad if something evil happens, but they should rather be happy with the good things that are present. If you are thrust into the obligation of having to help make things better, do what is permissible, and God will do what he wills. But if you want to go beyond this and mingle with the world, straighten every curve, cure every evil, and throw Satan out of the world, you will cause yourself nothing but labor and sorrow. You will accomplish no more than if you wanted to forbid the Elbe to flow. Human affairs refuse to be, and cannot be, governed by human will, but he who created all things also rules them by his will. Annotations on Ecclesiastes.[4]

The Vanity of Common Life. Jean de Serres: He notes great vanity also in the experience of common life. Human society is preserved by relationships of mutual exchange, and among the various social orders there is a harmony amid the difference and diversity—when people carry themselves as they ought to. But he teaches that so great is the envy that bursts into flame among people of every station that the arrows of jealously are especially concentrated on those who have handled their affairs best above all others. For so I understand the words "All labor and all rectitude in work"—that is, when a person so orders their affairs that they proceed according to the intention of the mind. The word *kišrôn* therefore indicates both industry and diligence, and also the happy outcome of one's labor. . . . But envy is a great hindrance to necessary and profitable things in life, yet often it follows hard on those who handle their matters actively and with good success. Therefore he suggests that there is great vanity in that kind of life, as is commonly said in the proverb "Envy follows riches," for the complaints of the envious are unrelenting. Thus, "potter is angry with potter," and so forth.[†] Commentary on Solomon's Ecclesiastes.[5]

[4]LW 15:63-65 (WA 20:75-76). [†]Hesiod, *Works and Days* 25.
[5]Serres, *Commentarius, in Solomonis Ecclesiasten*, 248-49. [†]Hesiod, *Works and Days* 25.

Envy Makes Little Things Appear Large. Michael Jermin: Having considered the sinful vanity of malice that oppresses right, the Preacher now considers the sinful vanity of envy, which opposes right action, saying, "I considered all travail and every right work . . . that for this a person is envied." When Abraham had rescued Lot and conquered those kings by whom he was taken prisoner, afterward the word of the Lord came to him, saying, "Fear not Abraham, I am your shield." If this had been spoken to him before the battle, it might have been done to encourage him, but being spoken after the battle and victory, these words seem to arm him against a new combat against envy, which his valiant deeds were about to bring upon him. For this is the difference between envy and other vices: the latter are cured by the good examples of others, but the goodness of others is that from which envy arises. Old Jacob, speaking of his son Joseph, says that "the archers have sorely grieved him, shot at him, and hated him," and St. Jerome, expounding these words, notes that "here envy is brought in with bow and arrows shooting at that which is spotless," where there is no spot for it to aim at.[†] Or else, as an archer sets up some white thing to be the mark at which he shoots, so it is the whiteness of some good thing against which the height of envy is carried. And therefore, when Jacob says, "an evil beast has devoured my son," he may seem to prophesy, since it was envy that had taken him away, and that is so evil a beast that it always opposes goodness. The Preacher here speaks of "all labor, and every right work": for if it be right, whatsoever it be, though never so small, it is by envy opposed. Envy will seek to hinder the labor in the performance [of any good deed], and will seek to overthrow the rightness of it when it is done. Indeed, it is the nature of envy to make little things appear to be great. For this reason it is reported by Panormitanus that a question was once raised in the court of Frederick the king as to what was good for eyesight. His physicians gave various answers, some saying one thing, others another. Sannizarius answered that envy was very good, and when his hearers smiled at this he explained: because envy makes all things appear bigger than they are.[‡] COMMENTARY UPON THE WHOLE BOOKE OF ECCLESIASTES.[6]

4:9-16 *The Benefits of Community*

A COMMENDATION OF SPIRITUAL COMMUNITY. DENIS THE CARTHUSIAN: This passage (4:9-12) praises life in community. To reinforce this commendation, the Lord and Savior sent his disciples out in pairs on their preaching mission. For this reason also the psalmist sings, "Behold, how good and pleasant it is when brothers dwell together in unity!" This is why those holy and well-tested fathers—Benedict, Bernard, Climacus, and Cassian—so strongly commended the cenobitic life, in which a multitude of people committed to the religious life might fight for God in holy obedience under the command of a spiritual father, and thus assure themselves of greater safety. Indeed, however sublime the life of a solitary hermit may be, they testify that it is beset by dangers and not appropriate for one who has not already been trained in all virtue, as the rule of St. Jerome wisely explains.[†] EXPOSITION OF THE BOOK OF ECCLESIASTES.[7]

COMMUNITY OF GOODS. MARTIN LUTHER: This is counsel from Solomon, in which he recommends a social existence and a community of goods. He commands us to use the things that are present and to work, not for ourselves alone but also for the benefit of others. Community is good for the preservation of things. A miser, however, cannot stand an associate and condemns the community of goods. He amasses things only for himself and is a regular dog in the manger. Such solitary accumulators, who are not human beings but beasts and dogs, are condemned by Solomon. It is more beautiful, he says, to live a social existence with a community of goods, "because if they fall . . . ."

The interpreters distort this passage by applying it to sin and confession. This is how they understand and interpret the text: If someone has fallen into sin and does not have a holy person to whom they can confess, they cannot rise to a life of godliness and grace. But it has already been shown that Solomon is speaking about the course of human life under the sun, in opposition to vain affliction. He is recommending human community and association in the enjoyment of things, against the solitary life of the miser. He wants to say, "The miser is of no use either to himself or to other people. No one can share his pleasure, because he does not live with anyone else and keeps his property all to himself; indeed, in having it he does not have it. Someone whose style of life is not so solitary, on the other hand, has certain definite advantages. Being himself of benefit to others, he also receives benefits from others." As I have said, this community serves to preserve and to increase goods. That is what it means when he adds, "He does not have anyone to lift him up" and "How can one be warm alone?" He does not have help, does not have counsel, does not have comfort in affliction. What does he have when he amasses things only for himself? He merely looks at his money as though it were a picture. ANNOTATIONS ON ECCLESIASTES.[8]

A COMMENDATION OF MARRIAGE. ANTONIO DEL CORRO: How much better by far, and how much wiser is it, I ask you, for one to take a companion and live together with courtesy and familiarity, doing good to one another in turn and sustaining friendship and goodwill, sharing one's possessions and spending them liberally on one's friends, spending time in pleasant conversation and other enjoyable recreations to ease the miseries of

---

[6]Jermin, *A commentary, upon the whole booke of Ecclesiastes*, 15; citing Gen 15:1; 49:23; 37:33. [†]Jermin cites Jerome's *Book of Hebrew Questions on Genesis*, but the relevant passage bears little resemblance to the quotation given here (PL 23:1008). [‡]Panormitanus (Nicolò de' Tudeschi, 1886–1446) was an Italian historian and jurist. The anecdote related here likely refers to the court of Frederick III of Sicily (1272–1337).

[7]DCOO 7:235; citing Ps 133:1. [†]Jerome did not write a monastic rule himself, but he did translate a number of passages from the Egyptian monk Pachomius (292–348), which came to be known as a "rule" (PL 23:59-86).

[8]LW 15:68-69 (WA 20:80-81).

this life! . . . This is why our high Creator and head Workman of all things, desiring to provide for humanity and seeing that a solitary life was not good, even in the first beginning of the world joining woman with man, with the aim that by mutual goodwill they might cherish and nourish one another, and make the other's happiness their study. For if two lie together, all cold is expelled and they warm one another; but one lying alone cannot easily escape the cold, or warm himself up. And then what good will his wealth do for such a miserable wretch, who avoids matrimony out of greed? What heat will his gold get him? What warmth will his silver bring him? A Sermon of King Solomon the Wise.[9]

Good Things Come in Pairs. John Cotton: Society is better than solitariness in all sorts of human affairs. Some think this passage speaks in praise of marriage, preferring it to the single life. But although that has its place here, marriage being one kind of society, yet it is not the case that marriage alone is intended here. Indeed, the proverb of a "threefold cord" does not fit so well with that. Polygamy is not preferred before digamy—that is, before the marriage of two, one man with one woman. First, in voluntary affairs, God would have two workmen put in charge of the ark: Bezalel and Oholiab. . . . In the body all instruments of action are made in pairs—for example, hands, feet, eyes, ears, legs, thighs—though there is only one head. This is because a person has liberty to consult with many heads in any business of importance. Indeed, if the business be urgent and requires haste, he does have another: his wife in his own family. In spiritual things, Christ sent forth his disciples two by two; Paul and Barnabas were sent out together by the Holy Ghost, and when they fell out, Paul took Silas, and Barnabas took Mark. This is why both a pastor and a teacher are appointed to assist one another for one congregation. In all duties two or three have a special assistance. A Brief Exposition.[10]

Work Without Worry. Antonio Brucioli: As he showed the vanity of avarice above, so now he turns to ambition. For many are born into regal authority, and yet they do not remain there. And many come out of prison to the throne and become rich. Others leave the royal life and become servants, so that we know that our efforts are nothing, and that our plans and our efforts accomplish nothing. And so Solomon teaches us to ignore that agitation and worry with which our heart is afflicted. It is certainly important that things are governed correctly, both in the family and in public, but we must avoid excessive worry and agitation over these things. So let us leave to God the world, and the place, and the time. Let no one think that Solomon deprecates virtuous human habits, only that he forbids excess cares and anxieties. The Ecclesiastes of Solomon.[11]

Poverty and Wisdom Often Go Together. John Trapp: "Better is a poor and wise child," such as was Joseph, David, Daniel, and his three comrades: apt to learn, ready to receive instruction, and as careful to follow it. And well does the Preacher join poverty with wisdom, for "somehow or other, poverty is the sister of talent," says Petronius.[†] And, "Poverty is the proper language of philosophy," and wisdom is undervalued little and set by.[‡] Those wisest of the Greeks were very poor: Aristides, Phocion, Pelopidas, Epaminondas, Socrates, Ephialtes. So were those worthies "of whom the world was not worthy; they wandered about in sheep skins and goat skins, being destitute." Sweet-smelling Smyrna was the poorest of all the seven churches, yet hath the richest price set on it. Lactantius died miserably poor; so did Theodorus Gaza, that learned Greek.[§] Of Archimedes thus sings Silius: "He was poor in this world's goods,

[9]Corro, *Sapientissimi regis Salomonis Concio*, 107-9.

[10]Cotton, *A Briefe Exposition upon Ecclesiastes*, 85-86; citing Ex 31:2, 6; Lk 10:1; Acts 13:2; Acts 15:39-40; Rom 12:7-8; Mt 18:20.

[11]Brucioli, *L'Ecclesiasto di Salomo*, E 4.

but to him the secrets of heaven and earth were revealed."◊ But I am fully of Aeneas Sylvius's judgment, that public figures should esteem wisdom as silver, noblemen as gold, princes as pearls.∆ A Commentary or Exposition upon Ecclesiastes.[12]

[12]Trapp, *A Commentary or Exposition upon Ecclesiastes*, 47; citing Heb 11:38; Rev 2:8-11. †Petronius, *Satyricon* 84.4 (LCL 15:244-45). ‡Apuleius, *Apologia* 18.2 (LCL 534:52). §Lactantius (c. 250–c. 325) was an early Christian writer and tutor to the sons of the Emperor Constantine; Theodore Gaza (c. 1398–c. 1475) was a Greek scholar who fled to Italy after the capture of his native city by the Turks. He was widely celebrated for his translations of Aristotle into Latin and for the assistance he gave to Western scholars seeking a better understanding of Greek. Despite this, he had difficulty making a living, and moved from court to court in search of patronage. Shortly after his death, Ermolao Barbo wrote to Pope Sixtus IV lamenting his loss and remarking that "that Greek man outdid all Latins in the task of writing and translating. . . . In my view, he is the only one to rival Antiquity itself." ◊Silius Italicus, *Punica* 14.443 (LCL 278: 296-97). ∆Aeneas Silvius Piccolomini (1405–1464) was an Italian humanist who later became Pope Pius II.

5:1-7 FEAR GOD

1[a]Guard your steps when you go to the house of
God. To draw near to listen is better than to offer
the sacrifice of fools, for they do not know that they
are doing evil. 2[b]Be not rash with your mouth, nor
let your heart be hasty to utter a word before God,
for God is in heaven and you are on earth.
Therefore let your words be few. 3For a dream
comes with much business, and a fool's voice with
many words.

4When you vow a vow to God, do not delay paying
it, for he has no pleasure in fools. Pay what you vow.
5It is better that you should not vow than that you
should vow and not pay. 6Let not your mouth lead
you[c] into sin, and do not say before the messenger[d]
that it was a mistake. Why should God be angry at
your voice and destroy the work of your hands? 7For
when dreams increase and words grow many, there is
vanity;[e] but[f] God is the one you must fear.

a Ch 4:17 in Hebrew **b** Ch 5:1 in Hebrew **c** Hebrew *your flesh* **d** Or *angel* **e** The Hebrew term *hebel* can refer to a "vapor" or "mere breath"; also verse 10 (see note on 1:2) **f** *Or For when dreams and vanities increase, words also grow many; but*

Overview: The first half of this chapter is concerned with matters of right worship and fidelity to vows, both issues of signal concern to Reformation-era interpreters. Martin Luther reads the charge to take care in approaching the house of God (Eccles 5:1) as an admonition to cleave to a middle path between legalism and antinomianism, while the radical Dirk Philips sees in the image of ritual purity a figure for the moral purity required by true discipleship. The Reformed Jean de Serres, by contrast, emphasizes the importance of right worship conducted in accordance with God's Word. On the matter of vows, Denis the Carthusian and Luther, both speaking from personal experience of monastic vows, illustrate the emerging gap between evangelical and Catholic on the binding of the individual conscience.

5:1-3 *Slow to Speak, Quick to Listen*

The Royal Road Is the Middle Path. Martin Luther: The reading of this book has the same effect on senseless people that the preaching of the gospel has on wicked people. For when the latter hear the righteousness of faith and Christian liberty being preached and the righteousness of works being denied, they soon draw the inference: "Then let us not do any works. In fact, let us sin! For faith is sufficient." On the other hand, if works and the fruits of faith are preached, they soon attribute justification to these and look for salvation from that source. Thus it is that the Word of God is always followed by these two effects, presumption and despair, so that it is extremely difficult to stick to the royal road. This little book has the same effects. For when senseless people hear this doctrine, that we should have such a quiet and peaceful heart that we commit everything to God, they draw this inference: "If everything is in the hand of God, we shall not do any works." In the same way others sin in the opposite direction by being excessively solicitous and wanting to measure and control everything in every way. But one should travel on the royal road. Let us work hard and do whatever we can in accordance with the Word of God; let us not, however, measure the work on the basis of our efforts, but commit every effort and plan and outcome to the wisdom of God. Therefore Solomon seems to me to be anticipating an objection here and addressing a salutary exhortation to those who are not traveling in the middle road but are either too negligent of their work or too concerned about it. He advises them to let themselves be governed by the Word of God and meanwhile to work diligently. Annotations on Ecclesiastes.[1]

Guidance on Prayer. Thomas Granger: Here he teaches us how we ought to pray, or to keep our foot or heart in prayer. "Do not be rash with your mouth." That is, when you are about to ask anything of God, or to give him thanks in prayer, do not let your tongue run before your wit; do not let your mind be carried away with roiling imaginations of many broken matters, and confused apprehensions, nor yet your affections unpurged from the scent of sensuality, pride, presumption, or boasting, like the Pharisees; do not babble forth ignorant and heartless formal speeches in the ears of God, as the hypocrites do, who think to be heard on account of the loudness of their noise and the multitude of their words. "And let not your heart be hasty to utter a thing before God." Do not be unadvised in your thoughts, with the intent in God's presence to ask or promise what you think to be good according to your own lust or liking, to give or take as it pleases yourself, as if whatever pleases you must also be pleasing to God. This is simply to doubt God's goodness, his promise of giving, and to limit his power. A Familiar Exposition.[2]

We Must Be Washed Before We Approach God. Dirk Philips: There was placed between the tent of witness and the altar a hand basin, and there was water to wash, for Aaron and his sons washed their hands and feet in it. For they had to wash themselves before entering the tent of witness or coming to the altar; thus the Lord commanded them. This signifies to us that all those who wished to go into the house of the Lord, in order to serve God or make a sacrifice or offering to the Lord, these had to cleanse themselves of all filthiness of spirit and the flesh, and lift up holy hands to God, and wash off with the waters of the Holy Spirit the evil lusts and desires that strive against the soul. For whoever desires to serve and sacrifice to God must do so with a clean heart and a good conscience, and with unfeigned faith, yes, in the Spirit and in truth. Otherwise it is uncleanness and an abomination before the Lord. The Enchiridion.[3]

True Happiness Consists in True Worship. Jean de Serres: "Guard your steps." The tenor of the discourse requires us to regard this verse as the beginning of the fifth chapter.† For it starts not only a new argument but an entirely new topic—indeed, the most important topic in the whole book, as it deals with true happiness. With the intention of urging this and setting it within an earnest fear of God (that is, true piety), he sets down a necessary preface, and diligently teaches how godliness ought to be set forth, so that instead of true religion we should not embrace its naked shadow and show. This new thought is knit and joined together with what has come before, so that we should not take the view of some interpreters, who think that it is a sentence cut off from the rest, with no connection to anything else. Therefore this is the meaning: I have explained in great detail what happiness is not, despite the fact that human reason imagines it to be located in various things or aspects of human experience; I have taught with sound reasons how far from the truth are all those idols, which simply reflect the shifting hues of human variety. Now it remains to show where true happiness lies. . . .

The first law or rule in truly and diligently establishing godliness is that we worship God in the church according to his Word, and that we abhor human fabrications; that we seek for saving doctrine in the church and its true ministry; and that we reverently hear the church when it teaches, wait on her voice, and do not embrace human inventions, but that we worship God with a pure and sound mind according to his Word, which is the rule of his will. For it is great folly and insanity for people to pay worship to whatever they pull

[1]LW 15:74-75 (WA 20:86-87).
[2]Granger, *A Familiar Exposition or Commentarie on Ecclesiastes*, 112-114.
[3]CRR 6:270*; citing Ex 30:17-18.

from their own brains. So this law commands two things for us: that we seek the Word of God in the church with a pure mind, and that we flee from human inventions when it comes to the worship of God. To "take heed of your steps when you enter the house of God" is to worship God with a pure and sound mind; or, to maintain a pure and sound mind in worshiping God. Commentary on Solomon's Ecclesiastes.[4]

Behaving in God's Presence. The English Annotations: He had gone up and down the world, from learning to pleasures, from pleasures to honors, from honors to thrones, to find happiness, and had met with nothing but vanity. Now he sends us to a fitter place to find it, the house of God, whether his temple or other synagogues where God is present with those that serve him. Here they shall find remedies against the vanity of other things and that which will stay and fix their hearts. Only we must take heed of putting vanity into God's worship, lest we be disappointed of our aims there as well as elsewhere. This caveat he gives us in the words "keep your foot" or "each foot." . . . It is serious advice about how you are to behave in God's presence, to look after your heart and affections, letting your heart be fixed, affections composed, and thoughts ordered, so that all is together within to serve him. It is a metaphor taken from people that walk in dangerous places, who take heed of their steps lest they stumble and fall, as well as an allusion to the speech of God to Moses. Annotations on Ecclesiastes 5:1.[5]

5:4-7 *Wisdom Regarding Vows and Dreams*

The Gravity of Religious Vows. Denis the Carthusian: The one who vows something when the urgency is imminent, and then when that necessity ceases grieves the vow and does not fulfill it, that person is an unbeliever. This is why it is foolish to vow things that are impossible; the same applies to vows concerning things that are indifferent to God. Moreover, it is evident from what has been said that it is better to do a good deed that one has vowed than a good deed one has not vowed. Let those religious who do not observe the substance of their vows consider how enormously and gravely they are sinning. Exposition of the Book of Ecclesiastes.[6]

Real and False Vows. Martin Luther: "When you vow a vow to God." This passage has really been thrown around in the church and in the kingdom of the pope, and it is almost the only one with which they urge and support monastic vows. We have spoken about this matter at greater length elsewhere.[†] We do not dispute whether vows should be paid or not paid but whether what they discuss are truly vows. Jerome and Lyra are agreed that a vow should be one that is possible and that redounds to the honor of God. A foolish vow they call something like picking up a piece of straw from the ground or scratching your head with your finger. Moses also lists the kinds of vows and which things may be vowed, namely, a field, a house, food, clothing, our own body, all of which are in our power. Thus the Jews would vow their soul or body to the priests, promising to serve them at some definite time. Beyond this, Moses has no perpetual vow, except for one that he calls anathema, namely, the vow of death, in the last chapter of Leviticus; whatever had been vowed was to be killed, whether it was from among human beings or cattle, as in the case of Jephthah in Judges 11. Therefore if the monks want to make such a thing of perpetual vows, they would soon be strangled—if, that is, they want to defend their vows on the basis of Moses. Otherwise all vows must be possible and temporary, as you could, for example, vow your body to the Lord, or a field, a meadow, a garment for a certain time, so that a priest or a Levite would use it. This method of vowing was very valuable for

[4]Serres, *Commentarius, in Solomonis Ecclesiasten*, 248-49. [†]In the Vulgate Bible, this verse was the concluding passage of Eccles 4; Serres's renumeration agrees with most modern translations.
[5]Downame, ed., *English Annotations*, 7B4v*; citing Ps 73:16; 4:6; 57:7; 103:1; Ex 3:5; 19:21; Josh 5:15.

[6]DCOO 7:239.

the Levites, to provide for them more easily and more comfortably. God established rules about these things in order to provide for them this way. But our vows are completely foolish, not to say wicked, because we vow poverty and obedience, which are commanded in the gospel and apply to all Christians. But the vow of virginity is impossible; therefore, on the basis of the judgment of Jerome and Lyra, these vows are null and void. Besides, this passage of Solomon seems to me to pertain obviously to those who deviate to the right, who upon hearing that their efforts do not avail do not want to do any works at all. For that is how a fool argues: "If I do not accomplish anything by my cares and efforts, I will not do anything. I will not pay even what I have vowed." In opposition to these despisers he says, "Do what God commands. I am not setting you free from toil, but commanding you to do what God has commanded. He has commanded, however, that if you vow you must pay what you have vowed. Therefore if you have vowed something and if you have something to pay it from, it must be paid." Summarize all of this as follows: "Listen, keep silent, and do what is to be done, what the Lord commands." Annotations on Ecclesiastes.[7]

Interpret Dreams with Care. John Trapp: As in the multitude of dreams, so in many words. There may be some matter in some of either, but neither is lacking in vanities. Dreams are of different sorts. Epicurus judged them all vain. The people of Telmessus, says Tertullian, held that no dreams were devoid of meaning.[†] But no wise person has ever doubted that some dreams are divine, some diabolical, and some natural, "the special support of natural oracles," as one might say, and good symptoms and indications of the natural constitution. That saying of the Philosopher has some truth in it, that a good person may be distinguished from a bad, though not by their sleep, yet by their dreams in their sleep.[‡] "But fear God." And so eschew this evil of fond babbling (in God's service especially), which is no less a vanity than plain doting, and procures divine displeasure. The one who does not fear God's wrath is sure to feel it. A Commentary or Exposition upon Ecclesiastes.[8]

Fearful Things Pass as Dreams. John Donne: All fearful things pass away as dreams, as vanities, to those who fear the Lord. They come at them, but in vain, if they are established in that fear. In Christ, there was no bone broken. In the one who fears the Lord, no constant purpose is ever shaken. Sermon on Psalm 34:11.[9]

[7]LW 15:79-80 (WA 20:92-93); citing Lev 27:14-25, 28-29. [†]See, for example, Luther's treatise *On Monastic Vows* (1521), LW 44:251-400.

[8]Trapp, *A Commentary or Exposition upon Ecclesiastes*, 57; citing Ps 90:11. [†]Tertullian, *De anima* 46. [‡]Aristotle, *Nicomachean Ethics* 1.13.

[9]Donne, *Works*, 5:285*.

5:8–6:12 The Futility of Wealth

[8]If you see in a province the oppression of the poor and the violation of justice and righteousness, do not be amazed at the matter, for the high official is watched by a higher, and there are yet higher ones over them. [9]But this is gain for a land in every way: a king committed to cultivated fields.[a]

[10]He who loves money will not be satisfied with money, nor he who loves wealth with his income; this also is vanity. [11]When goods increase, they increase who eat them, and what advantage has their owner but to see them with his eyes? [12]Sweet is the sleep of a laborer, whether he eats little or much, but the full stomach of the rich will not let him sleep.

[13]There is a grievous evil that I have seen under the sun: riches were kept by their owner to his hurt, [14]and those riches were lost in a bad venture. And he is father of a son, but he has nothing in his hand. [15]As he came from his mother's womb he shall go again, naked as he came, and shall take nothing for his toil that he may carry away in his hand. [16]This also is a grievous evil: just as he came, so shall he go, and what gain is there to him who toils for the wind? [17]Moreover, all his days he eats in darkness in much vexation and sickness and anger.

[18]Behold, what I have seen to be good and fitting is to eat and drink and find enjoyment[b] *in all the toil with which one toils under the sun the few days of his life that God has given him, for this is his lot. [19]Everyone also to whom God has given wealth and possessions and power to enjoy them, and to accept his lot and rejoice in his toil—this is the gift of God. [20]For he will not much remember the days of his life because God keeps him occupied with joy in his heart.*

6 *There is an evil that I have seen under the sun, and it lies heavy on mankind: [2]a man to whom God gives wealth, possessions, and honor, so that he lacks nothing of all that he desires, yet God does not give him power to enjoy them, but a stranger enjoys them. This is vanity;*[c] *it is a grievous evil. [3]If a man fathers a hundred children and lives many years, so that the days of his years are many, but his soul is not satisfied with life's good things, and he also has no burial, I say that a stillborn child is better off than he. [4]For it comes in vanity and goes in darkness, and in darkness its name is covered. [5]Moreover, it has not seen the sun or known anything, yet it finds rest rather than he. [6]Even though he should live a thousand years twice over, yet enjoy*[d] *no good—do not all go to the one place?*

[7]All the toil of man is for his mouth, yet his appetite is not satisfied.[e] *[8]For what advantage has the wise man over the fool? And what does the poor man have who knows how to conduct himself before the living? [9]Better is the sight of the eyes than the wandering of the appetite: this also is vanity and a striving after wind.*

[10]Whatever has come to be has already been named, and it is known what man is, and that he is not able to dispute with one stronger than he. [11]The more words, the more vanity, and what is the advantage to man? [12]For who knows what is good for man while he lives the few days of his vain[f] *life, which he passes like a shadow? For who can tell man what will be after him under the sun?*

a The meaning of the Hebrew verse is uncertain **b** Or *and see good* **c** The Hebrew term *hebel* can refer to a "vapor" or "mere breath"; also verses 4, 9, 11 (see note on 1:2) **d** Or *see* **e** Hebrew *filled* **f** The Hebrew term *hebel* can refer to a "vapor" or "mere breath" (see note on 1:2)

Overview: The second half of Ecclesiastes 5 and the entirety of Ecclesiastes 6 offer extended reflections on the role of money, power, and labor in human life—and their failure to satisfy the deepest human needs. Interpreters from all traditions in this period register and amplify the

Preacher's indignation at the oppression of the poor by the rich, though the admonition against wonder in Ecclesiastes 5:8 sets the tone for much of what follows: these injustices are evil, though not unexpected; they cannot be wholly cured in this life, but God will surely hold those who perpetrate them accountable. Antonio Brucioli agrees with Martin Luther in finding solace in the good gifts God gives us in the midst of these difficult conditions, while Jean de Serres balances pointed denunciations of avarice and *polypragmosynē*, or meddling in the affairs of others (one of Philipp Melanchthon's favorite themes in his commentary on Proverbs) with a moving description of the contentment that comes from faithful labor in one's vocation.

5:8-20 *The Vanity of Wealth*

Oppression Trains God's Elect. Denis the Carthusian: "If you see the oppression of the poor," which are carried out by the rich and the powerful, "and violent judgments," that is, censures, punishments, or other similar actions, which impious judges and rulers inflict on the weak and the powerless, "and subvert justice in the province," that is, oppressing the innocent and pursuing the righteous with persecutions, "do not wonder at this"; that is, do not marvel at such events with undue astonishment, confusion, or mistrust. For certain immature people, not yet sufficiently enlightened or practiced in the Scriptures, are wont to marvel, throw themselves into uproar, be greatly agitated and tied up in knots when they perceive the just, the wise, the innocent, and the saints to be afflicted, robbed, driven off, and slain by the worst of the wicked—as though the Scriptures *didn't* say, "Many are the afflictions of the righteous"; and, "Through many tribulations we must enter the kingdom of God"; and, "Blessed are those who suffer persecution for righteousness." For in this life the elect and the just undergo a purgation at the hands of the ungodly; they are drilled and sped on their way to the heavenly kingdom. Exposition of the Book of Ecclesiastes.[1]

Wicked Rulers Will Not Escape Judgment. Jean de Serres: "If you see the oppression of the poor." He spoke about this trial beginning in Ecclesiastes 3:16—namely, how it sometimes happens that ungodliness holds sway in the seat of justice and judgment; in other words, how law and equity are often broken by the magistrate (who ought to be their defender!) under the color of law, and how the innocent are wrongly punished by the very ones under whose guard and protection they ought to be safe from the injuries of wicked people. This trial also greatly troubled Job, David, and Jeremiah. He first touches on this when he says, "If you see a poor man"—who ought to be raised up by the help and protection of the magistrate—ground down "in a province" by the power of the mighty, or under pretense of law (this he calls *gēzel mišpāt*, that is, judicial plunder, the violation of justice itself), and by those who hold the highest authority. Do not be surprised and wonder whether it escapes God's notice, or whether he simply does not care, as though such things fell outside of the power and providence of God. Have you taken leave of your wits to wonder whether God has a care for human affairs, or whether he actually sees these outrages and confusions?

Yet human reason doubts the providence of God because of these disorders, and so Solomon responds with an answer to this doubt: the Most High certainly watches over those who are on high: he sees their deeds and watches what they do, and he will judge them—either now or in the future. And when it says, "those who are raised up over them," it refers to those who exercise authority over the poor, the vulnerable, and those with less power. For princes and powerful men imagine themselves to wield infinite power over those who are their inferiors, and no doubt they do occupy a higher position than their inferior—but God is higher than them. Why do they hold this power and

[1]DCOO 7:240-41; citing Ps 34:19; Acts 14:22; Mt 5:10.

authority? To maintain their own leisure? Certainly not, for God is the judge of the world. But he will execute the heaviest punishment on those who abuse their authority, and on that account he watches and notes their dealings. And not in vain does he watch them. Many ancient authorities have noted what the poet says: "Dreaded monarchs have power over their own flocks; monarchs themselves are under the power of Jove" (that is: God).[†]

To sum up, these outrages are not hidden from God, who is not only the creator of all things but also their moderator. For by his providence he governs all parts of the world, and especially human affairs. He has regard both for the godly and the ungodly, and therefore tyrants and other violators will not get off scot-free when they wrong those who are weaker, for they too will render an account of their whole lives to God, who is the highest lord and king. Therefore he warns us, "do not be amazed"—that is, we ought not to cling to this anxious and perplexing thought, or doubt God's providence, which shines forth with greater majesty and clarity when it wisely orders things that appear tangled and disordered, and constantly directs them to the best outcome. COMMENTARY ON SOLOMON'S ECCLESIASTES.[2]

PLOW WITH THE HORSES YOU HAVE. MARTIN LUTHER: After his treatise on piety he returns nicely to his catalog of vanities. He often repeats the same thing, as happens in sermons. Therefore he says, "I have said that you should fear God. Otherwise you will not do anything good. In fact, you will say that there is no God, unless you are fortified with the fear of God and the acknowledgment of the truth. For you will see the oppression of the poor and the subversion of justice. Then you will murmur, 'How unjustly these things happen!' and you will say, 'Where is God? Why does he put up with these things?'" It is against these thoughts and these offenses that Solomon is strengthening us. "As for you," he says, "fear God and think to yourself, 'This will have its Judge.' If you cannot improve the judge, think to yourself that such is the course of the world and that no one can bring it about that all judges should be just. This belongs only to God and the highest King." No one understands this except people who have been in public administration. I myself have seen and experienced in the monastery that many incompetent people there were promoted to the position of directing affairs or of holding office, a situation that cannot be corrected. Thus when our Staupitz wished and desired to promote the best men to all positions, he could not do so. "One must," he used to say, "plow with the horses one has."[†] Or, as the proverb says, "He who does not have horses must plow with oxen." That is how it is in human affairs. Sometimes there is a good prince, but he still cannot set all the judges straight or bring it about that all the officials and judges are good and just; nevertheless, he is obliged to have magistrates. Thus wise men are concerned and take care that the common people be provided with good laws and are obedient, but the latter only murmur and complain about the violence and incompetence of the judges. When you see such things, keep in mind that these are the vanities of the world, and do not flee from the world, as the monks flee into the desert. . . . Emperor Frederick III's famous saying is often quoted: "He who does not know how to dissemble does not know how to rule."[‡] You should add, "He who does not know how to dissemble does not know how to live." If you want to live in the world, learn to see this.

Is it a matter of doing nothing, then? By no means. One must act and work; but what you cannot bring about, you must dissemble. Thus a wise head of the household must dissemble many things and overlook the things that offend him. For it is impossible that everything be done rightly and without injustice. Therefore this book teaches you to have a quiet and peaceful heart in the affairs of this life, so that when you hear or see evil, you do not become indignant but say, "Such is the trouble in the course of the world. There is no other way here." On the other hand, when you see good

[2]Serres, *Commentarius, in Solomonis Ecclesiasten*, 313-16. [†]Horace, *Odes* 3.1.5-6 (LCL 33:140-41).

things, you should say, "Blessed be God, who governs things in such a way that he does not permit only evil to happen or to be committed, but mixes good with evil." Do what you can; commit the rest to God and bear it, in accordance with the proverb: "Whoever cannot lift a heavy stone should let it lie and lift a stone that he can pick up." Therefore when you see evil in princes, the abuse of vested authority by magistrates, wicked judgments by judges, the murmuring of the common people, quarrels among the wise, and so on, just keep in mind, "God will set these things straight." ANNOTATIONS ON ECCLESIASTES.[3]

REMEDIES AGAINST AVARICE. JEAN DE SERRES: Here Solomon sets down appropriate remedies against avarice, which tends to generate endless anxiety of mind. For the lust to possess has seized on the minds of all people and taken deep root inside. In this mad rage of desire the mind cannot help but be miserably tortured. It was necessary, therefore, that many reasons be gathered together so as to fortify our minds against so strong a poison, that by seeing and exploring the danger of avarice, we should come to loathe it more vehemently. The first reason comes by way of demonstrating the great harm that comes to "the one who loves silver," for the lust to possess is insatiable, and the love of money only increases as the money itself increases. And this indeed is a characteristic of sinful behavior, that the more one coaxes it, the more ferociously it rages and jeers. And indeed, the books of the heathen writers are full of such refutations against the mad intemperance of avarice.† Next he says the same thing in different words: "He that loves a multitude"—that is, of money (for *hāmôn* signifies wealth [in Hebrew], just as *copiae* signifies riches [in Latin])—is "without fruit"; that is to say, the fruitfulness of riches withers for them, for avaricious people do not use the present riches which they have, but are tormented with the desire of wealth to come. Therefore they undertake great labors, but at no profit to themselves, for they are always lacking, being poor in the midst of great wealth, and they cannot enjoy what is theirs any more than what is not. Thus they defraud themselves of the use of their own goods, which is the whole point of having riches in the first place. COMMENTARY ON SOLOMON'S ECCLESIASTES.[4]

WHEN RICHES BECOME A GALLOWS. THOMAS GRANGER: The unprofitableness of riches is figured by a gradation, thus: a person has not only no good by them, except to look on them (v. 11), but also they deprive them of their necessary and natural rest by night (v. 12); nor is this all they do, but they positively bring them to ruin often (v. 13). The former words include a comparison of evils among themselves, to illustrate this evil of riches—as if he should say: there are many infirmities and evils incident to humanity, and to his outward state, to increase vanity, anger, sorrow, grief, etc. Yet this is a sore evil (*ḥôlâ*), or evil disease—even a sickness to death—that a person should spend all their days in labor, depriving their body and mind of recreations, and such comforts as the use of riches bring, with the expectation that in their latter days their joy may be full and perfect, without any mixture of care or fear of want, either for themselves or for their children. But it falls out quite contrary to his expectation—namely, that those things which were gathered, kept, and preserved for their good should turn out to work for their destruction. This was the outcome of Haman's aspiration to promotion, honor, wealth, friendship, and so on. Little did he think that all his plots for honor and wealth should

[3]LW 15:83-84 (WA 20:96-98). †Johann von Staupitz (c. 1460–1524) was a Roman Catholic theologian and monk, the superior at the Augustinian order in Erfurt, and Luther's confessor. ‡The Latin maxim *qui nescit dissimulare, nescit imperare* has alternately been ascribed to the emperor Frederick III (1415–1493), or more frequently, to the French king Louis XI, "the Prudent" (1423–1483).

[4]Serres, *Commentarius, in Solomonis Ecclesiasten*, 325-26. †For example, see Plutarch's short treatise *On the Love of Wealth*, which describes avarice in similar terms: "Drink allays the desire of drink, and food is a remedy for hunger . . . but neither silver nor gold allays the craving for money, nor does the greed of gain ever cease from acquiring new gains." *Moralia* 523 (LCL 405:8-9).

have been a rope and a gallows to hang him on, when so many others had been hanged with less cost and labor. But the more cost, the greater the infamy; the higher the rise, the greater the fall. A Familiar Exposition.[5]

Enjoy God's Gifts and Use Them Well. Antonio Brucioli: This is the conclusion of the whole book, or at least of the argument set out in chapters 2 and 3. Solomon does not here condemn riches and power, nor does he prohibit us from acquiring them. But rather he teaches us that we must acknowledge them as gifts from God and be ready to lay down our cares, so that we wait on these things from God in faith and patiently endure their loss when he wills it. Therefore riches are not to be thrown away, because God has not given them so that we may toss them aside or abstain from their use; rather, we should make good use of them, and give to those who are in need. And this is the general theme and outlook of the whole book, that Solomon wants to warn us away from vain cares, so that we can gladly enjoy present things without undue worry about the future. And the one to whom God gives such a gift will not brood over the days of their life—that is, their heart is not troubled by cares and concerns for earthly things, nor for the future, because God fills their heart with joy. And so they have joy here in the midst of weariness, and surrounded by evils they enter paradise. But for those who are impious and miserly, and who do not follow this example and use well the things of this life, their torment begins here, and it will drag them to hell. The Ecclesiastes of Solomon.[6]

Summary of the Book. Martin Luther: This is the conclusion of this entire book or argument, which was also stated earlier in chapters 2 and 3. And here you see that Solomon does not condemn riches, nor does he forbid that we acquire riches or food or drink. But he calls these things gifts of God in order to teach us to put down our anxieties; then we shall wait for all of these things from God by faith and, when God wills, we shall surrender them with patience, just as Abraham gave his son back to God. Therefore riches are not to be rejected. Nor are they granted to us by God for the purpose of our rejecting them or abstaining from them, but rather so that we use them and distribute them to the poor. This statement is the interpreter of the entire book: Solomon intends to forbid vain anxieties, so that we may happily enjoy the things that are present and not care at all about the things that are in the future, lest we permit the present moment, our moment, to slip away. For this is his lot—that is, this is what he gets out of it. For he will not remember the days of his life—that is, his heart is not swollen with anxiety and care either about the things that are present or about the things that are in the future. Because God keeps him occupied with joy in his heart. In this way he has joy in his toil here, and here in the midst of evils he enters into paradise. On the other hand, wicked people and misers and as many as do not follow this example in using the things of this life begin already here to suffer torment and to be thrust down into hell. Annotations on Ecclesiastes.[7]

Fair Recompense. The English Annotations: God answers all his labors with joy and gives him such joy of heart as is a full compensation for his labor. As money is said to answer to all things in a proportionate value to them all, so shall his joy bear a full value to all the labor that was taken for it. There are other expositions, but this is the most genuine and natural. Annotations on Ecclesiastes 5:20.[8]

[5]Granger, *A Familiar Exposition or Commentarie on Ecclesiastes*, 124-25.
[6]Brucioli, *L'Ecclesiasto di Salomo*, G 1.
[7]LW 15:93 (WA 20:108).
[8]Downame, ed., *English Annotations*, 7C1v*; citing Eccles 10:19.

6:1-12 *Contentment in Life*

A Warning Against Overparenting. Jean de Serres: "There is an evil," indeed, a very great and most miserable calamity, and still many people are trapped in its snares. For this reason, he describes a rich man, lacking nothing for a pleasant and quiet life, who nevertheless is miserably ill at ease. The world is full of such people. . . . "A man to whom God has given." He sets out this misery (against which he has already warned us many times) that the avaricious person has no use for their own riches—indeed, they may as well be without them, since they are given by God to be used. Here he expands on the uselessness of riches in two ways, for neither can the avaricious person use their wealth while they are living (being such a tightwad), nor can their heirs (their children, that is) when they are dead, but often it falls to strangers. The hope of children, in whom parents seem in a certain sense to be reborn, thrusts so sharp a spur into the minds of people to pile up goods so that their children have the means to live honorably. But the Lord very often disappoints this hope, so as to demonstrate that children are his gift—and especially good children. Therefore, seeking to make provision for our children, we ought to set all our hopes and theirs in the immortal and omnipotent God, who according to his promise is not only our father but theirs as well. This is why it is crazy to obsess with worry over your children when you do not even know if they shall live or die. The poet says this very well: "He who, from regard to his heir, pinches and spares overmuch is next door to a madman."† Commentary on Solomon's Ecclesiastes.[9]

Missing Life's Pleasures. Martin Luther: "To see the sun" is Hebrew for "to enjoy things and take pleasure in them." For this physical life has the sun as a sort of very sacred divine power, one that is supremely necessary for moral people. Without it everything seems and is sad, as Christ also says: "He who walks in the darkness does not know where he goes. But if anyone walks in the day, he does not stumble, because he sees the light of this world." Therefore it is a most pleasant thing that the sun shines. But misers do not look at the light, they do not view the sun; that is, they do not think what a good thing light is, nor do they look at any creature as something to enjoy and to use well. For they have lost every consideration of the blessings, the creatures, and the things of God on account of their greed. They never see what an outstanding gift of God it is that the sun rises every day. They think of nothing, wonder at nothing, yearn for nothing—except money. In the same way the ambitious person looks at nothing except honors. The lover does not look at his own wife but is always looking at another woman. That is, such people do not enjoy the good creatures that are present now. Thus the wicked begin their hell in this life, because they are deprived of the use of all the creatures and gifts of God, so that they never see the sun, which we nevertheless have every day. In other words, they do not rejoice in the gifts of God but are always looking for something else. Annotations on Ecclesiastes.[10]

Work Is for the Body, Not the Soul. Cardinal Cajetan: Thus far he has argued as if on the basis of examples to support his conclusion [that human labors are vain]. Now, he argues as if on the basis of reason, because to all appearances it seems like human labor looks to the mouth—that is, a person's labor is repaid with food. For the work of every person is ordained to their sustenance, and thereby a person's good consists in food and drink, and the perception of the good from their own labor. "But his soul will not be filled with good things." According to the Hebrew, it should be: "and yet his soul will not be filled." To exclude the objection against the assumed proposition (namely, that all the labor of a person is for their mouth), he asserts that the soul will not be satisfied. For one

[9]Serres, *Commentarius, in Solomonis Ecclesiasten*, 337-38. †Horace, *Epistle* 1.5 (LCL 194:280).

[10]LW 15:96-97 (WA 20:112); citing Jn 12:35; 11:9.

may object by saying that the proposition is false, since there are many human labors that are not carried out for sustenance but for the sake of the soul, as evidenced by those who labor for honor, power, and so on. When faced with this objection he says, "and yet his soul will not be filled"—that is, he broadens the argument to say that "the appetite of the soul" will not be fulfilled; it is vain and will not attain to that which it desires. This is why a person's labor for the appetite of the soul is vain, since it does not satisfy the appetite. And so it remains that "all the labor of a person is for his mouth" inasmuch as they are pursuing their aim, and attaining that to which they were ordained: joy in their labor. For this they attain by eating and drinking, and by enjoying the good that comes from labor or wealth. The upshot of all this is that labor does not fulfill its aim relative to the soul (because it cannot offer the soul fulfilment), but relative to the mouth, as experience testifies. Therefore every person's labor is directed to their mouth by its very nature. The Parables of Solomon [and Ecclesiastes], Corrected by the Original Hebrew.[11]

To Each Their Allotted Share. Martin Luther: God assigns to each person their toil in accordance with their powers and in keeping with their calling. In German we say it this way: "Each one has their allotted share." To each one God has assigned their portion. A boy ought to toil in one way, a man in another; a magistrate ought to toil in one way, a private citizen in another. He wants you to be trained by means of infantile duties or labors, as though you were an infant, while the prince is trained with arduous and great ones. This is the source of the common saying: "Whatever one's official position is, that is the apron they receive." In this way, therefore, he calls us away from alien anxieties to our own business. Nor does he forbid toil. In fact, he declares that one must toil, but he wants you to do your duty happily in accordance with your assigned task and to leave other things to other people. He wants us to enjoy our pleasure, but in God, so that we do not abandon ourselves to pleasure when it is present, as the wicked do, nor grieve when it is absent but bear it with equanimity. You should, he says, have a happy spirit and an active body, but in such a way that you abide in your assigned place. Do not be like the envious person, who pursues what belongs to others: the merchant envies the soldier; the soldier counts his troubles and envies the merchant; the old man envies the youth. We turn our gaze away from our own real happiness, and with intense distress we look at the happiness of other people. No one is able to consider the good things they have or to be content with their lot; if they were to consider themselves, they would not long so much for what belongs to others. Annotations on Ecclesiastes.[12]

Contentment and Vocation. Jean de Serres: It is as though he were to say that all human labor is directed for the purpose of enabling the means and the ability to lead a comfortable life; but the avaricious person is so deranged as to be never satisfied. And so I ask you, what then is the point of their abundance, when there is no actual use of that which is over and above? Therefore, truly is it said, "Look out and be on guard against avarice, for one's life does not consist in abundant goods"; and, "Keep your life free from avarice, and be content with what you have." So long as we have what nature prescribes, which doubtless is very little—"if we have food and clothing, with these we will be content"—all the rest are useless burdens, the excrement of deranged desire. . . . Therefore I take the words "for the mouth" (*lĕpîhû*) as referring to those things that pertain to this life, and with which a person may nourish themselves *pour sa bouche*. Others interpret these words differently, taking them to refer to the manner and measure (which is indeed their usual signification in Scripture); the meaning

[11]Cajetan, *Parabolae Salomonis ad veritatem Hebraicam castigatae*, 335.

[12]LW 15:98 (WA 20:113-114).

would thus be that to each person there is appointed a certain measure, according to which they ought to labor, according to their vocation. For there are distinct duties for different persons and for different ages. A child ought to labor one way, a man another way; a magistrate one way, a person in private life another. So then this text calls us back from worrying about other people's business to consider our own duties, urging us cheerfully to apply ourselves to our own labors, being persuaded of God's goodness and content with our own estate. Finally, it condemns that busy meddling in other people's affairs (*polypragmosynē*) with which the greater part of humanity is sorely diseased. Both expositions are agreeable both to the language of the text and to the faith; the reader may choose either one. Commentary on Solomon's Ecclesiastes.[13]

God Preordains the Nature of Things. The English Annotations: The state, quality, order, condition, and everything belonging to the nature and being of [creation], everything externally happening to it is all preordained in the counsel and decree of God. He, by his immutable and irrefutable providence, has assigned to everyone his order and by how his wisdom disposes all things belonging to humanity. They are under his care and allowance, and therefore they ought not anxiously and solicitously to insist on provisions for the future. Rather, they should comfortably enjoy things present, and in a conscientious discharge of duty wait for a similar blessing and providence of God in the future, as they have experienced in the past. Annotations on Ecclesiastes 6:10.[14]

[13]Serres, *Commentarius, in Solomonis Ecclesiasten*, 340-41; citing Lk 12:15; Heb 13:5 1 Tim 6:8.

[14]Downame, ed., *English Annotations*, 7C3r*; citing Ps 33; 1 Sam 2:7; Acts 2:23; 4:18.

7:1-29 PRACTICAL WISDOM

[1]A good name is better than precious ointment,
and the day of death than the day of birth.

[2]It is better to go to the house of mourning
than to go to the house of feasting,

for this is the end of all mankind,
and the living will lay it to heart.

[3]Sorrow is better than laughter,
for by sadness of face the heart is made glad.

[4]The heart of the wise is in the house of mourning,
but the heart of fools is in the house of mirth.

[5]It is better for a man to hear the rebuke of the wise
than to hear the song of fools.

[6]For as the crackling of thorns under a pot,
so is the laughter of the fools;
this also is vanity.[a]

[7]Surely oppression drives the wise into madness,
and a bribe corrupts the heart.

[8]Better is the end of a thing than its beginning,
and the patient in spirit is better than the proud in spirit.

[9]Be not quick in your spirit to become angry,
for anger lodges in the heart[b] *of fools.*

[10]Say not, "Why were the former days better than these?"
For it is not from wisdom that you ask this.

[11]Wisdom is good with an inheritance,
an advantage to those who see the sun.

[12]For the protection of wisdom is like the protection of money,
and the advantage of knowledge is that wisdom preserves the life of him who has it.

[13]Consider the work of God:
who can make straight what he has made crooked?

[14]In the day of prosperity be joyful, and in the day
of adversity consider: God has made the one as well
as the other, so that man may not find out anything
that will be after him.
[15]In my vain[c] *life I have seen everything. There is a*
righteous man who perishes in his righteousness, and
there is a wicked man who prolongs his life in his
evildoing. [16]Be not overly righteous, and do not make
yourself too wise. Why should you destroy yourself? [17]Be
not overly wicked, neither be a fool. Why should you die
before your time? [18]It is good that you should take hold of
this, and from that withhold not your hand, for the one
who fears God shall come out from both of them.
[19]Wisdom gives strength to the wise man more
than ten rulers who are in a city.
[20]Surely there is not a righteous man on earth who
does good and never sins.
[21]Do not take to heart all the things that people say,
lest you hear your servant cursing you. [22]Your heart
knows that many times you yourself have cursed others.
[23]All this I have tested by wisdom. I said, "I will be
wise," but it was far from me. [24]That which has been
is far off, and deep, very deep; who can find it out?
[25]I turned my heart to know and to search out and
to seek wisdom and the scheme of things, and to know
the wickedness of folly and the foolishness that is
madness. [26]And I find something more bitter than
death: the woman whose heart is snares and nets, and
whose hands are fetters. He who pleases God escapes
her, but the sinner is taken by her. [27]Behold, this is
what I found, says the Preacher, while adding one
thing to another to find the scheme of things—
[28]which my soul has sought repeatedly, but I have not
found. One man among a thousand I found, but a
woman among all these I have not found. [29]See, this
alone I found, that God made man upright, but they
have sought out many schemes.

a The Hebrew term *hebel* can refer to a "vapor" or "mere breath" (see note on 1:2) **b** Hebrew *in the bosom* **c** The Hebrew term *hebel* can refer to a "vapor" or "mere breath" (see note on 1:2)

Overview: The first half of Ecclesiastes 7 recalls the genre of the book of Proverbs, with its compact aphorisms grouped loosely together by a common theme. Here Martin Luther and those who follow his world-affirming approach to the book find comfort in a catalog of practical wisdom set in counterpoint to the unceasing vanity of life's demands. By contrast, Jean de Serres emphasizes the wisdom that comes from living life in constant awareness of one's impending death. The second half of the chapter reverts to literary form, developing the theme of prudent moderation in response to life's unpredictability, and here our commentators continue to urge trust in God's providence. The admonition against being "over-righteous/just" receives classic treatment from Denis the Carthusian, who argues that while virtue itself cannot properly be excessive (since virtue is by definition a mean between extremes), the means and methods employed in pursuit of justice can be immoderate, or ill-suited to the social context in which one finds oneself. Luther, by contrast, appeals to the evangelical distinction between the righteousness of God and that of faith, arguing that a correct apprehension of the latter frees one to pursue one's worldly calling with moderation and common sense. Ecclesiastes 7:20, 29, highlight the persistent sin that characterizes the human condition, a feature of life noted by interpreters across the confessional range: the Anabaptist Dirk Philips notes the ongoing need for God's grace, Luther refutes the arguments of Erasmus and others in affirming free will, and Calvin defends the Augustinian conception of original sin.

7:1-13 *Wisdom and Folly Compared*

An Exhortation to Live Boldly. Martin Luther: This passage does not seem to be related by any logical connection to the preceding. To me this seems to be the point of this passage: Solomon wants to comfort the impatient in their fruitless efforts, just as heretofore he was concerned, after reciting a catalog of human vanities, to interject comfort and exhortation to fear God, urging our hearts to rise toward God, encouraging us to listen to the Word of God, not to be hasty in speaking, and so on. So here again he inserts an exhortation after he has completed a catalog; later on he will return to the catalog.

Therefore let this be a passage of exhortation or comfort inserted into the midst of the catalog of vain efforts and desires addressed to those who are impatient. For in this life the human heart experiences nothing but offenses and impatience. This is especially true of those who are the best of human beings, because, as he said above, "He who increases knowledge increases sorrow." Those who see and hear much have a great opportunity for sorrow and indignation, because they see and experience the things that bring injury to the heart. . . . Solomon is not speaking about foolish people, who do not care at all about wisdom and human affairs, but about the best of people, those who want to help human affairs, people such as those in public office and in the management of households. For those who administer public or private business come to experience the fraud and perfidy of human beings. This fact has frightened many people away from public office. Thus that old man in Terence thinks that he is fortunate never to have married.[†] By contrast, another says, "I married, and then what misery I had to behold! Children were born—still more trouble!" The human spirit is offended by all these things unless it has been forearmed by the Word of God. Therefore those who have seen these things exhort others as follows: "The one who has lived obscurely has lived well." But Christians should be exhorted to live in the very midst of the crowd, to marry, to govern their household, and so on. Moreover, when their efforts are hindered by the malice of others, they should bear it patiently and not cease their good works. Do not desert the battlefield but stick it out. Do not let yourself be broken by trouble or impatience, and do not let yourself be overcome by anger. Therefore this is a very good and joyful exhortation, yet one that no one but a Christian will listen to. Annotations on Ecclesiastes.[1]

[1]LW 15:105-6 (WA 20:122-23). [†]Terence, *Adelphi* 42-44.

Living in Readiness for Death. Jean de Serres: It is far better and more profitable to think soberly about death, and to weigh the incumbrances of the human condition, and to have experience of these trials both in ourselves and in others, than it is to fill our minds with delights, like those who give themselves to feasting—that is to say, to pleasure. For by the term "feasting" he indicates all kinds of voluptuousness, among which feasts have the chief place. Therefore Solomon's purpose is to recall them from the vanity of voluptuousness; and because all of us are impelled in this direction by our very nature, he places a bit in the mouth of the flesh's ferocity, so that it doesn't run off at a gallop when spurred on by these delights. Therefore, it will be a good remedy against the excesses of voluptuousness if we think well on the condition of human life, and consider how the body count ever rises—then we will not always be feasting and laughing! . . . After all, even one of the blind heathens has said that philosophy is a meditation on death.[†] No doubt we may say better and more truly that it is a most excellent gift of Christian truth diligently to think on death, with the aim that we should live within a state of readiness for death, when we will render an account of our lives to God. Commentary on Solomon's Ecclesiastes.[2]

Wise People Look to the End. The English Annotations: He proves sorrow is better, and more wholesome for the soul than laughter, by the choice and judgment of the wise and fools. That which the wise prefer is indeed better than that which fools choose, and the wise prefer spectacles, places, and occasions of sorrow while fools choose the contrary. Ergo, that is better than this. The wise consider the end of things and choose the most proper means to the best ends, while fools look only to the present and what is before their eyes. By "the house of mourning" we understand any place or object that occasions mourning, so the grave is called the house of ages, or humanity's long home. Annotations on Ecclesiastes 7:4.[3]

Affronts Cause Temporary Madness. John Trapp: "Surely oppression makes a wise person mad"—until such time, that is, as he has recollected himself and summoned the sobriety of his senses before his own judgment; till he has reasoned with himself and prayed himself out of his distemper, as David did in Psalm 73. Anger is a short madness, and fury a frenzy, and who is so apprehensive of an injury as the wise person? And who is so wise as not sometimes to be carried away by their passion to their cost? Oppression may draw forth actions from the meekest Moses that he may sorely repent, but he knows not how to remedy. Anger flips reason on its head even in the wisest sometimes, and especially in cases of calumny (for the eye and the good name will bear no jests, as the proverb has it). A person can bear a blow on the back more easily than a touch on the eye. You will find some, says Erasmus, that if death is threatened can despise it; but to be belied they cannot brook, nor from revenge constrain themselves. A Commentary or Exposition upon Ecclesiastes.[4]

Humility Leads to Patience and Trust. The English Annotations: His purpose is to show that patience is rooted in humility, and the less esteem people have of themselves, the more willing they are to endure what God inflicts and wait their time to be relieved of trouble. Pride and high-mindedness, in contrast, makes people willful and impatient of any opposition. Therefore, when God humbled David, we find how strong he was to bear the railing and cursing of Shimei. Annotations on Ecclesiastes 7:8.[5]

[2]Serres, *Commentarius, in Solomonis Ecclesiasten*, 360-61; [†]The basic idea is attributed to Plato, especially his allegory of the soul taking wing in the *Phaedo*, but the maxim itself is stated in Cicero, *Tusculan Disputations* 1.30.

[3]Downame, ed., *English Annotations*, 7C4r*; citing Eccles 12:5.

[4]Trapp, *A Commentary or Exposition upon Ecclesiastes*, 89.

[5]Downame, ed., *English Annotations*, 7C4r*; citing Prov 29:17; Ex 6:9; Prov 13:10; 2 Sam 16:11, 12; Hab 2:3, 4.

Against Nostalgia. Martin Luther: This is how the human heart customarily complains whenever it experiences the ingratitude of the world: "Things are worse than they used to be." But you, do not talk this way, for you are not asking or arguing the right way. Old men usually speak this way: "When I was a boy, everything was better." They are what the poet calls "glorifiers of times past."[†] But Solomon says, "This is false; things were never right." The reason you see and understand this only now is that as we grow, our experiences of things and our occasions to be angry grow also. A boy does not care and is not moved when someone cheats or murders someone else, but goes on playing, hunting, and riding; to his mind the highest of crimes is when someone steals another's marbles, and this makes him angry. But when he becomes the head of a household, then he is sensitive to the annoyance and unfaithfulness of his household, and he becomes angry if a horse breaks a leg or an ox is not properly fattened. Therefore the world has always been evil, but we have not always been in the world and are not now. When we were children, nothing disturbed us; we ourselves did indeed lead a more peaceful life, but the world has always been the same. To be sure, it is true that in one era wickedness erupts more than in another, but this happens because different situations and greater opportunities exist for it to erupt; the wickedness of the world, however, always remains the same. Julius Caesar shook up the whole world because he had a great opportunity to do so; if Esau or Absalom had had such an opportunity, they would have done the same thing. Therefore the evil in the world is always the same. See to it, then, that you have a peaceful and tranquil heart and that you do not get angry when you see this evil. You will never change the world, but see to it that you change into another kind of person. Annotations on Ecclesiastes.[6]

God's Judgments Are Beyond Human Understanding. Konrad Pellikan: The work of God is taught to be seen, but by what reason he corrects one and hardens another is beyond our judgment. Instead, let us join with Paul's great exclamation, "Who are you, O man, to answer back to God? Will the thing that is molded answer back to its molder?" And, "Oh, the depth of the riches and wisdom and knowledge of God!" But it is called "the work of God," not "works," for all things come to be from one single and unchangeable will, and that justly, though for a reason unknown to us. Nor should anyone be surprised by this, since we cannot even understand our own wills and actions, or discern their workings with certainty—how then do they think they can investigate the causes of the divine will? How can anyone know why he grants his grace to one and hardens another, why he gives Judas over to a reprobate mind and looks mercifully on Peter for his conversion, why he offers paradise to one thief, while passing over the other? It is certain that no one can be restored unless the grace of God prevenes, but it is possible for a person to be perverted according to the judgment of God—not without the evil will of the sinner and the good will of God, who orders all things well and does no one an injustice, for the Lord is the best and greatest of all. A Succinct and Universal Commentary on the Bible.[7]

7:14-29 *Upright and Fallen*

Why God Deals Out of Order. Jean de Serres: This seems to me to be the plain meaning of this passage: we must live in the day. That is, when our affairs prosper, we must give thanks to God and use his good gifts soberly; also, that we must not lay such great care on our minds that we be too much grieved, either with the sorrow of present troubles, or with the concern for miseries to come, and that we not be weighed down with such long and burdensome thoughts. Let us rather remember that such is the condition of this human

[6]LW 15:105-6 (WA 20:122-23). [†]Horace, *Ars poetica* 173.

[7]Pellikan, *Commentaria bibliorum et illa brevia quidem ac catholica*, 258r; citing Rom 9:20; 11:33.

life that it easily alternates between prosperity and adversity. Why then should we think ourselves to be free from the common lot of all mortals? Therefore, when God has given us peace in our affairs, let us not grow insolent and trample on others, being carried away with foolish confidence in our present condition. Nor let us meddle with things that are not our business, or neglect our calling and be slack in our duties, but instead let us use these circumstances wisely and justly, and fortify our souls against the storm that is to come. This is what it means to "be joyful in the day of prosperity"—that is, to enjoy God's benefits with a good conscience and thanksgiving.

But if adversity should come upon us, "In the day of adversity, consider"—that is, "consider" the judgments of God; carefully assess whether God may be punishing you, and when you understand the cause of the evil, repent and turn toward the Lord. Therefore he would have the minds of the faithful to be so prepared for calamities public and private that they should reverently discern the judgments of God and rest easy therein. For this considering is set against the rashness and insolence of human impatience, which rages so furiously and immoderately. But he adds a reason why that manifold and multifaceted wisdom of God effects such shifts and changes in human affairs when he says, "so that man may not find out anything that will be after him." God sends these turns of events so that people may understand that they do not have the power of governing themselves, but that the outcome of all our affairs is governed by the power and pleasure of God, which he can turn this way or that as he pleases.

Therefore it is not in our power either to maintain ourselves in prosperity or to remove ourselves from the storm of adversities. The providence of God has indeed set out certain secondary (or intermediate) causes, which he wants us to make use of; therefore, we should never conduct ourselves such that in prosperity we seek unlawful means, whether from rashness or arrogant curiosity, for this will surely carry us headlong into the most grievous miseries; or else in adversity that we flee into unlawful aids. Rather, we must firmly establish ourselves in the conviction that the providence of God is the ultimate rule over human affairs, and that it does so justly and wisely, despite the fact that we are unable to search out the causes of his works. For his ways are such that they cannot be discovered by us, nor does our weakness allow us entry to the innermost chambers of such mysteries. Therefore God deals out of order to cut off all opportunity for human reason to discover "anything that will be after him." Commentary on Solomon's Ecclesiastes.[8]

No Excess Virtue, Only Excess Striving. Denis the Carthusian: Justice is a virtue, and when it comes to justice, the more the better. So what does he mean in saying, "Do not be overjust"? I answer that justice is a virtue in itself, and thus there can be no direct excess, since its growth is its own completion; still, in the exercises or actions by which we reach justice, or progress in our development of this virtue (or in those actions that are thought to pertain to justice), excess and superfluity can occur, just as with respect to charity or self-control. Therefore, one ought not to wear oneself out with immoderate, indiscreet, and unsustainable vigils, fasts, disciplines, and the like, carried out for the love of obtaining or perfecting justice, or the desire to advance in charity or devotion. Nor ought one to go beyond justice, through too much rigor or austerity, but observe a middle path, indulging easily, and turn aside to lesser rigor rather than greater in the presence of one's neighbors. For moral virtue is a mediating term between two vicious extremes, and it is to be tempered by the elements of justice, just as this mode is described in Proverbs: "Set bounds to your prudence"; and in Jeremiah, "Because he did more than he could, for this reason [they] perished." Hence Chrysostom says, "Be austere when it comes to your own way of life, but compassionate with those of others."[†] Let yourself rarely be heard giving commands, but often be seen doing big things.

[8]Serres, *Commentarius, in Solomonis Ecclesiasten*, 378-81.

Severity (so Cicero says) is that by which judicial power or revenge is exercised more severely against someone. But what sort of intention ought to guide the corrections given by a just judge, this same Cicero makes clear when he says that, in correcting or avenging, these three rules must be followed, which the prince also must follow: first, that he may correct the one whom he punishes or rebukes; second, that his punishment should render the rest better; and third, that the unjust might be taken away, the rest may live more securely.[‡] But how much severity ought indeed to be avoided is evident from the words of Seneca, who confesses that "severity loses its potency by repeated correction."[§] Exposition of the Book of Ecclesiastes.[9]

On Governing with Discretion. Martin Luther: Here again it is necessary to watch Solomon closely, so that we do not suppose that he is speaking about the righteousness of God or the righteousness of faith. But he is speaking about political righteousness, so that you understand the "righteous man" to be the one who exacts righteousness from others, the one who wants to make people upright; such a man is a public official or the administrator of a household. "I have seen a righteous man," he says, "one who had outstanding laws and statutes. But when he began to enforce them and demanded that everything be done according to the rules, he accomplished nothing except that everything went backward." This is like what a certain idiot did: he was standing crooked in the sunlight and accusing his shadow of being crooked, although he did not straighten himself out meanwhile. This is how we are too. We see the speck that is in the eye of another, but do not notice the log that is in our own eye. In summary, "The highest law brings the deepest injustice."[†] Anyone who wants to govern everything according to the rules and to set everything straight in the state or in the household will have a lot of work but no results. On the other hand, someone else does not want to do anything and is a despiser of the enforcement of justice. Neither of these prevails. One must be neither wise nor unwise, neither righteous nor wicked. Then what is to be done? This will be the middle way: "Be not righteous overmuch." . . . That is, forget about the highest law; measure yourself by your own foot and sing, "Know thyself." Then you will find in your own breast a lengthy catalog of vices, and you will say, "Look, I myself am still unrighteous, and yet I am tolerated by God and am not banished by people. Then why am I so carried away with fury that I harshly require of others what I do not achieve myself?" This is what it means to be "righteous overmuch." The things of this world cannot bear it. . . .

"Be not wicked overmuch." This is the second part of the conclusion. See to it that just as you are not righteous overmuch, you are not wicked overmuch either. That is, do not despise and neglect all the duties of government committed to your charge, and do not permit everything to fall apart. It is good to overlook some things, but not to neglect all things. If wisdom does not succeed, that is no reason to go crazy with anger and revenge. Finally, do not give in to idleness, so that you do not want to care about anything. Do not behave like that wicked servant who buried his talent and did not want to trade with it at all. Well then, be just and let others be just with you; demand uprightness; persevere, regardless of the outcome. Why? "Why should you destroy yourself, or die before your time?" There is reason to fear that he may come suddenly and call you to judgment, as he took away the soul of the rich man at night when the rich man was not thinking about it. If this life were heavenly and angelic, nothing would happen unjustly; but our sinful nature cannot do anything but sin and be foolish. Anyone who does not know this has not yet learned about the world. We should think that here we are as though we were in a shipwreck or a fire, where one

[9]DCOO 7:253-54; citing Prov 23:4; Jer 48:36. [†]John Chrysostom, *Homiliae in Matthaeum* 43. [‡]Denis seems to be giving a loose paraphrase of broad themes in Cicero's conception of justice, rather than quoting any particular text. [§]Seneca, *De clementia* 22.3 (LCL 214:418).

must labor to snatch at least some brand from the fire when one cannot control or extinguish the whole fire. Therefore if you are in a household, be content to snatch even one person from the public fire of wicked people. If you are a teacher of children, labor to educate at least one of them and to bring him up properly. If you are a preacher of the gospel, do not preach as though you could gain all men for Christ, for not all heed the gospel; but if you convert three or four souls and lead them to Christ, like the tips of burning brands, give thanks. For one should not quit simply because so few are changed for the better to hear the preaching of the gospel. But do what Christ did: he rescued the elect and left the rest behind. This is what the apostles did also. It will not be better for you. You are foolish if you either presume that you alone can accomplish everything or despair of everything when it does not go your way. Annotations on Ecclesiastes.[10]

The Apostles Continued to Sin after Pentecost. Dirk Philips: Some persons have proposed that the apostles did not sin any more after Pentecost; yes, that they were not able to sin and that all who with the apostles have received the Spirit of the day of Pentecost (as they say) have come to the victory and are born again out of God so that they cannot sin any more. To this we reply that Scriptures includes all humanity under sin and knows no one (except Christ Jesus alone) as entirely free from sin. The Enchiridion.[11]

Uprightness in the Externals. Martin Luther: The scholastics have twisted this passage until the present day to prove the freedom of the will in opposition to grace.[†] This is contrary to Solomon's meaning, since Solomon throughout this book is speaking about bodily matters. As has already been said earlier, he is not instructing consciences before God, except that he occasionally refers to the fear of the Lord, but he is instructing human beings about political life, telling them to control their heart. The meaning, therefore, is this: God has placed humans into things, has given them certain works and a certain task. But men and women do not remain in these tasks, but by their lusts they seek for those that belong to someone else. God made humans upright, straightforward, to look at what is in front of them and before their eyes, that is, at the things that are present, and to be content with these. But men and women, forsaking this uprightness, argue about the things that are in the future. Therefore Solomon wants to say, "On the basis of my investigation I have found that no one lives content with their lot, but that everyone has crossed and oblique eyes." As Ovid said, "The crops in someone else's field are always more productive, and the neighbor's cattle have larger udders."[‡] And again, "The lazy ox wants to wear a saddle, and the riding horse wants to plow."[§] Peter had such eyes when he said, "What about this man?" Uprightness in external matters, therefore, consists in this, that everyone look straight ahead in their acting and in their ruling and that they not look elsewhere. But they have sought out many devices. That is, they occupy themselves with many plans and with anxious thoughts about how they will govern everything in the future, meanwhile neglecting the things that are present and that God has put before their very eyes. Thus a woman pursues a man's job, and a man pursues a woman's job. This statement, then, is a kind of final flourish in his discussion of human vanity. Annotations on Ecclesiastes.[12]

Humans Are Sinful by Choice, Not by Nature. John Calvin: Now away with those persons who dare write God's name on their faults, because we declare that humans are vicious by nature! They perversely search out God's handiwork in their own pollution, when they ought

[10]LW 15:121-24 (WA 20:141-44); citing Mt 7:3; 25:24-30; Lk 12:20; Amos 4:11; Rom 10:16. †Cicero, *De officiis* 1.10.33.
[11]CRR 6:283*; citing 1 Kings 8:46; Ps 143:2.

[12]LW 15:133 (WA 20:150-51); citing Jn 21:21. †Luther addressed these arguments at greater length in his treatise *Against Latomus*, LW 32:212-13. ‡Ovid, *Tristia* 5.12.23. §Horace, *Epistle* 1.14.43.

rather to have sought it in that unimpaired and uncorrupted nature of Adam. Our destruction, therefore, comes from the guilt of our flesh, not from God, inasmuch as we have perished solely because we have degenerated from our original condition. Let no one here grumble that God could have provided better for our salvation if he had forestalled Adam's fall. Pious minds ought to loathe this objection, because it manifests inordinate curiosity. Furthermore, the matter has to do with the secret of predestination, which will be discussed later in its proper place. Let us accordingly remember to impute our ruin to depravity of nature, in order that we may not accuse God himself, the Author of nature. True, this deadly wound clings to nature, but it is a very important question whether the wound has been inflicted from outside or has been present from the beginning. Yet it is evident that the wound was inflicted through sin. We have, therefore, no reason to complain except against ourselves. Scripture has diligently noted this fact. For Ecclesiastes says, "This I know, that God made humankind upright, but they have sought out many devices." Obviously, humanity's ruin is to be ascribed to humanity alone; for they, having acquired righteousness by God's kindness, have by their own folly sunk into vanity. INSTITUTES OF THE CHRISTIAN RELIGION.[13]

[13]LCC 20:253-54 (CO 2:184).

8:1–9:18 THE SUPERIORITY OF WISDOM

1 Who is like the wise?
And who knows the interpretation of a thing?

A man's wisdom makes his face shine,
and the hardness of his face is changed.

2 I say:[a] Keep the king's command, because of God's oath to him.[b] 3 Be not hasty to go from his presence. Do not take your stand in an evil cause, for he does whatever he pleases. 4 For the word of the king is supreme, and who may say to him, "What are you doing?" 5 Whoever keeps a command will know no evil thing, and the wise heart will know the proper time and the just way.[c] 6 For there is a time and a way for everything, although man's trouble[d] lies heavy on him. 7 For he does not know what is to be, for who can tell him how it will be? 8 No man has power to retain the spirit, or power over the day of death. There is no discharge from war, nor will wickedness deliver those who are given to it. 9 All this I observed while applying my heart to all that is done under the sun, when man had power over man to his hurt.

10 Then I saw the wicked buried. They used to go in and out of the holy place and were praised[e] in the city where they had done such things. This also is vanity.[f] 11 Because the sentence against an evil deed is not executed speedily, the heart of the children of man is fully set to do evil. 12 Though a sinner does evil a hundred times and prolongs his life, yet I know that it will be well with those who fear God, because they fear before him. 13 But it will not be well with the wicked, neither will he prolong his days like a shadow, because he does not fear before God.

14 There is a vanity that takes place on earth, that there are righteous people to whom it happens according to the deeds of the wicked, and there are wicked people to whom it happens according to the deeds of the righteous. I said that this also is vanity. 15 And I commend joy, for man has nothing better under the sun but to eat and drink and be joyful, for this will go with him in his toil through the days of his life that God has given him under the sun.

16 When I applied my heart to know wisdom, and to see the business that is done on earth, how neither day nor night do one's eyes see sleep, 17 then I saw all the work of God, that man cannot find out the work that is done under the sun. However much man may toil in seeking, he will not find it out. Even though a wise man claims to know, he cannot find it out.

9 But all this I laid to heart, examining it all, how the righteous and the wise and their deeds are in the hand of God. Whether it is love or hate, man does not know; both are before him. 2 It is the same for all, since the same event happens to the righteous and the wicked, to the good and the evil,[g] to the clean and the unclean, to him who sacrifices and him who does not sacrifice. As the good one is, so is the sinner, and he who swears is as he who shuns an oath. 3 This is an evil in all that is done under the sun, that the same event happens to all. Also, the hearts of the children of man are full of evil, and madness is in their hearts while they live, and after that they go to the dead. 4 But he who is joined with all the living has hope, for a living dog is better than a dead lion. 5 For the living know that they will die, but the dead know nothing, and they have no more reward, for the memory of them is forgotten. 6 Their love and their hate and their envy have already perished, and forever they have no more share in all that is done under the sun.

7 Go, eat your bread with joy, and drink your wine with a merry heart, for God has already approved what you do.

8 Let your garments be always white. Let not oil be lacking on your head.

9 Enjoy life with the wife whom you love, all the days of your vain[h] life that he has given you under the sun, because that is your portion in life and in your toil at which you toil under the sun. 10 Whatever your hand finds to do, do it with your might,[i] for there is no work or thought or knowledge or wisdom in Sheol, to which you are going.

11 Again I saw that under the sun the race is not to the swift, nor the battle to the strong, nor bread to the

wise, nor riches to the intelligent, nor favor to those with knowledge, but time and chance happen to them all. [12]*For man does not know his time. Like fish that are taken in an evil net, and like birds that are caught in a snare, so the children of man are snared at an evil time, when it suddenly falls upon them.*

[13]*I have also seen this example of wisdom under the sun, and it seemed great to me.* [14]*There was a little city with few men in it, and a great king came against it and besieged it, building great siegeworks against it.* [15]*But there was found in it a poor, wise man, and he by his wisdom delivered the city. Yet no one remembered that poor man.* [16]*But I say that wisdom is better than might, though the poor man's wisdom is despised and his words are not heard.*

[17]*The words of the wise heard in quiet are better than the shouting of a ruler among fools.* [18]*Wisdom is better than weapons of war, but one sinner destroys much good.*

a Hebrew lacks *say* **b** Or *because of your oath to God* **c** Or *and judgment* **d** Or *evil* **e** Some Hebrew manuscripts, Septuagint, Vulgate; most Hebrew manuscripts *forgotten* **f** The Hebrew term *hebel* can refer to a "vapor" or "mere breath"; also twice in verse 14 (see note on 1:2) **g** Septuagint, Syriac, Vulgate; Hebrew lacks *and the evil* **h** The Hebrew term *hebel* can refer to a "vapor" or "mere breath" (see note on 1:2) **i** Or *finds to do with your might, do it*

Overview: Ecclesiastes 8–9 deals with matters of political wisdom and worldly vocation, set against the backdrop of God's inscrutable providence. Michael Jermin and Jean de Serres celebrate the virtues of the wise person on a personal scale, while Philipp Melanchthon and Martin Luther take note of the specific forms of wisdom necessary to navigate political life. It may be true, as Jermin observes (quoting Philo), that the wise alone are true kings, but those who sit on thrones and bear the sword have an important role to play in God's providential governance of human affairs. Melanchthon stresses the duty to obey human governance, but only when it is attuned to divine law. Luther counsels patience when living under an unjust ruler, while Thomas Granger emphasizes the terrors of God's judgment against those who abuse their power to oppress the righteous. The opening verses of Ecclesiastes 9 reiterate the earlier doubts concerning the fate of the soul after death, and here the applications our commentators draw vary considerably. De Serres builds on the preceding discussion of the inscrutability of God's providence to argue that the Preacher is arguing on the basis of appearances, and appearances can be deceiving. Denis the Carthusian argues that the oblivion which engulfs the dead applies only to the *unjust* dead, while Luther reads the Preacher's apparent skepticism as a rejection of the cult of saints.

8:1-17 *The King's Command*

The Wise Are the Only True Kings. Michael Jermin: Philo speaking of wisdom says, "Who by searching can find out that good? What seas must he pass over? What islands must he pass into? To what shores must he go? With what nations is she to be found?"[†] And this the Preacher, having shown in the latter part of the former chapter by setting forth the difficulty of attaining wisdom and the rarity of the wise person, he begins this chapter with his excellence, saying, "Who is as the wise?" Who, though never so great in power, who though never so high in honor? Nay, who is rich in estate, who is great in power, who is high in honor but a wise person only? Philo therefore, speaking of the wise person, says that they alone are the true kings. . . .[‡] But to consider the manner of the Preacher's words, they being set down as a question show as it were that he could only admire them, and could not judge them. Commentary upon the Whole Booke of Ecclesiastes.[1]

[1]Jermin, *A commentary, upon the whole booke of Ecclesiastes*, 15. [†]Philo, *On the Change of Names* 35. [‡]The original quote has a slightly different sense: "Indeed, so good a thing is shepherding

True Modesty Is Seen in the Face. Jean de Serres: Human wisdom puffs a person up; by contrast, the wisdom of God gives a person true modesty. And it is about this kind of modesty that Solomon is concerned here. For this is the meaning of the words: that the power and efficacy of wisdom shines forth most clearly in this, that however much it raises the one endued with wisdom above others, nevertheless it so inclines them that the more they excel others in virtue and praise, the more modest they become. What, then, is the power of wisdom in a person? He says that it is this in particular, that they alter their countenance—that is, it takes all the harshness and violence out of their face and composes them in true and thoroughgoing modesty. Commentary on Solomon's Ecclesiastes.[2]

The King's Mouth and God's Calling. Philipp Melanchthon: "I observe the mouth of the king, and the words of the oath of God." This saying is very worthy of consideration and remembrance, and indeed it clearly shows that this book does not teach monastic idleness, as many have absurdly interpreted. But the king leads people in all necessary actions, and to many difficult and dangerous struggles; and lest there be license, he establishes the boundaries of human life and requires obedience. He commands that his subjects "observe his mouth," that is, the mandates of the king, but he adds this restriction: "and the words of the oath of God," that is, the law of God. For he also calls the law and oath elsewhere, because God sanctioned promises and threats by an oath. Therefore, there is no doubt that crimes are indeed punished, but punishments are mitigated by those who do penance; for this also is included in the oath. Let obedience be so ordered that first we obey the divine voice, which the mouth of the king ought to sound; next we obey the mandates of the king that do not conflict with the divine voice. This is congruent with that rule which states that we ought to obey God rather than humans. Now consider how this circumscribes a boundary around human life, not giving us license to indulge in all our desires, nor to be an idler or a busybody, but carry out the divine laws and the duties of the vocation in which you have been called by the king, without curiosity, or ambition, or any urge to stick your nose in someone else's business. Enarration on Ecclesiastes.[3]

Teachings on Patience, or Christian Fortitude. Jean de Serres: This section extends from this place (8:5) to chapter 9, verse 15. . . . There is certainly nothing greater or more difficult in this life than to overcome the wandering waves and storms of one's own heart. But because these bear down hard on us from every side all throughout our lives, there is no discussion more common or fertile with which our talk ought to be more occupied. For since there are so many different kinds of misery in this life, Solomon therefore arms us with new remedies against them. . . . And first of all he sets down a general rule: "Whoever keeps the commandment knows no evil thing." By "the commandment" he indicates the Word of God, by which alone we learn what is to be done and what left undone, and after what manner our lives are to be ordered. To know an "evil thing" is to feel and experience misery, or to be wrapped up in troubles and defeats. The gist of it is that in the Word of God, the faithful have true and certain rest and tranquility; no matter how much they are tossed about on great waves of calamities, the life-giving remedy is still to be set against all that ails us. . . . Yet Solomon's meaning here is not that the faithful shall be free from all troubles (for this runs contrary both to the Word of God and to experience), but rather that even though they be carried out onto the open sea of miseries, they shall remain unsinkable amid the

that it is justly ascribed not to kings only and wise men and perfectly cleansed souls but also to God the All-Sovereign" (*On Agriculture* 50; LCL 247:135). Philo's point is not that wise men alone are kings, but that both wise men and kings belong in the same exalted category.

[2]Serres, *Commentarius, in Solomonis Ecclesiasten*, 405; 401-2.

[3]CR 14:126; citing Acts 5:29.

waves, led as they are by this divine knowledge always lighting the way to safety, as a polestar. COMMENTARY ON SOLOMON'S ECCLESIASTES.[4]

HUMAN LIMITS LEAD TO DIFFICULTIES. THE ENGLISH ANNOTATIONS: Because one cannot foresee future events nor accurately judge the consequences of their actions, it is very difficult to avoid many of those miseries that attend them by reason of ignorance. There is one season and one manner of acting that would have been seconded with success if one could have foreseen it, but any other time, and other way of proceeding, would miscarry. Great, therefore, must be their miseries by reason of this ignorance, as there are a thousand ways to miss the mark, but only one to hit it. One cannot so much as appoint beforehand their own actions for the future, much less foresee the consequences or issues that will follow from it. None can foretell what will be but God alone. Only of this can a wise and holy person be sure, that whatever falls out shall be for their good, though it may be contrary to their desire and expectation. ANNOTATIONS ON ECCLESIASTES 8:7.[5]

BEARING WITH WICKED RULERS. MARTIN LUTHER: Now he returns to his catalog, as he once more enumerates the miseries caused by human vanity. "Among all these things that I have been reciting I have also seen that man lords it over human beings to their hurt." This should be referred to the person who is a subject; that is, it often happens that tyrants reign, but reign in such a way that they bring affliction on their subjects. And in spite of this the mouth of the king must be obeyed, and sedition must not be set in motion. For even if there is a good ruler, he still gets no thanks for it. Not only is there no thanks, but people themselves become worse, as is the case now with the rabble who have been set free from the laws and restrictions of the pope. Everyone wants tyranny to be abolished; but when they are set free, they cannot bear this either. Therefore he concedes that wicked magistrates exist in order to punish their subjects, but he also teaches that one should nevertheless put up with them. ANNOTATIONS ON ECCLESIASTES.[6]

SIC SEMPER TYRANNIS. THOMAS GRANGER: An exposition of the evils, or vanities, that follow tyranny—to wit, burial and oblivion. "And so I saw the wicked buried." Their wickedness profited them nothing; they were as gods, but they died like humans. And since they arrogated the glory of God to themselves, lived like beasts and were pitted like beasts, they tumbled into the grave or were even deprived of the honor of the grave, like Cononiah and Jezebel; and Ahab's blood was licked up by the dogs. There are many examples like this of emperors and popes, "who had come and gone from the holy place." This is an illustration of their misery by a comparison (or rather dissimilarity) between their place and dignity and their end. They went and came with pomp and terror to the place of judgment; they sat in majesty on the seat of judgment, which is the place of the Most Holy; they sat on the throne of God, and forgetting themselves to be but human beings, usurped the glory of God, like Nebuchadnezzar, Sennacherib, Antiochus, Herod, and antichrist did. Therefore so much the more remarkable was their later burial or end, the vanity of their pomp more evident, the pride of the wicked was more despicable, and their end made a testament to the endurance of human madness and misery. . . . Whereas in their lifetimes they wanted to be like gods, they died like humans, and were soon forgotten like beasts. They were not worthy to be thought on, nor spoken of, but their names rather to be clipped and curtailed, as that of Jeconiah, or cast into the ground to rot and be consumed with their corpses, and to be made

[4]Serres, *Commentarius, in Solomonis Ecclesiasten*, 410-12.
[5]Downame, ed., *English Annotations*, 7D2v*; citing Prov 27:1; Jas 4:14; Is 41:23; 44:7; 46:10; 1 Cor 3:22.
[6]LW 15:139 (WA 20:154).

documents to the living of their everlasting shame and contempt. A Familiar Exposition.[7]

Using the World's Foolishness Wisely. Martin Luther: "Then I saw the wicked buried." There is a similar passage in Amos 6:1: "Woe to you who are rich in Zion, who enter the house of Israel with pomp!" Entering the church, or the house of God, is a Hebrew figure of speech for holding office in the people of God. So it is that the Ammonites are forbidden to enter the assembly of God, that is, to have dominance in the Jewish state. The Ammonites could be among the people of God but could not hold office. Thus here, too, they were "in the holy place"—that is, they administered the state. This is why he says, "I saw the wicked buried"—that is, the tyrants extinguished and succeeded by a good prince, as David succeeded when Saul had been extinguished. But when the wicked have been set free from tyranny, they forget their liberation. Thus people simply do not recognize their blessings, as we have immediately forgotten Prince Frederick, the author of our peace. No one thinks what good things we have received through him and from what evil things we have been set free by him. We always want something else; we neglect and forget the things that are in the present. All of this is being said by Solomon so that we might learn to know the world and to use the foolishness of this world wisely. Therefore this book should especially be read by new rulers, who have their heads swollen with opinions and want to rule the world according to their own plans and require everything to toe the mark. But such people should first learn to know the world—that is, to know that it is unjust, stubborn, disobedient, malicious, and, in short, ungrateful. Let them be grateful if they can motivate even one percent to keep the laws. Thus our sectarians are not content with the good things in the present, the preaching of faith and the grace of the gospel; they disturb everything with their novel and vain teachings. Therefore it is Solomon's counsel that we should know this to be their vanity and should teach in opposition to it as much as we can. Finally, those whom we cannot convert to faith or keep by our admonitions, those we should let go; for the wicked become obdurate through continuous punishment. Annotations on Ecclesiastes.[8]

Enjoyment Above Curiosity. Jean de Serres: He notes another temptation here, that there is great disorder in life itself, as well as in our common death—namely, that often the godly have poor success in their endeavors, while the ungodly make out handsomely. This disorder he describes as "vanity." For what is more at variance with reason than that it should go ill for the good and well for the bad? Therefore human reason concludes that the faithful lose their labor in serving God, as the prophet says, "In truth, I have cleansed my heart in vain, and washed my hands in innocence." Against this doubt, Solomon sets down appropriate answers. "And I praised enjoyment." The first answer is that we must not indulge our curiosity thinking about these matters; rather, since no one can rightly give the cause of those disorders that trouble our lives, there is nothing better than to rid our minds of care for them, and cheerfully use the good things God gives us. . . . "Therefore," the second answer: if, he says, you seek to understand why things happen to people the way they do in this life, even if you were to concentrate all the sharpness of your intellect on the study and contemplation of such great secrets, spending all your labor and depriving yourself of sleep and the rest of life's comforts, still you will end up with a baffled mind, and all your labor of investigation will have been in vain. Therefore he warns us not to be wise according to the judgments of human reason, but rather in accordance with the Word of God, which is the true and solid wisdom. In sum, he indicates that it is impossible for us to understand the causes of things that fall one way or

[7]Granger, *A Familiar Exposition or Commentarie on Ecclesiastes*, 212-13; citing Jer 22:24.

[8]LW 15:139-40 (WA 20:155); citing Deut 23:3.

another in our common life—indeed, it is a vain thing to worry our minds investigating them out of curiosity. Rather, we must rest ourselves on the Word of God, and get our true answers from there. Commentary on Solomon's Ecclesiastes.[9]

Marveling at God's Wisdom. John Trapp: "When I applied my mind to know wisdom"—that is, the wisdom and other excellencies of God shining plainly and plentifully in ruling the affairs and ordering the disorders of the world to his own glory. "For also there is that neither day nor night sees." By day and by night I busied myself in this search, so that a little sleep served my turn all the while. "I never spend a day in idleness," says Seneca, "I appropriate even a part of the night for study."[†] I studied night and day, and followed it with all possible eagerness. Thuanus tells of a countryman of his whom he called Franciscus Vieta Fontenajus, a very learned man, that he was so set on his studies that for three days together sometimes he would sit close at it, without food or sleep, leaning only on his elbow to hold himself in place.[‡] Solomon seems by this text to have been as sharp set for finding out the way of divine administration, and the true reason of divine dispensations. But he got little further than to see that it far exceeded all human capacity and apprehension. "They who are more learned know," says a father, "and God grant you may understand more than I say."[§] A Commentary or Exposition upon Ecclesiastes.[10]

9:1-18 *Enjoyment Until Death Comes*

The Restlessness of the World. Martin Luther: Here one must be careful to remember the argument of the book, so that we do not listen to those who have applied this text to the question of humanity's worthiness of the hate or love of God and who wickedly teach that no one can be certain about grace. Solomon is speaking only about works that are done "under the sun," that is, among human beings in the administration of political affairs. Look, he says, how crooked the world is, where I find that there are those who govern justly and wisely, whose servants and subjects are in the hand of God and are blessed and protected by him, as was the case with Solomon and with David. And yet whether it is love or hate humankind does not know (I take both of these in an active sense); that is, "people are so depraved that they do not acknowledge as their benefactors even those just and wise people whose servants they see being governed and blessed by God; nor do they acknowledge either the love or the hate of these people." There is nothing they forget more rapidly than kindnesses. Solomon reigned wisely, in peace and with great wealth; but as soon as Solomon had died, they immediately began to complain about "the yoke of Solomon," and there was no remembrance of his deeds of kindness. Regardless of what the state of the world has been, it has always seemed intolerable to the world. Italy is an example of this to us; whether it has war or peace, it cannot bear it. In the time of peace they look for war, in time of war they yearn for peace. The world cannot stand on the things that are present, and it is always tormented by the things that are in the future. So it is that Germany is always looking for something new. When the gospel began, everyone ran to it eagerly; but once the gospel has prevailed, we are bored and forget the great blessings. Now there is a rush for the Sacramentarians;[†] but when they have grown old, people will become bored with them and will want something else. In short, the world cannot stand it, whether it is governed well or poorly. Those whom the Lord does not help in governing could not live even a single day without peril. Therefore if anyone wants to serve the world with wisdom, justice, or any other good

[9]Serres, *Commentarius, in Solomonis Ecclesiasten*, 417-19; citing Ps 73:13.
[10]Trapp, *A Commentary or Exposition upon Ecclesiastes*, 119. [†]Seneca, *Epistle* 8.2 (LCL 75:36-37). [‡]Jacques Auguste de Thou (1553–1617) was a French historian and statesman. François Viète (1540–1603) was a lawyer who served as privy councilor to two French kings and made important contributions to the study of algebra. [§]The unnamed father quoted here is Augustine, *Enarrations on the Psalms* 148.11 (PL 37:1945).

things, let them expect nothing from it except the worst. Thus David and Solomon, the best of kings, loved good people and hated evil people. But the people did not acknowledge their love and forgot all their kindnesses and good deeds. Therefore John wrote correctly, "the world lies in wickedness," because there is nothing there but ingratitude and utter wickedness. Annotations on Ecclesiastes.[11]

God's Grace Is Not Uncertain. John Calvin: The schoolmen most wickedly twist the testimony of Ecclesiastes, which they have continually on their lips: "No one knows whether they deserve hate or love." For, to pass over how this passage is erroneously translated in the Vulgate,[†] even children cannot miss what Solomon means by these words. That is, if anyone would judge by the present state of things, whom God pursues with hatred and whom he embraces in love, they labor in vain and trouble themselves to no profit, "since all things happen alike to righteous and impious, . . . to those who sacrifice victims and those who do not sacrifice." From this it follows that God does not everlastingly witness his love to those for whom he causes all things to prosper, nor does he always manifest his hate to those whom he afflicts. And he does this to prove the innate folly of humanity, since among things so necessary to know it is grasped with such great stupidity. As Solomon had written a little before, one cannot discern how the soul of a human being differs from the soul of a beast because both seem to die in the same way. If anyone would infer from this that the opinion that we hold concerning the immortality of souls rests on conjecture alone, should we not justly consider them insane? Are they sane who infer—since we can comprehend nothing by the physical beholding of present things—that there is no certainty of God's grace? Institutes of the Christian Religion.[12]

Do Not Be Deceived by Appearances. Jean de Serres: The third answer:[†] although reasons cannot always be offered for those troubles, nevertheless we must hold it certain that all things are most wisely governed by God. . . . "The righteous," according to the usage of the Scripture, is what he calls the faithful—those whom God has according to his mere grace accounted as righteous, since it is he who justifies the ungodly. This is what the apostle says when he reckons their faith in him as righteousness. He also imprints on them the testimonies of righteousness, as seen by the pure and innocent lives they lead, which are the pledges of their election. He calls them "wise" because they are enlightened with the true light of wisdom—that is, with the true knowledge of God and with piety, for it is in these that a true and sound wisdom consists. This is the main thrust of his answer, but he adds to it an accurate description of the fluctuating and uncertain condition of human existence, when he writes, "And yet" (for so I interpret the particle *gam*) "a person knows neither love nor hate." Although it is certain that God has a special care for the salvation of the faithful, yet such is the course of things as they fall out for people in this life that it cannot be judged on the basis of outward appearance who it is that God loves and whom he hates, for there is everywhere such a confused jumbling of things all together that the same outcome seems to obtain both for the godly and for the ungodly. So, for example, it often happens that depraved people pass their entire lives in wickedness, and yet at length they go to their death as if it were the end of the line for them, just as with others; all seem to be slain by death's dart in the same way. I read this all in one

[11]LW 15:144-45 (WA 20:158); citing 2 Chron 10:4; 1 Jn 5:19. [†]The term "sacramentarian" refers to those who denied the salvific power of the sacraments, or the real presence of Christ in the Eucharist. For Luther, this category included opponents such as Zwingli and Bucer, as well as the Anabaptists and other radicals.

[12]LCC 20:585-86 (CO 2:428-29); citing Eccles 3:19. [†]The Vulgate gives a slightly different sense for this passage: "All these things have I considered in my heart, that I might carefully understand them: there are just men and wise men, and their works are in the hand of God: and yet man knows not whether he be worthy of love, or hatred" (Eccles 9:1 Douay-Rheims).

context, from the first verse to the end of verse 6, and I think this to be the true meaning of these words: even though the outward appearance of things presents the eyes of human reason with infinite confusion, yet it is certain that the providence of God continually watches over the salvation and safety of the faithful. Commentary on Solomon's Ecclesiastes.[13]

The Just and Unjust Share the Sufferings of the World. John Donne: God, who knows best how to repair his own honor, suffers it, nay, appoints it, to be so, that the just and unjust are wrapped up in the same judgment. The corn is as much beaten in the threshing as the straw is; the just are as much punished here as the unjust. Because God in his infinite goodness has elected me from the beginning, therefore must he provide that I have a different manner of birth, or another manner of death, than the reprobate have? Must he provide that I be born into the world without original sin, as his son was, or that I go out of the world by being taken away, as Enoch was, or as Elijah? And though we have that one example of such a coming into the world, and a few examples of such goings out of the world, yet we have no example (not even in the Son himself) of passing through this world without taking part in the miseries and calamities of the world, common to the just and unjust, righteous and unrighteous. Sermon on Genesis 18:25.[14]

Fate of the Unjust Dead. Denis the Carthusian: "The living know that they will die," and thus in considering their own mortality they can correct their lives through penitence and prepare themselves for death; but "the dead know nothing more." Solomon is speaking about the *unjust* dead: he affirms that they know nothing more, and this is because they are in hell, in the same sense as he says later in this chapter, that there will be neither work, nor reason, nor wisdom, nor knowledge in hell. "Nor have they any more reward." Because they are damned, they are not in a state where merits or demerits are relevant. But in this life, even when living viciously, they experienced certain rewards, since for some kinds of good things that they have sometimes done, the faithful and just God has bestowed on them some temporal prosperity or a longer life. This is clear from the condemnation Abraham speaks to the rich man: "You have received your good things in life." Indeed, after this life those rewards cease. "For the memory of them is forgotten"; that is, God has forgotten them, such that he takes away his mercy from them forever, just as Job says: "Let mercy forget him, and may worms be his sweetness." "Their love also, and their hatred, and their envy are all perished"—that is, their inordinate and vicious affections, with which they loved certain things in a fleshly manner, while hating God and those who are just, these too are damned with them, nor can they gratify them. "They have no part in this world." They are cut off entirely from the body of the church, and they have no communication of charity or participation with the living, nor can they possess anything in this world. "And in the work that is done under the sun." That is, in works of piety that the living perform for the dead they have no share, because they are not helped by such intercessions. Exposition of the Book of Ecclesiastes.[15]

Quiet Enjoyment in Life, Willing Departure in Death. The English Annotations: By this knowledge they gain much, if they rightly improve it, for: (1) Hereby they are persuaded to repent and fit themselves to meet the king of terrors. (2) Hereby they are set to seriously consider how this unavoidable evil may be sweetened and sanctified to them that they may comfortably desire to depart and to be with Christ, which is best of all. (3) Hereby they are excited to

[13]Serres, *Commentarius, in Solomonis Ecclesiasten*, 419-22. †Serres is continuing the line of argument he began in Eccles 8:14, responding to doubts concerning God's providential ordering of the world.
[14]Donne, *Works*, 1:223*.
[15]DCOO 7:265-66; citing Lk 16:25; Job 24:20.

duty with more vigor when they look on this as the day of grace, the time of light, wherein only they can work. (4) Which seems most pertinent to this place, knowing that they shall die and that the present comforts of the world are for the living only and not for the dead, they set themselves to enjoy the good blessings of God here while they have time to enjoy them, and by cheerful and thankful enjoyment of present mercies, to prepare themselves for a happy dissolution. Godliness teaches us to both quietly enjoy the world and willingly leave it when God calls. Annotations on Ecclesiastes 9:5.[16]

Proof Against Prayers to the Saints. Martin Luther: The living, he says, know that they will die, and therefore in life they use this hope. Therefore they should not postpone acting or doing well from one day to the next, as do the fools and softies, who always pay attention to the examples of others and will not do right until they see others do right. But the dead know nothing, and they have no more reward. Jerome has clumsily distorted this passage to apply to the reward of the dead in purgatory.[†] Solomon seems to feel that the dead are asleep in such a way that they know nothing whatever. And I do not believe that there is a more powerful passage in Scripture to show that the dead are asleep and do not know anything about our affairs—this in opposition to the invocation of the saints and the fiction of purgatory.[‡] "They have no reward" is a Hebraism for what we would say in German this way: "It is all over for those who are dead." All that was theirs is nothing; they no longer do what would have been beneficial. As we read elsewhere, "There is a reward for your work," and Paul says, "Your labor is not in vain." "Their love and their hate." You must understand all of this in an active sense, as it was understood earlier, that all the good deeds they did by loving, obeying, and so on are handed over to oblivion. But when Jerome raises the quibble that although the dead do not know anything of what goes on in the world, they do know other things, namely, those that go on in heaven, this is an error, and a foolish one at that. And they have no more in the world any share—that is, they have no traffic with us. He describes the dead as unfeeling corpses. Therefore, he wants us to use life as much as is permitted and to work as much as we can. For we are forced to relinquish the larger part of the world to Satan and can scarcely gain a thousandth part of it for God. And so if your lion dies, you had better not kill your dog. Annotations on Ecclesiastes.[17]

Enjoy God's Good Gifts Without Worry. Jean de Serres: "Go, eat your bread with enjoyment." He first noted these things in 8:15; now, he gathers a general conclusion with striking illustrations, and the upshot is that curiosity is altogether vain and harmful; that it torments the mind on account of this life's outrages and confusions; that it is better to use the good gifts of God with a sober and cheerful heart and diligently apply ourselves, each one to their own calling. . . . "Go" therefore, he says, as if to say, Do not trouble your mind too greatly with these cares, but rather use and enjoy those things that are before you with an assured quietness of mind. As for things which befall people in this life that you cannot help, allow them to come and go as they flow. . . . In the same way Christ warned Martha not to busy herself

[16]Downame, ed., *English Annotations*, 7D4r*; citing 2 Cor 5:4; Phil 1:20; Job 9:4; Is 38:18, 19; Ps 118:17; Job 14:14; Ps 39:1, 4; 90:12.

[17]LW 15:147-48 (WA 20:160-61); citing 2 Chron 15:7; 1 Cor 15:58. [†]Jerome considers the view that Luther attributes to him in his comments on this passage, but he rejects it as "unsatisfactory," insisting on the view that the dead "can add neither to their virtues nor vices." Jerome, *Commentarius in Ecclesiasten*, in Richard J. Goodrich and David J. D. Miller, trans., *St. Jerome: Commentary on Ecclesiastes*, Ancient Christian Writers 66 (Mahwah, NJ: Paulist Press, 2012), 102. [‡]Luther expressed himself in various ways on the state of the soul after death. In many places (as here), he seems to imply that the soul sleeps after death until it is awakened at the last judgment—a view condemned not only by the Roman Catholic Church but also by many magisterial Protestant reformers, such as John Calvin (see below). In other writings, however, Luther seems to have held that the souls of the faithful pass directly into the conscious enjoyment of God.

with too much worry about her household tasks. "Eat, drink"—that is to say, freely use and enjoy life's good things.

"At all times let your garments be white." By these words he signifies that we must leave nothing undone for the enjoyment of a cheerful and pleasant life—namely, that cleanliness and elegance that make food and drink more enjoyable are not to be overlooked. For whereas some expound these words allegorically, reading them in reference to a simplicity of the heart—a true enough idea, and agreeable to faith—yet it strays from the proper meaning of this passage. And by "oil" he refers to sweet-smelling oil and other precious ointments, which were much used in the East. For God gives us not only those things that are necessary for the maintenance of our lives but also those things that contribute to honest and joyful pleasure, as is also shown in Psalm 104. Commentary on Solomon's Ecclesiastes.[18]

The Race Is Not to the Swift. John Trapp: Here the Preacher proves (what he had found true by experience) by the event of human endeavors, which are often frustrated, that nothing is in our power, but all carried on by a providence, which often crosses our likeliest projects, so that God may have the honor of all. Let a person be as swift as Asahel or Atalanta, yet they may not get the goal or escape the danger. The battle of Terwin, in France (fought by our Henry VIII), was called the "Battle of the Spurs" because many fled for their lives, who yet fell (as the men of Ai did) into the midst of their enemies. At Musselburgh Field, many of the Scots who were running away so strained themselves in their race that they fell down breathless and dead, whereby they seemed in running from their deaths to run to it, whereas two thousand of them who lay all day as dead got away safely in the night.[†] A Commentary or Exposition upon Ecclesiastes.[19]

Work Hard, but Commit the Work to God. Martin Luther: You should understand "time" here not to refer only to the end of life but to every appointed time and outcome; as though he were saying, "You should labor even though you do not know what will come of it." Therefore get an education; if God wills, he will grant success and fruit through your study. We should do the same in all the other affairs and business of life. We should labor but commit the outcome to God. For the time of success is hidden from us. "Like fish." He uses two lovely analogies to prove that things happen usually contrary to our plans and hope. A fish snaps at the bait and swallows the hook. Birds confidently enter and eat, with nothing further from their minds than a trap; and then suddenly they are captured. So it is that when we have chosen something good and hoped for it, we are deceived. And when it seems that something evil is impending, it is something good that is impending. In such a way do we stumble into things from which we then cannot extricate ourselves that we obviously do not know how we are deceived. All of this is so because the appointed time is unknown to us. There experience itself teaches us that human affairs are carried out not by our plans but usually contrary to our plans. This is the source of the statement of luckless people: "That is not what I had in mind!" Annotations on Ecclesiastes.[20]

God's Providence Disrupts Human Expectations. Jean de Serres: Great ends are often achieved by only a few, wholly contrary to the opinion and expectation of all. Themistocles, when the safety of Greece was beyond all hope, forsook Athens and overthrew the mighty host of Xerxes,

[18]Serres, *Commentarius, in Solomonis Ecclesiasten*, 425-27; citing Lk 10:38-41.
[19]Trapp, *A Commentary or Exposition upon Ecclesiastes*, 126-127.
[†]The Second Battle of Guinegate took place in August 1513 during the War of the League of Cambrai. A joint army of English and imperial troops surprised a force of heavy French cavalry, whose precipitous flight gave rise to the encounter being known as the "Battle of the Spurs." The Battle of Pinkie Cleugh, in September 1547, was the last pitched battle between English and Scots armies before the union of the crowns. Both battles represented dramatic turns of fortune involving the unexpected triumph of (apparently) overmatched forces.
[20]LW 15:152-53 (WA 20:164).

which hitherto had conquered all by the fear of his very name. Cyrus, with a very small beginning, won the largest empire of the Chaldeans. Alexander with a small army put to flight the great host of Darius and won the empire of the east. And so that I need not rehearse an infinite number of examples from memory from all nations and ages, my own poor country has, within these past few years, witnessed various spectacles issuing in unexpected outcomes during the furies of our civil war. And such is the providence with which God is wont to disrupt human enterprises, as Mary teaches so magnificently in her song and daily experience abundantly proves. Commentary on Solomon's Ecclesiastes.[21]

Christ's Wisdom Also Despised. Thomas Granger: The rich do wrong and are not reproved; they utter folly and are praised. The poor do right and are not favored; they speak wisely, and the response is, "What fellow is this?" When Christ taught in the temple, they said, "How does he know the Scriptures, seeing he never learned?" Here is a miracle, a plain evidence of divine power and extraordinary wisdom, yet they lightly pass it by, for they judge according to his outward appearance. They knew where he came from, so they spoke with contempt. So when he taught in a synagogue, while their minds were fixed on his speeches (for the novelty of his teaching commanded their attention), they say, "Where does he get these things? What wisdom is this that is given to him?" But when his poverty, lack of education, trade, parents, and kinsfolk come into their minds, they are offended: they yield no honor, afford no entertainment, they believe nothing, but turn back to their old bias. So Paul's gospel was despised by the slanting preachers of Corinth because his bodily presence was weak and his sermons without philosophy or rhetoric. He was poor, humble, and spiritual. So do our slanting badges nowadays, that suit themselves to people's humors, admiring persons for advantage, and making themselves as strange to their brethren as ruffians do to those who are grave, wise, and elderly. They show what spirit they come from, and which way they came in. A Familiar Exposition.[22]

[21]Serres, *Commentarius, in Solomonis Ecclesiasten*, 433-34.

[22]Granger, *A Familiar Exposition or Commentarie on Ecclesiastes*, 247-48; citing Jn 7:14-15; Mk 6:2-3.

10:1–12:14 LIVE IN LIGHT OF THE COMING JUDGMENT

1 Dead flies make the perfumer's ointment give off a stench;
so a little folly outweighs wisdom and honor.

2 A wise man's heart inclines him to the right,
but a fool's heart to the left.

3 Even when the fool walks on the road, he lacks sense,
and he says to everyone that he is a fool.

4 If the anger of the ruler rises against you, do not leave your place,
for calmness[a] will lay great offenses to rest.

5 There is an evil that I have seen under the sun, as
it were an error proceeding from the ruler: 6 folly is set
in many high places, and the rich sit in a low place. 7 I
have seen slaves on horses, and princes walking on the
ground like slaves.

8 He who digs a pit will fall into it,
and a serpent will bite him who breaks through a wall.

9 He who quarries stones is hurt by them,
and he who splits logs is endangered by them.

10 If the iron is blunt, and one does not sharpen the edge,
he must use more strength,
but wisdom helps one to succeed.[b]

11 If the serpent bites before it is charmed,
there is no advantage to the charmer.

12 The words of a wise man's mouth win him favor,[c]
but the lips of a fool consume him.

13 The beginning of the words of his mouth is foolishness,
and the end of his talk is evil madness.

14 A fool multiplies words,
though no man knows what is to be,
and who can tell him what will be after him?

15 The toil of a fool wearies him,
for he does not know the way to the city.

16 Woe to you, O land, when your king is a child,
and your princes feast in the morning!

17 Happy are you, O land, when your king is the son of the nobility,
and your princes feast at the proper time,
for strength, and not for drunkenness!

18 Through sloth the roof sinks in,
and through indolence the house leaks.

19 Bread is made for laughter,
and wine gladdens life,
and money answers everything.

20 Even in your thoughts, do not curse the king,
nor in your bedroom curse the rich,

for a bird of the air will carry your voice,
or some winged creature tell the matter.

11 *Cast your bread upon the waters,*
for you will find it after many days.

2 Give a portion to seven, or even to eight,
for you know not what disaster may happen on earth.

3 If the clouds are full of rain,
they empty themselves on the earth,

and if a tree falls to the south or to the north,
in the place where the tree falls, there it will lie.

4 He who observes the wind will not sow,
and he who regards the clouds will not reap.

5 As you do not know the way the spirit comes to
the bones in the womb[d] of a woman with child, so you
do not know the work of God who makes everything.

[6]In the morning sow your seed, and at evening withhold not your hand, for you do not know which will prosper, this or that, or whether both alike will be good.

[7]Light is sweet, and it is pleasant for the eyes to see the sun.

[8]So if a person lives many years, let him rejoice in them all; but let him remember that the days of darkness will be many. All that comes is vanity.[e]

[9]Rejoice, O young man, in your youth, and let your heart cheer you in the days of your youth. Walk in the ways of your heart and the sight of your eyes. But know that for all these things God will bring you into judgment.

[10]Remove vexation from your heart, and put away pain[f] *from your body, for youth and the dawn of life are vanity.*

12 *Remember also your Creator in the days of your youth, before the evil days come and the years draw near of which you will say, "I have no pleasure in them"; [2]before the sun and the light and the moon and the stars are darkened and the clouds return after the rain, [3]in the day when the keepers of the house tremble, and the strong men are bent, and the grinders cease because they are few, and those who look through the windows are dimmed, [4]and the doors on the street are shut—when the sound of the grinding is low, and one rises up at the sound of a bird, and all the daughters of song are brought low— [5]they are afraid also of what is high, and terrors are in the way; the almond tree blossoms, the grasshopper drags itself along,*[g] *and desire fails, because man is going to his eternal home, and the mourners go about the streets— [6]before the silver cord is snapped, or the golden bowl is broken, or the pitcher is shattered at the fountain, or the wheel broken at the cistern, [7]and the dust returns to the earth as it was, and the spirit returns to God who gave it. [8]Vanity*[h] *of vanities, says the Preacher; all is vanity.*

[9]Besides being wise, the Preacher also taught the people knowledge, weighing and studying and arranging many proverbs with great care. [10]The Preacher sought to find words of delight, and uprightly he wrote words of truth.

[11]The words of the wise are like goads, and like nails firmly fixed are the collected sayings; they are given by one Shepherd. [12]My son, beware of anything beyond these. Of making many books there is no end, and much study is a weariness of the flesh.

[13]The end of the matter; all has been heard. Fear God and keep his commandments, for this is the whole duty of man.[i] *[14]For God will bring every deed into judgment, with*[j] *every secret thing, whether good or evil.*

a Hebrew *healing* **b** Or *wisdom is an advantage for success* **c** Or *are gracious* **d** Some Hebrew manuscripts, Targum; most Hebrew manuscripts *As you do not know the way of the wind, or how the bones grow in the womb* **e** The Hebrew term *hebel* can refer to a "vapor" or "mere breath"; also verse 10 (see note on 1:2) **f** Or *evil* **g** Or *is a burden* **h** The Hebrew term *hebel* can refer to a "vapor" or "mere breath" (three times in this verse); see note on 1:2 **i** Or *the duty of all mankind* **j** Or *into the judgment on*

Overview: The final three chapters of the book gather together a variety of moral and prudential admonitions in proverbial form (Eccles 10:1–11:6), concluding with an extended meditation on the miseries of old age and the advantages of seeking God in one's youth (Eccles 11:7–12:14). Philipp Melanchthon takes what might be interpreted as a bit of worldly advice to bide one's time (Eccles 10:4) and uses it to urge pastors to expect opposition from "yes men" and stand firm. In similar fashion, Michael Jermin takes the apparent cynicism of Ecclesiastes 10:19, "money answers everything," as a lament for human corruption rather than a license for sharp practice. The familiar appeal to "cast your bread upon the waters" (Eccles 11:1) summons the eloquence of many of our commentators in expounding themes of generosity and God's promise to repay alms given in faith. In glossing this passage intertextually with reference to Proverbs 19:17 (a locus classicus for the traditional view of salvific almsgiving), Denis the Carthusian and Martin Luther display the ongoing relevance of these texts to the church's social and economic teachings; Melanchthon is the outlier here in reading the text as an explication of vocation rather than works of mercy. The book's concluding section contains the Preacher's thoughts on approaching old age, death, and future judgment, and he urges his readers to live in the light of providence while youth still affords the power to seek God. Both Cardinal Cajetan and Thomas Granger gloss the "light" that is "sweet to the eyes" (Eccles 11:7) as worldly prosperity. Cajetan warns that the light is fleeting, and so must be used to good purpose; Granger sharply inveighs against those who are dazzled by the light and cannot see further than their own immediate comfort. Melanchthon unpacks the sobering picture of old age as a warning against confidence in one's own powers of self-preservation, considerations congruent with the stress Granger and Jean de Serres place on the reality of God's impending judgment. The final admonition is to fear God and obey his commandments, a statement most of our commentators take as summarizing the book's main argument. Disagreement still remains on the matter of judgment, however. Unwilling to connect these imperatives directly with salvation, Luther reads the book's final warning of judgment as concerning proximate, this-worldly judgment: obey God's commandments because these commandments embody the wisdom required to live in the world God has made. Konrad Pellikan, on the other hand, may be taken as representative of the majority of our commentators, who view the Preacher's final words as pointing to eschatological judgment.

10:1-11:6 *Miscellaneous Proverbs*

A Fly in the Ointment. Jean de Serres: Such, he says, is the corruption and pestilence of this wicked folly that the one who is infected with it, no matter how great the gifts with which they are besides endowed, stinks shamefully; that is, those same gifts are altogether useless and destructive, and turn so much more to his greater condemnation. . . . Saul had excellent political gifts, as did Judas, but they were rotten flies in the ointment. Political gifts are certainly to be desired, but above all we ought to beg God for his Holy Spirit, a gift never to be repented of, a gift whose holy effect is a good conscience. Commentary on Solomon's Ecclesiastes.[1]

Faithful Leaders Stand Firm. Philipp Melanchthon: Even if for a time the envious triumph, whether sycophants or a boastful Thrasso,[†] do not be moved from acting justly, or give up your station on account of the perversity of their judgments, or from indignation. A good and faithful pastor is not moved by calumnies or vulgar clamors to desert the church, nor does he adjust himself to give countenance to wicked opinions, because in the meantime he will still be able to offer healing to many. Next follows a complaint deploring that common evil, and urging that since fools and the wicked often rule, it is easier in the court to be a yes man and parrot the moods of the lord rather than give wise and faithful counsel, as in these verses.

This life has mostly to the wicked befallen: "Yes men do best of all, blackmailers win the second prize."[‡] Enarration on Ecclesiastes.[2]

A Figure of Folly in Power. Thomas Granger: A particular explication of the evil or disorder before generally propounded is illustrated in these two verses: "Folly is set in great dignity, and the rich in a low place." Folly is a metonym of the adjunct, for a fool. By "fool" is not meant someone who is destitute of reason or understanding, but especially the one who has both but uses neither or abuses both. As the fruit of cracked or crazed reason is folly, so of corrupt or wicked reason also. There is more hope of a fool than of the one who is willful in their ways;

[1]Serres, *Commentarius, in Solomonis Ecclesiasten*, 442.
[2]CR 14:94-95. [†]A braggart captain in Terence, *Eunuchus* 3.1. [‡]Menander, fr. 223 (LCL 459:72-73).

corrupt or wicked wit is worse than a weak understanding. By "rich" is not meant wealthy, but rich in wisdom, understanding, discretion, and gifts to discharge the high calling of a prince or ruler, as it is said, that God gave to Saul another heart, and that was figured by the holy oil, with which the kings of Israel were anointed at their coronation. This is the complaint of Solomon, that unreasonable and reasonless men should sit on the throne and the bench. That such should reign and sit in the place of judgment is the secret judgment of God, either because people despise the goodness of God in his Word, and so he sets evil princes or children to rule over them, or else for their trial, that their faith may be tried under a wicked ruler. But it does not follow, as this complaint intimates, that either wicked or childish princes should be seditiously thrust out of their place and office, as Childeric king of France is said to have been by Pope Zacharias,[†] for that is nothing else but to offer violence to God, to pull the scourge out of his hand, which with patience we must bear. But we must rather look to the cause: our sins and hypocrisies. We must pray for patience and repentance, and pardon, and so remove evil with good, and not contend against God to increase our miseries. A Familiar Exposition.[3]

The Gravedigger's Warning. Martin Luther: Here Solomon inserts a kind of collection of proverbs, all of which he applies to the experience of governing human affairs. It is as though he were saying, "In human affairs, what these proverbs say is what happens. Whatever you undertake in human affairs, you will have the same experience as is described here: 'The one who digs a pit . . .'—that is, one does not get out of it without trouble. Similarly, governing people is the same as breaking through a wall, where it often happens that you are bitten by a serpent. Therefore even if evil things happen to you, do not be a quitter, but remember that it cannot be otherwise in human affairs." Governing human beings belongs only to God. Therefore anyone who has charge of administration should know that they are administering matters that cannot be controlled by any human counsel. The hearts of human beings do not lie in our own power. Only those who have the fear of God are easy to govern.

The proverb is taken from the experience of gravediggers, to whom it tends to happen that they will unknowingly fall into their pits. Thus governing human affairs is the same as digging a pit, where you should be forewarned that you will never be out of danger: for unless you are forewarned, you will fall into much greater and more unforeseen dangers. Dangers that one has foreseen do not strike as hard. Demipho in Terence's *Phormio* has wisely warned about this when he says, "Therefore when things are going well, all people should above all think about how they will bear the opposite kind of fate—danger, condemnation, exile."[†] A man returning from a journey should always consider the possibility that his son has committed some sin or that his wife has died or that his daughter has been taken ill. These are common things and can happen, and therefore this should not be something novel for his spirit. Whatever happens beyond your expectation you should regard as a gain, so that if something like this happens, you can say, "This is what I expected," and can recall that nothing is happening to you that is contrary to general human experience. In fact, if something good happens to you, you should regard it as your daily gain. Therefore one must not immediately quit digging, even though a careless person may fall in. Human life is filled with dangers. And just as in breaking through a wall there is often a danger that a hidden serpent will bite, so we must be careful in the administration of human affairs that we don't get hurt. But if you are bitten or get hurt, you must bear it; for what is happening to you is nothing new. Annotations on Ecclesiastes.[4]

---

[3]Granger, *A Familiar Exposition or Commentarie on Ecclesiastes*, 257-58; citing 1 Sam 10:9. [†]Childeric III (c. 717–754) was the last of the Merovingian kings. He was deposed in 743 by Pope Zacharias at the instigation of Pepin the Short.

[4]LW 15:160-61 (WA 20:171-72). [†]Terence, *Phormio* 241-43.

Do Not Break the Hedge of Unity. John Donne: The first thing that the householder in the parable [of the tenants] is noted to have done for his vineyard was "He hedged it in." That God has done for us in making us his church. He has inlaid us; he has hedged us in. . . . The one who breaks this hedge, the peace of the church, by their schism, the old serpent has bitten and poisoned and shall bite worse hereafter. If God, having thus severed us and hedged us in, expected grapes and we bring none, though we break no hedge here among ourselves, that is, no papist breaks in on us or no separatist breaks out from us, we enjoy security enough, yet even for our own barrenness, "God will take away the hedge and it shall be eaten up; he will break the wall and it will be trodden down." "Surely," says the prophet there, "the vineyard of the Lord of hosts is the house of Israel and the people of Judah are his pleasant plant." Surely we are the church which God has hedged in, but if we do not answer his expectation, certainly the confusion of the Gentiles at the last day (when they shall say to themselves of Christ, "Do you condemn us, and we do not know you?") shall not be so great as our confusion when we shall hear Christ say to us, whom he bred in his church, "I know not whence you are." Even this, that the ill use of his mercy of having been bred in his church, shall aggravate our condemnation then, shows the great benefit that we receive now that he takes care of us in his church. How many of the world would have lived ten times more Christianly than we do if they had but half the knowledge of Christ which we have? Sermon on Revelation 7:17.[5]

Wisdom and Labor Must Be United. The English Annotations: The fool puts all his strength into cleaving knotty wood with blunt tools, and all in vain. Instead, a little wisdom to whet their iron would make the work easier and more effectual. So here the fool, like an ignorant traveler, has lost their way and goes up and down to little purpose until they weary themselves, yet can never find the way to the city, something that otherwise could be easily done, because they lack skill or a guide to direct them. Where wisdom is wanting to direct our actions, labor will be endless, and we shall sooner weary ourselves than effect anything by blind endeavors. . . . True wisdom is to understand our way and make straight our paths for our feet to walk in, and to have the light shine on our ways, whatever relation we stand in, or whatever employment we are called to. Annotations on Ecclesiastes 10:15.[6]

Warning Against Immature Leadership. Jean de Serres: He spoke above concerning how we ought to conduct ourselves amid the dangers of a disordered and tyrannical rule; now he preaches on good governance and its opposite. For this reason I suppose that these two verses (16-17) and verse 20 have been set out of their places by the rabbis, as is apparent with the story set at the end of Judges, concerning the wife of the Levite who was defiled by the Benjaminites, in which mention is made of Phinehas the son of Eleazar, who could not have lived to such an age.[†] I am hesitant to change even a jot here, but if these verses are read in conjunction with verse 5, the thought flows more smoothly. "Woe to you, O land." He says that the land is unhappy with evil princes, and happy with good ones, for it is a great plague when those who ought to govern with goodness, justice, wisdom, and sobriety instead rush in like wolves to the ruin and destruction of human kind. "When your king is a child." He speaks not simply of those who are children in age (for kingdoms may in fact be governed very well by children, and on the contrary, they may be governed very ill by old men), but in wit and wisdom, such that they are carried headlong by evil counsel, as we are warned about in Isaiah and Hosea. Commentary on Solomon's Ecclesiastes.[7]

---

[5]Donne, *Works*, 4:56-57*; citing Mt 21:33; Is 5:8.

[6]Downame, ed., *English Annotations*, 7E3r*; citing Prov 14:8; Heb 12:13; Ps 5:8.

[7]Serres, *Commentarius, in Solomonis Ecclesiasten*, 454-55. [†]Serres is referring to Judg 20:27-28. The chronological issues raised by the narrative in Judges were well-known to Reformation-era

Beware Riotousness and Covetousness. Antonio del Corro: Now it is common in the courts of princes for one to see them not given to sobriety, temperance, and the common good, but continually preparing sumptuous feasts, making costly banquets for pleasure, laughing and making sport, not for necessity of nature; also, quaffing wine in unmeasurable bowls, not to quench their thirst, but for merriness, drunkenness, or mere madness. This immoderate riot of meat and drink, as well as the insolent expenses of sumptuous attire and costly apparel, arise from an infinite desire of possessing. For so great pleasures can neither be prepared nor maintained without much money and wealth. Thus they seek that they may spend, and when they have spent it seek to get more to make it up again. Thus covetousness engenders riotousness, and riotousness brings forth covetousness again. When these two have first crept into the commonwealth they will of necessity overthrow all. A Sermon of King Solomon the Wise.[8]

The Dangerous Power of Money. Michael Jermin: Having shown the hurt that comes to a land whose king is a child and whose princes eat in the morning, here the Preacher shows the good that arises in a land whose king is the son of nobles, whose princes eat in due season. So Cajetan joins this verse to the former, saying that these things belong to that blessed land spoken of before—namely, in abundance of bread, wine, and silver: "and abundance of bread is described by the expression, 'making bread for laughter.'"[†] For the original word, which is translated "feast," primarily signifies bread. Or else to refer this verse to that which goes immediately before it, as there the Preacher shows the mischief of laziness and sloth, so here we may understand him to show the benefit of labor and pains, from which come plenty (noted by "feasting" and "wine"), pleasure and delight (noted by laughter), wealth, and greatness of estate (noted by "money, which answers to all things"). That last part of the verse the Septuagint renders "all things by subjection obey money." And if it be understood with reference to those "kings whose sons are nobles," the words show how they bind their subjects to them by their humanity and alacrity in liberality. . . . Tremellius refers this verse to the ones preceding, but he reads the words in reference to those who voluptuously eat in the morning, whose buildings decay through sloth, and whose house falls in on account of idleness, since all is spent on luxurious living. He then reads the last part of the verse to indicate that their money makes all those things answer to their lustful desires. . . .

Our translation sets down the verse as if it were a sentence by itself, and as showing that whereas "a feast is made for laughter only, and wine is drunk to make merry only, that money serves for all things." The Preacher expresses the force of money by a *prosopopoeia*, and supposing the things to be endowed with speech and understanding, affirms money to give a satisfactory answer to whatsoever is asked, desired, commanded. Even if that which speaks is a great way off, yet money hears and answers to it. Seneca says that "about money there is much noise," but however much or great, money answers all.[‡] To make the sense more plain Pagine reads it, "money obtains all things"; Symachus reads it, "silver is profitable for all things." And this was the judgment of Verres, as Cicero sets it down: "all things can be done with money."[§] This is the same idea that the poet expresses: "Queen money gives nobility of birth, and beauty of body."[◊] This is why the prophet David, that he might show his great esteem for God and his great affection toward him, compares him with money and riches, saying, "I have rejoiced in the ways of your commandments as much as in all riches." Riches being held in such high regard and so beloved, he shows his regard and love for God to be much above it. And by whom is it honored so greatly? With whom is it so powerful? Aquinas answers, "All material things obey money, so far as the multitude of fools is

commentators; for a sample of the various solutions proposed, see RCS OT 4:446.

[8]Corro, *Sapientissimi regis Salomonis Concio*, 244-45.

concerned, who know no other than material goods, which can be obtained for money. But we should take our estimation of human goods not from the foolish but from the wise."[Δ] They are but fools therefore over whom money has so great a command; they are but fools who are so affected with it, as Gregory Thaumaturgus expounds this part of the verse: "By money they are drawn anywhere, being ready for a low price to do any vile and base thing."[††] Commentary upon the Whole Booke of Ecclesiastes.[9]

A Warning Against Listening Ears. Jean de Serres: Another effect of Christian wisdom (about which we spoke above in connection with verse 5) concerns how we ought to conduct ourselves under disorderly regimes. In this most wicked world we ought to exercise great caution, and if the morals of the ruler are distasteful to us we ought not to tell anyone, since this often exposes one to great danger. But he speaks in hyperbole when he says, "Speak no evil of the king, not even in your thought"—that is, be careful not to make yourself bear witness to those thoughts. . . . Yet he does not take away the holy liberty of the servants of God in reproving kings, when their calling requires it; but he shows every private person how discreetly and prudently they ought to carry themselves to avoid falling into danger, lest through foolish zeal they become ministers of reckless danger. He demonstrates the reason for this with an imaginary illustration: the power of kings is so great that even the very birds will tell them of things spoken or whispered in the ear within our most secret chambers. For they have spies everywhere, and their arms are long. Therefore we ought to take heed that we be wise as serpents and innocent as doves; to walk circumspectly, not as unwise, but as wise; to diligently pay attention to what is going on around us, and so be reminded to redeem the time, as the apostle says, because the days are evil. Commentary on Solomon's Ecclesiastes.[10]

The Sins of Authorities Are No Excuse for Rebellion. The English Annotations: Because, by occasion of such sins of misgovernment in evil princes, people might be very apt, through impatience of spirit, to break forth into disloyal thoughts and affection toward them, however, they might haply be restrained by fear of danger from seditious speeches or rebellious practices. He therefore concludes this whole argument with a strict prohibition on all hard and undutiful thoughts and risings of heart against rulers, notwithstanding their errors in government and corruption in living, not so much as secretly in their hearts to wrong them, both for the sake of conscience and for fear of wrath, as the apostle likewise directs. Annotations on Ecclesiastes 10:20.[11]

Works of Mercy. Denis the Carthusian: This is an admonition to works of spiritual and corporal mercy. "Cast your bread," that is, pour out corporal and spiritual refreshment, "upon the waters," that is, upon poor mendicants and those of your household who are needy, for they are like many waters, carrying you across to your ultimate end. Hence that saying in the Apocalypse, "The waters that you saw . . . are people and nations and tongues." And also this admonition in Isaiah: "Deal your bread to the hungry." And again, "Blessed are you who sow upon all the waters." "For you will find it after many days"—that is, you shall obtain the fruit and reward from it on the day of your death and judgment. "The one who is merciful to the poor lends to the Lord at interest." And this is why Tobit urges, "According to your ability, show mercy." "For thus you store up for yourself a good reward for the day of necessity. For alms deliver

[9]Jermin, *A commentary, upon the whole booke of Ecclesiastes*, 392-94; citing Ps 119:14. [†]Cajetan, *Parabolae Salomonis ad veritatem Hebraicam castigatae*, 377. [‡]Seneca, *De ira* 33. [§]Cicero, *In Verrem* 2.155. [◊]Horace, *Epistle* 1.4.35. [Δ]Aquinas, *Summa Theologiae* I-II, q. 2, a. 1, r. 1. [††]Oecolampadius, *In Ecclesiastem Solomonis Metaphrasis Divi Gregorii Neocaesariensis Episcopi*, 30.

[10]Serres, *Commentarius, in Solomonis Ecclesiasten*, 458-59; citing Eph 5:16.

[11]Downame, ed., *English Annotations*, 7E3v*; citing Rom 13:5.

from all sin, and from death, and will not suffer the soul to go into darkness. Alms will be a great confidence before the most high God to all those who give it." And so thus will Christ say to the merciful on the day of judgment, "Whatever you did to the least of these ones of mine, you did to me." Exposition of the Book of Ecclesiastes.[12]

Giving Generously. Martin Luther: "Cast your bread upon the waters." This again is a Hebraism, as Solomon abounds in figures of speech. He wants to say, "Be generous to everyone while you can; use your riches wherever you can possibly do any good." And he adds a promise: "For if you live long enough, you will receive back a hundredfold." So we read in Proverbs, "The one who is kind to the poor lends to the Lord"; so also Christ says, "Give, and it will be given to you"; and Paul says, "God loves a cheerful giver." Whoever wants to be poor, let them not give anything to others. Therefore he says, "Cast your bread"—that is, share your food, which the Lord has given to you. "Upon the waters"—that is, give it simply and generously, even though your kindness seems to you to perish and your bread seems to sink into the water. Solomon is using a metaphor, with which he merely wants to say, Being mortal yourself, feed those who are mortal. "For you will find it after many days"—that is, if you live long, you will find that bread which you have cast upon the waters. It is as though he were saying, The fact that you have been generous to others will not perish, even though it may seem to perish. Indeed, after a long time the Lord will grant bread. Psalm 37:26 says, "He is ever giving liberally and lending"; and again, "In the days of famine they have abundance." For God does not let himself be surpassed in generosity, but surpasses our generosity in endless ways. Annotations on Ecclesiastes.[13]

[12]DCOO 7:278; citing Rev 17:15; Is 58:6; Is 32:20; Prov 19:17; Tob 4:8, 10-12; Mt 25:40.

[13]LW 15:171 (WA 20:184); citing Prov 19:17; Lk 6:38; 2 Cor 9:7; Ps 37:19.

Entrust Your Labors to Providence. Philipp Melanchthon: This chapter casts a light on the whole book, for it demonstrates that these sermons are aimed at establishing a confirmation of the idea of providence and a refutation of the arguments that natural people have made to cast doubt on providence. Therefore it is the main argument that is placed here at the end: out of all these things, God will lead you into judgment. He expressly affirms that God judges and will judge human deeds, and he repeats this statement at the end of his sermon: "Fear God and obey his commands."

Having established this idea, that God will judge and that we should obey him according to his commandments, now consolations follow. When my mind doubts, what should I do? I see that many of my labors are ineffectual, and many people are ungrateful; I see hatred and hardships arising; should I remove myself from social life, or take myself away to solitary places, following that ancient maxim, "live unknown" (*lathe biōsas*)?[†] By no means! For earlier it was said, Work steadfastly at what God has given you to do. So he says, Obey his commandments and commit the outcome to God. Then you will not be broken by pain if adversities fall, but through these you will serve God, and by faith retain peace of mind, prayer, and hope. Be assured that that obedience is pleasing to God, and that your labors will not be altogether ineffectual, even if at times severe storms arise. Indeed, many great tumults troubled the reign of Moses, and the treachery of his own son troubled that of David. So we know that these things happen, and we ought not to lose hope, let our hearts be troubled, or fall away from prayer and our lawful duties, but rather we should think continually on this saying, "Commend your way to God and hope in him, and he will act." And this passage from Paul, "Your work is not in vain in the Lord." And Psalm 1: "His leaf does not wither." It is utterly necessary for all to understand this whole teaching and consolation in life, which indeed is handed down by God for this very reason, because reason is damaged by this confusion and led to doubt in God's care and help. This is the basic idea of the chapter—and indeed, of the whole book.

And this is what he says about the operations of God's governance: "Cast your bread upon the waters"—that is, let the teacher spread his teachings among the people like one casting bait into the water expects to catch fish, or one casting seeds elsewhere expects a harvest. So also a ruler spreads his labors in the way. For though some will perish, yet these labors will be of some use, and that usefulness will be understood by posterity. The government of Jeremiah was full of distress, but nevertheless it benefited all who came later. As long as there is occasion, continue to perform the duties of your calling, just as Paul commands us to redeem the time, because the days are evil. In other words, he orders them to take advantage of the opportunity, because in such miseries good counsels are often hindered. Enarration on Ecclesiastes.[14]

Give Freely, Expecting God to Repay. Jean de Serres: Here is a noble precept regarding the generosity of Christian charity in relieving the poor. The whole speech is figurative: "Cast your bread upon the waters"—that is, give liberally from your goods to the poor; show yourself a generous and ready giver of your wealth, and don't withdraw your hand from doing good when it appears you have no hope of being repaid. Rather, when it comes to helping the poor and those who stand in need of your assistance, cast them upon the face of the water as if they should be lost, even though you do not know what success your generosity may have. This is a hyperbolic way of speaking. For he does not remove prudential judgment, that considering matters wisely and diligently we should bestow a benefit on those whom we shall think worthy of our help, especially on those who are of the household of faith. But he does want us to understand that we must make no delay in helping the poor while we make curious inquiry as to who is worthy and who is unworthy. He would rather have our bread be "cast upon the waters," as though it should perish. . . . Even though it seems that what you have given is entirely lost, yet know this for certain: in the end you shall receive back again the benefit that you bestowed on the poor person, and that with interest. For God, to whom we owe ourselves and all that we have and who owes nothing to any creature, has given his promise as if he were the cosigner on the loan, and pledges us faithfully that he will pay us back again with great increase for everything we give to the poor in his name. Commentary on Solomon's Ecclesiastes.[15]

Do Good Before Evil Strikes. The English Annotations: Embrace the present opportunity to do good. You cannot foresee how soon you may be deprived of it, since you do not know what a day might bring forth. You may die and leave your wealth to those who will shut up their bowels against the poor. What they do shall not be put on your account, however. You are a steward of your estate no longer than for your own life, and therefore be your own executor, consider the wants of the poor at present and let not your bounty be only future. Perhaps God may prevent you another time from doing that good which he now puts into your hand. It is wisdom to do God's work in God's time. You yourself may fall into want and stand in need of help from others, therefore make yourself friends with mammon beforehand. Annotations on Ecclesiastes 11:2.[16]

11:7–12:14 *Youth Versus Old Age*

The Sun's Light Is Sweet, But Fleeting. Cardinal Cajetan: "The light is sweet, and it is delightful for the eyes to see the sun." The thought

[14]CR 14:94-95; citing Eccles 9:10; Ps 37:5 1 Cor 15:58; Ps 1:3; Eph 5:16. †A maxim attributed to Epicurus (see frag. 551) and frequently discussed by the ancient moralists. Plutarch, for example, devoted a short treatise to the question, *Is "Live Alone" a Wise Precept?* (*De latenter vivendo*; LCL 428:322-41).

[15]Serres, *Commentarius, in Solomonis Ecclesiasten*, 461-62; citing Gal 6:10.

[16]Downame, ed., *English Annotations*, 7E4v*; citing Jas 4:14; Prov 27:1; 3:27, 28; Lk 12:20.

is rendered differently in the Hebrew: "It is sweet and good for eyes to see the sun." Having finished the admonition concerning almsgiving, he moves on now to the fear of divine judgment, which is another good revelation to the mind. For just as almsgiving is a good exterior work, so fear of divine judgment is a good that inheres in the soul. First he discusses the time of future judgment; then he discusses the case to be pled at the judgment and declares that the time of trial will be after this life comparing the quality of the present life with the time after death. And so beginning from this life, he says that "the light of the present life is sweet, and it is good to see the sun." By this he means that the prosperity of the present life is sweet to humanity, and pleasant sensations delight the perception, just as the light of the sun that delights the eyes is well disposed for their good. "If a person live many years, and has rejoiced in them all, they must remember the darksome time, and the many days in which, when they shall come, the things past shall be accused of vanity." This is a continuation of the preceding idea, and it opens up its meaning more clearly. Although the present life may be sweet, let the one who lives for many years and always in joy remember that there will be many days of darkness (i.e., after death), and consider that everything that occurs in the present life is vanity. The Parables of Solomon [and Ecclesiastes], Corrected by the Original Hebrew.[17]

A Warning Against Thoughtless Ease. Thomas Granger: By "light" is meant worldly prosperity, just as in Isaiah: "Then shall your light break forth as the morning." By "the sun" is meant a happy outward estate, excelling all others, splendid and pompous, of which the whole world is enamored, as its only happiness, as in Job: "If I beheld the sun when it shined, or the moon walking in her brightness"—that is, if my heart was enamored of my flourishing estate, if I blessed myself for my wealth, power, and honor. To proceed, whereas Solomon before warned his readers from coveting earthly things and preferring self-love to charity and good works (so that he might more firmly establish this grace in their hearts), now he uproots the weeds of fleshly pleasures. He does this by bringing in the carnal person's objections on his own behalf . . . clinging to his dirty god Mammon, as crabs cleave to the rock and to one another when they are pulled away.

Ah! Even though a goodly inheritance is a sweet thing, it is a pleasant thing to be well-seated in a fertile soil, in a wholesome air, near to the river, not far from the city or market, to be free from all troubles and cares that poverty brings. What a heavenly life it is when a man need do nothing but walk about his grounds for his pleasure, oversee his workmen, look on his cattle, and so on (just as the covetous rich man did in Luke 12); when he is well-provided with the best household stuff and lodgings and able to make his friends welcome, to entertain a gentleman, to keep gentlemen company, to keep a couple of servants and a good gelding, to ride with credit and to change the fashion with the better sort, to have money always in his purse, to be able to do a favor for a friend or a gentleman at his request in need, to be able to maintain his wife in the style of a gentlewoman, and to bring up his children in learning for greater advancement. Ah, this is a lovely and desirable estate above all things, say what they will. . . . What a zealous man is this! How his bowels yearn with pity for the poor, and his poor minister! How he seeks first the kingdom of God and his righteousness! He means to be first, a covetous beast, to rake in money by any means, by hook or by crook, from church and the poor, and to leave his substance to his heir. But when the devils fetch him away and his heir roguishly wastes it all and is finally hanged, then shall his folly and madness be apparent. In the meantime nothing plagues him but "precise preachers," and they are his tormentors.† A Familiar Exposition.[18]

[17]Cajetan, *Parabolae Salomonis ad veritatem Hebraicam castigatae*, 381-82.

[18]Granger, *A Familiar Exposition or Commentarie on Ecclesiastes*, 301-3; citing Is 58:8; Job 31:26. †"Precise preachers," or "precision

Solomonic Irony. Jean de Serres: In view of life's vanity, we must live in the awareness that we are to die, and so we must use this life soberly and moderately, and not carry on so as to become intoxicated with life's pleasures. Now, this teaching applies to all people, but Solomon applies it in particular to the young, who through the vigor of their blooming age, combined with their lack of experience, do not think that they will ever die or that the strength of their youth will ever fail them. For this reason, they indulge more easily in immoderate pleasures. In another passage the sage also bids us rejoice, in the sense that we should use the good things of life cheerfully and gratefully.† But in this passage it is not to be so understood; the words run, "walk in the ways of your heart," which doubtless is not telling us to do whatever we want. Rather, we should understand this as a mocking (*eirōnikōs*) concession, as if he should say, "Have at it, young man, chase your pleasure and indulge yourself as much as you want. But know that in the end you must render accounts to God for your life." Commentary on Solomon's Ecclesiastes.[19]

Warnings and Promises. Philipp Melanchthon: Remember your Creator in prosperity and in adversity; obey him, rest in him and in his promises by faith, according to the promises that in his boundless goodness he has delivered to the church for the Mediator's sake. And know above all that when you call on him and desire to obey him, he will hear you; yet he will horribly punish those who defy him. Therefore he repeats the admonition about judgment and adds mention of old age and death, so that by this argument he may strengthen the assurances of providence, and exhort us to the fear of God, to faith and to obedience. There is no safety for those who despise God, for sickness and death make manifest our weakness. Even if you are drunk with fortune's favor and you have great hopes for the future, yet the hour of death will suddenly shake off these dreams. And if you have despised God in judgment, you will rush into everlasting wrath and eternal punishment. He gives this warning about death and judgment so as to draw us back from carnal security, and from doubts to the consideration of providence, to the fear of God, to faith and obedience.

There follows a figurative description of old age, which appears to have been taken from nature itself and from its physical signs. But not all of the metaphors are immediately obvious. "Before the sun and moon and stars are darkened"—that is, to the old the appearance of the entire natural world is duller and sadder. "And the clouds return with the rain"—that is, from time to time new miseries and new calamities arise; when one evil has passed, another comes, just as [Achilles] complains in Homer: "Thus for me does evil ever follow on evil."† Also, "Fear old age, for it does not come alone."‡ "When the guardians of the house tremble"—that is, the hands, because the nerves, tendons, and ligaments become more languid and feeble. "And the strong men are bent" in legs and thighs. "The grinders will be idle, and fewer": the teeth will grow weak and fall out. "When those who peer through the windows see dimly": the eyes grow weak. "The doors are closed": the lips become dry and flabby. "They shall rise at the voice of a bird": their sleep will be brief, for old people are easily woken by the rooster's crow. "The daughters of song are brought low": either the ears become deaf or the voice itself goes silent, because in the elderly there is less of spirits in the heart, and the lungs and trachea become weaker by cold humidity or dryness. "They shall fear high places in the way": they become afraid of heights. "The almond tree blossoms": gray hairs sprout up, like in the almond tree. "The locusts drag

men," were sardonic terms of abuse for preachers whose moral demands made their hearers uncomfortable. Richard Baxter gives voice to how these terms were often used against him and his fellow pastors: "Is it not almost the common voice of the nation in effect—'Give us our sports, and liberty of sinning; give us our readers, and singing men, our drunken preachers; give us our holydays and ceremonies, and the customs of our forefathers: away with these precise fellows; they are an eye-sore to us: these precise preachers shall not control us; this precise Scripture shall be no law to us'; and, consequently, this Christ shall not rule over us?" *The Practical Writings of Richard Baxter* (New Haven: Durrie & Peck, 1844), 2:317.

[19]Serres, *Commentarius, in Solomonis Ecclesiasten*, 470-71. †See Serres's comments on Eccles 9:7, above.

themselves along": the scapula and the hips are bent down—that is, the old men walk with a slump. And the shape of the exposed shoulder blades, and the hips, and the curved spine of the back is similar to that of the locust. "And desire fails": there is a loathing and nausea for food, drink, and other pleasures; because manhood is languishing, there is bad digestion, little good blood and spirits, and a little nourishment. Afterward he speaks of the interior ills. . . . This description of the old age and death is inserted here to remind readers of future judgment, just as he next repeats that saying: "God will bring all things to judgment," and so by means of this meditation on judgment, he aims to confirm our faith in providence, and arouse us to the fear of God, to prayers, and an earnestness in acting justly. Enarration on Ecclesiastes.[20]

Remember Death and Live Well. Jean de Serres: Some think that tender age grants a certain license for running riot, as though it were not yet the time to live wisely, just as nowadays many sneer at sober warnings. But against this, the sage warns that the time of living well is not to be put off for long, but that even in youth we ought to make a start of attaining wisdom. This is why it is fitting for the young to remember their Maker, for piety is the source and foundation of a good and blessed life. The time to think about such things is "before the evil days come," that is, before old age and the time of death draw near, and a late repentance; for if the occasion is missed, there is no opportunity to go back and recover the lost opportunity of doing good, or of recovering what has been lost. . . . The sum of this whole passage is that we must bear death continually in mind, so that living well, we may die well. Commentary on Solomon's Ecclesiastes.[21]

Necessity Is No Virtue. Henry Lok:

"Remember thy creator then, in these thy youthful days,
Ere crooked age all pleasure to thy loathed life denies."
And since though canst not shun death's fatall day,
And as the tree doth fall so shall it rise,
(Whilst yet thou mayest) prepare a quiet way
    Unto thy soul, which in such danger lies,
    If thou in time relief do not devise.

The earth and earthly things, do help deny
Heaven is the harbor, where thy soul doth dwell,
Let not thy hope on earth then longer stay,
But it and works thereof from heart expel,
    Delay no time in hope long life to have,
    Youth may, age must, ere long time go to grave.

To heaven thy progress though dost wish to make,
Then clothe thyself accordingly therefor,
The clogs of worldly love and lust forsake,
    And think them burdens to thee evermore,
    And in thy life, have lights of virtue store.

Let thought of thy Creator thee awake
From sins of youth, heart-burdensome in age,
Remember God account of thee will take,
If thy repentance not his wrath assuage,
    Yea leave thou sin, ere lust leave tempting thee,
    The abstinence else, cannot virtue be.

Ecclesiastes, Otherwise Called the Preacher.[22]

The Unfallen Spirit Returns to God. Balthasar Hubmaier: It is easy to note how the law is given in different ways: to the flesh for the recognition of its sins; to the spirit as an aid and witness against sin; to the soul as a light whereby it can see and learn the way of righteousness and flee sin and evil. Thus, when the flesh hears the law, it is frightened and its hair stands on end in terror. The spirit leaps for joy.† The believing soul thanks God and praises him for the lamp and light to his feet. For as the devil neither wishes to nor can do good, but is stuck in his evil, so likewise our flesh, since it has sinned out of willfulness when it saw the forbidden fruit was good to eat and was

[20]CR 14:141-44. †Homer, *Iliad* 19.290 (LCL 171:355). †Menander, *Sententiae* 802 and 830; Erasmus, *Adagia* 2.6.37 (CWE 33:309).
[21]Serres, *Commentarius, in Solomonis Ecclesiasten*, 473-74.

[22]Lok, *Ecclesiastes, Otherwise Called the Preacher*, 107.

appealing to the eyes and lovely to the sight. However, the soul did not sin out of its own willfulness but out of weakness and the impulse of the flesh since Adam did not want to grieve Eve, who was his flesh. And then he excused himself and said, "The woman you gave me for a mate, gave me from the tree and I ate." Only the spirit has remained upright in this fall; therefore it will return to the Lord who gave it. Freedom of the Will I.[23]

Don't Wait Until Old Age. The English Annotations: Our origin from the dust and our return to the dust should humble us and make us vile in our own eyes, and warn us to make haste to secure a better life before this is ended and not to put off endeavors toward it until old age, which we may well never attain to, and if we do, will bring itself work enough for us to do. Death is swift and uncertain. Sin, the longer lived in, is more hardened. Repentance is not in our call and command when we please. It is a work of the whole person and the whole life. The work deferred will be greater. The time to do it will be shorter. The strength to do it will be less. Bodily infirmities will disable spiritual actions. God will have less honor and service from us, and we shall have more sorrow and less comfort. Therefore remember your Creator, before the dust returns to the earth whence it came. Annotations on Ecclesiastes 12:7.[24]

The Vanity of False Rivals. Martin Luther: He concludes the book with the same saying with which he began it. He adds a recommendation of his teaching and an exhortation that we not be led astray by erring and varying doctrines but abide in that which has been prescribed. For this is a great source of misery, that when God has awakened his Word and good teachers, immediately heretics and wicked teachers arise, who divert the people to themselves with some sort of rivalry. Thus it was also the concern of the apostles to keep us in their doctrine. Even sound doctrine and the Word of God are forced to endure the perversity. When God has awakened his Word, right away there are heretics and apes who imitate the Word. Moses established the worship of God and certain ceremonies; immediately the apes followed him and erected idols. That is how it is in the arts too. If someone is a good poet, they are obliged to endure their Zoiluses.[†] If they are a good craftsman, they are followed by these pretenders. Thus all the arts have their imitators, that is, their destroyers. But worst of all is the fact that the crowd follows the foolish ones and prefers them to the genuine artists, as Christ said about them: "They will lead many astray." Solomon is complaining about that here. Annotations on Ecclesiastes.[25]

One Pastor, One Faith. Jean de Serres: Having finished his tractate on the advantage that comes from piety, he now concludes the whole disputation with a brief and orderly summary of the whole. We have said that this book was made up of three main parts: first, he taught by way of refutation (*anaskethastikos*), teaching that in all of human life there is no happiness to be found; second, that happiness is to be found in the fear of God; and third, he gave us clear and thorough description of the uses of piety. He reiterates these three parts of the book here in a brief summary (*anakephalaiōsis*): "vanity of vanities," as though he were to say, The arguments above have proved that happiness is nowhere to be found in human life, and he affirms that he has not taught this rashly. "And the more wise the preacher was"—not as if he would win authority for his teaching by the

[23]CRR 5:442-43*; citing Ps 119:105; Gen 3:6. [†]Hubmaier held a distinctive, trichotomous anthropology: the flesh, having been wholly corrupted by the fall, inclines only to evil; the soul is damaged by its association with the flesh, but still capable of free choice; the spirit, however, retains its capacity to delight in and respond to God's grace.
[24]Downame, ed., *English Annotations*, 7F2v*.

[25]LW 15:182-83 (WA 20:197); citing Mt 24:5. [†]Zoilus (c. 400–320 BC) was a cynic philosopher and literary critic who raised historical and moral objections against Homer's poems so harsh that he was given the nickname of *Homeromastix* (scourge of Homer) by contemporary critics.

authority of his own person (rather, the authority and dignity of his person depends rather on the teaching!), but from those things that he learned from experience, and from prudent and mature study. . . . "The preacher thought to find such words as might please." That is, words that should be received by the common consent of all people, whose authority should be credible in itself (*autopistos*). This is what he calls "the right Scripture" and "the words of truth," doubtless the words committed to writing by Moses by the very commandment of God, and by the inspiration of the Holy Spirit. Of these words, God is the author, Moses the minister, and the prophets the interpreters. Thus what he calls the "right Scripture" is what the apostle called "God-breathed" (*graphē theopneustos*), and this right Scripture is the foundation of all pure and sound teaching. "The words of the wise." For the Word of God contains axioms (*axiōmata*) and general doctrines, which the teachers of the orthodox church apply to the circumstances for particular people, places, and times, like one leading others to streams of water. Therefore he says, "The words of the wise are like pricks or goads and nails driven in," to sharpen and spur on the minds of people who respond with dullness to abstract doctrine; therefore, the teaching must be applied individually. This is why he calls the church's teachers "the wise" and "the lords" or "masters of gatherings" (*baʿălê ʾăsūppût*), because they write books from the pure Word of God for the church's use—not that they are the authors of the teachings, but only their ministers. Therefore he adds, "which are given by one pastor"—just as if he should say, Even though there may be many teachers in the church, yet they have received their teaching from one, on whom all of us ought to depend. And by this appellation, "one pastor," he indicates Moses, who was the minister of the law. But we must ascend up from Moses and the prophets to Christ, the true Teacher of his church, from whom alone both Moses and the prophets drew their teachings through the inspiration of the Holy Spirit. For just as he is the author of the holy Scriptures, so also is he their interpreter. This is why Peter says that no prophetic Scripture is a matter of private interpretation, and this is why Solomon desires all the faithful to depend on the one Pastor, and to beware of strange doctrine, for there is only one way, one truth, and one life—and one faith. Commentary on Solomon's Ecclesiastes.[26]

Obedience Is the Fruit of Godly Fear. Thomas Granger: The general conclusion of the whole scope of all Christian doctrine and exhortation. For all is but the mortification of the old person, and the quickening or renewing of the inner person, and these are both one: they are one motion and differ only in respect of the terms *a quo* and *ad quem*. For what is that which mortifies but life? The spirit of mortification enlivens, and the spirit of life mortifies at one and the same instant, in one action. . . . This is the substance of the conclusion, consisting of two precepts: the one concerns the inner person, or the affection; the other concerns the outward person, or the action. Concerning the first: by "fear" is meant a reverent awe of God's majesty, proceeding from faith, whereby through the feeling of his love, as well as the weight of his displeasure, we are afraid to offend him. . . . "And keep his commandments." This is the effect of true fear. The root is faith, the sap or juice is fear, the fruit is obedience. As is the inward person, so is the outward. The heart is deceitful, but the hypocrite cannot be hidden, for the tree shall be known by its fruit, not by its appearance or outward show—just as a wild tree makes a fairer show than many a good apple, yet the taste reveals the difference. Who is the one who in sincerity keeps the commandments? The one who sets God always before their face. Moreover, obedience can be either legal or evangelical, and Solomon speaks of the latter here. For both the curse and the rigorous exaction of the law are removed from those who believe, who are natural and freeborn children of God. In this time there

[26]Serres, *Commentarius, in Solomonis Ecclesiasten*, 486-88; citing 2 Pet 1:20.

are many masters but few doers; therefore shall they receive the greater condemnation. They would have good be done, so long as they themselves have no hand in it. Here is no fear of God, but a deceitful and wicked spirit, for such people only act in proportion to their fear. The one who does the commandments is true; the rest are babblers. A Familiar Exposition.[27]

Proximate Judgment. Martin Luther: Everything will finally come under judgment, whether good or evil. Prattlers, slanderers, and fools will eventually be confounded, and their dogmas will not endure. So Zoilus was finally thrown down alive from a rock, but Homer still remains the greatest of poets, regardless of all the Zoiluses and those who are even worse.[†] In this way all good authors, especially in sacred doctrine, have by the plan of God or the power of God persevered until now. "On account of every secret thing," that is, "on account of hypocrisy." For those apes put on a good appearance both in life and in doctrine. Thus Psalm 26:4 says, "I do not sit with dissemblers"; Christ calls them "hypocrites," and Paul says, "holding the form of religion." Therefore God will judge every work, so that what remains is genuine and the pretense under which they had hidden the work is removed. He is not speaking about the last judgment, however, but, as is usual in Scripture, about any judgments, whether those by which heretics are judged and punished or those by which other wicked people are judged. They all have their judgment and their time appointed by God that they are compelled to undergo. Thus the pope is being led to judgment today and has almost been judged. Thus also Arius and the other heretics were led to judgment, and the Lord revealed their shame, as Peter says, "in the time of investigation."[‡] Annotations on Ecclesiastes.[28]

Final Judgment. Konrad Pellikan: The aim of the entire book—and indeed, the end of all useful studies, and the explication of this whole book—is written here, that the most blessed outcome is simply to fear God—that is, to believe in him, to hope in him, and to love him; and to obey his commands. On this one thing the entirety of a person's being depends, and this alone our Creator demands, that for this our intention, trust, and striving should be single-minded. And this conclusion pertains to all and to everyone; that is, it contains all that God demands from humanity, and for which we are obliged and indebted to him. . . . We are certain, moreover, that we will give an account of these things to our Creator and our Judge, at whose seat we will all stand, when the Lord, the Son of Man, sits in the seat of his majesty, to pronounce judgment on the good and the wicked. Then everything will be made manifest that had been hidden for ages, and the thoughts of our hearts will be revealed. At that time the chosen lambs will be bidden to his right hand and the ungodly goats to the left; he will pronounce the benediction of eternal life on the former, and the latter will be punished with eternal damnation. A Succinct and Universal Commentary on the Bible.[29]

---

[27]Granger, *A Familiar Exposition or Commentarie on Ecclesiastes*, 337-43.

[28]LW 15:186-87 (WA 20:202-3); citing Mt 23:13-29; 2 Tim 3:5. [†]The Roman writer Vitruvius reports that although there were varied accounts of Zoilus's end, all agreed that that he had received his just deserts. It is not clear where Luther got his version of Zoilus's end, but clearly he agrees with the spirit of Vitruvius's account: "Some writers have said that he was crucified by [King Ptolemy] Philadelphus [in Alexandria]; others that he was stoned at Chios; others again that he was thrown alive upon a funeral pyre at Smyrna. Whichever of these forms of death befell him, it was a fitting punishment and his just due; for one who accuses men that cannot answer and show, face to face, what was the meaning of their writings, obviously deserves no other treatment." *De architectura* 7.9 (LCL 251:68-69). [‡]Luther's reference to the words of Peter is obscure, but may refer to 1 Pet 4:7; the allusion to Arius's "judgment" most likely refers to the well-known description of his death recounted by Athanasius in his letter to Serapion (*Epistle* 54), NPNF[2] 4:565.

[29]Pellikan, *Commentaria bibliorum et illa brevia quidem ac catholica*, 265v.

COMMENTARY ON SONG OF SONGS

Overview: Our commentators are all, without exception, in agreement with the long-standing patristic and medieval consensus that the Song of Songs should be read as a figurative representation of Christ's love for his people, though beyond this basic agreement, there is considerable diversity in approach. Most early modern commentators addressed a set of common themes in their introductory prefaces to the text, defending its place in the canon, warning against "carnal" exegesis of a lascivious nature, and identifying the basic theological themes of the poem. Though no early modern biblical commentaries of note actually reject the canonicity of the Song, the question is raised in more than a perfunctory manner, as the extracts from Erasmus and John Calvin illustrate. Though there is strong agreement on the legitimacy of figural interpretation, there is less agreement on how to approach the "plain meaning," or *sensus literalis*, of the text. Most pre-Reformation exegesis had denied that the Song had anything whatever to do with earthly, physical love, insisting on spiritual readings that altogether occluded any positive affirmation of human erotic desire. In other words, the Song was read as an "allegory of the poets," rather than as an "allegory of the theologians," as explained in the introduction to this volume. The continued influence of this tradition can be seen in Martin Luther's readiness to pounce on any hint at the Song's "amorous" content, though Erasmus's reply—in essence, "What's wrong with having a love song in the Bible?"—suggests the more positive evaluation of human sexuality that sometimes accompanied Renaissance humanism in this era. Calvin, though willing to part company with a junior colleague who read the text *exclusively* as a celebration of erotic love, could nevertheless concede that Scripture did in fact celebrate the joys of the marriage bed, though his continued discomfort with the "irregularity of the flesh"—even when "well regulated"—is striking. Most of our commentators, however, tend either to downplay the erotic and sexual imagery of the poem in favor of its spiritual meaning, or (more commonly) ignore it altogether. One exception to this trend is the Dutch Reformed scholar Hugo Grotius. For Grotius, it is the intimacies of the marriage bed that are veiled by the modest covering of figurative language, and while Grotius acknowledges the legitimacy of allegorical readings, he clearly views them as of secondary interest.

What of the allegorical readings themselves? The early Protestant writers collected here display a wide range of approaches. Most carry forward the venerable pre-Reformation traditions of reading the Song either as an allegory of Christ's love for the church (the "ecclesial allegory") or for the individual Christian (the "mystical allegory"), though there are new directions explored as well. The Reformed Hebraist Sebastian Münster signaled a new openness to reading the Song in light of the medieval Jewish exegetical tradition, and while his interpretations were generally in keeping with earlier Christian allegory, they were given an added depth by his engagement with the rabbis. Luther's explication of the Song as a figural representation of an ideal political order is (to my knowledge) unique in the history of the text's interpretation until the sixteenth century; afterward, it became the point of departure for Lutheran expositors (e.g., Veit Dietrich, Lucas

Osiander). Also noteworthy is the attempt on the part of English-speaking Puritan writers, such as John Cotton and Thomas Brightman, to read the Song as a "prophetical history," mapping out the fortunes of the church from the time of Solomon onward. All in all, these selections demonstrate both the unity and diversity of early Protestant interpretation of a profoundly beautiful and challenging text.

Amorous Allegories Common in Scripture. François Lambert: This Song is holy and wonderful, and truly spiritual, whatever it may seem on the surface. Indeed, though modest in size, it is full of mysteries and capable of explaining the loftiest things. So also, it is clear that those who have labored to diminish the authority of this text because it contains colloquies of mutual love between a bridegroom and his bride have wandered no small distance from the truth—as if it were not common for the Holy Spirit to represent the sincere love between God and the church under the type of a chaste marriage, or idolatry and impiety in the likeness of an adulterous woman (as Jeremiah 2–3 and Ezekiel 16 make perfectly clear)! If they find such fault with the sense of this book, because of what kisses, breasts, the womb, the navel, flower beds, and the rest call to mind, then why not also expunge the following passage: "You grew and arrived at the flower of womanhood. Your breasts grew large, and your hair sprouted . . ."?

Indeed, if according to the opinion of Paul in Ephesians 5 the pure marriage bed holds a great mystery in Christ and the church, and if kisses, the womb, the navel, and other such things belong to the sanctity of marriage, then it was necessary to be mindful of all of the above in order that the truth signified may fully be opened. Nor is it likely that the apostles, in whose time this book was received without doubt, would have failed to warn us, if it contained anything detracting from piety. On the contrary, when it comes to the things contained in this book, Paul does not hesitate to apply them even more effectively, comparing the mystery of Christ and the church with that of a husband and wife. Commentary on the Song of Songs.[1]

No Impropriety in an "Amatory" Song. Desiderius Erasmus: You [Luther] say that I satirize and ridicule the canon of the Jews. This is one source of slander. Another is that I make some jesting double-entendre when I call the Song of Songs "the Amatory Song."[†] A third is that I compare the Proverbs of Solomon and the Song with the two books of Esdras, Judith, and the stories of Susanna and of the dragon Bel. Here, where I never even dreamed of any offense, you think up three great crimes. I will quote the place from *A Discussion* so that you can better recognize that you have incriminated me without any justification. It goes as follows: "I do not think anyone would take exception to the authority of this work"—I am speaking of the book titled Ecclesiasticus—"because, as Jerome indicates, it was long ago not included in the canon by the Jews, since the church of Christ has accepted it into its canon with great unanimity. Nor do I see any reason why the Jews should have thought this book should be excluded from their canon, since they accept the Proverbs of Solomon and the Amatory Song. As for the fact that they did not accept into the canon the last two books of Esdras, the stories in Daniel about Susanna and the dragon Bel, Judith, Esther, and some other books but rather numbered them among the *hagiographa*, anyone who reads those books carefully can easily guess their motives. But in this work nothing of that sort strikes the reader." Up to this point I have quoted the words of *A Discussion*.

Do I satirize and ridicule the canon of the Jews because I say that it is not clear to me why they excluded Ecclesiasticus from the canon? . . . So much for the first crime. The second is just as shameless: I call the Song of Solomon the "Amatory Song." Suppose I had no more reason to call it that than that I wanted to, or in order to speak a purer Latin; where is the jesting double-entendre?

[1]Lambert, *In Cantica Canticorum Salomonis*, 1r-2v; citing Ezek 16:7.

Is it *not* an amatory song? Does "amatory" always have bad connotations? Now note the reason why I preferred to call it that: since two words are modified by the phrase "of Solomon," namely, "Proverbs" and "Song," if I had said "Song of Songs," the two genitives "of Solomon" and "of Songs" would not have fit well together, and I would have seemed to mean that Solomon wrote many other songs. If I had said simply "Song," someone might have suspected that I was talking about some song like the ones in the Psalms. And so from the subject matter of the work, I add the qualifier "amatory." As for me, I never thought worse of this Song than of Proverbs, of which I have the highest opinion. What, then, was the occasion for slandering me? . . . Now your third crime is manifestly groundless. For I do not compare Proverbs and the Song with the two books of Esdras or the stories of Susanna and of the dragon Bel, but with Ecclesiasticus, which treats subject matter similar to that of Proverbs. And in those that they rejected, I say that the careful reader will find something striking to show why they were not accepted, whereas in Ecclesiasticus there is no sign of such a striking reason. But if there is no striking reason in Ecclesiasticus, much less is there any in Proverbs or the Song. A Warrior Shielding a Discussion of Free Will Against the Enslaved Will by Martin Luther.[2]

[2]CWE 76:291-92. †In his *Bondage of the Will* (1525), Luther had taken umbrage at Erasmus's description of the Song of Songs as a "love song" (*canticum amatorium*) as well as the latter's tacit assumption that its place in the canon was no more (or less) secure than that of an "apocryphal" book such as Ecclesiasticus: "You [Erasmus] poke more than a little sarcastic fun at this when you compare Proverbs and the Song of Solomon (which with a sneering innuendo you call the 'Love Song') with the two books of Esdras, Judith, the story of Susanna and the Dragon, and Esther (which despite their inclusion of it in the canon deserves more than all the rest in my judgment to be regarded as noncanonical)" (LW 33:110). Though Luther never elaborated on his objection to Erasmus's description of the Song, one can infer from Luther's own exegesis of the text that he recoiled from the notion that the poem contained anything of an erotic nature. As the editors of the CWE dryly note, "perhaps Luther insinuated that a title analogous to Ovid's *Ars amatoria* might be thought improper" (CWE 76:292 n. 1060).

A Celebration of the Ideal Political Order. Martin Luther: Many commentators have produced all manner of interpretations of this song of King Solomon's—and they have been both immature and strange. But to get at the simplest sense and the real character of this book, I think it is a song in which Solomon honors God with his praises; he gives him thanks for his divinely established and confirmed kingdom and government; he prays for the preservation and extension of this his kingdom; and at the same time he encourages the inhabitants and citizens of his realm to be of good cheer in their trials and adversities and to trust in God, who is always ready to defend and rescue those who call on him.

Moses did the same in Exodus 15. He composed his song about the work being performed at that moment in the Red Sea; and all the songs found in holy Scripture deal with the stories of their own times.† Of this sort are the song of Deborah in Judges 5, the song of Hannah in 1 Samuel 2, and a good many others, including the majority of the psalms, with the exception of those that contain prophecies about Christ. Doubtless, therefore, Solomon, too, wrote his song about his own kingdom and government, which by the goodness of God he administered in the finest, happiest peace and the highest tranquility. All this will become clear from the text itself too.

Moreover, since every kingdom, principality, or state that has the Word and true worship of God is forced to sustain many afflictions—to be a laughingstock and abomination to the whole world, to dwell in the midst of enemies, and every single hour to await death like a sheep bound for the slaughter—such a kingdom or state is deservedly called "the people of God" and has every right to place this song, and Solomon's state, before itself as an example, to praise God in the same manner, to glory and rejoice in God, and to proclaim and marvel at his divine mercy and power, by which he protects his own against the snares of the devil and the tyranny of the world.

We use the psalms of David and the writings of the prophets in this way as examples, even though we are not David or the prophets, but because we have the same blessings in common with them—the same Word, Spirit, faith, and blessedness—and because we sustain the same dangers and afflictions on account of God's Word. So we rightly take over their voices and their language for ourselves, praising and singing just as they praised and sang. Thus any state in which there is the church and a godly prince can use this song of Solomon's just as if it had been composed about its own government and state.

And so from this Song of Songs, which Solomon sang about only his own state, there springs as it were a common song for all states that are "the people of God," that is, which possess the Word of God and worship reverently, which acknowledge and truly believe that the power of governments is established and ordained by God and that through this power God preserves peace, justice, and discipline, punishes the guilty, defends the innocent, and so on. They praise and proclaim God with thanksgiving for these great benefits. . . .

This is why this poem is called the Song of Songs, since it deals with matters of the loftiest and greatest kind—namely, with the divinely ordained governments, or with the people of God. It does not treat a story of an individual, as other songs in holy Scripture do, but an entire permanent kingdom, or people, in which God untiringly performs a host of staggering miracles and displays his power by preserving and defending it against all the assaults of the devil and the world.

What is more, he does not sing of these exalted matters in the common words that people ordinarily use, but he illustrates and adorns his theme with lofty and figurative words to such an extent that when the crowd hears them, it supposes that the subject treated is something very different.[‡] For this is the custom with kings and princes: they compose and sing amatory ballads that the crowd takes to be songs about a bride or a sweetheart, when in fact they portray the condition of their state and people with their songs. . . .

For we know that the purpose of the whole Scripture is this: to teach, reprove, correct, and train in righteousness, so that the person of God may be perfect for every good work, as Paul says in 2 Timothy 3:16-17. Those who fail to observe this purpose, even if they create the impression of erudition among the unlettered by their divinations, nevertheless are ignorant of the true essence of Scripture. . . . In the course of this exposition, therefore, we shall direct our reflections to the end that this book, too, may instruct us with doctrine useful for life, and second, with consolations.

For we shall never agree with those who think it is a love song about the daughter of Pharaoh beloved by Solomon. Nor does it satisfy us to expound it of the union of God and the synagogue, or like the tropologists, of the faithful soul.[§] For what fruit, I ask, can be gathered from these opinions? So even if this book, amid all the variety of Scripture, has had its place in the shadows until now, yet by pursuing a new path, we shall not depart from the substance of the thought even if we may perhaps err here and there in details.
A Brief but Altogether Lucid Exposition of the Song of Songs.[3]

[3]LW 15:191-95; WA 31.2:586-89. Luther's commentary on the Song of Songs was originally given as a series of lectures at the University of Wittenberg in 1530. Lecture notes by Luther's student Georg Rörer are reproduced in WA 31.2:586-759, along with the printed edition edited by Luther's colleague Veit Dietrich (who had also attended these lectures as a student) seven years later, *In Cantica Canticorum brevis, sed admodum dilucida enarratio* (Wittenberg: Johannes Lufft, 1539). [†]This is an important point for Luther, since he regards the poem not as allegory (as the term was understood by medieval theologians) but as nearer to what we would call "extended metaphor." Such an approach avoids, in Luther's view, the interpretive excesses of earlier writers by anchoring the text's deepest meaning in the original author's intent. However, this approach places the added demand on the interpreter of demonstrating that the text's figurative language would have been immediately recognized by its earliest readers. [‡]For Luther, the spiritual meaning of the Song is not a secret gnosis accessible only to the spiritual elite, nor is it a later distortion of the text's true meaning: the referent of Solomon's figurative language would have been instantly apparent to his first hearers. It is this perspicacity that for Luther sets the writings of Scripture apart from other writings, even writings of the same genre. [§]Luther alludes here to "tropology," one of the three "spiritual" senses of Scripture in medieval biblical interpretation. According to Nicholas of Lyra, a fourteenth-century commentator well-known to Luther, the spiritual sense of Scripture is threefold, "because if the matter signified by the words themselves refers to the significance of what the new law

A Figural Representation of Christ's Reign. John Calvin: In this psalm,[†] the grace and beauty of Solomon, his virtues ruling the kingdom, and also his power and riches are illustrated and described in terms of high commendation. More especially, as he had taken to wife a stranger out of Egypt, the blessing of God is promised to him in this relationship, provided the newly espoused bride, bidding adieu to her own nation, and renouncing all attachment to it, devote herself wholly to her husband. At the same time, there can be no doubt that under this figure the majesty, wealth, and extent of Christ's kingdom are described and illustrated by appropriate terms, to teach the faithful that there is no felicity greater or more desirable than to live under the reign of this king, and to be subject to his government.

This psalm is called "a song of loves," not, as some suppose, because it illustrates the fatherly love of God, as to the benefits he had conferred in such a distinguished manner on Solomon, but because it contains an expression of rejoicing on account of his happy and prosperous marriage. . . . But as the word "loves" [*amores*] is sometimes taken in a bad sense—and as even conjugal affection itself, however well regulated, has always some irregularity of the flesh mingled with it—this song is, at the same time, called *maskil*, to teach us that the subject here treated of is not some obscene or unchaste amours, but that, under what is here said of Solomon as a type, the holy and divine union of Christ and his church is described and set forth. Commentary on the Psalms.[4]

Not an Allegory of the Blessed Virgin. Desiderius Erasmus: All the ancients unanimously make the mystical Song of Solomon an allegory of Christ as groom and the church as bride. More modern writers have wrenched this into a reference to the most holy Virgin, Jesus' mother according to the flesh, but this requires no small degree of equivocation. They admit that the Song pertains to Christ and the church but say that it is not absurd to apply it through tropology to the mother of the groom, who holds first place among the brides of Christ. But all the souls of the pious are brides of Christ. After the head, which is Christ, Paul assigns first place in the body of the church to the apostles, who were the groom's nearest associates. It was a beautiful idea to attribute first place among the groom's associates to the Virgin Mother. But even when one accepts the extraordinary dignity of the most blessed Virgin and allows that even the majesty of the apostolic order yields to it, there are nevertheless in that Song things that it would hardly be modest to attribute to the most chaste Virgin, that is, in the way they sound to human ears. . . . I append no example of this phenomenon, because they will easily occur to anyone who has read this Song even once. In addition, there are some things there that do not fit a Virgin free from all stain of wrongdoing, such as, "I am black but beautiful," "Do not look at me that I am dusky," and "I looked for him and did not find him, the guards of the city found me." But however much one equivocates here, it is obvious that mystical Scripture has been twisted somewhat from its genuine sense contrary to the

[that is, the gospel] enjoins us to believe, then the allegorical sense is perceived; if, moreover, the words themselves refer to the significance of how we are to act, this is the moral or tropological sense; if, however, the words refer to the significance of what is to be hoped for in the way of future blessedness, this is the anagogical sense." Prologue to the *Glossa ordinaria*, PL 113:28CD; cited in Henri de Lubac, *Medieval Exegesis*, vol. 1, *The Four Senses of Scripture*, trans. Mark Sebanc (Grand Rapids, MI: Eerdmans, 1998), 271.

[4]CTS 5:173; CO 31:448-49. [†]Calvin never wrote a commentary on the Song of Songs, nor are there extant any sermons that he preached on the text. We have a good idea of how he would have approached its interpretation, however, thanks to a controversy that resulted in the expulsion of Sebastian Castellio from Geneva in 1544. Castellio, principal of the college Calvin had helped to found and a one-time boarder in the reformer's home, resigned his position and left the city over a combination of financial hardships and doctrinal differences with the city's ministers. In a letter drafted sometime after his departure, Calvin and his colleagues described with abhorrence Castellio's view that the Song of Songs was "a lascivious and obscene poem, in which Solomon describes his shameless acts of lovemaking" (CO 11:675). On the contrary, wrote Calvin, the Song of Songs is to be understood no differently from Psalm 45, in which "the beauty of Solomon and the adornment of his bride" are read as a figure for the mutual love between Christ and the church.

interpretation of all the ancients. The Evangelical Preacher.[5]

The Song of Solomon Is Repeated in Christ and His Congregation. Dirk Philips: In Christ and his congregation, the Song of Solomon about the king and his bride is spiritually repeated. Here the bridegroom, Christ, kissed his bride with the holy kiss of peace and is joyful because of her beauty and because of the costly fragrance of her ointments—that is, because of her inward gifts, virtues, and the anointment of the Holy Spirit with which she was adorned and anointed.

Here now it proceeds spiritually and in full power so that the bridegroom says to the bride, "My beautiful friend, come and see: the winter is past, the rain is gone and has passed by; the flowers have come forth in the land; spring has come forth; the turtledoves let themselves be heard in our land; the fig tree has received buds, the vines have blossomed and given forth a lovely fragrance." That is, the time of the law has run its course, the wrath of God is stilled, the punishment of the Lord is taken away, the joyful time of grace has come. The comforting gospel has been heard, the sweet fruits of righteousness blossom. The land has become fruitful in faith and in the knowledge of God, the plants of the Lord sprout forth. The branches on the vine of Jesus Christ get buds and give forth the sweet fragrance of life through the power of Christ that is in them. This indeed happened in the time of the first apostolic churches and still happens daily at the present time among all believers.

Here also are in a spiritual manner the sixty strong men out of the heroes of Israel round about the bed of Solomon, each with a sword on his hip because of the fear in the night—that is, round about the camp of Christ and his bride where they rest with each other in all sweetness, friendliness, and love of the Spirit. These are the ministers of the Word, the preachers of the gospel out of the strength in the faith, those who are elected in Israel. These are those who watch over the flock of Christ and are armed with the sword of the Spirit against the crafty attacks of Satan and against the pestilence that stalks in the darkness, against the arrows that fly in the night and are shot from the spirit of darkness, and so on. In summary, the whole of the highly esteemed Song of Solomon is spiritually repeated in Christ with his congregation. The Enchiridion.[6]

The Fitness of Allegory. Theodore Beza: This book has been reckoned by one common consent, both in the ancient church of the Israelites and also in the Christian church, not only among the number of those books dictated by the Holy Spirit and that ought to be the rule of our faith, but also as one of the most excellent and spiritual. Yet it has not been handled or read in the church like all the others, but rather it has been reserved for those who were further advanced in the knowledge of God and of a more stable judgment.

First, because it is written in a style entirely allegorical and enigmatic—that is, it presents our understanding with spiritual things by analogy with natural and corporal things—not everyone is able to understand it and be edified. Second, because this allegory is wholly grounded on the conjugal union of marriage, in which (to put it mildly) we find from start to finish many great faults and imperfections on the part of humanity, defects that have been rife ever since the entrance of sin into the world. Moreover, we know how these have daily increased, since humans have for so long given themselves over to all manner of filth and lasciviousness, which is nothing but a pollution of the caresses and chaste pleasures of marriage. Even though it has many defects, which the Lord must cover and tolerate in his great goodness, this does not negate what the apostle says in Hebrews 13:4, that "marriage should be honored by all, and the marriage bed be kept pure."

And thus you see that some, in consideration of the mischievousness of the world and the diverse ways of speech in this Song (which according to the simplicity of the time in which this book was

[5]CWE 68:920; citing Song 1:4-5; 3:1-3.

[6]CRR 6:340-41.

written might easily be abused), have been wary to expound it in the church, for fear that it would do more harm than good. Others have gone even further, and have been so bold—or rather presumptuous—as to remove this book from the canon of Scripture as being altogether profane, written by Solomon during the time of his dissolution.

As regards the first of these two, they are to be commended that they do not think it good that everyone should rashly be led to handle this book; as the apostle says in 1 Corinthians 3:2, we must begin with milk before we come to pure and solid meat. And this has been carefully observed both in this church and in others by faithful pastors.

But as for those who presume to condemn this book, they are no more to be listened to than those who directly oppose the Holy Spirit with an arrogance amounting to reckless abandon. For not only has the church in ancient times as well as more recently judged otherwise, this book being carefully expounded by the ancient Greek and Latin doctors (indeed, it was even read and used in contemplation more than any other book by monks in the monasteries, even though they solemnly foreswore any thoughts of women and marriage!), this same allegory of marriage is amply set forth for the same purpose in other books that, by common and perpetual consent, have always been regarded as divine and sacred.[†] This is especially clear in the fifth chapter of Ephesians, where the apostle uses the very same words uttered by Adam in the first institution of marriage—that is to say that the church is made flesh of flesh with Jesus Christ and bone of his bone. "This is," he says, "a great mystery." Finally, the Holy Spirit himself expounds the beginning of this book at the end of the Apocalypse.[‡] Therefore we should not take seriously the argument advanced by some that this book is not canonical because it is nowhere cited in the New Testament, for the similitudes taken from marriage in St. Paul and in the last chapter of the Apocalypse are taken from the Song. Besides, this same argument would allow us to condemn other books in the Old Testament that are received without contradiction.[§]

We must therefore hold to a middle way in the exposition of this book, handling it so as to edify the church of God. For God does not desire that anything he teaches us through the prophets and apostles should remain hidden away or kept secret, as though we should be content merely with having it written down, without searching out its meaning. The pagans carried on this way with their false religions, fearing that their abuses should be discovered if their mysteries became known; we also see this today in the practice of the false church, where the reading of the holy Scriptures in the common tongue is forbidden—even though the apostles and prophets have from the beginning of the world spoken and written in common and intelligible language so that they might be understood by all.

It is true, however, that the Holy Spirit has not always used the same style throughout, but has sometimes spoken quite plainly and sometimes obscurely—and yet always in such a way (as one of the ancient fathers rightly observes) as to temper obscurity with clarity. The aim in doing this is to sharpen our desire to search out that which at first we did not understand, and to treasure more dearly the secrets of his wisdom.[◊] This happens only after he has granted us the gift of knowing and understanding them through careful diligence in reading and drawing together various passages of Scripture.

And this is what we hope to do in the exposition of this book, by God's grace and supported by your prayers. For it is now about fifty years since God set up anew his Jubilee among us, causing the holy light of his gospel to shine in this part of the world, so that nothing as regards the gospel should now seem new or strange to us, as though we were still but tiny infants in understanding. On the contrary, we would be ashamed not to be numbered among those of whom it is spoken in the letter to the Hebrews, that they are trained in discerning good from evil.

Now in order to understand this book, it is necessary for us to know what moved the Holy Spirit to choose this analogy to marriage and to develop it so fully. For it is not as if the marriage relationship were without great imperfections, that the Lord might draw out the comparison rigorously in every detail. To put it briefly, this was because there is no relationship among human beings more sacred in obligation, nor more firmly binding in effect, than marriage. For all other contracts and bargains in which one person is obligated to another concern the goods of this world, and things that are external to the person. Or, if it is a question concerning the body, it does not involve a reciprocal obligation, where both parties have an equal interest, but may well be to the advantage of one and the disadvantage of the other. In the contract of marriage, however, the Lord himself acts as the principal author, and therefore this bond remains indissoluble, unless God himself should speak to the contrary, breaking this bond either by death or by some other of his ordinances. The obligation of both parties is so reciprocal that neither is free to do as he or she chooses, but rather the two become one person, as it were, through the union of marriage. Moreover, the effect of this union is more divine than human, as it issues in procreation. For through this contract God uses human beings as his instruments in performing a work that belongs properly to himself, engendering the members of whom his church is composed. . . .

The Holy Spirit therefore intends to represent something that in itself is incomprehensible—that is, the most intimate spiritual bond that exists between Jesus Christ and every faithful soul. The aim is to engender in the minds of believers (the assembly of whom is called the church) the knowledge of truth, together with all good and holy affections, so as to enliven them most fully and thus lead his church and assembly into true eternal life. And thus he could not choose a more proper comparison, nor a more effective model and pattern, than this union we see in marriage. Sermons on the First Three Chapters of the Song of Songs.[7]

The Wisdom of the Rabbis. Sebastian Münster: Rabbi Solomon, in his exposition of the Song of Songs, says that the author of this book, King Solomon, foresaw by the Holy Spirit that some of the people of Israel would fall away from the true God, to whom they had been betrothed in receiving the law, and would serve alien gods.[†] He intended to bear witness that they would find nothing of profit in the service of these gods, and to remind them how ahead of all the nations of the earth they were truly the special possession of God. "I will return to my former husband, for I was far better off with him than I am now." This fable, it is said, is told in the figure of a woman who abandons her faithful spouse. At length she regrets this, and greatly desiring his embraces again, she confesses her sins to him. He not only pardons her apostasy, sin, and adultery, but he actually makes beautiful her blackened and polluted appearance, adorns her with various jewels,

[7]Beza, *Sermons sur les trois premiers chapitres du Cantique des Cantiques, de Salomon*, 3-10; citing Eph 5:32; Heb 5:14. [†]Beza lists a number of intertextual parallels, all of which use marriage as figure for expressing spiritual truths, including Ps 45 (which he describes as a "summary and abridgment of this whole Song"); Is 62:1-6; Jer 3; Hos 1–2; Mt 25; Jn 3:29; Rom 7:1; 2 Cor 11:2. [‡]The reference given is "l'Apocalypse 17"; however, this cannot be correct, since this chapter deals exclusively with the Beast and the whore of Babylon. Beza must have been referring to Rev 22:17: "The Spirit and the bride say, 'Come!'" [§]Ecclesiastes and Esther are the only other books in the Hebrew Bible from which no citation or allusion is found in the New Testament. The canonicity of all three of these books was debated by the rabbis well into the second century AD; however, widespread use of the Septuagint in the early church may have insulated Christians from these controversies. [◊]Compare Beza's reasoning here with that of Augustine, who notes that "casual readers are misled by problems and ambiguities of many kinds, mistaking one thing for another. In some passages they find no meaning at all that they can grasp at, even falsely, so thick is the fog created by some obscure phrases. I have no doubt that this is all divinely predetermined, so that pride may be subdued by hard work and intellects which tend to despise things that are easily discovered may be rescued from boredom and reinvigorated." *De doctrina Christiana* 2.6.10; *On Christian Teaching*, trans. R. P. H. Green, Oxford World Classics (New York: Oxford University Press, 1997), 32.

pursues her with attentions, forgets his own injuries, offers her kisses, and loves only her. Therefore I have taken no offense in recording what this Rabbi Solomon thought about some particular texts—not that I approved of all of his observations . . . , but rather I offer them so that the Christian reader might have the opportunity of considering and searching out better things from these writings. The Song of Songs of Solomon.[8]

On the Benefits of Reading the Song. Lucas Osiander: The Song of Songs (in Hebrew, *Šir haššîrîm*) is known as the Most Excellent Song, or the Song of Solomon, the wisest of those who were king in Jerusalem. It is also known as the Song of Songs because the Holy Spirit desired in this song to sing of love, and the benefits of Christ's love for his church, which is in this world, and to display the desire of the church, which is won by Christ, whom it ardently loves. Therefore this oration is certainly figurative and poetic. There are mutual communications in this song between Christ, the bridegroom, and the church, his bride. And there are vicissitudes in this song, joys and complaints, because the church is exposed to the cross, afflictions, and various temptations, nor is she yet perfected in her knowledge of God and in charity. This little book may seem obscure, yet it can wonderfully strengthen us in conscience and in our love for Christ, who embraces us miserable sinners. And at the same time it ought to arouse us to return to Christ, our generous and sweet bridegroom. And in order that this dialogue may better be made visible, I will supply the names "Christ" and "Ecclesia" [in the text], but one must not inquire too closely about the rhetorical organization of this love song,[†] for it is all full of passions that drag the soul of the lover hither and yon. Song of Songs.[9]

A Song for All Seasons. John Cotton: It is to be wished that this book might be translated into verse or meter in every language, so that we might sing the Canticles, as the Hebrews did. This teaches us to strive for such a gracious frame of spirit that we might always be fitted to sing to God. This Song contains the estate of the church in both the best and the worst of times; yet Solomon can as well sing in the misery of the church as in her prosperity. . . . And though singing be chiefly fit and requisite in mirth, yet we should be fit also for a psalm in our affliction. But often we are too sullen to sing in our ill hours, and in our merry moods our spirits vanish away in carnal mirth and jolliness. But whatsoever the estate of the church may be, we should have our spirits as ready to sing as to pray. This also reproves that ancient law and custom of the synagogue, which prohibited young men (under thirty years of age) the reading and use of this book. But what age fitter for songs than cheerful youth? And further, the amorousness of the ditty will not stir up wantonness in any age, if the words are well understood; but rather, by inflaming with heavenly love, it will draw out and burn up all earthly and carnal lust, even as fire in the hand is drawn out by holding it to a stronger fire, or as the light and heat of the sun extinguishes a kitchen fire, so does heavenly love to Christ extinguish base kitchen lusts. . . .

This song admits more variety of interpretation than any other, and also of singular use: some have

[8]Münster, *Canticum Canticorum Solomonis*, 14r; citing Hos 2:7. [†]Rabbi Solomon Isaac of Troyes (1040–1105), also known by the popular acronym "Rashi," was perhaps the most influential Jewish commentator on the Hebrew Bible and the Babylonian Talmud during the Middle Ages. Münster freely borrowed from his work—not always (as here) with acknowledgment—and he was convinced that careful study of rabbinic exegesis was essential in coming at the plain sense of the Hebrew text. So deep was Münster's debt to this tradition that one critic (none other than Luther's foe at the Leipzig Dispute, Johann Eck) sneeringly dubbed him "Rabbi Münster."

[9]Osiander, *Canticum Canticorum*, 1246-47. [†]The *dispositio rhetorica* refers to a set of categories developed by ancient Roman authors such as Cicero and Quintilian to label the constituent parts of an address: e.g., the introduction (*exordium*), statement of the case (*narratio*), outline of major points (*divisio*). Renaissance humanists often deployed these categories in analyzing a wide range of ancient and modern texts, but Osiander here warns his readers not to expect any such schematic organization.

applied it to express the mutual affection and fellowship between Christ and every Christian soul; some between Christ and the Catholic Church; some to particular churches, from Solomon's time to the last judgment. There is holy and useful truth in each one of these interpretations, but the last most exceedingly magnifies the wonderful excellency of this Song, making it a divine abridgement of the *Acts and Monuments*[†] of the church. And that this book was chiefly penned to be such a historical prophecy or prophetical history may appear: First, by the correspondence or suitability of the words of this Song to the events of each age. Second, by the repetition of the same description, and other occurrences in diverse parts of this Song, which would be a needless tautology, if it were spoken of the same persons in the same time, as you may see if you compare Song 4:2 with 6:6, or 2:7 with 3:5, or 3:6 with 8:5. Third, by the diversity of descriptions of some persons, which would intimate and imply a contradiction, if they were not spoken of different times and of different persons.[‡] Fourth, by the sudden admiration of some new persons and occurrences.[§] A BRIEF EXPOSITION ON THE WHOLE BOOK OF CANTICLES.[10]

THE PLAN OF THE POEM. THOMAS BRIGHTMAN: The authority of this Song is declared by the inscription. Then he prosecutes his purpose in verse, which is wholly employed in describing the condition of the church, both as it was legal [i.e., under the Old Testament law], from the time of David to the death of Christ, in the first three chapters, and also as it is evangelical [i.e., under the law of the gospel], until the second coming of Christ, to the end of the book. The legal church is set forth in a diverse fortune, which for the sake of plainness we divide into three times. First, what it should be until the captivity, in the whole first chapter and the first two verses of the second. Second, what in the captivity itself, to the fifteenth verse of the same chapter. And last, what it should be afterward, to its last abrogation or dissolving, which reaches to the sixth verse of the fourth chapter. Before the captivity, beginning at his father David, he shows what condition [the church] enjoyed under him (vv. 1-2), and afterward under himself (v. 3). And from thence what it should be under his son, Rehoboam (vv. 4-9), under Abijah and Asa (vv. 9-11), under Jehoshaphat (v. 12), under Jehoram, Ahaziah, Joash, Amaziah, Uzziah, Jothan, and Ahaz (v. 13), under Hezekiah (v. 14), under Manasseh and Josiah (vv.15-16). COMMENTARY ON THE CANTICLES.[11]

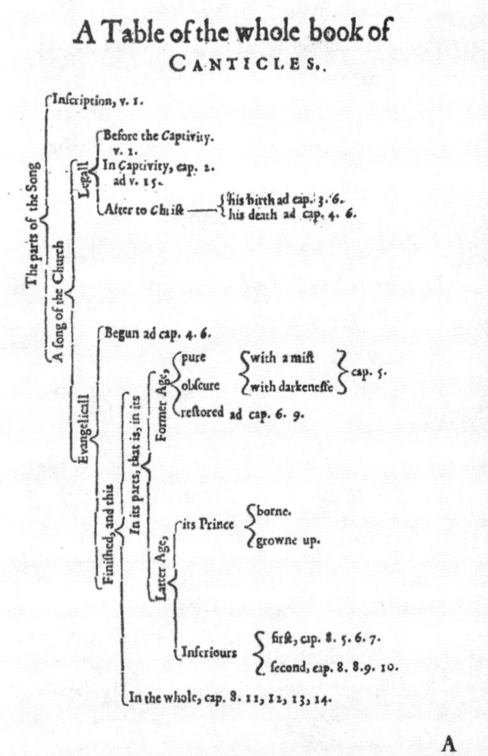

[10]Cotton, *Brief Exposition*, 3-11. [†]The allusion here is to John Foxe's *Actes and Monuments*, first published in 1563. Foxe's "Book of Martyrs," as it was (and is) popularly known, sets out a sort of Protestant version of "apostolic succession" through a line of martyrs stretching from the early church up to the Catholic persecutions of the sixteenth century. While Cotton's method differs from that of Foxe, in that he is not focused so consistently on martyrdom, he is clearly influenced by Foxe's narrative, and draws several of his own illustrations from the latter's work. [‡]A marginal note directs the reader to compare Song 3:3-6 with Song 5:7-9. [§]A marginal note cites Song 3:6; 6:10; 8:5.

[11]Brightman, *A Commentary on the Canticles or the Song of Salomon*, 980-81.

Timeless Mysteries. Richard Sibbes: Other books of Solomon lie more obvious and open to common understanding. But as none entered into the holy of holies but the high priest, so none can enter into the mystery of this Song of Songs, but those who have a closer communion with Christ. Songs, and especially marriage songs, serve to express humans' own joys and other praises. So this book contains the mutual joys and mutual praises between Christ and his church. And as Christ and his church are the greatest persons that partake of human nature, so whatever is excellent in the whole world is borrowed to set out the excellences of these two great Lovers. . . .

There are diverse things in this Song that a corrupt heart, to whom all things are defiled, may take offense. But "to the pure all things are pure." Such a sinful abuse of this heavenly book is far from the intention of the Holy Ghost, which is that by stooping low to us, to raise us higher to him. By taking advantage of the sweetest passage of our life (marriage) and the most delightful affection (love) in the sweetest manner of expression (by a song), he might carry up the soul to things of a heavenly nature. We see in summer that one heat weakens another, and a great light being near a little one draws away and obscures the flame of the other; so it is when the affections are taken up higher to their fit object, they die to all earthly things, while that heavenly flame consumes and wastes away all base affections and earthly desires. . . .

Let God's stooping to us occasion our rising up to him, for here the greatest things, the mystery of mysteries, the communion between Christ and his church, is set out in the familiar comparison of a marriage, so that we might better see it in the glass of a comparison. We cannot directly conceive of these things, yet even though we cannot look directly on the sun, we may still see its beams reflected on the water. Only our care must be not to look so much on the colors as the picture, and not so much on the picture as the person who is represented. . . .

Some think that Solomon, by a Spirit of prophecy, offers here a view of all the times, from his own age to the second coming of Christ, and sets down in this Song an abridgment of the various passages and periods of the church in different ages, containing diverse things that correspond to particular periods of the church.[†] But however this Song may contain a story of the church in different ages (and we do not deny this), yet this does not change the fact that most passages apply to the spiritual state of the church in every age, as most interpreters have thought. In this Song there is (1) a strong desire of the church for nearer communion with Christ; and then (2) some declining again in affection. (3) After this we have her recovery and regaining again of love; after this (4) the church falls again into a declining affection, and after this follows a further estrangement from Christ, which continues until (5) the church perceives Christ's constant affection for her, notwithstanding her unkind dealing, and cleaves to Christ more closely than before.

These passages agree with the experience of the best Christians in the state of their own lives. This observation must carry strength through this whole Song, that there is the same regard of the whole church, and of every particular member in regard of the highest privileges and graces that accompany salvation. Just as every drop of water in the ocean is water, and every spark in a flame is fire, there is the same respect of the part and the whole. And therefore as the whole church is the spouse of Christ, so is every particular Christian, and as the whole church desires still nearer communion with Christ, so does every particular member. Bowels Opened.[12]

The Veiled Intimacies of Marriage. Hugo Grotius: This song is called by the Hebrews *Excellentissimum carmen*, "The Most Excellent

[12]Sibbes, *Bowels Opened*, 1-5; citing Titus 1:15. [†]Likely a reference to the work of Thomas Brightman, whose commentary on the Song was first published in a Latin version in 1614, and grew in influence over the next generation. Cotton's sermons, published the following year (1642), pursue this line of interpretation.

Song," on account of the many elegant features that, in other forms of writing, are lost in translation. Now it is an *oarisus* (i.e., an intimate chat between spouses) between Solomon and the daughter of the king of Egypt, and also the conversations between two choruses—now the young men and now the virgins—who attend upon the marriage in the next chamber. Nuptial intimacies here lie hidden beneath the coverings of dignified words, and this is the reason why the ancient Hebrews did not want this book to be read, except by those preparing for marriage. It is believed, however, that Solomon, all the more that this work might long endure, artfully composed it in such a way that allegories (i.e., hidden meanings), illustrating the love of God for the people of Israel, could be uncovered without many distortions. This was the view of the Chaldean Paraphrast, and Maimonides allowed for no other.[†] Moreover, because this love was a type of Christ's love for the church, Christians applied their ingenuity to the words of this song, a praiseworthy effort. For even the apostles compared the union of Christ with the church to marriage. Annotations on the Old Testament.[13]

---

[13]Grotius, *Annotationes in Vetus Testamentum*, 267; citing Eph 5:32; 2 Cor 11:2; Rev 19:7-8. [†]The Chaldee Paraphrase is another term for the Aramaic Targum on the Song of Songs, an exegetical tradition that had probably crystallized by the seventh century.

1:1-4 THE BRIDE AND HER BELOVED

[1]The Song of Songs, which is Solomon's.
She[a]

[2]Let him kiss me with the kisses of his mouth!

For your love is better than wine;
[3]your anointing oils are fragrant;

your name is oil poured out;
therefore virgins love you.

[4]Draw me after you; let us run.
The king has brought me into his chambers.

Others

We will exult and rejoice in you;
we will extol your love more than wine;
rightly do they love you.

a The translators have added speaker identifications based on the gender and number of the Hebrew words

Overview: Commentary on the opening verses of the Song of Songs focuses on a number of critical issues that sets the tone for interpretation of the rest of the text. Opinion varies widely on the reason for the poem's title. Most agree with Luther that the book's title derives from the loftiness of its content, though Luther's view that the content is primarily an allegory of human government remained idiosyncratic. The view of Henry Ainsworth, that the Song treats of the drama of redemption, is nearer the mainstream of early Protestant interpretation. In contrast to most modern biblical scholarship, virtually all of our commentators accept without question the Solomonic authorship of the text. Starting from this assumption, commentary on the superscription tends to focus on placing the Song within the literary context of Solomon's career—particularly on how to situate the poem in relation to the account given in 1 Kings 11 of Solomon's fall into idolatry, an issue made particularly acute by the fact that this fall appears to have been precipitated by Solomon's excessive love for his many "foreign wives." Should the poem be read as holding forth the "innocent" love of the young Solomon as a figure for God's love for the church? Or do we hear the voice of an older, wiser Solomon (one who ostensibly had repented of his wayward lusts) warning his readers away from the delights of a merely physical erotic desire? No account is given in Scripture of any final (re-)conversion for Solomon, yet several of our exegetes (e.g., Richard Sibbes) seem to have regarded this as all but certain. Others (e.g., Johann Gerhard) were less sanguine, but left the matter open. One exception to this tendency is the Puritan divine Dudley Fenner, who argues that the mismatch between the virtuous lover of the Song and the historical Solomon is so great as to preclude any literal identification of the two.

Like most patristic and medieval commentators before them, Reformation-era interpreters attached great significance to the imagery of the kiss at the opening of the poem in verse 2. Most stressed its significance as a figure disclosing the grace, intimacy, and affection between Christ and his people, though several of our commentators (e.g., Theodore Beza) hasten to insist on the purely social, non-erotic character of the kiss. This passage also demonstrates the importance of intertextuality for interpretation during this period, as parallels are drawn between the kisses of the lovers in this text and numerous other kisses throughout Scripture, from Jacob kissing Rachel to Judas kissing Christ. Each of these kisses means something different, but the comparison our interpreters make between these gestures in different scriptural contexts serves as a point of departure for setting the Song of

Songs in its wider canonical context. Themes common to Reformation-era theology emerge quickly in exegesis of the poem's opening imagery. For example, François Lambert uses the imagery of the kiss to explicate a very "Lutheran" understanding of law and gospel, while Beza and the Westminster divines fasten on the language of the bridegroom's initiative in leading the bride into his chambers to emphasize the doctrine of election. All, however, are agreed in reading these opening images as bearing powerful witness to the unique intimacy Christ offers those whom he loves.

1:1 *Superscription*

The "Song of Songs." Martin Luther: This book derives its title either from the subject matter, because it deals with the greatest of all human works, namely, government; or else from the style, because it is written in the fashion of grand oratory. For the poem is entirely figurative, and figures of speech produce grand oratory. A Brief but Altogether Lucid Exposition of the Song of Songs.[1]

A Holy Collection. Antonio Brucioli: The inscription of this book is the Song of Songs, indicating that it contains songs far exceeding other songs in many holy mysteries, and they are called the songs of Solomon because he wrote them of the true Solomon, Jesus Christ, through his Holy Spirit. We read of many songs in the Scriptures, such as the songs of Moses, Deborah, Joshua, Anna, David, Habakkuk, and others, but this book is not just one song that Solomon sang, but many songs collected in one book and pertaining to one argument, in which is surely expressed the faith, charity, friendship, joy, delight, and various benefits—not without vehement affections!—with which our most merciful Redeemer pursues his elect with inexplicable graces. . . . Nor are we to look for any precise order in this dialogue, for real lovers are not concerned about such things, but rather whatever each does is taken in good part, and even errors and ignorance are received with grace and laughed at. The Song of Solomon.[2]

The Superlative Song. Henry Ainsworth: Songs and psalms are for the most part arguments of joy and gladness in those who sing, and of their praises, whom the songs concern. So this book, treating of humanity's reconciliation to God, and peace by Jesus Christ, with joy in the Holy Spirit, is called a song. Therefore, the faithful should learn to sing with understanding, making melody in their hearts to the Lord, when they feel themselves made partakers of his joy. And it is titled the Song of Songs, that is, the chief and most excellent song, just as Christ, whom it concerns, is called the King of kings and the Lord of lords; that is, the most high and mighty king, and supreme Lord of all. Solomon made a thousand songs and five, of all of which this was the most excellent—yea, and of all the songs in the Scriptures, for this celebrates the mysteries of Christ and his church, and the communion between them, more amply and more excellently than any other. Annotations upon the Song of Songs.[3]

The Eleventh Song. Sebastian Münster: *Šir haššîrîm.* The word *šîr* (song) is derived from the verb *šor* (he sang) and appears here as the first among a plurality. Rabbi Joseph enumerates ten songs in which God is glorified in this age and in the age to come.[†] First, Adam sang on the Sabbath day when his sin was forgiven him.[‡] The second was sung by Moses when the children of Israel crossed the Red Sea with dry feet. The third was sung by the children of Israel when water was brought forth [from the well of Beer] for them. The fourth was when Moses said, "Give

[1]LW 15:194; WA 31.2:593.

[2]Brucioli, *La Cantica di Salomo*, A-4.

[3]Ainsworth, *Annotations*, 2:681; citing Rev 19:16; 17:14; 1 Kings 4:32.

ear, O heavens." The fifth Joshua sang in battle, when the sun stood still at Gibeon. The sixth was sung by Barak and Deborah, when Sisera was handed over into the hands of Israel. The seventh Hannah the mother of Samuel sang. The eighth David sang, concerning all the signs and wonders that God had done for him. The ninth was by King Solomon.[§] The tenth was spoken by the captive children of Israel, when they were liberated from their bondage. The Song of Songs of Solomon.[4]

Solomon's Great Love. Richard Sibbes: It is called Solomon's Song, who (next to Christ) was the greatest son of wisdom that ever the church bred. His understanding was as great as the sand of the sea, and his affections (especially that of love) were as large—as we may see by his many wives, and by the delight he sought to take in all that nature could afford. This affection of love he misplaced, and this might have been his undoing, but that he was one beloved by God, who by his Spirit raised his soul to love objects of a higher nature. Here in this argument there is no danger for the deepest wit, or the largest affection—even that of a Solomon—to overreach, for the knowledge of the love of Christ to his church is above all knowledge. The angels themselves may admire it, though they cannot comprehend it. Bowels Opened.[5]

God's Penman. John Trapp: He was the penman, God the author. Of many other songs he was both author and instrument; not so of this, which the Chaldee Paraphrast here titles Songs and Hymns (in the plural, for the surpassing excellency of it) "which Solomon the prophet, the king of Israel, uttered by the spirit of prophecy, before the Lord, the Lord of all the earth."[†] A prophet he was, and is therefore now in the kingdom of heaven, notwithstanding his foul fall, from which he repented. For as it is not the falling into the water that drowns, but lying in it, so neither is it the falling into sin that damns, but dying in it. Solomon was also king of Israel, and surpassed all the kings of the earth in wealth and wisdom. Indeed, he was wiser than all people. And as he himself was a king, so he made this singular song (as David did in Psalm 45) concerning the King (Christ and his spiritual marriage to the church) who is also called Solomon and greater than Solomon. If therefore either the worth of the writer, or the weightiness of the matter may make to the commendation of any book, this wants for neither. There is a silly exception some take against this Song, as if it should not be canonical because God is not once named in it. But as often as the bridegroom is brought in speaking here, so often does Christ himself speak, who is "God blessed forever." Solomon made a thousand songs and five, but only this, as being the chief of all, and part of the holy canon, has been hitherto kept safe (when the rest are lost) in the cabinet of God's special providence, and in the chest of the Jews (God's faithful library keepers), it being not the will of our heavenly Father that any one hair of that sacred head should fall to the ground. Solomon's Book of All Virtues.[6]

---

[4]Münster, *Canticum Canticorum Solomonis*, 15v-r; Ps 92; Ex 15:1; Num 21:17; Deut 32:1; Josh 10:12; Judg 5:1; 1 Sam 2:1-2; 2 Sam 22:1; Is 30:29. [†]Münster is most likely referring to Rabbi Joseph Kimhi (c. 1105–1170), with whose works on Hebrew grammar and exegesis he was familiar. The Aramaic Targum on the Song of Songs observes that "ten songs were spoken in this world, this song being the best of them all." "The Aramaic Targum to Song of Songs," trans. Jay C. Treat, https://www.sas.upenn.edu/~jtreat/song/targum/. [‡]According to the midrash, Psalm 92 was written by Adam on the world's first Sabbath. According to one version of the story, Adam had disobeyed God on the very day of his creation, a Friday. He had been so terrified by the darkness of that first night, believing it to be a punishment for his sin, that when the sun rose the following morning, he broke forth in song: "It is good to give thanks to the Lord, to sing praises to your name, O Most High; to declare your steadfast love in the morning, and your faithfulness by night" (Ps 92:1-2). [§]Münster gives no reference for this song, but Jewish midrash typically identified it as Psalm 30, attributed to Solomon "at the dedication of the House of David."

[5]Sibbes, *Bowels Opened*, 3.

[6]Trapp, *Solomonis ΠΑΝΆΡΕΤΟΣ*, 174-75; citing 1 Kings 4:32; 2 Chron 9:22; 1 Kings 4:31; Song 3:11; Mt 12:42; Rom 9:5; 1 Kings 4:32; Rom 3:2; Jn 5:39. [†]The Chaldee Paraphrase is another term

Solomon Not the Subject. Dudley Fenner: I will in a word relate the chief ground that those who deny the authority of this book stand on when they say that this was a love and marriage song between Solomon and Pharaoh's daughter, Solomon's wife. How false this is shall appear in every part [of the Song], though these few [observations] shall serve at this time. First, if we consider the person of Solomon, how is it that he is compared to the spouse here praised and found in all things inferior to him? This appears plainly in 3:7-10. How is he so often brought in, as chaste as the dove, pleasing himself by wandering in the love of this one and no other, who yet had so many wives and concubines, who was drunk with the love of so many? Second, concerning the praise that is given to the bride or the woman, how can the diverse properties here mentioned apply to Pharoah's daughter, or any other queen? How is she compared with all who dwell under Solomon's curtain? How is she found seeking where the king feeds his flock? How is she found black, parched by the sun, afflicted by her brothers, or by the wall keepers? How does she wish him to be as like brother, whom she would bring into her mother's house, who taught and instructed her? How can these things agree with Pharaoh's daughter, or any queen of Solomon's, of whom none were subject to these infirmities, nor needed to ask or desire in such sort the bodily presence of Solomon? Third, how can one principal part of this book stand with this sentence? Which is that he both compares the marriage to a long day, when the shadows and darkness shall have passed away, and also that in the meantime he is in his hills of frankincense, and yet is desired and grants to be present still with her? Can this be reconciled by anyone's invention? . . . How can that open contradiction between the sixth chapter, where she is the only child of her mother, and the last chapter, where she has other sisters (and one sung to be without breasts!) be resolved, if not by that spiritual and mystical sense that we have delivered concerning the church? Because she is the Catholic Church, she is one; but as she is the heavenly Jerusalem above, she is the mother of us all, standing over many congregations, and thus with many sisters, and then of the Gentiles such a young one. The Song of Songs.[7]

Did Solomon Write the Song Before or After His Fall into Sin? Johann Gerhard: It is reported by the Holy Ghost concerning King Solomon, the author or poet of this Song, that in his youth he loved the Lord and walked in the statutes of David his father, and that he built a house for the Lord, namely, the temple in Jerusalem. But in his old age he consorted with foreign women (contrary to God's written command), and ensnaring him with love they turned his heart aside after strange gods, so that his heart was not wholly with the Lord his God, as the heart of his father David had been. . . . This raises the question of whether Solomon wrote this book before his fall into sin [*Sündenfall*] or afterward, when by true repentance he was again converted to the Lord his God. It is certain that Solomon did not write this book while he remained in the idolatrous and fleshly, forbidden love of foreign women, for "the mystery of the Lord is for those who fear him." "The fear of the Lord is the beginning of wisdom," but "wisdom will not enter a deceitful soul, or dwell in a body enslaved to sin." . . . And yet, it is not clear whether Solomon wrote this book before his fall or after his later conversion. For although there is no explicit account recorded in the Scriptures of his later conversion, still we may conclude, in keeping with several reasonable arguments and testimonies from the church's ancient teachers, that before the end of his life it is likely that Solomon was, through earnest repentance, converted to the true God of Israel and was saved.

On this assumption, some have held (especially the Jewish rabbis) that Solomon wrote both this Song and Ecclesiastes in his old age.† And some

for the Aramaic Targum on the Song of Songs, an exegetical tradition that had probably crystallized by the seventh century.

[7]Fenner, *The Song of Songs*, 15-16; citing Eccles 6:9; 8:8-10.

wish to prove this view by arguing that because the Song is placed after Ecclesiastes in the Bible, it must be assumed that this book was also written later. Now it is clear (they say) that Ecclesiastes was written after Solomon's fall because in that book he bemoans the vanity of this worthless and fleeting life, he recognizes the pleasures that one seeks in earthly things to be a seduction, and he warns with his own multifarious example that one should not have such love for the world and the things of the world as leads to this salaciousness, the lust of the eyes, and the pride of life. But this argument, which rests on the order of books in the Scriptures, is particularly weak, for neither the prophetic oracles nor the letters of the holy apostle are arranged in the order of their writing. . . .

So it is not yet clearly established that Solomon wrote Ecclesiastes in his old age after his fall into sin and subsequent conversion, for all of these admonitions which are set out in Ecclesiastes can just as easily be understood to have taken place prior to his fall from grace. Solomon says that his wisdom remained with him, but had he already fallen into sin, his divine and heavenly wisdom would not have remained with him. But had Solomon written Ecclesiastes after his fall, he would have given a report of his manifold lusts (to which he alludes in Eccles 2), and not forgotten his wives and concubines.

It is therefore likely and plausible that Solomon wrote the Song of Songs in his youth, namely, in the time when he loved the Lord and followed in the precepts of his father David. For this seems clear in 1 Kings 4 that long before he thought up the songs that he composed, that his heart was still rightly set on the Lord his God; the Song thus belongs to this period, before the account of his fall into sin is recorded in 1 Kings 11. Solomon was named Jedidiah ("beloved of the Lord"), "by the will of the Lord." We now understand the meaning of such names as being either active (i.e., because Solomon's love for the Lord was so extraordinary), or passive (i.e., because the Lord loved him to such an extraordinary degree), or relative (i.e., because he was so beloved by the people of Israel). It is certain that Solomon was no longer a "Jedidiah," one beloved of the Lord, when he fell into sin. God no longer loved him, but instead raised up an adversary to oppose him. And he also no longer loved God, for the true love of God is demonstrated by humble and willing obedience. And the people also loved him no longer, for after his fall into sin they lost their freedom because various enemies resisted Solomon. Therefore it is likely that this Song was written as a spiritual wedding song concerning the love between the heavenly bridegroom and his spiritual bride, when Solomon was still a true "Jedidiah," beloved by the Lord. For in this Song he is often a type of Christ, the heavenly bridegroom (the Hebrew word *dōd* signifies "loved one" or "friend," and this is the word from which Jedidiah is derived),[†] just as [Christ] was the true Solomon or King of freedom, because in this Song the heavenly Bridegroom is often represented by Solomon.

This is also the view taken by the book *Seder Olam*, that Solomon wrote this Song in his youth, when he still clung to the Lord with a holy and righteous love; the Proverbs were written in the years of his manhood, and Ecclesiastes in his old age, after his fall into sin and subsequent conversion.[§] "And this is also supported by something that is written about Solomon in the book of Sirach: All nations marveled at your songs (of which the Song of Songs is still extant), your proverbs (of which also the book of Proverbs remains), and your parables and interpretations (from which Ecclesiastes was compiled)." Altogether, it seems very likely that Solomon wrote all three books prior to his fall into sin. Postils on the Song of Songs.[8]

[8]Gerhard, *Postilla Salomonæa*, 3r-5v; citing 1 Kings 3:3; 6:2; 11:4; Ps 25:14; 3; Prov 1:9; Sir 1:16; Wis 1:4 1 Jn 2:15-16; Eccles 2:9; 2 Sam 12:25; 1 Kings 11:14, 23, 26; Jn 13:15, 15:10; Sir 47:18-21; 47:14-17.
[†]The final verdict on Solomon's character was never finally settled among premodern Jewish and Christian exegetes. Some held that his career represented a cautionary tale illustrating the dangers of excessive wealth, power, and lust, while others held out hope that he may have learned from his errors later in life. Jerome, for instance, working on the assumption of Solomonic authorship for both the Song and Ecclesiastes, detected in passages such as

1:2 *The Kisses of His Mouth*

The Kiss of Grace. François Lambert: Christ's betrothed asks for a kiss—namely, for love, grace, and peace. She asks for the remission of her sins, and that the grace of God might be merited for her through him. For she is terrified by the law, that is, by the commands, which she herself is unable to obey—or even pay heed to! Therefore she confesses her sin, desiring mercy. In short, terrified by the law, which she cannot keep, the gospel bids her hear a word comforting and lovely, of the forgiveness of sins through Christ. This is of course that well-known kiss that Adam, Eve, Abel, Noah, Abraham, David, and all the elect until the end have desired—and do desire—most ardently. Without a doubt nothing can boil up more hotly in the souls of the elect than to be made participants in the grace of that seed, namely, the seed of Christ, which crushed the head of the serpent, and which will receive the blessing of all nations. Again, this blessing is that by firmly trusting in him, one is made acceptable to God. Therefore she, believing in Christ and longing to be made gracious to God, asks for a kiss from the bridegroom. And Christ receives her, who through her faith has obtained grace from God. But one might object that whoever firmly trusts in the promise of God receives the kiss of peace and of grace; therefore, it is not by faith alone in Christ. We may respond that from the beginning no one has received grace from God except by becoming believers and participants in him who is God's fulness. Indeed, all of Scripture and revelation and all of the promises are accomplished for us in him. Accordingly, they only have true faith (by which one is justified) who, in Christ and on account of Christ, do not doubt that they fulfill this same word and these same promises in their own time. Commentary on the Song of Songs.[9]

The Kiss of Peace. Melchior Hoffman: In the Old Testament, the kiss of the mouth was a sign of love and peace, as is shown in Genesis 29, when Jacob kissed Rachel and Laban kissed Jacob, and the same in 2 Samuel 14, when Absalom received a kiss from David, that he might find peace and grace in his sight. The apostles also kept this sign of peace, as I hear in Romans 16: "Greet one another with a holy kiss." The same in 2 Corinthians 13, 1 Thessalonians 5, and 1 Peter 5: "Greet one another with the kiss of love." Judas Iscariot also used this kiss when he betrayed Christ in Matthew 26 and Luke 22.

The bride of Christ does not seek or desire such a physical or external kiss but rather a spiritual kiss. Christ also speaks to his people of this spiritual kiss in the parable in Luke 15, when he saw the father from the house, who embraced the prodigal son around the neck and kissed him. All sinners are represented in this one son, whom God the Father chose for his kingdom and whom God the Father kissed with his word of comfort. This is shown through Adam and Eve in Genesis 3, where God spoke to the snake: "I will put enmity between you and the woman, and between your seed and her seed. He will tread on your head and you will bite his heel." That was a very noble kiss of peace, through which kiss all the elect achieve and have achieved peace. Noah also felt this kiss, the same as Abraham and David. And it is a very comforting

Eccles 7:26 an allusion to Solomon's own experiences: "And I find something more bitter than death: the woman whose heart is snares and nets, and whose hands are fetters. He who pleases God escapes her, but the sinner is taken by her." ‡Gerhard is alluding to a term used in several places throughout the Song when the bride (or female speaker) describes her "beloved" (*dôd*): e.g., Song 1:13, 16; 2:3, 8-10, 16; 4:16; 5:2, 4-10. §The view Gerhard describes here is actually derived from the *Midrash Song of Songs Rabbah*, which says that "when a man is young, he composes songs; when he becomes an adult, he makes sententious remarks; when he becomes an old man he speaks of the vanity of things." *Midrash Rabbah*, trans. Maurice Simon (London: Soncino, 1939), 9:17. The *Seder Olam Rabbah*, a second-century rabbinic chronology written in Hebrew, held that "in Solomon's old age, close to his death, the holy spirit rested on him," and it was during this later period that he composed Proverbs, Song of Songs, and Ecclesiastes. *Seder Olam: The Biblical View of Biblical Chronology*, trans. Heinrich W. Guggenheimer (New York: Rowman and Littlefield, 1998), 144.

[9]Lambert, *In Cantica Canticorum Salomonis*, 7v-r; citing Gen 3:15; 22:18; Jn 1:16-18.

thing for him who hears and receives the right answer, as Proverbs 24 reads, the right answer kisses with lips. The Book of Song of Songs.[10]

The Kiss of Doctrine. Henry Ainsworth: The bride is the church espoused to Christ, and called "the wife of the Lamb," to whom she is to be presented "a chaste virgin." . . . However, before Christ came in our humanity, the church (according to the economical dispensation of God) was as a child in her youth, "under tutors and governors, until the time appointed of the father." . . . In this estate she continued till faith came, and then, she being dead to the law by the body of Christ, was to be married to another, "even to him who is raised from the dead, that she might bring forth fruit unto God." So, though our godly forefathers in the days of the prophets saw the promises afar off, and were persuaded of them, and embraced them, and all obtained testimony (and were glorious) through faith, yet they "received not the promise, God having provided some better thing for us, that they without us should not be perfected." Now, in Solomon's days, the church before Christ's coming had greatest glory, having the temple built, living under that most wise, rich, and peaceable king. . . . Even so, because Solomon was a prophet, he foresaw the ruin of his house and kingdom: in his book of Ecclesiastes he proclaimed all things under the sun to be vanity, and in this song he prophesied of the church and kingdom of Christ. And as he, with many other prophets, kings, and righteous people desired to see Christ, and to hear his words, but did not, so here he manifests his desire, and that of all the faithful, to enjoy the blessings and graces of Christ, saying, "Let him kiss me." By this, the church desires to have Christ manifested in the flesh, and to have the loving and comfortable doctrines of his gospel applied to her conscience, that she might not be always under the schoolmaster of the law (which works wrath), but might be infused with the grace of Christ, be reconciled to God, united to Christ, and have the feeling of his love toward her. For kissing is a token of love, and was used at the meeting and salutation of friends, just as David kissed Absalom in a sign of favor and reconciliation. And as we are willed "to kiss the Son," that is, to lovingly and gladly submit to and obey his commandments, so the church here prays first, that the Son would kiss her—that is, in love and kindness teach and apply to her the grace of his gospel. Annotations upon the Song of Songs.[11]

The Kiss of Wisdom. John Cotton: It is a prayer of the church or (which is the same thing) some chief member of it, for a pledge of Christ's sweet and familiar acquaintance, love, and fellowship with her. Kisses are pledges and incentives of love: "Men shall kiss his lips that answers upright words." This is the effect of upright answers, that human beings will kiss his lips. But God kissing a human's lips is the cause of humanity's answering upright words: his breathing into our mouths a right answer makes us speak accordingly. Just as, on the contrary, when one answers perversely, unjustly, or erroneously, then Satan has kissed them with his kisses—he has sent as a lying spirit into their mouths. "The kisses of his mouth" are more than the "kisses of his lips": the one is a silent gesture of love, the other implies also amiable speech, when Christ either puts wisdom and grace into our hearts, or speaks peace and comfort to our souls. . . . Whoever finds this wisdom finds Christ, the wisdom of the Father, in whom God is well pleased with us and in whom he (as it were) kisses us. This wisdom not only enables us to walk in a godly manner toward our salvation, but it also fits us to go in and out before our families, before our people, and so enlarges us to all the duties of our callings. To walk in the ways of this wisdom brings peace to our souls, and to those who live under us: "all her

[10] Hoffman, *Dat Boeck Cantica Canticorum*, 17-18; citing Rom 16:6; 1 Pet 5:14; Gen 3:15; 9:1-29; Prov 24:26.

[11] Ainsworth, *Annotations*, 681-82; citing Rev 21:9; 2 Cor 11:2; Gal 4:1-2; Rom 7:1-4; Heb 11:13, 39-40; 1 Kings 4:20, 25; Lk 10:24; Mt 13:17; Rom 4:15; 1 Pet 5:14; Lk 7:45; Ex 4:27; 18:7; 1 Thess 5:26; 2 Sam 14:33; Ps 2:12.

paths are peace." A Brief Exposition on the Whole Book of Canticles.[12]

The Kiss of Friendship. Theodore Beza: Now about this kissing that is spoken of here, we must note that human beings have a certain natural instinct to express their mutual love and friendship toward one another. Accordingly, they have used certain outward actions that have some agreeableness with what they would express within them, some after one fashion, others after another. For example, this custom of doffing the cap, or bowing the body. Likewise this kissing bears witness of the love and reverence one has for another, a gesture by which one makes oneself inferior to another to do them courtesy. Similar to this is the way one gives the hand to another, in witness that one is ready to make mutual delivery of their heart and all that they have. But among all other gestures, kissing seems to give the clearest representation of that which is within. For whereas the life of the body consists in respiration, and breathing is by the mouth, kissing is a sign that a person is ready to communicate and infuse their very soul into their friend. Sermons on the First Three Chapters of the Song of Songs.[13]

The Kiss of David's Reign. Thomas Brightman: First let us weight the words, and then let us see the application: kisses are sometimes taken for fair, mild, and pleasant words, as chidings and brawlings are compared to wounds, as Solomon says, "The wounds of a lover are more faithful than the flattering kisses of an enemy." The church then desired to be instructed with the words of her bridegroom, which she calls kisses, as the most assured pledges of the bridegroom's love; neither can anything be compared with this love. Therefore she prefers it before wine, which is chiefly esteemed among those things that taste most pleasant. For the comparisons of this song are taken from such things that chiefly tickle the senses, because our infirmity is such that we commonly feel no greater pleasure in this life than in those things that pertain to these inferior senses. This is the sum: the company of the faithful chiefly desire to be altogether overwhelmed in a most familiar conversation with Christ, and to be most plentifully instructed with the words of his mouth, which they confirm to be the greatest pleasure that can be.

Now for the application. Solomon begins from the church of his time, and he shows the face of it as it was in the reign of his father David in this and the next verse. Christ then by the mouth of David (bearing his type) kissed the church, instructing it with the sweetest odes, psalms, and songs, which in that time were most excellent above all others. David is called the sweet singer of Israel by the testimony of the Spirit, and the book of Psalms is a plentiful witness to this. Solomon also composed 1,005 songs, but very few of them are recorded in the sacred treasury. The prophets, which were many then (and at other times) chided very often, but they did not kiss: they reproved sins, they thundered out judgments, they terrified with threats. But this sweet singer of Israel poured out almost nothing but prayers, thanksgivings, promises, and exhortations. . . . With these kisses, which burned with love of the divine word and of all piety, the people then had no less desire to be embraced. Commentary on the Canticles.[14]

A Hidden Sign of Favor. Martin Luther: He speaks according to the custom of the people of that day. Among us kisses are held in less esteem. However, kisses are signs of love and favor. And so he says, "The Lord kisses me"—that is, "He shows favor to this government, he kisses it, he honors it with all manner of blessings and love." Now, to declare that a realm which to outward appearance was suffering all sorts of afflictions is God's own

[12]Cotton, *Brief Exposition*, 15-17; citing Prov 24:24; 1 Kings 22:23-24; Prov 3:1.

[13]Beza, *Sermons sur les trois premiers chapitres du Cantique des Cantiques, de Salomon*, 32-33.

[14]Brightman, *A Commentary on the Canticles or the Song of Salomon*, 981-82; citing Prov 27:6 2 Sam 23:1.

concern, that it is loved and cherished by God, is certainly the voice of faith. To outward appearance it is not obvious that he kisses the synagogue, but rather that he wounds it and hates it. A Brief but Altogether Lucid Exposition of the Song of Songs.[15]

Better than Wine. Antonio Brucioli: Seeing the abundant grace of her bridegroom toward her, she says, "Your love is better than wine"—that is, "better than the doctrine with which she was comforted by the ancient fathers." And so this is the sense of the verse: "I desire the kisses of your mouth," that is, my redemption, "because your teachings and your doctrine are my milk and food, giving me eternal life. They are better than the law, which only reminds me of my sin, and they are higher than all other teachings, which do not strengthen but rather kill the simple-minded, just as wine either inebriates or kills young children." The Song of Solomon.[16]

The Milk of the True Church Is Lovelier than Wine. Pilgram Marpeck: The children of the true Sarah suck the pure milk of her breasts, filled as they are by the Holy Spirit. They are lovelier than wine. Without deceit or wrong, the mother, the true Sarah, bears her children to the Father. The pure milk flows from her body as the bride and spouse of Christ through the fervent love and kiss of the Father. Her breasts are lovely and give sensible and pure milk. The Christian and Hagarite Churches.[17]

1:3 *Oil Poured Out*

The Aroma of Life. Isidore Clarius: "Oil poured out," or as the Hebrew has it, "Your name is oil emptied out," for when oil is poured out, and is transferred from vessel to vessel, then the scent is more fragrant. However, understand by "oil" a sweet-smelling and aromatic liquid. Therefore he foresees that the bride is to be wholly filled with divine goodness, and, as if from a long way off, an odor will be given off that, in the manner of the sweetest perfumes, would restore all things. This divine goodness the apostles carried with them and proclaimed, when they said, "We are the aroma of Christ" in "every place," for the Word of the Lord from Scripture is a summons to the peoples and nations, and his wondrous aroma draws the soul to Christ. The Song of Songs of Solomon.[18]

Christ the Anointed. Henry Ainsworth: By savor or smell is meant knowledge, understanding, sense, or feeling, as the apostle expounds it: "the savor of his knowledge." So a tree is said to bud through the smell or scent of water, and tow [flax] is broken "when it smells the fire," that is, feels it. Good ointments, or good oils, are precious and sweet ointments, wherewith special persons were anointed of old. . . . By this similitude the church here commends the graces of Christ, which he had, being full of the Holy Spirit, for his God had "anointed him with the oil of gladness above his fellows," and of him it is said, "The Spirit of the Lord is upon me, because he has anointed me to preach the gospel." . . . And the odor of these graces is smelled when the gospel preached is by sense or judgment perceived. "Your name is oil poured out." As Messiah and Christ is by interpretation "anointed," and he is called the oil or ointment in Isaiah 10:27, so by his name is meant his law, the doctrine of grace, or law of faith, as it is written, "The isles shall wait for his law," which is expounded, "The Gentiles shall trust in his name"; and the preaching of that grace is called the hearing of Christ's name before the Gentiles. Annotations upon the Song of Songs.[19]

The Name of the Lord. Johann Gerhard: The subject concerning which Solomon speaks

[15]LW 15:196 (WA 31.2:594).
[16]Brucioli, *La Cantica di Salomo*, A-7.
[17]CRR 12:555; citing 1 Pet 2:2.
[18]Isidore, *Canticum Canticorum Salomonis*, 5r; citing 2 Cor 2:14-15.
[19]Ainsworth, *Annotations*, 2:683; citing 2 Cor 2:14; Job 14:9; Judg 16:9; Heb 1:9; Lk 4:18; Is 61:1; Phil 1:9; Lk 9:45; Heb 5:14; Rom 3:27; Is 12:4; Mt 12:21; Acts 9:15.

here is the name of the heavenly bride. "Your name," he says about and to the heavenly bridegroom, "is an ointment that has been poured out." By this name of the heavenly bridegroom some ancient teachers of the church have understood the great name of God, the Lord "Jehovah," which is his own, proper name. Psalm 8: "You alone are called by the name the Lord"; "You alone are Jehovah by your name." Isaiah 42: "I the Lord—that is my name." For, because Christ is the true Son of God and thus also true God, this great name Jehovah or the Lord also certainly belongs to him, as the angel names him in the first Christmas sermon when he says, "To you is born today the Savior, who is Christ the Lord." Here Solomon says concerning this great name of the Bridegroom of our soul, "It is an ointment that has been poured out." For in the Old Testament this knowledge of the true God existed only among the Israelite people, as Psalm 76, Psalm 147, and Isaiah 31 state. Therefore, the great name of God is like an ointment sealed up in a bundle, just as the Son of God revealed himself in the flesh and brought forth from the bosom of the heavenly Father the hidden counsel of God concerning our salvation, as if the ointment has been poured out, and has brought forth the lovely aroma of the saving knowledge of God and spread it about throughout the entire world, as Christ thus conducted his holy office on earth. POSTILS ON THE SONG OF SONGS.[20]

1:4 *Into the King's Chambers*

THE FORCE OF GOD'S LOVE. ANTONIO BRUCIOLI: The church of the faithful cries out, "O God, draw me to you by the grace of your election, that after we have smelled this sweet aroma and enjoyed it, we may be fully united with you." And thus both the bride and her maidens, allured by the pleasant aroma of the bridegroom's ointments, run after him whom they love. And this drawing signifies a sort of violence, like one being hauled out of a deep pit with ropes. For the bride's flesh resists this drawing so long as she lives in the world, but God who draws her is able to overcome it. Therefore the bride desires him when she is drawn, and desires that he would never cease this drawing, knowing that otherwise she would not run after him. THE SONG OF SOLOMON.[21]

WE FOLLOW AFTER LOVE. PILGRAM MARPECK: In this time, we cannot lay claim to the fullness of love with its power to convince. But we can follow her path with sincere desire, and mark her footprints and tracks with earnestness, as love pleads with and speaks to love in the Canticle: "Draw me after you and let us make haste," and never to lose sight of her until we completely possess her in that day with Christ. For he who possesses her to the fullest degree possible in this time is merely given a greater desire for her, but can never see her form clearly as she has embraced them. She is like a stag or deer, which, when they see someone, quickly dash out of sight. Thus her return is swift to human eyes to grant them their desire to see her form and to prove with power why she is called love. CONCERNING THE LOVE OF GOD IN CHRIST.[22]

THE BRIDEGROOM ALWAYS MAKES THE FIRST MOVE. THEODORE BEZA: It may seem strange and even unseemly in this most chaste and pure virgin, that she should begin this way, since honesty itself prescribes and commands in every well-ordered marriage that the first words proceed from the man, and not from the maiden or woman whom he woos. I answer that indeed it is also the same in these spiritual engagements with regard to every faithful soul. For although the fiancée spoke first in this place, out of desire for her bridegroom, so also "the doe pants for the refreshment of the waters." Nevertheless, we must be careful not to think that this desire which opened her mouth had its origin in her. It is therefore the bridegroom who first

[20]Gerhard, *Postilla Salomonæa*, 127-28.

[21]Brucioli, *La Cantica di Salomo*, A-6.

[22]CRR 2:533*.

spoke to her and prepared her within to seek and to search after him, as it is said in Psalm 116: "I believed, and therefore I have spoken." And elsewhere, "With the heart one believes and is justified, and afterward one confesses with the mouth and is saved." And indeed, Ezekiel describes the beginning of this marriage contract, showing clearly that it proceeds not from the fiancée, whom he compares to a naked infant just coming out of her mother's womb, altogether bloody and foul. St. Paul explains this to us without figure in Ephesians 2, calling us wretched carrion, "dead in sin." And this is what the most righteous among us all must confess: that it is the Lord who first loved us, and therefore has washed us. He has chosen us, not for anything in ourselves—any more than we have made ourselves!—but in his well-beloved; not that we were already holy, but that we should be made holy. Sermons on the First Three Chapters of the Song of Songs.[23]

The Church in the Time of Solomon. Thomas Brightman: In this one little verse, Solomon describes the church during his reign, whose whole condition is divided into six members. First, this king drawing by his example and by the Spirit working together in the faithful. The first authority of his reign began with the published meeting at Gibeon.[†] Of what force was this attraction? There followed a most calm peace, such abundance of wealth as nowhere else, wisdom almost more than mortal. Glory that amazed all other kings, and (which exceeded all) a beholding next to God. These were enough to have drawn the most unwilling. But the people followed willingly: "We will run," they say, "after you." Second, it is taught here that the people drawn by the king's example fly with a swift course: he commanded the meeting at Gibeon, and they flocked there in great troops. Third, the chamber into which the bride is brought was that most magnificent temple built by Solomon. This house is the inner chamber—nay, rather the couch and bed (as it is afterward called) in which the bridegroom converses with the bride most intimately. Here Solomon brought the church, when for her sake he built and adorned it so beautifully, and especially by drawing the people into the temple on the day when he dedicated the house, going before them with sacrifices, prayer, and thanksgiving. Fourth and fitly is declared how joyful all the people were for those things, so happily begun and continued for many years. Lastly he says, "the upright love you." But why does he mention the upright, as though there were any in those times whose hearts were not sincere and sound? Indeed, he seems by these words to pass over privily those blessed times to a sorrowful falling away. We know how grievously Solomon fell in the last years of his reign, by bringing in strange wives. His heart was not found toward the Lord, but he followed Ashtaroth and Milcom, and built a high place for Chemosh and Molech. But did not many of his flattering courtiers run before, where they saw the king ready to decline? But the faithful and upright in heart remained firm in the truth, howsoever destitute of the king's authority. Here then we may behold the beginning and middle of his reign as very pleasant: the king leading and the people following, the temple built most magnificently, the great mirth and rejoicing of all people. But the most part in the end were defiled, yet the love of the upright was constant, though many fell away to idolatry. Commentary on the Canticles.[24]

The Free Response to Effectual Calling. Westminster Divines: All those whom God has predestinated to life, and those only, he is pleased, in his appointed time, effectually to call, by his Word and Spirit, out of that state of sin and death in which they are by nature, to grace and salvation, by Jesus Christ; enlightening their minds

[23]Beza, *Sermons sur les trois premiers chapitres du Cantique des Cantiques, de Salomon*, 28-30; citing Ps 42:1; 116:10; Rom 10:10; Ezek 16:4-6; Eph 2:5; Rev 1:5; 1 Jn 4:10; Ps 95; Eph 1:4.

[24]Brightman, *A Commentary on the Canticles or the Song of Salomon*, 984-85; citing 2 Chron 1:2; 1 Chron 1:13; 1 Kings 8; 11. [†]A reference to Solomon's dream and the gift of wisdom, which the text describes as having taken place at Gibeon (1 Kings 3:3-15).

spiritually and savingly to understand the things of God, taking away their heart of stone, and giving unto them an heart of flesh; renewing their wills, and, by his almighty power, determining them to that which is good, and effectually drawing them to Jesus Christ—yet so, as they come most freely, being made willing by his grace.† Westminster Confession of Faith.[25]

[25] *Westminster Confession of Faith*, chap. 10. †The last clause of the Westminster Assembly's statement on "effectual calling" cites Song 1:4 as the first prooftext. The implication is that the amorous response of the spouse to the bridegroom's call serves as an image for the free response of the individual Christian's soul to Christ's effectual call in regeneration.

1:5-7 THE BRIDE'S ALLURE

She

[5]*I am very dark, but lovely,*
O daughters of Jerusalem,

like the tents of Kedar,
like the curtains of Solomon.

[6]*Do not gaze at me because I am dark,*
because the sun has looked upon me.

My mother's sons were angry with me;
they made me keeper of the vineyards,
but my own vineyard I have not kept!

[7]*Tell me, you whom my soul loves,*
where you pasture your flock,
where you make it lie down at noon;

for why should I be like one who veils herself
beside the flocks of your companions?

Overview: Much of the commentary on these verses centers on the contrast between the outward "darkness" (or "blackness") of the bride and her continuing loveliness in the eyes of her beloved. All of our commentators agree that the bride's "darkness" is a superficial condition (that is, not an innate physical feature or supposed racial characteristic), though opinion varies widely on its cause: some take it to be the result of Satanic tumult (Martin Luther), or persecution (Theodore Beza), or God's chastisement for the church's own vices (John Cotton), though the more philologically oriented Sebastian Münster is content to point out how the language of the Hebrew text highlights the contrast between the rustic domesticity of the bride and the splendid "whiteness" of the royal tents. All of our interpreters, however, stress the condescension of the royal bridegroom who rescues his bride from the evils that beset her. Other exegetical problems include the hostility of the bride's brothers (or half brothers?) and her apparent perplexity at the bridegroom's absence (a theme that will recur throughout the poem). These poetic devices all highlight the asymmetry of the relationship between the bride and her beloved, providing fertile ground for figural representations of God's grace.

1:5 *Dark, but Lovely*

"Blackened" by Dust, but Washable. Sebastian Münster: Some say that *nā 'wâ* comes from the verb *ahw*, and signifies a shapeliness in the proportion of one's members.[†] "Kedar" refers to a tent-dwelling people in the desert. Therefore it says: even though I am black, I can still be washed and acquire the brightness of royal tents. For the "curtains of Solomon" simply indicates a white sheet stretched out onto a tent. The Song of Songs of Solomon.[1]

Outward Appearances Can Deceive. Martin Luther: "Although I am a state founded by God and adorned with the Word of God, yet I seem to be most wretched in appearance, there is

---

[1]Münster, *Canticum Canticorum Solomonis*, 16r. [†]Münster is addressing an issue that has worried commentators since the ancient period, the apparent contrast in the text between "blackness" and beauty. The LXX had rendered the text literally as, "Black I am and beautiful" (*Melaina eimi kai kalē*), but the Vulgate had interpreted this phrase as an adversative: "Black I am *but* beautiful" (*nigra sum sed formonsa*). Münster's translation at the beginning of his commentary follows the sense of the LXX: *Nigra sum ego & decora*. But here in the comments he still finds it necessary to explain the implied contrast by referring the bride's beauty to the proportions of her body, in contrast with a superficial "blackness" caused by exposure to the sun. Though he does not give credit here, this was the solution favored by the Jewish scholar Rashi.

no success, and there are very few who desire and maintain public peace. I seem to be not a state but some sort of rabble of seditious people. Do not be offended by this appearance. Turn your attention not to my blackness, but to the kiss that God offers me, and then you will see that I am comely and lovable. For although outwardly I suffer all manner of vexation, yet I am desirable on account of the Word and faith." The church, too, is similarly undesirable in appearance. It seems to be lacerated and wretchedly afflicted and exposed to the taunts of all people. But this is our consolation: that our salvation is anchored in the Word and faith, not in outward appearance. . . .

He continues to exhort in the face of scandals. He warns, "Do not stare at the part of me in which I am ugly, but fix your eyes on my beauty and grace, consider my virtues, not my vices." Moreover, the person who has learned this lesson should discover in the long run that they have learned and known the greatest art of all. For it is inbred in us that we are more disturbed by some single vice than by all the remaining virtues. Thus today those who are adjudged the wisest in the world are offended by the many evils, which they undeservedly impute to the gospel. Yet the magnitude of the blessings we have received from the gospel, both privately in human hearts and consciences and publicly in state and household, is appreciated by no one or by very few. For before the revelation of the gospel, what station of life was there, I ask, that people could assess correctly? Not husband, not wife, not children, not magistrates, not citizens, not menservants, not maidservants were sure that they were established in a way of life that was approved by God. So they all took refuge in the works of the monks. . . .

Moreover, this rule ought to be observed most diligently in private life as well: if a person banishes the blackness from their eyes, they will see a world full of God's mercy. Thus we read in Psalm 107:43, "Who is wise and will heed these things and understand the mercies of the Lord?" So in everyday human converse you will discover that no one is so bad that they do not possess innumerably many endowments. The heart, therefore, should be trained to admire the virtues in individual people rather than to be offended by their vices, if any. If someone has vices, the same person has his virtues too—they must, for they cannot abuse all the capacities they have received from nature! This argument will certainly help to preserve peace of heart. For if you direct your gaze only on the vices and the calamities that occur every day, the heart is necessarily tempted by impatience and hatred. Accordingly, since those evils and those troubles cannot be changed, change yourself and adopt a different outlook; keep your heart free and ignore the distresses at hand. As that excellent saying, which we have often used in Ecclesiastes, advises: "Let it go as it is going, since it wants to go as it is going."[†] But the present benefits and blessings are so numerous and so great that the godly person may easily forget the evils in comparison with them.

The sun signifies tribulation, as Christ indicates in the parable of the seed scorched by the sun. Similarly we read in Psalm 121:6: "The sun shall not smite you by day, nor the moon by night." Thus he is saying, Lest you be scandalized by any blackness whatsoever, I ask you now not to regard me as responsible for it. It is the sun that has blackened me. In other words, wherever the divine Word and ordinance are found, wherever there is some form of government, there the sun will come and inflict blackness. That is, the devil rises in opposition so that that Word or that state will appear on the verge of total failure. But do not be perturbed, Satan will not prevail. A Brief but Altogether Lucid Exposition of the Song of Songs.[2]

The Church Is Burned by Persecution, Not "Black" by Nature. Theodore Beza: It is nevertheless certain that the spouse speaks here of another kind of darkness—that is, of the outward ruin and scattering of the church by the fury of persecutions. This is the reason why many see no difference between the splendor of the

[2]LW 15:200-203 (WA 31.2:610-15); citing Mt 13:6. [†]The reference is obscure, perhaps an oblique restatement of Eccles 3:15.

kingdoms of this world and the spiritual beauty of that kingdom which is not of this world, and they allow themselves to be dazzled by outward luster. Either they do not enter the church at all, or if they do, they quickly remove themselves to return to their own vomit. In either case, they do not pay heed to this warning and advertisement not to rely or stand on the outward black and hideous appearance of the cross, but rather to weigh and consider carefully the true and native beauty of the church, even the midst of her great afflictions. Likewise, the Lord warns us that his kingdom "is not coming with things that can be observed," and he also says that "blessed is anyone who takes no offense at me." He, however, is called "a man of sorrows and grief," so disfigured that he is compared to a "worm of the earth." Nevertheless, the church must conform to him if it is to be the true church. Indeed, so far is the cross from obscuring the church's face that, on the contrary, it is the true mark, given only to true believers, that they suffer for the name of God. Sermons on the First Three Chapters of the Song of Songs.[3]

The "Blackness" of Rehoboam. Thomas Brightman: Having spoken before of the flourishing estate of the church, now the withering age follows, which is wholly prophetical, and so are the rest that follow. Brightness and light are tokens of mirth and gladness, and are so used in the Scriptures. Black and darkness are applied to grief and mourning. And truly, there happened mournful times soon after Solomon, when his son Rehoboam, by an indiscreet answer, drove ten tribes from the church. No wonder, then, that she mourned in black: a matter so full of offense that it might make the strongest to stagger and the weak to fall altogether. Commentary on the Canticles.[4]

The Church Suffers God's Chastisement. John Cotton: This shows us what it is that makes the church black, for its deformity stands in the fall and sins of the people and of the princes, in declining to idolatry in their folly, schisms, and rents from their mother; profaneness, apostasy, and rebellion in the church and commonwealth. These darken the fairest churches. If Solomon is going to set up other gods, God will set up foreign princes in his kingdom. If he and his people will serve other gods, God will cause his princes to draw foreign princes' chariots. If we be at unity with other gods, God will be at enmity with us. Second, this shows us that there may be a true, comely church in the midst of such deformities; indeed, the true church of God in the greatest darkness is always comely. The sins of princes and people cannot take away the church's comeliness. They may bring blackness on her, "like the tents of Kedar," but draw these curtains aside, and you shall find that God's church is comely, "like the curtains of Solomon." Therefore we should not run from the church because of her blackness, but run to her, and embrace her in her most sad defections. . . . [Finally], observe that the calamities of the church spring not out of the dust, but it is God that causes darkness on the church—yes, and to speak reverently, it is he who looks at her with a scorching eye; he searches her sins, and finding them out, he blasts her so that she is tanned and sunburned. If then it be God's hand, let us pity the church so much the more, and strive with God to renew the light of his countenance on her. A Brief Exposition on the Whole Book of Canticles.[5]

1:6 *My Mother's Sons Were Angry with Me*

The World Is a Cross for God's Children. Melchior Hoffman: The mother is Eve, who bore the children and placed them in the world, and in a congregation also ruled by the ruler of this world. These children, who remain in the first birth and have not yet come away and been made

[3]Beza, *Sermons sur les trois premiers chapitres du Cantique des Cantiques, de Salomon*, 90-91; citing 2 Pet 2:22; Lk 17:20; Mt 11:4, Lk 7:21; Is 53:3; Ps 22:6; Rom 8:29.

[4]Brightman, *A Commentary on the Canticles or the Song of Salomon*, 985.

[5]Cotton, *Brief Exposition*, 31-33.

black by the sun of Christ and its heat, are angry with those who have grasped the new birth and the blackness brought by Christ's sun. Christ also spoke of this in John 15: "You are not of the world, therefore the world hates you." And the psalmist also speaks in the 120th chapter: "I kept the peace, but when I spoke they began a quarrel." For as faith rises in the hearts of the elect, so does their speech, as we have in Psalm 116: "I believe, therefore I speak, but I am brought very low." This is what follows the sun's heat, for the sake of speaking of truth and righteousness. And the world is a cross for the children of God, and the children of God in turn are a cross for the world, as St. Paul also speaks of in Galatians 6. The Book of Song of Songs.[6]

Led into Idolatry. Isidore Clarius: "The sons of my mother fought against me." Or, "they urged me on"—that is, to sin. These were the impious among the people, the wicked prophets and kings who led the people to the observance of false religion, when they ought to have been keeping the Lord's vineyard free from danger. "They made me," she says, "a keeper in the vineyard"—that is, they made me serve idols, which are sometimes called vices. "My own vineyard I have not kept"—that is, she was not devoted solely to the worship of the true God, and therefore she has become black. The Song of Songs of Solomon.[7]

The Church's Two Half Brothers. Henry Ainsworth: "The sons of my mother," that is, either the children of the church, false brethren, false prophets, and deceivers; or inordinate lusts and sins that dwelt in her, and were conceived within her in the womb; for with both of these is the spouse of Christ afflicted. Of the first, David complains, "I am become a stranger to my brothers, and an alien to my mother's sons." And the apostle says, "Of your own selves shall people arise, speaking perverse things, to draw away disciples after them." . . . Such might be called the children of her mother (though not of her father), false brothers, among whom the saints are often in peril, who, pretending faith and godliness, dangerously oppose the same. . . . Of the second, the apostles tell us of "lusts that war in our members," "of fleshly lusts, which war against the soul," and these may be called our mother's children, because in sin and in iniquity we have been conceived and brought forth. This sin revives in us when the commandment of God comes, deceives us, and slays us, and under it we are sold, so that the good which we would, that we do not do. Annotations upon the Song of Songs.[8]

Hypocrites, Heretics, and Papists. John Trapp: Worldly people who are of the same human race that I am: these fretted at me, as Moab did at Israel (because they were of a different religion), or as Tobiah and his accomplices did at Nehemiah and his Jews—it was a quarrel enough to Jerusalem that it would not be miserable. Hypocrites and heretics especially are here understood (as some conceive), such as pretend to be children of the church, and her greatest friends, as the Donatists would be the only Christians, and after them the Novatian heretics called themselves the only Catholics. So did the Arians, and so do the papists, whose anger against the true children of the church is far hotter than Nebuchadnezzar's oven after it had been seven times heated for those three constant worthies [i.e., Shadrach, Meshach, and Abednego]. Solomon's Book of All Virtues.[9]

1:7 *Tell Me*

The Simple Adornment of Christ's Bride. Theodore Beza: The state of the church as represented in the preceding verse teaches us what

[6]Hoffman, *Dat Boeck Cantica Canticorum*, 28-29; citing Jn 15:19; Ps 120:7; 116:10.
[7]Isidore, *Canticum Canticorum Salomonis*, 6r.
[8]Ainsworth, *Annotations*, 2:687; citing Ps 69:8 Acts 20:30; Gal 2:4, 2 Cor 11:26; Jas 4:1; 1 Pet 2:11; Ps 41:7; Rom 7:9, 14, 19.
[9]Trapp, *Solomonis ΠΑΝΑΡΕΤΟΣ*, 184; citing Num 22:3-4; Neh 6:10-19.

she means to say here, when she turns her speech to the bridegroom: being so weary and tormented by her bastard brothers, and assuring herself of her spouse's love (however disheveled she may have been by their rough treatment), she now implores him to tell her where she may find him. She does this not only to be restored to her former condition, but to draw yet nearer to him than ever before, so that she may be more and more beautified by him. This is the sum of what is taught in this verse, containing a most excellent and most necessary doctrine—especially for our time, in which the question of the reestablishment of this poor bride (so miserably disfigured by false pastors) is so often debated. There is not a word here that does not have marvelous weight. Let us note, first of all, to whom she speaks and with what vehemence, and also what she means when she says, "O you whom my soul loves. . . ." She speaks to her bridegroom, her beloved, our Lord Jesus Christ, and she protests that she speaks without deception, and with the whole affection of her heart. And to induce him to answer, she makes mention of the entire amity that she bears for him. First of all, let us therefore learn that when the question concerns restoring the church of God after these desolations to her true form and splendor, there can be no question of seeking the manner and the means in our own heads, but rather we must address ourselves to God, to whom alone it falls to dress and adorn his spouse as he sees fit. If we do otherwise, we do nothing but disguise and disfigure her, now after one fashion and now after another, as we see has happened before in the Christian church, and well may happen again in our own time. For where else did this transformation in the Christian church come from, but that the successors of the first pastors established by the apostles, instead of keeping themselves to those simple and natural garments that the true apostles had cut out to clothe and adorn this bride, dressed her to their own liking? Some of these fashions and manners were obviously borrowed from Judaism, others from paganism itself; still others were invented by the whims of certain bishops. . . . And what is the outcome of all this? In this way our crafty enemy has served his purpose little by little—with the unwitting help of those who sought to do the opposite!—and at length has arrived at what was his goal all along: to transform the pure and chaste bride of the Lord into a painted whore. . . . The question today being the reform of the church . . . we are taught in this passage to have our recourse only to the wisdom of God as it has been precisely set down in his Word, doing nothing from our own heads, lest we offend in what we would amend. Sermons on the First Three Chapters of the Song of Songs.[10]

The Prayer of the Faithful Soul. Veit Dietrich: Here is a prayer, "My soul loves you"—that is, I have all trust and hope in you, dear God. But when my soul is so sick, and beset with such vexation, it appears that I have utterly lost my God, and he has forgotten me. Wherefore I beg of you, show me where I may find you, so that you may be with me and defend me from such troubles. For human wisdom is much too weak, when all these evils are arrayed against it. Therefore we have need of this prayer, because if God will not help we will range to and fro, but find certain help nowhere. The Song of Solomon.[11]

[10]Beza, *Sermons sur les trois premiers chapitres du Cantique des Cantiques, de Salomon*, 157-60.
[11]Dietrich, *Das Hohelied Salomonis*, 4-5.

1:8-11 The Bride and Her Beloved Delight in Each Other

He

[8]*If you do not know,*
O most beautiful among women,

follow in the tracks of the flock,
and pasture your young goats
beside the shepherds' tents.

[9]*I compare you, my love,*
to a mare among Pharaoh's chariots.

[10]*Your cheeks are lovely with ornaments,*
your neck with strings of jewels.

Others

[11]*We will make for you*[a] *ornaments of gold,*
studded with silver.

a The Hebrew for *you* is feminine singular

Overview: In this passage, the bridegroom addresses his bride through a series of suggestive metaphors. A majority of our commentators read these as various figures for the way in which Christ woos his people, drawing them into the life of grace. One exception, however, is Hugo Grotius, whose commentary often draws analogies between the imagery of the Song and various tropes in classical erotic poetry—in this instance, one of the odes of Horace. Most of our commentators, however, offer interpretations in keeping with the spirit of patristic and medieval allegory, though these readings are given added depth and complexity by their efforts to wrestle with the difficult syntax and vocabulary of the Hebrew text (especially in verse 9). A common theme among most of the interpretations is the comfort offered by the warlike imagery of the bridegroom's arrival.

1:8 *Follow in the Tracks of the Flock*

Christ's Sheep Are Rational Creatures. John Trapp: "If you know not, O fairest among women." So Christ is please to style her, even though she had called herself "black" and "sunburned." Nothing more commends us to Christ than humility and lowly-mindedness. For this reason, the daughter of Zion is compared to a comely and delicate woman, and her enemies to shepherds with their flocks. But false prophets also have their flocks, and seducers drag disciples after them. "Even wasps make combs, and even the Marcionites make churches," says Tertullian.[†] Wasps also have their honeycombs, and apes imitate human actions. These conventiclers the church must studiously decline, and not *viam per avia quaere* [to seek a pathless path], seek truth by wandering through the thicket of errors. . . .[‡] The spouse is here directed by the Arch-shepherd to repair to the "foddering places," to frequent the public assemblies: to tread in that sheep track; the footsteps of the flock, the Shepherd's tents. There Christ has promised to feed his lambs (that have golden fleeces, precious souls), to call them by name, as he did Moses, Cornelius, and so on, and to "teach them great and hidden things, such as they knew not." Also, to give them spiritual senses, and the ability to examine what is doctrinally propounded to them, to try before they trust (for all Christ's sheep are rational; they know his voice from the voice of a stranger), and to be fully persuaded of the truth that they take up and profess. Solomon's Book of All Virtues.[1]

[1]Trapp, *Solomonis ΠΑΝΆΡΕΤΟΣ*, 187; citing Song 1:5; 1 Pet 3:5 Jer 6:2-3; Acts 20:30; Jer 33:3. [†]Tertullian, *Against Marcion* 4.5.

1:9-11 *A Mare Among Pharaoh's Chariots*

Forced Servitude in Pharaoh's Army. Melchior Hoffman: God's cavalry is his spirits and angels, which we also have in 2 Kings 6, when Elisha's disciple saw the mountain filled with fiery horses and chariots. The bride is likened to these same horses and this same cavalry by Christ her bridegroom. Christ also spoke of this in Matthew 22: "God's elect will be like the angels." So Christ also compares the daughter of Zion to his rulers. And if she is presently among Pharaoh's chariots, that is in the kingdom of the devil and in the devil's congregation, nevertheless she shall soon be like the calvary of God and be led out of the darkness and the kingdom of the devil and the world and all that belongs to it. And if the ruler of this world presently uses and has used her for the sake of his own power and might, she shall nevertheless be released from this congregation and these chariots, and from these bonds and snares, and also led out of the darkness like St. Paul in Acts 9. The Book of Song of Songs.[2]

A Suitable Helper. Isidore Clarius: The phrase "I have compared you" is a Hebraism, meaning "I have accepted you as a partner," just as "Let us make for him a helper suitable for him"—namely, one agreeable to the partnership. When the chariots and horsemen of Pharaoh pursued you, at that time I took you for my spouse, friend, partner, and as one suitable for me. The Song of Songs of Solomon.[3]

A Playful Filly. Hugo Grotius: Horace says:

Who like a filly o'er the field
With playful spirit bounds, [and fears to yield
To hand of gentlest touch, or prove,
Wild as she is, the joys of wedded love.][†]

Annotations on the Old Testament.[4]

The Heavenly Host. Antonio Brucioli: He compares the happy bride of Christ, the most victorious king, to a troop of horses—that is, to the angels, because no one of understanding doubts that the angels are ministers of Christ. For this reason Christ speaks to his bride, saying, "O my friend, you were then most miserable, a prisoner of the devil and thus a stranger to me, but behold! I have now made you free and saved you, through my word and spirit, and I will so wonderfully glorify you that you shall be like the glorious host of my angels!" But in what way? In the chariots and power of Pharaoh the king of Egypt—that is, of the prince of darkness, the devil, and of sin, of death and of hell, all of which I have overcome for you, who trust in me. And this is said so that we may know that all those who are without Christ are like horses who draw the chariot of Pharaoh—that is, they are under the rule and guidance of him who drives the chariot, the devil. But all those who are with Christ are hitched to God's chariot, and are under his rule. The Song of Solomon.[5]

Equally Yoked in Faith. Theodore Beza. "My love, I compare you to the harness of one of Pharaoh's chariots."[†] This comparison may seem very strange, and yet it is perfectly appropriate, if we consider the sense to which it refers and not stretch it further. Even so, it is said figuratively that "the eagles gather themselves where there is a dead body," to show that the true church arrays herself in relation to her head, Jesus Christ, wherever she may be found.[‡] Now, it would be thought utterly absurd if one were to compare the children of God to carrion birds, or Jesus Christ (who is the holy of holies) to a cadaver. . . . So also in this passage the Spirit does not intend to compare his church to a horse or a mare, but because one of the principal

[†]Trapp cites this expression in connection with Junius (possibly Franciscus Junius, the sixteenth-century Reformed theologian), but the expression *viam per avia quaere* originates with the fourth-century grammarian Servius, who cites this example of an oxymoron in his commentary on book 9 of Virgil's *Aeneid*.

[2]Hoffman, *Dat Boeck Cantica Canticorum*, 32-33; citing Mt 22:30 Ps 2.

[3]Isidore, *Canticum Canticorum Salomonis*, 7r; citing Gen 2:18.

[4]Grotius, *Annotationes in Vetus Testamentum*, 267. [†]Horace, *Odes* 3.11.

[5]Brucioli, *La Cantica di Salomo*, A-14.

beauties of a woman is a straight and upright figure, with an agreeable expression (as it also specified in Ps 144:12, where the daughters are compared to high and straight pillars of great palaces), so the Holy Spirit wants to represent the excellence of the Lord's church, when she keeps to her true pastors, by means of bodily things. . . .

In addition, let us also note that this spouse is compared to a beautiful horse, and to a couple yoked together. This is an elegant simile, for in representing the church by this spousal figure, what else is signified but a company harnessed together?—two by two, as one might say, under the Lord's yoke. Thus we say to one another, not only in words, but also by example, "Come, let us ascend up the mountain of the Lord," with David, "I rejoiced when the said to me, 'we will go into the house of the Lord.'" In short, the whole Scripture is full of such exhortations, that together we should all aim at the same mark, not only in walking but in running, the stronger supporting the weaker one who is coupled with him. And this is the reason why it was ordained in the law that a person should not yoke a horse and an ass to labor together, for fear that one might draw the other under its feet. See what this holy assembly is, of which we have so singular a pattern, for the Holy Spirit took care in enumerating the apostles as six holy couples, and in sending them out two by two. Sermons on the First Three Chapters of the Song of Songs.[6]

Blessings in War and Peace. Martin Luther: "I have compared you, my love, to my cavalry of Pharaoh's chariots." This is an amplification of the foregoing consolation. But since there are some periods of war and others of peace, he also divides this amplification into two sections. This first section should be addressed to a period of affliction and the cross. In tribulation it seems to you that you have been abandoned and defeated. But I have compared you to my cavalry—that is, in my sight you are like a victorious cohort that is equipped to do battle, as are the chariots of Pharaoh, the mightiest of all kings. I think that mention is made of Pharaoh because of all those known to the Jews he was the most powerful king. This is a consolation of faith, a consolation that is a matter neither of experience nor of sight, for in Solomon's eyes his government is like a worm. Why? Because burdened and disturbed by evils and by its awareness of these evils, it deserts the Word and ignores all of its gifts. But if you look to the Word, all these assertions are perfect truth. It is therefore a most ample promise that God calls the government his friend; but it is not obvious. In appearance it seems rather as if God has deserted it.

"Your cheeks are comely like earrings, and your neck like strings of jewels." This is the second section of the amplification, dealing with the time of peace. For then the Word of God, which is lost or barely retained in tribulation, is present with us, then we are delighted by the gifts of the Spirit, which in the time of the cross are completely obliterated by our awareness of evils. We translate "earrings" because these ornaments are divided from each other and arranged in beautiful array. The Hebrew word elsewhere means "lines," or "rows." Moreover, earrings and "necklaces" are gifts of the Holy Spirit in the Word. They adorn our neck—that is, the Word is in public use, it is taught, read, heard, and the abundance of the divine promises is possessed everywhere. . . .

[6]Beza, *Sermons sur les trois premiers chapitres du Cantique des Cantiques, de Salomon*, 255, 261-62; citing Is 2:3; Ps 122:1; Gal 6:2; 1 Thess 5:14; Deut 22:10; Mt 10:2; Mk 6:7. †Beza's seemingly odd translation here reflects a notorious difficulty in the Hebrew, where "mare" (*sûsâ*) is singular and "chariots" (*rekeb*) is plural, thus: "I compare you to a mare with the chariots." Many translations (e.g., Vulgate, KJV) solve the infelicity by a collective term; compare with Luther's "cavalry of chariots." Beza, however, omits the mare altogether in his translation (though not in his exposition), postulating a "harness of one of Pharaoh's chariots" (French: *attellage de l'un des coches de Pharaon*). The choice is not without theological significance, as his exegesis (above) makes clear. ‡Mt 24:28. In taking for granted the figurative significance of this passage, Beza may have in mind the remarks of Calvin: "If birds have so great sagacity as to flock in great numbers from distant places to a single carcass, it would be disgraceful in believers not to assemble to the author of life, from whom alone they derive their actual nourishment." *Harmony of the Evangelists* (CC 17:144; CO 45:665).

"My Beloved is to me a bag of myrrh that lies between my breasts." Now he adds his commendation of the comfort and enlarges on the consolation with images of sweetness. "God is not far away, but he dwells in the midst of our life and is like a bag of myrrh in my bosom and in my embraces. That is, he cares for me, protects and comforts me. . . . In short, his feeling for me is like that of a bridegroom for his bride." It is to be noted, however, that these realities are not palpable. Rather, this consolation remains in the figure of a fragrance. These things are perceived only by smell, in order to express the mystery of faith, namely, that God dwells among his people through a fragrance, that is, through his Word and his name. The faith must needs be great that can believe these things regarding God, that he is between the breasts, that is, that he is very near and close to us, is not angry, and so on.

"Behold, you are beautiful, my love; behold, you are beautiful." After trial, when the consolation of the Word has taken hold of the heart, we not only feel that God loves and cherishes us, but we also feel that we please God, that we delight God, and that God takes care of us. In this way conscience and the Spirit give mutual testimony. Conscience feels that it pleases God, and so it praises God. The Holy Spirit approves this faith and in turn commends us. That is what you see expressed by this passage. A BRIEF BUT ALTOGETHER LUCID EXPOSITION OF THE SONG OF SONGS.[7]

A PROMISE OF VICTORY. HENRY AINSWORTH: The horse is a warlike beast, as God describes him in Job 39:19-35; and Solomon says, "The horse is prepared against the day of battle." "In the chariots of Pharaoh." Pharaoh's horses and chariots were highly sought after, as the Scriptures often show, and therefore were sought after by Solomon in his trading with Egypt. And the prophet says, "Woe to those who go down to Egypt for help, and stay on horses, and trust in chariots because they are many." And in Ezekiel 17:15, the king of Judah "sent his ambassadors into Egypt, that they might give him horses, and many people." For the meaning of this speech, it seems to be this: the church being sent forth by Christ into the footsteps of the flock to feed her kids besides the tents or dwellings of the shepherds was presently to look for troubles in itself; and in opposition at the hands of those companions mentioned in verse 7, and their flocks. And when God threatens wars against the daughter of Zion, he says, "The shepherds with their flocks shall come to her, they shall pitch their tents against her roughly." To comfort her, therefore, against such troubles, the Lord compares her to the troop of horses in Pharaoh's chariots, under this similitude promising her victory. ANNOTATIONS UPON THE SONG OF SONGS.[8]

YOKED IN SLAVERY. THOMAS BRIGHTMAN: This comparison of his love to a "mare" may seem a gross similitude to distressed lovers, but the counsel of the Spirit is most sweet and divine. We have seen in what case religion was left, as well among the two [remaining] tribes as among the dispersed remnants. This one verse touches the civil state, for what can be more servile than to be joined like a horse to a chariot, to draw at the driver's pleasure and against your will to endure the harness, the bridle, and the whip? Such was the condition of that kingdom, by whose aid and succor his "love" was protected. For in the fifth year of the reign of Rehoboam, when they had a little breathed after their former troubles, Shishak, the king of Egypt, made war on them, having twelve hundred chariots and a very great host. . . . This Shishak entered into the city and took away the treasures of the house of the Lord and the treasures of the king's house. He carried away also the shields of gold which Solomon had made. Behold the church now like a "mare" in the chariots of Pharaoh. COMMENTARY ON THE CANTICLES.[9]

[7]LW 15:206-209 (WA 31.2:622-30).

[8]Ainsworth, *Annotations*, 2:691; citing Prov 21:31; 2 Chron 1:16-17; Is 31:1; Acts 20:29-30; Gen 13:6-7, 26:14-15, 20-21; Ex 2:16-17; Jer 6:2-4.

[9]Brightman, *A Commentary on the Canticles or the Song of Salomon*, 988.

HARNESSED FOR BATTLE. VEIT DIETRICH: "I compare you, my friend, to my riding harness on Pharaoh's chariot." This also includes a comfort. When you are facing vexations and buffetings that make you fainthearted and threaten to overwhelm you, you sink right to the floor. But because you have God and his Word, then you are like a mighty riding harness, which charges through all the highways and byways. For as Christ says, "Even the gates of hell shall not prevail against it," so count on his Word as he praises the kingdom of Israel so admirably. Such praise goes to all governments guided by the Word of God; but that government which is not so guided, even though its wealth, property, power, or force be great, yet it is but a vain and fleeting endeavor, and cannot stand in the face of fiery ordeals and tribulation [*Anfechtung*]. This is certainly true. THE SONG OF SOLOMON.[10]

[10]Dietrich, *Das Hohelied Salomonis*, 5-6; citing Mt 16:18.

1:12-17 FRAGRANT AND BEAUTIFUL ALLURE

She

[12]*While the king was on his couch,*
my nard gave forth its fragrance.

[13]*My beloved is to me a sachet of myrrh*
that lies between my breasts.

[14]*My beloved is to me a cluster of henna blossoms*
in the vineyards of Engedi.

He

[15]*Behold, you are beautiful, my love;*
behold, you are beautiful;
your eyes are doves.

She

[16]*Behold, you are beautiful, my beloved, truly delightful.*
Our couch is green;

[17]*the beams of our house are cedar;*
our rafters are pine.

Overview: In this exchange between the bride and her bridegroom, the poet deploys a cascade of rich sensory images to express the mutual delight the lovers take in one another. Our commentators all make note of the intertextual associations of these images with other biblical passages, and some (e.g., Martin Luther, Theodore Beza) take special note of the fact that the poet focuses here on the sense of smell in particular. The figural significance of these images is interpreted in different ways, and our authors stress (or downplay) the erotic overtones of this sensual imagery to different degrees, but there is widespread agreement on the power of these verses in communicating the intimacy of the relationship between Christ and his people.

1:12 *My Nard Gave Forth Its Fragrance*

The Church's Fragrant Graces. Henry Ainsworth: Here the church speaks of the fruits and effects of Christ's former graces: how in her, and from her, so adorned by her beloved, the odor of the Spirit of God in her flowed forth and spread abroad to the delight of herself and others. By the king is meant Christ, as in verse 4; by his round table (which the Greek translates "his sitting down," which was typically done in a circle, or ring, as in 1 Sam 16:11) may be understood the spiritual banquet of Christ with his church, feeding her with his Word and graces. The "table of the Lord" signifies the communion between him and his people, as does also the supping of one with another. The spikenard is one of the pleasant fruits in the garden of the church, but here it seems to be the oil or ointment made of spikenard, which is very precious and which they used to pour out and anoint men with. This is what Mary anointed our Lord Jesus with, as "he sat at table with his friends, and the house was filled with the fragrance (or odor) of the ointment." Spiritually, it signifies the sweet-smelling fruits of repentance, faith, love, prayer, thanksgiving, and so on, which the church shows forth by the communion of Christ with her, but especially it signifies mortification and communion with Christ's death, burial, and resurrection, as that which Mary did to Christ was to anoint his body for burial. Annotations upon the Song of Songs.[1]

---

[1]Ainsworth, *Annotations*, 2:693-94; citing Mal 1:12; 1 Cor 10:21; Rev 3:20; Song 4:13-14; Jn 12:1-3; Rom 6:3-5; Mk 14:8; Jn 12:7.

The Powerful Aroma of Prayer. Veit Dietrich: Such consolation is not in vain, as if he wanted to say, "I was terribly afraid, when so many vexations and disasters struck me, that God had abandoned me," but he shows by his comfort and help that he is gracious to me. "And my *nard*," that is, "my prayer gives off its aroma and is heard, for I see that God is again most friendly to me and acts utterly in my best interest, and he is like a fragrant flower or precious balm between my breasts." The Song of Solomon.[2]

The Power of Aroma over Taste. Theodore Beza: But let us note that the bride adds that, being so near to the bridegroom in this banquet, her "spikenard gave off its aroma." The herb we call spikenard was held in particular regard in former times among the people of the east as a perfume that they specifically used at their banquets, as is clearly to be seen in the Gospel history. Where truly and visibly the church banqueted with her bridegroom in the person of the apostles and Mary, and perfumed him in such a way that it might even appear that Solomon spoke in this text in a prophetic spirit. But since this is more subtle than certain, we must search for another sense in this passage to make our profit. Therefore let us learn here that it is not enough to be called to this banquet, but we must enter in and sit down; otherwise, our invitation serves only to our condemnation, as alas today more than ever we see people so bewitched with the cares and vanities of this world that there are very few who will think on this banquet, though they are invited daily. And it shall happen to them as is spoken in Matthew 22:7-8. For again, it is not enough to enter in and sit down, but our perfume must also give off its aroma.

But some will say that we should rather eat and drink to be satisfied, and here is no mention made of drink or meat. Let us therefore note that in this banquet there is no question of refreshing the belly, which would require meat and drink, but rather the question concerns the spiritual life, and therefore mention is made of the aroma of the bride's spikenard, of myrrh and clusters of camphor. The reason for this is that there are no sensible things more fitting to signify spiritual realities than the odors, which are received in the head after so subtle a manner. And this exposition is neither far-fetched nor less certain, for this is the very style of Scripture, as we will show throughout. Sermons on the First Three Chapters of the Song of Songs.[3]

Reprieve Under King Asa. Thomas Brightman: You have heard before that the gifts of the Spirit are foreshadowed by ointments, and spikenard (which is chief among ointments) rightly betokens the most excellent gifts. Therefore, while the king sat, the spouse as it were opening a box perfumed all the neighborhood by breathing out most holy graces. But if any ask who the prophet says sat at this repast, behold King Asa, surrounded by a large garland of Jews and Israelites in that assembly, where he made borders of gold with studs of silver. A covenant was made; but what mirth of a banquet could be compared with this delight? Furthermore, the joy in sacrificing (which was great at that time) had the holy pleasure of banqueting conjoined to it by the law. As concerning the smell of the spikenard, how pleasant was it to make a covenant among so many people, to worship the Lord with all their heart, and with all their mind. Many of Ephraim, Manasseh, and Simeon, stirred up by the sweetness of this smell, came to Asa, seeing the Lord his God to be with him, as it is said in 2 Chronicles 15:9. Therefore, whatsoever is spoken of the church in the reign of Asa is contained in these three little verses. Commentary on the Canticles.[4]

---

[2]Dietrich, *Das Hohelied Salomonis*, 6.

[3]Beza, *Sermons sur les trois premiers chapitres du Cantique des Cantiques, de Salomon*, 285-87; citing Lk 7:37; Jn 12:3.

[4]Brightman, *A Commentary on the Canticles or the Song of Salomon*, 990.

1:13-16 *A Sachet of Myrrh*

The Bitterness of Myrrh. Antonio Brucioli: Certainly it is high praise for the bridegroom, that apart from him the bride has no good odor at all. And so she desires, or rather she knows, that she possesses Christ, and that Christ must always dwell with her as a sachet of myrrh. Myrrh is certainly bitter, but it has the sweetest aroma, and it preserves from corruption. And truly the Spirit of the bridegroom brings such things to pass in the faithful. First he brings bitterness on them, as the knife of merit pierces their soul. Second, he pours out the aroma of his sweet ointments. Third, he preserves them from corruption, granting eternal life to those who believe in him, as is said in John 3. And just as Moses lifted up the snake in the desert, so also must the Son of Man be lifted up, so that whoever believes in him will not perish, but have eternal life. And clearly this myrrh is a bitter thing, signifying harsh and difficult tribulations. But seeing that all of these things loom over her for the sake of her beloved, she consoles herself with these words, trusting that she will be given the grace manfully to endure all things. Therefore she does not describe these things that she must bear on account of her love a burden, but a bundle, or rather a little sachet, because the afflictions of this world are not to be compared with the future glory which will be revealed in us. The Song of Solomon.[5]

The Figure of a Fragrance. Martin Luther: Now he adds his commendation of the comfort and enlarges on the consolation with images of sweetness. "God is not far away, but he dwells in the midst of our life and is like a bag of myrrh in my bosom and in my embraces. That is, he cares for me, protects and comforts me, and so on. In short, his feeling for me is like that of a bridegroom for his bride." It is to be noted, however, that these realities are not palpable. Rather, this consolation remains in the figure of a fragrance. These things are perceived only by smell, in order to express the mystery of faith—namely, that God dwells among his people through a fragrance, that is, through his Word and his name. The faith must needs be great that can believe these things regarding God, that he is between the breasts—that is, that he is very near and close to us, and is not angry. A Brief but Altogether Lucid Exposition of the Song of Songs.[6]

Room for Only One. Isidore Clarius: Next it is told how I had left behind my odor from the flocks when God gave to me a skillfully made sachet of myrrh—that is, the temple, where God remained in his ark. The ark was carried between two poles, as if being placed between the breasts, for these protruding poles resembled breasts. Or, simply understand "My beloved is like a sachet of myrrh, which is held between the breasts" to mean that my beloved is fastened to my heart; otherwise, he would not be my beloved, if anything else besides him could be set there. The Song of Songs of Solomon.[7]

The Intimacy of the Marriage Bed. John Trapp: It is the manner of maids to wear nosegays of sweet flowers in their bosoms, and to make no small account of them. Myrrh is marvelously sweet and savory, but nowhere near as sweet as the Lord Christ is to those that have spiritual senses. This is who the spouse places between her breasts, there the sweet savor may ascend into her nostrils. Again, myrrh has a bitter root. Christ seems bitter at first, because of afflictions, but "if we suffer with him, we shall also reign together with him." Third, myrrh was very precious: this is why the wise men offered it to Christ at his birth. Christ is so esteemed by his people, "chosen and precious," that as wise merchants they sell everything to purchase him. Last, myrrh is of a preserving nature, and was therefore made use of at funerals. Likewise, Christ does by his Spirit's heat exsiccate or dry up the

[5]Brucioli, *La Cantica di Salomo*, B-9-10; citing Rom 8:18.

[6]LW 15:208 (WA 31.2:628).

[7]Isidore, *Canticum Canticorum Salomonis*, 8v.

superfluity of our degenerate nature, whereby body and soul are preserved to eternal life; so, after our bodies are turned to dust, he still preserves a substance that he will raise again at the last day. . . .

"He shall lie all night between my breasts."[†] This is Christ's proper place: "My son, give me your heart." Christ should dwell in the heart by faith. But too often he is shut out, and adultery is found "between the breasts." There they carried the signs of their idolatry (as the papists now do their crucifixes) to testify that the idol had their hearts. But what did the martyr Mr. Bradford say in a certain letter?[‡] "As the wife will keep her bed only for her husband, although in other things she is content to have fellowship with others—for example, to speak, sit, eat, drink, go. . . . So our consciences (which are Christ's wives) must needs keep the bed—that is, God's sweet promises, alone for ourselves and our husband to meet together, to embrace and laugh together, and to be joyful together. If sin, the law, the devil, or anything else would creep into the bed, and lie there and complain to your husband Christ, immediately you shall see him play the part of Phinehas."[§] SOLOMON'S BOOK OF ALL VIRTUES.[8]

THE MANIFOLD SYMBOLISM OF MYRRH. JOHANN GERHARD: Observe what is proclaimed, what then the spiritual bride boasts about this her bridegroom. She says, "My friend is a small bundle of myrrh." The Hebrew word (*mōr*), which has been preserved in the Latin and German languages, is used both for the myrrh tree and also for the fruit of the myrrh tree. The myrrh tree is also described as a lowly tree or shrub that grows especially abundantly in Arabia, not unlike a thorn bush, whose leaves and shrubs emit a lovely fragrance from the same tree. If in the springtime it sways back and forth, especially in the north wind and the south wind or is also scored by the inhabitants of the same land, a sap flows out, which runs together thereafter and is brought into receptacles, to use not only for incense but also for medicine inside the body. This drop of myrrh or myrrh is (1) very bitter, as it thereafter in the holy language got its name, and because of its bitterness the godless soldiers "mixed with myrrh" the drink that was given to the Lord Christ in his passion. (2) It also emits a strong, pleasant aroma. Athenaeus explains that it was determined that all ointments get their name from myrrh, as *myron* [Greek for "sweet ointment"] is so named as it is pronounced as if it were *myrrhon* [i.e., myrrh], because myrrh surpasses all aromas because of the fragrance of its smell.[†] Compare then "The beds were sprinkled with myrrh" that they might emit a lovely smell and what Wisdom says in Sirach 24:15: "I gave off a lovely scent like the best myrrh." (3) It is used to clean and heal wounds and injuries. (4) It drives out the bad dampness from which the major illnesses arise, if it is used internally and taken into the body. (5) It soothes pains. (6) It strengthens the heart; therefore, it was previously customary that those who had a weak heart smeared the chest with myrrh oil; see Athenaeus, in his last book, chapter fifteen. And finally, (7) it preserves the bodies of the dead from decomposition and worms. Anselm says on this passage, "Myrrh is a most bitter object and so bodies anointed with it remain intact because worms do not approach them because of their excessive

[8]Trapp, *Solomonis ΠΑΝΆΡΕΤΟΣ*, 191-92; citing Ps 45:8; Prov 7:17; Mk 15:23; 2 Tim 2:12; 1 Pet 2:6; Mt 13:44; Jn 19:39; Prov 23:26; Eph 3:17; Hos 2:2. [†]The Hebrew verb translated in the ESV as "lies" often carries the implication of "lying" or "staying" overnight (e.g., Gen 19:2; 24:23; Num 22:8; Josh 3:1), thus the KJV's translation of this passage (which Trapp follows) as, "A bundle of myrrh is my well beloved unto me; he shall lie *all night* betwixt my breasts." In other contexts, however, the same verb simply means "to lie" or "to remain," and modern translations tend to favor this simpler rendition. [‡]John Bradford (1510–1555) was a Protestant minister appointed as an itinerant preacher by Bishop Nicholas Ridley. He was later imprisoned in the Tower of London with Ridley, Hugh Latimer, and Thomas Cranmer, prior to his execution by burning during the reign of Mary I. He was celebrated as a martyr in the *Actes and Monuments* of John Foxe, to which the letter from which Trapp here quotes was printed as an appendix. *Acts and Monuments*, ed. John Pratt, 3rd ed. (London: Georgy Seely, 1870), 7:264. [§]A reference to the story in Num 25:6-13, which recounts an incident in which Phinehas killed with a spear an Israelite and his Midianite wife. Phinehas is commended for his zeal and credited with turning back the Lord's anger (Num 25:11).

bitterness."[‡] That is therefore the properties and power of myrrh, which can be found in the shrub and its leaves as well as in the fruit of the tree—although even more in the fruit than in the leaves. And because the Hebrew word (*mōr*) is used both for the shrub and the leaves of the myrrh as well as the fruit of the tree and the myrrh oil prepared out of the sap or gum, it suggests that all these meanings together can all apply here. Postils on the Song of Songs.[9]

1:17 *Our Bed Is Green*

Green and Flourishing. Henry Ainsworth: "Our bed" or "Our bedstead." Beds were used either to rest and sleep on, or to sit on when eating and feasting, as we do at tables. And figuratively the place of offering sacrifices is called a bed. "Our bed is green," or flourishing and fruitful; for it is not meant so much of color, as of flourishing growth, and increase. This word, when applied to men and women, means a prosperous and flourishing estate, as when Nebuchadnezzar said, "I was at rest in my house, and green (or flourishing) in my palace." And David compares himself to "a green (or flourishing) olive tree in the house of God," where the Greek [Septuagint] translates it "a fruitful olive." By this the church signifies that by her communion with Christ (whether by the similitude of bed or board) she became flourishing and fruitful, as it is said of those who are planted in the Lord's house: "They shall still bring forth fruit in hoary age, they shall be fat and green." And this is the nature of the Gospel, where it is received by faith, that it "brings forth fruit" and makes people "fruitful in every good work, and increasing in the knowledge of God." It may here also signify the increase of the children of the church, which are begotten by the immortal seed of the Word, through the power of Christ, giving a blessing to its ministry. Annotations upon the Song of Songs.[10]

The Restoration of God's House. John Cotton: It is an ornament of the church to restore her with beams of cedar, and her walls, or galleries, with fir. Cedar is famous for durability, enduring even to eternity, says Pliny.[†] Fir is acceptable for its sweetness, and while it grows, for its height, straightness, and perpetual greenness. Solomon's house or temple was of old a lively type, partly: first, of the human body of Christ, the temple of the deity; second, of the mystical body of Christ, his church or congregation. Christ's human body never decays, and therefore it needs no repairing. His mystical body the church, if it falls into decay through corruption of doctrine or worship, may be most fitly repaired: first, by laying into the walls of the church such solid and eternal truths of God as may hold up the walls of the building. Thus Luther restored the church by laying this beam of cedar, the doctrine of free justification by Christ. Second, by setting up such worship and works for the people to walk in, as are truly sweet and amiable in God's sight. Springing from a fresh and green sincerity, growing up to the heavens, these are like galleries of fir, whereas vows of perfection, and works of supererogation, and all other relics and rags of popery, are no better than rotten and moth-eaten wood, fit fuel for the fire. A Brief Exposition on the Whole Book of Canticles.[11]

---

[9]Gerhard, *Postilla Salomonæa*, 304-5; citing Mk 15:2; Prov 7:17. [†]Athenaeus was a third-century-AD Greek grammarian and rhetorician. Gerhard summarizes a discussion of the etymology of perfumes in the *Deipnosophistae* 15.688. [‡]Anselm of Laon (c. 1050–1117) was an early scholastic theologian and commentator whose cathedral school in Laon became one of the most influential centers of "secular" learning outside a monastic setting prior to the rise of the universities. Anselm and his school were early contributors to the *Glossa ordinaria*, but the *Enarrationes in Cantica canticorum* from which Gerhard is quoting here was a separate commentary that was very influential among later interpreters (PL 162:1195).

[10]Ainsworth, *Annotations*, 2:695-96; citing Ps 122:3-4 Esther 1:5-6; Amos 6:4; Ezek 23:41; Is 57:7; Dan 4:4; Ps 92:13-14; Col 1:6, 10.

[11]Cotton, *Brief Exposition*, 48-49; citing 1 Cor 3:16. [†]Pliny the Elder (AD 23–79) notes in his *Natural History* (8.11) that the wood of the cedar tree "lasts forever, for which reason it is that they have long been in the habit of using it for making the statues of the gods" (LCL 370:130-31).

2:1-7 THE LAVISH BANQUET BETWEEN LOVERS

1I am a rose[a] of Sharon,
a lily of the valleys.

He

2As a lily among brambles,
so is my love among the young women.

She

3As an apple tree among the trees of the forest,
so is my beloved among the young men.

With great delight I sat in his shadow,
and his fruit was sweet to my taste.

4He brought me to the banqueting house,[b]
and his banner over me was love.

5Sustain me with raisins;
refresh me with apples,
for I am sick with love.

6His left hand is under my head,
and his right hand embraces me!

7I adjure you,[c] O daughters of Jerusalem,
by the gazelles or the does of the field,

that you not stir up or awaken love
until it pleases.

a Probably a bulb, such as a crocus, asphodel, or narcissus **b** Hebrew *the house of wine* **c** That is, I put you on oath; so throughout the Song

Overview: Another rich succession of images provokes a wide range of interpretation from our commentators. There is some disagreement as to who is speaking in Song of Song 2:1. Some (e.g., François Lambert) take it to be the voice of the bridegroom (i.e., Christ), describing his own perfections, while most take it to be the voice of the bride celebrating her lover's beauty. Most of our commentators pick up on the Hebrew text's description of the "house of wine" in Song of Song 2:4 ("banqueting house" in the ESV), though opinion varies as to its significance. Most interpret these images as a sign of the bridegroom's lavish provision for the happiness of his betrothed, pointing to the building contrast between the fruit of apples in verse 3 and fruit of the vine in verse 4. The English Puritans Henry Ainsworth and (especially) John Trapp emphasize the subjective dimension: the ravishing love of Christ makes his true followers appear inebriated in the sight of the unbelieving world. The embraces described in Song of Songs 2:6 are generally viewed as affirmations of Christ's tender love, however Martin Luther (and following him, Veit Dietrich) uses the reference to "left" and "right" hands as an opportunity to elaborate on the distinction. between God's two kingdoms, the church and the state. The adjuration to the daughters of Jerusalem (v. 7) sustains a wide variety of interpretation. Most follow the Vulgate's "beloved" rather than the more abstract "love" favored by most modern translations, with the result that the bridegroom appears to be guarding his beloved's slumber. The "gazelles or the does" whom he calls to witness are glossed alternately as angels (Lambert) or as the Gentiles whom Christ sought to woo (John Cotton). Several creative explanations are offered to explain the bridegroom's solicitude for the bride's slumber, but only Hugo Grotius insinuates that their rest may be the natural result of exhaustion from their union.

2:1-2 *A Rose of Sharon, a Lily Among Thorns*

Christ, the Flower of the World's Beauty. François Lambert: It should be carefully noted that at the very end of the last chapter the church's desirable bed is described as unpolluted and green. And indeed, here it is described less with greenery as with flowers, the point of which is to illustrate its verdure and beauty. They bloom in the morning and pass away; when evening falls, they harden and wither. Its flowers are, first of all, the bridegroom himself: "There shall come forth a rod out of the root of Jesse, and a flower[†] shall rise up out of his root." And its flowers are the flowers of honors and riches.

The bridegroom himself is called "the flower of the field" (or earth), because no human effort can make it arise. But coming into the world solely by the operation of the Holy Spirit, he assumed flesh from the unsullied Virgin. Likewise, he is not inappropriately called "the flower of the field" (or world), because you know that all the beauty of the world (signified by the flower) is situated in him. We are all certainly wretched, deformed little worms, fallen every one; but he himself alone is the most excellent flower of all, and his Spirit is marvelously effective, for they alone flourish who believe and trust in him with a pure heart. And the "field" in which wheat springs up is the appropriate place for this, for wheat is the most prominent and beautiful flower in the field. Therefore Christ is the wheat, or the seed of wheat, which died for our salvation and rising again bore eternal flowers and fruit, and he continually offers to his chosen ones innumerable of the sweetest fruits of his Spirit. Rightly, therefore, does he say, "I am the flower," who from the stump of Jesse was sprung up, the beautiful and lovely flower of the field (that is, of the world), which is the great assembly of his chosen ones. Finally, he added, "and the lily of the valley." What else can we understand by "valley" except genuine believers, those who are truly humble? For they are the valleys that are completely filled and raised up, as opposed to the "hills"—that is, the proud. As Isaiah says, "Every valley shall be exalted, and every mountain and hill shall be made low." And in Luke, "Every valley shall be filled." The lily of these valleys is the brightness and glory of Christ, who casts down rulers and the disobedient proud from their thrones, and exalts the believing humble. Commentary on the Song of Songs.[1]

The Church's Vulnerable Beauty. Henry Ainsworth: This is thought by some to be the speech of Christ, by others to be spoken by the church. The latter seems most probably, and is so expounded by the Chaldean Paraphrast.[†] If we understand it of Christ, it signifies the excellence of the graces in himself, which he readily communicates with his people. If of the church, it shows her graces received from Christ, whereby she is lovely and delightful, for sweet odor and beauty. "The rose of Sharon." In Greek, "the flower of the field," but Sharon is the name of a very fruitful place or plain, where David's herd of cattle were fed. The prophet mentions "the excellence of Carmel and Sharon," and when he threatens desolation he says, "Sharon is like a wilderness." But promising mercy to his people, he says, "Sharon shall be like a fold of flocks." The rose is the queen of flowers, most commendable for sweetness and beauty; so the lily, mentioned next, is glorious and amiable: "even Solomon in all his glory was not arrayed like one of these." "The lily is next in nobility to the rose," says Pliny.[‡] "Of the valleys, or of the low (or deep) places." These also were fruitful places, where the king's herds were fed. And as roses and lilies growing in Sharon and these valleys had more moisture than those that grew on hills and mounts, so this signifies the blessed estate of the church in Christ, by whose grace it is in low and base estate made sweet and amiable like the rose and lily. As the prophet says, "The wilderness and the dry place

[1]Lambert, *In Cantica Canticorum Salomonis*, 31v-r; citing Ps 89:6; Is 11:1 Sir 24:23; Is 40:4; Lk 3:5. [†]Lambert is quoting from the Vulgate, in which the same Latin word (*flos* = "flower") appears in both passages. Most modern English translations render the Hebrew *nēṣer* as "branch," not "flower."

shall be glad for them, and the desert shall rejoice and blossom as the rose." . . . But as here is mentioned the plain of Sharon, and the valleys, which were open places where cattle fed, and not enclosed gardens, so by this may be signified how the church is exposed to persecution, to be plucked at by all who pass by the way and trodden down, and eaten by beasts. And this the words following do more confirm. Annotations upon the Song of Songs.[2]

God's Protection of Princes and Magistrates. Martin Luther: "I am a rose of the field, a lily of the valleys."[†] This is a complaint in which he describes the danger. He does so by employing a contrast. Flowers that are nurtured inside walls and enclosures are safe from harm from both human and beast. But we, he says, are like a rose in an open field—anyone has access to it. I do not deny that I am a flower, I acknowledge the gift of the state that God has given me—but oh, that this flower had a hedge around it! For who could count all the dangers to which we are exposed in the midst of the nations, like those who dwell in an open field? In this light we can call the magistrate "a flower of the field" on account of the innumerable dangers to which he is exposed. He names the flower that grows on a lower level the lily of the valleys, perhaps to distinguish between the higher and lower magistrates. For the fact that there are various species of flowers can also be applied to the diversity of gifts in a sound state. The state itself has the consolation that it is a rose. However, even if it appears from the world's point of view to lack a hedge and stand unprotected, yet so long as it retains the Word and worship of God, it is surrounded and hedged about by the fiery chariots that Elisha showed his servant. Daniel, too, demonstrates that the angels are the guardians of the state. But only the faithful discern these protections. A Brief but Altogether Lucid Exposition of the Song of Songs.[3]

A Figure of Christ's Two Natures. Theodore Beza: In this passage, the bridegroom (who is Jesus Christ) reveals his excellence to our understanding, comparing himself to two flowers, the rose and the lily. . . . And not without reason was this comparison chosen by the Holy Spirit. For if we consider flowers very closely, we will find that among all creatures that we see here below with our eyes, there are none more admirable, none that more seem to have been sent down from heaven rather than to have come forth from the earth, than a flower, however small it may appear. And this is so whether we consider the pure and delicate material from which they are made, or the astonishing workmanship that appears in them, or the colors with which they are draped, or the sweet smell that proceeds from them, or finally, the fruits and seeds that spring from them according to their infinitely diverse kinds. Thus, it requires only the smallest flower to convict all the atheists and mockers of the world of the infinite power and wisdom of God. And thus it is not without reason that the Lord says that all the glory and splendor of Solomon cannot compare with a lily of the fields. . . .

Therefore I say that this analogy, taken from these two flowers that are beautiful and fragrant above all others, is marvelously adapted to represent this bridegroom to us, as if it were in a beautiful and resplendent mirror. There is nothing more white and clean than the whiteness of a lily, also called the lily of the valley because it grows in such places. And who else approaches the purity and justice of him in whom there was never found any blemish, either within or without, of him who

[2]Ainsworth, *Annotations*, 2:696-97; citing Hos 14:7; 1 Chron 27:29; Is 35:2; 33:9; 65:10; Mt 6:29; 1 Chron 27:9; Is 35:1. [†]The Chaldee Paraphrase is another term for the Aramaic Targum on the Song of Songs, an exegetical tradition that had probably crystallized by the seventh century. [‡]Pliny the Elder, *Naturalis historia* 21.5.

[3]LW 15:211-12 (WA 31.2:635-37); citing 2 Kings 6:17. [†]Luther follows the Septuagint and Vulgate in rendering the Hebrew *šārôn* as a common noun. The Authorized Version (1611) took it as a proper noun, and many modern translations have followed suit. Luther follows the Vulgate in his transcription, "flower of the field" (*flos campi* in Latin), though in his exegesis he identifies the flower more specifically as a rose (*rosa*).

is the holy of holies, the only one whose justice and innocence was able to appease the wrath of God? This may also be said of the white rose, but if we prefer instead to compare this bridegroom to the scarlet rose, or the color of the carnation, he will again be represented to us, not according to that divine nature, which, considered in itself, is invisible and incomprehensible, but rather insofar as he is the Son of God manifested (that is, made visible and truly human) in our bodily nature. For among all the colors of the world, just as the dye of the scarlet rose is the most excellent that may be found, so also there is none that represents more truly the color of human flesh, very lively and moderately colored.

What then is this scarlet rose? It is the great mystery of our religion, namely, the true Son of God "manifested in flesh, vindicated in spirit, seen by angels, preached among nations, believed in throughout the world, and taken up in glory." This is that firstborn brother, "the fairest of all men"; this is our sovereign high priest, "holy, blameless, undefiled, separated from sinners, and exalted above the heavens," "crowned with glory and honor," with a "name above every name." But how did he arrive at such an exalted place? By suffering his death—"even death on a cross." Such was he when Pilate, after having him scourged, brought him before the people and said, "Behold the man!" Such was he when, bathed in his own blood on the cross, he was wounded for our sins, bruised for our iniquities, and disfigured for our transgressions. And where then was the beauty of that rose? To be sure, it was obscured from view and effaced "for a little while," and for a little while this bridegroom became "more vile than a worm of the earth." But then that obedience is more beautiful and pleasant to God than sacrifice, and there was never such obedience as on the cross. It thus follows that this rose even then appeared before God in perfect splendor and beauty, notwithstanding the fact that it was dyed in blood—not a dye that stains, but one that takes away the stains of the whole world. This seems to have been represented figurally by the Holy Spirit—quite contrary to the intention of Pilate and Herod—both by the purple robe in which Pilate clad him when he was all bloody from scourging (this corresponds to the scarlet rose) and by the white robe that Herod put on him in mockery (this corresponds to the lily).[†] What is more, even today: if this rose had not appeared before God the Father, to be seen and smelled by him before, during after this bloody oblation—even to all eternity—there would never have been any bride for this bridegroom—that is to say, neither church nor eternal happiness.

And what is it that we do every day, whether it be in the hearing and receiving of the Word, and giving thanks to God, or whether it be in the celebration of the holy Supper, but refresh the memory of Christ's death and passion? It is not that we offer him up as a sacrifice once again (for this would be to deny the reality of his once-for-all oblation), but rather we present him as being, if I may say so, still sacrificed every day, and still all covered with blood, insofar as we set his death and passion between us and God as the sole foundation for our faith and our hope. Therefore, let us know that unless we present to the Father this red rose and this pure lily, neither we nor our prayers will be agreeable to him. Sermons on the First Three Chapters of the Song of Songs.[4]

2:3 *As an Apple Tree*

A Prophecy of the Captivity. Thomas Brightman: Hitherto the state of the church until they were carried way captive by Nebuchadnezzar. Now, the captivity follows, whose first comfort is rest granted to the miserable remnant that (when the rest were carried away) had leave

[4]Beza, *Sermons sur les trois premiers chapitres du Cantique des Cantiques, de Salomon*, 320-26; citing Lk 12:27; 1 Tim 3:16; Rom 8:29; Ps 45:2; Heb 7:26; Heb 2:9; Phil 2:9; 2:8; Is 53:5; Heb 2:9; Ps 22:6; 1 Sam 15:22; Jn 19:5; Lk 23:11. [†]Most modern English translations interpret the Greek adjective *lampros* (Lk 23:11) as relating to a quality other than color: the KJV, for example has "a gorgeous robe," and the NIV makes it "elegant." The Vulgate, however, had given *alba vesta*, or "white robe," and in his French translation of 1535, Pierre Robert Olivétan had followed suit with a *vestement blanc*.

granted to remain in their own country. This comfort is declared by the similitude of an apple tree, which is but a low tree: neither in length of body nor in far-spreading limbs can it compare with many others, yet her fruit excels many others in profit and pleasantness. The similitudes are always fitted to the times and the diverse conditions that the church enjoys; this apple tree signifies Gedaliah, whom Nebuchadnezzar made governor over the people who were left in the land. He was low in regard of the tallness of former kings, or of those high cedars that flourished in the Babylonian mountains, yet in shadow he was very pleasant, and in fruit wholesome, so that all the scattered church flocked under his covering, especially when he had joined the prophet Jeremiah to his. For now were the cedar beams and the fir rafters broken, and no leave granted to remain, no not in the rubbish of the city. Commentary on the Canticles.[5]

2:4 *His Banner Over Me Was Love*

The Hospitality of God's House. Isidore Clarius: "The king led me into his wine cellar," or, as the Hebrew has it, "in his house of wine," and "he marked me with his charity," or, "the banner of his charity is over me." The king has brought me to an inn, where many who wish to feast are gathering, which is a sign of charity. . . . And this house to which he led her, namely, a house of refreshment, is called a house of wine, and it was filled with apostles when they were getting drunk. And this emblem of charity is said to have been in this house as a sign that the house of the church should be a house of charity or love for its guests. The Song of Songs of Solomon.[6]

The Fortifying Effect of Feasting on God's Word. John Trapp: "He brought me to the banqueting house." In Hebrew, "to the house of wine," where he gives me that which is better than apple drink. As the sufferings of Christ abound in us, so our consolation also abounds by Christ. The lower that ebb, the higher this tide, as is to be seen in the martyrs, who went as merrily to die as ever they did to dine, and sang in the flames, and felt no more pain than if they had laid on beds of roses. This their persecutors counted as stupidity and vainglory, but they knew not the power of the Spirit and the force of faith. As Mr. Philpot to scoffing Morgan, who coming to confer with him, asked,[†]

> "How do you know that you have the Spirit of God?"
>
> Mr. Philpot answered, "By the faith of Christ that is in me."
>
> "Ah, by faith," said Morgan, "do you now? I think rather it is the spirit of the buttery[‡] that your fellows have had who have been burned before you, who were drunk the night before they went to their death, and I think went drunk to it."
>
> At this, Philpot replied, "It appears by your conversation that you are better acquainted with the spirit of the buttery than of God. I think you are more like a scoffer in a play than a reasonable doctor to instruct one. You have the spirit of illusion and sophistry, which is not able to countervail the Spirit of truth. You are but an ass in the things of God. God shall surely rain fire and brimstone on such scorners of his Word and blasphemers of his people as you are."

The same censure was passed on Nicholas Burton, martyr in Spain, who because he went cheerfully to the stake, and embraced death with all gladness and patience, his tormentors and enemies said that the devil had his soul, before he came to the fire, and therefore his sense of feeling was past.[§] These carnal creatures do not meddle with the true Christian's joy, neither do they know the privy armor of proof (the joy of faith) that he has a triple shield about his heart, making him insuperable, and therefore more than a conqueror. True grace has a fortifying, comforting virtue, which the world

[5]Brightman, *A Commentary on the Canticles or the Song of Salomon*, 996-97; citing 2 Kings 25:22; Jer 40.
[6]Isidore, *Canticum Canticorum Salomonis*, 10v-r.

knows nothing of. Just as true gold comforts and strengthens the heart, gold made by alchemy does not. And as a person who by good fare and plenty of the best wines has their bones filled with marrow and their veins with good blood and a fresh spring of spirits, can endure to go with less clothes than another, because they are well-lined within, so it is with a heart that, by often feasting with Christ in his ordinances, and by often reading and ruminating on the Scriptures (called here the "banqueting house" or "wine cellar," as most think) has got a great deal of joy and peace. Such a one will go through troubles and make nothing of them, even though outward comforts utterly fail. Solomon's Book of All Virtues.[7]

Christ's Love is a Call to Arms. Lucas Osiander: "He brought me into the cellar of wine, he set in order charity in me." The Hebrew reads, "and his banner over me is charity." Christ gladdens the heart of the church with a spiritual happiness, and he declares with the greatest clarity that he loves us with a burning passion. His love raises our frightened minds, as if raising a banner that rouses his soldiers to action. Song of Songs.[8]

2:5-6 *His Left Hand*

The Embrace of God's Left Hand. Martin Luther: "O that his left hand were under my head, and that his right hand embraced me!" This, too, is a figure drawn from the love of bride and groom. It is a holy and lawful love, and therefore Satan hates it and tries to impede it even though it is the font of procreation and education. Furthermore, he includes here two special blessings belonging to this people: the kingdom, or government, which he calls the left hand, and the priesthood, or worship of God. These embraces, he says, make it possible for this rose to endure the thrust of wild beasts and brambles, since it is wholly within the embrace of God, whether you look at the church or the kingdom, for the Word of God is in both. This awareness, or better, this faith, Solomon would like to stir up in other men too. A Brief but Altogether Lucid Exposition of the Song of Songs.[9]

The Comfort of Christ's Embrace. Henry Ainsworth: "His left hand." Understand "is under my head"; or prayerwise, "let it be under my head." The church by faith beholds the help of Christ himself in the ministry of his Word and Spirit sustaining her, outwardly and inwardly, as with the left and right hand: upholding her head, folding about and comforting her heart, as a loving husband does his wife in her sorrow and sickness. As the apostle says, the Lord "nourishes and cherishes" his church. . . . "Under my head," as a pillow to rest on. By sins and afflictions, "the whole head is sick, and the whole heart faint." By the righteousness of Christ, and consolations of his

[7]Trapp, *Solomonis ΠΑΝΆΡΕΤΟΣ*, 203-4; citing 2 Cor 1:5; Rom 8:35; Hab 3:17. †Trapp reproduces this exchange almost verbatim from the 1563 edition of Foxe's *Actes and Monuments*. John Philpot (1516–1555) was erstwhile archdeacon of Winchester, burned at Smithfield in December 1555. Morgan Philipps (d. 1570), who assisted in the interrogation, was a Catholic priest who fled to the Continent after the accession of Elizabeth I and assisted in the foundation of the English College at Douai. ‡A place for storing liquor. §An English merchant, Nicholas Burton was burned at the stake by the Inquisition in Seville for professing the Protestant faith. See John Foxe, *Acts and Monuments* (1563) 5:1813.

[8]Osiander, *Canticum Canticorum*, 1252.

[9]LW 15:215-16 (WA 31.2:648-49). Luther frequently uses the image of God's "two hands" in his writings in connection with his "two kingdoms" theology (*Zwei-Reiche-Lehre*). God's "right hand" refers to the preaching of the gospel and the ministry of Word and sacrament, while God's "left hand" refers to the administration of civil government by the magistrate. As David Steinmetz explains, "The two governments refer to the two ways in which God governs the world. God governs the Church though the gospel, a government from which all modes of coercion are excluded; and he governs the world through law and coercion, a government which cannot achieve its ends through the persuasive preaching of love. These two spheres of existence and two modes of government must be distinguished, even though they intersect in every Christian believer." Luther's interpretation of this passage neatly encapsulates this view: Solomon's left hand is under the head of the beloved, providing firm physical support, while the right hand offers caresses. God's two hands thus perform distinct works, and the work of the right hand is dependent on the work of the left. David C. Steinmetz, "Luther and the Two Kingdoms," in *Luther in Context*, 2nd ed. (Grand Rapids, MI: Baker Academic, 2002), 115.

Spirit, our sins are forgiven, and our consciences comforted. This grace is felt, when by the ministration of the Word, the flagons and apples mentioned in verse 5 are applied to the repentant believing sinner, who says, when their flesh and their heart is consumed and fails, "The rock of my heart, and my portion, is God forever." "His right hand," which teaches him fearful things, so both his hands, even all that Christ is, his Godhead and his manhood, his life, death, resurrection, ascension; his weakness, power, and glory, are employed for the comfort and salvation of his church. "Does embrace me," or "let embrace me." It is a speech of faith, or prayer (as in 1:2, "let him kiss me") concerning the fruition of Christ's love and graces. For to embrace or fold the arms about one is (as kissing) a sign of love. In this sense we are counseled to embrace the wisdom of God. This commends the love of Christ, which does not leave his church in her sickness, sins, and infirmities, but comes to her, comforts her, and sustains her with his own hands, in manifestation of all love, compassion, and kindness, and rejoices in her, as "the bridegroom rejoices over the bride," and keeps her safe from evil. It sets forth also the church's faith and thankfulness, which sees Christ present in his doctrine and ordinances, and his ministry, as if he were crucified before her and rejoices before others for his love and help. Annotations upon the Song of Songs.[10]

2:7 *I Charge You*

The Bride's Rest Guarded by Angels. François Lambert: The church of God rests and gains surpassing peace in every sense, so long as she feels the bridegroom's left hand, without doubting that she will, at the appointed time, experience ineffable delights at his right hand. Moreover, the bridegroom protects her sweet quiet and rest in the Lord, watching over her so that nothing may disturb her.† And indeed, so long as the Lord bestows on her his peace, no one can take it from her. For even in the midst of fires, adversity, and the cross, Christ's true believers have peace. Therefore, desiring to give the church peace, he orders the young women concerning her: "I adjure you, daughters of Jerusalem." Gazelles and deer are the swiftest of runners; by these are signified the most ardent spirits of the holy angels, who are constantly in the fields for us—that is, they hasten to the assemblies of the faithful, they are concerned for us and watch over us, they attend to us and minister to us, as it says in Psalm 90: "He has given his angels charge over you, to keep you in all your ways." And Hebrews 1 says that "they are all ministering spirits, sent to minister to them who shall receive the inheritance of salvation." These are the ones who guard the bride, and prevent her from being disturbed by anyone. Commentary on the Song of Songs.[11]

Judgment Is Coming and the Bride Will Be Awoken. David Joris: Let us be victorious and become completely full of light and spiritual, or our work, which has begun before this day, will be for naught, as it is written. For the ordained time must come to an end and all things will be fulfilled. For this the church of God, the bride herself, prays for her entrance and day. He will not wake her up before this, until, I say, it has become her own will, lust, desire, and greatest pleasure. Therefore can those who do not work strongly and forcefully on behalf of the kingdom presume it will not come upon them? No. Therefore, make your reckoning. When the number is fulfilled, Zion will declare her number closed. These will be all those who have desired and fulfilled the law of Christ and of the Lord. Pay close attention. Hear, Hear,

[10]Ainsworth, *Annotations*, 2:700; citing Eph 5:29; Is 1:5; 1 Jn 2:12, 3:24; Rom 14:17; Ps 73:26; 45:5; Prov 4:7; Is 62:5; Gal 3:1; 2 Cor 1:3-5.

[11]Lambert, *In Cantica Canticorum Salomonis*, 36v-r; citing Ps 90:11; Heb 1:14. †Modern translations of the Hebrew text typically render the end of Song 2:7 as referring to love in the abstract: "I adjure you . . . that you not stir up or awaken love until it pleases" (ESV). Lambert, however, follows the Vulgate reading, where the feminine noun *dilectam* suggests that the bridegroom is speaking of the bride: "that you not stir up or awaken the beloved until she pleases."

Hear, Great Wonder, Great Wonder, Great Wonder.[12]

Idleness Grieves the Spirit. Dudley Fenner: The fellowship of Christ is declared by the fruits of his spiritual presence (vv. 6-16), and by the very nature of it (v. 16). The effects or fruits of his communion or fellowship are double: first, the present comfort and rest she has with him (vv. 6-7), and second, the other fruits of his presence, in the ordering of his church (vv. 8-15). . . . And [her fellowship with Christ] is further declared by the fruit in her, which is a vehement charge to all her members and friends whom she receives into her fellowship. This, for the form and manner, is so weighty that it is bound with an oath[†]—or rather, an adjuration—for it is very necessary that they follow an honest calling appointed of God and fit for them in looking, as Rachel to her father's herds,[‡] and in taking honest and profitable recreation: not to awaken Christ by grieving the Spirit, wherewith we are sealed in our redemption, through vanity, filthiness, wantonness in words, apparel, gestures, or in anything that is idle and without fruits of edification. The Song of Songs.[13]

Witness of the Prophets. Viktorin Strigel: The fathers and prophets are called gazelles and deer. For these animals are often devoured by wolves or dogs, for the principal lights of the church certainly sustain the most grievous calamities, according to the counsel of God. The Three Books of Solomon.[14]

Enduring Suffering with Patience. John Cotton: I adjure you . . . I make you swear by the roes, and by the hinds of the field, not by them as persons you are to swear by, but by those for whose sake, and by whose means they are to understand themselves bound as by a solemn oath no to stir up or awake my love—that is, not to provoke Christ to exercise his church by any change of their estate, until it shall please him.

These roes and hinds are wild and fearful creatures, easily and swiftly running away, yet otherwise they are willing to feed with the sheep. Such were the Gentiles at that time willing to converse with the Jews, and to come toward religion. Yet if the estate of the church should have proved more troublesome by any indiscreet or offensive carriage of the Jews, they would soon have started back from fellowship with them. For their sakes, therefore, the church charges her daughters, as by an oath, not to seek deliverance prematurely, before the time that Christ had appointed, lest it turn to the disturbance of her peace and to driving away such Gentiles as were coming to be proselytes.

This may first let us see that notwithstanding the reformation of religion, Christ may be pleased rather to live abroad in the fields than at home, where the people would willingly assemble. The house of God was now repaired and the bed green, and the church invites Christ to come in to her, yet he prefers rather to call her abroad. So we may see that notwithstanding the purity and simplicity of Christ's worship, yet Christ is not bound to any place: if things were completely reformed, even so he might leave us and go into the wild field. Rome has long doted on Peter's chair, and Jerusalem might as well have bragged of her privileges as any other place, but Christ left them. We must therefore never rest in any outward estate, for Christ may leave us. The Palatinate has been as reformed as any church in its doctrine, and they might say that "their bed was green," and that "their beams were of cedar and their rafters of fir," yet God has left them—for do we think that if God had been there, these things that have happened to

[12]CRR 7:142-43*; citing Mt 24; Mk 14; Lk 21; 1 Pet 3:11-14; Song 3:5; 8:4.

[13]Fenner, *The Song of Songs*, 32. †In a marginal note, Fenner references Neh 10:30-33, where the returning exiles make a solemn pledge not to give their sons or daughters in marriage to foreigners. ‡In a marginal note, Fenner references Gen 29:6. This passage relates the story of Jacob's first encounter with Rachel. The implication seems to be that just as Rachel's diligence in tending her father's flock sets the stage for Jacob's courtship, so also the bride's attendants should be equally diligent in attending to their edifying duties.

[14]Strigel, *Salomonis Libri Tres, Proverbia, Ecclesiastes, Canticum*, 276-77.

them now would have befallen?[†] A Brief Exposition on the Whole Book of Canticles.[15]

An "Oath" by the Church's Oppressors. Thomas Brightman: The "daughters of Jerusalem" are the citizens of the church. The roes and hinds are those nations that held the church in captivity. The meaning of this verse is as though she should have said, "I require you, daughters of Jerusalem, that you swear to me by the roes and hinds of the field, that if by your fault you drive away my love from my embrace, those roes and hinds shall avenge it on you with deserved punishment." Not that it is lawful to swear by enemies, or by any other than God, but figuratively by the form of an oath, she teaches that it should be as certain that the citizens of the church should avoid all grievous offences, with no less diligent heed (namely, for fear of the enemies among whom they lived) than if a covenant had been undertaken on that matter and confirmed by an oath. Thus, the history of this oath is the rest of the time of the captivity. Commentary on the Canticles.[16]

Love's Rhythm. Hugo Grotius: "Do not arouse or awaken love." Theocritus:

[Sleep, breathing love and desire into each other's breasts,]
and do not forget to wake at dawn.
[We too shall come back in the morning,
when after roosting the first cock raises his feathered neck and crows.
Hymen, O Hymenaeus, may you take pleasure in this marriage!]

Annotations on the Old Testament.[17]

[15]Cotton, *Brief Exposition*, 59-61; citing Song 1:16-17. [†]The Palatinate was a German territory on the upper Rhine that played a leading role in the "second reformation," a wave of reforming activity that swept northern Europe in the latter half of the sixteenth century. The Counts Palatine Frederick III ("the Pious," r. 1559–1576) and Frederick IV (r. 1583–1610) created a safe haven for reform-minded refugees from across the region, and under their protection the University of Heidelberg became an intellectual center for Reformed theology. The aggressive policies of Frederick V (r. 1610–1623) proved disastrous for the Reformed churches in Germany, however, when his acceptance of the Bohemian crown in 1619 set off the Thirty Years' War. Spanish imperial troops invaded the lower Palatinate in 1620, and shortly after the fall of Heidelberg in 1622, Frederick's territories were transferred to Duke Maximilian I of Bavaria, an ardent Catholic, who moved aggressively to establish the Counter-Reformation in his newly acquired lands.

[16]Brightman, *A Commentary on the Canticles or the Song of Salomon*, 999.

[17]Grotius, *Annotationes in Vetus Testamentum*, 268. As he often does, Grotius compares the imagery of the Song with secular erotic poetry, citing only a very short extract, and expecting his reader to fill in the remainder. In this instance, the extract is from Theocritus's *Idyll* 18, the closing lines of a pastoral poem where a newlywed couple are sent off to bed after lengthy celebrations (LCL 28:265-67).

2:8-17 THE BRIDE ADORES HER BELOVED

[8]*The voice of my beloved!*
Behold, he comes,

leaping over the mountains,
bounding over the hills.

[9]*My beloved is like a gazelle*
or a young stag.

Behold, there he stands
behind our wall,

gazing through the windows,
looking through the lattice.

[10]*My beloved speaks and says to me:*

"Arise, my love, my beautiful one,
and come away,

[11]*for behold, the winter is past;*
the rain is over and gone.

[12]*The flowers appear on the earth,*
the time of singing[a] *has come,*

and the voice of the turtledove
is heard in our land.

[13]*The fig tree ripens its figs,*
and the vines are in blossom;
they give forth fragrance.

Arise, my love, my beautiful one,
and come away.

[14]*O my dove, in the clefts of the rock,*
in the crannies of the cliff,

let me see your face,
let me hear your voice,

for your voice is sweet,
and your face is lovely.

[15]*Catch the foxes*[b] *for us,*
the little foxes

that spoil the vineyards,
for our vineyards are in blossom."

[16]*My beloved is mine, and I am his;*
he grazes[c] *among the lilies.*

[17]*Until the day breathes*
and the shadows flee,

turn, my beloved, be like a gazelle
or a young stag on cleft mountains.[d]

a Or *pruning* **b** Or *jackals* **c** Or *he pastures his flock* **d** Or *mountains of Bether*

Overview: This passage finds the bride waiting with anticipation for the return of her beloved. She hears his voice ringing in the wilderness and sees his approach from far away, and she imagines his words of comfort to her on his return. Many of our commentators note the bride's ability to recognize the voice of her beloved, and connect this with many other passages in Scripture that indicate a readiness on the part of God's people to respond to his Word. Opinions vary on the reason for the bridegroom's separation from his bride, though most of our interpreters connect this image in some way to the experience of God's people longing for closer intimacy with the Lord. For some, these images point to historical events, such as the bondage of the Hebrews in Egypt (Isidore Clarius) or the later Babylonian captivity (John Cotton). For most, however, it is a more general image of the way in which God's Word meets us in our moral and spiritual desolation. Several of the other images in this passage are also often remarked on. Modern commentators point to the imagery of the bridegroom peering in at the bride's window (Song 2:9) as evidence of a clandestine love affair, possibly between young (presumably unmarried!) lovers. Our interpreters prefer to read these images allegorically, as figures of the way in which Christ governs the world at a certain distance, through his Word (Martin Luther), or as representing the as yet unconsummated relationship between Christ and his people under the old covenant (Theodore Beza). Some also draw attention to the imagery of the "little foxes," pointing to the spiritual dangers that persist in the relationship, even as the lovers' intimacy grows ever closer. If one common theme emerges from these interpreters, it is the growing ardor of the bride's longing for union with her spouse, even as she remains painfully aware of the distance that remains and the dangers that threaten to divide her from her love.

2:8 *The Voice of My Beloved!*

The Lord Makes Haste to Deliver. Isidore Clarius: The bride tells primarily of love. "I remember," she says, "when he came to me, in the time when I was in Egypt, as one who leaps over hills, and making haste along on his way, he cut short the time of my captivity in Egypt, with the speed of gazelles and stags. He stood as one behind a wall, like one contemplating the sky through the window." For this reason it says, "I have seen the affliction of my people who are in Egypt." The Song of Songs of Solomon.[1]

God's Word Makes Peaceable Subjects. Veit Dietrich: This is a prayer of thanksgiving, as though Solomon were saying, "Praise God that I have a peaceful kingdom!" Nothing else matters when God by his Word comes across all the hills and mountains—that is, when it is heard throughout the whole country, even as a deer will remain in its place, but also leaps to and fro. This same Word makes the king's subjects loyal, silent, and obedient. The Song of Solomon.[2]

Christ's People Recognize His Voice. Henry Ainsworth: Here the spouse breaks out and rejoices to hear the bridegroom's voice, and signifies to her friends the comforts that she has thereby, expressing her soul's sickness and grief when he withdrew himself and kept silence. By "the voice" is meant the word of his grace, the preaching of the gospel, which she knows to be his and receives with joy, as Christ's sheep are said to hear and to know the voice of the Shepherd, and not a stranger. In this sense, he said before Pilate, "Everyone that is of the truth, hears my voice"; and they did not know "the voices of the prophets," that is, their doctrines; and "today, if you shall hear his voice, harden not your hearts." This voice is heard before his coming, to prepare the hearers to receive him; as John the Baptist, who prepared the way before Christ, is called "the voice of a crier." Annotations upon the Song of Songs.[3]

A Warning Against Monastic Slumber. Theodore Beza: We left the bride in the repose of her meditation, altogether ravished in ecstasy. She is now awakened from her slumber by the bridegroom—not to trouble her, but to lead her, as it were, from one pleasure to another. This is similar to natural sleep, which taken in sufficient measure has the effect of refreshing a person and reviving their vigor. But if they indulge in too much sleep they become slack and lazy, and ultimately they are drawn into an utterly corrupt way of life. So it is with this spiritual rest, which the soul enjoys when it is drawn aside by itself to meditate on the graces of God and attend to secret prayer, whether by night or by day, according to the example of David in many of the psalms. But if a person tries to make of this meditation a "contemplative life" (falsely called "evangelical"),[†] they commit two errors, which little by little lead to a third, and this is their undoing. For first, a person withdraws themselves from the principal duty of a Christian, which is to serve their neighbor according to their

[1]Isidore, *Canticum Canticorum Salomonis*, 11v; citing Ex 3:7.
[2]Dietrich, *Das Hohelied Salomonis*, 9.
[3]Ainsworth, *Annotations*, 2:701; citing Jn 10:3-4; 18:37; Acts 13:27; Heb 3:7; Mk 1:2-3.

vocation. But this cannot be done if a person sequesters themselves from others and does not apply their mind to any actions that are not specially and particularly focused on themselves. Rather, we ought to apply all the knowledge we have, both in divine and in human matters, to the mutual advancement of one another. Second, by this sort of continual contemplation it is impossible for a person to avoid eventually becoming a dreaming fop and a fanatic—especially if they add to this an austerity of life without good measure. And at last, after they have become thus deluded and fanatical, they persuade themselves little by little, not only of that false and damnable opinion concerning merits, but also that they have finally arrived at perfection—having passed beyond paradise itself! I say nothing of the hypocrisy and stinking filth that, under the color of this mode of life, has appropriated the name "religion." . . . But let us now go out of this sewer[‡] and return to the bride, who is now awakened by her bridegroom and summoned to the other part of the Christian life—that is to say, the other kind of conversation with her spouse. In other words, she is now called to practice what she has learned and meditated on. For what else could this mean, "to arise and come with me," but that the bridegroom now directs the course of the bride's life according to her vocation, in conformity to the commandments of God? SERMONS ON THE FIRST THREE CHAPTERS OF THE SONG OF SONGS.[4]

A PROPHECY OF CHRIST'S DELIVERANCE THROUGH CYRUS. JOHN COTTON: "The voice of my beloved." This was the report of Cyrus coming to besiege Babel, and his mustering together of many nations to that service. This rumor was discerned by the faithful to be the accomplishment of the prophecies given them before, of deliverance by Cyrus. And therefore the church, hearing this rumor, suddenly acknowledges in it the promise and voice of Christ. . . . "He stands behind the wall," laying siege to the walls of Babylon. "He looks forth at the windows," that is, he gives some glimpse of hope of further enlargement to the church. "He shows himself through the lattice." As in the original, any place burned through in the siege of Babel, when Cyrus diverted the course of the Euphrates another way, which before came through the midst of the city. Burning up the reeds and drying up the water passages, he showed himself through the place, and entered the city.

"My beloved spoke and said to me, Rise up my love, my fair one, and come away." That is, Cyrus made open proclamation for my departure out of Babel, and return into my own country. Though Cyrus was a heathen, and did not know Christ the beloved, yet the church in Cyrus saw the hand and voice of Christ, using Cyrus as an instrument for deliverance. . . . This teaches us that in all the instruments of the church's deliverance, we should see and discern Christ speaking and working in them. See here the church looks not at Cyrus so much but at Christ in him. Do they hear a rumor of a deliverance? It is the voice of Christ, and it must be a strong voice that Christ is the author of. The wisest, Daniel, Shadrach, Meshach, and Abednego, they say it is Christ, and all the rest yield and the church sees Christ come skipping. Does it see Cyrus about the walls? She sees Christ there. Does she see Cyrus showing himself through the lattice? She sees Christ there. Does she see when he is possessed there, and makes

[4]Beza, *Sermons sur les trois premiers chapitres du Cantique des Cantiques, de Salomon*, 372-74; citing Mt 6:6. [†]The "contemplative life" and the "evangelical life" were two of the most common names for monasticism in medieval Christianity. The former term highlighted the contrast between monasticism and the "active life," while the latter alluded to a distinction between the commands of the law, which are binding on all Christians, and counsels of "evangelical perfection," which apply only to a select few. The Protestant reformers were virtually unanimous in rejecting both of these distinctions. [‡]The word Beza uses for the monastic life, *cloaque*, is reminiscent of the word Luther had used in Table Talk years earlier, when he had remarked that the Holy Spirit granted him his revolutionary insight into justification by faith alone *auff diser cloaca*—literally, "on the toilet" (WA Tr 3:228; no. 3232)! Scholars have debated whether Luther intended this remark literally or whether he meant that his new perspective came to him when he was still mired in his old life of monastic "works righteousness." In any event, many of Luther's later followers and cobelligerents would, like Beza, concur in the unflattering association of monasticism with the unspeakable filth of the sewer.

proclamation to them to go up again to Jerusalem? She looks at it as Christ's voice, saying, "Arise my love, my fair one, and come away."

So the Holy Ghost teaches that whatever favor anyone shows to the church, it is Christ that does it. So take it that if any good befall the church, it is Christ that does it. If any lead into captivity—Nebuchadnezzar, or any other—it is Christ that leads her into a wine cellar. If there be any rumor or work of deliverance, it is Christ that comes leaping and skipping. So in all the calamities, and in all the blessings that befall the church, ascribe all to Christ. The same hand that gave, the same hand takes away. God turned the captivity of Job, and God turned again the captivity of his people. This is a wonderful stay to God's church, and to every member of it, for humanity cannot bring it into captivity, or bring it out again. Humanity's hand cannot bring hard things on the church, nor bring her out again from them, for if it were in human hands, or in Satan's, or in our own hands, it would not go well with us. But being in Christ's hands alone, it may be a stay and a comfort. A Brief Exposition on the Whole Book of Canticles.[5]

2:9 *My Beloved Is Like a Gazelle*

The Deliverance of Cyrus. Thomas Brightman: The first part of this verse declares the swiftness of the coming of Cyrus; the later part describes his presence, and that by three circumstances: his standing behind the wall, his looking through the window, and showing himself through the gates. All of which sets forth to us the besieging of Babylon by Cyrus and Darius, for quickly passing over the mountains and hills, his tents were pitched around the walls of Babylon. There Cyrus stood a while behind the wall, doubting what to do. His retinue urged him on, yet nothing prospered after his desire. At length, "he looked forth through the lattices—that is, he took crafty counsel and considered secretly how he might gain the city, and turning the river Euphrates, he brought his army into the city by the channel so secretly that the city was taken before any force of battery was felt. Neither should anyone marvel that the name of "Beloved" is given to this heathen king, for whatsoever the church has, the Beloved himself gives it, but he uses diverse instruments, on whom he bestows his own name, that all help may be properly understood to be of him whose name the instruments bear. Commentary on the Canticles.[6]

Entering in at the Window. Sebastian Münster: "Looking through the lattice." Rather, "entering in [through the lattice]." The Hebrew *mēṣîṣ* is a *hiphil* participle from the root *ṣûṣ*, which means to flower or to bud,[†] or in this context, that which was hidden in the branches budding into the open air. This is actually a transumption [taking one thing for another] for "looking out for" or "sticking up his head." The Song of Songs of Solomon.[7]

Christ Returns to Comfort His People. John Trapp: "My beloved is like a roe, or a young hart" for sweetness and swiftness, as in the previous verse. His help seems long, because we are short. At the opportune time he will not be wanting to those who wait for him. The lion seems to leave her young ones till they have almost killed themselves with roaring and howling, but at last she relieves them, and so they become the more courageous. God seems to forget his people sometimes, but it is so that they may the better remember themselves and remind him. He seems

[5]Cotton, *Brief Exposition*, 66-68, 73-75.

[6]Brightman, *A Commentary on the Canticles or the Song of Salomon*, 999.

[7]Münster, *Canticum Canticorum Solomonis*, at 2:9. [†]*The Hebrew and Aramaic Lexicon of the Old Testament* gives two entries for this Hebrew verb: (1) "start to bud, blossom," and (2) "gaze." Most modern English translations use the latter in this context, but Münster seems to have favored the former, suggesting a scene where the bridegroom figuratively "sprouts up" outside the bride's window, and possibly enters in. Ludwig Koehler, Walter Baumgartner, and Johann J. Stamm, *The Hebrew and Aramaic Lexicon of the Old Testament*, trans. and ed. under the supervision of Mervyn E. J. Richardson, 4 vols. (Leiden: Brill, 1994–1999).

here to have taken a long journey, and to be at a great distance from them, when as indeed he is as near us as once he was to Mary Magdalen after his resurrection, but she was so bleary-eyed that she could not see him. If he at any time should absent himself for trial of our faith and love to him, and to let us know how ill we can be without him, yet he is no further off than behind some wall or screen. Or if he get of our doors from us, yet he looks in at the window to see how we take it, and soon after he shows himself through the lattice, that we may not altogether despond or despair of his return. Indeed, he "flourishes" or "blossoms" through the lattices, like some flower or fruit tree that grows under a window and sends a sweet scent into the room, or perhaps some pleasant branches.† This is to teach that Christ comes not to his people without profit, and comfort to their souls. Solomon's Book of All Virtues.[8]

The Hidden Presence of the Word. Martin Luther: By means of his Word he leaps from one city to another so that everywhere the effect of his ministration may be felt among women and men. By the metaphor of the stag and the gazelle Solomon signifies the progress of the Word, because it spreads its effects to distant places with great swiftness.

"Behold, there he stands behind our wall, gazing in at the windows, looking through the lattice." Here he once more indicates that he has all these possessions in faith. For such a reminder is the Holy Spirit's custom when he preaches the gifts of God so splendidly, in order that we may understand that he is speaking about joy of conscience, not about carnal consolation. "No one has seen God at any time," but faith is our veil in such a fashion that we with certainty possess the things promised and yet do not see or feel them. Accordingly, what he has said about the groom, that he leaps from hill to hill like a stag and is present everywhere, keeping all things within his governance and oversight, all this he now refers to faith—that God is truly present, but yet he cannot be seen, he stands behind the wall, he is not perceived by our eyes nor felt by our hand. Thus Christ is present to his church through the Word and sacraments, but he is not perceived by the eyes. And for those who are occupied in the business of state there is certainly need of this comfort. For although it is impossible to alleviate all ills, however much you want to, we must not on that account think that God does not take care of governments. He is indeed present, yet as one who stands behind the wall and gazes at us through the lattice.

"My beloved speaks and says to me." He now says more softly what he has just been saying in an apparently rather sharp fashion. He stands behind the wall, he seems sometimes to have deserted his people, but he does not stand silent. He speaks with me and comforts me so that I may bear patiently whatever vicissitudes befall me from time to time. "Arise, hasten, my love." These are words of the greatest sweetness. In them the groom answers his bride as she toils and yet perseveres in faith, in the hope that she will hold fast the sure confidence that she is the beloved of her God even at the very moment when she seems deserted by God. The Jewish realm was certainly shaken violently enough by a host of calamities, and yet the voice of the bridegroom constantly bore witness to his signal love for his people—even later during the captivity. "My fair one, and come away." The stress is on the pronoun "my." It is as if he were saying, "You are fair in my eyes, even though you are utterly contemptible in the world's sight." This beauty is located first and foremost in the Word and gifts of the Holy Spirit and then in the external administration, or government, established by God on the finest laws. A Brief but Altogether Lucid Exposition of the Song of Songs.[9]

Christ the Summer, Flowers the People, the Spirit the Dove. Pilgram Marpeck: My dearest ones, observe this text carefully with spiritual eyes. Although the words are brief, their

[8]Trapp, *Solomonis ΠΑΝΆΡΕΤΟΣ*, 211. †See Münster's explanation of the Hebrew in the previous selection.

[9]LW 15:217-19 (WA 31.2:654-59).

understanding and meaning in the Holy Spirit are great. Flesh and blood can and will never attain to it. For the Lord will call his bride in no other form than in the adornment of the virtue of Christ, since the storm, winter, and rain—that is, the time of sin and sleeping, are past and gone; their affliction and tribulation is over. For we had nowhere to flee in the storm of our sin until Christ came down, the true summer, in which alone all the flowers can bloom.

These flowers are the people who, before the advent of Christ, remained stuck with their root in the earth through sin, without blossom or fruit. Indeed, although they were sweet, friendly, and happy people, like the fig tree and the vine they had neither buds nor blossoms before the summer—that is, before the advent of the man Jesus Christ, who is the true day, light, and summer of the world. Yes, not until this true sun let the lowliness of the winter of our sin and again appeared in the presence of the Father in the heights in glory and power. Before that, the sun of the Father shines on humankind as arid ground with the righteousness of the law through wrath, but no fruit was found in humankind because of the heat of the Father's wrath. But when the sun Christ Jesus appeared on earth in weakness as true man, the seed of woman and the race of man, then only man began to bloom, fig tree and vine developed buds and blossoms, but without fruit before the setting of this sun, Jesus Christ. Through this setting, the heat of the day, the Father's wrath, has cooled. Until the time of the resurrection and ascension of Christ, the bridegroom reveled with his bride under flowers, buds, blossoms, and roses as a foretaste and shadow until the brightness or the spring should come. When the turtledove, that is, the Holy Spirit, was heard, then only the first and earliest fruits were borne. The blossoms ceased with the appearance of the fruit, the shadow shrank away through the sun of union and reconciliation to bring fruits to God through the beautiful dawn. This is also the sealing of the Holy Spirit in the forgiveness of sins with the cool dew of grace. My dearest ones, the highest ornament and adornment of love is therefore the preserving of the unity in the Holy Spirit, for without this unity there is no sincere love. The Unity of the Bride of Christ.[10]

The Dividing Wall Not Yet Broken Down. Theodore Beza: The bride adds here that the bridegroom kept himself behind the wall and was only visible through the lattice, and this ought to be taken as setting forth the distinction between the old covenant and the new. For it is true that there was never any other mediator between God and humankind but only the Bridegroom of this spouse (who is the church). It is also very true that as regards its effect, Jesus Christ suffered from the beginning of the world, and thus it follows that the faith of the fathers and our own is one and the same faith. But as regards the manner and measure of the manifestation of this knowledge of salvation, there have been two covenants. The old one had, from the beginning, an end—that is, it was ordained to last no longer than the real coming of the Savior and the plain exhibition and declaration of the doctrine of salvation, which is the gospel. During the old covenant, therefore, the Lord spoke many times and in diverse ways, not of another doctrine, but in a different fashion: both to the patriarchs prior to the law, and afterward in another manner under the law through shadows and figures, of which Jesus Christ was the substance and the body. . . . The bridegroom therefore came to his spouse, not so as to kiss her with the kisses of his own mouth, which is the last pledge in consummation of the marriage. Rather, he kept himself "behind the wall," as if to say, "Look at me, the one who has not forgotten you, but will certainly keep his promises in his own time, without failing you in anything, no matter what difficulties present may come between us." And this is confirmed by the whole sacred history of the time preceding the advent of Jesus Christ in the flesh.

Therefore, by this wall we must understand first of all whatever was lacking in the old covenant in comparison with the new, and this in two respects.

[10]CRR 2:524-25*.

For not only that the effect of the faith of the ancient fathers was dependent on that which was still to be executed, and which really was executed for our salvation by Jesus Christ come in the flesh . . . , but this mystery was also foreshadowed to them by diverse figures in the law, which is here compared to a wall that must first be crossed over so that the two may see one another and be joined more closely. Moreover, as is divinely expressed by the apostle in the epistle to the Galatians, the accomplishment of all righteousness and the satisfaction for our sins being not yet actually come (though by faith these were present before God and to the eyes of the faithful), there was still a very thick wall between this bridegroom and this bride. Second, the Lord having chosen this one people for himself, separated them from all the other peoples of the earth, both with regard to the principal point, the covenant of salvation, and also with regard to the governance of Israel. This separation lasted until the wall was broken down and the blessing of Jacob was accomplished, in which he calls the Messiah (the bridegroom, that is) "the expectation of the nations." . . .

It is therefore no wonder that this bride makes mention of a wall, considering her condition as it was then and would remain until the coming of the bridegroom in the flesh. But she adds this word, "lattice," to show that this wall is not of a sort as to utterly prevent the bridegroom from being from the other side, nor is it like the walls that separate the wicked from God. Rather, it was the sort of wall that had open windows in it, or as if it were recessed with a grate. For such was the ancient covenant made with Abraham, and afterward renewed in the time of Moses with a thousand ceremonies, that even though it was obscure, still the ancient fathers beheld with Abraham "the day of the Lord and rejoiced in it." Sermons on the First Three Chapters of the Song of Songs.[11]

[11]Beza, *Sermons sur les trois premiers chapitres du Cantique des Cantiques, de Salomon*, 384-87; citing Rev 13:8; Heb 11:1-40; 1:1; 10:1; Col 2:17; 1 Cor 10:4, 11; Gal 4:24; Song 1:2; Eph 2:12; Gen 49:10; Jn 8:56.

2:10-11 *For Behold, the Winter Is Past*

The Spiritual Winter of the Law. Melchior Hoffman: The Israelites have been in the winter and in the night—that is, in the law and the shadows. For the spiritual winter of the soul is the law, which freezes the soul or causes it to grow cold and kills whoever is not clothed by the bride of the Lamb and the light of faith, by which she was preserved. When Christ with his apostles let the sun's rays shine and the warm south wind blow and took away the cold rain of the law, that was the joyful day and the summer of grace in full force, when Christ sent for his bride, received her and took her up, comforted and quickened her with all loving intention, enlightened, and glorified her. And he said, The law, or the cold rain, is gone away, it is all past, and dear summer is at hand—the light day and bright sunshine, the warm wind. The flowers, he says, have appeared in the land. These flowers were Christ's apostles, who gave off all manner of attractive aromas, and wholesome and nourishing. As stated above, the bride desires these flowers, so that she might be strengthened and quickened by them. These were very noble flowers and their strength is still to be enjoyed today. The Book of Song of Songs.[12]

2:12-15 *Catch Us the Foxes*

The Fox-Like Craftiness of the Devil. Martin Luther: "Since you are persevering in purity of doctrine and holy worship, practice it in the place I have designated. Sing and teach, praise and give thanks. For your face and your voice delight me." Indeed, all the works of believers are gratifying and pleasing to God. These are consoling words. But now immediately a little fox that stirs up fresh troubles will be provided. For even though Satan is totally contaminated, it is not his custom to seek ashes or other ugly places to sit in, but instead he chooses the very cleanest spots. He wants to be among the children of God, as he is in

[12]Hoffman, *Dat Boeck Cantica Canticorum*, 49-50.

Job 1. Accordingly he stirs up false brethren in the church and seditious citizens in the state. We need therefore to walk cautiously, as Solomon goes on to warn.

"Catch us the foxes, the little foxes, that spoil the vineyards." We have seen above that the vineyard is the people of God, as Isaiah 5 also shows. So it is easy to understand who are the foxes whose capture he urges. He speaks of two classes of foxes: foxes and little foxes, in order to indicate the existence of a double danger from astute and malicious people in both government and the church. The little foxes are false brethren in the church, and also heresies that at first worm their way in so that they can be detected only with difficulty. But those who disrupt public affairs give themselves away immediately by their seditious plans, like bigger foxes, which cannot as readily conceal themselves.

"For our vineyards are in blossom." See how wily Satan is. He seizes the moment when he can do the greatest damage! So under the papacy everything was calm; but after the Word began to be disseminated, seditions and heresies sprang up that spoiled the ripening fruit of the gospel, while previously both states and churches appeared to be enjoying a profound peace. The more certain, therefore, the effect of the Word is shown to be, the more careful we must be not to yield ground to Satan's wiles. A Brief but Altogether Lucid Exposition of the Song of Songs.[13]

Nibbling Foxes Cannot Destroy Christ's Fellowship with His Church. John Cotton: Restrain the enemies of the church, of greater or lesser power, such as were the Samaritans. These spoiled the vines, hindered the proceeding of the building of the temple, and the peace of the church. And therefore Tobiah said truly of himself and his fellows, that they, as foxes going upon the weak foundation of the walls of Jerusalem, might easily demolish them. Yet these foxes in the end were taken and restrained: first, partly by the edict of Darius, and second, partly by the hanging of Haman and his sons and the destruction of some other of the Jews' enemies. . . . Observe that the church will always be troubled with some enemies. There will always be some Sanballat, or Tobiah, or some other to be nibbling at the church of God. Do not wonder at this, for this will always be so. But observe regarding these enemies of the church: First, they shall deal subtly and craftily with her. Second, they may disturb and hinder her peace and proceedings, but (third) they shall in the end be restrained, as in Revelation 19:20. Therefore let such foxes know the time will come when Christ will either take them, and chain them, and bind them up, as he did Sanballat, Tobiah, and Shethar-bozenai, or else hang them up, as he did Haman and his sons. Let people then take heed that they do not push at the church, for God will either chain them up, or hang them out of the way.

"My beloved is mine and I am his." The church enjoys familiar and comfortable communion with Christ, now that these enemies have been quelled. "She feeds among the lilies." That is, among pure and fair Christians, all corruptions being weeded out, both of strange wives, of usury, of the Levites' maintenance and ministration, and profanation of the Sabbath. . . . Last, here we may see, when the enemies of the church are restrained or destroyed, and corruptions weeded out of it, the church then enjoys sweet, safe, and full fellowship with the Lord Jesus, and he with her: he gives her pledges of his favor, and she gives him pledges of pure worship. He feeds her with his ordinances, and she him with her sacrifices. And if any would procure Christ such sacrifices, let them first weed out their own sins, such as usury, wicked marriages, profanations of God's Sabbaths, and so on. Such churches shall be sweet, and much sweet solace shall they enjoy one with another, Christ with them and they with him. A Brief Exposition on the Whole Book of Canticles.[14]

[13]LW 15:221 (WA 31.2:662-64).

[14]Cotton, *Brief Exposition*, 72-74, 78-80; citing Neh 4:3.

2:16-17 *My Beloved Is Mine and I Am His*

Christ Present in the Flesh. Melchior Hoffman: Here the bride is fully united with Christ and has completed her race. And the little flock is all gathered and brought in a congregation to Christ the Shepherd. And time is up and completed; Christ and the bride are one thing, and so she says, heartened, that he is hers and she is his. This bridegroom grazes among the roses—that is, among the congregations. Roses here are understood to be Christian congregations. They can also be understood as apostolic teachers, as in 2 Esdras 2.[†] Among these roses Christ grazed in the time of the apostles and God's Word, until the day became cool and the heat of the blazing sun and the rays of the clear bright Word went away, and the cross was spoken of and highlighted. For when God's Word goes out clear and bright in the light of the sun, then the noble heat is at hand. But when it goes down, and night, which is the children of the devil and the darkness, takes the upper hand, it wakes the shadows that follow in its wake and becomes very cool, so that God's Word loses its heat for as long as Christ grazes among the congregations. But when the course is ended and completed, his grazing is over, for the congregation has finished the course. The Book of Song of Songs.[15]

Christ Present Through Faith. Theodore Beza: Someone may object that this bridegroom had not yet come when the bride spoke in this way. On the contrary: faith cannot be without the one to whom she tends as her only end, and who also has her foundation in him who gives and forms faith (that is, Jesus Christ, true God and true man, not God only or man only). And again the church cannot be without faith, since faith is the church's essential form. If Jesus Christ, true God and true man, were not in the church from the very moment of the promise made to Adam, then not only was there no faith, but no church at all. And yet the humanity of Jesus Christ did not actually begin prior to his conception by the power of the Holy Spirit in the womb of the most blessed virgin. This I admit, but I say with the Scripture that Jesus Christ (a name that carries the quality of a unique mediator, that which is absolutely and necessarily required; in other words, that he be considered and apprehended by faith as true God and true man in one single person), not only was, but was also sacrificed from the beginning of the world, seeing that the church, being elected from all eternity, was not saved except by him. And these things are easily seen in light of what is said in Hebrews 11:1—namely, that faith (that is, this gift of God by which every faithful soul is assured of his salvation through the only Mediator, Jesus Christ, who is true God and true man) causes that which the believer does not yet possess except by hope to be present to him in reality, and shows him (that is, in the spirit of the believer) what he does not yet see. Therefore the humanity of Jesus Christ, without which he would not be our Mediator, nor the object of our faith, was not in nature in Solomon's time, nor for many centuries after; nevertheless, he was really and effectually present through the eyes of faith. . . . This is what the bride meant in the following verse, when she prays that the bridegroom "will return as the wind of the day arises, and the shadows flee." In effect, she describes her condition as one of "shadows," a time when the bridegroom did not show himself, but rather under the shadows and figures of the ceremonial law "the substance of things hoped for"—that is, Jesus Christ—appeared "but from a distance." Not that the light from this shadow was insufficient to lead the saints into the light of glory, seeing that light, according to their measure, was called "the bosom of Abraham." Nevertheless, this light was dim by

[15]Hoffman, *Dat Boeck Cantica Canticorum*, 54-56; citing Gen 1; Jn 1. [†]2 Esdras is an apocalyptic book ascribed to the biblical Ezra, but likely authored in the first or second century AD. Jerome had included it (along with 4 Esdras) in the book of Ezra, but most Protestant writers relegated it to apocryphal status. The passage in question reads, "I will send you help: my servants Isaiah and Jeremiah. According to their counsel I have consecrated and prepared for you twelve trees loaded with various fruits, and the same number of springs flowing with milk and honey and seven mighty mountains on which roses and lilies grow; by these I will fill your children with joy" (2:18-19).

comparison to that great day which brought the bridegroom to us in person, and when he declared openly to us and in detail the "whole counsel of God" his Father touching on our salvation. He also continued to reveal himself to us by his apostles, and still does so—even to the very consummation of the world—through his true pastors and teachers. Therefore we must distinguish this "shadow of the night" from the "shadow of death" mentioned in Isaiah 9:2, wherein we are all of us born. Sermons on the First Three Chapters of the Song of Songs.[16]

Fleeing the Fall of Spiritual Darkness. Melchior Hoffman: Night once again spreads out over the world and the children of the world, who are in the night. For through human teachings it truly becomes night again, and false teachings strongly encroach and increase such that the wicked let themselves be seen, as happened after the time of the apostles and will now happen mightily again in these times. Thus it was the bride's desire in that time that Christ should turn back away from the cleft mountains, like a quick young hart or deer, and not be near them. These cleft mountains are the congregations that have separated themselves from the right way of truth. They can also be understood to be the teachers who separate themselves from the kingdom of God, which a third of our teachers will now separate themselves from in these last times. And the little child of God's Word will again be snatched up to God in his throne or kingdom, and the bridegroom will return. And wisdom will return again to its place and the trees will give off blooms of human wisdom, as after the time of the apostles. This has now happened since the summer and since the time of the apostles, and this prophecy is very nicely laid out. The Book of Song of Songs.[17]

[16]Beza, *Sermons sur les trois premiers chapitres du Cantique des Cantiques, de Salomon*, 456-59; citing Heb 11:1, 13; Lk 16:22; Jn 15:15; Mt 13:17; Eph 4:11; Eph 2:1.

[17]Hoffman, *Dat Boeck Cantica Canticorum*, 57-58; citing Rev 12; Mt 24; Mk 13; Lk 21; Joel 3; Mt 25; 2 Esdras 5.

3:1-5 THE BRIDE'S DREAM

[1]*On my bed by night*
I sought him whom my soul loves;
I sought him, but found him not.

[2]*I will rise now and go about the city,*
in the streets and in the squares;

I will seek him whom my soul loves.
I sought him, but found him not.

[3]*The watchmen found me*
as they went about in the city.

"Have you seen him whom my soul loves?"

[4]*Scarcely had I passed them*
when I found him whom my soul loves.

I held him, and would not let him go
until I had brought him into my mother's house,
and into the chamber of her who conceived me.

[5]*I adjure you, O daughters of Jerusalem,*
by the gazelles or the does of the field,

that you not stir up or awaken love
until it pleases.

Overview: Here the poem takes an abrupt turn, as the bride languishes in separation from her beloved. In general, our commentators all agree in seeing this as an image of separation from Christ, the heavenly Bridegroom, though there is some difference as to whether the image points to the private experience of the interior soul, or to a historical period of wandering or decline. Most of our commentators favor the latter view: Isidore Clarius identifies this fearful interlude with the forty years of Israel's wandering in the desert, whereas John Cotton and Thomas Brightman associate it with the period of Seleucid tyranny prior to the Maccabean revolt. Theodore Beza holds that periods of such forgetfulness have occurred periodically throughout sacred history, but with especially frequency since the time of Constantine. Veit Dietrich and Melchior Hoffmann, however, see in this passage an image of the individual soul's struggle to remain faithful when Christ appears absent and the devil is given a free hand.

3:1 *On My Bed by Night*

Inquire of the Appointed Watchmen. Isidore Clarius: This is the place where I felt destitute and abandoned, so that it did not now seem possible to say, "Our bed is green." Rather, it should be called a bed of sorrow, not of pleasure. In this bed every night I sought, grieving, after the one whom my soul loves, but I did not find him. That is to say, he was angry with a sinful people, now rebelling, now murmuring. It was like nighttime to me, when all my members were in the darkness of sin. Impatient of the delay, in the manner of love-struck women who seek in every place after a lost love, so I wandered about the gloomy desert for forty years, seeking but not finding a way to be reconciled. In the midst of this anxiety, I fell among "the watchmen," Moses and Aaron, who were guardians of the city—that is, of my fellow citizens. I asked them whether they had seen him whom my soul loves—that is, I hoped to employ them in being reconciled to my bridegroom. Truly not, they answered me. But he is only away that they might lead me into the Promised Land, though they themselves could not enter.

"Scarcely had I passed them." After their death—that is to say, in the time of Joshua, who truly was a type of Jesus—I found him whom my soul loves, and I experienced his favor. I held on to the one I had found, nor did I depart so long as I found the Lord in that place, but I made a tabernacle to the God of Jacob, and indeed "I brought it into my mother's house"—that is to say, into the ancient land of my ancestors, in which Abraham, Isaac, and Jacob had once lived. This account can be applied as follows so that the character of the Christ's church may be strengthened, and also the souls of the faithful: when it seems that the bridegroom has been snatched away, she recalls better times, in which there was reconciliation after anger, and receiving this record of faithfulness, she does not despair. In the meantime, observe that we must inquire of the watchmen and sentries of our souls and pay heed to them, to learn how we may find the bridegroom, and what may be useful. Observe then what follows: "scarcely had I passed them," that is, soon after they had been questioned (for they cannot do it all, but it is enough that they remind of the way, and point like a finger to the source), "I found him whom my soul loves." The Song of Songs of Solomon.[1]

The Church's Bed of Affliction. Henry Ainsworth: The church now shows the greater afflictions into which she fell, through want of feeling the presence and comforts of Christ. While she thought herself sure of her beloved, and laid herself down as on the bed of ease, supposing him to be with her, she misses his company, and seeking him by solitary meditation, did not find him. Thus we may understand this place, comparing it with 5:2-3. . . . The "bed" sometimes signifies tribulation, as in Revelation 2:22, which may also be implied here—that is, the church sought and waited for the Lord, in the way of his judgments. . . . "The night." The time of solitary and earnest meditation, as also of affliction, are signified by "the night." . . . So in Isaiah 36:9, "With my soul have I desired thee in the night; yea, with my spirit within me, will I seek thee early." . . . For neglect of taking hold on grace when it is offered, or not keeping it when it is received, God often withdraws the light of his countenance, to stir up zeal and fervency in his children. Annotations upon the Song of Songs.[2]

The Dangers of Drowsiness. Theodore Beza: In the previous chapter we saw the gracious encounter when the bridegroom caressed his bride and spoke with her in a delightful repose, this despite the expectation of a still more intimate arrival, when the Bridegroom should come like the bright sun arising to illuminate the world, and when the figures and shadows of the law should come to an end. . . . It seemed at that time that all was best in the world: the temple of the Lord had been completed in great magnificence and its service well established, and the estate of the realm was wisely administered by Solomon; indeed, we must say that the church was then resplendent in glory, and all the people lived in great repose. The same may also be said of the state of the church during the time of Joshua, when the people were brought into the rest of the Lord, as the Lord himself describes it. But what? This did not last long, as Moses had predicted and we see described—or rather, painted most divinely—in this passage. This passage contains a doctrine altogether necessary for our own time, so that we may not be deceived into damaging our salvation. For the Christian church is fallen from age to age into that miserable state described in Matthew 13:13-25. Little by little, her excessive ease has led her into a deep sleep, with the result that the enemy has set up his seat and arranged it to his wishes in the very middle of the house of God, as the apostle predicted. And when today the Lord would awaken her, the most part are so bleary-eyed that they cannot or will not open them; others are in so deep a slumber that though they are roused with

[1] Isidore, *Canticum Canticorum Salomonis*, 14v-r; citing Song 1:16.

[2] Ainsworth, *Annotations*, 2:701; citing Is 26:8; Ps 63:7; 119:55; 127:2-4; Prov 1:24, 28; Mic 3:4; Jer 11:10-11.

great strokes of the whip, still they lay their head down again upon the pillow. . . .

But where does this fault come from? Not on the Lord's side, but the wretchedness of men and women, who cannot order themselves aright, neither in prosperity nor in adversity, neither in poverty, nor in abundance. But if we compare both of these extremes, we shall find both by reason and by experience that the way of rest, accompanied with prosperity and abundance, is the more dangerous. For adversity and need stir up and awaken the most insensible to think on a remedy, and for this reason it is said that necessity is the occasion for the invention of the arts and sciences. But prosperity and abundance lull even the best to sleep: witness Adam and Eve before their miserable fall, and Solomon who was so wise—in short, the whole history of the truly Christian, apostolic, and catholic church, which flourished under St. Peter and St. John, "who had neither gold nor silver," but distributed to others in the midst of their poverty, beginning at daybreak, the true riches which God had committed to them. So also under St. Paul, who lived and nourished others by the labor of his hands, preaching to them by night and by day, and that with tears. But ever since the peace granted by Constantine, accompanied by abundance, the mother of ambition and of dissolution, she never ceased her decline as regards heavenly things until now, though as regards the world she has grown great. For how can the kingdom of God and of the world agree, seeing as how they are so contrary to one another? Thus we see how a short nap leads to a deep slumber, not only in this person or that, but in the church as a whole, and that in less than a wink she is turned away from her betrothed. Sermons on the First Three Chapters of the Song of Songs.[3]

Judas Maccabeus a Type of Christ. John Cotton: "By night." That is, in time of darkness and public calamity, when Antiochus Epiphanes, the "little horn, which waxed exceeding great," wasted the pleasant land and cast some of the host and stars of heaven to the ground.[†] He took away the daily sacrifice, and trod down the sanctuary and cast down the truth to the ground. He robbed the temple, murdered the people, spoiled the city, and made laws for profaning the Sabbath, for offering swine's flesh, and for neglecting circumcision. He set up the statues of Jupiter Olympias, the abomination of desolation in the holy place. He burned the books of the Law and made it death to have a Testament. He broke down the altar and set up another, and he put to death women who had caused children to be circumcised, hanging the children on the necks of their mothers.[‡]

"In my bed." Not "in my bed" of ease and sloth (as some take it), for what ease could the church take in the night time of calamity? But "in my bed," that is, in the place and duties of God's worship, the temple and the ordinances. "I sought him whom my soul loves." I desired and endeavored to have fellowship with Christ, "but I found him not," the sanctuary being polluted and the daily sacrifice taken away, and profane idols set up in the place. "In the streets of the city"—that is, in the open assemblies of the faithful, in the synagogues, in the cities of Judea and Jerusalem. But behold, there are altars erected to idols, and incense burned, and the books of Law cast into the fire—behold, the citizens of Jerusalem all fled and gone, and the rest going in precession to Bacchus.[§] A Brief Exposition on the Whole Book of Canticles.[4]

[3]Beza, *Sermons sur les trois premiers chapitres du Cantique des Cantiques, de Salomon*, 466-67, 470-71; Ps 95:11 Deut 32:15; 2 Thess 2:3-5; Acts 3:6; 5:21; 20:31-34; Lk 18:36; Jas 4:4.

[4]Cotton, *Brief Exposition*, 84-85; citing Dan 8:9. [†]Antiochus IV (r. 175–164 BC), the Seleucid ruler who took to himself the epithets *theos* (god) and *ephiphanes* (manifest), outraged his Judean subjects by plundering the temple in Jerusalem and abrogating many of the Jews' ancestral customs, actions that sparked the revolt described in the books of First and Second Maccabees. Cotton's reading of the imagery in Song of Songs 3 is remarkable for the way it weaves together canonical, deuterocanonical, and even secular history in a tapestry of typological interpretation. The description of Antiochus's actions in this paragraph are a loose paraphrase of the description of the "little horn" of Dan 8:9-12. [‡]This catalog of horrors is drawn from 1 Macc 1:23-58. [§]1 Macc 1:57-58; 1:40; 2 Macc 6:7.

When God Withdraws, the Devil Advances. Veit Dietrich: This is a lamentation by the bride, who has lost her bridegroom. For the devil cannot run riot when the Word of God is there, yet he seeks with all his might to wreak havoc. Now and then God withdraws himself—that is, he leaves the devil room, as is often done in wartime maneuvers. When this happens, the best thing is not to lie still, but rather to seek the bridegroom, and find him in the Word that is preached by the watchmen. Then you will finally receive comfort and find the bridegroom again. The Song of Solomon.[5]

3:2-3 *I Will Rise Now and Go About the City*

Awakening from the Darkness of Sin. Melchior Hoffman: The rising of the bride is the act of waking up from the vanity of darkness and sin—that is, she desists from sin and with spirit, heart, and courage learns to recognize and hate this same sin and darkness. St. Paul speaks of this rising in Ephesians 5: "Wake up, you who sleep, stand up from the dead and Christ will be your light." I also find this rising in Romans 13 and in Daniel 12. Many of those who sleep in the dust of the earth will rise up. This rising is now at hand, and all the elect will rise out of all sin and unrighteousness and our eyes will be opened concerning sinful living and false dealings. The city of which the bride speaks is the congregation of Satan, in which congregation the bride did not find Christ. The streets on which she went here and there are false teachings, and on these streets she also did not find Christ. For as Christ is a path to life, as in John 14, so also is the devil's false teaching a path and street to death, on which we wander toward damnation. The Book of Song of Songs.[6]

The Blessings of Solomon's Reign. Martin Luther: Up to this point we have listened to Solomon singing in general terms about his state, in which he maintained that worship of God which God himself had established. At this point he begins to digress somewhat in order to carry his account down to his own period and to his own person. For this reason we shall interpret almost all the following verses as pertinent to Solomon himself. . . . "The watchmen found me, as they went about in the city. . . ." The guards are the judges and princes. "Among them," he says, "I was looking for what I desired, namely, peace and tranquility. But I found peace neither under Saul and David nor before them under the judges. Whenever a new judge or a new king was given, hope sprang up that the ills of the state would be cured, but I did not find it until I went a little further and came to Solomon. There I finally found what I was looking for, as his name also promises." As I said before, I take all these statements to be about the person of Solomon. Under his rule the kingdom enjoyed an abundant flowering of peace and every kind of blessing. Yet here these words are not to be taken as if he were writing a hymn of praise to himself. For they are all spoken in the person of the state, as it acknowledges the divine blessings that God has granted through the godly magistrate and gives thanks to God for them. This is the manner in which we are to take the hymn of praise to Solomon written in this chapter. A Brief but Altogether Lucid Exposition of the Song of Songs.[7]

Levitical Watchmen. John Cotton: "The watchmen that go about the city." These are the Levites, who answered her with silence, but a little later she found succor at Modin, for the priests Mattathias and his sons Judas, Jonathan, and Simon, and the rest that went about to repair the ruins of the church and commonwealth. To these the faithful church repaired, and finding deliverance and comfort by Judas [Maccabeus]

[5]Dietrich, *Das Hohelied Salomonis*, 11.

[6]Hoffman, *Dat Boeck Cantica Canticorum*, 61-63; citing Eph 5:14; Rom 13:11.

[7]LW 15:223-24 (WA 31.2:666-68).

especially—or rather by Christ in him—she did not leave him until she had brought him into the temple, where she soon after cleansed the sanctuary and restored the purity of God's worship.[†] Thus again they found Christ in a typical Savior,[‡] held him by faith, and with courage and zeal, brought him into the temple and sanctuary, "the house and chamber of her mother"—that is, of the former church of Israel, or of the catholic church, for the church of the former ages is the mother of the latter, or the whole church is the mother of each part in usual phrase of Hebrew speech: the temple is the house of both, the sanctuary is the chamber of her that bore her. A Brief Exposition on the Whole Book of Canticles.[8]

3:4-5 *I Found Him Whom My Soul Loves*

The Ardor of Love Restored. Lucas Osiander: "The watchmen found me, who guard the city." I said to them, when I came upon them, "Have you seen him whom my soul loves?" Not one of you can show me where my bridegroom is? But they neither saw him, nor could they point me to him. This is what happened to Christians afflicted and tested under the papacy, who had no fit ministers of the church from whom they could receive true and solid consolation regarding the grace and mercy of Christ. Therefore "scarcely had I passed them by, when I [finally] found him whom my soul loves." Thus Christ returns to us in his own time—that is, our hearts are given consolation through the gospel, that we might be tranquil in soul and perceive in our hearts the testimony of the Holy Spirit that we are in the grace of God and that Christ by his favor has made us whole. "I held on to him, I will not let him go until I bring him into the house of my mother, and into the chamber of her that bore me." That is, the hearts of the pious, after receiving consolation, burn more hotly with love for Christ, and cling to him ever more closely. Also, he proposes that the greatest gift he desires to give is never to lose Christ again (as was done before), but to remain in his presence through grace and continuously to experience his great mercy and benevolence. Song of Songs.[9]

Conjugal Cohabitation. John Trapp: "Until I had brought him into my mother's house." That is, into my conscience, say some (where faith dwells, and Christ by faith), into the synagogues of the Jews say others, or into the congregations of the Gentiles. They do best who understand it of the catholic church, the supernal Jerusalem, that mother of us all, figured by Sarah, where Christ has most delightful dwelling, a comfortable commemoration, and (as it were) conjugal cohabitation with his spouse. Solomon's Book of All Virtues.[10]

A Charged Invitation. Hugo Grotius: Theocritus:

[Just look; there's such a pain in my heart.
If only I could turn into a buzzing bee]
and come into your cave [through the ivy and fern
that hide you!]

Annotations on the Old Testament.[11]

Peace Until the Coming of the Messiah. Thomas Brightman: This verse shows that there should be no great trouble in the church from the time of the Maccabees till the birth of Christ, as was said in the end of the former verse. Now there should be silence and a tolerable rest, whereby the saints might be defended in their true studies from fear of their enemies, which are here noted by "roes and hinds" of the field. For though they were come home, out of the enemies' land and settled in their

[8]Cotton, *Brief Exposition*, 85-86. [†]1 Macc 3:6-8; 4:42, 46. [‡]By "typical savior," Cotton indicates any one of a number of historical figures whose actions make them *types* of Christ. See Cotton's remarks on Cyrus as a type of Christ in his exegesis of 2:8, above.

[9]Osiander, *Canticum Canticorum*, 1256.

[10]Trapp, *Solomonis ΠΑΝΑΡΕΤΟΣ*, 220; citing Rom 10:10; Gal 4:19; Gal 4:24-26.

[11]Grotius, *Annotationes in Vetus Testamentum*, 270. Grotius draws another analogy with a passage in Theocritus (*Idyll* 3.12-14; LCL 28:61), one highly charged with innuendo.

own proper seats, yet they found at home all places full of enemies. Now the Romans oppressed them, and Herod's tyranny bridled them. These wild "roes" caused God's people to worship him more diligently, and to be the more careful, lest with any noise of apparent impiety (which only disturbs our beloved from his rest) she should lose the enjoyment of him in any way. Commentary on the Canticles.[12]

[12]Brightman, *A Commentary on the Canticles or the Song of Salomon*, 1011.

3:6-11 THE BRIDEGROOM ARRIVES FOR THE WEDDING

[6]What is that coming up from the wilderness
like columns of smoke,

perfumed with myrrh and frankincense,
with all the fragrant powders of a merchant?

[7]Behold, it is the litter[a] of Solomon!
Around it are sixty mighty men,
some of the mighty men of Israel,

[8]all of them wearing swords
and expert in war,

each with his sword at his thigh,
against terror by night.

[9]King Solomon made himself a carriage[b]
from the wood of Lebanon.

[10]He made its posts of silver,
its back of gold, its seat of purple;

its interior was inlaid with love
by the daughters of Jerusalem.

[11]Go out, O daughters of Zion,
and look upon King Solomon,

with the crown with which his mother crowned him
on the day of his wedding,
on the day of the gladness of his heart.

a That is, the couch on which servants carry a king **b** Or *sedan chair*

Overview: The bride in the poem, having endured a night of fearful separation from her beloved, now regains her equanimity upon his return, rejoicing in the glory of his triumphal procession. Our radical commentators understand this in reference to the individual soul or congregation: thus, for Melchior Hoffman, the wilderness refers either to the world in general or to the suffering that always assaults true faith; for Dirk Philips, the imagery of the sixty "strong ones" signifies those who are strong in faith within the congregation. Others read the imagery with reference to specific historical events: for Theodore Beza, the arrival of Solomon is a figure for the advent of Christ; for John Cotton and Thomas Brightman, John the Baptist; for Martin Luther, it is the fame of the kingdom of Solomon that spread across the ancient world. Still other commentators are less concerned with any particular historical referent, dwelling instead on the ways in which aspects of Solomon's reign foreshadow the reign of Christ in the new age.

3:6 *Who Is This Coming Up from the Wilderness?*

The Church's Flight to the Wilderness. Melchior Hoffman: The wilderness is understood in two ways: the wilderness of which the bridegroom speaks is understood to be the world; but the bride breaks forth and breaks out from the world, and she refrains from all that belongs to the world and its ruler and turns to God, in the true spiritual wilderness. There the cross and suffering follow close behind; as St. Paul says in 2 Timothy 3, that "those who desire to live godly lives must suffer persecution." Christ in his glory also had to endure his cross and suffering. And God also speaks of such persecution in Zechariah 13, how he will lead his children through fire and prove them like gold, burn them like silver, and he will acknowledge them as his children, and they will call on him as their Lord and God. The bride of God and Christ must be well burned by the heat of such a fire, so that she becomes an atrocity to the world, but to God and Christ a noble perfume of myrrh.

The myrrh is understood to be the cross and suffering. So when the bride is in the right heat [that is, the fire in which God will purify her], concerning which St. Peter writes, the smell and perfume of myrrh can rise to God and to Christ, and a noble perfume can be offered to God. And a person who has been strengthened into such myrrh desists from sin. The perfume of incense is the prayer of the saints. It wafts without ceasing from the bride of Christ to her bridegroom. And her heart, spirit, and resolve burn at all times with God's Spirit and Word. That same perfume rises day and night from her heart and mouth, and it is the scent of all manner of merchants' spices and flowers of God's Word that rises from the bride. And if anyone asks the bridegroom what it is, it is such a perfume as the world does not recognize. It is not bad, but rather very precious, lovely, and pleasant, and a noble, lasting perfume of noble salves.

For such a person suffering is not difficult, so long as they acknowledge Christ the lovely bridegroom. He offers his suffering to God the Father through Christ along with his whole heart, spirit, and resolve, and he praises God with all his works, words, and deeds, without ceasing. This is joy, delight, and the highest peace. In such a heart can be found the true myrrh and perfume of incense and all herb and spices of God's mighty Word and truth. And what becomes the heart becomes the mouth also, as Christ says concerning his bride. The Book of Song of Songs.[1]

The Strong Ones Are the Strong in Faith. Dirk Philips: It serves well to notice the figure from the sixty strong ones who stood around the bed of Solomon, of the strong ones in Israel, and each one had his sword at his side on account of the fear in the night. This signifies that round about the congregation of the Lord Jesus Christ stand those who are strong in the faith, who are equipped with the armor of God to protect the congregation through the help of God before all the horrors of the night, that is, before the errors and spirits of darkness which are secretly round about to deceive the simple. Answer to Sebastian Franck, citing Song 3:6.[2]

The Bridegroom's Delight in the Bride. Theodore Beza: It follows in our text, "Who is this that rides from the desert like palms of smoke?" Whereupon we may first ask what person is alluded to in this verse. Some think that these are the "daughters of Jerusalem" who are addressed here, but there is no reason for this. It is therefore the bridegroom who speaks, conversing with his bride in her mother's chamber and magnifying the graces he had bestowed on her. And this very change of person (that is, that he addressed his speech as if to a third person, even though he was speaking to her) displays a wonderful grace. Neither must we take this as a demand, as if the bridegroom was inquiring after something he did not know, but rather we should take it as an expression of admiration for the good grace of his bride. Therefore he compares her to a high, straight pillar, like the palm trees of that region, or like a column of vapor rising upward from the mountains of the desert. And proceeding with the analogy, he also says of this vapor that the bride is so perfumed with all sorts of excellent odors that scent rises up even to heaven. Such then is this comparison, which seems to be derived from this image, that a multitude marching and coming together from any place resembles a cloud, as the apostle says in Hebrews 12:1. For however the bride is introduced here, speaking in this Song of one person only, it must yet be understood as referring to the whole company of the faithful, joined together in one body, and vivified by the same Spirit, as is described for us in Act 4:32. Sermons on the First Three Chapters of the Song of Songs.[3]

[1]Hoffman, *Dat Boeck Cantica Canticorum*, 61-63; 2 Tim 3:12; Rev 5; 8; Ps 1.

[2]CRR 6:451*.

[3]Beza, *Sermons sur les trois premiers chapitres du Cantique des Cantiques, de Salomon*, 535-36.

John the Baptist Is a Type for Christian Ministers. John Cotton: "Who is this that comes out of the wilderness?" This is a description of John the Baptist, and of the church gathered by his ministry in the wilderness. This is set forth: first, by the admiration and inquisitiveness of the old synagogue after him and his baptism . . . ; second, by the place of his arising, and the church with him, in the wilderness; third, by the manner of arising, like pillars of smoke that arise from fire, as the church arose from the zeal and fervency of John's ministry, and ascend on high, as the propagation of the church, spreading eventually to Jerusalem . . . ; fourth, by the excellent fragrance and sweetness of the graces that perfumed him, preserving from putrefaction. Such was the powerful zeal of John and his ministry, strongly fragrant as myrrh, preserving his hearers from pharisaical hypocrisy. Frankincense is likewise a strong fragrance, and chiefly used in making holy incense, by which prayer was signified. This intimates the fragrancy and fervency of his prayers, who taught all his disciples to pray.

This is first to show us that God can raise up a church even in the wilderness, to the admiration of observers, and so he can raise up our neighbor churches, now brought to a wilderness. This may comfort us in regard of them, for though they be now desolate, yet we may hope a time will come when they shall rise again. Second, see here a part of the duty of ancient Christians, not to malign the graces of God in those who come after them, but to admire them: "Who is it that comes out of the wilderness?" Third, this shows what gifts and graces are most requisite in a minister: zeal in his ministry, fervency in prayers, and all sorts of sweet graces to season and direct all sorts of his people in their individual callings, as John did when the people came and said, "'What shall we do?' He answered and said, 'The one who has two coats, let them give to the one who has none.'" . . . So John was perfumed with graces for all people, for people must not come into the ministry with judgment and learning alone, for these may come from nature, but they must come perfumed with graces to keep themselves and others from putrefaction—yes, they must labor for those graces that will give a strong scent to save themselves and others. A Brief Exposition on the Whole Book of Canticles.[4]

The Church at the Time of Christ's Birth. Thomas Brightman: Hitherto has been shown the condition of the church before the birth of Christ, now what it should be while he lived on the earth. This description contains a prophecy, especially of things done from the conception of Christ until thirty years of his age, when the beauty of the church should cause admiration in the beholders. "Who is this?" they say, which seem to be the words of the legal church, wondering at the excellent smell of the new smoke stirred up. For at this time, the church in outward form was twofold: the legal continued yet, and the evangelical was newly begun. Her threefold propriety was: her admirable coming out of the desert; her smoky enlarging and increase; and last, her sweet smell. She came first out of the desert, by the message of the angel to the Virgin Mary, living then in Nazareth of Galilee, a solitary place compared to others more frequented. She was then divinely revealed to Elizabeth in the mountains of Judea, as she testified when Mary came to see her. This report is compared to pillars of smoke, for as smoke goes before the flame, breaking forth and arising up like branched pillars, yet quickly disperses and vanishes in the air, no matter how thick it be, so shall we find this report and people's expectations altogether like this. As by the prophecy of Zacharias of raising up a horn of salvation in the house of David, confirmed by miracles, as well that of a son born to him in his old age, and of his speech restored after ten months. What fear came upon all the inhabitants of the hill country? This smoke arising in the wilderness, how pleasantly it smelled to all the godly waiting for the

[4]Cotton, *Brief Exposition*, 87-89, 95-96; citing John 1:19; Lk 3:15; 3:2-4; Mk 1:3-4; Mt 3:5-6; Song 1:13; Mt 3:10; Ex 30:34; Ps 141:2; Lk 11:1; 3:10-14.

consolation of Israel, yet folded up in such thick obscurity that people could not see the greatest part of it, and where the thing they desired so much would end up. But afterward by the former when the shepherds and the wise men came seeking for the newborn King, all Jerusalem was troubled. Then the branched smoke flew upward, breaking forth with such force, by reason of the increased heat, that it ascended like a pillar, yet this smoke quickly vanished. Not that the church ever failed, but because this rumor ceased, there was so deep a silence from that time until the baptism of John, as if all these things had vanished into smoke. But who can declare how sweet this rumor was to all the godly thirsting for the Messiah? Simeon, taking the child in his arms and praising God very joyfully, desired to die, having obtained that which was most to be desired in this life. And truly all myrrh, frankincense, and all manner of perfumes are unsavory in comparison to this sweetness. Commentary on the Canticles.[5]

3:7-10 *Look! It Is Solomon's Carriage*

The Fame of the Jewish Kingdom. Martin Luther: This text has been made into a hymn concerning the Blessed Virgin[†]—obviously so that there may nowhere be any lack of evidence by which to establish the incredible ignorance and blindness of our adversaries! There is no reference here to the Blessed Virgin. It is the Jewish kingdom as it existed under Solomon that is described and commended in such elegant and poetic figures. We may paraphrase: The state and kingdom under Solomon was so very fragrant that all the neighboring realms were filled with the sweetness of its odor, or the celebrity of its fame. It is thus fitly compared to a column of smoke that rises from aromatic incense and fills the whole palace. And by the sweetness of this most pleasing odor the queen of the South was invited to come to Solomon. . . . Listing various sorts of aromatic substances and saying that the smoke rises from them suggests that various gifts have been resident in this people, wisdom, prudence, patience, faith. . . .

"King Solomon made himself a palanquin." The section of the hymn of praise that we have heard so far is nothing else but a thanksgiving for the litter—that is, for the people. Now here he mentions the palanquin, or seat, which Solomon made for himself. However, he does not intend us to think he is saying this of the materials, but he is comparing to the seat, or palanquin, those laws and judgments by which Solomon governs his people. He praises them for their marks of great distinction: "of gold," that is, wisdom; "of silver," that is, eloquence; "of purple," that is, the ardor of love; "from the cedar of Lebanon," that is, freedom from corruption, so that they might be stable and fixed. But for what purpose? "For the sake of the daughters of Jerusalem." Not for the sake of the Gentiles but for the sake of the people of God. A Brief but Altogether Lucid Exposition of the Song of Songs.[6]

Solomon's Temple Prefigures Christ's Reign. Melchior Hoffman: King Solomon is Christ, who was symbolized by the one Christ allowed to build for him a tabernacle, or throne, or litter, as I understand it. But the fact that he says he allowed it to be made for himself, rather than saying that he made it himself, is because Christ is honoring his heavenly Father here and recognizing him as Creator, Maker, and one God of glory and power. I see this in Luke 1, when the angel says to

[5]Brightman, *A Commentary on the Canticles or the Song of Salomon*, 1011-12; citing Lk 1:69; 2:18; Mt 2:3; Lk 2:29.

[6]LW 15:225-26 (WA 31.2:669-72). [†]Texts from the Song of Songs were applied to the Blessed Virgin in many liturgical settings, so it is difficult to know exactly which hymn Luther has in mind here. The imagery of a rising column of smoke in Song 3:6 was sometimes taken to signify the bodily assumption of Mary into heaven, a suggestion attributed to Jerome in a pseudepigraphic letter to Paula and Eustochium: "And rightly is [the Virgin] represented as a pillar of smoke, for she is slender and delicate, worn thin by divine disciplines, and consumed within as a burnt offering by the ardor of holy love." PL 30:129d. For more on Marian readings of the Song of Songs in medieval exegesis, see E. Ann Matter, *The Voice of My Beloved: The Song of Songs in Western Medieval Christianity* (Philadelphia: University of Pennsylvania Press, 1990), 151-77.

Mary, "He will give him the throne of his father David, and of his reign there will be no end." I also find this throne in Revelation 3, where Christ is seated on it. It is his Father's throne, as also in Psalm 45. So here now is understood the throne or tabernacle, that is the host of angels, apostles, preachers, and shepherds of the New Testament, who are compared to the noble wood of Lebanon. They are cut out of the wood of the devil's kingdom and by his Spirit God makes them into a tabernacle for Christ. For Psalm 19 speaks of this in another way, that the eternal heavens are a tabernacle of Christ, or Christ's sun, and in the heavens his course is prepared and his reign is fulfilled.

The silver pillars are understood to be the apostolic preachers of the New Testament, who spread the gospel of Christ here and there through parables and allegories. These silver pillars are also explained in the preface to Matthew. The gold is likened to the Word, illuminated and uncovered by Luther, and God's Spirit in Luther. I also find this in the preface to Matthew. But the purple seat is made of yellow silk, red silk, rosy red silk, strong white silk, and with gold mixed in. This is also laid out in the preface to Matthew. The decorations are understood to be all God's elect, on whom Christ has his throne. And the elect are represented in the throne, as God says in Psalm 2: "I have installed my king on my holy mountain Zion." This mountain is the congregation of Zion and Israel, that is now the throne of God or Christ and is for him a seat, or litter, or a dwelling or tabernacle. I find this throne or tabernacle in 1 Kings 10 and 2 Chronicles 9. It had six steps, and on each step two golden lions. The six steps are the twelve kingdoms of Israel and the twelve golden lions are the twelve patriarchs and apostles of the two testaments. I hear more about this throne in Revelation 4.

But the beautiful decoration was for the sake of the daughter of Jerusalem. This is the reason that Zion and the elect people of God were so beautifully composed in this throne of God and his apostles, as above with the sixty strong men. And Christ is such a noble cornerstone and foundation for the sake of all daughters, and believers of all tribes and congregations, or people of every tongue and nation. And we also through faith build ourselves into a foundation of Christ, and so bear Christ and his apostolic spirits as our throne and kingdom, and also as our crown with its stars. We are his foundation and he, along with his apostles, is our foundation and cornerstone or ornament. The Book of Song of Songs.[7]

3:11 *Go Out, O Daughters of Zion, and Look upon King Solomon*

Solomon Governs with the Consent of the People. Martin Luther: This little section, too, is extremely fitting for this hymn of praise. It is as if he were saying, "I have shown you what sort of kingdom God has given you under Solomon and the magnitude of the gifts that have been lavished on you, in that both at home in the state you have laws and judgment and abroad you have peace. Now do this also: notice how these gifts had their beginning. Solomon did not seize his kingdom through tyranny, but his mother crowned him—that is, the kingdom was committed to him by the consent of the whole people. Therefore revere and esteem him, and give God thanks for these his gifts that he has lavished on you so richly under this king." A Brief but Altogether Lucid Exposition of the Song of Songs.[8]

Solomon Foreshadows Christ as Peacemaker. Johann Gerhard: Solomon says, "Go out, you daughters of Zion, and look upon King Solomon." The evangelist John has described in chapter 12 how this very same thing was fulfilled on Palm Sunday at the royal entrance of the Lord Christ. There he reports that many people from the city of Jerusalem "went to meet the Lord Christ with palm branches and cried out to him,

[7]Hoffman, *Dat Boeck Cantica Canticorum*, 64-67; citing Lk 1:32-33; Ps 2:6; Rev 12; 21.
[8]LW 15:226 (WA 31.2:673).

'Hosanna! Blessed is he who comes in the name of the Lord, a king of Israel.'" I wish, therefore, on this occasion to set before us this saying of Solomon and to explain it briefly and simply. . . .

In the saying just read there are two items presented to us by the Holy Spirit. The first is the presentation of the Messiah, the King. This was the Messiah promised to us in the Old Testament, but fulfilled now, presented as a king with his crown. The second is the serious encouragement to receiving this king worthily. The daughters of Zion—and in their name, all of us—are exhorted that we should go out to meet this our king and behold him.

In the first portion we have examined the first subject, who should be understood in this very passage by this King Solomon. The Jews want to understand such a reference to refer to the earthly King Solomon, which David begat with Bathsheba and who followed him in the kingdom. But we Christians understand here by King Solomon none other than the Messiah who had been promised at that time. For, first of all, there are all the same arguments that prove that in this Song of Songs of Solomon the earthly King Solomon, the next heir to the throne of David, and his spouse, the daughter of Pharaoh, the king of Egypt, are not being treated, but rather the heavenly Solomon, namely, Christ Jesus, and his spiritual bride, the Christian church. . . .

Second, Solomon was a type of the Messiah, the heavenly Solomon, as Christ teaches us when he speaks about himself in this way in Matthew 12 and Luke 11: "The queen of the South came from the end of the earth in order to hear Solomon's wisdom, and behold, here is more than Solomon." Third, the name of Solomon also beautifully points to Christ. For Solomon means "peaceable," and Christ is now the true Prince of Peace. "He is our peace." His kingdom is a kingdom of peace, as Zechariah 9 prophesied about him: "He will teach peace among the heathen; I will abolish the chariots from Ephraim and the war horses from Jerusalem and the battle bow will be broken." Augustine comments on Psalm 71 [72]: "Solomon means 'peacemaker,' and through this sort of word he corresponds very well and most truly to Christ, since through him, our Mediator, we are turned from being enemies and reconciled to God when we accept the forgiveness of sins."[†] Solomon was also named Jedidiah—"dear to the Lord" or "beloved of the Lord"—by the prophet Nathan. Christ is the true Jedidiah, the most beloved Son of the heavenly Father, in whom we all must be beloved. As a result we should experience God's favor and love again. Postils on the Song of Songs.[9]

[9]Gerhard, *Postilla Salomonæa*, 3-4; citing Jn 12:13; Mt 12:42; Lk 11:31; Is 9; Eph 2:14; Zech 9:10; 2 Sam 12:24; Mt 3:17; Eph 1. [†]Augustine, *City of God* 17.8 (LCL 415:282-83).

4:1-8 THE BEAUTY OF THE BRIDE

He

[4]*Behold, you are beautiful, my love,*
behold, you are beautiful!

Your eyes are doves
behind your veil.

Your hair is like a flock of goats
leaping down the slopes of Gilead.

[2]*Your teeth are like a flock of shorn ewes*
that have come up from the washing,

all of which bear twins,
and not one among them has lost its young.

[3]*Your lips are like a scarlet thread,*
and your mouth is lovely.

Your cheeks are like halves of a pomegranate
behind your veil.

[4]*Your neck is like the tower of David,*
built in rows of stone;[a]
on it hang a thousand shields,
all of them shields of warriors.

[5]*Your two breasts are like two fawns,*
twins of a gazelle,
that graze among the lilies.

[6]*Until the day breathes*
and the shadows flee,

I will go away to the mountain of myrrh
and the hill of frankincense.

[7]*You are altogether beautiful, my love;*
there is no flaw in you.

[8]*Come with me from Lebanon, my bride;*
come with me from Lebanon.

Depart[b] *from the peak of Amana,*
from the peak of Senir and Hermon,

from the dens of lions,
from the mountains of leopards.

a The meaning of the Hebrew word is uncertain **b** Or *Look*

OVERVIEW: Contemporary readers are often puzzled at the string of similes that unfold in the first half of this chapter, appearing more comical than erotic to modern sensibilities. Reformation-era interpreters, as we have seen, often downplayed the erotic dimensions of the text, seeking without embarrassment to draw edifying figural applications to Christian dogma and piety. Isidore Clarius notes the special aptitude of the female form in representing various graces, a sample of which are cataloged below. Thomas Brightman, who consistently applies his historical-apocalyptic method throughout the text, regards the description of the bride's beauty here as a fitting allusion to the purity of the church in its earliest age, when she beheld the Bridegroom incarnate with the eyes of the body. Several of our commentators find the imagery of teeth a fitting representation of the church's leadership, which masticates the Word of truth (Melchior Hoffman, Martin Luther, Johann Gerhard). Other traditional exegetical motifs—for example, breasts as sources of nourishment and delight, or the Marian reading of the tower imagery—continue to capture interpreters' imaginations, but despite the diversity in allegorical detail, all our commentators agree that these verses serve to heighten the beguiling beauty of Christ's bride.

4:1-3 *Beholding the Beauty of the Beloved*

THE GRACEFULNESS OF THE BRIDE. ISIDORE CLARIUS: Since this *epithalium* proposes to trace out for our imaginations a figure, either of the church or of some faithful soul, under the guise of bodily things, in this passage and in the following that figure is contemplated as though it were the members of a beautiful woman, from which grace especially tends to shine forth. By "your eyes" is indicated those who rank first among the people, for the eyes hold a place of primacy in the body. "Within your locks," it adds, in order to make the metaphor more graceful, because locks of hair add grace to the eyes.[†] However, among the Hebrews, "within your locks" is interpreted as "within your encampment," where the people were gathered, as if they were locks of hair.[‡] "Your hair is as flocks of goats." This refers to the weak among the people. They are, it says, like "flocks of goats, which descend from Mt. Galaad."[§] This is understood [as referring to the time] when Jacob came from Mesopotamia.[◊]

"Your teeth." Your soldiers are, it says, also strong: all of them are uninjured, and there is not a bad one among them. So undoubtedly it happens in the church of Christ, that no one of any rank is without their own splendor and beauty, so long as they profess Christ from the heart. "Your lips are like a scarlet thread." Lips are commended for this color. This signifies grace of conversation, and constancy in speech. Or, some think (not foolishly) that this alludes to the red cord that Rahab let down, and kept faith with the people [of Israel]. "Your cheeks are like a piece of pomegranate." For redness of the cheeks indicates how bashfulness and modesty render the face of the church beautiful, especially in the period of her youth. The Song of Songs of Solomon.[1]

The Bite of Apostolic Teaching. Melchior Hoffman: The teeth of Christ's bride are understood to be all the apostolic teachers standing before the face of Christ. And the false teachers are also called teeth, as are the devil's godless teachers. And God's people and elect are eaten by these apostolic teachers and preachers, as we have St. Peter in Acts 10, who received a vision that he should slaughter and eat with Cornelius along with his companions. The slaughter happened at God's command, so that they were killed, choked, and with the gospel they were then eaten by the apostolic teacher into the flesh of Christ and the people of God, and into the everlasting kingdom. In this way the apostles of the devil also eat the unbelievers into the devil's kingdom and into everlasting damnation.

As above he likened the teachers to hair and to the flock of shorn goats, so he also likens them to the teeth of such a flock and sees that they are coming out of the water. The teeth, or teachers, came to be washed and purified through the true inner baptism, which happened through fire and the spirit, and they are all purified through the death and bloodshed of Christ. Through it they are born anew and made rightly fruitful, after they have died and come up through the water, which is understood to be the true baptism, that was signified in this figure or sign.

But since all bear twins, and no tooth is unfruitful, it is understood that the two twins are the Old and New Testament, each of which bore and put in place apostolic teachers. And that Old and New Testament bring out from their heart, and are pregnant with, these same teachers. And afterward the two twins are likened to the breasts, which are mentioned above in the first chapter.

[1]Isidore, *Canticum Canticorum Salomonis*, 17v; citing Gen 31; Josh 2:21. [†]As noted in the introduction, Isidore is one of the first early modern commentators to depart from the Latin Vulgate and correct the text from Hebrew sources, and in this passage, the payoff is evident. Most modern commentaries have rendered the Hebrew "behind your veil," where Jerome's Latin had been obscure: *absque eo quod intrinsecus latet* (besides what is hid within). Isidore, working from the Hebrew and consulting medieval rabbinic commentaries, anticipates the KJV's "within thy locks." [‡]According to Rashi, "Within your kerchief, your hair is beautiful and glistens with brilliance and whiteness like the hair of white goats descending from the mountains, whose hair gleams in the distance. And in the allegorical sense, [it is said of] the congregation of Israel that within your camps and your tents, even the empty ones among you are as dear to Me as Jacob and his sons, who streamed down to descend from Mount Gilead when Laban overtook them there." *The Complete Jewish Bible with Rashi Commentary*, Chabad.org, https://www.chabad.org/library/bible_cdo/aid/16448/jewish/Chapter-4.htm. [§]The Vulgate has "come up from Mount Galaad." [◊]In Gen 31, Jacob parts company from Laban, setting out for "the hill country of Gilead" (Gen 31:18), driving his flocks and his little ones on ahead of him.

Through these teachers Christ the Word of God is also eaten and chewed, as Christ called himself food and drink in John 6. In this way Christ eats his own through the teachers and they eat him in turn through the teachers, so that they are all of one faith, spirit, and essence, which is sufficiently touched on in the twelfth chapter of Daniel. The Book of Song of Songs.[2]

The Incisive Power of the Word. Martin Luther: "Your hair is like a flock of goats that are shorn on Mount Gilead." Perhaps he is alluding to the passage in Genesis 31:25, because Jacob camped with his flocks in Gilead on his way back from Mesopotamia. However, it seems more likely to me that he is reflecting on the name of the mountain. Gilead means "mount of testimony." With this name he alludes to the temple, where the sacrifices and the other cultic acts were carried out. He compares the hair not simply to goats but to a flock of goats in order to signify the concord and agreement of those who teach among the people. Therefore he also calls the goats shorn, not because they have been clipped, but because the hairs are as even as if they had been combed.[†]

"Your teeth are like a flock of shorn ewes that have come up from the washing." As you know, one commends whiteness in teeth, darkness in eyes. Just as the image of the hair displays the agreement of the teachers among themselves, so also we see that the teeth are arranged in order and give each other help, as it were. But the function of the teeth is to bite. It is also required of a teacher that he should be powerful in arguing and convincing. However, this should be carried out in such a way that the teeth nevertheless remain white—that is, it should be done without acrimony, without bitterness and hatred, as seeking correction, not revenge. This kingdom, he says, has teachers like this.

"All of which bear twins, and not one among them is barren." He adds this in order to show forth the fruit of their ministry. For twins are brought forth whenever souls are first terrified by the law and then are raised up again by the promises, or the gospel. In the same fashion, those who rightly divide the Word see the fruit of their teaching in the church. For it simply cannot happen that teaching should go on in the church without bearing fruit, just as the text says, "not one among them is barren." A Brief but Altogether Lucid Exposition of the Song of Songs.[3]

The Church's Teachers Break Up Spiritual Food. Johann Gerhard: What is said in Solomon's Song of Songs about the spiritual bride can be conveniently accommodated and applied to either the entire church in common, as St. Paul speaks of her in 2 Corinthians 11: "I have betrothed you to a man in order that I might bring a pure virgin to Christ." Or to each individual believing soul in particular, as it stands concerning her in the Revelation 22: "The Spirit and the Bride say, 'Come, Lord Jesus.'" There is even such an opportunity with this statement of praise by which the heavenly bridegroom praises the beauty of his spiritual bride: "Your teeth are like a flock of sheep with shorn wool that come from their watering hole, which all at once bear twins, and there is not a barren one among them." For if we interpret this statement of praise to refer in common to the entire Christian church, one can readily understand the teeth on this spiritual body of Christ to refer to the teachers of the church, since teeth not only help people to formulate speech, which elegantly fits teachers and preachers since through them God the Lord speaks to the church and the church through them speaks to others. They also

[2]Hoffman, *Dat Boeck Cantica Canticorum*, 71-72; citing Rev 9:8; Ps 3:7; Rev 1; Jn 3:16.

[3]LW 15:228-29 (WA 31.2:677-80); citing 2 Tim 2:15. [†]Luther seems to be indulging in a little wordplay here: the Latin word for "shorn" (*tonsa*) is the same word used for the distinctive haircut worn by men in monastic orders. Luther himself had abandoned the tonsure when he left the Augustinian order in the 1520s, and he regarded such external marks of holiness as "sheep's clothing." See, for example, his answer to Jerome Emser (LW 39:192). Given his identification of the "flock" in this passage with the Levitical priesthood, it is hardly surprising that he wishes to avoid any confusion that holiness is a function of a haircut.

serve the purpose of letting a person chew and grind the foods that they want to take into themselves, so that they can digest the same thereafter in their stomach all the better—which also elegantly fits the teachers of the church, since they should rightly divide the Word of truth, the heavenly food for the soul and break up this bread of life for their hearers, so that those who are still tender and weak in the faith can understand it. POSTILS ON THE SONG OF SONGS.[4]

CHRIST PRAISES HIS BRIDE'S BEAUTY. THOMAS BRIGHTMAN: In the last verse of the former chapter was taught how the solemnity of the marriage began. Now the bridegroom in his own words shows how the bride was adorned. All of this is but to let us see the state and condition of the church, which Christ himself chose present here on earth, whose first arising was like a pillar of smoke but after he began his office, he came forth in a most divine glorious show, as sliding from heaven. She is first commended for her eyes, for by the sight of the eyes is often understood judgment and understanding. She was commended for this by Christ himself, who announced those eyes to be blessed that saw the things which the bride then saw. He also gave thanks to his Father, that he had hid these things from the wise and prudent, but revealed them to babes. Her eyes were dove's eyes—that is, chaste and bashful, looking only on her own husband, as demonstrated by the words of Peter himself (when others fell away), who declared that he knew not where else to go. Yet though these eyes were clear, they were within her locks—that is, they were so covered with hair that the brightness of them was somewhat hindered, the multitude of the faithful being condemned and despised. This dove-like chastity of the bride was so covered that she seemed a disorderly company to the proud Pharisees: "Do any of the elders, or of the Pharisees believe on him? But this common people that know not the law are accursed." Yet this sight was not so sharp at first, but grew by degrees; it was always pure and true, but small in the beginning: they were ignorant of the death of Christ, and much more of his resurrection. His doctrine also was often little understood: "Are you without understanding?" Neither does he upbraid them only that once with ignorance and dullness, for their hair hanging scattered and disorderly hindered their sight.

Her second praise is of the hair itself, that she might not be thought deformed by it. Now this hair indicates the whole multitude of the faithful of those times, fitly set forth by their number: her comparison to a flock of goats may be understood (if I am not deceived) partly of that which goes before, and partly of that which follows. Before, the godly Israelites scattered through the ten tribes are called goats, whose flocks are said to be less and thinner, because they scatter themselves and do not keep together, as sheep do (as Varro says in his second book of husbandry[†]). Christ, indeed, had many hearers, but few amongst them who truly believed; of many called, few were chosen. The head on whom the faithful depend is Christ, and to be with him then was thought to be a great danger, as the goats hang on the sides of Mt. Gilead, or any other steep hill or rock. "If any did confess him to be Christ, he should be cast out of the Synagogue." Therefore Nicodemus dared not be seen on this mountain of Gilead in the daytime. Such was the condition of the church at that time: her piety quick of understanding and chaste, but covered with hair and hid from the world; not having yet obtained ripeness, it was thin and reproachful, not daring to join together without great danger. COMMENTARY ON THE CANTICLES.[5]

4:4-5 *Your Neck, Your Breasts*

MARY, THE TOWER OF DAVID, DEFENDS HER SON. ARCANGELA TARABOTTI: In Mary alone did the Holy Trinity entrust the mystery of the

[4]Gerhard, *Postilla Salomonæa*, 153-54; citing 2 Cor 11:2; Rev 22:17; 2 Tim 2:15; Lam 4.

[5]Brightman, *A Commentary on the Canticles or the Song of Salomon*, 1017-18; citing Lk 10:23, 21; Jn 6:68; 7:48-49; Mt 15:26; Song 1:8; Jn 9:22. [†]Varro, *Rerum rusticarum* 2.3.9.

incarnation; in her alone for nine months did the Holy Trinity entrust within her sealed womb heaven's most precious treasure—to confound men's treacherous tongues, croaking their usual lies about "women's loquaciousness." Men's foolhardy dreams devised impossible machinations; one woman alone, declaring herself the handmaid of the Lord, became a strong tower, reaching beyond the stars and making them a crown for herself: "the tower of David, which is built with bulwarks: a thousand bucklers hang on it, all the armor of valiant men." If the Holy Spirit was the Architect and Builder of this tower, will it not be fully armed? Not only was Mary a treasure chest of God's secrets, a tower that reached the heavens, but also a temple within a temple within which are adored all the wonders of the Almighty God Most High. Paternal Tyranny.[6]

Ornament and Use. Henry Ainsworth: These are both for ornament and for use, as both experience in nature and the Scriptures show. For God says to his church, "You arrived at full adornment; your breasts were formed, . . ." and he also shows their use, that her children and lovers "may nurse and be satisfied from her consoling breast." So here the "breasts" of Christ's spouse are compared to "roes" for pleasantness, to "fawns," or young roes, for smallness, to "twins" for equalizing, and to roes feeding among the lilies, as in fat and sweet pasture. This signifies how the church is fruitful in good works and words of comfort, and communication of all God's blessings, so that by her loving affection, wholesome doctrines, sweet consolations, and gracious beneficence her children are delighted, and sucking "the sincere milk of the Word, do grow thereby." Annotations upon the Song of Songs.[7]

[6]Tarabotti, *Paternal Tyranny*, 126*. The Litany of Loreto, approved by Pope Sixtus V in 1587, speaks of Mary as the tower of David. A justification for this title can be found in John Henry Newman, *Meditations and Devotions* (London: Longmans, Green, 1916), 99-101.

[7]Ainsworth, *Annotations*, 2:713-14; citing Ezek 16:7; Is 66:11; 1 Pet 2:2.

4:6-8 *You Are Altogether Beautiful, My Love*

Otherworldly Beauty. Melchior Hoffman: This beauty comes, as stated above, when the bride turns wholly around and stands, alone in hope, submitted to Christ her Bridegroom in patience and longsuffering and in longing and praying for the sake of the Bridegroom. She has no comfort or confidence in anything that belongs to the world or to the ruler of this world, nor any haughtiness of the eyes. In this way the bride is purified of all spots and flaws, and all the muck of the world and the children of the world, and all creatures of and everything that belongs to the world. Nor does she have any mean wrinkles or evil inclination to cunning or bitterness or any haughtiness of the eyes. These wrinkles are all far from her and cannot be found on her. The Book of Song of Songs.[8]

Christ Calls His Mother at Her Death. Chiara Matraini: When the time had come for the purest mother of the Son of God to loose herself from her bodily limbs and receive the prize and crown of infinite glory, her beloved and most sweet Son made it known to her through his usual ambassador, the archangel Gabriel, that she soon had to leave these our worldly miseries and ascend to heaven, above all the choirs of angels, to enjoy the happiness prepared for her by her most loving Son. Hearing the longed-for news, the Blessed Virgin thanked the supreme and merciful God for his divine grace and very humbly and joyfully prepared herself for her journey, receiving the most holy sacraments to fulfill all the evangelical commandments and directions. Among these is the teaching concerning being prepared and ready for death, something for which she felt no grief, nor did she fear devils, nor the sentence of judgment, since she knew she had never sinned in any way. On the contrary, she even rejoiced, and felt remarkable happiness, as she was to be with Christ,

[8]Hoffman, *Dat Boeck Cantica Canticorum*, 77.

her sweetest and beloved son who, calling her, said to her, "Come from Libanus, my spouse, come from Libanus, Come," inviting her with such dear and sweet words to leave the world and rise up to his longed-for presence. As she heard herself called so sweetly, she breathed her most holy soul out of her body and felt great and incredible sweetness in the parting. Brief Discourse.[9]

[9]Colonna, Matraini, and Marinella, *Who Is Mary?*, 115.

4:9-16 MY LOVE IS A GARDEN

9 You have captivated my heart, my sister, my bride;
you have captivated my heart with one glance of your eyes,
with one jewel of your necklace.

10 How beautiful is your love, my sister, my bride!
How much better is your love than wine,
and the fragrance of your oils than any spice!

11 Your lips drip nectar, my bride;
honey and milk are under your tongue;
the fragrance of your garments is like the fragrance of Lebanon.

12 A garden locked is my sister, my bride,
a spring locked, a fountain sealed.

13 Your shoots are an orchard of pomegranates
with all choicest fruits,
henna with nard,

14 nard and saffron, calamus and cinnamon,
with all trees of frankincense,

myrrh and aloes,
with all choice spices—

15 a garden fountain, a well of living water,
and flowing streams from Lebanon.

16 Awake, O north wind,
and come, O south wind!

Blow upon my garden,
let its spices flow.

She

Let my beloved come to his garden,
and eat its choicest fruits.

Overview: This passage raises interesting exegetical challenges for our interpreters, in terms of both the narrative voice and the imagery it deploys. Many Reformation-era expositors were troubled by the intense language of passion associated with the voice of the bridegroom here—recall that in classical philosophy, the "passions" represent not merely an intense experience of emotion but one that overpowers the reason and distorts the will. Accordingly, our interpreters struggle to make sense of the notion that a text referring to Christ would indicate his heart being "stolen," as though against his will. François Lambert avoids the difficulty by an adroit translation, and then pivots to a very "Lutheran" contrast between faith and good works. Thomas Brightman continues his historical-apocalyptic schema, associating the imagery with a scene in the middle chapters of the Acts of the Apostles. John Trapp gets nearer the mark with his translation, preserving the passionate character of the Hebrew, but explains in good Augustinian/Reformed fashion that what really "ravishes" Christ's heart is the perception of his own Word taking root in the believing soul. The imagery of the garden in the closing verses of the chapter provides ample scope for allegorical elaboration. John Cotton's elaboration of ten periods of persecution may seem contrived to modern readers, but many of the details of his exegesis apply more broadly beyond the specific historical circumstances he had in mind. Contrast the specificity of Cotton's allegorizing with the more generalized reflections on the doctrine of providence in Richard Sibbes, and it is clear that the two approaches are not so far removed.

4:9-11 *You Have Stolen My Heart*

The Bride's Adornments Come from Faith. François Lambert: The bride's eyes are the senses, and the judgments of God's Spirit, as we stated at the beginning of this chapter. The throat signifies faith; a necklace is placed about her throat, and what can this be aside from faith, since works come from faith? Then the bride has two eyes, because so long as she lives in the flesh, she has need of both spiritual and carnal judgment. The first is pleasing to Christ, the second displeasing, because it is contrary to it, from which she will be completely free when the old Adam is slain and the tabernacle of the body is dissolved by death. She also has two necklaces: one of the true faith, the other a counterfeit. The latter is hypocrisy—that is, work that appears to be good on the surface but does not come from faith; the former is truly good work, which is from faith. The first is acceptable to the bridegroom; the other he hates intensely. Commentary on the Song of Songs.[1]

The Church in Antioch. Thomas Brightman: This "eye" and "chain"[†] are the church of Antioch enclosed within the mountains of Amana and Lebanon. By the labor and diligence of Paul and Barnabas, and the working of the Spirit, the bridegroom was with good cause ravished with this eye, which shined with great light. Yet the beauty of this eye chiefly glistened when the church withstood those who were arguing to keep the law joined with Christ, and when Barnabas and Paul maintained that faith alone in Christ was sufficient to salvation in the synod of the apostles at Jerusalem. And then was the chain hung about her neck, when she was first called a Christian. The humanity of Christ was before the neck of the church, now the name of Christ is the chain around that neck. And being a Gentile, yet she is now a sister to the Jewish church. And to show that she is as dear to him as the Jewish church, he calls her also his spouse. Commentary on the Canticles.[2]

Christ Ravished by His Own Handiwork. John Trapp: "You have ravished my heart." You have caught it and carried it from me, so that I am least master of it, for "the heart is where it loves, and not where it lives."[†] The Hebrew is, "you have behearted me," as we might say that one is beheaded, behipt, and so on. You have robbed me of my heart, and set yourself in its place; "your love is fixed in the table of my heart," so the Chaldee[‡] expounds it. . . . And surely when the saints hide Christ's words in their hearts, as his mother Mary did, when they give themselves wholly up to it, as the Macedonians do, so that the Word of Christ "indwells richly in them in all wisdom," and he by his Spirit puts "his laws into their minds" so that they assent to them, and "into their hearts" so that they consent to them, and have the comfort, feeling, and fruit of them, then is his heart ravished with his own handiwork—then is he so far in love with such a soul as that, like Esther, she may have anything she wants from the king. "The king can do nothing against you"—Christ seriously says this. His heart has become a very "lump of love" toward his sister, as near to him in consanguinity as his spouse is in affinity. So Christ is endeared to all his people in all manner of near relations. For whosoever does the will of his Father is his brother, and sister, and mother. Solomon's Book of All Virtues.[3]

[1]Lambert, *In Cantica Canticorum Salomonis*, 67r-68v; citing Gal 5:17.

[2]Brightman, *A Commentary on the Canticles or the Song of Salomon*, 1023; citing Eccles 4:8; Acts 15; 11:26. [†]The KJV renders this end of this verse, "With one of thine eyes, with one chaine of thy neck."

[3]Trapp, *Solomonis ΠΑΝΆΡΕΤΟΣ*, 255; citing Col 3:16; Heb 8:10; Jer 38:5; Mt 12:50. [†]Numerous early modern sources (including Trapp) mistakenly attribute this saying to Augustine; however, Bernard of Clairvaux is the actual source (SChr 457:276). [‡]The Chaldee Paraphrase is another term for the Aramaic Targum on the Song of Songs, an exegetical tradition that had probably crystallized by the seventh century.

4:12-15 *You Are a Garden Locked Up*

The Purity of Synagogue and Church Preserved. Martin Luther: Another praiseworthy characteristic of this people! He commends the people because they are bound by most excellent laws, regulated by circumcision and other rites, and what is most important of all, sealed by the promises, by which they are distinguished from all other people. In the same way we Christians are now sealed by the Word, baptism, and the sacrament of the altar, by which we are distinguished from all other races, not just before the world, but rather in God's own judgment. A Brief but Altogether Lucid Exposition of the Song of Songs[4]

Living Water Quenches Thirsty Hearts. David Joris: Hear, O you fruitful good trees of righteousness planted at the flowing waters. These were meant to divide up into many lovely rivers, in order to moisten all lovely places. And to gladden, I say, the thorny, dry places. Namely, the thirsty, believing hearts that cry and weep for the quiet, running, clear water, which flows under the threshold of God. It flows out of the sides into all the larger waters, in order to make healthy all living animals therein. A Blessed Instruction for the Hungering, Burdened Souls.[5]

The Church in an Age of Persecution. John Cotton: After the church is gathered by the ministry of the apostles, next follows a representation of the church under the ten persecutions, which is here described: first, by her restraint, second, by her privacy, and third, by her fruitfulness, refreshing and watering others, and fourth, by her prayer in this condition. . . .[†]

"A garden." The church is here so called, as in verse 13, an "orchard," or as it is in the original, a "paradise," as if this were the Garden of Eden.[†] All the world is like a wilderness, or at least a wild field, but the church is God's garden or orchard, in these three respects: First, as the garden of paradise was the habitation of Adam in the state of innocence, so is the church of all those who are renewed into innocence. Second, as in that garden were all manner of pleasant and wholesome herbs and trees growing, so in the church are all manner of useful and savory spirits. Third, as a man walks in his garden to refresh himself, so does Christ walk in his church, and he calls his friends there to walk with him.

"A spring, a fountain." Not because the church is the fountain of grace, but because, Christ being in it, it is the spring or fountain of the waters of life for all. "A garden, spring, fountain enclosed, shut up, sealed." Not by a pale or wall of defense by Christian magistrates, but rather shut up by restraint, for the word signifies to enclose or shut up, as with locks and fetters. Again, the church prays for the enlargement of the flowing of her spices, and therefore her present shutting up was uncomfortable to her. The church was then said to be shut up, first, because under the persecutions it was shut up in prisons, and other places of punishment, as under locks and fetters. Second, because the church was then assembled in private, closed places—woods, dens, and so on—and not in the open places of towns or cities. Third, because it was shut up from free access of foreigners, people without. Neither were the emperors willing that their subjects should come to them, nor the church willing to admit all promiscuously.

"Your plants." That is, your children or members, as an orchard of pomegranates, camphor, spikenard, saffron, calamus, cinnamon. The children of the church are compared to these wholesome and sweet fruits, trees, and herbs in two ways: First, because the virtues of these fruits and spices are especially seen when they are cut and poured out, or beaten, burned, or bruised. So it is with the graces of God's children: they are chiefly exercised by the hard dealing of persecutors. Second, there was in the faithful who were persecuted a resemblance to the virtues of these [particular] fruits and spices.

[4]LW 15:234 (WA 31.2:695-96).
[5]CRR 7:252*.

"Pomegranates" repress and restrain the heat of choler, the malignity of fevers, the looseness of the belly; they also comfort the stomach and the bowels, and they prevent fainting and swooning.[§] "Camphor" delights and strengthens the spirits with its sweetness of smell; it cheers up the mind, helps the stone, and restrains ulcers. "Spikenard" prevents distillations from the head, strengthens the stomach, digests cold humors, and helps conception. "Saffron" thins phlegm, helps lethargy, coughs, and pleurisy, aids digestion, comforts the heart, and redresses the rottenness of other parts, which it also strengthens. "Calamus" helps the passage of urine and the faults of the reins,[◊] and it helps the womb and conception. "Cinnamon" strengthens and cheers the spirits and the mind; it dries up rotten matter, helps against poison, and it warms and strengthens the stomach for digestion. "Frankincense" restrains and helps ulcers, gout, fluxes of the blood, and it cleans and heals wounds and ulcers. "Myrrh" refreshes the brain, dries up superfluous humors, helps straightness of breath, restrains ulcers and itchiness, and fills ulcers and wounds with flesh. "Aloes" cleanse tough phlegm and choler, dry up raw and cold humors, preserve the rest from putrefaction, open obstructions, and strengthen the stomach strongly.

Suitable to the virtues of these fruits and spice, persecution bred and stirred up in the faithful grace of similar efficacy, restraining heats of emulation, contention, and ambition; repressing ulcers of malignity and disaffection to one another; healing the coldness, hypocrisy, and rottenness of their spirits; staying distillations of cold raw matters, dropping from the head bishops of Rome; also strengthening their appetite for the word, comforting the faint-hearted, and knitting the members together.

"A fountain of gardens." . . . For the church, pouring out her confessions and martyrdoms for the truth, propagated and watered many churches, for *sanguis martyrum* was *semen ecclesiae*, a "well of living waters."[Δ] The church was not then dried up, but plentifully stored with the graces of the Spirit, "streams from Lebanon." A Brief Exposition on the Whole Book of Canticles.[6]

4:16 *Awake, North Wind*

Christ Orders All for the Good of His Church. Richard Sibbes: We see here that Christ sends forth his Spirit to command all means, under the name of "north" and "south wind," to further the fruitfulness of his church. The wind is nature's fan; what winds are to the garden, the Spirit of Christ is to the soul in the use of means. From this comparison we may observe that all creatures stand in obedience to Christ, as ready at a word, whenever he speaks to them. They are all as it were asleep until he awakes them. He can call for the wind out of his treasures when he pleases, for he holds them in his fist. This should comfort all those who are Christ's that they are under one who has all creatures at his beck under him, to do them service, and at his check, to do them no harm. This drew the disciples in admiration to say, "What manner of man is this, that even the winds and the seas obey him?" And cannot the same power still

[6]Cotton, *Brief Exposition*, 130-34; citing Zach 13:1; Ps 87:7; Jn 4:10. [†]Cotton's reference to the "ten persecutions" echoes John Foxe's description of the sufferings of the early church under the Roman Empire. Drawing on the *Magdeburg Centuries* and Eusebius of Caesarea's *Ecclesiastical History*, Foxe enumerated ten periods of persecution, beginning with the emperor Nero in AD 67 and concluding with the emperor Diocletian in 303. [‡]The Hebrew *gan* is used both for the "locked garden" of Song 4:12 and of the "Garden of Eden" in Gen 2. Association between the two gardens was a commonplace in patristic and medieval exegesis. [§]In medieval and early modern medical lore, choler was one of the four bodily humors, associated with yellow bile. An excess of choler was thought to produce a peevish, irascible temperament. [◊]An archaic term for the kidneys, thought to be the seat of the affections or strong emotion; thus Sir Philipp Sidney renders Ps 7:10: "Thou righteous proofes to hartes and reines dost send." [Δ]Cotton alludes to the famous line often attributed to Tertullian (160–220), "The blood of the martyrs is the seed of the church." The actual line in Tertullian's *Apology* reads, "The oftener we are mown down by you, the more in number we grow; the blood of Christians is seed" (*Apology* 50.13; ANF 3:55). Foxe, in the 1583 edition of his *Actes and Monuments*, gives a slightly different version of the quotation: "Tertullian hath well sayde, that the bloud of Martyrs is the seed of the Gospell" (2133). The precise origin of the quotation *sanguis martyrum semen ecclesiae* is obscure, but it well captures the spirit of Tertullian's argument.

the winds and waves of the churches and states, and cause a sudden calm if (as the disciples did) we awake him with our prayers?

Second, we see here that Christ speaks to winds contrary to one another, both in regard of the coasts from whence they blow and in their quality. But both agree in this, that both are necessary for the garden. From this we see that the courses that Christ takes, and the means that he uses with his church may seem contrary, but by a wise ordering all agree in the wholesome issue. A prosperous and an afflicted condition are contrary; a mild and a sharp course may seem to cross one another. Yet sweetly they agree in this, that as the church needs both, so Christ uses both for the church's good. The north is a nipping wind, and the south is a cherishing wind, therefore the south wind is more welcome and sweet after the north wind has blown. Nevertheless, all things are ours: "Paul, Apollos, Cephas, things present and to come, life, death . . . ." And, "all things work together for good" to us, being in Christ. So it is the manifold wisdom of Christ makes use of such variety of conditions, and so it is that the Spirit of Christ is mild in some people's ministries and sharp in others—nay, in the very same minister, as the state of the soul they have to deal with requires.

Sometimes again the people of God need purging, and sometimes refreshing. For this reason the Spirit of God carries itself suitably to both conditions, and the Spirit in the godly themselves draws good out of every condition, sure as they are that all winds blow them good; were it not for their good, no winds would blow on them. But in regard to these times of ours, by long peace and plenty we grow cold, heavy, and secure, we need all kinds of winds to blow on us, and all little enough. Time was when we were more quick and lively; but now the heat of our spirits are abated. We must therefore take heed of it, and "quicken those things that are ready to die," or else instead of the north and south wind, God will send an east wind that shall dry up all.

Again, if Christ can raise or lay, bind up or let loose all kinds of winds at his pleasure, then if means be wanting or fruitless it is he who says to the clouds, "Do not rain," and to the winds, "Do not blow." Therefore, we must acknowledge him in want or plenty of means. The Spirit of Christ in the use of means is a free agent, sometimes blowing strongly, sometimes more mildly, sometimes not at all. No creature has these winds in a bag at command. Therefore it is wisdom to yield to the gales of the Spirit, though in some other things (as Solomon observes) it may hinder to observe the winds, yet here it is necessary and profitable to observe the winds of the Spirit.[†] Bowels Opened.[7]

[7]Sibbes, *Bowels Opened*, 6-9; citing Mt 8:27; 1 Cor 3:22; Rom 8:28; Rev 3:2; Hos 13:15. [†]Sibbes is referring to Eccles 11:4: "He that observeth the wind shall not sow; and he that regardeth the clouds shall not reap," a passage that warns against being paralyzed by a fear of natural forces beyond one's control. Sibbes acknowledges the practical wisdom inherent in the proverb, while setting it in the wider context of a trust in God's providence.

5:1-8 TOGETHER IN THE GARDEN OF LOVE

He

[1]*I came to my garden, my sister, my bride,*
I gathered my myrrh with my spice,
I ate my honeycomb with my honey,
I drank my wine with my milk.

Others

Eat, friends, drink,
and be drunk with love!

She

[2]*I slept, but my heart was awake.*

A sound! My beloved is knocking.

"Open to me, my sister, my love,
my dove, my perfect one,

for my head is wet with dew,
my locks with the drops of the night."

[3]*I had put off my garment;*
how could I put it on?

I had bathed my feet;
how could I soil them?

[4]*My beloved put his hand to the latch,*
and my heart was thrilled within me.

[5]*I arose to open to my beloved,*
and my hands dripped with myrrh,

my fingers with liquid myrrh,
on the handles of the bolt.

[6]*I opened to my beloved,*
but my beloved had turned and gone.

My soul failed me when he spoke.

I sought him, but found him not;
I called him, but he gave no answer.

[7]*The watchmen found me*
as they went about in the city;

they beat me, they bruised me,
they took away my veil,
those watchmen of the walls.

[8]*I adjure you, O daughters of Jerusalem,*
if you find my beloved,

that you tell him
I am sick with love.

Overview: The exegesis of this passage is complicated by disagreements over where the section ends, and who is speaking. For many of our commentators, 5:1 belongs at the end of chapter 4, and represents a climactic moment of bliss where the lovers are united in a garden of delights; 5:2 thus opens a new sequence, which finds the lovers separated once again. Others follow the chapter separation and view the bride's slumber in verse 2 as made possible by the bridegroom's presence within the garden. No matter which approach they take, all of our commentators focus their attentions on explaining the scene's horticultural imagery, often with dramatically different results. Konrad Pellikan, for example, sees this imagery as pointing to the eschatological consummation of Christ's fellowship with his elect; Martin Luther, however, sees the garden as the civic space in which faithful Christians exercise their vocations. Many of our commentators are concerned to qualify the passage's imagery commending drunkenness, and John Trapp manages to do so without sounding dour. Beginning in verse 2, our commentators seek to locate the account of the bride's slumber within a wider narrative frame. Richard Sibbes expounds this passage according to what the medievals called the "mystical sense," as pertaining to the spiritual struggle within the soul of individual Christians.

Luther, by contrast, continues with his political scheme of interpretation, applying it to the various ills that beset even the best-ordered polities. Thomas Brightman and John Cotton see in this episode a coded reference to the post-Constantinian church, which, having been brought into the garden of sound teaching by the ministry of the church fathers, now fell into drowsiness and decay in the centuries that followed. One result of this fall into superstition was the bride's abandonment of her "garment" (Song 5:3), which John Calvin and Brightman read as an image of Christ's imputed righteousness.

5:1 *I Came to My Garden*

A Vision of the Saints' Future Bliss. Konrad Pellikan: Now the soul's bridegroom, Christ, ascending to the heavens speaks to his bride, the church, "I entered into my garden by the dispensation of the flesh, into my Father's kingdom, which he gave to me and to my friends. I will recline there at the table with the elect, and I will eat and drink of the fruits of the vine, ambrosia and nectar. There I will offer you the myrrh I have gathered with its aromas; I will return to you a share of all my good things, and I will make you to share in my priceless goods. For now, instead of the bitter gall of the most bitter death I suffered for you, I eat from of the honeycomb of happiness, and I enjoy the most delicious honey of the glory of God the Father, at whose right hand I now sit, drinking the wine of infinite joy and eating the fat of all delicacies. Therefore come, you blessed by my Father, enter into the kingdom prepared for you by my Father and won by my merits, and remain here with me forever in happiness. Rejoice with me in blessedness, and I will give you eternal life, and every good and perfect gift." A Succinct and Universal Commentary on the Bible.[1]

Testimony of a Clean Conscience. Martin Luther: You, my God, have planted this garden, this government; therefore come, tend and conserve it with your Word and Spirit, lest it perish from neglect. Eat of its noblest fruits—that is, make it clear to us by your presence that all these things please you. . . . "I have come into my garden." The prayer has been heard. For he indicates that he is present and tests everything and that everything pleases him. This is the testimony of conscience that godly people experience in their office and calling; when they serve their calling, they can affirm with certainty that God approves their works and is pleased by them, even if they are somewhat negligent in certain respects, for remission of sins is not excluded here either. A Brief but Altogether Lucid Exposition of the Song of Songs.[2]

Holy Drunkenness. John Trapp: By Christ's friends here understand those earthly angels, the saints whom he cheers up and encourages to fall to it lustily, and by a *sancta crapula* [holy drunkenness], as Luther calls a holy gluttony,[†] to lay on, to feed hard, and to fetch hearty drafts till they be even "drunk with love" (as the Hebrew here has it), being ravished with the love of God, where they are sure to find it (as in honeypots) the deeper the sweeter. Those who eat like this are called Christ's friends, and those who drink like this his beloved, as Gregory rightly observes here.[‡] And the only ones who do this are those who hear the Word with delight, turn it into juice and blood, mix it and incorporate it, as it were, into their very souls, and are so deeply affected with it that, like drunken people, they forget and let go of all other things, that they may retain it and practice it. People like this are not drunk with wine, which leads to excess, but filled with the Holy Ghost. Solomon's Book of All Virtues.[3]

[1]Pellikan, *Commentaria bibliorum et illa brevia quidem ac catholica*, 269v.

[2]LW 15:236 (WA 31.2:703).

[3]Trapp, *Solomonis ΠΑΝΑΡΕΤΟΣ*, 269; citing Jn 15:14; Is 41:8; Jas 2:23; Eph 5:16. [†]Commenting on Gen 49:12 ("His eyes shall be red with wine"), Luther remarks, "It is the voice and the glory of the churches that we have been bound to the vine in order that we

5:2 *I Slept, but My Heart Was Awake*

A Confession and a Correction. Richard Sibbes: The church, as she consists of a double principle, flesh and spirit mingled together in all parts, as darkness and light in the twilight and dawning of the day—so here she expresses her condition in regard to both parts: so far as she was carnal, she slept; so far as she was spiritual, she was awake. In this mixed condition, the flesh for the present prevailed, but still the Spirit had his working: "She slept, but her heart waked." The words contain a confession ("I sleep"), and a correction ("but my heart wakes"). She has a double aspect: one to the ill (her sleeping), the other to her good (her heart in some degree awakened). The Spirit of God is a discerning Spirit; he discovers what is flesh and what is spirit.

We must not imagine this sleep to be that dead sleep all people are in by nature, nor that judicial sleep, that spirit of slumber that is a further degree of that natural sleep, to which God gives up some as a seal of their desperate condition. Rather, what is meant here is that sleep which arises out of the remainder of unsubdued corruption and is now prevailing in the church over her better part. Flesh and spirit have both their intercourse in us, as Moses and Amalek had; unless we stand on our guard, the flesh will get the upper ground, as we see here. The best are no further safe than they are watchful. . . .

You see here then first of all in this correction that Christians have two principles in them: that which is good and that which is evil. From the latter issues the weakness of actions and affections; they are all mixed, as are the principles from which they come forth. We may observe further that Christians may know how it is with themselves, though they be mixed of flesh and spirit, for they have a distinguishing knowledge and judgment, whereby they know both the good and the evil in themselves. In a dungeon where there is nothing but darkness . . . they can see nothing. But where there is a supernatural principle, where there is this mixture, there the light of the Spirit searches the dark corners of the heart. A person who has the Spirit knows both: they know themselves and their own heart. The Spirit has a light of its own, even as reason does. How does reason know what it knows? By a reflex act inbred in the soul. If a person in their natural state [i.e., unregenerate] may reflect on their condition and know what they know, what they think, what they do, may not the soul that is raised to a higher estate know as much? Undoubtedly it may. Besides, we have the Spirit of God, which is light, and self-evidencing, it shows us where it is and what it is. The work of the Spirit may sometimes be hindered, as in times of temptation, and then I confess that a person may look wholly on corruption, and so mistake themselves, in judging by that which they see present in themselves, and not by the other principle that is concealed for a time within them. But a Christian, when they are not in such a temptation, know their own estate, and can distinguish between the principles in them, of the flesh and spirit, grace and nature. . . .

God's children never totally fall from grace; though they sleep, yet their hearts are awake. The prophet Isaiah, speaking of the church and children of God, says, "It shall be as a tree, as an oak whose substance is in them, when they cast their leaves." Though you see neither fruit, nor leaves, still there is life in the root: "the seed remains in them." There is always a seed remaining, for it is an immortal seed by which we are begotten. Peter, when he denied his master, was like an oak that was weather-beaten, yet there was still life in the root, for without a doubt, Peter loved Christ

may be made drunk with the Holy Spirit. . . . For we are not drunk with the wine that makes life dissolute and disordered; but this is a holy drunkenness [*sancta crapula*] by which we become accustomed to salutary discipline and diligence in the control of our morals for this life and for fleeing fornications and promiscuous lusts to such an extent that we abstain even from the slightest cursing with the tongue and have a tongue that blesses, heals, and comforts. For Christians do not execrate, curse, or swear falsely, as drunkards and madmen are accustomed to do; but a wholesome life results from that drunkenness, when Christians keep themselves from all vices and crimes and only proclaim and praise the wonderful works of God." LW 8:252-52. ‡Gregory of Nyssa, *Homilies on the Song of Songs* (hom. 10).

from his heart. . . . This is a sound doctrine and comforting; it agrees with Scripture and with the experience of God's people. We must therefore not lose it, but make use of it against the time of temptation. There are some pulses that indicate life in the sickest person; so also there are some breathings and spiritual motions of the heart that will comfort in such times. These two never fail on God's part: his love, which is unchangeable, and his grace, which is a fruit of his love. And two on our part: the impression of that love, and the gracious work of the new creature. "Christ never dies" (says the apostle): as he never dies in himself (after his resurrection), so he never dies in his children. There is always spiritual life. Bowels Opened.[4]

A Prophecy of Future Suffering. Martin Luther: A new section begins here. Up to this point he has been describing the very lovely period of peace that flourished under Solomon and has been expressing his thanks for it. Now he looks forward to times to come and sees that because of the sins of the people both the government and the priesthood are to be afflicted in turn by various ills. For just as there are changes of weather, so war follows peace, happiness follows sorrow, consolation follows affliction—and then some new affliction follows consolation. Solomon deals with these alternations almost to the end of this book and gives a general description of the trials that are to come. "This is the way it must always be in this kingdom; from time to time we shall be tested, exercised by various calamities, and so on."

"I sleep, and my heart is awake." "I sleep—I am now enjoying a deep peace, I am secure, and everything is calm. Nonetheless, my heart is awake, for I see the sins of the people, I see God threatening evils through his Word. And so I am anxious about the evil to come. . . ." "The voice of my beloved as he knocks!" This is where the cross begins. "The voice of one knocking" is a voice of terror bent on purging clean, lest in her smugness she lose her present possessions. For the cross is necessary and useful for us. "He who loves his son increases his whippings," he says in Proverbs. "Open to me, my love, . . . for my head . . . ." This is an accusation against the bride. "The peace that you have enjoyed up to this point has made you slothful. You lie in bed and let me stand drenched by the night rains outside the doors; that is, you neglect me, you administer the government and the priesthood with equal negligence. My head and all my locks are wet; that is, your leaders in both realms go unheeded. . . ." "I have put off my garment." "I am lying down naked, I cannot get up." This signifies not only the guilt of neglecting the Word, but also rebellion. On account of her sins, she does not wish to obey God submissively in his visitation. She does not want to lose her peace, but she persists in her sins nevertheless. A Brief but Altogether Lucid Exposition of the Song of Songs.[5]

The Constantinian Fall. Thomas Brightman: This drowsiness crept in in the time of Constantine, when a gasping heaviness with a continual desire of sleeping so oppressed the spouse that the sharpest-sighted pastors could not use their outward senses: not perceiving how ambition crept in among the bishops, and not only that, but now they began to consecrate temples to saints, earnestly to seek their relics, to worship them with prayers, and to believe that prayers made in the honor of saints at their sepulchers did much profit. Who could now tell whether the church was sleeping or waking, who neither loathed nor perceived such things? When Constantine was dead, Christ found the church asleep, and sought by all means to stir her up, both by knocking and calling. He knocked by persecutions in the times of Constans, Julian, and Valens, of whom, though Julian was a professed enemy, the other two exceeded him in cruelty. After their tyrannical reign, God stirred up Valentinian in the West, by whom Christ lovingly called his spouse, that returning to her former integrity she should

[4]Sibbes, *Bowels Opened*, 90-91, 107-8, 112-13; citing Is 6:13.

[5]LW 15:237-38 (WA 31.2:705-7); citing Prov 13:24.

open and let him in. Then taking away Valens, he called more earnestly at both doors, as it were, as well in the West as in the East, by Gratian and Theodosius the elder, and after by Arcadius and Honorius, then by Theodosius the Younger and Valentinian III. And last (that there might be four pair, as it were, answerable to the four voices: my sister, my love, my dove, my undefiled one) by Marcian alone in the East. These emperors studied and labored very religiously to defend and enlarge true religion, but the church was all in the fault, who having these helps prepared would not use them to recover her former brightness. To this readiness of the emperors was added the voice of the most excellent bishops and best learned men of that time: as Basil, Gregory, Nazianzen, Ambrose, Jerome, Chrysostom, Augustine, and other lights of that time. But seeing that his profession of love could not move her, he tried shutting the doors at night. "My head," he says, "is filled with dew, and my locks with the drops of night." The locks of hair signified before the congregation of the faithful, among whom true religion was now so much decayed by new and foolish ceremonies, borrowed partly from the Jews and Gentiles, and partly invented out of their own idle brains, that the grass is scarce more covered with drops of dew in the night than the church was at that time with superstitions. Commentary on the Canticles.[6]

Medieval Superstition. John Cotton: Constantine came into the church and enjoyed its fellowship, partaking of all its parts. He also richly endowed it, so that the church and all her friends ate and drank abundantly of wealth, preferments, and so on, and for this reason she fell into a deep sleep. . . .

"I sleep, but my heart wakes." Now follows [5:2–6:4] the description of the estate of the church from Constantine's time to the time of the restoration of the gospel and reform of the church by the ministry of Luther, and other recent divines. After Constantine had largely endowed the church with peace, wealth, and honor, it fell into a state of carnal security. . . . The church, overflowing with abundance of prosperity in Constantine's time, neglected the purity and power both of doctrine and of worship, and received corruptions, such as prayers to saints, building of temples to them, superstitions regarding their relics, the worship of images, ceremonies annexed to the sacraments, choice of meats, affecting and applauding monkish life, purgatory, and so on.

"My heart wakes." The church was still awake: First, to hearty devotion, according to their knowledge of it (and beyond it). Second, to discern such gross heresies as quenched the heart and life of Christianity, such as the impiety of Arius, denying the godhead of Christ; of Macedonius and Eunomius, denying the personhood of the Holy Ghost; of Nestorius, dividing the persons in Christ; of Eutyches, confounding their natures. But other straw and stubble built on the foundation they neglected.

"It is the voice of my beloved that knocks, saying, 'Open!'" Christ used good means to awaken his spouse, and to raise her up from this carnal security. First, he called to her in the voice of various good divines, who complained of the intolerable burden of human inventions that defiled common Christians. Christ complains of this here: his locks and hair were full of the drops of the night, drops that the coldness of religion and the darkness of ignorance had engendered. Second, he knocked by means of the blows that Constantius, Valens, and Julian gave to the church: the two former persecuted the orthodox bishops, ministers, and other Christians in favor of the Arians, while Julian made a flat apostasy from the church and subtly supplanted the nursing of religion. A Brief Exposition on the Whole Book of Canticles.[7]

Against Soul Sleep. The Thirty-Three Articles: Observe that perishable, sinful flesh and blood cannot possess the eternal, imperishable, but

[6]Brightman, *A Commentary on the Canticles or the Song of Salomon*, 1031-32.

[7]Cotton, *Brief Exposition*, 139-44.

it must be renewed and glorified by God through the death and resurrection. Just as when a person falls into a deep sleep, and their heart, soul, or body does not sleep as completely as the body, so also the spirit or soul of human beings does not die or pass away with the body, but is and remains an immortal spirit. Death, Hell, and Damnation.[8]

Spiritual Wakefulness. Johann Gerhard: But what does "to awaken" and "to be awake" mean? How must one arrange matters so that one follows the admonition of Christ and of the holy apostles, and so that one could also say with the spiritual bride, "My heart is awake"? Some have wanted to understand this to refer to the alertness of the body and of the soul at the same time, as cognate words are used also among the Greeks to refer to both kinds of being awake (*agrypnein/grēgorein*). And there can be no doubt that also in the sleep of the body one ought to maintain a proper limit, since those who are too dedicated to sleep are negligent in the performance of the work to which they have been called. But in our brief passage we have the clearest explanation that this wakefulness should be properly understood of the alertness of the heart or of the soul, which Christ also teaches when he says in the gospel of the next Sunday in the series, "So now be awake"—or awaken—"at all times." But if it is not possible to be awake at all times in the body, because sleep is necessary for the preservation of the nature of a human being, then also staying awake bodily must be of little value, if spiritual awakening or the watching of the heart is not present. Postils on the Song of Songs.[9]

5:3-5 *I Had Put Off My Garment*

Forgiveness Not a License for Sin. John Calvin: It is the most worthless of slanders to say people are invited to sin, when we affirm the free forgiveness of sins in which we assert righteousness consists. For we say that it is of such great value that it cannot be paid for by any good of ours. Therefore, it can never be obtained except as a free gift. Now for us indeed it is free, but not so for Christ, who dearly bought it at the cost of his most sacred blood, apart from which there was no ransom of sufficient worth to satisfy God's judgment. When people are taught this, they are made aware that they cannot do anything to prevent the shedding of his most sacred blood as often as they sin. Furthermore, we say that our foulness is such that it can never be cleansed except by the fountain of this purest blood. Ought not those who hear these things to conceive a greater dread of sin than if it were said that they are cleansed by the sprinkling of good works? And if they have any sense of God, how can they but dread, once purified, to wallow once more in the mire, so as to disturb and poison, as much as they can, the purity of this fountain? "I have washed my feet," says the believing soul according to Solomon, "how shall I defile them anew?" Institutes of the Christian Religion.[10]

Casting Off the Coat of Christ's Imputed Righteousness. Thomas Brightman: It was a great negligence in the spouse to give herself to so much sleep, but pardon her heaviness. Why did she not open when he knocked and called? Was she so buried in sleep that she did not hear him? It is plainly seen that she answered him quickly. But was she so benumbed that she could neither move hands nor feet? Neither was that the matter. But when she heard and might open, she made an idle excuse: "I have put off my coat," she says, "and washed my feet." The coat is Christ and his only imputed righteousness; but as soon as we look on ourselves and seek righteousness in the perfection of our own virtue, we spoil ourselves of this garment, and our filthiness appears presently to God and the angels. And so we may wash our feet with other waters, that we may seem to ourselves most clean. So much was the doctrine of free justification by Christ alone decayed

[8]CRR 11:255*; citing 1 Cor 15:50; Acts 7:59; Ps 31:6; Wis 3:1; Mt 10:28.
[9]Gerhard, *Postilla Salomonæa*, 26.
[10]LCC 20:801-2.

at that time, and another means of washing and purging the feet found out besides him, that one coming to Christ by faith alone was commonly believed without danger of defiling. Commentary on the Canticles.[11]

Superstition, Not Apostasy. John Cotton: Thus upon slight pretense the church refuses to open to Christ: she pretends that religion and the worship of God would appear too naked, if it were not clothed with comely human inventions; how then should she in so naked a manner open to Christ? Human inventions do not clothe religion, or the church professing it with any comely ornaments, but, as it were, with warm blankets, lap her and lull her asleep in the bed of perfunctory worship and carnal security. I do not think that the church acknowledges she has cast off her garments of Christ's righteousness, for then how should she remain the spouse of Christ? Indeed, how then should her heart have been otherwise than asleep too? But she only pleads that she should appear too naked if she should open to Christ, if she should worship him in the simplicity and nakedness of his simple ordinances.

"I have washed my feet." Not with the laver of regeneration, for that would have been no impediment, but rather a furtherance to the pure worship of God. Rather, she had washed her feet, she had cleansed her conversation from defilements of secular affairs; she had taken up a devout regard of virginity, of hermit-like or monkish solitary retirement. Having been "cleansed" and "washed" in these devices, she cannot betake herself to worship the Lord in his simple ordinances, and in the ways of her calling, without some "defilement." Thus marriage and worldly business (though both are allowed by God) seem to be a defilement, in comparison to her more strict and superstitious devotion. A Brief Exposition on the Whole Book of Canticles.[12]

[11]Brightman, *A Commentary on the Canticles or the Song of Salomon*, 1032-33.
[12]Cotton, *Brief Exposition*, 144-46.

5:6-8 *My Beloved Is Gone!*

Wounded by Idolatry. Thomas Brightman: These watchmen differ much from those in 3:3, who (it is likely) knew where the bridegroom had gone and where he might be found again. For she asks them whether they saw him, but she says nothing to these, assured of their ignorance, and would have been glad to have passed them by in safety. Likewise, those former watchmen, though they could give her no help (sailing in the same vessel) yet did not lay violent hands on her. But these beat and wound her, and reproachfully take away her veil. They are far different in courtesy and in humanity, yet their common name shows some similarity in their office. For this reason they are the rulers and governors, emperors, bishops, prelates, and persons of such rank, as the event plainly teaches. For as soon as the truth began to appear, in what shameful a manner was she received by the wicked world, and especially those who would be accounted watchmen of the city? She was smitten with reproaches, lies, and cursings in the time of Gregory II, by whom Leo Isaurus was excommunicated for putting down the worship of images.[†] But at the Council of Nicaea under Constantine (son of Leo) and Irene his mother (by compulsion or instigation of Pope Adrian and Torasius, bishop of Constantinople) in 788 she was cruelly wounded.[‡] The watchmen within the city are the ecclesiastical teachers and rulers; the keepers of the walls, the civil governors. But in the time of Theodora, the empress, and Michael, her son, the veil was taken away, so that the church had neither priest nor magistrate to defend her. These were the times when the spouse kept to her bed and was never seen abroad for many years: the worst times that ever she endured. She was much troubled in mind (her heart failing her) in the wine cellar; as before, but then she was supplied with flagons and apples—nay, her beloved came quickly to her and embraced her, who was ready to fall, in both his arms. But here she is "smitten and wounded, her veil taken away and laid for dead"; no flagons or apples, or hope of her beloved's coming, for no man dares speak or look freely to testify his will, much less to reach out a helping hand to the truth lying prostrate. The common harlot of Rome may then see how far she is estranged from this spouse, who boasts so much of her visibility since her first beginning. Commentary on the Canticles.[13]

[13]Brightman, *A Commentary on the Canticles or the Song of Salomon*, 1034-35; citing Eccles 3:3; 2:4-5. †Pope Gregory II (669–731) was viewed with suspicion by Reformed churchmen such as Brightman not only for his role in suppressing the iconoclasts but also for his rejection of imperial meddling in church affairs, often seen as a step along the path to papal monarchy. Leo III "the Isaurian" (685–741) was Byzantine emperor during a period when the empire still had footholds in Italy, even as it was being pressured on its eastern flank by the expansionist Umayyad Empire. Beginning in 726, Leo issued a series of edicts banning the use of images in public worship, but he encountered fierce resistance, especially in Italy and Greece. ‡The Second Council of Nicaea, which concluded in October 787, is regarded as the seventh "ecumenical council" by the Roman Catholic and Orthodox Churches. The council was nominally convoked by the emperor Constantine VI (r. 780–797), though it was his mother Irene (whom Calvin called "a wicked Proserpine") who in fact orchestrated the council and its outcome, owing to the emperor's minority. Among its twenty-two canons were decrees affirming the veneration of images in Christian worship, mandating the placement of relics in all churches, and ordering the confiscation of iconoclastic writings. Calvin's negative evaluation of the Second Council of Nicaea can be found in *Institutes* 1.11.14.

5:9–6:3 THE BRIDE PRAISES HER BELOVED

Others

9 *What is your beloved more than another beloved,*
O most beautiful among women?

What is your beloved more than another beloved,
that you thus adjure us?

She

10 *My beloved is radiant and ruddy,*
distinguished among ten thousand.

11 *His head is the finest gold;*
his locks are wavy,
black as a raven.

12 *His eyes are like doves*
beside streams of water,

bathed in milk,
sitting beside a full pool.[a]

13 *His cheeks are like beds of spices,*
mounds of sweet-smelling herbs.

His lips are lilies,
dripping liquid myrrh.

14 *His arms are rods of gold,*
set with jewels.

His body is polished ivory,[b]
bedecked with sapphires.[c]

15 *His legs are alabaster columns,*
set on bases of gold.

His appearance is like Lebanon,
choice as the cedars.

16 *His mouth*[d] *is most sweet,*
and he is altogether desirable.

This is my beloved and this is my friend,
O daughters of Jerusalem.

Others

6 *Where has your beloved gone,*
O most beautiful among women?

Where has your beloved turned,
that we may seek him with you?

She

2 *My beloved has gone down to his garden*
to the beds of spices,

to graze[e] *in the gardens*
and to gather lilies.

3 *I am my beloved's and my beloved is mine;*
he grazes among the lilies.

a The meaning of the Hebrew is uncertain **b** The meaning of the Hebrew word is uncertain **c** Hebrew *lapis lazuli* **d** Hebrew *palate* **e** Or *to pasture his flock*; also verse 3

Overview: This passage begins a lengthy celebration of the bridegroom's beauty, which the bride offers in response to the inquiries of her companions. Antonio Brucioli notices a parallel between the bride's loquacity on this topic and the church's teaching office, while others puzzle over the fact that the bride is still viewed as lovely, despite her disheveled appearance. Here political allegory aligns with the mystical allegory in elaborating a figural representation of Christ's manifold beauties, the inner workings of grace through tribulations (Martin Luther), and the human response to antecedent grace (Richard Sibbes). Our historical-apocalyptic commentators, Thomas Brightman and John Cotton, trace in these verses the history of the Western church from the heroes of the Middle Ages who resisted papal corruption up to the dawn of the Reformation.

5:9–6:1 *What Is Your Beloved More Than Another Beloved?*

The Church's Teaching Office. Antonio Brucioli: It is not possible for the young maidens (the daughters of Jerusalem), whom the church loves best, to understand what the bridegroom is like unless they first hear. And so here in this passage they ask about his condition and qualities, inquiring earnestly. Thus the faithful people of God earnestly desire to receive instructions from the church, and be informed by her about their beloved (for it is the church's job alone to define these things), provided always that she does so by the tenor and prescript of God's Word, which is her only life and measuring rod. The Song of Solomon.[1]

A Borrowed Beauty. Richard Sibbes: The question is asked, "What is your beloved more than another's beloved, O though fairest among women?" What! Now "fair," when her veil was taken away? Now "fair" when the watchmen abased her? Now "fair" when she was disgraced? Yes, now fair and now fair, and in the sight of Christ, who calls her "the fairest among women." So that under all disgraces, infirmities, and scandals, under all the shame that rises in the soul upon sin, under all these clouds there is an excellency of the church: she is "the fairest among women," notwithstanding all these. . . .

Where does this fairness come from, under such seeming foulness and disgrace? It comes from without; it is a borrowed beauty. By nature we lie in our blood; there must be a beauty put on us. We are fair with the beauty that we have out of Christ's wardrobe. The church shines in the beams of Christ's righteousness: she is not born thus fair, but newborn fairer. The church of Christ is all-glorious, but it is within, not seen by the world. She has a life, but it is a hidden life: "Our glory and our life is hidden in Christ." It is hidden sometimes from the church itself, who sees only her deformity and not her beauty, her death but not her life, because her life is hid. Here is a mystery of religion: the church is never more fair than when she judges herself to be most deformed; never more happy than when she judges herself to be miserable; never more strong than when she feels herself to be weak; never more righteous than when she feels herself to be most burdened with the guilt of her own sins. Bowels Opened.[2]

Longing for the Hidden God. Martin Luther: "What is your beloved more than another beloved?" Or rather, "beloveds." They want to know whom she has as her beloved, that she prefers him to all other beloveds and even though she is deserted does not want to turn to other defenses and aids. This is the sort of question people will ask who are directed and instructed not by the Spirit of God but by their own reason. Here, then, she begins a long figurative description of the sort of beloved she has. Now that she has lost him, she describes him for the first time. We are all like this—we are blasé about the blessings we have in our possession, and we neglect them. But when they are snatched from our sight, we seek them enviously, as the poet says.[†]

"My Beloved is all radiant and ruddy." This is a figurative description of God, not as he is in his majesty, but as he is in his Word and worship—that is, a God clothed and adorned by the kingdom and the priesthood in this people. The "radiance" indicates happiness, since on festival days they used to wear dazzling garments. The "ruddiness" means love. It is as if she were saying, "When the priesthood and kingdom were still standing unimpaired, we abounded in very excellent gifts by which God testified to us of his love toward us. Thus everything used to be full of joy and gladness; but now, with the government disrupted and all those excellent gifts taken away, we mourn in wretchedness." Such is life. Those who have the Word of God have a loving, consoling, gladdening, and beneficent God. But the people complain that they

[1]Brucioli, *La Cantica di Salomo*, [158].

[2]Sibbes, *Bowels Opened*, 320-22; citing Ezek 16:1-2; Col 3:3.

have lost all these things. A Brief but Altogether Lucid Exposition of the Song of Songs.[3]

Passion in the Particulars. Richard Sibbes: We will take that which is safe, because we will have sure footing (as near as we can) in this mystical portion of Scripture. What is that "white and ruddy"? Why does the church set forth the spiritual excellences of Christ by that which is most outwardly excellent and most beautiful? Because of all complexions, the mixed complexion of these two colors, "white and ruddy," is the purest and the best; therefore she sets out the beauty and the spiritual excellence of Christ as a beauty arising from a mixture of the two. . . . In a word, then, this carnation color, "white and ruddy," may be understood of that excellent and sweet mixture that makes such a gracefulness in Christ: in him there is a wonderful purity and holiness, and yet a wonderful weakness; there is God, the great God, and a piece of earth, of flesh, in one person—a bloody, pierced body, and a glorious, shining body; humility and glory; justice, wonderful justice, and yet exceeding love and mercy; justice to his enemies, mercy to his children. . . .

Now you may ask, why is she so exact in reckoning up so many particulars of her beloved—his head, locks, eyes, lips, and such like? Why it is from the greatness of her affection. A large heart always has large expressions. When we are barren in our expressions toward Christ, and of good things, where does this come from but narrow, poor affections? Therefore she had suitable expressions. . . .

Then she shows her particular care and study, to be exact in this knowledge of Christ, to rip him up and anatomize him thus from head to foot. This show that she had studied Christ well before she could attain this excellence; so should it be the study and care of every Christian to study the excellences of Christ, not only in the gross—that is, to say as much as you have in the creed (i.e., he was born for us of the Virgin Mary, was crucified, dead, and buried, etc.), which every child can say—but to be able to particularize the high perfections and excellences of Christ, as the church does here—that is, to study his nature, offices, the state he was in, and how he carried himself in his humiliation and exaltation, what good we have by both states; redemption by his abasement; application of it by his advancement. What he did for us on earth, what he does for us in heaven; what he does for us in justification, adoption, sanctification, and in the glory to come. Study everything and warm the heart with meditation on them. Bowels Opened.[4]

Glimmers of Christ's Beauty in the Medieval Church. John Cotton: The Christians, the daughters of Jerusalem, from this day forward to the days of Peter Waldo (from whom the Waldenses took their name)[†] were very ignorant of Christ, and therefore they ask who he was, and how he was better than another. But instead of him they magnified the church: holy mother church was all in all with them. They acknowledged her to be fairest among women, though they see nothing in Christ better than in another.

"My beloved is white and ruddy." Thus Peter Waldo, a citizen of Lyons, opened Christ to the daughters of Jerusalem, to the children of the church, setting before them the white innocence of his true holiness and the ruddy scarlet dye of his death. The righteousness and death of Christ plainly yet powerfully opened by him brought many to behold Christ and to profess him. When persecution was stirred up against them by the bishop of Rome they were dispersed into many places, yet they multiplied exceedingly. And being then called Albigenses,[‡] in many battles they fought against the soldiers that Pope Innocent III had sent against them, led by Simon Montfort and many others signed with the cross. In many of

[3]LW 15:239-40 (WA 31.2:613-14). [†]"We reject virtue when it is alive; then, when it's removed from our sight, we long to have it back, jealous creatures that we are." Horace, *Odes* 3.24.30-32; LCL 33:199.

[4]Sibbes, *Bowels Opened*, 326-28, 353-54.

these battles the Albigenses prevailed, helped by Raymond of Toulouse and Peter of Aragon, though afterward they were overcome and scattered further into many places of Christendom. So in regard to these troops of many thousands, Christ is here called the standard-bearer, as the word signifies, or "the choice of ten thousand." Again, at that time Christ may be said to be white and ruddy in regard of his members, who were then white with innocence of life, yet ruddy, enduring persecution.

"His head is as the most fine gold." Christ comes now to be described in his members more particularly: this head of gold Christ showed on the earth in the person of Frederick, the second emperor of Rome, a prince of much purity and worth, as a head of the church of fine gold.[§] He contended with many popes about the headship of the church, advanced the headship of Christ, and of himself and his vicegerents above the counterfeit head of the pope's supremacy. He wrestled for Christ against them which much difficulty, yet he prevailed, so that even in the popish schools his election of God was agreed and consented to by many. . . .

"His cheeks are as a bed of spices, as sweet flowers; his lips like lilies, dropping sweet smelling myrrh." "Cheeks" imply the outward face of the faithful church, for the cheeks are a place most conspicuous, which shows that the faithful of those times were as beds of spices and sweet flowers—that is, not gathered into any set garden, as afterward in Luther's time,[◊] but scattered here and there, yet of sweet and precious savor in the nostrils of Christ. . . . The doctrine of the church at those times was such, like "myrrh," served to preserve the faithful from putrefaction: "That which you have already, hold fast till I come." In the primitive apostolic church her lips dropped like a honeycomb, being of strong, sweet relish to delight and nourish to full growth. But the lips of this church drop myrrh rather than honey; they preserved some truth of grace, but did not yield any abundant nourishment to procure increase to the church. A Brief Exposition on the Whole Book of Canticles.[5]

The Strength of the Church in Bohemia. Thomas Brightman: The beginning of this verse sets forth the nether parts, whose chief praise consists in strength and stability. All would fail, unless that which upholds were sufficient to bear the weight. For this reason the bridegroom stands immoveable on such strong bases, and lest we should think that his strength lacks beauty, lo! the feet are of gold, so that from the crown of the head to the sole of the feet, he shines with infinite glory and majesty. Yet there is no doubt but that these things belong also to history: therefore these two golden bases, on which the marble pillars are set, seem to point out Jan Hus and Jerome of Prague. As is the perpetuity of marble, such was their constancy to endure death willingly for the truth's sake, enduring a trial by fire, as the purest gold.

[5]Cotton, *Brief Exposition*, 153-58; citing Rev 2:25; Eccles 4:11. [†]The term "Waldenses" refers to a group of radical reform movements originating in the Piedmont valleys of what is now northern Italy in the late twelfth century. Initially inspired by a figure called Valdes in the earliest sources (the Christian name "Peter" appeared later) who abandoned his family and property to pursue a life of apostolic poverty, the movement quickly came under suspicion and was condemned by the Council of Verona in 1184. Also known as the "Poor men of Lyons," the movement was characterized by a rejection of ecclesiastical hierarchy, itinerant lay preaching, voluntary poverty, and works of charity. Some surviving Waldensian groups in the southwest Alps merged with the new Reformed churches in the latter half of the sixteenth century, and Protestant historians such as Matthias Flacius and John Foxe described them as proto-Protestant martyrs. [‡]Cotton here follows the lead of John Foxe and John Bale, both of whom conflate the Albigensians with the Waldensians. In reality, the two movements originated separately, and there is little evidence of cross-pollination. The Albigensians (also known as the Cathars) shared many of the beliefs that made the Waldensians appealing to later Protestants (e.g., biblicism and an emphasis on preaching over sacramental worship); however, they were far more radical in their rejection of orthodox Christian teaching, positing a radical dualism with strong similarities to varieties of ancient Gnosticism and Manichaeism. [§]Frederick II (1194–1250) was a flamboyant ruler who worked to expand imperial power at the expense of papal prerogatives. He was twice excommunicated by the papacy: once by Pope Gregory IX for failing to fulfill his crusade vow, and a second time by the Council of Lyons for, among other things, "despising the power of the keys." [◊]See Cotton's comments on Song 6:2.

They differed from the popelings in many things, but this chiefly bit the mitered fathers: that they gravely reprehended their wicked and lascivious lives. This was the ulcer that could not endure scratching, which made them rage so fiercely against them. This was about the year 1415. The other member of the verse, "his countenances as Lebanon, excellent as the cedars." His countenance is seen here on earth in the true knowledge of Christ, and by his true worship, which he himself has appointed. Now the "spouse," comparing it to "Mount Lebanon," shows by this that there should be so great an increase of knowledge and renewed worship, that the profession of Christ should continue as firm as the hills themselves, and as the cedars of Lebanon exceed other trees in length, so should true religion excel all scratching and pricking superstitions in reverend majesty, which most fitly agrees with the times presently following, when the Bohemians shook off the Romish yoke, in 1420. Now first began the Word to be truly preached, the sacraments to be administered in both kinds, wicked superstitions to be rooted out, monasteries to be beaten down, and the priests constrained to till the land or yield some better fruit. Commentary on the Canticles.[6]

6:2-3 *My Beloved Has Gone Down to His Garden*

Testing Produces Hope. Martin Luther: At this point, consolation returns. For she sees that she has not been altogether deserted by the bridegroom, but that he has gone down into his garden, to tend the garden and gather roses—that is, to increase his gifts to the people even further. For when God deserts us, he does not do it out of anger or hatred toward us, but he is pruning his vine so that it will bring forth fruit more richly. The bride is speaking here about the fruit of trial, the fruit we bring forth in faith and good works through many tribulations. A Brief but Altogether Lucid Exposition of the Song of Songs.[7]

Grace Begets Grace. Richard Sibbes: We see here a growth in the desires of the daughters of Jerusalem, and from this we learn that grace, though it be in never so small a proportion at the first, is still growing. . . . Nothing is smaller than grace at the first, nothing in the world so little in proportion. The kingdom of heaven is compared to a grain of mustard seed—that is, the work of grace in the heart, as well as in the preaching of the gospel, is little. It is true of the work of grace, as well as of the word of grace, that it is like a grain of mustard seed at first. "What is your beloved?" inquires the church at first, but when she hears of the excellency of Christ, then "Where has your beloved gone?" Grace begets grace, there is a connection and knitting together in religion, good things beget good things. It is a strange thing in religion, how great a matter arises from a little beginning. The woman of Samaria had but a small beginning of grace, and yet she presently drew many of her neighbors to believe in Christ. Likewise Andrew: as soon as he was converted he finds his brother Simon and tells him that he had found the Messiah, and so brings him to Christ. . . . Paul speaks of his bonds, how the noise of them was in Caesar's court, and many believed the very report; although this is not a working cause, yet it may be a preparing, inducing, leading cause to such things, from one thing to another, till there follows this change and full conversion.

You see here the daughters of Jerusalem growing; therefore let us labor to be under good means. Some of the Romanists and others who are ill-affected and grounded in that point, they think that the efficacy of grace is, as we call it, from the congruity, fitness, and proportion of the means to the heart and will of human beings, and it is for this reason that God converts one and not another, because there is a congruous and fit offering of means to him, when one is fitly disposed and

[6]Brightman, *A Commentary on the Canticles or the Song of Salomon*, 1040-41.

[7]LW 15:243 (WA 31.2:720-21); citing Jn 15:2.

another is not fitly disposed. Therefore there follows not upon it effectual calling. So that the virtue of the means offered depends on the suitableness and fitness in the party to whom the means are offered, and not on the power and blessing of God. Indeed, this is plausible, and goes down very roundly with many weak persons, but this is a false and gross error, for unless God by his Holy Spirit does the work through these means, no planting and watering will bring any increase and change the heart and mind. There were greater means in Christ's time, when he performed these miracles, than at any time before, yet all those could not convert that froward generation. And it was Moses' complaint in the wilderness, where they had an abundance of means, that "God has not given you a heart to perceive, and eyes to see, and ears to hear until this day." When a person is planted under good means, and frequents them, then ordinarily it pleases God by the inward workings of his own powerful Spirit to work great matters; but those who keep out of God's reach, that will not come into places where they may hear good things, there is no hope of them: though there be many ill fish in the net, yet there is no hope to catch those that are outside the net. So those that are kept out of all opportunities and occasions whereby God's Spirit may work on them, there is no hope of them. Bowels Opened.[8]

Christ Returns to His Garden in the Reformation. John Cotton: "My beloved is gone into his garden." The Holy Ghost in these words descends to set forth the state of the church reformed by the ministry of Luther and other late divines. This reformed church is described in various ways, first as by Christ's visitation of her. . . . Here she is compared to a garden, being stored with a variety of godly people, like sweet flowers set in order, some teaching and some hearing. Second, it was fenced in as with a hedge, pale, or wall, by the protection of Frederick, the good Duke of Saxony.[†] Third, it was a place where Christ walked (as we do in our gardens) to refresh himself and his friends.

"Is gone down into his garden." That is, Christ descends from those famous cities and eminent places, like Rome and Constantinople, into a mean country city. "To the beds of spices." Because in Germany at that time, many Christians were called and sorted into several beds and companies in different places, though not attempting at first to be so many gardens—that is, separate churches. "To feed in the gardens." In process of time, these several beds of spices (i.e., companies of Christians) grew up to the fashion of just and full churches in Zurich, Strasbourg, Basel, Berne, and Geneva, besides those in Hesse and Prussia.

"I am my beloved's and my beloved is mine." These words imply four things: First, that the church had familiar fellowship with Christ in his holy public ordinances, especially in the main doctrine of pardon of sins by Christ's blood alone, and of justification by faith. Second, that she enjoyed this fellowship with him before the time of her deliverance out of a Babylonian or Romish captivity, for the same words are used for the deliverance out of Babel as for enjoying God's ordinances in their own country, but with this difference: there, the church says, "My beloved is mine, and I am his," because he delivered her out of Babel before he gave her the free use of his ordinances; but here the church says, "I am my beloved's and my beloved is mine," because she first found Christ in his ordinances, before she enjoyed deliverance from subjection to Rome. For Luther preached against the pope's pardons before he rejected the supremacy of the pope. Third, their open profession of their fellowship with Christ, when the princes of Germany openly protested against the Mass and other corruptions in the church and avowed the defense of the Reformation that had begun (whence they were afterward called Protestants). Fourth, Christ's gracious protection of those churches, especially in their first beginnings. For how should Luther (a poor friar) have attempted and gone through with so great a work,

[8]Sibbes, *Bowels Opened*, 396-99; citing Mt 13:31; Jn 1:40-42; Phil 1:13; Deut 29:4.

against such great and general opposition, and in the end die quietly in his bed, if Christ had not held him, as it were, in his arms?

"You are beautiful as Tirzah." Tirzah was the chief city of the kingdom of Israel, after they had separated themselves from Judah, until Samaria was afterward built. The city and its governors (the people having recourse to it for judgment, rather than Jerusalem) were at first in disgrace and obloquy with the Jews for their schism and separation from the house of David at Jerusalem, and for her rebellion against the king of Judah. But this did not diminish her beauty, because this separation was from God. Afterward Tirzah lost her beauty by erecting the golden calves, and falling off (not only from the idolatry of Solomon, in which they did well) from the true worship of God, which was restored and continued in the temple of Jerusalem. But Solomon hear speaks of Tirzah while she retained her beauty, and indeed the reformed churches were in this way similar to Tirzah: at first in disgrace and obloquy for their separation from Rome and rebellion against the emperor and other princes, and yet beautiful nevertheless, because this separation was from God, in regard of the idolatries of the church of Rome, which indeed were greater than those of Solomon. Thus the Duke of Saxony and the Landgrave of Hesse were proscribed as rebels against the emperor, and yet their cause was beautiful and good.[‡] The faithful at that time in England were burned in King Henry VIII's days as heretics and refractory subjects, or rebels, yet they were beautiful in God's sight.

"Comely as Jerusalem." In process of time, the church wore out the suspicion and disgrace of heresy, separation, and rebellion, and was countenanced and adorned by royal laws in the days of King Edward VI, and by laws of the empire tolerating the Protestant princes, so that the church seemed as Jerusalem, the state of princes, the true church of God, and at unity also within itself, and in this its comeliness consisted. For as Jerusalem had once been three cities—Zion, Salem, and Millo—and all three were knit together into one Jerusalem, so the three differences between Lutherans and Calvinists in doctrine and discipline were all compacted together at Geneva in brotherly love, in the harmony of their confessions. A Brief Exposition on the Whole Book of Canticles.[9]

The Self-Giving Nature of Faith. Richard Sibbes: The church you see here, though she stood out a while against all Christ's invitation and knocking, yet at length she is brought to yield herself up wholly to Christ, and to renounce herself. God takes this course with most—yes, in a manner with all his people, before they go out of this world—to lay all high things low, to beat down every high thought and imagination which exalts itself against him, that they may give themselves and all they have to Christ, if he calls for it. For the one who does not do this is not worthy of Christ. . . .

Now this follows on apprehension of Christ being ours: "I am my beloved's, because my beloved is mine first." There are four reasons why Christ must be given to us, before we can give ourselves to him by this self-resignation: (1) Because he is the chief spring of all good affections, which he must plant in us, loving us, before we can love him. (2) Because love descends; though it be of a fiery nature, yet in this it is contrary, for love descends, whereas fire ascends. The superior first loves the inferior; Christ must descend in his love to us, before we can ascend to him in our affections. (3) Because our nature is such that we cannot love but when we know ourselves to be loved first; therefore God is indulgent to us in this, and that we may love him he manifests his love first to us. (4) Because we are naturally conscious of our guilt, we are full of fears. Therefore, if the soul is not fully

[9]Cotton, *Brief Exposition*, 169-76; citing 1 Kings 14:17; 15:33. [†]Frederick "the Wise" of Saxony (1463–1525) was Luther's protector during the early years of his reforming movement at Wittenberg. [‡]Henry IV, "the Pious" (1473–1541), introduced Lutheranism into Ducal Saxony upon the death of his brother George in 1539; Philipp I, "the Magnanimous" (1504–1567) was an early and ardent supporter of Luther's cause.

persuaded first of Christ's love, it runs away from him, as Adam did from God and as Peter from Christ: "Depart from me, for I am but a sinful man." So the soul of every person would say, if first it were not persuaded of God's love in Christ: "Who among us shall dwell with the everlasting burning?" Therefore, to prevent that disposition of soul that would rise out of the sense of guilt and unworthiness, God first speaks to us in Christ, at length saying to our souls, "I am your salvation." After this the soul, first finding his love, loves him back again, of whom it finds itself so much beloved, so that our love is but a reflection of his: "I am my beloved's, because my beloved is mine." Bowels Opened.[10]

The Triumphant Assumption of the Virgin Mother. Chiara Matraini: After the blessed soul of the virgin and mother of the Son of God had left her incorruptible body, it pleased the high and divine majesty that immediately after her death she should rise again and be assumed body and soul into the eternal and happy homeland. To which she went, victorious and triumphant over the most powerful enemies of the world, on the chariot of the infinite multitude of angels, and clothed in the immense light of heavenly glory, and crowned with the most shining stars of singular virtues. Pleasant and sweetest perfumes through good works and most holy examples breathed forth around her, and when she entered, the holy angels saw her so very marvelous and extraordinary beauty, and the exceeding triumph and glory with which she entered the most happy kingdom, and how much light and splendor she spread all around her, that each, filled with wonder and marvel, inquired of the others what marvelous woman this was, since she appeared to some of them through her light, like the dawn, the moon, and the sun. Others, because of her great power, compared her to an army set in array, yet others, marveling that she gave forth such an abundance of the sweetest scents, compared her with the vapor of most precious spices, and some others, noting the great abundance of delights and graces that she brought with her, never ceased to ask what an incomparable woman was this, who rose from the desert above the sacred and celestial spheres with so much glory, since it was something quite extraordinary and new to them to see a pure creature rise above all the choirs of angels and saints, and be placed at the right hand of the Son of God, and be crowned by him with a rich and precious crown, and made Empress of the Universe. Brief Discourse.[11]

[10]Sibbes, *Bowels Opened*, 437-39; citing 1 Jn 4:10, 19; Lk 5:8; Is 33:14.

[11]Colonna, Matraini, and Marinella, *Who Is Mary?*, 117.

6:4–7:13 BRIDE AND GROOM DELIGHT IN EACH OTHER

He

4 *You are beautiful as Tirzah, my love,*
lovely as Jerusalem,
awesome as an army with banners.

5 *Turn away your eyes from me,*
for they overwhelm me—

Your hair is like a flock of goats
leaping down the slopes of Gilead.

6 *Your teeth are like a flock of ewes*
that have come up from the washing;

all of them bear twins;
not one among them has lost its young.

7 *Your cheeks are like halves of a pomegranate*
behind your veil.

8 *There are sixty queens and eighty concubines,*
and virgins without number.

9 *My dove, my perfect one, is the only one,*
the only one of her mother,
pure to her who bore her.

The young women saw her and called her blessed;
the queens and concubines also, and they praised her.

10 *"Who is this who looks down like the dawn,*
beautiful as the moon, bright as the sun,
awesome as an army with banners?"

She

11 *I went down to the nut orchard*
to look at the blossoms of the valley,

to see whether the vines had budded,
whether the pomegranates were in bloom.

12 *Before I was aware, my desire set me*
among the chariots of my kinsman, a prince.[a]

Others

13b *Return, return, O Shulammite,*
return, return, that we may look upon you.

He

Why should you look upon the Shulammite,
as upon a dance before two armies?[c]

7 *How beautiful are your feet in sandals,*
O noble daughter!

Your rounded thighs are like jewels,
the work of a master hand.

2 *Your navel is a rounded bowl*
that never lacks mixed wine.

Your belly is a heap of wheat,
encircled with lilies.

3 *Your two breasts are like two fawns,*
twins of a gazelle.

4 *Your neck is like an ivory tower.*
Your eyes are pools in Heshbon,
by the gate of Bath-rabbim.

Your nose is like a tower of Lebanon,
which looks toward Damascus.

5 *Your head crowns you like Carmel,*
and your flowing locks are like purple;
a king is held captive in the tresses.

6 *How beautiful and pleasant you are,*
O loved one, with all your delights![d]

7 *Your stature is like a palm tree,*
and your breasts are like its clusters.

8 *I say I will climb the palm tree*
and lay hold of its fruit.

Oh may your breasts be like clusters of the vine,
and the scent of your breath like apples,

[9]*and your mouth*[e] *like the best wine.*
She

It goes down smoothly for my beloved,
gliding over lips and teeth.[f]

[10]*I am my beloved's,*
and his desire is for me.

[11]*Come, my beloved,*
let us go out into the fields
and lodge in the villages;[g]

[12]*let us go out early to the vineyards*
and see whether the vines have budded,

whether the grape blossoms have opened
and the pomegranates are in bloom.

There I will give you my love.

[13]*The mandrakes give forth fragrance,*
and beside our doors are all choice fruits,

new as well as old,
which I have laid up for you, O my beloved.

a Or *chariots of Ammi-Nadib* **b** Ch 7:1 in Hebrew **c** Or *dance of Mahanaim* **d** Or *among delights* **e** Hebrew *palate* **f** Septuagint, Syriac, Vulgate; Hebrew *causing the lips of sleepers to speak*, or *gliding over the lips of those who sleep* **g** Or *among the henna plants*

Overview: This section contains a series of emotionally charged exchanges between the lovers, in which they deploy a rapid succession of evocative imagery. There is wide agreement among our commentators that the bridegroom's appreciation of the bride's beauty—despite her bedraggled condition—represents Christ's condescending love for his people despite their sinful condition. Yet there is ample scope for creative exegesis of the text's detailed imagery. For example, in Song of Songs 6:8 the elaboration of Solomon's wives, concubines, and maidens by number proves fertile ground for theologically charged numerology. In Song of Songs 6:11, mention of a visit to the nut orchard reminds Martin Luther of the demands of pastoral visitation, while for John Cotton, the hardness of the fruit brings to mind the stubborn resistance of Jews to the gospel—unfortunately, a common Christian trope in early modern Europe. Observing the thinly veiled reference to genitalia in Song of Songs 7:1, Luther nevertheless rejects the view that adolescents should be prevented from reading the Song, insisting that the onus is on young men to remember that women are God's creation, and should thus be treated accordingly. In the following verse, Johann Gerhard gives a surprisingly sympathetic account of Ambrose's "Mariological" reading of the passage, allowing that since the text refers figurally to the church and Mary is a member of that group, it is legitimate to refer the imagery to her at one remove. Throughout these verses the historical-apocalyptic school nears the end of its historical narrative, connecting the poem's imagery to events current at the time of writing and in the future.

6:4-7 *You Are Beautiful, My Love*

A Dwelling Fit for a King. Henry Ainsworth: The bride having found and being reconciled to Christ is here commended by him for her manifold graces, by which she was beautified. . . . Tirzah was a city in Canaan, not far from Samaria, where one of the thirty-one kings whom Joshua conquered dwelt. Afterward the kings of Israel kept their courts in it. By interpretation, Tirzah signifies "grateful," "well-pleasing," or "acceptable," and so the Greek translates it as "pleasure," or "favorable acceptation," which shows it to be a goodly, pleasant place, such as kings delight to dwell in.[†] A similar beauty is here ascribed to the bride being made fair and acceptable by Christ her beloved in Ephesians 1:6 and 5:27. Annotations upon the Song of Songs.[1]

[1]Ainsworth, *Annotations*, 728; citing Josh 12:24; 1 Kings 14:7. [†]The LXX reads, "You are fair, my companion, as pleasure [*eudokia*]."

The Terrible Beauty of Christ's Bride. Antonio Brucioli: How is it that the chaste spouse of Christ is benevolent and full of grace, unless by Christ's spirit, in whom she believes? And so he rightly calls her "beautiful" and "comely." And he calls her his "love" or "friend" by grace, since by nature she did not deserve this love from the bridegroom. But by grace she was comely and fair, because he elected and chose her, dressed and adorned her, and so loved her that he provided most abundantly all things necessary for her salvation. And because Jerusalem was in the time of King Solomon richer than any other city in gold, silver, mighty warriors, peace, joy, and an abundance of all bodily and temporal goods, therefore there was no better way to set for the beauty of the church than by comparing it to Jerusalem, the city of God—especially since the church is without doubt a city of God, full of every spiritual good. Not only is the church beautified, and adorned with every grace and virtue, which shine in her, but also is she terrible—or rather, majestic and magnificent, made invincible by the power of the bridegroom, and always triumphing over all the world and its wicked inhabitants. The Song of Solomon.[2]

Wars of Religion. Thomas Brightman: The last age of the restored church is "terrible as an army with banners." She shall bestow all her time in warlike preparations and undertakings. For the hellish furies will not suffer her enemies to rest, neither will she endure herself to be rent and torn by the wolves, but resist the injury with an armed hand. In this way she will become fearful to her enemies, as she has done these many years in England, France, and the Low Countries. But this is nothing to that terror that shall shortly follow when Antichrist himself and his ensign-bearer (the king of Spain) and all who carry his mark shall be so destroyed by the spouse that no mention of them shall remain. Commentary on the Canticles.[3]

6:8-10 *There Are Sixty Queens*

Three Types of Faithful Soul. Konrad Pellikan: This passage must be understood in the most religious sense. The bridegroom of the whole church, both his ancient people and the new, chooses for himself a great many souls, whom he has adorned with excellent gifts as queens and made them into a glorious assembly; through them his glory is greatly increased throughout the world. He chose a greater number of people of lower rank, whom he beautified with less glory; however, he was most intimately known to them by his grace, and delighted to keep them as concubines, even though he did not honor them with gifts so great, lest they seem to be queens, like the former. In the third place are the common people of faith, who have been chosen by the grace of Christ for beatitude without number. Over all these is Solomon the peaceable king, and the lover of their souls, just as Christ the Lord has chosen and established faithful souls in their varying degrees for his own glory—not scantily, but perfect in number: for though both sixty and eighty are perfect numbers, their worth is increased still more when even a denarius is added. Now all souls become a heavenly bride through the Word of the Lord, but in three degrees, just as the good earth yields fruit in three degrees: good, better, and best. For that fruit is good which guarantees the betrothal and the grace of a completed union to the bridegroom, and its return is eternal life.

But there is only one Spirit of Christ our Lord, not only uniquely exalted in love and honor by virtue of his enjoyment of the Godhead and without any sin, but also through personal unity

Modern commentators are divided on whether the Hebrew *trṣh* should be translated as a proper noun (i.e., the city mentioned in Josh 12:24), or as a common noun. The Vulgate reading had followed the LXX, but in the early modern period Christian Hebraists came to a variety of conclusions. Ainsworth's solution seems to aim at a compromise, translating as a proper noun, while drawing a theological conclusion based on the broader meaning.

[2]Brucioli, *La Cantica di Salomo*, [163-64].

[3]Brightman, *A Commentary on the Canticles or the Song of Salomon*, 1040-41.

was he assumed in Christ by the Word of God, so that he could never have displeased the Word of God. This Spirit alone is the most innocent dove, ignorant of offense, but yet knowing how to make satisfaction to the heavenly Father for the sins of all the faithful with inexpressible groans. In this Spirit alone is perfection and the consummation of grace, out of whose fulness all who are accepted receive—but not according to their measure. A Succinct and Universal Commentary on the Bible.[4]

Three Types of Church. Thomas Brightman: Having spoken so fully of the church restored, some things are now briefly set down, particularly in these two verses (6:8-9), where he divides the various congregations into three ranks, according to their degrees of purity—namely, queens, concubines, and virgins or maids. And she that comes nearest to truth and holiness, the bridegroom holds her dearest; for this reason, the queens are mighty and flourishing churches, which excel the rest in purity. The concubines are of a lower rank; they are admitted to the bed, but far from the honor and excellency of the lawful wives, having no dower themselves, nor are their children to inherit. The virgins are in the lowest places, as servants and handmaids. Altogether estranged from any familiar acquaintance, they have employment in the house, and they have victuals and clothing; they are reckoned to be of their master's household, but are not partakers of his goods; they labor not for themselves, but for their masters. It is also to be observed that the queens are numbered, and so are the concubines; but the virgins (as of no reckoning) are without number.

This division into such different degrees happened about the year 1563, when John Brentius and James Andrewes rent the church in pieces with that unlucky controversy concerning the monstrous ubiquity.[†] It was before sown by Luther, but he restrained contention about it as long as he lived. But Brentius revived it, and three years after, Illyricus and other doctors out of far countries came to Antwerp and renewed that error, whereby the face of the church, even in her infancy, was miserably defiled. Besides, Anabaptists and Libertines, Antitrinitarians, new Arians, and I know not what other monsters, which wasted and spoiled Transylvania and the regions thereabouts. The English, Irish, Scottish, Belgians, Genevese, Swiss, and Rhenish are flourishing (God be praised!) with the dignity of queens. The German, Danish, Thuringian, and Swedish churches, and others cleaving to their opinions, have taken a crown to themselves and have got the place of concubines. Among the virgins I reckon the Anabaptists, Libertines, Antitrinitarians, Arians, and the like, which now altogether miserably waste and destroy Moravia, Polonia, Hungary, Transylvania, and a great part of Denmark. To these may be added the filthy Roman sink, wherever it is dispersed. We have seen the whole Song marvelous up to this point, but especially now, when we come to things present. Behold then the condition of the restored truth, into what different degrees she at length should fall by a great separation. The Spirit foretold a lamentable success: this age feels it, and every day plainly threatens a further departure. Commentary on the Canticles.[5]

[4]Pellikan, *Commentaria bibliorum et illa brevia quidem ac catholica*, 269v.

[5]Brightman, *A Commentary on the Canticles or the Song of Salomon*, 1047-48. [†]Brightman is referring to a controversy that broke out between Lutheran and Reformed divines concerning Christology and the Lord's Supper. In 1563, the elector Palatine Frederick III introduced Calvinist theology into his territory, sparking tensions with his Lutheran neighbor, Duke Christoph of Würtemberg. The following year a colloquy was held at the abbey of Maulbronn, in which the senior Lutheran theologians, Jakob Andreae (1528–1590) and Johannes Brenz (1499–1570), argued vigorously in defense of Luther's view that Christ's human nature partook fully of his divine characteristics, such as omnipresence (i.e., ubiquity). The Palatinate theologians argued from the Reformed position that "the finite is not capable of bearing the infinite," a theological axiom with wide-ranging implications for Christology, sacramentology, and worship. The colloquy failed to provide any resolution to the controversy, only deepening the mutual suspicion between Lutheran and Reformed princes and theologians, as well as fueling intra-Lutheran controversies between the Philippists (known by their adversaries as "crypto-Calvinists"), who favored a more conciliatory

6:11-13 *I Went Down to the Orchard*

The Fruit of the Word Obscured by Various Evils. Martin Luther: New trial follows on the heels of consolation. Up to this point he has been praising his kingdom and giving thanks for it, for he sees his dove—that is, in every city he sees some good people whose godliness and way of life he approves. Now he turns his attention to another group, and he sees that there is such a huge crowd of ungodly people that by comparison there seem to be no godly or good people. It is ever thus: vices move hearts more vehemently. So special strength is required here, strength which the Spirit of God supplies so that one is not crushed by the appearance of all those evils.

"I went down," he says, "into my garden." "I acted as bishop and visitor to see the effects of my government, and lo! so great was the number of the ungodly that I was constrained to say: 'I did not know,' or 'I did not recognize,' that is, 'I did not recognize my dove.'" For when we add up the numbers, the preponderance of the ungodly is so great that there seem to be no godly people at all. The same thing happens to us when we visit the churches: we find so many vices everywhere that a man might well despair of the fruit of the Word. And yet that dove remains, even though it is hard to see, because it is hidden by a multitude of evils. A Brief but Altogether Lucid Exposition of the Song of Songs.[6]

The Hardness of the Jews. John Cotton: The Jewish synagogues are called a "garden of nuts" because of the hardness and blindness of their hearts, like a hard nut shell surrounding the kernel. "To see the fruits of the valleys." Valleys lying in the shade between two mountains bring forth their fruit late; so the Jews are late in bringing forth fruit for Christ. "To see whether the vine flourished, and the pomegranates budded." The Jews are like a garden of nuts because of the hardness of their hearts, but when their conversion shall be wrought, they will be like vines and pomegranates, bringing forth sweet and wholesome fruits for the refreshment of God and humankind. A Brief Exposition on the Whole Book of Canticles.[7]

7:1 *How Beautiful Are Your Feet*

The Joy of Returning Exiles. Thomas Brightman: A particular description of each member is here begun from beneath, for such shall the progress of things be. Up till now, the beginning was always made from the head. The place of the eyes, teeth, and temples: because the first beginnings were more famous and sooner perceived, as in the doctors and the administration appointed. But now, in a wonderful manner, the feet shall be first converted, and shall begin to stand and walk in the right way, as some notable reason shall show why such a thing should be done. He therefore admires the beauty of her feet, because it was truly a thing full of admiration. A shoe is applied in the Scriptures to three significations: to mirth, speed, and liberty. It was a sign of mirth, which we know because they either put them off of their own accord, as when "David ascended to the Mount of Olives, his head covered and barefoot," or they were constrained against their wills, as captives to the victors, who led them naked and barefoot. Speed has somewhat a more plain efficacy, for the one who is shod treads more boldly, and does not fear pebbles or thorns. Therefore God, when he assured a speedy return to his people, promised to bring it to pass that they shall go with shoes on their feet. It was also to the Israelites a sign of liberty, or rather of obtaining their redeemed inheritance, whereas putting off the shoe was for a reproach. And for this reason, it seems that God commanded Moses to put off his

interpretation of the Augsburg Confession on these points, and the Wittenberg theologians, who did not. For more on this debate, see Richard Cross, "Lutheran and Reformed Debates in the Early 1560s," in *Communicatio Idiomatum: Reformation Christological Debates* (New York: Oxford University Press, 2019), 141-65.

[6]LW 15:246-47 (WA 31.2:730-31).

[7]Cotton, *Brief Exposition*, 195-96.

shoe as he drew near him, to remind us how base a condition flesh is before him. All the significations agree: the mirth of the people returning, their speed of returning, and the recovery of their ancient inheritance, will without doubt be a matter of wonderful glory and of great admiration, so that worthily the nations may cry out, "How beautiful are your feet!" Commentary on the Canticles.[8]

On the Holy Spirit's Style of Allegory. Martin Luther: It is said that among the Jews it was forbidden for adolescents to read this book. There are some who suppose that this prohibition was designed to prevent adolescents becoming inflamed to lust by reading it. For myself, however, I think it was forbidden rather for its difficulty, for since it speaks politically throughout, it seems to be of no value to the young, who as yet have no use for worldly affairs. For even adolescents are capable of hearing and speaking about young women without concupiscence if they regard them as God's creation. And the Holy Spirit has a chaste mouth and a pure heart. Accordingly, he is here speaking about the genital members as about his own creation, which our flesh and concupiscence misuse by their own fault, not by that of the Holy Spirit. I say this so that no one will be offended by this text, which seems to be rather amatory.

It is to be noted that when the Holy Spirit uses allegories, his attention is more on the use of a thing than on its form. So here he makes mention of the reproductive organs like the belly, navel, thighs, and so on in order to describe the fruitfulness of this people. Broader thighs are commended in young women because they are better fitted for childbearing. Solomon is therefore speaking about spiritual birth in this people, that the youth is being prepared for ministry in church and state. Among us schools are "thighs" of this sort. And for this reason we say that Germany is unfortunate because it lacks such a fitting and elegant junction of the thighs—its schools are lying deserted. A Brief but Altogether Lucid Exposition of the Song of Songs.[9]

The Jews Return from Exile. John Cotton: This chapter, to the end of 8:4, describes a fourfold estate of the Jewish church, when they shall be converted to the Lord: first, as it shall be gathered and established (7:1-5); second, as it shall be grown up to her full stature and maturity (7:6-7); third, as it shall be further enlarged by the access of the Gentiles (7:8-10); fourth, as it shall multiply and stretch itself into the country villages, and throughout the land of Israel (7:11–8:4). . . .

"How beautiful are your feet with shoes, O prince's daughter!" In her feet shod with shoes there is a threefold beauty, for it implies: First, a return from captivity, for bare feet is a sign of going into captivity. Secondly, her challenging and recovery of her former inheritance in Israel. Third, her walking in that peace of conscience which the gospel prepares. In contrast, the one who walks barefoot either grows a think, brawny skin on the soles of their feet, or if their feet are more tender, they prick them ever and anon with thorns, or little sharp stones as scruples. A conscience not furnished with true peace either grows senseless and brawny, or else scrupulous and anxious. All the three things are beautiful and glorious, but on the contrary, it is a great disturbance and deformity to go into captivity, to sell and forgo a man's inheritance, to walk unquietly and uncomfortably. And if it be beautiful and glorious to return out of bodily captivity, and to recover the earthly inheritance, how much more is it, together with these outward things, to join a return out of spiritual captivity with recovery of an everlasting inheritance, as the Jews shall do at their conversion? A Brief Exposition on the Whole Book of Canticles.[10]

[8]Brightman, *A Commentary on the Canticles or the Song of Salomon*, 1057-58; citing 2 Sam 15:30; Is 20:4; 11:15; Deut 25:9-10; Ex 3:5; Is 52:12-15.

[9]LW 15:246-47 (WA 31.2:736-37).

[10]Cotton, *Brief Exposition*, 205-8; citing Deut 25:9; Ruth 4:7-8.

7:2-10 *I Am My Beloved's*

The Umbilical Cord of Faith. Melchior Hoffman: I understand the navel to be faith, which causes the inner person to grow. For just as children in their mothers' womb receive what they need to grow through the navel, so also do the spiritual children of God through the spiritual navel, that is, faith, which the elect have without end for eternity, which the roundness signifies. And the navel of such a faith has no lack or flaw for drinking godly wisdom and words. However it does not behoove such a faith that it should merely carry drink, but rather in such faith there is a spring of life, that always wells up to eternal life. The Book of Song of Songs.[11]

A Figure of Mary's Womb. Johann Gerhard: The words of our text that we are treating are words of the maidens or "playmates" of the spiritual bride, as they are called in Psalm 45, in which, while they wait in service on her and accompany her, they praise and laud her according to the most distinguished members of her body. For they praise the beauty of her gait or feet, her loins, her navel, her stomach, her breasts, her neck, her nose, her head, and her hair. They compare her stomach to a completely round, piled-up "heap of wheat surrounded with roses" or as it properly reads in the holy language (*baššôšanîm*) "with lilies," not only because of the form and appearance and also because of the pure white clothes, but rather also because of chastity and purity, which is indicated through the white, pure, blooming lilies. But Solomon in these words does not look to the external beauty and purity as much as to the inner, spiritual beauty and purity. For as the bride of whom he speaks is a spiritual bride, therefore also her beauty and purity is a spiritual beauty and purity.

The early church father Ambrose interpreted these words to refer to the holy Virgin Mary, the mother of the Messiah, when he thus wrote in the *Book Concerning the Education of the Virgin,* "In the womb of Mary a heap of wheat and the grace of the lily flower sprouted forth, because she was bearing Christ, a grain of wheat and a lily."[†] The body of Mary is compared to a heap of wheat surrounded with lilies, because she bore into the world the selfsame one who is the true, fruitful, "grain of wheat" and "the lilies in the valley." We certainly do not want to reject this interpretation. For although in the Song of Songs of Solomon the matter that is being discussed is not concerning the holy Virgin Mary, the mother of Christ, but rather the Christian church in general or each believing soul as the spiritual bride of Christ, nonetheless, because the holy, praiseworthy Virgin Mary is also a true, living member of the Christian church and because her soul through true faith in Christ is also married with him in a spiritual manner and has become his dear, spiritual bride, thus what is said in this Song of Songs about the Christian church in general can also be applied to her in particular as a true member of the church. For in addition, this also would come into play: that Mary was a type of the Christian church in many aspects and especially in that she here is praised in the spiritual bride—namely, that she at the same time became a fruitful mother and remained a pure virgin. Now it is not uncustomary that that which was spoken from the prefigured is interpreted to refer to the type. Therefore, that which is said here about the spiritual bride—her body is like a heap of wheat surrounded with lilies—that can also be applied, so to speak, to Mary, the mother of the Messiah, as she who was exalted to this honor above all other images of women, that not only the spiritual fruitfulness and spiritual virginity were together in her—which also can be found in other members of the Christian church—but rather that also bodily fruitfulness and bodily virginity was found in her together through a special and wondrous work of grace done by God. These

[11]Hoffman, *Dat Boeck Cantica Canticorum,* 113-14; citing Jn 4.

words of Solomon can be not unaptly applied to this fact. Postils on the Song of Songs.[12]

7:11-13 *Let Us Go Out to the Vineyards*

Prayer for the Word to Go Forth. Martin Luther: Here the bride entreats a new gift, for which she will later give thanks. Under Solomon the kingdom of Israel reached its greatest extent, since he ruled over the peoples of Edom, Palestine, Syria, and Moab. Since she still has many other peoples abroad (this is what she means by "the fields"), the bride prays that the bridegroom will give his grace that they, too, may be governed rightly and that the Word may be extended to the neighboring peoples. A Brief but Altogether Lucid Exposition of the Song of Songs.[13]

The Fruitfulness of God's Presence. David Joris: Blessed are you, O you of the earth, rejoice in the heavens, which pour out their riches and fullness on you, to the help and trust, to the glory and joy of the burdened who dwell therein. For they who have lain alone in the long desert will yet appear pleasant, verdant, and joyful. The field will blossom just like a lily and open like a rose. And it will smell of the sweetness of pleasant-smelling herbs and overflowing blossoms, just like the powder of an apothecary's fire. The mandrake and all the good, holy fruits will grow to overflowing and increase on the earth, which will be renewed and refreshed in mercy. This is that the earnest love, truth, and righteousness of God will do. He will certainly dwell therein and remain eternally unchanged. Pay attention, the mouth of the Lord has spoken it. A Blessed Instruction for the Hungering, Burdened Souls.[14]

A Late-Blooming Harvest. Thomas Brightman: "Mandrakes," says Pliny, have a strong smell, but he gives no commendation of the scent, but mention is made of it only to show its budding and growth.[†] It is a cold herb, drowsy and late-blooming; it seems that it grew in the fields in the land of Canaan. They are also opposed in this place to those more delicate fruits that are planted near the house, as well for delight as for more easy keeping. The new and old fruits have a plain meaning: an excellent division of the citizens seems to be set forth here, where some are far scattered in remote colonies, like mandrakes growing in the open fields, while others are like domestic, milder fruit, which by vicinity or near neighborhood yield more plentiful delights. Some again are newly fresh planted into the church, like mandrakes, cold and late-blooming herbs springing more slowly. Such shall the Jews be lastly called, who shall more lately shake off their drowsiness. Some are elder, who shall yield their names to the first calling, and spend their time in the received truth somewhat before the rest shall come in. This shall be a most pleasant sight to the elders, when they shall see religion not decaying with age—which, alas, we behold to our grief, as if the fulness of the Gentiles did now approach, every later generation in their degrees falling away from the sanctity of their parents. Commentary on the Canticles.[15]

---

[12]Gerhard, *Postilla Salomonæa*, 268-69; citing Jn 12:24; Song 2:1; Hos 11; Mt 2. [†]Ambrose, *De institutione virginis liber unus* 14.89; PL 16:326.

[13]LW 15:252-53 (WA 31.2:768).

[14]CRR 7:252*; citing Is 35:1-2.

[15]Brightman, *A Commentary on the Canticles or the Song of Salomon*, 1066-67; citing Gen 30:14. [†]Pliny the Elder, *Naturalis historia* 25.147-50. Contrary to Brightman's assertion, Pliny describes the mandrake as having a strong and noxious aroma, though he catalogs a number of reported uses for its juice or crushed leaves.

8:1-14 THE BRIDE LOOKS FOR HER BELOVED

1 *Oh that you were like a brother to me*
who nursed at my mother's breasts!

If I found you outside, I would kiss you,
and none would despise me.

2 *I would lead you and bring you*
into the house of my mother—
she who used to teach me.

I would give you spiced wine to drink,
the juice of my pomegranate.

3 *His left hand is under my head,*
and his right hand embraces me!

4 *I adjure you, O daughters of Jerusalem,*
that you not stir up or awaken love
until it pleases.

5 *Who is that coming up from the wilderness,*
leaning on her beloved?

Under the apple tree I awakened you.

There your mother was in labor with you;
there she who bore you was in labor.

6 *Set me as a seal upon your heart,*
as a seal upon your arm,

for love is strong as death,
jealousy[a] *is fierce as the grave.*[b]

Its flashes are flashes of fire,
the very flame of the Lord.

7 *Many waters cannot quench love,*
neither can floods drown it.

If a man offered for love
all the wealth of his house,
he[c] *would be utterly despised.*

Others

8 *We have a little sister,*
and she has no breasts.

What shall we do for our sister
on the day when she is spoken for?

9 *If she is a wall,*
we will build on her a battlement of silver,

but if she is a door,
we will enclose her with boards of cedar.

She

10 *I was a wall,*
and my breasts were like towers;

then I was in his eyes
as one who finds[d] *peace.*

11 *Solomon had a vineyard at Baal-hamon;*
he let out the vineyard to keepers;
each one was to bring for its fruit a thousand
pieces of silver.

12 *My vineyard, my very own, is before me;*
you, O Solomon, may have the thousand,
and the keepers of the fruit two hundred.

He

13 *O you who dwell in the gardens,*
with companions listening for your voice;
let me hear it.

She

14 *Make haste, my beloved,*
and be like a gazelle

or a young stag
on the mountains of spices.

a Or *ardor* **b** Hebrew *as Sheol* **c** Or *it* **d** Or *brings out*

Overview: The concluding dialogue in the last chapter of the Song is viewed by most of our commentators as depicting the church's love for Christ in a more mature state, having been tested by affliction, persecution, and separation from her beloved, for whom she continues to long. Most of our commentators see in these verses a foreshadowing of a wider spread of the Christian faith throughout the world as the bride grows in stature and in beauty, forsaking the wilderness to join the bridegroom on the mountains of spice. The early imagery of the bride's pre-nubile condition is most commonly glossed as a flashback to the immaturity or incompleteness of the faith received in earlier eras, though Thomas Brightman, cleaving to a strictly chronological sequence in his historical-apocalyptic account, concludes that the "little sister" is a rival to the bride, the people of Islam. The concluding wish of the bride to join her beloved on the mountains is interpreted variously as a wish for Christ's abiding presence with his people in this world (Antonio Brucioli), for an escape from the snares of heresy and corrupt teaching (Melchior Hoffman), or for the eschatological consummation of Christ with his people (John Trapp).

8:1-2 *Oh That You Were Like a Brother to Me*

Public Displays of Affection. Antonio Brucioli: Christ is indeed like a brother to those who are in the congregation of the faithful, as he says in Mark 3:35: "Whoever does the will of God, he is my brother, and my sister, and mother." So also Paul calls him "firstborn among many brothers." And he was made like a brother when he took on flesh, and was in outward appearance like us human beings. Now as every brother—that is to say, every faithful person—sucks the breasts of his mother the church, which begat him by the Word of God, and receives aid and comfort of her charity and love—so in the same way Christ, although indeed he did not receive any comfort from her breasts, yet nevertheless we may truly say that he did "suck her breasts" because he took delight and comfort in them. For the two breasts signify love and charity, as has been explained above. And this husband Christ is he whom the church desires to find in the streets of the city—that is to say, among the multitudes of peoples—because it is her earnest desire that if it be possible she may be seen and be known to everyone by faith. And so at last, to the honor and glory of God, and for the example to others, she desires to "kiss him," that is, humbly to request God's favor and grace through Christ, and so the bride here in this passage appears willing to confess herself in front of everyone to be a most wretched, vile, and miserable sinner, making daily intercessions and prayers to God through Christ for his merciful favor. This is why she asks permission to kiss him publicly in the streets. The Song of Solomon.[1]

The Gentiles Will Be Led into God's House. Martin Luther: We said at the beginning that this book of Solomon was a sort of hymn in which he sings the divine blessings shown to his people through the Word and expresses his thanks for them. Here he appears to begin his conclusion to this canticle and to pray for the future spread of the kingdom. For he gazes forward to the time of Christ, when the Word and the worship of God would be spread throughout the whole world. This is similar to the prayer in the psalm: "Strengthen, O God, what you have wrought in us."

"O that someone would give you to me as my little brother, one who nurses at my mother's breast, that I might meet you outside and kiss you!" The sense is, "O our God, expand this kingdom into infinity." It is already "outside in the field," that is, in the neighboring tribes, and it longs to expand even beyond that. He pictures the bridegroom as an infant sucking at its mother's breast. For if you look at other realms into which he was to be introduced, God seemed to be like a little baby in this people. So she says, "You are like a child sucking his mother's milk. Who will give me the privilege that I may see you introduced abroad to all peoples through the word of the gospel?" She adds, "That I might kiss you." To "kiss" is to give the Word, to

[1]Brucioli, *La Cantica di Salomo*, [175]; citing Rom 8:29.

possess the gospel. "When these things take place," she says, "men will no longer despise me. Now we are a contemptible people. But then there will be some in every kingdom of the whole world who will revere and praise me, who will embrace the worship of God and believe the Word of God." A Brief but Altogether Lucid Exposition of the Song of Songs.[2]

Brotherhood Restored. Thomas Brightman: Everything now at length fully perfected, and all the faithful Jews fitted into one body of Christ, their affection is wonderful, made clear by the contrast with the former Jews, with whom Christ in times past had to do in the earth. With wondrous skill, with one and the same labor, he sets forth both the accursed hatred of these, as the willing and ready love of those new citizens. The old Jews despised and refused Christ coming in the flesh and showing himself a brother; but there shall be nothing better to those, nothing that they shall more desire, than that they may enjoy the favor of his presence, for by this the horrible wickedness of despising the Son of God by their elders may be recompensed by their faith and diligence in holy duties. The old Jews sought only his death, but fled and did not follow him (when he taught in the streets) with kisses, but with reproaches. All familiarity with him was regarded as a reproach and blame; Nicodemus was constrained by fear to seek private conference with him by night. These shall diligently seek him wheresoever he should be, and finding him shall worship him with great reverence. Commentary on the Canticles.[3]

8:3-4 *I Adjure You, O Daughters of Jerusalem*

The Lure of False Teaching. Melchior Hoffman: This urging is shown in the second, third, and fifth chapters, that the bride should not be awakened by false human teaching of flesh and blood. The cross does not harm the bride the stronger she becomes, and mightier in the Spirit. She finds no unrest of heart or conscience there. But false teaching brings the bride out of her peaceful state of mind and being and brings her unrest, a bad conscience, and a lack of peace in her spirit and heart. For this reason Christ her Bridegroom threatens, terrifies, and forbids all congregations, so that no one should bring his bride to such an awakening and thus stimulate her. The Book of Song of Songs.[4]

Waiting Patiently on Providence. Konrad Pellikan: It is a comfort and assurance that the absence of the Bridegroom may now be tolerated with equanimity, and the grace of his calling and his appearance may be expected, since this will come about not by human deserving, but the will of divine providence. For it is by grace, and not from the works that the Gentiles are called, and the church is sanctified and united to the Bridegroom. A Succinct and Universal Commentary on the Bible.[5]

8:5 *Who Is That Coming Up from the Wilderness?*

From the Garden to the Wilderness. Melchior Hoffman: The one who comes out of the wilderness and leans on the bridegroom is the bride, who with the cross fought to the end in the world. This world is a ferocious wilderness, and since no comfort, no help, and nothing good or cheerful can be found there any longer, the bride turns herself entirely out of the wilderness and toward her bridegroom Christ. She places all her comfort and confidence in Christ the bridegroom, sets out in his strength and builds herself on him with her whole heart, courage, and faith.

[2]LW 15:254-54 (WA 31.2:750-51); citing Ps 68:28.
[3]Brightman, *A Commentary on the Canticles or the Song of Salomon*, 1069.
[4]Hoffman, *Dat Boeck Cantica Canticorum*, 123.
[5]Pellikan, *Commentaria bibliorum et illa brevia quidem ac catholica*, 271r.

The apple tree of which the bridegroom speaks I find in Genesis 3—the tree of life, and the tree of the knowledge of good and evil in the middle of the garden. Under this tree our mother Eve bore and placed us into death, and also under this tree Eve the mother sickened, where she began such toil and labor as a bearer of children. So under this tree, through her defection to the devil's teaching, she came to nothing, and her children came to death.

And here Christ says that he has awakened his bride under this tree, so that she rose up from the dead, as St. Paul also saw concerning those who sleep in death: "Wake up you who sleep, stand up from the dead, and Christ will be your light." This is also found in a similar fashion in Daniel 12. Christ has awakened his bride through his Word and enlightened her with his Spirit and gospel. They have received Christ, the light of the sun, and have become a day and a light in Christ. As St. Paul also says, "You were once darkness, but now you are a light in the Lord." The Book of Song of Songs.[6]

The Church of the Wilderness. John Cotton: In these words the Holy Ghost sets out the calling and estate of two other churches, after the calling of the Jews: the one arising out of the wilderness (8:5-7), and the other, a little sister (8:8-10), together with the estate of the whole church, as it shall then stand, from that time to the end of the world (8:11-14). . . .

Who these churches should be, that remain to be called after the conversion of the Jews and Gentiles, we cannot conceive any more fitly than the churches of Assyria, and second of Egypt, of which we read in Isaiah 19:23-25. When a church shall be elected among the Jews, signified by Ezekiel's goodly temple, the water of God's Spirit shall flow from there eastward, going down into the desert, and spreading itself far and near. This desert, or wilderness, eastward from Judah, is the wilderness of Arabia, and spiritual graces shall be conveyed there from Jerusalem, and from there into the east countries, so that the Assyrians and others may be gathered and converted. It is for this reason that the church arising from the wilderness of Arabia is said to "lean" on her beloved with an Arabian word, as when the Holy Ghost was to speak of the Babylonian captivity (or "winter") being passed, he used the Babylonian or Chaldean word.[†] So then, when the churches of Judea shall see such a good church spring from small help out of the wilderness of Arabia, beyond their expectation, they shall say of her, "Who is this that comes out of the wilderness, leaning on her beloved?" That is, trusting by faith on him, and thereby attaining and enjoying fellowship with him. For "to lean" describes an act of faith, or trusting, and this gesture implies a familiar love. A Brief Exposition on the Whole Book of Canticles.[7]

The Heathens Ascending. Johann Gerhard: The ascension or ascent of the spiritual bride out of the wilderness. In these words the Christian church as the dear bride of Christ is portrayed beforehand in the picture of a beautiful, well-adorned virgin who comes up out of the desert and ascends to the city of Jerusalem. For the adjacent places around the city of Jerusalem were mountainous and the city itself was founded on a raised mountain—namely, on Mount Zion and Moriah. Thus came about this manner of speaking that whoever wanted to draw near to Jerusalem, the holy Scriptures thus spoke that he ascended to Jerusalem or went up, as also Christ said to his disciples, "See, we are going up to Jerusalem."

However, the city of Jerusalem, in which Solomon wrote this Song of Songs, was presented to us in the holy Scripture as a type of the Christian church, while the wilderness, which lay not so far from Jerusalem, was presented to us as a type of heathendom. Because Solomon saw in the Spirit that thereafter the then-promised Messiah, Christ

[6]Hoffman, *Dat Boeck Cantica Canticorum*, 124-25; citing Eph 5:14; Jn 1; Eph 5:8.

[7]Cotton, *Brief Exposition*, 243-47; citing Ezek 47:1-9. [†]Compare Song 2:11. Cotton views these *hapax legomena* in Song 2:11 and Song 8:5 as giving clues to the deeper, theological significance of the imagery.

Jesus, would gather a church out of the heathen in the New Testament, which would be led and brought as a spiritual bride to Christ, the heavenly Bridegroom, therefore he spoke here that the spiritual bride of Christ would be like a beautiful, well-adorned virgin, who would ascend from the desert and would hasten up to the city of Jerusalem, to show that in the New Testament also heathendom would set out for the church and for the kingdom of the Messiah. Therefore, also John the Baptist and Christ himself wanted to spend time first in the wilderness before they began their ministry of preaching. Indeed, they made the beginning of their preaching in the wilderness because now the time was at hand that also heathendom should and would set out to the church of God and to the kingdom of Christ. Postils on the Song of Songs.[8]

8:6-7 *Set Me as a Seal upon Your Heart*

Christ the True Seal on Our Consciences. Melchior Hoffman: Christ Jesus is the true seal with which our conscience will be sealed, with the strength of God's Word, which will be a seal for it. This seal will sustain the spirit and courage of the elect, along with the arm, or all the strength and might of the faithful. The arm is understood as strength and power. "Love is as strong as death." Just as death vanquished all the world and brought it to itself, so Christ through his love has called all his elect back out of death and into life and bought his own with his suffering and death. Just as hell is jealous for its own and holds them dear, and is therefore greatly envious of those who would steal them from him, so too is Christ's love that of a strongly envious and jealous lover, so that anyone who seeks to lay a hand on his bride lays a hand on him, as in Matthew 25. As firmly as death leads to death, so firmly does Christ lead to life. As jealous as death is for hell, so jealous is Christ for heaven. And this love cannot be wiped out; as hell will not be robbed of its own, so too will life not be robbed of its own. And this love for his own, which arose and still arises in Christ, is unfathomable, like a burning fire, like a stark mountain burning fiercely, which cannot be extinguished. This is the love of Christ, a flame of the Father and of the exalted Godhead, the flame is the Holy Ghost and love itself, mightily jealous. The Book of Song of Songs.[9]

We Must Love Others with God's Unquenchable Love. Dirk Philips: This is now the principal teaching and highest command of our Lord Jesus Christ, that we shall have love for one another just as he has loved us. And this love is not only in words, but lies in power and truth and must be shown in deeds. For since God is love, as John says, so it is powerful and, according to Solomon's word, stronger than death and firmer than hell, for love is fiery and a flame of the Lord, that waters also cannot extinguish love, nor streams drown it. Epistle to Four Cities.[10]

The Passion of the Bride's Love. John Trapp: Love is itself a passion, and it delights to show itself in suffering for the one it loves—yes, though it were to pass through a thousand deaths for the sake of the beloved. And this is here offered as a reason why the bride first awakened Christ, and now desires to be so closely knit to him, to be "set as a seal on his hand," even on his heart, for the love of Christ constrains her and lays so hard on her, that she could do nothing less than beg such a favor of him. . . . And surely to account Christ precious as a tree of life, although we be fastened to him as to a stake to be burned, this is love. And this our labor of love cannot be vain in the Lord. Solomon's Book of All Virtues.[11]

[8]Gerhard, *Postilla Salomonæa*, 869; citing Lk 19:28; Zech 9; Gal 4; 2 Cor 11:2; Mt 3; Mt 4.

[9]Hoffman, *Dat Boeck Cantica Canticorum*, 125-26; citing Exod 20; Deut 5.

[10]CRR 6:479*; citing Jn 15:12; 1 Jn 3:8.

[11]Trapp, *Solomonis ΠΑΝΆΡΕΤΟΣ*, 325.

8:8-10 *We Have a Little Sister*

Israel Longs for the Maturation of God's Reign Through the Word. Martin Luther: I pointed out above that at the end of this canticle Solomon looks forward to the spiritual kingdom of Christ, because a future kingdom was expected far wider and greater than the physical kingdom of the Jewish people. And it is beyond doubt that these expectations were frequently and thoroughly discussed in everyday conversations. But in this process a misconception arose. The crowd thought that the kingdom of the Christ would be a physical kingdom. They did not understand that Christ would reign through the Word in such a way that the kingdoms of the world would still run their course. Solomon, then, is saying, "If we look at the extent of the kingdom which Christ will institute through the new covenant, we will be right to compare our present people to a little girl who does not yet have breasts—that is, it is not yet mature enough to preach a gospel that is to be spread throughout the whole world." The further significance of the complaint put forward here is this: it is a sort of common voice of all the prophets and saints of the people of the law, yearning for a release from the prison of the law into the broad freedom of the gospel, that God would bring to fruition the promises made about Christ. . . .

"What shall we do for our sister . . . ?" How intense is the emotion of a heart aflame with the expectation of the coming Christ! As Christ himself says in the Gospel, "Verily, I tell you that many kings and prophets desired to see and hear what you see and hear, but they neither saw nor heard it." So here Solomon, in the person of all the saints, asks, "What shall we do?" It is as if he were saying, "How great and how joyous will the shape of those times be?" He adds, "On the day when she is to be spoken for." The very lovely meaning and one that is not at all obscure is this: the kingdom of Christ is located only in the Word. For he does not say, "on the day when she is to be adorned, when she is to be led into the wedding chamber," but "when she is to be spoken for," namely, in the sweet preaching of the gospel by the apostles and Christ himself. By this preaching she will be taught about the grace of God and the remission of sins.

It is as if he were saying, "Today is not a day for speaking but for keeping silent. We are still caught in the prison of the law and see only a sort of distant glimmer of the Word to be revealed, the Word through which the kingdom of Christ will be spread abroad into the whole world." A Brief but Altogether Lucid Exposition of the Song of Songs.[12]

The Muslims Laid Waste. Thomas Brightman: He comes now to the calling of a new nation, which we said was another of the younger sisters. Our divines suppose these to be the words of the old church, and her wishes to us Gentiles. But we have seen this prophecy many years ago, carried beyond the age of that old church, and now exercised in the farthest borders of our earthly habitation. Isaiah seems to teach who this people may be in the latter times approaching; he joins three nations in a common profession of the truth: the Assyrians, Jews, and Egyptians. Of the Jews and Assyrians, the Paranymph[†] has spoken before, and seems to have reserved the Egyptians for the last, a nation that truly embraced Christ many ages since and was in times past very famous for churches much frequented. Yet without a doubt, the former times are not here described, but times yet to come, as the course of things sufficiently shows. . . . But Joel says that Egypt shall be desolate, and Zechariah says that her scepter shall be removed. It is thus very likely that all Muslims shall be destroyed there, before those places shall obtain the kingdom of Christ: but this blotting out of the wicked does not signify an utter destruction, but a laying the way open to better inhabitants, yielding their power and authority to Christ's government. Commentary on the Canticles.[13]

[12]LW 15:259-60 (WA 31.2:760-62); citing Lk 10:24.
[13]Brightman, *A Commentary on the Canticles or the Song of Salomon*, 1073; citing Is 19:18-23; Joel 3:19; Zech 10:11.[†] Paranymphs are attendants of the bride and groom at a

8:11-12 *My Very Own Vineyard Is Before Me*

Christ Claims His Treasure. Melchior Hoffman: The thousand silver coins are understood to be the thousand coins or pieces of silver that Christ received from the faithful apostolic shepherds, who presented Christ with all the money along with the fruits. And it is rightly understood that, as Solomon had a thousand wives, so Christ as the spiritual Solomon should receive a thousand congregations, with all the gifts and adornments of grace.

And each congregation is likened here to a silver penny, as I also hear in Matthew 25. They all, through God's Word and gospel, proverbs, parables, and allegories, are described in a word: they become a silver piece, a coin, a treasure and possession, a bread, a drink, a great quantity of wheat, a sheaf of wheat, a field of wheat, a mountain, a dove, a young woman, a garden, a spirit, a woman, a castle, a rose, a horse, and similar things in a human fashion are compared to God's congregation, as also a herd of sheep.

But as to those shepherds who retain the two hundred congregations with their fruits, or the two hundred pennies or pieces of silver, it is understood that they signify the false shepherds, who rob and steal these congregations from Christ. This is like it happened with the false apostles, who at first serve Christ and wish to bring the people to him and in this way receive a debt from Christ. They rob and steal these people from him, as happened with the false apostles and will now happen again in these times, that a third of our current teachers will fall away again and be stolen along with a great host. Just as well! It is as God foreordained, that such blasphemers should be given to the shepherds with false natures and not to Christ, the true Shepherd. The Book of Song of Songs.[14]

The Church Is a Vineyard. Johann Gerhard: In the Gospel of the next Sunday in the series,[†] Matthew 20, as also in Matthew 21, Mark 12, Luke 13 and 20, Christ presents us the situation of the Christian church here on earth in the form of a parable drawn from the vineyard. That not only Solomon now, but also Moses, David, the holy prophets, and Christ himself so often and so many times compared the church of God to a vineyard happened not only because of the abundance of vineyards in Palestine (although one does indeed take parables readily from common and well-known objects) but also and especially because of its aptness, because of the fitting comparison that is found between a vineyard and the church of God:

1. In its value. For just as there is nothing more noble among all the estates of land and field than a beautiful, well-laid-out vineyard, which a diligent father of the house holds dear and valuable and spends much time on the same throughout the year, so God the Lord holds nothing on earth dearer or more welcome than his dear church, since the Son of God purchased it for him through his own blood, whom he [God the Father] permitted to build it with all diligence and work therein. Solomon himself makes this reason clear when he speaks in the person of the heavenly Solomon, Christ Jesus, "My vineyard is for me," as we wish hereafter to hear further about.

2. In the necessity of its being planted. A vineyard does not grow by itself, as grass grows on the plain. It also does not bring forth any sweet, delicious fruits unless it is planted, laid out and built. Accordingly, we human beings cannot now after the fall bring forth any sweet fruits pleasing to God unless God the Lord plants and sets us in the vineyard of his church. Before that happens we bear purely acrid, unripe grapes.

3. In the variety of labor. One must work the whole year in the vineyard: now one has to remove branches, now chop them, now trim them, now prop them up with stakes, now bind them, now scale off leaves, because one task follows another. Therefore, also in the church of God there is

wedding. Here, Brightman is connecting the words of the bride's friends in 8:8-9 to the prophesy in Isaiah 19:18-23.

[14]Hoffman, *Dat Boeck Cantica Canticorum*, 130-32; citing Rev 12; Mt 24; Lk 21; Joel 3.

always work to do. Because in this life sin still dwells in the flesh of the regenerate, which are vines in the vineyard, one must always work through the word on them that they will not become a mass of wild tendrils, as John 15:2 says, "My heavenly Father will trim every branch that bears fruit so that it may bear more fruit." Postils on the Song of Songs.[15]

The Coming of the Bridegroom. John Cotton: "My vineyard which is mine, is before me." That is, I do not let out my vineyard to others, but I tended it always myself. Let Solomon take his thousands for the fruits of his vineyard, and the reapers their hundreds; I will not do so, but take all the pains to keep my vineyard, and reap all the gains of its fruit for myself. The meaning is that when Christ has gathered together all these churches of the Jews, Assyrians, Egyptians, and neighboring nations, he will then keep his church with his mighty power, that neither dragons, nor wild boars, nor foxes shall thereafter root it up or make havoc of it, as in times past they have done. This is expressly foretold, and shall come to pass after the destruction of Leviathan, the great Turk.

"You that dwell in the gardens." The participle being of the feminine gender shows that it is the church, not Christ, that is here spoken to, who is said to "dwell in the garden." That is, in the particular churches, as the sea dwells in each particular national sea (e.g., the German Sea, the Spanish Sea, the Baltic Sea). So also the Catholic Church is divided into particular churches, or the Jewish mother church dwells by her authority and directions in all other churches. "The companions hearkening to your word (or voice) cause me to hear it." So the words in the original imply either that the church would have the mother church of the Jews take care of all other Christian churches and give direction to them—and yet not as handmaids, but as companions—or else if the words be read, "the companions hearken to your voice," they imply that after the calling of these churches, this shall be their constant estate to the world's end: First, they shall embrace one another as companions, not claiming Romish supremacy. Second, they shall hearken to the voice and directions of the mother church (in Solomon's days, for wisdom to him). Third, they shall continue in calling upon the name of Christ without dissipation or interruption to the end.

"Make haste, my beloved." This is the prayer of all the churches. Now that all things are accomplished that the prophets and apostles have foretold, that Christ would hasten his last coming as swiftly and quickly as the swiftest of the creatures, "the roe, or young hart," to take them up with himself into the highest of heavens of the mountains of spices, where are all manner of spices, where are all manner of sweet and fragrant and pleasing things, even fulness of joy at God's right hand for evermore. Thus is the end of the Revelation, "The Spirit and the Bride," and every faithful soul says in like sense, "Come Lord Jesus, come quickly." A Brief Exposition on the Whole Book of Canticles.[16]

8:13-14 *Make Haste, My Beloved*

The Church Longs for Christ's Continuing Presence. Antonio Brucioli: This "mountain of spices" is the church, and therefore the lesser and particular churches are called "mountains of spices." Christ wanted to hear the bride speak, and the bride answered him by uttering words of perfect charity, by which it appears how zealous she is for Christ's glory and the knowledge of his truth, and also how enflamed she is with desire for the salvation of all people. And this, in short, is the meaning of those words, "O my beloved, fly away": as a man flies away in great haste, or as does and young bucks skit nimbly along the tops of the hills—so must you make haste, and do not delay in

[15]Gerhard, *Postilla Salomonæa*, 268-69; citing Acts 20; Is 5:2.
[†]Septuagesima Sunday, the ninth Sunday before Easter and the Sunday when Mt 20:1-16 was the traditional Gospel reading.

[16]Cotton, *Brief Exposition*, 255-57; citing Is 27:1-3; Ps 16:11; Rev 22:17-20.

coming to the mountains of spices—that is, to come both to the church universal, and also to be present and give aid to the particular churches, lest it chance that they may be forced to receive someone else besides you, and so estrange themselves from you and perish eternally. Therefore, gentle Christ, come quickly, to help and succor, to direct and guide us into the right way, the way which leads to life everlasting. The Song of Solomon.[17]

The Church Longs for the Time of Grace. Melchior Hoffman: It is the bride's desire that Christ should flee like a hind or deer, or like a young hart. So quickly shall he come away from all the godless and from the host of antichrists. For the bride is united with Christ in peace, and the course is completed, as is the time of grace. The time of works is past. It is the bride's desire that Christ should wish to remain up on the mountains of spices or herbs. Here the bride once again calls God's congregation the many mountains that bear spices or herbs, which noble spices are the apostolic teachers, as shown above in the sixth chapter. And the nourishing roses, among which Christ the deer or young hart grazed are the noble herbs and noble spices of the congregation, from which the power and spirit of the Word drips and flows. Just as Christ also above in the fourth chapter calls his congregation myrrh mountains, and in the same way calls many preachers hills or small mountains. Oh that we all might be such mountains and herbs of faith and strength, so help us God through Jesus Christ our Savior. Amen. The Book of Song of Songs.[18]

The Church Longs for Heaven. John Trapp: Just as this book began with a wish, so it ends: "The entire life of a good Christian is a holy desire."[†] He loves, and longs, and looks for Christ's second appearance, and even spends and exhales himself in continual sallies and egressions of affection to him in the meanwhile. He has taken some turns with Christ on those "mountains of spice" (so heaven is called, for its inconceivable height and sweetness), he has tasted of the grapes of this celestial Canaan. So he is as eager for that as once the Gauls were for Italy, when they had once tasted of the sweet wine of those grapes that grew there. The old character of God's people was that they waited for the consolation of Israel, Christ's first coming. Now they long as much for his second, as the engaged maid does for her marriage, the apprentice for his freedom, the captive for his ransom, the traveler for his inn, the mariner for the haven—"looking for and hasting the coming of that day of God." Solomon's Book of All Virtues.[19]

[17]Brucioli, *La Cantica di Salomo*, [183].

[18]Hoffman, *Dat Boeck Cantica Canticorum*, 133.

[19]Trapp, *Solomonis ΠΑΝΆΡΕΤΟΣ*, 174-75; citing 2 Pet 3:12.

[†]Augustine, *In Epistolam Ioannis ad Parthos tractatus decem* 4.6 (PL 35:2009).

Map of Europe at the Time of the Reformation

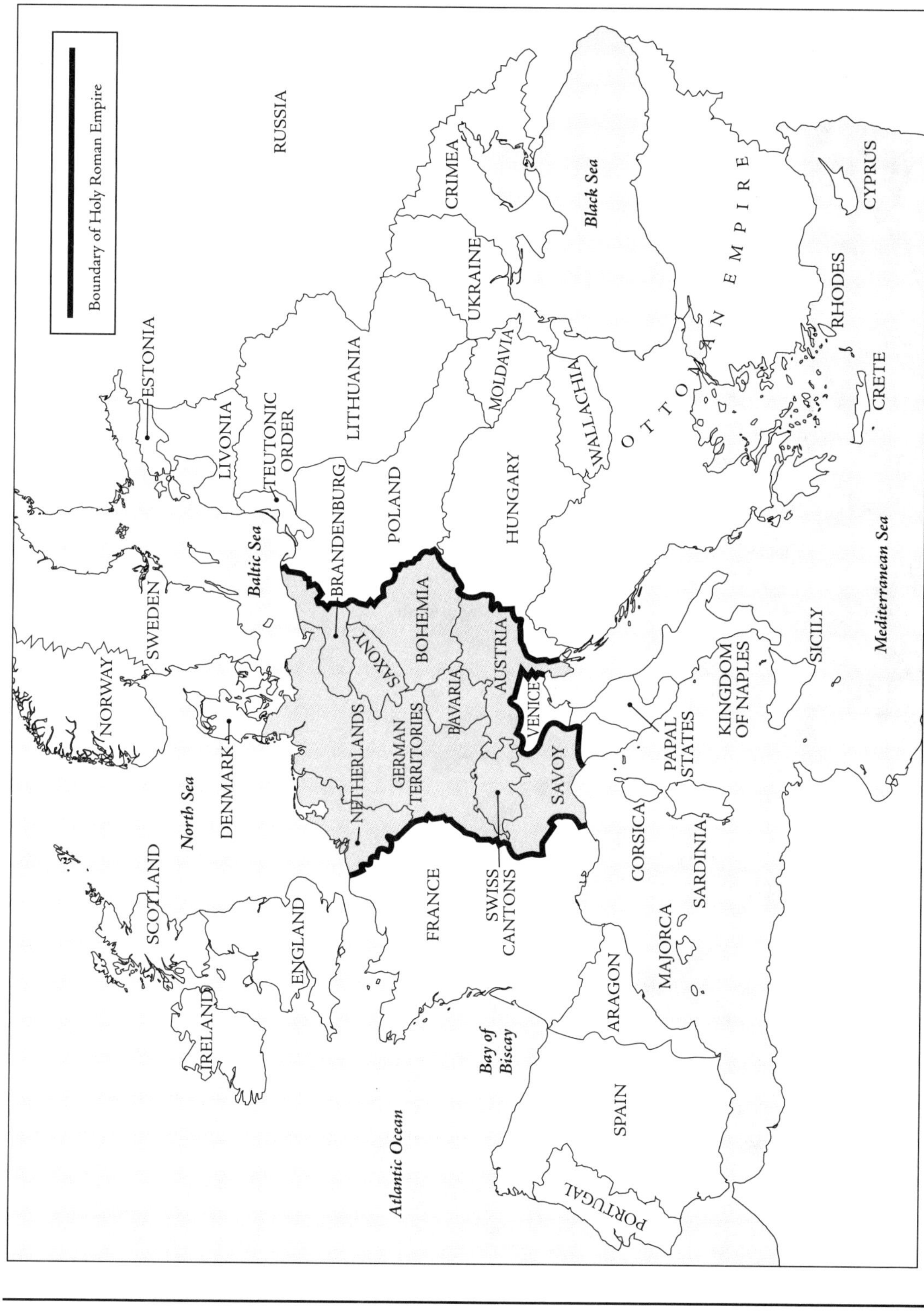

Timeline of the Reformation

	German Territories	France	Spain	Italy	Switzerland	Netherlands	British Isles
1309–1377		Babylonian Captivity of the Papacy					
1337–1453		d. Nicholas of Lyra Hundred Years' War	b. Paul of Burgos (Solomon ha-Levi)(d. 1435) Alonso Tostado (1400–1455)				Hundred Years' War
1378–1415		Western Schism (Avignon Papacy)		Western Schism			
1384							d. John Wycliffe
1414–1418					Council of Basel (1431–1437)		
1415				Council of Constance; d. Jan Hus; Martin V (r. 1417–1431); Council of Florence (1438–1445)			
1450	Invention of printing press						
1452				b. Leonardo da Vinci (d. 1519)			
1453				Fall of Constantinople			
1455–1485	b. Johannes Reuchlin (d. 1522)						War of Roses; rise of House of Tudor
1456	Gutenberg Bible						
1460				Pope Pius II issued *Execrabilis*			
1466		b. Jacques Lefèvre d'Étaples (d. 1536)					
1467						b. Desiderius Erasmus (d. 1536)	b. John Colet (d. 1519)
1469	b. Antoius Broickwy von Königstein (d. 541)						
1470				b. Santes Pagninus (d. 1541)			b. John (Mair) Major (d. 1550)
1475				b. Michelangelo (d. 1564)			
1478	b. Wolfgang Capito (d. 1541)		Ferdinand and Isabella	b. Jacopo Sadoleto (d. 1547)			b. Thomas More (d. 1535)

	German Territories	France	Spain	Italy	Switzerland	Netherlands	British Isles
1480	b. Balthasar Hubmaier (d. 1528); b. Andreas Bodenstein von Karlstadt (d. 1541)						
1481–1530			Spanish Inquisition				
1482					b. Johannes Oecolampadius (d. 1531)		
1483	b. Martin Luther (d. 1546)						
1484	b. Johann Spangenberg (d. 1550)				b. Huldrych Zwingli (d. 1531)		
1485	b. Johannes Bugenhagen (d. 1554)						b. Hugh Latimer (d. 1555)
1486	r. Frederick the Wise, Elector (d. 1525); b. Johann Eck (d. 1543)						
1488	b. Otto Brunfels (d. 1534)						b. Miles Coverdale (d. 1568)
1489	b. Thomas Müntzer (d. 1525); b. Kaspar von Schwenckfeld (d. 1561)						b. Thomas Cranmer (d. 1556)
1491	b. Martin Bucer (d. 1551)		b. Ignatius Loyola (d. 1556)				
1492			Defeat of Moors in Grenada; Columbus discovers America; expulsion of Jews from Spain	Alexander VI (r. 1492–1503)			
1493	b. Justus Jonas (d. 1555)						
1494							b. William Tyndale (d. 1536)
1496	b. Andreas Osiander (d. 1552)					b. Menno Simons (d. 1561)	
1497	b. Philipp Melanchthon (d. 1560); b. Wolfgang Musculus (d. 1563) b. Johannes (Ferus) Wild (d. 1554)						

	German Territories	France	Spain	Italy	Switzerland	Netherlands	British Isles
1498				d. Girolamo Savonarola	b. Conrad Grebel (d. 1526)		
1499	b. Johannes Brenz (d. 1570) b. Justus Menius (d. 1558)			b. Peter Martyr Vermigli (d. 1562)			
1500			b. Charles V (–1558)				
1501	b. Erasmus Sarcerius (d. 1559)						
1502	Founding of University of Wittenberg			Julius II (r. 1503–1513)		b. Frans Titelmans (d. 1537)	
1504					b. Heinrich Bullinger (d. 1575)		
1505	Luther joins Augustinian Order			b. Benedict Aretius (d. 1574)			
1506		b. Augustin Marlorat (d. 1562)		Restoration of St. Peter's begins			
1507				Sale of indulgences approved to fund building			
1508	b. Lucas Lossius (d. 1582)						
1509		b. John Calvin (d. 1564)					r. Henry VIII (–1547)
1510	Luther moves to Rome			b. Immanuel Tremellius (d. 1580)			b. Nicholas Ridley (d. 1555)
1511	Luther moves to Wittenberg						
1512				Sistine Chapel completed			
1512–1517				Fifth Lateran Council; rejection of conciliarism			
1513	Luther lectures on Psalms			r. Pope Leo X (–1521)			b. John Knox (d. 1572)
1515	Luther lectures on Romans	r. Francis I (–1547); b. Peter Ramus (d. 1572)					
1516		Est. French National Church (via Concordat of Bologna)		Concordat of Bologna		Publication of Erasmus's Greek New Testament	
1517	Tetzel sells indulgences in Saxony; Luther's Ninety-five Theses						

	German Territories	France	Spain	Italy	Switzerland	Netherlands	British Isles
1518	Heidelberg Disputation; Luther examined by Cajetan at Diet of Augsburg			Diet of Augsburg			
1519	Leipzig Disputation	b. Theodore Beza (d. 1605)	Cortés conquers Aztecs; Portuguese sailor Magellan circumnavigates the globe		Zwingli appointed pastor of Grossmünster in Zurich; b. Rudolf Gwalther (d. 1586)		
1520	Publication of Luther's "Three Treatises"; burning of papal bull in Wittenberg		Coronation of Charles V	Papal Bull v. Luther: *Exsurge Domine*			
1521	Luther excommunicated; Diet/Edict of Worms—Luther condemned; Luther in hiding; Melanchthon's *Loci communes*	French-Spanish War (–1526)	French-Spanish War; Loyola converts	Papal excommunication of Luther			Henry VIII publishes *Affirmation of the Seven Sacraments* against Luther; awarded title "Defender of the Faith" by Pope
1521–1522	Disorder in Wittenberg; Luther translates New Testament						
1521–1525		First and Second Habsburg–Valois War					
1522	Luther returns to Wittenberg; Luther's NT published; criticizes Zwickau prophets; b. Martin Chemnitz (d. 1586)		Publication of Complutensian Polyglot Bible under Cisneros		Sausage Affair and reform begins in Zurich under Zwingli		b. John Jewel (d. 1571)
1523	Knight's Revolt	Bucer begins ministry in Strasbourg	Loyola writes Spiritual Exercises	r. Pope Clement VII (–1534)	Iconoclasm in Zurich		
1524	Luther criticizes peasants; d. Johann von Staupitz					Erasmus's disputation on free will	
1524–1526	Peasants' War						
1525	Luther marries; execution of Thomas Müntzer; publication of Luther's *Bondage of the Will*				Abolition of mass in Zurich; disputation on baptism; first believers' baptism performed in Zurich		

	German Territories	France	Spain	Italy	Switzerland	Netherlands	British Isles
1526					Zurich council mandates capital punishment of Anabaptists	Publication of Tyndale's English translation of NT	
1527	d. Hans Denck (b. c. 1500) d. Hans Hut (b. 1490) b. Tilemann Hesshus (d. 1588)			Sack of Rome by mutinous troops of Charles V	First Anabaptist executed in Zurich; drafting of Schleitheim Confession		
1528	Execution of Hubmaier						
1529	Second Diet of Speyer; evangelical "protest"; publication of Luther's catechisms; Marburg Colloquy; siege of Vienna by Turkish forces	Abolition of mass in Strasbourg			d. Georg Blaurock (b. 1492)		Thomas More appointed chancellor to Henry VIII
1530	Diet of Augsburg; Confession of Augsburg	d. Francois Lambert (Lambert of Avignon) (b. 1487)	Charles V crowned Holy Roman Emperor				
1531	Formation of Schmalkaldic League				d. H. Zwingli; succeeded by H. Bullinger		
1532		Publication of Calvin's commentary on Seneca; conversion of Calvin	b. Francisco de Toledo (d. 1596)				
1533	b. Valentein Weigel (d. 1588)	Nicholas Cop addresses University of Paris; Cop and Calvin implicated as "Lutheran" sympathizers	b. Juan de Maldonado (d. 1583)				Thomas Cranmer appointed as Archbishop of Canterbury; Henry VIII divorces
1534	First edition of Luther's Bible published	Affair of the Placards; Calvin flees d. Guillame Briçonnet (b. 1470)		Jesuits founded; d. Cardinal Cajetan (Thomas de Vio) (b. 1469)			Act of Supremacy; English church breaks with Rome
1535	Bohemian Confession of 1535; Anabaptist theocracy at Münster collapses after eighteen months				b. Lambert Daneau (d. 1595)		d. Thomas More; d. John Fisher

	German Territories	France	Spain	Italy	Switzerland	Netherlands	British Isles
1536	Wittenberg Concord; b. Kaspar Olevianus (d. 1587)				First edition of Calvin's *Institutes* published; Calvin arrives in Geneva (–1538); First Helvetic Confession	Publication of Tyndale's translation of NT; d. W. Tyndale	d. A. Boleyn; Henry VIII dissolves monasteries (–1541)
1537					Calvin presents ecclesiastical ordinances to Genevan Council		
1538					Calvin exiled from Geneva; arrives in Strasbourg (–1541)		
1539		Calvin publishes second edition of *Institutes* in Strasbourg		d. Felix Pratensis			Statute of Six Articles; publication of Coverdale's Great Bible
1540				Papal approval of Jesuit order			d. Thomas Cromwell
1541	Colloquy of Regensburg	French translation of Calvin's *Institutes* published	d. Juan de Valdés (b. 1500/1510)		d. A. Karlstadt; Calvin returns to Geneva (–1564)		
1542	d. Sebastian Franck (b. 1499)			Institution of Roman Inquisition			War between England and Scotland; James V of Scotland defeated; Ireland declared sovereign kingdom
1543	Copernicus publishes *On the Revolutions of the Heavenly Spheres*; d. Johann Eck (Johann Maier of Eck) (b. 1486)						
1545–1547	Schmalkaldic Wars; d. Martin Luther			First session of Council of Trent			b. Richard Bancroft (d. 1610)
1546	b. Johannes Piscator (d. 1625)						
1547	Defeat of Protestants at Mühlberg	d. Francis I; r. Henri II (–1559)					d. Henry VIII; r. Edward VI (–1553)
1548	Augsburg Interim (–1552) d. Caspar Cruciger (b. 1504) b. David Pareus (d. 1622)						

	German Territories	France	Spain	Italy	Switzerland	Netherlands	British Isles
1549	d. Paul Fagius (b. 1504)	d. Marguerite d'Angoulême (b. 1492)			Consensus Tigurinus between Calvin and Bullinger		First Book of Common Prayer published
1550	b. Aegidius Hunnius (d. 1603)						
1551–1552				Second session of Council of Trent			
1552	d. Sebastian Münster (b. 1488) d. Friedrich Nausea (b. c. 1496)						Book of Common Prayer revised
1553	d. Johannes Aepinus (b. 1449)				Michael Servetus executed in Geneva		Cranmer's Forty-Two Articles; d. Edward VI; r. Mary I (d. 1558)
1554							Richard Hooker (d. 1600)
1555	Diet of Augsburg; Peace of Augsburg establishes legal territorial existence of Lutheranism and Catholicism b. Johann Arndt (d. 1621)	First mission of French pastors trained in Geneva				b. Sibbrandus Lubbertus (d. 1625)	b. Lancelot Andrewes (d. 1626) b. Robert Rollock (d. 1599); d. Hugh Latimer; d. Nicholas Ridley d. John Hooper
1556	d. Pilgram Marpeck (b. 1495) d. Konrad Pellikan (b. 1478) d. Peter Riedemann (b. 1506)		Charles V resigns			d. David Joris (b. c. 1501)	d. Thomas Cranmer
1557							Alliance with Spain in war against France
1558			d. Charles V				b. William Perkins (d. 1602); d. Mary I; r. Elizabeth I (–1603)
1559		d. Henry II; r. Francis II (–1560); first national synod of French reformed churches (1559) in Paris; Gallic Confession		First index of prohibited books issued	Final edition of Calvin's *Institutes*; founding of Genevan Academy	b. Jacobus Arminius (d. 1609)	Elizabethan Settlement

	German Territories	France	Spain	Italy	Switzerland	Netherlands	British Isles
1560	d. P. Melanchthon	d. Francis II; r. Charles IX (1574); Edict of Toleration created peace with Huguenots	d. Domingo de Soto (b. 1494)		Geneva Bible		Kirk of Scotland established; Scottish Confession
1561-1563				Third session of Council of Trent			
1561						Belgic Confession	
1562	d. Katharina Schütz Zell (b. 1497/98)	Massacre of Huguenots begins French Wars of Religion (–1598)					The Articles of Religion—in Elizabethan "final" form (1562/71); publication of Latin edition of Jewel's *Apology*
1563	Heidelberg Catechism						
1564				b. Galileo (d. 1642)	d. J. Calvin		b. William Shakespeare (d. 1616); publication of Lady Ann Bacon's English translation of Jewel's *Apology*
1566	d. Johann Agricola (b. 1494)			Roman Catechism	Second Helvetic Confession		
1567						Spanish occupation	Abdication of Scottish throne by Mary Stuart; r. James VI (1603–1625)
1568						d. Dirk Phillips (b. 1504) Dutch movement for liberation (–1645)	*Bishops' Bible*
1570		d. Johannes Mercerus (Jean Mercier)		Papal Bull *Regnans in Excelsis* excommunicates Elizabeth I			Elizabeth I excommunicated
1571	b. Johannes Kepler (d. 1630)		Spain defeats Ottoman navy at Battle of Lepanto				b. John Downame (d. 1652)
1572		Massacre of Huguenots on St. Bartholomew's Day		r. Pope Gregory XIII (1583–1585)		William of Orange invades	b. John Donne (d. 1631)
1574		d. Charles IX; r. Henri III (d. 1589)					

	German Territories	France	Spain	Italy	Switzerland	Netherlands	British Isles
1575	d. Georg Major (b. 1502); Bohemian Confession of 1575						
1576		Declaration of Toleration; formation of Catholic League		b. Giovanni Diodati (d. 1649)		Sack of Antwerp; Pacification of Ghent	
1577	Lutheran Formula of Concord						England allies with Netherlands against Spain
1578	Swiss Brethren Confession of Hesse d. Peter Walpot		Truce with Ottomans				Sir Francis Drake circumnavigates the globe
1579			Expeditions to Ireland			Division of Dutch provinces	
1580	Lutheran Book of Concord						
1581			d. Teresa of Avila				Anti-Catholic statutes passed
1582				Gregorian Reform of calendar			
1583							b. David Dickson (d. 1663)
1584		Treaty of Joinville with Spain	Treaty of Joinville; Spain inducted into Catholic League; defeats Dutch at Antwerp			Fall of Antwerp; d. William of Orange	
1585	d. Josua Opitz (b. c. 1542)	Henri of Navarre excommunicated		r. Pope Sixtus V (–1590)			
1586							Sir Francis Drake's expedition to West Indies; Sir Walter Raleigh in Roanoke
1587	d. Johann Wigand (b. 1523)	Henri of Navarre defeats royal army					d. Mary Stuart of Scotland
1588		Henri of Navarre drives Henri III from Paris; assassination of Catholic League Leaders	Armada destroyed				English Navy defeats Spanish Armada
1589		d. Henri III; r. Henri (of Navarre) IV (–1610)	Victory over England at Lisbon				Defeated by Spain in Lisbon
1590		Henri IV's siege of Paris		d. Girolamo Zanchi (b. 1516)			Alliance with Henri IV

	German Territories	France	Spain	Italy	Switzerland	Netherlands	British Isles
1592	d. Nikolaus Selnecker (b. 1530)						
1593		Henri IV converts to Catholicism					Books I-IV of Hooker's *Laws of Ecclesiastical Polity* published
1594		Henri grants toleration to Huguenots					
1595		Henri IV declares war on Spain; received into Catholic Church		Pope Sixtus accepts Henri IV into Church			Alliance with France
1596		b. René Descartes (d. 1650) b. Moïse Amyraut (d. 1664)					
1597							Book V of Hooker's *Laws of Ecclesiastical Polity* published
1598		Edict of Nantes; toleration of Huguenots; peace with Spain	Treaty of Vervins; peace with France				
1600	d. David Chytraeus (b. 1531)						
1601							b. John Trapp (d. 1669)
1602					d. Daniel Toussain (b. 1541)		
1603							d. Elizabeth I; r. James I (James VI of Scotland) (–1625)
1604	d. Cyriacus Spangenberg (b. 1528)						d. John Whitgift (b. 1530)
1605						b. Rembrandt (d. 1669)	Guy Fawkes and gunpowder plot
1606							Jamestown Settlement
1607							b. John Milton (d. 1674)
1608							
1610		d. Henri IV; r. Louis XIII (–1643)	d. Benedict Pererius (b. 1535)			The Remonstrance; Short Confession	

	German Territories	France	Spain	Italy	Switzerland	Netherlands	British Isles
1611							Publication of Authorized English Translation of Bible (AV/KJV); George Abbot becomes Archbishop of Canterbury (–1633)
1612							b. Richard Crashaw (d. 1649)
1616							b. John Owen (d. 1683)
1617							b. Ralph Cudworth (d. 1689)
1618–1619						Synod of Dordrecht	
1618–1648	Thirty Years' War						
1620							English Sepratists land in Plymouth, Massachusetts
1621							d. Andrew Willet (b. 1562)
1628							Puritans establish Massachusetts Bay colony
1633	d. Christoph Pelargus (b. 1565)						Laud becomes Archbishop of Canterbury
1637	d. Johann Gerhard (b. 1582)					*Statenvertaling*	
1638							d. Joseph Mede (b. 1638)
1640				Diodati's Italian translation of Bible published			
1642–1649							English civil wars; d. Charles I; r. Oliver Cromwell (1660)
1643		d. Louis XIII; r. Louis XIV (–1715)					
1643–1649							Westminster Assembly
1645							d. William Laud (b. 1573)

	German Territories	France	Spain	Italy	Switzerland	Netherlands	British Isles
1648		Treaty of Westphalia ends Thirty Years' War					Books VI and VIII of Hooker's *Laws of Ecclesiastical Polity* posthumously published
1656	d. Georg Calixtus (b. 1586)						
1658							d. Oliver Cromwell
1659							Richard Cromwell resigns
1660							English Restoration; r. Charles II (–1685)
1662							Act of Uniformity; Book VII of Hooker's *Laws of Ecclesiastical Polity* posthumously published
1664						d. Thieleman Jans van Braght (b. 1625)	d. John Mayer (b. 1583)
1671							d. William Greenhill (b. 1591)
1677							d. Thomas Manton (b. 1620)
1678						d. Anna Maria von Schurman (b. 1607)	
1688							Glorious Revolution; r. William and Mary (-1702); d. John Bunyan (b. 1628)
1691							d. Richard Baxter (b. 1615)

BIOGRAPHICAL SKETCHES OF REFORMATION-ERA FIGURES AND WORKS

This list is cumulative, including all the authors cited in the Reformation Commentary on Scripture to date as well as other people relevant to the Reformation and Reformation-era exegesis. For works consulted, see "Sources for Biographical Sketches," p. 495.

Cornelius À Lapide (1567–1637). Flemish Catholic biblical exegete. A Jesuit, Lapide served as professor of Holy Scripture and Hebrew at Louvain for twenty years before taking a similar role in Rome, where he taught until his death. He is best known for his extensive commentaries on the Scriptures. Encompassing all books of the Bible except Job and the Psalms, his work employs a fourfold hermeneutic and draws heavily on the work of patristic and medieval exegetes.

Thomas Adams (1583–1653). Anglican minister and author. He attended the University of Cambridge where he received his BA in 1601 and his MA in 1606. Following his ordination in 1604, Adams served as curate at Northill in Bedfordshire. In 1611, he became vicar of Willmington. Three years later he served the parish of Wingrave, Buckinghamshire, where he remained until 1618. From 1618 to 1623 Adams was preacher at St. Gregory by St. Paul's. He also served as chaplain to Henry Montague, First Earl of Manchester, and Lord Chief Justice of England. Among his most important works are the *Happiness of the Church* (1618) and an extensive commentary on 2 Peter (1638).

Johannes Aepinus (1499–1553). German Lutheran preacher and theologian. Aepinus studied under Martin Luther,* Philipp Melanchthon* and Johannes Bugenhagen* in Wittenberg. Because of his Lutheran beliefs, Aepinus lost his first teaching position in Brandenburg. He fled north to Stralsund and became a preacher and superintendent at Saint Peter's Church in Hamburg. In 1534, he made a diplomatic visit to England but could not convince Henry VIII* to embrace the Augsburg Confession.* His works include sermons and theological writings. Aepinus became best known as leader of the Infernalists, who believed that Christ underwent torment in hell after his crucifixion.

Johann Agricola (c. 1494–1566). German Lutheran pastor and theologian. An early student of Martin Luther,* Agricola eventually began a controversy over the role of the law, first with Melanchthon* and then with Luther himself. Agricola claimed to defend Luther's true position, asserting that only the gospel of the crucified Christ calls Christians to truly good works, not the fear of the law. After this first controversy, Agricola seems to have radicalized his views to the point that he eliminated Luther's *simul iustus et peccator* ("at the same time righteous and sinful") paradox of the Christian life, emphasizing instead that believers have no need for the law once they are united with Christ through faith. Luther responded by writing anonymous pamphlets against antinomianism. Agricola later published a recantation of his views, hoping to assuage relations with Luther, although they were never personally reconciled. He published a commentary on Luke, a series of sermons on Colossians, and a massive collection of German proverbs.

Henry Ainsworth (1571–1622/1623). English Puritan Hebraist. In 1593, under threat of persecution, Ainsworth relocated to Amsterdam, where he served as a teacher in an English congregation. He composed a confession of faith for the community and a number of polemical and exegetical works, including annotations on the Pentateuch, the Psalms and Song of Songs.

Henry Airay (c. 1560–1616). English Puritan professor and pastor. He was especially noted for his preaching, a blend of hostility toward Catholicism and articulate exposition of English Calvinism. He was promoted to provost of Queen's College Oxford (1598) and then to vice chancellor of the university in 1606. He disputed with William Laud* concerning Laud's putative Catholicization of the Church of England, particularly over the practice of genuflection, which Airay vehemently opposed. He also opposed fellow Puritans who wished to separate from the Church of England. His lectures on Philippians were his only work published during his lifetime.

Albert the Great (1201–1280). German theologian, philosopher, scientist, and ecclesiastic. Albert was born in Lauingen, located in the Bavarian-Swabian region. After completing his studies at Padua, Albert joined the Dominicans in 1220s. Upon finishing further theological studies at Cologne, Albert became a conventual lecturer during the 1230s at Hildesheim, Freiberg (Saxony), Regensburg, and Strasbourg. In the early 1240s, Albert was sent to Paris where he became a master of theology, and regent of the university in 1245. He served as regent until 1248. While at Paris, Albert commenced his paraphrases of Aristotle's works. Furthermore, Albert authored a systematic theology, and lectured on the four Gospels and nine books of the Old Testament. Albert is best known for having taught Thomas Aquinas,* who, as his assistant, transcribed his course on the works of Dionysius and Aristotle's *Nicomachean Ethics.*

Alexander (Ales) Alesius (1500–1565). Scottish Lutheran theologian. Following the martyrdom of his theological adversary Patrick Hamilton (c. 1504–1528), Alesius converted to the Reformation and fled to Germany. In 1535 Martin Luther* and Philipp Melanchthon* sent him as an emissary to Henry VIII* and Thomas Cranmer.* He taught briefly at Cambridge, but after the Act of Six Articles reasserted Catholic sacramental theology he returned to Germany, where he lectured at Frankfurt an der Oder and Leipzig. Alesius composed many exegetical, theological and polemical works, including commentaries on John, Romans, 1–2 Timothy, Titus and the Psalms.

Robert Allen (fl. 1596–1612). English Protestant clergyman and writer. Allen is known only by his writings, which reveal few biographical details except that he was a minister and he wrote from London and Suffolk. His works include a theological summary of Proverbs and Ecclesiastes, an exposition of the Gospel, and a catechism.

Andreas Althamer (c. 1500–1539). German Lutheran humanist and pastor. Forced from the chaplaincy at Schwäbisch-Gmünd for teaching evangelical ideas, Althamer studied theology at Wittenberg before serving as a pastor in Eltersdorf, Nuremberg, and Ansbach. A staunch Lutheran, he contended against Reformed theologians at the 1528 disputation at Bern and delivered numerous polemics against Anabaptism. He also composed an early Lutheran catechism, published at Nuremberg in 1528.

William Ames (1576–1633). English Puritan theologian. Heavily influenced by William Perkins* while at Cambridge, Ames was unable to find employment in the English church due to his Puritan commitments. Most of his life was spent in exile in the Netherlands, where he served as chaplain to English forces at The Hague and was the pastor of a small congregation. Best known as a controversialist during his early career, Ames was the theological advisor to the president of the Synod of Dort (1618–1619) and was later installed as chair of theology at the University of Franeker in Friesland. *The Marrow of Theology* (1627) is viewed as a model of seventeenth-century Puritan theology.

Moïse Amyraut (1596–1664). French Reformed pastor and professor. Originally intending to be a lawyer, Amyraut turned to theology after an encounter with several Huguenot pastors and having read Calvin's* *Institutes.* After a brief stint as a parish pastor, Amyraut spent the majority of his career at the Saumur Academy. He was well known for his irenicism and ecumenicism (for example, in advocating intercommunion with Lutherans). Certain aspects of his writings on justification, faith, the covenants and especially predestination proved controversial among the Reformed. His doctrine of election is often called hypothetical universalism or Amyraldianism, stating that Christ's atoning work was intended by God for all human beings indiscriminately, although its effectiveness for salvation depends on faith, which is a free gift of God given only to those whom God has chosen from eternity. Amyraut was charged with grave doctrinal error three times before the National Synod but was acquitted each time. Aside from his theological treatises, Amyraut published paraphrases of almost the entire New Testament and the Psalms, as well as many sermons.

Anabaptists of Trieste (1539). Following a meeting between Swiss Brethren and the Hutterites at Steinabrunn on December 6, 1536, around 140 radicals were arrested and imprisoned in Falkenstein Castle. After six weeks in captivity, the ninety men of the group were forced to march to Trieste to be sold as galley slaves. Twelve days after arrival, all but twelve prisoners managed to escape and return to Moravia, where they published a confession of their beliefs.

Jakob Andreae (1528–1590). German Lutheran theologian. Andreae studied at the University of

Tübingen before being called to the diaconate in Stuttgart in 1546. He was appointed ecclesiastical superintendent of Göppingen in 1553 and supported Johannes Brenz's* proposal to place the church under civil administrative control. An ecclesial diplomat for the duke of Württemberg, Andreae debated eucharistic theology, the use of images, and predestination with Theodore Beza* at the Colloquy of Montbéliard (1586) to determine whether French Reformed exiles would be required to submit to the Formula of Concord.* Andreae coauthored the Formula of Concord. He and his wife had eighteen children.

Lancelot Andrewes (1555–1626). Anglican bishop. A scholar, pastor and preacher, Andrews prominently shaped a distinctly Anglican identity between the poles of Puritanism and Catholicism. He oversaw the translation of Genesis to 2 Kings for the Authorized Version.* His eight-volume collected works—primarily devotional tracts and sermons—are marked by his fluency in Scripture, the Christian tradition and classical literature.

Thomas Aquinas (1225–1274). Dominican medieval theologian. Thomas Aquinas was born into a noble family in Rocasecca, Italy. In 1230 Thomas's father sent him to the abbey at Monte Casino as a child oblate. When, at age fourteen, Thomas was given the choice between taking his final vows and leaving, he chose to go to Naples to study at the school recently founded by the Holy Roman Emperor. While studying at Naples, Thomas came into contact with the Dominicans, and joined this order in 1244. Although his family objected to his decision at first, to the point of actually imprisoning Thomas, they came to accept his decision the following year. Afterwards, Aquinas traveled to Paris where he began his formal studies under Albert the Great (1200–1280). Aquinas followed his teacher to Cologne in 1248 where he was ordained a priest, and completed his course in theology. Four years later, he was appointed a bachelor in the Dominican convent in Paris where he lectured on Peter Lombard's (1096–1160)* *Sentences*. In 1256, Thomas was incepted as a master of the sacred page, and he taught in Paris until 1259. In 1261, he was appointed lecturer at a school in Orvieto. Four years later, Aquinas was transferred to Rome, and in 1268 returned to Paris. In 1272, the Dominican order appointed Aquinas to start a new school in Naples. A mystical experience reportedly caused Aquinas to abruptly cease his writing. Aquinas died at a monastery in Fossanova. In addition to his major works, *Summa Theologia* and *Summa Contra Gentiles*, Aquinas's voluminous corpus includes extensive commentaries on Jeremiah, Lamentations, Isaiah, Job, and an incomplete one on the Psalms. Aquinas also wrote commentaries on the Gospels of Matthew and John as well as the Pauline Epistles. Furthermore, at the request of the pope, Aquinas produced the *Catena Aurea*, a commentary on the four Gospels consisting of exegetical statements by the Latin and Greek fathers. One of the most significant features of Aquinas's biblical commentaries is his emphasis on the literal meaning of a Scriptural text. As a representation of medieval Catholic theology, Aquinas's theology was regularly challenged by the Protestant reformers.

Benedict Aretius (d. 1574). Swiss Reformed professor. Trained at the universities of Bern, Strasbourg and Marburg, Aretius taught logic and philosophy as well as the biblical languages and theology. He advocated for stronger unity and peace between the Lutheran and Reformed churches. Aretius joined others in denouncing the antitrinitarian Giovanni Valentino Gentile (d. 1566). He published commentaries on the New Testament, as well as various works on astronomy, botany and medicine.

Aristotle (388–322 BC). Ancient Greek philosopher and scientist. Aristotle was born in Stagira, Chalkdice, northern Greece. He is considered the "Father of Western Philosophy" along with his teacher, Plato, because his teaching produced the bases for almost every discipline studied in the Western world. After his father's death while he was still a child, Aristotle was raised by his guardian, Proxenus of Atarneus. At the age of about eighteen, Aristotle joined Plato's Academy in Athens, where he remained until his was thirty-seven. Aristotle's writings cover a wide range of subjects: physics, biology, zoology, metaphysics, logic, ethics, aesthetics, poetry, theater, music, rhetoric, psychology, linguistics, and politics. Shortly after Plato's death, King Philip II of Macedonia requested his services as a tutor to his son, Alexander the Great. Aristotle began tutoring the young prince in 343 BC. While teaching Alexander, Aristotle was able to acquire hundreds of books for the library of what would become his Lyceum. Aristotle's work profoundly shaped scholarship during the Middle Ages and early modern period as his logic was employed in the exegesis of Scripture and formation of theology. Among the major theologians who incorporated Aristotle's methods into their theological systems was Thomas Aquinas.* Aristotle's methods and categories would also be utilized by many Protestant theologians throughout the sixteenth and seventeenth centuries.

Jacobus Arminius (1559–1609). Dutch Remonstrant pastor and theologian. Arminius was a vocal critic of high

Calvinist scholasticism, whose views were repudiated by the Synod of Dordrecht. Arminius was a student of Theodore Beza* at the academy of Geneva. He served as a pastor in Amsterdam and later joined the faculty of theology at the university in Leiden, where his lectures on predestination were popular and controversial. Predestination, as Arminius understood it, was the decree of God determined on the basis of divine foreknowledge of faith or rejection by humans who are the recipients of prevenient, but resistible, grace.

Johann Arndt (1555–1621). German Lutheran pastor and theologian. After a brief time teaching, Arndt pastored in Badeborn (Anhalt) until 1590, when Prince Johann Georg von Anhalt (1567–1618) began introducing Reformed ecclesial policies. Arndt ministered in Quedlinberg, Brunswick, Eisleben and Celle. Heavily influenced by medieval mysticism, Arndt centered his theology on Christ's mystical union with the believer, out of which flows love of God and neighbor. He is best known for his *True Christianity* (1605–1609), which greatly influenced Philipp Jakob Spener (1635–1705) and later Pietists.

John Arrowsmith (1602–1659). English Puritan theologian. Arrowsmith participated in the Westminster Assembly, and later taught at Cambridge. His works, all published posthumously, include three sermons preached to Parliament and an unfinished catechism.

Articles of Religion (1562; revised 1571). The Articles underwent a long editorial process that drew from the influence of Continental confessions in England, resulting in a uniquely Anglican blend of Protestantism and Catholicism. In their final form, they were reduced from Thomas Cranmer's* Forty-two Articles (1539) to the Elizabethan Thirty-Nine Articles (1571), excising polemical articles against the Anabaptists and Millenarians as well as adding articles on the Holy Spirit, good works and Communion. Originating in a 1535 meeting with Lutherans, the Articles retained a minor influence from the Augsburg Confession* and Württemberg Confession (1552), but showed significant revision in accordance with Genevan theology, as well as the Second Helvetic Confession.*

Anne Askew (1521–1546). English Protestant martyr. Askew was forced to marry her deceased sister's intended husband, who later expelled Askew from his house—after the birth of two children—on account of her religious views. After unsuccessfully seeking a divorce in Lincoln, Askew moved to London, where she met other Protestants and began to preach. In 1546, she was arrested, imprisoned and convicted of heresy for denying the doctrine of transubstantiation. Under torture in the Tower of London she refused to name any other Protestants. On July 16, 1546, she was burned at the stake. Askew is best known through her accounts of her arrests and examinations. John Bale (1495–1563), a bishop, historian and playwright, published these manuscripts. Later John Foxe (1516–1587) included them in his *Acts and Monuments*, presenting her as a role model for other pious Protestant women.

Mary Astell (1666–1731). English writer and philosopher. Astell received an informal education from her uncle, a clergyman. Left almost penniless after the death of her parents, she settled in London, where she made her career as a writer. She is best known for her proto-feminist works, including *A Serious Proposal to the Ladies* (1694, 1697), *Some Reflections on Marriage* (1700), and *The Christian Religion, as Professed by a Daughter of the Church of England* (1705). In these works she argues for the moral and intellectual equality of the sexes and the need for women to receive a similar education to men so that they can navigate the world by themselves. Retiring from writing, Astell spent her final decades organizing a charity school for girls in Chelsea backed by the Society for the Propagation of Christian Knowledge.

Augsburg Confession (1530). In the wake of Luther's* stand against ecclesial authorities at the Diet of Worms (1521), the Holy Roman Empire splintered along theological lines. Emperor Charles V sought to ameliorate this—while also hoping to secure a united European front against Turkish invasion—by calling together another imperial diet in Augsburg in 1530. The Evangelical party was cast in a strongly heretical light at the diet by Johann Eck.* For this reason, Philipp Melanchthon* and Justus Jonas* thought it best to strike a conciliatory tone (Luther, as an official outlaw, did not attend), submitting a confession rather than a defense. The resulting Augsburg Confession was approved by many of the rulers of the northeastern Empire; however, due to differences in eucharistic theology, Martin Bucer* and the representatives of Strasbourg, Constance, Lindau and Memmingen drafted a separate confession (the Tetrapolitan Confession). Charles V accepted neither confession, demanding that the Evangelicals accept the Catholic rebuttal instead. In 1531, along with the publication of the Augsburg Confession itself, Melanchthon released a defense of the confession that responded to the Catholic confutation and expanded on the original articles. Most subsequent Protestant confessions followed the general structure of the Augsburg Confession.

Augustine of Hippo (354–430 AD). North African bishop and theologian. Augustine was born in Thagaste

(Ahras, Algeria), a small town in the Roman province to Numidia, the son of a Christian mother, Monica, and a non-Christian father, Patricius, a local official of modest means. Enabled by local patronage, Augustine received a classical education, which afforded him the opportunity to pursue advanced training in rhetoric at Carthage. Upon completing his education at Carthage, Augustine taught rhetoric there as well as in Rome and Milan, where he was appointed official rhetorician of that city. Inspired by his reading of Cicero's *Hortensius*, Augustine embarked upon a quest for wisdom. While in Carthage, Augustine was repulsed by the seemingly simplistic Christianity he encountered, and therefore joined the Manicheans. Having become disillusioned by the Manichaeans' failure to lead him to the wisdom they promised, Augustine was eventually drawn to orthodox Christianity by the preaching of Ambrose (340–397) and his reading of the Neo-Platonist philosopher Plotinus (204–270). As a result of his conversion in 386, Augustine abandoned his secular ambitions in favor of a celibate life fully committed to intellectual and spiritual devotion to God. Towards this end, Augustine returned to north Africa to establish a semi–monastic community. However, in 391, while visiting Hippo Regius, he was forcibly ordained into the priesthood, and made bishop of that church in 396. In addition to his many duties as a bishop, Augustine engaged in controversies against the Manicheans, Donatists, and Pelagians, which took up the remainder of his life and career. He died in 430 while the Vandals besieged Hippo. Among his many works, Augustine devoted several to exegesis. He outlines exegetical principles in his *De Doctrina Christiana* ("On Christian Doctrine"), and he authored extensive series of homilies on most of the books of the New Testament as well as the Old Testament books of Psalms and Genesis (incomplete). During the Reformation era, both Catholic and Protestant theologians appealed to and engaged with Augustine's theology, especially his emphases upon original sin and humanity's need for God's grace.

Authorized Version (1611). In 1604 King James I* commissioned this new translation—popularly remembered as the King James Version—for uniform use in the public worship of the Church of England. The Bible and the Apocrypha was divided into six portions and assigned to six companies of nine scholars—both Anglicans and Puritans—centered at Cambridge, Oxford and Westminster. Richard Bancroft, the general editor of the Authorized Version, composed fifteen rules to guide the translators and to guard against overly partisan decisions. Rather than offer an entirely fresh English translation, the companies were to follow the Bishops' Bible* as closely as possible. "Truly (good Christian Reader)," the preface states, "we neuer thought from the beginning that we should need to make a new Translation, nor yet to make of a bad one a good one . . . but make a good one better, or out of many good ones, one principall good one, not iustly to be excepted against: that hath bene our endeauour, that our mark." Other rules standardized spelling, dictated traditional ecclesial terms (e.g., *church*, *baptize* and *bishop*), and allowed only for linguistic marginal notes and cross-references. Each book of the Bible went through a rigorous revision process: first, each person in a company made an initial draft, then the company put together a composite draft, then a supercommittee composed of representatives from each company reviewed these drafts, and finally two bishops and Bancroft scrutinized the final edits. The text and translation process of the Authorized Version have widely influenced biblical translations ever since.

Gervase Babington (1549/1550–1610). English Anglican bishop. Born into an influential family, Babington studied at Cambridge and spent time as a preacher at the university and as prebendary of Hereford Cathedral before serving, in turn, as bishop of Llandaff, Exeter, and Worcester. He published a number of sermons, expositions of the Ten Commandments and Lord's Prayer, and notes on Genesis, Exodus, and Leviticus.

Robert Bagnall (b. 1559 or 1560). English Protestant minister. Bagnall authored *The Steward's Last Account* (1622), a collection of five sermons on Luke 16.

Friedrich Balduin (1575–1627). German Lutheran theologian. After spending time in the pastorate at Freiberg and Oelsnitz, Balduin was appointed professor of theology at Wittenberg in 1604, where he remained until the end of his life. He also served as head of the theology faculty, superintendent of churches, and assessor of the consistory. Known for his commitment to Lutheran orthodoxy, Balduin's major works include a commentary on the Pauline letters and writings on exegesis, homiletics, and casuistry.

John Ball (1585–1640). English Puritan theologian. Ball was a respected educator. He briefly held a church office until he was removed on account of his Puritanism. He composed popular catechisms and tracts on faith, the church and the covenant of grace.

John Barlow (1580/1581?–1629/1630). English Protestant minister. Educated at Oxford, Barlow ministered in Plymouth, Halifax, and Chester. A number of his sermons have been preserved, including his teachings on 2 Timothy 1 and 1 Thessalonians 4:18.

Thomas Bastard (c. 1565–1618). English Protestant minister and poet. Educated at Winchester and New College, Oxford, Bastard published numerous works, including collections of poems and sermons; his most famous title is *Chrestoleros* (1598), a collection of epigrams. Bastard was alleged to be the author of an anonymous work, *An Admonition to the City of Oxford*, which revealed the carnal vices of many clergy and scholars in Oxford; despite denying authorship, he was dismissed from Oxford in 1591. Bastard was recognized as a skilled classical scholar and preacher. He died impoverished in a debtor's prison in Dorchester.

Jeremias Bastingius (1551–1595). Dutch Reformed theologian. Educated in Heidelberg and Geneva, Bastingius pastored the Reformed church in Antwerp for nearly a decade until the Spanish overran the city in 1585; he later settled in Dordrecht. He spent the last few years of his life in Leiden on the university's board of regents. He wrote an influential commentary on the Heidelberg Catechism that was translated into English, Dutch, German and Flemish.

Johann (Pomarius) Baumgart (1514–1578). Lutheran pastor and amateur playwright. Baumgart studied under Georg Major,* Martin Luther* and Philipp Melanchthon* at the University of Wittenberg. Before becoming pastor of the Church of the Holy Spirit in 1540, Baumgart taught secondary school. He authored catechetical and polemical works, a postil for the Gospel readings throughout the church year, numerous hymns and a didactic play (*Juditium Salomonis*).

Richard Baxter (1615–1691). English Puritan minister. Baxter was a leading Puritan pastor, evangelist and theologian, known throughout England for his landmark ministry in Kidderminster and a prodigious literary output, producing 135 books in just over forty years. Baxter came to faith through reading William Perkins,* Richard Sibbes* and other early Puritan writers and was the first cleric to decline the terms of ministry in the national English church imposed by the 1662 Act of Uniformity; Baxter wrote on behalf of the more than 1700 who shared ejection from the national church. He hoped for restoration to national church ministry, or toleration, that would allow lawful preaching and pastoring. Baxter sought unity in theological, ecclesiastical, sociopolitical and personal terms and is regarded as a forerunner of Noncomformist ecumenicity, though he was defeated in his efforts at the 1661 Savoy Conference to take seriously Puritan objections to the revision of the 1604 Prayer Book. Baxter's views on church ministry were considerably hybrid: he was a paedo-baptist, Nonconformist minister who approved of synodical Episcopal government and fixed liturgy. He is most known for his classic writings on the Christian life, such as *The Saints' Everlasting Rest* and *A Christian Directory*, and pastoral ministry, such as *The Reformed Pastor*. He also produced *Catholick Theology*, a large volume squaring current Reformed, Lutheran, Arminian and Roman Catholic systems with each other.

Thomas Becon (1511/1512–1567). English Puritan preacher. Becon was a friend of Hugh Latimer,* and for several years chaplain to Archbishop Thomas Cranmer.* Becon was sent to the Tower of London by Mary I and then exiled for his controversial preaching at the English royal court. He returned to England upon Elizabeth I's* accession. Becon was one of the most widely read popular preachers in England during the Reformation. He published many of his sermons, including a postil, or collection of sermon helps for undertrained or inexperienced preachers.

Belgic Confession (1561). Written by Guy de Brès (1523–1567), this statement of Dutch Reformed faith was heavily reliant on the Gallic Confession,* although more detailed, especially in how strongly it distances the Reformed from Roman Catholics and Anabaptists. The Confession first appeared in French in 1561 and was translated to Dutch in 1562. It was presented to Philip II (1527–1598) in the hope that he would grant toleration to the Reformed, to no avail. At the Synod of Dordrecht* the Confession was revised, clarifying and strengthening the article on election as well as sharpening the distinctives of Reformed theology against the Anabaptists, thus situating the Dutch Reformed more closely to the international Calvinist movement. The Belgic Confession in conjunction with the Heidelberg Catechism* and the Canons of Dordrecht were granted official status as the confessional standards (the Three Forms of Unity) of the Dutch Reformed Church.

Robert Bellarmine (1542–1621). Italian Catholic cardinal. A Jesuit, Bellarmine first taught at Louvain before being appointed chair of polemical theology at the Roman College. Much of Bellarmine's career was devoted to the refutation of Protestant teachings, and his three volume work, the *Controversies* (1586–93), was widely disseminated in the post-Tridentine era as the foremost refutation of the evangelical message. He was influential in the official revision of the Vulgate* text during the reign of Pope Clement VIII (1536–1605), with the resulting version, the Sixto-Clementine Vulgate, providing the basic biblical text for Catholics until Vatican II. Bellarmine is also a controversial figure in the history of science. Appointed to the Holy Office, also known as the

Inquisition, by Pope Paul V (1550–1621), it was he who examined Galileo Galilei (1564–1642) and ordered him to treat heliocentrism as a hypothesis rather than a reality, believing the evidentiary threshold had not yet been met. Later in his career, Bellarmine's attention turned to works on devotion and piety, and include his extensive commentary on the Psalms (1611).

Bernard of Clairvaux (1090–1153). French abbot and theologian. Born the son of a Bugundian knight, Bernard became interested in the new reforming movement at Citeaux, and thus abandoned his preparation for a secular career in favor of monastic life there. Towards this end, Bernard persuaded thirty-one of his friends and relatives to follow him to Citeaux, and join the Cistercian order. Among this group were four of Bernard's brothers. In 1115, Bernard went with others of his order to found a Cistercian monastery at Claivaux. Bernard's austere approach to the monastic life attracted many followers to the point that by the time of his death there were sixty-eight Cistercian houses. Throughout his career, Bernard preached, mediated theological disputes, and advised. Bernard is best known for having preached the Second Crusade (1147–1150) as well as advising his former student, Pope Eugenius III (r. 1145–1153), and engaging in theological controversies with Peter Abelard (1079–1142) and Gilbert of Poitiers (1085–1154). One of the distinguishing characteristics of Bernard's theology is his Christocentric mysticism. Among Bernard's most important works are his treatises *On Consideration* and *On Loving God* along with his *Sermons on the Song of Songs* as well as many other sermons on the liturgical year and other subject. Many of the reformers in the sixteenth century cited Bernard extensively, especially Martin Luther* and John Calvin*.

Richard Bernard (1568–1641). English Puritan minister. A moderate Puritan, Bernard eschewed separation from the Church of England, spending the majority of his career in parish ministry at Batcombe, Somerset. Many of his works, including a handbook for pastors and a household catechism, were well received and printed numerous times during his lifetime.

Theodore Beza (1519–1605). French Reformed pastor and professor. Beza was compatriot and successor to John Calvin* as moderator of the Company of Pastors in Geneva during the second half of the sixteenth century. He was a noteworthy New Testament scholar whose *Codex Bezae* formed the basis of the New Testament section of later English translations. A leader in the academy and the church, Beza served as professor of Greek at the Lausanne Academy until 1558, at which time he moved to Geneva to become the rector of the newly founded Genevan Academy. He enjoyed an international reputation through his correspondence with key European leaders. Beza developed and extended Calvin's doctrinal thought on several important themes such as the nature of predestination and the real spiritual presence of Christ in the Eucharist.

Theodor Bibliander (1504?–1564). Swiss Reformed Hebraist and theologian. Professor of Old Testament at the Zurich Academy from 1531, Bibliander published two Hebrew grammars, a collection of letters by Zwingli* and Oecolampadius*, commentaries on Isaiah, Ezekiel, and Nahum, a Latin translation of the Qur'an, and a tract warning Christians against the threat of Islam. He taught a universalist view of predestination, arguing that God saved all people unless they rejected divine grace. Following a dispute with double-predestinarian Peter Martyr Vermigli*, he was forced into retirement in 1560.

Thomas Bilson (1546/1547?–1616). English Anglican Bishop and theologian. A celebrated preacher and theologian, Bilson served as canon of Winchester Cathedral and warden of Winchester College before becoming bishop of Worcester. He held this position for only one year, however, before his appointment to the wealthier see of Winchester. As an advisor to King James I,* he preached at his coronation, and he was involved with the publication of the 1611 Authorized Version,* being part of the Cambridge company responsible for translating the Apocrypha, the author of part of the front matter, and one of the text's final editors. His extant writings defend the episcopacy against Erastianism, condemn rebellion, and argue for a literal understanding of Christ's descent into hell.

Hugh Binning (1627–1653). Scottish Presbyterian theologian. At the age of eighteen, Binning became a professor of philosophy at the University of Glasgow. In his early twenties he left this post for parish ministry, and died of consumption a few years later. His commentary on the Westminster Confession and a selection of his sermons were published after his death.

Samuel Bird (d. 1604). Anglican minister and author. A native of Essex, Bird matriculated at Queen's College, Cambridge, where he received his BA in 1570 and his MA in 1573, at which time he was also elected a fellow of Corpus Christi College, Cambridge. For reasons unknown, Bird resigned his fellowship sometime in 1576. He spent nearly the entirety of his post-university career as rector of St. Peter's in Ipswich until his death in 1604. Among Bird's major works are *A Friendlie Communication or Dialogue Betweene Paule and Demas, wherein is Disputed*

How We are to Use the Pleasures of This Life (1580), *Lectures upon the 11. Chapter of Hebrews and upon the 38. Psalme* (1598), and *Lectures upon the 8 and 9 Chapters of the Second Epistle to the Corinthians* (1598).

Bishops' Bible (1568). Anglicans were polarized by the two most recent English translations of the Bible: the Great Bible (1539) relied too heavily on the Vulgate* and was thus perceived as too Catholic, while the Geneva Bible's* marginal notes were too Calvinist for many Anglicans. So Archbishop Matthew Parker (1504–1575) commissioned a new translation of Scripture from the original languages with marginal annotations (many of which, ironically, were from the Geneva Bible). Published under royal warrant, the Bishops' Bible became the official translation for the Church of England. The 1602 edition provided the basis for the King James Bible (1611).

Christopher Blackwood (1607/1608–1670). English Baptist pastor. Initially an Anglican priest, Blackwood served at the parishes of Stockbury and Rye until Puritan sympathies led him to migrate to New England. Returning to England, he pastored briefly at Cranbrook until Baptist preaching caused him to leave the established church, be rebaptized, and serve as a pastor of a General Baptist congregation in Staplehurst. Joining the Parliamentary Army in their goal to evangelize Ireland, he helped plant a number of Baptist churches and pastored at Wexford, Kilkenny, and Dublin. His numerous writings include treatises on baptism and repentance, a catechism, and a commentary on the first ten chapters of Matthew.

Georg Blaurock (1492–1529). Swiss Anabaptist. Blaurock (a nickname meaning "blue coat," because of his preference for this garment) was one of the first leaders of Switzerland's radical reform movement. In the first public disputations on baptism in Zurich, he argued for believer's baptism and was the first person to receive adult believers' baptism there, having been baptized by Conrad Grebel* in 1525. Blaurock was arrested several times for performing mass adult baptisms and engaging in social disobedience by disrupting worship services. He was eventually expelled from Zurich but continued preaching and baptizing in various Swiss cantons until his execution.

Bohemian Confession (1535). Bohemian Christianity was subdivided between traditional Catholics, Utraquists (who demanded Communion in both kinds) and the *Unitas Fratrum*, who were not Protestants but whose theology bore strong affinities to the Waldensians and the Reformed. The 1535 Latin edition of this confession—an earlier Czech edition had already been drafted—was an attempt to clarify and redefine the beliefs of the *Unitas Fratrum*. This confession purged all earlier openness to rebaptism and inched toward Luther's* eucharistic theology. Jan Augusta (c. 1500–1572) and Jan Roh (also Johannes Horn; c. 1490–1547) presented the confession to King Ferdinand I (1503–1564) in Vienna, but the king would not print it. The *Unitas Fratrum* sought, and with slight amendments eventually obtained, Luther's advocacy of the confession. It generally follows the structure of the Augsburg Confession.*

Bohemian Confession (1575). This confession was an attempt to shield Bohemian Christian minorities—the Utraquists and the *Unitas Fratrum*—from the Counter-Reformation and Habsburg insistence on uniformity. The hope was that this umbrella consensus would ensure peace in the midst of Christian diversity; anyone who affirmed the 1575 Confession, passed by the Bohemian legislature, would be tolerated. This confession was, like the Bohemian Confession of 1535, patterned after the Augsburg Confession.* It emphasizes both justification by faith alone and good works as the fruit of salvation. Baptism and the Eucharist are the focus of the sacramental section, although the five traditional Catholic sacraments are also listed for the Utraquists. Though it was eventually accepted in 1609 by Rudolf II (1552–1612), the Thirty Years' War (1618–1648) rendered the confession moot.

Samuel Bolton (1606–1654). English Anglican minister. Bolton served a number of parishes in London before being elected to the Westminster Assembly. He spent the remainder of his career as master of Christ's College, Cambridge. A number of his writings were published, including works on sin, the sacraments, and Christian freedom.

Book of Common Prayer (1549; 1552). After the Church of England's break with Rome, it needed a liturgical manual to distinguish its theology and practice from that of Catholicism. Thomas Cranmer* drafted the Book of Common Prayer based on the medieval Roman Missal, under the dual influence of the revised Lutheran Mass and the reforms of the Spanish Cardinal Quiñones. This manual details the eucharistic service, as well as services for rites such as baptism, confirmation, marriage and funerals. It includes a matrix of the epistle and Gospel readings and the appropriate collect for each Sunday and feast day of the church year. The 1548 Act of Uniformity established the Book of Common Prayer as *the* authoritative liturgical manual for the Church of England, to be implemented everywhere by Pentecost 1549. After its 1552 revision, Queen Mary I banned it; Elizabeth I* reestablished it in 1559, although it was rejected by Puritans and Catholics alike.

The Book of Homilies (1547; 1563; 1570). This collection of approved sermons, published in three parts during the reigns of Edward VI and Elizabeth I,* was intended to inculcate Anglican theological distinctives and mitigate the problems raised by the lack of educated preachers. Addressing doctrinal and practical topics, Thomas Cranmer* likely wrote the majority of the first twelve sermons, published in 1547; John Jewel* added another twenty sermons in 1563. A final sermon, *A Homily Against Disobedience*, was appended to the canon in 1570. Reprinted regularly, the *Book of Homilies* was an important resource in Anglican preaching until at least the end of the seventeenth century.

Martin (Cellarius) Borrhaus (1499–1564). German Reformed theologian. After a dispute with his mentor Johann Eck,* Borrhaus settled in Wittenberg, where he was influenced by the radical Zwickau Prophets. He travelled extensively, and finally settled in Basel to teach philosophy and Old Testament. Despite his objections, many accused Borrhaus of Anabaptism; he argued that baptism was a matter of conscience. On account of his association with Sebastian Castellio (1515–1563) and Michael Servetus (1511–1553), some scholars posit that Borrhaus was an antitrinitarian. His writings include a treatise on the Trinity and commentaries on the Torah, historical books, Ecclesiastes and Isaiah.

Sigmund Bosch (unknown). German Anabaptist hymn writer. An elder in the Swiss and South German Anabaptist churches, Bosch collaborated with Pilgram Marpeck* in his ministry. He is known to have composed three hymns and a letter on the end times, which he addressed to the congregation in Austerlitz.

John Bourchier (d. 1660). English Puritan parliamentarian. Bourchier served as a justice of the peace in Yorkshire until imprisoned at the outbreak of the English Civil War. After his release, he was elected as the member of parliament for Ripon, and in this capacity he served as a judge at the trial of Charles I and signed the king's death warrant. Deemed too ill for trial with the other regicides, he died soon after the Restoration of the monarchy under Charles II.

John Bowle (d. 1637). Anglican pastor. After matriculating from Cambridge, Bowle was household pastor to Sir Robert Cecil (1563–1612) and held a pastorate at Tilehurst in Berkshire. He was appointed dean of Salisbury in 1620 and bishop of Rochester in 1629.

John Boys (1571–1625). Anglican priest and theologian. Before doctoral work at Cambridge, Boys pastored several parishes in Kent; after completing his studies he was appointed to more prominent positions, culminating in his 1619 appointment as the Dean of Canterbury by James I.* Boys published a popular four-volume postil of the Gospel and epistle readings for the church year, as well as a companion volume for the Psalms.

John Bradford (1510–1555). English Reformer, prebendary of St. Paul's, and martyr. Bradford was born in Blackley, Manchester, to an affluent family. After grammar school, Bradford at first began legal studies at the Inner Temple in London. However, while there, he heard the preaching of a fellow student, and thus converted to an evangelical faith. This conversion caused Bradford to abandon his study of law and enroll at St. Catherine's Hall, Cambridge, to study theology. He completed his MA in 1549, and in the same year, received an appointment of fellow at Pembroke Hall, Cambridge. In August, 1550, Bishop Nicholas Ridley ordained Bradford a deacon, and appointed him his personal chaplain. Bradford's exceptional preaching moved King Edward VI to select him as his chaplain and prebendary at St. Paul's Cathedral. After Mary Tudor succeeded her half-brother to throne, Bradford was tried and convicted of heresy on January 31, 1555. He was executed at the stake on July 1 of the same year.

Anne Bradstreet (1612–1672). English-American Puritan poet. Born in Northampton, Bradstreet married at sixteen and emigrated to the Massachusetts Bay Colony, of which both her father and husband would serve as governors. Mother to eight children, Bradstreet also wrote poetry. Much of her verse reflects on marriage, children, and her Puritan faith. While her writing received a mixed reception from contemporaries, many of whom viewed poetry as outside a woman's purview, she is today celebrated as the most significant early English poet in North America.

Thieleman Jans van Braght (1625–1664). Dutch Radical preacher. After demonstrating great ability with languages, this cloth merchant was made preacher in his hometown of Dordrecht in 1648. He served in this office for the next sixteen years, until his death. This celebrated preacher had a reputation for engaging in debate wherever an opportunity presented itself, particularly concerning infant baptism. The publication of his book of martyrs, *Het Bloedigh Tooneel of Martelaersspiegel* (1660; *Martyrs' Mirror*), proved to be his lasting contribution to the Mennonite tradition. *Martyrs' Mirror* is heavily indebted to the earlier martyr book *Offer des Heeren* (1562), to which Braght added many early church martyrs who rejected infant baptism, as well as over 800 contemporary martyrs.

David Bramley (unknown). English lay preacher. Two works by Bramley survive, an exposition of Matthew 11:25 and a treatise arguing for the acceptance of lay preachers without university training like himself. On both tracts, he is identified simply as a "Preacher of the Gospel."

Johannes Brenz (1499–1570). German Lutheran theologian and pastor. Brenz was converted to the reformation cause after hearing Martin Luther* speak; later, Brenz became a student of Johannes Oecolampadius.* His central achievement lay in his talent for organization. As city preacher in Schwäbisch-Hall and afterward in Württemberg and Tübingen, he oversaw the introduction of reform measures and doctrines and new governing structures for ecclesial and educational communities. Brenz also helped establish Lutheran orthodoxy through treatises, commentaries and catechisms. He defended Luther's position on eucharistic presence against Huldrych Zwingli* and opposed the death penalty for religious dissenters.

Guillaume Briçonnet (1470–1534). French Catholic abbot and bishop. Briçonnet created a short-lived circle of reformist-minded humanists in his diocese under the sponsorship of Marguerite d'Angoulême. His desire for ecclesial reform developed throughout his prestigious career (including positions as royal chaplain to the queen, abbot at Saint-Germain-des-Prés and bishop of Meaux), influenced by Jacques Lefèvre d'Étaples.* Briçonnet encouraged reform through ministerial visitation, Scripture and preaching in the vernacular and active study of the Bible. When this triggered the ire of the theology faculty at the Sorbonne in Paris, Briçonnet quelled the activity and departed, envisioning an ecclesial reform that proceeded hierarchically.

William Bridge (1600?–1670). English Puritan minister. Bridge ministered in Norfolk and Essex until excommunicated as a Nonconformist and exiled, leading him to Rotterdam, where he copastored a church with Jeremiah Burroughs.* Returning to England, he was a member of the Westminster Assembly and pastored at Great Yarmouth until ejected from the ministry by the Act of Uniformity (1662). Many of Bridge's sermons were published during his life, and he also composed a number of works designed to encourage struggling believers.

Walter Bridges (unknown). English Anglican minister. Three works are attributed to Bridges. Two were published anonymously, a sermon on Joab before the House of Commons and a catechism for those taking the Eucharist, while a third, a sermon on unity given before the Lord Mayor and Aldermen of London, names him and his position as preacher at St. Dunstans-in-the-East, London.

Thomas Brightman (1562–1607). English Puritan pastor and exegete. Under alleged divine inspiration, Brightman wrote a well known commentary on Revelation, influenced by Joachim of Fiore (d. 1202). In contrast to the putatively true churches of Geneva and Scotland, he depicted the Church of England as a type of the lukewarm Laodicean church. He believed that the Reformation would result in the defeat of the Vatican and the Ottoman Empire and that all humanity would be regenerated through the spread of the gospel before Christ's final return and judgment.

Hugh Broughton (1549–1612). English Puritan Hebraist and theologian. Following his time as a student and fellow at Cambridge, Broughton established himself as a scholar and preacher in London. His first work, *A Concent of Scripture* (1588), an attempt to harmonize the chronology of Scripture, caused significant controversy and led him to spend much of the next two decades traveling throughout Europe. On the Continent, he built a reputation in disputes with numerous Jewish, Catholic, and Protestant scholars and helped to plant an English Reformed church in Amsterdam, a congregation he may also have pastored for a time. Broughton's extensive writings include comments on numerous aspects of the Old Testament and New Testaments, a genealogy of Christ, and an explication of Christ's descent into hell.

Robert Browne (c. 1550–1633). English Nonconformist minister. While drawn to Puritan teachings, Browne began his career within the Church of England, ministering in London and Cambridge. Convinced that more radical reformation was needed outside the constraints of the state, Browne is recognized as the first to found a separatist church, establishing a congregation in Norwich, with those who followed him becoming known as Brownists. After a brief imprisonment, he left for Middelburg in the Netherlands, gathering a church based on the principles he espoused in his two most important works, *A Treatise of Reformation Without Tarrying* (1582) and *The Life and Manners of All True Christians* (1582), which set forth the foundations of congregationalist church government. Browne did not remain a separatist, however, and after a few years returned to England and reentered the Church of England, serving as a school headmaster and pastoring in Northamptonshire.

Antonio Brucioli (c. 1498–1566). Italian Protestant humanist and translator. Born in Florence, Brucioli and other humanists fled to Lyon after implication in a conspiracy to assassinate Guilio de' Medici (1478–1534, later Pope Clement VII r. 1523–1534). After publishing a series of philosophical dialogues, he returned to Florence, only to be expelled for involvement in further political intrigues, anticlerical writings, and suspected Lutheranism. Settling in Venice, Brucioli established a publishing house and began a prodigious printing program. Best known for rendering the first translation of the Scriptures into Italian directly from Hebrew and Greek, he also composed introductions and commentaries on the books of the Bible and published translations of philosophers such as Cicero, Pliny, and Aristotle. His writings on Scripture were scrutinized for their Protestant teachings, particularly with regard to the sacraments, and he was called before the Inquisition three times. The first time, Brucioli was fined and exiled from Venice; the second, his writings were banned and burned; and the third, he was imprisoned and left to die penniless upon release.

Otto Brunfels (c. 1488–1534). German Lutheran botanist, teacher and physician. Brunfels joined the Carthusian order, where he developed interests in the natural sciences and became involved with a humanist circle associated with Ulrich von Hutten and Wolfgang Capito.* In 1521, after coming into contact with Luther's* teaching, Brunfels abandoned the monastic life, traveling and spending time in botanical research and pastoral care. He received a medical degree in Basel and was appointed city physician of Bern in 1534. Brunfels penned defenses of Luther and Hutten, devotional biographies of biblical figures, a prayer book, and annotations on the Gospels and the Acts of the Apostles. His most influential contribution, however, is as a Renaissance botanist.

Martin Bucer (1491–1551). German Reformed theologian and pastor. A Dominican friar, Bucer was influenced by Desiderius Erasmus* during his doctoral studies at the University of Heidelberg, where he began corresponding with Martin Luther.* After advocating reform in Alsace, Bucer was excommunicated and fled to Strasbourg, where he became a leader in the city's Reformed ecclesial and educational communities. Bucer sought concord between Lutherans and Zwinglians and Protestants and Catholics. He emigrated to England, becoming a professor at Cambridge. Bucer's greatest theological concern was the centrality of Christ's sacrificial death, which achieved justification and sanctification and orients Christian community.

Johannes Bugenhagen (1485–1558). German Lutheran pastor and professor. Bugenhagen, a priest and lecturer at a Premonstratensian monastery, became a city preacher in Wittenberg during the reform efforts of Martin Luther* and Philipp Melanchthon.* Initially influenced by his reading of Desiderius Erasmus,* Bugenhagen grew in evangelical orientation through Luther's works; later, he studied under Melanchthon at the University of Wittenberg, eventually serving as rector and faculty member there. Bugenhagen was a versatile commentator, exegete and lecturer on Scripture. Through these roles and his development of lectionary and devotional material, Bugenhagen facilitated rapid establishment of church order throughout many German provinces.

Henry Bull (d. 1575?). English Protestant theologian and martyrologist. Little is known about Bull's circumstances after he was expelled from Magdalen College, Oxford, for snatching the censer from the hand of a priest officiating Mass. A committed reformer, he edited, translated, compiled, and published a number of Protestant works, including a book of prayers and meditations and writings by John Hooper* and Martin Luther.* He also worked alongside John Foxe* in the compilation of *Acts and Monuments*, while Miles Coverdale's* *The Letters of the Martyrs* is largely Bull's work.

Heinrich Bullinger (1504–1575). Swiss Reformed pastor and theologian. Bullinger succeeded Huldrych Zwingli* as minister and leader in Zurich. The primary author of the First and Second Helvetic Confessions,* Bullinger was drawn toward reform through the works of Martin Luther* and Philipp Melanchthon.* After Zwingli died, Bullinger was vital in maintaining adherence to the cause of reform; he oversaw the expansion of the Zurich synodal system while preaching, teaching and writing extensively. One of Bullinger's lasting legacies was the development of a federal view of the divine covenant with humanity, making baptism and the Eucharist covenantal signs.

Heinrich Bünting (1545–1606). Lutheran theologian and pastor. Bünting was born in Hanover, Germany, and studied theology at the University of Wittenberg, where he graduated in 1569. Upon finishing his studies at Wittenberg, Bünting became a pastor at Lemgo, where he was dismissed in 1575. Afterward he moved to Gronau an der Leine, where he served until his appointment as superintendent in Goslar. However, due to controversy over some of his teachings, Bünting was relieved of his position in 1600, retiring thereafter to Hanover, where he lived the remainder of his life. Bünting's most notable work is his *Itinerarium Sacrae Scripturae* (1581), a summary of biblical geography. Throughout this treatise, Bünting follows the travels of various major biblical figures, highlighting their theological as well as exegetical importance. When published, the *Itinerarium Sacrae Scripturae* was the most complete summary of biblical geography. Among the work's distinctive features is its collection of maps.

John Bunyan (1628–1688). English Puritan preacher and writer. His *Pilgrim's Progress* is one of the best-selling English-language titles in history. Born to a working-class family, Bunyan was largely unschooled, gaining literacy (and entering the faith) through reading the Bible and such early Puritan devotional works as *The Plain Man's Pathway to Heaven* and *The Practice of Piety*. Following a short stint in Oliver Cromwell's parliamentary army, in which Bunyan narrowly escaped death in combat, he turned to a preaching ministry, succeeding John Gifford as pastor at the Congregational church in Bedford. A noted preacher, Bunyan drew large crowds in itinerant appearances and it was in the sermonic form that Bunyan developed his theological outlook, which was an Augustinian-inflected Calvinism. Bunyan's opposition to the Book of Common Prayer and refusal of official ecclesiastical licensure led to multiple imprisonments, where he wrote many of his famous allegorical works, including *Pilgrim's Progress, The Holy City, Prison Meditations* and *Holy War.*

Michelangelo Buonarroti (1475–1564). Italian Catholic artist and poet. Michelangelo was born in Florence but spent the majority of his career in Rome, completing artworks commissioned by the popes of the early sixteenth century. One of the most recognized artists of all time, his artworks include the *Pietà* (1499), *David* (1501–1504), the ceiling of the Sistine Chapel (1508–1512), *Moses* (1515), and the *Last Judgment* (1536–1541), which remain famous and have done much to shape Western aesthetics. Toward the end of his life, his interests shifted toward architecture, culminating with his contributions to the designs of St. Peter's Basilica in Rome. Michelangelo is thought to have been devoutly Catholic throughout his life, but recent scholarship has considered the complexity of his relationship with the Catholic Reformation and the Protestant movement.

Jeremiah Burroughs (c. 1600–1646). English Puritan pastor and delegate to the Westminster Assembly. Burroughs left Cambridge, as well as a rectorate in Norfolk, because of his nonconformity. After returning to England from pastoring an English congregation in Rotterdam for several years (1637–1641), he became one of only a few dissenters from the official presbyterianism of the Assembly in favor of a congregationalist polity. Nevertheless, he was well known and respected by presbyterian colleagues such as Richard Baxter* for his irenic tone and conciliatory manner. The vast majority of Burroughs's corpus was published posthumously, although during his lifetime he published annotations on Hosea and several polemical works.

William Burton (d. 1616). English Puritan minister. Burton first ministered in Norwich, where he was present for the burning of Francis Kett (d. 1589) for Arianism. He later pastored in Bristol, Reading, and London. Throughout his life, he published a number of his sermons and treatises as well as a brief catechism.

Anthony Cade (d. 1641). Anglican pastor. Cade served as tutor and chaplain to George Villiers, First Duke of Buckingham (1592–1628), a close confidante of King James I* before holding a number of pastoral positions in Leicestershire and Northamptonshire.

Cardinal Cajetan (Thomas de Vio) (1469–1534). Italian Catholic cardinal, professor, theologian and biblical exegete. This Dominican monk was the leading Thomist theologian and one of the most important Catholic exegetes of the sixteenth century. Cajetan is best-known for his interview with Martin Luther* at the Diet of Augsburg (1518). Among his many works are polemical treatises, extensive biblical commentaries and most importantly a four-volume commentary (1508–1523) on the *Summa Theologiae* of Thomas Aquinas.*

Georg Calixtus (1586–1656). German Lutheran theologian. Calixtus studied at the University of Helmstedt where he developed regard for Philipp Melanchthon.* Between his time as a student and later as a professor at Helmstedt, Calixtus traveled through Europe seeking a way to unite and reconcile Lutherans, Calvinists and Catholics. He attempted to fuse these denominations through use of the Scriptures, the Apostles' Creed, and the first five centuries, interpreted by the Vincentian canon. Calixtus's position was stamped as syncretist and yielded further debate even after his death.

John Calvin (1509–1564). French Reformed pastor and theologian. John Calvin was born in Noyon, France. After receiving his primary education in the aristocratic family of Charles de Hangest, he attended the University of Paris to prepare for further study of theology. However, after completing his BA degree, as per his father's instructions, Calvin proceeded to the study of the law at Orleans of Bourges. While at Orleans, Calvin's interests in Greek and Latin literature were reawakened. Upon his father's death, Calvin resumed his study of classical literature at the newly founded College of Royal Readers in Paris under the direction of Guillaume Bude. The product of these studies was his commentary on Seneca's *De Clementia* (1532).

Sometime between 1533 and 1534 Calvin experienced a "sudden conversion" due largely to the influence to Martin Luther's 1520 treatises. Calvin's embracing of an evangelical faith forced him to flee France. From there he went to Basel, where he wrote the first edition of his *Institutes of the Christian Religion* in 1536. The *Institutes* became a theological dogmatics for the Reformed churches. Calvin spent most of his career in Geneva (excepting a three-year ministry in Strasbourg with Martin Bucer*). In Geneva, Calvin reorganized the structure and governance of the church and established an academy that became an international center for theological education. He was a tireless writer, revising his *Institutes* several times, and authoring theological treatises as well as biblical commentaries. Calvin is also known for his debates with his contemporaries, including Michael Servetus, whose anti-Trinitarian views led to his execution in Geneva in 1553. Calvin also maintained friendly correspondence with many reformers, including Melanchthon* and Bullinger*, the latter of whom he was able to come to an agreement with regarding the presence of Christ in the Lord's Supper with the signing of the *Consensus Tigurinus* in 1551, which brought a degree of unity between Geneva and Zurich and to the Reformed tradition. One of the foremost figures during the Reformation period, Calvin has an extensive exegetical and theological legacy.

Wolfgang Capito (1478?–1541). German Reformed humanist and theologian. Capito, a Hebrew scholar, produced a Hebrew grammar and published several Latin commentaries on books of the Hebrew Scriptures. He corresponded with Desiderius Erasmus* and fellow humanists. Capito translated Martin Luther's* early works into Latin for the printer Johann Froben. On meeting Luther, Capito was converted to Luther's vision, left Mainz and settled in Strasbourg, where he lectured on Luther's theology to the city clergy. With Martin Bucer,* Capito reformed liturgy, ecclesial life and teachings, education, welfare, and government. Capito worked for the theological unification of the Swiss cantons with Strasbourg.

Pietro Carnesecchi (1508–1567). Italian humanist. Carnesecchi rose in the papal bureaucracy under Medici patronage, but after the death of Clement VII* he began to deviate from Catholic orthodoxy, aligning himself with Juan de Valdés.* While he retained relations with the established church, he also read Protestant works by theologians such as Luther,* Calvin,* and Bucer,* and his only extant doctrinal writing defends Bucer's view of the Eucharist over that of Zwingli.* Carnesecchi was able to avoid arrest by the Inquisition for a time, and his condemnation to death in absentia was pardoned under Pope Pius IV (1499–1565). However, Pius V (1504–1572) was a longtime opponent of Carnesecchi, and upon his election to the papal office, reopened the case and those of a number of others suspected of Protestant leanings. While seeking refuge in Florence, Carnesecchi was betrayed to the Inquisition by Cosimo I de' Medici, and following trial he was beheaded.

François Carrière (d. 1665). French Catholic theologian. A Franciscan doctor of theology, Carrière composed a commentary on the whole Bible, a summary of Catholic doctrine, and a history of the papacy.

John Carter (1554–1635). English Puritan minister. After graduating from Cambridge, Carter served as vicar at Bramford, Suffolk, until disputes over his Puritanism within the congregation led him to be moved to the nearby parish of Belstead.

Denis the Carthusian (1402/1403–1471). Belgian Catholic theologian and mystic. Denis studied philosophy and theology at the University of Cologne before entering the Carthusian monastery at Roermond, where he spent most of his career in strict seclusion. A prodigious writer, his work spanned diverse genres, including popular devotional works, scholastic summaries of Lombard* and Aquinas,* and dogmatic works on numerous topics, including Mary, ecclesiology, and morality. Denis also produced commentaries on every book of the Bible.

Thomas Cartwright (1535–1606). English Puritan preacher and professor. Cartwright was educated at St. John's College, Cambridge, although as an influential leader of the Presbyterian party in the Church of England he was continually at odds with the Anglican party, especially John Whitgift.* Cartwright spent some time as an exile in Geneva and Heidelberg as well as in Antwerp, where he pastored an English church. In 1585, Cartwright was arrested and eventually jailed for trying to return to England despite Elizabeth I's* refusal of his request. Many acknowledged him to be learned but also quite cantankerous. His publications include commentaries on Colossians, Ecclesiastes, Proverbs and the Gospels, as well as a dispute against Whitgift on church discipline.

Mathew Caylie (unknown). English Protestant minister. Caylie authored *The Cleansing of the Ten Lepers* (1623), an exposition of Luke 17:14-18.

Jan Cents (Unknown). Dutch Anabaptist. Believed to be a leader of the Anabaptist congregation in Amsterdam, Cents was the first signer and possibly author of a confession intended to unite Frisian and High German Mennonites.

John Chardon (d. 1601). Irish Anglican bishop. Chardon was educated at Oxford. He advocated Reformed doctrine in his preaching, yet opposed those Puritans who rejected Anglican church order. He published several sermons.

Christian Chemnitz (1615–1666). German Lutheran theologian. Grandnephew of Martin Chemnitz,* Christian Chemnitz was principal at the high school in Jena before serving the church as a deacon and archdeacon in Weimer and Braunschweig then as superintendent in Eisenach. Returning to Jena, he received his doctorate and replaced John Major as professor of theology, also serving as dean of the theology faculty and rector of the university. He wrote on numerous biblical, pastoral, and controversial topics, with his works including a defense of Lutheranism, instructions for young ministers, and a series of sermons on judgement.

Martin Chemnitz (1522–1586). German Lutheran theologian. A leading figure in establishing Lutheran orthodoxy, Chemnitz studied theology and patristics at the University of Wittenburg, later becoming a defender of Philipp Melanchthon's* interpretation of the doctrine of justification. Chemnitz drafted a compendium of doctrine and reorganized the structure of the church in Wolfenbüttel; later, he led efforts to reconcile divisions within Lutheranism, culminating in the Formula of Concord*. One of his chief theological accomplishments was a modification of the christological doctrine of the *communicatio idiomatium*, which provided a Lutheran platform for understanding the sacramental presence of Christ's humanity in the Eucharist.

David Chytraeus (1531–1600). German Lutheran professor, theologian and biblical exegete. At the age of eight Chytraeus was admitted to the University of Tübingen. There he studied law, philology, philosophy, and theology, finally receiving his master's degree in 1546. Chytraeus befriended Philipp Melanchthon* while sojourning in Wittenberg, where he taught the *Loci communes*. While teaching exegesis at the University of Rostock Chytraeus became acquainted with Tilemann Heshusius,* who strongly influenced Chytraeus away from Philippist theology. As a defender of Gnesio-Lutheran theology Chytraeus helped organize churches throughout Austria in accordance with the Augsburg Confession.* Chytraeus coauthored the Formula of Concord* with Martin Chemnitz,* Andreas Musculus (1514–1581), Nikolaus Selnecker* and Jakob Andreae.* He wrote commentaries on most of the Bible, as well as a devotional work titled *Regula vitae* (1555) that described the Christian virtues.

Isidorus Clarius (1495–1555). Italian Catholic humanist, biblical scholar, and bishop. As a leading Benedictine monk, Clarius sought reform the Roman Catholic Church from within. He participated in the commission that composed the *Consilium de Emendanda Ecclesia* (1536), and as bishop of Foligno, he sought to put many of its recommendations into action, demanding moral reform and consistent preaching from the clergy while reorganizing the charitable work of his diocese. Clarius was also open to rapprochement with Protestants. In 1540, he published *Adhortatio ad Concordiam* seeking compromise with the Lutherans, and his annotated revision of the Vulgate text (1542) interacted with Lutheran and Reformed scholars. This confessional openness was scrutinized after Clarius's death, and his edition of the Vulgate was included in the *Index Librorum Prohibitorum* (1557). For his work on the text of Scripture, however, he is recognized by name in the introduction to the 1611 King James Bible.

David Clarkson (1622–1686). English Puritan theologian. After his dismissal from the pastorate on account of the Act of Uniformity (1662), little is known about Clarkson. At the end of his life he ministered with John Owen* in London.

Robert Cleaver (1571–1613). English Puritan pastor. Cleaver served as rector at Drayton in Oxfordshire until silenced by Archbishop Richard Bancroft for advocating Nonconformity. Despite opposition from ecclesiastical authorities, Cleaver enjoyed a reputation as an excellent preacher. His published works include sermons on Hebrews 4 and Song of Songs 2 as well as one on the last chapter of Proverbs. Cleaver also authored *The Parsimony of Christian Children*, which contained a defense of infant baptism against Baptist criticisms.

George Close (unknown). English Protestant preacher. A series of Close's sermons on Matthew 16 were copied and published while he served as a reader at St. Antholin, London.

Michael Cobabus (d. 1686). German Lutheran theologian and mathematician. Trained in philosophy, mathematics, and theology at the University of Rostock, Cobabus remained in the city, serving as rector of the city school until appointed professor of mathematics at the university. He later received a doctorate in theology from the University of Griefswald and exchanged his position in the Rostock mathematics faculty for a professorship in theology.

Johannes Cocceius (1603–1669). German Reformed theologian. Cocceius first served as professor of biblical philology in his hometown of Bremen before moving to Franeker, where he taught Hebrew and theology, and finally to Leiden, where he spent the majority of his career as professor of theology. Cocceius is perhaps best remembered for his exposition of Reformed federal theology, defining the relationship between humanity and God in terms of progressive covenants. His critics, chief among them Gisbertus Voetius (1589–1676), argued that Cocceius's view of salvation history ignored the unity of the Scriptures and spiritualized the Old Testament. His other writings are extensive, including commentaries on all the books of the Bible, an influential Hebrew and Aramaic lexicon, and numerous works on theology, ethics, and philology.

John Colet (1467–1519). English Catholic priest, preacher and educator. Colet, appointed dean of Saint Paul's Cathedral by Henry VII, was a friend of Desiderius Erasmus,* on whose classical ideals Colet reconstructed the curriculum of Saint Paul's school. Colet was convinced that the foundation of moral reform lay in the education of children. Though an ardent advocate of reform, Colet, like Erasmus, remained loyal to the Catholic Church throughout his life. Colet's agenda of reform was oriented around spiritual and ethical themes, demonstrated in his commentaries on select books of the New Testament and the writings of Pseudo-Dionysius the Areopagite.

Vittoria Colonna (1490–1547). Italian Renaissance poet. Born into a noble family, Colonna was betrothed at three years of age to Fernando d'Ávalos (1489–1525), and they married in 1509. D'Ávalos was largely absent on military campaigns during their marriage, while she exercised his governorship of Benvenuto and became involved in the literary circles of Rome and Naples. One of the most important writers of her age, her friends included Pietro Bembo (1470–1547), Marguerite de Navarre,* and Michelangelo Buonarroti.* Writing primarily in the Petrarchan style, Colonna's reputation as a poet grew after the death of her husband, and much of her poetry was dedicated to his memory. Spiritual concerns form a major element of Colonna's writings, promoting contemplation and the ascetic life. While denied her desire to take holy orders in widowhood, Colonna spent much of her life residing in religious communities, and she was actively involved in movements seeking their improvement, collaborating with reformers such as Reginald Pole,* Juan de Valdés,* and Bernardo Ochino.*

Gasparo Contarini (1483–1542). Italian statesman, theologian and reform-minded cardinal. Contarini was an able negotiator and graceful compromiser. Charles V requested Contarini as the papal legate for the Colloquy of Regensburg (1541), where Contarini reached agreement with Melanchthon* on the doctrine of justification (although neither the pope nor Luther* ratified the agreement). He had come to a similar belief in the priority of faith in the work of Christ rather than works as the basis for Christian life in 1511, though unlike Luther, he never left the papal church over the issue; instead he remainied within it to try to seek gentle reform, and he adhered to papal sacramental teaching. Contarini was an important voice for reform within the Catholic Church, always seeking reconciliation rather than confrontation with Protestant reformers. He wrote many works, including a treatise detailing the ideal bishop, a manual for lay church leaders, a political text on right governance and brief commentaries on the Pauline letters.

Michel Cop (c. 1501–1566). Swiss Protestant pastor. Son of the physician to Francis I* and childhood friend of John Calvin,* Cop was a cathedral canon until fleeing France after his brother Nicholas's (c. 1501–1566) inaugural sermon as rector of the University of Paris was declared heretical for its Lutheran themes. Cop spent some time in Basel before settling in Geneva, where he served as a pastor, taught Calvin Hebrew, and published a sermon series on Proverbs and Ecclesiastes.

Christoph Corner (1518–1594). German Lutheran theologian. Professor of philosophy, rhetoric, and theology at the University of Frankfurt, Corner participated in the drafting of the Formula of Concord.* He also served as superintendent of churches in Mark Brandenberg.

Antonio del Corro (1527–1591). Spanish Reformed pastor and theologian. After encountering the ideas of Martin Luther* and other reformers, Corro abandoned the Hieronymite order. Leaving Spain to avoid charges of heresy, he traveled through Europe, spending time in Geneva and Lausanne before pastoring churches in France and the Low Countries. The arrival of Spanish armies in the Netherlands saw Corro and his family relocate to England, where he pastored a church of Spanish exiles in London and taught at Temple Church and Oxford. Corro courted controversy throughout his career, entering into debates with a wide array of Protestant theologians. In England, he was suspended from his pastorate for slander and examined a number of times for heresy, with some finding suggestions of Arianism in his Christology. Although these charges were never upheld, they clouded his later career and legacy.

Antonius Corvinus (1501–1553). German Lutheran theologian and administrator. After meeting Luther* and Melanchthon,* Corvinus left the humanist circle of Erasmus* to serve as a pastor in cities including Goslar, Witzenhausen, and Pattensen. A signatory of the Schmalkald Articles,* much of his career was devoted to constructing the organizational apparatus of the Lutheran church, and he established disciplinary procedures and church orders for numerous cities in northern Germany. His expository postils on the Gospels, Epistles, Psalms, and Genesis were also distributed widely in order to aid preachers of the region.

John Cosin (1594–1672). Anglican preacher and bishop. Early in his career Cosin was the vice chancellor of Cambridge and canon at the Durham cathedral. But as a friend of William Laud* and an advocate for "Laudian" changes, he was suspected of being a crypto-Catholic. In 1640 during the Long Parliament a Puritan lodged a complaint with the House of Commons concerning Cosin's "popish innovations." Cosin was promptly removed from office. During the turmoil of the English Civil Wars, Cosin sojourned in Paris among English nobility but struggled financially. Cosin returned to England after the Restoration in 1660 to be consecrated as the bishop of Durham. He published annotations on the Book of Common Prayer* and a history of the canon.

John Cotton (1584–1652). New England Puritan minister. Cotton was born to Puritan parents in Derby, England. He entered Trinity College, Cambridge, graduating with his bachelor's degree in 1603. Afterward, Cotton became a fellow at Emmanuel College, Cambridge, which at the time was heavily influenced by Puritanism. There, Cotton finished his master's degree in 1606. Cotton then served as head lecturer, dean, and catechist for the college. It was in this period that he heard the preaching of Richard Sibbes,* which proved instrumental in Cotton's personal conversion. Cotton received a bachelor of divinity in 1610 from Cambridge and was shortly thereafter ordained into the priesthood of the Church of England. However, Cotton's increasing nonconformity brought him into conflict with episcopal authorities, which prompted him to move to the colony of Massachusetts in July 1633. Upon his arrival, he immediately assumed a position of leadership as the teacher of the First Church of Boston. Throughout his tenure, Cotton exerted significant influence in the civic and ecclesiastical affairs of the colony. He continued in his ministry at First Church until his death on December 23, 1652. Over the course of his ministry, Cotton wrote nearly forty works. Among these were the *Keys of the Kingdom of Heaven, and the Power Thereof* (1644) and *Exposition upon the Thirteenth Chapter of Revelation* (1655).

Council of Constance (1414–1418). Convened to resolve the Western Schism, root out heresy and reform the church in head and members, the council asserted in *Sacrosancta* (1415) the immediate authority of ecumenical councils assembled in the Holy Spirit under Christ—even over the pope. Martin V was elected pope in 1417 after the three papal claimants were deposed; thus, the council ended the schism. The council condemned Jan Hus,* Jerome of Prague (c. 1365–1416) and, posthumously, John Wycliffe. Hus and Jerome, despite letters of safe conduct, were burned at the stake. Their deaths ignited the Hussite Wars, which ended as a result of the Council of Basel's concessions to the Bohemian church. The council fathers sought to reform the church through the regular convocation of councils (*Frequens*; 1417). Martin V begrudgingly complied by calling the required councils, then immediately disbanding them. Pius II (r. 1458–1464) reasserted papal dominance through *Execrabilis* (1460), which condemned any appeal to a future council apart from the pope's authority.

Council of Trent (1545–1563) Convoked by Pope Paul III (r. 1534–1549) with the support of Charles V*, the nineteenth ecumenical council was convened in the northern Italian city of Trent. Attended primarily by Italian clerics, it met in three distinct phases. Beginning in December 1545, during its first eight sessions, the council issued doctrinal decrees, asserting the authority of tradition alongside Scripture, the authenticity of the Vulgate, the prerogative of the church in interpretation, and the necessity of human cooperation in the work of salvation. Ecclesial abuses were also addressed, as attempts were made to eliminate absenteeism and pluralism and devolve power from Rome to bishoprics and parishes. The council was suspended following the outbreak of the plague in Trent in March 1547. A number of Protestant delegates were present during the second phase of the council, which met between May 1551 and April 1552 under the supervision of Pope Julius III (r. 1550–1555). The primary achievement of this period of the council was the clarification of teachings on the seven sacraments, with transubstantiation, the objective efficacy of the Eucharist, and the necessity of auricular confession confirmed as dogma. Reconvened by Pope Pius IV (r. 1559–1565) in 1561, the third phase of the council addressed the relationship between bishops and Rome, resulting in affirmations of the divine appointment of the church hierarchy and the obligation of bishops to reside in their dioceses. Clerical education, the regulation of marriage, and teachings on purgatory, indulgences, the use of images, and the saints were also addressed.

Miles Coverdale (1488–1568). Anglican bishop. Coverdale is known for his translations of the Bible into English, completing William Tyndale's* efforts and later producing the Great Bible commissioned by Henry VIII* (1539). A former friar, Coverdale was among the Cambridge scholars who met at the White Horse Tavern to discuss Martin Luther's* ideas. During Coverdale's three terms of exile in Europe, he undertook various translations, including the Geneva Bible*. He was appointed bishop of Exeter by Thomas Cranmer* and served as chaplain to Edward VI. Coverdale contributed to Cranmer's first edition of the Book of Common Prayer.*

William Cowper (Couper) (1568–1619). Scottish Puritan bishop. After graduating from the University of St. Andrews, Cowper worked in parish ministry for twenty-five years before becoming bishop. As a zealous Puritan and advocate of regular preaching and rigorous discipline, Cowper championed Presbyterian polity and lay participation in church government. Cowper published devotional works, sermon collections and a commentary on Revelation.

Benjamin Coxe (fl. 1646). English Baptist minister. Coxe began his career in the Church of England, ministering at parishes in Devonshire, Bedford, and Coventry. After preaching against infant baptism, he was challenged to a public debate by Richard Baxter.* Coxe lost and was briefly arrested after refusing to leave the city. Following his release, he joined a congregation of Anabaptists in London.

Walter Cradock (1606–1659). Welsh Anglican minister. Cradock was born in Llangwm, Monmouthshire, Wales. After completing his education at the University of Oxford, Cradock assumed his first position as curate at Peterson-super-Ely, Glamorgan. In 1633, Cradock, along with some other Welsh ministers, was reported to Archbishop William Laud* and the Court of High Commission for preaching nonconformity and for refusing the *Book of Sports*. In 1634 Cradock traveled throughout Wexham and Herefordshire encouraging the establishment of Welsh Nonconformist congregations. Cradock later became pastor of an Independent congregation at Llanfair Waterdine in 1639. When the English Civil War began, Cradock and his conventicle moved to Bristol, but when Royalist forces came to occupy the city, he and some of his group departed for All-Hallows-the-Great, where he preached regularly with Henry Jessey (1603–1663). In 1641, Cradock was among the group of preachers for Wales commissioned by the Long Parliament. Later, he served as regular preacher for the Barebones Parliament. Throughout this period, Cradock was an ardent supporter of Oliver Cromwell. Cradock lived the remainder of his life quietly while ministering to a congregation at Llangwm. Throughout his career, Cradock authored a number of devotional works, among which were *Gospel Liberty* (1648) and *Gospel Holiness* (1655).

Thomas Cranmer (1489–1556). Anglican archbishop and theologian. Cranmer supervised church reform and produced the first two editions of the Book of Common Prayer.* As a doctoral student at Cambridge, he was involved in the discussions at the White Horse Tavern. Cranmer contributed to a religious defense of Henry VIII's* divorce; Henry then appointed him Archbishop of Canterbury. Cranmer cautiously steered the course of reform, accelerating under Edward VI. After supporting the attempted coup to prevent Mary's assuming the throne, Cranmer was convicted of treason and burned at the stake. Cranmer's legacy is the splendid English of his liturgy and prayer books.

Richard Crashaw (1612–1649). English Catholic poet. Educated at Cambridge, Crashaw was fluent in Hebrew, Greek and Latin. His first volume of poetry was *Epigrammatum sacrorum liber* (1634). Despite being born into a Puritan family, Crashaw was attracted to Catholicism, finally converting in 1644 after he was forced to resign his fellowship for not signing the Solemn League and Covenant (1643). In 1649, he was made a subcanon of Our Lady of Loretto by Cardinal Palotta.

Herbert Croft (1603–1691). Anglican bishop. As a boy Croft converted to Catholicism; he returned to the Church of England during his studies at Oxford. Before the English Civil Wars, he served as chaplain to Charles I. After the Restoration, Charles II appointed him as bishop. Croft ardently opposed Catholicism in his later years.

John Crompe (d. 1661). Anglican priest. Educated at Cambridge, Crompe published a commentary on the Apostles' Creed, a sermon on Psalm 21:3 and an exposition of Christ's passion.

Oliver Cromwell (1599–1658). Commander of the Parliamentary forces during the English Civil War. Lord Protector of the Commonwealth of England, Scotland, and Ireland. Cromwell was born in Huntingdon, East Anglia, the only surviving son of Robert Cromwell. In 1616, he enrolled at the University of Cambridge as a fellow commoner. However, he withdrew from the university the following year due to his father's death. He represented Huntingdon in Parliament in 1628, and later Cambridge in the Short and Long Parliaments. During the Civil War, he commanded the Parliamentary forces, which he led to victory at the Battles of Marston Moor (1644) and Naseby (1645). After the execution of King Charles I in 1649, he became a member of the Council of State. It was at this time that the monarchy was abolished. In 1653, he was elevated to the position of Lord Protector of the Commonwealth. He declined the crown, though it was offered him in 1657. As Lord

Protector, he endeavored to lead the postwar recovery, suppress military resistance, and advance British influence throughout Europe and the world. Moreover, he promoted a limited religious toleration in the kingdoms of England, Scotland, and Ireland. After his death in 1658, his son Richard (1626–1712) succeeded him as Lord Protector. However, due to incompetence, Richard was forced to resign, which paved the way for the Restoration of the monarchy in 1660 with the ascension of Charles II (1630–1685) to the throne. One year after the Restoration, Oliver Cromwell's body was disinterred from Westminster Abbey, hung on the gallows at Tyburn, and cast into an unmarked grave.

Caspar Cruciger (1504–1548). German Lutheran theologian. Recognized for his alignment with the theological views of Philipp Melanchthon,* Cruciger was a scholar respected among both Protestants and Catholics. In 1521, Cruciger came Wittenberg to study Hebrew and remained there most of his life. He became a valuable partner for Martin Luther* in translating the Old Testament and served as teacher, delegate to major theological colloquies and rector. Cruciger was an agent of reform in his birthplace of Leipzig, where at the age of fifteen he had observed the disputation between Luther and Johann Eck.*

Elisabeth Cruciger (c. 1500–1535). German Lutheran hymnist. Following her conversion to Lutheranism, Cruciger left the Praemonstratensian order and relocated to Wittenberg, where she married Caspar Cruciger.* While her authorship has been contested, recent scholarship has assigned Cruciger the place of the first female Lutheran hymnist for her composition of "Lord Christ is the Only Son of God" (Herr Christ der einig Gotts Sohn) (1524).

Ralph Cudworth (d. 1624) English Protestant minister. Father of noted Cambridge Platonist Ralph Cudworth (1617–1688), the elder Cudworth was a fellow of Emanuel College, Cambridge and rector of Aller in Somersetshire.

Marguerite d'Angoulême (1492–1549). French Catholic noblewoman. The elder sister of King Francis I of France, Marguerite was the Queen of Navarre and Duchess of Alençon and Berry. She was a poet and author of the French Renaissance. She composed *The Mirror of a Sinful Soul* (1531)—condemned by the theologians of the Sorbonne for containing Lutheran ideas—and an unfinished collection of short stories, the Heptaméron (1558). A leading figure in the French Reformation, Marguerite was at the center of a network of reform-minded individuals that included Guillame Briçonnet,* Jacques Lefèvre d'Etaples,* Gérard Roussel (1500–1550) and Guillame Farel (1489–1565).

Jakob Dachser (1486–1567). German Anabaptist theologian and hymnist. Dachser served as a Catholic priest in Vienna until he was imprisoned and then exiled for defending the Lutheran understanding of the Mass and fasting. Hans Hut* rebaptized him in Augsburg, where Dachser was appointed as a leader of the Anabaptist congregation. Lutheran authorities imprisoned him for nearly four years. In 1531 he recanted his Radical beliefs and began to catechize children with the permission of the city council. Dachser was expelled from Augsburg as a possible insurrectionist in 1552 and relocated to Pfalz-Neuberg. He published a number of poems, hymns and mystical works, and he versified several psalms.

Jean Daillé (1594–1670). French Reformed pastor. Born into a devout Reformed family, Daillé studied theology and philosophy at Saumur under the most influential contemporary lay leader in French Protestantism, Philippe Duplessis-Mornay (1549–1623). Daillé held to Amyraldianism—the belief that Christ died for all humanity inclusively, not particularly for the elect who would inherit salvation (though only the elect are in fact saved). He wrote a controversial treatise on the church fathers that aggravated many Catholic and Anglican scholars because of Daillé's apparent demotion of patristic authority in matters of faith.

Lambert Daneau (1530?–1595). French Reformed pastor and theologian. After a decade of pastoring in France, following the St. Bartholomew's Day Massacre, Daneau fled to Geneva to teach theology at the Academy. He later taught in the Low Countries, finishing his career in southern France. Daneau's diverse works include tracts on science, ethics and morality as well as numerous theological and exegetical works.

John Davenant (1576–1641). Anglican bishop and professor. Davenant attended Queen's College, Cambridge, where he received his doctorate and was appointed professor of divinity. During the Remonstrant controversy, James I* sent Davenant as one of the four representatives for the Church of England to the Synod of Dordrecht.* Following James's instructions, Davenant advocated a *via media* between the Calvinists and the Remonstrants, although in later years he defended against the rise of Arminianism in England. In 1621, Davenant was promoted to the bishopric of Salisbury, where he was generally receptive to Laudian reforms. Davenant's lectures on Colossians are his best-known work.

William Day (1605–1684). Anglican theologian. Born and raised in Windsor, Berkshire, Day received his early education from Eton College. Afterward, he matriculated at King's College, Cambridge, where he was elected a fellow in 1624. Day received his BA in 1629, and MA in 1632. In 1635, Day was incorporated MA at Oxford and in 1637 became vicar of Mapledurham, Oxfordshire. Throughout his long career, Day conformed to all the ecclesiastical changes dictated by the government through the Restoration, during which he retained his vicarage. Finally, Day was made divinity reader at the King's Chapel, Windsor Chapel. He published two commentaries, *An Exposition of the Book of the Prophet Isaiah* (1654) and *A Paraphrase and Commentary upon the Epistle of St. Paul to the Romans* (1666).

Defense of the Augsburg Confession (1531). See *Augsburg Confession.*

Hans Denck (c. 1500–1527). German Radical theologian. Denck, a crucial early figure of the German Anabaptist movement, combined medieval German mysticism with the radical sacramental theology of Andreas Bodenstein von Karlstadt* and Thomas Müntzer.* Denck argued that the exterior forms of Scripture and sacrament are symbolic witnesses secondary to the internally revealed truth of the Sprit in the human soul. This view led to his expulsion from Nuremberg in 1525; he spent the next two years in various centers of reform in the German territories. At the time of his death, violent persecution against Anabaptists was on the rise throughout northern Europe.

Stephen Denison (unknown). English Puritan pastor. Denison received the post of curate at St. Katherine Cree in London sometime in the 1610s, where he ministered until his ejection from office in 1635. During his career at St. Katherine Cree, Denison waded into controversy with both Puritans (over the doctrine of predestination) and Anglicans (over concerns about liturgical ceremonies). He approached both altercations with rancor and rigidity, although he seems to have been quite popular and beloved by most of his congregation. In 1631, William Laud* consecrated the newly renovated St. Katherine Cree, and as part of the festivities Denison offered a sermon on Luke 19:27 in which he publicly rebuked Laud for fashioning the Lord's house into a "den of robbers." Aside from the record of his quarrels, very little is known about Denison. In addition to *The White Wolf* (a 1627 sermon against another opponent), he published a catechism for children (1621), a treatise on the sacraments (1621) and a commentary on 2 Peter 1 (1622).

Arthur Dent (d. 1607). English Puritan preacher. Ordained in the Church of England, Dent ministered in Essex, where he made his Puritan sympathies clear and was disciplined for refusing to wear a surplice and make the sign of the cross. He published a number of works, including an exposition of the Articles of Faith and an exposition of Revelation targeted against the Roman Catholic Church.

Marie Dentière (1495–1561). Belgian Reformed theologian. Dentière relinquished her monastic vows and married Simon Robert (d.1533), a former priest, in Strasbourg. After Robert died, she married Antoine Froment (1508–1581), a reformer in Geneva, and became involved in the reform of that city. Her best-known writings are a tract addressed to Marguerite d'Angoulême,* the *Very Useful Epistle* (1539), in which she espoused the evangelical faith and the right of women to interpret and teach scripture, and a preface to Calvin's sermon on 1 Timothy 2:8-12. Dentière is the only woman to have her name inscribed on the International Monument to the Reformation in Geneva.

Edward Dering (c. 1540–1576). English Puritan preacher. An early Puritan, Dering's prospects of advancement in the Elizabethan church were effectively ended after a sermon in front of the Queen in which he described her as an "untamed and unruly heifer" while criticizing the state of the church and clergy. While continuing with intemperate and critical attacks throughout his career, Dering established himself as a preacher at St. Paul's Cathedral in London, where he became known for his pastoral concern and desire to teach the assurance of salvation.

Jean D'Espagne (1591–1659). French Independent pastor. After leading churches at Orange and the Hague, D'Espagne departed under accusations of immorality and settled in London, where he pastored a French congregation. A fractious figure, he led a group that separated from the established French congregation and entered into numerous controversies. Many of his extant writings are targeted toward errors he perceived in the theology and practice of others.

David Dickson (1583?–1663). Scottish Reformed pastor, preacher, professor and theologian. Dickson defended the Presbyterian form of ecclesial reformation in Scotland and was recognized for his iteration of Calvinist federal theology and expository biblical commentaries. Dickson served for over twenty years as professor of philosophy at the University of Glasgow before being appointed professor of divinity. He opposed the imposition of Episcopalian measures on the church in Scotland and was active in political and ecclesial venues to protest and prohibit such influences. Dickson was removed from his academic post following his refusal of the oath of supremacy during the Restoration era.

Veit Dietrich (1506–1549). German Lutheran preacher and theologian. Dietrich intended to study medicine at the University of Wittenberg, but Martin Luther* and Philipp Melanchthon* convinced him to study theology instead. Dietrich developed a strong relationship with Luther, accompanying him to the Marburg Colloquy (1529) and to Coburg Castle during the Diet of Augsburg (1530). After graduating, Dietrich taught on the arts faculty, eventually becoming dean. In 1535 he returned to his hometown, Nuremberg, to pastor. Later in life, Dietrich worked with Melanchthon to reform the church in Regensburg. In 1547, when Charles V arrived in Nuremberg, Dietrich was suspended from the pastorate; he resisted the imposition of the Augsburg Interim to no avail. In addition to transcribing some of Luther's lectures, portions of the Table Talk and the very popular *Hauspostille* (1544), Dietrich published his own sermons for children, a manual for pastors and a summary of the Bible.
Louis de Dieu (1590–1642). Dutch Reformed pastor and linguist. Committed to his pastoral and teaching ministry in Leiden, Dieu turned down the opportunity to teach theology and Old Testament at the University of Utrecht. He published grammars of Hebrew (1626) and Persian (1639); a comparative grammar of Hebrew, Aramaic, and Syriac (1628); and a collection of writings on the New Testament text.
Giovanni Diodati (1576–1649). Italian Reformed theologian. Diodati was from an Italian banking family who fled for religious reasons to Geneva. There he trained under Theodore Beza;* on completion of his doctoral degree, Diodati became professor of Hebrew at the academy. He was an ecclesiastical representative of the church in Geneva (for whom he was a delegate at the Synod of Dordrecht*) and an advocate for reform in Venice. Diodati's chief contribution to the Italian reform movement was a translation of the Bible into Italian (1640–1641), which remains the standard translation in Italian Protestantism.
John Dod (c. 1549–1645). English Puritan pastor. Over the course of his lengthy pastoral career (spanning roughly sixty years), Dod was twice suspended for nonconformity and twice reinstated. A popular preacher, he published many sermons as well as commentaries on the Ten Commandments and the Lord's Prayer; collections of his sayings and anecdotes were compiled after his death.
John Donne (1572–1631). Anglican poet and preacher. Donne was born into a strong Catholic family. However, sometime between his brother's death from the plague while in prison in 1593 and the publication of his *Pseudo-Martyr* in 1610, Donne joined the Church of England. Ordained to the Anglican priesthood in 1615 and already widely recognized for his verse, Donne quickly rose to prominence as a preacher—some have deemed him the best of his era. His textual corpus is an amalgam of erotic *and* divine poetry (e.g., "Batter My Heart"), as well as a great number of sermons.
Dordrecht Confession (1632). Dutch Mennonite confession. Adriaan Cornelisz (1581–1632) wrote the Dordrecht Confession to unify Dutch Mennonites. This basic statement of Mennonite belief and practice affirms distinctive doctrines such as nonresistance, shunning, footwashing, and the refusal to swear oaths. Most continental Mennonites subscribed to this confession during the second half of the seventeenth century.
Johann George Dorsche (1597–1659). German Lutheran theologian. Dorsche pastored briefly at Entzheim before being called to Strasbourg, where he earned his doctorate, was appointed professor of theology, and served as a preacher at the cathedral. He spent the last five years of his life as professor of theology at the University of Rostock. Dorsche published a number of theological works as well as commentaries on the Gospels and Hebrews.
John Downame (c. 1571–1652). English Puritan pastor and theologian. See *English Annotations.*
Charles Drelincourt (1595–1669). French Reformed pastor, theologian and controversialist. After studying at Saumur Academy, Drelincourt pastored the Reformed Church in Paris for nearly fifty years. He was well known for his ministry to the sick. In addition to polemical works against Catholicism, he published numerous pastoral resources: catechisms, three volumes of sermons and a five-volume series on consolation for the suffering.
The Dutch Annotations (1657). See *Statenvertaling.*
Daniel Dyke (d. 1614). English Puritan preacher. Born of nonconformist stock, Dyke championed a more thorough reformation of church practice in England. After the promulgation of John Whitgift's* articles in 1583, Dyke refused to accept what he saw as remnants of Catholicism, bringing him into conflict with the bishop of London. Despite the petitions of his congregation and some politicians, the bishop of London suspended Dyke from his ministry for refusing priestly ordination and conformity to the Book of Common Prayer.* All of his work was published posthumously; it is mostly focused on biblical interpretation.
John Eachard (unknown). English Anglican minister. After graduating with his master of arts from Trinity College, Cambridge, Eachard was the vicar at Darsham in

Suffolk. At least two of his sermons, one on Matthew 3:10 and another on Revelation 12:11, were published in his lifetime.

Johann Eck (Johann Maier of Eck) (1486–1543). German Catholic theologian. Though Eck was not an antagonist of Martin Luther* until the dispute over indulgences, Luther's Ninety-five Theses (1517) sealed the two as adversaries. After their debate at the Leipzig Disputation (1519), Eck participated in the writing of the papal bull that led to Luther's excommunication. Much of Eck's work was written to oppose Protestantism or to defend Catholic doctrine and the papacy; his *Enchiridion* was a manual written to counter Protestant doctrine. However, Eck was also deeply invested in the status of parish preaching, publishing a five-volume set of postils. He participated in the assemblies at Regensburg and Augsburg and led the Catholics in their rejection of the Augsburg Confession.

Edward VI of England (1537–1553). English monarch. Son of Henry VIII* and Jane Seymour (1508–1537), Edward ascended to the throne as a minor, leaving the practical power of the monarchy in the hands of those appointed by the Regency council as Lord Protector of the Realm, first, his uncle, Edward Seymour, duke of Somerset (1500–1552), and afterwards, John Dudley, duke of Northumberland (1504–1553). Under Somerset and Northumberland, and with Thomas Cranmer* installed as Archbishop of Canterbury, the eclectic reforms made during the reign of Henry VIII were drawn into the service of a thoroughly Protestant transformation. During the reign of Edward, communion in two kinds was instituted, all services were held in the vernacular, and a series of ecclesiastical visitations oversaw the suppression of Catholic religion. Alongside the flood of Protestant refugees from the continent that sheltered in the kingdom, the publication of the revised Book of Common Prayer*, the Book of Homilies* and the Forty-Two Articles (1553) helped establish the future direction of Anglicanism.

Elizabeth I of England (1533–1603) English monarch. The daughter of Henry VIII* (r. 1509–1547) and Anne Boleyn (c. 1501–1536), Elizabeth outwardly conformed to Catholicism during the reign of her sister Mary I (r. 1553–1558), but her Protestant upbringing encouraged the hopes of many reformers upon her accession in 1558. With the 1559 Elizabethan Settlement, Elizabeth redefined England as a Protestant country, with the Act of Supremacy asserting the monarch as the head of the English church, and the Act of Uniformity establishing the 1559 *Book of Common Prayer** as the valid order of service within the realm. However, Elizabeth resisted the aggressive persecution of Catholics for political reasons, while also allowing some traditional vestments, furniture and ceremonies to be retained. Her moderate and pragmatic reforms frustrated many who wished for more thorough change and led to the emergence of the Puritan movement. Elizabeth faced numerous threats during her reign, including the machinations of Scottish Catholics and claims to the throne of Mary Stuart (1542–1547), leading to her rival's imprisonment and execution in 1587; the attempted invasion of England by Spain, which culminated in the celebrated defeat of the Spanish Armada in 1588; and a Catholic rebellion in Ireland that was suppressed during the Nine Years War (1594–1603). Elizabeth never married, and was succeeded on the throne by James I* following her death in 1603.

Edward Elton (1569–1624). Puritan minister. Elton served as pastor of St. Mary Magdalen's Church in Bermondsey, Surrey. Richard Baxter* praised him for his exegetical works, among which were *Three Excellent Pious Treatises in Sundry Sermons upon the Whole Seventh, Eighth, and Ninth Chapters of the Epistle to the Romans* and *An Exposition of the Epistle of St. Paul to the Colossians*.

English Annotations (1645; 1651; 1657). Under a commission from the Westminster Assembly, the editors of the English Annotations—John Downame* along with unnamed colleagues—translated, collated and digested in a compact and accessible format several significant Continental biblical resources, including Calvin's* commentaries, Beza's* *Annotationes majores* and Diodati's* *Annotations*.

Desiderius Erasmus (1466–1536). Dutch Catholic humanist and pedagogue. Erasmus, a celebrated humanist scholar, was recognized for translations of ancient texts, reform of education according to classical studies, moral and spiritual writings and the first printed edition of the Greek New Testament. A former Augustinian who never left the Catholic Church, Erasmus addressed deficiencies he saw in the church and society, challenging numerous prevailing doctrines but advocating reform. He envisioned a simple, spiritual Christian life shaped by the teachings of Jesus and ancient wisdom. He was often accused of collusion with Martin Luther* on account of some resonance of their ideas but hotly debated Luther on human will.

George Estey (c. 1560–1601). English Anglican priest. After graduating from Cambridge, Estey was ordained in the Church of England and served as vicar of St. Mary in Bury St. Edmunds, Suffolk.

Paul Fagius (1504–1549). German Reformed Hebraist and pastor. After studying at the University of Heidelberg, Fagius went to Strasbourg where he perfected his Hebrew under Wolfgang Capito.* In Isny im Allgäu (Baden-Württemberg) he met the great Jewish grammarian Elias Levita (1469–1549), with whom he established a Hebrew printing press. In 1544 Fagius returned to Strasbourg, succeeding Capito as preacher and Old Testament lecturer. During the Augsburg Interim, Fagius (with Martin Bucer*) accepted Thomas Cranmer's* invitation to translate and interpret the Bible at Cambridge. However, Fagius died before he could begin any of the work. Fagius wrote commentaries on the first four chapters of Genesis and the deutero-canonical books of Sirach and Tobit.

Guillaume Farel (1489–1565) French Reformed preacher and theologian. At the vanguard of the French Reformation, Farel was a student of Jacques Lefèvre d'Étaples* and member of Archbishop Briçonnet's* circle in Meaux until his desire for more rapid change saw him depart in 1523 to preach the Protestant message in Basel, Montbéliard, Strasbourg, Bern, and Aigle. During this period of his ministry, he composed the first French Protestant book, an evangelical commentary on the Lord's Prayer and the Apostle's Creed, as well as the first French Confession of Faith. A catalyst in Geneva's acceptance of the Reformation in 1536, it was Farel who persuaded Calvin* to settle in the city. After he and Calvin were banished from Geneva in 1538, Farel accepted the pastorate in Neuchâtel, a position he held until his death while continuing to travel and support the Reformation in the French-speaking lands.

John Fary (unknown). English Puritan pastor. Fary authored *God's Severity on Man's Sterility* (1645), a sermon on the fruitless fig tree in Luke 13:6-9.

Margaret Fell (1614–1702). English Quaker. Known as the "Mother of Quakerism," Fell was born at Dalton-in-Furness in northern England. The daughter of a local judge, she married Thomas Fell, who was a judge as well as a member of Parliament, representing Lancashire. In 1652, under the preaching of George Fox (1624–1691), Fell and her daughters became members of the Society of Friends (the Quakers). From that time onward, she became a pivotal figure in the subsequent development of the Quaker movement. Throughout her extensive correspondence to powerful members of the nobility, including King Charles II (r. 1660–1685), she pleaded for the release of imprisoned Quakers. Fell was arrested in 1664 for leading Quaker meetings and for her refusal to swear the Oath of Obedience, and she was sentenced to four and a half years imprisonment. After her release, she married George Fox in 1669, her first husband having died eleven years earlier. In addition to her advocacy for incarcerated Quakers, Fell enhanced the work of the Quaker Women's Meeting, which consisted of caring for the sick and elderly as well as orphans and prisoners. Her exegetical works include *For Mannaseth Ben Israel* and *A Loving Salutation to the Seed of Abraham*, both published in 1656, and translated into Hebrew (the latter believed to have been translated by the Jewish philosopher Benedict Spinoza). Moreover during her imprisonment, she authored her most famous treatise, *Women's Speaking Justified, Proved and Allowed of by the Scriptures*.

Dudley Fenner (1558?–1587). English Puritan minister. Fenner ministered briefly in Kent before following his mentor Thomas Cartwright* to Antwerp, where he was ordained in the Reformed church. After pastoring the English congregation alongside Cartwright, Fenner returned to his previous congregation in Kent, but he was soon suspended and arrested for refusing to conform to the Book of Common Prayer* and Thirty-Nine Articles.* Once released, he returned to the Low Countries, spending the remainder of his career leading an English congregation in Middelburg. He composed devotional and polemical writings as well as commentaries on Song of Songs and Philemon.

William Fenner (1600–1640). English Puritan pastor. After studying at Cambridge and Oxford, Fenner ministered at Sedgley and Rochford. Fenner's extant writings, which primarily deal with practical and devotional topics, demonstrate a zealous Puritan piety and a keen interest in Scripture and theology.

Charles Ferme (1566–1617). Scottish Reformed pastor and educator. After studying and teaching at the University of Edinburgh, Ferme pastored in Philorth, where he later served as the principal of a newly chartered university. The reconstitution of the episcopacy brought challenges for Ferme, and his resistance saw him imprisoned a number of times, including a three-year incarceration on the Isle of Bute. His only extant writing is a logical analysis of Romans.

Henry Ferne (1602–1662). English Protestant minister. Ferne ministered at a number of parishes in the north of England before serving as an extraordinary chaplain to Charles I* after earning his doctorate of divinity. A committed Royalist, he left official ministry during the Civil War (1642–1651), though he often preached, wrote a number of theological treatises against the Roman Catholics, and accompanied the king on a number of occasions. After the Restoration, Ferne served as master at Trinity College, Cambridge, and dean of Ely Cathedral before becoming bishop of Chester.

Richard Ferrers (Unknown). English poet. Ferrers is remembered for his poem *The Worth of Woman* (1622), defending the equality and value of women.

First Helvetic Confession (1536). Anticipating the planned church council at Mantua (1537, but delayed until 1545 at Trent), Reformed theologians of the Swiss cantons drafted a confession to distinguish themselves from both Catholics and the churches of the Augsburg Confession.* Heinrich Bullinger* led the discussion and wrote the confession itself; Leo Jud, Oswald Myconius, Simon Grynaeus and others were part of the assembly. Martin Bucer* and Wolfgang Capito* had desired to draw the Lutheran and Reformed communions closer together through this document, but Luther* proved unwilling after Bullinger refused to accept the Wittenberg Concord (1536). This confession was largely eclipsed by Bullinger's Second Helvetic Confession.*

John Fisher (1469–1535). English Catholic bishop and theologian. This reputed preacher defended Catholic orthodoxy and strove to reform abuses in the church. In 1521 Henry VIII* honored Fisher with the title *Fidei Defensor* ("defender of the faith"). Nevertheless, Fisher opposed the king's divorce of Catherine of Aragon (1485–1536) and the independent establishment of the Church of England; he was convicted for treason and executed. Most of Fisher's works are polemical and occasional (e.g., on transubstantiation, against Martin Luther*); however, he also published a series of sermons on the seven penitential psalms. In addition to his episcopal duties, Fisher was the chancellor of Cambridge from 1504 until his death.

Matthias Flacius (1520–1575). Lutheran theologian. A native of Croatia, Matthias Flacius commenced his studies at the University of Tubingen, and completed them at Wittenberg, where through Luther's influence, he embraced the university's evangelical theology. Flacius began his career as instructor of Hebrew at the University of Wittenberg in 1544, and remained in this post until 1549. As a devoted follower of Luther's teachings, Flacius sought to defend them in their purity which drove him and Nikolaus von Amsdorf as leaders of the Gnesio-Lutherans to oppose the more moderate positions of Philipp Melanchthon and his sympathizers, the Philippists, in several controversies concerning the role of free will and good works in justification as well as relations with Calvinism. After serving as a professor at the University of Jena (1557–1561), Flacius spent the remainder of his life as an independent scholar, frequently moving from one city to another to escape persecution. Flacius died in Frankfurt am Main in 1575. His important exegetical works are *De vocabula Dei* (1549), *Clavis Scripturae Sacrae* (1567), and *Glossa Novi Testamenti* (1570). Flacius also published two historical works, *Catalogus Testium Veritatis* (1556) and the *Magdeburg Centuries*.

Marcantonio Flaminio (1498–1550). Italian humanist and poet. Flaminio was dependent on patronage, and he spent much of his life in the houses of noble benefactors in Bologna, Genoa, and Verona. While he never left the Roman church, he was drawn to intellectual currents that sought reform. In Naples, he participated in an intellectual circle that included Juan de Valdés* and Pietro Carnesecchi* before joining the house of Cardinal Pole* in Viterbo. Alongside his poetry and humanistic writings, Flaminio also edited one of the most significant Italian texts of the Reformation, Benedetto de Mantova's* *The Benefit of Christ* (1543).

John Flavel (c. 1630–1691). English Puritan pastor. Trained at Oxford, Flavel ministered in southwest England from 1650 until the Act of Uniformity in 1662, which reaffirmed the compulsory use of the Book of Common Prayer. Flavel preached unofficially for many years, until his congregation was eventually allowed to build a meeting place in 1687. His works were numerous, varied and popular.

Giovanni Battista Folengo (1490–1559). Italian Catholic exegete. In 1528 Folengo left the Benedictine order, questioning the validity of monastic vows; he returned to the monastic life in 1534. During this hiatus Folengo came into contact with the Neapolitan reform-minded circle founded by Juan de Valdés.* Folengo published commentaries on the Psalms, John, 1–2 Peter and James. Augustin Marlorat* included Folengo's comment in his anthology of exegesis on the Psalms. In 1580 Folengo's Psalms commentary was added to the Index of Prohibited Books.

John Forbes (1568?–1634). Scottish Reformed pastor. While minister at Alford in Aberdeenshire, Forbes was appointed moderator of the Presbyterian Aberdeen Assembly, which met against the orders of King James I.* Refusing to accept the monarch's jurisdiction, he was exiled to the Continent and settled in the Netherlands, where he pastored English congregations at Middleburg and Delft until forced out under the reforms of Archbishop Laud.*

Formula of Concord (1577). After Luther's* death, intra-Lutheran controversies between the Gnesio-

Lutherans (partisans of Luther) and the Philippists (partisans of Melanchthon*) threatened to cause a split among those who had subscribed to the Augsburg Confession.* In 1576, Jakob Andreae,* Martin Chemnitz,* Nikolaus Selnecker,* David Chytraeus* and Andreas Musculus (1514–1581) met with the intent of resolving the controversies, which mainly regarded the relationship between good works and salvation, the third use of the law, and the role of the human will in accepting God's grace. In 1580, celebrating the fiftieth anniversary of the presentation of the Augsburg Confession to Charles V (1500–1558), the *Book of Concord* was printed as the authoritative interpretation of the Augsburg Confession; it included the three ancient creeds, the Augsburg Confession, its Apology (1531), the Schmalkald Articles,* Luther's *Treatise on the Power and Primacy of the Pope* (1537) and both his Small and Large Catechisms (1529).

John Foxe (1516–1587). English Protestant martryrologist, historian. John Foxe was born in Boston, Lincolnshire. After completing his early education, Foxe became a fellow at Magdalen College, Oxford, where he completed his BA degree in 1537, and MA in 1543. Also he was lecturer in logic from 1539 to 1540. However, in 1545, Foxe was forced to resign from Magdalen because he had adopted Protestant beliefs. After leaving Oxford, Foxe became tutor to the children of the Earl of Surrey. During this time Foxe made the acquaintance of John Bale (1495–1562) who fostered his interest in history. When Mary Tudor ascended the throne of England in 1553, Foxe fled to the continent. While there, Foxe traveled to Frankfurt, where in 1555 he met Edmund Grindal (1519–1583), who had been composing accounts of Protestant martyrs. Foxe later joined Grindal in Basel, where he translated his narratives into Latin. Foxe published the book resulting from his labors in Basel in 1559. After Elizabeth I* succeeded to the throne in the same year, Foxe returned to England. Upon his return he began working with the printer, John Day, who published the first English edition of Foxe's work. This voluminous work, *The Acts and Monuments*, underwent four editions during the remainder of the author's lifetime. *The Acts and Monuments* contributed significantly to the development of the national identity and piety of Elizabethan England. Shorter versions of this work are known simply as *Foxe's Book of Martyrs*.

Francis I of France (1494–1547). French monarch. Francis ascended to the French throne following the death of Louis XII (1462–1515), who was both his cousin and father-in-law. Much of Francis's reign was dominated by warfare. In Italy, victory over the Swiss allowed him to assert his dynastic claim to the Duchy of Milan, and extract liberties for the French church from Pope Leo X* through the Concordat of Bologna. His campaign against Charles V* was less successful, however, as Milan was lost and following defeat at the Battle of Pavia, Francis was taken prisoner. His release was negotiated by his sister, Marguerite d'Angouleme*, though he reneged in its terms once reaching safety, ensuring continued conflict with the Holy Roman Emperor throughout his reign. Francis fostered humanistic learning within his kingdom, and while he resisted Lutheran and other evangelical thought, he gave some space for its expression, giving protection to scholars such as those gathered around his sister and Bishop Guillaume Briçonnet* at Meaux. His desire for social order saw him take increasingly strident steps against the Reformation, however, particularly after his bedchamber was pamphleted during the Affair of the Placards, and the final years of his reign saw a significant increase in attempts to reassert Catholic doctrine and stamp out Protestantism with persecution.

Sebastian Franck (1499–1542). German Radical theologian. Franck became a Lutheran in 1525, but by 1529 he began to develop ideas that distanced him from Protestants and Catholics. Expelled from Strasbourg and later Ulm due to his controversial writings, Franck spent the end of his life in Basel. Franck emphasized God's word as a divine internal spark that cannot be adequately expressed in outward forms. Thus he criticized religious institutions and dogmas. His work consists mostly of commentaries, compilations and translations. In his sweeping historical *Chronica* (1531), Franck supported numerous heretics condemned by the Catholic Church and criticized political and church authorities.

Leonhard Frick (d. 1528). Austrian Radical martyr. See *Kunstbuch*.

John Frith (1503–1533). English reformer, author, and martyr. Frith was born in Westerham, Kent. He was the son of Richard Frith, the innkeeper of the White Horse Inn. After receiving his earlier education at Sevenoaks Grammar School and Eton College, Frith matriculated at Queen's College, Cambridge, where Stephen Gardiner (1497–1555), future bishop of Winchester, and opponent of the English Reformation, was his tutor. Frith graduated with his BA degree in 1525, having obtained proficiency in Latin and mathematics. While still a student, Frith met Thomas Bilney (1495–1531), who most likely introduced him to evangelical faith. After graduating, Frith became a junior canon at Christ Church, Oxford. However, while at Oxford, Frith along with nine others was imprisoned in a fish cellar for possessing what ecclesiastical authorities considered "heretical books." Upon his release, Frith traveled to the Continent, where he assisted William Tyndale* with his translation work. Also while on the Continent, Frith translated some antipapal polemical works, and authored *A Disputation of Purgatory*. Upon Frith's return to England in 1532, he was arrested and imprisoned several times for publicly preaching against transubstantiation and purgatory. Eventually, Frith was imprisoned in the Tower of London, and later transferred to Newgate Prison. He was burned at the stake on July 4, 1533.

Libert Froidmont (1587–1653). Belgian philosopher, scientist, and theologian. A childhood friend of Cornelius Jansen (1585–1638), Froidmont entered the Society of Jesus and his early career was focused on philosophy and the sciences, teaching at Antwerp, Saint-Michel, and Louvain. Drawn to the rigorous but controversial Augustinianism of Jansen, Froidmont earned his doctorate in theology in 1628 and succeeded Jansen as chair of theology at Louvain. While publishing a number of theological and exegetical works, including a commentary on Paul's letters, Froidmont was also active in the scientific and philosophical debates of his era. He published against Nicolas Copernicus (1473–1543) and Galileo Galilei (1564–1642), whom he argued were wrong but not heretical, and was one of the first to engage with the thought of René Descartes (1596–1650).

William Fulke (1538–1589). English Protestant theologian. Responsible for preaching and lecturing on Old Testament and other subjects, William Fulke courted controversy during his tenure as fellow at Cambridge. He was briefly expelled for his advocacy of Vestarians and later resigned until acquitted of being in an incestuous marriage. He left Cambridge to serve as chaplain to Robert Dudley, Earl of Leicester (1532–1588), returning almost a decade later as master of Pembroke College. He is best remembered as a controversialist and was the author of numerous anti-Catholic tracts.

Thomas Fuller (1608–1661). English Protestant minister. Fuller, the son of a minister, graduated from Cambridge, and his early career was overseen by his uncle John Davenant,* who secured his nephew a number of pastoral positions. Known for his wit and moderation, Fuller was a chaplain in the Royal army during the Civil War (1642–1651), and he served as an extraordinary chaplain to King Charles II (1630–1685) after the Restoration. He composed a number of exegetical and pastoral works, but he is primarily remembered for his historical writings. These include histories of the Crusades and the church in England as well as a biographical dictionary, the *History of the Worthies of England* (1622).

Gallic Confession (1559). This confession was accepted at the first National Synod of the Reformed Churches of France (1559). It was intended to be a touchstone of Reformed faith but also to show to the people of France that the Huguenots—who faced persecution—were not seditious. The French Reformed Church presented this confession to Francis II (1544–1560) in 1560, and to his successor, Charles IX (1550–1574), in 1561. The later Genevan draft, likely written by Calvin,* Beza* and Pierre Viret (1511–1571), was received as the true Reformed confession at the seventh National Synod in La Rochelle (1571).

Geneva Bible (originally printed 1560). During Mary I's reign many English Protestants sought safety abroad in Reformed territories of the Empire and the Swiss Cantons, especially in Calvin's* Geneva. A team of English exiles in Geneva led by William Whittingham (c. 1524–1579) brought this complete translation to press in the course of two years. Notable for several innovations—Roman type, verse numbers, italics indicating English idiom and not literal phrasing of the original languages, even variant readings in the Gospels and Acts—this translation is most well known for its marginal notes, which reflect a strongly Calvinist theology. The notes explained Scripture in an accessible way for the laity, also giving unlearned clergy a new sermon resource. Although controversial because of its implicit critique of royal power, this translation was wildly popular; even after the publication of the Authorized Version (1611) and James I's* 1616 ban on its printing, the Geneva Bible continued to be the most popular English translation until after the English Civil Wars.

Johann Gerhard (1582–1637). German Lutheran theologian, professor and superintendent. Gerhard is considered one of the most eminent Lutheran theologians, after Martin Luther* and Martin Chemnitz.* After studying patristics and Hebrew at Wittenberg, Jena and Marburg, Gerhard was appointed superintendent at the age of twenty-four. In 1616 he was appointed to a post at the University of Jena, where he reintroduced Aristotelian metaphysics to theology and gained widespread fame. His most important work was the nine-volume *Loci Theologici* (1610–1625). He also expanded Chemnitz's harmony of the Gospels *(Harmonia Evangelicae)*, which was finally published by Polykarp Leyser (1552–1610) in 1593. Gerhard was well-known for an irenic spirit and an ability to communicate clearly.

George Gifford (c. 1548–1600). English Puritan pastor. Gifford was suspended for nonconformity in 1584. With private support, however, he was able to continue his ministry. Through his published works he wanted to help develop lay piety and biblical literacy.
George Gifford (d. 1620). English Puritan minister. A celebrated preacher in Maldon, Essex, Gifford was removed from the pulpit when he refused to subscribe to Articles of Conformity drawn up by Archbishop John Whitgift.* Allowed to continue ministry in the office of lecturer, he also served as a representative for Essex at Puritan synods. He published numerous works, including a primer for common Christians, a dialogue between a Catholic and a Protestant, and two works on witchcraft.
Anthony Gilby (c. 1510–1585). English Puritan translator. During Mary I's reign, Gilby fled to Geneva, where he assisted William Whittingham (c. 1524–1579) with the Geneva Bible.* He returned to England to pastor after Elizabeth I's* accession. In addition to translating numerous continental Reformed works into English—especially those of John Calvin* and Theodore Beza*—Gilby also wrote commentaries on Micah and Malachi.
Bernard Gilpin (1517–1583). Anglican theologian and priest. In public disputations, Gilpin defended Roman Catholic theology against John Hooper (c. 1495–1555) and Peter Martyr Vermigli.* These debates caused Gilpin to reexamine his faith. Upon Mary I's accession, Gilpin resigned his benefice. He sojourned in Belgium and France, returning to pastoral ministry in England in 1556. Gilpin dedicated himself to a preaching circuit in northern England, thus earning the moniker "the Apostle to the North." His zealous preaching and almsgiving roused royal opposition and a warrant for his arrest. On his way to the queen's commission, Gilpin fractured his leg, delaying his arrival in London until after Mary's death and thus likely saving his life. His only extant writing is a sermon on Luke 2 confronting clerical abuses.
Paul Glock (c. 1530–1585). German Radical preacher. A teenage convert to Hutterite Anabaptism, Glock spent nineteen years imprisoned at Hohenwittlingen, unwilling to recant. While incarcerated, he wrote hymns, a confession and defense of his beliefs, and numerous letters that proved influential in the development of Anabaptist thought. After helping extinguish a fire at the prison in 1576, Glock was freed and settled with the Brethren in Moravia.
Glossa ordinaria. This standard collection of biblical commentaries consists of interlinear and marginal notes drawn from patristic and Carolingian exegesis appended to the Vulgate*; later editions also include Nicholas of Lyra's* *Postilla*. The *Glossa ordinaria* and the *Sentences* of Peter Lombard (c. 1100–1160) were essential resources for all late medieval and early modern commentators.
Franciscus Gomarus (1563–1641). Dutch Reformed theologian and pastor. A religious refugee at an early age, Gomarus's family was forced to leave Bruges for the Palatinate, with Gomarus receiving a Reformed education at Strasbourg, Neustadt, Oxford, Cambridge, and Heidelberg. He pastored at Frankfurt am Main until becoming professor of theology at the University of Leiden, where he came into extended conflict with colleague Jacobus Arminius* over predestination. Gomarus left Leiden in protest when Conradus Vorstius,* a follower of Arminius with Socinian tendencies, was appointed over his objections. Gomarus then pastored briefly at Middelburg before teaching at the Reformed academy at Saumur and the University of Groningen. Representing the university at the Synod of Dordrecht,* Gomarus was a leading opponent of Remonstrant theology and a key figure in ensuring their censure.
Robert Gomersall (1602–1646?). English Protestant minister and dramatist. Little is known of Gomersall's life beyond his graduation from Oxford and entrance into the ministry. He published a number of poetic and dramatic works, including a tragedy on the life of Italian prince Ludovicio Sforza (1452–1508) and a poetic meditation on Judges 19–20.
Thomas Goodwin (1600–1679). Puritan minister. Goodwin was born October 5, 1600, in Norfolk. After receiving his early education from local schools, Goodwin matriculated at Christ College, Cambridge, which was a prime center of Puritan influence. He graduated with the BA degree in 1616 and MA in 1620. Upon receiving his MA, Goodwin became a fellow and lecturer at the university. In October 1620, Goodwin experienced a profound conversion on his twentieth birthday. After his conversion, Goodwin joined the Puritan party at Cambridge. He was licensed to preach in the Church of England in 1625. Three years later, Goodwin became lecturer at Trinity Church. He served as vicar of this church from 1632 to 1634. Unwilling to comply with Archbishop William Laud's* directives for conformity, Goodwin was forced to resign all of his ecclesiastical and academic positions, and leave Cambridge. During the remainder of the 1630s, due to John Cotton's* influence, Goodwin came to adopt the principles of Independency. In 1639, in order to escape the increasing restrictions of unauthorized preachers, Goodwin fled to the Nether-

lands, where he worked with other English Independent exiles. In 1641, Goodwin returned to England per Parliament's request, and preached before it on April 27, 1642. Goodwin was later appointed a delegate to the Westminster Assembly. In the Assembly, Goodwin proved himself to be one of the foremost advocates of Independency. After the Westminster Assembly adjourned, Goodwin was appointed a lecturer at Oxford, and a year later became president of Magdalen College. Furthermore, Goodwin served as an advisor to Oliver Cromwell (1599–1658) and as the Lord Protector's Oxford commissioner. Goodwin also tended to Cromwell on his deathbed. In addition to his university and advisory duties, Goodwin pastored an Independent church at Oxford. Notably, Goodwin was one of the primary authors of the Savoy Declaration of Faith (1658), which served as the confession of faith for the Independent/Congregational churches. When Charles II ascended to the throne of England in 1660, Goodwin withdrew from Oxford to London, where he pastored an Independent congregation until his death at the age of eighty. Throughout his career, Goodwin produced an enormous literary corpus, which includes many exegetical works. Best known among these are his expositions of Ephesians and Revelation.

Marie le Jars de Gournay (1565–1645). French Catholic writer and editor. Born into the minor nobility, the early death of Gournay's father led her family to relocate to their estate in Picardy, where she taught herself Latin and Greek. After reading the *Essais* (1580) of Michel de Montaigne (1533–1592), she committed herself to a life of literature and became active in the intellectual circles of Paris. While she translated many classical writings, she is best known for her editorial work on Montaigne's essays and her advocacy for the rights of women, laid out in a number of writings including *The Equality of Men and Women* (1622) and *The Ladies' Grievance* (1626).

Simon Goulart (1543–1628) French Reformed pastor, translator, and theologian. Goulart spent most of his career as a pastor in Geneva and its surrounds, particularly at the city parish of St. Gervais, and was the leader of the Company of Pastors during the last decades of his life. A prolific translator, he published numerous French editions of classical, patristic, and contemporary works from diverse authors including Plutarch, Seneca, Chrysostom, Cyprian, Tertullian, Beza*, Perkins* and Vermigli*. He also composed numerous devotional writings, important histories of early French Protestantism, and polemical treatises supporting the Huguenot cause.

Thomas Granger (1578–1627). English Protestant pastor. After completing his studies at Cambridge, Granger ministered to congregations at Butterwick and Horbling in Lincolnshire.

Conrad Grebel (c. 1498–1526). Swiss Radical theologian. Grebel, considered the father of the Anabaptist movement, was one of the first defenders and performers of believers' baptism, for which he was eventually imprisoned in Zurich. One of Huldrych Zwingli's* early compatriots, Grebel advocated rapid, radical reform, clashing publicly with the civil authorities and Zwingli. Grebel's views, particularly on baptism, were influenced by Andreas Bodenstein von Karlstadt* and Thomas Müntzer.* Grebel advocated elimination of magisterial involvement in governing the church; instead, he envisioned the church as lay Christians determining their own affairs with strict adherence to the biblical text, and unified in volitional baptism.

William Greenhill (1591–1671). English Puritan pastor. Greenhill attended and worked at Magdalen College. He ministered in the diocese of Norwich but soon left for London, where he preached at Stepney. Greenhill was a member of the Westminster Assembly of Divines and was appointed the parliament chaplain by the children of Charles I. Oliver Cromwell included him among the preachers who helped draw up the Savoy Declaration. Greenhill was evicted from his post following the Restoration, after which he pastored independently. Among Greenhill's most significant contributions to church history was his *Exposition of the Prophet of Ezekiel.*

Catharina Regina von Greiffenberg (1633–1694). Austrian Lutheran poet. Upon her adulthood her guardian (and half uncle) sought to marry her; despite her protests of their consanguinity and her desire to remain celibate, she relented in 1664. After the deaths of her mother and husband, Greiffenberg abandoned her home to debtors and joined her friends Susanne Popp (d. 1683) and Sigmund von Birken (1626–1681) in Nuremberg. During her final years she dedicated herself to studying the biblical languages and to writing meditations on Jesus' death and resurrection, which she never completed. One of the most important and learned Austrian poets of the Baroque period, Greiffenberg published a collection of sonnets, songs and poems (1662) as well as three sets of mystical meditations on Jesus' life, suffering and death (1672; 1683; 1693). She participated in a society of poets called the Ister Gesellschaft.

Lady Jane Grey (1537–1554). English Protestant monarch, sometimes known as "the Nine Days Queen." The eldest daughter of Henry Grey and Frances Brandon, the daughter of Henry VIII's* younger sister Mary, Jane received an extensive Protestant and humanist education. She married Lord Guildford Dudley (c. 1535–1554), son of Edward VI's* chief minister John Dudley, Duke of Northumberland (1504–1553). Seeking to avoid succession by Edward's Catholic half-sister Mary I, Edward and Northumberland conspired to alter the order of succession, naming Jane as heir in the king's will. Following Edward's death, Jane reluctantly took the crown on July 9, 1553, but Northumberland and other Protestants were unable to raise adequate support for her claim and the Privy Council proclaimed Mary queen on July 19. Upon Mary's accession, Jane was imprisoned in the Tower of London and after trial was executed alongside her husband for treason. A handful of her writings exist demonstrating her religious affections, while the story of her martyrdom is prominent in John Foxe's *Acts and Monuments*.

Edmund Grindal (c. 1519–1583). English Anglican archbishop. Grindal began his career in the church as chaplain to Nicholas Ridley* and King Edward VI* until forced to exile in Strasbourg during the reign of Mary I.* Returning to England upon the accession of Elizabeth I,* Grindal helped set the direction for the Church of England, participating in the 1559 Westminster Conference and serving as a member of the committee revising the liturgy. A moderate reformer, he reluctantly became bishop of London despite concerns over continuing Roman practices such as the wearing of vestments and the use of wafer bread for communion. His tenure as archbishop of York was marked by disputes with Presbyterians who wished to abolish the episcopacy and prayer book. Grindal was appointed Archbishop of Canterbury in 1575, but a conflict with Queen Elizabeth I hampered his ability to make change. He refused her request to suppress the "prophesyings" of Puritan clergy and meetings for theological discussion and sermon preparation. After addressing a remonstrance to the queen, he refused to resign, and he was stripped of the administrative power of his position until his death.

Hugo Grotius (1583–1645). Dutch lawyer, statesman, and humanist. Grotius began practicing law at The Hague in 1599, was appointed Advocate-General of the Fisc for the provinces of Holland, Zeeland, and West Friesland in 1607 and in 1613 became pensionary of Rotterdam. As debates between Calvinists and Arminians came to national significance, Grotius sided with the Remonstrants, especially in his rejection of Reformed arguments for the independence of the church, defending the right of the state to appoint ministers and adjudicate over matters of doctrine. Following the victory of Maurice of Orange (1567–1635) over Grotius's patron Johan van Oldenbarnevelt (1547–1619) and the condemnation of Arminianism at the Synod of Dordrecht* (1618–1619), Grotius was imprisoned, though only briefly, as he escaped in a book chest and fled to Paris. Unable to secure return from exile, Grotius became a Swedish ambassador to France while seeking religious toleration and the establishment of a Christian republic. A number of his works from this period, in particular *De Jure Belli ac Pacis* (On the law of war and peace, 1625) made a significant contribution to the establishment of international law.

Argula von Grumbach (c. 1490–c. 1564) German Lutheran noblewoman. Grumbach, an attendant of Queen Kunigunde of Austria (1465–1520), was one of the first women to publish in support of the Reformation. She is best known for letters from 1523 and 1524 written in defense of Arsacius Seehofer (1503–1545), a lecturer at the university of Ingolstadt accused of Lutheranism. For unknown reasons, Grumberg ceased to publish after 1524, although her private correspondence after this time demonstrates a continued effort to support evangelical reform.

Johann Jacob Grynaeus (1540–1617). Swiss Reformed theologian. Raised Lutheran, Grynaeus replaced his father as pastor at Rotelen. After becoming professor of Old Testament at Basel, however, Grynaeus caused conflict by embracing Reformed theology. He avoided controversy by spending two years at the University of Heidelberg. Upon his return to Basel, his opponents had largely died, and he was made superintendent of the church in the city and professor of New Testament. Grynaeus aligned the Basel church with his Reformed convictions and reorganized the city's educational system while preaching regularly and composing numerous theological, exegetical, and practical works.

William Guild (1586–1657). Scottish Reformed minister and theologian. Guild was born in Aberdeen and educated at Marischal College. He was licensed to preach in 1605 and ordained to serve as minister of the parish of King Edward in 1608. In 1617, Guild joined the protest for the liberties of the Scottish national church. While in Edinburgh, Guild met the acquaintance of Bishop Lancelot Andrewes,* who was accompanying King James VI/I* on his royal visit to the city. Moreover, Guild dedicated his best-known work, *Moses Unveiled* (1620), to both Andrewes and the king. He was later appointed chaplain to Charles I, and shortly thereafter received the degree of doctor of divinity. In 1631, Guild was given his second charge in Aberdeen. When he assumed this charge,

Guild expressed his support for episcopacy. He signed the National Covenant in 1638 with some conditions. However, when in 1640 an army came to Aberdeen to enforce full subscription to the Covenant, Guild fled to the Netherlands. After returning to Scotland later that year, he was appointed Guild Principal for King's College Aberdeen, but was deprived of this post by Oliver Cromwell's (1599–1658) military commissioners in 1651. Following his deprivation, Guild lived in retirement until his death in Aberdeen.

Rudolf Gwalther (1519–1586). Swiss Reformed preacher. Gwalther was a consummate servant of the Reformed church in Zurich, its chief religious officer and preacher, a responsibility fulfilled previously by Huldrych Zwingli* and Heinrich Bullinger.* Gwalther provided sermons and commentaries and translated the works of Zwingli into Latin. He worked for many years alongside Bullinger in structuring and governing the church in Zurich. Gwalther also strove to strengthen the connections to the Reformed churches on the Continent and England: he was a participant in the Colloquy of Regensburg (1541) and an opponent of the Formula of Concord.*

Matthias Hafenreffer (1561–1619). German Lutheran theologian. After holding pastoral positions in Herenberg, Ehingen, and Stuttgart, Hafenreffer was appointed professor of theology at Tübingen, a position he held for more than twenty-five years. He composed exegetical works on Nahum, Habakkuk, and Ezekiel, a number of polemical works, and a theological *loci communes* that served as a common textbook within the Lutheran churches for much of the seventeenth century.

Henry Hall (unknown). English Protestant preacher. A fellow of Trinity College, Cambridge, Hall preached and published a sermon given before the House of Commons in 1644 on Matthew 11:12.

Joseph Hall (1574–1656). English Anglican bishop and controversialist. After studying at Cambridge, Hall courted controversy with a series of satires before entering the ministry of the Church of England. As a pastor, Hall served parishes in Suffolk and Essex and was chosen by James I* as an English delegate at the Synod of Dordrecht.* Upon his return, Hall was appointed bishop of Exeter and later transferred to the see of Norwich, where, despite his low-church preferences, his defense of the episcopacy saw him convicted of praemunire by the Puritan parliament and imprisoned in the Tower of London for a short time with a number of other bishops. Hall's literary output was extensive and included controversial tracts against the Brownists and Arminians, treatises on virtue and union with Christ, and numerous devotional works.

Hans Has von Hallstatt (d. 1527). Austrian Reformed pastor. See *Kunstbuch*.

Henry Hammond (1605–1660). Anglican priest. After completing his studies at Oxford, Hammond was ordained in 1629. A Royalist, Hammond helped recruit soldiers for the king; he was chaplain to Charles I. During the king's captivity, Hammond was imprisoned for not submitting to Parliament. Later he was allowed to pastor again, until his death. Hammond published a catechism, numerous polemical sermons and treatises as well as his *Paraphrase and Annotations on the New Testament* (1653).

Jörg Haug (Unknown) German Anabaptist leader. Haug was a radical preacher during the 1525 Peasant's Revolt and composed a tract entitled *A Christian Order of a True Christian* (1524) enumerating seven degrees of faith reached by Christians.

Peter Hausted (d. 1645). Anglican priest and playwright. Educated at Cambridge and Oxford, Hausted ministered in a number of parishes and preached adamantly and vehemently against Puritanism. He is best known for his play *The Rival Friends*, which is filled with invective against the Puritans; during a performance before the king and queen, a riot nearly broke out. Haustead died during the siege of Banbury Castle.

Erhart Hegenwald (Unknown). Swiss Protestant teacher and doctor. A teacher at the Pfäffen Monastery in St. Gallen and at the Schola Carolina in Zurich, Hegenwald recorded the minutes of Zwingli's* First Zurich Disputation in 1523. Correspondence demonstrates he remained in contact with the Zurich reformers while he studied medicine at Wittenberg, and after graduating in 1526, he may have practiced as a physician in Frankfurt.

Heidelberg Catechism (1563). This German Reformed catechism was commissioned by the elector of the Palatinate, Frederick III (1515–1576) for pastors and teachers in his territories to use in instructing children and new believers in the faith. It was written by theologian Zacharias Ursinus (1534–1583) in consultation with Frederick's court preacher Kaspar Olevianus* and the entire theology faculty at the University of Heidelberg. The Heidelberg Catechism was accepted as one of the Dutch Reformed Church's Three Forms of Unity—along with the Belgic Confession* and the Canons of Dordrecht—at the Synod of Dordrecht,* and became widely popular among other Reformed confessional traditions throughout Europe.

Ursula Hellrigel (b. c. 1521). Austrian Anabaptist. Imprisoned for her heterodox beliefs at 17, authorities sought Hellrigel's recantation, but she refused to acquiesce. After five years she was released from prison and exiled from the Tyrol. The thirty-sixth hymn in the first known Anabaptist hymnal, the *Ausbund* (1654), is commonly attributed to her.

Niels Hemmingsen (1513–1600). Danish Lutheran theologian. Hemmingsen studied at the University of Wittenberg, where he befriended Philipp Melanchthon.* In 1542, Hemmingsen returned to Denmark to pastor and to teach Greek, dialectics and theology at the University of Copenhagen. Foremost of the Danish theologians, Hemmingsen oversaw the preparation and publication of the first Danish Bible (1550). Later in his career he became embroiled in controversies because of his Philippist theology, especially regarding the Eucharist. Due to rising tensions with Lutheran nobles outside of Denmark, King Frederick II (1534–1588) dismissed Hemmingsen from his university post in 1579, transferring him to a prominent but less internationally visible Cathedral outside of Copenhagen. Hemmingsen was a prolific author, writing commentaries on the New Testament and Psalms, sermon collections and several methodological, theological and pastoral handbooks.

Henry IV of France (1553–1610). French monarch. Son of Jeanne of Navarre* and Antoine de Bourbon (1518–1562), Henry's religious loyalties wavered throughout his life. Raised Protestant at the behest of his mother, he practiced Catholicism while attending the Valois court. After his mother's death in 1572, Henry succeeded her as King of Navarre and soon afterwards married Margaret of Valois (1553–1615), the daughter of Henry II of France (1519–1559) and Catherine de' Medici (1519–1589). Their wedding provided the occasion for the St. Bartholomew's Day Massacre, when Catholic forces seized the opportunity to decimate the Huguenot leadership gathered to celebrate the nuptials in Paris, leading to an outbreak of mob violence that devastated the Huguenot movement. A great proportion of the Protestants in France were killed in the weeks that followed the wedding, while many others, including Henry, reconverted to Catholicism. In 1576, Henry escaped the influence of the Valois court, returned his allegiance to Protestantism and took a leadership role amongst the Huguenots. Following the assassination of Henry III of France (1551–1589), Henry was the presumptive heir, but French Catholics were unwilling to accept his rule and Henry was unable to assert his prerogative outside Huguenot strongholds. In 1593, therefore, Henry converted again to Catholicism, with legend claiming he justified his decision with the phrase "Paris is worth a mass." Over the following years, Henry established his authority throughout his kingdom, and while remaining Catholic, provided some relief to Protestants, particularly through the Edict of Nantes (1598), essentially ending the Religious Wars. Henry's pragmatic reign ended with his assassination by a Radical Catholic in 1610.

King Henry VIII of England (1491–1547). English monarch. The second son of Henry VII (r. 1485–1509) and Elizabeth of York (1466–1503), Henry VIII succeeded his father to the English throne, his elder brother Edward having died in 1502. Soon after accession, he married his brother's widow, Catherine of Aragon (1485–1536). Following several stillbirths and the birth of a daughter, Mary, Henry, who was desperate for a male heir to head off dynastic challenges, wished separation from Catherine in order to marry Anne Boleyn (c. 1501–1536). Believing his marriage cursed as it transgressed the commands in Leviticus against marrying a brother's widow, Henry sought dispensation from the church for his annulment and remarriage. While the case was first heard by a papal legate in England, it was transferred to Rome upon the order of Pope Clement VII*, who wished to placate Charles V, Catherine's nephew, whose troops had recently sacked Rome and held the pope under house arrest. Henry asserted praemunire, arguing that as king, he was supreme in his own kingdom. With the formation of the Reformation Parliament in 1529, the legislative process to disentangle the English Church from the Roman was begun. The issue of Henry's divorce was finalized in 1533, after Thomas Cranmer* became Archbishop of Canterbury and declared his marriage to Catherine invalid. While Henry's divorce, assertion of royal supremacy, and subversion of Catholic institutions gave impetus to English Protestantism, Henry's beliefs remained essentially Catholic, and these continued to be enforced by law. He ultimately married six times, and was succeeded by Edward VI*, his son by his third wife, Jane Seymour (1508–1537). Elizabeth I*, Henry's daughter by Anne Boleyn, later became Queen and with the Elizabethan Settlement in 1559, redefined England as a Protestant country.

George Herbert (1593–1633). Anglican minister, theologian, and poet. Herbert was born in Montgomery Powys, Wales, on April 3, 1593, to a noble family. After completing his early education at Westminster School, Herbert matriculated at Trinity College, Cambridge, in 1609. He graduated with both his bachelor's and master's degrees. Shortly thereafter Herbert was elected a fellow of the college, and then became Reader of Rhetoric. From 1620 to 1627, Herbert was Public Orator for the University of Cambridge. In 1624, Herbert was elected to Parliament. However, after the death of King James I,* and of his other major patrons, Herbert withdrew from politics to pursue a career in the church. Toward this end, Herbert was ordained to the priesthood of the Church of England in 1630, and appointed rector of Fugglestone St. Peter and later Bemerton St. Andrews in Wiltshire near Salisbury. While at St. Andrews, Herbert composed his collection of poems titled *The Temple* and his guide for rural ministers, *A Priest to the Temple, or The Country Parson: His Character and Rule of Holy Life*. Twice a week Herbert traveled to Salisbury, where he attended services at Salisbury Cathedral. Following the services, Herbert would compose music with the cathedral musicians. Herbert died of consumption in 1633.

Tilemann Hesshus (1527–1588). German Lutheran theologian and pastor. Hesshus studied under Philipp Melanchthon* but was a staunch Gnesio-Lutheran. With great hesitation—and later regret—he affirmed the Formula of Concord.* Heshuss ardently advocated for church discipline, considering obedience a mark of the church. Unwilling to compromise his strong convictions, especially regarding matters of discipline, Hesshus was regularly embroiled in controversy. He was expelled or pressed to leave Goslar, Rostock, Heidelberg, Bremen, Magdeburg, Wesel, Königsberg and Samland before settling in Helmstedt, where he remained until his death. He wrote numerous polemical tracts concerning ecclesiology, justification, the sacraments and original sin, as well as commentaries on Psalms, Romans, 1–2 Corinthians, Galatians, Colossians and 1–2 Timothy, and a postil collection.

Edo Hilderich (1533–1599). German Lutheran historian and theologian. Hilderich (also named Hildericus) was born to a noble family in Frisia. After attending a local school, Hilderich went on to the University of Wittenberg, where he received the degree of master of philosophy in 1556. Among his teachers was Philipp Melanchthon.* In 1559, Hilderich was appointed to the Faculty of Arts at Wittenberg. He also served as professor of mathematics at the University of Jena from 1564 until 1567, when he resigned the post in order to return to the arts faculty at Wittenberg, of which he became dean in 1570. Three years later he became rector of the academy in Magdeburg, and went from there to the University of Frankfurt in 1575. In 1577, Hilderich became professor of history and Hebrew at Frankfurt. Following the expulsion of the Reformed theologians from the University of Heidelberg in 1578, he went there to be the second professor of theology and Hebrew language. He received his doctorate at Heidelberg a year later. However, Hilderich's refusal to sign the Formula of Concord resulted in removal from his post. On June 3, 1581, he accepted the professorship of theology at the University of Altdorf, where he later became rector in 1582, and professor of Hebrew in 1584. Hilderich's most important exegetical work is his *Oratio de politia et hierarchia populi Iudaici*, published in 1570, in which he traces the history of ancient Israel's government.

Samuel Hieron (1576?–1617). English Puritan minister. After graduating from Cambridge, Hieron became a minister in the Church of England and gained a reputation as a popular preacher in London before becoming the vicar at Modbury in Devonshire. Many of his sermons were published during his lifetime, and he also composed treatises on prayer and the value of Scripture.

Cornelis Hoen (c. 1460–1524). Dutch humanist, jurist, and theologian. A lawyer at the Court of Holland at the Hague, Hoen was prosecuted in 1523 over his sympathy for the evangelical message. He proposed a symbolic interpretation of Christ's presence in the Eucharist justified with reference to Matthew 24:23 in an influential, posthumously-published treatise.

Melchior Hoffman (1495?–1543). German Anabaptist preacher. First appearing as a Lutheran lay preacher in Livonia in 1523, Hoffman's claim to direct revelation, his perfectionist teachings and his announcements that the end of the world would occur in 1533 saw him alienated from both Lutheran and Reformed circles. After converting to Anabaptism in Strasbourg in 1530, a city he claimed would rise as the spiritual Jerusalem, Hoffman escaped brief arrest and fled to the Netherlands, where his preaching made him the first to bring the radical faith to the Low Countries. Believing himself to be Elijah, Hoffman gathered numerous followers, including future Anabaptist leaders Obbe Philips* and Jan Mathijs (d. 1534), until his arrest in Strasbourg in 1533, whereupon he was imprisoned for the final decade of his life. A tendency toward mystical allegory and apocalyptic exegesis supported by direct revelation is found in his writings, which include commentaries on Romans, Revelation, and Daniel 12 alongside numerous tracts, pamphlets, and letters.

Nathaniel Holmes (1599–1678). English Puritan theologian. Educated at Oxford, Holmes was a preacher in the Anglican Church until his millenarian views led him to establish an independent congregation. His publications include defenses of infant baptism and

exclusive psalmody; treatises against witchcraft, usury, and astrology; and a commentary on the Song of Solomon.
Christopher Hooke (unknown). English Puritan physician and pastor. Hooke published a treatise promoting the joys and blessings of childbirth (1590) and a sermon on Hebrews 12:11-12. To support the poor, Hooke proposed a bank funded by voluntary investment of wealthy households.
Richard Hooker (c. 1553–1600). Anglican priest. Shortly after graduating from Corpus Christi College Oxford, Hooker took holy orders as a priest in 1581. After his marriage, he struggled to find work and temporarily tended sheep until Archbishop John Whitgift* appointed him to the Temple Church in London. Hooker's primary work is *The Laws of Ecclesiastical Polity* (1593), in which he sought to establish a philosophical and logical foundation for the highly controversial Elizabethan Religious Settlement (1559). The Elizabethan Settlement, through the Act of Supremacy, reasserted the Church of England's independence from the Church of Rome, and, through the Act of Uniformity, constructed a common church structure based on the reinstitution of the Book of Common Prayer.* Hooker's argumentation strongly emphasizes natural law and anticipates the social contract theory of John Locke (1632–1704).
Thomas Hooker (1586–1647). English-American Puritan Preacher. Hooker ministered at churches in Surrey and Essex and established a school to teach pastors until threatened with arrest as Archbishop Laud* worked to suppress Puritanism. Fleeing to Holland and then New England, he pastored a church in New Town (later Cambridge), Massachusetts before playing an important role in the foundation of Hartford, Connecticut and assisting with the composition of the state constitution.
John Hooper (d. 1555). English Protestant bishop and martyr. Impressed by the works of Huldrych Zwingli* and Heinrich Bullinger,* Hooper joined the Protestant movement in England. However, after the Act of Six Articles was passed, he fled to Zurich, where he spent ten years. He returned to England in 1549 and was appointed as a bishop. He stoutly advocated a Zwinglian reform agenda, arguing against the use of vestments and for a less "popish" Book of Common Prayer.* Condemned as a heretic for denying transubstantiation, Hooper was burned at the stake during Mary I's reign.
John Hoskin (unknown). English Protestant preacher. Hoskin published a sermon on Matthew 18:23 in 1610 in which he is identified as a minister of God's Word and student of divinity.
Rudolf Hospinian (Wirth) (1547–1626). Swiss Reformed theologian and minister. After studying theology at Marburg and Heidelberg, Hospinian pastored in rural parishes around Zurich and taught secondary school. In 1588, he transferred to Zurich, ministering at Grossmünster and Fraumünster. A keen student of church history, Hospinian wanted to show the differences between early church doctrine and contemporary Catholic teaching, particularly with regard to sacramental theology. He also criticized Lutheran dogma and the Formula of Concord*. Most of Hospinian's corpus consists of polemical treatises; he also published a series of sermons on the Magnificat.
Hans Hotz (dates unknown). Swiss Anabaptist leader. Born in Grüningen, near Zurich, Hotz was an associate of Georg Blaurock.* He defended Anabaptism as spokesman for the Swiss Brethren at disputations in Zofingen (1532) and Bern (1538).
John Howson (1557?–1632). English Anglican bishop. Howson held a number of pastoral positions in Oxfordshire before becoming vice chancellor of Oxford University. An opponent of Puritanism, he was appointed bishop of Oxford in 1619, and then to the bishopric of Durham in 1628, where he was an advocate for the reform program of Archbishop Laud.*
Caspar Huberinus (1500–1553). German Lutheran theologian and pastor. After studying theology at Wittenberg, Huberinus moved to Augsburg to serve as Urbanus Rhegius's* assistant. Huberinus represented Augsburg at the Bern Disputation (1528) on the Eucharist and images. In 1551, along with the nobility, Huberinus supported the Augsburg Interim, so long as communion of both kinds and regular preaching were allowed. Nevertheless the people viewed him as a traitor because of his official participation in the Interim, nicknaming him "Buberinus" (i.e., scoundrel). He wrote a number of popular devotional works as well as tracts defending Lutheran eucharistic theology against Zwinglian and Anabaptist detractions.
Balthasar Hubmaier (1480/5–1528). German Radical theologian. Hubmaier, a former priest who studied under Johann Eck,* is identified with his leadership in the peasants' uprising at Waldshut. Hubmaier served as the cathedral preacher in Regensberg, where he became involved in a series of anti-Semitic attacks. He was drawn to reform through the early works of Martin Luther*; his contact with Huldrych Zwingli* made Hubmaier a defender of more radical reform, including believers' baptism and a memorialist account of the Eucharist. His involvement in the Peasants' War led to his extradition and execution by the Austrians.

Aegidius Hunnius (1550–1603). German Lutheran theologian and preacher. Educated at Tübingen by Jakob Andreae (1528–1590) and Johannes Brenz,* Hunnius bolstered and advanced early Lutheran orthodoxy. After his crusade to root out all "crypto-Calvinism" divided Hesse into Lutheran and Reformed regions, Hunnius joined the Wittenberg theological faculty, where with Polykarp Leyser (1552–1610) he helped shape the university into an orthodox stronghold. Passionately confessional, Hunnius developed and nuanced the orthodox doctrines of predestination, Scripture, the church and Christology (more explicitly Chalcedonian), reflecting their codification in the Formula of Concord.* He was unafraid to engage in confessional polemics from the pulpit. In addition to his many treatises (most notably *De persona Christi*, in which he defended Christ's ubiquity), Hunnius published commentaries on Matthew, John, Ephesians and Colossians; his notes on Galatians, Philemon and 1 Corinthians were published posthumously.

Jan Hus (d. 1415). Bohemian reformer and martyr. This popular preacher strove for reform in the church, moral improvement in society, and an end to clerical abuses and popular religious superstition. He was branded a heretic for his alleged affinity for John Wycliffe's writings; however, while he agreed that a priest in mortal sin rendered the sacraments inefficacious, he affirmed the doctrine of transubstantiation. The Council of Constance* convicted Hus of heresy, banned his books and teaching, and, despite a letter of safe conduct, burned him at the stake.

Hans Hut (1490–1527). German Radical leader. Hut was an early leader of a mystical, apocalyptic strand of Anabaptist radical reform. His theological views were shaped by Andreas Bodenstein von Karlstadt,* Thomas Müntzer* and Hans Denck,* by whom Hut had been baptized. Hut rejected society and the established church and heralded the imminent end of days, which he perceived in the Peasants' War. Eventually arrested for practicing believers' baptism and participating in the Peasants' War, Hut was tortured and died accidentally in a fire in the Augsburg prison. The next day, the authorities sentenced his corpse to death and burned him.

George Hutcheson (1615–1674). Scottish Puritan pastor. Hutcheson, a pastor in Edinburgh, published commentaries on Job, John and the Minor Prophets, as well as sermons on Psalm 130.

Roger Hutchinson (d. 1555). English reformer. Little is known about Hutchinson except for his controversies. He disputed against the Mass while at Cambridge and debated with Joan Bocher (d. 1550), who affirmed the doctrine of the celestial flesh. During the Marian Restoration he was deprived of his fellowship at Eton because he was married.

Andreas Hyperius (1511–1564). Dutch Protestant theologian. After a peripatetic humanist education that encompassed studies in theology, canon law, and medicine, Hyperius became professor of theology at Marburg in 1541 and held this position until his death. Often viewed as mediating between Lutheran and Reformed thought, Hyperius was particularly concerned with the practical application of theology, demonstrated in his composition of the first Protestant text on homiletic method.

Abraham Ibn Ezra (1089–c. 1167). Spanish Jewish rabbi, exegete and poet. In 1140 Ibn Ezra fled his native Spain to escape persecution by the Almohad Caliphate. He spent the rest of his life as an exile, traveling through Europe, North Africa and the Middle East. His corpus consists of works on poetry, exegesis, grammar, philosophy, mathematics and astrology. In his commentaries on the Old Testament, Ibn Ezra restricts himself to *peshat* (see *quadriga*).

Valentin Ickelshamer (c. 1500–1547). German Radical teacher. After time at Erfurt, he studied under Luther,* Melanchthon,* Bugenhagen* and Karlstadt* in Wittenberg. He sided with Karlstadt against Luther, writing a treatise in Karlstadt's defense. Ickelshamer also represented the Wittenberg guilds in opposition to the city council. This guild committee allied with the peasants in 1525, leading to Ickelshamer's eventual exile. His poem in the Marpeck Circle's *Kunstbuch** is an expansion of a similar poem by Sebastian Franck.*

Arthur Jackson (1593?–1666). English Presbyterian minister. Known for his pastoral concern, Jackson served at a number of parishes in London. Imprisoned briefly for his support of the Royalist cause, after the Restoration, he was ejected from ministry following the 1662 Act of Uniformity. Jackson's primary works are a series of annotations of many books of the Old Testament.

Thomas Jackson (1579–1640). Anglican theologian and priest. Before serving as the president of Corpus Christi College at Oxford for the final decade of his life, Jackson was a parish priest and chaplain to the king. His best known work is a twelve-volume commentary on the Apostles' Creed.

King James I of England (VI of Scotland) (1566–1625). English monarch. The son of Mary, Queen of Scots, James ascended to the Scottish throne in 1567 following his mother's abdication. In the Union of the Crowns (1603), he took the English and Irish thrones after the death of his cousin, Elizabeth I.* James's reign was tumultuous and tense: Parliament and the nobility often opposed him, church factions squabbled over worship forms and ecclesiology, climaxing in the Gunpowder Plot. James wrote treatises on the divine right of kings, law, the evils of smoking tobacco and demonology. His religious writings include a versification of the Psalms, a paraphrase of Revelation and meditations on the Lord's Prayer and passages from Chronicles, Matthew and Revelation. He also sponsored the translation of the Authorized Version*—popularly remembered as the King James Version.

Cornelius Jansen (1585–1638). Dutch Catholic bishop and theologian. Jansen studied and taught in France and Holland, joining the theological faculty of the University of Leuven after receiving his doctorate. He later became bishop of Ypres. An ardent Augustinian, his posthumously published work *Augustinus* (1640) caused great controversy by advocating for the utterly gratuitous character of God's grace in opposition to the teachings of Jesuit Luis de Molina (1536–1609), which put greater emphasis on human choice. Due to its perceived Protestant leanings, *Augustinus* was judged heretical, and Jansen's followers, known as Jansenists, took up his cause in a series of conflicts that carried on into the eighteenth century.

Jeanne of Navarre (1528–1572) French Reformed noblewoman. Daughter of Henry II, King of Navarre (1503–1555) and Marguerite d'Angoulême*, Jeanne was forced into a strategic marriage at age 12 by her uncle, Francis I* to William, Duke of Cleves (1516–1592). Shifting political alignments allowed her an annulment after four years and in 1548 she wed the first Prince of the Blood, Antoine de Bourbon (1518–1562). Jeanne took the throne of her father, and after making a public announcement of her conversion to the evangelical faith, established a Reformed community at Béarn. A regular correspondent of reformers such as Calvin* and Beza* and an advocate for the reformation of her lands, Jeanne nevertheless remained largely neutral and advocated tolerance during the first years of religious war. At the outbreak of the Third War of Religion (1569–1570), however, she recognized her moderate position was untenable, and from the Protestant stronghold of La Rochelle served as political head for the Huguenot cause alongside Gaspard de Coligny (1519–1572), commander of the Huguenot armed forces.

Michael Jermin (1591–1659). English Protestant pastor. Jermin's early career was spent on the Continent, where he served as chaplain for Elizabeth Stuart, queen of Bohemia (1596–1662) and earned a doctorate of divinity from the University of Leiden. Returning to England, he earned a second doctorate at Oxford before becoming chaplain to Charles I* and serving as rector of St. Martin, Ludgate. A Royalist, he was deprived of his living during the English Civil War (1642–1651), and while he continued to preach occasionally, he was forced to survive on charity.

John Jewel (1522–1571). Anglican theologian and bishop. Jewel studied at Oxford where he met Peter Martyr Vermigli.* After graduating in 1552, Jewel was appointed to his first vicarage and became the orator for the university. Upon Mary I's accession, Jewel lost his post as orator because of his Protestant views. After the trials of Thomas Cranmer* and Nicholas Ridley,* Jewel affirmed Catholic teaching to avoid their fate. Still he had to flee to the continent. Confronted by John Knox,* Jewel publicly repented of his cowardice before the English congregation in Frankfurt, then reunited with Vermigli in Strasbourg. After Mary I's death, Jewel returned to England and was consecrated bishop in 1560. He advocated low-church ecclesiology, but supported the Elizabethan Settlement against Catholics and Puritans. In response to the Council of Trent, he published the *Apoligia ecclesiae Anglicanae* (1562), which established him as the apostle for Anglicanism and incited numerous controversies.

St. John of the Cross (Juan de Yepes y Álvarez) (1542–1591). Spanish Catholic mystic. Born into poverty, Álvarez entered the Carmelite order in Medina del Campo, where, after studying theology at Salamanca, he met the famed mystic Teresa of Ávila (1515–1582). Drawn to her vision of the contemplative life, with two others, he established the first house of Discalced (barefoot) Carmelite Friars and became a leader in the Catholic reform movement. An exceptional administrator and spiritual leader, for more than twenty years, John of the Cross sought to return his order to its original vision of asceticism and prayer while establishing many new reformed Carmelite houses. He encountered significant resistance in his work for renewal, however, and spent nine months imprisoned and tortured by his Carmelite superiors. Considered among the foremost poets in Spanish literary history, his poems, including *The Spiritual Canticle*, *Ascent of Mount Carmel*, and *The Dark Night of the Soul* demonstrate his overriding desire for spiritual growth and closeness to God.

Francis Johnson (1562–1618). English Brownist pastor. A popular Puritan preacher at Cambridge, Johnson was arrested for slander and factitiousness after a sermon criticizing the ecclesiastical hierarchy and the comfortable lives of the ministers at the school. Retracting some of his statements, he was released and expelled from Cambridge. While pastoring an English church in the Netherlands, he came across writings from followers of Robert Browne* and became convinced of the need to separate from the established church and commit to congregational church polity, but his attempts to institute these changes in the church led to his firing. Returning to England, Johnson became pastor of the Brownist church in London, for which he was arrested numerous times until he convinced the Privy Council to allow him to found a Brownist church in Newfoundland. The expedition was canceled, however, and he returned to the Netherlands, where he pastored separatist churches, some alongside Henry Ainsworth* and John Smyth,* until his death.

Justus Jonas (1493–1555). German Lutheran theologian, pastor and administrator. Jonas studied law at Erfurt, where he befriended the poet Eobanus Hessus (1488–1540), whom Luther* dubbed "king of the poets"; later, under the influence of the humanist Konrad Muth, Jonas focused on theology. In 1516 he was ordained as a priest, and in 1518 he became a doctor of theology and law. After witnessing the Leipzig Disputation, Jonas was converted to Luther's* cause. While traveling with Luther to the Diet of Worms, Jonas was appointed professor of canon law at Wittenberg. Later he became its dean of theology, lecturing on Romans, Acts and the Psalms. Jonas was also instrumental for reform in Halle. He preached Luther's funeral sermon but had a falling-out with Melanchthon* over the Leipzig Interim. Jonas's most influential contribution was translating Luther's *The Bondage of the Will* and Melanchthon's *Loci communes* into German.

Robert Jones. A pseudonym; see Thomas Lushington.

William Jones (1561–1636). Anglican minister and theologian. After teaching at Cambridge, Jones ministered at East Bergholt in Suffolk for forty-four years, publishing a commentary on Philemon and Hebrews and tracts on suffering, the nativity, and arrangements to be made before one's death.

David Joris (c. 1501–1556). Dutch Radical pastor and hymnist. This former glass painter was one of the leading Dutch Anabaptist leaders after the fall of Münster (1535), although due to his increasingly radical ideas his influence waned in the early 1540s. Joris came to see himself as a "third David," a Spirit-anointed prophet ordained to proclaim the coming third kingdom of God, which would be established in the Netherlands with Dutch as its *lingua franca*. Joris's interpretation of Scripture, with his heavy emphasis on personal mystical experience, led to a very public dispute with Menno Simons* whom Joris considered a teacher of the "dead letter." In 1544 Joris and about one hundred followers moved to Basel, conforming outwardly to the teaching of the Reformed church there. Today 240 of Joris's books are extant, the most important of which is his *Twonder Boek* (1542/43).

Jörg Haugk von Jūchsen (unknown). German Radical preacher. Nothing is known of Haugk's life except that during the 1524–1525 Peasants' War in Thuringia, he was elected as a preacher by the insurrectionists in his district. He composed one extant tract, titled *A Christian Order of a True Christian: Giving an Account of the Origin of His Faith*, published in 1526 but likely written before the Peasants' War. While lacking reference to most distinctive Anabaptist doctrines, this pamphlet became popular among radicals as it set out the stages of Christian growth toward perfection.

Andreas Bodenstein von Karlstadt (Carlstadt) (1486–1541). German Radical theologian. Karlstadt, an early associate of Martin Luther* and Philipp Melanchthon* at the University of Wittenberg, participated alongside Luther in the dispute at Leipzig with Johann Eck.* He also influenced the configuration of the Old Testament canon in Protestantism. During Luther's captivity in Wartburg Castle in Eisenach, Karlstadt oversaw reform in Wittenberg. His acceleration of the pace of reform brought conflict with Luther, so Karlstadt left Wittenberg, eventually settling at the University of Basel as professor of Old Testament (after a sojourn in Zurich with Huldrych Zwingli*). During his time in Switzerland, Karlstadt opposed infant baptism and repudiated Luther's doctrine of Christ's real presence in the Eucharist.

Edward Kellett (d. 1641). Anglican theologian and priest. Kellett published a sermon concerning the reconversion of an Englishman from Islam, a tract on the soul, and a discourse on the Lord's Supper in connection with Passover.

David Kimchi (Radak) (1160–1235). French Jewish rabbi, exegete and philosopher. Kimchi wrote an important Hebrew grammar and dictionary, as well as commentaries on Genesis, 1–2 Chronicles, the Psalms and the Prophets. He focused on *peshat* (see *quadriga*). In his Psalms commentary he attacks Christian interpretation as forced, irrational and inadmissible. While Sebastian Münster* censors and condemns these arguments in his *Miqdaš YHWH* (1534–1535), he and many other Christian commentators valued Kimchi's work as a grammatical resource.

Moses Kimchi (Remak) (1127–1190). French Jewish rabbi and exegete. He was David Kimchi's* brother. He wrote commentaries on Proverbs and Ezra-Nehemiah. Sebastian Münster* translated Kimchi's concise Hebrew grammar into Latin; many sixteenth-century Christian exegetes used this resource.

Andreas Knöpken (c. 1468–1539). German Lutheran pastor. Knöpken worked in Pomerania as assistant to Johannes Bugenhagen* before relocating to Riga. Here he served as pastor of St. Peter's, and after a brief setback that saw him return to his previous position, he returned and won a disputation before the authorities, which allowed him to undertake the evangelical reform of the city. Knöpken oversaw the reorganization of the churches and schools, composed the church order, wrote a commentary on Romans, and arranged a number of hymns based on the Psalms.

John Knox (1513–1572). Scottish Reformed preacher. Knox, a fiery preacher to monarchs and zealous defender of high Calvinism, was a leading figure of reform in Scotland. Following imprisonment in the French galleys, Knox went to England, where he became a royal chaplain to Edward VI. At the accession of Mary, Knox fled to Geneva, studying under John Calvin* and serving as a pastor. Knox returned to Scotland after Mary's death and became a chief architect of the reform of the Scottish church (Presbyterian), serving as one of the authors of the Book of Discipline and writing many pamphlets and sermons.

Antonius Broickwy von Königstein (1470–1541). German Catholic preacher. Very little is known about this important cathedral preacher in Cologne. Strongly opposed to evangelicals, he sought to develop robust resources for Catholic homilies. His postils were bestsellers, and his biblical concordance helped Catholic preachers to construct doctrinal loci from Scripture itself.

Kunstbuch. In 1956, two German students rediscovered this unique collection of Anabaptist works. Four hundred years earlier, a friend of the recently deceased Pilgram Marpeck*—the painter Jörg Probst—had entrusted this collection of letters, tracts and poetry to a Zurich bindery; today only half of it remains. Probst's redaction arranges various compositions from the Marpeck Circle into a devotional anthology focused on the theme of the church as Christ incarnate (cf. Gal 2:20).

Osmund Lake (c. 1543–1621). English Pastor who ministered at Ringwood in Hampshire.

Thomas Lamb (d. 1686). English Nonconformist minister. Lamb earned a living as a soap boiler while serving as a teaching elder and occasional preacher at a congregational church in London. Convicted of the necessity of adult baptism and the invalidity of infant baptism, he formed a Particular Baptist congregation and led this church for four years before rejoining the Church of England as a layman, retracting his former teachings and becoming a vocal opponent of separatism. Toward the end of his life, he turned to philanthropy, seeking to improve the lives of the poor and prisoners and to further the religious education of children.

François Lambert (Lambert of Avignon) (1487–1530). French Reformed theologian. In 1522, after becoming drawn to the writings of Martin Luther* and meeting Huldrych Zwingli,* Lambert left the Franciscan order. He spent time in Wittenberg, Strasbourg, and Hesse, where Lambert took a leading role at the Homberg Synod (1526) and in creating a biblically based plan for church reform. He served as professor of theology at Marburg University from 1527 to his death. After the Marburg Colloquy (1529), Lambert accepted Zwingli's symbolic view of the Eucharist. Lambert produced nineteen books, mostly biblical commentaries that favored spiritual interpretations; his unfinished work of comprehensive theology was published posthumously.

Eitelhans Langenmantel (d. 1528). German Radical writer. The son of the mayor of Augsburg, Langenmantel was converted to Anabaptism and was rebaptized by Hans Hut* in 1527. Arrested for his heterodox views later that year, he was freed after accepting the validity of infant baptism during a debate, but after renouncing his recantation in 1528, he was rearrested and beheaded. Seven tracts he composed during 1526 and 1527 survive, focusing on the Lord's Supper and the moral life.

Emilia Lanier (1569–1645). English poet. The daughter of a musician at the court of Elizabeth I,* she received a humanist education at the home of Susan Bertie, Countess of Kent (b. 1554). Following a long affair with Henry Carey (1526–1596), Lord Chamberlain to the queen, and after conceiving a child, she married a distant cousin, Alfonso Lanier (unknown). She is best known for a book of poetry written in the hope of securing a patron, *Salve Deus Rex Judaeorum* (1611), which contains a number of protofeminist themes. Modern scholars have also suggested she may be the "Dark Lady" who appears in a number of William Shakespeare's (1564–1616) sonnets.

Hugh Latimer (c. 1485–1555). Anglican bishop and preacher. Latimer was celebrated for his sermons critiquing the idolatrous nature of Catholic practices and the social injustices visited on the underclass by the aristocracy and the individualism of Protestant government. After his support for Henry's petition of divorce he served as a court preacher under Henry VIII* and Edward VI. Latimer became a proponent of reform following his education at Cambridge University and received license as a preacher. Following Edward's death, Latimer was tried for heresy, perishing at the stake with Nicholas Ridley* and Thomas Cranmer.*

William Laud (1573–1645). Anglican archbishop, one of the most pivotal and controversial figures in Anglican church history. Early in his career, Laud offended many with his highly traditional, anti-Puritan approach to ecclesial policies. After his election as Archbishop of Canterbury in 1633, Laud continued to strive against the Puritans, demanding the eastward placement of the Communion altar (affirming the religious centrality of the Eucharist), the use of clerical garments, the reintroduction of stained-glass windows, and the uniform use of the Book of Common Prayer.* Laud was accused of being a crypto-Catholic—an ominous accusation during the protracted threat of invasion by the Spanish Armada. In 1640 the Long Parliament met, quickly impeached Laud on charges of treason, and placed him in jail for several years before his execution.

Ludwig Lavater (1527–1586). Swiss Reformed pastor and theologian. Under his father-in-law Heinrich Bullinger,* Lavater became an archdeacon in Zurich. In 1585 he succeeded Rudolf Gwalther* as the city's Antistes. He authored a widely disseminated book on demonology, commentaries on Chronicles, Proverbs, Ecclesiastes, Nehemiah and Ezekiel, theological works, and biographies of Bullinger and Konrad Pellikan.*

Laws and Liberties of the Inhabitants of Massachusetts (1647). North American colonial constitution. The first printed set of laws in the American colonies, the 1647 *Laws and Liberties of the Inhabitants of Massachusetts* was a revision of the *Massachusetts Body of Liberties* (1641), a legal code collected by Puritan minister Nathaniel Ward (1578–1652). The *Laws and Liberties* codified Puritan expectations of doctrine and morality, and included provision for the punishment for heresy, stipulating banishment for Anabaptism. The majority of the document consists of practical clauses addressing general and specific aspects of communal and commercial life.

John Lawson (unknown). Seventeenth-century English Puritan. Lawson wrote *Gleanings and Expositions of Some of Scripture* (1646) and a treatise on the sabbath in the New Testament.

Jacques Lefèvre d'Étaples (Faber Stapulensis) (1460?–1536). French Catholic humanist, publisher and translator. Lefèvre d'Étaples studied classical literature and philosophy, as well as patristic and medieval mysticism. He advocated the principle of *ad fontes*, issuing a full-scale annotation on the corpus of Aristotle, publishing the writings of key Christian mystics, and contributing to efforts at biblical translation and commentary. Although he never broke with the Catholic Church, his views prefigured those of Martin Luther,* for which he was condemned by the University of Sorbonne in Paris. He then found refuge in the court of Marguerite d'Angoulême, where he met John Calvin* and Martin Bucer.*

Edward Leigh (1602–1671). English Puritan biblical critic, historian and politician. Educated at Oxford, Leigh's public career included appointments as a Justice of the Peace, an officer in the parliamentary army during the English Civil Wars and a member of Parliament. Although never ordained, Leigh devoted himself to the study of theology and Scripture; he participated in the Westminster Assembly. Leigh published a diverse corpus, including lexicons of Greek, Hebrew and juristic terms, and histories of Roman, Greek and English rulers. His most important theological work is *A Systeme or Body of Divinity* (1662).

John Lightfoot (1602–1675). Anglican priest and biblical scholar. After graduating from Cambridge, Lightfoot was ordained and pastored at several small parishes. He continued to study classics under the support of the politician Rowland Cotton (1581–1634). Siding with the Parliamentarians during the English Civil Wars, Lightfoot relocated to London in 1643. He was one of the original members of the Westminster Assembly, where he defended a moderate Presbyterianism. His best-known work is the six-volume *Horae Hebraicae et Talmudicae* (1658–1677), a verse-by-verse commentary illumined by Hebrew customs, language and the Jewish interpretive tradition.

Wenceslaus Linck (1482–1547). German Lutheran theologian and preacher. As dean of the theology faculty at the University of Wittenberg and successor to Johannes von Staupitz* as the prior of the Augustinian Monastery, Linck worked closely with Martin Luther* and attended the Heidelberg Disputation with him. He replaced Staupitz as vicar-general of the Augustinian order in 1520 in Germany, a capacity in which he pronounced all members free from their vows before renouncing the order himself. After periods of ministry in Munich and Altenburg, Linck settled in Nuremberg, where he became known as an exemplary preacher and an advisor to cities undertaking Protestant reform. He published a significant number of sermons and practical tracts as well as a paraphrase and annotations on the Old Testament.

Henry Lok (1553?–1608?). English Puritan poet. Patronized by Sir Robert Cecil (1563–1612), Lok served the secretary of state as a foreign agent, working to gather intelligence in Scotland, southern France, and Spain. After falling out of favor, Lok served at least two sentences in debtors' prison and died penniless. He published two works: a collection of devotional sonnets and a paraphrase of Ecclesiastes.

Peter Lombard (1095–1160). Scholastic theologian, bishop of Paris. Though little is known about his life, some records indicate that Lombard came from the region of Novara in Lombardy. Bernard of Clairvaux* patronized his studies at Reims, and later recommended him for further study at St. Victor in Paris. In 1144, Lombard participated in an examination of the writings of Gilbert of Poitiers for heresy. Lombard became a canon at Notre Dame in 1145, and an archdeacon there in 1156. Meanwhile he spent a year and a half in Rome as an assistant to Theobald, bishop of Paris. Lombard was elected bishop of Paris in 1159. He died less than a year later. Lombard's most important work was the *Four Books of the Sentences*, which served as the standard textbook for theology throughout the remainder of the Middle Ages, and at the beginning of the early modern period. Additionally, Lombard produced commentaries on the Psalms and Pauline epistles.

Johannes Lonicer (1499–1569). German Lutheran theologian and linguist. After studying in Erfurt and Wittenberg, Lonicer renounced his Augustinian vows. He briefly taught Hebrew at the University of Freiburg, but controversy saw him flee to Strasburg, where he worked with a printer, translating some early Lutheran vernacular works into Latin. At the opening of the University of Marburg, Lonicer was appointed to teach Greek and Hebrew, and he later also served as professor of theology.

Lucas Lossius (1508–1582). German Lutheran teacher and musician. While a student at Leipzig and Wittenberg, Lossius was deeply influenced by Melanchthon* and Luther,* who found work for him as Urbanus Rhegius's* secretary. Soon after going to work for Rhegius, Lossius began teaching at a local gymnasium (or secondary school), *Das Johanneum*, eventually becoming its headmaster. Lossius remained at *Das Johanneum* until his death, even turning down appointments to university professorships. A man of varied interests, he wrote on dialectics, music and church history, as well as publishing a postil and a five-volume set of annotations on the New Testament.

Sibrandus Lubbertus (c. 1555–1625). Dutch Reformed theologian. Lubbertis, a key figure in the establishment of orthodox Calvinism in Frisia, studied theology at Wittenburg and Geneva (under Theodore Beza*) before his appointment as professor of theology at the University of Franeker. Throughout his career, Lubbertis advocated for high Calvinist theology, defending it in disputes with representatives of Socinianism, Arminianism and Roman Catholicism. Lubbertis criticized the Catholic theologian Robert Bellarmine and fellow Dutch reformer Jacobus Arminius*; the views of the latter he opposed as a prominent participant in the Synod of Dordrecht.*

Thomas Lushington (1590–1661). English Anglican minister. Best known as the tutor of polymath Sir Thomas Browne (1605–1682), Lushington also served as a chaplain to Richard Corbet, bishop of Oxford. Committed to the program of Archbishop Laud,* he lost his position during the English Civil Wars and retired to write. Most of his works were published anonymously or pseudonymously, including a translation of a commentary on Hebrews by Polish theologian Johannes Crellius (1590–1633) as G. W. and a series of sermons given at Oxford as Robert Jones.

Martin Luther (1483–1546). German Lutheran priest, professor, and theologian. Martin Luther was born in Eisleben, Saxony, to an entrepreneurial minor. Upon completing his earlier education at Eisenach, Luther matriculated at the University of Erfurt where he completed his BA in 1502, and MA in 1505. While at Erfurt, Luther studied the philosophy of William of Ockham (1285–1347), and his disciple, Gabriel Biel (1420–1495). After receiving his MA, Luther proceeded to the study of law. However, a number of events culminating in his promise to St. Anne (the patron saint of minors) to become a monk compelled Luther to withdraw from law school and join the Augustinian monastery at Erfurt in 1505. At this monastery, Luther was ordained a priest. Later, the Augustinians sent Luther to the University of Wittenberg to study theology. In 1512, Luther received his doctorate, and took up the post of lecturer in Bible at Wittenberg, a position he would hold the rest of his life. While a professor at this university, Luther reinterpreted the doctrine of justification. Convinced that righteousness comes only from God's grace, he disputed the sale of indulgences with his *Ninety-Five Theses*, which he reportedly posted to the door of All Saints' Church in Wittenberg on October 31, 1517. Luther's positions brought conflict with Rome. He challenged the Mass, transubstantiation, and communion in one kind, and his denial of papal authority led to excommunication. Though Luther was condemned by the Diet of Worms, Frederick III, the Elector of Saxony, provided him safe haven. Luther later returned to Wittenberg with public order collapsing under Andreas Bodenstein von Karlstadt* and steered a more cautious path of reform. Among his most influential works are three treatises published in 1520: *To the Christian Nobility of the German Nation*, *On the Babylonian Captivity of the Church*, and *On the Freedom of a Christian*. His rendering of the Bible and liturgy in the vernacular, as well as his hymns and sermons, proved extensively influential.

Georg Major (1502–1574). German Lutheran theologian. Major was on the theological faculty of the University of Wittenberg, succeeding as dean Johannes Bugenhagen* and Philipp Melanchthon.* One of the chief editors on the Wittenberg edition of Luther's works, Major is most identified with the controversy bearing his name, in which he stated that good works are necessary to salvation. Major qualified his statement, which was in reference to the totality of the Christian life. The Formula of Concord* rejected the statement, ending the controversy. As a theologian, Major further refined Lutheran views of the inspiration of Scripture and the doctrine of the Trinity.

John (Mair) Major (1467–1550). Scottish Catholic philosopher. Major taught logic and theology at the universities of Paris (his alma mater), Glasgow and St Andrews. His broad interests and impressive work drew students from all over Europe. While disapproving of evangelicals (though he did teach John Knox*), Major advocated reform programs for Rome. He supported collegial episcopacy and even challenged the curia's teaching on sexuality. Still he was a nominalist who was critical of humanist approaches to biblical exegesis. His best-known publication is *A History of Greater Britain, Both England and Scotland* (1521), which promoted the union of the kingdoms. He also published a commentary on Peter Lombard's *Sentences* and the Gospel of John.

Juan de Maldonado (1533–1583). Spanish Catholic biblical scholar. A student of Francisco de Toledo,* Maldonado taught philosophy and theology at the universities of Paris and Salamanca. Ordained to the priesthood in Rome, he revised the Septuagint under papal appointment. While Maldonado vehemently criticized Protestants, he asserted that Reformed baptism was valid and that mixed confessional marriages were acceptable. His views on Mary's immaculate conception proved controversial among many Catholics who conflated his statement that it was not an article of faith with its denial. He was intrigued by demonology (blaming demonic influence for the Reformation). All his work was published posthumously; his Gospel commentaries were highly valued and important.

Thomas Manton (1620–1677). English Puritan minister. Manton, educated at Oxford, served for a time as lecturer at Westminster Abbey and rector of St. Paul's, Covent Garden, and was a strong advocate of Presbyterianism. He was known as a rigorous evangelical Calvinist who preached long expository sermons. At different times in his ecclesial career he worked side-by-side with Richard Baxter* and John Owen.* In his later life, Manton's Nonconformist position led to his ejection as a clergyman from the Church of England (1662) and eventual imprisonment (1670). Although a voluminous writer, Manton was best known for his preaching. At his funeral in 1677, he was dubbed "the king of preachers."

Benedetto da Mantova (c. 1495–c. 1556). Italian Catholic monk. Benedetto entered the Benedictine order in Mantua and served as dean at San Giorgio Maggiore in Venice. At San Nicolò l'Arena on Mt. Etna, he became acquainted with Waldensian and Protestant thought, which influenced his composition of *The Benefit of Christ*, one of the most significant Italian writings of the Reformation. Marcantonio Flaminio* was asked to rewrite the text in more elegant prose before its anonymous publication in 1543, and although the work drew the ire of the Inquisition, Benedetto's authorship was not uncovered during his lifetime. His increasingly radical spiritualism saw him arrested in Padua, though nothing of his later life is known.

Felix Mantz (d. 1527). Swiss Anabaptist Leader. An early supporter of Zwingli* in Zurich, Mantz's frustration with the pace of the magisterial Reformation led him to found an independent congregation, the Swiss Brethren, with Conrad Grebel,* Georg Blaurock,* and others. Mantz and Grebel represented the Brethren in two disputations with Zwingli over infant baptism in 1525. Defeated, the Brethren refused to cease meeting and rebaptizing adults, which they considered a first baptism, leading to suppression by the Zurich authorities. Mantz was able to spread his message for a time, traveling through a number of Swiss regions despite several arrests. Imprisoned by the Zurich authorities in March 1526 with Grebel and Blaurock, he briefly escaped, but having returned to his practice of believers' baptism, he was executed by drowning, the punishment for Anabaptism, in January 1527.

Lucrezia Marinella (1571–1653). Venetian poet and writer. While famous for her writings, very little is known of Marinella's personal life. As was expected of a women of her class, she spent most of her life in seclusion, and she did not participate in public life. She married a physician, but the fact that she had two children is only known from her will. Marinella's writings spanned a number of subjects, including, philosophy, religious poetry, and proto-feminist texts on the abilities of women and their place in society. Perhaps her best-known work is *The Nobility and Excellence of Women and the Defects and Vices of Men* (1600), in which she argues for the moral and intellectual superiority of women.

Augustin Marlorat (c. 1506–1562). French Reformed pastor. Committed by his family to a monastery at the age of eight, Marlorat was also ordained into the priesthood at an early age in 1524. He fled to Geneva in 1535, where he pastored until the Genevan Company of Pastors sent him to France to shepherd the nascent evangelical congregations. His petition to the young Charles IX (1550–1574) for the right to public evangelical worship was denied. In response to a massacre of evangelicals in Vassy (over sixty dead, many more wounded), Marlorat's congregation planned to overtake Rouen. After the crown captured Rouen, Marlorat was arrested and executed three days later for treason. His principle published work was an anthology of New Testament comment modeled after Thomas Aquinas's* *Catena aurea in quatuor Evangelia*. Marlorat harmonized Reformed and Lutheran comment with the church fathers, interspersed with his own brief comments. He also wrote such anthologies for Genesis, Job, the Psalms, Song of Songs and Isaiah.

Pilgram Marpeck (c. 1495–1556). Austrian Radical elder and theologian. During a brief sojourn in Strasbourg, Marpeck debated with Martin Bucer* before the city council; Bucer was declared the winner, and Marpeck was asked to leave Strasbourg for his views concerning paedobaptism (which he compared to a sacrifice to Moloch). After his time in Strasbourg, Marpeck traveled throughout southern Germany and western Austria, planting Anabaptist congregations. Marpeck criticized the strict use of the ban, however, particularly among the Swiss brethren. He also engaged in a christological controversy with Kaspar von Schwenckfeld.*

Stephen Marshall (c. 1594–1655). English Presbyterian minister. Known for his Nonconformist preaching, Marshall pastored in Essex before appearing on the national stage prior to the Civil War (1642–1651). An advocate of armed rebellion against a lawful sovereign over religious matters, he preached before Parliament a number of times, was a member of the Westminster Assembly, and served as lecturer at St. Margaret's, Westminster. He also ministered to Archbishop Laud* and Charles I* before their executions.

Gregory Martin (1542?–1582). English Catholic priest and translator. After studying at Oxford, Martin tutored the sons of the Duke of Norfolk until leaving for the college of Douai, where he received his doctorate. He taught for two years at the English college in Rome before returning to the college of Douai, which was temporarily based at Rheims. While he composed a number of polemical writings, he is best known as the primary translator of the Douai-Rheims Bible, an English translation of the Vulgate with commentary and notes intended to provide a Catholic alternative to the influx of Protestant annotated English Bibles. The New Testament was published at Douai in 1582 and the Old Testament at Rheims in 1609–1610.

Mary I of England (1516–1558). English monarch. Daughter of Henry VIII* and his first wife Catherine of Aragon (1509–1553), Mary was raised in the strict Catholicism of her mother. Her succession of Edward VI, her half-brother, was briefly contested by Lady Jane Grey*, daughter of Henry VIII's younger sister, in whom Protestants placed their hopes, but unable to raise adequate support, this challenge was quickly dismissed. Upon her ascent, Mary set about the task of restoring the Catholic religion, a reversal of royal policy that was positively received by much of the populace. While able to reestablish relations with the Pope and reassert the mass and other aspects of Catholicism, the impoverishment of the church following the dissolution of the monasteries and the closure of the chantries was difficult to overcome. Other aspects of popular piety, including the cult of the saints, pilgrimages, and the doctrine of purgatory, were not restored during her reign. Mary looms large in the Protestant imagination, and her persecution of evangelicals led to the moniker "Bloody Mary." The accounts of martyrs such as Thomas Cranmer*, Hugh Latimer*, and Nicholas Ridley* were immortalized in John Foxe's (1516–1587) *Acts and Monuments** and became a mainstay of Protestant propaganda.

Johannes Mathesius (1504–1565). German Lutheran theologian and pastor. After reading Martin Luther's* *On Good Works*, Mathesius left his teaching post in Ingolstadt and traveled to Wittenberg to study theology. Mathesius was an important agent of reform in the Bohemian town of Jáchymov, where he pastored, preached and taught. Over one thousand of Mathesius's sermons are extant, including numerous wedding and funeral sermons as well as a series on Luther's life. Mathesius also transcribed portions of Luther's Table Talk.

Chiara Matraini Contarini (1514–1604). Italian Catholic poet. Widowed at twenty-seven, Matraini became active in the literary circles of Lucca and Pescia. Her early published works were composed on secular topics, and include love poetry, songs, a reflection on warfare, and a translation of Isocrates's (436–338 BC) *Ad Demonicum*. Later in her life, she wrote on spiritual topics, publishing a series of spiritual meditations, reflections on the penitential psalms, and a treatise on Mary.

Anthony Maxey (d. 1618). Anglican minister. Maxey was born in Essex and educated at Westminster School. After completing his early education at Westminster, Maxey matriculated at Trinity College, Cambridge, in 1578. Maxey graduated Cambridge with the BA (1581), MA (1585), BD (1594), and DD (1608) degrees. However, he was unable to obtain a fellowship at Trinity. King James I* appointed Maxey as his chaplain and dean of Windsor on June 21, 1612. Maxey was also inducted into the Order of the Garter. He died on May 3, 1618. Maxey's published works consist of three sermons: *The Churches Sleep*; *The Golden Chain of Man's Salvation*; and *The Fearful Point of Hardening*.

John Mayer (1583–1664). Anglican priest and biblical exegete. Mayer dedicated much of his life to biblical exegesis, writing a seven-volume commentary on the entire Bible (1627–1653). Styled after Philipp Melanchthon's* *locus* method, Mayer's work avoided running commentary, focusing instead on textual and theological problems. He was a parish priest for fifty-five years. In the office of priest Mayer also wrote a popular catechism, *The English Catechisme, or a Commentarie on the Short Catechisme* (1621), which went through twelve editions in his lifetime.

Joseph Mede (1586–1638). Anglican biblical scholar, Hebraist and Greek lecturer. A man of encyclopedic knowledge, Mede was interested in numerous fields, varying from philology and history to mathematics and physics, although millennial thought and apocalyptic prophesy were clearly his chief interests. Mede's most important work was his *Clavis Apocalyptica* (1627, later translated into English as *The Key of the Revelation*). This work examined the structure of Revelation as the key to its interpretation. Mede saw the visions as a connected and chronological sequence hinging around Revelation 17:18. He is remembered as an important figure in the history of millenarian theology. He was respected as a mild-mannered and generous scholar who avoided controversy and debate, but who had many original thoughts.

Philipp Melanchthon (1497–1560). German Lutheran educator, reformer, and theologian. Philipp Melanchthon was born in the Palatinate, the son of an armorer. He attended the Latin school in Pforzheim, where he lived with the sister of Johannes Reuchlin* to whom he was related by marriage. Having completed his early education, Melanchthon went on to attend the University of Heidelberg, where he received his BA in 1511. Afterwards, he earned his MA from the University of Tubingen in 1514. In 1518, Reuchlin recommended Melanchthon for the new professorship of Greek at the University of Wittenberg, where he remained for the rest of his life. There, Melanchthon taught Greek, rhetoric, and logic. Melanchthon is known as the partner and successor to Martin Luther* in reform in Germany and for his pioneering *Loci Communes*, which served as a theological textbook. Melanchthon participated with Luther in the Leipzig disputation, helped implement reform in Wittenberg, and was a chief architect of the Augsburg Confession.* Later, Melanchthon and Martin Bucer* worked for union between reformed and Catholic churches. On account of Melanchthon's ecumenical disposition and his modification of several of Luther's doctrines, he was held in suspicion by some.

Andrew Melville (1545–1622). Scottish Reformed theologian. Melville was born at Baldovie on August 1, 1545, to an evangelical family. After finishing his early education at Montrose Grammar School, he matriculated at St. Mary's College, St. Andrews, in 1559. Melville graduated St. Andrews in 1564, after which he traveled to Paris, where he studied Greek, Hebrew, mathematics, and other languages. While in Paris, Melville came under the influence of Petrus Ramus,* whose pedagogical methods he would later utilize in Scotland. From there, he proceeded to Poitiers to study law. There, he became regent of the College of St. Marceon. However, when Poitiers came under siege, Melville departed the city for Geneva, where Theodore Beza* warmly received him. Shortly after Melville's arrival in Geneva, he assumed the chair of humanities at the academy. Melville remained in this position at the academy until 1573, when he returned to Scotland. In 1574, Melville was appointed principal of the College of Glasgow. While in this post, Melville led in the reform of the college's curriculum, and engaged in ecclesiastical controversy. He served on the committee that drafted the Second Book of Discipline, and was elected moderator of the General Assembly in 1578. In 1580, Melville became principal of St. Mary's College, St. Andrews, where he initiated the same types of reform as he did at Glasgow. Throughout his career, Melville denounced royal ecclesiastical supremacy, arguing strongly for the autonomy of the national church. For this he was summoned to the Privy Council in Edinburgh in 1584 on the possible charge of treason for his resistance to royal ecclesiastical authority. Though they could not charge Melville with sedition, the Privy Council still determined to consign him to trial, but Melville managed to escape to England. While in England, he visited Puritan leaders at Oxford and Cambridge. He also lectured on Genesis in London. Melville returned to Scotland in 1585, and became rector of the University of St. Andrews in 1590. He was eventually deprived of this rectorship in 1587 for his opposition to episcopacy. In 1606, along with several ministers, he was summoned to appear before Hampton Court, where he gave some uncompromising speeches. These speeches resulted in Melville's imprisonment in several places, including the Tower of London. Melville was released from the Tower on April 19, 1611, and from there traveled to France. Having arrived in France, Melville proceeded through Paris and Rouen to Sedan, where he assumed the chair of theology. He remained in Sedan until his death in 1622. Melville authored an extensive literary corpus, which includes a commentary on Romans.

Justus Menius (1499–1558). German Lutheran pastor and theologian. Menius was a prominent reformer in Thuringia. He participated in the Marburg Colloquy and, with others, helped Martin Luther* compose the Schmalkald Articles.* Throughout his career Menius entered into numerous controversies with Anabaptists and even fellow Lutherans. He rejected Andreas Osiander's (d. 1552) doctrine of justification—that the indwelling of Christ's divine nature justifies, rather than the imputed alien righteousness of Christ's person, declared through God's mercy. Against Nikolaus von Amsdorf (1483–1565) and Matthias Flacius (1520–1575), Menius agreed with Georg Major* that good works are necessary to salvation. Osiander's view of justification was censored in Article 3 of the Formula of Concord*; Menius's understanding of the relationship between good works and salvation was rejected in Article 4. Menius translated many of Luther's Latin works into German. He also composed a handbook for Christian households and an influential commentary on 1 Samuel.

Johannes Mercerus (Jean Mercier) (d. 1570). French Hebraist. Mercerus studied under the first Hebrew chair at the Collège Royal de Paris, François Vatable (d. 1547), whom he succeeded in 1546. John Calvin* tried to recruit Mercerus to the Genevan Academy as professor of Hebrew, once in 1558 and again in 1563; he refused both times. During his lifetime Mercerus published grammatical helps for Hebrew and Chaldean, an aid to the Masoretic symbols in the Hebrew text, and translated the commentaries and grammars of several medieval rabbis. He himself wrote commentaries on Genesis, the wisdom books, and most of the Minor Prophets. These commentaries—most of them only published after his death—were philologically focused and interacted with the work of Jerome, Nicholas of Lyra,* notable rabbis and Johannes Oecolampadius.*

Thomas Mocket (1602–1670?). British Puritan minister. Mocket ministered in Wales and England, publishing numerous works, including a catechism, a tract on the duties of Christians, and an excursus on the celebration of Christmas.

Peter Moffett (d. 1617). English Protestant clergyman. Rector at Fobbing, Essex, Moffett published a commentary on the Song of Solomon and a sermon on 1 Timothy 1:16.

Ambrose Moibanus (1494–1554). German Lutheran bishop and theologian. Moibanus helped reform the church of Breslau (modern Wroclaw, Poland). He revised the Mass, bolstered pastoral care and welfare for the poor, and wrote a new evangelical catechism.

Olympia Morata (1526/27–1555). Italian Protestant humanist and theologian. Daughter of a humanist scholar, her father taught in the court of Ferrara, and she was raised alongside Anna d'Este (1531–1607), daughter of Protestant Renée of France (1510–1574) and later wife of Francis, Duke of Guise (1519–1563), a central antagonist in the St. Bartholomew's Day Massacre. A precocious scholar, Morata's classical, humanist, and biblical studies drew her toward the evangelical currents of the court, but these Protestant leanings also raised the constant suspicion of the Inquisition. In 1550, Morata married Andreas Grundler (unknown), a German Protestant doctor, and moved to his native Schweinfurt, where, facing limited opportunities due to her gender, she continued her studies and privately tutored in Greek and the classics. She developed an extensive correspondence with friends, especially noblewomen she had met at court, and Protestant leaders including Luther*, Melanchthon* and Matthias Flacius (1520–1575), whom she asked to translate some of Luther's work into Italian. Most of Morata's writings were destroyed during the siege of Schweinfurt in 1553–1554, and while she was able to resettle in Frankfurt, she died of tuberculosis soon afterwards. In her writings that survived the siege, her scholarly erudition is clear, and her letters demonstrate a ministerial care for her correspondents and desire for the spread of the Reformation message.

Thomas More (1478–1535). English Catholic lawyer, politician, humanist and martyr. More briefly studied at Oxford, but completed his legal studies in London. After contemplating the priesthood for four years, he opted for politics and was elected a member of Parliament in 1504. A devout Catholic, More worked with church leaders in England to root out heresy while he also confronted Lutheran teachings in writing. After four years as Lord Chancellor, More resigned due to heightened tensions with Henry VIII* over papal supremacy (which More supported and Henry did not). Tensions did not abate. More's steadfast refusal to accept the Act of Supremacy (1534)—which declared the King of England to be the supreme ecclesial primate not the pope—resulted in his arrest and trial for high treason. He was found guilty and beheaded with John Fisher (1469–1535). Friends with John Colet* and Desiderius Erasmus,* More was a widely respected humanist in England as well as on the continent. Well-known for his novel *Utopia* (1516), More also penned several religious treatises on Christ's passion and suffering during his imprisonment in the Tower of London, which were published posthumously.

Henry Morley (d. 1616). English Protestant preacher. Morley published a sermon of the cleansing of the leper given at St. Paul's Cathedral in London during an outbreak of the plague in 1603.

Sebastian Münster (1488–1552). German Reformed Hebraist, exegete, printer, and geographer. After converting to the Reformation in 1524, Münster taught Hebrew at the universities of Heidelberg and Basel. During his lengthy tenure in Basel he published more than seventy books, including Hebrew dictionaries and rabbinic commentaries. He also produced an evangelistic work for Jews titled *Vikuach* (1539). Münster's *Torat ha-Maschiach* (1537), the Gospel of Matthew, was the first published Hebrew translation of any portion of the New Testament. Despite his massive contribution to contemporary understanding of the Hebrew language, Münster was criticized by many of the reformers as a Judaizer.

Thomas Müntzer (c. 1489–1525). German Radical preacher. As a preacher in the town of Zwickau, Müntzer was influenced by German mysticism and, growing convinced that Martin Luther* had not carried through reform properly, sought to restore the pure apostolic church of the New Testament. Müntzer's radical ideas led to expulsions from various cities; he developed a highly apocalyptic theology, in which he heralded the last days that would establish the pure community out of suffering, prompting Müntzer's proactive role in the Peasants' War, which he perceived as a crucial apocalyptic event. Six thousand of Müntzer's followers were annihilated by magisterial troops; Müntzer was executed.

John Murcot (1625–1654). English Puritan pastor. After completing his bachelor's at Oxford in 1647, Murcot was ordained as a pastor, transferring to several parishes until in 1651 he moved to Dublin. All his works were published posthumously.

Simon Musaeus (1521–1582). German Lutheran theologian. After studying at the universities of Frankfurt an der Oder and Wittenberg, Musaeus began teaching Greek at the Cathedral school in Nuremberg and was ordained. Having returned to Wittenberg to complete a doctoral degree, Musaeus spent the rest of his career in numerous ecclesial and academic administrative posts. He opposed Matthias Flacius's (1505–1575) view of original sin—that the formal essence of human beings is marred by original sin—even calling the pro-Flacian faculty at Wittenberg "the devil's latrine." Musaeus published a disputation on original sin and a postil.

Wolfgang Musculus (1497–1563). German Reformed pastor and theologian. Musculus produced translations, biblical commentaries and an influential theological text, *Loci communes Sacrae Theologiae* (*Commonplaces of Sacred Theology*), outlining a Zwinglian theology. Musculus began to study theology while at a Benedictine monastery; he departed in 1527 and became secretary to Martin Bucer* in Strasbourg. He was later installed as a pastor in Augsburg, eventually performing the first evangelical liturgy in the city's cathedral. Displaced by the Augsburg Interim, Musculus ended his career as professor of theology at Bern. Though Musculus was active in the pursuit of the reform agenda, he was also concerned for ecumenism, participating in the Wittenberg Concord (1536) and discussions between Lutherans and Catholics.

Georg Mylius (1548–1607). German Lutheran pastor and theologian. Mylius began his career as a preacher in Augsburg, rising to superintendent of the churches in the city after receiving his doctorate in theology. He was arrested and ejected from the city by the Catholic-dominated council for his opposition to the Gregorian calendar, returning briefly to learn of the death of his pregnant wife and child. After grieving in Ulm, Mylius spend the remainder of his career as a preacher and professor of theology at Wittenberg, with a brief hiatus teaching at Jena.

Hans Nadler (unknown). German Radical layperson. An uneducated and illiterate needle salesman, after receiving baptism from Hans Hut* in 1527, Nadler sought to share the faith with those he met during his extensive travels. He is remembered through the records of his arrest and examination, recorded by a court reporter, which give insight into his beliefs and activities as a committed Anabaptist layperson, whereby he affirmed believer's baptism, the spiritual reception of the Eucharist, and nonresistance.

Friedrich Nausea (c. 1496–1552). German Catholic bishop and preacher. After completing his studies at Leipzig, this famed preacher was appointed priest in Frankfurt but was run out of town by his congregants during his first sermon. He transferred to Mainz as cathedral preacher. Nausea was well connected through the German papal hierarchy and traveled widely to preach to influential ecclesial and secular courts. Court preacher for Ferdinand I (1503–1564), his reform tendencies fit well with royal Austrian theological leanings, and he was enthroned as the bishop of Vienna. Nausea thought that rather than endless colloquies only a council could settle reform. Unfortunately he could not participate in the first session of Trent due to insufficient funding, but he arrived for the second session. Nausea defended the laity's reception of the cup and stressed the importance of promulgating official Catholic teaching in the vernacular.

Melchior Neukirch (1540–1597). German Lutheran pastor and playwright. Neukirch's pastoral career spanned more than thirty years in several northern German parishes. Neukirch published a history of the Braunschweig church since the Reformation and a dramatization of Acts 4–7. He died of the plague.

Nicholas of Lyra (1270–1349). French Catholic biblical exegete. Very little is known about this influential medieval theologian of the Sorbonne aside from the works he published, particularly the *Postilla litteralis super totam Bibliam* (1322–1333). With the advent of the printing press this work was regularly published alongside the Latin Vulgate and the *Glossa ordinaria*. In this running commentary on the Bible Nicholas promoted literal interpretation as the basis for theology. Despite his preference for literal interpretation, Nicholas also published a companion volume, the *Postilla moralis super totam Bibliam* (1339), a commentary on the spiritual meaning of the biblical text. Nicholas was a major conversation partner for many reformers though many of them rejected his exegesis as too literal and too "Jewish" (not concerned enough with the Bible's fulfillment in Jesus Christ).

John Norden (1547–1625). English devotional writer. Norden was born at Somerset, and in 1564 entered Hart Hall, Oxford where he graduated with his BA in 1568, and MA in 1573. Norden spent most of his life Middlesex, moving later to St. Giles in the Fields in 1619, where he remained until his death in 1625. Throughout his life, Norden distinguished himself also as a cartographer, chorographer, and antiquarian. His best known devotional work was his Progress of Piety (1596).

Alexander Nowell (1517–1602). Anglican theologian. Born in Lancashire, Nowell was educated at Brasenose College, Oxford where he shared a room with the future martyrologist John Foxe. Nowell was elected a fellow at the same college, where he spent thirteen years. In 1543, he was appointed master of Westminster School, and in December, 1551, a prebendary of Westminster Abbey. Though elected to the House of Commons in 1553, Nowell was permitted to assume his seat because as a prebendary, he had a seat in Convocation. Because of his evangelical convictions, Nowell lost prebendary in 1554, after which he fled to the Continent, traveling first to Strasbourg, and then to Frankfurt. When Elizabeth I ascended the throne, Nowell returned to England where he afterwards served as chaplain to Edmund Grindal. In 1561 Nowell became Dean of St. Paul's Cathedral, a post which he held until his death. Nowell's best known work was his Catechism originally written in Latin (1563), and translated into English by Thomas Norton in 1570.

Bernardino Ochino (1487–1564). Italian Reformed theologian. After serving as vicar general of the Franciscan order, Ochino left the foundation of the Capuchins, where he assisted in the composition of their constitution and served as vicar general. A famed preacher, his teaching came to the attention of the Inquisition as it began to reflect the thought of Juan de Valdés. Summoned to Rome in 1542, he fled to Geneva with Peter Martyr Vermigli* where his Reformed orthodoxy, tinged with Franciscan mysticism, was brought into the open. Following his flight, Ochino led an unstable life, with brief stays in Basel, Strasbourg, and Augsburg before moving to England with Vermigli in 1548 where he was able to compose a significant treatise against the Roman church. His doctrinal orthodoxy was questioned by the pastor of the Italian congregation in London, but his case left unresolved when he departed for Geneva, then Basel and Zurich, at the accession of Mary*. As pastor of a congregation of Italian refugees in Zurich, Ochino courted considerable controversy. He refused to have his works approved by the city magistrates before publication, and his opponents alleged that his Dialogi XXX (1563) included questionable teachings on the Trinity and divorce while seeming to advocate polygamy. Expelled from Zurich in 1563, he died in Moravia the following year.

Charles Odingsells (d. 1637). English Protestant preacher. Odingsells published two sermons on prophesying and miracles from Matthew 7 given at Langar in Nottinghamshire.

Johannes Oecolampadius (Johannes Huszgen) (1482–1531). Swiss-German Reformed humanist, reformer and theologian. Oecolampadius (an assumed name meaning "house light") assisted with Desiderius Erasmus's* Greek New Testament, lectured on biblical languages and exegesis and completed an influential Greek grammar. After joining the evangelical cause through studying patristics and the work of Martin Luther,* Oecolampadius went to Basel, where he lectured on biblical exegesis and participated in ecclesial reform. On account of Oecolampadius's effort, the city council passed legislation restricting preaching to the gospel and releasing the city from compulsory Mass. Oecolampadius was a chief ally of Huldrych Zwingli,* whom he supported at the Marburg Colloquy (1529).

Kaspar Olevianus (1536–1587). German Reformed theologian. Olevianus is celebrated for composing the Heidelberg Catechism and producing a critical edition of Calvin's *Institutes* in German. Olevianus studied theology with many, including John Calvin,* Theodore Beza,* Heinrich Bullinger* and Peter Martyr Vermigli.* As an advocate of Reformed doctrine, Olevianus oversaw the shift from Lutheranism to Calvinism throughout Heidelberg, organizing the city's churches after Calvin's Geneva. The Calvinist ecclesial vision of Olevianus entangled him in a dispute with another Heidelberg reformer over the rights of ecclesiastical discipline, which Olevianus felt belonged to the council of clergy and elders rather than civil magistrates.

Josua Opitz (c. 1542–1585). German Lutheran pastor. After a brief stint as superintendent in Regensburg, Opitz, a longtime preacher, was dismissed for his support of Matthias Flacius's (1520–1575) view of original sin. (Using Aristotelian categories, Flacius argued that the formal essence of human beings is marred by original sin, forming sinners into the image of Satan; his views were officially rejected in Article 1 of the Formula of Concord.*) Hans Wilhelm Roggendorf (1533–1591) invited Opitz to lower Austria as part of his Lutheranizing program. Unfortunately Roggendorf and Opitz never succeed in getting Lutheranism legal recognition, perhaps in large part due to Opitz's staunch criticism of Catholics, which resulted in his exile. He died of plague.

Lucas Osiander (1534–1604). German Lutheran pastor. For three decades, Osiander—son of the controversial Nuremberg reformer Andreas Osiander (d. 1552)—served as pastor and court preacher in Stuttgart, until he fell out of favor with the duke in 1598. Osiander produced numerous theological and exegetical works, as well as an influential hymnal.

John Owen (1616–1683). English Puritan theologian. Owen trained at Oxford University, where he was later appointed dean of Christ Church and vice chancellor of the university, following his service as chaplain to Oliver Cromwell. Although Owen began his career as a Presbyterian minister, he eventually departed to the party of Independents. Owen composed many sermons, biblical commentaries (including seven volumes on the book of Hebrews), theological treatises and controversial monographs (including disputations with Arminians, Anglicans, Catholics and Socinians).

Ephraim Pagitt (1575–1647). English Protestant minister. Pagitt ministered at St. Edmunds in London until forced into retirement for his Royalist tendencies during the Civil War (1642–1646). Some of his later writings demonstrate sympathy for Presbyterian theology, and he became an opponent of Baptists and other sectarians. His most popular writing was *Heresiography* (1662), in which he set out to catalog the heretics he identified within the church.

Santes Pagninus (c. 1470–1541). Italian Catholic biblical scholar. Pagninus studied under Girolamo Savonarola* and later taught in Rome, Avignon and Lyons. He translated the Old Testament into Latin according to a tight, almost wooden, adherence to the Hebrew. This translation and his Hebrew lexicon *Thesaurus linguae sanctae* (1529) were important resources for translators and commentators.

Johann Pappus (1549–1610). German Lutheran theologian. After a decade as a teacher of Hebrew and professor of theology at the Strasbourg academy, Pappus was appointed president of the city's company of pastors. Despite resistance from the Reformed theologian Johann Sturm (1507–1589), he led the city away from its Swiss Reformed alliances and toward subscription to the Lutheran Formula of Concord. A talented humanist, Pappus published more than thirty works on controversial, theological, historical, and exegetical subjects.

David (Wängler) Pareus (1548–1622). German Reformed pastor and theologian. Born at Frankenstein in Lower Silesia, Pareus studied theology at Heidelberg under Zacharias Ursinus (1534–1583), the principal author of the Heidelberg Catechism.* After reforming several churches, Pareus returned to Heidelberg to teach at the Reformed seminary. He then joined the theological faculty at the University of Heidelberg, first as a professor of Old Testament and later as a professor of New Testament. Pareus edited the *Neustadter Bibel* (1587), a publication of Martin Luther's* German translation with Reformed annotations—which was strongly denounced by Lutherans, especially Jakob Andreae* and Johann Georg Sigwart (1554–1618). In an extended debate, Pareus defended the orthodoxy of Calvin's exegesis against Aegidius Hunnius,* who accused Calvin of "judaizing" by rejecting many traditional Christological interpretations of Old Testament passages. Towards the end of his career, Pareus wrote commentaries on Genesis, Hosea, Matthew, Romans, 1 Corinthians, Galatians, Hebrews and Revelation.

Catherine Parr (1512–1548). The last of King Henry VIII's* six wives, Catherine Parr was Queen Consort to Henry from 1543 until his death in 1547. She enjoyed a close relationship with two of her step children, Elizabeth and Edward (the future Queen Elizabeth I* and King Edward VI), involving herself extensively in their education. Having married three more times after the death of Henry VIII, Catherine died in 1548. Her published works are *Psalms or Prayers* (1543) and a *Lamentation of a Sinner* (1548).

Paul of Burgos (**Solomon ha-Levi**) (c. 1351–1435). Spanish Catholic archbishop. In 1391 Solomon ha-Levi, a rabbi and Talmudic scholar, converted to Christianity, receiving baptism with his entire family (except for his wife). He changed his name to Paul de Santa Maria. Some have suggested that he converted to avoid persecution; he himself stated that Thomas Aquinas's* work persuaded him of the truth of Christian faith. After studying theology in Paris, he was ordained bishop in 1403. He actively and ardently persecuted Jews, trying to compel them to convert. In order to convince Jews that Christians correctly interpret the Hebrew Scriptures, Paul wrote *Dialogus Pauli et Sauli contra Judaeos, sive Scrutinium Scripturarum* (1434), a book filled with vile language toward the Jews. He also wrote a series of controversial marginal notes and comments on Nicholas of Lyra's* *Postilla*, many of which criticized Nicholas's use of Jewish scholarship.

Christoph Pelargus (1565–1633). German Lutheran pastor, theologian, professor and superintendent. Pelargus studied philosophy and theology at the University of Frankfurt an der Oder, in Brandenburg. This irenic Philippist was appointed as the superintendent of Brandenburg and later became a pastor in Frankfurt, although the local authorities first required him to condemn Calvinist theology, because several years earlier he had been called before the consistory in Berlin under suspicion of being a crypto-Calvinist. Among his most important works were a four-volume commentary on *De orthodoxa fide* by John of Damascus (d. 749), a treatise defending the breaking of the bread during communion, and a volume of funeral sermons. He also published commentaries on the Pentateuch, the Psalms, Matthew, John and Acts.

Konrad Pellikan (1478–1556). German Reformed Hebraist and theologian. Pellikan attended the University of Heidelberg, where he mastered Hebrew under Johannes Reuchlin. In 1504 Pellikan published one of the first Hebrew grammars that was not merely a translation of the work of medieval rabbis. While living in Basel, Pellikan assisted the printer Johannes Amerbach, with whom he published some of Luther's* early writings. He also worked with Sebastian Münster* and Wolfgang Capito* on a Hebrew Psalter (1516). In 1526, after teaching theology for three years at the University of Basel, Huldrych Zwingli* brought Pellikan to Zurich to chair the faculty of Old Testament. Pellikan's magnum opus is a seven-volume commentary on the entire Bible (except Revelation) and the Apocrypha; it is often heavily dependent upon the work of others (esp. Desiderius Erasmus* and Johannes Oecolampadius*).

William Pemble (1591–1623). Puritan theologian and author. Pemble was born in Egerton, Kent. He was educated at Magdalen College, Oxford, where he graduated with his BA degree in 1614. Afterward he moved to Magdalen Hall, where he became a reader and tutor in divinity. He received his MA in 1618. Primarily a Hebrew scholar, Pemble authored commentaries on Ecclesiastes (1629), the first nine chapters of Zechariah (1629), and portions of Ezra, Nehemiah, and Daniel. Pemble also wrote *An Introduction to the Worthy Receiving the Sacrament* (1628), as well as treatises on predestination and justification. He died of a fever on April 14, 1623.

Benedict Pererius (1535–1610). Spanish Catholic theologian, philosopher and exegete. Pererius entered the Society of Jesus in 1552. He taught philosophy, theology, and exegesis at the Roman College of the Jesuits. Early in his career he warned against neo-Platonism and astrology in his *De principiis* (1576). Pererius wrote a lengthy commentary on Daniel, and five volumes of exegetical theses on Exodus, Romans, Revelation and part of the Gospel of John (chs. 1–14). His four-volume commentary on Genesis (1591–1599) was lauded by Protestants and Catholics alike.

William Perkins (1558–1602). English Puritan preacher and theologian. Perkins was a highly regarded Puritan Presbyterian preacher and biblical commentator in the Elizabethan era. He studied at Cambridge University and later became a fellow of Christ's Church college as a preacher and professor, receiving acclaim for his sermons and lectures. Even more, Perkins gained an esteemed reputation for his ardent exposition of Calvinist reformed doctrine in the style of Petrus Ramus,* becoming one of the first English reformed theologians to achieve international recognition. Perkins influenced the federal Calvinist shape of Puritan theology and the vision of logical, practical expository preaching.

François Perrault (1577–1657). French Reformed pastor for over fifty years. His book on demonology was prominent, perhaps because of the intrigue at his home in 1612. According to his account, a poltergeist made a commotion and argued points of theology; a few months later Perrault's parishioners slew a large snake slithering out of his house.

Dirk Philips (1504–1568). Dutch Radical elder and theologian. This former Franciscan monk, known for being severe and obstinate, was a leading theologian of the sixteenth-century Anabaptist movement. Despite the fame of Menno Simons* and his own older brother Obbe, Philips wielded great influence over Anabaptists in the Netherlands and northern Germany where he ministered. As a result of Philips's understanding of the apostolic church as radically separated from the children of the world, he advocated a very strict interpretation of the ban, including formal shunning. His writings were collected and published near the end of his life as *Enchiridion oft Hantboecxken van de Christelijcke Leere* (1564).

Obbe Philips (1500–1568). Dutch radical leader. Trained as a physician, Philips was drawn to mystical Anabaptism, as taught by Melchior Hoffman (1495–1543) in his hometown of Leewarden. After adult rebaptism and ordination, he preached in Amsterdam, Delft, Appingedam, and Grongen, and he ordained other leaders including his brother Dirk Philips*, David Joris*, and Menno Simmons*. Disillusioned with the growth of revolutionary, enthusiastic, and apocalyptic elements within Anabaptism and unable to reconcile any visible church with the church of God, Philips withdrew from the radical movement in 1540, after which nothing is known of his life. His only extant writing, entitled *The Confession of Obbe Philips*, was published after his death and recounts elements of the history of the Anabaptist movement and defends his departure from the movement.

James Pilkington (1520-1576). Protestant bishop of Durham and Elizabethan author. Born in Lancashire, Pilkington received his early education at Manchester Grammar School. Afterwards, he entered Pembroke College, Cambridge, and later transferred to St. John's College, Cambridge, from where he graduated with his BA degree in 1539, and MA in 1542. Pilkington was appointed vicar of Kendal in 1545, but resigned this position shortly thereafter in order to return to Cambridge. While there, Pilkington was granted a license to preach, and was awarded the degree of Bachelor of Theology in 1551. In this same year, Pilkington became president of the college. When Mary Tudor succeeded her half-brother, Edward VI, in 1553, Pilkington fled to the Continent where he traveled to Zurich, Geneva, Frankfurt, and Strasbourg. He returned to England in 1559 when Elizabeth I ascended the throne of England. After returning to England, Pilkington became Regius Professor of Divinity at Cambridge and after, bishop of Durham in 1560. Pilkington's major work was his voluminous commentary on the Prophet Haggai.

Charles Pinner (Unknown). English Protestant pastor. Pinner studied at New College, Oxford, and served as rector at Wootton Bassett in Wiltshire. His extant writings include two sermons on 1 Timothy and two on 1 Peter.

Hector Pinto (c. 1528–1584). Portuguese Catholic theologian and exegete. A member of the order of Saint Jerome, Pinto taught theology and Scripture at the Universities of Sigüenza and Coimbra. A respected theologian and exegete, he published commentaries on Daniel, Nahum, Jeremiah, and Isaiah and an influential devotional work, *The Image of the Christian Life*.

Caritas Pirckheimer (1466–1532). German Catholic nun. Sister of famed humanist Wilibald Pirckheimer (1470–1530), Caritas received a humanistic education before entering the Franciscan convent at Nuremberg. Extolled by Erasmus* as one of the most learned women in Europe, Pirckheimer served as abbess at the advent of the Reformation, and her experiences are recorded in a journal covering the pivotal years of 1524–1528. While Nuremberg accepted Lutheran theology under the leadership of the city council and preachers such as Andreas Osiander (1498–1552), Pirckheimer defended the right of her order to continue in their vocation. She ultimately won a concession after a visit from Philipp Melanchthon* in 1525, who recommended that the council allow those who wished to remain in the cloister to live out their vows in peace.

Johannes Piscator (1546–1625). German Reformed theologian. Educated at Tübingen (though he wanted to study at Wittenberg), Piscator taught at the universities of Strasbourg and Heidelberg, as well as academies in Neustadt and Herborn. His commentaries on both the Old and New Testaments involve a tripartite analysis of a given passage's argument, of scholia on the text and of doctrinal loci. Some consider Piscator's method to be a full flowering of Beza's* "logical" scriptural analysis, focused on the text's meaning and its relationship to the pericopes around it.

Amandus Polanus von Polansdorf (1561–1610). German Reformed educator and theologian. Polanus spent his career as an educator, serving as a tutor for noble families and a teacher at the Bohemian Brethren school in Moravia before earning his doctorate and becoming professor of Old Testament and later dean of the theological faculty at the University of Basel. His best-known work is the *Syntagma theologiae christianae* (1609), a compendium of Reformed dogmatics.

Constantino Ponce de la Fuente (1502–1559). Spanish Protestant theologian and preacher. A priest in Seville, Ponce de la Fuente was a critic of the established church and associated with the evangelical circle in the city. A popular preacher, he authored a catechism and a number of books on doctrine and the Christian life that focused on the work of Christ. Charged with heresy by the Inquisition, he admitted to the authorship of a number of heretical writings and died in prison awaiting trial while his works were added to the Index of Prohibited Books.

Matthew Poole (1624–1679). English Nonconformist minister. Having made known his preference for simplicity in worship, Matthew Poole was rector of St Michael-le-Querne until the passing of the 1662 Act of Uniformity led him to resign. Living off his inheritance, he preached occasionally and composed some brief tracts but devoted much of his effort to the compilation of Latin biblical commentary in the *Synopsis criticorum* (1669) and the composition of his own annotations on Scripture. He died in Amsterdam, having fled London during the Popish Plot (1678–1681). He believed his life was in danger for his anti-Catholic writings as part of a Catholic conspiracy to kill Charles II, which was ultimately revealed as a fiction concocted by Titus Oates (1649–1705).

Thomas Porter (d. 1667). English Anglican minister. A graduate of Christ's College, Cambridge, Porter ministered in Flintshire in Cheshire and at Whitchurch in Shropshire. Among his published works are a sermon on Matthew 5:13 and a response to antitrinitarian John Knowles (fl. 1646–1668).

Gabriel Powell (1575–1611). Puritan minister. Powell was born at Ruabon in Denbigshire in 1575. Having completed his studies at Jesus College, Oxford, Powell became master of the free-school in Ruthen. During his tenure at Ruthen, Powell closely studied the writings of the church fathers as well as philosophy, and afterward endeavored to publish several works based on this research. Finding his present location to be a hinderance to his literary objectives, Powell relocated to Oxford, entering St. Mary's Hall, where he finished his anticipated projects. Powell is chiefly known for his literary debate with Thomas Bilson (1547–1619) concerning Christ's descent into hell. Later, Richard Vaughan (1550–1607), bishop of London, appointed Powell his domestic chaplain. Powell died on December 31, 1611. In addition to many controversial and polemical works, Powell wrote a commentary on Romans 1.

Vavasor Powell (1617–1670). Welsh Puritan minister and author. Powell was born at Knucklas, Radnorshire, Wales. After completing his education at Jesus College, Oxford, Powell returned to Wales to assume the position of a local schoolmaster. During this time, Powell came under the influence of Walter Cradock's* preaching as well as the writings of Richard Sibbes* and William Perkins,* resulting in his conversion to Puritanism. Soon thereafter he became an itinerant preacher, traveling throughout Wales. He was arrested twice for nonconformity. During the Civil War, Powell first preached in London, and shortly thereafter pastored an Independent congregation in Wales. On December 26, 1641, Royalist forces arrested and imprisoned Powell. In 1646, as victory for the Puritans appeared inevitable, Powell was released, and allowed to return to Wales, having received a letter of endorsement from the Westminster Assembly. Back in Wales, Powell played a prominent role in the Westminster Assembly's 1650 commission for the better propagation of the gospel throughout Wales. In 1653, Powell returned to London, where he preached at St. Ann Blackfriars. It was at this time that Powell denounced Oliver Cromwell (1599–1658) for assuming the position of Lord Protector. For this reason, he was arrested and imprisoned. At the Restoration in 1660, Powell was again arrested and imprisoned for unauthorized preaching for seven years. Though released in 1667, Powell was once more arrested and incarcerated. He remained in custody until his death on October 27, 1660. Powell authored many poems and a concordance to the Bible.

Felix Pratensis (d. 1539). Italian Catholic Hebraist. Pratensis, the son of a rabbi, converted to Christianity and entered the Augustinian Hermits around the turn of the sixteenth century. In 1515, with papal permission, Pratensis published a new translation of the Psalms based on the Hebrew text. His *Biblia Rabbinica* (1517–1518), printed in Jewish and Christian editions, included text-critical notes in the margins as well as the Targum and rabbinic commentaries on each book (e.g., Rashi* on the Pentateuch and David Kimchi* on the Prophets). Many of the reformers consulted this valuable resource as they labored on their own translations and expositions of the Old Testament.

John Preston (1587–1628). Puritan minister and author. Preston was born at Upper Heyford, Northamptonshire, on October 27, 1587. He studied philosophy at King's College and Queen's College, Cambridge, earning his bachelor's degree in 1607. He became a fellow at Queen's in 1609, and a prebendary at Lincoln Cathedral a year later. During this period, Preston studied medicine and astronomy. In 1611, he received the MA degree. Sometime afterward, he experienced a conversion under the preaching of John Cotton.* After his conversion, Preston went on to study theology, concentrating mainly on Thomas Aquinas,* Duns Scotus, and William of Ockham. From there, he proceeded to the reformers, especially John Calvin.* Preston was appointed court chaplain in 1615. In this position he was influential in the promotion of Puritans to high civil office. Preston later assumed the positions of dean and catechist at Queen's College, Cambridge, where he distinguished himself by preaching a series of sermons that formed the basis of his body of divinity. In 1622, he received the degree of bachelor of divinity, becoming thereafter master of Emmanuel College, Cambridge. While at Emmanuel, Preston participated in the conflict between Calvinism and Arminianism. Moreover, in the same year, Preston succeeded John Donne* as preacher at Lincoln's Inn. Two years later, Preston accepted the lectureship at Trinity Church. He died at the age of forty in 1628. Throughout his prodigious career, Preston authored a sizable corpus, which includes published sermons on Romans.

Quadriga. The *quadriga*, or four senses of Scripture, grew out of the exegetical legacy of Paul's dichotomy of letter and spirit (2 Cor 3:6), as well as church fathers like Origen (c. 185–254), Jerome (c. 347–420) and Augustine* (354–430). Advocates for this method—the primary framework for biblical exegesis during the medieval era—assumed the necessity of the gift of faith under the guidance of the Holy Spirit. The literal-historical meaning of the text served as the foundation for the fuller perception of Scripture's meaning in the three spiritual senses, accessible only through faith: the allegorical sense taught what should be believed, the tropological or moral sense taught what should be done, and the anagogical or eschatological sense taught what should be hoped for. Medieval Jewish exegesis also had a fourfold interpretive method—not necessarily related to the *quadriga*—called *pardes* ("grove"): *peshat*, the simple, literal sense of the text according to grammar; *remez*, the allegorical sense; *derash*, the moral sense; and *sod*, the mystic sense related to Kabbalah. Scholars hotly dispute the precise use and meaning of these terms.

Edward Rainbow[e] (1608–1684). Anglican minister, scholar, and bishop. Rainbow was born at Lincolnshire on April 20, 1608. After completing his education, Rainbow matriculated at Corpus Christi College, and later transferred to Magdalene College, Cambridge, where he graduated with the BA (1627), MA (1630), BD (1637), and DD (1643). He was elected a fellow at Magdalene in 1633 and a master there in 1642. In 1630, Rainbow accepted the mastership of the Kirton-in-Lindsey but shortly afterward moved to London. In 1632, Rainbow took holy orders and preached his first sermon in April of that year. His first appointment was that of curate of Savoy Hospital. Rainbow was recalled to Cambridge in 1633 and elected a fellow. Four years later he became dean of Magdalene and master of the same college in 1642. Though dismissed from his mastership by Parliament in 1650, Rainbow was restored to it in the year of the Restoration (1660). At the same time, he was appointed chaplain to the king. In 1661, Rainbow became dean of Peterborough, and appointed vice chancellor of Cambridge a year later. Rainbow was elected bishop of Carlisle in 1664. As bishop, Rainbow led in the systemic reform of his diocese. Rainbow died March 26, 1684. His published works consist of three published sermons and an incomplete treatise, *Verba Christi*.

Petrus Ramus (1515–1572). French Reformed humanist philosopher. Ramus was an influential professor of philosophy and logic at the French royal college in Paris; he converted to Protestantism and left France for Germany, where he came under the influence of Calvinist thought. Ramus was a trenchant critic of Aristotle and noted for his method of classification based on a deductive movement from universals to particulars, the latter becoming branching divisions that provided a visual chart of the parts to the whole. His system profoundly influenced Puritan theology and preaching. After returning to Paris, Ramus died in the Saint Bartholomew's Day Massacre.

Rashi (Shlomo Yitzchaki) (1040–1105). French Jewish rabbi and exegete. After completing his studies, Rashi founded a yeshiva in Troyes. He composed the first comprehensive commentary on the Talmud, as well as commentaries on the entire Old Testament except for 1–2 Chronicles. These works remain influential within orthodox Judaism. Late medieval and early modern Christian scholars valued his exegesis, characterized by his preference for peshat (see quadriga).

Reformatio Legum Ecclesiasticarum (1552). Under the leadership of Archbishop of Canterbury Thomas Cranmer,* Edward VI* established a committee of thirty-two bishops, theologians, and lawyers including Nicholas Ridley,* John Hooper,* Peter Martyr Vermigli,* Matthew Parker (1504–1575), and William Cecil (1520–1598) to align the laws of the English church with Reformed theology and English civil law. Completed in 1552, it touched on diverse topics, including church organization, doctrine and heresy, qualifications for ministry, and marriage and divorce. It was brought before Parliament in 1553, where it was blocked by John Dudley, Duke of Northumberland (1504–1553), who wished to decrease church powers, and then dropped upon the accession of Mary I. A manuscript of the proposal revised by John Foxe (1516/1517–1587) was published in 1671, and while some elements of the Reformatio Legum Ecclesiasticarum were adopted under Elizabeth I, thoroughgoing reform of ecclesiastical law was not brought about until the *Book of Canons* (1604).

Remonstrance (1610). See *Synod of Dordrecht.*

Johannes Reuchlin (1455–1522). German Catholic lawyer, humanist and Hebraist. Reuchlin held judicial appointments for the dukes of Württemberg, the Supreme Court in Speyer and the imperial court of the Swabian League. He pioneered the study of Hebrew among Christians in Germany, standing against those who, like Johannes Pfefferkorn (1469–1523), wanted to destroy Jewish literature. Among his many works he published a Latin dictionary, an introductory Greek grammar, the most important early modern Hebrew grammar and dictionary (*De rudimentis hebraicis*; 1506), and a commentary on the penitential psalms.

Edward Reynolds (1599–1676). Anglican bishop. Reynolds succeeded John Donne* as the preacher at Lincoln's Inn before entering parish ministry in Northamptonshire. During the English Civil Wars, he supported the Puritans because of his sympathy toward their simplicity and piety—despite believing that Scripture demanded no particular form of government; later he refused to support the abolition of the monarchy. Until the Restoration he ministered in London; afterward he became the bishop of Norwich. He wrote the general thanksgiving prayer which is part of the morning office in the *Book of Common Prayer.**

Urbanus Rhegius (1489–1541). German Lutheran pastor. Rhegius, who was likely the son of a priest, studied under the humanists at Freiburg and Ingolstadt. After a brief stint as a foot soldier, he received ordination in 1519 and was made cathedral preacher in Augsburg. During his time in Augsburg he closely read Luther's* works, becoming an enthusiastic follower. Despite his close friendship with Zwingli* and Oecolampadius,* Rhegius supported Luther in the eucharistic debates, later playing a major role in the Wittenberg Concord (1536). He advocated for peace during the Peasants' War and had extended interactions with the Anabaptists in Augsburg. Later in his career he concerned himself with the training of pastors, writing a pastoral guide and two catechisms. About one hundred of his writings were published posthumously.

Lancelot Ridley (d. 1576). Anglican preacher. Ridley was the first cousin of Nicholas Ridley,* the bishop of London who was martyred during the Marian persecutions. By Cranmer's* recommendation, Ridley became one of the six Canterbury Cathedral preachers. Upon Mary I's accession in 1553, Ridley was defrocked (as a married priest). Ridley returned to Canterbury Cathedral after Mary's death. He wrote commentaries on Jude, Ephesians, Philippians and Colossians.

Nicholas Ridley (c. 1502–1555). Anglican bishop. Ridley was a student and fellow at Cambridge University who was appointed chaplain to Archbishop Thomas Cranmer* and is thought to be partially responsible for Cranmer's shift to a symbolic view of the Eucharist. Cranmer promoted Ridley twice: as bishop of Rochester, where he openly advocated Reformed theological views, and, later, as bishop of London. Ridley assisted Cranmer in the revisions of the Book of Common Prayer.* Ridley's support of Lady Jane Grey against the claims of Mary to the throne led to his arrest; he was tried for heresy and burned at the stake with Hugh Latimer.*

Peter Riedemann (1506–1556). German Radical elder, theologian and hymnist. While traveling as a Silesian cobbler, Riedemann came into contact with Anabaptist teachings and joined a congregation in Linz. In 1529 he was called to be a minister, only to be imprisoned soon after as part of Archduke Ferdinand's efforts to suppress heterodoxy in his realm. Once he was released, he moved to Moravia in 1532 where he was elected as a minister and missionary of the Hutterite community there. His

Account of Our Religion, Doctrine and Faith (1542), with its more than two thousand biblical references, is Riedemann's most important work and is still used by Hutterites today.

John Robinson (1576–1625). English Puritan pastor. After his suspension for nonconformity, Robinson fled to the Netherlands with his congregation, eventually settling in Leiden in 1609. Robinson entered into controversies over Arminianism, separation and congregationalism. Most of his healthy congregants immigrated to Plymouth in 1620; Robinson remained in Leiden with those unable to travel.

John Rogers (1505–1555). English Protestant Bible translator. Rogers was born in Deritend, Birmingham. After receiving his early education at the Guild School of St. John the Baptist, Rogers matriculated at Pembroke Hall, Cambridge, where he graduated with the BA degree in 1526. He served as rector of Holy Trinity the Less in London from 1532 to 1534, when he left for the Continent to serve as chaplain to the English merchants of the Company of the Merchant Adventurers. It was at this time that he met William Tyndale,* under whose influence he came to embrace an evangelical faith. After Tyndale's death, Rogers completed his late colleague's translation of the Old Testament, which had ended with 2 Chronicles, by adding Miles Coverdale's translation of the remainder, including the Apocrypha. The resulting work, known as the "Matthew Bible" (Rogers published it under the pseudonym "Thomas Matthew") was published in 1537. It has the distinction of being the first complete English Bible translated essentially from the original languages to be printed. "Matthew's Bible" served as the basis for the Great Bible (1540), which in turn was used by those who prepared the Bishops' Bible (1568), on which later the King James Version (1611) was produced. In 1540, Rogers enrolled at the University of Wittenberg, where he became close friends with Philipp Melanchthon.* During his three years at Wittenberg, Rogers was a superintendent of the Lutheran Church in northern Germany. When Rogers returned to England in 1548, he published a translation of Melanchthon's *Considerations of the Augsburg Interim*, and later served in a variety of ecclesiastical roles. Rogers was burned at the stake for heresy during the reign of Mary Tudor on February 4, 1555.

Nehemiah Rogers (1593–1660). Anglican priest. After studying at Cambridge, Rogers ministered at numerous parishes during his more than forty-year career. In 1643, he seems to have been forced out of a parish on account of being a Royalist and friend of William Laud.* Rogers published a number of sermons and tracts, including a series of expositions on Jesus' parables in the Gospels.

Richard Rogers (1550?–1618). English Presbyterian minister. Rogers spent much of his career as lecturer at Wethersfield, Essex, where he was well-known as a Nonconformist. His writings, which include an introduction to the Christian life and a commentary on the book of Judges, demonstrate his Puritan leanings.

Thomas Rogers (d. 1616). Anglican theologian and translator. Rogers attended Christ Church, Oxford, where he completed his BA degree in 1573 and MA in 1576. Later he served as rector of Horrigner in Suffolk, and chaplain to Archbishop of Canterbury, Richard Bancroft. He died at Horringer and was buried in his church. Among his many works were an exposition of the Thirty-Nine Articles as well as a paraphrase of the Psalms and a translation of Niels Hemmingsen's commentary on Psalm 84.

Robert Rollock (c. 1555–1599). Scottish Reformed pastor, educator and theologian. Rollock was deeply influenced by Petrus Ramus's* system of logic, which he implemented as a tutor and (later) principal of Edinburgh University and in his expositions of the Bible. Rollock, as a divinity professor and theologian, was instrumental in diffusing a federalist Calvinism in the Scottish church; he lectured on theology using the texts of Theodore Beza* and articulated a highly covenantal interpretation of the biblical narratives. He was a prolific writer of sermons, expositions, commentaries, lectures and occasional treatises.

David Runge (1564–1604). German Lutheran theologian. First appointed professor of Hebrew at the University of Greifswald, Runge supported and later replaced his father in teaching philosophy and theology. After receiving his doctorate, he was named to the theological faculty at Wittenberg, where he also served as dean and rector of the university.

Johann Rurer (1480–1542). German Lutheran pastor. Rurer was court chaplain to Margrave Casimir of Brandenberg–Kulmbach (1481–1527), and the first Protestant pastor in Ansbach. Conflict over church order and his desire for reform led to his expulsion, but he was recalled after Casimir's death by his successor, George (1484–1543), who sought a throughgoing Lutheran reformation of the town and appointed Rurer preacher at the collegiate church.

Samuel Rutherford (1600–1661). Scottish Reformed theologian. Rutherford was born in Nisbet, Roxburghshire. After completing his early education at Jedborough, Rutherford enrolled at the University of Edinburgh, where he received his MA degree in 1621. In 1623,

Rutherford was appointed professor of humanities at Edinburgh. Two years later, he was dismissed from his position on account of misbehavior with the woman who would later be his wife. Sometime after this incident, he underwent a spiritual conversion. In 1625, Rutherford commenced the study of theology at Edinburgh. Upon finishing his studies, Rutherford was called to pastor a church in Antwoth by Solway in Kirkcudbrightshire. Throughout his ministry, Rutherford proved to be an ardent opponent to episcopacy. For this, he was summoned to appear before the Court of High Commission in 1630. Despite the court's warnings to cease and desist, Rutherford continued his nonconformity. Rutherford also participated extensively in the Arminian controversy, writing treatises against Arminius as well as the Jesuits. Since Rutherford's virulent opposition to Arminianism placed him in direct opposition with the English episcopacy, he was once again summoned by the Court of High Commission in 1636. After a three-day trial, Rutherford was deprived of his ministerial office and ordered not to preach anywhere in Scotland. Meanwhile he was confined to Aberdeen. In 1638, when the National Covenant was signed and Presbyterianism restored in Scotland, Rutherford left Aberdeen and assumed the post of professor of theology at St. Mary's College, St. Andrews. Later, Rutherford served as a commissioner to the Westminster Assembly, where he contributed to the discussions related to the Shorter Catechism. In 1647, Rutherford returned to Scotland, where he was appointed principal of St. Mary's College, and rector of the university in 1651. After the monarchy was restored, Rutherford was charged with treason, and deprived of all his ecclesiastical and university positions. He died on March 30, 1661. Throughout his career, Rutherford published many sermons and theological works, most famous of which is *Lex Rex* (The law is king), a treatise arguing against the divine right of kings.

Jacopo Sadoleto (1477–1547). Italian Catholic Cardinal. Sadoleto, attaché to Leo X's court, was appointed bishop in 1517, cardinal in 1536. He participated in the reform commission led by Gasparo Contarini.* However, he tried to reconcile with Protestants apart from the commission, sending several letters to Protestant leaders in addition to his famous letter to the city of Geneva, which John Calvin* pointedly answered. Sadoleto published a commentary on Romans that was censored as semi-Pelagian. His insufficient treatment of prevenient grace left him vulnerable to this charge. Sadoleto emphasized grammar as the rule and norm of exegesis.

Alfonso Salmerón (1515–1585). Spanish Catholic exegete and theologian. While studying at the Sorbonne, Salmerón met Ignatius Loyola (1491–1556) and, with five others, took a vow of poverty and service to church and pope. After ministering in France, the group traveled to Rome, where they were given papal approval to form the Society of Jesus. Salmerón helped write the constitutions of the order, and following the priorities of the Jesuits, spent much of his career focused on education. He lectured throughout Italy, served briefly on the faculty of the University of Ingolstadt, and, in Naples, founded one of the first Jesuit colleges. He also undertook a number of missions as a papal emissary and served as a papal theologian at all three meetings of the Council of Trent. His primary works are his commentaries on the New Testament, which cover the Gospels, Acts, and Paul's letters.

Heinrich Salmuth (1522–1576). German Lutheran theologian. After earning his doctorate from the University of Leipzig, Salmuth served in several coterminous pastoral and academic positions. He was integral to the reorganization of the University of Jena. Except for a few disputations, all of Salmuth's works—mostly sermons—were published posthumously by his son.

Robert Sanderson (1587–1663). Anglican bishop and philosopher. Before his appointment as professor of divinity at Oxford in 1642, Sanderson pastored in several parishes. Because of his loyalty to the Crown during the English Civil Wars, the Parliamentarians stripped Sanderson of his post at Oxford. After the Restoration he was reinstated at Oxford and consecrated bishop. He wrote an influential textbook on logic.

Edwin Sandys (1519–1588). Anglican bishop. During his doctoral studies at Cambridge, Sandys befriended Martin Bucer.* Having supported the Protestant Lady Jane Grey's claim to the throne, Sandys resigned his post at Cambridge upon Mary I's accession. He was then arrested and imprisoned in the Tower of London. Released in 1554, he sojourned on the continent until Mary's death. On his return to England he was appointed to revise the liturgy and was consecrated bishop. Many of his sermons were published, but his most significant literary legacy is his work as a translator of the Bishop's Bible (1568), which served as the foundational English text for the translators of the King James Bible (1611).

Erasmus Sarcerius (1501–1559). German Lutheran superintendent, educator and pastor. Sarcerius served as educational superintendent, court preacher and pastor in Nassau and, later, in Leipzig. The hallmark of Sarcerius's reputation was his ethical emphasis as exercised through ecclesial oversight and family structure; he also drafted disciplinary codes for regional churches in Germany. Sarcerius served with Philipp Melanchthon* as Protestant delegates at the Council of Trent, though both withdrew prior to the dismissal of the session; he eventually became an opponent of Melanchthon, contesting the latter's understanding of the Eucharist at a colloquy in Worms in 1557.

Michael Sattler (c. 1490–1527). Swiss Radical leader. Sattler was a Benedictine monk who abandoned the monastic life during the upheavals of the Peasants' War. He took up the trade of weaving under the guidance of an outspoken Anabaptist. It seems that Sattler did not openly join the Anabaptist movement until after the suppression of the Peasants' War in 1526. Sattler interceded with Martin Bucer* and Wolfgang Capito* for imprisoned Anabaptists in Strasbourg. Shortly before he was convicted of heresy and executed, he wrote the definitive expression of Anabaptist theology, the Schleitheim Articles.*

Girolamo Savonarola (1452–1498). Italian Catholic preacher and martyr. Outraged by clerical corruption and the neglect of the poor, Savonarola traveled to preach against these abuses and to prophesy impending judgment—a mighty king would scourge and reform the church. Savonarola thought that the French invasion of Italy in 1494 confirmed his apocalyptic visions. Thus he pressed to purge Florence of vice and institute public welfare, in order to usher in a new age of Christianity. Florence's refusal to join papal resistance against the French enraged Alexander VI (r. 1492–1503). He blamed Savonarola, promptly excommunicating him and threatening Florence with an interdict. After an ordeal by fire turned into a riot, Savonarola was arrested. Under torture he admitted to charges of conspiracy and false prophecy; he was hanged and burned. In addition to numerous sermons and letters, he wrote meditations on Psalms 31 and 51 as well as *The Triumph of the Cross* (1497).

Leupold Scharnschlager (d. 1563). Austrian Radical elder. See *Kunstbuch*.

Leonhard Schiemer (d. 1528) Austrian radical martyr. Troubled by the hypocrisies he experienced, Scheimer left the Franciscan order and spent a period of time wandering. Attracted to the teachings of Hans Hut* after hearing him debate Balthasar Hubmaier* in Moravia, he was rebaptized and traveled widely throughout Austria and Southern Germany, spreading the Anabaptist message until he was arrested in Rattenberg, where he was condemned to death and beheaded. A number of his essays and hymns survive, dispersed among the *Kunstbuch** and other collections of radical writings.

Hans Schlaffer (c. 1490–1528). Austrian Radical martyr. Drawn by Luther's theology, Schlaffer resigned his priesthood in 1526 only to turn to Anabaptism soon afterward. While contemporaries recognized his ability as a preacher, he never settled in a ministry position. He spent time among Radical congregations in Freistadt, Nicholsburg, Augsburg, Nuremberg, and Regensburg before his arrest in Schatz, where he was executed. Nine writings by Schlaffer remain, most of which were composed during his imprisonment. They include confessions of his beliefs and devotional works, which have been preserved among Hutterite churches.

Schleitheim Articles (1527). After the death of Conrad Grebel* in 1526 and the execution of Felix Manz (born c. 1498) in early 1527, the young Swiss Anabaptist movement was in need of unity and direction. A synod convened at Schleitheim under the chairmanship of Michael Sattler,* which passed seven articles of Anabaptist distinctives—likely defined against both magisterial reformers and other Anabaptists with less orthodox and more militant views (e.g., Balthasar Hubmaier*). Unlike most confessions, these articles do not explicitly address traditional creedal interests; they explicate instead the Anabaptist view of the sacraments, church discipline, separatism, the role of ministers, pacifism and oaths. Throughout the document there is a resolute focus on Christ's example. Also referred to as the Schleitheim Confession and the Schleitheim Brotherly Union, the Schleitheim Articles are considered the definitive statement of Anabaptist theology, particularly regarding separatism.

Schmalkald Articles (1537). In response to Pope Paul III's (1468–1549) 1536 decree ordering a general church council to solve the Protestant crisis, Elector John Frederick (1503–1554) commissioned Martin Luther* to draft the sum of his teaching. Intended by Luther as a last will and testament—and composed with advice from well-known colleagues Justus Jonas,* Johann Bugenhagen,* Caspar Cruciger,* Nikolaus von Amsdorf (1483–1565), Georg Spalatin (1484–1545), Philipp Melanchthon* and Johann Agricola*—these articles provide perhaps the briefest and most systematic summary of Luther's teaching. The document was not adopted formally by the Lutheran Schmalkald League, as was hoped, and the general church council was postponed for several years (until convening at Trent in 1545). Only in 1580 were the articles officially received, by being incorporated into the *Book of Concord* defining orthodox Lutheranism.

Sebastian Schmidt (1617–1696). German Lutheran theologian. After serving as pastor in Entzheim and rector of the high school in Lindau, Schmidt became professor of theology at Strasbourg. His body of writings is extensive and includes commentaries on many of the Pauline letters, Hebrews, John, and Jeremiah.

Dietrich Schnepff (1525–1586). German Lutheran pastor and theologian. Schnepff taught briefly at the city school in Tübingen while working toward his theological doctorate before taking pastorates in Derendingen and Nürtingen. Returning to Tübingen as professor of theology, Schnepff also took on additional roles as rector of the university and pastor of the Collegiate Church.

Anna Maria van Schurman (1607–1678). Dutch Reformed polymath. Van Schurman cultivated talents in art, poetry, botany, linguistics and theology. She mastered most contemporary European languages, in addition to Latin, Greek, Hebrew, Arabic, Farsi and Ethiopian. With the encouragement of leading Reformed theologian Gisbertus Voetius (1589–1676), van Schurman attended lectures at the University of Utrecht—although she was required to sit behind a wooden screen so that the male students could not see her. In 1638 van Schurman published her famous treatise advocating female scholarship, *Amica dissertatio . . . de capacitate ingenii muliebris ad scientias*. In addition to these more polemical works, van Schurman also wrote hymns and poems, including a paraphrase of Genesis 1–3. Later in life she became a devotee of Jean de Labadie (1610–1674), a former Jesuit who was also expelled from the Reformed church for his separatist leanings. Her *Eucleria* (1673) is the most well known defense of Labadie's theology.

Kaspar von Schwenckfeld (1489–1561). German Radical reformer. Schwenckfeld was a Silesian nobleman who encountered Luther's* works in 1521. He traveled to Wittenberg twice: first to meet Luther and Karlstadt,* and a second time to convince Luther of his doctrine of the "internal word"—emphasizing inner revelation so strongly that he did not see church meetings or the sacraments as necessary—after which Luther considered him heterodox. Schwenckfeld won his native territory to the Reformation in 1524 and later lived in Strasbourg for five years until Bucer* sought to purify the city of less traditional theologies. Schwenckfeld wrote numerous polemical and exegetical tracts.

Scots Confession (1560). In 1560, the Scottish Parliament undertook to reform the Church of Scotland and to commission a Reformed confession of faith. In the course of four days, a committee—which included John Knox*—wrote this confession, largely based on Calvin's* work, the Confession of the English Congregation in Geneva (1556) and the Gallic Confession.* The articles were not ratified until 1567 and were displaced by the Westminster Confession (1646), adopted by the Scottish in 1647.

Abraham Scultetus (1566–1625). Silesian Reformed theologian. Scultetus spent the majority of his career in service of the Palatinate, holding a number of pastoral roles before becoming court preacher to Elector Frederic V (1596–1632). Appointed professor of theology at Heidelberg in 1618, he represented the Palatinate at the Synod of Dordrecht* (1618–1619), where he opposed the theology of the Remonstrants. Scultetus is often vilified for encouraging Reformed Frederic V to take the crown of Lutheran Bohemia, an act that led to war and the defeat of Frederic V, but his exegetical, historical, and pastoral teachings nevertheless garnered significant respect from his contemporaries.

Second Helvetic Confession (1566). Believing he would soon die, Heinrich Bullinger* penned a personal statement of his Reformed faith in 1561 as a theological will. In 1563, Bullinger sent a copy of this confession, which blended Zwingli's and Calvin's theology, to the elector of the Palatinate, Frederick III (1515–1576), who had asked for a complete explication of the Reformed faith in order to defend himself against aggressive Lutheran attacks after printing the Heidelberg Confession.* Although not published until 1566, the Second Helvetic Confession became the definitive sixteenth-century Reformed statement of faith. Theodore Beza* used it as the organizing confession for his *Harmonia Confessionum* (1581), which sought to emphasize the unity of the Reformed churches. Bullinger's personal confession was adopted by the Reformed churches of Scotland (1566), Hungary (1567), France (1571) and Poland (1571).

Obadiah Sedgwick (c. 1600–1658). English Puritan minister. Educated at Oxford, Sedgwick pastored in London and participated in the Westminster Assembly. An ardent Puritan, Sedgwick was appointed by Oliver Cromwell (1599–1658) to examine clerical candidates. Sedgwick published a catechism, several sermons and a treatise on how to deal with doubt.

Nikolaus Selnecker (1530–1592). German Lutheran theologian, preacher, pastor and hymnist. Selnecker taught in Wittenberg, Jena and Leipzig, preached in Dresden and Wolfenbüttel, and pastored in Leipzig. He was forced out of his post at Jena because of suspicions that he was a crypto-Calvinist. He sought refuge in Wolfenbüttel, where he met Martin Chemnitz* and Jakob Andreae.* Under their influence Selnecker was drawn away from Philippist theology. Selnecker's shift in theology can be seen in his *Institutio religionis christianae* (1573). Selnecker coauthored the Formula of Concord* with Chemnitz, Andreae, Andreas Musculus (1514–1581), and David Chytraeus.* Selnecker also published lectures on Genesis, the Psalms, and the New Testament epistles, as well as composing over a hundred hymn tunes and texts.

Jean de Serres (1540–1598). French Reformed pastor and historian. Serres fled France under persecution and studied at Lausanne and Geneva before being called to the Genevan parish of Jussy. After publishing a commentary on the French civil wars, he was disciplined and deposed for abandoning his ministry. Relocating to Lausanne, Serres became principal of the college and published a three-volume translation of Plato's works then moved to reform the College of Nimes. He became an advisor to King Henry IV* and was given the title "Historian of France." In this role, he sought resolution of the civil wars and composed a short history of France.

Short Confession (1610). In response to some of William Laud's* reforms in the Church of England—particularly a law stating that ministers who refused to comply with the Book of Common Prayer* would lose their ordination—a group of English Puritans immigrated to the Netherlands in protest, where they eventually embraced the practice of believer's baptism. The resulting Short Confession was an attempt at union between these Puritans and local Dutch Anabaptists ("Waterlanders"). The document highlights the importance of love in the church and reflects optimism regarding the freedom of the will while explicitly rejecting double predestination.

Richard Sibbes (1577–1635). English Puritan preacher. Sibbes was educated at St. John's College, Cambridge, where he was converted to reforming views and became a popular preacher. As a moderate Puritan emphasizing interior piety and brotherly love, Sibbes always remained within the established Church of England, though opposed to some of its liturgical ceremonies. His collected sermons constitute his main literary legacy.

Menno Simons (c. 1496–1561). Dutch Radical leader. Simons led a separatist Anabaptist group in the Netherlands that would later be called Mennonites, known for nonviolence and renunciation of the world. A former priest, Simons rejected Catholicism through the influence of Anabaptist disciples of Melchior Hoffmann and based on his study of Scripture, in which he found no support for transubstantiation or infant baptism. Following the sack of Anabaptists at Münster, Simons committed to a nonviolent way of life. Simons proclaimed a message of radical discipleship of obedience and inner purity, marked by voluntary adult baptism and communal discipline.

Henry Smith (c. 1550–1591). English Puritan minister. Smith stridently opposed the Book of Common Prayer* and refused to subscribe to the Articles of Religion,* thus limiting his pastoral opportunities. Nevertheless he gained a reputation as an eloquent preacher in London. He published sermon collections as well as several treatises.

John Smyth (d. 1612). English Baptist minister. Ordained as an Anglican clergyman, Smyth served as a lecturer in Lincoln, but left the established church for a separatist congregation in Gainsborough. Moving to Amsterdam, he began to follow the teachings of Jacobus Arminius* and led a group to break away from the English Reformed congregation, undertake rebaptism, and form their own church. He soon decided he did not have the authority to establish a church and baptize, but trying to lead his congregation on another course saw him excommunicated with a number of his close followers. This smaller group was rejected when they attempted to join a Mennonite congregation, and so were forced to form another congregation, which dissolved after Smyth's death. Smyth wrote a number of the earliest English treatises expressing Baptist principles including *The Differences of the Churches of the Separation* (1608) and *The Character of the Beast* (1609). He also wrote a reflection on the Lord's Prayer, *A Paterne of True Prayer* (1605).

Domingo de Soto (1494–1560). Spanish Catholic theologian. Soto taught philosophy for four years at the University in Alcalá before entering the Dominican order. In 1532 he became chair of theology at the University of Salamanca; Soto sought to reintroduce Aristotle in the curriculum. He served as confessor and spiritual advisor to Charles V, who enlisted Soto as imperial theologian for the Council of Trent. Alongside commentaries on the works of Aristotle and Peter Lombard (c. 1100–1160), Soto commented on Romans and wrote an influential treatise on nature and grace.

Fausto Sozzini (1539–1604). Italian theologian. Without a formal education, Sozzini used his inherited wealth to travel widely throughout Europe after his family came under the suspicion of the Inquisition for Lutheranism. Spending time in Lyons, Zurich, and Geneva, he published his first work, an explanation of the prologue to John's Gospel, claiming Christ was not divine, but a human worthy of respect due his divinely appointed office. Returning to Italy, Sozzini served at the Florentine court of Isabella de Medici (1542–1576) for more than a decade, departing for Basel, then Transylvania and Poland after her death. His thoroughgoing rationalism saw him elevate human reason over divine revelation and traditional doctrine. He rejected the doctrine of the Trinity and Nicene orthodoxy, instead arguing that Christ was not divine and did not make atonement for humanity, but rather served as a model of victory over death for all people.

Cyriacus Spangenberg (1528–1604). German Lutheran pastor, preacher and theologian. Spangenberg was a staunch, often acerbic, Gnesio-Lutheran. He rejected the Formula of Concord* because of concerns about the princely control of the church, as well as its rejection of Flacian language of original sin (as constituting the "substance" of human nature after the fall). He published many commentaries and sermons, most famously seventy wedding sermons (*Ehespiegel* [1561]), his sermons on Luther* (*Theander Luther* [1562–1571]) and Luther's hymns (*Cithara Lutheri* [1569–1570]). He also published an analysis of the Old Testament (though he only got as far as Job), based on a methodology that anticipated the logical bifurcations of Peter Ramus.*

Johann Spangenberg (1484–1550). German Lutheran pastor and catechist. Spangenberg studied at the University of Erfurt, where he was welcomed into a group of humanists associated with Konrad Muth (1470–1526). There he met the reformer Justus Jonas,* and Eobanus Hessius (1488–1540), whom Luther* dubbed "king of the poets." Spangenberg served at parishes in Stolberg (1520–1524), Nordhausen (1524–1546) and, by Luther's recommendation, Eisleben (1546–1550). Spangenberg published one of the best-selling postils of the sixteenth century, the *Postilla Teütsch*, a six-volume work meant to prepare children to understand the lectionary readings. It borrowed the question-answer form of Luther's *Small Catechism* and was so popular that a monk, Johannes Craendonch, purged overt anti-Catholic statements from it and republished it under his own name. Among Spangenberg's other pastoral works are *ars moriendi* ("the art of dying") booklets, a postil for the Acts of the Apostles and a question-answer version of Luther's *Large Catechism*. In addition to preaching and pastoring, Spangenberg wrote pamphlets on controversial topics such as purgatory, as well as textbooks on music, mathematics and grammar.

John Spilsbury (1593–1668). English Baptist pastor. A cobbler by trade, Spilsbury left congregationalism to found the first Particular Baptist church in London, teaching a theology that attempted to fuse Reformed teachings on the covenant and particular atonement with the Anabaptist demand for adult baptism upon confession of faith. He composed a number of works on baptism and may have been an author of the 1644 London Baptist Confession of Faith.

Georg Spindler (1525–1605). German Reformed theologian and pastor. After studying theology under Caspar Cruciger* and Philipp Melanchthon,* Spindler accepted a pastorate in Bohemia. A well-respected preacher, Spindler published postils in 1576 which some of his peers viewed as crypto-Calvinist. To investigate this allegation Spindler read John Calvin's* *Institutes*, and subsequently converted to the Reformed faith. After years of travel, he settled in the Palatinate and pastored there until his death. In addition to his Lutheran postils, Spindler also published Reformed postils in 1594 as well as several treatises on the Lord's Supper and predestination.

Statenvertaling (1637). The Synod of Dordrecht* commissioned this new Dutch translation of the Bible ("State's Translation"). The six theologians who undertook this translation also wrote prefaces for each biblical book, annotated obscure words and difficult passages, and provided cross-references; they even explained certain significant translation decisions. At the request of the Westminster Assembly, Theodore Haak (1605–1690) translated the *Statenvertaling* into English as *The Dutch Annotations Upon the Whole Bible* (1657).

John Stalham (d. 1681). English Puritan minister. Stalham likely ministered in Edinburgh before becoming vicar of Terling in Essex. An opponent of Quakerism who sought to remove disreputable ministers from their pulpits, Stalham himself lost his position with the 1662 Act of Uniformity, leading him to found a congregational church in the same village.

Johann von Staupitz (d. 1524). German Catholic theologian, professor and preacher. Frederick the Wise summoned this Augustinian monk to serve as professor of Bible and first dean of the theology faculty at the University of Wittenberg. As Vicar-General of the Reformed Augustinian Hermits in Germany, Staupitz sought to reform the order and attempted unsuccessfully to reunite with the conventional Augustinians. While in Wittenberg, Staupitz was Martin Luther's* teacher, confessor and spiritual father. He supported Luther in the early controversies over indulgences, but after releasing Luther from his monastic vows (to protect him), he distanced himself from the conflict. He relocated to Salzburg, where he was court preacher to Cardinal Matthäus Lang von Wellenburg (d. 1540) and abbot of the Benedictine monastery. Staupitz wrote treatises on predestination, faith and the love of God. Many of his sermons were collected and published during his lifetime.

Peter Sterry (d. 1672). English Puritan theologian. Associated with the Cambridge Platonists, Sterry was closely aligned with the Parliamentarians during the English Civil War, serving as chaplain to Robert Greville (1607–1643) and Oliver Cromwell.* After the execution of Charles I, he was appointed preacher to the Council of State and asked to examine its ministers. Cast out from influence after Cromwell's death, Sperry spent the last years of his career writing and tutoring private students.

Petrus Stevartius (1549–1624). German Catholic theologian. A Jesuit, Stevartius spent most of his career as professor of exegesis at the University of Ingolstadt, also serving as rector and procurator. He also established a library for the school and an orphanage in the city. His writings include commentaries on most Pauline letters and James and a defense of the Jesuits.

Michael Stifel (1486–1567). German Lutheran mathematician, theologian and pastor. An Augustinian monk, Stifel's interest in mysticism, apocalypticism and numerology led him to identify Pope Leo X as the antichrist. Stifel soon joined the reform movement, writing a 1522 pamphlet in support of Martin Luther's* theology. After Luther quelled the fallout of Stifel's failed prediction of the Apocalypse—October 19, 1533 at 8 a.m.—Stifel focused more on mathematics and his pastoral duties. He was the first professor of mathematics at the University of Jena. He published several numerological interpretations of texts from the Gospels, Daniel and Revelation. However, Stifel's most important work is his *Arithmetica Integra* (1544), in which he standardized the approach to quadratic equations. He also developed notations for exponents and radicals.

John Stoughton (1593?–1639). English Puritan minister. Stoughton pastored at Aller in Somerset and St. Mary Aldermanbury in the city of London. A Puritan, he was briefly arrested by Archbishop Laud, accused of financially supporting the Puritan cause. A collection of his sermons and other writings was published after his death.

Viktorin Strigel (1524–1569). German Lutheran theologian. Strigel taught at Wittenberg, Erfurt, Jena, Leipzig and Heidelberg. During his time in Jena he disputed with Matthias Flacius (1520–1575) over the human will's autonomy. Following Philipp Melanchthon,* Strigel asserted that in conversion the human will obediently cooperates with the divine will through the Holy Spirit and the Word of God. In the Weimar Disputation (1560), Strigel elicited Flacius's opinion that sin is a substance that mars the formal essence of human beings. Flacius's views were officially rejected in Article 1 of the Formula of Concord*; Strigel's, in Article 2. In 1567 the University of Leipzig suspended Strigel from teaching on account of suspicions that he affirmed Reformed Eucharistic theology; he acknowledged that he did and joined the Reformed confession on the faculty of the University of Heidelberg. In addition to controversial tracts, Strigel published commentaries on the entire Bible (except Lamentations) and the Apocrypha.

William Strode (1602–1645). English Anglican minister, dramatist, and poet. A Royalist and an opponent of Puritanism, Strode spent most of his life around Oxford, where he studied and then served as a public orator and canon of Christ Church. A popular poet, he also preached a number of times before the king and had a number of his plays performed at court.

William Strong (d. 1654). English Independent minister. Forced to leave his ministry in Dorset by Royalists during the Civil War, Strong built a reputation as a preacher in London, ministering to an independent congregation at St. Dunstan's-in-the-West. Many of his sermons were published, as well as treatises on communion with God and the covenants.

Johann Sutell (1504–1575). German Lutheran pastor. After studying at the University of Wittenberg, Sutell received a call to a pastorate in Göttingen, where he eventually became superintendent. He wrote new church orders for Göttingen (1531) and Schweinfurt (1543), and expanded two sermons for publication, *The Dreadful Destruction of Jerusalem* (1539) and *History of Lazarus* (1543).

Swiss Brethren Confession of Hesse (1578). Anabaptist leader Hans Pauly Kuchenbecker penned this confession after a 1577 interrogation by Lutheran authorities. This confession was unusually amenable to Lutheran views—there is no mention of pacifism or rejection of oath taking.

Synod of Dordrecht (1618–1619). This large Dutch Reformed Church council—also attended by English, German and Swiss delegates—met to settle the theological issues raised by the followers of Jacobus Arminius.* Arminius's theological disagreements with mainstream Reformed teaching erupted into open conflict with the publication of the *Remonstrance* (1610). This "protest" was based on five points: that election is based on foreseen faith or unbelief; that Christ died indiscriminately for all people (although only believers receive salvation); that people are thoroughly sinful by nature apart from the prevenient grace of God that enables their free will to embrace or reject the gospel; that humans are able to resist the working of God's grace; and that it is possible for true believers to fall away from faith completely. The Synod ruled in favor of the Contra-Remonstrants, its Canons often remembered with a TULIP acrostic—total depravity, unconditional election, limited atonement, irresistible grace, perseverance of the saints—each letter countering one of the five Remonstrant articles. The Synod also officially accepted the Belgic Confession,* Heidelberg Catechism* and the Canons of Dordrecht as standards of the Dutch Reformed Church.

Arcangela Tarabotti (1604–1652). Italian Catholic nun. At the age of eleven, Tarabotti entered a Benedictine convent as a student-boarder; three years later her father forced her to take monastic vows. The dignity of women and their treatment in the male-controlled institutions of early modern Venice concerned Tarabotti deeply. She protested forced cloistering, the denial of education to women, the exclusion of women from public life and the double standards by which men and women were judged. Tarbotti authored numerous polemical works and an extensive correspondence.

Johannes Tauler (c. 1300–1361). German mystical theologian. A Dominican friar and disciple of Meister Eckhart (c. 1260–c. 1328), Tauler spent most of his career as a mendicant preacher in Strasburg and Basel. Known through a collection of about eighty German sermons, Tauler taught a practical spirituality, accessible to those outside the cloister and intended to draw his audience to deeper contemplation of the divine nature.

Richard Taverner (1505–1575). English Puritan humanist and translator. After graduating from Oxford, Taverner briefly studied abroad. When he returned to England, he joined Thomas Cromwell's (1485–1540) circle. After Cromwell's beheading, Taverner escaped severe punishment and retired from public life during Mary I's reign. Under Elizabeth I,* Taverner served as justice of the peace, sheriff and a licensed lay preacher. Taverner translated many important continental Reformation works into English, most notably the Augsburg Confession* and several of Desiderius Erasmus's* works. Some of these translations—John Calvin's* 1536 catechism, Wolfgang Capito's* work on the Psalms and probably Erasmus Sarcerius's* postils—he presented as his own work. Underwritten by Cromwell, Taverner also published an edited version of the Matthew Bible (1537).

Francis Taylor (1590–1656). English Presbyterian minister. After graduating from Cambridge, Taylor served as vicar of Yalding in Kent and rector of Clapham in Surrey. He was a member of the Westminster Assembly of Divines and was a member of the College of Six Preachers at Canterbury Cathedral.

Jeremy Taylor (1613–1667). Anglican theologian, preacher, and author. Son of a barber, Taylor studied at Cambridge before the patronage of Archbishop Laud* drew him into the work of the English church. After serving as chaplain to Laud and King Charles I (1600–1649), he entered parish ministry. Following the outbreak of the Civil War (1642–51), his commitment to the Royalist cause saw him imprisoned at least three times. Withdrawing to Wales, he ran a school preparing students for university while serving as chaplain to the earl of Carbery. Known for his skill as a writer, it was here that Taylor composed many of his best known works, including his popular devotional manuals, *The Rules and Exercises of Holy Living* (1650), and *The Rules and Exercises of Holy Dying* (1651). After the Restoration, Taylor was made Bishop of Down and Connor in Ireland and served as vice-chancellor of the University of Dublin.

Thomas Taylor (1576–1633). English Puritan pastor. Taylor ministered in Watford and Reading before becoming minister at St. Mary Aldermanbury in the city of London. He wrote more than fifty works on diverse topics, including a commentary on Titus, a response to the Gunpowder Plot, and an explanation of the role of the law under the gospel.

Thomas Taylor (1576–1632). Puritan minister and commentator. Taylor was born in Richmond, Yorkshire. He was educated at Christ's College, Cambridge, where he earned the degrees of Bachelor of Arts (1595) and Master of Arts (1598). Prior to entering pastoral ministry, Taylor served as a fellow and lecturer in Hebrew at the university. Throughout his academic career, Taylor was significantly influenced by the writings of William Perkins.* At the age of twenty-five, Taylor preached a virulent sermon against the papacy before Queen Elizabeth I.* As a Puritan, Taylor denounced the ecclesiastical policies of Archbishop Richard Bancroft.* In 1612, Taylor became minister of a church in Watford, Hertfordshire. While serving this charge, Taylor preached regularly in Berkshire and Reading. Moreover, Taylor formed and led a Puritan seminary, where he personally trained Nonconformist preachers. In the early 1620s, Taylor served as a chaplain to Edward Conway (1564–1631), secretary of state under James VI/I* (1566–1625). In 1625, Taylor was called to be curate and lecturer at St. Aldermanbury, London. While there, he organized and ran another Puritan seminary. Two years later, Taylor joined several other Puritans' efforts to send relief to oppressed Reformed ministers on the Continent. Taylor retired from his labors in 1630 due to ill health. He died of pleurisy in 1632. His main works include *Christ Revealed; or The Old Testament Explained* and *An Exposition of Titus*.

Teresa of Ávila (1515–1582). Spanish monastic reformer and mystical theologian. Born into a wealthy merchant family, Teresa entered the Carmelite order at Ávila in 1535. While Teresa initially enjoyed the lax practices of the convent, reading devotional literature caused her to deepen her spirituality, and in 1555 she began to have visions of God and claimed to have mystical union with him. Convinced the monastic life required complete withdrawal, Teresa could no longer tolerate the practices of her Carmelite cloister and founded the Discalced Carmelites with John of the Cross* (1542–1591) in 1562, which was committed to enclosure and strict asceticism. By her death, she had personally founded fourteen houses for her new order despite significant resistance from Carmelite leaders. She also wrote extensively. Her best-known works are *The Way of Perfection* (1577), a method for the contemplative life, and *The Interior Castle* (1577), a manual for spiritual growth.

Thirty-Nine Articles. See *Articles of Religion*.

Thomas Thorowgood (1595–1669). English Puritan pastor. Thorowgood was a Puritan minister in Norfolk and the chief financier of John Eliot (1604–1690), a Puritan missionary among the Native American tribes in Massachusetts. In 1650, under the title *Jews in America, or, Probabilities that Americans be of that Race*, Thorowgood became one of the first to put forward the thesis that Native Americans were actually the ten lost tribes of Israel.

Thirty-Three Articles (1617). Frisian Anabaptist confession. Also known as the "Confession of Faith According to God's Word," the Thirty-Three Articles was composed by members of the Old Frisians, a Dutch Mennonite sect, at a time when they were coming into conflict with other Anabaptist groups.

John Tillinghast (1604–1655). English Puritan minister. Tillinghast began his ministry in the Church of England, pastoring two congregations in Sussex until he moved to London and became an independent, leading him to pastor Puritan congregations in Suffolk and Norfolk. He was a member of the Fifth Monarchists, a millenarian Puritan sect that believed the political upheaval of their time was ushering in the kingdom of Christ.

Frans Titelmans (1502–1537). Belgian Catholic philosopher. Titelmans studied at the University of Leuven, where he was influenced by Petrus Ramus.* After first joining a Franciscan monastery, Titelmans realigned with the stricter Capuchins and moved to Italy. He is best known for his advocacy for the Vulgate and his debates with Desiderius Erasmus* over Pauline theology (1527–1530)—he was deeply suspicious of the fruits of humanism, especially regarding biblical studies. His work was published posthumously by his brother, Pieter Titelmans (1501–1572).

Francisco de Toledo (1532–1596). Spanish Catholic theologian. This important Jesuit taught philosophy at the universities of Salamanca and Rome. He published works on Aristotelian philosophy and a commentary on Thomas Aquinas's* work, as well as biblical commentaries on John, Romans and the first half of Luke. He was also the general editor for the Clementine Vulgate (1598).

John Tombes (1603–1676). English Baptist pastor. After leaving Oxford, Tombes held many pastoral positions in Anglican churches throughout the Midlands until founding a Baptist church in Bewdley, Worcestershire. He left this congregation following a debate with Richard Baxter,* leading him to take on a number of pastoral positions in Herefordshire while continuing to seek public debates and writing against Quakerism and Roman Catholicism.

Laurence Tomson (1539–1608). English Reformed politician and translator. Tomson was born in Northhamptonshire and educated at Magdalen College, Oxford. He graduated with his BA degree (1559) and MA degree (1564). Tomson was a fellow at Magdalen until he resigned in 1569. Prior to this resignation, Tomson was part of a diplomatic delegation to France. From 1575 to 1587, Tomson served in the House of Commons and attended the royal court at Windsor in 1582. He went on further embassies throughout Europe, where he occasionally lectured on Hebrew. Tomson died on March 29, 1608. Tomson's chief exegetical contribution was his revised text and annotations of the New Testament of the Geneva Bible.

Edward Topsell (d. 1638?). English Protestant minister. Topsell held a number of pastoral posts in Sussex, Dorset, and the Midlands before being appointed perpetual curate of St. Botolph's, Aldersgate, in the city of London. While he composed a number of religious works, including his lectures on Ruth, which were so popular they appeared in three editions, he is primarily remembered for his two illustrated works on natural history, which cataloged four-footed animals and serpents.

Alonso Tostado (1400–1455). Spanish Catholic bishop and exegete. Tostado lectured on theology, law and philosophy at the University of Salamanca, in addition to ministering in a local parish. Tostado entered into disputes over papal supremacy and the date of Christ's birth. Tostado's thirteen-volume collected works include commentaries on the historical books of the Old Testament and the Gospel of Matthew.

Daniel Toussain (1541–1602). Swiss Reformed pastor and professor. Toussain became pastor at Orléans after attending college in Basel. After the third War of Religion, Toussain was exiled, eventually returning to Montbéliard, his birthplace. In 1571, he faced opposition there from the strict Lutheran rulers and was eventually exiled due to his influence over the clergy. He returned to Orléans but fled following the Saint Bartholomew's Day Massacre (1572), eventually becoming pastor in Basel. He relocated to Heidelberg in 1583 as pastor to the new regent, becoming professor of theology at the university, and he remained there until his death.

John Trapp (1601–1669). Anglican biblical exegete. After studying at Oxford, Trapp entered the pastorate in 1636. During the English Civil Wars he sided with Parliament, which later made it difficult for him to collect tithes from a congregation whose royalist pastor had been evicted. Trapp published commentaries on all the books of the Bible from 1646 to 1656.

Immanuel Tremellius (1510–1580). Italian Reformed Hebraist. Around 1540, Tremellius received baptism by Cardinal Reginald Pole (1500–1558) and converted from Judaism to Christianity; he affiliated with evangelicals the next year. On account of the political and religious upheaval, Tremellius relocated often, teaching Hebrew in Lucca; Strasbourg, fleeing the Inquisition; Cambridge, displaced by the Schmalkaldic War; Heidelberg, escaping Mary I's persecutions; and Sedan, expelled by the new Lutheran Elector of the Palatine. Many considered Tremellius's translation of the Old Testament as the most accurate available. He also published a Hebrew grammar and translated John Calvin's* catechism into Hebrew.

Richard Turnbull (d. 1593). English minister. A preacher in London, Richard Turnbull published sermons on James, Jude, and Psalm 15.

William Tyndale (Hychyns) (1494–1536). English reformer, theologian and translator. Tyndale was educated at Oxford University, where he was influenced by the writings of humanist thinkers. Believing that piety is fostered through personal encounter with the Bible, he asked to translate the Bible into English; denied permission, Tyndale left for the Continent to complete the task. His New Testament was the equivalent of a modern-day bestseller in England but was banned and ordered burned. Tyndale's theology was oriented around justification, the authority of Scripture and Christian obedience; Tyndale emphasized the ethical as a concomitant reality of justification. He was martyred in Brussels before completing his English translation of the Old Testament, which Miles Coverdale* finished.

John Udall (1560?–1592). English Puritan pastor. Udall began his pastoral career in the Anglican parish of Kingston-upon-Thames, becoming known for his preaching and Puritan convictions, particularly his rejection of the episcopacy. While facing discipline for his views, he published anonymous and pseudonymous pamphlets critical of the established church alone and with friends, leading to his losing his position in London and relocating to Newcastle, where he continued in ministry and criticism. Udall was arrested under suspicion of complicity in publishing the critical tracts and, unwilling to deny that he wrote them, was convicted and sentenced to death. The death sentence was not carried out, however, and he remained in prison almost two years until pardoned, but died soon after release.

Guillaume du Vair (1556–1621). French Catholic priest, lawyer, and writer. While du Vair took holy orders in his youth, much of his life was spent serving the state as a counselor of the parliament of Paris, a representative of King Henry IV both in France and abroad, and as Keeper of the Seals, the highest legal office in the country. The last four years of his life were spent as the bishop of Lisieux. His studies on Epictetus and the Stoics, and attempts to relate Stoicism to the Christian faith, were influential in the dissemination of this philosophy during the seventeenth and eighteenth centuries. He also wrote significant works on politics, the moral life, prayer, and the use and abuse of the French language.

Juan de Valdés (1500/10–1541). Spanish Catholic theologian and writer. Although Valdés adopted an evangelical doctrine, had Erasmian affiliations and published works that were listed on the Index of Prohibited Books, Valdés rebuked the reformers for creating disunity and never left the Catholic Church. His writings included translations of the Hebrew Psalter and various biblical books, a work on the Spanish language and several commentaries. Valdés fled to Rome in 1531 to escape the Spanish Inquisition and worked in the court of Clement VII in Bologna until the pope's death in 1534. Valdés subsequently returned to Naples, where he led the reform- and revival-minded Valdesian circle.

Henry Vaughan (1617/1618–1661). English Protestant preacher. Possibly a student at Christ's College, Cambridge, Vaughan published a sermon on Matthew 5:20 given to the House of Commons.

Thomas Venatorius (c. 1490–1551). German Lutheran theologian, mathematician, and humanist. Following a humanistic education, Venatorius spent the majority of his career in Nuremberg, where he advocated for reform as the head of the city's school system and as a preacher and pastor in the city's churches. His theological and pastoral works include one of the first Protestant works on ethics, a short catechism, and a commentary on 1 Timothy. He also edited the first Greek edition of

Archimedes's writings and translated Aristophanes's *Plutus*.

Peter Martyr Vermigli (1499–1562). Italian Reformed humanist and theologian. Vermigli was one of the most influential theologians of the era, held in common regard with such figures as Martin Luther* and John Calvin.* In Italy, Vermigli was a distinguished theologian, preacher and advocate for moral reform; however, during the reinstitution of the Roman Inquisition Vermigli fled to Protestant regions in northern Europe. He was eventually appointed professor of divinity at Oxford University, where Vermigli delivered acclaimed disputations on the Eucharist. Vermigli was widely noted for his deeply integrated biblical commentaries and theological treatises.

Matthieu Virel (fl. 1561–1595). French Reformed pastor and theologian. Only two episodes from Virel's life are known: he preached the reformation message at Namur in 1561, and sixteen years later he pastored a French congregation in Basel. He published two known works: an excursus on the calendar and a brief summary of the Christian religion.

Pierre Viret (1511–1571). Swiss Reformed pastor and teacher. Converted to Protestantism at the University of Paris, Viret returned to his hometown, Orbe, where Guillaume Farel* brought him into ministry. Preaching also at Payerne and Neuchâtel, Viret's success in spreading the Reformed faith led to an assassination attempt before he and Farel sought to reform Geneva. Soon after the Genevan Assembly voted to accept the Reformation, Viret relocated to Lausanne, where he established the Reformed faith, served as chief pastor, and founded a Reformed academy. After almost twenty-five years, he was exiled from the city, spending a short time pastoring and teaching in Geneva until establishing himself in southern France, where he brought the evangelical faith to Lyons, pastored, and served as an advisor to Jeanne d'Albret, the queen of Navarre (1528–1572).

Juan Luis Vives (1492?–1540). Spanish Catholic humanist. Born into a Jewish family but baptized Catholic, Vives spent most of his life outside Spain following the persecution of his family by the Inquisition. After studying in Paris, he lived in Bruges, where he became part of the intellectual circle around Erasmus,* and taught at Oxford toward the end of his life. Vives largely avoided entering into religious controversies, and his works received a mixed reception from both Catholics and Protestants. He is best known for his educational and social writings, including an influential Latin primer, works on pedagogy and women's education, and arguments for pacifism and poor relief.

Gisbertus Voetius (1589–1676). Dutch Reformed theologian. Voetius pastored at Vlijmen and Heusden and served as the youngest delegate at the Synod of Dordrecht* before becoming professor of theology and Oriental languages at the University of Utrecht. While Voetius's writings demonstrate concern for missions, practical piety, and personal purity, he also entered into numerous theological controversies during his career. His Reformed commitments led to ongoing conflicts with Arminians and Catholics, and he sought to uphold the importance of the Old Testament against Johannes Cocceius's (1603–1669) formulation of the covenants. He also entered into debate with René Descartes (1596–1650) and his followers, arguing from an Aristotelian perspective that to accept Cartesian skepticism was to reject biblical truth and the Christian tradition.

Conradus Vorstius (1569–1622). Dutch Arminian-Socinian theologian. A student of David Paraeus* and Johannes Piscator,* Vorstius's Socinian tendencies emerged during his tenure as professor of theology at Steinfurt. After an apology and examination, he was allowed to replace Arminius* as professor of theology at Leiden though never permitted to teach, as his questioning of the doctrine of atonement and the eternity, foreknowledge, and omnipresence of God drew wide censure, ultimately from King James I of England.* Exiled to Gouda and deposed at the Synod of Dordrecht,* Vorstius published numerous theological works and a commentary on the Pauline letters.

Vulgate. In 382 Pope Damasus I (c. 300–384) commissioned Jerome (c. 347–420) to translate the four Gospels into Latin based on Old Latin and Greek manuscripts. Jerome completed the translation of the Gospels and the Old Testament around 405. It is widely debated how much of the rest of the New Testament was translated by Jerome. During the Middle Ages, the Vulgate became the Catholic Church's standard Latin translation. The Council of Trent recognized it as the official text of Scripture.

George Walker (1581–1651). Puritan minister. Walker was born at Hawkshead, Lancashire, and educated at St. John's College, Cambridge. After graduating Cambridge, Walker moved to London, where he became rector of St. John the Evangelist on Watling Street in 1614. He served this parish for nearly forty years. Throughout his ministry, Walker showed himself to be an ardent opponent of the papacy and practices within the Church of England that he deemed not sufficiently reformed. Toward this end, Walker engaged numerous disputations and literary debates with both conformists and Catholics. For his sermons that were critical of the Church of England, he was summoned to appear before Archbishop Laud in 1635 and the Star Chamber in 1638, which fined and imprisoned him for twelve weeks. On another occasion, Walker was incarcerated for as long as two years for his nonconformity until released by the Long Parliament. In 1643, Walker was selected to serve in the Westminster Assembly and to participate in the trial of Laud. Walker died in London. Among his many published sermons and polemical works is a treatise on justification.

Thomas Walkington (d. 1621). Anglican minister and author. Born in Lincoln, he was educated at Cambridge, graduating with his BA in 1597 and his MA in 1600. Walkington was elected a fellow at St. John's College, Cambridge, in 1602. Later, he received a BD from Oxford and a DD from Cambridge. He served as rector of parishes in Northamptonshire, Lincolnshire, and Middlesex. A prolific author, Walkington published works on diverse subjects. Among his biblical works are *An Exposition of the First Two Verses of the Sixth Chapter to the Hebrews in form of a Dialogue* (1609) and *Theologicall Rules to Guide Us in the Understanding and Practice of Holy Scripture* (1615).

Peter Walpot (d. 1578). Moravian Radical pastor and bishop. Walpot was a bishop of the Hutterite community after Jakob Hutter, Peter Riedemann* and Leonhard Lanzenstiel. Riedemann's *Confession of Faith* (1545; 1565) became a vital authority for Hutterite exegesis, theology and morals. Walpot added his own *Great Article Book* (1577), which collates primary biblical passages on baptism, communion, the community of goods, the sword and divorce. In keeping with Hutterite theology, Walpot defended the community of goods as a mark of the true church.

Richard Ward (c. 1601–1684). English Anglican pastor. Educated at Cambridge and St. Andrews, Ward pastored in London and Essex. His published writings include a commentary on Matthew and an explanation of the Solemn League and Covenant (1643), which allied Scottish Covenanters and English Parliamentarians during the First English Civil War (1642–1646).

Thomas Watson (d. 1686). English Puritan pastor. After graduating from Cambridge, Watson became pastor of St. Stephen Walbrook in the city of London, a pulpit he served for twenty years, though he was imprisoned for a year for his part in the plot of Christopher Love (1618–1651) to restore Charles II to the throne. A well-respected preacher, Watson was expelled from official ministry by the 1662 Act of Uniformity, though he continued to preach in private until his retirement. While Watson published many sermons and devotional works, he is perhaps best known for *A Body of Divinity* (1692), a series of sermon on the Westminster Catechism.

Valentin Weigel (1533–1588). German Lutheran pastor. Weigel studied at Leipzig and Wittenberg, entering the pastorate in 1567. Despite a strong anti-institutional bias, he was recognized by the church hierarchy as a talented preacher and compassionate minister of mercy to the poor. Although he signed the Formula of Concord,* Weigel's orthodoxy was questioned so openly that he had to publish a defense. He appears to have tried to synthesize several medieval mystics with the ideas of Sebastian Franck,* Thomas Müntzer* and others. His posthumously published works have led some recent scholars to suggest that Weigel's works may have deeply influenced later Pietism.

Hieronymus Weller von Molsdorf (1499–1572). German Lutheran theologian. Originally intending to study law, Weller devoted himself to theology after hearing one of Martin Luther's* sermons on the catechism. He boarded with Luther and tutored Luther's son. In 1539 he moved to Freiburg, where he lectured on the Bible and held theological disputations at the Latin school. In addition to hymns, works of practical theology and a postil set, Weller published commentaries on Genesis, 1–2 Samuel, 1–2 Kings, Job, the Psalms, Christ's passion, Ephesians, Philippians, 1–2 Thessalonians and 1–2 Peter.

Westminster Assembly (1643–1652). English church council. Called by English Parliament to advise on church reform, the Westminster Assembly was made up of more than 120 clergymen, thirty parliamentary observers, and a delegation from the Church of Scotland. Beginning with a review of the Articles of Religion,* the most heated debates were undertaken over ecclesiology, as factions argued for presbyterianism, congregationalism, Erastianism, and episcopalianism, with the council ultimately recommending presbyterianism to the parliament. Much of the legacy of the assembly is held in the major documents it produced, the *Directory for Public Worship* (1644), *The Form of Presbyterial Church Government* (1645), the *Westminster Confession of Faith* (1646), the *Shorter Catechism* (1647), and the *Larger Catechism* (1648), which became foundational for the English and Scottish churches and many of the Reformed denominations.

William Whitaker (1547/1548–1595). English Puritan theologian. Whitaker spent most of his career at Cambridge, where he served as Regius Professor of Divinity and master of St. John's College. While his tenure was occasionally opposed due to his Puritanism, he was nevertheless widely respected, and he published numerous significant works on topics including the Protestant doctrine of Scripture, original sin, grace, and ecclesiastical authority. He also drafted the Lambeth Articles (1595), a proposed addendum to the Thirty-Nine Articles* endorsing double predestination, but the changes were rejected by Elizabeth I*.

John Whitgift (1530–1604). Anglican archbishop. Though Whitgift shared much theological common ground with Puritans, after his election as Archbishop of Canterbury (1583) he moved decisively to squelch the political and ecclesiastical threat they posed during Elizabeth I's* reign. Whitgift enforced strict compliance to the Book of Common Prayer,* the Act of Uniformity (1559) and the Articles of Religion.* Whitgift's policies led to a large migration of Puritans to Holland. The bulk of Whitgift's published corpus is the fruit of a lengthy public disputation with Thomas Cartwright,* in which Whitgift defines Anglican doctrine against Cartwright's staunch Puritanism.

Johann Wigand (1523–1587). German Lutheran theologian. Wigand is most noted as one of the compilers of the *Magdeburg Centuries*, a German ecclesiastical history of the first thirteen centuries of the church. He was a student of Philipp Melanchthon* at the University of Wittenburg and became a significant figure in the controversies dividing Lutheranism. Strongly opposed to Roman Catholicism, Wigand lobbied against innovations in Lutheran theology that appeared sympathetic to Catholic thought. In the later debates, Wigand's support for Gnesio-Lutheranism established his role in the development of confessional Lutheranism. Wigand was appointed bishop of Pomerania after serving academic posts at the universities in Jena and Königsburg.

Thomas Wilcox (c. 1549–1608). English Puritan theologian. In 1572, Wilcox objected to Parliament against the episcopacy and the Book of Common Prayer,* advocating for presbyterian church governance. He was imprisoned for sedition. After his release, he preached itinerantly. He was brought before the courts twice more for his continued protest against the Church of England's episcopal structure. He translated some of Theodore Beza* and John Calvin's* sermons into English, and he wrote polemical and occasional works as well as commentaries on the Psalms and Song of Songs.

Johann (Ferus) Wild (1495–1554). German Catholic pastor. After studying at Heidelberg and teaching at Tübingen, this Franciscan was appointed as lector in the Mainz cathedral, eventually being promoted to cathedral preacher—a post for which he became widely popular but also controversial. Wild strongly identified as Catholic but was not unwilling to criticize the curia. Known for an irenic spirit—criticized in fact as *too* kind—he was troubled by the polemics between all parties of the Reformation. He preached with great lucidity, integrating the liturgy, Scripture and doctrine to exposit Catholic worship and teaching for common people. His sermons on John were pirated for publication without his knowledge; the Sorbonne banned them as heretical. Despite his popularity among clergy, the majority of his works were on the Roman Index until 1900.

Andrew Willet (1562–1621). Anglican priest, professor, and biblical expositor. Willet was a gifted biblical expositor and powerful preacher. He walked away from a promising university career in 1588 when he was ordained a priest in the Church of England. For the next thirty-three years he served as a parish priest. Willet's commentaries summarized the present state of discussion while also offering practical applications for preachers. They have been cited as some of the most technical commentaries of the early seventeenth century. His most important publication was *Synopsis Papismi, or a General View of Papistrie* (1594), in which he responded to many of Robert Bellarmine's critiques. After years of royal favor, Willet was imprisoned in 1618 for a month after presenting to King James I* his opposition to the "Spanish Match" of Prince Charles to the Infanta Maria. While serving as a parish priest, he wrote forty-two works, most of which were either commentaries on books of the Bible or controversial works against Catholics.

Thomas Wilson (d. 1586). English Anglican priest. A fellow of St John's, Cambridge, Wilson fled to Frankfurt to escape the Marian Persecution. After his return to England, he served as a canon and Dean of Worcester.

George Wither (1588–1667). English poet, satirist, and hymn writer. Wither was born in Bentworth, Hampshire. After finishing his early education under the tutelage of a local minister, Wither continued his studies at Magdalen College, Oxford. Afterward, he studied law at the Inns of Chancery. Wither commenced his literary career with the publication of an elegy on the occasion of the death of Henry Frederick, Prince of Wales (1594–1612). Most of Wither's literary works consist of satirical pamphlets for which he was regularly arrested, imprisoned, and released. He fought in the Parliamentary Army during the Civil War. A conforming Anglican, Wither composed numerous hymns as well as translations of the Psalms. Two of Wither's major works are *Preparation to the Psalter* (1619), in which he explores various literary aspects of the Bible, and *Hymns and Songs of the Church* (1622/1623). He died in London.

John Woolton (c. 1535–1594). Anglican bishop. After graduating from Oxford, Woolton lived in Germany until the accession of Elizabeth I.* He was ordained as a priest in 1560 and as a bishop in 1578. Woolton published many theological, devotional and practical works, including a treatise on the immortality of the soul, a discourse on conscience and a manual for Christian living.

John Wycliffe (c. 1330–1384). English theologian, philosopher, and reformer known as "the Morning Star of the Reformation." While holding benefices from a number of parishes, Wycliffe spent the majority of his career at Oxford, where he studied, taught, and served as head of Balliol College. His early work focused on logic and metaphysics, but after entering into the service of John of Gaunt, Duke of Lancaster (1340–1399) and serving as a royal envoy to discuss taxes with papal representatives, Wycliffe turned his attention to more practical concerns. His criticism of papal power and wealth drew initially civil and ecclesiastical approval, but application of his principle that any headship profiting the governor rather than the governed is illegitimate to the English church brought controversy and censure. This criticism increased as he rejected transubstantiation, criticized monasticism, argued along Augustinian lines that only the invisible body of the elect constituted the true church, that Scripture belongs to the body of the elect rather than the institutional church, and that as many leaders of the visible church were likely reprobate, their offices and sacraments were invalid. While dismissed from Oxford in 1381, powerful defenders protected Wycliffe from further consequences during his lifetime, but he was condemned as a heretic at the Council of Constance (1515), whence he was exhumed and his remains burned. While largely condemned by contemporaries, Wycliffe, and his followers, the Lollards, are often viewed as forerunners of the Reformation who prepared the way for the tumult of the sixteenth century.

Girolamo Zanchi (1516–1590). Italian Reformed theologian and pastor. Zanchi joined an Augustinian monastery at the age of fifteen, where he studied Greek and Latin, the church fathers and the works of Aristotle and Thomas Aquinas.* Under the influence of his prior, Peter Martyr Vermigli,* Zanchi also imbibed the writings of the Swiss and German reformers. To avoid the Inquisition, Zanchi fled to Geneva where he was strongly attracted to the preaching and teaching of John Calvin.* Zanchi taught biblical theology and the *locus* method at academies in Strasbourg, Heidelberg, and Neustadt. He also served as pastor of an Italian refugee congregation. Zanchi's theological works, *De tribus Elohim* (1572) and *De natura Dei* (1577), have received more attention than his commentaries. His commentaries comprise about a quarter of his literary output, however, and display a strong typological and christological interpretation in conversation with the church fathers, medieval exegetes, and other reformers.

Katharina Schütz Zell (1497/98–1562). German Reformed writer. Zell became infamous in Strasbourg and the Empire when in 1523 she married the priest Matthias Zell, and then published an apology defending her husband against charges of impiety and libertinism. Longing for a united church, she called for toleration of Catholics and Anabaptists, famously writing to Martin Luther* after the failed Marburg Colloquy of 1529 to exhort him to check his hostility and to be ruled instead by Christian charity. Much to the chagrin of her contemporaries, Zell published diverse works, ranging from polemical treatises on marriage to letters of consolation, as well as editing a hymnal and penning an exposition of Psalm 51.

Martha Elizabeth Zitter (Unknown). German Catholic nun. Zitter entered the Ursuline convent in Erfurt during her teenage years. Most of what is known about her is drawn from a letter she composed to her mother, explaining her decision to leave the order and become Lutheran, which focuses on aspects of her vows and Roman Catholic piety she believes to be unbiblical. Despite this public departure from the Roman church, however, Zitter returned toward the end of her life.

Ulrich Zwingli (1484–1531). Swiss Reformed humanist, preacher and theologian. Zwingli studied at the University of Vienna, and afterwards the University of Basel, where he received his BA and MA in 1504 and 1506. Ordained in September 1506, Zwingli became priest of the church in Glarus where he taught himself Greek, and read deeply in the church fathers. During this period, Zwingli was also greatly impacted by the writings of Desiderius Erasmus*. In 1516, Zwingli accepted the position of priest at the Benedictine Abbey at Einsiedeln in Schwyz, where he intently studied the Greek New Testament, and learned Hebrew. When he became a preacher in the city cathedral at Zurich, Zwingli enacted reform through sermons, public disputations, and conciliation with the town council, abolishing the Mass and images in the church. Zwingli broke with the lectionary preaching tradition, instead preaching serial expository biblical sermons. He later was embroiled in controversy with Anabaptists over infant baptism and with Martin Luther* at the Marburg Colloquy (1529) over their differing views of the Eucharist. Zwingli, serving as chaplain to Zurich's military, was killed in the Second Battle of Kappel.

SOURCES FOR BIOGRAPHICAL SKETCHES

General Reference Works

Allgemeine Deutsche Biographie. 56 vols. Leipzig: Duncker & Humblot, 1875–1912; reprint, 1967–1971. Accessible online via deutsche-biographie.de/index.html.

Baskin, Judith R., ed. *The Cambridge Dictionary of Judaism and Jewish Culture*. New York: Cambridge University Press, 2011.

Benedetto, Robert, ed. *The New Westminster Dictionary of Church History*. Vol. 1. Louisville: Westminster John Knox Press, 2008.

Bettenson, Henry and Chris Maunder, eds. *Documents of the Christian Church*. 3rd ed. Oxford: Oxford University Press, 1999.

Betz, Hans Dieter, Don Browning, Bernd Janowski and Eberhard Jüngel, eds. *Religion Past & Present: Encyclopedia of Theology and Relgion*. 13 vols. Leiden: Brill, 2007–2013.

Bremer, Francis J. and Tom Webster, eds. *Puritans and Puritanism in Europe and America: A Comprehensive Encyclopedia*.
2 vols. Santa Barbara, CA: ABC-CLIO, 2006.

Ghisalberti, Alberto Maria, ed. *Dizionario Biografico degli Italiani*. 100 vols. Istituto della Enciclopedia italiana, Roma, 1960–2020. Online edition available at treccani.it.

Gritsch, Eric W. *A History of Lutheranism*. Minneapolis: Fortress Press, 2002.

Haag, Eugene and Émile Haag. *La France protestante ou vies des protestants français*. 2nd ed. 6 vols. Paris: Sandoz & Fischbacher, 1877–1888.

Hillerbrand, Hans J., ed. *Oxford Encyclopedia of the Reformation*. 4 vols. New York: Oxford University Press, 1996.

Kolb, Robert, and Timothy J. Wengert, eds. *The Book of Concord: The Confessions of the Evangelical Lutheran Church*. Translated by Charles Arand et al. Minneapolis: Fortress, 2000.

McKim, Donald K., ed. *Dictionary of Major Biblical Interpreters*. Downers Grove, IL: InterVarsity Press, 2007.

Müller, Gerhard, et al., ed. *Theologische Realenzyklopädie*. Berlin: Walter de Gruyter, 1994.

Neue Deutsche Biographie. 28 vols. projected. Berlin: Duncker & Humblot, 1953–. Accessible online via deutsche-biographie.de/index.html.

New Catholic Encyclopedia. 15 vols. New York: McGraw-Hill, 1967; 2nd ed., Detroit: Thomson-Gale, 2002.

Oxford Dictionary of National Biography. 60 vols. Oxford: Oxford University Press, 2004.

Pelikan, Jaroslav. *The Christian Tradition*. 5 vols. Chicago: University of Chicago Press, 1971–1989.

Stephen, Leslie, and Sidney Lee, eds. *Dictionary of National Biography*. 63 vols. London: Smith, Elder and Co., 1885–1900.

Terry, Michael, ed. *Reader's Guide to Judaism*. New York: Routledge, 2000.

Wordsworth, Christopher, ed. *Lives of Eminent Men connected with the History of Religion in England*. 4 vols. London: J. G. & F. Rivington, 1839.

Additional Works for Individual Sketches

Akin, Daniel L. "An Expositional Analysis of the Schleitheim Confession." *Criswell Theological Review* 2 (1988): 345-70.

Astell, Mary. *The Christian Religion, as Professed by a Daughter of the Church of England*. Edited by Jacqueline Broad. Toronto: Iter Inc and the Center for Reformation and Renaissance Studies, 2013.

Bald, R. C. *John Donne: A Life*. Oxford: Oxford University Press, 1970.

Beeke, Joel, and Randall J. Pederson. *Meet the Puritans*. Grand Rapids: Reformation Heritage Books, 2006.

Bireley, Robert, *The Refashioning of Catholicism, 1450–1700*, Washington, DC: Catholic University of America Press, 1999.

Blok, P. J., and P. C. Molhuysen, eds. *Nieuw Nederlandsch Biografisch Woordenboek*. 10 vols.

Brackney, William H. *A Genetic History of Baptist Thought: With Special Reference to Baptists in Britain and North America*. Atlanta: Mercer University Press, 2004.

———. *Historical Dictionary of the Baptists*. 2nd ed. Lanham, MD: Scarecrow, 2009.

Brook, Benjamin. *The Lives of the Puritans*. 3 vols. London: James Black, 1813. Reprint, Pittsburgh, PA: Soli Deo Gloria, 1994.

Brown, Peter. *Augustine of Hippo: A Biography*. Berkeley & Los Angeles, CA: University of California Press, 1967.

Burke, David G. "The Enduring Significance of the KJV." *Word and World* 31, no. 3 (2011): 229-44.

Campbell, Gordon. *Bible: The Story of the King James Version, 1611–2011*. Oxford: Oxford University Press, 2010.

Cathcart, William. *The Baptist Encyclopaedia*. 3 vols. Philadelphia: Louis H. Everts, 1881.

Charles, Amy. *A Life of George Herbert*. Ithaca, NY: Cornell University Press, 1977.

Christian, Jacob. *The Sovereign Map: Theoretical Approaches to Cartography Throughout History*. Chicago: University of Chicago Press, 2006.

Coffey, John. *Politics, Religion, and the British Revolutions: The Thought of Samuel Rutherford*. Cambridge: Cambridge University Press, 1997.

Colish, Marcia. *Peter Lombard*, 2 vols. Leiden, Netherlands: Brill, 1993.

Culpepper, Scott. *Francis Johnson and the English Separatist Influence: The Bishop of Brownism's Life, Writings, and Controversies*. Macon, GA: Mercer University Press, 2011.

Doornkaat Koolman, J ten. "The First Edition of Peter Riedemann's 'Rechenschaft.'" *Mennonite Quarterly Review* 36, no. 2 (1962): 169-70.

Emerson, Everett H. *John Cotton*. New York: Twayne, 1990.

Fischlin, Daniel and Mark Fortier, eds. *Royal Subjects: Essays on the Writings of James VI and I*. Detroit: Wayne State University Press, 2002.

Fishbane, Michael A. "Teacher and the Hermeneutical Task: A Reinterpretation of Medieval Exegesis." *Journal of the American Academy of Religion* 43, no. 4 (1975): 709-21.

Friedmann, Robert. "Second Generation Anabaptism as Illustrated by the Walpot Era of the Hutterites." *Mennonite Quarterly* 44, no. 4 (1970): 390-93.

Frymire, John M. *The Primacy of the Postils: Catholics, Protestants, and the Dissemination of Ideas in Early Modern Germany*. Leiden: Brill, 2010.

Furcha, Edward J. "Key Concepts in Caspar von Schwenckfeld's Thought, Regeneration and the New Life." *Church History* 37, no. 2 (1968): 160-73.

Gordon, Bruce, *The Swiss Reformation*. Manchester: Manchester University Press, 2002.

Greaves, Richard L. *Society and Religion in Elizabethan England*. Minneapolis: University of Minnesota, 1981.

Greiffenberg, Catharina Regina von. *Meditations on the Incarnation, Passion, and Death of Jesus Christ*. Edited and translated by Lynne Tatlock. The Other Voice in Early Modern Europe. Chicago: University of Chicago Press, 2009.

Grendler, Paul. "Italian biblical humanism and the papacy, 1515-1535." In *Biblical Humanism and Scholasticism in the Age of Erasmus*. Edited by Erika Rummel, 225-76. Leiden: Brill, 2008.

Haemig, Mary Jane. "Elisabeth Cruciger (1500?–1535): The Case of the Disappearing Hymn Writer." *Sixteenth Century Journal* 32, no. 1 (2001): 21-44.

Harpley, W., ed. *Report and Transactions of the Devonshire Association for the Advancement of Science, Literature and Art* 24 (July 1882). Plymouth: William Brendon and Son, 1892.

Heiden, Albert van der. "Pardes: Methodological Reflections on the Theory of the Four Senses." *Journal of Jewish Studies* 34, no. 2 (1983): 147-59.

Hendrix, Scott H., ed. and trans. *Early Protestant Spirituality*. New York: Paulist Press, 2009.

Hobbs, R. Gerald. "Is Abbot Isidore Also Among the Prophets?": Protestant Influences upon the Annotated Bible of Isidore Clarius." *Renaissance and Reformation*. New series, 17, No. 1 (Winter 1993): 53-71.

Hvolbek, Russell H. "Being and Knowing: Spiritualist Epistelmology and Anthropology from Schwenckfeld to Böhme." *Sixteenth Century Journal* 22, no. 1 (1991): 97-110.

Kahle, Paul. "Felix Pratensis—a Prato, Felix. Der Herausgeber der Ersten Rabbinerbibel, Venedig 1516/7." *Die Welt des Orients* 1, no. 1 (1947): 32-36.

Kelly, Joseph Francis. *The Ecumenical Councils of the Catholic Church: A History*. Collegeville, MN: Liturgical Press, 2009.

Koop, Karl, ed. *Confessions of Faith in the Anabaptist Tradition 1527–1660*. Translated by Cornelius J. Dyck et al. CRR 11. Kitchener, ON: Pandora Press, 2006.

Lake, Peter. *The Boxmaker's Revenge: "Orthodoxy", "Heterodox" and the Politics of the Parish in Early Stuart London*. Stanford, CA: Stanford University Press, 2001.

Lane, Anthony N. S. *Calvin and Bernard of Clairvaux*. Princeton, NJ: Princeton Theological Seminary, 1996.

Lane, Belden C. *Ravished by Beauty: The Surprising Legacy of Reformed Spirituality*. Oxford: Oxford University Press, 2011.

Lee, Jason K. *The Theology of John Smyth* (Macon, GA: Mercer University Press, 2003).

Lockhart, Paul Douglas. *Frederick II and the Protestant Cause: Denmark's Role in the Wars of Religion, 1559–1596*. Leiden: Brill, 2004.

Lubac, Henri de. *Medieval Exegesis: The Four Senses of Scripture*. 3 vols. Translated by Mark Sebanc and E. M. Macierowski. Grand Rapids: Eerdmans, 1998–2009.

Manetsch, Scott, *Calvin's Company of Pastors: Pastoral Care and the Emerging Reformed Church, 1536–1609*. Oxford: Oxford University Press, 2013.

Manschereck, Clyde Leonard. *Melanchthon, the Quiet Reformer*. New York: Abingdon, 1958.

Marinella, Lucrezia. *The Nobility and Excellence of Women and the Defects and Vices of Men*. Edited and translated by Anne Dunhill. Chicago: University of Chicago Press, 1999.

Matheson, Peter, *Argula von Grumbach: A Woman's Voice in the Reformation*. Edinburgh: T&T Clark, 1995.

McGuire, Daniel Patrick. *The Difficult Saint: Bernard of Clairvaux and his Tradition*. Collegeville, MN: Cistercian Publication, 1991.

McKinley, Mary B. "Volume Editor's Introduction." In *Epistle to Marguerite of Navarre and Preface to a Sermon by John Calvin*, edited and translated by Mary B. McKiney. Chicago: University of Chicago Press, 2004.

M'Crie, Thomas. *The Life of Andrew Melville*. 2 vols. Edinburgh: William Blackwood, 1819.

Norton, David. *A Textual History of the King James Bible*. New York: Cambridge University Press, 2005

Nuttall, Geoffrey. *The Welsh Saints, 1640–1660: Walter Cradock, Vavasor Powell, Morgan Llwyd*. Cardiff: University of Wales Press, 1957.

Oberman, Heiko A. *Luther: Man Between God and the Devil*. New York, NY: Doubleday, 1989.

O'Meara, Thomas F. *Albert the Great: Theologian and Scientist*. Chicago: New Priory Press, 2013.

Packull, Werner O. "The Origins of Peter Riedemann's Account of Our Faith." *Sixteenth Century Journal* 30, no. 1 (1999): 61-69.

Papazian, Mary Arshagouni, ed. *John Donne and the Protestant Reformation: New Perspectives*. Detroit: Wayne State University Press, 2003.

Paulicelli, Eugenia. "Sister Arcangela Tarabotti: Hair, Wigs and Other Vices." In *Writing Fashion in Early Modern Italy: From Sprezzatura to Satire*, by idem, 177-204. Farnham, Surrey, UK: Ashgate, 2014.

Pragman, James H. "The Augsburg Confession in the English Reformation: Richard Taverner's Contribution." *Sixteenth Century Journal* 11, no. 3 (1980): 75-85.

Rashi. *Rashi's Commentary on Psalms*. Translated by Mayer I. Gruber. Atlanta: Scholars Press, 1998.

Raynor, Brian. *John Frith: Scholar and Martyr*. Kent, UK: Pond View Books, 2000.

Reid, Jonathan A. *King's Sister—Queen of Dissent: Marguerite of Navarre (1492–1549) and her Evangelical Network*. Leiden: Brill, 2009.

Schmidt, Josef, "Introduction" in Johannes Tauler, *Sermons*. New York: Paulist Press, 1985, 1-34.

Smith, Hannah. "Mary Astell, *A Serious Proposal to the Ladies* (1694), and the Anglican Reformation of Manners in Late-Seventeenth-Century England." In *Mary Astell: Reason, Gender, Faith*, edited by William Kolbrenner and Michal Michelson, 31-48. New York: Routledge, 2007.

Spinka, Matthew. *John Hus: A Biography*. Princeton, NJ: Princeton University Press, 1968.

———. *John Hus at the Council of Constance*. New York: Columbia University Press, 1968.

———. *John Hus and the Czech Reform*. Hamden, CT: Archon Books, 1966.

Steinmetz, David C. *Reformers in the Wings: From Geiler von Kayserberg to Theodore Beza*. Oxford: Oxford University Press, 2000.

———. "The Superiority of Pre-Critical Exegesis." *Theology Today* 37, no. 1 (1980): 27-38.

Stjerna, Kirsi. *Women of the Reformation*. Malden, MA: Blackwell Publishing, 2009.

Synder, C. Arnold. "The Confession of the Swiss Brethren in Hesse, 1578." In *Anabaptism Revisited: Essays on Anabaptist/Mennonite Studies in Honor of C. J. Dyck*. Edited by Walter Klaassen, 29-49. Waterloo, ON; Scottdale, PA: Herald Press, 1992.

———. "The Schleitheim Articles in Light of the Revolution of the Common Man: Continuation or Departure?" *Sixteenth Century Journal* 16, no. 4 (1985): 419-30.

Thornton, Wallace. *John Foxe and His Monument: A Theological-Historical Perspective*. Birmingham, AL: Aldersgate Heritage Press, 2013.

Todd, Margo. "Bishops in the Kirk: William Cowper of Galloway and the Puritan Episcopacy of Scotland." *Scottish Journal of Theology*, 57 (2004): 300-312.

Tschackert, Paul. "Varel, Edo Hilderich of." In *General German Biography* (ADB). Volume 39. Leipzig: Duncker & Humblot, 1895.

Van Liere, Frans. *An Introduction to the Medieval Bible*. New York: Cambridge University Press, 2014.

Voogt, Gerrit. "Remonstrant-Counter-Remonstrant Debates: Crafting a Principled Defense of Toleration after the Synod of Dordrecht (1619–1650)." *Church History and Religious Culture* 89, no. 4 (2009): 489-524.

Wabuda, Susan. "Henry Bull, Miles Coverdale, and the Making of *Foxe's Book of Martyrs*." In *Martyrs and Martyrologies: Papers Read at the 1992 Summer Meeting and the 1993 Winter Meeting of the Ecclesiastical History Society*, edited by Diana Wood, 245-58. Oxford: Blackwell, 1993.

Wallace, Dewey D. Jr. "George Gifford, Puritan Propaganda and Popular Religion in Elizabethan England." *Sixteenth Century Journal* 9, no. 1 (1978): 27-49.

Wawrykow, Joseph P. *The Westminster Handbook to Thomas Aquinas*. Louisville, KY: Westminster John Knox, 2005.

Wendel, Francois. *Calvin: The Origins and Development of His Religious Thought*. New York: Harper & Row, 1963.

Wengert, Timothy J. "'Fear and Love' in the Ten Commandments." *Concordia Journal* 21, no. 1 (1995): 14-27.

Wiesner-Hanks, Merry, ed. *Convents Confront the Reformation: Catholic and Protestant Nuns in Germany*. Translated by Joan Skocir and Merry Wiesner-Hanks. Milwaukee: Marquette University Press, 1996.

———. "Philip Melanchthon and John Calvin against Andreas Osiander: Coming to Terms with Forensic Justification." In *Calvin and Luther: The Continuing Relationship*, edited by R. Ward Holder, 63-87. Göttingen: Vandenhoeck & Ruprecht, 2013.

Wilkinson, Robert J. *Tetragrammaton: Western Christians and the Hebrew Name of God*. Leiden: Brill, 2015.

Yarnell, Malcolm. "Christopher Blackwood: Exemplar of the Seventeenth-Century Particular Baptists." *Southwestern Journal of Theology* 57, no 2 (Spring 2015): 181-205.

BIBLIOGRAPHY

Primary Sources and Translations Used in This Volume

Ainsworth, Henry. *Annotations upon the five bookes of Moses, the booke of the Psalmes, and the Song of Songs, or, Canticles*. 2 vols. Glasgow: Blackie and Son, 1846. First published London: M. Flesher and J. Haviland, 1627. Digital copy online at http://archive.org.

Beza, Theodore. *Ecclesiastes Solomonis concio ad populum habita, de vita sic instituenda, ut ad veram aeternamque felicitatem perveniatur*. Geneva, 1588. Digital copy online at www.e-rara.ch.

———. *Sermons sur les Trois Premiers Chapitres du Cantique des Cantiques, de Salomon*. Geneva, 1586. Digital copy online at www.e-rara.ch.

Brenz, Johannes. *Ecclesiastes Salomonis, cum commentarijs Ioannis Brentij, per Hiobem Gast e Germano in Latinum tralatus, & per autorem, quantum ad sententiarum cognitionem satis est, restitutus*. Hagenau, 1529. Digital copy online at daten.digitale-sammlungen.de.

Brightman, Thomas. *A commentary on the Canticles or the Song of Salomon wherein the text is analised, the native signification of the words declared, the allegories explained, and the order of the times whereunto they relate observed*. London, 1644. Digital copy online at EEBO.

Bromiley, G. W., ed. and trans. *Zwingli and Bullinger*. LCC 24. Philadelphia: Westminster, 1953.

Broughton, Hugh. *A comment upon Coheleth or Ecclesiastes framed for the instruction of Prince Henri our hope*. Amsterdam, 1605. Digital copy online at Google Books.

Brucioli, Antonio. *La Cantica di Salomo, tradotta dalla ebraica verita in lingua toscana, & con nuovo commento dichiarato*. Venice, 1536. Digital copy online at www.bsb-muenchen.de.

Cajetan, Cardinal (Thomas de Vio). *Parabolae Salomonis ad veritatem Hebraicam castigatae, & per reuerendissimum Dominum D. Thomam de Vio Caietanum, Cardinalem sancti Xisti, ordinis Praedicatorum enarrate: recens iampridem in lucem editae, sed nunc multò vltra archetypum elimatiores*. Lyons, 1545. Digital copy online at Google Books.

Calvin, John. *Calvin's Tracts*. Translated by Henry Beveridge. 3 vols. Edinburgh: Calvin Translation Society, 1844–1851.

———. *In librum Psalmorum, Iohannis Calvini Commentarius. Ioannis Calvini Opera quae supersunt omnia* 32-32. Edited by G. Baum, E. Cunits and E. Reuss. Brunswick, 1891.

———. *Institutio Christianae Religionis in libros quatuor . . .* 1559. *Ioannis Calvini Opera quae supersunt omnia* 2. Edited by G. Baum, E. Cunits, and E. Reuss. Brunswick, 1864.

———. *Vivere apud Christum non dormire animis sanctos qui in fide Christi decedunt, quae vulgo Psychopannychia dicitur* (1534). *Ioannis Calvini Opera quae supersunt omnia* 5. Edited by G. Baum, E. Cunits and E. Reuss. Brunswick, 1866.

Cartwright, Thomas. *Commentarii succincti & dilucidi in Proverbia Salomonis*. London, 1632. Digital copy online at http://archive.org.

———. *In librum Salomonis, qui inscribitur Ecclesiastes cum metaphrasi, homiliae, quae et iusti commentarii loco esse possint*. London, 1604. Digital copy online at EEBO.

Cleaver, Robert. *A Briefe Explanation of the Whole Booke of the Proverbs of Salomon*. London, 1615. Digital Copy Online at EEBO.

Cop, Michel. *Sur les Proverbes de Salomon, exposition familiere, en forme de briefves homilies, contenans plusieurs sainctes exhortations convenables au temps present*. Geneva, 1556. Digital copy online at www.e-rara.ch.

Corro, Antonio del. *Sapientissimi regis Salomonis concio de summo hominis bono, quam Hebraei Cohelet, graeci & Latini Ecclesiasten vocant in Latinam linguam ab Antonio Corrano Hispalensi versa, & ex eiusdem praelectionibus paraphrasi illustrata*. London, 1579. Digital copy online at EEBO.

Cotton, John. *A brief exposition of the whole book of Canticles, or, Song of Solomon*. London: Philipp Nevil, 1642. Digital copy online at Google Books.

———. *A briefe exposition with practicall observations upon the whole book of Ecclesiastes by that late pious and worthy divine*. London, 1654. Digital copy online at EEBO.

Denys the Carthusian. *Enarrationes in Quinque Libros Sapientiales*. In *Doctoris Ecstatici Dionysii Cartusiani Opera Omnia*. 42 vols. Montreuil-sur-Mer, 1896–1913.

Dietrich, Veit. *Das Hohelied Salomonis*. Ansbach: Brügel, 1845. First published in *Summaria uber die gantze Bibel, das Alte vnd Newe Testament*. Nuremberg, 1548. Digital copy online at Google Books.

Dod, John. *A Plaine and Familiar Exposition of the Ninth and Tenth Chapters of the Proverbs of Salomon*. London, 1606.

———. *A Plaine and Familiar Exposition of the Eleventh and Twelfth Chapters of the Proverbs of Salomon*. London, 1608.

———. *A Plaine and Familiar Exposition of the Thirteenth and Fourteenth Chapters of the Proverbs of Salomon*. London, 1609.

———. *A Plaine and Familiar Exposition of the Fifteenth, Sixteenth, and Seventeenth Chapters of the Proverbs of Salomon*. London, 1609.

Erasmus, Desiderius. *Adages*. CWE 30-36. Toronto: University of Toronto Press, 2016–2017.

———. *The Praise of Folly and Other Writings*. Translated by Robert M. Adams. New York: Norton, 1989.

———. *A Warrior Shielding a Discussion of Free Will Against the Enslaved Will by Martin Luther, book one / Hyperaspistes liber unus*. CWE 76. Toronto: University of Toronto Press, 1999.

Fenner, Dudley. *The Song of songs that is, the most excellent song which was Solomons, translated out of the Hebrue into Englishe meeter, vvith as little libertie in departing from the wordes, as any plaine translation in prose can vse: and interpreted by a short commentarie*. Middleburgh, 1587. Digital copy online at EEBO.

Gerhard, Johann. *Postilla Salomonæa, Das ist Erklärung etlicher Sprüche auß dem Hohenlied Salomonis*. Jena, 1652.

Gifford, George. *Eight sermons, vpon the first foure chapters, and part of the fifth, of Ecclesiastes Preached at Mauldon*. London, 1589. Digital copy online at EEBO.

Granger, Thomas. *A familiar exposition or commentarie on Ecclesiastes. Wherein the worlds vanity, and the true felicitie are plainely deciphered*. London, 1621.

Grotius, Hugo. *Annotationes in Vetus Testamentum*. Amsterdam, 1644.

Hoffman, Melchior. *Dat Boeck Cantica canticorum, edder, dat hoge leedt Salomonis*. Kiel, 1529. Digital copy online at http://aleph.nkp.cz.

Isidore Clarius of Brescia. *Canticum Canticorum Salomonis, ad Hebraicam veritatem nunc demum emendatum, adiectis scholiis ex arcanis hebræorum erutis, quae in primis Christi, et ecclesiae misteria breviter explicent*. Ferrara, 1544.

Jermin, Michael. *Paraphrasticall Meditations, by way of Commentarie upon the Whole Booke of the Proverbs of Solomon*. London, 1638. Digital copy online at EEBO.

Junius, Franciscus. *Observationes in Willerami Abbatis Francicam paraphrasin Cantici canticorum*. Amsterdam, 1655. Digital copy online at Google Books.

Lambert, François. *In Cantica Canticorum Salomonis, libellum quidem sensibus altiss. in quo sublimia sacri Coniugii mysteria, quae in Christo et Ecclesia sunt, pertractantur, Francisci Lamb. Auenionensi Commentarii*. Strasbourg, 1524. Digital copy online at http://digitale.bibliothek.uni-halle.de.

Lavater, Ludwig. *In librum Proverbiorum siue Sententiarum Solomonis Regis sapientissimi, Ludouici Lauateri Tigurini Commentarii*. Zürich, 1562. Digital copy online at www.bsb-muenchen.de.

Lok, Henry. *Ecclesiastes, otherwise called The preacher Containing Salomons sermons or commentaries (as it may probably be collected) vpon the 49. Psalme of Dauid his father*. London, 1597. Digital copy online at EEBO.

Luther, Martin. *D. Martin Luthers Werke, Kritische Gesamtausgabe*: [Schriften]. 73 vols. Weimar: Hermann Böhlaus Nachfolger, 1883–2009. Digital copy online at http://archive.org.

———. *In Cantica Canticorum, breuis, sed admodum dilucida enarratio*. Wittenberg, 1539.

———. *Luther's Works* [American edition]. 82 vols. projected. St. Louis: Concordia, www.cph.org; Philadelphia: Fortress, 1955–1986; 2009–. Used by permission. All rights reserved.

Marinella, Lucrezia. *Exhortations to Women and to Others If They Please*. Edited and translated by Laura Benedetti. Toronto: Iter and the Center for Reformation and Renaissance Studies, 2012.

Melanchthon, Philipp. *Enarratio brevis Concionum Libri Salomonis, cuius Titulus est Ecclesiastes*. Wittenberg, 1551. Digital copy online at Google Books.

———. *Explicatio Proverberium Salomonis, in schola Witembergensi dictata*. Wittenberg, 1555. CR 14:1-88.

———. *Nova scholia Philipppi Melanchthonis, in Prouerbia Salomonis, adiusti penè commentarii modum conscripta*. Haganau, 1531. Digital copy online at www.bsb-muenchen.de.

Moffett, Peter. *A Commentary upon the Whole Booke of the Proverbs of Salomon, the second time perused, much enlarged, and newly published for the aedification of the Church of God*. London, 1596. Digital copy online EEBO.

Münster, Sebastian. *Canticum Canticorum Salomonis, Latine iuxta Hebraicum contextum per Sebastianum Munsterum translatum, atque annotationibus aliquot nonnihil illusratum*. Basel, 1525. Digital copy online at www.bsb-muenchen.de.

Oecolampadius, Johannes. *In Ecclesiastem Solomonis Metaphrasis Divi Gregorii Neocaesariensis Episcopi*. Augsburg, 1520. Digital copy online at diglib.hab.de.

Osiander, Lucas. *Esdras, Nehemias, Esther, Iob, Psalterium, Proverbia Salomonis, Ecclesiastes, & Canticum Canticorum: iuxta Veterem seu Vulgatam Translationem omnia ad Hebraeam Veritatem emendata....* Tübingen, 1578. Digital copy online at Google Books.

Pellikan, Konrad. *Commentaria bibliorum et illa brevia quidem ac catholica*. Vol. 4, *In quo continentur scripta reliqua, quae vocant hagiographa, libri videlicet quinque, Iob, Psalterium, Parabolae, Ecclesiastes, & Cantica Salomonis, comment. Chuon. Pel. ministri ecclesiae Tigurinae illustrati*. Zürich, 1534.

Piscator, Johann. *Commentarii in omnes libros Veteris Testamenti: antehac aliquoties separatim editi, nunc vero in unum volumen collecti*. Herborn, 1644. Digital copy online at Google Books.

Serres, Jean de. *Joannis Serrani Commentarius, in Solomonis Ecclesiasten. Quo commentario ultilissimae concionis methodus, sententia, usus, breviter et perspicue explicantur*. Geneva, 1580. Digital copy online at www.e-rara.ch.

Sibbes, Richard. *Bowels Opened: Or, A Discovery of the Neare and Deare Love, Union and Communion betwixt Christ, and the Church, and consequently betwixt Him and every beleeving Soule. Delivered in divers Sermons on the fourth, fifth and sixth Chapters of the CANTICLES*. London: George Edwards, 1641. Digital copy online at http://archive.org.

Strigel, Viktorin. *Salomonis Libri Tres, Proverbia, Ecclesiastes, Canticum*. Leipzig, 1565. Digital copy online at Google Books.

Tarabotti, Arcangela. *Paternal Tyranny*. Edited and translated by Letizia Panizza. Chicago: University of Chicago Press, 2004.

Taylor, Francis. *An Exposition with Practicall Observations upon the Three First Chapters of the Proverbs: Grammaticall, Rhetoricall, Logicall, and Theologicall, As they were delivered in severall Expository Lectures at Christ-Church in Canterbury*. London, 1655.

Trapp, John. *Solomonis ΠΑΝΆΡΕΤΟΣ: commentarie upon the books of Proverbs, Ecclesiastes, and the Song of Songs*. London, 1650. Digital copy online at Google Books.

Zwingli, Ulrich. *Commentary on the True and False Religion*. Translated by Samuel Macauley Jackson. Durham, NC: Labyrinth Press, 1981.

———. *De Vera et falsa religione*. Zürich, 1530. First published Zürich, 1525. Digital copy online at www.e-rara.ch.

———. *Von Klarheit und Gewissheit des Wortes Gottes*. Zürich, 1524. First published Zürich, 1522. Digital copy online at www.e-rara.ch.

Author and Writings Index

Subject Index

Scripture Index